HANDBOOK OF
EARLY CHILDHOOD EDUCATION

Handbook of
EARLY
CHILDHOOD
EDUCATION

EDITED BY

Robert C. Pianta

Associate Editors
W. Steven Barnett
Laura M. Justice
Susan M. Sheridan

THE GUILFORD PRESS
New York   London

© 2012 The Guilford Press
A Division of Guilford Publications, Inc.
72 Spring Street, New York, NY 10012
www.guilford.com

Printed in the United States of America

This book is printed on acid-free paper.

Last digit is print number: 9 8 7 6 5 4 3 2 1

Library of Congress Cataloging-in-Publication Data

Handbook of early childhood education / edited by Robert C. Pianta . . . [et al.].
    p. cm.
    Includes bibliographical references and index.
    ISBN 978-1-4625-0337-7 (hardcover)
    1. Early childhood education—United States—Handbooks, manuals, etc.   I. Pianta, Robert C.
    LB1139.25.H33 2012
    372.210973—dc23
                                                         2011028803

To Ann
—R. C. P.

About the Editor

Robert C. Pianta, PhD, is Dean of the Curry School of Education at the University of Virginia, where he is also the Novartis Professor of Education and Director of the Center for Advanced Study of Teaching and Learning. A former special education teacher, Dr. Pianta's research focuses on investigating the effects of schooling on children's social and academic outcomes, and on improving school and classroom experiences through teachers' professional development. His team of education researchers has developed the Classroom Assessment Scoring System™, an observational measure that has been tested and proven effective in several large national studies and is being utilized by every Head Start program in the United States. Dr. Pianta is Editor of the *Journal of School Psychology* and the author of more than 400 journal articles, chapters, and books in the areas of early childhood development, transition to school, school readiness, and parent–child and teacher–child relationships. He consults regularly with federal agencies, foundations, and universities.

Associate Editors

W. Steven Barnett, PhD, is Board of Governors Professor and Director of the National Institute for Early Education Research at Rutgers, The State University of New Jersey. His research investigates the economics of early care and education, including costs and benefits, the long-term effects of preschool programs on children's learning and development, and the distribution of educational opportunities. Dr. Barnett has authored or coauthored over 160 publications, including the series of *State Preschool Yearbooks* providing annual, state-by-state analyses of progress in public PreK.

Laura M. Justice, PhD, is a clinical speech–language pathologist and applied researcher in early childhood language and literacy development, educational interventions, and communication disorders. She is Professor in the College of Education and Human Ecology at The Ohio State University, where she also directs the Children's Learning Research Collaborative, a research unit within the School of Teaching and Learning. Dr. Justice has published more than 100 articles and chapters on early education and language/literacy development and intervention, and has authored or edited 10 books, including *Language Development from Theory to Practice, Communication Disorders: A Contemporary Perspective,* and *Scaffolding with Storybooks.* She is a Founding Editor of *EBP Briefs* and past Editor of the *American Journal of Speech–Language Pathology.*

Susan M. Sheridan, PhD, is George Holmes University Professor of Educational Psychology at the University of Nebraska, where she is also Director of the Nebraska Center for Research on Children, Youth, Families, and Schools and of the National Center for Research on Rural Education. Her research interests include early childhood intervention, school readiness, parent engagement and partnerships, and parent–teacher (conjoint) behavioral consultation. Dr. Sheridan has written more than 100 books, chapters, and journal articles on these and related topics. She is a Fellow of Division 16 of the American Psychological Association and past President of the Society for the Study of School Psychology.

Contributors

W. Steven Barnett, PhD, National Institute for Early Education Research, Rutgers, The State University of New Jersey, New Brunswick, New Jersey

Clive R. Belfield, PhD, Department of Economics, Queens College, City University of New York, Flushing, New York

Elena Bodrova, PhD, Mid-Continent Research for Education and Learning, Denver, Colorado

W. Thomas Boyce, MD, College for Interdisciplinary Studies and Faculty of Medicine, University of British Columbia, Vancouver, British Columbia, Canada

Sue Bredekamp, PhD, early childhood education consultant, Cheverly, Maryland

Mindy Sittner Bridges, PhD, Life Span Institute, University of Kansas, Lawrence, Lawrence, Kansas

Virginia Buysse, PhD, Frank Porter Graham Child Development Institute, University of North Carolina at Chapel Hill, Chapel Hill, North Carolina

Claire E. Cameron, PhD, Center for the Advanced Study of Teaching and Learning, University of Virginia, Charlottesville, Virginia

Brandy L. Clarke, PhD, Nebraska Center for Research on Children, Youth, Families, and Schools, University of Nebraska–Lincoln, Lincoln, Nebraska

Douglas H. Clements, PhD, Department of Learning and Instruction, University at Buffalo, State University of New York, Buffalo, New York

Keely D. Cline, PhD, Department of Human Development and Learning, East Tennessee State University, Johnson City, Tennessee

Carolyn T. Cobb, PhD, Frank Porter Graham Child Development Institute, University of North Carolina at Chapel Hill, Chapel Hill, North Carolina

Maureen A. Conroy, PhD, Department of Special Education, School Psychology, and Early Childhood Studies, University of Florida, Gainesville, Florida

Karen E. Diamond, PhD, Department of Human Development and Family Studies, Purdue University, West Lafayette, Indiana

Celene E. Domitrovich, PhD, Prevention Research Center, Pennsylvania State University, University Park, Pennsylvania

Jason T. Downer, PhD, Center for Advanced Study of Teaching and Learning, University of Virginia, Charlottesville, Virginia

Dale J. Epstein, PhD, Frank Porter Graham Child Development Institute, University of North Carolina at Chapel Hill, Chapel Hill, North Carolina

Ellen Frede, PhD, Acelero Learning, New York, New York

Allison H. Friedman, MEd, Steinhardt School of Culture, Education, and Human Development, New York University, New York, New York

Eugene E. García, PhD, Office of the Provost, Arizona State University, Phoenix, Phoenix, Arizona

Cristina Gillanders, PhD, Frank Porter Graham Child Development Institute, University of North Carolina at Chapel Hill, Chapel Hill, North Carolina

Walter S. Gilliam, PhD, Yale Child Study Center, Yale University, New Haven, Connecticut

Stacie G. Goffin, EdD, Goffin Strategy Group, LLC, Washington, DC

Shelley Gray, PhD, Department of Speech and Hearing Science, Arizona State University, Tempe, Tempe, Arizona

Megan R. Gunnar, PhD, Institute of Child Development, University of Minnesota, Minneapolis, Minneapolis, Minnesota

Bridget K. Hamre, PhD, Center for Advanced Study of Teaching and Learning, University of Virginia, Charlottesville, Virginia

Mary Louise Hemmeter, PhD, Department of Special Education, Vanderbilt University, Nashville, Tennessee

Tiffany P. Hogan, PhD, Department of Special Education and Communication Disorders, University of Nebraska–Lincoln, and Neurogenetic Communication Disorders Consortium, University of Nebraska Medical Center, Lincoln, Nebraska

Diane M. Horm, PhD, Early Childhood Education Institute, College of Education, University of Oklahoma–Tulsa, Tulsa, Oklahoma

Jason T. Hustedt, PhD, Department of Human Development and Family Studies, University of Delaware, Newark, Delaware

Marilou Hyson, PhD, Department of Applied Developmental Psychology, George Mason University, Fairfax, Virginia

Tanya B. Ihlo, PhD, Nebraska Center for Research on Children, Youth, Families, and Schools, University of Nebraska–Lincoln, Lincoln, Nebraska

Iheoma Iruka, PhD, Frank Porter Graham Child Development Institute, University of North Carolina at Chapel Hill, Chapel Hill, North Carolina

Faiza M. Jamil, MEd, Center for Advanced Study of Teaching and Learning, University of Virginia, Charlottesville, Virginia

Laura M. Justice, PhD, School of Teaching and Learning, College of Education and Human Ecology, Ohio State University, Columbus, Ohio

Lisa L. Knoche, PhD, Nebraska Center for Research on Children, Youth, Families, and Schools, University of Nebraska–Lincoln, Lincoln, Nebraska

Cynthia Lamy, EdD, National Institute for Early Education Research, Rutgers, The State University of New Jersey, New Brunswick, New Jersey

Jamie M. Lawler, MA, Institute of Child Development, University of Minnesota, Minneapolis, Minneapolis, Minnesota

Deborah J. Leong, PhD, Department of Psychology, Metropolitan State College of Denver, Denver, Colorado

Christine A. Marvin, PhD, Department of Special Education and Communication Disorders, University of Nebraska–Lincoln, Lincoln, Nebraska

Julia E. Moore, MS, Prevention Research Center, College of Health and Human Development, Pennsylvania State University, State College, Pennsylvania

Susan B. Neuman, EdD, Department of Educational Studies, School of Education, University of Michigan, Ann Arbor, Michigan

Jelena Obradović, PhD, School of Education, Stanford University, Stanford, California

Robert C. Pianta, PhD, Curry School of Education, University of Virginia, Charlottesville, Virginia

Ximena A. Portilla, BA, School of Education, Stanford University, Stanford, California

Douglas R. Powell, PhD, Department of Human Development and Family Studies, Purdue University, West Lafayette, Indiana

Sara E. Rimm-Kaufman, PhD, Curry School of Education, University of Virginia, Charlottesville, Virginia

Sharon Ritchie, EdD, Frank Porter Graham Child Development Institute, University of North Carolina at Chapel Hill, Chapel Hill, North Carolina

Sharon Ryan, EdD, Graduate School of Education, Rutgers, The State University of New Jersey, New Brunswick, New Jersey

Mesut Saçkes, PhD, Research and Development Unit, Balikesir Provincial Directorate of National Education, Balikesir, Turkey

Julie Sarama, PhD, Department of Learning and Instruction, University at Buffalo, State University of New York, Buffalo, New York

Susan M. Sheridan, PhD, Nebraska Center for Research on Children, Youth, Families, and Schools, University of Nebraska–Lincoln, Lincoln, Nebraska

Ross A. Thompson, PhD, Department of Psychology, University of California, Davis, Davis, California

Jeffrey Trawick-Smith, EdD, Center for Early Childhood Education, Eastern Connecticut State University, Willimantic, Connecticut

Kathy Cabe Trundle, PhD, School of Teaching and Learning, College of Education and Human Ecology, Ohio State University, Columbus, Ohio

Shannon B. Wanless, PhD, Program of Applied Developmental Psychology, Department of Psychology in Education, School of Education, University of Pittsburgh, Pittsburgh, Pennsylvania

Marcy Whitebook, PhD, Center for the Study of Child Care Employment, Institute for Research on Labor and Employment, University of California, Berkeley, Berkeley, California

Pamela J. Winton, PhD, Frank Porter Graham Child Development Institute, University of North Carolina at Chapel Hill, Chapel Hill, North Carolina

Preface

There is a widespread belief that early childhood education is one of the best solutions for providing educational opportunities for all children regardless of race or social class (Heckman & Masterov, 2007). This belief, and the accompanying evidence, has transformed research, program development, and policymaking in the field over the past 20 years. As a field of scientific inquiry, early childhood education is at the nexus of basic developmental science, policy research and analysis, and the applied disciplines of education and prevention science. The field has become one of the most vibrant areas of scientific activity in terms of the connections among scientific advances and theory, program design, policy, and classroom practices. Moreover, the quality of scientific inquiry has improved at all levels, and the research now includes descriptive population-level studies and rigorous controlled evaluations of innovative programs, as well as highly controlled analyses of scaled-up interventions and smaller scale laboratory-based work that fuels conceptual advances and new applications. It is precisely this nexus of science, application, and policy that is represented in the chapters in this volume and that warrants a handbook as a way to document and package this knowledge.

Rapid advances are taking place now in neuroscience and policymaking that directly involve early childhood education. New understandings of very basic developmental processes now inform classroom practices and interventions to promote children's self-regulation, as well as policies around school readiness assessment and curricular choice. At a more macro level, states and the federal government have taken a keen interest in advancing the ways in which investments in early childhood education also advance children's school readiness; accountability, human capital management systems, and scaled-up quality rating and improvement systems are now present in Head Start and the vast majority of the states. In nearly all cases, these shifts in knowledge, practice, and policy are being driven by a connection between science and the field. This handbook is the outgrowth of this high level of scientific and applied activity, situated in a context of pressing national importance, a shifting demography, and the continuing challenges of poverty and inequity.

Perhaps in no context have the connections among public policy, early childhood practices, and research been more evident than in recent presidential and gubernatorial elections; candidates have relied on available evidence to make arguments for expansion and refinement of early education programs as a means of addressing serious concerns about achievement and learning in the early grades and inequities in society at large. In most instances, the argument is based on research on the role of early education in enhancing children's competencies.

The argument made in many circles—including policymakers at state and federal levels, advocacy, program planning, and development—is that early childhood education is a means to address concerns that an unacceptably large number of children are already, by 5 years of age, lacking in competencies fundamental to their school success—notably in the areas of spoken language and literacy, self-regulation, social-relational competence, and early math. The long-term effects of early gaps in achievement and social functioning are so pronounced that effective and efficient interventions targeted toward these gaps in early childhood are essential not only to the developmental success of children but also to the economic and social health of communities. Early childhood education is viewed as a means by which policymakers can address these issues, as both small experimental studies and quasi-experimental studies of large-scale programs have shown consistently positive effects of exposure to preschool. Findings of long-term effects in the United States have been replicated by studies in a wide range of other countries around the globe, indicating that in broad terms the results are highly generalizable.

Who can benefit from educationally effective preschool programs? All children have been found to benefit from high-quality preschool education. Claims that preschool programs only benefit boys or girls, or one particular ethnic group, or just children in poverty do not hold up across the research literature as a whole. Children from lower-income families do tend to gain more from good preschool education than do more advantaged children. However, the educational achievement gains for nondisadvantaged children are substantial, perhaps 75% as large as the gains for low-income children. Some concerned with reducing the achievement gap between children in poverty and others might conclude that preschool programs should target only children in poverty. Such an approach ignores evidence that disadvantaged children appear to learn more when they attend preschool programs with more advantaged peers, and they also benefit from peer effects on learning in kindergarten and the early elementary grades when their classmates have attended quality preschool programs.

But we must come to grips with the magnitude of effects, whether short or long term. All of the major evaluations show that early childhood education programs produce only *modest* effects overall, with somewhat greater effects for low-income children, and some evidence that gains last through early grades. Typical child care has considerably smaller short- and long-term effects than more educationally focused programs such as selected Head Start programs or higher-quality preschool programs linked to public education. And across studies and program models/features, effects range from near zero to almost a standard deviation on achievement tests (the size of the achievement gap for poor children). There is no evidence whatsoever that the average run-of-the-mill preschool program produces benefits in line with what the best programs produce. Thus, on average, the nonsystem that is preschool in the United States narrows the achievement gap by about 30%. It is abundantly evident that the wide variation in program design, models, curricula, staffing, auspices, funding, and level of educational aims plays a major role in the rather small, albeit significant and meaningful, impacts of preschool on child development.

Because the wide-ranging and diverse experiences in preschools are not, in aggregate, producing the level and rate of skills gains required for children to be ready for school, some have argued that simply enrolling more children in more programs, although helpful, will not close, or even narrow in noticeable ways, the skills gap at school entry. Instead, investments (in research, program development, and policy initiatives) are urgently needed to enhance substantially the positive effects of existing and expanding educational offerings on the very child outcomes in which skills gaps are so evident. The key challenges to heightening the impact of programs are to align policy with research, to identify gaps in the science, and then to close these gaps in the knowledge base while acting on points of alignment. It is within this reality that the chapters of this volume are situated and provide a basis for the next generation of research, practice, and policymaking.

This handbook tackles the challenges of both summarizing recent work in an incredibly active field, and positioning those summaries to shape the future. The four major sections into which chapters are organized reflect large frames of reference, activity, and need. To start, there is simply no question that early education is now a sector of U.S. public education, a feature of the national opportunity structure. The first section of this volume, edited by W. Steven Barnett, provides a contemporary and critical look at this landscape of opportunity, evaluating issues such as access, investment, assets, demography, and poverty. A major area of scientific work over the past decade has been the design and evaluation of curricula in early education—some specific to domains of development such as literacy and math, and others more general approaches to fostering developmental progress. The second section, edited by Laura M. Justice, draws together chapters by leading investigators and innovators that collectively should begin to put to rest the vexing question "What early childhood curricula are effective to promote school readiness?" In the third section, edited by Susan M. Sheridan, the focus shifts to social development and the larger family context in which early education is situated. Perhaps one of the unique features of early education is its explicit emphasis on the whole child and the critical connections to and role of the family for fostering child development. Again, recent scientific advances drive the focus and content of these chapters, with direct implications for the field. Finally, in the fourth major section, chapters address the range of contemporary issues that frame and at times constrain and shape the scientific and applied problems faced in the field. The increasing numbers of children with identified special needs must be addressed with inclusive and effective educational supports; teacher preparation, credentialing, and certification supports must be redesigned and improved; and the need for innovations in preservice and inservice preparation are outlined as critical directions for future work.

In summary, this handbook captures the contemporary realities and knowledge base in early childhood education in chapters that collectively provide a lens and framework for shaping future work in the field. As in the prior decade, this work is likely to take place at the intersection of science, practice, and policy—a nexus of ideas, activity, and debate that we hope shapes a more effective and equitable system of opportunities for the nation's young children.

Reference

Heckman, J. J., & Masterov, D. V. (2007). The productivity argument for investing in young children. *Review of Agricultural Economics, 29,* 446–493.

Acknowledgments

No project of this scope and scale is ever the result of any one person's work. In this case, the volume simply would not exist without the participation and leadership of three of the leading scholars in early education as Associate Editors. I don't need to describe the contributions to the field made by Steve Barnett, Laura Justice, and Sue Sheridan; their own current work itself would make for a terrific handbook. As section editors, Steve, Laura, and Sue secured, reviewed, and edited chapters from the finest authors in the field, ensuring that the topics are relevant and the work is contemporary. Any praise garnered by this volume is entirely due to their efforts and the efforts of the authors. Of course, I am deeply indebted to the many authors who took the time and effort to prepare chapters. Many worked on tight deadlines, and each worked through successive drafts to produce chapters that stand on their own as examples of first-rate analysis and scholarship. I also appreciate that many authors are friends and collaborators who chose to assist with this project.

I also want to extend thanks to Craig Thomas and his colleagues at The Guilford Press. Craig's patience and steadfast guidance have been a terrific asset to this project, and the Guilford staff members have been responsive and efficient.

And thanks are also owed to my many colleagues and collaborators at the University of Virginia's Center for Advanced Study of Teaching and Learning. Our work over the past years is truly a collective effort and the result of a great amount of cooperation in the service of larger goals. It has been a unique privilege to work with such talented people.

Finally, I owe many thanks to Jeanne Stovall, my executive assistant, coach, and navigator. Jeanne's attention to detail, communication, and insistence on top-notch products are responsible for the quality of my professional work. I simply cannot put a value on Jeanne's effort and contributions.

ROBERT C. PIANTA, PhD
University of Virginia

Contents

PART IV. BUILDING SYSTEMS OF EFFECTIVE EARLY INTERVENTION SUPPORTS: Meeting the Needs of Diverse Children and the Adults Who Serve Them

PART I

EARLY EDUCATION OPPORTUNITIES IN THE UNITED STATES

CHAPTER 1

Early Education in the United States

Programs and Access

Dale J. Epstein and W. Steven Barnett

Since the mid-1960s, enrollment rates of 3- and 4-year-olds in early education programs have increased dramatically. In 1965, 3- and 4-year-olds attending a public preschool program numbered approximately 127,000. By 2009, enrollment in public preschool had risen to 2.7 million (U.S. Department of Education, National Center for Education Statistics [USDOE, NCES], 2010b). This increase in enrollment is a reflection of not only more working families but also public and private responses to an increase in evidence of the benefits of quality early education programs on children's learning and development (Adams, Zaslow, & Tout, 2007). Today, most children enter kindergarten having already participated in some type of early education program (Barnett & Yarosz, 2007).

The public response has been to fund a variety of programs at the federal, state, and local levels. Two major federal early childhood initiatives have their roots in the mid-1960s. The Head Start program began in 1965 and Early Head Start in 1995. Head Start targets low-income children ages 3–5 and their families, with a focus on providing comprehensive services that include education, health, nutrition, and social services. The Early Head Start program serves low-income infants and toddlers and their families. These federal programs are available in every state, and though it basically targets children in families at or below 100% of the federal poverty level, children in some circumstances, including those with special needs, do not have to meet the income guidelines. Head Start and Early Head Start have seen major increases in their funding levels in recent years through both the American Recovery and Reinvestment Act (ARRA) and the regular appropriations process for fiscal year (FY) 2011. ARRA alone provided $2.1 billion, though it remains to be seen whether future appropriations will be sufficient to maintain expanded enrollments.

Child care subsidies (Child Care and Development Fund [CCDF]) have also grown over the last few years, with funding increasing by almost $1.7 billion since 2008. These subsidies provide low-income parents with funds to select a child care center for their children. Child care centers vary greatly with respect to their quality and populations served, but in general refer to full-day, 5-day-a-week programs intended to care for children while their parents are working (Kamerman & Gatenio-Gabel, 2007). These increases seen in federal investments have helped to continue to provide access to children, especially children who are most at risk.

States have also taken an active role and interest in developing and financing prekindergarten (PreK) education programs, greatly fueling this growth of early education programs, particularly during the past two decades (Barnett et al., 2010; Mitchell, 2001). By fall 2009, state PreK initiatives enrolled almost 1.3 million children in 40 U.S. states. Total public spending on these initiatives topped $6.2 billion, including a commitment of $5.4 billion in state funds alone. While state PreK initiatives vary greatly across the United States, they share a number of common features (Barnett et al., 2010). First and foremost, they are funded and administered by state government, following specified state regulations. They focus primarily on education for 3- and 4-year-olds rather than parent education or workforce development. These initiatives are not designed primarily to serve children with disabilities or to offer child care, though coordination with state special education and, to a lesser extent, child care systems is an important component of PreK initiatives. State PreK initiatives offer group-based learning experiences to children at least 2 days per week and are always voluntary for parents.

This chapter provides an overview of access to early education programs in the United States, with a particular focus on state-funded PreK initiatives that drive publicly funded PreK education, as well as a review of Head Start and child care programs. We begin by presenting research on the impact and effectiveness of early education programs in the United States. Next, we describe overall trends of early education programs, as well as the current status of state PreK, Head Start, and child care, focusing on access and quality standards. Our review of state PreK initiatives is supported by data from the eighth in a series of intensive annual surveys of state PreK conducted by the National Institute for Early Education Research (Barnett et al., 2010). Last, we present a discussion of policy issues related to the administration of early childhood education programs in the United States.

Impacts of Early Education Programs on Young Children

Early education programs typically aim to improve children's academic skills including improving language and early literacy abilities, as well as developing knowledge and skills that relate to math and science. Also important is the development of children's social and emotional skills, as many are entering a group environment for the first time. An array of research has found that preschool education programs can produce substantive gains in children's development and that these can persist well into the school years. Two randomized trials of public preschool programs dating back to the 1960s are especially informative when examining the research, even though these programs differ somewhat in their features compared to larger-scale state PreK initiatives offered today (Barnett, 2008).

The first of these studies is the well-known High/Scope Perry Preschool Study (Schweinhart et al., 2005). Most children participated in the Perry Preschool program for 2 years, beginning at age 3, but some had only 1 year at age 4. Although similar in many ways to today's part-day state PreK programs, the teacher–child ratio was much more intensive 1:6 or 7. The initial effects of this intervention on children's language and cognitive abilities were very impressive, about 0.90 standard deviation. Though effects on IQ were not persistent, there were persistent effects in literacy and math, as well as other positive outcomes, such as better teacher-reported classroom and personal behavior, fewer special education placements, and higher high school graduation rates (Berrueta-Clement, Schweinhart, Barnett, Epstein, & Weikart, 1984; Schweinhart, Barnes, & Weikart, 1993).

In the second study, conducted by the Institute for Developmental Studies (IDS; Deutsch, Deutsch, Jordan, & Grallow, 1983; Deutsch, Taleporos, & Victor, 1974; Jordan, Grallow, Deutsch, & Deutsch, 1985), 402 children were randomly assigned to a 1-year public PreK program beginning at age 4, or to a control group. Classes of 17 children were staffed by one teacher and one aide. By the end of the PreK year, estimated effects on measures of cognitive and language abilities were more than 0.40 standard deviation. An estimated effect of 0.20 standard deviation in these areas remained evident at least through third grade.

An early methodologically rigorous study of public school preschool focusing on a larger-scale initiative also dates back to the 1960s—the Chicago Parent–Child Center (CPC) study (Reynolds, 2000). CPC programs operate within Chicago's public school system, and study participants attended half-day preschool programs for 2 years starting at age 3, or for 1 year starting at age 4. There were also kindergarten and elementary school follow-on components for the CPC participants in this study. Classes of 18 children were staffed by a certified teacher and a teacher assistant; parent outreach and support were also provided. Initial effects of the CPC program by kindergarten varied by type of measure but were in the range of 0.35 to 0.77 standard deviation (with effects of 0.20 to 0.65 standard deviation for a single year of attendance). Long-term positive impacts of the CPC program include higher test scores through middle school, increased high school graduation rates, and reduced rates of arrests and special education placements. These findings from the CPC study are especially important because they essentially replicate the findings of the Perry Preschool study in the context of a more broadly available, and somewhat less intensive, public preschool initiative (Barnett, 2008).

Recently, many other studies have provided evidence on the impact of early education programs (see Barnett, 2008; Camilli, Vargas, Ryan, & Barnett, 2010). However, many of the studies suffer from methodological weaknesses, and few have evaluated the effects of state preschool programs (Gilliam & Zigler, 2000, 2004). Gormley and colleagues (Gormley, Gayer, Phillips, & Dawson, 2005; Gormley, Phillips, & Gayer, 2008) have conducted rigorous research on the state PreK classrooms in Tulsa, Oklahoma. These studies applied a regression discontinuity approach to address the problem of selection bias, and found effects on literacy and math achievement of 0.36 to 0.99 standard deviation. Effects were only modestly smaller for children who did not qualify for free or reduced-price school lunches than for those who did. Researchers at the National Institute for Early Education Research have taken a similar approach to estimate the initial effects of state-funded PreK on children's cognitive abilities in eight states (Barnett, Howes, & Jung, 2008; Hustedt, Barnett, Jung, & Goetze, 2009; Hustedt, Barnett, Jung, & Thomas, 2007; Wong, Cook, Barnett, & Jung, 2008). Average effect sizes across these eight states at kindergarten entry were 0.23 for cognitive and language ability, 0.31 for mathematics, and 0.79 for print awareness. Last, two recent studies conducted on state PreK in Tennessee, one a randomized trial and the other using a regression discontinuity approach, found substantial positive effects on preschool-age children's literacy, language, and mathematics skills after attending just 1 year of PreK (Lipsey, Farran, Hofer, Bilbrey, & Dong, 2011).

Effectiveness of Early Education Programs

Regardless of the setting, it is critical to examine the educational effectiveness of early education programs. While no specific formula guarantees educational effectiveness for all children who participate in early education programs, research has shown that certain features are linked to substantial gains in preschoolers' learning and development. Four main features seem particularly important (Barnett & Ackerman, 2011; Frede, 1998), and our later discussion of quality compares these components across state PreK, Head Start, and child care programs. First, early childhood teachers should be well educated and well paid. Given what the field expects of them, a bachelor's degree may be necessary to prepare early education teachers in both public and nonpublic settings fully, as is the case in public kindergarten programs (Bowman, Donovan, & Burns, 2001). It is reasonable to expect that preschool teachers should have an educational attainment comparable to that of kindergarten teachers. Second, teaching and instruction should be intentional, using a well-planned curriculum that helps children understand how to be successful in a school setting. Third, class sizes and teacher–child ratios in preschool education programs should be structured to allow children to work in small groups or individually with teachers. Finally, teachers need strong mentoring and supervision to guide their instruction and interactions with students.

As we discuss later on, there is great variation in early education programs in terms of quality standards set at the program level. "Professional capacity" is a term that refers to the skills and knowledge held by both individuals and their organizations (Johnson & Thomas, 2004). Simply put, public schools, private child care providers, and Head Start may each have different capacities to offer educationally effective early education programs that provide the greatest benefits to children. Each type of auspice stands to make valuable contributions to a broader system of early education (Barnett & Ackerman, 2011). For example, state PreK initiatives in public settings offer substantial organizational capacity, stricter educational standards for teachers that focus on bachelor's degrees and certification, and higher salaries. They are also experienced in aligning instruction to statewide standards (Council of Chief State School Officers and National Governors Association, n.d.) Furthermore, public schools already serve large numbers of preschoolers with disabilities each year and can more easily integrate these children into regular education program when also serving children who do not have special needs or educational difficulties. Some drawbacks of public schools as sites for PreK programs include teachers whose cultural backgrounds are less likely to reflect those of their students, potential obligations to make sacrifices in the interest of a larger system that is not focused specifically on early childhood (Barnett & Ackerman, 2011), and a lack of capacity to respond quickly and inexpensively to needs for new facilities (Sussman & Gillman, 2007).

Benefits of Head Start's model include the greater resources it receives as a product of federal funding, an increased emphasis on hiring more qualified teachers, small class sizes, comprehensive services, and program standards that are consistent across all sites nationwide. Nevertheless, Head Start teachers receive much lower salaries than their public school counterparts, even those with bachelor's degrees, and the emphasis on providing comprehensive services for young children may reduce the educational emphasis of the programs (Barnett & Ackerman, 2011).

Access

Although enrollment in early education programs continues to rise, variations in participation rates by child and family demographics can still be seen, and it is important to consider the effects these have on participation rates (Barnett & Yarosz, 2007; Ranck, 2003). As of 2005, 60% of white 4-year-olds attended some type of child care program; 7% of these children were enrolled in a Head Start program, while the rest were in another type of center-based care such as preschool, early learning centers, or nursery schools (USDOE, NCES, 2010a). Similarly, 62% of black children at age 4 attended a center-based program, but in contrast to white children, 25% of black children were enrolled in a Head Start program. Fewer Hispanic 4-year-olds were enrolled in center-based programs (49%), although almost 20% of them attended Head Start (USDOE, NCES, 2010a).

Differences in access to child care, preschool, and Head Start can also be seen when looking at family income levels. Of children under the age of 6, 35% of children living above the poverty level are in center-based care compared to only 26% of children living at or below the poverty level (USDOE, NCES, 2006). At age 4 alone, 51% of children from families below the poverty level were in center-based programs in 2005, while 59% of children at or above the poverty level were in these programs. Of the 4-year-olds in some type of center-based care, 26% of children living below the poverty level attended Head Start, compared to only 8% of children living at or above the poverty level, a reflection of program eligibility requirements (USDOE, NCES, 2010a). These patterns of participation by income suggest that young children in poverty still attend center-based programs at lower rates than middle- or higher-income families (Barnett & Yarosz, 2007). Next, we present recent evidence of access to center-based care on three main early education programs—state PreK, Head Start, and child care.

State-Funded PreK Programs

As of the 2009–2010 school year, 1,292,310 children were enrolled in state-funded PreK programs (Barnett et al., 2010). These initiatives were available in 40 U.S. states, with some states offering multiple distinct PreK initiatives aimed at different groups of children. The vast majority of the children enrolled in state PreK were 4-year-olds, with 27% of all 4-year-olds in the country being served. Four percent of the nation's 3-year-olds were also enrolled in state PreK in the 2009–2010 school year. Overall enrollment in state PreK has continued to increase annually, dating back to at least the 2001–2002 school year, when we began collecting this type of data. However, during the 2009–2010 school year, total enrollment barely increased from the prior year, reflecting a large slowdown in this trend due to the recession (Barnett et al., 2010).

Enrollment and Eligibility Criteria in State PreK Programs

For all state PreK initiatives, age is the primary eligibility criterion, with programs offering enrollment to 4-year-olds who will be eligible for kindergarten the following year. Oklahoma continues to be the state that serves the greatest percentage of its 4-year-old population, with 71% of all 4-year-olds in the state enrolled. During the 2009–2010 school year, five other states served more than half of their 4-year-olds in their state PreK programs: Florida (68%), West Virginia (55%), Georgia (55%), Vermont (52%), and Wisconsin (52%). Twenty-four of the 40 states with PreK initiatives also offered enrollment to 3-year-olds, though always to a lesser degree than they offered enrollment to 4-year-olds. States that enrolled the greatest percentages of 3-year-olds were Illinois (19%), New Jersey (18%), Vermont (17%), Nebraska (11%), Kentucky (10%), and California (10%). All of the other states served fewer than 10% of their 3-year-olds in state PreK (Barnett et al., 2010). Table 1.1 provides state-by-state enrollment information for each state offering a PreK initiative.

In addition to age determining eligibility, most states also use other criteria, such as income and risk factors. Family income limits are most common, as states set maximum income levels to target programs to the most financially disadvantaged. In at least 27 of the 40 states with PreK initiatives, state income limits are used to determine eligibility for at least some subset of the enrolled children (Barnett et al., 2010). Some states use other risk factors to determine PreK eligibility as well, such as low levels of parent education, disability or developmental delay, or having non-English-speaking family members (Barnett, Friedman, Hustedt, & Stevenson Boyd, 2009). A smaller but growing group of states has begun offering universally available PreK programs that are intended (now or in the future) to be available to all 4-year-olds statewide—including Florida, Georgia, Illinois, Iowa, New

TABLE 1.1. Access to State-Funded PreK Programs in 2009–2010

State	Percent of children enrolled in state PreK (2009–2010)			Number of children enrolled in state PreK (2009–2010)		
	4-year-olds	3-year-olds	Total (3s and 4s)	4-year-olds	3-year-olds	Total (3s and 4s)
Alabama	6.2%	0.0%	3.1%	3,870	0	3,870
Alaska	1.9%	0.0%	1.0%	200	0	200
Arizona	4.2%	0.0%	2.1%	4,319	0	4,319
Arkansas	41.1%	8.6%	24.8%	16,583	3,481	20,064
California[a]	17.1%	9.6%	13.4%	92,255	52,172	144,427
Colorado	20.4%	6.1%	13.2%	14,749	4,448	19,197
Connecticut	12.8%	7.2%	10.0%	5,440	3,068	8,508
Delaware	7.1%	0.0%	3.6%	843	0	843
Florida	68.1%	0.0%	33.7%	155,877	0	155,877
Georgia	54.6%	0.0%	27.2%	81,177	0	81,177
Illinois	30.7%	18.8%	24.8%	54,149	33,302	87,451
Iowa	38.1%	1.4%	19.4%	15,032	583	15,615
Kansas	23.9%	0.0%	11.8%	9,463	0	9,463
Kentucky	29.4%	9.7%	19.5%	16,742	5,557	22,299
Louisiana	32.3%	0.0%	17.0%	20,348	0	20,348
Maine	25.3%	0.0%	12.6%	3,605	0	3,605
Maryland	35.2%	0.0%	17.5%	26,147	0	26,147
Massachusetts[b]	14.0%	3.6%	8.8%	10,657	2,811	13,468
Michigan	16.1%	0.0%	8.0%	19,781	0	19,781
Minnesota[b]	1.4%	0.9%	1.2%	1,053	679	1,732
Missouri	3.9%	1.6%	2.7%	3,035	1,296	4,331
Nebraska	27.4%	10.6%	19.0%	7,147	2,803	9,950
Nevada	2.1%	1.0%	1.5%	820	390	1,210
New Jersey	27.0%	18.1%	22.6%	29,960	19,875	49,835
New Mexico	16.1%	0.0%	8.1%	4,848	0	4,848
New York	45.3%	0.1%	22.6%	107,712	215	107,927
North Carolina	23.9%	0.0%	11.9%	31,197	0	31,197
Ohio	2.4%	1.1%	1.8%	3,535	1,666	5,201
Oklahoma	70.7%	0.0%	35.1%	37,356	0	37,356
Oregon	8.3%	5.0%	6.6%	4,009	2,451	6,460
Pennsylvania[b]	16.9%	4.6%	10.7%	24,980	6,816	31,796
Rhode Island	1.1%	0.0%	0.5%	126	0	126
South Carolina	37.9%	2.8%	20.1%	22,818	1,745	24,563
Tennessee	21.4%	0.8%	10.9%	17,603	649	18,252
Texas	46.8%	5.2%	25.9%	192,594	21,578	214,172
Vermont[b]	52.1%	17.4%	35.1%	3,374	1,082	4,456
Virginia	14.3%	0.0%	7.1%	14,944	0	14,944
Washington	7.4%	1.8%	4.5%	6,411	1,615	8,026
West Virginia	55.3%	8.6%	31.7%	11,522	1,823	13,345
Wisconsin[b]	51.5%	1.1%	26.1%	36,724	780	37,504

Note. Data are derived from Barnett et al. (2010). Ten states are omitted because they did not offer state PreK during the 2009–2010 school year. They are Hawaii, Idaho, Indiana, Mississippi, Montana, New Hampshire, North Dakota, South Dakota, Utah, and Wyoming.
[a]In California, the number and percent of 3- and 4-year-olds served reflects a change from prior years in the number of programs included in the California State Preschool Program.
[b]At least one program in these states did not break down total enrollment figures into specific numbers of 3- and 4-year-olds served. As a result, the figures in this table are estimates.

York, Oklahoma, and West Virginia. Illinois is the only state that has committed to providing a universally available state PreK program for 3-year-olds.

Location and Operation of PreK Programs

Although state PreK initiatives are all publicly financed, and controlled and administered at the state level, states frequently partner with private organizations to operate state PreK programs. This not only takes advantage of existing early childhood facilities and staff but also benefits from the ability of the private sector to grow quickly. Each of the 40 states with PreK initiatives allows both public schools and private providers to receive state PreK funds (Hustedt & Barnett, in press). While the majority of children attend programs located in public schools, other private agencies (e.g., Head Start, private child care providers, faith-based agencies) are involved, but the degree to which private agencies participate varies from state to state.

We estimate that 67% of all children enrolled in state PreK during the 2008–2009 school year were served in public school settings. As recently as the 2003–2004 school year, 76% of all state PreK enrollees attended classrooms in the public schools. This decrease in public school enrollment reflects a national trend toward growing enrollment levels in private settings as state PreK programs become more widely available across the United States. For example, in 2002, West Virginia's PreK initiative served all enrolled children at public school sites (Barnett, Hustedt, Robin, & Schulman, 2004), but by 2009, this initiative had grown considerably, and more than two-thirds of the children were enrolled in private settings. These changes come in the context of a 10-year phase-in process toward making PreK available to all 4-year-olds in West Virginia by the 2012–2013 school year (Cavalluzzo, Clinton, Holian, Marr, & Taylor, 2009).

Other states, including Texas and Kentucky, offer state PreK programs that are primarily based in the public schools but may also be provided in a much more limited manner in non-public-school settings such as Head Start (Barnett, Epstein, Friedman, Sansanelli, & Hustedt, 2009). These states are not able to provide enrollment breakdowns by type of school setting, and for the current purposes we estimate that in such cases all PreK children are enrolled in public schools. Even using less conservative estimates in which we assume that 10% of state PreK children in these states are enrolled in private settings, it still has little impact on the national average. As a result, the best current estimate is that about two-thirds of children attending state PreK programs are served directly in the public schools.

Head Start Programs

Across the country during the 2009–2010 school year, Head Start and Early Head Start programs served approximately 950,000 children, 755,000 of which were 3- and 4-year-olds (Barnett et al., 2010). However, while programs are located in every state, accessibility continues to be a critical issue as there are many more children who qualify than the number of slots available. Therefore, many children who would benefit from an early education program do not have access to one. Similar to state PreK programs, there is wide variability by state in the percentage of children enrolled in Head Start. For example, while Nevada enrolls only 4% of 4-year-olds and 3% of 3-year-olds in Head Start, Mississippi enrolls 34% of 4-year-olds and 26% of 3-year-olds. Only some of this variation across states is due to differences in state poverty rates. Head Start enrollments also may be influenced by the extent of state PreK provision and by the collaboration between state PreK programs that partner with Head Start programs. Differences can also be seen in program operating schedules because not all Head Start programs serve children for a full day or for 5 days per week. For example, Idaho and Wyoming enroll only 1% of their children in full-day, 5-day per week programs, while other states such as Alabama, Florida, and Georgia enroll over 90% of their children in full-day, 5-day per week Head Start programs.

Child Care Programs

Over 11 million children under the age of 5 are in some type of child care arrangement across the United States, either in child care centers, with family members, or in a family child care home (National Association of Child Care Resource and Referral Agencies [NAC-CRRA], 2010). However, due to the multitude of programs available to young children and lack of reporting, it is difficult to track these data nationally. Excluding children in state PreK center-based programs, Head Start, or special education programs, approximately 33% of 3-year-olds and 35% of 4-year-olds were in either a local public school program, a private child care program, or a center-based program during the 2008–2009 school year (Barnett, Epstein, et al., 2009). It is estimated that, on average, children are in child care programs 36 hours per week, with one-third of children in multiple child care arrangements (NACCRRA, 2010). Of the children who are receiving child care subsidies, over 60% are enrolled in child care centers rather than family child care homes or alternative child care. Preschool-age children who have subsidies are even more likely to be enrolled in a child care center in the United States (Child Care Bureau, 2009).

Other Programs: Special Education and Local Preschool Initiatives

Special education programs are another important component of access to early childhood education initiatives in the public schools. During the 2009–2010 school year, more than 425,000 children received publicly funded special education services at ages 3 and 4, though some of these children received those services through state PreK programs and are included in the state PreK enrollment counts reported previously (Barnett et al., 2010; Data Account-ability Center, 2010). Special education programs are funded through a combination of federal, state, and local sources. In the 2009–2010 school year, preschool special education funding (Individuals with Disabilities Education Act [IDEA] Part B, Section 619) at the federal level was $574 million, which included funds from ARRA. For FY 2011, the federal budget for preschool special education was reduced to $374 million. There is great variability from state to state in percentages of children served, likely because states do not use identical sets of eligibility guidelines (Hustedt & Barnett, in press). Overall, we estimate that 3% of the nation's 4-year-olds and 3% of the nation's 3-year-olds receive special education services, in addition to those already counted as part of state PreK programs (Barnett et al., 2010). A few states, most notably Kentucky and Wyoming (which does not offer a state PreK program), have preschool special education programs that are much larger than the national average in terms of the percentage of the population served; they appear to serve a substantial number of children at risk of developmental delay. In addition, states such as Kentucky and West Virginia serve all of their children with disabilities in their state PreK programs, while other states serve very few children with disabilities in their PreK programs.

When combining state PreK and special education programs, over 325,000 3-year-olds (8%) and almost 1,295,000 4-year-olds (31%) are enrolled in these initiatives. When adding in Head Start enrollment numbers, enrollment is seen to be even higher. Fourteen percent of 3-year-olds and 40% of 4-year-olds in the United States are enrolled in state PreK, special education, or Head Start programs. Nevertheless, even when combining all of these programs, more than half of all children in the country are not enrolled in one of these public initiatives. When examining enrollment trends by state, Oklahoma continues to be a national leader, surpassing all other states, with 86% of 4-year-olds being served in state PreK, special education, or Head Start and 71% of children being served in state PreK alone. Florida and West Virginia follow, serving 78% of their 4-year-olds in one of these three programs. Table 1.2 presents state-by-state enrollment data on 3- and 4-year-olds in PreK, special education, and Head Start programs.

In addition to the publicly funded early childhood program already discussed, there are programs designed and administered at the local level, including local programs that make use of Title I and other federal funding streams. It is difficult to estimate the number of children enrolled because these locally developed programs are not required to report their preschool enrollment to state or federal agencies.

Quality Standards

When considering accessibility to an early education program, quality programs standards must also be addressed. The issue of accessibility is not just whether a child can attend an early education program, but instead whether a child has access to a quality program. Research on early educational programs has found links to quality regarding positive effects on children's development, academic success, and other outcomes that yield economic benefits to society. In establishing and expanding early childhood programs, decisions have to be made about program standards that facilitate the provision of high-quality learning environments to all children. However, often the standards that may lead to the highest quality environments are also the most costly to implement, such as teacher qualifications and teacher–child ratios. Other quality standards such as having comprehensive early learning standards, providing meals, and conducting health screenings are less costly to provide and are therefore more commonly implemented.

Early childhood programs vary greatly in their policies regarding quality standards, as well as how they are enforced and implemented. State-funded PreK programs each have their own policies at the state level and can therefore greatly differ. Head Start, on the other hand, follows guidelines and regulations developed at the federal level that must be implemented in all programs across the country, regardless of location. Last, child care programs have the most variability because regulations are determined at the local level and can be dependent on accreditation guidelines.

State-Funded PreK Programs

The National Institute for Early Education Research conducts an annual survey that tracks 10 quality standards in state-funded PreK programs. These 10 standards and the benchmarks for "adequate" performance on each are presented in Table 1.3 (Barnett et al., 2010). It is important to note that these quality standards and benchmarks are not judged to be of equal importance nor are the areas of focus all-inclusive. However, each of these standards is judged to contribute to the educational effectiveness of an early childhood program.

Teacher Qualifications

While findings may not be conclusive, a considerable body of research indicates that children whose lead teachers have bachelor's degrees and specializations in PreK education have better academic outcomes (Barnett, 2003; Burchinal, Cryer, Clifford, & Howes, 2002). Some researchers suggest that the evidence indicates teacher qualifications do not strongly contribute to preschool student learning for a variety of reasons (Early et al., 2005; Mashburn

TABLE 1.2. Enrollment of 3- and 4-Year-Olds in State PreK, Preschool Special Education, and Federal and State Head Start

| | PreK + PreK special education | | | | PreK + PreK special education + Head Start[a] | | | |
| | 3-year-olds | | 4-year-olds | | 3-year-olds | | 4-year-olds | |
State	Number enrolled	Percent of state population	Number enrolled	Percent of state population	Number enrolled	Percent of state population	Number enrolled	Percent of state population
Alabama	1,412	2.3%	6,006	9.7%	6,734	10.8%	14,696	23.7%
Alaska[b]	420	4.0%	856	8.3%	1,299	12.4%	2,037	19.9%
Arizona	3,520	3.4%	9,658	9.4%	8,456	8.2%	20,795	20.2%
Arkansas	6,184	15.3%	20,054	49.7%	9,847	24.5%	24,199	60.0%
California[b, c]	68,261	12.6%	115,708	21.5%	97,168	17.9%	168,949	31.4%
Colorado	7,266	10.0%	18,803	26.0%	10,359	14.3%	23,124	32.0%
Connecticut	5,232	12.3%	8,067	18.9%	7,854	18.4%	11,183	26.2%
Delaware[d]	620	5.2%	1,628	13.8%	1,299	10.9%	2,181	18.4%
Florida	7,511	3.2%	160,002	69.9%	19,575	8.5%	178,285	77.8%
Georgia	883	0.6%	83,991	56.5%	11,792	9.6%	93,212	62.7%
Hawaii	658	3.8%	850	5.1%	1,465	8.4%	2,424	14.5%
Idaho	918	3.7%	1,360	5.6%	1,656	6.7%	3,562	14.7%
Illinois	36,327	20.5%	60,653	34.4%	50,112	28.5%	77,920	44.5%
Indiana	4,677	5.2%	6,089	7.0%	8,671	9.7%	12,942	14.8%
Iowa	2,082	5.1%	16,932	42.9%	4,480	10.9%	20,145	51.1%
Kansas	2,493	6.2%	13,094	33.1%	4,840	12.0%	16,087	40.7%
Kentucky	5,557	9.7%	17,275	30.4%	10,457	20.1%	24,600	45.5%
Louisiana[b]	2,054	3.6%	22,224	35.2%	12,372	21.9%	30,135	47.8%
Maine[b]	969	6.8%	4,640	32.5%	1,843	12.4%	6,051	42.4%
Maryland	3,322	4.4%	30,352	40.8%	7,725	10.5%	34,361	46.2%
Massachusetts	6,359	8.2%	14,710	19.3%	10,506	13.6%	19,743	25.9%
Michigan	5,881	4.8%	26,436	21.5%	16,027	13.0%	44,085	35.4%
Minnesota[d]	3,973	5.5%	5,999	8.5%	7,342	10.2%	11,061	15.4%
Mississippi	1,767	4.1%	2,969	6.9%	11,619	26.9%	15,776	36.8%
Missouri	4,235	5.3%	8,380	10.7%	9,741	12.5%	15,851	20.2%
Montana	320	2.6%	599	5.0%	1,817	14.9%	2,624	22.1%
Nebraska	3,396	12.9%	7,726	29.6%	4,799	18.2%	9,960	38.2%
Nevada	1,910	4.7%	3,224	8.1%	3,030	7.4%	4,536	11.4%
New Hampshire	865	5.5%	1,120	7.1%	1,368	8.8%	1,812	11.4%
New Jersey	24,140	22.0%	35,916	32.3%	29,892	27.5%	43,108	38.8%
New Mexico	1,657	5.5%	7,240	24.0%	4,521	15.1%	11,282	37.4%
New York[b]	20,219	8.4%	121,266	51.0%	35,460	14.8%	141,413	59.4%
North Carolina	4,119	3.1%	35,633	27.3%	9,657	7.3%	45,367	34.8%
North Dakota	414	4.8%	573	7.1%	1,379	16.1%	1,899	23.7%
Ohio	7,019	4.8%	11,463	7.9%	20,293	13.7%	28,813	19.4%
Oklahoma	1,436	2.7%	37,356	70.7%	7,780	14.4%	44,370	85.8%
Oregon	4,478	9.1%	6,700	13.8%	6,741	13.7%	10,307	21.3%
Pennsylvania[b, d]	14,338	9.6%	33,985	23.0%	23,403	15.6%	47,284	32.0%
Rhode Island	685	5.7%	1,119	9.6%	1,190	9.9%	2,201	18.9%
South Carolina[b]	3,504	5.6%	23,985	39.8%	8,958	14.5%	29,232	48.6%
South Dakota	612	5.3%	921	8.0%	1,895	16.5%	2,815	24.5%
Tennessee	2,843	3.4%	20,264	24.6%	7,183	8.5%	29,052	35.3%
Texas	30,219	7.3%	199,108	48.4%	58,225	14.0%	233,343	56.7%

(cont.)

TABLE 1.2. *(cont.)*

| State | PreK + PreK special education | | | | PreK + PreK special education + Head Start[a] | | | |
| | 3-year-olds | | 4-year-olds | | 3-year-olds | | 4-year-olds | |
	Number enrolled	Percent of state population	Number enrolled	Percent of state population	Number enrolled	Percent of state population	Number enrolled	Percent of state population
Utah	2,123	3.9%	3,180	6.1%	3,370	6.5%	6,650	12.8%
Vermont	1,525	24.5%	3,957	61.1%	1,862	29.4%	4,457	68.8%
Virginia[b]	3,751	3.5%	19,345	18.5%	7,885	7.5%	25,859	24.4%
Washington	4,563	5.1%	11,121	12.8%	8,231	9.5%	17,665	20.3%
West Virginia	1,875	8.8%	11,889	57.1%	3,611	18.6%	15,780	78.4%
Wisconsin[d]	4,201	5.8%	39,030	54.8%	9,667	13.4%	44,527	62.5%
Wyoming	845	10.7%	1,269	16.7%	1,324	16.8%	1,976	26.0%
50 states	326,153	7.7%	1,294,725	31.0%	600,774	14.2%	1,682,414	40.3%

Note. Data are derived from Barnett et al. (2010).
[a]This figure includes federally funded and state funded Head Start enrollment.
[b]These states serve special education children in their state PreK programs but were not able to provide an unduplicated count for at least one of their programs. Estimations were based on the average percentage of special education students in state PreK and enrollment numbers for each program.
[c]In California, the increase in the number and percentage of 3- and 4-year-olds served reflects a change in the number of PreK programs included in the California State Preschool Program.
[d]These states serve special education children in their state-funded Head Start PreK programs but were not able to provide an unduplicated count for the Head Start program. Estimations were based on the percentage of children with individualized education plans as reported by the program information report.

et al., 2008). Others emphasize that only programs employing highly educated, well-paid teachers have been found to produce very large gains for students on broad measures of learning and development in randomized trails (Barnett, 2011). Furthermore, continued teacher professional development is crucial for success in the classroom. In order to require these high levels of teacher qualifications in public early childhood programs, states typically need to offer supports and incentives, such as higher salaries, scholarships, and mentors, to encourage teachers to obtain the necessary degrees. This often is costly, and states vary in the emphasis placed on teacher training and degrees as is evident in current policies for public PreK programs.

TABLE 1.3. Quality Standard Benchmarks

Early childhood program policy	Quality standard benchmark
Early learning standards	Comprehensive
Teacher degree	At least a BA
Teacher specialized training	Specializing in PreK
Assistant teacher degree	CDA or equivalent
Teacher inservice	At least 15 hours/year
Maximum class size	20 or lower
Staff–child ratio	1:10 or better
Screening/referral and support services	Vision, hearing, health; at least one support service
Meals	At least one/day
Monitoring	Site visits

Note. Benchmarks are derived from Barnett et al. (2010).

While most state-funded early education programs have policies requiring PreK specialization and professional development, many states still do not require teachers to have bachelor's degrees. Out of the 52 distinct state-funded PreK initiatives offered in 40 states during the 2009–2010 school year, only 27 initiatives required all lead teachers to have a bachelor's degree, while 45 required specialization in early childhood education. This difference reflects the fact that many states not requiring a bachelor's degree do require a Child Development Associate (CDA) credential, which is a specialization in early childhood education. Similar to requiring specialization in early childhood education, 44 state PreK initiatives required at least 15 hours per year of professional development.

Though state PreK programs continue to increase the quality requirements for lead teachers, very few have strict educational requirements for assistant teachers. Similar to research supporting the need for high-quality lead teachers, findings indicate a relationship between assistant teachers' qualifications and their effectiveness in the classroom (Barnett, 2003; Bowman et al., 2001; Burchinal et al., 2002). Therefore, it is troubling that there is a lack of emphasis on developing requirements for assistant teachers. During the 2009–2010 school year, only 16 state-funded PreK initiatives required assistant teachers to have at least a CDA or equivalent. This is an increase of only five initiatives since the 2001–2002 school year, two of which were new pilot PreK programs during the 2009–2010 school year, indicating virtually no progress in this area. As children enter state PreK programs, especially our most at-risk children, it is critical that all adults present in the classroom be prepared to serve these children.

When examining state-funded PreK programs in general, policies and program standards apply equally to all types of auspices in which the program is located. However, in some states there are key differences in educational requirements for teachers depending on location. Thirteen of the 40 states with state PreK programs have initiatives with different degree requirements for lead teachers in public settings compared to teachers in nonpublic settings. While the actual program requirements are different in each state, all 13 of these initiatives require lead teachers in public school settings to have a bachelor's degree (BA), whereas for nonpublic settings degree requirements range from no degree to an associate's degree (AA) or a CDA. On the other hand, 27 states have initiatives that apply the same degree requirements to lead teachers in both public and nonpublic settings, though some require a minimum of an AA for all teachers and others require a BA for all. Last, a few state-funded PreK initiatives currently operate only in public school settings, all of which require lead teachers to have a BA: the Kansas At-Risk program, the Louisiana 8(g) program, the Pennsylvania K4 and school-based PreK (SBPK) programs, and the South Carolina 4K program.

For assistant teachers, almost all state-funded PreK initiatives require the same educational requirements regardless of program location. There are district differences in requirements for assistant teachers in initiatives in only six states—Massachusetts, New York, Pennsylvania, Tennessee, Vermont, and Virginia.

Other Program Standards in State PreK

In addition to teacher qualifications, it is important to understand what other standards are in place to determine the quality of a program. As of the 2009–2010 school year, all but three state PreK initiatives had comprehensive early learning standards. Of those three without early learning standards, one of them, California, has already developed comprehensive standards, but they are not expected to be implemented until the 2010–2011 school year (Barnett et al., 2010). Early learning standards provide a framework for programs to ensure that all areas of children's learning and development are covered in the classrooms.

Comprehensive early learning standards should cover all areas as identified by the National Education Goals Panel (1991)—children's physical well-being and motor development, social–emotional development, approaches toward learning, language development, and cognition and general knowledge.

Other aspects of program structure such as class size and staff–child ratios are important determinants of program effectiveness. Research suggests that young children perform better in classrooms with fewer students and low staff–child ratios, especially disadvantaged children (Barnett, 1998; Bowman et al., 2001; Frede, 1998). Smaller classes with more adults present allow for more teacher–child interactions and individualized attention, resulting in both short- and long-term academic and social–emotional gains. It is recommended that to enhance program quality and, in turn, effectiveness, early childhood programs should have a maximum class size of 20, with at least two adults in the classroom, creating a 1:10 staff–child ratio or lower. For the 2009–2010 school year, 44 out of 52 state-funded PreK initiatives met both of these benchmarks. Texas and Pennsylvania's K4 programs continue to be the only state-funded PreK initiatives not to set limits on maximum class size and staff–child ratios. While Maine, Ohio, and Wisconsin 4K programs do set limits, they do not meet the recommendations of 20 or fewer children and a 1:10 staff–child ratio.

Good nutrition and health are directly related to brain development and learning (Shonkoff & Phillips, 2000). Moreover, early detection of health, vision, and hearing problems can prevent or ameliorate later developmental and learning issues. It is recommended that early education programs serve at least one meal a day, and that meals follow U.S. Department of Agriculture Child and Adult Care Food Program nutritional guidelines. However, less than half (24 of 52) the state-funded PreK initiatives in the United States require at least one meal a day. More state PreK initiatives (36 of 52) require screenings and referrals for at least vision, hearing, and health for all children enrolled in these initiatives.

Last, while it is important to have policies in place regarding quality standards, it is critical to conduct monitoring activities aimed at ensuring that programs are correctly and successfully implementing these standards. Unfortunately, unless programs are held accountable, not all of them take the necessary steps to create high-quality learning environments for young children. The majority of PreK initiatives (40 of 52) conduct site visits along with other monitoring activities to ensure that all programs are meeting the required quality standards. However, 12 initiatives still do not have such statewide provisions in place to hold programs accountable for meeting the minimum required standards. Moreover, due to the current economic climate, some states are getting rid of this provision, as it is costly to monitor programs, even though it is necessary to ensure that program quality standards are being met.

Over the last decade, state PreK initiatives have worked to increase levels of quality in their classrooms through implementing new policies. However, as noted earlier, some states are making more progress and reaching their goals faster than others. It is important that all programs provide the necessary resources to create high-quality learning environments so that all young children have a chance to reach their potential.

Head Start Programs

As noted earlier, Head Start programs are required to follow Head Start Performance Guidelines for their program standards. States may, however, supplement Head Start funding to implement higher standards or otherwise enhance program quality in ways that can lead to differences across states in Head Start services. All programs offer health screenings and referrals, including, but not limited to, vision, hearing, height/weight, immunizations, developmental, and dental. Programs also require an array of services for families, as well as for English language learners. Class sizes are limited to 20 children, with a staff–child ratio of 1:10.

Teacher Qualifications

The recent Head Start Reauthorization Act of 2007 set forth new mandates on teacher qualifications, indicating an emphasis on improving program quality. The Act requires that by 2011, all lead teachers must have a minimum of an AA degree, and by 2013, 50% must have at least a BA degree. Currently lead teachers are required to only have a CDA. Moreover, by 2013, all assistant teachers must have a CDA or be enrolled in a program to obtain a CDA, AA, or BA within 2 years. During the 2009–2010 school year, approximately 53% of lead teachers had a BA degree or higher, 32% had an AA degree, 12% had a CDA, and 3% had no credentials (Office of Head Start Program Information Report [PIR], 2010). In comparison, only 7% of assistant teachers had a BA, 15% had an AA, and 33% had a CDA, while 45% had no credentials (Head Start PIR, 2010).

Child Care Programs

The quality of a child care program can be thought of in terms of two main domains, structural quality (i.e., program features such as class size and ratio, teacher education and training, curriculum and health standards) and process quality (i.e., classroom activities, interactions and relationships between peers and adults) (Karoly, Ghosh-Dastidar, Zellman, Perlman, & Fernyhough, 2008). Structural quality facilitates the latter, and is more easily regulated and monitored. In order to ensure that child care programs are high-quality, multiple strategies need to be used. Most child care centers across the United States are licensed and regulated by states in terms of health and safety standards, staff–child ratio and group size, and nutrition standards, which are monitored through annual inspections, though there is wide variation in the regulations states set (Kamerman & Gatenio-Gabel, 2007). Other strategies that can be used to promote quality can include the use of a quality rating system (QRS) or quality rating improvement system (QRIS), to evaluate program and child outcomes, set program standards, and engage in independent accreditation (Karoly, 2009). Nevertheless, there is inconsistent use of these strategies, and quality across child care programs is uneven, typically with the most disadvantaged children attending low-quality programs (Karoly, 2009).

It is estimated that across the United States there are over 120,000 child care centers. However, only about 10% are accredited (NACCRRA, 2010); that is, they have gone through a comprehensive review process and have been found to meet specific quality program standards. In addition, while the majority of states limit staff–child ratios to 1:10 for 3-year-olds, other states (e.g., New York and North Dakota) have ratios as low as 1:7. On the flip side, states such as Georgia, North Carolina, and Texas have staff–child ratios as high as 1:15 in classrooms for their 3-year-olds. There is more variation in staff–child ratios for 4-year-olds. Florida sets a standard of 1:20 in classrooms for 4-year-olds, while New York remains low with a 1:8 staff–child ratio (Barnett et al., 2010).

Child care group size also varies by state. For example, Georgia sets their maximum group size at 30 and 36 in classes for 3- and 4-year-olds, respectively, whereas Mississippi and North Dakota set their maximum group sizes at 14 and 20 in classes for 3- and 4-year-olds, respectively. In addition, 16 states do not regulate group size, instead only setting staff–child ratios for their programs (2008 Child Care Licensing Study; National Child Care Information and Technical Assistance Center [NCCIC], 2010).

Teacher Qualifications

In the majority of states, teachers are not required to have previous experience or training in working with young children in child care programs. Only eight states mandate some type of prior experience, typically only 1 year. In six states, teachers are not even required to complete an orientation before entering the classroom (NACCRRA, 2010). Furthermore, most states do not require teachers to have specialized training in early childhood education. Sixteen out of 50 states have created specialized training requirements for teachers. Of those 16 states, Hawaii, Illinois, Minnesota, New Jersey, and Vermont require teachers to have a CDA, while the other states vary in their requirements, although many require vocational child care training (2008 Child Care Licensing Study; NCCIC, 2010). This lack of requirements for teacher qualifications is particularly troublesome given the large number of 3- and 4-year-olds enrolled in child care programs across the country, many of which may vary greatly in quality.

Conclusions and Policy Issues

Early education programs, and state PreK initiatives in particular, have continued to expand significantly over the past two decades. However, due to the effects of the recession and budget cuts over the past few years, access to these initiatives is slowing down at a time when young children need early education programs the most. While state-funded PreK continues to grow, there is a noticeable decrease in annual enrollment growth, although it should be noted that there is tremendous variation from state to state with respect to availability and quality. Nevertheless, while some states (such as Oklahoma) have model programs that succeed in combining wide availability, high standards for quality, and adequate funding, these are the exception (Barnett et al., 2010). Therefore, it would be extremely beneficial if the federal government had a program to incentivize states to focus their efforts on creating high-quality, accessible preschool programs, so that all children have the opportunity to have a quality early education. Increased financial support from the federal government would allow states to reach a higher level of consistency in the early childhood programs that are offered.

Current federal policy relies on Head Start to provide a quality program for children in poverty and on the CCDF to support largely custodial child care. However, even with all of these programs, many children, especially those most at risk, are still unable to attend an early education program because there are not enough programs and slots available to meet the growing demand. Moreover, this demand will increase as the effects of the recession continue to take a toll on households and more children become eligible.

Even without increased financial support, there are steps that the federal government could take during the economic downturn to promote a better integrated system of early childhood education in the United States. One recommendation is to reduce the amount of Head Start regulations on programs, so that states are better able to align their Head Start and state PreK programs promoting stronger collaboration efforts. In addition, the federal government could help states merge state PreK and child care funds to raise the quality of the standards in the program, while reducing unnecessary duplication of services. Both of these recommendations should help to maximize efficient use of the state and federal early childhood systems that are already in place and reduce the current silo effect of early education programs in the United States.

Nevertheless, with more involvement from the federal government in early education and states growing their PreK programs, two key questions emerge and must be addressed.

First, how will collaboration and coordination be handled across existing programs that currently have distinct missions—including special education, Head Start, child care, and state PreK? As part of the most recent Head Start reauthorization, early learning councils are required to be developed to address these missions. It is crucial that all programs, including state PreK programs, fully participate in this process. State-funded PreK programs have the potential to serve as a hub for services across different types of auspices, as already seen in some states. Second, how will publicly funded early childhood programs fit into the new educational policy promoted by the Obama administration through its Race to the Top initiative that began providing new federal funds to state public school systems in 2010? In order to serve America's young children best by providing access to quality early education programs, it is imperative that these initiatives work together to ensure the success of every child's future.

References

Adams, G., Zaslow, M., & Tout, K. (2007, May). *Early care and education for children in low-income families: Patterns of use, quality, and potential policy implications, Paper 4.* Retrieved April 15, 2011, from *www.urban.org/uploadedpdf/411482_early_care.pdf.*

Barnett, W. S. (1998). Long-term effects on cognitive development and school success. In W. S. Barnett & S. S. Boocock (Eds.), *Early care and education for children in poverty: Promises, programs, and long-term results* (pp. 11–44). Albany: State University of New York Press.

Barnett, W. S. (2003). Better teachers, better preschools: Student achievement linked to teacher qualifications. *Preschool Policy Matters, 2.* New Brunswick, NJ: National Institute for Early Education Research, Rutgers University.

Barnett, W. S. (2008). *Preschool education and its lasting effects: Research and policy implications.* Boulder, CO/Tempe, AZ: Education and the Public Interest Center, University of Colorado, & Education Policy Research Unit, Arizona State University.

Barnett, W. S. (2011). Minimum requirements for preschool teacher educational qualifications. In E. Zigler, W. Gilliam, & W. S. Barnett (Eds.), *The pre-K debates: Current controversies and issues* (pp. 48–54). Baltimore: Brookes.

Barnett, W. S., & Ackerman, D. J. (2011). Public schools as the hub of a mixed delivery system of early care and education. In E. Zigler, W. Gilliam, & W. S. Barnett (Eds.), *The pre-K debates: Current controversies and issues* (pp. 126–130). Baltimore: Brookes.

Barnett, W. S., Epstein, D. J., Carolan, M. E., Fitzgerald, J., Ackerman, D. J., & Friedman, A. H. (2010). *The state of preschool 2010: State preschool yearbook.* New Brunswick, NJ: National Institute for Early Education Research, Rutgers University.

Barnett, W. S., Epstein, D. J., Friedman, A. H., Sansanelli, R. A., & Hustedt, J. T. (2009). *The state of preschool 2009: State preschool yearbook.* New Brunswick, NJ: National Institute for Early Education Research, Rutgers University.

Barnett, W. S., Friedman, A. H., Hustedt, J. T., & Stevenson Boyd, J. (2009). An overview of prekindergarten policy in the United States: Program governance, eligibility, standards, and finance. In R. C. Pianta & C. Howes (Eds.), *The promise of pre-K* (pp. 3–30). Baltimore: Brookes.

Barnett, W. S., Howes, C., & Jung, K. (2008). *California's state pre-K program: Quality and effects on children's learning* (Working paper). New Brunswick, NJ: National Institute for Early Education Research, Rutgers University.

Barnett, W. S., Hustedt, J. T., Robin, K. B., & Schulman, K. L. (2004). *The state of preschool: 2004 state preschool yearbook.* New Brunswick, NJ: National Institute for Early Education Research, Rutgers University.

Barnett, W. S., & Yarosz, D. J. (2007). *Who goes to preschool and why does it matter?* (Preschool Policy Brief, 15). New Brunswick, NJ: National Institute for Early Education Research, Rutgers University.

Berrueta-Clement, J. R., Schweinhart, L. J., Barnett, W. S., Epstein, A. S., & Weikart, D. P. (1984). *Changed lives: The effects of the Perry Preschool Program on youths through age 19.* Ypsilanti, MI: High/Scope Press.

Bowman, B. T., Donovan, M. S., & Burns, M. S. (Eds.). (2001). *Eager to learn: Educating our pre-schoolers.* Washington, DC: National Academy Press.

Burchinal, M. R., Cryer, D., Clifford, R. M., & Howes, C. (2002). Caregiver training and classroom quality in child care centers. *Applied Developmental Science, 6,* 2–11.

Camilli, G., Vargas, S., Ryan, S., & Barnett, W. S. (2010). Meta-analysis of the effects of early education interventions on cognitive and social development. *Teachers College Record, 112*(3), 579–620.

Cavalluzzo, L., Clinton, Y., Holian, L., Marr, L., & Taylor, L. (2009). *West Virginia's progress toward universal prekindergarten* (Issues & Answers Report, REL 2009–No. 070). Washington, DC: U.S. Department of Education, Institute of Education Sciences, National Center for Education Evaluation and Regional Assistance, Regional Educational Laboratory Appalachia.

Child Care Bureau, Administration for Children and Families, U.S. Department of Health and Human Services. (2009). FFY 2008 CCDF data tables (preliminary estimates). Retrieved April 15, 2011, from *www.acf.hhs.gov/programs/ccb/data/ ccdf_data/08acf800_preliminary/list.htm.*

Council of Chief State School Officers & National Governors Association. (n.d.). Common core state standards initiative. Retrieved January 30, 2010, from *www.corestandards.org.*

Data Accountability Center. (2010). Individuals with Disabilities Education Act (IDEA) data: Part B Child Count 2008. Retrieved January 12, 2010, from *www.ideadata.org/partbchildcount. asp.*

Deutsch, M., Deutsch, C. P., Jordan, T. J., & Grallow, R. (1983). The IDS program: An experiment in early and sustained enrichment. In Consortium for Longitudinal Studies (Ed.), *As the twig is bent: Lasting effects of preschool programs* (pp. 377–410). Hillsdale, NJ: Erlbaum.

Deutsch, M., Taleporos, E., & Victor, J. (1974). A brief synopsis of an initial enrichment program in early childhood. In S. Ryan (Ed.), *A report on longitudinal evaluations of preschool programs: Vol. 1. Longitudinal evaluations* (pp. 49–60). Washington, DC: Office of Child Development, U.S. Department of Health, Education, and Welfare.

Early, D., Barbarin, O., Bryant, D., Burchinal, M., Chang, F., Clifford, R., et al. (2005). *Prekinder-garten in eleven states: NCEDL's multi state study of pre-kindergarten and study of state wide early education programs (SWEEP)* (NCEDL Working Paper). Chapel Hill, NC: National Center for Early Development and Learning.

Frede, E. C. (1998). Preschool program quality in programs for children in poverty. In W. S. Barnett & S. S. Boocock (Eds.), *Early care and education for children in poverty* (pp. 77–98). Albany: State University of New York Press.

Gilliam W. S., & Zigler, E. F. (2000). A critical meta-analysis of all evaluations of state-funded preschool from 1977 to 1998: Implications for policy, service delivery and program evaluation. *Early Childhood Research Quarterly, 15,* 441–473.

Gilliam, W. S., & Zigler, E. F. (2004). *State efforts to evaluate the effects of prekindergarten: 1977 to 2003.* New Haven, CT: Yale University Child Study Center.

Gormley, W. T., Jr., Gayer, T., Phillips, D., & Dawson, B. (2005). The effects of universal pre-K on cognitive development. *Developmental Psychology, 41,* 872–884.

Gormley, W. T., Jr., Phillips, D., & Gayer, T. (2008). Preschool programs can boost school readiness. *Science, 320,* 1723–1724.

Hustedt, J. T., & Barnett, W. S. (in press). Private providers in state pre-K: Vital partners. *Young Children.*

Hustedt, J. T., Barnett, W. S., Jung, K., & Goetze, L. D. (2009). *The New Mexico PreK Evaluation: Results from the initial four years of a new state preschool initiative: Final report.* New Brunswick, NJ: National Institute for Early Education Research, Rutgers University.

Hustedt, J. T., Barnett, W. S., Jung, K., & Thomas, J. (2007). *The effects of the Arkansas Better Chance Program on young children's school readiness.* New Brunswick, NJ: National Institute for Early Education Research, Rutgers University.

Johnson, H., & Thomas, A. (2004). Professional capacity and organizational change as measures of educational effectiveness: Assessing the impact of postgraduate education in development policy and management. *Compare: A Journal of Comparative Education, 34*, 301–314.

Jordan, T. J., Grallow, R., Deutsch, M., & Deutsch, C. P. (1985). Long-term effects of early enrichment: A 20-year perspective on persistence and change. *American Journal of Community Psychology, 13*(4), 393–415.

Kamerman, S. B., & Gatenio-Gabel, S. (2007). Early childhood education and care in the United States: An overview of the current policy picture. *International Journal of Child Care and Education Policy, 1*(1), 23–34.

Karoly, Lynn A. (2009). Preschool adequacy and efficiency in California: Issues, policy options, and recommendations. Santa Monica, CA: RAND Corporation. Retrieved from *www.rand.org/pubs/monographs/MG889.*

Karoly, Lynn A., Ghosh-Dastidar, B., Zellman, G. L., Perlman, M., & Fernyhough, L. (2008). Prepared to learn: The nature and quality of early care and education for preschool-age children in California. Santa Monica, CA: RAND Corporation. Retrieved from *www.rand.org/pubs/technical_reports/TR539.*

Lipsey, M., Farran, D., Hofer, K., Bilbrey, C., & Dong, N. (2011). *The effects of the Tennessee Voluntary Pre-Kindergarten Program: Initial results.* Nashville, TN: Peabody Research Institute, Vanderbilt University.

Mashburn, A. J., Pianta, R. C., Hamre, B. K., Downer, J. T., Barbarin, O. A., Bryant, D., et al. (2008). Measures of classroom quality in prekindergarten and children's development of academic, language, and social skills. *Child Development, 79*(3), 732–749.

Mitchell, A. W. (2001). *Education for all young children: The role of states and the federal government in promoting prekindergarten and kindergarten.* (FCD Working paper). New York: Foundation for Child Development.

National Association of Child Care Resource and Referral Agencies (NACCRRA). (2010). Child care in America: 2010 state fact sheets. Retrieved from *www.naccrra.org/publications/naccrra-publications/publications/state_fact_bk_2010_all_070710.pdf.*

National Child Care Information and Technical Assistance Center (NCCIC) & the National Association for Regulatory Administration (NARA). (2010). The 2008 Child Care Licensing Study. Retrieved from *nccic.acf.hhs.gov/resource/state-requirements-child-staff-ratios-and-maximum-group-sizes-child-care-centers-2008.*

National Educational Goals Panel. (1991). *The Goal 1 Technical Planning Subgroup report on school readiness.* Washington, DC: Author.

Office of Head Program Information Report. (2010). Retrieved May 1, 2011, from *eclkc.ohs.acf.hhs.gov/PIR.*

Ranck, E. R. (2003). Access to programs. In D. Cryer & R. M. Clifford (Eds.), *Early childhood education and care in the USA* (pp. 47–63). Baltimore: Brookes.

Reynolds, A. J. (2000). *Success in early intervention: The Chicago Child–Parent Centers.* Lincoln: University of Nebraska Press.

Schweinhart, L. J., Barnes, H. V., & Weikart, D. P. (1993). *Significant benefits: The High/Scope Perry Preschool Study through age 27.* Ypsilanti, MI: High/Scope Press.

Schweinhart, L. J., Montie, J., Xiang, Z., Barnett, W. S., Belfield, C. R., & Nores, M. (2005). *Lifetime effects: The High/Scope Perry Preschool Study through age 40* (Monographs of the High/Scope Educational Research Foundation, No. 14). Ypsilanti, MI: High/Scope Press.

Shonkoff, J. P., & Phillips, D. A. (Eds.). (2000). *From neurons to neighborhoods: The science of early childhood development.* Washington, DC: National Academy Press.

Sussman, C., & Gillman, A. (2007). *Building early childhood facilities: What states can do to create supply and promote quality* (Preschool Policy Brief, No. 14). New Brunswick, NJ: National Institute for Early Education Research, Rutgers University.

U.S. Department of Education, National Center for Education Statistics (USDOE, NCES). (2006). Early Childhood Program Participation Survey of the National Household Education Surveys Program (ECPP-NHES:2005). Retrieved from *nces.ed.gov/programs/digest/d10/tables/dt10_053.asp.*

U.S. Department of Education, National Center for Education Statistics (USDOE, NCES). (2010a). Early Childhood Longitudinal Study, birth cohort 9-month–kindergarten restricted-use data file and electronic codebook. Retrieved from *nces.ed.gov/programs/digest/d10/tables/dt10_055.asp.*

U.S. Department of Education, National Center for Education Statistics (USDOE, NCES). (2010b). Preprimary Enrollment, 1965, 1970, and 1975. U.S. Department of Commerce, Census Bureau, Current Population Survey (CPS), October, 1980 through 2009. Retrieved from *nces.ed.gov/programs/digest/d10/tables/dt10_052.asp.*

Wong, V. C., Cook, T. D., Barnett, W. S., & Jung, K. (2008). An effectiveness-based evaluation of five state prekindergarten programs. *Journal of Policy Analysis and Management, 27*(1), 122–154.

CHAPTER 2

Early Childhood Care and Education

Enrollment Patterns and Expenditures

Clive R. Belfield

The policy agenda to improve early childhood care and education (ECCE) for families has gained significant momentum over the last decade. Research has demonstrated the substantial developmental benefits of early education (Barnett & Belfield, 2006). And public funding has increased: By 2005, annual state spending was $3.1 billion, up from $2.7 billion in 2001, with Head Start federal funding at $6.8 billion and funding for means-tested child care assistance through Temporary Assistance for Needy Families (TANF), Child Care and Development Fund (CCDF), and Social Services Block Grant (SSBG) a further $7.7 billion (Administration for Children and Families [ACF], 2008; Magnuson, Meyers, & Waldfogel, 2007, Table 1; National Institute of Early Education Research [NIEER], 2006). Families can now access child care and early education from a range of public and private agencies (see Besharov & Higney, 2006). At issue here is whether and how these changes have altered patterns of family behaviors in relation to ECCE.

There is a substantial literature on families' reliance on ECCE, as well as some research on expenditures on ECCE. (By ECCE we mean any form of nonfamily care for children before kindergarten.) The pattern is complex. For children ages 0–4, there are approximately equal proportions in the primary care of parents, relatives, nonrelatives, and organized facilities (Blau & Currie, 2006, Table 1). However, most families rely on multiple modes of care. And a binary classification masks significant variation in who pays for care, the price of care, and the amounts of care across family characteristics, such as marital status, maternal employment, and age of child (Rosenbaum & Ruhm, 2007).[1]

However, there has been limited research for the 2000s. Almost exclusively, studies of ECCE patterns use data from the (early) 1990s and rely on expenditures reported in the Survey of Income and Program Participation (SIPP). Clearly, these studies cannot identify the impacts of recent developments in policies, as noted earlier, or indeed any labor market or demographic changes. To address all these developments, we use data on early child care and education from the 1995, 2001, and 2005 National Household Education Surveys (NHES). These harmonized surveys collect detailed information on child care enrollment and expenditures across a national sample of families. They allow us to examine patterns of expenditure and behaviors for a recent cohort, and compare this cohort to earlier ones.

The structure of the chapter is as follows. First, we summarize the extensive evidence from existing literature and describe a model of how ECCE patterns and expenditures are determined. We then report descriptive information on the patterns of ECCE participation across the decade beginning in 1995. Next, we estimate the determinants of ECCE hours using a regression equation for each year: The goal is to see how the influences of various family characteristics have changed over the period. We then perform a parallel exercise for ECCE expenditures, documenting overall patterns, then estimating the determinants of expenditures over time. In the conclusion we discuss the policy implications of these results.

Patterns of ECCE Participation and Expenditures

Evidence from the 1990s

Participation and expenditure patterns of ECCE are complex. Families rely on multiple sources—relatives, nonrelatives, and centers—at a range of intensities and prices net of subsidies. Also, ECCE choices are sensitive to family characteristics.

ECCE participation is often modeled as a binary indicator as to the primary child care arrangements for the family with a focus on who enrolls in center-based care. Blau and Currie (2006) report that primary child care arrangements for children ages 0–4 are evenly split between parents, relatives, nonrelatives, and center-based care, and that this split has stayed approximately stable from 1985 to 1999. However, focusing just on 4-year-olds, Bainbridge, Meyers, Tanak, and Waldfogel (2005) document how preschool enrollment grew substantially between 1986 and 2000, from 23 to 65%. Many families rely on more than one form of ECCE: Binary indicators of primary arrangements may therefore mask changes in overall usage patterns as families substitute across the options.

Generally, preschool participation (to any extent) is a function of maternal education and employment (positively); the age of the child (positively); and region (depending on state policies for ECCE). There are also income effects—preschool is a normal good. But the effect of income is muted at lower levels because very low-income families are eligible for subsidies, so the income–enrollment relationship is approximately flat for families with below-median income. Moreover, these relationships seem to exhibit a high degree of stability, at least over the 1990s (Bainbridge et al., 2005; Barnett & Yarosz, 2007; Smith, 2000).

For ECCE expenditures, it is important to consider both absolute expenditures and prices per hour net of subsidies. Families make decisions about spending jointly with labor market decisions. In order to obtain sufficient hours of ECCE, working mothers may rely on multiple arrangements (or select lower quality, cheaper provision).[2] Some families are eligible for public subsidies (e.g., through Head Start), but these subsidies may be insufficient.[3] Some families rely on relatives, who typically provide ECCE at very low prices. But relatives typically cannot provide sufficient, regular care to allow mothers to work (and may expect reciprocal help). Other family members, including fathers, may reduce the need for ECCE, but many mothers are single and so have a greater need for ECCE as well as a lesser ability to afford it. Relatedly, as mothers participate more intensely in the labor market, they may face a rising price for child care to cover all the necessary working hours.

Binary indicators from the 1996–1999 SIPP for employed mothers show that 39% of families do not pay anything for care for their children ages 0–5 (Rosenbaum & Ruhm, 2007). Using earlier SIPP data (1992–1993), Connelly and Kimmel (2003a, Table 1) report that 47% of single mothers do not pay for care for children ages 0–5. However, it is unclear what the fraction is for all families, or how it might have changed since.[4] Connelly and Kimmel (2003a) report weekly expenditures in 1992–1993 for children ages 0–5 by single mothers at $58 (only for those reporting any expenditures); Blau and Currie (2006) calculate it at $76 by 1999 (including children up to age 14). For total expenditures on ECCE, Rosenbaum and Ruhm (2007) estimate these as 4.9% of aftertax income for families with children ages 0–6. However, the distribution is highly skewed: for 1 in 10 families, ECCE expenditures are over 15% of net income. These data, too, are from the 1990s.[5] In addition, expenditures vary across type of ECCE: Connelly and Kimmel (2003b, Table 4) report that weekly expenditures are highest for center-based care, then home-based care (care by nonrelatives), and lowest for care by relatives. The same ranking is found by Rosenbaum and Ruhm but with larger gaps: Expenditures per hour are five times higher for nonrelative care and seven times higher for center-based care than for care by relatives. Both studies find differential effects by marital status. Connelly and Kimmel (2003b) also report differences across employment status.

There is evidence that public subsidies do influence participation without increasing family spending on ECCE: Using Current Population Survey (CPS) data, Magnuson and colleagues (2007) describe increases in access concomitant with a substantial, real increase in ECCE subsidies and Head Start funding per child.[6] They conclude that "nearly half of the increase in enrollment in formal child care among low-income children may be attributed to the expansions in public funding" (p. 49). However, and perhaps unsurprisingly, Magnuson and colleagues find that the subsidy effect is strongest for 3- and 4-year-olds. Indeed, these subsidies may substantially offset any income effects on ECCE spending: Rosenbaum and Ruhm (2007) report no impact on the share of income spent on ECCE by level of socioeconomic status.

Hence, a full understanding of ECCE choices by families should consider all the types of ECCE on which families might rely; account for private expenditures net of subsidies by families, both in total and per hour of ECCE; and recognize that the patterns are likely to differ according to the age of the child (his or her school class), the mother's employment status, and her marital status. Potentially, many of these elements may have changed over the last decade.

The ECCE Market

To formalize our explanations of ECCE participation and expenditures, we depict ECCE as a set of interlinked markets. Based on their characteristics and their work decisions, families express a demand for ECCE for each year prior to kindergarten. Separate demand functions are likely across the types of ECCE supplied in the market. A range of suppliers of ECCE is available: These include private centers and nonrelatives who charge fees, relatives who require nominal payments, and government providers who charge no fees. These demand and supply functions may serve to illuminate changes in the quantities and prices of ECCE over time.

We might anticipate considerable changes in the demands of families for preschool over the last decade. First, if mothers' labor market participation rates have changed, either because of the economic boom of the late 1990s or welfare reforms implemented in the mid-1990s, the demand for all forms of ECCE will increase. (A similar effect would occur if the number of single mothers has increased.) Other demand-side changes may shift families toward particular forms of ECCE. Increasingly, preschool is becoming recognized as an important opportunity for children to develop and learn academic and social skills; this might motivate families to invest more and at an earlier age in center-based ECCE, at the expense of nonrelative and even relative care.

On the supply side, the salient change is, of course, the expansion of state programs for 3- and 4-year-olds. We can interpret this as a reduction in the demand for any form of paid care. A final consideration is whether the technology of center-based ECCE has changed: Because it is a labor-intensive service industry with some regulatory burdens, center-based preschool programs may suffer from Baumol's "cost disease" (i.e., greater than average inflation). This might lead families to rely more on unregulated care, either by relatives or nonrelatives.

With this market framework, we can predict ECCE patterns—both quantities and prices—when there is an expansion of government-subsidized programs for children just before they enter kindergarten (the 4-year-old class). In programs for the 4-year-old class, which are now relatively more expensive, the dominant effect is likely to be the inward shift in demand for any form of private ECCE. This should reduce the quantity and price of private and nonrelative ECCE, with reductions differing by the extent to which public ECCE is an effective substitute for the other types of ECCE at this age, and the extent to which families in private ECCE are eligible for public ECCE. However, the expansion of programs for the 4-year-old class is likely to affect the ECCE markets for younger children: Supply will shift toward the 4-year-old class and so raise the prices families face for ECCE for younger children. If this shift is coupled with an increase in the demand for ECCE for younger children, the price change will be magnified.

Data

We investigated these predictions using data from the NHES of 1995, 2001, and 2005. These surveys include an ECCE module, with an extensive set of questions on early education enrollments, hours, and expenditures across all types of child care, as well as information on the care providers (see Hagedorn, Montaquilla, Carver, & O'Donnell, 2006). We note that the questions are about expenditures, from which we calculate hourly prices; strictly, therefore, these are not the costs of ECCE (i.e., they are not quality-adjusted).[7] The surveys in these 3 years are harmonized, such that identical questions are asked in each year (the first ECCE module, in 1991, followed a different format). Thus, we obtain standardized information such that comparisons across the decade can be made.[8]

We restrict our analysis to families that report on all children who are too young to be eligible for kindergarten. To better model ECCE choices, we use information on the date of birth of the child to assign him or her by age cohort: infants/toddlers (ages 0–2); 2-year-old class (becoming 3 during the academic year); 3-year-old class (becoming 4 during the academic year); and 4-year-old class (becoming 5 during the academic year).[9] This is consistent with the composition of school cohorts, so the 4-year-olds are those children who will enter kindergarten in the following year (not those born in the same calendar year). An additional advantage of the NHES is that it collects information on child care enrollments and expenditures for all families, regardless of mother's employment status (in contrast to the SIPP). Our sample sizes are 7,490 children in the 1995 survey, 6,472 in the 2001 survey, and 6,895 in the 2005 survey. Sampling weights are available for the 2001 and 2005 data to ensure the surveys are nationally representative.[10]

As a preliminary exercise, we can look directly at the characteristics of the mothers. If these are unchanged, it is unlikely that ECCE expenditures will change much also. Table 2.1 shows in the top two rows the similarity in the samples of mothers across the surveys in terms of marital status and educational activity. Across the ages and years, 73–78% of the sample is married; as well, the percentages reporting education (being in school or college) as their main activity are stable at 11–13%. Also, as shown in the final row of Table 2.1, the number of hours worked by mothers does not appear to show any trend (ranging from

TABLE 2.1. Maternal Characteristics in 1995, 2001, and 2005

	Ages 0–2			2-year-old class			3-year-old class			4-year-old class		
	1995	2001	2005	1995	2001	2005	1995	2001	2005	1995	2001	2005
Married	73	75	77	73	74	78	73	75	77	74	75	77
In school (main activity)	12	11	13	11	12	12	11	12	11	11	12	13
Works full time	37	42	40	42	46	41	42	44	40	42	47	40
Works part time	14	15	15	13	13	16	14	17	17	16	15	19
Hours of work	18	19	19	19	21	19	20	21	19	20	21	20
N	3,141	2,720	2,994	1,470	1,372	1,338	1,549	1,345	1,522	1,566	1,241	1,275

Note. Data from NHES ECPP 1995/2001/2005 survey. Classes are based on respondents turning 3/4/5 during academic year (September–August). Hours of work includes all mothers, regardless of work status.

18–21 hours per week). Table 2.1 does show a slight increase in maternal employment over the decade. But there is no clear trend: Maternal labor market participation rates appear highest in 2001, and the changes in employment are partially driven by changes in the fraction of mothers who are working part time. These results raise the possibility that changes in the ECCE market are unlikely to have generated a large change in maternal employment elasticities.

Patterns of ECCE Participation, 1995–2005

ECCE Types and Total Hours of Participation

We begin by reporting basic patterns of ECCE participation. Table 2.2 reports simple measures of access/participation in ECCE and hours of reliance on each type across the decade.

The top panel of Table 2.2 shows ECCE by type and uses mutually exclusive categories for each child: A child is designated as in formal center-based ECCE regardless of duration; for those with no formal care, children are designated as either relative or nonrelative care if the hours per week exceed 20; otherwise, they are in full family care. For very young children (age 0–2), the proportion of families who use no formal ECCE is close to 90% and has fallen only slightly over the decade from 1995 to 2005. For each year that children age this proportion falls by 15–20 percentage points; by the time children are in the 4-year-old class, only 26–35% use no formal ECCE. This age-related trend is mirrored in participation rates in private fee-paying ECCE centers: As the children age, this proportion increases by 10 percentage points per annum. Other types are only relevant for the older groups: Head Start serves 8% of the 3-year-old class and 12–16% of the 4-year-old class; and special education ECCE is a small fraction of all ECCE, rising approximately 1 percentage point for each year of age.

Notably, there is one significant change in the patterns of ECCE across the decade: Whereas in 1995 only 9% of families with children in the 4-year-old class had access to subsidized ECCE (in either a public or private center), by 2005 the proportion doubled to 18%. This movement appears across the decade, with the proportion at the midpoint year (2001) approximately halfway. This result is consistent with a large expansion in public funding for ECCE immediately before entry to kindergarten. However, this increase in subsidized center-based care has not come from substitution away from private ECCE: instead it is almost completely reflected in declining rates of families with no formal ECCE (down from

TABLE 2.2. Provision of ECCE in 1995, 2001, and 2005

Per child	Ages 0–2			2-year-old class			3-year-old class			4-year-old class		
	1995	2001	2005	1995	2001	2005	1995	2001	2005	1995	2001	2005
ECCE type (%)												
Head Start	0	1	1	1	3	2	8	8	8	16	12	13
Special education	0	0	0	1	0	1	2	2	3	2	3	5
Private–fees	8	10	13	20	23	27	34	35	34	38	40	38
Private–no fee	2	2	2	3	3	3	4	4	3	3	4	6
Public	0	0	0	0	1	0	2	4	3	6	12	12
Family	60	62	61	48	48	50	34	34	36	29	20	21
Relative care	16	13	12	13	13	9	9	8	9	5	6	4
Nonrelative care	14	12	10	14	10	8	8	7	4	5	3	2
Hours per week												
Relatives	7	6	6	6	6	4	6	5	5	4	6	5
Nonrelatives	6	5	4	6	5	4	4	4	3	3	3	2
Center-based	3	4	5	7	8	9	10	12	11	11	16	16
Total	16	15	15	19	19	18	19	21	19	19	24	23
N	3,141	2,720	2,994	1,470	1,372	1,338	1,549	1,345	1,522	1,566	1,241	1,275

Note. Data from NHES ECPP 1995/2001/2005 survey. Survey sampling weights FEWT applied; 1995 survey unweighted. Head Start identified as Head Start attendance with no stated fee and no family expenditure above $3,000pa (2005 dollars). Special education identified as any center-based care, any identified disability (not "other") or any disability provision from state or local government and no family expenditure above $3,000pa (2005 dollars). Private identified as any center-based care not in a public school; fee or no fee based on statement about how much household pays. Public identified as the residual of Head Start, special education, and private, assuming positive answer to "any center-based care." Hours rounded to nearest unit.

35 to 26%). This might lead us to expect big changes in labor market participation rates for mothers who previously were taking care of the children, even as the evidence from Table 2.1 shows that this change in labor market participation is not easily discernible. Interestingly, families with younger children (age 0–2 and the 2-year-old class) have increased their enrollments in center-based ECCE by 5–7 percentage points over the decade. Two explanations are plausible. One is that these families may be "closing the gap" such that more children have no period in which they are only in the care of the immediate family; mothers may be less likely to exit the labor market to care for their young children if they sense that they will be quickly rejoining it when subsidized preschool becomes available (see rates in Attanasio, Low, & Sanchez-Marcos, 2008). Alternatively, families may be able to afford care in 1 year if they are not having to pay for it in subsequent years.

For families with no formal ECCE, there is also a change over the decade. For children younger than the 4-year-old class, the proportion relying on only family care is constant across the decade per child's age. Congruent with the shift noted earlier, however, family care fell significantly for the 4-year-old class, from 29% in 1995 to 21% by 2005. The proportions relying on relatives or nonrelatives have also fallen over the decade but mainly for the younger age groups. In 1995, for example, 30% of families with infants relied on relatives or nonrelatives; by 2005, it was 22%. By the time children are in the 4-year-old class, the rate of care by relatives or nonrelatives is sufficiently small that further declines over time will be hard to detect. Thus, the expansion of public programs for the 4-year-old class appears to have benefited families who previously only used family care.

The bottom panel of Table 2.2 shows hours per week of ECCE. The first point to note is that families rely on care by relatives, by nonrelatives, and at centers. For infants, especially, average hours of care are spread almost evenly across the three types. Thus, it is an oversimplification to designate families into one mode of care. Families average 4–6 hours of care from relatives and 2–6 hours of care from nonrelatives per week. These numbers are very stable across the decade and decline only slightly as children age. In contrast, hours in center-based ECCE rise significantly with the age of the child, from 3–5 hours for very young children to 11–16 hours for the 4-year-old class. By the time of the 4-year-old class, care by relatives and nonrelatives is a relatively trivial proportion of all ECCE. Commensurate with the data from the top panel of Table 2.2, the main trend over the decade is the extra 4–5 hours per family per week of publicly funded, center-based ECCE for the 4-year-old class of 2005 over the 4-year-old class of 1995.

We can compare these figures to those reported by families in the Early Childhood Longitudinal Study—Birth Cohort (ECLS-B), which surveyed children born in 2001 when they were age 9 months, then age 2 years, and then during their preschool year (4-year-old class). The initial sample was 10,700 children, with an oversample of low birthweight children. This survey is considerably more detailed than the NHES rounds but it does include similarly structured questions with regard to ECCE. Importantly, it is approximately contemporaneous with the NHES 2005 cohort.

Broadly, the frequencies in the ECLS-B correspond to those in the NHES 2005.[11] At age 2, 51% of the ECLS-B cohort are in family care, which tallies almost exactly with the 50% reported in NHES 2005 in Table 2.2. However, the ECLS-B shows larger proportions of 2-year-olds in relative or nonrelative care—and so fewer in center-based care—than the NHES does. In the preschool year [4-year-old class], the ECLS-B [NHES 2005] yields a distribution of: 13% [13%] in Head Start; 19% [21%] in family care; 46% [61%] in center-based care; and 20% [6%] in relative/nonrelative care.

Patterns by Marital Status and Maternal Employment

To show more clearly the patterns by family characteristics, we report ECCE patterns by child's age, marital status (single mother or married), and maternal employment status (not employed, part time, and full time). Figure 2.1 shows hours of ECCE per week. Two features stand out. First, total hours of ECCE are clearly determined: They are higher for single parents, higher as mothers participate in the labor market, and higher as children age. Second, almost all families rely on some ECCE: Even the least reliant grouping, not employed married mothers, averages approximately 8 hours of ECCE per week.

Figures 2.2–2.4 show weekly hours of ECCE for each of the three modes. Figure 2.2 (ECCE hours by relatives) shows a clear pattern with respect to marital status and maternal employment. As mothers work, they require more care from relatives. Single mothers rely more on care by relatives. Also, families with very young children rely on relatives more (beyond age 2 there is no age-of-child effect on care by relatives). There is no clear trend over the decade in reliance on care by relatives.

Figure 2.3 shows disaggregated patterns of care by nonrelatives. Maternal employment leads to more hours of ECCE by nonrelatives. But there is no clear difference across marital status. For married mothers, however, there is a shift away from care by nonrelatives as children age. At the same time, the ECCE–employment gradient is much steeper for married mothers. Again, there appears to be no clear pattern over time.

Finally, Figure 2.4 shows hours of care in ECCE centers. These histograms mirror very closely those for total hours of ECCE: There are strong differences across employment status and children's ages. However, the gap between married families and single mothers is smaller than the overall gap in Figure 2.1. There is some indication that ECCE hours are more "regularized" by 2005, with more uniform "steps" according to age of child and with the pattern for single mothers more closely resembling that of married mothers. This trend might be consistent with a public system that now makes access more directly a function of need.

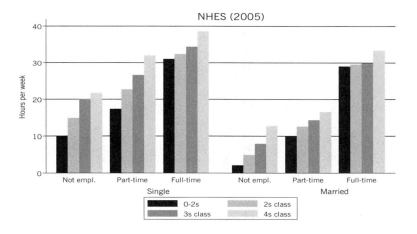

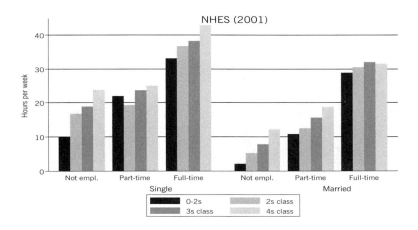

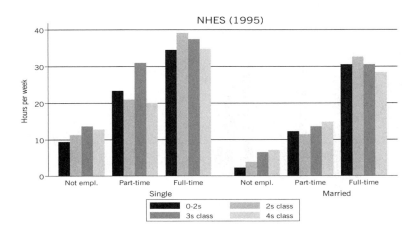

FIGURE 2.1. Hours of ECCE per week.

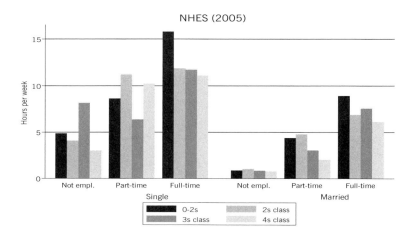

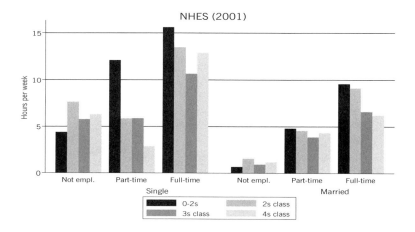

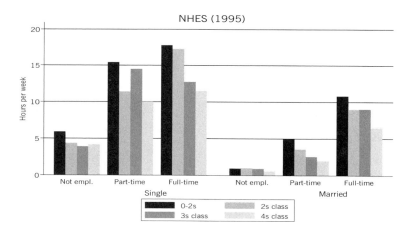

FIGURE 2.2. Hours of ECCE by relatives per week.

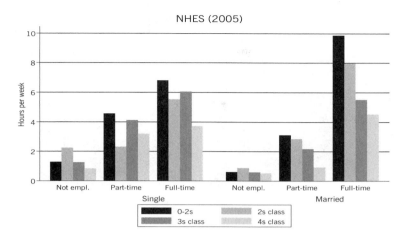

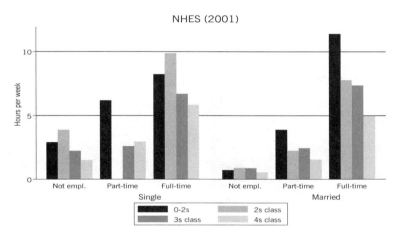

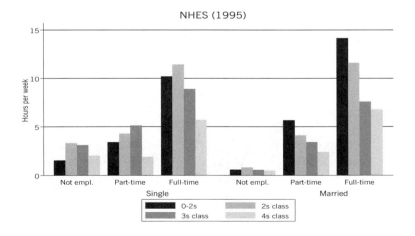

FIGURE 2.3. Hours of care by nonrelatives per week.

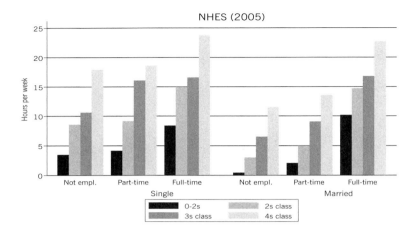

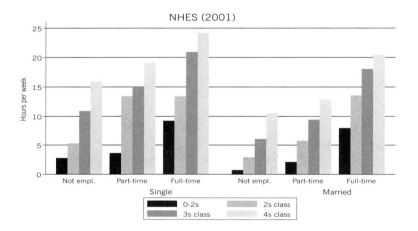

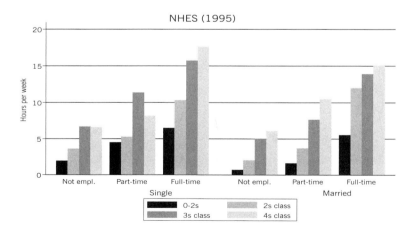

FIGURE 2.4. Hours of care in centers per week.

Modeling ECCE Hours

Given the multiple influences on ECCE hours, we now estimate the determinants of hours in a series of regression equations. These equations are estimated separately for each year and correspond approximately to the models reported by Rosenbaum and Ruhm (2007, Table 5).[12] We include all families in the equations, even those who report no ECCE in each year. However, to better identify any trends in reliance on center-based ECCE we estimate a model to determine total ECCE hours and center-based ECCE hours separately.

The results are given in Table 2.3. Total hours of ECCE are higher with household income, if the mother is working, if the child is African American, if the mother is college educated or in school, if the mother is not married, and if the child is older. The effect of maternal employment is particularly large, perhaps suggesting that small policy changes in available hours are unlikely to influence female labor supply. Household size effects are also evident. But there is no effect of family income until the fifth quintile of families.

There has been a change over the decade in how important some of these factors are (but not for household income or marital status). Notably, the age-of-child gradient is steeper. In 1995, there was no difference in hours of ECCE for any age except infants, who received approximately 2 fewer hours of ECCE per week (controlling for other variables). By 2001 and extending to 2005, there was a clear age-of-child gradient: Compared to infants, each year of child age is associated with an additional 2 hours of ECCE. Thus, controlling for family characteristics, there has been a shift toward formal ECCE over the decade. But this shift appears to be heavily concentrated in the additional hours of the 4-year-old class children. Similarly, the maternal education gradient is steeper: Having a mother who is more highly educated means more hours in ECCE in 2005 than it did in 1995. Possibly, these families are better able to access publicly provided ECCE programs or they have higher incomes.

A similar pattern is evident when we estimate the determinants of center-based hours. The same influences on total hours are found for determining center-based hours as for the total hours of ECCE. Notably, the age-of-child gradient has steepened over time; this causes the steepening total hours gradient.[13] Also, in 1995, the highest two quintiles rely on center-based care more; by 2005, an income effect is only evident for the top quintile. Last, African American families are, by 2005, more likely to use ECCE centers.

ECCE Expenditures, 1995–2005

Basic Patterns of ECCE Expenditures

We now consider private expenditures on ECCE, both in total and per hour. Table 2.4 describes overall patterns of private expenditure on ECCE across the decade. All figures are reported in 2005 dollars.

The first indicator is the percentage of families making non-zero payments for ECCE. This fraction rises from one-third for very young children to over one-half by the 3-year-old and 4-year-old classes. Notably, 31% of families are paying something for ECCE for their infants, even as 84% are classified as not having any formal ECCE (Table 2.2). This affirms that the mutually exclusive classification system may not be informative: Many parents rely on the informal ECCE market and so use multiple types of ECCE. Over the decade, however, the fraction spending any amount is almost entirely unchanged.

The second panel shows annual private spending, both for all families and for families with non-zero spending. Both rows show an increase in spending over the decade. But this is driven by higher spending by families who spend non-zero amounts: By 2005, families who

TABLE 2.3. Total Hours of ECCE and Center–Based Hours of ECCE in 1995, 2001, and 2005

	Total hours			Center-based hours		
	1995	2001	2005	1995	2001	2005
Household income: Quintile 2	−0.0878	1.277	−0.755	0.603	0.396	−0.528
	(0.585)	(0.815)	(0.887)	(0.439)	(0.582)	(0.706)
Household income: Quintile 3	0.0398	1.166	−0.0788	0.684	0.339	−0.728
	(0.548)	(0.840)	(0.994)	(0.423)	(0.670)	(0.829)
Household income: Quintile 4	1.862***	2.395***	2.821***	1.963***	0.822	1.239
	(0.578)	(0.855)	(0.961)	(0.453)	(0.694)	(0.828)
Household income: Quintile 5	4.519***	5.692***	5.144***	3.718***	4.086***	3.341***
	(0.715)	(0.852)	(1.028)	(0.610)	(0.731)	(0.911)
Household size (age < 7)	−0.948***	−0.758*	−1.389***	−0.929***	−0.719**	−0.715**
	(0.212)	(0.426)	(0.418)	(0.150)	(0.301)	(0.296)
Household size (age > 6)	0.544***	−0.933***	−0.457*	−0.593***	−0.882***	−0.815***
	(0.195)	(0.254)	(0.273)	(0.135)	(0.186)	(0.203)
Mother works full time	25.44***	23.22***	21.26***	6.387***	7.026***	8.338***
	(0.400)	(0.549)	(0.618)	(0.318)	(0.417)	(0.501)
Mother works part time	9.015***	7.417***	6.321***	1.359***	1.444***	1.077**
	(0.459)	(0.578)	(0.695)	(0.322)	(0.420)	(0.491)
Black	1.805***	4.279***	3.803***	0.736	3.291***	3.653***
	(0.641)	(0.930)	(1.009)	(0.544)	(0.777)	(0.864)
Hispanic	−0.802*	0.520	0.662	−1.854***	−0.827	−0.397
	(0.476)	(0.624)	(0.661)	(0.378)	(0.510)	(0.558)
Other race	1.038	2.621**	−0.482	−0.0442	0.881	1.117
	(0.782)	(1.109)	(1.327)	(0.647)	(0.870)	(1.036)
Mother: High school graduate	1.600***	0.447	2.970***	0.677*	−0.0195	0.855
	(0.498)	(0.802)	(0.905)	(0.346)	(0.611)	(0.655)
Mother: College degree +	3.936***	1.618*	5.235***	2.875***	1.348*	3.004***
	(0.648)	(0.913)	(1.022)	(0.505)	(0.774)	(0.776)
Mother mainly in school	8.592***	5.008***	5.541***	3.882***	4.083***	4.699***
	(0.594)	(0.789)	(0.840)	(0.504)	(0.684)	(0.761)
Mother married	−5.021***	−6.189***	−4.871***	−1.775***	−1.999***	−1.753***
	(0.495)	(0.699)	(0.807)	(0.418)	(0.559)	(0.663)
2-year-old class	2.294***	2.818***	2.285***	3.586***	3.707***	3.995***
	(0.454)	(0.634)	(0.675)	(0.388)	(0.519)	(0.609)
3-year-old class	2.787***	4.642***	4.311***	6.313***	7.424***	6.512***
	(0.462)	(0.610)	(0.714)	(0.411)	(0.530)	(0.563)
4-year-old class	2.081***	7.582***	6.593***	7.431***	11.03***	10.57***
	(0.486)	(0.709)	(0.722)	(0.393)	(0.549)	(0.603)
R^2	0.460	0.413	0.395	0.197	0.216	0.244
Observations	7,490	6,472	6,895	7,490	6,472	6,895

Note. Data from NHES ECPP 1995/2001/2005 survey. Equations estimated using ordinary least squares (OLS). Controls also included for mother's age (and square); sex of child (1); region (4); poverty rate of local area (1); and urban status (1). For 2001 data, household size age cutoff is 10, not 7. Standard errors in parentheses.
***$p < 0.01$; **$p < 0.05$; *$p < 0.1$.

were spending something were spending more than in 1995. However, much of the increase in private spending is for the youngest children. From 1995 to 2005, annual average real spending for non-zero spenders for young children ages 0–2 or in the 2-year-old class rose by 30% (from $3,790 to $4,780). For those in the 3-year-old class, it rose by 17% and for those in the 4-year-old class it rose by only 6% (from $3,300 to $3,530). Yet the evidence from Table 2.2 shows that the demand for ECCE has gone up at least as fast for the 4-year-old class as for infants. Thus, if demand changes are not explaining the differential trends in expenditure, supply changes must be. In fact the result is consistent with the existence of a set of ECCE markets, interlinked by age of child, where government intervention is influential. Government intervention in the form of expanded public preschool programs for 4-year-olds introduced in the early 2000s has made available a supply of subsidized ECCE. This subsidized system has partially offset the trend of rising private expenditures for the 4-year-old classes caused by rising demand. Also, we cannot rule out the other possibility: The expansion of preschool programs for the 4-year-old classes may have attracted away suppliers from the early years, increasing the wage that must be paid to obtain care for these young children.

The third panel of Table 2.4 shows expenditures per hour on average and for each of the three modes of care. As with earlier research, the cost per hour of care by relatives is much lower than that for ECCE by nonrelatives and in centers. Indeed, for the 4-year-old class, care by relatives (at $1.20 per hour) costs one-sixth of that for nonrelatives ($7.20 per hour). This ratio is close to that reported earlier from Rosenbaum and Ruhm (2007). However, the NHES data suggest that care by nonrelatives is the most expensive per hour, not center-based care.

Spending per hour has risen significantly over the decade; this explains the rise in total expenditures. Spending per hour on care by relatives does not show a clear trend over the decade, but it is a very small amount compared to the other options. Spending per hour on nonrelatives has increased significantly over the decade for all ages of children by, on average, $1.60 more per hour. Similarly, hourly spending on center-based care has risen over the decade except for the 4-year-old class (and very young infants). Again, this result is consistent with public programs holding the price of center-based ECCE down, at least when set against an overall trend of rising prices for care outside of family members.

Finally, the bottom panel of Table 2.4 shows the percentage of ECCE spending by type. This shows the importance of center-based care for infants. Even though few infants are enrolled, spending on center-based care is between 25 and 43% of total spending. By the 4-year-old class, center-based ECCE is up to three-quarters of all spending.

As with participation, it is also possible to cross-check these figures against those reported by families in the ECLS-B. Across the preschool ECLS-B sample, 49% of respondents report spending any amount on ECCE; this approximates the 53–55% in the NHES surveys. The average private spending per annum in the ECLS-B is very close to that derived from the NHES surveys. For the preschool ECLS-B sample, the average amount spent per family (including those who spend nothing) is $1,900, which is almost exactly the same as the $1,960 for the 2005 NHES 4-year-old class. Similarly, the average amount spent by families who spend any amount is $3,870 compared to the estimate of $3,530 reported in Table 2.4. Given differences in sampling frames, as well as slight differences in question format and ages of the children, these spending amounts are remarkably consistent.

Expenditures by Maternal Marital Status and Employment

As with patterns of ECCE, we anticipate significant differences in expenditures on ECCE according to family structure and maternal labor force participation. Figures 2.5–2.9 show

TABLE 2.4. Spending on ECCE in 1995, 2001, and 2005

Per child	Ages 0–2			2-year-old class			3-year-old class			4-year-old class		
	1995	2001	2005	1995	2001	2005	1995	2001	2005	1995	2001	2005
% spending > 0	33	35	31	44	45	43	53	55	53	53	59	55
Private spending per annum[a]												
All families	1,250	1,460	1,480	1,500	1,690	1,940	1,740	2,030	2,020	1,740	1,980	1,960
If spending > 0	3,790	4,240	4,780	3,380	3,780	4,470	3,310	3,670	3,840	3,300	3,380	3,530
Spending per hour (if > 0)[a]												
Average	4.20	5.30	5.40	4.00	4.20	5.00	3.60	4.00	4.60	3.60	3.60	3.70
Relatives	2.60	2.20	1.80	2.00	1.70	2.00	1.50	1.90	2.70	2.10	1.10	1.20
Nonrelatives	4.70	7.40	8.00	5.00	5.60	6.30	6.10	6.50	9.60	6.30	9.30	7.20
Center-based	4.70	4.80	4.70	4.20	5.00	5.30	3.60	3.80	4.80	3.60	3.50	3.90
% of ECCE spending on:												
Relatives	17	15	9	12	11	6	10	9	9	9	7	6
Nonrelatives	58	51	47	44	35	33	33	31	24	29	25	18
Center-based	25	35	43	44	54	61	57	59	67	62	68	76
N	3,141	2,720	2,994	1,470	1,372	1,338	1,549	1,345	1,522	1,566	1,241	1,275

Note. Data from NHES ECPP 1995/2001/2005 survey. Survey sampling weights FEWT applied; 1995 survey unweighted. Classes are based on respondents turning 3/4/5 during academic year (September–August).
[a]2005 dollars; spending in 1995/2001 adjusted to 2005 dollars using Consumer Price Index (CPI). Total spending rounded to nearest $10; spending per hour rounded to nearest $0.10.

patterns of spending disaggregated by child's age, by maternal marital status, and by maternal employment. These figures illustrate how the overall patterns in Table 2.4 may mask underlying influences.

Annual total spending (Figure 2.5) reflects the pattern of usage of ECCE described earlier: It is strongly and independently influenced by child's age, marital status, and maternal employment status. (The possible exception is that total expenditures by single mothers do not differ significantly if the mothers are either not employed or employed part time). Comparing full-time working mothers, there is a notable difference in annual expenditures by marital status: Married mothers spend significantly more on ECCE.

Looking across the decade, the big difference in total expenditures only appears for one group—married mothers who are employed full time. Regardless of the age of the child, these mothers are spending approximately $3,500 in 2005. Adjusted for inflation, no married mother working full time was spending in excess of $3,000 in 1995. In contrast, single mothers working full time were spending approximately $2,000 in 1995 and the same amount in 2005. Thus, additional spending on ECCE appears to be driven by married mothers who work full time.

Spending per hour is given in Figure 2.6. The numbers show how married families pay much more per hour for ECCE than single mothers do. It also shows that spending per hour is broadly flat across maternal employment status, at least for single mothers. No matter how many hours are required, expenditure per hour is flat (and low). For married mothers, a decreasing cost curve can be delineated: As the family demands more hours, the average amount paid per hour falls.

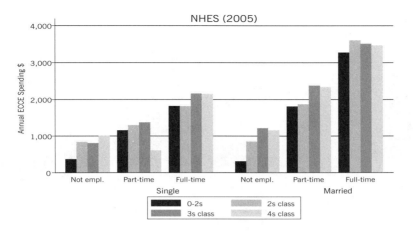

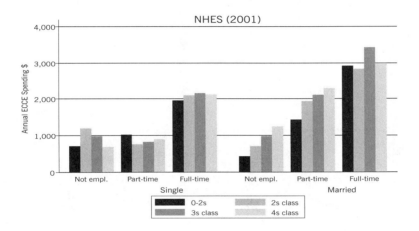

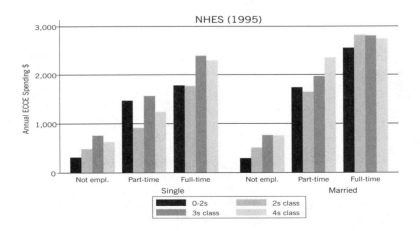

FIGURE 2.5. Annual total spending on ECCE.

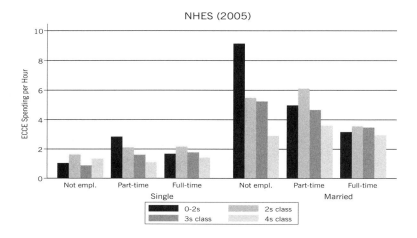

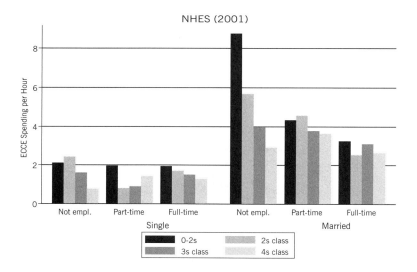

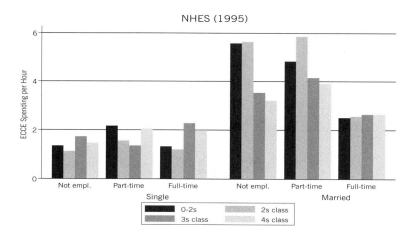

FIGURE 2.6. ECCE spending per hour.

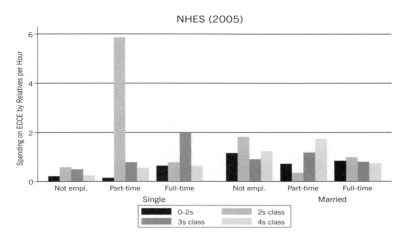

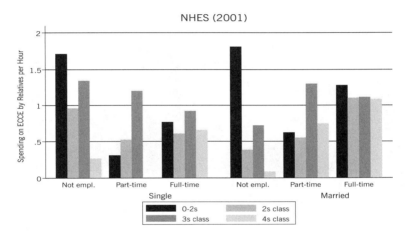

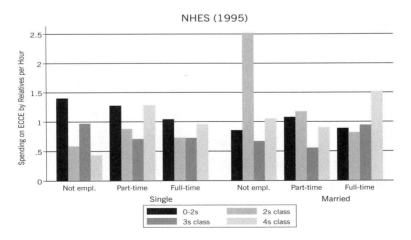

FIGURE 2.7. Spending per hour on care by relatives.

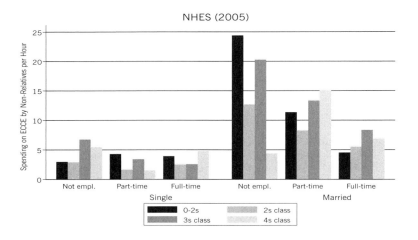

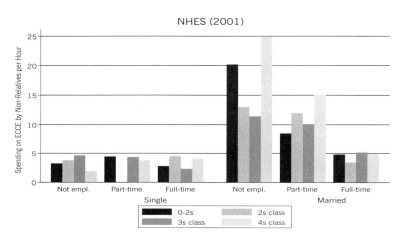

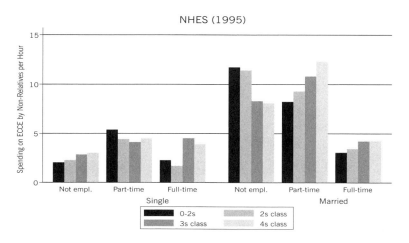

FIGURE 2.8. Spending per hour on care by nonrelatives.

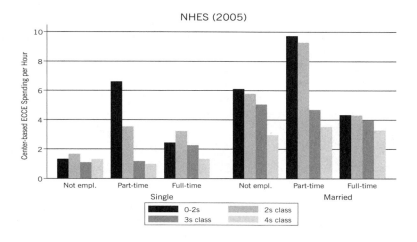

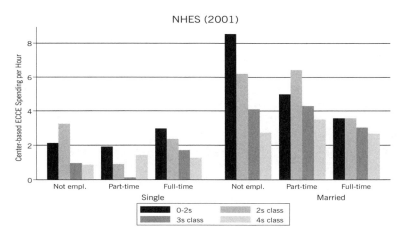

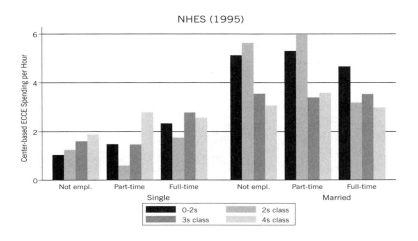

FIGURE 2.9. Spending per hour on center-based ECCE.

Figure 2.7 shows spending per hour on ECCE by relatives. No pattern is clear, not least because spending per hour is so low. Similarly, there is no clear pattern regarding spending per hour on nonrelatives, as depicted in Figure 2.8. For both types of care there do not appear to be any observable trends across the decade.

Finally, Figure 2.9 shows that spending per hour on center-based ECCE is higher for married families but shows no pattern with respect to maternal employment status. Looking across the decade, expenditures per hour by full-time working, married mothers are unchanged between 1995 and 2005. Thus, the higher spending of this group must be due to more hours of ECCE being required.

Determinants of ECCE Expenditures

To see how particular family circumstances influence ECCE expenditures, we estimate a series of regression equations for each year. These equations include the same set of variables as those in Table 2.3 and so correspond approximately to the specifications in Rosenbaum and Ruhm (2007, Table 5).[14] One important consideration is that our equations are for expenditures only on one child and not all children in the family.

The first equation in Table 2.5 predicts the share of household income spent on ECCE. There is a set of consistent effects on expenditure shares. Specifically, shares are lower if the household includes more persons over age 6 or if the family is Hispanic. Shares are higher if the mother works, either full or part time; if the mother is more highly educated; and if the mother is in school. The expenditure share grows progressively with the age of the child. But there is no effect of marital status on expenditure shares. Only some of our coefficients have the same sign as those from Rosenbaum and Ruhm (2007), notably, mother's education is positively associated with the fraction spent on ECCE. Other results are discrepant (e.g., marital status).[15]

Of most interest are the changes over the decade. In 1995, minority families spent a higher fraction of their income on ECCE than white families; by 2005 this differential was significantly diminished (with no difference for black families). In 1995, all working mothers and mothers in school spent significantly more of their income on ECCE; by 2005, these disparities were much smaller. Finally, Table 2.5 also shows that the burdens on families with children in the 3-year-old and 4-year-old classes were much lower by 2005.

Rosenbaum and Ruhm (2007) draw attention to the plight of families with the heaviest burden of payment for ECCE (i.e., those in the top 10% in terms of expenditure shares). We replicate their specification in Table 2.5 by estimating the determinants of being in this top decile of expenditure shares. We find that minority families are less likely to be in this category. However, we also find that these high spenders tend to be highly educated, with older children, and more likely to be married. These relationships suggest that the highest spenders are exercising choices for higher-quality ECCE rather than being overly burdened with "unaffordable" ECCE.

The probability that a family pays anything for ECCE is estimated in the first panel of Table 2.6. (As shown in Table 2.2, this divides the families into two approximately equal-size groups.) Spending is associated positively with household income, whether the mothers works (either full or part time) or is in school, and negatively with being married. There is also an age gradient: As children age, the probability of spending increases, but the gradient is quite flat for the 3-year-old and 4-year-old classes. Overall, the coefficients are consistent over the decade.

For the families that do spend any non-zero amount on ECCE, the second panel of Table 2.6 shows how this amount varies with family attributes.[16] This equation is a better measure of how family expenditure patterns for ECCE are determined, with 22–33% of the variance explained. There are strong effects of household income, maternal employment, and mother's education (college) on spending levels (the last of these is also reported by

TABLE 2.5. Share of Household Income Spent on ECCE in 1995, 2001, and 2005

	Expenditure share			Indicator for families at or above 90th percentile of expenditure share		
	1995	2001	2005	1995	2001	2005
Household size (ages < 7)	−0.0136*** (0.00349)	0.00343 (0.00391)	−0.00685 (0.00526)	−0.00672 (0.00413)	−0.0100* (0.00532)	−0.0170*** (0.00596)
Household size (ages < 6)	−0.0188*** (0.00303)	−0.0183*** (0.00257)	−0.0153*** (0.00332)	−0.0171*** (0.00357)	−0.0197*** (0.00373)	−0.0132*** (0.00406)
Mother works full time	0.183*** (0.00651)	0.153*** (0.00643)	0.191*** (0.00820)	0.148*** (0.00955)	0.117*** (0.0105)	0.118*** (0.0116)
Mother works part time	0.130*** (0.00822)	0.0859*** (0.00825)	0.0982*** (0.0105)	0.120*** (0.0165)	0.0816*** (0.0188)	0.0840*** (0.0185)
Black	−0.0152* (0.00874)	0.0210** (0.00864)	0.0261** (0.0106)	0.00381 (0.00936)	0.0100 (0.0127)	0.0204 (0.0141)
Hispanic	−0.0178** (0.00801)	−0.0458*** (0.00839)	−0.0371*** (0.0103)	−0.000943 (0.00898)	0.0210* (0.0113)	0.00690 (0.0112)
Other race	−0.0177 (0.0120)	−0.0252** (0.0115)	−0.0373** (0.0177)	−0.0229* (0.0117)	−0.00973 (0.0138)	−0.0169 (0.0177)
Mother: High school graduate	0.0293*** (0.00902)	−6.40e-05 (0.00893)	0.0800*** (0.0132)	−0.00341 (0.00946)	−0.0215* (0.0112)	0.0326** (0.0147)
Mother: College degree +	0.0660*** (0.0106)	0.0263** (0.0104)	0.106*** (0.0148)	0.000849 (0.0117)	−0.0247** (0.0118)	0.0479** (0.0196)
Mother mainly in school	0.0798*** (0.00813)	0.0366*** (0.00810)	0.0497*** (0.00994)	0.0794*** (0.0132)	0.0320** (0.0128)	0.0399*** (0.0154)
Mother married	−0.0482*** (0.00723)	−0.0577*** (0.00711)	−0.0655*** (0.00911)	−0.0996*** (0.0109)	−0.110*** (0.0136)	−0.0876*** (0.0151)
2-year-old class	0.0372*** (0.00750)	0.0165** (0.00716)	0.0482*** (0.00923)	0.0181* (0.00936)	0.00424 (0.00980)	0.0184 (0.0118)
3-year-old class	0.0536*** (0.00731)	0.0439*** (0.00723)	0.0792*** (0.00911)	0.0122 (0.00922)	0.0105 (0.0103)	0.0169 (0.0111)
4-year-old class	0.0548*** (0.00738)	0.0497*** (0.00748)	0.0766*** (0.00958)	0.0107 (0.00926)	0.0159 (0.0114)	0.000967 (0.0116)
Observations	7,490	6,472	6,895	7,490	6,472	6,895

Note. Data from NHES ECPP 1995/2001/2005 survey. Expenditure share equation estimated using Tobit function. Indicator equation estimated using probit equation; marginal effects reported. Controls also included for mother's age (and square); sex of child (1); region (4); poverty rate of local area (1); and urban status (1). For 2001 data, household size age cutoff is 10, not 7. Standard errors in parentheses.
***$p < 0.01$; **$p < 0.05$; *$p < 0.1$.

Rosenbaum & Ruhm, 2007). But there is no independent effect of marital status. The age gradients are also notable. Unlike for any spending, with which child age is positively associated, total spending shows a negative association with child age. As the child ages through the classes, the amount of spending goes down.

Many variables influence spending in a consistent way across the years 1995 to 2005. Specifically, the influences of household income, household size, maternal employment, and maternal schooling are unchanged between 1995 and 2005. (Racial characteristics and marital status are not influential in any year). However, a stronger age gradient has developed over the decade: As the child ages, the amount spent (by those who spend anything) falls. In 1995, a parent with a child in the 4-year-old class spent 17% less than a parent of an infant; by 2005, this spending gap was double, at 34%. Thus, the specifications in Table 2.6 support the notion that, controlling for a set of covariates, additional public funding for ECCE has alleviated spending pressure in the years immediately before kindergarten.

TABLE 2.6. Any ECCE Costs and Expenditure on ECCE in 1995, 2001, and 2005

	Any ECCE costs			Log expenditure (non-zero spending)		
	1995	2001	2005	1995	2001	2005
Household income: Quintile 2	0.0120 (0.0229)	0.0814*** (0.0276)	0.0141 (0.0333)	0.0967 (0.0616)	0.202*** (0.0746)	0.221*** (0.0784)
Household income: Quintile 3	0.0373* (0.0216)	0.114*** (0.0295)	0.101*** (0.0373)	0.182*** (0.0544)	0.339*** (0.0750)	0.297*** (0.0818)
Household income: Quintile 4	0.168*** (0.0222)	0.211*** (0.0291)	0.250*** (0.0358)	0.234*** (0.0564)	0.378*** (0.0744)	0.468*** (0.0787)
Household income: Quintile 5	0.294*** (0.0271)	0.341*** (0.0284)	0.358*** (0.0368)	0.584*** (0.0662)	0.682*** (0.0788)	0.696*** (0.0869)
Household size (ages < 7)	−0.0359*** (0.00825)	−0.0307** (0.0130)	−0.0282* (0.0168)	−0.0849*** (0.0193)	0.00734 (0.0276)	−0.0539** (0.0252)
Household size (ages > 6)	−0.0377*** (0.00750)	−0.0463*** (0.00827)	−0.0311** (0.0123)	0.00309 (0.0178)	−0.0470*** (0.0162)	−0.0554*** (0.0200)
Mother works full time	0.469*** (0.0126)	0.449*** (0.0154)	0.399*** (0.0187)	0.640*** (0.0404)	0.605*** (0.0566)	0.585*** (0.0473)
Mother works part time	0.323*** (0.0175)	0.251*** (0.0231)	0.182*** (0.0247)	0.328*** (0.0516)	0.274*** (0.0650)	0.342*** (0.0598)
Black	−0.0726*** (0.0210)	−0.0129 (0.0284)	0.00535 (0.0329)	−0.0219 (0.0422)	−0.0788 (0.0615)	0.0372 (0.0527)
Hispanic	−0.0734*** (0.0184)	−0.0516** (0.0219)	−0.0188 (0.0234)	0.0257 (0.0389)	0.0368 (0.0481)	0.0843 (0.0517)
Other race	−0.0953*** (0.0271)	−0.0768** (0.0315)	−0.107*** (0.0363)	−0.0538 (0.0605)	0.115* (0.0620)	0.153* (0.0901)
Mother: High school graduate	0.109*** (0.0202)	−0.00499 (0.0280)	0.0929*** (0.0354)	−0.0413 (0.0557)	−0.00371 (0.0759)	0.204* (0.111)
Mother: College degree +	0.221*** (0.0256)	0.0763** (0.0334)	0.163*** (0.0402)	0.199*** (0.0626)	0.211*** (0.0796)	0.414*** (0.118)
Mother mainly in school	0.218*** (0.0224)	0.118*** (0.0274)	0.113*** (0.0292)	0.152*** (0.0460)	0.0266 (0.0537)	0.144*** (0.0526)
Mother married	−0.0561*** (0.0187)	−0.0883*** (0.0234)	−0.0606** (0.0292)	−0.0154 (0.0399)	−0.0744 (0.0459)	0.0607 (0.0544)
2-year-old class	0.136*** (0.0180)	0.104*** (0.0218)	0.136*** (0.0257)	−0.0621* (0.0363)	−0.147*** (0.0466)	−0.108** (0.0455)
3-year-old class	0.217*** (0.0177)	0.232*** (0.0214)	0.232*** (0.0256)	−0.161*** (0.0365)	−0.239*** (0.0410)	−0.227*** (0.0427)
4-year-old class	0.215*** (0.0181)	0.268*** (0.0224)	0.231*** (0.0276)	−0.168*** (0.0375)	−0.290*** (0.0460)	−0.339*** (0.0460)
R^2				0.224	0.279	0.329
Observations	7,490	6,472	6,895	3,252	2,953	2,938

Note. Data from NHES ECPP 1995/2001/2005 survey. Any ECCE costs estimated using probit equation; marginal effects reported. Log expenditure equation estimated using OLS. Controls also included for mother's age (and square); sex of child (1); region (4); poverty rate of local area (1); and urban status (1). For 2001 data, household size age cutoff is 10, not 7. Standard errors in parentheses.
***$p < 0.01$; **$p < 0.05$; *$p < 0.1$.

Conclusions

ECCE provision for families is a patchwork of different modes of care at varying prices per hour. Families with young children therefore rely on many forms of ECCE depending on the ages of their children, their employment opportunities, and the composition of their household. As such, it is difficult to draw a single, consistent picture of ECCE.

Nevertheless, we can identify several important changes over the decade from 1995 to 2005. First, there has been a doubling of the percentage of 4-year-old class children in no-fee public or private ECCE; this has largely been a result of families who previously had no ECCE being able to access the formal ECCE market. For the average child in a 4-year-old class, though, this has only amounted to 4–5 extra hours of ECCE per week. Second, although the numbers of families paying for ECCE has remained stable over the decade, the amount spent by spenders has increased significantly. The largest increases in spending were for two subgroups: families with very young children and married mothers who worked full time. These two conclusions are consistent with a scenario in which an expanded preschool system has allowed families to access ECCE in the 4-year-old class without an undue financial burden. Potentially, the expanded preschool program has caused the increase in financial burden for families with younger children. Finally, additional spending on ECCE reflects both higher prices per hour and/or more hours of ECCE. Notably, married families spend significantly more per hour on ECCE than do single mothers, independent of the child's age and the mother's employment status.

These findings suggest several policy conclusions. First, public policy should recognize that many families rely on multiple modes of ECCE. This patchwork system is unlikely to be efficient or provide consistent quality for children; it is also likely to be precarious, as each mode of ECCE may be uncertain in duration, price, and availability. Given existing patterns of ECCE, it is almost impossible to conceive that care by relatives and nonrelatives can meet families' needs in any comprehensive way. Second, publicly funded ECCE does offset the need for private expenditures, but this is within the context of rising private expenditures. Third, the proportions of families with very young children in ECCE are growing. At issue is whether the existing supply of ECCE is appropriate for these children (see Loeb, Bridges, Bassok, Fuller, & Rumberger, 2007). More broadly, however, policy changes must address the growth in demand over the decade from 1995 to 2005 and whether this trend continues into the next decade.

Notes

1. In addition, there is a large, long-standing literature on how the costs of ECCE influence maternal labor supply (Heckman, 1974; Powell, 2002). Blau and Currie (2006, Table 5) summarize 20 estimates of the elasticity of maternal employment with respect to child care costs. The elasticities range between −0.02 and −3.60, with significant differences by marital status, employment intensity, family income, and type of care. Other research has examined the relationship between welfare status and child care availability (Barnett & Masse, 2007; Gennetian, Crosby, Huston, & Lowe, 2004). In a companion paper, we estimate maternal employment elasticities over time.

2. Using National Longitudinal Survey of Youth (NLSY) data from 1988 to 1992, Baum (2002) examines the path into work and reliance on ECCE for low-income mothers as their child age.

3. For mothers who are working, the subsidies almost certainly are incomplete: Preschools typically only run for 180 days per year and finish at 2:00–3:00 P.M. Also, many families are not eligible for subsidies until the child is 3 or 4 years old.

4. Blau and Currie (2006, Table 3B) show that the percentage with zero expenditure fell by one-third between 1985 and 1999. But their figures are for working mothers with children ages 0–14.

5. Blau and Currie (2006) show that the amount paid per week per family has fallen from $90 to $76 per week (1999$) even as that amount paid as percent of income has risen from 6.6 to 7.5% (Table 3B). Again, these figures are for employed mothers with children under age 14 as reported in the SIPP. Using Current Employment Statistics (CES) data, Kaushal, Gao, and Waldfogel (2007) find that the total expenditures of low-education single mothers were relatively unaffected by welfare reform in 1996. The composition of expenditures did shift toward work-related expenditures. However, the analysis pooled all children under age 18 within households, such that ECCE expenditures were only a very small fraction of total expenditures. Han and Waldfogel (2001) also use the SIPP to calculate prices per hour.

6. Cascio (2009) finds powerful effects from the introduction of publicly funded kindergarten, with families switching away from private programs toward public ones. Cascio also finds that the labor supply of single mothers with the youngest child age 5 was significantly affected (with married mothers largely unaffected).

7. Higher expenditures per hour may reflect higher quality child care, rather than higher cost. No independent information on the quality of the ECCE provision is available in NHES.

8. As noted above, these data are rarely used, although see Barnett and Yarosz (2004) and Swenson (2007) for descriptive analysis.

9. That is, a child who was born in November 2000 is in the 4-year-old class and a child born in February 2000 is in the 3-year-old class. Our use of this age classification may explain some of the discrepancies with earlier work. For example, Blau and Currie (2006, Table 1) report a significantly lower fraction of children aged 4 in center-based care compared to our estimate for the 4-year-old class.

10. Weights are not available for the 1995 NHES, but the weights do not materially affect the results for the later surveys. So we assume that the weights are not driving our results. Also, it is possible that parents are misreporting their ECCE and that this is especially prevalent among low-income or low-education parents. However, such misreporting may be offset by the format of the NHES questionnaires. Specifically, parents are asked several variations of the same question and are asked to give follow-up information on their responses; there are also questions that cross-check against initial questions.

11. Frequencies reported here for ECLS-B are unweighted. Full tabulations from the ECLS-B are available from the author.

12. The differences between our estimates and those of Rosenbaum and Ruhm (2007) are subtle—variables such as ages of children must be interpreted with caution. Also, we are able to include household income and labor market participation directly in our equations. Regional indicators are available in the NHES but they are too crude to be used as proxies for availability of ECCE.

13. Looking at total hours of ECCE, the impact of being employed full time is less in 2005 than in 1995 (21 vs. 25). But that result does not hold up for center-based ECCE hours: The impact of being employed full time is higher in 2005 than in 1995 (6 vs. 8).

14. For the expenditure share equations, we exclude family income.

15. This result may be explained by an association between number of children and household size.

16. As a robustness check, we also estimated these log expenditure equations with a Heckman selection equation for non-zero spending. The coefficients are not materially altered when a selection correction is implemented, so for ease of presentation we reported the uncorrected equation results here. (Details available from the author.)

References

Attanasio, O., Low, H., & Sanchez-Marcos, V. (2008). Explaining changes in female labor supply in a life-cycle model. *American Economic Review, 98*, 1517–1552.

Bainbridge, J., Meyers, M. K., Tanak, S., & Waldfogel, J. (2005). Who gets an early education?: Family income and the enrollment of three- to five year olds from 1968 to 2000. *Social Science Quarterly, 86*, 724–745.

Barnett, W. S., & Belfield, C. R. (2006). Early childhood development and social mobility. *Future of Children, 16*(2), 73–98.

Barnett, W. S., & Masse, L. (2007). Comparative benefit–cost analysis of the Abecedarian program and its policy implications. *Economics of Education Review, 26,* 113–125.

Barnett, W. S., & Yarosz, D. J. (2007). Who goes to preschool and why does it matter? (Preschool Policy Matters, No. 15). New Brunswick, NJ: National Institute for Early Education Research, Rutgers University. Retrieved April 29, 2011, from *nieer.org/resources/policybriefs/15.pdf.*

Baum, C. (2002). A dynamic analysis of the effect of child care costs on the work decisions of low-income mothers with infants. *Demography, 39,* 139–164.

Besharov, D., & Higney, C. A. (2006). *Federal and state child care expenditures (1997–2003): Rapid growth followed by steady spending* (Report to the U.S. Department of Health and Human Services, University of Maryland Working Paper). Baltimore: University of Maryland.

Blau, D., & Currie, J. (2006). Pre-school, day care, and after-school care: Who's minding the kids? In E. Hanushek & F. Welch (Eds.), *Handbook of the economics of education* (Vol. 2, pp. 1163–1278). Amsterdam: North-Holland.

Cascio, E. U. (2009). Maternal labor supply and the introduction of kindergartens into American public schools. *Journal of Human Resources, 44,* 140–170.

Connelly, R., & Kimmel, J. (2003a). The effect of child care costs on the employment and welfare recipiency of single mothers. *Southern Economic Journal, 69,* 498–519.

Connelly, R., & Kimmel, J. (2003b). Marital status and full-time/part-time work status in child care choices. *Applied Economics, 35,* 761–777.

Gennetian, L., Crosby, D. A., Huston, A. C., & Lowe, E. D. (2004). Can child care assistance in welfare and employment programs support the employment of low-income families? *Journal of Policy Analysis and Management, 23,* 723–743.

Hagedorn, M., Montaquilla, J., Carver, P., & O'Donnell, K. (2006). National Household Education Surveys Program of 2005. Washington, DC: U.S. Department of Education, NCES.

Han, W., & Waldfogel, J. (2001). Child care costs and women's employment: A comparison of single and married mothers with pre-school-aged children. *Social Science Quarterly, 82,* 552–567.

Heckman, J. J. (1974). Effects of child-care programs on women's work effort. *Journal of Political Economy, 82,* 136–163.

Kaushal, N., Gao, Q., & Waldfogel, J. (2007, September). Welfare reform and family expenditures: How are single mothers adapting to the new welfare and work regime? *Social Service Review,* pp. 369–396.

Loeb, S., Bridges, M., Bassok, D., Fuller, B., & Rumberger, R. (2007). How much is too much?: The influence of preschool centers on children's social and cognitive development. *Economics of Education Review, 26,* 52–66.

Magnuson, K. A., Meyers, M. K., & Waldfogel, J. (2007, March). Public funding and enrollment in formal child care in the 1990s. *Social Service Review,* pp. 47–83.

Powell, L. (2002). Joint labor supply and childcare choice decisions of married mothers. *Journal of Human Resources, 37,* 108–128.

Rosenbaum, D. T., & Ruhm, C. J. (2007). Family expenditures on child care. *B.E. Journal of Economic Analysis and Policy, 7.* Retrieved April 30, 2011, from *www.bepress.com/bejeap/vol7/iss1/art34.*

Smith, K. (2000). Who's minding the kids?: Child care arrangements, Fall 1995 (Current Population Reports, Series P70). Washington, DC: U.S. Department of Commerce.

Swenson, K. (2007). *Child care arrangements in urban and rural areas.* Washington, DC: U.S. Department of Health and Human Services.

CHAPTER 3

Investments in Early Education

Resources at the Federal and State Levels

Jason T. Hustedt, Allison H. Friedman, and W. Steven Barnett

M ost children in the United States now participate in an early childhood education program during the year immediately prior to kindergarten (Barnett & Yarosz, 2007), and some participate in programs with an educational focus for 2 or more years prior to kindergarten entry. Enrollment increases in early education programs over time have also been accompanied by substantial increases in government spending. In spite of overall patterns of growth in enrollment and spending, early childhood education in the United States is widely acknowledged as a "non-system" because different initiatives serve a variety of different objectives and are not well coordinated with each other (Barnett & Hustedt, 2011; Satkowski, 2009).

Early childhood initiatives that currently exist are usually supported by funding streams tied to specific goals at the federal, state, or local levels. It can be challenging to integrate funding streams when the goals of separate initiatives cannot be easily aligned. As a result, the types of programs available to children vary tremendously from state to state and even within individual communities. Some children have access to high-quality early childhood programs that are available at no cost to their families because they have low-income status or reside in specific states or towns. Other children from similar communities lack access to publicly funded programs and can only participate in the types of early childhood experiences that their parents have the resources to provide.

This chapter offers an overview of major federal and state investments in early childhood. Our emphasis is mainly on initiatives supported by public funds. Although private child care providers play an extremely important role in the overall landscape of early childhood education programs, they are a focus of this chapter only to the extent that they partner with publicly funded initiatives. Since federal and state initiatives typically aggregate financial data from program sites on an annual basis, in general this information is publicly available. However, private child care providers—including family day care homes, church-run programs, and even larger child care centers supported mostly by parent tuition—may have little reason to report financial information or lack a convenient means of doing so. As a result, it is much more difficult to estimate investments in early education that are supported through private funds.

We begin with an overview of the numerous federal investments in early education. Next, we summarize state-specific investments and provide detailed estimates of spending amounts needed for each state to provide high-quality preschool programs to 3- and 4-year-old children using different enrollment scenarios. A complementary fiscal analysis is provided for federal Head Start programs operating in each state. We conclude by discussing the current status of funding for early education and projections for the upcoming decade.

Federal Investments in Early Education

The federal government made its initial investment in large-scale early childhood programs in the mid-1960s by creating Project Head Start. Head Start grew out of the War on Poverty during the Johnson administration, and is a comprehensive child development program primarily designed to serve preschool-age children from low-income families. Head Start began as a summer program in 1965, and was implemented on a very broad scale from the outset. This new initiative received $96.4 million in federal funds to serve 561,000 children its first summer (U.S. Department of Health and Human Services, 2010b). By fiscal year 1966, more than 730,000 children were enrolled. While Head Start has remained a major force in early childhood education since its inception, this initial growth was not sustained. Though inflationary spending increases continued to take place almost every year, enrollment levels dropped below half a million children by 1970, then remained relatively stable for the next two decades before increasing again.

Federal efforts to make early childhood initiatives more broadly available in the early 1970s were unsuccessful. Both the U.S. House and Senate passed the Comprehensive Child Development Act of 1971, which would have provided voluntary early childhood care and education programs for children nationwide (Zigler, Gilliam, & Jones, 2006). However, this measure was ultimately vetoed by President Nixon. Its failure meant that the federal government's role in early childhood education would remain limited to targeted programs such as Head Start rather than focusing on initiatives available to all interested families. Ultimately, this more circumscribed involvement by the federal government allowed states to play leading roles in the establishment and delivery of preschool education programs (Barnett, Brown, Finn-Stevenson, & Henrich, 2007), much as states and localities have historically taken primary responsibility for the delivery of K–12 education.

In recent years, the role of the U.S. Congress has been to help establish policy priorities supporting the design and implementation of early childhood programs at the state and local levels (Kamerman & Gatenio-Gabel, 2007). Federal initiatives intended to meet specific goals (e.g., providing child care for working families) are then complemented by state or local initiatives that extend the federal goals or address additional, more localized goals. In this context, it is not surprising that a multitude of programs has emerged to support various aspects of early childhood care and education. In fact, there are dozens of initiatives just at the federal level (Barnett & Masse, 2003). However, Head Start is relatively unique among these initiatives because it is delivered as a consistent package of early childhood services that all grantees must offer. Most other federal initiatives are best viewed as funding streams that can be used to support a variety of different early childhood services in different locations.

Head Start

More than four decades after its inception, Head Start remains the federal government's major center-based early childhood initiative. During fiscal year 2010, Head Start received a federal appropriation of $7.2 billion to support an enrollment of just more than 900,000 children (U.S. Department of Health and Human Services, 2010b). These figures represent funding and enrollment for both Head Start and Early Head Start but do not reflect an additional $2.1 billion appropriated through the American Recovery and Reinvestment Act of 2009 (ARRA) and available for 2 years beginning with fiscal year 2009. As a comprehensive child development program, Head Start focuses on meeting young children's needs across several different developmental domains, offering educational, social, health, and nutritional services to enrolled children and their families. Head Start services are delivered through center-based programs, as well as visits to families' homes. In order to qualify for Head Start, families typically must have incomes below 100% of the federal poverty level (FPL). Up to 10% of Head Start slots are reserved for children with disabilities. Effective with the most recent Head Start reauthorization, eligibility criteria have been expanded to include children in families with incomes up to 130% FPL, provided that all children from needier families in a community have already been served (Improving Head Start for School Readiness Act, 2007).

Head Start is available to children from ages 3 to 5. However, a companion initiative, Early Head Start, was established in 1994 and extends Head Start services to infants and toddlers from birth to age 3, as well as to pregnant mothers. Federal funding for Early Head Start programs represented about 10% of the total Head Start budget in fiscal year 2009, allowing about 66,000 infants and toddlers to be served (U.S. Department of Health and Human Services, 2010b). Historically, the funding available for Head Start and Early Head Start programs has not been sufficient to serve all income-eligible families. Now that eligibility has been extended to families at slightly higher income levels, it is unlikely that demand for Head Start programs can be met without substantial additional funding commitments.

Title I

Title I funding through the Elementary and Secondary Education Act (ESEA, 1965; also currently known as No Child Left Behind) is another potential source of federal support for early childhood education programs. Title I funds are distributed to schools based on percentages of children who are economically disadvantaged, and can be used to offer a broad range of educational services that help to ensure children a high-quality education at every age level (Gayl, Young, & Patterson, 2010; Matthews & Ewen, 2010). Nearly all school districts in the United States and more than half of all individual public schools receive Title I funds, with the majority of the money distributed to elementary schools (Stullich, Eisner, & McCrary, 2007). Local education agencies have significant authority to make decisions about how Title I funds can be used in individual schools (Matthews & Ewen, 2010). Even though these funds have not been widely used in support of early childhood education programs, the broad availability and flexibility of Title I money make this an important potential source of funds for preschool education programs. Schools choosing to offer Title I preschool programs can make them available schoolwide if at least 40% of children in the school are in poverty; otherwise, preschool programs may be offered only to specific children who are considered academically at risk (Gayl et al., 2010). Currently, it is difficult to estimate precise amounts of Title I spending that are specific to preschool-age children.

In recent years, annual spending of $400 million may be a reasonable estimate. Temporary recovery funds through ARRA made an additional $13 billion in Title I funds available for children at all ages beginning in 2009 (Matthews & Ewen, 2010).

Early Childhood Special Education

The federal government also provides funding for special education and related services for young children through the Individuals with Disabilities Education Act (IDEA; 1997). Under IDEA Part B, Section 619, by the 1991–1992 school year, all states were required to offer a free and appropriate education for children ages 3 to 5 with disabilities. This age range includes children in preschool education programs, as well as those in kindergarten. In addition to the requirement to serve all children with disabilities, states may, at their discretion, enroll children who have developmental delays. Perhaps due to differences in how states define eligibility, there is great variability from state to state in the percentages of young children enrolled in federally funded preschool special education programs. Nationally, about 4% of 3-year-olds and 6% of 4-year-olds were enrolled in preschool special education during the 2009–2010 school year, sometimes in conjunction with their participation in a state preschool or Head Start program (Barnett et al., 2010). The percentages of 3-year-olds receiving special education services ranged from 2% in Alabama, Georgia, and Texas, to 11% in Wyoming, while percentages of 4-year-olds enrolled ranged from 3% in Texas to as high as 17% in Wyoming.

The total fiscal year 2010 appropriation for IDEA Part B special education programs across the United States was $374 million (U.S. Department of Education, 2010). This does not include additional ARRA funding of $400 million available beginning in fiscal year 2009 for 2 years. In general, federal funding for special education has not kept up with inflation or enrollment increases—as a result, state and local governments pay the vast majority of the costs associated with these services. While it is difficult to estimate the current cost of preschool special education, state and local spending may be as high as $6 billion annually, in addition to any federal spending (Barnett & Hustedt, 2011).

Special education services for infants and toddlers from birth through age 2 are provided through Part C of IDEA. In order to enroll in an IDEA Part C program, children must have developmental delays or conditions that put them at high risk of developmental delay. States have discretion to specify eligibility requirements for these early intervention programs, just as they do with programs for preschoolers under Part B. National Part C participation rates are somewhat lower than Part B participation rates, with about 2.4% of children under age 3 receiving Part C services in 2005 (Hebbeler et al., 2007). On average, children receive services that are fairly modest, with a median of 1.5 hours per week delivered in home or center-based settings. In fiscal year 2010, the federal appropriation for IDEA Part C programs across the United States was $439 million (U.S. Department of Education, 2010). An additional $500 million in ARRA funding was available for 2 years beginning in fiscal year 2009. Again, federal spending on early intervention programs is considerably less than the total cost. Estimated state and local spending for Part C early intervention programs is approximately $3 billion (Barnett & Hustedt, 2011).

Child Care Subsidies

Another important component of the overall federal investment in early education is the child care subsidy system, financed through the Child Care and Development Fund (CCDF, also referred to as the Child Care and Development Block Grant, or CCDBG) and Temporary

Assistance to Needy Families (TANF). Both initiatives target low-income families with children from birth to age 13. In order to qualify for CCDF, families must be employed and must fall below 85% of the median income level in their state. For goals related to early childhood, families qualify for TANF on the basis of being needy, using criteria specified at the state level (Greenberg & Schumacher, 2003). TANF and CCDF each provide states with base funding amounts, with additional federal funds provided to states if they also meet "maintenance of effort" (MOE) requirements by spending their own funds.

TANF was created as part of welfare reform in 1996 as a replacement for the Aid to Families with Dependent Children program, and is a more broad-based family support initiative than CCDF, which focuses specifically on child care. While, in some circumstances, states may use TANF money to fund child care or preschool education directly, states also may transfer as much as 30% of their annual TANF awards to CCDF. Because CCDF regulations apply to funds transferred from TANF, it is possible to use these TANF transfer funds to serve families who would not ordinarily qualify for child care under TANF requirements. CCDF money may be used to fund child care for age-eligible children through vouchers to parents or grants to child care providers (Greenberg & Schumacher, 2003).

Quality standards under CCDF are determined by the states, and are variable as a result. However, aggregated data provide general information about the types of services children receive. During fiscal year 2008, more than 1.6 million children were served by CCDF, and nearly two-thirds of them were age 5 or younger. The majority of children in CCDF (61%) attended child care centers, although 27% attended family child care homes. Vouchers were the method of payment for 88% of participating children. An estimated 22% of children participated in settings that were not required to follow licensing regulations (U.S. Department of Health and Human Services, 2010a). In recent years, CCDF has been flat funded at about $5 billion per year for children through age 13. Beyond this dedicated CCDF funding, $2 billion was transferred to CCDF from TANF in fiscal year 2007, and $1.2 billion in TANF funds were spent directly on child care. In addition to base CCDF appropriations and TANF transfers to CCDF, $2 billion in ARRA funding was available for 2 years beginning in fiscal year 2009 (Matthews, 2009). Although these spending figures are not specific to early childhood, it can be estimated that the majority of CCDF spending is directed toward children age 5 and younger, based on the proportion of children served in CCDF who are in this age group.

Other Federal Supports for Early Education

There are several other types of federal initiatives that support early childhood education and care more indirectly. Among these initiatives, the largest investment is made in the form of tax credits by the U.S. Treasury, through the Dependent Care Assistance Program (DCAP) and Child and Dependent Care Tax Credit (CDCTC). Both the DCAP and CDCTC can be used by families with children up to age 13 who participate in child care. Employees who enroll in the DCAP may set aside as much as $5,000 of their annual income to pay for child care. DCAP accounts are exempt from both federal and state taxes. The CDCTC provides parents with reimbursements up to $3,000 per child per year for a maximum of two children. This progressive tax credit has reimbursement rates starting at 35% of qualifying child care expenses for families with annual incomes below $15,000. The reimbursement rate then drops by 1% per $2,000 in income beyond the $15,000 threshold, with a minimum rate of 20% for families with incomes above $43,000. Unlike Head Start and child care subsidies, the CDCTC tends to benefit middle-income families, as lower-income families have fewer tax liabilities. President Obama has proposed changing the structure of the reimbursement rate so that it reaches 20% for families with incomes over $113,000. In recent years, about 6.5 million families have claimed the CDCTC on their tax returns, with an average claim of about $535 per year (Urban Institute & Brookings Institution, 2010). As with several of the spending figures discussed previously, this total includes reimbursements for qualifying children at all age ranges and is not specific to early childhood.

Another federal initiative that provides indirect support for early education is the Child and Adult Care Food Program (CACFP), one of several nutrition and food programs operated by the U.S. Department of Agriculture. The CACFP provides reimbursement for meals and snacks offered in participating child care centers and family day care homes, as well as afterschool programs, emergency shelters, and small numbers of adults in nonresidential daytime care. While the CACFP is open to most child care providers and to all children with eligible providers, individual children from low-income families and centers serving large proportions of such children are targeted for higher reimbursement rates. However, recent analyses suggest that many children from low-income families still lack access to the CACFP due to program eligibility requirements or nonparticipation by their child care centers (Gordon, Kaestner, Korenman, & Abner, 2010). In fiscal year 2009, the CACFP served about 1.9 billion meals, 97% of which were provided in child care and family day care settings. Total CACFP spending was $2.5 billion (Oliveira, 2010). A breakdown of costs by children's ages was not found, but if the percentage of costs were comparable to that for CCDF, a potentially conservative estimate is that children under age 5 would account for about $1.4 billion.

An additional federal investment in early childhood began in the form of a new home visiting initiative included in the Patient Protection and Affordable Care Act, as part of health care reform in 2010. The federal home visiting initiative helps states establish programs for pregnant women, infants, and young children through kindergarten, as well as parents of infants and young children. Programs employ staff such as nurses and social workers who visit participants' homes and provide training on areas including improved mother and child health and improved school readiness and achievement. The initial funding level for home visiting was $100 million in fiscal year 2010, with planned increases over the upcoming years totaling a $1.5 billion federal investment by the end of fiscal year 2014 (Pew Center on the States, 2010).

Finally, the Department of Defense (DOD) offers child care to children up to age 13 whose parents are in the military, as well as to children of military retirees and civilian employees. The DOD programs operate in child care centers and family day care homes, and are often promoted as a model for the private sector because of their high quality. However, only a small fraction of eligible children are served, with roughly 100,000 children under age 5 enrolled.

Summarizing Federal Investments in Early Education

The federal government makes a significant investment in initiatives that directly or indirectly support early childhood education. However, this broad array of initiatives serves disparate goals, and different initiatives are not currently well integrated. Federal early childhood initiatives range from comprehensive multigenerational programs for children and parents in poverty to relatively small tax credits that mostly benefit middle-income families. We estimate that the federal government invested a total of $19.6 billion on initiatives related to early childhood education during fiscal year 2010. Table 3.1 presents a summary of estimated spending amounts for the components of these initiatives most closely related to early childhood.

TABLE 3.1. Federal Early Education Programs Serving Children under Age 5 and Estimated Funding

Program	Federal agency responsible	Estimated funding, fiscal year 2010
Head Start (excluding Early Head Start)	Health and Human Services	$6.7 billion[a]
Early Head Start	Health and Human Services	$1.0 billion[a]
Title I preschool	Education	$500 million
Preschool special education (IDEA Part B, Sect. 619)	Education	$574 million[a]
Early intervention for infants and toddlers with disabilities (IDEA Part C)	Education	$632 million[a]
Child care subsidies (CCDF)	Health and Human Services	$5.7 billion[a]
Tax credits (CTCDC and DCAP)	Treasury	$2.2 billion (minimum estimate)
Child care food program	Agriculture	$1.4 billion
Home visiting	Health and Human Services	$100 million
DOD child care	Defense	$750 million
Total		$19.6 billion

Note. Sources for fiscal year 2010 funding amounts are as provided in the text.
[a]Includes additional American Recovery and Reinvestment Act Funds for fiscal year 2010.

State Investments in Early Education

As noted previously, several federal early childhood initiatives rely heavily on state matching funds to carry out their missions, especially those providing child care subsidies and special education. In addition to the federal programs available nationwide, state governments have made major investments in early childhood education by developing their own statewide programs. Conservatively, these investments totaled about $17 billion in additional funds for state-funded prekindergarten (PreK), preschool special education, early intervention, and child care subsidy programs. Of these four early childhood investment strategies, state PreK is the most substantial state and local investment in early childhood that does not supplement or mirror an existing federal program (Barnett & Hustedt, 2011; Hustedt & Barnett, 2011). The total state investment in PreK programs exceeded $5.4 billion in fiscal year 2010, not including additional federal or local funds contributed. Almost 1.3 million children were enrolled across 40 states, representing 4% of 3-year-olds and 27% of 4-year-olds in the United States (Barnett et al., 2010).

State PreK initiatives share a number of common features: They offer center-based education programs to children prior to kindergarten eligibility and are administered by state government agencies following common sets of statewide standards. Despite these key similarities, there are vast differences from state to state in terms of target audiences, availability, and quality standards. State PreK initiatives run the gamut from those available only to a subset of the most at-risk children to those available to nearly all children statewide. Quality standards are minimal in some states and very high in others (Barnett et al., 2010). These wide variations in the types of PreK programs are accompanied by wide variations in state spending levels for children, and even in the fiscal models used to generate state PreK funds.

Fiscal Approaches Used in State-Funded PreK

A common state PreK fiscal model involves simply allocating a set amount of the state budget toward PreK education. California, Illinois, and New York are among the states that make substantial annual investments in PreK using this type of model. However, because this approach does not provide a recurring funding stream specific to PreK, annual allocations may be subject to economic downturns and shifts in priorities. For example, in 1998, New York began offering a Universal Prekindergarten initiative intended to make voluntary PreK available to all 4-year-olds statewide. After more than a decade of uneven growth, this goal was revised under the administrations of previous Governors Spitzer and Paterson, and full phase-in of Universal Prekindergarten in New York is now set for the 2016–2017 school year (Barnett et al., 2010; Cochran, 2009; Winning Beginning New York, 2010). Instead of relying on the outcomes of the annual budget allocations process, other states have chosen to embed PreK funding within existing education funding formulas or to create new revenue streams supporting PreK.

School Funding Formulas

A number of states fund their public PreK initiatives in the same way they appropriate funds for K–12 education, using school funding formulas. Under this approach, PreK is viewed as a downward extension of public education programs for older children. Thus, PreK education is linked to states' dedicated K–12 funding streams, which have large constituencies and are relatively stable even in difficult budgetary times (Stone, 2008). A major advantage of using school funding formulas to support growing state PreK programs is that this approach triggers funding increases as enrollment rises. There is a clear path to expansion for growing state PreK programs because enrollment can increase as needed, without first securing larger state appropriations.

In recent years, two states have been especially successful in using school funding formulas to make PreK initiatives widely available: Oklahoma and West Virginia. Oklahoma established a PreK program for Head Start–eligible children and then in 1998 used the state school funding formula as a lever to move from this targeted program toward a voluntary PreK program available to all 4-year-olds. By 2010, 71% of Oklahoma's 4-year-olds were enrolled, using more than $167 million in state funds. West Virginia also started with a smaller state PreK program until 2002, when it began a 10-year phase-in toward offering PreK to all 4-year-olds in the state. By 2010, West Virginia had enrolled 55% of 4-year-olds statewide in its PreK initiative, using more than $76 million in state funds to support these children as well as 9% of the state's 3-year-olds. In both states, the use of the school funding formula made new PreK funds attractive to school districts with declining K–12 enrollments and revenues (Barnett et al., 2010; Cavalluzzo, Clinton, Holian, Marr, & Taylor, 2009; Gormley & Phillips, 2003). However, as school funding formulas provide additional funding for each additional child enrolled, this particularly flexible funding approach is by no means limited to states where K–12 enrollment is on the decline.

State Lotteries

A number of states in the southern United States use lottery proceeds to fund PreK (Mitchell, 2009). Georgia was the first state to do so, beginning in 1993. During its initial years,

Georgia's PreK program expanded quickly, although growth stalled in 2000 (Southern Education Foundation, 2008). More recently, North Carolina financed PreK expansion using a new education lottery. While the lottery permitted rapid initial growth, state administrators faced challenges to further expansion a few years after the lottery began (Cobb, 2009). Although lotteries offer an innovative source of PreK funds, this approach has important drawbacks. As illustrated in Georgia and North Carolina, while lottery funds allow for initial expansion of PreK initiatives, they may not permit ongoing growth. Also, most U.S. states have already instituted lotteries that have designated beneficiaries (Stone, 2008), perhaps limiting the availability of this option to states that do not have lotteries.

Other State PreK Finance Strategies

Other approaches to state PreK finance vary greatly in terms of long-term sustainability. Rhode Island's use of federal Title I funds to supplement a state allocation for its new demonstration PreK program (Barnett et al., 2010) is an especially promising model. As discussed earlier, Title I funds are accessed by the majority of public elementary schools across the United States. Although not yet widely utilized for preschool programs, Title I funds are available at a minimum to support PreK for children at risk—and, in high-poverty schools, for all preschool-age children. Because Title I funds are stable, widely accessible, and can be paired with funding for established state and local initiatives to expand PreK services, this is a promising funding strategy worth exploring in many states.

While a number of other creative funding approaches have been used by state PreK initiatives, these approaches are less promising as models for other states because they lack sustainability over time. Ohio and Louisiana have made significant investments of federal TANF funds in state PreK. This strategy was especially problematic in Ohio, where one of the state's PreK initiatives was ultimately eliminated because the state was no longer able to use TANF funds to support it. Kansas and other states have used money from the federal tobacco settlement to support PreK, but this source of revenue will eventually be phased out. Yet another finance approach for state PreK involves "sin taxes" on alcohol, tobacco, or gambling (Barnett et al., 2010; Mitchell, 2009). While sin taxes may produce an initial influx of revenue, they also provide a disincentive to continue engaging in the taxed activity, potentially reducing the availability of PreK revenues over time.

Spending Estimates in State-Funded PreK

In the following section, we provide spending data for each of the 40 states currently operating PreK initiatives, along with estimates of the additional investments needed to offer high-quality PreK programs in each state. These data are drawn from surveys of state administrators conducted by the National Institute for Early Education Research (NIEER; Barnett et al., 2010), and provide a vivid illustration of the differences across states in PreK spending. Across all U.S. states, the total investment in PreK education was $6.2 billion in fiscal year 2010. State funds represented more than $5.4 billion of this total, and federal and local funding streams comprised the remainder. When NIEER began collecting information on state PreK spending in fiscal year 2002, states spent $2.4 billion on their PreK initiatives, less than half their 2010 contributions before adjusting for inflation. After adjusting for inflation, the increase in state PreK spending since 2002 is approximately $1.7 billion in 2010 dollars.

Trends in Spending for State-Funded PreK

Growth in state PreK spending has been sustained for many years, but it slowed during the recent economic downturn. From fiscal year 2009 to fiscal year 2010, there was a $25 million decrease in state funding before adjusting for inflation, or a $30 million decrease in state funding after adjusting for inflation.[1] This decrease marks the first time since 2002 that total state PreK spending declined from the previous year. In comparison, between fiscal years 2008 and 2009, state spending increased by $446 million before adjusting for inflation, and between fiscal years 2007 and 2008 state spending increased by $871 million.

Although many states supplement the investment of state funds with federal and/or local dollars, not all states are able to report the amounts of these additional sources of funding. Between fiscal year 2009 and fiscal year 2010, *all reported spending on state PreK* (including state, as well as federal and local contributions, to the extent known) increased by $61 million before adjusting for inflation, or $55 million after adjusting for inflation. As the state component of this spending actually declined from the previous year, this reflects an approximately $75 million increase in federal and local contributions during fiscal year 2010, before adjusting for inflation. Whether this increase is due to actual growth in federal and local spending or better tracking and reporting of spending data is currently unknown.

While total spending amounts help quantify the overall magnitude of each state's investment, per-child spending amounts are also useful, as they take into account the number of children served in each state and thus provide a common metric for cross-state comparisons. During fiscal year 2010, states spent an average of $4,212 per child, a decrease of $114 per child after adjusting for inflation. Including all reported federal and local contributions, per-child spending was $4,831 in 2009–2010, a decrease from the previous year of $57 per child after adjusting for inflation. Given the general expectation that higher per-child spending levels permit higher-quality PreK programs, these decreases raise concerns. However, they are consistent with longer-term trends. Excluding any federal and local contributions, state per-child spending for PreK initiatives decreased during seven of the nine fiscal years for which we have data, from an inflation-adjusted starting point of $4,719 per child in fiscal year 2002.

As shown in Table 3.2, states vary widely in both their total and per-child contributions to state PreK. For example, in fiscal year 2010, California and Texas each spent more than $790 million on their state PreK initiatives. In comparison, both Alaska and Rhode Island spent less than $2 million, including state, federal, and local dollars. Arizona contributed less than half a million dollars to its state-funded PreK program in fiscal year 2010, and eliminated it for the following year. Ten states—Hawaii, Idaho, Indiana, Mississippi, Montana, New Hampshire, North Dakota, South Dakota, Utah, and Wyoming—did not invest in a state PreK initiative at all.

In terms of per-child spending amounts, New Jersey and Connecticut reported spending more than $10,000 per child enrolled. In New Jersey, state funds comprised the entire $11,578 per-child amount, whereas state funds in Connecticut amounted to $9,297 per child, and local funds covered the remainder. However, not all states funded their state PreK initiatives at these high levels. Five states—Arizona, Nebraska, Kansas, Florida, and Nevada—each spend less than $3,000 per child when including all reported funding.

Funding Needed for a High-Quality Program

Variations in per-child spending reflect differences in both states' abilities to fund high-quality programs and in what it costs to provide an education program in each individual

TABLE 3.2. Overview of State PreK Spending in Fiscal Year 2010

State	Total state PreK spending	State $ per child enrolled in preschool	Change in state spending from 2001–2002 to 2009–2010 (2010 dollars)	Change in state per-child spending from 2001–2002 to 2009–2010 (2010 dollars)	Total all reported spending on state PreK[a]	All reported $ per child enrolled in PreK[a]	Quality standards checklist sum (max. 10)
Alabama	$17,585,880	$4,544	$13,764,705	−$510	$17,585,880	$4,544	10
Alaska	$1,700,000	$8,500	$1,700,000	$8,500	$1,700,000	$8,500	10
Arizona	$494,687	$115	−$12,944,514	−$3,028	$4,719,770	$1,093	3
Arkansas	$111,000,000	$5,414	$102,159,847	$2,622	$171,973,151	$8,388	9
California	$796,320,978	$5,410	$30,587,624	−$560	$819,950,497	$5,571	4
Colorado	$45,246,206	$2,321	$23,794,526	$186	$73,252,182	$3,757	6
Connecticut	$83,301,663	$9,297	$28,358,482	$66	$93,547,400	$10,441	6
Delaware	$5,727,800	$6,795	−$166,724	−$198	$5,727,800	$6,795	8
Florida	$391,819,943	$2,514	$391,819,943	$2,514	$391,819,943	$2,514	3
Georgia	$341,470,922	$4,206	$15,535,022	−$917	$341,935,357	$4,212	9
Hawaii	$0	$0	$0	$0	$0	$0	No program
Idaho	$0	$0	$0	$0	$0	$0	No program
Illinois	$295,267,954	$3,371	$69,439,954	−$889	$295,267,954	$3,371	9
Indiana	$0	$0	$0	$0	$0	$0	No program
Iowa	$48,634,416	$3,092	$38,117,274	−$1,439	$58,964,238	$3,749	7.7
Kansas	$23,564,928	$2,490	$17,368,428	−$288	$23,564,928	$2,490	7.2
Kentucky	$69,187,530	$3,103	$5,432,430	−$502	$140,261,553	$6,290	9
Louisiana	$95,757,442	$4,706	$52,890,240	−$995	$97,757,442	$4,804	8.9
Maine	$6,443,614	$1,787	$3,414,214	−$316	$13,826,444	$3,835	5
Maryland	$107,619,200	$4,116	$62,112,757	$1,876	$252,179,702	$9,645	9
Massachusetts	$52,462,817	$3,895	−$80,279,983	−$2,750	$52,462,817	$3,895	6
Michigan	$87,128,000	$4,405	−$29,710,450	−$8	$87,128,000	$4,405	7
Minnesota	$13,682,074	$7,301	−$7,940,208	−$936	$13,682,074	$7,301	9
Mississippi	$0	$0	$0	$0	$0	$0	No program
Missouri	$13,215,441	$3,051	−$7,439,559	−$263	$13,215,441	$3,051	9
Montana	$0	$0	$0	$0	$0	$0	No program

State							
Nebraska	$11,922,004	$1,163	$10,131,904	-$2,566	$21,218,373	$2,070	6
Nevada	$3,338,875	$2,710	$1,584,107	-$1,352	$3,338,875	$2,710	7
New Hampshire	$0	$0	$0	$0	$0	$0	No program
New Jersey	$576,996,173	$11,578	$213,630,514	$1,668	$576,996,173	$11,578	8.8
New Mexico	$16,542,407	$3,412	$15,164,966	$1,772	$16,542,407	$3,412	8
New York	$378,107,213	$3,503	$32,342,513	-$1,484	$378,107,213	$3,503	6
North Carolina	$163,451,644	$5,239	$154,501,144	-$1,979	$244,085,049	$7,824	10
North Dakota	$0	$0	$0	$0	$0	$0	No program
Ohio	$22,243,792	$3,902	-$140,724,201	-$3,003	$22,243,792	$3,902	2
Oklahoma	$167,245,396	$4,477	$80,730,092	$1,134	$293,412,975	$7,853	9
Oregon	$54,897,578	$8,435	$16,892,378	-$1,842	$54,897,578	$8,435	8
Pennsylvania	$189,808,021	$5,924	$189,808,021[b]	$5,924[b]	$189,808,021	$5,924	5.3
Rhode Island	$700,000	$5,556	$700,000	$5,556	$1,150,000	$9,127	10
South Carolina	$35,513,846	$1,446	$3,052,156	-$583	$79,683,628	$3,244	6.2
South Dakota	$0	$0	$0	$0	$0	$0	No program
Tennessee	$81,657,785	$4,445	$61,002,785	-$3,216	$104,487,513	$5,688	9
Texas	$791,378,304	$3,686	$210,284,304	-$258	$791,378,304	$3,686	4
Utah	$0	$0	$0	$0	$0	$0	No program
Vermont	$17,790,714	$3,980	$15,890,454	$2,082	$17,790,714	$3,980	4
Virginia	$63,078,873	$4,221	$37,230,049	-$177	$93,974,015	$6,288	7
Washington	$54,716,348	$6,817	$19,883,186	$954	$54,716,348	$6,817	9
West Virginia	$76,617,241	$5,521	$46,507,621	$1,127	$130,640,325	$9,413	8
Wisconsin	$128,960,062	$3,282	$60,213,337	-$1,562	$197,960,062	$5,038	5.1
Wyoming	$0	$0	$0	$0	$0	$0	No program
50 states	$5,442,597,771	$4,212	$1,746,839,340	-$691	$6,242,953,938	$4,831	

[a]These figures reflect state, federal, and local dollars spent on state PreK initiatives. Some state PreK programs are entirely funded by state dollars. Others are funded by a combination of funding streams. However, not all states are able to report total amounts of local and federal dollars used to fund their PreK programs. Therefore, for some states, these numbers may be an underestimation of actual spending.

[b]While Pennsylvania did have a state-funded PreK program in fiscal year 2002, the state could not provide spending information for the program. As a result, the change calculated here is an overestimate reflecting an increase from zero in fiscal year 2002.

state. Gault, Mitchell, and Williams (2008) calculated annual per-child spending amounts necessary at different levels of quality, taking into account class sizes, teacher qualifications, and length of the school day. Based on these data from Gault and colleagues and additional adjustments for each state's cost of living (Taylor & Fowler, 2006), we estimated the per-child spending amounts needed in each state to support a high-quality part-day (3-hour) and/or full-day (6-hour) program. In states offering both part- and full-day programs, a weighted estimate was calculated, based on the proportion of children currently enrolled in part- and full-day programs. The unadjusted full-day estimate to fund a PreK program sufficiently is $7,454, and the unadjusted half-day estimate is $4,071 (Gault et al., 2008).

Also, for purposes of these estimates, *high-quality PreK programs* were defined as initiatives meeting the 10 research-based benchmarks on which NIEER has tracked state PreK policy since 2002. These benchmarks reflect minimum practices necessary for a high-quality preschool program. Four of the 10 quality standards concern teacher qualifications, two relate to structural elements of the classroom, and two more relate to comprehensive support services offered to enrolled children and families. The final benchmark elements relate to the availability of comprehensive early learning standards and a state monitoring process aimed at ensuring that all state PreK standards are met. While each of these quality standards is essential to ensure effective practices, they do not all carry equal weight. More details about the NIEER benchmarks are provided in Barnett and colleagues (2010).

Costs of Improving Quality in Existing State PreK Programs

Table 3.3 shows estimates of per-child spending necessary to fund high-quality PreK adequately in each state, based on current operating schedules in each state PreK program. In fiscal year 2010, only 17 states appeared to provide sufficient funding for high-quality PreK programs meeting all 10 NIEER quality benchmarks, based on current operating schedules. Despite the availability of sufficient funding, only three of these states—Alaska, Rhode Island, and North Carolina—actually offered PreK programs at this level of quality. Five additional adequately funded states (Arkansas, Kentucky, Maryland, Minnesota, and Oklahoma) met nine of the quality standards. While Vermont and Maine adequately funded their programs, they only met four and five quality benchmarks, respectively. Of the 17 states that adequately funded their preschool programs, these two states have the lowest per-child spending levels, at less than $4,000 per child.

Among the remaining 33 states that do not appear to fund their PreK programs adequately, there is a wide range in the additional funding needed. Massachusetts, which met six quality benchmarks, needs almost $5,000 more per child to fund its program adequately. Georgia and Missouri, two states that met nine quality benchmarks, are each estimated to need at least $3,000 more per child to fund their programs adequately. On the other end, Ohio, which met two quality benchmarks, is estimated to need only $400 more per child to meet all 10 benchmarks. These findings suggest that some states are more efficient at allocating resources to create high-quality programs. Unfortunately, not all states can provide a complete report of federal and local funding amounts used to supplement the states' own funds. As a result, our calculations may underestimate the number of states that adequately fund their PreK programs.

We estimate that states would need to invest a total of $8.15 billion in order to fund high-quality PreK programs adequately at current enrollment levels and operating schedules. This would represent an increase of more than $1.9 billion above current state PreK spending levels from all reported sources. Because the majority (85%) of children enrolled in state PreK programs are age 4, the majority of the $8.15 billion would be spent on programs for 4-year-olds. However, this estimate does not take into account the funds that would be needed in the 10 states not presently offering state-funded PreK, spending for children not currently enrolled in the other 40 states, or spending to convert current half-day slots to full-day slots.

Costs of Improving Quality in Existing Programs and Offering Full-Day Schedules

During fiscal year 2010, only seven states provided full-day programs to all students enrolled in state PreK, although an additional 20 states offered a mixture of both full- and part-day programs. Assuming that high-quality options are available, families may prefer full-day programs to part-day programs because they offer more hours of care and better match parents' work schedules. Table 3.3 also provides state-specific estimates of the per-child spending needed to fund high-quality, full-day PreK programs adequately. Only 10 states can be verified to fund full-day PreK programs at a level sufficient to meet all 10 quality standards. Among these states, two currently offer only part-day programs, and five currently offer a mixture of full- and part-day programs. Of the 30 states offering state PreK but not providing sufficient funds for high-quality, full-day PreK programs, six states would need to spend at least $5,000 more per child in order to do so. Included among these states are New York, Illinois, and Florida, which have especially large populations of preschool-age children.

We estimate that states would need to spend $10.8 billion annually in order to fully fund full-day, high-quality programs at current enrollment levels. This represents an additional $2.75 billion investment beyond our estimate of the funds needed to serve all currently enrolled students at the current (half-day or full-day) operating schedule. This is an increase of almost $4.6 billion beyond fiscal year 2010 funding levels. However, it is still likely to underestimate the needed funding because it does not take into account the states not currently offering state PreK. This figure may also be an underestimate because some programs, both full- and part-day, currently provide PreK fewer than 5 days per week. In these states, the calculated per-child spending figure represents the funding amount for fewer than 5 days; therefore, additional funding would be needed to offer PreK programming 5 days per week.

Costs of Enrolling All 3- and 4-Year-Olds in Poverty

The previous $10.8 billion estimate reflects sufficient funding for children *currently served* by state PreK. However, only 27% of 4-year-olds and 4% of 3-year-olds nationwide are enrolled in such programs (Barnett et al., 2010). Additionally, only six states serve a majority of 4-year-olds, and no states enroll more than 20% of 3-year-olds. Therefore, an important goal should be to improve access to high-quality early childhood programs. The majority of state-funded PreK initiatives are targeted to children meeting specific criteria, based on income and/or other risk factors. Only a few states—including Oklahoma, Florida, West Virginia, and Georgia—offer programs designed to be available to all families that wish to enroll their 4-year-olds. Even when Head Start and special education enrollment are included, only Oklahoma serves more than 80% of 4-year-olds, and no state serves more than 30% of 3-year-olds. As mentioned previously, although the federal Head Start program makes a major investment in early childhood education for young children in poverty, it does not have sufficient resources to serve all eligible children. Since estimates suggest that approximately 40–60% of qualifying children are enrolled in Head Start, a sizable population of children living in poverty (perhaps 1.5 million 3- and 4-year-olds) are not enrolled in Head Start and could benefit from improved access to state PreK.

TABLE 3.3. Estimates of Spending Needed to Serve Children in High-Quality State PreK Programs (2010 Dollars)

State	Estimate of per-child funding needed to meet NIEER benchmarks[a]		Total $ needed to fund a high-quality program based on the estimate of per-child spending and current enrollment[b]		Additional $ needed to fund a high-quality program based on the estimate of per-child spending, current enrollment, and current all reported spending		Total $ needed to serve all children living in poverty in a high-quality program	Total $ needed to serve all children in the state in a high-quality program
	Current operating schedule	Full-day program	Current operating schedule	Full-day program	Current operating schedule	Full-day program	Full-day program	Full-day program
Alabama	$7,222 F	$7,222	$27,948,224	$27,948,224	$10,362,344	$10,362,344	$219,847,620	$761,323,688
Alaska	**$4,274** P	**$7,824**	$1,700,000	$1,700,000	$0	$0	$15,580,786	$136,095,754
Arizona	$4,438 F/P	$7,551	$19,167,722	$32,612,141	$14,447,952	$27,892,371	$341,697,722	$1,359,634,880
Arkansas	**$6,784** F	**$6,784**	$171,973,151	$171,973,151	$0	$0	$127,658,217	$438,789,542
California	$6,362 F/P	$9,037	$936,390,970	$1,330,155,719	$116,440,473	$510,205,222	$1,778,255,172	$8,568,834,602
Colorado	$4,319 P	$7,906	$84,193,739	$154,135,622	$10,941,557	$80,883,440	$208,829,815	$1,022,880,706
Connecticut	**$8,300** F/P	**$9,065**	$93,547,400	$93,547,400	$0	$0	$101,991,905	$668,545,532
Delaware	$4,579 P	$8,383	$5,727,800	$7,066,896	$0	$1,339,096	$27,820,312	$174,906,022
Florida	$4,358 F/P	$7,632	$679,311,966	$1,189,600,452	$287,492,023	$797,780,509	$717,669,898	$3,180,685,449
Georgia	$8,093 F	$8,093	$656,968,770	$656,968,770	$315,033,413	$315,033,413	$478,427,911	$2,186,641,924
Hawaii	$4,265 P	$7,808	NA	NA	NA	$0	$20,423,157	$232,273,321
Idaho	$3,625 P	$6,637	NA	NA	NA	$0	$50,128,717	$287,202,893
Illinois	$4,647 P	$8,508	$407,021,135	$745,143,956	$111,753,181	$449,876,002	$467,203,232	$2,629,136,761
Indiana	$3,999 P	$7,321	NA	NA	NA	$0	$276,452,704	$1,120,319,932
Iowa	$4,093 F/P	$6,902	$64,378,797	$108,568,587	$5,414,559	$49,604,349	$89,318,723	$485,630,673
Kansas	$3,809 P	$6,974	$36,049,203	$65,996,194	$12,484,275	$42,431,266	$83,094,763	$468,699,396
Kentucky	**$4,425** F/P	$7,281	$140,261,553	$162,360,465	$0	$22,098,912	$181,965,258	$729,796,745
Louisiana	$7,147 F	$7,147	$145,423,527	$145,423,527	$47,666,085	$47,666,085	$185,567,349	$679,348,529
Maine	**$3,759** P	$6,882	$13,826,444	$24,808,145	$0	$10,981,701	$24,191,876	$162,755,838
Maryland	**$6,980** F/P	**$8,913**	$252,179,702	$252,179,702	$0	$0	$113,794,732	$1,181,307,551
Massachusetts	**$8,859** F/P	$8,970	$119,313,012	$120,801,652	$0	$68,338,835	$125,929,892	$1,214,972,210
Michigan	$5,503 F/P	$8,047	$108,854,843	$159,186,097	$66,850,195	$72,058,097	$407,914,695	$1,623,146,980
Minnesota	**$4,352** P	$7,967	$13,682,074	$14,929,441	$21,726,843	$1,247,367	$152,492,169	$997,020,504
Mississippi	$3,740 P	$6,846	NA	NA	NA	$0	$101,643,108	$381,635,030

Missouri	$6,477 F/P	$7,456	$28,051,887	$32,290,686	$14,836,446	$19,075,245	$245,269,847	$1,009,725,610
Montana	$3,331 P	$6,098	NA	NA	NA	$0	$27,807,189	$117,365,171
Nebraska	$3,808 P	$6,972	$39,025,061	$71,444,173	$17,806,688	$50,225,800	$38,371,858	$326,463,687
Nevada	$4,479 P	$8,201	$5,518,630	$10,103,097	$2,179,755	$6,764,222	$111,303,771	$605,270,537
New Hampshire	$4,190 P	$7,671	NA	NA	NA	$0	$32,050,996	$215,481,982
New Jersey	$8,882 F/P	$9,311	$576,996,173	$576,996,173	$0	$0	$255,723,055	$1,829,847,121
New Mexico	$3,949 P	$7,229	$19,143,154	$35,045,860	$2,600,747	$18,503,453	$107,736,382	$349,164,624
New York	$6,016 F/P	$9,221	$649,288,832	$995,202,930	$271,181,619	$617,095,717	$717,174,982	$3,693,190,530
North Carolina	**$7,780 F**	$7,780	$244,085,049	$244,085,049	$0	$0	$460,859,520	$1,836,084,090
North Dakota	$3,610 P	$6,609	NA	NA	NA	$0	$10,456,775	$85,558,341
Ohio	$4,312 P	$7,894	$24,579,005	$44,997,411	$2,335,213	$22,753,619	$420,971,537	$1,941,719,268
Oklahoma	**$5,583 F/P**	$6,930	$293,412,975	$293,412,975	$0	$0	$115,319,583	$622,009,653
Oregon	**$4,114 P**	$7,532	$54,897,578	$54,897,578	$0	$0	$121,771,727	$647,256,312
Pennsylvania	$6,999 F/P	$7,855	$224,268,957	$251,703,618	$34,460,936	$61,895,597	$348,563,949	$1,990,680,102
Rhode Island	$8,328 F	$8,328	$1,150,000	$1,150,000	$0	$0	$30,288,538	$166,587,908
South Carolina	$4,769 F/P	$7,430	$117,140,947	$182,494,363	$37,457,319	$102,810,735	$211,163,469	$798,683,020
South Dakota	$3,424 P	$6,269	NA	NA	NA	$0	$19,921,060	$112,136,545
Tennessee	$7,576 F	$7,576	$139,176,072	$139,176,072	$34,688,559	$34,688,559	$281,253,017	$1,111,937,105
Texas	$5,697 F/P	$8,155	$1,223,111,718	$1,750,818,629	$431,733,414	$959,440,325	$1,550,133,005	$6,058,587,943
Utah	$4,125 P	$7,552	NA	NA	NA	$0	$69,052,190	$717,773,103
Vermont	$3,849 F/P	$6,972	$17,790,714	$31,162,710	$13,371,996	$13,371,996	$16,191,451	$73,640,379
Virginia	$8,800 F/P	$8,923	$131,507,200	$133,339,509	$37,533,185	$39,365,494	$233,416,986	$1,692,854,349
Washington	$4,907 F/P	$8,560	$54,716,348	$68,699,620	$0	$13,983,272	$233,753,067	$1,352,152,832
West Virginia	**$6,331 F/P**	$6,979	$130,640,325	$130,640,325	$0	$0	$52,286,183	$241,598,979
Wisconsin	**$4,273 P**	$7,823	$197,960,062	$307,349,929	$0	$109,389,867	$136,804,773	$977,565,262
Wyoming	$3,645 P	$6,673	NA	NA	NA	$0	$9,419,952	$78,196,776
50 states			$8,150,380,720	$10,820,116,847	$1,907,426,782	$4,577,162,909	$12,154,964,592	$58,445,696,248

aStates offering only full-day programs are indicated by an F. States offering only part-day programs are indicated by a P. States that offer both full- and part-day programs are indicated by F/P. For these programs, a weighted estimate of per-child spending was calculated. **Bolded** numbers indicate states that are verified to adequately fund their program to meet the 10 NIEER quality standards at either their current operating schedule or for a full-day program.
bSome states spent more per child than the estimate of sufficient per-child spending. For these states, current spending levels are reported in the column with estimates for full-day programs.

We estimate that states would need more than $12 billion to offer full-day, high-quality PreK programs targeted to all 3- and 4-year-olds in poverty who do not already attend Head Start. This is an increase of almost $6 billion over current state PreK funding levels. Because more 4-year-olds than 3-year-olds enroll in Head Start, a greater number of 3-year-olds in poverty would need to enroll in state PreK. Accordingly, in this estimate, more than 50% of the spending ($6.4 billion) would be directed toward serving 3-year-olds, and $5.8 billion would be used to serve 4-year-olds. Due to a current emphasis on serving 4-year-olds in state-funded PreK initiatives, approximately 85% of total state PreK funds are used to serve 4-year-olds. The spending now directed toward 4-year-olds in state PreK is almost sufficient to cover all 4-year-olds living in poverty nationwide. However, there is a large discrepancy between current funding for 3-year-olds in state PreK and funding needed to serve all 3-year-olds living in poverty. An additional $5.6 billion would be needed.

Also, our estimate of $12 billion may understate total costs to the extent that states continue serving non-poor children currently enrolled in their programs, in addition to serving all children in poverty. This may increase the amount needed to serve 4-year-olds more than the amount needed to serve 3-year-olds, since more non-poor 4-year-olds than 3-year-olds currently attend state PreK. Additionally, targeted programs generally do not define risk solely based on income eligibility. For example, states often use additional eligibility guidelines, such as having a non-English-speaking family, teen parent, or disability. Therefore, additional funding could be necessary if states chose to define at-risk status more broadly.

Costs of Offering Universally Available Programs to 3- and 4-Year-Olds

Even more funding would be needed to offer universal programs to all preschool-age children whose parents wish to enroll them. More than $58 billion would be needed to serve all 3- and 4-year-olds not currently enrolled in Head Start or special education in full-day, high-quality state PreK programs in all 50 states. Of this $58 billion, approximately $30 billion would be needed to serve 3-year-olds and approximately $28 billion to serve 4-year-olds because fewer 3-year-olds are already served in Head Start and special education programs. This total estimate is more than 10 times the amount that states now spend on state PreK, and it would be extremely challenging to attain this level of investment, even by coordinating federal and local funding streams with state funds. However, the $58 billion figure is likely an overestimate of the total amount needed because some parents would choose to keep their children at home, and others would choose to enroll them in family day care or private, tuition-based programs. Data from the National Household Education Surveys suggest that only 75% of 4-year-olds and 51% of 3-year-olds enroll in some type of center-based care (Barnett, 2011), though these numbers would be expected to rise if more parents had access to high-quality free (or subsidized) preschool.

Spending Estimates in Federal Head Start

Next, we offer state-specific spending estimates for federal Head Start as a complement to our state PreK spending estimates. Even with a budget of $7.2 billion in fiscal year 2010, it is likely that Head Start only serves 40–60% of eligible children. Since eligibility criteria have recently been extended from 100% FPL to 130% FPL in certain circumstances (Improving Head Start for School Readiness Act, 2007), the federal funding level needed to serve all eligible children has increased as well. As shown in Table 3.4, the total amount of federal funds received by Head Start agencies in each state varies greatly, ranging from a total of more than $1 billion in California to just over $15 million in Vermont. The Head Start funding amount tends to be correlated with both the total number of 3- and 4-year-olds and the number of 3- and 4-year-olds living in poverty in each state. For example, the five states (California, Texas, New York, Florida, and Illinois) receiving the highest Head Start funding amounts also have the largest populations of 3- and 4-year-olds and the largest numbers of young children in poverty. Almost 40% of federal Head Start funding was directed toward these five states, and approximately 55% of 3- and 4-year-olds living in poverty reside in these states (Barnett et al., 2010; U.S. Census Bureau, 2009; U.S. Department of Health and Human Services, 2010c). Thus, it seems that federal Head Start allocations are generally proportional to the need in a state.

However, spending per child enrolled in Head Start varies by state. In most states, per-child spending amounts in Head Start are greater than per-child spending amounts in state PreK, but Head Start programs also provide more comprehensive services than most state PreK programs (Barnett & Robin, 2006). Nationwide, federal Head Start spending averaged $9,198 per child served, more than double the average state spending in state PreK initiatives. Federal Head Start spending per child ranged from $7,026 in Mississippi to $12,267 in Vermont. This $5,000 discrepancy is difficult to explain given that the program requirements for Head Start are federally mandated rather than state-specific. While Head Start centers can differ in the hours per day and days per week that programs are offered, this may not fully explain differences between the two extremes in Mississippi and Vermont. For example, only 25% of Vermont Head Start students attended full-day programs 5 days per week, while 80% of Mississippi Head Start students did so (Barnett et al., 2010; U.S. Department of Health and Human Services, 2010c). Per-child Head Start spending and the percentage of children enrolled in full-day, 5-day per week programs are not correlated. Another possible explanation for between-state differences in per-child Head Start funding may be differences in the cost of living in each state. For example, it may cost less in Mississippi than in Vermont to provide Head Start services, and this may explain the discrepancy in per-child spending amounts.

When a cost of living index was used to covert each state's per-child spending to the same scale, Head Start programs in Mississippi are estimated to receive $7,925 per child and those in Vermont, to receive $13,588 per child. Even after this adjustment, there is great variation between states in the federal Head Start per-child spending amount, and the gap between Mississippi and Vermont increases slightly. Additionally, across the 50 states, the range in per-child spending increases after this adjustment, with Illinois spending $7,635 per child and Vermont spending $13,588 per child. It does not seem that differences in costs of living and of providing education between states can explain the differences in per-child Head Start spending. Also, after this adjustment, higher per-child spending is still not related to serving more children in full-day, 5-day per week programs. For example, Idaho has high per-child spending levels but only serves 1% of children in programs with this type of operating schedule.

Again, Head Start serves only part of its eligible population. Therefore, while spending levels are generally high for each child enrolled, estimates of spending for each Head Start–eligible child tend to be lower, suggesting a need for additional funding to serve all children living in poverty. Because Head Start serves more 4-year-olds than 3-year-olds, estimates of spending per child in poverty are lower for 3-year-olds. While nationally an average of $9,198 is spent per child enrolled in federal Head Start programs, only $3,215 is spent per income-eligible 3-year-old, and $4,599 is spent per income-eligible 4-year-old. These figures may even overestimate the amount spent per income-eligible child because they are based on 100% FPL rather than the current eligibility criterion of 130% FPL once all children at 100% FPL are served. In New Mexico, the Head Start per-child spending amount was approximately $10,000. However, Head Start spending per eligible 3-year-old

TABLE 3.4. Head Start Current and Needed Spending (2010 Dollars)

State	Federal actual Head Start spending	Federal spending per child enrolled in Head Start	Estimate of spending per child enrolled in Head Start adjusted for the cost of living	Percent of children in full-day, 5-day-per-week programs	Head Start spending per 3-year-old living in poverty[a]	Head Start spending per 4-year-old living in poverty[a]	Total $ needed to serve children living in poverty in Head Start
Alabama	$128,795,386	$7,978	$8,531	92%	$2,535	$4,215	$305,091,252
Alaska	$26,088,946	$11,197	$11,051	5%	$7,606	$9,167	$34,643,433
Arizona	$190,893,444	$10,251	$10,483	2%	$2,211	$4,778	$554,218,348
Arkansas	$79,686,440	$7,496	$8,531	97%	$3,325	$3,365	$178,501,824
California	$1,023,119,647	$10,382	$8,871	26%	$3,059	$5,261	$2,529,129,675
Colorado	$86,426,170	$8,772	$8,568	12%	$2,207	$3,479	$270,191,438
Connecticut	$58,684,386	$9,536	$8,123	54%	$3,685	$4,541	$136,297,681
Delaware	$15,322,257	$9,582	$8,827	10%	$5,031	$2,923	$38,626,653
Florida	$343,981,599	$9,457	$9,569	93%	$2,473	$3,726	$1,048,589,680
Georgia	$201,990,482	$8,892	$8,485	93%	$3,037	$2,702	$624,992,254
Hawaii	$25,564,131	$9,503	$9,399	37%	$5,108	$7,489	$37,566,918
Idaho	$37,102,374	$10,300	$11,985	1%	$1,923	$6,442	$93,930,190
Illinois	$318,393,527	$8,413	$7,635	35%	$3,772	$5,087	$608,007,381
Indiana	$115,065,187	$8,443	$8,906	18%	$1,771	$3,570	$373,944,971
Iowa	$59,193,525	$8,806	$9,852	46%	$2,861	$4,580	$143,026,069
Kansas	$60,402,087	$8,792	$9,735	20%	$2,926	$5,509	$133,807,768
Kentucky	$126,735,890	$8,326	$8,830	23%	$3,405	$4,329	$270,240,015
Louisiana	$167,769,210	$8,054	$8,702	78%	$4,934	$4,287	$291,796,002
Maine	$32,153,323	$11,215	$12,585	14%	$3,530	$14,352	$54,572,051
Maryland	$89,282,638	$9,288	$8,047	51%	$5,813	$4,480	$162,878,355
Massachusetts	$123,525,886	$10,499	$9,038	36%	$5,112	$8,250	$200,763,686
Michigan	$285,081,505	$8,286	$7,951	6%	$3,057	$5,558	$551,711,052
Minnesota	$99,705,881	$8,941	$8,666	6%	$3,341	$4,922	$215,245,613
Mississippi	$182,385,869	$7,026	$7,925	80%	$6,019	$7,136	$194,070,875
Missouri	$138,784,655	$8,583	$8,889	34%	$2,786	$4,144	$346,918,724

Montana	$40,141,416	$9,663	$12,238	6%	$4,659	$7,998	$63,140,109
Nebraska	$45,235,012	$9,964	$11,036	18%	$3,791	$8,909	$76,839,738
Nevada	$33,886,592	$11,589	$10,913	7%	$2,030	$2,490	$174,149,731
New Hampshire	$15,520,982	$10,734	$10,805	6%	$2,204	$4,680	$52,434,300
New Jersey	$151,222,061	$10,504	$8,712	90%	$4,448	$4,360	$361,121,979
New Mexico	$78,047,977	$9,661	$10,320	26%	$3,560	$4,732	$181,049,280
New York	$500,805,950	$10,979	$9,194	56%	$4,603	$5,395	$1,094,680,671
North Carolina	$182,226,238	$9,580	$9,509	89%	$1,683	$4,017	$652,684,357
North Dakota	$29,354,771	$10,008	$11,695	10%	$8,584	$11,605	$29,034,501
Ohio	$286,301,051	$7,962	$7,788	18%	$3,472	$4,697	$559,552,589
Oklahoma	$125,121,754	$8,145	$9,076	60%	$4,045	$6,889	$197,355,313
Oregon	$98,816,871	$11,524	$11,815	13%	$4,480	$5,459	$225,924,753
Pennsylvania	$265,563,416	$9,180	$9,025	44%	$3,800	$5,311	$532,981,286
Rhode Island	$25,013,144	$10,685	$9,907	10%	$2,461	$13,193	$48,348,772
South Carolina	$103,567,326	$8,459	$8,791	91%	$3,032	$2,987	$291,069,524
South Dakota	$38,038,186	$9,689	$11,934	7%	$5,879	$9,643	$48,104,838
Tennessee	$139,485,096	$8,699	$8,866	69%	$2,178	$3,965	$388,940,294
Texas	$635,812,037	$8,688	$8,227	73%	$2,653	$3,013	$1,945,246,175
Utah	$51,267,889	$8,821	$9,020	3%	$2,100	$6,928	$104,644,008
Vermont	$15,125,641	$12,267	$13,588	25%	$3,069	$10,074	$35,342,232
Virginia	$118,228,838	$9,062	$7,843	65%	$2,462	$5,280	$293,043,670
Washington	$163,359,624	$11,389	$10,274	11%	$3,477	$6,397	$377,250,944
West Virginia	$58,127,999	$7,956	$8,804	5%	$3,328	$7,128	$87,740,976
Wisconsin	$118,438,485	$8,609	$8,499	9%	$4,712	$5,233	$205,590,683
Wyoming	$15,605,794	$9,191	$10,635	1%	$9,551	$5,891	$20,623,912
50 states	$7,350,448,596	$9,198			$3,215	$4,599	$17,320,764,816

ᵃThis calculation is based on multiplying the total Head Start spending in the state by the percentage of the Head Start enrollment that is 3 or 4 years old and then dividing this by each state's number of 3- and 4-year-olds in poverty.

was $3,560, and spending per eligible 4-year-old was $4,732. In Alaska, the Head Start per-child spending was just over $11,000. However, spending per eligible 3-year-old was $7,606, and spending per eligible 4-year-old was $9,167. While our data do not allow us to determine whether one state serves a greater percentage of children living in poverty, our findings do suggest that some states (e.g., Alaska) fund slots for larger percentages of income-eligible children than other states (e.g., New Mexico).

Because of this discrepancy and the estimate that 40–60% of eligible children are served in Head Start, it is important to estimate the total funding Head Start would need to serve all children at or below 100% FPL. Twenty-two percent of 3- and 4-year-olds nationwide live below 100% FPL. We estimate that the federal government would need to invest over $17 billion to serve all children in poverty at the current per-child spending rate for Head Start in each state. This represents a $10 billion increase over current federal Head Start funding levels, with about 57% of this additional spending directed toward slots for 3-year-olds. However, if Head Start continues to serve children between 100 and 130% FPL, then $10 billion underestimates the additional amount needed. It seems unlikely given the current fiscal situation that the federal government will be able to fully fund Head Start anytime soon. However, many state preschool initiatives are targeted to very similar at-risk populations and therefore reduce the number of children Head Start would need to cover.

Conclusions and Projections for the Future

Public investments in early childhood education at both the federal and state levels are substantial and support numerous initiatives. In 2010, the federal government invested nearly $20 billion in programs that provide a range of services, including center-based early education, special education, child care subsidies, and nutritious meals. State governments contributed at least $17 billion more toward early education, much of it geared toward programs modeled on federal initiatives, but also including $5.4 billion in funds for state PreK initiatives. Federal and local investments in state PreK initiatives totaled another $0.8 billion during fiscal year 2010. Yet, in general, there has been little coordination across different initiatives at the federal level, and little coordination of state PreK initiatives with federal early childhood initiatives.

Not surprisingly, early childhood policies and fiscal approaches used to support early education by the states are also quite variable. In most cases, current state PreK funding levels are inadequate to support high levels of quality in the classroom consistently. We estimate that states would need to invest a total of $8.15 billion per year to provide sufficient funding to bring their current PreK initiatives to high levels of quality, and $10.8 billion annually to offer high-quality, full-day programs to the children currently enrolled. It would likely cost states more than $12 billion per year to offer high-quality, full-day programs to all 3- and 4-year-olds in poverty who do not currently attend federal Head Start. Alternatively, we estimate that for Head Start to enroll *all* 3- and 4-year-olds in poverty, a $17 billion federal investment would be required. Finally, if state PreK systems offered high-quality, full-day programs to all 3- and 4-year-olds in the United States not already attending Head Start, the projected cost of those state initiatives would total perhaps $58 billion annually.

The current lack of consistency in available funding streams, and the inadequacy of spending levels to support broadly available, high-quality early childhood programs, may impact the organizations providing the services, as well as the children being served. Research by Sandfort, Selden, and Sowa (2008) suggests that different types of policy tools used at the state level have differential impacts on the organizational capacity of providers.

For example, providers receiving grants (the Head Start model) had greater management capacity than providers receiving contracts (often used in state PreK) or vouchers (common in child care), possibly due to the stability of grant funds and greater support for infrastructure compared to the other two models examined. Also, considerable research is still needed to examine child outcomes associated with participation in state PreK, especially since state PreK initiatives are characterized by such vast differences in policy approaches and the adequacy of state funds to support high-quality PreK programming. A growing body of methodologically rigorous research (e.g., Gormley, Gayer, Phillips, & Dawson, 2005; Wong, Cook, Barnett, & Jung, 2008) shows that higher-quality state PreK programs in states such as Oklahoma and New Jersey produce positive impacts on young children's cognitive development.

While finding the money to provide high-quality early education to all 3- and 4-year-olds may seem like an insurmountable challenge, currently even more is spent per grade on public K–12 education. On average, nationwide, almost $47 billion annually is spent on each grade of K–12 education, with approximately $23 billion coming from state funds (National Education Association, 2010). Based on our estimates, the per-grade spending needed to offer high-quality, full-day PreK amounts to $29 billion. This potential investment seems more feasible when compared to K–12 expenditures per grade. Additionally, cost–benefit research suggests that the return on investment for every dollar invested in high-quality early education programs will be greater than for K–12 education (Barnett, 2008; Barnett & Masse, 2007; Temple & Reynolds, 2007).

Since it is likely that the trend toward expansion of state PreK will continue during the current decade, coordination across different early education initiatives at the federal and state levels is critically important. Recent actions by the federal government suggest a willingness to make new investments aimed at encouraging this coordination. The 2007 Head Start reauthorization law (Improving Head Start for School Readiness Act, 2007) includes a new requirement for each state to have an Advisory Council on Early Childhood Education and Care, charged with responsibility to look for ways to collaborate and coordinate across state and federal funding streams for early childhood. Initial federal funding for these Councils was appropriated through ARRA in 2009 (Satkowski, 2009). Another opportunity involves the Early Learning Challenge Fund, which passed the U.S. House before being dropped from legislation in 2009, was proposed again in the U.S. Senate in March 2011, and ultimately revised and issued as a federal Race to the Top grant competition in August 2011. States selected for Race to the Top–Early Learning Challenge grants will receive federal funds aimed at enrolling more children from low-income and disadvantaged backgrounds in high-quality programs and at promoting statewide integration of early learning services (U.S. Department of Education and U.S. Department of Health and Human Services, 2011).

Both the early childhood Advisory Councils and the Race to the Top–Early Learning Challenge hold great promise for better integration of federal and state investments in early education, due to their emphasis on coordination and collaboration across current initiatives. However, both state and federal governments will have important issues to consider as they foster this increased collaboration. For example, should state PreK programs be available only to children with certain risk factors such as poverty, or be more broadly available to the general population? Should programs be available on a part- or full-day basis? How does the mission of the federal Head Start program, which already serves a sizable proportion of children in poverty, fit with the missions of state-specific initiatives that also serve children from low-income families? Each of these questions merits serious consideration in the future as state and federal governments seek to maximize the benefits that can be derived from their investments in early education.

Note

1. In July 2009, the California State Preschool Program Act consolidated a number of separate initiatives into the California State Preschool Program. Although all programs now meet NIEER's criteria for state PreK, only some of the programs previously did so. Additional funding for early childhood programs not previously meeting the criteria for state PreK initiatives is not included when calculating spending changes in California or the United States between 2009 and 2010, as this funding does not represent an increase in the state's contribution to state PreK.

References

American Recovery and Reinvestment Act of 2009, Public Law No. 111-5, 123 Stat. 181 (2009).

Barnett, W. S. (2008). Why governments should invest in early education. *CESifo DICE Report, 6*(2), 9–14.

Barnett, W. S. (2011). Four reasons the United States should offer every child a preschool education. In E. F. Zigler, W. S. Gilliam, & W. S. Barnett (Eds.), *The pre-K debates: Current controversies and issues* (pp. 34–39). Baltimore: Brookes.

Barnett, W. S., Brown, K. C., Finn-Stevenson, M., & Henrich, C. (2007). From visions to systems of universal prekindergarten. In J. L. Aber, S. J. Bishop-Josef, S. M. Jones, K. T. McLearn, & D. A. Phillips (Eds.), *Child development and social policy: Knowledge for action* (pp. 113–128). Washington, DC: American Psychological Association.

Barnett, W. S., Epstein, D., Carolan, M., Fitzgerald, J., Ackerman, D., & Friedman, A. H. (2010). *The state of preschool 2010: State preschool yearbook.* New Brunswick, NJ: National Institute for Early Education Research, Rutgers University.

Barnett, W. S., & Hustedt, J. T. (2011). Improving public financing for early learning programs. *Preschool Policy Brief, 23.* New Brunswick, NJ: National Institute for Early Education Research, Rutgers University.

Barnett, W. S., & Masse, L. N. (2003). Funding issues for early childhood education and care programs. In D. Cryer & R. M. Clifford (Eds.), *Early childhood education and care in the USA* (pp. 137–165). Baltimore: Brookes.

Barnett, W. S., & Masse, L. N. (2007). Early childhood program design and economic returns: Comparative benefit–cost analysis of the Abecedarian program and policy implications. *Economics of Education Review, 26*(1), 113–125.

Barnett, W. S., & Robin, K. B. (2006). *How much does quality preschool cost?* (NIEER Working Paper). New Brunswick, NJ: National Institute for Early Education Research, Rutgers University.

Barnett, W. S., & Yarosz, D. J. (2007). *Who goes to preschool and why does it matter?* (Preschool Policy Brief No. 15). New Brunswick, NJ: National Institute for Early Education Research, Rutgers University.

Cavalluzzo, L., Clinton, Y., Holian, L., Marr, L., & Taylor, L. (2009). *West Virginia's progress toward universal prekindergarten* (Issues & Answers Report, REL 2009–No. 070). Washington, DC: U.S. Department of Education, Institute of Education Sciences, National Center for Education Evaluation and Regional Assistance, Regional Educational Laboratory Appalachia.

Cobb, C. (2009). North Carolina's More at Four Prekindergarten Program: A case study of funding versus quality and other issues in large-scale implementation. In R. C. Pianta & C. Howes (Eds.), *The promise of pre-K* (pp. 123–144). Baltimore: Brookes.

Cochran, M. (2009). Implementing large-scale prekindergarten initiatives: Lessons from New York. In R. C. Pianta & C. Howes (Eds.), *The promise of pre-K* (pp. 145–167). Baltimore: Brookes.

Elementary and Secondary Education Act of 1965, Public Law No. 107-116, 20 U.S.C. A. § 6301 *et seq.* (1965).

Gault, B., Mitchell, A., & Williams, E. (2008). *Meaningful investments in pre-K: Estimating the per-child costs of quality programs.* Washington, DC: Institute for Women's Policy Research.

Gayl, C. L., Young, M., & Patterson, K. (2010). *Tapping Title I: What every school administrator should know about Title I, pre-K and school reform.* Washington, DC: Pre-K Now.

Gordon, R. A., Kaestner, R., Korenman, S., & Abner, K. (2010). *The Child and Adult Care Food Program: Who is served and what are their nutritional outcomes?* (NBER Working Paper No. 16148). Cambridge, MA: National Bureau of Economic Research.

Gormley, W. T., Jr., Gayer, T., Phillips, D., & Dawson, B. (2005). The effects of universal pre-K on cognitive development. *Developmental Psychology, 41,* 872–884.

Gormley, W. T., Jr., & Phillips, D. (2003). *The effects of universal pre-K in Oklahoma: Research highlights and policy implications* (CROCUS Working Paper No. 2). Washington, DC: Center for Research on Children in the United States, Georgetown University.

Greenberg, M., & Schumacher, R. (2003). *Financing universal pre-kindergarten: Possibilities and technical issues for states in using funds under the Child Care and Development Fund and Temporary Assistance for Needy Families Block Grant.* Washington, DC: Center for Law and Social Policy.

Hebbeler, K., Spiker, D., Bailey, D., Scarborough, A., Mallik, S., Simeonsson, R., et al. (2007). *Early intervention for infants and toddlers with disabilities and their families: Participants, services, and outcomes.* Menlo Park, CA: SRI International.

Hustedt, J. T., & Barnett, W. S. (2011). Financing early childhood education programs: State, federal, and local issues. *Educational Policy, 25*(1), 167–192.

Improving Head Start for School Readiness Act of 2007, Public Law No. 110-134, § 11, 121 Stat. 1411 (2007).

Individuals with Disabilities Education Act Amendments of 1997, Public Law No. 105-17, 20 U.S.C. A. §§ 1400 *et seq.* (1997).

Kamerman, S. B., & Gatenio-Gabel, S. (2007). Early childhood education and care in the United States: An overview of the current policy picture. *International Journal of Child Care and Education Policy, 1,* 23–34.

Matthews, H. (2009). *Child care assistance in 2007.* Washington, DC: Center for Law and Social Policy.

Matthews, H., & Ewen, D. (2010). *FAQ: Using Title I of ESEA for early education.* Washington, DC: Center for Law and Social Policy.

Mitchell, A. (2009). Models for financing state-supported prekindergarten programs. In R. C. Pianta & C. Howes (Eds.), *The promise of pre-K* (pp. 51–63). Baltimore: Brookes.

National Education Association. (2010). Rankings and estimates: Rankings of the states 2010 and estimates of school statistics 2001. Retrieved February 15, 2011, from *www.nea.org/assets/docs/he/nea_rankings_and_estimates010711.pdf.*

Oliveira, V. (2010). *The food assistance landscape: FY 2009 annual report* (Economic Information Bulletin No. 6–7). Washington, DC: U.S. Department of Agriculture, Economic Research Service.

Patient Protection and Affordable Care Act of 2010, Public Law No. 111-148, § 2951, 124 Stat. 119 (2010).

Pew Center on the States. (2010). Federal health care reform legislation: Home visiting summary. Retrieved March 3, 2011, from *www.pewcenteronthestates.org/uploadedfiles/wwwpewcenteronthestatesorg/initiatives/home_visiting/hv_health_care_reform_summary_final.pdf.*

Sandfort, J., Selden, S. C., & Sowa, J. E. (2008). Do government tools influence organizational performance?: Examining their implementation in early childhood education. *American Review of Public Administration, 38,* 412–438.

Satkowski, C. (2009). *The next step in systems-building: Early Childhood Advisory Councils and federal efforts to promote policy alignment in early childhood.* Washington, DC: New America Foundation.

Southern Education Foundation. (2008). *Time to lead again: The promise of Georgia Pre-K.* Atlanta: Author.

Stone, D. (2008). *Funding the future: States' approaches to pre-K finance 2008 update.* Washington, DC: Pre-K Now.

Stullich, S., Eisner, E., & McCrary, J. (2007). *National assessment of Title I final report. Volume I: Implementation.* Washington, DC: National Center for Education Evaluation and Regional Assistance, Institute of Education Sciences, U.S. Department of Education.

Taylor, L., & Fowler, W. (2006). *A comparable wage approach to geographic cost adjustment.* Washington, DC: Institute of Education Sciences, U.S. Department of Education.

Temple, J. A., & Reynolds, A. (2007). Benefits and costs of investments in preschool education: Evidence from the Child–Parent Centers and related programs. *Economics of Education Review, 26*(1), 126–144.

Urban Institute and Brookings Institution, Tax Policy Center. (2010). Historical Dependent Care credits. Retrieved February 1, 2011, from *www.taxpolicycenter.org/taxfacts/displayafact.cfm?docid=180.*

U.S. Census Bureau. (2009). American Community Survey public use microdata. Retrieved from *www.census.gov/acs/www.*

U.S. Department of Education. (2010). FY 2011 Department of Education justification of appropriation estimates to Congress. Retrieved January 19, 2011, from *www2.ed.gov/about/overview/budget/budget11/justifications/index.html.*

U.S. Department of Education and U.S. Department of Health and Human Services. (2011). Race to the Top–Early Learning Challenge executive summary. Retrieved September 13, 2011, from *www2.ed.gov/programs/racetothetop-earlylearningchallenge/exec-summ.pdf.*

U.S. Department of Health and Human Services, Administration for Children and Families, Office of Child Care. (2010a). FFY 2008 CCDF data tables. Retrieved January 24, 2011, from *www.acf.hhs.gov/programs/ccb/data/ccdf_data/08acf800/list.htm.*

U.S. Department of Health and Human Services, Administration for Children and Families, Office of Head Start. (2010b). Head Start program fact sheet fiscal year 2010. Retrieved December 29, 2010, from *eclkc.ohs.acf.hhs.gov/hslc/head%20start%20program/head%20start%20program%20factsheets/fheadstartprogr.htm.*

U.S. Department of Health and Human Services, Administration for Children and Families, Office of Head Start. (2010c). Head Start program information report. Retrieved January 7, 2011, from *eclkc.ohs.acf.hhs.gov/hslc/head%20start%20program/program%20administration%20_%20accountability/progam%20information%20report.*

Winning Beginning New York. (2010). 2010 state budget update. Retrieved March 16, 2011, from *www.winningbeginningny.org/documents/2010_state_budget_update.pdf.*

Wong, V. C., Cook, T. D., Barnett, W. S., & Jung, K. (2008). An effectiveness-based evaluation of five state prekindergarten programs. *Journal of Policy Analysis and Management, 27*(1), 122–154.

Zigler, E., Gilliam, W. S., & Jones, S. M. (2006). *A vision for universal preschool education.* New York: Cambridge University Press.

CHAPTER 4

Accountability and Program Evaluation in Early Education

Walter S. Gilliam and Ellen Frede

The federal Government Performance and Results Act of 1993 heralded a new era of accountability for public-funded programs, mandating evidence of effectiveness for programs and services funded through public money. Not long after that, many private foundations echoed this demand for accountability and formal evidence. Foundations began moving away from responsive giving, in which funding is given in response to program requests, toward more strategic systems of funding in order to achieve measurable outcomes across several funded initiatives. All of these changes in the expectations of grant recipients are in the context of increased fiscal responsibility and belt-tightening across the nation, made more acute in the current faltering economy. In order for programs and services for young children and families to survive in this new culture, evidence of program quality and effectiveness are of paramount importance as a way to convince funders to continue investing in these programs, whether those funders are public or private.

Programs that rely on public funds increasingly have been held accountable for demonstrating their effectiveness. Early education programs are no exception. In many states, formal evaluation of program implementation and impact is mandated in the state legislation authorizing early education. However, most states have not formally evaluated the impacts of their state-funded prekindergarten programs, and most states that have conducted such evaluations have relied on less than rigorous methods of estimating program effects (Gilliam & Ripple, 2004; Gilliam & Zigler, 2000; Ripple, Gilliam, Chanana, & Zigler, 1999). A review of the long-term cognitive and academic impacts of both model (Perry Preschool Program, Abecedarian Program, etc.) and large-scale public (state prekindergarten, Head Start, etc.) preschool programs found that in many cases public programs had weaker effects than the often higher-quality and better-implemented model programs, highlighting the need for scientifically valid evaluations of the effectiveness of these large-scale public programs (Barnett, 1995, 1998).

There is a clear need to design and implement accountability systems to ensure that investments in young children are well spent. Broad interest in the overlapping issues of child and classroom assessment, accountability, and program evaluation is evident in recent publications such as the combined position statement of the National Association for the Education of Young Children (NAEYC) and the National Association of Early Childhood Specialists in State Departments of Education (NAECS/SDE) (2003) and the report of the National Task Force on Early Childhood Accountability (Schultz & Kagan, 2007). In addition, the convergence of interest in programs for young children and the large accountability movement are apparent in other initiatives, such as the now-abandoned Head Start National Reporting System (Tarullo et al., 2008), which required that every Head Start child be assessed at the beginning and end of the program year, and efforts by organizations such as the Data Quality Campaign to ensure that early childhood data are included in statewide child-level databases (Laird, 2009).

What Is Program Evaluation?

"Program evaluation" is a systematic process of describing the components and outcomes of an organized intervention or service, with the aim at improving the quality of the services received or documenting the program's beneficial impacts. Evaluations, like the programs and clients themselves, can take many forms, ranging from careful yet relatively straightforward descriptions of the quantity and quality of the services being provided to very elaborate and rigorous studies of the effectiveness of these services. Of course, the more rigorous the evaluative methods, the more confidence one can have that any observed beneficial outcomes indeed were caused by participation in the program.

Evaluation is always a process of comparing. These comparisons may focus on aspects of the services being delivered, the outcomes observed in the participating children and families, or both. At the more complex end, causal inferences can be made by comparing client outcomes to a benchmark designed to represent what the outcomes might have been had the client not participated in the program. This comparison benchmark, referred to as the "counterfactual" by some program evaluators, might include demographically similar children and families who were not provided access to the program or even the level of functioning of the participating clients before they participated in the program compared to their functioning following the program.

These evaluative comparison, however, do not always need to focus on showing direct programmatic impacts. Rather, evaluation methods might focus on comparing child and family outcomes or aspects of the program's service quality and quantity to some idealized criteria. For example, a perfectly valid and useful application of program evaluation is simply to define what the program designers and implementers believe are the necessary components of the program in order to achieve the desired outcomes, then measure how closely what is being implemented matches what was intended. In this case, evaluation questions may include "How much contact is needed?" and "How good does the relationship need to be between the providers and the clients?" In cases where the service has been well defined or manualized, the evaluative questions might include "How closely must the program follow the prescribed processes?" After answering these questions, the evaluation might turn to measuring how closely the program as it is being implemented resembles the program as it was intended.

Other criteria might include defining how children and families should look upon exiting the program, with programmatic success defined on the basis of how much child and family exit measures resemble the desired status of participants after the program. For example, with family support programs that aim to reduce the degree of parental stress, an outcome goal might be that caregivers participating in the program will report levels of parental stress that are within the typical range of caregivers. Of course, the utility of an outcome goal such as this rests on the assumption that caregivers report elevated levels of parental stress before the support intervention and that the intervention itself targets the reduction of parental stress, possibly by providing direct support to caregivers or creating social networks in which caregivers may obtain assistance.

Program Evaluation as a Vehicle for Accountability

Policymakers, the early childhood profession, and other stakeholders in young children's lives share the responsibility to engage regularly in program evaluation (NAEYC & NAECS/ SDE, 2003). Prior to charting a course for program evaluation as part of an accountability system, however, state officials and other decision makers must consider the purposes of the evaluations and the audiences to which they are addressed (Patton, 2008). Purposes for program evaluation may vary from obtaining data to inform high-stakes decisions, such as determining program funding or child placement, to measuring program quality and/or children's progress for program improvement purposes. Audiences may include policymakers, educators, researchers, and the public in general. Whatever the case, well-conceived program evaluation is a valuable source of information that informs decision making in what Campbell (1991) referred to as an "experimenting society," which strives to implement and test rigorously new initiatives.

Both the purpose of program evaluation and the audience(s) affect what should be measured and how it should be measured. For example, if the legislature wants to know whether the money is spent as intended, then accountability may include expenditure analyses, as well as child outcome studies. For that to happen, however, it is critical that the program standards and desired outcomes already be established (Patton, 2008). If, on the other hand, the accountability question is whether the program is producing adequate child progress, then child learning standards need be agreed upon (Darling-Hammond, 2010), and the relationship between classroom implementation and child progress should be established. Curriculum and teaching must be examined and program standards that detail criteria for program operations, such as administrator credentials or community involvement, are necessary if program implementation is to be assessed.

The major issues in accountability and assessment can be broadly distilled down to the following: (1) designing the accountability system to be valid and useful for multiple purposes, and (2) ensuring that the assessment instruments are valid, administered reliably, and measure useful and appropriate accomplishments.

Designing the Accountability System

State child assessment systems, especially those designed and operated by departments of education and administered in the public schools, typically yield data for accountability; however, great caution should be taken in forming conclusions about program effects using such data (Nichols & Berliner, 2007). The question is whether it is possible to develop a comprehensive system that provides information for instructional decision making and for broad-scale program evaluation that is more efficient and less burdensome than separate systems for each purpose. It is easy to think of (1) improving practice, (2) providing accountability, and (3) conducting program evaluations as if they were completely separate objectives. Perhaps this is because we tend to associate these with separate audiences (e.g., providers vs. policymakers) and different levels and processes of decision making (classroom vs. funding/administrative levels). Rather than thinking about these as separate objectives, it may be possible to think of them as components of one system.

The main purpose of all child assessments should be to further educational goals by informing efforts to improve the effectiveness of the services provided to children and families. Assessments may be used by teachers to make classroom- and child-specific decisions regarding educational strategies. Also, assessments may be used by administrators and other decision makers to judge the overall impact of the early education system (or parts of it) and where changes could be made to improve effectiveness. Either way, the goal is to use test data to inform decisions about how to improve the educational services provided. Therefore, any early childhood assessment system—whether its focus is at the child, classroom, or larger systemic levels—should have a clearly delineated path running from the data to mechanisms for generating recommendations for clear and observable changes in educational service provision.

A comprehensive statewide assessment system used for multiple purposes should be multilevel and include more than child assessment data. Information needs to be gathered to inform practice at individual child, classroom (children and teachers), program (administrator qualifications and practices, as well as other kinds of program support; e.g., coaches, parent involvement) and state levels, if it is to be useful for the purposes of instructional assessment, accountability, and program evaluation.

The timing of the examination of key research questions is essential. Often administrators and policymakers are anxious to determine whether an initiative is having the desired effect, but as McCall cautions, "Service programs often needed two or three cohorts of participants for service professionals to learn and refine the implementation of the program before participants benefited (Fixsen et al., 2005)—a validation of Campbell's (1987) admonition "to evaluate no program before it's proud" (2009, p. 4). Appropriate evaluation often begins by developing an understanding of the landscape of early education services in a state—what programs are available, who has access, and who is attending. This could include information on who accesses programs and who leaves programs, when, and why.

In addition to establishing that the services are being used by the intended participants, treatment fidelity should be established to ensure that the program is being implemented as intended. Too often in program evaluations, treatments are labeled without any verification, what Patton (2008) refers to as "the problem of labeling the black box" (p. 142). For example, a program may report using a particular curriculum or that they are basing teaching practices on the state standards, and without verification the labels become reified. In an evaluation of a state preschool program, Frede and Barnett (1992) found that the program had beneficial effects on children's learning *only after* they controlled for fidelity of implementation of the curriculum. In a national evaluation of implementation and effects of the Comprehensive Child Development Program, Gilliam, Ripple, Zigler, and Leiter (2000) found marked variation in implementation across sites. Implementing a process evaluation will not only ameliorate the problem pointed out by Patton but it can also provide insight into the programmatic needs and the cost associated with planning technical assistance, if necessary.

With the rise in state-funded PreK programs (Barnett, Epstein, Friedman, Sansanelli, & Hustedt, 2009) and quality rating improvement systems (QRIS; National Child Care Information Center, 2007), statewide multilevel data collection efforts have become more common. Rigorously designed effectiveness studies that include information on program quality should be one aspect of a comprehensive program evaluation system once the program has reached a reasonable level of treatment fidelity. To date, the majority of state evaluations of preschool programs have been less than rigorous in terms of scientific standards, with many having flaws that severely limits interpreting the results (Gilliam & Zigler, 2000, 2004). For all research designs, more information is better. This may include child and family background data, health histories and maternal education, attendance records, information on previous out-of-home care, pretest data, and data on programs. If reporting on subgroups is desirable, then the sample has to be large enough to allow for it. Often, it is only after nonsignificance is found that it is learned the sample is too small to detect the expected effects of the program on the entire population or on subgroups. This problem can be avoided by predetermining the size of the samples needed to detect the smallest effects of interest.

In the following section, we describe the pros and cons of commonly used research designs for systemwide evaluation. The first three options described below rely on identifying nonequivalent groups of children for comparison to the treatment group. The groups are nonequivalent because whether or not a child attended preschool was determined by characteristics of the children or families. Often programs limit eligibility based on family income or other risk factors. When the space available is insufficient for all applicants, programs may prioritize enrollment based on measures or perceptions of child and family need. Using a first-come, first-served approach is likely to lead to systematic differences in the skills and educational aspirations of parents in the two groups. Even when programs do not explicitly select children, unless there is a lottery or other random assignment procedure, it must be assumed that program enrollment does not happen randomly. It cannot be assumed that haphazard enrollment is the same as random assignment.

This problem raised by the use of nonequivalent group designs is known as "selection bias." It is one of the most difficult problems encountered when estimating the effects of educational programs on children's learning and development. Note that the problem does not arise if all we are interested in is whether children meet a specified criterion. For example, a state might decide that all children who attend the PreK program should know 10 letters, be able to count to 20, and have five friends at entry to kindergarten. In such a framework, decision makers are not interested in whether the program produced those results. Leaving aside the question of whether these are appropriate goals, it is a relatively simple task to determine if they have been achieved, and no comparison group at all is required. However, if we wish to know how much the PreK program contributed to the achievement of these goals, we face a much more difficult task. Simple comparisons of children who did and did not attend the PreK program will confound differences between the two groups that influence those outcomes with the effects of the program. Adjusting for a pretest measure on these outcomes and for family background characteristics does not necessarily ameliorate the problem.

In summary, without random assignment, the treatment and no-treatment comparison groups are likely to be inherently different before the treatment is provided *in ways that are not measured, or inadequately measured, and are related to children's learning and development.* For example, if enrollment is first-come, first-served, then using a waiting list for the comparison group could confound program participation with organizational skills or educational aspirations of parents that also influence the child's learning and development. If the comparison group is composed of children whose parents did not seek enrollment, then we must consider whether the determinants of enrollment are likely to include factors that would also influence child development, for example, how much importance parents ascribe to achievement, parents' perceptions of a specific child's need for PreK, parents' willingness and ability to provide early education in the home, and access to other sources of early education in the community. In principle, we could statistically model all of these processes and selection into PreK programs to eliminate the bias. However, we know little about the complex selection processes that take place in PreK or later in school. For example, one researcher has shown that third-grade learning is predicted equally well by the quality of the third- and fourth-grade teachers (Rothstein, 2009). Such a pattern would result only from systematic assignment of children to teachers rather than teacher effects.

In many studies with nonequivalent groups, it is difficult to rule out what Campbell (1976) referred to as "plausible rival hypotheses." For example, if the selection criterion for a targeted intervention is children from low-income homes in which the home language is not English, then some evaluators might choose a comparison group of low-income English speakers. If achievement test scores in English are comparable between the two groups at the end of the treatment, it is tempting to attribute the relative gain to the effects of the program. However, the non-English-speaking families might be more recent immigrants who are highly motivated to learn English and emphasize to the child the importance of learning English quickly, perhaps even requiring the child to speak only English at home. Parents in these families might attend adult education programs to learn English and infuse what they are learning into interactions with their children. The basis for ruling out such alternatives would be stronger if more were known about household activities or if it were known that prior to offering the program (or in other places without PreK programs) children in similar families did not score comparably to native English speakers at kindergarten entry.

We briefly describe each of five major design approaches below.

Utilizing Extant Data

State personnel and others often use extant data, such as statewide tests at third grade, to compare preschool attendees to those who did not attend. This may seem like a logical use of these data, and it may be appealing because it is fairly inexpensive, particularly if the database already includes information on whether children attended preschool or not. However, there are several issues with this approach. The first is the selection bias discussed earlier, which is a threat for either targeted or universal programs (parents choose even when programs do not). The second is that other factors influence who ends up in the two groups (preschool treatment and no preschool) at third grade and who does not. In some states a significant number of children may not take the test at all. Some children may be absent because of illness, irregular attendance generally, or even encouragement from the school. Some children may be excused by virtue of their lack of facility in English, or because they are in special education (reasons that are increasingly prohibited but not necessarily unknown). Some children are retained in grade and do not take the third-grade test with their age cohort; it is not an acceptable solution to this problem simply to omit such children from the comparison or to add in their scores from testing 1 or more years later. If the preschool and comparison groups differ with respect to these characteristics, then the absence of test scores for these children biases the estimates. This attrition problem is especially troubling when it is differential across the two groups of preschool attendees and nonattendees, particularly because it can be expected that an effective PreK program causes these differences—increasing later attendance, improving children's English language abilities, and decreasing grade retention and special education. As Barnett (1993) has shown, the gradual differential loss of children in the two groups results in the test scores of those left in the groups becoming more similar over time (as a higher percentage of low-scoring children are cumulatively lost from the comparison group). Finally, children are also added and subtracted to the population tested at third grade by families moving into and out of a school district, city, or state. Those who move in or out are unlikely to be comparable to those who are there at PreK and stay through third grade.

Extant data also have been used recently in interrupted time series designs to compare results on the National Assessment of Educational Progress (NAEP) between annual cohorts in fourth graders who would have been age 4 before state-funded preschool was initiated with cohorts in which many of the children might have attended preschool (e.g.,

Olsen & Snell, 2006). This approach faces all of the threats just discussed from bias due to differential attrition plus the additional problem of populations changing over time. Failure to recognize that the changing composition of the population might over time affect scores for the population as the whole can lead to serious misinterpretations of the data. Also, in this case, Olsen and Snell selectively chose years and a test (reading not math) that enhanced the appearance of support for the conclusion that preschool had no effects (Barnett, 2006). This is another kind of selection bias, the selection of data points after reviewing them so as to "prove" a desired point of view. Barnett has shown that in Georgia, where well over 60% of the children attend state-funded preschool, a simple comparison of aggregated NAEP data for 1998 (before universal PreK) to that for 2002–2005 (after universal PreK) might be misinterpreted to show that preschool has had no lasting effects. However, the educationally at-risk proportion of the population had grown disproportionately faster during that period. When NAEP scores were disaggregated by ethnic group, it could be seen that every group was actually scoring better after preschool was initiated than before. Of course, this approach is also threatened by the potential for other changes in the schools (textbook selection or the approach to teaching reading in third grade), communities (an economic recession or unusually bad flu season), or families (increased divorce rates) to affect test scores.

Nonequivalent Groups, Posttest Only at Kindergarten Entry

This design compares children beginning at kindergarten entry. As with the extant data approach, this design brings problems of potential selection bias that arise because the groups may differ inherently. It improves on the use of later test data, in that children are tested directly and determination of the group to which children belong is likely to be more accurate. In addition, the potential added attrition biases over time are limited to those children who are lost during the course of a year, and not over a longer period of time. The extent of the attrition problem is likely to be affected by the extent of academic redshirting and use of readiness testing to delay kindergarten entry. When local matches within small communities can be made to provide a comparison group, then the degree of bias may not be overwhelming, but this is an undeniably risky approach.

Nonequivalent Groups Pre- and Posttest in Preschool

In another common design, nonequivalent groups are identified and assessed before the beginning of the preschool program, and growth is compared at the end of the preschool year. This requires either a waiting list for entry into the program or some other method of identifying children who are not enrolled in the program at the time of program enrollment, so both groups can be pretested. Some selection bias may be reduced by the use of a pretest and more statistical power for detecting what can be modest effects is provided; selection bias due to unmeasured differences between groups remains a threat unless it is reasonable to assume that all differences between the groups are captured by the pretest score. Experience suggests that this is not a reasonable assumption.

Regression-Discontinuity Design

This research design seeks protection against selection bias beyond that offered by a pretest or simply controlling for family background in a statistical analysis. The regression-discontinuity design (RDD) approach depends on the ability to identify a variable that predicts group membership but is not associated with any characteristics of the children and families. For example, if age, family income, or a test score is used to determine who is admitted to a program from among the applicants, then that cutoff can be used to define groups and employed in a statistical model to estimate program effects (Barnett, Frede, Mobasher, & Mohr, 1988; Cook, 2008; Gormley, Gayer, Phillips, & Dawson, 2005). With a strict age cutoff, for example, children just entering preschool can be used as a control for children who are entering kindergarten and already had preschool the year before. The analyses statistically estimate the effects of age on test scores but look for a bump, or discontinuity, in the line relating age to test score exactly at the age cutoff. This bump provides an unbiased estimate of the treatment effect provided that no other characteristics of the child and family vary suddenly at just that age, and that the model correctly captures the relationship between age and test score. It is important to have a sufficient number of children enrolled to provide confidence in the estimates at the point of the discontinuity, and it is best conducted when the population participating in the program is reasonably stable from one year to the next (e.g., there is no significant expansion in the provision of the preschool program from the prior year in the communities participating in the study). Confidence in RDD studies is also increased if children can be assessed very early in the school year and substantial numbers of children who enroll in preschool do not leave the program before entering kindergarten.

Randomized Trial

Randomized trials in which children are assigned by random chance either to the preschool program or a control group have a number of strong points, including the ease with which they are interpreted and explained. They offer the strongest protection against selection bias (Campbell & Boruch, 1975). Randomized trials also require a smaller sample size to detect a given effect size than any of the other designs. Two circumstances work well for randomization: when there are more children to serve than slots available, or during a planned expansion. Of course, randomized trials can fall victim to attrition, as can any of the other designs. In addition, children assigned to the treatment group may fail to participate, and those assigned to the control group may access the service. Control group children may also access a near substitute, which is more or less of a problem depending on whether the goal is to estimate the effect of the program compared to no treatment or compared to what the children would access without the program.

Limitations in Current Prekindergarten Evaluations Conducted by States

Evaluations of state-funded prekindergarten programs range from simple to highly complicated (Gilliam & Zigler, 2000, 2004). The 69 evaluation reports that document the 20 PreK evaluations between 1978 (the year of the first released state PreK evaluation) and 2003 provide useful information regarding how states have evaluated the effectiveness of early education programs. Evaluations were identified for 20 different state-funded PreK systems operating in 18 states. Complete reports were obtained for all evaluations, and program evaluators were contacted directly when additional information or clarification was needed. Of the 20 evaluations reviewed, 11 were conducted by third-party evaluators, sometimes in collaboration with the state departments of education, and the rest were conducted solely by research staff at the state agency administering the program. Third-party evaluators often were affiliated with one of the state's public universities. Private consultants and educational research foundations also were contracted by states to evaluate their programs. Several methodological characteristics of these studies are described below and presented in Table 4.1.

TABLE 4.1. Methodological Characteristics of State-Funded Prekindergarten Evaluations

State	No. of cohorts	Pretest	Grade levels assessed	Type of contrast group[a]	Sample size[b]	Outcomes measured[l]
AR	1	Yes	PreK	None	P = 175	1
CT	3	Yes[k]	PreK–3	Varies[j]	P = 264	1,3,5,9,10
DC	4	No	PreK–5	M[f]	Cohort 1 = 22 pairs; cohorts 2–4 = 112–234 pairs	1,3,6,7
DE	1	Yes	PreK	None	P = 490	1
FL	3	Yes	PreK–4	E$_{no}$	Cohorts 1–3: P ≈ 500–700, C ≈ 400–700	1,3,5–7,9–11
GA	2	No	K–1	M[f]	Cohort 1: P = 111, C = 111; cohort 2: P = 267, C = 267	1,5,7,9–11
GA-UPK	1	Yes	PreK–K	NN[i]	P = 353; Head Start = 134; child care = 143	1,3–5,7,11
KA	1	No	K–1	None	P = 738	1
KY	6	Yes	PreK–4	Cohorts 1, 2, 6 = RC; Cohorts 3–5 = E[c]	Cohorts 1–6: P ≈ 120–320, C ≈ 30–200	1–3,5,10
LA-8(g)	2	Yes	PreK	None	Nearly all enrolled children (~ 1,500 each cohort)	1
LA-4	2	Yes	PreK	None	Cohort 1 = 1,358; cohort 2 = 3,711	1
MD	1	No	K; 3; 5; 8; 9, 10	RC	P = 416, C = 476	1,5,7–10
MI	1	No	K–4	E$_{no}$[d]	P = 351, C = 279	1,5,7,9–11
NJ-Abb	1	Yes	PreK	NN	P = 1,488	1,3
NY-EPK	5	Yes	PreK–6	WL[e]	Cohorts 1–5: P ≈ 1,000–1,900, C ≈ 57–1,700	1,5,7,9,10
OK	2	Yes	PreK–K	E[h]	Total N = 2,396	1
SC	3[f]	No	1–3	Cohort 1 = E; cohort 3 = RC	Cohort 1: P ≈ 600–721, C ≈ 2,500–4,700; cohort 3: P ≈ 3,000, C ≈ 4,000	1,7,9,10
TX	1	No	PreK–3	E	P ≈ 1,499–46,379, C ≈ 396–43,589[g]	7,9–11
VT	1	No	K–2	None	P = 280	1,6,9,10
WA	3	No	PreK–7	M	Cohort 1 = 250 pairs; cohort 2 = 156 pairs; cohort 3 = 946 pairs	1,3,4,6,10,11

[a] M, program-eligible nonattendees matched to participants on some characteristics; E, program-eligible nonattendees; E$_{no}$, program-eligible nonattendees who have attended no other form of preschool; NN, participants were compared to national norms from tests; WL, program-eligible children who were on a wait list; RC, random classmates.

[b] P, prekindergarten participants; C, comparisons.

[c] Due to difficulties with attrition, eligible nonattendees were replaced in each cohort as needed with random classmates beginning in kindergarten.

[d] Participants must have attended the program 100 of 151 program days.

[e] Two types of "wait-listed" children were used depending on the variable and cohort.

[f] Only results for the first and third cohorts of the South Carolina evaluation could be located.

[g] Exact numbers depend on the specific outcome being measured.

[h] The Oklahoma study used a quasi-experimental regression-discontinuity design.

[i] Comparisons were also made to gains by children in Head Start and in privately obtained child care.

[j] A kindergarten comparison group was added to the design for Cohort 3 during the 2001–2002 school year. The obtained evaluation report only includes data for Cohorts 1 and 2.

[k] A pretest was used only in Cohort 2.

[l] 1, developmental skills; 2, self-perceived competence; 3, behavior problems; 4, child health; 5, school attendance; 6, grades; 7, school-administered achievement tests; 8, school dropout; 9, grade retention; 10, special education referral or placement; 11, parental involvement.

Number of Cohorts, Length of Follow-Up, and Number of Subjects

Most studies evaluated multiple cohorts of children and followed participants prospectively beginning in their PreK year. Many, however, recruited children once they enrolled in kindergarten, when a comparison group could be located most easily. The median length of follow-up was second grade. Maryland followed children until their 10th grade, the farthest of the state evaluations. The number of subjects varied significantly by state: Some evaluations relied on individual assessment of representative samples, whereas others relied mostly on school-collected data that existed for all students. To recruit samples, evaluators typically selected school districts or building sites to represent various regions of the state, then randomly selected subjects at the classroom level. This created nested designs, but the statistical analyses never accounted for this feature. Most study attrition rates ranged from less than 10% to about 25% per year, rather similar to the 20% rate typical for evaluations of programs serving at-risk families (Gomby, 1999).

Comparison Groups and Study Designs

No state evaluation randomly assigned children to program and control groups; therefore, all resorted to some less rigorous comparison group.

Evaluation Designs for Targeted Prekindergarten Programs

Of the 20 evaluations identified in Table 4.1, all but two were of programs targeting children from low-income families or some other risk status for educational failure. These 18 evaluations of targeted PreK programs used a variety of designs and comparison groups.

All six of the evaluations without comparison groups (Arkansas, Delaware, Kansas, Louisiana 8(g), Louisiana LA4, and Vermont), are severely limited methodologically. These designs used a single-group pretest–posttest (and in two cases no pretest was given) with non-nationally normed instruments in an attempt to demonstrate positive growth associated with participation in the program. In all six of these evaluations, children were determined to have improved in their skills, but, unfortunately, there is no way to attribute any of the growth to the effects of PreK participation as opposed to simple maturation. In some cases, posttest results of PreK participants were compared to some valued benchmarks for the program or the schools. This can be useful in order to determine whether children are leaving the program with the desired skill levels or to target services, but this methodology simply cannot support even the most tenuous of causal inferences. Other methodological flaws plagued several of these six evaluations. These flaws include using tests that have not been validated or normed and requiring PreK teachers to administer the evaluation measures on their own children, introducing the potential for significant bias in the ratings. Because of these extreme limitations, these six evaluations were excluded from further description and presentation of findings.

In the 12 remaining evaluations of targeted PreK programs, at least one of five different types of comparison groups was used: waitlisted comparisons, matched program-eligible nonattendees, nonmatched program-eligible nonattendees, program-eligible nonattendees who did not attend any other preschool program, and random classmates who may or may not have been eligible for the program.

Arguably, of the comparison groups used, the *waitlist comparison* provided the best test of the program, since comparison children and their families were both eligible for services and motivated to apply for the program. Unfortunately, the only program to employ this comparison was the evaluation of the New York State Experimental Prekindergarten Program, which was by far the most outdated state evaluation (University of the State of

New York & New York State Education Department, 1977). Use of the three other comparison groups of program-eligible nonattendees may have introduced a self-selection bias to the results, since families of comparison children were not motivated to seek placement in the program being evaluated. The *matched program-eligible nonattendee comparison* attempts methodologically to control some of this bias by matching the two groups on related variables (e.g., gender; ethnicity; parent education and occupational level; and some type of proxy for family income, such as eligibility for free or reduced lunch at school). The *program-eligible nonattendee comparison* is even less rigorous, since comparison children, though eligible for the program, may have significantly differed from participants in many ways. The comparison group that arguably provides the least stringent test of the program is the one that used *program-eligible nonattendees who did not attend any other preschool program*, since the families of comparison children were not motivated to seek preschool programming for their children. Furthermore, in Michigan, the participants were required to have attended the program at least two-thirds of the total number of program days (100 of 150 days). Stipulating that the participant children must have attended the program at least minimally, and that the comparison children could not have participated in a similar program, may bias studies toward finding positive results. However, one could also argue that it is unfair to test the effectiveness of a program by using participants who have not participated in at least some minimal way or by comparing outcomes to children who may have attended similar programs (Gilliam et al., 2000).

Three evaluations used *random elementary school classmates* as comparisons. Despite this method of selecting comparisons, the two groups in Maryland were comparable in ethnicity, age, gender, family composition, and father's educational and occupational level, but differences in maternal educational and occupational level slightly favored preschool participants. In Kentucky and South Carolina, random classmate comparisons were used only for certain cohorts or at certain grade levels. Additionally, in three of Kentucky's six cohorts, a program-eligible nonattendee comparison group was initially recruited, then changed to random classmates over the course of yearly follow-ups as a result of serious attrition rates in the comparison group. This practice, of course, makes it difficult to determine the nature of the comparison group in the follow-up years and precludes a longitudinal treatment of the data.

Evaluation Designs for Universal Prekindergarten Programs

The two evaluations of universal PreK programs—the Georgia and Oklahoma studies— deviated from the earlier types of contrast. Universal programs create a special challenge in terms of locating suitable comparison groups. Because the saturation rates of these universal programs are relatively high—of all state-funded PreK programs, Oklahoma (71.0%) and Georgia (53.4%) serve the highest percentage of their states' 4-year-olds (Barnett et al., 2009)—the comparison pool is relatively small, and many of the children not served by these programs may be served by other preschool programs operating in the state.

The Oklahoma Early Childhood Four-Year-Old Program evaluation (Gormley & Gayer, 2003; Gormley & Phillips, 2003), conducted in the Tulsa Public Schools (TPS), used a very sophisticated design and analysis to deal with this problem. The TPS use an age cutoff to determine eligibility to enter the program: Only children with a birthday earlier than September 1 can enroll in the program, and children born after that date must wait 1 year. Taking advantage of this arbitrary entry criterion, the evaluators designed a quasi-experimental regression-discontinuity study that tested differences in predicted probabilities of test scores based on a bilateral quadratic parametric fit. This design allowed for a comparison of children who barely met the cutoff versus those that barely missed it, and preliminary analyses verified the demographic comparability of the groups. Given the difficulty of identifying and recruiting a suitable comparison group for an evaluation of a universally accessible program, this designed provided an excellent means for estimating program impacts.

Rather than seek a method for providing a true counterfactual for participation in the PreK program, the Georgia Universal Prekindergarten Program (UPK) evaluation (Henry et al., 2003) focused on contrasting the PreK children with two samples of children served in Head Start and in community-based child care programs obtained by the parents. Overall, two different types of analyses were employed to contrast these three groups: (1) comparing posttest scores among these three groups at the end of the preschool year, and (2) comparing pretest to posttest gain scores during the preschool year and into the beginning of kindergarten. Also, by using several tests that have national norms, the evaluators were able to benchmark children's performance in all three groups against national norms for several of the child outcomes being assessed.

Using the first analytic strategy described earlier, the Georgia evaluators attempted to document program effects by comparing at the end of the preschool year and the beginning of the kindergarten year child outcome scores for PreK participants to those for children who attended Head Start and children who attended private, community-based child care centers. At the end of the PreK year and at the beginning of kindergarten, Georgia UPK children outscored Georgia Head Start students across most measures. However, children who attended private, community-based child care centers typically outscored both groups. Unfortunately, simply comparing child scores at the end of a program says nothing about the degree to which these exit scores were the result of the intervention, and contrasting three service options (Georgia UPK, Head Start, and privately obtained child care) results in a serious underestimation of the effects of the Georgia UPK because of the lack of a no-treatment comparison (Abbott-Shim & Lambert, 2003).

Because the Georgia UPK posttest-only comparisons described earlier did not provide the data necessary to estimate changes due to the intervention, the evaluators used gain scores to attempt to document program impacts. Across the several measures used in this evaluation, only four measures for which analyses were conducted had national normative data. By using the national norms built into these tests, the evaluators were able to assess whether PreK participants showed a gain in these areas during the course of the PreK program that exceeded normative expectations. Statistically significant pretest (collected near the beginning of the 4-year-old preschool year) to posttest (collected near the end of the year) differences were reported for the Georgia UPK participants across all four measures: pretest to the end of PreK on the Peabody Picture Vocabulary Test (PPVT-3), Letter–Word Identification, and the Oral and Written Language Scales (OWLS), and from pretest to kindergarten entry on the PPVT-3, Letter–Word Identification, and Applied Problems (Henry et al., 2003, Table 5.1, p. 45). Although these differences were labeled "statistically significant," the report does not indicate the type of analyses used, the test statistics, or the level of significance. Furthermore, since standard deviations were not reported anywhere in the report (Abbott-Shim & Lambert, 2003), it was not possible to determine accurately the standardized effect size. Assuming that the sample standard deviations are the same as the test standard deviations for the instruments used, standardized effect sizes ranged from 0.13 on Letter–Word Identification to 0.29 on the PPVT-3, both at the end of the prekindergarten year. Although apparently no statistical tests compared the Georgia UPK gains to those in either Head Start or privately obtained child care, gain scores across these three groups appeared rather similar. One exception was a +7.04 point pretest-to-kindergarten entry gain on the PPVT-3 for the Head Start sample, which results in an estimated effect size of 0.47 (assuming that the sample standard deviations approximate the test's normative standard deviation). Significant pretest–posttest gains on non-normed measures were reported in the Georgia UPK evaluation, but it is impossible to know the degree to which these differences reflect simple maturation unrelated to PreK participation.

Domains of Outcomes Assessed and Instruments Used

As in Gilliam and Zigler (2000), outcomes were categorized in one of 11 domains, and most states tracked outcomes in more than one domain (see Table 4.1). (For a complete list of the 62 different measures used, see Gilliam & Zigler, 2004.) A large number of tests and procedures were used in these 20 evaluations. Several of them are well-known, psychometrically valid instruments. In many cases, however, relatively unknown tests were used, with little data provided in the evaluation reports regarding their reliability and validity.

What Can Be Learned from State Evaluations?

There are many methodological weaknesses in many of these evaluations, and some are so flawed as to weaken significantly any ability to draw solid conclusions about program effects. These methodologically fatal flaws include practices that build-in a strong evaluator bias (e.g., relying solely on PreK teacher reports in a pretest–posttest design), as well as basing results solely on single-group pretest–posttest analyses without attempting to control for maturation and other factors. Gilliam and Zigler (2000) provide several recommendations for PreK program evaluation, including choosing appropriate and realistic outcomes and validated measures, obtaining the most comparable contrast group possible, using process evaluations to guide and contextualize outcome evaluations, and other suggestions that may help guide program evaluations in this area.

Evaluations of Universal Prekindergarten Programs

Evaluating a universally accessible program presents major methodological challenges, since adequate comparison groups may be hard to locate. Two universal PreK program evaluations used very different approaches to dealing with this problem. In Georgia, gain scores for UPK participants were compared to national norms on the tests used, an approached used in the Head Start Family and Child Experiences Survey (FACES) national evaluation (Zill et al., 2003) and to contrast groups of children who have attended either Head Start or privately obtained child care. The use of these national norms to serve as a sort of control group, though common in this type of research, has several limitations. The most noteworthy limitation is that there is little evidence to suggest that the national norms of these tests adequately reflect the learning trajectory of the particular students who may be participating in the program. This is a major problem for evaluations of programs that serve at-risk populations (e.g., Head Start and most of the state PreK programs that target services to low-income children) because the populations served by these programs vary in significant ways from the national norms used in these tests—norms that were derived from a national sample of children across all socioeconomic levels. Though the use of these national norms in evaluating universally accessible programs is not ideal, the population served by universally accessible PreK programs may match these norms more closely.

The Oklahoma UPK evaluation, in contrast to the Georgia UPK evaluation, utilized the arbitrary birthday cutoff that the program uses (September 1) to analyze differences in children who were able to attend the program because their birthday fell before September 1 versus children who did not attend because their birthday fell after that date, and controlled for any age differences between the two groups. The Oklahoma design and analytic strategy allowed the evaluators to provide well-supported findings about the impact of the program, without denying services to a control group or using national normative data that may not reflect adequately the sample being studied. This approach holds significant promise for evaluating UPK programs.

Ensuring That Assessments Are Valid and Useful

There are many potential benefits to an assessment system. However, rather than measuring what we value, it may be more accurate to say that we all too often value what we measure. Whatever is measured tends to become a focus of concern for preschool providers, policymakers, and the public. Therefore, assessment systems have the potential for driving much of what goes on in early education classes, simply by increasing the saliency of the measured areas of the curriculum relative to the unmeasured (or less well measured) areas.

In the absence of a clear mechanism for utilizing assessment data to create meaningfully beneficial changes in educational services at the classroom level (where they are experienced by children), it is hard to imagine any assessment system as being effective. For assessment systems used by teachers for classroom learning proposes, the true test of effectiveness is whether the assessment results actually lead to changes in teaching behaviors that improve children's learning. Likewise, the test of effectiveness for assessment systems used by administrators and decision makers should also be whether they yield data that lead to meaningful improvements in the educational system. The "effectiveness" of any data collection system depends as much on how the data are *used* as it does on how they were *collected*. No system can be efficient unless it is first effective. Therefore, it seems advisable to focus first on ensuring that any system or systems of data collection lead to a clear mechanism that improves services.

As with program evaluation design, the intended purpose should determine the type of assessment being administered (Meisels, 1994). Different types of tests are designed for different purposes and have different levels of constraint on the test administration and questions asked; that is, they vary in how formal and structured the test situation is. Screening tests, which are widely used at kindergarten entry and in preschool, are easy and quick to administer but have relatively low predictive power because they are designed only to identify children who may need further and more complex diagnostic assessment. The purpose of diagnostic testing is to determine whether children are in need of special education, and to guide teachers and others in planning instruction. Readiness tests are, according to Meisels (1999), the equivalent of achievement tests administered at entry to a program to determine whether a child has the skills necessary to benefit from the program. Information from readiness tests can be used to modify a program or individualize instruction to enhance its effectiveness with each student—making the program ready for the children rather than the other way around. Achievement tests are given in the middle or end of a program to determine what the child has gained from participation in that program. Less formal methods of assessment can be used for similar purposes and include parental report, direct observation of children in their natural settings and routine activities, and systematic collection and analysis of work samples.

In a recent policy report, Darling-Hammond (2010, p. 1) sets out the following recommendations for any assessment system:

The Student Assessment System should

- address the depth and breadth of standards as well as all areas of the curriculum, not just those that are easy to measure
- consider and include all students as an integral part of the design process, anticipating their particular needs and encouraging all students to demonstrate what they know and can do
- honor the research indicating that students learn best when given challenging content and provided with assistance, guidance, and feedback on a regular basis

- employ a variety of appropriate measures, instruments, and processes at the classroom, school, and district levels, as well as the state level. These include multiple forms of assessment and incorporate formative as well as summative measures
- engage teachers in scoring student work based on shared targets

All high-stakes testing is controversial, since it represents a snapshot of ability, and this has even led some colleges and universities to halt use of Scholastic Aptitude Tests (SATs) in admissions. High-stakes testing of young children is even more controversial, leading the National Association of Elementary School Principals (1990), the National Association of State Boards of Education (1988), the NAECS/SDE (2000), and the NAEYC (2003) to criticize universal standardized testing of children under third grade for the following reasons:

- Development in early childhood is variable and rapid, and unevenly impacted by experience and environmental factors.
- Young children are not consistent in showing their abilities. Contexts and how questions are asked can greatly affect their performance.
- By virtue of their lack of experience and age, young children don't understand the need to perform well.
- The long-term predictive validity of tests of young children is not very high.
- The results are not typically very useful to parents and teachers unless a very extensive and, therefore, expensive test is administered.
- Standardized tests don't provide information about what a child can do in his or her normal environment, only what he or she can or can't do in a highly constrained situation.
- Results of tests can be misused to deny children access to programs, to determine funding for programs, and to reward or punish teachers.

An additional reason that high-stakes, on-demand tests are questionable is that there is no common definition of readiness or achievement goals for preschool or kindergarten. Meisels (1999) points out that educational philosophy greatly influences how readiness is defined, which in turn impacts the choice of instrument.

The merits and limitations of sampling are the converse of those of assessing all children. In sampling, the merit is that one can get data representative of the whole (assuming the sample was well drawn) at a fraction of the cost, time, and child–staff burden (potentially allowing resources to go toward more in-depth assessment, external assessors, and beefed up reliability training to improve the veracity of the data); the limitation is that one does not have data on all of the children that can be used for instructional planning. In testing all of the children, the merit is that instructional planning data are readily available for all (assuming a good test was used for the purpose and that the teachers/staff are suitably skilled at using such data for this purpose); the limitation is that it is incredibly expensive in monetary cost, time, and child–staff burden. Attempts to offset the cost and time often come at the expense of the veracity of the data (by limiting the resources spent on external assessors, reliability training, and adequate data coding and management systems) and by reducing the amount of time spent in assessment by using tests that are too cursory to provide detailed, useful information on learning and development.

For statewide or large-scale assessment, we recommend matrix sampling in which children are selected randomly, and specific domains are chosen randomly for each child. This design allows one to select the sample size necessary for valid results, while dividing between selected children the full burden of the comprehensive assessment—minimizing the overall child assessment burden, as well as the burden for any one specific child. In order to make sure that enough sample is available to form valid conclusions about children and subgroups, stratification and perhaps oversampling techniques can be used.

External assessors administering direct/standardized child assessment tools can generate data to improve instruction, and provide for accountability and program evaluation. However, that data should only inform professional development and program improvement efforts at a state or large program level. Typically, results should *not* be used to make inferences about the effectiveness of teachers, curriculum, or other elements of instruction at the individual child or classroom level. It may provide an acceptable basis for inferences about effectiveness at the classroom level if it is part of a very rigorous design that includes random assignment of children to classrooms. At the child level, many safeguards need to be in place, and only a few specific assessment tools are comprehensive and likely to measure state standards. Typically it is best not to use teachers to administer on-demand tests for children. It can pervert teaching and lead to incorrect conclusions, especially if teachers believe that their job, pay, or program is in jeopardy. (An exception to this might be made if the assessment is comprehensive within a domain, but the training demands to do this on a large scale would probably not be worth it.)

Teacher-generated observational assessments of children's progress that are used to improve instruction can also be used for accountability or program evaluation purposes if the system implemented has proven validity that meets the same standards as those expected for standardized "on-demand" assessments. Knowledgeable and well-prepared teachers are the best source of information about children's development, but "report cards" and other checklists that do not have rigorous requirements for data-based conclusions based on systematic observation and documentation over time are regularly found to be inaccurate. The primary purpose of performance-based assessment using teacher ratings is to inform teaching, and these ratings should only be used for program evaluation and other purposes when there is sufficient psychometric information to ensure that both the instrument *and* the administration are valid and reliable (Riley-Ayers, Frede, Jacobs, & Stevenson-Boyd, 2008). Some essential caveats to this include the following:

1. The aggregated results of performance-based assessment should be used for program improvement and overall program evaluation, *not* high stakes decision making for teachers or programs, nor should assessments of individuals be the sole source of information for placement of children (e.g., referral to special education).
2. Teachers must be trained to an acceptable level of reliability. This means every teacher who administers the instrument.
3. Methods must be in place to ensure that drift does not occur in scoring over time.
4. Teachers should be supported in using the data to inform instruction.

When constructing assessment systems the special case of English language learners must be considered. Choice of instruments depends to a large extent on the language of instruction and the purpose of the assessment. If the teachers only speak English, then the instructional utility of knowing more about the child's ability in the home language is limited. And if the language of instruction is English, then, for program evaluation purposes, it may be appropriate to use only English assessments. But this is unclear from the research: How much transference from the home language to English or vice versa do emergent bilinguals do? In our program evaluations, we test in both languages whenever necessary and feasible (most assessments only exist in English and sometimes Spanish). Assessment should be conducted in the language of instruction; thus, if the child is in a bilingual setting, bilingual assessments should be administered. Some new assessments (Early Mathematics Assessment System [EMAS]: Ginsburg, 2008; Lens on Science: Greenfield, Dominguez, Fuccillo, Maier,

& Greenberg, 2009) can be administered *bilingually*; that is, the trained bilingual assessor uses the appropriate language throughout the test, responding to the child. Direct translations of English assessments are typically not psychometrically sound (Espinosa, 2010).

Conclusions

Programs should perform evaluations both intensively and extensively. For intensive evaluation, the program should conduct, or contract for, a well-designed, scientific study collecting data from a sample of program sites. For extensive evaluation, all program sites should collect data on program implementation and children's development. The intensive evaluation should be designed to provide valid estimates of the effectiveness of the program with sufficient precision to guide decisions about the program, and should be adequately funded and last long enough for this purpose. The programwide data collection should provide data for teachers and program managers to use to improve teaching and learning. Both types of information can be used together to hold local agencies and providers accountable for performance. Ideally, local accountability suggests that local agencies and providers contract with outside assessors, or that the state supply them. Practically, local accountability is likely to be based on self-monitoring, with teachers collecting program implementation and child progress data that monitor the achievement of benchmarks, with the understanding that child assessment data may only weakly support inferences about program effectiveness. If a program is effective statewide, and classroom quality in a particular location is comparable to the state average, while children's abilities at kindergarten entry seem satisfactory, then the local program may be judged effective locally. It is our obligation to children, parents, taxpayers, and other stakeholders to ensure that the programs we provide live up to their promise and use data-based decision making to improve their effectiveness continuously. It is also imperative that, as we reach the benchmarks set for improvement, we revise the standards, so that we constantly raise the bar and improve programs and services for young children.

References

Abbott-Shim, M., & Lambert, R. (2003). *Review of the "Report of the Findings from the Early Childhood Study."* Unpublished manuscript, Georgia State University, Atlanta, and University of North Carolina at Charlotte.

Barnett, W.S. (1993, May 19). Does Head Start fade out? *Education Week*. Retrieved February 27, 2010, from *nieer.org/resources/research/battleheadstart.pdf*.

Barnett, W. S. (1995). Long-term effects of early childhood programs on cognitive and school outcomes. *The Future of Children, 5*(3), 25–50.

Barnett, W. S. (1998). Long-term effects on cognitive development and school success. In W. S. Barnett & S. S. Boocock (Eds.), *Early care and education for children in poverty* (pp. 11–44). Albany: State University of New York Press.

Barnett, W. S. (2006). A review of the Reason Foundation's report on preschool and kindergarten (NIEER Working paper). New Brunswick, NJ: National Institute for Early Education Research, Rutgers University. Retrieved February 27, 2010, from *nieer.org/docs/?docid=150*.

Barnett, W. S., Epstein, D. J., Friedman, A. H., Sansanelli, R., & Hustedt, J. T. (2009). *The state of preschool: 2009 state preschool yearbook.* New Brunswick, NJ: National Institute for Early Education Research, Rutgers University.

Barnett, W. S., Frede, E., Mobasher, H., & Mohr, P. (1988). The efficacy of public preschool programs and the relationship of program quality to efficacy. *Educational Evaluation and Policy Analysis, 12*, 169–181.

Campbell, D. T. (1976). *Assessing the impact of planned social change* (Occasional Paper Series, Paper #8). Hanover, NH: Public Affairs Center, Dartmouth College.

Campbell, D. T. (1991). Methods for an experimenting society. *American Journal of Evaluation, 12*(3), 223–260.

Campbell, D. T., & Boruch, R. F. (1975). Making the case for randomized assignment to treatments by considering the alternatives: Six ways in which quasi-experimental evaluations in compensatory education tend to underestimate effects. In C. A. Bennet & A. A. Lumsdaine (Eds.), *Evaluation and experiment* (pp. 195–296). New York: Academic Pres.

Cook, T. D. (2008). Waiting for life to arrive: A history of the regression-discontinuity design in psychology, statistics, and economics. *Journal of Econometrics, 142*(2), 636–654.

Darling-Hammond, L. (2010). Performance counts: Assessment systems that support high-quality learning. Washington, DC: Council of Chief State School Officers. Available at *www.ccsso.org/publications/details.cfm?publicationid=381.*

Espinosa, L. M. (2010). Assessment of young English language learners. In E. Garcia & E. Frede (Eds.), *Developing the research agenda for young English language learners* (pp. 119–142). New York: Teachers College Press.

Frede, E., & Barnett, W. S. (1992). Developmentally appropriate public school preschool: A study of implementation of the High/Scope curriculum and its effects on disadvantaged children's skills at first grade. *Early Childhood Research Quarterly, 7,* 483–499.

Gilliam, W. S., & Ripple, C. H. (2004). What can be learned from state-funded preschool initiatives?: A data-based approach to the Head Start devolution debate. In E. Zigler & S. J. Styfco (Eds.), *The Head Start debates* (pp. 477–497). Baltimore: Brookes.

Gilliam, W. S., Ripple, C. H., Zigler, E. F., & Leiter, V. (2000). Evaluating child and family demonstration initiatives: Lessons from the Comprehensive Child Development Program. *Early Childhood Research Quarterly, 15,* 41–59.

Gilliam, W. S., & Zigler, E. F. (2000). A critical meta-analysis of all impact evaluations of state-funded preschool from 1977 to 1998: Implications for policy, service delivery and program evaluation. *Early Childhood Research Quarterly, 15,* 441–473.

Gilliam, W. S., & Zigler, E. F. (2004). State efforts to evaluate the effects of prekindergarten: 1977–2003. New Haven, CT: Yale University. Retrieved September 12, 2011, from *nieer.org/resources/research/StateEfforts.pdf.*

Ginsburg, H. P. (2008). *Early Mathematics Assessment System (EMAS).* New York: Author.

Gomby, D. S. (1999). Understanding evaluations of home visitation programs. *The Future of Children, 9*(1), 27–43.

Gormley, W., Gayer, T., Phillips, D., & Dawson, B. (2005). The effects of universal Preschool on cognitive development. *Developmental Psychology, 41,* 872–884.

Gormley, W. T., & Gayer, T. (2003). Promoting school readiness in Oklahoma: An evaluation of Tulsa's pre-k program (CROCUS Working Paper #1). Washington, DC: Georgetown University, Center for Research on Children in the United States. Available at *www.crocus.georgetown.edu/working.paper.1.pdf.*

Gormley, W. T., & Phillips, D. (2003). The effects of universal pre-k in Oklahoma: Research highlights and policy implications (CROCUS Working Paper #2). Washington, DC: Georgetown University, Center for Research on Children in the United States. Available at *www.crocus.georgetown.edu/working.paper.2.pdf.*

Greenfield, D. B., Dominguez, M. X., Fuccillo, J. M., Maier, M. F., & Greenberg, A. C. (2009, April). *Development of an IRT-based direct assessment of preschool science.* Paper presented at the biennial meeting of the Society for Research in Child Development, Denver, CO.

Henry, G. T., Henderson, L. W., Ponder, B. D., Gordon, C. S., Mashburn, A. J., & Rickman, D. K. (2003). *Report of the findings from the Early Childhood Study: 2001–02.* Atlanta: Georgia State University, Andrew Young School of Policy Studies.

Laird, E. (2009, May). Connecting the dots: Making longitudinal data work for young children (Data Quality Campaign). Retrieved February 10, 2010, from *www.dataqualitycampaign.org/files.*

McCall, R. B. (2009). Evidence-based programming in the context of practice and policy. *SRCD Social Policy Report, 23*(3), 3–18. Retrieved from *www.srcd.org/spr.html.*

Meisels, S. J. (1999). Assessing readiness. In R.C. Pianta & M. Cox (Eds.), *The transition to kindergarten* (pp. 39–66). Baltimore: Brookes.

Meisels, S. J., with Atkins-Burnett, S. (1994). *Developmental screening in early childhood: A guide* (4th ed.). Washington, DC: National Association for the Education of Young Children.

National Association for the Education of Young Children. (2003). *Early childhood curriculum, assessment, and program evaluation: Building an effective, accountable system in programs for children birth through age 8.* Washington, DC: Author.

National Association for the Education of Young Children (NAEYC) & National Association of Early Childhood Specialists in State Departments of Education (NAECS/SDE). (2003). *Early childhood curriculum, child assessment and program evaluation: Building an accountable and effective system for children birth through age eight* (A joint position statement of NAEYC and NAECS/SDE). Washington, DC: NAEYC.

National Association of Early Childhood Specialists in State Departments of Education. (2000). *Still unacceptable trends in kindergarten entry and placement.* Washington, DC: Author.

National Association of Elementary School Principals. (1990). *Early childhood education and the elementary school principal: Standards for quality programs for young children.* Alexandria, VA: Author.

National Association of State Boards of Education. (1988). *Right from the start: The report of the NASBE Task Force on Early Childhood Education.* Alexandria, VA: Author.

National Child Care Information Center. (2007). Child Care Bulletin 32. Washington, DC: U.S. Department of Human Services, Administration for Children and Families, Child Care Bureau. Retrieved February 16, 2011, from *nccic.acf.hhs.gov/files/resources/issue32.pdf.*

Nichols, S. L., & Berliner, D. C. (2007). *Collateral damage: How high-stakes testing corrupts America's schools.* Cambridge, MA: Harvard Education Press.

Olsen, D., & Snell, L. (2006). *Assessing proposals for preschool and kindergarten: Essential information for parents, taxpayers and policymakers.* Los Angeles: The Reason Foundation.

Patton, M. Q. (2008). *Utilization-focused evaluation* (4th ed.). Newbury Park, CA: Sage.

Riley-Ayers, S., Frede, E., Jacobs, G., & Stevenson-Boyd, J. (2008, June). *Improving teaching through standards-based systematic assessment: Development of the Early Learning Scale.* Paper presented at the National Institute for Early Childhood Professional Development, New Orleans, LA.

Ripple, C. H., Gilliam, W. S., Chanana, N., & Zigler, E. (1999). Will fifty cooks spoil the broth?: The debate over entrusting Head Start to the states. *American Psychologist, 54,* 327–343.

Rothstein, J. (2009). Student sorting and bias in value-added estimation: Selection on observables and unobservables. *Education Finance and Policy, 4,* 537–571.

Schultz, T., & Kagan, S. L. (2007). Taking stock: Assessing and improving early childhood learning and program quality (Report of the National Early Childhood Accountability Task Force). Retrieved September 12, 2011, from *ccf.tc.columbia.edu/pdf/task_force_report.pdf.*

Tarullo, L. B., Vogel, A. C., Aikens, N., Martin, E. S., Nogales, R., & Del Grosso, P. (2008, December). Implementation of the Head Start National Reporting System: Spring 2007 final report. Princeton, NJ: Mathematica. Retrieved February 10, 2011, from *www.mathematica-mpr.com/publications/pdfs/earlychildhood/headstart_nrs2007.*

Todd, P. E., & Wolpin, K. I. (2007). The production of cognitive achievement in children: Home, school, and racial test score gaps. *Journal of Human Capital, 1,* 91–136.

University of the State of New York & New York State Education Department. (1977). *Preliminary report of findings: Evaluation of the New York State Experimental Prekindergarten Program.* Albany: Authors.

Zill, N., Resnick, G., Kim, K., O'Donnell, K., Sorongon, A., McKey, R. H., et al. (2003, May). *Head Start FACES 2000: A whole-child perspective on program performance—Fourth progress report.* Washington, DC: U.S. Department of Health and Human Services.

CHAPTER 5

More Than Teachers

The Early Care and Education Workforce

Sharon Ryan and Marcy Whitebook

If you ask anyone working in the field who is the early childhood care and education workforce you are likely to get a range of answers. Some people will say caregivers, while others might mention family day care providers, kindergarten teachers, administrators, teaching assistants, and the like. If the same question is asked of someone working beyond the walls of the school, center, or home, then the answer might be mental health professionals, early interventionists, advocates, professional development consultants, teacher educators, or researchers. In general, people tend to define who works in early education and care from their particular vantage points, which are shaped by the sector in which they work and their role in the field (Whitebook & Austin, 2009). This lack of definitional clarity is perhaps not surprising given that, unlike other professions, the early childhood field has no nationally agreed-upon vocabulary to delineate the various job roles associated with the work of educating young children (Kagan, Kauerz, & Tarrant, 2008).

The knowledge base of the early education and care workforce does little to help with this state of affairs. Most studies concentrate on those who work hands-on with children on a daily basis within a particular sector. For example, there are studies of teachers in publicly funded prekindergarten (Gilliam & Marchesseault, 2005; Ryan & Ackerman, 2005), teachers and teaching assistants in child care (e.g., Whitebook, Howes, & Phillips, 1990) and family day care providers (Kontos, Howes, Shinn, & Galinsky, 1995). Yet the education of preschool-age children occurs across all of these sectors and is enacted by many other workers in addition to those directly caring for children.

This chapter reviews the research base on the preschool workforce in the United States. We define the "preschool workforce" as those individuals working in a program offering early care and education to children 0–5 years of age. Our aim in this chapter is to describe what is known about the characteristics, work environments, and practices of early childhood professionals both within and beyond the classroom door and what the research suggests about their ability to provide high-quality preschool programs. After outlining the methods and data sources typically used to measure and describe the workforce, we examine what is known about three differing sets of roles—those who work directly with children in an instructional capacity, those who lead preschool programs, and those who work in infrastructure positions. This chapter concludes with a discussion of the workforce development problems that impede high-quality services for children, and the types of research and policies that could contribute to their amelioration. We contend that without careful attention to the early care and education workforce in more holistic, sustained, and systematic ways, the potential of preschool programs to level the playing field for all children will not be realized.

Studying the Early Childhood and Care Workforce

In order to study the early childhood workforce, researchers have conceptualized the work of educating young children in differing ways, employing a range of data sources and methods.

Conceptualizing the Workforce

To understand the early childhood workforce, researchers have typically looked at two sets of variables, staff characteristics and the work environment. Collecting individual demographic information such as ethnicity, languages spoken, qualifications, and years of experience provides insights into general staffing patterns and how these patterns change over time. For example, by examining early childhood workforce data extracted from the Current Population Survey over a period of 25 years, Herzenberg, Price, and Bradley (2005) found that the qualifications of early childhood teachers and administrators had declined relative to the workforce as a whole. Demographic information, therefore, helps policymakers plan for future shortages in the labor pool, as well as identify particular issues concerning the quality of the workforce.

Information about the adult work environment, such as the structure of the work (i.e., compensation, benefits, and teacher–child ratios), as well as process variables (e.g., workplace policies, leadership, and professional development), offer important insights into the conditions that mediate job performance. Many early childhood studies for example, have found that the low wages associated with care work are linked to program stability and quality, teacher behavior, and child outcomes (Gable, Rothrauff, Thornburg, & Mauzy, 2007; National Institute of Child Health and Human Development [NICHD] Early Child Care Research Network, 2000; Phillips, Mekos, Carr, McCartney, & Abbott-Shim, 2000; Whitebook, Howes, & Phillips, 1990, 1998; Whitebook & Sakai, 2004). Collecting this kind of information can provide policymakers and administrators with insights into the kinds of environments that contribute to staff stability and quality in early care and education settings.

In addition to workplace information and demographic data, a new line of inquiry explores the dynamic nature of the relationship between the workplace and those who work in it. Organizational theorists (e.g., Leana, Appelbaum, & Shevchuk, 2009; Wrzesniewski & Dutton, 2001) and researchers in early education working from this orientation (Ryan & Lancaster, 2008; Whitebook & Ryan, 2011) have begun to examine the way people make sense of, and craft, their work. From this job-crafting perspective, work is something learned through socialization into a community of practice (Lave & Wenger, 1991) and constructed through the actions of individuals working in a particular context. This newer line of inquiry focuses on not only job satisfaction but also how individuals enact early education and care work to improve the fit between the job and their own understanding of the work. In one study, Ryan and Lancaster (2008) found that teachers in child care craft their work more frequently than assistant teachers, and that job crafting behavior varies by auspice. While limited research on job crafting in early childhood education exists, by understanding how structural and process elements in the workplace interact with the agency of teaching staff, it may be possible to identify which components of the workplace are essential for improved job performance.

Sources of Workforce Data

Researchers interested in workforce demographics and trends at a national level draw on datasets that are updated regularly and managed by the federal government. Workforce data are available from the Bureau of Labor Statistics (BLS), which looks at industries at both individual and occupation levels. The Current Population Survey (CPS) is conducted monthly on 50,000 households by the Bureau of the Census, offering information about the employment status of individuals age 16 years and over. Conducted yearly, the American Community Survey (ACS) collects data on individual community members' education, job status, wages and benefits, and demographic characteristics. Wage data are available from the Occupational Employment Statistics series (BLS/OES). There are also national datasets on early education that are used to make estimates about the early childhood workforce, such as the Early Childhood Longitudinal Survey (ECLS), which provides information on adult:child ratios. The Early Childhood supplement of the National Household Education Survey (NHES) provides information on parents' reported use of child care. Similarly, Head Start collects annual workforce data as part of its Program Information Report (PIR). While the workforce is not the only focus of these education datasets, information collected on early childhood program arrangements enables researchers to make inferences about the number of teaching staff in different kinds of programs.[1]

The advantage of these national datasets is that they collect workforce information from large, nationally representative samples and are highly reliable (Brandon, Stutman, & Maroto, 2009). However, no single source provides an accurate account of the size and character of the early care and education workforce (Brandon et al., 2002). Moreover, most of these national surveys do not make it possible to discern the differences in qualifications and working conditions in differing sectors of the field (Bellm & Whitebook, 2006). In the ACS, for instance, the term *preschool teacher* is used to identify anyone working with 3- and 4-year-olds, yet the qualifications and working conditions of a teacher working in a public PreK program are quite different from those of someone working with 4-year-olds in child care. With the aim of addressing these issues, some researchers have attempted to come up with new methods to make estimates about the workforce on which policymakers can rely. In a collaboration between the Center for the Child Care Workforce and the Human Services Policy Center, for example, researchers used child care demand data derived from the NHES Early Childhood Supplement and the Early Childhood Longitudinal Study and compared this information with supply data of child care workers (Brandon et al., 2002). This research led to a larger national estimate of the workforce serving children ages 0–5 years than had previously been calculated.

In order to predict staffing demands across sectors and to create professional development plans, some states and local communities have conducted their own studies to gather more accurate information about the workforce. The National Child Care Information and Technical Assistance Center provides a list of some 20 state studies conducted over the past decade, although this list is not exhaustive. These studies vary in terms of roles and workforce variables targeted for collection and analysis, but nearly all use survey methodologies to gain a glimpse into instructional roles in a particular sector (e.g., child care, family day care, after school hours care). Although not all states have conducted studies of their early care and education workforce, the available state data tend to provide more useful information about education, tenure, wages, demographics, education, and qualifications for a broad set of job roles. In the California Early Care and Education Workforce Study (Whitebook et al., 2006), for example, 1,800 licensed family day care providers and 1,921 center directors were surveyed over the telephone about a number of key variables, including participants' professional preparation to serve English language learners and special needs populations, in addition to workforce demographics, wages and turnover, and educational attainment.

With the need for updated workforce data, nearly half the states now use workforce registries to help with policy and programming decisions. Early childhood registries are usually linked to a state's career system and collect a wide variety of information that includes qualifications and professional development training, as well as job role and title for a number of differing roles in the workforce. While more cost-effective than funding statewide research studies, most registries are not mandatory and only look at segments of the early care and education worker population (e.g., child care workers in licensed family day care and center-based care). Thus, registries are a good place to start to learn about a state's early care and education workforce, but the information available cannot be used to determine the quantity or quality of the entire preschool workforce (Kipnis & Whitebook, 2011).

Although there are regularly updated data on the early childhood workforce at both state and national levels, the research base on the early childhood workforce is not extensive, and what we know about the workforce is uneven. Typically, researchers collect workforce data via interview or survey; therefore, the accuracy of the data collected relies on how those working in early education self-identify their jobs, working conditions, and characteristics. As a consequence, more is known about workforce characteristics than about what these programs are like for the adults who work in them. In what follows, we review the available research about different members of the early care and education workforce.

Who Constitutes the Early Childhood Workforce?

For the purposes of this review, we are defining "workforce" broadly as the group of individuals working in some capacity to provide education and care services to 0- to 5-year-olds. Our review therefore covers research that examines the work of direct caregivers and leaders, as well as individuals in a variety of roles working in infrastructure organizations on behalf of early childhood programs. For the most part, we try to provide a national picture of what is known about each of these different groups of early childhood workers, although in some cases we feature state data because they are all that is available. Each section of the review begins with a brief description of the research base, then examines extant research on workforce demographics and work environments for each of these groups of early childhood professionals. To the extent possible, we examine the research base for linkages between workforce variables and the quality of care and education young children receive.

Direct Caregivers

Individuals who work on a regular basis with young children for pay include center- or school-based teachers and teaching assistants, family child care providers, nannies, informal caregivers who receive public dollars, and paid friends and relatives. Some of the earliest information about the preschool teaching workforce comes from studies of child care that have statistically related natural variation in program features with program quality and child outcomes (e.g., Helburn, 1995; Kontos et al., 1995; Travers & Goodson, 1980; Whitebook et al., 1990; Willer et al., 1991). Most of these studies used either onsite interviews or questionnaires with child care staff (mostly teachers and directors) to gather workforce information (qualifications, compensation, demographics, turnover rate) that was then examined in relation to program variables (e.g., staff–child ratio, sector/auspice, group size), observed classroom quality and teacher sensitivity scores, and child outcome data.

The most extensive study of the child care workforce remains the National Child Care Staffing Study (Whitebook et al., 1990, 1998; Whitebook, Phillips, & Howes, 1993), a longitudinal study that began in 1988 and concluded 9 years later. Unlike many studies of child care quality that examine workforce data by asking program directors or administrators for wage data, teacher demographic information, and working conditions, researchers collected data from 1,309 teachers, 444 assistant teachers, and 227 center directors across five states. Data were collected on a large number of workplace variables that extended beyond typical indicators such as qualifications, compensation, and turnover to include work environment data (e.g., benefits, professional satisfaction, and job satisfaction). These data were examined in relation to program characteristics and to child outcomes in a subsample of centers.

In the ensuing years since the National Child Care Staffing Study, public and investment interest in early education has increased as a result of ever-increasing numbers of women entering the workforce and evidence that high-quality early education programs can contribute to children's academic success (Barnett, 2008; Saluja, Early, & Clifford, 2002). As a result there has been an expansion in services, particularly publicly funded prekindergarten programs (Barnett et al., 2010) and, concomitantly, the need to recruit and retain early childhood education staff (Bellm & Whitebook, 2006). Expansion of early childhood education programs has also brought increasing standards for teachers in some sectors. For example, the last reauthorization of Head Start requires that 50% of lead teachers in Head Start programs obtain a bachelor's degree (BA) and teaching credential by 2013 (Improving Head Start for School Readiness Act of 2007). Similarly, in the 37 states utilizing a mixed service delivery system of prekindergarten, 17 of them require teachers to have a BA (Barnett et al., 2010). In response to these factors, several studies have been conducted to estimate the number and characteristics of the preschool teaching workforce (Brandon et al., 2009; Gilliam & Marchesseault, 2005; Herzenberg et al., 2005; Saluja et al., 2002).

Across these differing programs of research, there is some consistency in findings related to characteristics of the caregiver workforce and work environments.

Caregiver Characteristics

Utilizing both supply and demand data from national datasets Brandon and colleagues (2009) estimate that the workforce comprises 2.2 million paid workers. In a typical work week, most of the care for preschool-age children is provided in center-based arrangements, with 500,000 caregivers working with children ages 3–5. While the largest proportions of caregivers work in child care centers, 78,802 individuals working with 3- to 5-year-olds are in public prekindergarten programs. An additional 101,471 caregivers work in preschool classrooms in Head Start programs. It is also estimated that 80,247 family day care providers and 312,047 paid relatives are caring for children ages 3–5. For children under 3 years of age, there is an increase in the numbers receiving care in home-based arrangements. Brandon and colleagues estimate that approximately 78,120 family day care providers care for infants, and another 92,037 care for toddlers. In contrast, approximately 11,536 caregivers work with infants and toddlers in Early Head Start programs.

The majority of paid caregivers are white females whose mean age is 39 years. While women of color, often from diverse linguistic backgrounds, comprise much, and in some states, the majority, of the early childhood workforce, there is a higher proportion of white teachers in public school programs compared to child care and Head Start (Gilliam & Marchesseault, 2005; Saluja et al., 2002; Whitebook, 2010). However, Saluja and colleagues (2002) found that in classrooms where 75% or more of children are from one racial group, there was a higher proportion of caregivers of the same ethnicity. State workforce studies also suggest that ethnicity of caregivers varies by job title. In California, assistant teachers are more likely to be women of color, and able to speak a language other than or in addition to English, while lead teachers are more likely to be white women and to speak English only (Whitebook et al., 2006).

Herzenberg and colleagues (2005) found that 30% of early childhood teachers in 2000–2003 had a BA. However, the dataset on which this estimate relies does not include teachers in public school settings, the fastest growing sector of the field, in which the vast majority of teachers have a BA. Teachers with BAs are more likely to be older (Herzenberg et al., 2005; Whitebook et al., 2006) and working in public schools, while the least educated are more likely to be working in Head Start, for-profit centers, or family day care (Gilliam & Marchesseault, 2005: Herzenberg et al., 2005; Saluja et al., 2002).

Given the way data have been collected, it is typically difficult to breakdown caregiver characteristics for different job titles. Information of this type is usually gathered at the state rather than the national level. The information available suggests that caregiver qualifications and characteristics vary by job title, by state, and within regions of a state (Kagan et al., 2008). Gilliam and Marchesseault (2005), for example, found that the majority of teaching assistants in public prekindergarten programs had a high school diploma, 17% had a Child Development Associate credential (CDA), and approximately 24% had an associate's degree. However, Pennsylvania was the only state prekindergarten program in which none of the assistant teachers had an associate's degree. Thus, it can be concluded that early learning practitioners are as likely to have completed a BA as they are to have yet earned their high school diploma or general equivalency degree (GED), and most are somewhere in between in terms of educational attainment. This wide variation is concerning given that the research base indicates the quality of care and instruction in center- and home-based programs is higher when teachers hold a BA than when they do not (Burchinal, Cryer, Clifford, & Howes, 2002; Kelley & Camilli, 2007; Whitebook et al., 1990; Whitebook & Ryan, 2011).

Work Environment

As mentioned previously, the work environment includes the structure of work (e.g., compensation, paid leave and hours worked), as well as work processes (e.g., professional development opportunities). Most of what we know about the work environment of direct caregivers relates to compensation and turnover; the research on professional development opportunities and life on the job is still somewhat limited.

WAGES AND COMPENSATION

In general, the wages of preschool teachers are low whether one looks at studies of child care from the 1980s or at the first decade of the 21st century. According to the most recent statistics from the U.S. Department of Labor, Bureau of Labor Statistics (2008), child care workers earn an average hourly wage of $9.73, but this wage may range from $7.40 to $11.97. In contrast, preschool teachers earn an average of $16.19, with a range of $9.47 to

$16.63. However, Gilliam and Marchesseault (2005) also found that 18.7% of prekinder-garten teachers nationwide at the time of the study had a second job to improve their earn-ings. As Herzenberg and colleagues (2005) and Brandon and colleagues (2009) point out, early childhood teachers with a college degree earn about two-thirds of what women college graduates earn in other fields.

The National Child Care Staffing Study (Whitebook et al., 1990) found that most child care teachers earned minimal employment benefits, with only 1 in 3 staff members receiv-ing health coverage, and 1 in 5 receiving some type of pension benefit. Nine years later, in their follow-up study, Whitebook and colleagues (1998) found that more centers offered health coverage, although many centers only paid full benefits for their most qualified staff. Despite another decade having passed Herzenberg and colleagues (2005) have reported sim-ilar results, with only 1 in 4 all center-based teachers receiving health benefits, and 1 in 5 teachers participating in employer-sponsored pensions.

Healthy, responsive adults are essential to children's optimal development and ability to learn (Center on the Developing Child at Harvard University, 2009; National Forum on Early Childhood Policy and Programs, 2008; National Scientific Council on the Developing Child, 2004). Yet given the wages and working conditions, many early childhood teachers experience persistent poverty, ill health, and depression, all conditions that can prevent adults from meeting the needs of young children. Higher than average indicators of depres-sion found among early care and education teachers and providers are associated with com-promised interactions with the children they teach (Gilliam, 2008; Hamre & Pianta, 2004; Whitebook & Sakai, 2004).

Given the lower wages and benefits associated with being a preschool teacher and their potential detrimental effects on caregiver well-being, it is not surprising that staff stability and turnover are ongoing issues. Based on state studies, the lowest rates of staff turnover are typically found in public school programs where the wages are higher and the workforce receives better benefits. In center-based care, turnover has been found to be lower when the center is a not-for-profit site that is able to use sources of funding aside from parent fees to provide higher wages (Helburn, 1995; Whitebook et al., 1998; Whitebook & Sakai, 2004). Turnover impacts everyone in a center (Kagan et al., 2008; Whitebook & Bellm, 1999), limiting quality of care and ability to improve (Whitebook & Sakai, 2004). Consistency of caregiving, especially in the earliest years, is crucial to children's development, and teacher turnover has been found to impact negatively on children's attachment security and behav-ior (Whitebook et al., 1990). Early childhood teachers work in teams, and teacher perfor-mance, particularly for those less experienced, is positively related to opportunities to make decisions about practice in collaboration with coworkers (Leana et al., 2009).

PROFESSIONAL DEVELOPMENT

In the K–12 sector it is widely recognized that regardless of experience or qualifications, teachers require ongoing professional development to continue to improve practice and to be effective (Fullan, 2001). Models of professional development have shifted from one-shot, decontextualized workshops to more individualized approaches such as learning communi-ties and coaching that provide supports for teachers to try out new ideas in practice (Lave & Wenger, 1991; Warren-Little, 2001). Given the wide variation in formal qualifications and education of caregivers, it might be assumed that early care and education work envi-ronments would utilize a range of approaches to support their workers ability to learn and improve on the job.

Many work environments do not offer the supports that encourage and allow for more effective teacher practices, such as paid planning time and professional development opportunities. Paid opportunities for early childhood teachers to meet with other teachers at times that do not require simultaneous child supervision, as well as guidance from experienced and trained mentors and supervising teachers, are identified by teachers themselves as necessary scaffolding for best practices (Lobman, Ryan, & McLaughlin, 2005; Whitebook, Gomby, Bellm, Sakai, & Kipnis, 2009). Available data suggest, however, that most professional development continues to be offered through workshops and on topics that are often unrelated to the practical needs of caregivers. Approximately one-third of all early childhood staff members are likely to have a child with special needs in their program, and one-fifth of the workforce are responsible, for children from homes where English is not the family's home language (Brandon et al., 2009), yet these topics are less likely to be accessed as part of noncredit training (Lobman et al., 2005; Whitebook et al., 2006). Thus, while recent studies suggests that early childhood education (ECE) professional development that involves coaching leads to more changes in teacher behavior than programs implemented without coaching (Pianta, Mashburn, Downer, Hamre, & Justice, 2008; Ramey & Ramey, 2008), coaching and mentoring opportunities are much less available for ECE teachers (Whitebook & Ryan, 2011). Even teachers working in the better-resourced publicly funded prekindergarten sector do not all benefit from mentoring support (Barnett et al., 2010).

As can be seen the available data on those providing direct care and education services to young children come from a wide variety of sources and vary considerably in the information provided. Thus, if anything can be concluded from the knowledge base to date, it is that the preschool teaching workforce is characterized by immense variation. What we do know is that teacher characteristics and working conditions vary by auspice or sector. Regardless of auspice or sector, however, one thing shared by the vast majority of early care and education teachers is that the wages and benefits are inadequate (Whitebook, 2010).

Leaders

ECE leaders are those who have responsibility for overseeing an early childhood program, such as directors, site administrators, teacher-directors and, with the integration of public prekindergarten with the K–12 sector, principals and superintendents. Leaders are the gatekeepers to quality because they set the tone for what is expected in terms of teaching interactions and child outcomes (Bella & Bloom, 2003; Kagan et al., 2008). Research on K–12 and ECE indicates that leadership style and preparation of directors and principals contribute to the climate of professional learning in a school or center and related teacher development (Howes, James, & Ritchie, 2003; Lower & Cassidy, 2007; Robinson, Lloyd, & Rowe, 2008; Vu, Jeon, & Howes, 2008; Whitebook et al., 2009; Whitebook, Sakai, Gerber, & Howes, 2001; Zaslow, Tout, Halle, Whittaker, & Lavelle, 2010).

Despite recognition of the importance of leadership to program and instructional quality, the research base on these members of the workforce is limited. Most studies of early childhood leadership focus on directors (Bella & Bloom, 2003; Bloom & Sheerer, 1992) and much of what is known about such personnel is derived from studies of child care quality. Some states include director data as part of their workforce studies (e.g., California: Whitebook et al., 2006; Illinois: Fowler, Bloom, Talan, Beneke, & Kelton, 2008) focusing mostly on demographics, education levels, specialized training, and compensation. A small group of studies has examined director professional development needs and opportunities (Bloom & Sheerer, 1992; Lower & Cassidy, 2007; Ryan, Whitebook, Kipnis, & Sakai, 2011; Whitebook, Ryan, Kipnis, & Sakai, 2008). Although many prekindergarten programs are governed by state and local education authorities, to date there are few studies about the role of principals and/or superintendents in early education programs. Available information tends to be anecdotal (e.g., Marietta, 2010), describing how school leaders help to advocate for prekindergarten in their contexts. Despite the limited research base, some patterns emerge about the characteristics and work environments of ECE leaders that have implications for the field.

Leader Characteristics

Most ECE leaders are white females who tend to be older than teachers and caregivers in their programs, with many nearing retirement age (Bellm & Whitebook, 2006; Herzenberg et al., 2005). Tenure of center administrators also tends to be longer than that of teaching staff. While program directors are more likely to have a BA, the younger the administrator the less likely they are to have a college degree (Herzenberg et al., 2005). This trend is concerning given that studies of child care quality have found that directors with higher educational qualifications tend to lead programs with higher classroom quality scores (Helburn, 1995; Phillips, Howes, & Whitebook, 1991; Vu et al., 2008; Whitebook & Sakai, 2004). Moreover, level of education has been found to be related to the quality of administrative practices of child care directors (Lower & Cassidy, 2007).

Work Environments

Very little research is available on the work environment for ECE leaders, although higher-quality centers, most often not-for-profit sites, have been found to employ directors with longer tenure, more years of formal ECE training, and more prior experience in child care programs (Helburn, 1995; Vu et al., 2008; Whitebook & Sakai, 2004).

Increasingly, preschool programs are seen as a key strategy for addressing achievement gaps between children of different economic, cultural, and linguistic backgrounds (Whitebook et al., 2008). As a consequence, many directors are working in mixed service delivery systems, negotiating multiple sets of policies, managing a range of budgetary and personnel considerations, and ensuring that the instructional quality of their programs readies children for school. Unfortunately, the salaries of leaders in child care, prekindergarten, and Head Start programs do not reflect the complexities of this work. According to the National Bureau of Labor Statistics, the average annual salary for a child care or preschool director in 2010 was $50,410, whereas an elementary school principal earned an annual salary of $89,990.

While many states now have early learning standards, and education and professional development expectations for preschool teachers, few have similar standards for their ECE leaders. For example, in New Jersey, prekindergarten teachers must have a BA and preschool to third grade (P–3) certification, but directors are not required to have any specialized qualifications other than completing a one-time Director's Academy, which consists of 45 hours of training in child care center administration, management, and leadership. On the other hand, school leaders are typically required to have advanced training and formal qualifications in supervision and administration, although they may know little about the education of children younger than 5 years old (Goffin & Means, 2009).

It is not clear from the research whether early childhood worksites provide compensation and professional development opportunities for their leaders. However, directors who receive specialized training in areas such as management skills, and interpersonal communication report being able to perform their job more effectively (Bella & Bloom, 2003; Ryan et al., 2011). A qualitative study of directors leading programs within a publicly funded, mixed-delivery preschool system (Ryan et al., 2011), found that directors need not only training in administrative skills but also updated knowledge about early childhood education. One of the few studies (Rice & Costanza, 2011) available on the professional development of school leaders of prekindergarten programs suggests that specific training can lead to improved communication between school leaders and directors of Head Start and child care programs. Thus, it would seem that ECE leaders want and benefit from targeted training, but because the few studies to date rely on self-reports, further research is needed to help identify the kinds of professional development and preparation that ensure program improvement.

Infrastructure Personnel

In addition to onsite leaders and those in instructional roles, the early childhood workforce includes a number of individuals who work on behalf of children but in support roles. Some of these roles are teacher-leader positions such as curriculum coaches and mentors (Mangin, 2005). Teacher-leaders are exemplary teachers who use their extensive experience and understandings of ECE to provide technical assistance to help teachers learn new curriculum and teaching approaches (Pianta et al., 2008; Ryan & Hornbeck, 2004; Ryan, Hornbeck, & Frede, 2004). Aside from teacher-leaders who visit sites scaffolding teacher learning over time, there are infrastructure personnel involved in the professional development and preparation of teachers in some way as teacher educators, trainers, or consultants. Infrastructure staff also may serve as the liaison between families and services and programs or they may be advocates representing the field to the public and policymakers (Whitebook, Sakai, & Kipnis, 2010).

All of these workers are essential to the field, but little is known about their characteristics, education, work environments, or professional development needs. There is no single national dataset that encompasses the range of infrastructure roles; instead differing roles are embedded within differing occupations (e.g., teacher educator in education administrator). However, a handful of state and local studies provide some insights into this segment of the workforce.

One of the few studies available on this group of individuals that looks across roles and organizations was conducted by the Center for Child Care Employment (Whitebook et al., 2010). A sample of 1,588 staff members working in child care resource and referral agencies, First Five Commissions,[2] and local child care coordination agencies across the state were surveyed to elicit information about worker demographics and professional development needs. In general the staff in these organizations were middle-aged, well-educated females, with nearly two-thirds of staff having a BA degree or higher. Those infrastructure staff members with a BA or higher were paid much higher than instructional staff with similar education in Californian child care settings, having an average hourly wage of $28.61. Nearly half of these infrastructure workers were people of color, and the majority had worked in their organizations for more than 5 years. Although well educated, less than one-fourth of these individuals had a specialized degree related to early childhood. However, approximately 50% had experience working directly with young children in center- or home-based care and reported leaving direct care typically because of low wages. Not surprisingly, given their backgrounds, nearly half of the workers surveyed reported desiring more knowledge and training in child development, while those working in supervisory roles within these organizations said that additional training in management and supervision would be helpful to their work.

Several studies have also looked at the work of those in professional development roles, whether in higher education, public schools and resource and referral agencies, or out in the field as teacher-leaders. While higher education is the focus of another chapter in this volume (see Hyson, Horm, & Winton, Chapter 26, this volume), it is important to note that a few studies (Hyson, Tomlinson, & Morris, 2009; Lobman, Ryan, McLaughlin, & Ackerman,

2004) have examined the characteristics of early childhood teacher educators and the work contexts of higher education. These studies find a striking lack of ethnic and racial diversity among teacher educators, in stark contrast to the students they serve (Maxwell, Lim, & Early, 2006; Whitebook, Bellm, Lee, & Sakai, 2005). Nearly one-third of faculty members in upper-division and graduate ECE teacher preparation programs were reported to have no experience working with children prior to kindergarten age, and many did not have specific ECE academic preparation. Early childhood programs within institutions of higher education also employ fewer full-time faculty and have higher faculty-to-student ratios than other departments on their campuses (Maxwell et al., 2006; Whitebook et al., 2005), suggesting that many teacher education programs are hampered in their ability to structure programs that reflect professional wisdom and research about high-quality teacher preparation (Lobman, Ryan, & McLaughlin, 2005; Maxwell et al., 2006; Whitebook et al., 2005; Whitebook & Ryan, 2011).

A similar portrait emerges relative to the characteristics of those providing professional development. Lobman and colleagues (2004) found that instructors hired by school districts, and resource and referral agencies to lead early childhood workshops were mostly white and held a master's degree or higher. In contrast to higher education faculty, however, the majority of workshop instructors in this study reported having qualifications in ECE or a related field and prior experience working with 3- and 4-year-olds.

While little is known about the work environments of those whose main role is to provide professional development for practitioners working with young children, two studies of early childhood teacher-leaders provide a glimpse into the challenges of providing professional development in centers on an ongoing basis. A time use study (Ryan et al., 2004) of 35 early childhood mentor teachers, whose role was to provide curriculum assistance and professional development to child care and Head Start staff working in the state-funded prekindergarten program, revealed that despite being highly experienced as teachers, with an average of 16 years experience, mentors were underprepared for their leadership roles. Having not received any professional preparation for their role, the teacher-leaders tended to spend more of their work time on administrative duties or preparing for trainings they intended to give than actually providing onsite guidance to teaching staff.

A follow-up case study with one of these teacher-leaders (Ryan & Hornbeck, 2004) illustrates further the need for role clarification and training for this kind of work because the teacher-leader spent most days involved with a minimum of 10 different activities, many of them administrative tasks requested by her supervisors that prevented her from working onsite with teachers. Appointed to the role of teacher-leader after only 3 years in the classroom, this woman also struggled with her role as curriculum leader helping teachers to learn new practices because many of the teachers with whom she worked, while less educated, had many more years of experience in the classroom. Together, these studies suggest that teacher-leaders may require additional training in adult development and different strategies for helping other teachers improve on the job.

In summary, the research on ECE infrastructure roles is very small and mostly descriptive. The studies reviewed here indicate that even when these personnel are highly educated, not all of these workers have experience or qualifications appropriate to their ECE positions. These roles involve leadership of a different kind than has been associated with the ECE leadership roles to date. Curriculum coaches, professional development providers, and teacher educators are primarily expected to help others change their practice, and are less engaged in management tasks and formal supervision. While the studies reviewed here provide a glimpse into the characteristics and work contexts of some of these individuals that may help them enact their leadership work, further research is clearly needed if we are to ensure that these staff members can do their jobs effectively.

Taking the Early Care and Education Workforce Seriously: Challenges and Possibilities

The early childhood workforce is essential to children's learning and development. Yet, while the field of early childhood care and education continues to expand, minimal research attention has been given to those who work with young children or to help caregivers and leaders to become better at their work. Put simply, early care and education staff have been missing in action (Ryan & Goffin, 2008). As a consequence, the research base is uneven, with much more known about those who are in the classroom working with children, especially lead teachers. The lack of research attention to leaders and infrastructure staff is concerning given that many who work directly with children have variable qualifications and need on-the-job support to improve in their interactions with children. At the same time, the information on direct caregivers in early care and education settings is more informative about the workforce on some issues and roles than others. The limitations of the current knowledge base point to four key issues—compensation, ongoing learning, building a workforce pipeline, and creating an effective research agenda—that require policy attention.

Adequately Compensating the Early Childhood Workforce

No matter where one works in early childhood care and education, it is rare to be rewarded well for the work. Compared to other service professions, wages are low, often decoupled from educational attainment, and benefits are often nonexistent. To obtain increased compensation teachers who have a BA degree or higher more often than not choose to leave the classroom (Whitebook et al., 2010). To be sure, knowledgeable professionals are needed in leadership and infrastructure roles, but not at the risk of losing well-trained teachers in classrooms to other fields entirely (Whitebook, 2010). For the most part, only when salaries are built into the cost of programs, such as publicly funded prekindergarten in states such as New Jersey and Oklahoma, is it possible to ensure professional compensation based on educational attainment for those who work with children on a daily basis.

However, comparable pay with other educational sectors based on experience and qualifications is not all that matters. The research base on caregivers shows that health benefits, retirement plans, and the like are often absent in the early care and education workplace. Providing benefits encourages staff to stay in the field and ensures that they are supported to do their job well. For the majority of ECE teachers, assistant teachers, and family day care providers who do not have education or credentials that offer a pathway out of the classroom, the lack of benefits and compensation are inherently problematic. In addition to high turnover and its negative consequences, the higher likelihood of caregiver illness and depression related to poverty wages and inadequate sick leave and health coverage contribute to poorer quality of care and education for children (Center on the Developing Child at Harvard University, 2009).

Policymakers at all levels need to support the well-being of practitioners with a living wage and critical benefits, and to provide comparability in salaries among members of the birth to 5 years and K–3 workforce with equivalent education. The federal and state governments can promote experimentation with new approaches to financing, substituting charters or contracts for vouchers, for example, or helping to tie higher reimbursement to staff compensation approaches that can provide more ongoing support for staff (Whitebook, 2010). Continued comprehensive inattention to resolving the compensation issue will not lead to the healthy, committed, and educated ECE staff necessary to ensure children's well-being across all sectors of the early childhood care and education system.

Supporting Learning and Improvement

Regardless of role or qualifications, education and ongoing learning is necessary for all ECE and care staff to be able to perform and improve at their work. The ECE workforce is characterized by enormous variation in qualifications and the availability of job-related training and professional development. Differing standards and public investments for different sectors of the field have resulted in inequitable opportunities for learning and improvement. Most of the research to date is concentrated around determining the baseline of formal education needed to be a teacher of young children (Bogard, Traylor, & Takanishi, 2008; Early et al., 2007), paying scant attention to the quality of formal education that teachers receive and work environments that support their ongoing learning (Whitebook & Ryan, 2011). At the same time, the focus on caregivers' qualifications to perform their work has diverted attention away from the education and professional development needs of leaders and infrastructure staff. While a large proportion of individuals in these roles have higher qualifications, these qualifications are not necessarily suited to their work in early care and education, and little is known about their work environments. Yet, paradoxically, leaders and infrastructure staff are those charged with the task of educating and supervising caregivers in their instructional work.

To ensure the best for children and families, policymakers and organizational leaders must make investments in the education and professional development of the workforce as a whole. Such an education initiative involves making professional development opportunities—on the job and in the community—more widely available and accessible to *all* teachers, leaders, and infrastructure personnel working in the field. Attention to the quality of professional development is essential, so that one-shot workshops on irrelevant content do not predominate. Instead, professional development investments must be targeted to particular levels of expertise, and offer opportunities for reflection and testing out ideas in practice, with appropriate guidance and support.

For professional development to be effective, early education and care practitioners need a respectful and rewarding work environment that provides time to learn, plan, and improve. Yet the adult environment is overlooked in most workforce studies and in current policies. Licensing in many states sidesteps these issues; federal and state workforce standards, such as paid breaks, are routinely ignored in early childhood settings, and if quality rating and improvement system (QRIS) criteria address work environment issues, they are typically set at a low level (Austin & Whitebook, 2011; Whitebook, 2010). Even teachers and leaders who have experienced the best preparation and support for ongoing learning cannot demonstrate their competence absent a respectful and rewarding workplace.

Building a Pipeline for a Qualified and Diverse Early Care and Education Workforce

In addition to targeted professional development and work environments that support and sustain ongoing learning, policy attention must also be given to creating a pipeline of qualified ECE workers. The extant research suggests that formal education is linked to quality and job performance for most segments of the population. Yet recent national estimates of the qualifications of the workforce suggest that fewer individuals are entering the field with any formal qualifications (Herzenberg et al., 2005). This trend is all the more concerning given that turnover remains a constant issue for the field. At the same time, a higher proportion of leaders and infrastructure staff, those who tend to have BA degrees or higher, are closer to retirement age. In addition to this aging trend among those with more formal education, the majority of women in the workforce with higher qualifications are also predominantly white. In order to build a pipeline of qualified and diverse ECE workers, policymakers can build on some exemplars from within the field and from outside in K–12 education to promote educational access and degree attainment (Chu, Martínez-Griego, & Cronin, 2010; Whitebook, Kipnis, Sakai, & Almaraz, 2011).

To encourage current and future members of the workforce to improve their qualifications and continue to learn, policy should strengthen the link between salaries and degree attainment. There are various state models that can inform such efforts, such as WAGES, REWARD, and similar programs, in which teachers and caregivers receive ongoing bonuses for their educational achievements. Similarly, policymakers can draw on models that have already been shown to work with practitioners, such as TEACH (Whitebook, 2010). Financial reward for education and professional development might also be built into state QRIS criteria, but as yet they are limited (Austin & Whitebook, 2011). However, such strategies must cut across sectors and funding sources, so that there is a system for all members of the early education and care workforce within a state, not just certain sectors.

In an effort to recruit and retain ECE practitioners and providers, policymakers need to institute mentoring and induction programs both for those new to the field and for those who have had little professional development despite considerable experience. For K–12 teachers, federal law requires states to have induction programs for new teachers, over and above requirements for earning degrees, and public dollars are dedicated to this. The federal government is already moving in the direction of dedicating more resources to mentoring for Head Start practitioners, and this is a good start toward ensuring that every practitioner has the opportunity to work with a seasoned and skilled mentor—one who has been trained on how to work with adults—within a certain time period after employment begins. However, mentoring should not be sector specific, but should be built into workforce initiatives at the state and federal levels as one aspect of the work environment for new and even seasoned practitioners. Mentoring initiatives can also be part of onsite training for those in leadership and infrastructure roles to help them acclimate to the demands and tasks associated with working in these differing roles.

Another strategy that can be drawn from the K–12 sector is that of leadership preparation. Leadership programs and standards exist across every state for school leaders and are linked to improved compensation. However, few states consider the competencies required to be a leader in early care and education, and few programs of early childhood leadership exist in higher education (Goffin & Means, 2009; Whitebook & Austin, 2009). Moreover, most of the existing ECE leadership programs do not focus on the range of leadership roles (mentors, teacher-leaders, professional development providers, etc.) in the field of early care and education. Policymakers need to invest in creating or adapting higher-education programs that are responsive to the leadership development needs of the field as a whole. In doing so, public resources should be provided to support women from diverse linguistic and cultural backgrounds in differing sectors of the field as they participate in early care and education leadership programs. Investing in a cadre of diverse leaders who are educated in adult learning, organization change and contemporary knowledge about children's development, and early childhood curriculum and policy will help to ensure that caregivers and teachers receive the guidance needed to develop in their work as professionals.

Developing a Comprehensive Workforce Research Agenda

The review encompassed in this chapter illustrates the piecemeal nature of the research base on the early care and education workforce. Much of the work to date has been conducted on direct caregiving roles, but most research focuses on lead teachers, with less known about family day care providers and assistant teachers. The research base on leaders and those in infrastructure roles is limited to small studies, usually state-based or qualitative in nature. Across all studies of the workforce, information about the work environments that structure and support what individuals do on behalf of young children is uneven. A comprehensive research agenda is desperately needed to build our knowledge about how best to invest in preparing, supporting, and rewarding the workforce for continuing improvement (Whitebook, 2010).

In developing and carrying out this research agenda, policymakers, practitioners, and researchers must come together to identify the key questions to be addressed at a systems level that cover all roles and all sectors. The focus must include three critical ingredients—compensation, preparation and professional development, and work environments that support adult learning—to generate evidence to guide efforts to ensure an ongoing supply of educated and diverse workers for the field. In doing so, attention must be paid to the quality of information provided by existing national and state data sources, and how they might be refined to provide more accurate and relevant data that can inform policy and practice. This research agenda must also include a dissemination strategy, so that evidence can inform improvements across sectors and beyond individual states. Some of this important work has already begun with Early Learning Councils, the National Association for the Education of Young Children workforce initiative, national longitudinal data systems, and state workforce registries. Given that more is known about the gaps in the research base than about the necessary inputs and processes that ensure a qualified, committed, and diverse workforce, these initiatives need to be coordinated and expanded in a national vision for young children and those who work on their behalf.

In conclusion, it is not possible to build a 21st-century vision as long as workforce issues in early care and education remain mired in 20th-century attitudes that working with very young children is something women do naturally (Whitebook, 2010). Informed by scientific evidence and promising practices, it is time to craft a 2020 ECE Workforce vision that dismantles more than a century of assumptions about the value and skill of working with and on behalf of young children (Whitebook, 2010). By giving the same research and policy attention to those who teach, lead, and support as we have to programs and to children's outcomes, it might finally be possible to have a profession in which people are educated, rewarded, and valued for the work they do.

Notes

1. For a detailed discussion of the uses and limitations of national datasets for knowledge about the early childhood workforce, please refer to Bellm and Whitebook (2006).
2. In 1998, California voters passed Proposition 10, adding a 50-cent per pack cigarette tax to create First 5 California (also know as the California Children and Families Commission), which funds education, health care, child care, and other programs related to children from birth through age 5. First 5 California distributes 80% of these funds to the state's 58 counties, all of which have created local First 5 Commissions to address local needs. The amount of funding provided to each county First 5 Commission is based on the area's birth rate.

References

Austin, L., & Whitebook, M. (2011). *Staff preparation, reward, and support: Are quality rating and improvement systems addressing these key ingredients necessary for change?* Berkeley: Center for the Study of Child Care Employment, Institute for Research on Labor and Employment, University of California at Berkeley.

Barnett, W. S. (2008). *Preschool education and its lasting effects: Research and policy implications*. Boulder, CO/Tempe, AZ: Education and the Public Interest Center and Education Policy Research Unit.

Barnett, W. S., Epstein, D. J., Carolan, M. E., Fitzgerald, J., Ackerman, D. J., & Friedman, A. (2010). *The state of preschool 2010: State preschool yearbook*. New Brunswick, NJ: National Institute for Early Education Research, Rutgers University.

Bella, J., & Bloom, P. J. (2003). *Zoom: The impact of early childhood leadership training on role perceptions, job performance and career decisions*. Wheeling, IL: Center for Early Childhood Leadership.

Bellm, D., & Whitebook, M. (2006). *Roots of decline: How government policy has de-educated teachers of young children*. Berkeley: Center for the Study of Child Care Employment, University of California at Berkeley.

Bloom, P. J., & Sheerer, M. (1992). The effect of leadership training on child care program quality. *Early Childhood Research Quarterly, 7*, 579–594.

Bogard, K., Traylor, F., & Takanishi, R. (2008). Teacher education and PK outcomes: Are we asking the right questions? *Early Childhood Research Quarterly, 23*(1), 1–6.

Brandon, R., Maher, E., Burton, A., Whitebook, M., Young, M., Bellm, D., et al. (2002). *Estimating the size and components of the U.S. child care workforce and caregiving population*. Washington, DC: Center for the Child Care Workforce.

Brandon, R., Stutman, T., & Maroto, M. (2009). *The economic value of early care and education for young children*. Washington, DC: Human Services Policy Center.

Burchinal, M. R., Cryer, D., Clifford, R. M., & Howes, C. (2002). Caregiver training and classroom quality in child care centers. *Applied Developmental Science, 6*(1), 2–11.

Center on the Developing Child at Harvard University. (2009). Maternal depression can undermine the development of young children: Working Paper No. 8. Cambridge, MA: Author. Retrieved from *www.developingchild.harvard.edu*.

Chu, M., Martínez-Griego, B., & Cronin, S. (2010). A Head Start/college partnership: Using a culturally and linguistically responsive approach to help working teachers earn degrees. *Young Children, 65*(4), 24–27.

Early, D. M., Maxwell, K. L., Burchinal, M., Alva, S., Bender, R. H., Bryant, D., et al. (2007). Teachers' education, classroom quality, and young children's academic skills: Results from seven studies of preschool programs. *Child Development, 78*(2), 558–580.

Fowler, S., Bloom, P. J., Talan, T. N., Beneke, S., & Kelton, R. (2008). *Who's caring for the kids?: The status of the early childhood workforce in Illinois–2008*. Wheeling, IL: McCormick Tribune Center for Early Childhood Leadership.

Fullan, M. (2001). *The new meaning of educational change* (3rd ed.). New York: Teachers College Press.

Gable, S., Rothrauff, T. C., Thornburg, K. R., & Mauzy, D. (2007). Cash incentives and turnover in center-based child care staff. *Early Childhood Research Quarterly, 22*(3), 363–378.

Gilliam, W. S. (2008). *Implementing policies to reduce the likelihood of preschool expulsion* (Foundation for Child Development Policy Brief, Advancing PK–3, No. 7). New York: Foundation for Child Development.

Gilliam, W. S., & Marchesseault, C. M. (2005). *From capitols to classrooms, policies to practice: State funded prekindergarten at the classroom level: Part I. Who's teaching our youngest students?: Teacher education and training, experience, compensation and benefits and assistant teachers*. New Brunswick, NJ: National Institute for Early Education Research, Rutgers University.

Goffin, S. G., & Means, K. M. (2009). *Leadership in early childhood care and education: A view of the landscape*. Washington, DC: Goffin Strategy Group.

Hamre, B., & Pianta, R. (2004). Self-reported depression in nonfamilial caregivers: Prevalence and associations with caregiver behavior in child care settings. *Early Childhood Research Quarterly, 19*(2), 297–318.

Helburn, S. (Ed.). (1995). *Cost, quality, and child outcomes in child care centers: Technical report*. Denver: University of Colorado, Center for Research in Economic and Social Policy.

Herzenberg, S., Price, M., & Bradley, D. (2005). *Losing ground in early childhood education: Declining workforce qualifications in an expanding industry, 1979–2004.* Washington, DC: Economic Policy Institute.

Howes, C., James, J., & Ritchie, S. (2003). Pathways to effective teaching. *Early Childhood Research Quarterly, 18*(1), 104–120.

Hyson, M., Tomlinson, H. B., & Morris, C. (2009). Quality improvement in early childhood teacher education: Faculty perspectives and recommendations for the future. *Early Childhood Research and Practice, 11*(1). Available at *ecrp.uiuc.edu/v11n1/hyson.html.*

Improving Head Start for School Readiness Act of 2007, Public Law 110-134, 42 USC 9801 *et seq.* (Dec. 12, 2007).

Kagan, S., Kauerz, K., & Tarrant, K. (2008). *The early care and education teaching workforce at the fulcrum: An agenda for reform.* New York: Teachers College Press.

Kelley, P., & Camilli, G. (2007). *The impact of teacher education on outcomes in center-based early childhood education programs: A meta-analysis* (NIEER Working Paper). New Brunswick, NJ: National Institute for Early Education Research, Rutgers University.

Kipnis, F., & Whitebook, M. (2011). *Workforce information: A critical component of state early care and education data systems.* Berkeley: Center for the Study of Child Care Employment, University of California, Berkeley.

Kontos, S., Howes, C., Shinn, M., & Galinsky, E. (1995). *Quality in family child care and relative care.* New York: Teachers College Press.

Lave, J., & Wenger, E. (1991). *Situated learning: Legitimate, peripheral participation.* Cambridge, UK: Cambridge University Press.

Leana, C., Appelbaum, E., & Shevchuk, I. (2009). Work process and quality of care in early childhood education: The role of job crafting. *Academy of Management Journal, 52*(6), 1169–1192.

Lobman, C., Ryan, S., & McLaughlin, J. (2005). Reconstructing teacher education to prepare qualified preschool teachers: Lessons from New Jersey. *Early Childhood Research and Practice, 7*(2).

Lobman, C., Ryan, S., McLaughlin, J., & Ackerman, D. J. (2004). *Educating Preschool Teachers: Mapping the Teacher Preparation and Professional Development System in New Jersey.* New York: Foundation for Child Development.

Lower, J. K., & Cassidy, D. (2007). Child care work environments: The relationship with learning environments. *Journal of Research in Childhood Education, 22*(2), 189–204.

Mangin, M. M. (2005). Distributed leadership and the culture of schools: Teacher leaders' strategies for gaining access to classrooms. *Journal of School Leadership, 15*(4), 456–484.

Marietta, G. (2010). *PreK–3rd: How superintendents lead change* (PreK–3rd Policy to Action Brief No. 5). New York: Foundation for Child Development.

Maxwell, K. L., Lim, C.-I., & Early, D. M. (2006). *Early childhood teacher preparation programs in the United States: National report.* Chapel Hill: University of North Carolina, FPG Child Development Institute.

National Forum on Early Childhood Policy and Programs. (2008). Workforce development, welfare reform, and child well-being: Working Paper #7. Cambridge, MA: Center on the Developing Child at Harvard University. Retrieved from *www.developingchild.harvard.edu.*

National Institute of Child Health and Human Development (NICHD) Early Child Care Research Network. (2000). Characteristics and quality of child care for toddlers and preschoolers. *Applied Developmental Science, 4*(3), 116–125.

National Scientific Council on the Developing Child. (2004). *Young children develop in an environment of relationships* (Working Paper No. 1). Cambridge, MA: Center on the Developing Child at Harvard University. Available online at *www.developingchild.net/pubs/wp/young_children_environment_relationships.pdf.*

Phillips, D., Howes, C., & Whitebook, M. (1991).Child care as an adult work environment. *Journal of Social Issues, 47*, 49–70.

Phillips, D., Mekos, D., Carr, S., McCartney, K., & Abbott-Shim, M. (2000). Within and beyond the classroom door: Assessing quality in child care centers. *Early Childhood Research Quarterly, 15*(4), 475–496.

Pianta, R. C., Mashburn, A. J., Downer, J. T., Hamre, B. K., & Justice, L. (2008). Effects of web-mediated professional development resources on teacher–child interaction in pre-kindergarten classrooms. *Early Childhood Research Quarterly, 23*(4), 431–451.

Ramey, S. L., & Ramey, C. T. (2008). Establishing a science of professional development for early education programs: The Knowledge Application Information Systems theory of professional development. In L. M. Justice & C. Vukelich (Eds.), *Achieving excellence in preschool literacy instruction* (pp. 41–63). New York: Guilford Press.

Rice, C., & Costanza, V. (2011). Building early learning leaders: New Jersey's Prek–3rd leadership training: A case study. Retrieved from Association for Young Children website at *www.acnj.or/ main.asp?uri=1003&di=1941*.

Robinson, V., Lloyd, C., & Rowe, K. (2008). The impact of leadership on student outcomes: An analysis of the differential effects of leadership types. *Educational Administration Quarterly, 44*(5), 635–674.

Ryan, S., & Ackerman, D. J. (2005). Using pressure and support to create a qualified workforce. *Education Policy Analysis Archives, 13*(23). Retrieved November 5, 2007, from *epaa.asu.edu/ epaa/v13n23*.

Ryan, S., & Goffin, S. G. (2008). Missing in action: Teaching in early care and education. *Early Education and Development, 19*(3), 385–395.

Ryan, S., & Hornbeck, A. (2004). Mentoring for quality improvement: A case study of a mentor teacher in the reform process. *Journal of Research on Childhood Education, 19,* 78–95.

Ryan, S., Hornbeck, A., & Frede, E. (2004). Mentoring for change: A time use study of teacher consultants in preschool reform. *Early Childhood Research and Practice, 6*(1). Retrieved from *ecrp. uiuc.eu/v6n1/ryan.html*.

Ryan, S., & Lancaster, D. (2008, March). *Working in child care: The mediating role of organizational practices on teaching and learning.* Paper presented at the annual meeting of the American Educational Research Association, New York.

Ryan, S., Whitebook, M., Kipnis, F., & Sakai, L. (2011). Professional development needs of directors leading in a mixed service delivery preschool system. *Early Childhood Research and Practice.*

Saluja, G., Early, D. M., & Clifford, R. M. (2002). Demographic characteristics of early childhood teachers and structural elements of early care and education in the United States. *Early Childhood Research and Practice, 4*(1). Online journal available at *ecrp.uiuc.edu/v4n1/saluja.html*.

Travers, J., & Goodson, B. (1980). *Research results of the national day care study.* Cambridge, MA: Abt Associates.

U.S. Department of Labor, Bureau of Labor Statistics. (2008). National Compensation Survey: Occupational Earnings in the United States, 2008. Available online at *www.bls.gov/ncs/ncswage2008. htm.*

Vu, J., Jeon, H., & Howes, C. (2008). Formal education, credential or both: Early childhood program classroom practices. *Early Education and Development, 19*(3), 479–504.

Warren-Little, J. (2001). Professional development in pursuit of school reform. In A. Lieberman & L. Miller (Eds.), *Teachers caught in the action: Professional development that matters* (pp. 23–44). New York: Teachers College Press.

Whitebook, M. (2010, May). *Listening and learning about early learning: The early learning workforce and professional development.* Paper presented at meeting of U.S. Departments of Education and Health and Human Services, Denver, CO.

Whitebook, M., & Austin, L. (2009). *Leadership in early childhood: A curriculum for emerging and established agents of change.* Berkeley: Center for the Study of Child Care Employment. University of California, Berkeley.

Whitebook, M., & Bellm, D. (1999). *Taking on turnover: An action guide for child care center teachers and directors.* Washington, DC: Center for the Child Care Workforce.

Whitebook, M., Bellm, D., Lee, Y., & Sakai, L. (2005). *Time to revamp and expand: Early childhood teacher preparation programs in California's institutions of higher education.* Berkeley: Center for the Study of Child Care Employment, University of California at Berkeley.

Whitebook, M., Gomby, D., Bellm, D., Sakai, L., & Kipnis, F. (2009). *Preparing teachers of young children: The current state of knowledge, and a blueprint for the future.* Berkeley: Center for the

Study of Child Care Employment, Institute for Research on Labor and Employment, University of California at Berkeley.

Whitebook, M., Howes, C., & Phillips, D. A. (1990). *The National Child Care Staffing Study: Final report. Who cares?: Child care teachers and the quality of care in America*. Washington, DC: Center for the Child Care Workforce.

Whitebook, M., Howes, C., & Phillips, D. A. (1998). *Worthy work, unlivable wages: The National Child Care Staffing Study, 1988–1997*. Washington, DC: Center for the Child Care Workforce.

Whitebook, M., Kipnis, F., Sakai, L., & Almaraz, M. (2011). *Learning together: A study of six B.A. Completion Cohort Programs in Early Care and Education: Year 3*. Berkeley: Center for the Study of Child Care Employment, University of California at Berkeley.

Whitebook, M., Phillips, D., & Howes, C. (1993). *National Child Care Staffing Study revisited: Four years in the life of center-based child care*. Oakland, CA: Child Care Employee Project.

Whitebook, M., & Ryan, S. (2011). *Degrees in context: Asking the right questions about preparing skilled and effective teachers of young children*. New Brunswick, NJ: National Institute for Early Education Research, Rutgers University.

Whitebook, M, Ryan, S., Kipnis, F., & Sakai, L. (2008). *Partnering for preschool: A study of center directors in New Jersey's mixed delivery Abbott programs*. Berkeley: Center for the Study of Child Care Employment, University of California at Berkeley.

Whitebook, M., & Sakai, L. (2004). *By a thread: How child care centers hold on to teachers, how teachers build lasting careers*. Kalamazoo, MI: Upjohn Institute for Employment Research.

Whitebook, M., Sakai, L., Gerber, E., & Howes, C. (2001). *Then and now: Changes in child care staffing, 1994–2000*. Washington, DC: Center for the Child Care Workforce, and Berkeley: Center for the Study of Child Care Employment, University of California at Berkeley.

Whitebook, M., Sakai, L., & Kipnis, F. (2010). *Beyond homes and center: The workforce in three California early childhood infrastructure organizations*. Berkeley: Center for the Study of Child Care Employment, University of California at Berkeley.

Whitebook, M., Sakai, L., Kipnis, F., Lee, Y., Bellm, D., Almaraz, M., et al. (2006). *California early care and education workforce study: Licensed child care centers: Statewide 2006*. Berkeley: Center for the Study of Child Care Employment, University of California at Berkeley.

Willer, B., Hofferth, S., Kisker, E., Divine-Hawkins, P., Farquhar, E., & Glantz, F. (1991). *The demand and supply of child care in 1990: Joint findings from the National Child Care Survey 1990 and a profile of child care settings*. Washington, DC: National Association for the Education of Young Children.

Wrzesniewski, A., & Dutton, J. E. (2001). Crafting a job: Renvisioning employees as active crafters of their work. *Academy of Management Review, 26*, 179–201.

Zaslow, M., Tout, K., Halle, T., Whittaker, J., & Lavelle, B. (2010). *Toward the identification of features of effective professional development for early childhood educators: Literature review*. Washington, DC: Child Trends.

CHAPTER 6

Restructuring and Aligning Early Education Opportunities for Cultural, Language, and Ethnic Minority Children

Cristina Gillanders, Iheoma Iruka, Sharon Ritchie,
and Carolyn T. Cobb

The U.S. education system continues the struggle to increase the educational attainment of the population as a whole and reduce the opportunity inequity between advantaged children and those children who are more vulnerable. In spite of decades of educational reform to address the achievement gap, including the establishment of No Child Left Behind, we still face persistent disparities between minority and nonminority students, poor and non-poor students, and dual language learners and native English speakers. The 2009 Report Card on Reading from the National Assessment of Educational Progress (2010) shows no significant change in reading across student groups for grades 4 and only somewhat higher scores across most groups for grade 8 since 2007. A study of achievement and economic consequences in the United States found that we face an education achievement gap when compared to other countries, as well as a persistent achievement gap by race and income within our own country (McKinsey & Company, 2009). Achievement as early as fourth grade can be linked to life outcomes. In short, McKinsey and Company (2009) assert that this loss of human capital amounts to a "permanent recession."

Our purpose in this chapter is to examine how restructuring the early education of young children can address the needs of vulnerable children, specifically those who are poor and come from cultural, language, and ethnic minority families. The grade and age range between prekindergarten and grade 3 (PreK–3, or ages 3–8) is increasingly the focus of diverse policy groups, professional organizations, funders, and initiatives intent upon improving school experiences and achievement for all children. For example, the first of 10 recommendations from the College Board as part of their College Completion Agenda is to "provide a program of voluntary preschool education, universally available for children from low income families" (Lee & Rawls, 2010). The U.S. Chamber of Commerce (2010) emphasized the need for early childhood education in building a high-quality workforce:

"Achieving a world-class education system and creating a highly-skilled workforce begins with high-quality early learning opportunities" (p. 1).

However, nationally, there appears to be more conversation about PreK–3 than there is meaningful, coherent implementation of PreK–3 across states and school districts. Exceptions like Montgomery County, Maryland, stand as rare examples of implementing a comprehensive PreK–3 approach (Marietta, 2010). In addition to recognizing the need to target resources to the "Red Zone" (a largely urban, high-poverty, mostly Hispanic and African American children district), Montgomery County crafted a districtwide strategy around early learning that focused on the following: more time for learning, including afterschool and summer programs; incorporation of evidence-based practices and use of monitoring assessments; continuity throughout the early years; and collaboration with families and communities around early learning. A few states such as Ohio and North Carolina have worked on pilot initiatives to address "ready schools" (ETR Services, 2010; Ohio Department of Education and Ohio Association of Elementary School Administrators, 2008) that focus more on schools being ready for children than children being ready for school, aligning early care and education with early elementary schools, attending to meaningful home–school–community partnerships, and better preparing the workforce to address the educational and social needs of young children. Also, several states such as New Jersey, North Carolina, and Maryland have established offices that oversee prekindergarten through grades 2 or 3 but continue to face the challenge of how to integrate these offices with the rest of the education department and really ensure that they are supportive of school improvement and transformation efforts statewide that critically focus on the early years.

Any new approach to education must address and make headway against the education inequity between vulnerable and nonvulnerable children. A core value for education is to "even the playing field"; however, U.S. schools and the education system have failed children of color and children from economically disadvantaged families. On average, racial and cultural minority children, compared to European American children in almost every major urban school system are not achieving (Murrell, 2002). Among the many factors that contribute to this reality are less educated and not multicultural and culturally responsive teachers (Sleeter, 2001); low teacher expectations (Gay, 2004); inability to engage families (Comer, 1986; Epstein, 1992; U.S. Department of Education, 2001); and a dearth of multicultural education (Banks, 1993; Gay, 2004). Despite increasing pressure on schools and districts to close the achievement gap, we continue to see cultural and ethnic minority children left further behind, especially African American and Latino males (Chall & Snow, 1988; Council of Great City Schools, 2010; Dupree, Spencer, & Bell, 1997; Garcia Coll & Magnuson, 2000; Murrell, 2002). Disadvantaged children, specifically, racial, ethnic, language minority, and children from low-income families, are more likely to enter kindergarten behind their middle-class European American peers; to have lower achievement in reading and math; and to be assigned disproportionately to special education classrooms; even when their incomes are similar African Americans and Latinos/as score lower than European Americans on standardized tests (Bondy & Ross, 1998; Bowman, Donovan, & Burns, 2001; Knapp & Associates, 1995; National Center for Education Statistics, 2001; Ray, Aytch, & Ritchie, 2010; Riegle-Crumb, 2006). Furthermore, in the last decade, the dropout rates for Latino children have not shown a similar reduction to that of other ethnic minority groups, including African Americans (Aud, Fox, & KewalRamani, 2010; Lee, 2002). Thus, as important as it is to ensure that all children are progressing and learning, critical attention is needed on the most vulnerable children.

The kind of restructuring we discuss in this chapter is not limited to a mere incorporation of PreK classrooms into the elementary school system or schools, but rather a reconceptualization of early education that includes changes in the curriculum, instructional practices, and home–school partnerships. Our argument is that the PreK–3 approach should receive the sophisticated scrutiny required to avoid simplistic answers to complex questions. The goal for the PreK–3 approach must be well-articulated school reform focused on changing the school experience for all children, but especially children who are the most vulnerable.

The Case for PreK–3

The early years of schooling may be the key to long-term success for students, as well as positive and cost-effective social and economic outcomes for both students and society, yet recent research reveals that the quality of schooling at these ages is poor or at best variable, with vulnerable children likely to attend low-quality programs and schools. Specifically, ethnic minority children and children living in poverty are more likely to attend programs and schools with teachers who lack subject content knowledge, who have lower academic achievement, and are inexperienced (Peske & Haycock, 2006). In addition, researchers have shown that inadequate schools are part of a larger ecology that includes poverty, racism, low-wage jobs, and unsafe housing (Dupree et al., 1997; Garcia Coll et al., 1996; McLoyd, 1990, 1998)—all factors that jeopardize children's development and family functioning. For example, the National Center for Early Development and Learning (NCEDL) conducted a multistate study of prekindergartens and found wide variation in the quality of environments and instruction (Clifford et al., 2005; Pianta et al., 2005). In another study using the NCEDL data, Early and colleagues (2010) found that for almost two-thirds of a school day, observers saw no teacher–child interaction, and that most of the observed interactions focused on routine, maintenance activities, especially in classrooms of children from racial and ethnic minority backgrounds and low income. Stuhlman and Pianta (2009) analyzed profiles of over 800 first-grade classrooms across the United States in terms of the emotional climate and instructional dimensions of quality. Classrooms were classified as high quality, mediocre quality, low quality, or positive emotional climate/lower academic demand. The types of classrooms varied widely both within and across schools. "Children whose preschool achievement scores were lowest, whose ethnicity was non-white, and who were from poor or working-poor families were about twice as likely to be in the low overall quality classrooms than they were to be in the high overall quality classrooms" (p. 337). These findings make it clear that the foundations for success are *not* in place.

Although numerous research studies find that high-quality early education experiences lead to better academic and social outcomes for children, prekindergarten programs or similar interventions alone cannot ensure maximized learning for our most vulnerable students. Kauerz (2006) and Shore (2009) argue that benefits of prekindergarten may begin to fade by third or fourth grade without sustained quality instruction through the primary grades. Others have argued that the impact of early childhood programs, such as Head Start, may not be sustained because of the low-quality schools into which Head Start children are likely to transition (Currie & Thomas, 2000; Garces, Thomas, & Currie, 2002).

The premise for PreK–3 education is that coherent, high-quality instructional approaches across the PreK–3 span will result in positive outcomes for children throughout their early years, and an increased likelihood that children will complete grade 3 prepared to succeed at increasingly difficult academic curricula. In *The Case for Investing in PreK–3rd Education: Challenging Myths about School Reform*, Shore (2009) makes a case for "a more reasoned approach to school reform—one that builds a solid foundation for learning by providing coordinated, enhanced learning opportunities every year from Pre-Kindergarten (for three- and four-year-olds) through Third Grade" (p. 2). Guernsey and Mead (2010) present the New America Foundation's case for a new education contract for the primary grades of education. They note that numerous studies provide evidence of the longer-term benefits and outcomes both for the child and society with multiyear, high-quality programs across the early grades, for example, the High/Scope Perry Preschool Study (Schweinhart et al., 2005); the Carolina Abecedarian Project (Campbell & Ramey, 1995; Pungello et al., 2010); the Chicago Child–Parent Centers (CPC; Reynolds, Wang, & Walberg, 2003) study; and dimensions of PreK–3 available in the Early Childhood Longitudinal Study—Kindergarten Cohort (ECLS-K; Reynolds, Magnuson, & Ou, 2006). Long-term benefits include higher rates of high school graduation and college attendance, and less risk of teen parenthood or involvement with the criminal justice system. Magnuson, Ruhm, and Waldfogel (2007) found that prekindergarten makes a difference for children, with some indication that effects diminished in first or second grade only to return in third grade ("sleeper effects"). They also found that in the early elementary grades, high-quality experiences (small class size and time spent on early reading instruction) could help children who did not attend prekindergarten or were behind at kindergarten to catch up by third grade. Other early grade experiences that resulted in later achievement for children included full-day kindergarten, amount of time devoted to instruction during the school day, low mobility across schools (i.e., consistent learning environment), attention to both socioemotional and cognitive skills, and quality of interactions with teachers. Together, this evidence strongly suggests the need for a coherent approach to educating children from prekindergarten through third grade.

What Is Needed in Order for Vulnerable Children to Succeed in PreK–3?

In this chapter we argue that the PreK–3 approach truly has the potential to address the needs of all children, especially those who live in poverty and/or come from ethnic and language minority backgrounds. As described earlier, an emphasis on the early years, a high-quality early education experience, and a coherent approach to early schooling can have a positive impact on children's later educational experiences. Moreover, numerous studies have pointed out that vulnerable children are more likely to benefit from quality early educational experiences than are advantaged children (e.g., Burchinal, Peisner-Feinberg, Bryant, & Clifford, 2000; Burchinal, Roberts, Zeisel, Hennon, & Hooper, 2006; Caughy, DiPietro, & Strobino, 1994; Peisner-Feinberg et al., 2001; Vandell et al., 2010). However, even high-quality programs sometimes struggle to address the needs of the most vulnerable children. What structures, practices, and values make the PreK–3 experience especially beneficial for these children?

Children from ethnic minority backgrounds are in a "double-jeopardy situation" (García, 2010). All children make transitions from home to school. However, children from ethnic, language, and culture minority backgrounds encounter an additional discontinuity between their home and a school modeled on the beliefs, values, and practices of the majority culture (García, 2010). Educators are well aware that ethnic minority children often experience more risk factors than European American middle-class children and are therefore at greater risk of underachievement and more subject to inequities in education. A recent report from the National Center on Education Statistics notes that ethnic minority children are likely be poor; to live in a single-parent, female-headed household (predominantly African American children); to have a less educated mother and unqualified teachers; and are more likely to be suspended or expelled, absent, or to drop out (Aud et al., 2010). Additionally, children from immigrant families, compared to children from native-born families, are more likely to be poor; to have a parent with limited English proficiency; to have limited access to health care, justice, and other social institutions; and to have a father who has not graduated from high school (40 vs. 12%) (Hernandez, Denton, & Macartney, 2008). However, these same communities possess strengths about which there may be less general awareness. Children from immigrant families are more likely than those from native-born families to live with both parents (84 vs. 76%), to live in homes with four or more siblings (19 vs. 14%), and to live with their grandparents (10–20 vs. 5%). Similarly, the African American family compared to other families is more spiritual and has a complex extended formal and informal family structure (Littlejohn-Blake & Anderson Darling, 1993; Utsey, Bolden, Lanier, & Williams, 2007). These strengths-based characteristics have the potential to provide additional support, nurturing, and psychological well-being for cultural and ethnic minority children.

Strengths of culturally diverse families are often overlooked by schools, which tend to focus instead on risk factors and challenges. Schools need the knowledge and support that would help them to ameliorate rather than exacerbate risks, and the ability to make use of rather than ignore families' strengths. Lee (2003) has identified schools' common misconceptions about minority children and their families:

(a) a singular pathway for child and adolescent development, and by extension for learning, based on studies of European and European-American children and adolescents; (b) life course challenges of ethnic and racial minority youth are fundamentally pathological, rather than normative; (c) home and community experiences of such youngsters, particularly those living in persistent poverty, are viewed as deficits to be overcome by school, rather than as resources on which to build; (d) to attend to race and ethnicity explicitly in cultural socialization as preparation for learning is simply polemic and is not relevant to majority children; and (e) racial and ethnic minorities are, on the whole, homogenous and fundamentally different from the majority. (p. 6)

These assumptions have led schools, first, to believe that children from minority backgrounds need to be "fixed" because their development does not follow the same pathways as children from the majority culture (Gutierrez, Morales, & Martínez, 2009; Gutierrez & Rogoff, 2003). Second, their home and community experiences are too often viewed through a lens of cultural deprivation rather than cultural difference that emphasizes "difference" as unique rather than deviant (Souto-Manning, 2010). Too often, attempts to consider children's race and ethnicity are based on general and stereotypical assumptions about particular racial and ethnic minority groups rather than on the particular social and cultural practices of the children's families and communities (Gutierrez & Rogoff, 2003). This lack of genuine knowledge of family and community cultural practices ensures that the "fix" is divorced from children's reality.

Therefore, the "double-jeopardy situation" of ethnic minority children lies not only in the prevalence of their risk factors but also the failure of schools to recognize that children's participation in home cultural practices is rich and can be a resource for schools. Rather than attempting to "fix" or "remediate" children's learning and development, schools can enrich children's experiences, so that children are able to participate actively in different cultural contexts (Gutierrez et al., 2009). This means that schools need deliberately to build cultural bridges between children's backgrounds and the learning required to succeed in school (García, 2010).

Schools' failure to build cultural bridges is in part a result of modernization. Previous generations of children learned to become participants in a community by collaborating in ongoing activities such as farming, weaving, fishing, and so forth, so that their learning was situated in the authentic use of the skills. During the industrial revolution, schools became "assembly line factories" (Rogoff, Goodman-Turkanis, & Bartlett, 2001) in which children were expected to learn at a similar pace, be grouped according to their age, and learn content and skills isolated from their authentic uses in the community. Schools have stubbornly remained the same through the centuries and have perpetuated the social inequalities of society (Cole, 2010). A restructuring of early education would involve a return to an education in which children can collaboratively participate in the ongoing activities of their communities, families, and schools.

Although the reconceptualization of the role of schools as a bridge between different cultural experiences is not unique to the PreK–3 approach (e.g., González, Moll, & Amanti, 2005; Ladson-Billings, 1995; Rogoff et al., 2001), we believe that the PreK–3 structure is particularly well situated to facilitate the construction of these bridges because of the following:

1. For most children prekindergarten is the first time they and their families encounter the school culture. This makes it a natural place to establish meaningful connections between home and school experiences that can continue throughout schooling.
2. A PreK–3 approach draws on the science of child development. Recent thinking on developmental science addresses the critical importance of foundational processes in children's learning (Ritchie, Maxwell, & Bredekamp, 2009). Building bridges necessitates viewing development as a cultural process (Rogoff, 2003), which depends on understanding how foundational processes such as positive relationships and executive function develop in different cultural contexts.
3. A PreK–3 approach also emphasizes teacher knowledge of how children learn academic content (math, literacy, science, etc.) and acquire knowledge. Schools need to focus specifically on how the lives of cultural and ethnic minority children can become integrated into the curriculum through culturally responsive practices.

In the next section we detail our thinking about the impact of home–school partnerships, foundational processes, and culturally responsive teaching within the PreK–3 framework.

Home–School Partnerships

In order to establish a cultural bridge between home and school, schools need to make deliberate efforts to engage families as contributors to children's learning. To achieve this goal, the first step is for schools to establish positive relationships with parents beginning at the prekindergarten level that are sustained throughout the early elementary years. Generally schools have not been successful in engaging low-income minority parents in traditional parent involvement activities. Teachers often complain about the lack of participation in school by low-income ethnic minority parents despite their efforts to involve them (Bernhard, Lefebvre, Kilbride, Chud, & Lange, 1998; De Gaetano, 2007; Goldenberg, 1987; Lawson, 2003). In many cases, schools' efforts to involve parents are school-centric (Lawson, 2003) and based on the belief system and lives of European American middle-class families. Little consideration is given to ethnic minority parents' beliefs, goals, interests, and life circumstances. In fact, rather than include them, school-centric involvement strategies can exclude ethnic minority parents (Lareau & Horvat, 1999) and undervalue their nontraditional forms of involvement in their children's education, such as helping with homework or talking with their children about school (Gutman & McLoyd, 2000; Henderson & Mapp, 2002). These forms of involvement are often not recognized because they don't fit with traditional models of involvement (Scribner, Young, & Pedroza, 1999). Even when families engage in more traditional ways, the efforts of cultural and ethnic minority families remain unrecognized. For example, Wong and Hughes (2006) found that though African American families reported higher levels of positive perceptions, communication with school, school-based involvement, and shared responsibility with schools than whites and English-speaking and Spanish-speaking Latinos, teachers rated their alliance with African American families lower than that with white or Latino families. Although African American families reported the highest level of communication with school and school-based involvement, teachers in this study viewed African American families as the least involved of the four ethnic groups. Thus, issues of bias and perception must be honestly confronted in order to strengthen the value and impact of home–school partnership for children's success.

Early childhood educators have emphasized home–school collaboration more strongly than elementary school educators. Parents appear more willing to participate in their children's school during the preschool years. It is hard to untangle whether that is because their children are younger or because the school culture changes as their children grow older. Engaging racial and ethnic minority parents is both especially important and difficult given that many parents have experienced cultural and racial discrimination, and consequently distrust social institutions (Auerbach, 2007; Rowley, Helaire, & Banerjee, 2010). The PreK–3 approach offers a powerful opportunity to establish strong home–school partnerships. The 5-year span provides time to build trust and promote engagement through demonstrated interest by educators in family goals, beliefs and aspirations, and home practices, and an improved ability to give families knowledge and experiences about what happens in schools and classrooms, and the reasoning behind it.

Foundational Processes

Teachers need a thorough understanding of what needs to be in place and sustained in order for children to maximize their learning opportunities. In this section we highlight the foundational processes of positive student–teacher relationships and executive function. We believe that teachers who focus on these areas better prepare vulnerable children for more complex learning in the future.

Positive Teacher–Child Relationships

Research from the past 15 years strongly points to the association between teacher–child relationships and children's academic (Burchinal, Peisner-Feinberg, Pianta, & Howes, 2002; Hamre & Pianta, 2001; Pianta, Nimetz, & Bennett, 1997; Pianta & Stuhlman, 2004) and social development (Birch & Ladd, 1997; Iruka, Burchinal, & Cai, 2010; Ladd, Birch, & Buhs, 1999; Peisner-Feinberg et al., 2000, 2001). It is possible that children who see teachers as supportive are more likely to pursue goals valued by teachers, such as engagement in academic activities (Hamre & Pianta, 2005), and children who trust and like teachers may be more motivated to succeed (Cicchetti & Lynch, 1993). It appears that this construct holds true for ethnic minority boys, children who have been retained, and those identified as "at risk." Minority boys who experienced close relationships demonstrated higher academic achievement, fewer disciplinary infractions, and fewer school suspensions through eighth grade (Hamre & Pianta, 2001). Although behavior problems alone do not predict school success or failure, the teacher–child relationships and, specifically, the levels of conflict within the relationships do predict later school success. Pianta and Steinberg (1992) found a similar outcome while studying children who were retained by their teachers. They found that children were differentially promoted based on the closeness of the teacher–child relationships, such that children who were promoted had closer teacher–child relationships than children who were retained. Hamre and Pianta (2005) identified children in kindergarten at risk for developing conflictual teacher–child relationships but found that the risk was moderated by the emotional support provided by the teachers. Not surprisingly, at-risk children who were placed in classrooms with low emotional support were particularly vulnerable to developing conflictual teacher–child relationships (Hamre & Pianta, 2005). Birch and Ladd (1997) also found that children who experienced dependent and conflictual relationships with their teachers had poor academic performance, negative school attitudes, and less positive engagement with the school environment; lacked self-directedness and cooperative participation in the classroom; and avoided school.

Other studies indicate that teachers may view cultural and ethnic minority children's behavior and ability differently than that of their white peers (Chang et al., 2007; Murray, Murray, & Wass, 2008), which may impact the teacher–child relationship. A teacher can misinterpret a child's behavior as problematic when this behavior might be congruent with his or her cultural contexts. Successful development of positive relationships between teachers and children from minority backgrounds requires that teachers have some understanding of the children's language and cultural background. Chang and colleagues (2007) found that teachers who spoke more Spanish in the classroom rated their relationships with Spanish-speaking dual language learners as closer than did teachers who spoke less Spanish. In addition, teachers who depended more on English gave higher ratings of problem behaviors and teacher–child conflict to Spanish-speaking children. Furthermore, an understanding of the children's sociocultural background might help teachers find avenues toward positive teacher–child relationships that might be different or require additional steps to those used for European American, middle-class children. For example, in a case study of a prekindergarten English-speaking teacher who established positive relationships with the Latino children in her class, Gillanders (2007) found that she used strategies such as providing responsive individualized attention, being consistent and firm, and supporting children's positive behaviors—strategies that have been reported as conducive to positive teacher–child relationships with most children (Howes & Ritchie, 2002). In addition, she also used strategies that incorporated children's culture and language, such as learning songs and words in Spanish. Similarly, Davis (2003) has also emphasized, "Black males in general share this desire for a more personal connection with teachers" (p. 531), and their relationship with teachers plays a significant role in children's learning and achievement.

These studies emphasize the notion that relationships are pivotal for children's development, transitions, and success (Bronfenbrenner & Morris, 1998). Many of these ideas are based on attachment theory, which emphasizes the role of secure attachment between children and mothers in providing a foundation for children to explore and interact with their environment and others (Ainsworth, 1969; Bowlby, 1958, 1988). Attachment theory can also be used to think about student–teacher relationships (Zionts, 2005). Similar to parents, teachers can serve as a secure base during children's navigation of unfamiliar settings, such as children's transition from home to school, grade to grade, or school to school. Successfully navigating these transitions is essential to children's academic and social adjustment during their first exposure to formal schooling. For vulnerable children, these relationships and their consequences are even more critical.

Executive Function

"Executive function" is the interaction of inhibitory control that helps children resist temptation and distraction, and gives them the opportunity to make good choices instead of acting habitually or without thought; working memory that allows children to hold and utilize information; and cognitive flexibility that helps them adjust to change (Diamond, Barnett, Thomas, & Munro, 2007). Within the structure and culture of school, children who have poor executive function enter into a cycle of negativity. Their impulsive behavior gets them in trouble, their limited ability to hold onto knowledge makes them unsuccessful participants, and change is a source of stress and anxiety. Their teachers' expectations of uncontrolled behavior and poor academic results are fulfilled, and the children feel increasingly negative about themselves. Blair (2002) describes the ideal early school environment as one that attends to both the processes of acquiring knowledge and the emotional climate that optimizes learning and development. This environment ultimately supports active engagement, motivation, and a sense of capability. Support for this comes from a study of school readiness and self-regulation involving children in Head Start (Blair & Razza, 2007). The study's findings suggest that self-regulation results from the balance and coordination of emotional and cognitive systems. Turner and Johnson (2003) also found that low-income African American children's mastery motivation, an aspect of executive function, was directly linked to their language skills; number, letter, and word identification; and counting, number concepts, and numerical problem solving, supporting the notion that these foundational skills may play a part in children's early learning and later academic success.

Though studies have found that young children from low-income families are often less regulated and engaged when offered new and/or challenging tasks than children from higher-income families, these studies often fail to take into account the relationships between children and teachers, and their sociocultural experiences in the schools, classrooms, homes, and communities that impact their ability to regulate and attend. These abilities are subsequently related to school disengagement and dropout (Evans & Rosenbaum, 2008; Howse, Lange, Farran, & Boyles, 2003; Malakoff, Underhill, & Zigler, 1998).

Given the contribution of executive function to academic success, and the persistent failure of schools to meet the needs of vulnerable children, schools need to reframe their approaches to take advantage of children's sociocultural contexts that promote the development of executive function. For example, Carlson and Meltzoff (2008) found that low socioeconomic status (SES) bilingual children can perform executive function tasks at levels comparable to their middle-class monolingual peers even though they might perform at lower levels in verbal ability. The authors assume that their bilingual ability helps them compensate for their lower verbal ability and acquire executive function at levels comparable to their monolingual counterparts. Furthermore, although less studied, specific child-rearing cultural practices might contribute to the development of executive function. Because of their sociohistorical experiences of racism, prejudice, and disenfranchisement, and the cultural focus on respect and authority, African American families may prepare their children for the bias they may experience (Boykin & Toms, 1985; Frabutt, Walker, & MacKinnon-Lewis, 2002; Hughes, 2004; Hughes & Chen, 1997). As a consequence, this might potentially limit children's opportunities to engage actively and emotionally in their environment, especially in an environment that may not understand their culture and needs, which in turn may minimize children's ability to strengthen their executive function skills. More research, however, is needed to uncover the sociocultural factors that influence the development of this foundational process, so that schools can promote better cultural bridges to provide more opportunities for children to develop their executive function skills.

As the education system focuses more and more on math and literacy achievement for young children, it has in turn neglected to focus on the approaches and activities that promote the development of executive function, a skill and ability applicable to all aspects of children's learning and development, including math, literacy, science, and the development of positive peer relationships. Bodrova and Leong (2007) postulate that concentrating on improving executive function in young children, particularly those at risk, rather than focusing nearly exclusively on math and literacy instruction, may reduce referrals for special education, discipline, suspension, and retention, and, consequently, school failure and dropout; that is, understanding how vulnerable children's unique experiences impact their attention, and how their processing skills impact their learning and engagement, may truly address their needs.

Culturally Responsive Classrooms

The goal of coordinating children's PreK–3 experiences is to recognize when the gulf between experiences is too great for children to navigate successfully and make changes. The cultural discontinuity between the home lives of many children who come from poverty or minority backgrounds and the dominant culture of schools makes for a very large gulf indeed. Many teachers may unintentionally accept and/or promote forms of discrimination (Delpit, 2006; Smith, Moallem, & Sherrill, 1997). Teachers often fear "saying the wrong thing" and avoid the often taboo topic of race, retreating to the false security of "color blindness" that ultimately devalues diverse students' contributions to the classroom environment. Teachers who may not engage in important dialogue with children regarding race may never establish a safe community for children to reflect, learn, and appreciate racial differences (Howard & Denning del Rosario, 2000). Additionally, color blindness can affect teachers' attitudes and expectations, which in turn affect the students' academic outcomes (Barnes, 2006; Howard & Denning del Rosario, 2000). This is concerning because children's negative perceptions and attitudes about competence become stronger and harder to reverse as they progress through school (Valeski & Stipek, 2001).

Research suggests that teachers should, in fact, be engaged in the exact opposite of "color blindness" by providing culturally responsive learning environments that recognize, promote, and support the differences between their students (Barnes, 2006). Scheurich's (1998) research on highly successful elementary schools serving vulnerable children indicates that the development of shared beliefs by educators and families who work within their own community contexts are paramount. He suggests that, in general, these successful schools share four beliefs: (1) All children can succeed at high academic levels; (2) relationships with children must be based on love, appreciation, and respect; (3) the child's culture and first language are highly valued; and (4) the school exists for and serves families and the community.

Souto-Manning (2010) poses an essential question: "How can children's roles be pedagogically reframed and become meaningful strengths to curriculum and teaching in classrooms?" (p. 150). To put this in practice, Souto-Manning used a home visitation model to help teachers experience, understand, and value home and community literacy practices, and ultimately employ them within their own classrooms. Through this engaged learning, teachers found that the Latino families participating in the study struggled with defined starting and ending times for the home visits. This observation gave teachers a new lens through which to view children's difficulty leaving activities and transitioning without the opportunity to complete their work. Using this cultural lens, teachers became more flexible and provided the children with more choice, insisting less on time structure. They learned to step back and watch how children negotiated their own learning rather than insist upon their own style, which in turn resulted in children being more engaged and willing to take risks (Souto-Manning, 2010).

Gloria Ladson-Billings (1995) reveals the centrality of culturally relevant pedagogy for "the academic success of African American and other children who have not been well served by our nation's public schools" (p. 159) by discussing how children's culture and experiences were incorporated in their learning in her 3-year study of successful teachers of African American students. Some examples of culturally relevant pedagogical practices include use of rap music to incorporate literacy concepts and terminologies; use of African

American boys' social power in the school to make them leaders in the classroom through positive interactions; incorporation of parents' and community members' knowledge and skills to be valued and used as role models; and valuing children's language and form of expression while also teaching "Standard American English."

In classrooms using the Tools of the Mind approach that focuses on developing executive function in children, teachers "wallpaper" the classrooms with photographs from children's homes, specifically, with pictures in kitchens, dining rooms, and living rooms (Bodrova & Leong, 2007). Children are encouraged to pay attention to the details in the different photographs and emulate them in their dramatic play. Children begin to identify their own cultures and the cultures of others through the negotiation of scenarios based on difference.

In a project focused on parental involvement in mathematics education, Civil (2007) developed a program for low-income ethnic and language minority parents, teachers, and children based on the theory that household and community knowledge provide resources for mathematics education in the classroom. In the "building a garden module," parents contributed both soil and seeds, and knowledge about gardening. The teacher drew from this knowledge and developed a lesson around the geometry of garden design. Children became active participants in solving problems, such as how to find the area of the garden's irregular shape or graphing the growth of an amaryllis.

There are far too few examples of specific culturally responsive teaching and practices. More work is needed to determine paradigms that are most effective in engaging and incorporating ethnic minority children's lives and experiences. Meaningful education occurs when students perceive its relationship to them and are engaged in their education. An ultimate goal of using culturally responsive practices in the classroom is to allow children to become engaged in their learning. Some children are already disengaged as early as kindergarten. In fact, research suggests that children form academic trajectories early in their school careers that tend to be stable and difficult to change over the course of their schooling (Alexander & Entwistle, 1993), and that children's patterns of engagement and achievement formed during the first 3 years of school may impact these academic trajectories (Hamre & Pianta, 2001). Alexander, Entwistle, and Horsey (1997) found that once students' performance patterns and conduct habits are established, their ideas about school and self take shape, subsequently fueling others' judgments of their competence and character, leading students to be assigned to "niches" in the system. It is far more difficult for a student to become reengaged in school when his or her early school experiences included retention, discipline, and labeling (Alexander et al., 1997).

Schlechty (2002) outlines five types of engagement by children in classrooms: authentic, ritual, and passive engagement, and retreatism and rebellion. "Authentically engaged students see meaning in what they are doing and that meaning is connected to ends or results that truly matter to the student" (p. 10). However, students can also be authentically engaged because they see a link between what is being done and a goal that has significant consequence for them. Ritualized students do the work and carry out the activity, oftentimes with diligence and persistence, but they are doing the activity for reasons not associated with the task itself. The passively engaged student sees no meaning in the activity but does the work to avoid negative consequences. Retreating students are not engaged in the task but they do not disrupt the engagement of others, while a rebellious student refuses to do the activity and acts in ways that disrupt others.

Meaningful education is conveyed by the real presence of an educator in the lives of students, both through his or her own absorption and knowledge, and his or her relationship with students based on personal interest and knowledge of their current lives and backgrounds, as well as a belief that children are capable constructors of knowledge, and that educators and families are co-constructors with them. These beliefs are conveyed through an educator's ability to help students see that learning directly links them to the things they care about, and their idea of the future. Educators need the support and development necessary to help them understand that the creation of environments and activities that result in authentic engagement are under their control and strongly impact the success of their students.

Barriers Related to System Issues

How can we accomplish a PreK–3 approach as described earlier? What are the barriers to achieve this kind of schooling? The systems that run early childhood (birth to age 5), public schools (PreK–grade 12), and postsecondary education are essentially separate. There are attempts to coordinate across them using entities such as "Education Cabinets" (i.e., state-level collaboration across agencies and organizations that serve young children), but these efforts typically do not include early childhood education or change the structural nature of the systems. Early childhood care (birth to age 5) is funded and run primarily by Departments of Health and Human Services at the national and state level. The U.S. and state-level Departments of Education have the primary responsibility to fund K–12, and typically prekindergarten. Other programs, such as Head Start, have funding from Health and Human Services departments and are administered by local grantees but may have more formal ties to education or health and human services across states. Figure 6.1, using prekindergarten funding in North Carolina as an example, shows that the funding lines increasingly begin to cross each other the closer they get to the providers of services, suggesting the challenge that local deliverers of services might face in accessing and leveraging funds. Policies that guide these funding streams are not coordinated to ensure smooth services and transitions for children as they move across years and programs. Some states have worked to coordinate funding, to make policies consistent where possible, and to serve children across multiple settings. In North Carolina, for example, the NC Department of Public Instruction's More at Four PreK Program, the NC Partnership for Children (independent nonprofit), and the NC Department of Human Services, Division of Child Development blend funding for prekindergarten children served in multiple private and public settings, share funding streams, and issue joint contracts to blend funds for early childhood teacher scholarships, health insurance, and the like.

Data to support knowledge about children as they move from the earliest years into the public school setting may be either nonexistent or at best fragmented, and often do not include the basic demographics of the families. Use of data across these systems varies as well. A push for accountability, coupled with the lack of good data in the early grades, has led schools to seek simplistic answers to improving third-grade test scores. School have increased demands and expectations of younger children, and base curriculum and instructional decisions on ill-conceived notions that children's educational and developmental needs are the same regardless of their age or background.

One attempt to address the lack of coordinated and useable data is the Data Quality Campaign (DQC), a national, collaborative effort to encourage and support state policymakers to improve the availability and use of high-quality education data to improve student achievement. The collaborative effort of several major national policy organizations, supported by national foundations (e.g., Gates, Casey, Lumina, Dell, Pew) supports the development of longitudinal student-level databases and the policies and programs that support them. (More information can be found at *www.dataqualitycampaign.org/about.*) To extend these databases to include the early years, the Early Childhood Data Collaborative (ECDC; 2010) was established to support state policymakers' efforts to build and use

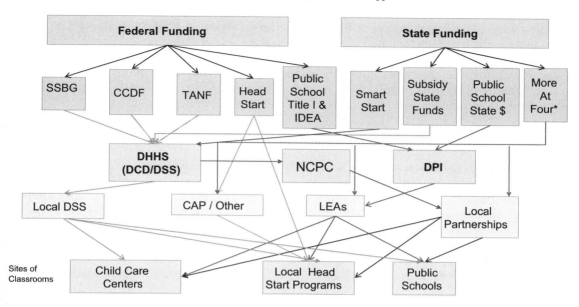

FIGURE 6.1. Sources and flow of state and federal funding for prekindergarten assistance: North Carolina. More at Four funding flows from the Local Smart Start Partnerships, LEAs, and CAPS to the classroom sites. *Note.* SSBG, Social Services Block Grant; CCDF, Child Care Development Fund; TANF, Temporary Assistance for Needy Families; DHHS, Department of Health and Human Services; DCD/DSS, Division of Child Development/Division of Social Services; NCPC, North Carolina Partnership for Children; DPI, Department of Public Instruction; CAP, community action programs; LEAs, local education agencies.

coordinated early childhood education (ECE) data systems that also link to K–12 systems. The DQC and its related organizations also participate in this Collaborative. Data systems from four areas of ECE are included: child care (birth–age 13); early intervention programs (birth–age 3); early childhood special education (ages 3–5), Early Head Start (birth–age 3), and Head Start (ages 3–5); and prekindergarten (ages 3–5).

Standards for the education and development of children in the preschool years typically do not align with the K–12 standards. The new Common Core Standards Initiative (available at *www.corestandards.org*), led by the National Governors Association and the Council of Chief State School Officers, has been endorsed by 38 states. These standards are intended to provide clear and comprehensive expectations for all states, but at this point, they typically address only K–12 and postsecondary education, leaving out prekindergarten and other early childhood education. Complaints include a structure that starts at the college level and moves backward through the grade levels, rather than one that builds on the needs and strengths of young children and moves upward. Both Florida and Massachusetts are working to align their prekindergarten standards to the Common Core State Standards. Similarly, curriculum linkages at the state level between early childhood and K–12 typically are nonexistent or inadequate. Many states have early learning standards for prekindergarten, and some are developing infant/toddler standards. But none of these provide clear and appropriate vertical alignment across developmental and educational levels.

With the focus on streamlining and aligning funding, services, data, curricula, and standards, there is a continued need to examine whether these efforts to remove barriers to a PreK–3 approach take into consideration the impact on vulnerable children. For example, would the curriculum linkages ensure that culturally relevant pedagogical practices are prominent and clearly articulated, and supported through the early years? Are alignment of services and funding examined to ensure that schools and programs serving the most vulnerable children are receiving priority and support? Though the goal of the PreK–3 approach is to enhance the learning of all children, critical attention is needed to address the needs of vulnerable children who are often impacted most by an ineffective system.

Barriers in Teacher Preparation and Workforce

Race, social class, and culture must be central to conversations about effective teacher preparation. Teacher preparation must embody a social justice agenda that pushes educators to take responsibility for responding to the conditions that perpetuate inequities for racial minority children and children in poverty. We know a lot about what teachers need to know and be able to do in order to be effective. Scholars argue that teachers who understand how learning occurs are better able to select and develop curriculum that supports the learning process (Bransford, Darling-Hammond, & LePage, 2005). Teachers who understand child development and learning are more likely to select learning experiences, tasks, materials, and instructional strategies that meet children where they are, maintain their motivation, and move them toward greater competence (Horowitz et al., 2005). Historically, ECE teacher preparation programs have emphasized child development, whereas preparation programs for elementary school teachers have emphasized academic content (e.g., math, literacy). Research has shown that children are more successful when their teachers understand *both* development *and* content (Siraj-Blatchford, Sylva, Muttock, Gilden, & Bell, 2002), and that varied use of strategies is the hallmark of a versatile teacher, who is able to select among teaching approaches to match students' learning styles and competencies (de Kruif, McWilliam, Ridley, & Wakely, 2000; Kontos & Wilcox-Herzog, 1997).

Most teacher preparation programs seriously lack the ability to prepare teachers for the skills detailed earlier. Similarly, schools of education are being regulated and prescribed so strongly that, just like their colleagues within schools, they are hindered from responding to the individual needs of their students and the contexts into which they will be moving. In addition, the overwhelming majority of elementary teachers are white women. Eighty-three percent of these teachers are white, 7% are African American, and 8% are Hispanic (U.S. Department of Education, 2001).

There are attempts to ameliorate these problems. For example, the Teacher Education and Compensation Helps (T.E.A.C.H.) Early Childhood® Project addresses the issues of undereducation, poor compensation, and high turnover within the early childhood workforce by giving scholarships to child care workers and prekindergarten teachers to complete course work in early childhood education and to increase their compensation (Child Care Services Association, 2010). Yet despite years of efforts, we have made little headway in attracting and recruiting minority scholars into the field of education or providing the skills that allow teachers to meet the instructional and emotional needs of a culturally and ethnically diverse classroom.

Reframing How We Think About and Look at the Early Years

How do we transform schools in order to utilize fully our knowledge about what works for young children, especially cultural, language, and ethnic minority children and children living in poverty? Policy advocates, professional organizations, and selected states and districts are beginning to rethink and reframe how the early years of education should look (e.g., Guernsey & Mead, 2010). A more seamless and integrated educational continuum from

PreK–3 will better ensure that the barriers to successful education of our most vulnerable children are eliminated, and that we help these children arrive at third grade achieving at grade level and ready for success throughout their educational career.

Important components of the PreK–3 educational continuum to consider in reframing the early years of education include better coordination across different governance systems for PreK–3 and the ages/grades on either side of this continuum. Thus, policies for areas such as program standards, funding, curriculum, and teacher preparation cannot be made independently. Funding streams need better coordination and must start with federal policy across the Departments of Education and Health and Human Services. In the meantime, school systems must find ways to leverage the existing resources to the maximum extent feasible. Clifford, Crawford, Stebbins, Reszka, and Coatney (2009) illustrate a model of financing a PreK–3 school using funding already available to schools. Haskins and Barnett (2010) recently suggested that trial of innovations be conducted by waiver of existing regulations around policies and funding.[1] But perhaps the most important systems challenges are changing the learning climate, instructional and classroom experiences, and teacher and leader skills in implementing a seamless education for our most vulnerable children grades PreK–3. Culturally responsive environments ensure continuity for young children as they enter early care and education (Thorp & Sanchez, 1998). Development of strong, positive racial and cultural identities has been found to contribute to positive school outcomes for students from racial/ethnic minority groups (Spencer & Markstrom-Adams, 1990), enabling students to maintain a healthy sense of identity and to demonstrate resilience (Darling-Hammond & Bransford, 2005).

FirstSchool

FirstSchool is an innovative systems approach to early schooling for vulnerable 3- to 8-year-old children that focuses on collaboration across multiple systems, agencies, and people; the use of data and inquiry to guide and monitor progress and change; and a commitment to seamless education across the PreK–3 span. Ultimately our goal is for teachers to improve the academic, socioemotional, and behavioral functioning of the most vulnerable children by prioritizing the ideas we detailed earlier: home–school partnerships; foundational processes; and culturally responsive practice. We believe this will result in positive teacher-child relationships, self-regulated and autonomous children, and families and children who experience themselves and their heritage as valuable and accomplished. We believe that this will result in decreased negative and/or punitive interactions, retentions, and special education referrals.

In our work in schools throughout the United States we have encountered the same challenges that we have described throughout this chapter. We have observed the following:

- A lack of alignment between children's educational experiences from prekindergarten to elementary school.
- Overrepresentation of children from minority backgrounds in special education, discipline, suspension, and retention.
- Early childhood teachers who do not utilize content-driven curricula because they perceive them as not responsive to individual children's development.
- Elementary school teachers who are required to follow a rigid prescriptive curriculum that is remote from children's everyday experiences.
- School administrators who are overwhelmed by pressures of accountability, and who seek answers that too often focus solely on narrow measures of children's academic development at the expense of other developmental domains.

- School-centric family involvement strategies that overlook families' experiences as resources of children's learning.
- A lack of acknowledgment and value of ethnic minority children's culture, language, and experiences as resources in their learning process.

Currently we are partnering with four schools in North Carolina and four in Michigan. All schools are struggling to meet adequate yearly progress, and all serve high proportions of children and families who live in poverty. Six of the eight schools serve high proportions of African American and Latino students. These schools share our values and goals, and have demonstrated a commitment to self-reflection.

In FirstSchool, we respond to these issues by working with educators within professional learning communities to focus on the practice of reflective thinking, to learn more about the children in their classrooms, and to design and improve supportive learning environments and opportunities for them. We help schools effectively use data as the basis for making instructional and curricular changes that support the needs of each child and help shift from a focus on teaching to a focus on learning. Full participation requires a willingness to engage in ongoing inquiry and to question what contributes to patterns of success and failure in classrooms and schools, as well as across subgroups of children. This requires commitment to a long-term effort and buy-in at the school and district level. It requires a secure and supportive administrative environment that allows, encourages, and guides teachers to identify their challenges and to work with colleagues and families to address these problems.

Schools have a variety of data sources that provide information about how the children in the school are achieving. FirstSchool helps schools organize and view their own data in order to seek information about the struggling learners in their school. FirstSchool also collects additional data that provide educators with new lenses through which to view instructional practices and home–school partnerships.

Instructional Practices

In order to address alignment across the PreK–3 span and examine the classroom experiences of children, the FirstSchool Snapshot (Ritchie et al., 2010) calculates the amount of time that children spend in specific activity settings, engage in content, and experience teaching approaches throughout the day. By showing how children experience each PreK–3 classroom within a school, these data provoke dialogue around issues such as the change in children's experiences as they move from grade to grade, the amount of time that children spend in transitions, and the balance of content and teaching approaches across the day and across literacy and mathematics instruction. Teachers use these data to stimulate conversations that focus on their own philosophy of instruction; on the federal, state, and local mandates that constrain or support their philosophy; and on the professional development they need in order to make progress in areas that prove difficult.

We detail below features of the Snapshot that were infrequently experienced by the children in the classroom, and that attracted teachers' interest and attention: flexibility, oral language and vocabulary development, strategies for teaching dual language learners, and didactic and scaffolded teaching approaches.

Flexibility

Teachers who are flexible in their responses to children—that is, teachers who nurture students' interests, give students opportunities to make choices, and do not attempt unduly to control student activity—are allowing children to regulate their own learning (Jang, Reeve,

& Deci, 2010). Initially teachers were concerned that flexibility would mean losing control in their classrooms. We began to explore the possibilities for teachers to provide students with clear instructions, expectations, procedures, and order, without controlling their students' every action or ignoring student interests (Jang et al., 2010). Some teachers were willing to examine the arbitrary rules in their classrooms that too often meant boys, especially African American boys, were in trouble instead of thriving. They exchanged rigid rules—such as sitting "crisscross applesauce," hands in your lap, and silent—for choice about where to sit, stand, and lie down while working, and engaged children in interesting observations as they moved through the school. They examined previously unchallenged practices and took risks to change their focus to improve the school experiences of the most vulnerable children.

Oral Language and Vocabulary Development

It is clear that it is important for children to develop oral language skills at an early age because of its implications for later reading and academic achievement (Dickinson, McCabe, Anastasopoulos, Peisner-Feinberg, & Poe, 2003; Dickinson & Tabors, 2001). In particular, vocabulary knowledge is one of the strongest predictors of academic achievement beginning as early as the third grade (Storch & Whitehurst, 2002). Children who have home environments rich in oral language opportunities are at an advantage when they enter school because they have larger vocabularies and more developed conceptual backgrounds. Despite what we know about the importance of vocabulary development and oral language expression, it does not appear to receive a lot of attention in the classroom. Data from FirstSchool classrooms bear this out. On average, children were engaged in oral expression for about 14% of the day (approximately 56 minutes) and intentional vocabulary building for about 2% of the day (approximately 8 minutes).

Strategies for Dual Language Learners and Didactic and Scaffolded Teaching Approaches

Strategies to support dual language learners were rarely seen (e.g., strategic use of the home language, use of comprehensible input, explicit vocabulary instruction). Didactic teaching, through which teachers provided information without input from children, occurred on average about three times more frequently than a scaffolded approach that provided children with opportunities to talk about what they heard, learned, and understood, or gave them the chance to link their learning with previous knowledge or their own life experiences. The lack of reciprocal conversation impacts not only academic development but also the development of relationships between students and teachers.

The reality we encountered as we explored these data with the teachers is that the prescriptive/scripted curricula that predominate, particularly in the schools with high minority populations, force a pace that is unresponsive to the actual learning, understanding, and sociocultural contexts of the students. Teachers know they are not meeting the needs of their students, but they regularly report that they fear reprisal if they do not comply with program demands. Prescriptive programs were developed for teachers who needed additional support as they honed their own skills. Despite the shortcomings of prescriptive curricula, this instruction is sometimes more valuable than the instruction these teachers are prepared to offer on their own. As has been found in other studies (e.g., Justice, Mashburn, Hamre, & Pianta, 2008), teachers are able to implement a prescribed curriculum with a high degree of procedural fidelity; however, this does not ensure high-quality instruction.

Untangling state, district, and individual school mandates and expectations is especially daunting. It is very difficult to tell just exactly where the authority lies and where there is room for flexibility and negotiation. Too often schools resort to the most expedient solution, without sufficiently considering what they may be sacrificing to its implementation. It can be difficult to find the entry point for discussing how to promote the instructional practices that we know support children's learning.

In one of our schools, the principal has agreed that addressing these issues is important. Rather than tackling work across the entire PreK–3 span, it was decided that the development of the first-grade team into a highly productive professional learning community would be a strong first step. The first-grade team is developing a plan to move from prescriptive curricula to practices that are more responsive to the individual academic and social needs of the children. Team members' goals are to use their professional knowledge to integrate the individual programs they currently use into cohesive learning opportunities rather than isolated skills building; to use the programs as resources rather than scripts; to have children's interests and background knowledge serve as a basis to drive instruction; to identify and master the effective programs and eliminate those that are duplicative or inadequate; and to develop a daily schedule that supports development of relationships and time for meaningful interactions. FirstSchool supports their efforts to identify, digest, and apply research that supports their goals and direction, and facilitates a negotiation process between the teachers and the administrators.

Home–School Partnerships

With an emphasis on using data for school change, FirstSchool encourages schools purposefully to find out about the beliefs, goals, practices, culture, and language of ethnic minority parents. Through the use of focus groups, led by a person outside of the school who is of the same ethnicity as the parents, we were able to uncover parents' beliefs about their role in children's education, their views about the schools' invitations to participate, beliefs and practices that promote their children's learning, and their life circumstances that facilitate or hinder their ability to support children's learning (Hoover-Dempsey & Sandler, 1997). Because this information was obtained directly from the parents, the schools are using the data to design home–school partnerships that address the particular needs of the population they are serving.

In one school we learned that a group of Latino mothers wanted to create a soccer team for the children in the school. A soccer team could provide children with an outdoor activity that they could not have outside of the school due to issues of safety and cost. Also, as recent immigrants, these mothers felt isolated, and by attending soccer matches in the school they could develop social networks with other parents. We learned from a group of African American single mothers that a major concern was the lack of male role models in their boys' lives. Finally, both the Latino and the African American mothers often felt frustrated when helping their children with homework. Although they viewed it as their responsibility to help their children, they frequently could not understand the instructions or they felt overwhelmed by the amount of homework assigned. Sharing this information has helped schools design more appropriate activities that engage all parents, not just a few. As a result, schools are developing strategies that not only fulfill the schools' goals but also are more attuned to the parents' goals and aspirations for their children.

The implementation of FirstSchool is in its first year. We are discovering both new problems and reasons for hope at every turn. We are working to help schools achieve the mindset that they are responsible for meeting the needs of each child who enters the school, and an ability and willingness across the schools to determine pathways for creating a sustained approach to pedagogy, programs, and policies based on shared beliefs about the educational and social needs of young children. As FirstSchool develops and expands, there will continue to be a need for research on practices that support a year's worth of progress each year for every child, regardless of circumstances or background.

Conclusion

In this chapter we have made the case that the PreK–3 approach is well situated to address the needs of vulnerable children in this country. In addition, we have explicitly called for a reconceptualization of the early education of young children, so that the failures of previous educational structures are not incorporated into the PreK–3 approach. As FirstSchool continues and evolves, there will be a need for additional research and evaluation on practices to improve the learning and development of ethnic minority and poor children, and explicit examination of the assumption that what works for European American, middle-class children works for everybody.

Why is implementation of comprehensive PreK–3 reform lagging behind the rhetoric nationwide? The reasons include accountability systems that push schools toward inappropriate results-based strategies, lack of knowledge about the high-quality research supporting PreK–3 systemic approaches, and early childhood and elementary educational systems that are not aligned or linked across various educational components (e.g., standards, teacher credentialing, vertical curriculum alignment, smooth transitions, funding streams, and data systems). When the latest research tells us that only 10% of poor children experience high-quality instruction consistently throughout the elementary school years, and that only 7% of students in the early grades have consistently stimulating classroom experiences (Pianta, Belsky, Houts, & Morrison, 2007), we must accept the challenge to make dramatic changes in the education of both our teachers and our students. It is essential that we scrutinize the negative educational climate that has emerged from what often feels like a desperate grab for simple answers, and make transparent the high-pressure environment that too many teachers and young students experience on a daily basis. The strong national commitment to improved student achievement must be redirected from simplistic measurement and grading of schools and teachers to more comprehensive and evidence-based restructuring and alignment. The policy and funding changes that improve alignment, and changes in accountability systems at state levels, will take time and continuing advocacy.

Note

1. For a summary of the discussion in this book and comments by readers, see Lisa Guernsey's Early Ed Watch Blog at New American Foundation, October 28, 2010 (*earlyed.newamerica.net/blogposts/2010/proposed_waiving_rules_in_return_for_innovations_in_early_ed-39158*).

References

Ainsworth, M. D. S. (1969). Object relations, dependency, and attachment: A theoretical review of the infant–mother relationship. *Child Development, 40,* 969–1025.

Alexander, K. L., & Entwistle, D. R. (1993). Entry into schools: The beginning school transition and educational stratification in the U.S. *Annual Review of Sociology, 19,* 401–423.

Alexander, K. L., Entwisle, D. R., & Horsey, C. S. (1997). From first grade forward: Early foundations of high school dropouts. *Sociology of Education, 70,* 87–107.

Aud, S., Fox, M., & KewalRamani, A. (2010). *Status and trends in the education of racial and ethnic groups* (NCES 2010-015). Washington, DC: U.S. Department of Education, National Center for Education Statistics.

Auerbach, S. (2007). From moral supporters to struggling advocates: Reconceptualizing parent roles in education through the experience of working-class families of color. *Urban Education, 42*(3), 250–283.

Banks, J. A. (1993). The canon debate, knowledge construction, and multicultural education. *Educational Researcher, 22*(5), 4–14.

Barnes, C. J. (2006). Preparing preservice teachers to teach in a culturally responsive way. *Negro Educational Review, 57,* (1–2), 85–93.

Bernhard, J., Lefebvre, M., Kilbride, K., Chud, G., & Lange, R. (1998). Troubled relationships in early childhood education: Parent–teacher interactions in ethnoculturally diverse child care settings. *Early Education and Development, 9*(1), 5–28.

Birch, S. H., & Ladd, G. W. (1997). The child–teacher relationship and children's early school adjustment. *Journal of School Psychology, 35,* 61–79.

Blair, C. (2002). School readiness: Integrating cognition and emotion in a neurobiological conceptualization of child functioning at school entry. *American Psychologist, 57,* 111–127.

Blair, C., & Razza, R. C. (2007). Relating effortful control, executive functional and false belief understanding to emerging math and literacy ability in kindergarten. *Child Development, 78*(2), 647–663.

Bodrova, E., & Leong, D. J. (2007). *Tools of the mind: The Vygotskian approach to early childhood education* (2nd ed.). Upper Saddle River, NJ: Pearson Education.

Bondy, E., & Ross, D. D. (1998). Confronting myths about teaching Black children: A challenge to teacher educators. *Teacher Education and Special Education, 21*(4), 241–254.

Bowlby, J. (1958). The nature of the child's tie to his mother. *International Journal of Psychoanalysis, 39,* 350–373.

Bowlby, J. (1988). *A secure base: Parent–child attachment and healthy human development.* New York: Basic Books.

Bowman, B., Donovan, S., & Burns, S. (2001). *Eager to learn: Educating our preschoolers.* Washington, DC: National Academy Press.

Boykin, A., & Toms, F. (1985). Black child socialization: A conceptual framework. In H. P. McAdoo (Ed.), *Black children: Social, educational, and parental environments* (pp. 33–51). Thousand Oaks, CA: Sage.

Bransford, J. D., Darling-Hammond, L., & LePage, P. (2005). Introduction. In L. Darling-Hammond & J. D. Bransford (Eds.), *Preparing teachers for a changing world: What teachers should learn and be able to do* (pp. 1–39). San Francisco: Jossey-Bass.

Bronfenbrenner, U., & Morris, P. (1998). The ecology of developmental processes. *Handbook of child psychology: Vol. 1. Theoretical models of human development* (5th ed., pp. 993–1028). Hoboken, NJ: Wiley.

Burchinal, M., Peisner-Feinberg, E., Bryant, D., & Clifford, R. (2000). Children's social and cognitive development and child-care quality: Testing for differential associations related to poverty, gender, or ethnicity. *Applied Developmental Science, 4*(3), 149–165.

Burchinal, M., Roberts, J., Zeisel, S., Hennon, E., & Hooper, S. (2006). Social risk and protective child, parenting, and child care factors in early elementary school years. *Parenting: Science and Practice, 6*(1), 79–113.

Burchinal, M. R., Peisner-Feinberg, E., Pianta, R., & Howes, C. (2002). Development of academic skills from preschool through second grade: Family and classroom predictors of developmental trajectories. *Journal of School Psychology, 40*(5), 415–436.

Campbell, F. A., & Ramey, C. T. (1995). Cognitive and school outcomes for high-risk African-American students at middle adolescence: Positive effects of early intervention. *American Educational Research Journal, 32*(4), 743–772.

Carlson, S., & Meltzoff, A. (2008). Bilingual experience and executive functioning in young children. *Developmental Science, 11*(2), 282–298.

Caughy, M. O., DiPietro, J., & Strobino, M. (1994). Day-care participation as a protective factor in the cognitive development of low-income children. *Child Development, 65,* 457–471.

Chall, J. S., & Snow, C. E. (1988). School influences on the reading development of low-income children. *Harvard Educational Newsletter, 4*(1), 1–4.

Chang, F., Crawford, G., Early, D., Bryant, D., Howes, C., Burchinal, M., et al. (2007). Spanish-speaking children's social and language development in pre-kindergarten classrooms. *Early Education and Development, 18*(2), 243–269.

Child Care Services Association. (2010). T.E.A.C.H. Early Childhood® Project—North Carolina. Retrieved from *www.childcareservices.org/ps/teach.html.*

Cicchetti, D., & Lynch, M. (1993). Toward an ecological/transactional model of community violence and child maltreatment: Consequences for children's development. *Psychiatry: Interpersonal and Biological Processes, 56,* 96–118.

Civil, M. (2007). Building on community knowledge: An avenue to equity in mathematics education. In N. S. Nasir & P. Cobb (Eds.), *Improving access to mathematics: Diversity and equity in the classroom* (pp. 105–117). New York: Teachers College Press.

Clifford, R., Barbarin, O., Chang, F., Early, D., Bryant, D., Howes, C., et al. (2005). What is pre-kindergarten?: Characteristics of public pre-kindergarten programs. *Applied Developmental Science, 9*(3), 126–143.

Clifford, R. M., Crawford, G. M., Stebbins, H., Reszka, S. S., & Coatney, B. (2009). Financing services for 3- and 4-year olds in a preK–3rd school (Issues in PreK–3rd Education No. 2). Chapel Hill: University of North Carolina, FPG Child Development Institute, FirstSchool.

Cole, M. (2010). Education as an intergenerational process of human learning, teaching, and development. *American Psychologist, 65*(8), 796–807.

Comer, J. P. (1986). Parent participation in the schools. *Phi Delta Kappan, 67,* 422–446.

Council of Great City Schools. (2010). Beating the odds: An analysis of student performance on state assessments and NAEP. *Individual District Profiles.* Retrieved from *www.cgcs.org/publications/achievement.aspx.*

Currie, J., & Thomas, D. (2000). School quality and the long-term effects of Head Start. *Journal of Human Resources, 35,* 755–774.

Darling-Hammond, L., & Bransford, J. (2005). *Preparing teachers for a changing world: What teachers should learn and be able to do.* San Francisco: Jossey-Bass.

Davis, J. E. (2003). Early schooling and academic achievement of African American males. *Urban Education, 38*(5), 515–537.

De Gaetano, Y. (2007). The role of culture in engaging Latino parents' involvement in school. *Urban Education, 42*(2), 145–162.

de Kruif, R. E. L., McWilliam, R. A., Ridley, S. M., & Wakely, M. B. (2000). Classification of teachers' interaction behaviors in early childhood classrooms. *Early Childhood Research Quarterly, 15,* 247–268.

Delpit, L. (2006). *Other people's children: Cultural conflict in the classroom.* New York: New Press.

Diamond, A., Barnett, W. S., Thomas, J., & Munro, S. (2007). Preschool program improves cognitive control. *Science, 318*(5855), 1387–1388.

Dickinson, D. K., McCabe, A., Anastasopoulos, L., Peisner-Feinberg, E., & Poe, M. D. (2003). The comprehensive language approach to early literacy: The interrelationship among vocabulary, phonological sensitivity, and print knowledge among preschool-aged children. *Journal of Educational Psychology, 95*(3), 465–481.

Dickinson, D. K., & Tabors, P. O. (2001). *Beginning literacy with language.* Baltimore: Brookes.

Dupree, D., Spencer, M. B., & Bell, S. (1997). African American children. In G. Johnson-Powell & J. Yamamotoa (Eds.), *Transcultural child development: Psychological assessment and treatment* (pp. 237–268). New York: Wiley.

Early Childhood Data Collaborative. (2010, August). Getting started: 10 fundamentals of coordinated state early care and education data systems. Retrieved December 8, 2010, from *dataqualitycampaign.org/resources/details/1016.*

Early, D. M., Iruka, I. U., Ritchie, S., Barbarin, O. A., Winn, D. C., Crawford, G. M., et al. (2010). How do pre-kindergarteners spend their time?: Gender, ethnicity and income as predictors of experiences in pre-kindergarten classrooms. *Early Childhood Research Quarterly, 25,* 177–193.

Epstein, J. (1992). School and family partnerships. In M. Alkin (Ed.), *Encyclopedia of educational research* (6th ed., pp. 1139–1151). New York: Macmillan.

ETR Services, LLC. (2010, April). *Ready Schools Cross-Cutting Evaluation Report.* Durham, NC: Author.

Evans, G., & Rosenbaum, J. (2008). Self-regulation and the income-achievement gap. *Early Childhood Research Quarterly, 23*(4), 504–514.

Frabutt, J., Walker, A., & MacKinnon-Lewis, C. (2002). Racial socialization messages and the quality of mother/child interactions in African American families. *Journal of Early Adolescence, 22*(2), 200–217.

Garces, E., Thomas, D., & Currie, J. (2002). Longer-term effects of Head Start. *American Economic Review, 92*(4), 999–1012.

García, E. E. (2010). Developing and learning in more than one language: The challenges and opportunities for transitions in early education settings. In S. L. Kagan & K. Tarrant (Eds.), *Transitions for young children: Creating connections across early childhood systems* (pp. 93–106). Baltimore: Brookes.

Garcia Coll, C., Lamberty, G., Jenkins, R., McAdoo, H. P., Crnic, K., Wasik, B. H., et al. (1996). An integrative model for the study of developmental competencies in minority children. *Child Development, 67,* 1891–1914.

Garcia Coll, C. T., & Magnuson, K. (2000). Cultural differences as sources of developmental vulnerabilities and resources. In J. P. Shonkoff & S. J. Meisels (Eds.), *Handbook of early childhood interventions* (pp. 94–114). New York: Cambridge University Press.

Gay, G. (2004). Multicultural curriculum theory and multicultural education. In J. A. Banks & C. M. Banks (Eds.), *Handbook of research in multicultural education* (2nd ed., pp. 30–49). San Francisco: Jossey-Bass.

Gillanders, C. (2007). An English-speaking prekindergarten teacher for young Latino children: Implications of the teacher–child relationship on second language learning. *Early Childhood Education Journal, 35*(1), 47–54.

Goldenberg, C. (1987). Low-income Hispanic parents' contributions to their first-grade children's word-recognition skills. *Anthropology and Education Quarterly, 18*(3), 149–179.

González, N., Moll, L., & Amanti, C. (2005). *Funds of knowledge: Theorizing practices in households, communities, and classrooms.* Mahwah, NJ: Erlbaum.

Guernsey, L., & Mead, S. (2010, March). *The next social contract for the primary years of education.* Washington, DC: New America Foundation.

Gutierrez, K. D., Morales, P. Z., & Martínez, D. C. (2009). Re-mediation literacy: Culture, difference, and learning for students from nondominant communities. *Review of Research in Education, 33,* 212–245.

Gutierrez, K. D., & Rogoff, B. (2003). Cultural ways of learning: Individual traits or repertoires of practice. *Educational Researcher, 32,* 19–25.

Gutman, L., & McLoyd, V. (2000). Parents' management of their children's education within the home, at school, and in the community: An examination of African-American families living in poverty. *Urban Review, 32*(1), 1–24.

Hamre, B. K., & Pianta, R. C. (2001). Early teacher–child relationships and the trajectory of children's school outcomes through eighth grade. *Child Development, 72*(2), 625–638.

Hamre, B. K., & Pianta, R. C. (2005). Can instructional and emotional support in the first-grade classroom make a difference for children at risk for school failure? *Child Development, 76*(5), 949–967.

Haskins, R., & Barnett, W. S. (Eds.). (2010). *Investing in young children: New directions in federal preschool and early childhood policy.* Washington, DC: Center on Children and Families at Brookings & National Institute of Early Education Research.

Henderson, A., & Mapp, K. (2002). *A new wave of evidence: The impact of school, family, and community connections on student achievement: Annual synthesis, 2002.* Austin, TX: National Center for Family and Community Connections with Schools (SEDL).

Hernandez, D., Denton, N., & Macartney, S. (2008). The lives of America's youngest children in immigrant families. *Zero to Three, 29*(2), 5–12.

Hoover-Dempsey, K. V., & Sandler, H. M. (1997). Why do parents become involved in their children's education? *Review of Educational Research, 67*(1), 3–42.

Horowitz, F. D., Darling-Hammond, L., Bransford, J., Comer, J., Rosebrock, K., Austin, K., et al. (2005). Educating teachers for developmentally appropriate practice. In L. Darling-Hammond

& J. Bransford (Eds.), *Preparing teachers for a changing world* (pp. 88–125). San Francisco: Jossey-Bass.

Howard, T. C., & Denning del Rosario, C. (2000). Talking race in teacher education: The need for racial dialogue in teacher education programs. *Action in Teacher Education, 21*(4), 127–137.

Howes, C., & Ritchie, S. (2002). *A matter of trust: connecting teachers and learners in the early childhood classroom.* New York: Teachers College Press.

Howse, R., Lange, G., Farran, D., & Boyles, C. (2003). Motivation and self-regulation as predictors of achievement in economically disadvantaged young children. *Journal of Experimental Education, 71*(2), 151–174.

Hughes, D. (2004). Correlates of African American and Latino parents' messages to children about ethnicity and race: A comparative study of racial socialization. *American Journal of Community Psychology, 31*, 15–33.

Hughes, D., & Chen, L. (1997). When and what parents tell children about race: An examination of race-related socialization among African American families. *Applied Developmental Science, 1*(4), 200–214.

Iruka, I., Burchinal, M., & Cai, K. (2010). Long-term effect of early relationships for African American children's academic and social development: An examination from kindergarten to fifth grade. *Journal of Black Psychology, 36*(2), 144–171.

Jang, H., Reeve, J., & Deci, E. (2010). Engaging students in learning activities: It is not autonomy support or structure but autonomy support and structure. *Journal of Educational Psychology, 102*(3), 588–600.

Justice, L., Mashburn, A., Hamre, B., & Pianta, R. (2008). Quality of language and literacy instruction in preschool classrooms serving at-risk pupils. *Early Childhood Research Quarterly, 23*(1), 51–68.

Kauerz, K. (2006, January). *Ladders of learning: Fighting fade-out by advancing PK–3 alignment* (Issue Brief No. 2). Washington, DC: New America Foundation Early Education Initiative.

Knapp, M. S., & Associates. (1995). *Teaching for meaning in high-poverty classrooms.* New York: Teachers College Press.

Kontos, S., & Wilcox-Herzog, A. (1997). Influences on children's competence in early childhood classrooms. *Early Childhood Research Quarterly, 12*(3), 247–262.

Ladd, G. W., Birch, S. H., & Buhs, E. S. (1999). Children's social and scholastic lives in kindergarten: Related spheres of influence? *Child Development, 70*(6), 1373–1400.

Ladson-Billings, G. (1995). But that's just good teaching!: The case for culturally relevant pedagogy. *Theory Into Practice, 34*, 159–165.

Lareau, A., & Horvat, E. (1999). Moments of social inclusion and exclusion: Race, class, and cultural capital in family–school relationships. *Sociology of Education, 72*(1), 37–53.

Lawson, M. (2003). School–family relations in context: Parent and teacher perceptions of parent involvement. *Urban Education, 38*(1), 77–133.

Lee, C. D. (2003). "Every shut eye ain't sleep": Studying how people live culturally. *Educational Researcher, 32*(5), 6–13.

Lee, J. M., & Rawls, A. (2010). The college completion agenda 2010: Progress report. Retrieved from *completionagenda.collegeboard.org/sites/default/files/reports_pdf/progress_report_2010.pdf.*

Lee, Y. (2002). Racial and ethnic achievement gap trends: Reversing the progress toward equity? *Educational Researcher, 31*(1), 3–12.

Littlejohn-Blake, S., & Anderson Darling, C. (1993). Understanding the strengths of African American families. *Journal of Black Studies, 23*(4), 460–471.

Magnuson, K. A., Ruhm, C., & Waldfogel, J. (2007). The persistence of preschool effects: Do subsequent classroom experiences matter? *Early Childhood Research Quarterly, 22*(1), 18–38.

Malakoff, M., Underhill, J., & Zigler, E. (1998). Influence of inner-city environment and Head Start experience on effectance motivation. *American Journal of Orthopsychiatry, 68*(4), 630–638.

Marietta, G. (2010, August). Lessons in early learning: Building an integrated PreK–12 system in Montgomery County public schools (Educational Reform Series). Retrieved December 8, 2010, from *www.pewtrusts.org/uploadedfiles/wwwpewtrustsorg/reports/pre-k_education/pkn_montgomery_county_report_final.pdf?n=8226.*

McKinsey & Company. (2009). The economic impact of the achievement gap in America's schools: Summary of findings. Retrieved December 8, 2010, from *www.mckinsey.com/app_media/ images/page_images/offices/socialsector/pdf/achievement_gap_report.pdf*.

McLoyd, V. C. (1990). The impact of economic hardship on black families and children: Psychological distress, parenting, and socioemotional development. *Child Development, 61*, 311–346.

McLoyd, V. C. (1998). Socioeconomic disadvantage and child development. *American Psychologist, 53*, 185–204.

Murray, C., Murray, K. M., & Wass, G. A. (2008). Child and teacher reports of teacher–student relationship: Concordance of perspectives and associations with school adjustment in urban kindergarten classrooms. *Journal of Applied Developmental Psychology, 29*, 49–61.

Murrell, P. C., Jr. (2002). *African-centered pedagogy: Developing schools of achievement for African American children*. Albany: State University of New York Press.

National Assessment of Educational Progress. (2010, April). *Reading 2009: The National Assessment of Educational Progress at grades 4 and 8*. Washington, DC: Institute of Educational Sciences, U.S. Department of Education.

National Center for Education Statistics. (2001). *Education achievement and black–white inequality*. Washington, DC: U.S. Department of Education.

Ohio Department of Education and Ohio Association of Elementary School Administrators. (2008, September). *Strong beginnings, smooth transitions, continuous learning: A ready schools research guide for elementary school leadership*. Columbus: Ohio Department of Education and Ohio Association of Elementary School Administrators.

Peisner-Feinberg, E. S., Burchinal, M. R., Clifford, R. M., Culkin, M. L., Howes, C., Kagan, S. L., et al. (2000). *The children of the cost, quality and child outcomes study go to school* (Technical Report). Chapel Hill: University of North Carolina at Chapel Hill & FPG Child Development Institute.

Peisner-Feinberg, E. S., Burchinal, M. R., Clifford, R. M., Culkin, M. L., Howes, C., Kagan, S. L., et al. (2001). The relation of preschool child-care quality to children's cognitive and social developmental trajectories through second grade. *Child Development, 72*(5), 1534–1553.

Peske, H. G., & Haycock, K. (2006). Teaching inequality: How poor and minority students are shortchanged on teacher quality. Retrieved August 7, 2007, from *www2.edtrust.org/edtrust/ press+room/teacherquality2006.htm*.

Pianta, R. C., Belsky, J., Houts, R., & Morrison, F. (2007). Opportunities to learn in American's elementary classrooms. *Science, 315*, 1795–1796.

Pianta, R. C., Howes, C., Burchinal, M., Bryant, D., Clifford, R., Early, D., et al. (2005). Features of pre-kindergarten programs, classrooms, and teachers: Do they predict observed classroom quality and child–teacher interactions? *Applied Developmental Science, 9*, 144–159.

Pianta, R. C., Nimetz, S. L., & Bennett, E. (1997). Mother–child relationships, teacher–child relationships, and school outcomes in preschool and kindergarten. *Early Childhood Research Quarterly, 12*, 263–280.

Pianta, R. C., & Steinberg, M. (1992). Teacher–child relationships and the process of adjusting to school. In R. C. Pianta (Ed.), *Beyond the parent: The role of other adults in children's lives* (pp. 61–80). San Francisco: Jossey-Bass.

Pianta, R. C., & Stuhlman, M. W. (2004). Teacher–child relationships and children's success in the first years of school. *School Psychology Review, 33*(3), 444–458.

Pungello, E., Kainz, K., Burchinal, M., Wasik, B., Sparling, J., Ramey, C., et al. (2010). Early educational intervention, early cumulative risk, and the early home environment as predictors of young adult outcomes within a high-risk sample. *Child Development, 81*(1), 410–426.

Ray, A., Aytch, L., & Ritchie, S. (2010). *Kids like Malik, Carlos, and Kiana: Culturally responsive practice in culturally and racially diverse schools*. Unpublished manuscript.

Reynolds, A., Magnuson, K., & Ou, S. R. (2006). *PK–3 education: Programs and practices that work in children's first decade*. New York: Foundation for Child Development.

Reynolds, A. J., Wang, M. C., & Walberg, H. J. (Eds.). (2003). *Early childhood programs for a new century*. Washington, DC: Child Welfare League of America.

Riegle-Crumb, C. (2006). The path through math: Course sequences and academic performance at the intersection of race–ethnicity and gender. *American Journal of Education, 113*(1), 101–122.

Ritchie, S., Maxwell, K. L., & Bredekamp, S. (2009). Rethinking early schooling: Using developmental science to transform children's early school experiences. In O. A. Barbarin & B. H. Wasik (Eds.), *Handbook of child development and early education: Research to practice* (pp. 3–13). New York: Guilford Press.

Ritchie, S., Weiser, B., Kraft-Sayre, M., Mason, E., Crawford, G., & Howes, C. (2010). *Emerging academics snapshot.* Chapel Hill: University of North Carolina at Chapel Hill.

Rogoff, B. (2003). *The cultural nature of human development.* New York: Oxford University Press.

Rogoff, B., Goodman-Turkanis, C., & Bartlett, L. (2001). *Learning together: Children and adults in a school community.* New York: Oxford University Press.

Rowley, S., Helaire, L., & Banerjee, M. (2010). Reflecting on racism: School involvement and perceived teacher discrimination in African American mothers. *Journal of Applied Developmental Psychology, 31*(1), 83–92.

Scheurich, J. J. (1998). Highly successful and loving, public elementary schools populated mainly by low-SES children of color: Core beliefs and cultural characteristics. *Urban Education, 33*(4), 451–491.

Schlechty, P. (2002). *Working on the work.* San Francisco: Jossey-Bass.

Schweinhart, L. J., Montie, J., Xiang, A., Barnett, W. S., Gelfield, C. R., & Nores, M. (2005). *Lifetime effects: The HighScope Perry preschool study through age 40.* Ypsilanti, MI: HighScope Educational Research Foundation.

Scribner, J. D., Young, M. D., & Pedroza, A. (1999). Building collaborative relationships with parents. In P. Reyes, J. D. Scribner, & A. P. Scribner (Eds.), *Lessons from high-performing Hispanic schools: Creating learning communities* (pp. 36–60). New York: Teachers College Press.

Shore, R. (2009). *The case for investing in PreK–3rd education: Challenging myths about school reform* (PreK–3rd Policy to Action Brief No. 1). New York: Foundation for Child Development.

Siraj-Blatchford, I., Sylva, K., Muttock, S., Gilden, R., & Bell, D. (2002). *Researching effective pedagogy in the early years* (Research Brief No. 356). Norwich, UK: Queen's Printer.

Sleeter, C. E. (2001). *Culture, difference and power.* New York: Teachers College Press.

Smith, R., Moallem, M., & Sherrill, D. (1997). How preservice teachers think about cultural diversity: A closer look at factors which influence their beliefs towards equality. *Educational Foundations, 11*(2), 41–61.

Souto-Manning, M. (2010). Challenging ethnocentric literacy practices: (Re) Positioning home literacies in a Head Start classroom. *Research in Teaching of English, 45*(2), 150–178.

Spencer, M., & Markstrom-Adams, C. (1990). Identity processes among racial and ethnic minority children in America. *Child Development, 61*(2), 290–310.

Storch, S. A., & Whitehurst, G. J. (2002). Oral language and code-related precursors to reading: Evidence from a longitudinal structural model. *Developmental Psychology, 38,* 934–937.

Stuhlman, M. W., & Pianta, R. C. (2009). Profiles of educational quality in first grade. *Elementary School Journal, 109*(4), 323–342.

Thorp, E., & Sanchez, S. (1998). The use of discontinuity in preparing early educators of culturally, linguistically, and ability-diverse young children and their families. *Zero to Three, 18*(6), 27–33.

Turner, L., & Johnson, B. (2003). A model of mastery motivation for at-risk preschoolers. *Journal of Educational Psychology, 95*(3), 495–505.

U.S. Chamber of Commerce. (2010). *Why business should support early childhood education.* Washington, DC: Institute for a Competitive Workforce, U.S. Chamber of Commerce.

U.S. Department of Education. (2001). *Family involvement in children's education: An idea book* (Abridged version). Jessup, MD: Office of Educational Research and Improvement.

Utsey, S., Bolden, M., Lanier, Y., & Williams, O. (2007). Examining the role of culture-specific coping as a predictor of resilient outcomes in African Americans from high-risk urban communities. *Journal of Black Psychology, 33*(1), 75–93.

Valeski, T., & Stipek, D. (2001). Young children's feelings about school. *Child Development, 72*(4), 1198–1213.

Vandell, D., Belsky, J., Burchinal, M., Steinberg, L., Vandergrift, N., & NICHD Child Care Research Network. (2010). Do effects of early child care extend to age 15 years?: Results from the NICHD study of early child care and youth development. *Child Development, 81*(3), 737–756.

Wong, S., & Hughes, J. (2006). Ethnicity and language contributions to dimensions of parent involvement. *School Psychology Review, 35*(4), 645–662.

Zionts, L. T. (2005). Examining relationships between students and teachers: A potential extension of attachment theory? In K. A. Kerns & R. A. Richardson (Eds.), *Attachment in middle childhood* (pp. 231–254). New York: Guilford Press.

CHAPTER 7

Language, Culture, and Early Education in the United States

Eugene E. García

Some 2 to 3 million children, ages 0–8, in the United States who are learning English as a second language form quite diverse cultural backgrounds, with many living in immigrant families (García & Jensen, 2009a). How we define these children and the labels we ascribe can be confusing. Several terms are used in the literature to describe U.S. schoolchildren whose native language is other than English. The term "language minority" is used to describe U.S. children whose native language and family culture are other than English, and who reside in a family culture in which that language serves as the major mode of communication (García, 2005). In this chapter, a variant of this term is utilized, "dual language/cultural learner," and its abbreviation (DLCL), as a way of emphasizing students' learning and progress in two languages at early ages of language development within a developmental cultural context aligned with a heritage language other than English. A recent analysis of young children identified as speaking a language other than English in the United States indicates that most children under age 8 (85%) who live in predominantly non-English environments are also exposed in a substantial manner to English, and to diverse cultural circumstances in which English and a heritage language are present (Hernández, Denton, & Macartney, 2008). The DLCL term emphasizes and strategically recognizes that integrating children's knowledge, skills, and abilities related to two languages and cultures is central to the educational practices needed in early learning environments to improve their educational opportunities.

This chapter addresses the significant issues related to the early education of DLCL children, with a concern for bringing to light the latest research information on these issues. It necessarily focuses on Latino and recent U.S. immigrant populations primarily because the research portfolio on these groups is more prevalent. More specifically, the chapter achieves the following:

- Provides a brief overview of the demography of DLCL children and families.
- Describes the educational circumstances of our youngest DLCLs.
- Provides a review of programs and best practices that have demonstrated effectiveness in enhancing overall development and early academic achievement, including issues related to instruction, programs, teachers, and family engagement.

The Demographic Reality

The overall child population speaking a non-English native language in the United States rose from 6% in 1979 to 14% in 1999 (García & Jensen, 2009a; National Clearinghouse for English Language Acquisition, 2006), and the number of DLCL students in K–12 schools has been estimated to be over 14 million (August, 2006). The representation of these students in U.S. schools has its highest concentration in early education. Therefore, young DLCLs (ages 0–8 years) have been the fastest growing student population in the country over the past few decades, due primarily to increased rates in (legal and illegal) immigration, as well as high birthrates among immigrant families (García & Frede, 2010).

While a majority comes from Spanish-speaking immigrant families, these students represent many cultural groups and more than 350 languages. Most of these children have cultural "roots" in Latino immigrant families (Capps et al., 2005). Nationally, Spanish was the native language of some 77% of DLCL children during the 2008–2009 school year. The Caribbean, East Asia, and Europe (combined with Canada and Australia) each accounts for 10–11% of the overall population of children from immigrant families; Central America, South America, Indochina, and West Asia each accounts for 5–7% of the total; and the former Soviet Union and Africa each accounts for 2–3%. At least 3 in 4 children in immigrant families are born in the United States (Capps et al., 2005). Just as immigrant families are settling in new destinations in response to labor demands (Zúñiga & Hernández-León, 2005), these students are increasingly attending school in states that previously served few to none of these children in the 1980s and previous decades. While immigrant families continue to be concentrated in California, Texas, New York, Florida, Illinois, and New Jersey, seven states experienced over 100% increases from 1990 to 2000 in the number of children from immigrant families attending grades PreK–5, including Nevada, North Carolina, Georgia, Nebraska, Arkansas, Arizona, and South Dakota (Capps et al., 2005). Nevada, Nebraska, and South Dakota, respectively, saw increases of 354, 350, and 264% in their young DLCL populations.

A Focus on Latino DLCL Children and Families

Recently much national attention has been given to the burgeoning Latino population in the United States and, concurrently, the development of an extended research base regarding the intersection of language, culture, and schooling (García, 2005; National Task Force on the Early Childhood Education of Hispanics, 2007). The rapid growth is due to both an expanding wave of immigration from Latino countries and the relatively high birthrate among Latino families living in the United States. The high birthrate magnifies the demographic significance of the 6.8 million young Latino children (ages 0–8) living in this country, who account for 20% of all young children, while Latinos as a whole account for only 12.5% of the country's population (Hernández, Macartney, & Denton, 2010). Meanwhile, the high proportion of Hispanic children from often-underprivileged immigrant families reemphasizes the fact that too many face circumstances related to low levels of school readiness and achievement. In combination, these facts make clear the urgent imperative for the nation's school system to adapt and find better ways to serve the largest and fastest growing group of children (Hernández et al., 2010; Ramirez & de la Cruz, 2003).

Based on national demographic data (and considering each statistic separately), a Latino child is most likely American born (88%), of Mexican descent (65%), living in California (31%) with both parents (77%), at least one of whom is an immigrant (64%), in a low-income family (58%), and is likely at least somewhat proficient in English (70%). His or her family is probably low-income (58%) and the mother probably did graduate high school but has no college degree (47%). However, this hypothetical child, despite having been categorized as Latino, belongs to a very diverse group of individuals with widely varying nationalities, generational status, and socioeconomic status (SES) levels.

Most young children of Latino descent come from immigrant families, as do the majority of DLCL children in this country. In the year 2000, 64% of Latino children were either immigrants themselves (first-generation Americans) or were U.S.-born children of immigrants (second-generation American). Of these 64%, most (88%) fit the latter category (Hernández et al., 2010). The other 36% were third-generation Americans and beyond. As expected, immigration status is a category in which much variability is found. The likelihood that a given child will be from an immigrant family depends heavily on the family's national heritage. For Latinos, roughly 90% of Dominican, Central American, and South American families are immigrant families. By comparison, about two-thirds of Mexican and Cuban youngsters belong to immigrant families. Puerto Rican children are the least likely to belong to immigrant families, with nearly half having two native-born parents.

Latino families past and present arrive from a large number of countries and represent many different cultures. In 2000, the U.S. statistical breakdown by national heritage for all Latino children under age 8 was as follows: Mexicans, 65.2%; Puerto Ricans, 9.3%; Central Americans, 7.2%; South Americans, 5.5%; Dominicans, 2.3%; Cubans, 2.3%; and all other Latinos, 8% (Hernández et al., 2010). Other demographic studies suggest that these percentages have remained steady throughout the recent past (Martin et al., 2005).

It is important to note that the educational attainment patterns of the parents of young Hispanics vary substantially based on immigration status. At the national level, in 2000, native-born mothers of young Latino children were over 50% more likely than immigrant mothers to hold a college degree (12.4 and 8.0%, respectively), were almost twice as likely to have finished high school (63.8 and 37.7%, respectively), and were more than eight times as likely to have progressed beyond the eighth grade (95.5 and 62.2%, respectively) (Hernández et al., 2008). The educational attainment of Latino fathers also varies with their immigration generational status. All Latino immigrant fathers are less likely to attain a high school diploma than native-born Latino fathers. Twenty-four percent of native-born fathers of Mexican descent did not have a high school diploma in 2000. The percentage for immigrant Latino fathers was 66%.

Reardon and Galindo (2006) point out that the parental educational circumstances are most disadvantaged for first- and second-generation students of Mexican Central American origins. First- and second-generation Mexican students are three times as likely to have parents with less than a high school education as third-generation and beyond Mexican students. Furthermore, Mexican American mothers are the least likely to hold a college degree, with only 6.2% having a college degree in 2000. In that year, young children of Mexican descent had a 51.4% probability of having a mother without a high school diploma. This is the case for 49.9% of Central American children, 35.5% of Dominican children, 29.5% of Puerto Rican children, and 17.1% of South American children. Cubans, who make up the smallest percentage of Hispanics in the country, had the highest level of education. More than one-fourth (29.2%) of young Cuban children have mothers who have attained a college degree, and 84.6% had mothers who graduated high school, figures that are very similar to those for white mothers (30.2 and 91.1%, respectively) and well above the national averages (23.8 and 81.8%, respectively) (Hernández et al., 2010).

Given the lower average level of education for the parents of young Latino children, it is perhaps unsurprising that Latino children experience very high levels of poverty in America. More than one-fourth (26%) of Latino children age 8 or younger live below the poverty line, and more than half (58%) come from low-income families (those with incomes less than twice the national poverty line). This compares to only 9% of white children living below the poverty line, and 27% of white children belonging to low-income families.

Notably, the pattern of economic success mirrors that of educational attainment with respect to immigration status and cultural heritage. Young Latino children with immigrant families (63%) are 31% more likely to live in poverty or under low-income conditions compared to those with native-born parents (48%). Mothers of young Mexican American children, who have the lowest average educational attainment among Latino cultural heritage groups, also showed the lowest rates of economic success, with 68% of their children living in low-income families (Hernández et al., 2010).

The population of Latino children is indeed diverse in terms of generational status, cultural heritage, the economic success of their families, and the ultimate education attained by their parents. These facts, combined with the overall unequal numbers and growth rates of Latino in different regions, means that policymakers, administrators, and teachers all face their own unique set of challenges as they prepare to serve this large and rapidly growing population. I have focused on the Latino DLCL population solely because the recent explosion of data on Latinos allows such a focus. However, these data might be somewhat applicable to other DLCL children, since they also are likely to be living in immigrant circumstances (with developmental contexts of more than one language and culture), within in families with low education capital (limited successful education background), and overrepresented in situations of family poverty. Overall, these populations of students presents a new set of challenges to our implementation of early education in this country.

Acquiring Another Language

As the study of early language has morphed from a consideration of habits (Skinner, 1957) and innate structures (Chomsky, 1959) to an interlocking study of linguistic, psychological, and social domains, language and its many parts—phonology, morphology, syntax, pragmatics, vocabulary, word literacy, text literacy, and reading comprehension—must be analyzed in terms of not only its mechanics (e.g., word attack, reading fluency) but also context (e.g., person-to-person interactions, relationships, activity settings). In the case of DLCLs and second language learning, this necessitates an understanding of bilingualism, and of the cognitive and sociocultural factors that play an important role in second language acquisition.

Research on the bilingual development of young children over the past three decades suggests that linguistic structures (i.e., phonology, morphology, and syntax) between languages influence one another, and that bilingualism is heavily influenced by the environments in which children develop. For these reasons, bilingualism cannot be viewed simply as "the arithmetic sum of two languages" (García, 2005, pp. 21–38).

A child is usually described as a "balanced bilingual" when he or she possesses age-appropriate competence in both languages. The amount of early exposure and opportunity to explore both languages also determines the type of bilingualism a child develops. For instance, a child who is exposed to English and Spanish at relatively comparable amounts in the home and given adequate opportunity to use both is likely to develop simultaneous bilingual proficiency. Whereas, another child exposed only to Spanish in the home and English in school will develop the two languages sequentially—either rapidly or successively, depending on the amount of opportunities to experiment with and use the second language (Genesee, 2010).

It is often the case that young bilinguals in the United States do not develop their native language beyond early conversational skills learned in the home. Many Latino immigrant children, for example, lose native language proficiency at the expense of developing English skills. Several studies have been conducted with young Latino children and their families to explore the various factors that influence Spanish maintenance even as English skills are being developed (Hammer, Miccio, & Wagstaff, 2003; Lee & Samura, 2005; López, 2005; Pérez-Bazán, 2005). They found native language maintenance to be a result of interacting personal and family factors. While Latino immigrant children inevitably gain proficiency in English through interaction with the larger community, proficiency in Spanish was found to be associated with the quality and quantity of Spanish use in the home (Pérez-Bazán, 2005). Spanish maintenance also has been found to be related with parent education levels, with higher levels associated with greater bilingual and Spanish proficiency (López, 2005), opportunities for native language use (Lee & Samura, 2005), as well as attitudinal and motivational features (López, 2005).

In order for language-minority students to succeed in academic settings and perform well in comparison to their peers, they need strong English skills. For a large number of DLCLs, this means acquiring them in a second language. Krashen (1985) maintains that in order for this to happen, the learner needs to be exposed to "comprehensible input," which is input that is "*slightly* ahead of a learner's current state of grammatical knowledge" (Gass & Selinker, 2001, p. 200; emphasis added). In other words, input needs to be both meaningful and understandable, at the same time that it provides some new grammatical knowledge to the learner. "The teacher's main role, then, is to ensure that students receive comprehensible input" (Gass & Selinker, 2001, p. 201).

Another important aspect of second language development is the duration required to attain proficiency: How long does it take second language learners to attain English proficiency? Research shows that the answer to this question depends on how it is posed in reference to oral or academic English proficiency (Collier, 1989, 1995; Cummins, 1981; Mitchell, Destino, & Karam, 1997). "Oral proficiency" generally precedes academic proficiency, and refers to the development of conversational vocabulary, grammar, and listening comprehension. "Academic proficiency" refers to various skills, including word reading, spelling, reading fluency, reading comprehension, and writing.

Reporting on data from 5,585 DLCLs from four different school districts (two from the San Francisco Bay Area and two from Canada) to address the question of duration, Hakuta, Goto Butler, and Witt (2000) analyzed various forms of English proficiency as a function of length of exposure to English. Their study plotted English proficiency as a function of length of residence, which was calculated by subtracting age at immigration from present age. They found that oral proficiency took 3–5 years to develop, and academic English proficiency required 4–7 years. Moreover, socioeconomic factors tended to slow the rate of acquisition. Studies assessing the duration of English acquisition have been conducted mostly with school-age children.

Rather than stipulating time limits for DLCLs to attain English skills, it has been suggested that education policy and practices should continue to identify and leverage children's abilities, and provide empirically sound instructional and curricular practices to help children succeed academically, with the understanding that the development of satisfactory English skills requires a number of years. Historically, school districts and states have approached the language development and education of DLCLs in very different ways. Unfortunately, these approaches typically are not influenced by rigorous research but by politics and ideology (García & Jensen, 2009a).

Several theories have been presented over the past few decades to explain how young children learn a second language, and ways in which linguistic properties between the first and second language interact. "Transfer" theories are currently the most commonly cited frameworks used to explain second language acquisition and the relationships between linguistic properties of the first and second languages. García and Jensen (2009b) assert that language skills from the first language transfer to the second. Theoretically, then, the acquisition and development of first and second languages are interdependent (Cummins, 1981, 2000). In other words, development of the first language can influence—either by facilitating or inhibiting—development in the second. However, according to this theoretical orientation, not all aspects of second language development are affected by the first language. Cummins (2000) explains how language that is contextually embedded (e.g., casual, culturally laden social communication) and cognitively undemanding (i.e., automatic and overlearned interaction) does not lend itself well to transfer; that is, language skills involved in day-to-day interpersonal communication are not developmentally interdependent. Language that is contextually reduced and cognitively demanding, on the other hand, is developmentally interdependent. Thus, transfer is much more likely to occur. This means that higher-order cognitive skills, such as academic language, are more developmentally interdependent and amenable to transfer between languages. A broad range of variables has been found to moderate cross-linguistic processes (Genesee, 2010). Moderators include factors such as proficiency level in both the first and the second language, the quality and quantity of first language use in the home, socioeconomic status, generational status, instructional approaches, and individual factors such as personality (Genesee, Geva, Dressler, & Kamil, 2006).

Sociocultural theorists posit that the psychology of the individual learner is deeply shaped by social interaction—in essence, that both children and those with whom they interact are engaged in the process of constructing knowledge primarily through social activity. Knowledge, therefore, is created between individuals primarily through social interaction. Higher-order mental processes, the tendency to look at things in certain ways, and values themselves are produced by shared activity and dialogue (Rogoff, 1990). In a broader sense, these social interactions are highly determined by culture and directly affect language, cognitive, and social development, as well as the acquisition of any new knowledge and behavior—that phenomenon we call "learning."

Educators of DLCL children often find this theoretical framework helpful because it conceives of learning as an interaction between individual learners and an embedding context. This context may be as immediate as the social environment of the classroom or as indirect as the traditions and institutions that constitute the history of an educational system. Contexts and many other factors come into play whenever teachers and students interact. Important contexts for teaching and learning range from (1) close detailed instruction of individual learners and (2) concern for the social organization of classrooms to (3) a consideration of the cultural and linguistic attributes of teachers, students, and peers. These contexts interweave, and we can follow their strands to gain a new understanding of the relationship among language, culture, and cognition.

It is useful, therefore, to conceive of co-occurring linguistic, cognitive, and social character of a child's development as inherently interrelated (García, 2005; García & Frede, 2010). As children develop their ability to use language, they absorb more and more understanding of social situations and improve their thinking skills. This in turn allows them to learn how to control their own actions and thoughts. It is through a culturally bound and socially mediated process of language development that children construct mental frameworks (or schemas) for perceiving the world around them. If language is a tool of thought, it follows that as children develop more complex thinking skills, the mental representations through which language and culture embody the child's world play a significant role. This perspective is especially important for young children negotiating two or more languages (Hammer, Miccio, & Rodriguez, 2004).

Unfortunately, educational policy and practice discussions regarding the education of bilingual students are often overly simplistic and focus solely on linguistic deficiencies (i.e., limited English skills) (García, 2005; García & Jensen, 2009b; Rolstad, Mahoney, & Glass, 2005; Stritikus, 2001; Tharp & Gallimore, 1989). They tend to neglect the complex interweaving of students' cultural, linguistic, and cognitive development. In their study of the possible effects of language on cognitive development, Hakuta, Ferdman, and Diaz (1987) recognized the importance of acknowledging these three important strands in children's development, and addressing them in schools. They concluded that most of the variance in cognitive growth directly relates to the way in which society affects and manipulates cognitive capacities. Therefore, cultural and contextual sensitivity theories that examine the social and cultural aspects of cognitive development would best serve immigrant student populations (García, 2005; García & Frede, 2010).

Educational Circumstances

The academic performance patterns of DLCL students as a whole cannot be adequately understood without considering their social and economic characteristics in comparison with native English speakers, in addition to the institutional history of U.S. schools (Jensen, 2008). While a great deal of socioeconomic variation exists among DLCLs, they are more likely than native English-speaking children, on average, to live in poverty and to have parents with limited formal education (García & Cuellar, 2006). In addition, DLCL students are more likely to be an ethnic/racial minority (Capps et al., 2005). Each of these factors—low income, low parent education, and ethnic/racial minority status—decreases group achievement averages across academic areas, leading to the relatively low performance of DLCL students.

In their analyses of a national dataset of academic performance in early elementary school, Reardon and Galindo (2006) found reading and mathematics achievement patterns from kindergarten through third grade to vary based on home language environments among Latino students. Those living in homes categorized as "primarily Spanish" or "Spanish only" lagged further behind white children than did Latinos who lived in homes where primarily English or English only was spoken. Given the associations among educational risk factors for DLCL students, the impact of language background on achievement outcomes should be contextualized. The interrelationship of risk variables has been documented in several reports (Collier, 1987; Jensen, 2007). In a separate analysis of the same national dataset, Jensen (2007) compared Spanish-speaking kindergarteners to their general education peers on a number of outcomes, including SES, parent education, and mathematics achievement. He found that Spanish-speaking kindergartners, on average, scored four-fifths of a standard deviation lower than the general body of kindergartners in mathematics. They also fared less well, an entire standard deviation below their peers, in terms of SES and maternal educational attainment. Nearly half of the kindergarteners from Spanish-speaking homes had mothers who had not completed high school.

Thus, rather than pointing to one or two student background factors that account for the low achievement in DLCL students, it should be understood that educational risk, in general, is attributable to myriad interrelated out-of-school factors, including parent education levels, family income, parent English language proficiency, mother's marital status at the time of birth, single- versus dual-parent homes, and, immigrant generational status (National Center for Educational Statistics, 1995; National Task Force on the Early Childhood Education for Hispanics, 2007). The more risk factors to which the child is subject, the lower the probability that the child will do well in school in terms of learning and attainment in the standard educational environment. Because DLCL children, on average, exhibit three of the five risk factors at higher rates than do native English speakers, they are generally at greater risk for academic underachievement (Hernández et al., 2008). Using Census 2000 data, Capps and colleagues (2005) found that 68% of DLCL PreK–5 students lived in low-income families, compared to 36% of English-proficient children. The percentages changed to 60 and 32%, respectively, for sixth- to 12th-grade students. Moreover, 48% of DLCL PreK–5 children and 35% of DLCLs in the higher grades had a parent with less than a high school education, compared to 11 and 9%, respectively, of English-proficient children in the same grades (Capps et al., 2005).

Language, Schooling, and Best Practices

Best-Fit Program Features for DLCLs

There are many possible program options for young children learning English as a second language. These carry various titles, including transitional bilingual education, maintenance bilingual education, 90-10 bilingual education, 50-50 bilingual education, developmental bilingual education, dual-language learning, two-way immersion, English as a second language, English immersion, sheltered English, structured English, submersion, and so forth. These programs differ in the way in which they use the native language and English during instruction (Ovando, Collier, & Combs, 2006). They also differ in terms of theoretical rationale, language goals, cultural goals, academic goals, student characteristics, ages served, entry grades, length of student participation, participation of mainstream teachers, teacher qualifications, and instructional materials (García, 2005; Genesee, 1999, 2010). The extent to which a program is successful depends on local conditions, choices, and innovations.

Because sociodemographic conditions differ, and local and state policies demand assorted objectives from their schools and teachers, no single program works best in every situation. When selecting a program, one of the most fundamental decisions should be whether bilingual proficiency is an objective. Clearly, given the cognitive and economic advantages of bilingual proficiency in a world that is becoming increasingly globalized, promoting bilingualism is an intuitive ambition (García & Jensen, 2006). However, the development of balanced bilingualism depends on state and local policies, as well as the availability of teachers and course curricula to meet the need. Indeed, the feasibility of bilingual promotion varies between schools.

A critical feature that should be considered when selecting a program designed for DLCLs is optimizing individual achievement and literacy development. Academic performance continues to be the driving force behind educational policy reform and practice in the United States, and programs developed for young DLCLs should strive to reduce achievement gaps. It is additionally important, however, that programs support the development of the whole child, simultaneously sustaining the cognitive, social, emotional, and psychological development. Therefore, a holistic approach is especially important during the early years (i.e., PreK–3) of schooling (Zigler, Gilliam, & Jones, 2006).

Heritage Language and Culture

Decades of research support the notion that children can competently acquire two or more languages (Genesee, 2010). The acquisition of these languages can be but need not be parallel; that is, the qualitative character of one language may lag behind, surge ahead, or develop equally with the other language. Moreover, the relationship of linguistic properties between languages is quite complex. Several theories have been put forward to explain how language and literacy develop for young children managing two or more linguistic systems. Currently, among the available theoretical approaches, transfer theory is most widely accepted to explain the language development of DLCLs. This theoretical position asserts that language skills from the first language transfer to the second. In like manner, errors or interference in second language production occur when grammatical differences between the two languages are present. However, not all aspects of second language development are affected by the first language. Language that is contextually embedded and cognitively undemanding—or automatic, overlearned interaction—does not lend itself well to transfer. This is the language involved in day-to-day interpersonal communication. Research shows that contextually reduced and cognitively demanding linguistic skills, on the other hand, transfer between languages (August & Shanahan, 2006; Genesee, 1999). Higher-order cognitive skills relevant to academic content are more developmentally interdependent and, therefore, amenable to transfer.

Bringing together the disciplines of psychology, semiotics, education, sociology, and anthropology, sociocultural theory has become an important way of understanding issues of language, cognition, culture, human development, and teaching and learning (García, 2005). This approach posits that children's linguistic, cognitive, and social characteristics are fundamentally connected and interrelated. A child's basic cognitive framework is shaped by his or her native language, early linguistic experiences, and cultural context. Children from non-English-speaking homes often must adjust their cognitive and linguistic representations to negotiate social exchanges within the school environment. Though research in this area is limited, extant best practices (Goldenberg, Rueda, & August, 2006) suggest that bridging home–school sociocultural differences can enhance students' engagement and level of participation in classroom instruction. Because home linguistic interactions (which vary by SES indicators such as parent education) and teacher practices, perspectives, and expectations influence the development of literacy skills; children whose teachers recognize and take full advantage of home resources (including child's home language and cultural practices) and parental supports tend to experience more optimal outcomes.

Given the demographic circumstances of young DLCL children in the United States, the development of school programs and practices that recognize the conditions and strengths of DLCL children and families is crucial. For example, because 3 in 4 young Latino children are exposed to Spanish in the home, and even more are exposed to Spanish through relatives and/or neighbors, ways in which these programs integrate language in teaching and learning are important. Currently, young Latino children, on average, lag substantially behind their Asian American and white peers in terms of academic achievement; differences are quite large at the beginning of kindergarten, and the gap closes very little thereafter. Within the Latino population, first- and second-generation children and those of Mexican and Central American origins demonstrate the lowest achievement levels, influenced by multiple out-of-school factors, including SES, low parent education, limited English proficiency of parents, and other home circumstances (National Task Force on Early Childhood Education for Hispanics, 2007).

Children's culture and related educational practices in the home are important to evaluate because they bear on children's early cognitive development and, therefore, influence school readiness and sustained academic performance (García & Cuellar, 2006). The amount of language (regardless of the particular linguistic system) used in the home has been found to be strongly associated with early literacy and cognitive development. More specifically, research indicates that the amount of "extra" talk between caretakers and their children, book reading, and parent–child interactions (i.e., reading, telling stories, singing) influence early development. This is an important consideration because low-income families are less likely, on average, to engage in these activities; DLCL parents are less likely than non-DLCL parents to read, tell stories, and sing to their children (National Task Force on the Early Childhood Education for Hispanics, 2007).

Schooling program options for young DLCLs differ in terms of their goals, requirements for staff competency, and the student populations they are meant to serve. The effectiveness of a given program depends on local conditions, choices, and innovations. In terms of student achievement outcomes, meta-analyses and best-evidence syntheses suggest that programs supporting bilingual approaches to curriculum and instruction are favorable to English-only or English immersion programs. These programs provide sound instruction in both Spanish and English (García, 2005).

Driven by sociocultural notions of language and learning, dual language (DL or two-way immersion) programs—a particular approach to bilingual education—integrate language-minority and language-majority students in the same classroom. Educators in DL programs use English-plus-Spanish (EPS) approaches to teach both languages through course content. Studies suggest that students (from multiple-language backgrounds) in DL programs perform at equal levels as their peers and, in many cases, outperform those in other programs (García & Jensen, 2006). Preliminary evidence suggests that prekindergarten programs (for students 3- and 4-years old) can increase early learning for young DLCL children (García & Miller, 2008). High-quality prekindergarten programs can improve school readiness for young Latino children and decrease achievement differences between racial/ethnic groups at kindergarten entry (National Task Force on the Early Childhood Education for Hispanics, 2007).

High-Quality Instructors

High-quality teachers/instructors for DLCLs are critical (Freedson, 2010). However, data from teachers instructing these children indicate that these teachers are not well prepared to meet students' needs (National Center for Education Statistics, 2001). Responding to this lack of preparedness, the literature on teacher preparation has begun to develop conceptual frameworks regarding competencies essential for teachers working with DLCLs. A series of conceptual pieces has recently emerged that identifies aspects of the knowledge base, skills base, and attitudes and dispositions necessary to work effectively with DLCLs (Ballantyne, Sanderman, & Levy, 2008; Lucas & Grinberg, 2008; Lucas, Villegas, & Freedson-González, 2008). According to Lucas and Grinberg (2008), teachers should have language-related experience, linguistic knowledge, and opportunities to participate programs that collaboratively prepare teachers across disciplines to instruct DLCLs in mainstream classrooms. In order to be prepared effectively, they argue, teachers of DLCLs need specialized training within these particular areas.

Current research on preparation to teach DLCLs reports inconsistencies in the way teachers are prepared, due to state mandates (e.g., Proposition 203 in Arizona, Proposition 227 in California) and other, larger policy implications (e.g., No Child Left Behind, Reading First). Gandara, Rumberger, Maxwell-Jolly, and Callahan (2003) report that variations in the preparation of DLCL teachers stem from the impact of these larger social policies and state initiatives. Nevertheless, there are common factors reported on practices necessary to teach DLCLs effectively. In their synthesis of the research on effective practices for DLCLs,

Waxman and Tellez (2002) reported several strategies, including collaborative learning communities, multiple representations, building on prior knowledge, instructional conversation, culturally responsive instruction, and technology-rich instruction. They argue that these practices must be used simultaneously. Similar to the work of Lucas and colleagues (2008), Lucas and Grinberg (2008) purport that teachers need specialized preparation that includes language-related experience and linguistic knowledge.

In the larger body of research on teacher preparation, Darling-Hammond (2006) summarized common features of exemplary teacher education programs. Four of the seven common features speak specifically to the preparation of teachers working with DLCLs:

- A common, clear vision of good teaching permeates all coursework and clinical experiences.
- Curriculum is grounded in knowledge of child and adolescent development, learning, social contexts, and subject matter pedagogy, taught in the context of practice.
- Extended clinical experiences are carefully developed to support the ideas and practices presented in simultaneous, closely interwoven coursework.
- Explicit strategies help students confront their own deep-seated beliefs and assumptions about learning and students, and learn about the experiences of people different from themselves.

Darling-Hammond and Bransford (2005) identified three general areas of knowledge that teachers must acquire:

- Knowledge of learners and how they learn and develop within social context.
- Conceptions of curriculum and social purposes of education.
- An understanding of teaching.

In a review of the most recent research on the preparation of teachers for DLCLs, common factors are similar in high-quality teacher preparation, as noted by Darling-Hammond (2006) and Darling-Hammond and Bransford (2005). Table 7.1 illustrates these common factors (García, Arias, Harris Murri, & Serna, 2010).

The research in Table 7.1 indicates the knowledge needed for teaching and working with DLCLs, and the broader literature indicates the knowledge teachers need to acquire

TABLE 7.1. Preparing Teachers for DLCL Children/Students

Prepared credentialed teachers (Villegas & Lucas, 2002a)	General areas of acquired knowledge for teacher (Darling-Hammong & Bransford, 2005)	Knowledge related to English learners (Lucas & Grinberg, 2008; Merino, 2007; Lucas, Villegas, & Freedson-Gonzáles, 2008; Téllez & Waxman, 2006)
• Build on what students already know • Understand how students construct knowledge • Demonstrate a sociocultural consciousness • Know about the lives of their students • Affirm the views of students	• Knowledge of learners and how they learn and develop within a social context • Conceptions of curriculum and social purposes of education • Understanding of teaching	• Students' funds of knowledge • Connections between language, culture, and identity • Sociocultural factors situated in communities, classrooms, and schools • Families, communities and the role of home culture impacting school outcomes • Culturally responsive classrooms, instruction, and cultural sensitivity

in order to be effective teachers. However, what is important to point out is the absence of the specific competencies of the English learner's knowledge. In order to address the needs of DLCL students, teacher preparation programs must also address these areas within the schools and communities.

Research suggests the influence of teachers' attitudes and beliefs on their expectations of DLCLs, interaction, and instructional practices (García-Nevarez, Stafford, & Arias, 2005; Reeves, 2004; Youngs & Youngs, 2001). Youngs and Youngs (2001) found that teachers who had taken foreign language classes were significantly more positive toward teaching DLCLs than teachers who had not taken a course. García (2005) argues for a "pedagogy of empowerment," a responsive pedagogy that expands students' knowledge beyond their own immediate experiences, while using those experiences as a sound foundation for appropriating new knowledge. He characterizes the schoolwide and teacher practices that reflect this pedagogy. Included in the schoolwide practices is a school vision that values diversity, professional collaboration, and teacher practices that focus on language development through meaningful interactions and communications, and awareness of the role of language and language policy in schools. A conceptual framework for teacher preparation for DLCLs needs to situate this knowledge, as well as these features and factors, within the living communities and schools.

Through their review of the research and work with teachers in culturally and linguistically diverse classrooms, Villegas and Lucas (2002a, 2002b) purport that in order to become culturally responsive teachers, teachers must develop a "sociocultural consciousness," recognizing that each individual's "perspective reflects his or her location in the social order" (2002a, p. 42). In her review of the research and her work with national projects, Gay (2002) defines culturally responsive teaching as

> using the cultural characteristics, experiences, and perspectives of ethnically diverse students as conduits for teaching them more effectively. It is based on the assumption that when academic knowledge and skills are situated within the lived experiences and frames of reference of students, they are more personally meaningful, have higher interest appeal, and are learned more easily and thoroughly. (p. 106)

Therefore, it is important to consider the beliefs and values that impact teachers' teaching practices.

Culturally responsive teaching practices must be grounded in an understanding of student's background (Gay, 2000; Ladson-Billings, 1994; Villegas & Lucas, 2002a). Villegas and Lucas (2002b) report common characteristics of culturally responsive teaching practices, which include building on what students already know, understanding how students construct knowledge, demonstrating a sociocultural consciousness, knowing and understanding about the lives of their students, and affirming the views of students. These practices cannot be conducted in isolation; rather, they must be supported and situated within specific learning communities. In teacher preparation programs, this speaks to field placements in which prospective teachers may actively participate in the community within which they teach and their students live. Research strongly suggests the benefits of such culturally diverse field placements (Zeichner, 1996) that provide opportunities for prospective teachers to change the way they are thinking about their students.

Responsive Learning Communities

The learning environments that are considered essential to the development of a responsive pedagogy are referred to as "effective schooling" (Freedson, 2010; García, 1999, 2001,

2005). The focus on the social, cultural, and linguistic diversity represented by students in today's public schools further challenges us to consider the theoretical and practical concerns relative to ensuring educational success for diverse students; that is, responsive learning communities must necessarily address issues of diversity in order to maximize their potential and to sustain educational improvement over time. To further examine this challenge, Figure 7.1 summarizes the conceptual dimensions for high-performing, responsive learning communities.

The provision of high-quality programs across the PreK–3 spectrum necessitates high-quality teachers. This means teachers are bilingual/multilingual so that they can communicate with children and families, and knowledgeable regarding the cultural and linguistic circumstances of these children and families. Indeed, research shows that the transfer of academic skills between languages is heightened and early achievement outcomes increases for young bilingual and emergent bilingual students when teachers use the heritage language in the classroom (Jensen, 2007). The most successful teachers are fluent in both languages, understand learning patterns associated with second language acquisition, have a mastery of appropriate instructional strategies (i.e., cooperative learning, sheltered instruction, differentiated instruction, and strategic teaching), and have strong organizational and communication skills. With these skills, teachers are able to interact with parents appropriately and encourage them to engage in literacy activities with their children at home, and to find out as much detail as possible about the linguistics backgrounds of their students to develop creative and accurate assessments of the children's linguistic ability and development.

Schoolwide Practices

- A vision defined by the acceptance and valuing of diversity
- Treatment of classroom practitioners as professionals/colleagues in school development decisions
- Characterized by collaboration, flexibility, enhanced professional development
- Elimination (gradual or immediate) of policies that seek to categorize diverse students, thereby rendering their educational experiences as inferior or limiting for further academic learning
- Reflection of and connection to surrounding community—particularly with the families of the students attending the school

Teacher/Instructional Practices

- Bilingual/bicultural skills and awareness
- High expectations of diverse students
- Treatment of diversity as an asset to the classroom
- Ongoing professional development on issues of cultural and linguistic diversity and practices that are most effective
- Bases of curriculum development to address cultural and linguistic diversity:
  1. Attention to and integration of home culture/practices
  2. Focus on maximizing student interactions across categories of English proficiency, academic performance, regency of immigration, and so forth.
  3. Regular and consistent attempts to elicit ideas from students for planning units, themes, activities
  4. Thematic approach to learning activities—with the integration of various skills, events, and learning opportunities
  5. Focus on language development through meaningful interactions and communications combined with direct grammatical skills building in content-appropriate contexts

---

FIGURE 7.1. Conceptual dimensions of addressing cultural and linguistic diversity in responsive learning communities.

Family Engagement

As discussed earlier in this chapter, DLCL immigrant children often start school under disadvantaged academic circumstances; however, the literature has shown that immigrant families posses positive attributes that are likely to work as a safeguard against these risk factors (National Task Force for Early Childhood Education of Hispanics, 2007). For example, familism, a foundational attribute in Latino and many immigrant families, expresses important values such as family identification, obligation, and support (García et al., 2009). Familism has been found to affect immigrant students' academics positively (Valenzuela & Dornbusch, 1994).

Another important attribute is the high percentage of intact families within the immigrant community. Mexican immigrant families have the highest percentage of intact families compared to all immigrant and U.S.-born families, including white families (Hernández et al., 2008). The generational status of Latino families is important in understanding the variability in intact families within the immigrant community. For instance, in 2000, this was 86% for Mexican American children from immigrant families and 65% for Mexican American children in native-born families. The following percentage pairs represent (immigrant and native) group: Puerto Ricans, 64 and 52%; Central Americans, 81 and 52%; Cubans, 85 and 71%; Dominicans, 66 and 33%; and South Americans, 85 and 67%. Importantly, research shows that children who grow up in stable, two-parent households, compared to children who lack these attributes, achieve higher levels of education, earn higher incomes, enjoy higher occupational status, and report less symptoms of depression, even after researchers control for parental income and education (Amato, 2005). Specifically, for immigrant Mexican American families, it has been suggested that the high rate of intact marriages contributes to Mexican American children's high levels of psychological well-being (Crosnoe, 2006). Moreover, Latino children often live in households that include nuclear and extended family. This affects Latino children positively. Immigrant households that include grandparents and other extended family members are conducive to communal caregiving and familywide participation in children's early learning experiences (Buriel & Hurtado-Ortiz, 2000).

Family engagement in children's education has been documented in the academic literature as important in the academic well-being of children (Barrera & Warner, 2006; Lee & Bowman, 2006; Raikes et al., 2006). Using Early Childhood Longitudinal Study—Kindergarten Cohort (ECLS-K) data, Qiuyun (2006) studied the effects of involvement of language-minority parents in their children's academic outcomes (reading, math, and science) and socioemotional outcomes in the K–3 years. The findings suggest that DLCLs with less parent involvement through the early academic years lagged behind their DLCL peers from the beginning of kindergarten through the end of third grade.

Promising Programs in Working with DLCL Families

AVANCE and Project FLAME (Family Literacy: Aprendiendo, Mejorando, Educando) have been found to have a positive effect on Latino immigrant parental involvement in education and Latino children's early achievement. AVANCE, a nonprofit organization established in 1973 with the mission of strengthening families within at-risk communities through effective parent education and support programs, is a parent–child education program that focuses on parent education, early childhood development, brain development, literacy, and school readiness. The program largely supports Latino immigrant families under conditions of economic stress in underserved communities, and aims to prepare parents to be supporters and role models to help their children to succeed in school.

The AVANCE (2007) program, with chapters throughout Texas and in Los Angeles, California, is a 9-month course built on the assumption that parents can improve their parenting skills, that they are the most influential teachers and role models for their children, and that the years between childbirth and age 3 are critical to influencing a child's educational success.

The program serves parents with children from 0–3 years of age and operates in housing projects, schools, and community centers. AVANCE instructors make parents aware of the learning and development their children undergo, including the emotional, physical, social, and cognitive processes. This awareness-raising practice is based on the discussion of topics that range from the importance of effective discipline and nutrition to reading and math. Parents are also encouraged to attend classes in literacy, learn English, and prepare for the general equivalency degree (GED) examination.

A program that came about with the purpose to improve the parent involvement and academic achievement of children of parents with limited English proficiency, Project FLAME (Family Literacy: Aprendiendo, Mejorando, Educando; Rodriguez-Brown & Shanahan, 1989), is housed at the University of Illinois, Chicago, and is carried out in public schools. The program model has been circulated nationally to over 50 sites to train family literacy professionals. It was specifically developed in support of a more comprehensive educational intervention aimed at DLCL children. FLAME offers wide-ranging services to mostly immigrant and Spanish-speaking Latino families with children between ages 3 and 9, with the purpose of increasing parents' abilities to provide literacy opportunities for their children and to act as a positive literacy models for their children; improving parents' literacy skills, so that they may efficiently initiate, encourage, support, and extend their children's learning; and improving the relationship between parents and school officials. An important aspect of Project FLAME is the emphasis on using the language in which the parents feel the most comfortable.

Following are some of the skills that target Latino parents and ways in which the program has improved Latino children's early education. For example, parents learn what types of books are appropriate for the age of their children, and are encouraged to reach out in the community to access literacy materials and create literacy centers at home. Parents are also provided with English as a second language courses and encouraged to engage in reading and writing activities with their children. Through workshops in the program parents learn the value of interacting with their children in activities such as talking, singing, and playing. The program emphasizes talking with children about books. In order to improve parent–school communication, parents learn what school personnel expect from their children academically and are encouraged to volunteer in their children's classroom. Through the participation with the program, children's knowledge of basic concepts, letters, and print awareness increase. Furthermore, Latino parents' involvement activities, such as volunteering and implementing teacher suggestions, also increase (Rodriguez-Brown, 2009).

In a quasi-experimental study, children who did not attend preschool but whose parents attended FLAME were compared to children who attended a state-funded preschool program, but whose parents did not partake in FLAME. The children were compared in terms of their print awareness, recognition of lower and uppercase letters, and knowledge of basic concepts via the Boehm Test. All children came from similar socioeconomic backgrounds, and most of their families asserted that Spanish was their dominant language. On the pretest, the children who attended the state-sponsored preschool outperformed the FLAME children, but on the posttest no differences were detected. This was after adjustment for the preexisting differences between the FLAME and the comparison groups. The fact that this study included a comparison group was important, indicating that improvements among the

FLAME children were due to their parents' participation in the FLAME project (Rodriguez-Brown & Mulhern, 1993).

It has begun to be clear that family engagement of DLCL students is positively associated with academic performance (Rodriguez-Brown, 2009). Again, this relationship seems to be strongest in the early grades (García & Miller, 2008). Family engagement programs can help parents and family members contribute to the academic growth of students through linguistically and culturally responsive strategies (García, Scribner, & Cuellar, 2009). This set of understandings, particularly for this population, is valuable in constructing educational interventions of the highest caliber.

Conclusion

For our youngest language-minority children, ages 3–8 years, understanding early learning parameters is critically important in building a solid foundation for future educational success. These DLCL children not only offer us some unique challenges but also the greatest opportunities to intervene with families as partners in ways that will enhance their present educational circumstances. In this chapter we have attempted to review those educational circumstances, to provide some clearer direction with regard to program and program attributes that "work" for these children, and to identify what are becoming promising best practices.

To summarize, any intervention for DLCL children must draw heavily on critical elements of theory research and practice to achieve the following three goals:

1. Provide students with a learning environment that optimizes both language development and the acquisition of content-specific knowledge.
2. Provide teachers with the instructional support needed to maximize student potential.
3. Improve and expand on how parents and families contribute to the academic growth of their children.

In Support of Goal 1

• *Objective*: Refrain from "English-only" instruction that embeds teaching of the "mechanics" of the English language into academic content.

• *Rationale*: To be effective, teachers must provide a classroom environment with ample opportunity for students to practice academic language in thoughtful and meaningful ways in both the heritage language of the child/family and in English (Espinosa, 2010). The intervention must structure instruction so as to support a curriculum that adheres to the volume of second language learning research, suggesting that optimal learning occurs when students are taught language "mechanics" within rigorous and academically focused instruction (see August, Goldenberg, & Rueda, 2010; August & Shanahan, 2006; García, 2005; Valdes, 2009).

In Support of Goal 2

• *Objective*: Provide professional development focused on teaching methods that reflect best practices in the area of DLCL language and academic development.

• *Rationale*: A vast body of research has documented a direct link between DLCL students' achievement and the expertise and experience of their classroom teacher (Freedson, 2010; García, 2005). Do teachers have specific training related to and experience in teaching DLCLs? Do they use instructional strategies that are specifically responsive to students acquiring English in academic contexts? Do they receive the continuous professional development and classroom-related support they need to determine the effect their instruction has on student outcomes? Are they given the support they need to use regular authentic assessments of student achievement to assess this impact? The proposed intervention uses the knowledge-base regarding the relationship between teacher factors and student success to enhance teachers' capacity to increase academic achievement in their students (García, 2005).

In Support of Goal 3

• *Objective*: Implement family engagement programs whose effectiveness in promoting parental engagement is well documented.

• *Rationale*: Recently published research has begun to make clear that parental engagement with DLCL students is positively associated with academic performance (Rodriguez-Brown, 2009). Again, this relationship seems to be strongest in the early grades (García & Miller, 2008). Parental engagement programs can assist parents in contributing to the academic growth of their students through linguistically and culturally responsive strategies (García et al., 2009).

Of course, a teaching and learning community that is responsive to the dynamics of social, cultural, and linguistic diversity within the broader concerns for high academic achievement requires particular learning that encompasses the same critical elements. While considerable work has been devoted to restructuring schools and changing the fundamental relationships among school personnel, students, families, and community members, seldom have these efforts included attention to the unique influences of the linguistic and sociocultural dimensions of these same relationships and structures.

A knowledge base put forward in this overview recognizes that academic learning has its roots in processes both out of school and in school. Diversity is perceived and acted on as a resource for teaching and learning instead of a problem. A focus on what students bring to the schooling process generates a more asset/resource-oriented approach. This redirection or "transformation" considers a search for and documentation of particular implementations of principles of teacher development that serve a diverse set of educational environments. An understanding of how individuals with diverse sets of experiences, packaged individually into cultures, "make meaning," and communicate and extend that meaning, particularly in social contexts we call schools, makes a huge difference for immigrant children and their families. Such a mission requires in-depth treatment of the processes associated with producing diversity and issues of socialization in and out of schools, coupled with a clear examination of how such understanding is actually transformed into pedagogy and curriculum that results in high academic performance and overall social well-being for all students.

References

Amato, P. (2005). The impact of family formation change on the cognitive, social and emotional wellbeing of the next generation. *The Future of Children, 15,* 76–96.

AVANCE. (2007). About AVANCE. Retrieved October 4, 2007, from *www.avance.org.*

August, D. (2006). Demographic overview. In D. August & T. Shanahan (Eds.), *Report of the National Literacy Panel on Language Minority Youth and Children*. Mahwah, NJ: Erlbaum.

August, D., Goldenberg, C., & Rueda, R. (2010). Restrictive state language policies: Are they scientifically based? In P. Gandara & M. Hopkins (Eds.), *Forbidden languages: English learners and restrictive language policies* (pp. 139–158). New York: Teachers College Press.

August, D., & Shanahan, T. (2006). *Developing literacy in second language learners: Report of the National Literacy Panel on Language-Minority Children and Youth*. Mahwah, NJ: Erlbaum.

Ballantyne, K., Sanderman, A., & Levy, J. (2008). *Educating English language learners: Building teacher capacity*. Washington, DC: National Clearinghouse for English Language Acquisition.

Barrera, J. M., & Warner, L. (2006). Involving families in school events. *Kappa Delta Pi Records, 42*(2), 72–75.

Buriel, R., & Hurtado-Ortiz, M. T. (2000). Child care practices and preferences of native-and foreign-born Latina mothers and Euro-American mothers. *Hispanic Journal of Behavioral Sciences, 22*(3), 314–331.

Capps, R., Fix, M. E., Murray, J., Ost, J., Passel, J. S., & Hernandez, S. H. (2005). The new demography of America's Schools: Immigration and the No Child Left Behind Act. Retrieved July 2, 2010 from *www.urban.org/url.cfm?id=311230*.

Chomsky, N. (1959). A review of B. F. Skinner's *Verbal Behavior. Language, 35*(1), 26–58.

Collier, V. (1987). Age and rate of acquisition of second language for academic purposes. *TESOL Quarterly, 21*, 617–641.

Collier, V. (1989). How long?: A synthesis of research on academic achievement in a second language. *TESOL Quarterly, 23*, 509–531.

Collier, V. P. (1995). Acquiring a second language for school. *Directions in Language and Education, 1*(4), 1–27.

Crosnoe, R. (2006). *Mexican roots, American schools: Helping Mexican immigrant children succeed*. Palo Alto, CA: Stanford University Press.

Cummins, J. (1981). The role of primary language development in promoting educational success for language minority students. In California State Department of Education (Ed.), *Schooling and language minority students: A theoretical framework* (pp. 3–50). Los Angeles: National Dissemination and Assessment Center.

Cummins, J. (2000). *Language, power and pedagogy: Bilingual children in the crossfire*. Clevedon, UK: Multilingual Matters.

Darling-Hammond, L. (2006). *Powerful teacher education: Lessons from exemplary programs*. San Francisco: Jossey-Bass.

Darling-Hammond, L., & Bransford, J. (Eds.). (2005). *Preparing teachers for a changing world: What teachers should learn and be able to do*. San Francisco: Jossey-Bass.

Espinosa, L. M. (2010). Classroom teaching and "best practices" for young English language learners. In E. E. García & E. C. Frede (Eds.), *Young English language learners: Current research and emerging directions for policy and practice* (pp. 143–164). New York: Teachers College Press.

Freedson, M. (2010). Educating preschool teachers to support English language learners. In E. E. García & E. C. Frede (Eds.), *Young English language learners: Current research and emerging directions for policy and practice* (pp. 165–183). New York: Teachers College Press.

Gandara, P., Rumberger, R., Maxwell-Jolly, J., & Callahan, R. (2003). English learners in California schools: Unequal resources, unequal outcomes. *Educational Policy Analysis Archives, 11*(36). Retrieved July 30, 2010, from *epaa.asu.edu/ojs/article/viewfile/264/390*.

García, E. (1999). *Student cultural diversity: Understanding and meeting the challenge* (2nd ed.). Boston: Houghton Mifflin.

García, E., & Jensen, B. (2009a). The demographic imperative: Educating English language learners. *Educational Leadership, 66*(7), 9–13.

García, E., & Jensen, B. (2009b). Early educational opportunities for children of Hispanic origins. *Social Policy Report, 23*(2), 1–17.

García, E. E. (2001). *Rethinking school reform in the context of cultural and linguistic diversity: Creating a responsive learning community*. Berkeley: University of California.

García, E. E. (2005). *Teaching and learning in two languages: Bilingualism and schooling in the United States.* New York: Teachers College Press.

García, E. E., Arias, M. B., Harris Murri, N. J., & Serna, C. (2010). Developing responsive teachers: A challenge for a demographic reality. *Journal of Teacher Education, 61*(1–2), 132–143.

García, E. E., & Cuellar, D. (2006). Who are these linguistically and culturally diverse students? *Teachers College Record, 108*(11), 2220–2246.

García, E. E., & Frede, E. C. (Eds.). (2010). *Young English language learners: Current research and emerging directions for policy and practice.* New York: Teachers College Press.

García, E. E., & Jensen, B. T. (2006). Dual-language programs in the US: An alternative to monocultural, monolingual education. *Language Magazine, 5*(6), 30–37.

García, E. E., & Miller, L. S. (2008). Findings and recommendations of the National Task Force on Early Childhood Education for Hispanics. *Child Development Perspectives, 2*(2), 53–58.

García, E. E., Scribner, K., & Cuellar, D. (2009). Latinos and early education. In E. L. Grigovenko & R. Takanishi (Eds.), *Immigration, diversity and immigration* (pp. 95–111). New York: Routledge.

García-Nevarez, A. G., Stafford, M. E., & Arias, B. (2005). Arizona elementary teachers' attitudes toward English language learners' and the use of Spanish in classroom instruction. *Bilingual Research Journal, 29*(2), 295–318.

Gass, S. M., & Selinker, L. (2001). *Second language acquisition: An introductory course.* Mahwah, NJ: Erlbaum.

Gay, G. (2000). *Culturally responsive teaching: Theory, research and practice.* New York: Teachers College Press.

Gay, G. (2002). Preparing for culturally and responsive teaching. *Journal of Teacher Education, 53*(2), 106–116.

Genesee, F. (Ed.). (1999). *Program alternatives for linguistically diverse students.* Berkeley: Center for Research on Education, Diversity and Excellence (CREDE), University of California.

Genesee, F. (2010). Dual language development in preschool children. In E. E. García & E. C. Frede (Eds.), *Young English language learners: Current research and emerging directions for policy and practice* (pp. 59–79). New York: Teachers College Press.

Genesee, F., Geva, E., Dressler, C., & Kamil, M. (2006). Synthesis: Cross-linguistic relationships. In D. August & T. Shanahan (Eds.), *Report of the national literacy panel on language minority youth and children* (pp. 161–187). Mahwah, NJ: Erlbaum.

Goldenberg, C., Rueda, R., & August, D. (2006). Synthesis: Sociocultural contexts and literacy development. In D. August & T. Shanahan (Eds.), *Report of the National Literacy Panel on Language Minority Youth and Children.* Mahwah, NJ: Erlbaum.

Hakuta, K., Ferdman, B. M., & Diaz, R. M. (1987). Bilingualism and cognitive development: Three perspectives. In S. Rosenberg (Ed.), *Advances in applied psycholinguistics: Vol. II. Reading, writing and language learning* (pp. 284–319). Cambridge, UK: Cambridge University Press.

Hakuta, K., Goto Butler, Y., & Witt, D. (2000). How long does it take English learners to attain proficiency? (Policy Report 2000-1). Berkeley: University of California Linguistic Minority Research Institute.

Hammer, C. S., Miccio, A. W., & Wagstaff, D. A. (2003). Home literacy experiences and their relationship to bilingual preschoolers' developing English literacy abilities: An initial investigation. *Language, Speech, and Hearing Services in Schools, 34,* 20–30.

Hammer, C. S., Miccio, A., & Rodriguez, B. (2004). Bilingual language acquisition and the child socialization process. In B. Goldstein (Ed.), *Bilingual language development and disorders in Spanish–English speakers* (pp. 21–52). Baltimore: Brookes.

Hernández, D., Macartney, S., & Denton, N. A. (2010). A demographic portrait of young English language learners. In E. E. García & E. C. Frede (Eds.), *Young English language learners: Current research and emerging directions for policy and practice* (pp. 10–41). New York: Teachers College Press.

Hernández, D. J., Denton, N. A., & Macartney, S. E. (2008). Children in immigrant families: looking to America's future. *Social Policy Report: A Publication of the Society for Research in Child Development, 22*(3), 1–24.

Jensen, B. T. (2007). The relationship between Spanish use in the classroom and the mathematics achievement of Spanish-speaking kindergartners. *Journal of Latinos and Education, 6*(3), 267–280.

Jensen, B. T. (2008). Immigration and language policy. In J. M. González (Ed.), *Encyclopedia of bilingual education*. Thousand Oaks, CA: Sage.

Krashen, S. (1985). *The input hypothesis: Issues and implications*. New York: Longman.

Ladson-Billings, G. (1994). *The dreamkeepers: Successful teachers for African-American children*. San Francisco: Jossey-Bass.

Lee, J., & Bowman, N. (2006). Parent involvement, cultural capital, and the achievement gap among elementary school children. *American Education Research Journal, 43*(2), 193–218.

Lee, J. S., & Samura, M. (2005, September). *Understanding the personal, educational, and societal factors that lead to additive bilingualism*. Paper presented at the annual conference of the American Educational Research Association, Montreal, Quebec, Canada.

López, L. (2005). *A look into the homes of Spanish-speaking preschool children*. Paper presented at the 5th International Symposium on Bilingualism, Barcelona, Spain.

Lucas, T., & Grinberg, J. (2008). Responding to the linguistic reality of mainstream classrooms: Preparing all teachers to teach English language learners. In M. Cochran-Smith, S. Feiman-Nemser, & D. J. McIntyre (Eds.), *Handbook of research on teacher education* (3rd ed., pp. 606–636). New York: Routledge.

Lucas, T., Villegas, A. M., & Freedson-González, M. (2008). Linguistically responsive teacher education. *Journal of Teacher Education, 59*(4), 361–373.

Martin, J. A., Hamilton, B. E., Sutton, P. E., Ventura, S. J., Menacker, F., & Munson, M. S. (2005). Births: Final data for 2003. *National Vital Statistics Report, 52*(2), 1–114.

Merino, B. (2007). Identifying critical competencies for teachers of English learners. *UCLMRI Newsletter, 16*, 1–8.

Mitchell, D., Destino, T., & Karam, R. (1997). *Evaluation and English language development programs in Santa Ana Unified School District: A report on data system reliability and statistical modeling of program impacts*. Riverside: University of California, California Educational Research Cooperative.

National Center for Education Statistics. (1995). *Approaching kindergarten: A look at preschoolers in the United States* (National household survey). Washington, DC: U.S. Department of Education, Office of Educational Research and Improvement.

National Center for Education Statistics. (2001). The condition of education 2001. Washington, DC: National Center of Education Statistics, U.S. Department of Education. Retrieved May 18, 2009, from *nces.ed.gov/programs/coe/2001/essay/index.asp*.

National Clearinghouse for English Language Acquisition. (2006). *The growing numbers of limited English proficient students: 1993-94–2003/04*. Washington, DC: Office of English Language Acquisition (OELA), U.S. Department of Education.

National Task Force on Early Childhood Education for Hispanics. (2007). Para nuestros ninos: Report of expanding and improving early education for Hispanics—Main report. Tempe, AZ: National Task Force on Early Childhood Education for Hispanics. Retrieved August 6, 2007, from *www.ecehispanic.org/work/expand_mianreport.pdf*.

Ovando, C., Collier, V., & Combs, V. (2006). *Bilingual and ESL classrooms: Teaching in multicultural contexts* (4th ed.). New York: McGraw-Hill.

Pérez-Bazán, M. J. (2005). *Input rate: The pacemaker of early bilingual acquisition*. Paper presented at the 5th International Symposium on Bilingualism, Barcelona, Spain.

Qiuyun, L. (2006, April). *Beyond cultural deficit approach: Disentangling language minority parents' involvement in early grades*. Paper presented at the annual meeting of the American Educational Research Association, San Francisco.

Raikes, H., Alexander Pan, B., Luze, G., Tamis-LeMonda, C. S., Brooks-Gunn, J., & Constantine, J. (2006). Mother–child bookreading in low-income families: Correlates and outcomes during the first three years of life. *Child Development, 77*(4), 924–953.

Ramirez, R., & de la Cruz, P. (2003). *The Hispanic population in the United States: March, 2002*. Washington, DC: U.S. Census Bureau.

Reardon, S. F., & Galindo, C. (2006). *Patterns of Hispanic students' Math and English literacy test scores* (Report to the National Task Force on Early Childhood Education for Hispanics). Tempe: Arizona State University.

Reeves, J. (2004). Like everybody else: Equalizing educational opportunity for English language learners. *TESOL Quarterly, 38*(1), 43–66.

Rodriguez-Brown, F. V. (2009). *The home–school connection: Lessons learned in a culturally and linguistically diverse community.* New York: Routledge.

Rodriguez-Brown, F. V., & Mulhern, M. M. (1993). Fostering critical literacy through family literacy: A study of families in a Mexican-immigrant community. *Bilingual Research Journal, 17* (3/4), 1–16.

Rodriguez-Brown, F. V., & Shanahan, T. (1989). *Literacy for the limited English proficient child: A family Approach.* Chicago: University of Illinois.

Rogoff, B. (1990). *Apprenticeship in thinking: Cognitive development in social context.* Oxford, UK: Oxford University Press.

Rolstad, K., Mahoney, K., & Glass, G. V. (2005). The big picture: A meta-analysis of program effectiveness research on English language learners. *Educational Policy, 19*(4), 572–594.

Skinner, B. (1957). *Verbal behavior.* Englewood Cliffs, NJ: Prentice-Hall.

Stritikus, T. (2001). From personal to political: Proposition 227, literacy instruction, and the individual qualities of teachers. *International Journal of Bilingual Education and Bilingualism, 4*(5), 291–309.

Téllez, K., & Waxman, H. (Eds.). (2006). *Preparing quality educators for English language learners.* Mahwah, NJ: Erlbaum.

Tharp, R. G., & Gallimore, R. (1989). Rousing schools to life. *American Educator, 13*(2), 20–25, 46–52.

Valdes, G. (2009). Commentary: Language, immigration and the quality of education: Moving toward a broader conversation. In T. G. Wiley, J. S. Lee, & R. W. Rumberger (Eds.), *The education of language minority immigrants in the United States* (pp. 164–173). Bristol, UK: Multilingual Matters.

Valenzuela, A., & Dornbusch, S. M. (1994). Families and social capital in the academic achievement of Mexican origin and Anglo adolescents. *Social Science Quarterly, 75,* 18–36.

Villegas, A. M., & Lucas, T., (2002a). *Educating culturally responsive teachers: A coherent approach.* Albany: State University of New York Press.

Villegas, A. M., & Lucas, T. (2002b). Preparing culturally responsive teachers: Rethinking the curriculum. *Journal of Teacher Education, 53,* 20–32.

Waxman, H. C., & Tellez, K. (2002). *Research synthesis on effective teaching practices for English language learners.* Philadelphia: Temple University, Mid-Atlantic Regional Educational Laboratory, Laboratory for Student Success. (ERIC Document Retrieval No. ED474821)

Youngs, C., & Youngs, G. (2001). Predictors of mainstream teachers' attitudes toward ESL students. *TELL Quarterly, 35,* 97–120.

Zeichner, K. (1996). Educating teachers for cultural diversity. In K. Zeichner, S. Melnick, & M. L. Gomez (Eds.), *Currents of reform in preservice teacher education* (pp. 133–175). New York: Teachers College Press.

Zigler, E., Gilliam, W. S., & Jones, S. M. (2006). *A vision for universal preschool education.* Cambridge, UK: Cambridge University Press.

Zúñiga, V., & Hernández-León, R. (Eds.). (2005). *New destinations: Mexican immigration in the United States.* New York: Russell Sage Foundation.

CHAPTER 8

Poverty Is a Knot,
and Preschool Is an Untangler

Cynthia Lamy

Head Start Started as Poverty Fighting

Head Start, the federally funded preschool program begun in 1964, was meant to fight poverty. It began as a key component of President Lyndon Johnson's War on Poverty, with the serious intent to end the poverty of the children who attended as they reached adulthood (Zigler & Muenchow, 1992). Why would policymakers have believed that an early childhood program could fight poverty? Two relatively new ideas related to child development, made possible the concept that preschool could end poverty. How so? The dawning recognition of the importance of *environmental context* for children's cognitive development was beginning to eclipse a more genetic, biologically based concept of intelligence. If a child's environmental context, physical or psychological, could influence his or her development, then intervention would be possible, since context is so much more amenable to intervention than are genetic traits. Also, new recognition of the importance of *early experience* to child development, the nature of this experience forming the foundation of a trajectory of development, with the power to set children on a particular life course for better or worse, brought the years of early childhood to the attention of interventionists, educators, and policymakers.

These theoretical underpinnings allowed for the new and thrilling possibility that an early childhood intervention could be expected to produce lasting impacts that could lift children out of poverty decades later. Poverty-stricken families, unable to provide those early, enriching experiences that middle-class families so much more easily afford for their children, would have access to a program that would even the playing field. Their children would enter kindergarten ready for school and on course for the long-term educational success that is the ticket out of poverty. The children's educational success would translate into higher adult earnings, and their poverty would be history.

Other new concepts contributed to the foundational pillars of the Head Start model. The recognition of the interrelatedness of developmental domains in early childhood informed a "whole child" approach that allowed Head Start directly to provide for any of the children's

158

physical or psychological needs, including medical, dental, and mental health services, along with nutritious meals, in support of the children's cognitive and social development. A child with a toothache or a grumbling stomach, or a big problem weighing on his or her mind is very unlikely to be learning up to potential. And a recognition of the particular importance of the family context to children's academic success meant that programs to help parents, whether to encourage their own educational pursuits or employment goals, or to relieve the stress of parenting under the very difficult circumstances of poverty, could be implemented alongside the more child-focused part of the programs. While maintaining a politically important focus on children in poverty—children innocent of any wrongdoing that might have made poverty their own fault—the argument could be made that a more knowledgeable and less stressed mother was in a better position to support the academic development of her child.

Head Start has faced much criticism over the years. The congressional mandate to evaluate the effects of Head Start, a mandate that currently continues, has given rise to several important studies of its effectiveness (see Resnick, 2010, for a succinct history). The majority of studies overall have reported that, within a few years, the initial positive effects of Head Start on children's school-related outcomes are no longer found, although various study flaws tend to render the findings uncertain (Barnett, 1995). The latest and most rigorous study, the 2010 Head Start Impact Study, found immediate effects of Head Start, positive though moderate, across many, varied areas of children's development. Yet most of the effects were no longer found by the end of first grade (Administration for Children and Families, 2010). Not surprisingly, this study also had its flaws. It is important to note, however, that very little is known about the adult outcomes of Head Start children, though some findings suggest very moderate, positive, long-term impacts on education, earnings, and crime (Garces, Thomas, & Currie, 2000; Ludwig & Miller, 2005).

Based on these findings over many studies and many years, was it wrong to think that a preschool program could fight poverty? It may be that the average Head Start program does not produce the impact required to create the lifelong trajectory of education-related success needed to fight poverty for children who attend. There are several hypotheses as to why this may be true. Though average Head Start classroom quality is reported to be good (Resnick, 2010; Zill et al., 2003), it may be that program quality remains too low to produce the needed impact. It may also be that as children live their childhoods and adolescent years in poverty-stricken neighborhoods and schools, their experiences subsequent to Head Start function to erase the good that the program has done. Researchers have long considered this to be the chief possibility (Lee & Loeb, 1995; McKey et al., 1985; Ramey et al., 2000). Given the small to moderate immediate effects found by so many studies over many years, it does not seem likely that the Head Start experience overall has lifted many children out of poverty. However, other important studies on the effects of high-quality early childhood programs do indeed indicate that preschool can fight poverty.

The Three Longitudinal Studies

Three rigorous, longitudinal studies provide strong evidence of the potential for high-quality early childhood programs to impact children's developmental trajectories significantly, improving their educational attainment, their health, and, eventually their adult economic success. These studies, the Perry Preschool Study, the Abecedarian Study, and the Chicago Child–Parent Study, are well known and have been extensively described in the literature (Campbell & Ramey, 1995; Campbell, Ramey, Pungello, Sparling, & Miller-Johnson, 2002; Reynolds, Temple, & Ou, 2010; Reynolds, Temple, Robertson, & Mann, 2002; Schweinhart et al., 2005). These studies, too, are not without flaws and negative critiques. For instance, the Perry and Abecedarian studies, though methodologically rigorous, enrolled and followed relatively small numbers of children, and the interventions took place now decades ago. The Chicago study did not randomize families and children into groups but followed a much larger sample of enrolled preschool experiment and no-preschool controls, and used more current measures; being more recent interventions, the programs themselves may currently be more relevant. The most recent Perry Study follow-up found the original study children at age 40, while the Abecedarian and Chicago studies each followed up their original cohorts of children into their early 20s. For each study, differences between preschool and nonpreschool groups are striking.

Each study can report substantially improved educational outcomes for the preschool group of children. Both in the Perry and Chicago studies preschoolers were much more likely to graduate high school (65 vs. 45% for Perry; 79 vs. 71% for Chicago), while the Abecedarian preschoolers were much more likely to have attended college (36 vs. 14%). Both the Abecedarian and Chicago studies found significantly lower grade retention for children in their preschool group across the school years, approximately 40% lower than for nonpreschool children, while all three studies found that special education placement for children in their preschool group was also significantly lower, at approximately half the rate for the nonpreschool children.

Moreover, each study found remarkable differences in many other aspects of the children's lives as they matured into adulthood. For instance, Abecedarian and Chicago preschoolers grew up to hold more skilled employment. Two of the three studies (Perry and Chicago) found substantially less criminal activity for children in the preschool group: The Perry preschoolers were much less likely ever to have been convicted of a crime at age 40 (28 vs. 52%), and the Chicago preschoolers had fewer felony arrests at age 24 (16.5 vs. 21%). Findings on the impact of the Perry and Abecedarian programs on long-term health outcomes have recently been found (Muennig et al., 2011; Muennig, Schweinhart, Montie, & Neidell, 2009), and many other significant differences between groups across these studies, outcomes related to teenage childbearing, important purchases such as cars and houses, and the extent of welfare use, are extensively detailed elsewhere.

It is important not to overstate the case. The children of these studies, as a group, still went on to experience educational failure and social problems at higher rates than would be expected for a nonpoor population. Preschool did not eradicate poverty from their lives. Despite this, it is clear that the children who attended these programs grew up to earn more, to own more, to be healthier and less likely to fall into crime, to have fewer babies as teenagers, and to spend less time on welfare. With this evidence we can say that while early childhood programs may not be the only weapon needed to win a war on poverty, high-quality programs can certainly fight poverty and win a few key battles.

State Programs Provide Recent Evidence of Strong, Immediate Impact

High-quality early childhood programs can fight poverty for the children who attend them, but can we implement preschool programs of high enough quality and of large enough enrollment capacity to allow these programs to fulfill their promise on a broader scale? Research results of children's kindergarten and early elementary school achievement from a handful of state studies are beginning to shed some light on this question. Regression-discontinuity studies implemented in a handful of states with high-quality state-administered preschool programs indicate immediate and substantial increases in children's test scores.

At kindergarten entry, sample children attending the state preschool programs of Arkansas, California, New Mexico, Michigan, New Jersey, Oklahoma, South Carolina, and West Virginia were found on average to have higher vocabulary and math scores than their peers who had not yet attended preschool (Barnett, Jung, Frede, Hustedt, & Howes, 2011). Vocabulary scores are on average 22% of a standard deviation higher and math scores are 39% of a standard deviation higher.

Single-state studies also provide local evidence. Additional evidence from Oklahoma, a state implementing a high-quality program serving about 70% of 4-year-olds, indicates that children arrive at kindergarten scoring substantially higher on early math and literacy tests, and that while all children gain significantly, children from families in poverty gain more (Gormley, 2010). New Mexico's state preschool program, begun in 2005 and serving about 4,000 primarily low-income children, has been evaluated annually for its impact on children's kindergarten entry test scores. These evaluations find consistent impacts on children's early vocabulary and math scores at kindergarten entry (Hustedt, Barnett, & Friedman, 2010).

A few states are beginning to collect evidence of the impact of preschool on children's school success continuing into elementary school. New Jersey has implemented a very high-quality preschool program for 3- and 4-year-olds across the 30 or so poorest school districts in the state (known as the Abbott Districts), and significant improvements due to preschool in a rigorous longitudinal study were found in children's second-grade achievement scores, along with significant decreases in grade retention for the preschool group of children (Frede, Barnett, Jung, Lamy, & Figueras, 2010; Frede, Jung, Barnett, & Figueras, 2009). Preschool increased scores by between 0.20 and 0.30 effect size, with grade retention cut by one-third to one-half, depending on the length of the preschool experience. And results from a rigorous longitudinal study of the impact of the Arkansas state preschool program, also a program of high quality and wide reach, indicates that the preschool group of children at the end of first grade continued to outscore their nonpreschool peers significantly, though moderately (Hustedt, Barnett, & Jung, 2008). From these results we can say that some state investments in high-quality preschool are producing important benefits well into elementary school.

Will these test score increases fade with time? Subsequent studies will have to tell us. However, the larger effect sizes, found at later ages than those found for Head Start, and the decreases in grade retention, provide some support for the expectation that high-quality state-level early childhood programs can produce meaningful impacts on children's long-term educational outcomes—impacts that fight poverty.

High-Quality Preschool
Has a More Complex Relationship with Poverty

The mechanisms by which preschool impacts children's adult outcomes are multifaceted and not completely understood (Barnett, Young, & Schweinhart, 1998; Heckman, Malofeeva, Pinto, & Savelyev, 2010). High-quality preschool may improve the life chances of children in poverty through an immediate, direct influence on the children cognitively or socially, or some combination thereof. Additionally, the impact may be due in some part to the experience of early success that catalyzes subsequent successes over time, or through a direct impact on parents that filters through to the children, or some combination of both. Perhaps some part of the impact is additionally a result of higher expectations of children's success—expectations of the children for themselves, or expectations of others for the children, or both. In any case, it is clear that excellent early childhood programs *change* children and parents, especially those children and parents living in poverty, and that through that change children are set on a life course with a higher probability of success.

There may be even more mechanisms through which preschool could fight poverty. To understand what those mechanisms might be, let us consider the nature of developmental risk for children in poverty.

Poverty as Contextual Risk to Child Development

Poverty is like a knot of risk around children. A "risk" is defined here as a *factor that jeopardizes a child's chances for success in our society*. While risks to child development are present to some extent in every developmental context, whether children are from wealthier or poorer families, risks to child development are much more prevalent in a context of poverty. As the number of risks in the childhood context increases, the probability that a child will suffer some developmental or educational trauma or failure, such as incarceration or high school dropout, also increases (Sameroff, Bartko, Baldwin, Baldwin, & Seifer, 1998; Sameroff & Chandler, 1975; Sameroff, Seifer, Baldwin, & Baldwin, 1993; Zill & West, 2001). Singly, each risk factor may be expected to contribute some amount of risk to child development, though a single risk typically does not cause developmental or educational derailment.

It is very important to know that most children have some "protections" that contribute to their resiliency in the face of risk (Garmezy & Rutter, 1983; Werner & Smith, 1982). Here, "protections" are defined as *those factors that support children's chances for successful development*. For instance, a loving adult in a child's life is a very important protection, but a special skill or a strong interest that brings a child some positive attention and direction could also function to protect a child from risk. For children growing up in a context of poverty, protections are fewer and more fragile than those for children in more advantageous environments.

We know that when the number of risks, widely specified, in the early family context reaches three or four, children typically are unable to succeed educationally or socially, falling prey with much higher probabilities as adults to many pathologies, such as drug abuse, mental illness, and chronic disease (Felitti et al., 1998). While the number of risks impacting children is of vital concern, the qualitative nature of those risks is not simply to pile up in number, but to combine, interact, and strengthen (McLoyd, 1990)—hence, the concept of poverty as a knot of risks around children. We can think of preschool as one element that works to untangle children from poverty's knot.

Preschool and Family Risks

Head Start and other early childhood models of high quality provide essential supports for the family context. Many of the risks to child development that exist in the family context have been well documented, such as single-mother family structure, low maternal educational attainment, maternal depression, and a detrimental parenting style, among others. Low family income is well known as a fundamental risk for children of any age, but especially for young children, with serious long-term impacts on their academic and social outcomes (Duncan & Brooks-Gunn, 2000; Linver, Brooks-Gunn, & Kohen, 2002). Low family income not only influences a young child's development through a reduction in the quality of the home learning environment and through increased parental stress, which increases the likelihood of nonoptimal parenting (Duncan & Brooks-Gunn, 2000; McLoyd,

1998), but it also has been found to have some impact outside these channels (Dearing, McCartney, & Taylor, 2001). Whatever the mechanisms, increased family income is very important to young children in poverty. As the income-to-needs ratio becomes positive for families in poverty, these increases have been found to offset risks to children's development, both academic and social (Dearing, McCartney, & Taylor, 2001, 2006; Huston et al., 2001; MacMillan, McMorris, & Kruttschnitt, 2004), with proportional improvements for children as income rises. Spending less time in poverty also improves children's outcomes (Smith, Brooks-Gunn, & Klebanov, 1997).

One immediate impact of subsidized early childhood programs for children and families in poverty is increased probability of employment for the families of enrolled children, generally estimated at about 15%, with some estimates running much higher for families with more difficulty finding and keeping jobs (Matthews, 2006). This new employment increases family income, concurrently improving children's long-term probabilities for more optimal outcomes. Therefore, the increased probability of employment for the parents of enrolled children is another mechanism for the impact of preschool on the poverty of those children, immediately and into the future.

We have mentioned that high-quality early childhood programs change children and parents, especially those living in poverty. Another avenue by which early childhood programs may decrease the probability of risk in the family context around children in poverty, thereby improving their chances of life success, is improved parenting. An extensive literature links parenting with children's academic and social outcomes (Baumrind, 1991; McLoyd, 1990; Steinberg, Lamborn, Darling, Mounts, & Dornbusch, 1994), and we know that Head Start can produce small but meaningful improvements in parenting, with long-term effects (Administration for Children and Families, 2010; Love et al., 2005). Especially when early childhood programs pair up with strong, validated parenting intervention models, evidence indicates that early childhood programs can significantly reduce parental harshness, physical discipline, and authoritarian style, and increase communication, praise, and patience for those parents who attend (Baydar, Reid, & Webster-Stratton, 2003; Webster-Stratton, 1998). More optimal parenting is very important to children in poverty. To illustrate, Webster-Stratton, Rinaldi, and Reid (2009), controlling for important covariates, found that whereas 9% of adolescents whose moms had improved their parenting while the adolescents were preschoolers had any involvement with law enforcement, 32% of adolescents whose moms had not been able to improve their parenting became delinquent. Preschool's beneficial effect on parenting improves children's chances for academic and life success, fighting poverty for those children.

Risk in the School Context

From a systems perspective, creating positive change in the nature of a cohort of children and families about to enter an educational system should to some extent create positive change across the whole educational system. Preschool, then, may potentially have an even more complex effect on poverty than a multifaceted early impact on children and families. Preschool may also have the potential to improve children's life chances through an impact on the educational systems that surround those children. How so? Let us think for a moment about educational systems as a context for risk to child development.

The school context is not often thought of as a contributor of major risk to child development, even though it is often in the school context that children's developmental failures are most noticeable. But the educational systems in which children in poverty enroll may contribute their own set of risks to the development of those children. What are these risks? They include negative teacher–student relationships, poorly qualified teachers and administrators, detrimental attitudes of the school staff toward the children and their families, low expectations for student success, and school administrative policies, among others.

The teacher–student relationship is far and away the most important aspect of the school environment from a child's perspective (Hamre & Pianta, 2005; Pianta, 1999; Pianta, La Paro, Payne, Cox, Bradley, 2002), and most adults, from parents to educational researchers, understand that the teacher–student relationship has the power to encourage or discourage a child's educational success. Researchers find that teachers who maintain warm, emotionally supportive relationships with the children in their classrooms are accessible to those students as an important resource for both academic and social learning, and that those children tend to show more motivation to learn, more engagement in the learning process, and more social competence in the classroom (Howes, 2000; Wu, Hughes, & Kwok, 2010). This is especially important for children who are in poverty or are otherwise at risk for educational failure, for whom a warm, responsive teacher can contribute to increases in academic skills and achievement scores (Burchinal, Peisner-Feinberg, Pianta, & Howes, 2002; Gordon, Kane, & Staiger, 2006; Hamre & Pianta, 2001; Hughes, Luo, Kwok, & Lloyd, 2009).

In high-poverty schools, staff members are more likely to be underqualified (Boyd, Goldhaber, Lankford, & Wyckoff, 2007; Jacob, 2007; Peske & Haycock, 2006). Inadequately qualified teachers contribute risk to child development through their reduced ability to teach academic subjects due to lack of content knowledge and poor pedagogical skills. However, highly qualified education professionals bring not only content expertise but also many other skills to the job. They are knowledgeable about child development and skilled in classroom management techniques, and they are aware of the importance of a positive emotional climate in the classroom and take care to maintain it. Underqualified teachers, who are more likely to be stressed and to lack strong skills to teach their students and manage their classrooms, often err toward a controlling or punitive style that is unsupportive of children's learning (Hamre, Pianta, Downer, & Mashburn, 2008).

Hopeless or disrespectful attitudes of school staff members toward students and their families, or low expectations for the children's academic success are risks to children's development, as these attitudes disengage students from the learning process in the classroom (Espinosa & Laffey, 2003). But when low expectations inform educational and administrative policies, then school or district policies that should reflect strong support for children's academic and social development and achievement may instead begin to reflect a systemic need for the maintenance of control and the status quo. For instance, less qualified teachers are hired (Boyd, Lankford, Loeb, Rockoff, & Wyckoff, 2008; Heck, 2009; Jacob, 2007) because hiring policies support disciplinary objectives rather than the need for a highly qualified teaching staff to implement new and creative ideas for greater educational success.

What Do These Risks Have to Do with Preschool?

High-quality preschool has not only the capacity to mitigate the risk to children found in family systems but also the potential to mitigate the risk to children's development found in school systems, especially high-poverty school systems, as indicated in Figure 8.1. How might preschool influence school systems to decrease these risks? There are several possible mechanisms.

Through positive change in the nature of the children themselves as they become more cognitively and socially ready for school, those who have attended a high-quality preschool

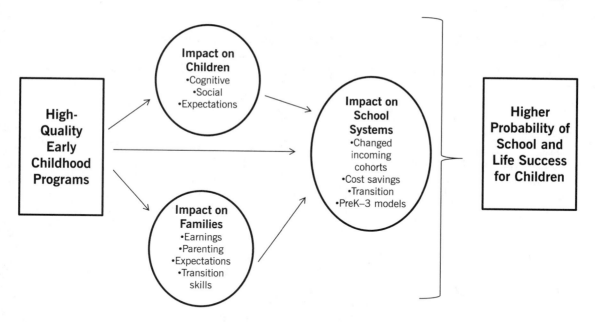

FIGURE 8.1. Potential mechanisms for the impact of high-quality early childhood programs on children's academic and life success.

stress high-poverty school systems less. For instance, research indicates that kindergarten is a particularly challenging year for teachers, who must take in children from varied preschool backgrounds and experiences, and prepare them all for the increased academic and behavioral standards of first grade; between one-third and one-half of kindergarten teachers in high-poverty districts report that the majority of their students have trouble behaviorally and academically in the classroom (Rimm-Kaufmann, Pianta, & Cox, 2000). However, kindergarten teachers recognize and appreciate the importance of high-quality preschool to improve children's chances for kindergarten success (LoCasale-Crouch, Mashburn, Downer, & Pianta, 2008; Rimm-Kaufman et al., 2000) and to influence positively the relationship between a child and a kindergarten teacher. This has very important ramifications for children's school success.

As we noted earlier, high-quality preschool has been found to reduce the number of students retained in a grade or requiring special services during their school careers. Fewer preschool children requiring grade retention or special educational services reflects less stress in the system overall. But the decreased need for these costly interventions also produces cost savings for school systems, especially for high-poverty districts. School districts with fewer children in these more expensive circumstances can save a substantial amount of money, with estimated total cost savings between 2 and 4% of the annual educational budget when most of the children entering the school system have experienced high-quality preschool (Belfield, 2004). Moreover, expenses related to vandalism, school security, and general disciplinary issues are also likely be lower, and efficiencies related to positive peer effects driven by large cohorts of children who enter kindergarten more ready to learn also reduce costs (Belfield, 2004). Even without reaching an appreciable percentage of the school district budget, these cost savings can easily amount to sizable sums that, redirected from remediation and intervention activities, can instead fund policies and activities in the support of educational excellence for children in poverty.

Additional mechanisms that illuminate the influence of preschool on subsequent educational systems include the concept of transition to kindergarten and comprehensive, extended models of care and education that integrate into elementary school some of the best policies and practices of preschool, such as preschool–third grade (PreK–3) educational models.

Transition to Kindergarten

Transition has long been an important concept related to high-quality preschool. As researchers began reporting the phenomenon of the fade out of the higher test scores of Head Start children, attention shifted to practices in the early elementary school grades, especially kindergarten, that might contribute to the fading of those immediate, early benefits. Evidence suggests that a smooth transition from preschool to kindergarten, for children and parents, improves children's school success (Reynolds, Magnuson, & Ou, 2010; Schulting, Malone, & Dodge, 2005).

Transition, in theory and practice, ranges from simpler to more complex concepts and structures (Bohan-Baker & Little, 2002; Kagan & Neuman, 1998). Often, transition activities to bridge the year between preschool and kindergarten consist of a small set of narrowly defined activities—late school year visits by the preschoolers to kindergarten classrooms, or a fun activity at the elementary school to introduce the children and parents to the school and to key staff, such as the principal. These activities may contribute to a smoother transition from preschool to kindergarten simply by putting children and parents more at ease. Even so, a small number of simple, short-term transition activities do not produce a lasting effect on children's school success, or carry the long-term impact of best-practice preschool into elementary schools.

However, transition activities that are part of an extended process to engage families more intensively through a wider variety of opportunities for involvement have been found to produce positive outcomes for children (Bohan-Baker & Little, 2002; Kraft-Sayre & Pianta, 2000; Pianta, Rimm-Kaufman, & Cox, 1999; Shulting et al., 2005), including fewer problem behaviors in the classroom. Also, families offered a wider variety and more meaningful opportunities for school involvement tend to increase their engagement with the school and their children's schooling. Intensive, extended transition activities, including preschool contacts with both children and families, preschool–elementary school staff connections, summer children's peer connections, home visits, parent support groups, home–school learning activities, home–school information sharing, and Parent–Teacher Association (PTA) chapters, are more likely to be found in schools with a stronger socioecological and developmentally appropriate theoretical stance on the development and education of young children.

Schools that offer meaningful, extended opportunities for families and school staff to support the transition of children to formal schooling are more likely to be grounded in an assumption of the importance of collaborative working relationships between families, schools, and the broader community, especially local early care and education programs (Kraft-Sayre & Pianta, 2000; Rimm-Kaufman & Pianta, 2000). The assumption of the importance of the family–school relationship allows for, even compels schools to reach out to families as their most important educational collaborators. This educational stance creates a more positive environment for family–school interactions and produces a supportive environment in which family needs are more likely to be addressed without disrespect, and family strengths are more likely to be noted and appreciated. These positive school characteristics—extended, intensive transition activities, a family-friendly environment, best-practice theoretical grounding—decrease the likelihood of school-based risks to child development, particularly those arising from negative, disrespectful attitudes and expectations toward both the families of the children and the children themselves.

While research has found that the beneficial effect of transition activities is even more pronounced for children and families in poverty, high-poverty schools are less likely to provide them (LoCasale-Crouch et al., 2008; Ramey et al., 2000; Schulting et al., 2005). It is devilishly difficult for schools in poverty areas to develop and to institutionalize more positive practices. However, families that have been encouraged by high-quality preschool experiences to recognize the possibility and importance of educational success for their children, and their role in their child's progress, may be more likely to collaborate with their child's teachers. Perhaps even a small amount of direct positive experience with the families, as teachers and administrators come into contact with the families through whatever transition activities the school provides, can better inform school staff of the challenges and strengths of families and create the possibility for more effective, supportive relationships.

Best-practice transition is meant to increase children's readiness for entry into the more formal schooling of kindergarten and beyond, and to encourage positive interactions between families and schools. In doing so, it can continue the positive change in the children and families that began in preschool and provide an avenue in which families can show support for their child's schooling, while mitigating detrimental attitudes and expectations of school staff. However, while best-practice transition may to some extent signal a school's readiness to be the kind of environment in which children can best learn and thrive, it cannot guarantee that promise after transition activities end, usually by the end of kindergarten or first grade.

PreK–3 Models:
A Stronger Influence of Early Education on Later Education

Recent attempts to move the field of elementary education toward more comprehensive, developmental educational models include efforts to align aspects of high-quality preschool models with elementary school policies and practices, especially through comprehensive PreK–3 models (Reynolds, Magnuson, & Ou, 2010). Educational models such as James Comer's Yale School Development Program (SDP), or Zigler and Finn-Stevenson's 21st Century Schools (21C) include important aspects of alignment between some best preschool policies/practices and formal elementary schooling, and these and other similar models may also function to some extent to decrease risks to children that are found in the school context. However, while Comer's model includes a strong family–school–community focus (Comer, Joyner, & Ben-Avie, 2004), and 21C brings excellent early childhood programs into public school buildings (Zigler & Finn-Stevenson, 2007), neither model is meant specifically to extend the fundamental concepts and best early childhood policies or practices into subsequent schooling. A comprehensive PreK–3 model is designed specifically to do that.

The implementation of comprehensive PreK–3 models in high-poverty elementary schools would bring to those schools a developmental, research-based foundation across several aspects of the educational process (Sadowski, 2006; Shore, 2009). These fundamental concepts include the importance of a positive working relationship with families, as we discussed earlier. Other key fundamentals include a thorough knowledge of child development and its principles; the use of research-based, well-designed curricula aligned across content areas and developmental domains, and across subsequent years of schooling;

appropriate, relevant, and formative assessments of both children and classroom quality; and meaningful professional development.

The strong grounding of child development in the model and the use of research-based tools mean that teachers of young children implementing a PreK–3 model must be well educated and have specialized expertise (Bogard, Traylor, & Takanishi, 2008). Moreover, an important tenet of child development is equal consideration and respect for all children and families regardless of social or ethnic background; thus, better educated teachers with specialized expertise in early childhood education will be less likely to bring detrimental and hurtful attitudes into the classroom. When schools strive to implement a comprehensive PreK–3 model of education, highly knowledgeable and qualified teachers and administrators who respect the development and learning of all children, and who have the ability to use research-based curricula and assessment tools, and to employ ongoing, meaningful professional support, decrease the likelihood of the presence of risks that poorly qualified teachers and administrators bring to children in high-poverty districts.

Moreover, best-practice assessment in early childhood not only measures children's progress but also allows for authentic, observational assessment of children in classrooms (e.g., the Work Sampling System; Meisels, Jablon, Marsden, Dichtelmiller, & Dorfman, 2001), and is often used to inform classroom practices and professional development activities. High-quality preschools often use well-known early childhood assessment tools that are tightly linked to research-based curriculum models (e.g., the High/Scope Curriculum and the Child Observation Record; the Creative Curriculum and the Individual Child Profile). This comprehensive, coordinated approach to teaching and learning for children and teachers is a hallmark of excellent early education. In many schools, but especially in high-poverty schools, student assessments do not link meaningfully to educational processes or loop back relevantly into classroom practice, and curricula found in high-poverty schools are more often out of date than curricula in nonpoor schools. Therefore, in high-poverty schools, administrative efforts toward the strong implementation of a comprehensive PreK–3 model would decrease the risks related to administrative decisions on topics such as curricula, assessment, and professional development, that institutionalize the risks so often found in the classroom context for children in poverty.

Is There a Research Base for a PreK–3 Model of Education?

There are no impact studies of currently implemented PreK–3 models. However, the findings of the Abecedarian and Chicago studies, both of which included preschool-plus components in which important aspects of the preschool model were extended well into the elementary school grades, provide important information. Both studies have preschool-only and preschool-plus participant groups. The Abecedarian Study's preschool-plus group received home and classroom visits from a home–school resource teacher who supported the use of developmentally appropriate classroom activities and provided extensive parent advocacy through second grade. Results indicate that the group of children who received this extended intervention scored significantly higher than the preschool-only group in reading achievement through age 15, with higher scores, though nonsignificant, in reading achievement continuing through age 21 (Campbell & Ramey, 2010). The Chicago Study's preschool-plus group members received an instructional approach aligned to their preschool experience, smaller class sizes with a teacher's aide, and intensive parent supports, through third grade. The children in the preschool-plus group outscored their preschool-only peers and were less often retained in grade and held back, with differences between the groups still apparent at the age 24 follow-up (Reynolds, Magnuson, & Ou, 2010).

These findings reveal the value of developmentally appropriate, aligned educational experiences through the first 3 years of elementary school for children's long-term educational success, extending the benefits of high-quality early childhood programs into later childhood and more effectively fighting poverty for children. However, the knot of poverty-related risks around children—and, in fact, around schools—can be quite tight and seem almost impervious to loosening. It is important to know that improving the policies and practices of schools tangled up in poverty's risks is a difficult challenge. The National Head Start/Public School Early Childhood Transition Demonstration Project, a large study of the implementation of continued early childhood best practices through third grade, was meant to study the effects of improved educational practices in early elementary school on children's academic achievement. The transition program was a PreK–3 model that comprised developmentally appropriate classroom curricula and more supportive educational environments, along with family supports provided by specially trained Head Start family service workers. The program encouraged transition activities and close working relationships between Head Start programs and public elementary schools.

The most important finding of the national study, however, was that implementation of the program was highly problematic. Even in schools where administrators reported that they strongly valued improvements to their early elementary practices, teachers were often unable or unwilling to implement the changes, and administrators were often unable to manage the improvements successfully. School district poverty was a clear barrier to the successful implementation of the PreK–3 model, and teachers and administrators needed extensive support over time to create robust change in their schools. Given these implementation failures, it is not surprising that no impacts on children's scores were found overall (Ramey et al., 2000), though in one study site that strongly implemented the family support component of the PreK–3 model, significant increases in children's school attendance and academic and social skills were still found 1 year after the end of the program, at the end of fourth grade (Lamy, 2002).

The press toward comprehensive PreK–3 models of education—a continuous, energetic press—may alert educators in high-poverty schools to the existence of better methods of relating to families and educating young children, and to the possibility of successful change for them, with the collaboration of knowledgeable, experienced, and accessible early childhood professionals. It makes good sense, and research evidence suggests, that this press toward deeper expertise and higher quality through the implementation of PreK–3 educational models in the early elementary grades will fight poverty for the children who attend those schools.

Summary

We have discussed in this chapter the potential of high-quality early childhood programs to reduce the poverty of children. Decades ago, Head Start was created to fight poverty by intervening in the early contexts and experiences of children and families in poverty. Time has not refuted the veracity of Head Start's foundational concepts—that early experience is formative, that very young children are embedded in important contextual environments exerting strong influence on their development, and that young children are best cared for and educated in the whole and not in domain-specific parts. Though a vast body of research tells us that Head Start may falter in its ability to provide intensive enough educational interventions to produce strong effects, early childhood programs of high-enough quality do indeed change the course of children's lives. Several states across the country have taken up the challenge to implement high-quality preschool for large numbers of children, and recent studies indicate substantially increased early academic achievement for the children who attend those programs, raising the probability that state-level programs may fight poverty for those children in the long term.

It is the higher probability of risk to child development in high-poverty environments that ties children to poverty as they grow to adulthood. What loosens the knot of multiplying, interacting, strengthening risks around children, untangling them from poverty's ties, becomes poverty fighting. Studies indicate that high-quality early childhood programs decrease risks found in the family context by increasing the probability of employment and by improving parenting. But to the extent that the best of early education's policies and practices can penetrate subsequent systems of formal education, especially in high-poverty districts, it can also mitigate the impact of risks to child development found within those schools. How?

By creating positive change in cohorts of preschoolers and their parents, students transitioning from high-quality early childhood programs into high-poverty educational systems simply stress the systems less, easing the job of the teachers and reducing the need for costly remediation. Less need for remedial services saves schools substantial sums that may be redirected toward more positive educational activities. By smoothing the transition to kindergarten, families are encouraged to collaborate in the education of their children, and school staff members may develop a more balanced view of family strengths and challenges, decreasing risks to children arising from detrimental attitudes and low expectations in the classroom. By introducing fundamental aspects of high-quality early education through the implementation of comprehensive PreK–3 educational models, the best of early childhood policy and practice may be integrated into elementary schools, and the poverty-fighting power of excellent early childhood programs is extended into later childhood.

The integration of these policies and practices, including a thorough knowledge of child development and its principles; the use of research-backed educational tools, such as assessment instruments and curricula; and feedback loops linking classroom quality and professional development lowers the probability of school-based risks to child development so often found in high-poverty schools. These risks—negative teacher–student relationships, underqualified teachers and administrators, negative attitudes and low expectations, and school administrative policies that institutionalize risk in the system—combine and interact with other risks found in the family context, making it much more difficult for children to grow up and out of poverty. When these risks are embedded in schools, best practices for the education of young children are much more difficult to implement, but for children in poverty these best practices are even more important. Therefore, the community of early childhood experts, benefiting from a long tradition of rigorous and improving research, must continuously and energetically press for the implementation of best early childhood policies and practices not only within existing early childhood programs but also extended into the early elementary school years.

References

Administration for Children and Families. (2010). *Head Start impact study: Final report*. Washington, DC: U.S. Department of Health and Human Services.

Barnett, W. S. (1995). Long-term effects of early childhood programs on cognitive and school outcomes. *The Future of Children, 5*(3), 25–50.

Barnett, W. S., Jung, K., Frede, E., Hustedt, J., & Howes, C. (2011). *Effects of eight state prekindergarten programs on early learning*. New Brunswick, NJ: National Institute for Early Education Research, Rutgers University.

Barnett, W. S., Young, J., & Schweinhart, L. (1998). How preschool education influences long-term cognitive development and school success. In W. S. Barnett & S. S. Boocock (Eds.), *Early care and education for children in poverty: Promises, programs, and long-term results* (p. 167). Albany: State University of New York Press.

Baumrind, D. (1991). The influence of parenting style on adolescent competence and substance use. *Journal of Early Adolescence, 11*(1), 56–95.

Baydar, N., Reid, M. J., & Webster-Stratton, C. (2003). The role of mental health factors and program engagement in the effectiveness of a preventive parenting program for Head Start mothers. *Child Development, 74*(5), 1433–1453.

Belfield, C. (2004). *Early childhood education: How important are the cost-savings to the school system?* New York: Teachers College, Columbia University.

Bogard, K., Traylor, F., & Takanishi, R. (2008). Teacher education and PK outcomes: Are we asking the right questions? *Early Childhood Research Quarterly, 23,* 1–6.

Bohan-Baker, M., & Little, P. M. D. (2002). *The transition to kindergarten: A review of current research and promising practices to involve parents.* Cambridge, MA: Harvard Family Research Project.

Boyd, D., Goldhaber, D., Lankford, H., & Wyckoff, J. (2007). The effect of certification and preparation on teacher quality. *The Future of Children, 17*(1), 45–68.

Boyd, D., Lankford, H., Loeb, S., Rockoff, J., & Wyckoff, J. (2008). The narrowing gap in New York City: Teacher qualifications and its implications for student achievement in high poverty schools. *Journal of Policy Analysis and Management, 27*(4), 793–818.

Burchinal, M., Peisner-Feinberg, E., Pianta, R., & Howes, C. (2002). Development of academic skills from preschool through second grade: Family and classroom predictors of developmental trajectories. *Journal of School Psychology, 40*(5), 415–436.

Campbell, F. A., & Ramey, C. T. (1995). Cognitive and school outcomes for high-risk African-American students at middle adolescence: Positive effects of early intervention. *American Educational Research Journal, 32*(4), 743–772.

Campbell, F. A., & Ramey, C. T. (2010). Carolina Abecedarian Project. In A. J. Reynolds, A. J. Rolnick, M. M. Englund, & J. A. Temple (Eds.), *Childhood programs and practices in the first decade of life: A human capital integration* (pp. 76–98). New York: Cambridge University Press.

Campbell, F. A., Ramey, C. T., Pungello, E. P., Sparling, J. J., & Miller-Johnson, S. (2002). Early childhood education: Young adult outcomes from the Abecedarian project. *Applied Developmental Science, 6,* 42–57.

Comer, J., Joyner, E. T., & Ben-Avie, M. (2004). *Six pathways to healthy child development and academic success.* Thousand Oaks, CA: Corwin Press.

Dearing, E., McCartney, K., & Taylor, B. (2001). Change in family income-to-needs matters more for children with less. *Child Development, 72,* 1779–1793.

Dearing, E., McCartney, K., & Taylor, B. (2006). Within-child associations between family income and externalizing and internalizing problems. *Developmental Psychology, 42*(2), 237–252.

Duncan, G., & Brooks-Gunn, J. (2000). Family poverty, welfare reform, and child development. *Child Development, 71,* 188–196.

Espinosa, L., & Laffey, J. M. (2003). Urban primary teacher perceptions of children with challenging behaviors. *Journal of Children and Poverty, 9*(2), 135–156.

Felitti, V., Anda, R., Nordenberg, D., Wiliamson, D. F., Spitz, A. M., Edwards, V., et al. (1998). Relationship of child abuse and household dysfunction to many of the leading causes of death in adults: The Adverse Childhood Experiences (ACE) study. *American Journal of Preventive Medicine, 14,* 245–258.

Frede, E., Barnett, W. S., Jung, K., Lamy, C., & Figueras, A. (2010). Abbott Preschool Program Longitudinal Effects Study: Year one findings. In A. J. Reynolds, A. J. Rolnick, M. M. Englund, & J. A. Temple (Eds.), *Childhood programs and practices in the first decade of life: A human capital integration* (pp. 214–234). New York: Cambridge University Press.

Frede, E., Jung, K., Barnett, W. S., & Figueras, A. (2009). *The APPLES Blossom: Abbott Preschool Program Longitudinal Effects Study (APPLES) preliminary results through 2nd grade.* New Brunswick, NJ: National Institute for Early Education Research.

Garces, E., Thomas, D., & Currie, J. (2000). Longer term effects of Head Start (RAND Working Paper Series 00-20). Santa Monica, CA: RAND Corporation.

Garmezy, N., & Rutter, M. (1983). *Stress, coping and development in children.* New York: McGraw-Hill.

Gordon, R., Kane, T., & Staiger, D. (2006). *Identifying effective teachers using performance on the job* (Discussion Paper 2006-01). Washington, DC: The Brookings Institution.

Gormley, W. (2010). Small miracles in Tulsa: The effect of universal Pre–K. In A. J. Reynolds, A. J. Rolnick, M. M. Englund, & J. A. Temple (Eds.), *Childhood programs and practices in the first decade of life: A human capital integration* (pp. 188–198). New York: Cambridge University Press.

Hamre, B., & Pianta, R. C. (2001). Early teacher–child relationships and the trajectory of children's school outcomes through eighth grade. *Child Development, 72*(2), 625–638.

Hamre, B., & Pianta, R. C. (2005). Can instructional and emotional support in the first grade classroom make a difference for children at risk of school failure? *Child Development, 76*(5), 949–967.

Hamre, B., Pianta, R. C., Downer, J. T., & Mashburn, A. J. (2008). Teachers' perceptions of conflict with young students: Looking beyond problem behaviors. *Social Development, 17*(15), 115–136.

Heck, R. H. (2009). Teacher effect and student achievement: Investigating a multilevel cross-classified model. *Journal of Educational Administration, 47*(2), 227–249.

Heckman, J., Malofeeva, E., Pinto, R., & Savelyev, P. (2010, June 2). *Understanding the mechanisms through which an influential early childhood program boosted adult outcomes.* Presentation at the Measuring Education Outcomes: Moving from Enrollment to Learning Conference at the Center for Universal Education at Brookings, Brookings Institution, Washington, DC.

Howes, C. (2000). Social-emotional classroom climate in child care, teacher–child relationship and children's second grade peer relationships. *Social Development, 9,* 191–204.

Hughes, J., Luo, W., Kwok, O., & Lloyd, L. (2009). Teacher–student support, effortful engagement, and achievement: A 3-year longitudinal study. *Journal of Educational Psychology, 100*(1), 1–14.

Hustedt, J., Barnett, W. S., & Friedman, A. H. (2010). *The New Mexico Preschool Evaluation: Impacts from the fourth year (2008–2009) of New Mexico's state-funded Pre-K program.* New Brunswick, NJ: National Institute for Early Education Research, Rutgers University.

Hustedt, J., Barnett, W. S., & Jung, K. (2008). *Longitudinal effects of the Arkansas Better Chance Program: Findings from kindergarten and first grade.* New Brunswick, NJ: National Institute for Early Education Research, Rutgers University.

Huston, A. C., Duncan, G. J., Granger, R., Bos, J., McLoyd, V., Mistry, R., et al. (2001). Work-based antipoverty programs for parents can enhance the school performance and social behavior of children. *Child Development, 72,* 318–336.

Jacob, B. (2007). The challenges of staffing urban schools with effective teachers. *The Future of Children, 17*(1), 129–154.

Kagan, S. L., & Neuman, M. J. (1998). Lessons from three decades of transition research. *Elementary School Journal, 98*(4), 365–379.

Kraft-Sayre, M. E., & Pianta, R. C. (2000). *Enhancing the transition to kindergarten: Linking families, schools and children.* Charlottesville: National Center for Early Development and Learning, University of Virginia.

Lamy, C. (2002). Implementing research in the real world: An account of a Head Start intervention and its effects on children's school success through fourth grade. *National Head Start Association Dialog, 6*(1), 53–70.

Lee, V., & Loeb, S. (1995). Where do Head Start attendees end up?: One reason why preschool effects fade out. *Education Evaluation and Policy Analysis, 17*(1), 62–82.

Linver, M. R., Brooks-Gunn, J., & Kohen, D. E. (2002). Family processes as pathways from income to young children's development. *Developmental Psychology, 38,* 719–734.

LoCasale-Crouch, J., Mashburn, A., Downer, J. T., & Pianta, R. (2008). Pre-kindergarten teachers' use of transition practices and children's adjustment to kindergarten. *Early Childhood Research Quarterly, 23*(1), 124–139.

Love, J., Kisker, E., Ross, C., Raikes, H., Constantine, J., Boller, K., et al. (2005). The effectiveness of Early Head Start for 3 year old children and their parents: Lessons for policy and programs. *Developmental Psychology, 41*(6), 885–901.

Ludwig, J., & Miller, D. (2005). Does Head Start improve children's life chances?: Evidence from a regression discontinuity design (Institute for Research on Poverty Discussion Paper No. 1311-05). Madison: University of Wisconsin–Madison.

MacMillan, R., McMorris, B. J., & Kruttschnitt, C. (2004). Linked lives: Stability and change in maternal circumstances and trajectories of anti-social behavior in children. *Child Development, 75*, 205–220.

Matthews, H. (2006). *Child care assistance helps families work. A review of the effects of subsidy receipt on employment.* Washington, DC: Center for Law and Social Policy.

McKey, R. H., Condelli, L., Ganson, H., Barrett, B. J., McConkey, C., & Plantz, M. C. (1985). The impact of Head Start on children, families and communities (Department of Health and Human Services Publication No. OHDS 85-31193). Washington, DC: U.S. Government Printing Office.

McLoyd, V. (1990). The impact of economic hardship on black families and children: Psychological distress, parenting and socioemotional development. *Child Development, 61*, 311–346.

McLoyd, V. (1998). Socioeconomic disadvantage and child development. *American Psychologist, 53*, 185–204.

Meisels, S. J., Jablon, J. R., Marsden, D. B., Dichtelmiller, M. L., & Dorfman, A. B. (2001). *The work sampling system.* New York: Pearson Early Learning.

Muennig, P., Robertson, D., Johnson, G., Campbell, F., Pungello, E., & Neidell, M. (2011). The effect of an early education program on adult health: The Carolina Abecedarian Project randomized controlled trial. *American Journal of Public Health, 101*(3), 512–516.

Muennig, P., Schweinhart, L., Montie, J., & Neidell, M. (2009). Effects of a prekindergarten educational intervention on adult health: 37-year follow-up results of a randomized controlled trial. *American Journal of Public Health, 99*(8), 1431–1437.

Peske, H., & Haycock, K. (2006). *Teaching inequality: How poor and minority students are shortchanged on teacher quality.* Washington, DC: The Education Trust.

Pianta, R. C. (1999). *Enhancing relationships between children and teachers.* Washington, DC: American Psychological Association.

Pianta, R. C., La Paro, K. M., Payne, C., Cox, M. J., & Bradley, R. (2002). The relation of kindergarten classroom environment to teacher, family, and school characteristics and child outcomes. *Elementary School Journal, 102*(3), 225–238.

Pianta, R. C., Rimm-Kaufman, S. E., & Cox, M. J. (1999). Introduction: An ecological approach to kindergarten transition. In R. C. Pianta & M. J. Cox (Eds.), *The transition to kindergarten.* Baltimore: Brookes.

Ramey, S. L., Ramey, C. T., Phillips, M. M., Lanzi, R. G., Brezausek, C., Katholi, C. R., et al. (2000). *Head Start children's entry into public school: A Report on the National Head Start/Public School Early Childhood Transition Demonstration Study.* Birmingham: CIVITAN International Research Center, University of Alabama at Birmingham.

Resnick, G. (2010). Project Head Start: Quality and links to child outcomes. In A. J. Reynolds, A. J. Rolnick, M. M. Englund, & J. A. Temple (Eds.), *Childhood programs and practices in the first decade of life: A human capital integration* (pp. 121–156). New York: Cambridge University Press.

Reynolds, A. J., Magnuson, K. A., & Ou, S. (2010). Preschool-to-third grade programs and practices: A review of research. *Children and Youth Services Review, 32*(8), 1121–1131.

Reynolds, A. J., Temple, J. A., & Ou, S. (2010). Impacts and implications of the Child–Parent Center preschool program. In A. J. Reynolds, A. J. Rolnick, M. M. Englund, & J. A. Temple (Eds.), *Childhood programs and practices in the first decade of life: A human capital integration* (pp. 168–187). New York: Cambridge University Press.

Reynolds, A. J., Temple, J. A., Robertson, D. L., & Mann, E. A. (2002). Age 21 cost–benefit analysis of the Title I Chicago Child–Parent Centers. *Educational Evaluation and Policy Analysis, 24*(4), 267–303.

Rimm-Kaufman, S., & Pianta, R. (2000). An ecological perspective on the transition to kindergarten: A theoretical framework to guide empirical research. *Journal of Applied Developmental Psychology, 21*(5), 491–511.

Rimm-Kaufman, S., Pianta, R., & Cox, M. J. (2000). Teachers' judgments of problems in the transition to kindergarten. *Early Childhood Research Quarterly, 15*(2), 147–166.

Sadowski, M. (2006). Core knowledge for PK–3 teaching: Ten components of effective instruction (PreK–3rd Action Brief No. 5). New York: Foundation for Child Development.

Sameroff, A., Bartko, W., Baldwin, A., Baldwin, C., & Seifer, R. (1998). Family and social influences on the development of child competence. In M. Lewis & C. Feiring (Eds.), *Families, risk and competence* (pp. 161–186). Mahwah, NJ: Erlbaum.

Sameroff, A., & Chandler, M. (1975). Reproductive risk and the continuum of caretaker casualty. In F. D. Horowitz, M. Hetherington, S. Scarr-Salopatek, & E. G. Siegal (Eds.), *Review of child development psychology* (Vol. 4, pp. 187–244). Chicago: University of Chicago Press.

Sameroff, A., Seifer, R., Baldwin, A., & Baldwin, C. (1993). Stability of intelligence from preschool to adolescence: The influence of social and family risk factors. *Child Development, 64*, 80–97.

Schulting, A., Malone, P., & Dodge, K. (2005). The effect of school-based kindergarten transition policies and practice on child academic outcomes. *Developmental Psychology, 41*(6), 860–871.

Schweinhart, L., Monti, J., Xiang, Z., Barnett, W. S., Belfield, C., & Nores, M. (2005). Lifetime effects: The High/Scope Perry Preschool Study through age 40 (Monographs of the High/Scope Educational Research Foundation, No. 14). Ypsilanti, MI: High/Scope Press.

Shore, R. (2009). The case for investing in PreK–3rd education: Challenging myths about school reform (PreK–3rd Action Brief No. 1). New York: Foundation for Child Development.

Smith, J., Brooks-Gunn, J., & Klebanov, P. K. (1997). The consequences of living in poverty for young children's cognitive and verbal ability and early school achievement. In G. J. Duncan & J. Brooks-Gunn (Eds.), *Consequences of growing up poor* (pp. 132–189). New York: Russell Sage Foundation.

Steinberg, L., Lamborn, S., Darling, N., Mounts, N., & Dornbusch, S. (1994). Over-time changes in adjustment and competence among adolescents from authoritative, authoritarian, indulgent and neglectful families. *Child Development, 65*, 754–770.

Webster-Stratton, C. (1998). Preventing conduct problems in Head Start children: Strengthening parenting competencies. *Journal of Consulting and Clinical Psychology, 66*(5), 715–730.

Webster, Stratton, C., Rinaldi, J., & Reid, J. (2009). Long-term outcomes of Incredible Years Parenting Programs: Predictors of adolescent adjustment. Seattle: University of Washington. Retrieved April 21, 2011, from *www.incredibleyears.com/library/items/long-term-outcomes-of-iy-parenting-pgrm_7-7-09.pdf*.

Werner, E. E., & Smith, R. S. (1982). *Vulnerable, but invincible: A longitudinal study of resilient children and youth.* New York: McGraw-Hill.

Wu, J., Hughes, J., & Kwok, O. (2010). Teacher–student relationship quality type in elementary grades: Effects on trajectories for achievement and engagement. *Journal of School Psychology, 48*(5), 357–387.

Zigler, E., & Finn-Stevenson, M. (2007). From research to policy and practice: The school of the 21st century. *American Journal of Orthopsychiatry, 77*(2), 175–181.

Zigler, E., & Muenchow, S. (1992). *Head Start: The inside story of America's most successful educational experiment.* New York: Basic Books.

Zill, N., Resnick, G., Kim, K., O'Donnell, K., Sorongon, A., McKey, R. H., et al. (2003). *Head Start FACES 2000: A whole child perspective on program performance.* Washington, DC: Department of Health and Human Services.

Zill, N., & West, J. (2001). Entering kindergarten: A portrait of American children when they begin school: Findings from the Condition of Education 2000 (NCES No. 2001-035). Washington, DC: U.S. Department of Education, National Center for Education Statistics.

PART II

INSTRUCTION AND CURRICULUM IN EARLY EDUCATION SETTINGS

Impacts on Young Children's Preacademic Outcomes

CHAPTER 9

Promoting Lower- and Higher-Level Language Skills in Early Education Classrooms

Mindy Sittner Bridges, Laura M. Justice, Tiffany P. Hogan, and Shelley Gray

Learning the complexities of language is one of the most important and observable achievements of early childhood. A multidimensional aspect of children's development, language comprises a set of rule-governed, basic developmental processes (or domains) that begin to emerge at the time of birth (if not before), then rapidly develop over the next 6 years (see Pence & Justice, 2007). Children's language skills during early childhood are closely related to a number of other developmental domains, including social competence (Fujiki, Brinton, Isaacson, & Summers, 2001), literacy development (National Institute of Child Health and Human Development [NICHD] Early Child Care Research Network, 2005; Scarborough, 1990), and self-regulation (Fujiki, Brinton, & Clarke, 2002). An individual's language skills provide the means for efficient communication with others and therefore, across the entire lifespan, provide the mechanism for meeting very basic communicative needs (e.g., to request, to reject), and for engaging in a range of daily living contexts, including home, school, and community.

For a majority of children the development of language occurs rapidly and in a predictable sequence. However, there are a variety of known risk factors, both environmental and genetic, that have the potential to alter and slow this natural developmental course, thereby affecting not only the pace of language acquisition but also other aspects of development closely linked to language (e.g., Justice, Bowles, Pence Turnbull, & Skibbe, 2009). For instance, children who receive relatively little linguistic input, due to either a physical disability (e.g., significant hearing loss) or understimulating caregiving environments, may experience significant lags in their language development compared to other children. This can lead to lags in development of other skills, such as social competence and prereading abilities. Nonetheless, researchers have identified a number of important ways in which early lags in language development can be prevented or mitigated, including implementation of interventions within early education classrooms.

This chapter is organized to describe language skills warranting special attention within early education settings that are known to be malleable through intervention. In the first section, we describe various domains of language and identify the difference between lower- and higher-level language skills. We also examine how specific language skills contribute to social and academic success. In the second section we discuss different approaches for teaching higher- and lower-level language skills, and describe a possible scope and sequence of instruction that may be utilized in early education settings.

Domains of Language

Historical Conceptualizations

Three decades ago Bloom and Lahey's (1978) conceptualization of language as a three-domain system provided a parsimonious approach to describing children's early developments in language. Bloom and Lahey described language as comprising three interrelated domains; within each, children must internalize specific rules: form, content, and use. *Form* includes the "building blocks" of language: phonology, morphology, and syntax. *Phonology* involves the rules governing sound structure, *morphology* involves the rules governing word constructions, and *syntax* involves the rules governing sentence constructions. *Content* can be conceptualized as the rules governing vocabulary words and their associated meanings, and is synonymous with the term *semantics*. *Use*, also referred to as *pragmatics*, refers to rules governing the communicative intent of language. Knowledge of the differences among these three domains of language, as well as their interrelations, allows one to describe more fully the course of language acquisition and identify more precisely areas of language in which a given child may exhibit a developmental weakness or impairment.

Form: Phonology, Morphology, and Syntax

Phonology refers to the rules governing sound structure, specifically the use of individual sounds within languages. These individual sounds are called *phonemes* and are the smallest unit of contrastive meaning in language. An example of a phoneme is the sound /b/ that one hears in the beginning of the word *bit*. Note that changing the initial phoneme of this word from /b/ to /p/ changes the meaning of the word entirely, despite the fact that the two words (*bit, pit*) are produced almost identically.

Standard American English has approximately 39 phonemes; of these, 15 are vowels and 24 are consonants. It is important to note that the sounds of a spoken language are not equivalent to the letters (or *graphemes*) in an alphabetically based written language, such as English or Spanish. Alphabet letters do correspond to specific sound(s) (e.g., the sound /f/ corresponds to the letter *f*), but not all alphabet letters are restricted to one associated phoneme. For example, in English, the letter *c* is associated with two phonemes in English: the /k/ sound heard in the beginning of the word *cat* as well as the /s/ sound heard in the beginning of the word *circle*. The use of letters to represent individual speech sounds (*written language*) emerged long after humans began to use speech sounds to represent their internal thoughts to others (*oral language*).

Phonological awareness, a familiar term to many educators, refers to one's ability to attend to and manipulate phonemes in oral language and can be measured by asking children to complete tasks such as rhyming or identifying the initial sound in a spoken word. Knowing the correspondences between letters and sounds is referred to as *letter–sound knowledge* and, while it relies on one's phonological awareness, it is a different developmental construct. For instance, a child may exhibit phonological awareness but have little knowledge of letter–sound correspondences. Many early educators are interested in supporting children's development of phonological awareness and letter–sound knowledge, given that these are important foundations of beginning reading skill (Calfee, Lindamood, & Lindamood, 1973; Catts, Fey, Zhang, & Tomblin, 2001; Torgesen, Wagner, & Rashotte, 1994); therefore, it is important to recognize the distinctiveness of closely related terms such as *phonology, phonological awareness*, and *letter–sound knowledge*, so that each is attended to instructionally in early education settings.

Grammar, a language domain often highlighted in child development literature, particularly as it relates to children with language disorders, is an umbrella term encompassing both morphology and syntax. Both components are part of an overarching set of rules that define how words, or parts of words, are combined in ways that conform to the rules of a particular language. It is regrettable that so many adults dislike discussing grammar (at least from our experience as university faculty who have taught courses in language development) because grammar is a very important aspect of children's language growth that has strong linkages with other aspects of language (e.g., vocabulary; see Dixon & Marchman, 2007), as well as later reading achievement (Adlof, Catts, & Lee, 2010; Muter, Hulme, Snowling, & Stevenson, 2004). Although grammar is considered a relatively resilient aspect of language development, grammar deficits are a hallmark of childhood language disorders (which affect about 7–10% of young children; see Tomblin et al., 1997). It is important for early educators to understand grammar—comprising both morphology and syntax—so that they can provide instruction in their classrooms to stimulate this particular aspect of language development.

Morphology is the rules that govern the structure of words. A *morpheme* is a basic unit of meaning and can be a stand-alone word (e.g., *boy*) or a prefix or suffix that adds meaning (e.g., the *-s* in the word *boys* to mark plurality or the *-ing* in the word *walking* to mark the present progressive state of the verb). The former type of morpheme is called a *free morpheme*, and the latter is a *bound morpheme*. Bound morphemes include both derivational and inflectional morphemes. A *derivational morpheme* can be added to a word to devise another word, such as *pre-* added to the word *school* to form *preschool*. In this case, the morpheme provides information about the semantics, or meaning, of the word: by adding *pre-* to the word *school*, we know more about the particular type of school (i.e., it is a school for very young children). *Inflectional morphemes* are those that add grammatical meaning to a word; such morphemes include the plural *-s*, the possessive marker *-'s*, the past tense marker *-ed*, and the present progressive marker *-ing*. The ability to produce and comprehend morphemes in language is called *morphological awareness*. Good morphological awareness allows children to expand their vocabulary greatly by adding inflections onto known base words (e.g., *school, schooling, schooled, preschool*); additionally, the ability to use morphemes correctly allows children to express their ideas in a more precise manner. For example, when a child says "They walked" (vs. "They walk"), he or she is conveying important information about the timing of an event. The ability to communicate precisely is critical for using language to meet both social and academic needs.

Syntax refers to the rules that govern the internal organization of sentences; that is, syntactic rules dictate that words in a particular language must be in a prescribed order. A remarkable aspect of syntax is that a minimal number of rules allows one to combine words in an infinite number of correct sentences. Additionally, these rules provide listeners or readers important information related to the meaning of a sentence. Consider, for instance, the sentences "The boy kissed the girl" and "The boy was kissed by the girl." The two sentences include almost the same set of words, and the word order is similar. However, the meanings are very different, and it is implicit knowledge of active and passive sentences that allows one to discern the important distinction in meaning.

Content: Semantics

Learning to recognize or produce the label for objects is one of the most exciting language accomplishments of early childhood. The infant's first expression of a word, often the name of a salient caregiver (*Mama, Dada*), is typically cause for celebration. Semantics, or rules governing the content of language, involve the rules related to individual word meanings, as well as word combinations. Most children acquire knowledge of vocabulary words quickly, with relatively little effort, as adults around them label objects, actions, and attributes (Bloom, 2000). By the beginning of kindergarten children may know approximately 3,500 word meanings (Biemiller & Slonim, 2001).

Word knowledge includes literal meanings, such as the understanding that a "cat" is a furry, four-legged animal that is often a household pet. However, it is important for children to comprehend figurative meanings of word combinations as well. Take, for example, the phrase "zip it." The literal meaning of this involves moving a zipper on an article of clothing to achieve closure. However, it is imperative that an elementary school child also realizes that the figurative meaning is "quit talking." The ability to comprehend such figurative language is an important academic skill, especially as children begin to encounter figurative language in print and social contexts.

Use: Pragmatics

The use of language is often termed *pragmatics* and involves rules governing the social use of language. Pragmatics is often described as involving three major communicative skills: using language for different intentions; changing language according to the needs of a communication partner; and following rules for conversation, storytelling, and narration (American Speech–Language–Hearing Association, 2010). The latter skill emphasizes the importance of narration and is too often an underemphasized aspect of language development within early education settings. Narrative production and comprehension is the child's ability to express and understand language at the discourse level, whereby words and sentences are organized to form coherent sequences of events or ideas. Narrative ability is one of the most "ecologically valid ways in which to measure communicative competence" because narratives form the basis of many childhood speech acts (Botting, 2002, p. 1). Narratives typically follow a flexible but organized sequence; generally, stories share some common features, such as a setting, a plot, a conflict, and a resolution. The ability to generate and produce narratives begins in the preschool years and increases through the elementary school years; mastery of narratives is a critical language skill that is predictive of academic success, particularly as related to reading comprehension (Beck, Omanson, & McKeown, 1982).

Lower- and Higher-Level Language Skills

In the previous section we provided a general primer of the major domains of language, all of which are in an active state of development during the course of early childhood. For instance, with respect to the domain of phonology, enormous growth in phonology occurs between birth and age 5. Whereas at 6 months an infant is using only a few sounds to babble (typically /m/ and /b/), by 5 years the typical child is wholly intelligible and uses most, if not all, of the phonemes in his or her native language to produce an infinite number of words.

In general, we have largely focused on describing what might be called basic or "lower-level" language skills, so named because they emerge relatively quickly and easily for the majority of children during the course of early childhood and form the foundation for a host of other "higher-level" skills. By about age 6 a child's form, content, and use of language represent automatized processes that occur very efficiently. For instance, a typical first grader is readily able to draw upon automatized phonological, lexical, and grammatical processes accurately to comprehend the sentence: "After we read this story together, we're going to make a list of all the adjectives that describe Arthur, so you really need to pay attention."

Higher-level language skills are layered upon lower-level language skills and are especially important when using language for complex purposes such as problem-solving, reasoning, and inferencing. Higher-level skills are particularly important for reading comprehension, especially the comprehension of more complex written materials. Theory and research demonstrate that, among mature readers, one's skills in reading comprehension approximate one's listening comprehension (Perfetti, 2007). Based on this "simple view" of reading, among the most critical determinants of listening comprehension are an individual's language skills, transcending both lower- (i.e., automatic) and higher-level (i.e., integrative) processes (Perfetti, 2007). Higher-order language skills are processes that are considered to be less automatic and instead play more of an integrative role in comprehension (Cain, Oakhill, & Bryant, 2004; Perfetti, 2007). Higher-level language skills that particularly influence skilled comprehension include *inferencing, comprehension monitoring*, and use of *text structure knowledge*, collectively and variously referred to as "higher-level meaning construction skills" and "higher-level factors in comprehension" (respectively, Cain et al., 2004; Perfetti, Landi, & Oakhill, 2005).

In simple terms, inferencing allows one to "fill in the gaps" in language. To understand written or spoken language readers need to be able to go beyond the literal meaning of words by linking main ideas from the text and using general knowledge to provide additional information that is not explicitly stated. The ability to make inferences relies heavily on possessing the appropriate schema, or background knowledge, to comprehend spoken or written text. An additional higher-order language skill, comprehension monitoring, involves the capacity to reflect on one's own comprehension, and in addition, the ability to detect incongruities within a text. It is important to note that a failure to notice problems or inconsistencies in text may stem from lack of general knowledge instead of a failure to monitor inconsistencies. Finally, knowledge of text structure is considered another higher-level language skill. Children need the ability to produce and comprehend both narrative and expository text to be successful readers. These three higher-order skills involve the integration of numerous language processes, and often children with language delays or disorders have limited abilities in these higher-level processes.

Both lower- and higher-order language skills are used to construct meaning of connected text. The automatic, lower-order language skills are used to construct the literal meanings of a text, referred to by some as the *textbase* (Kintsch & Kintsch, 2005). Theoretically, when lexical representations are well specified and coherently organized—that is, *verbally efficient* (Perfetti, 2007)—one is able to draw upon the higher-level language resources to engage in higher-level comprehension of text. This higher-level comprehension involves creating a mental model of the text that integrates the text with one's prior knowledge and organizes its multiple propositions into an integrated whole (Kintsch & Kintsch, 2005). Creation of a mental model of a text—a *situation model*—draws upon the higher-level language skills that are not resource-cheap, so to speak, but are particularly crucial to higher level comprehension because of the *integrative* role they play (Cain et al., 2004; Perfetti, 2007). Indeed, measures of each of these three higher-level language skills explain significant amounts of unique variance in 8- to 11-year-old children's reading comprehension, even when controlling for lower-level language skills and other factors such as working memory and word-reading abilities (Cain et al., 2004).

Risk and Resilience in Early Language Development

One of the most widely-researched risk factors related to language development is familial socioeconomic status (SES), typically defined by family income level or maternal education. Early language development is rooted in the communication interactions that young children have with others, particularly their caregivers. In a seminal study Hart and Risley (1995) highlighted the importance of a child's home environment for providing language experiences to promote language development. They examined the home environment and language abilities of children from families of various SES levels. Children of families in the highest SES level heard approximately four times more vocabulary words than children in families with the lowest SES level. This difference in vocabulary was related to the children's language and cognitive skills at age 3 years and to expressive language at age 9 years, with the children from the lowest SES exhibiting, on average, the lowest language scores.

An additional risk factor associated with SES is the quality of early child care. Research has shown that quality teacher–child interactions, as well as the quantity and quality of teacher language use, can positively influence children's language development (Girolametto & Weitzman, 2002; Mashburn et al., 2008). For instance, children who are naturally exposed to more exemplars of complex syntax in their preschool classroom, such as that embedded within teachers' talk to students, have better grammar comprehension compared to children exposed to fewer exemplars of complex syntax (Huttenlocher, Vasilyeva, Cymerman, & Levine, 2002). Although these results are encouraging, many parents cannot afford to send their children to quality preschools; thus, their children miss quality interactions that serve to increase their language abilities. At the same time, parents may select preschools for their children on the basis of other factors, such as cost and convenience, rather than the quality of the interactions children experience.

Beyond SES, many types of developmental disability are accompanied by delays or disorders in language development, with several of the most common related to intellectual disabilities. Regulations for the Individuals with Disabilities Education Act (IDEA; 2004) define individuals with intellectual disabilities as those who score below 70 on an intelligence test and have accompanying "deficits in adaptive behavior" that "adversely affect a child's educational performance." Down syndrome, a genetic disorder associated with an extra chromosome 21, is one of the most common causes of intellectual disability. Down syndrome is associated with numerous behavioral features, but language is one of the most impaired domains of functioning and is the most prohibitive barrier to academic success and to inclusion by peers. Individuals with Down syndrome typically show decreased language performance across language domains, but have particular difficulty with language production and syntax (Roberts, Price, & Malkin, 2007).

Another disorder with associated language deficits is autism. Because manifestations of autism vary greatly among individuals, the disorder is often referred to as autism spectrum disorder (ASD). An ASD diagnosis is based on the presence of deficits in three areas: communication ability, social interaction, and repetitive and stereotyped behaviors (American Psychiatric Association, 1994). Language abilities among children with autism range from no verbal language to the ability to participate in conversations but difficulty with the higher-order aspects of language. Children with ASD often use language in idiosyncratic, repetitive ways and have difficulty initiating or reciprocating in conversational interactions. Those with higher-level language skills may have difficulty comprehending abstract language or making inferences (Rice, Warren, & Betz, 2005). Children with higher language ability are often diagnosed with a form of autism called Asperger syndrome. Although many aspects of their language are relatively well developed, individuals with this particular form of autism have substantial problems with social interaction that greatly affect their ability to develop and maintain peer relationships.

Specific language impairment, or SLI, a developmental disability associated with decreased language abilities, is defined as language disorder in the absence of frank neurological, sensorimotor, nonverbal cognitive, or socioemotional deficits (see Watkins & Rice, 1994). A hallmark of SLI in English-speaking children is a delay or deficit in the use of grammar, particularly as related to grammatical morphemes (e.g., plural -*s*, past tense -*ed*). Specifically, children with SLI omit morphemes long after their peers with typical language development show consistent production of these morphemes. Language difficulties may become apparent early in life and typically remain throughout childhood and into adolescence. Although the most widely noted deficit is grammar, other domains of language are typically affected by SLI (see Leonard, 2000). A diagnosis of SLI puts children at greater risk for later academic difficulties, particularly reading disabilities (Bishop & Adams, 1990; Catts, Adlof, Hogan, & Weismer, 2005). Additionally, these language difficulties most likely influence peer interactions, with research indicating that children with SLI have trouble initiating and responding to peers (Hadley & Rice, 1991) and are typically more withdrawn than their peers with typical language development (Fujiki, Brinton, Isaacson, & Summers, 2001).

Instructional Objectives in Language

The language domains discussed thus far in this chapter provide a framework for developing a scope of instruction that ensures an emphasis on language development within the early education setting. The term *scope* refers to the breadth of instructional objectives to be addressed during teaching. Instructional objectives describe the desired learning outcomes of instruction and provide the means to move a child to competence in a given language ability. In this section we discuss objectives across language skills discussed earlier in this chapter, to include both lower-level skills (syntax, morphology, vocabulary) and higher-level skills (inferencing, comprehension monitoring, text structure knowledge). Table 9.1 includes a possible scope of instruction that could be implemented within early childhood and kindergarten classrooms.

Grammar (Syntax and Morphology)

Because grammatical skills in preschool are highly predictive of later reading achievement and provide a foundation for higher-level language skills (e.g., Scarborough, 1990), educators should include specific classroom instruction related to this language ability. One instructional objective targeting grammatical competence is using a variety of phrase structures, such as prepositional phrases, noun and verb phrases, and adjectival phrases. This objective can be made developmentally appropriate for younger preschool students by eliciting production of noun phrases that include the following: a determiner or article, an adjective, and a noun (e.g., *the big cow*). A more complex indicator for kindergarten students might be to use prepositional phrases (e.g., *over the hill*).

As children acquire more complex language skills, they begin to modulate their utterances by producing a wider array of grammatical morphemes (Brown, 1973). An appropriate objective for young children is understanding and producing morphemes, such as plurals and past tense. A preschool indicator could involve use of plural markers (i.e., *ducks*), while a more advanced indicator might require the correct use of past tense -*ed* (i.e., *kicked*).

TABLE 9.1. Instructional Objectives across Lower- and Higher-Level Language Domains

Language skill	Instructional objectives
Syntax	1. Use a variety of verbs to signal changes in tense 2. Use a variety of phrase structures (prepositional phrases, noun phrases, adjectival phrases) 3. Use and respond to a variety of question types
Morphology	1. Comprehend and produce grammatical morphemes (plural, past tense) 2. Comprehend and produce common derivational affixes 3. Comprehend and produce compound words (e.g., superman)
Vocabulary	1. Use abstract nouns and verbs 2. Distinguish shades of meaning 3. Produce definitions for words
Inferencing	1. Comprehend and produce questions about mental states and motives 2. Comprehend and produce questions about causes of events 3. Generate predictions about future events
Comprehension monitoring	1. Summarize narratives 2. Summarize information in expository texts 3. Comprehend nonverbal information in narratives and expository text
Text structure knowledge	1. Identify key story elements (i.e., setting, characters, plot, theme) 2. Identify key differences between text structures of narrative and expository text 3. Retell a story including main story grammar elements

Vocabulary

The one aspect of oral language that is often incorporated into general classroom instruction is vocabulary, and indeed there is a strong correlation between vocabulary knowledge and general reading ability (e.g., NICHD Early Child Care Research Network, 2005; Stanovich, 1986; Stanovich, Cunningham, & Freeman, 1984). However, young children have vastly diverse vocabularies (Biemiller & Slonim, 2001), and those differences place many children at risk for difficulties in learning to read and comprehend text. Recent research has shown that direct instruction does have a positive effect on young children's vocabulary knowledge (e.g., Justice, Meier, & Walpole, 2005; NICHD Early Child Care Research Network, 2005; Penno, Wilkinson, & Moore, 2002). Teaching children to distinguish between shades of meaning is one way to provide direct instruction in vocabulary. The ability to discern subtle meanings in words becomes increasingly important as text in expository books or narratives becomes more complex. To promote this skill a teacher could ask students to distinguish the differences among nouns within a common category. When discussing flowers in a garden, for instance, children could learn names of various types of flowers, such as *roses, tulips,* and *daisies*. A more difficult indicator would be to distinguish the difference between verbs that can be used to describe movement. These words, such as *run, walk, stroll*, and *prance*, all involve someone moving from one place to another, but the way in which this movement is accomplished is vastly different.

Inferencing

Recall that inferencing involves predicting or deducing something that is not explicitly stated. An inference contrasts sharply with literal language, in that it requires some sort of prior or world knowledge to deduce meaning. A literal discussion of text emphasizes recalling facts that were directly presented in text or accompanying pictures, whereas an inferential discussion goes beyond that which is directly stated. Research has shown that preschool-age children are able to engage in inference making (van den Broek et al., 2005; van Kleeck, 2006); thus, objectives related to inferencing should be part of early childhood classroom instruction. One objective that focuses on such skills requires children to answer questions related to a character's mental state or actions that are not explicitly stated in the text. An example of a question that taps inferential abilities is "How do you think the bird felt when he couldn't find his mother?" A similar type of question requires that children answer questions regarding what course of action a character might take (e.g., "Where do you think the bird should go now?"). These types of questions motivate children to use their background knowledge or reasoning skills to provide a feasible answer.

Comprehension Monitoring

Good readers are typically aware of their comprehension as they listen to or read written text, and when they experience difficulty, they automatically use a variety of strategies to increase their comprehension (Pressley & Afflerbach, 1995). However, young children are likely to have a difficult time monitoring their comprehension independently. Because of this, instructional objectives related to comprehension monitoring should be included in early childhood instruction. One method for encouraging comprehension monitoring is to ask children to summarize a story. *Summarizing* requires that children identify the most salient parts of a story and then retell that information in their own words. Asking a child periodically to summarize parts of a storybook will help alert the child to parts of the story that he or she did not understand. Children can also be asked to summarize information learned in an expository text.

Text Structure

Text structure refers to the characteristics of written material, as well as the way ideas in a text are constructed and organized. Researchers suggest that increasing students' knowledge about text structure facilitates their ability to attend to the most salient details in the text, thereby increasing comprehension (e.g., Carnine & Kinder, 1985; Gersten, Fuchs, Williams, & Baker, 2001). One relevant objective centers on knowledge of important parts of a fictional narrative, often called *story grammar*. Story grammar elements were formulated by Stein and Glenn (1979) to categorize the various elements used by children to comprehend and generate stories. In its simplest form, story grammar element consists of a main character, his or her problem, his or her attempts to solve the problem, and events that lead to a resolution or ending (Mandler & Johnson, 1977; Stein & Trabasso, 1982). There is empirical evidence that instruction in story grammar components is effective in improving comprehension of narrative text (e.g., Carnine & Kinder, 1985; Dimino, Gersten, Carnine, & Blake, 1990). A specific objective for young children related to story grammar is retelling a story aloud using the key story elements. As children become increasingly aware of the essential components of a story, they are more likely to understand a novel story and be able to include the important parts when composing their own story.

The former objective focused on teaching elements related to fictional narratives. Expository texts are typically not as widely used as narratives in early childhood and primary classrooms; however, recent work has shown the importance of expository texts for building background knowledge (Williams, Stafford, Lauer, Hall, & Pollini, 2009). Expository text is generally more difficult to understand and remember than narrative text, primarily because the content in expository text is less familiar and the structure is more difficult than that in narrative texts (Kucan & Beck, 1997). However, scholars have argued for increased use of expository text in early childhood and primary grade classrooms (e.g., Caswell & Duke, 1998; Pappas, 1991; Williams, 2005). One objective related to assisting young children in learning from nonfiction texts is to teach differences in features between this type of text and narrative texts. For example, teachers can point out that narratives include story grammar elements such as characters and problems, but expository texts focus on information and include elements such as compare–contrast.

Approaches to Teaching
Lower- and Higher-Level Language Skills

Once an instructional scope and sequence is established, educators need an arsenal of empirically validated instructional techniques they can use to teach objectives across the language domains. Research across many decades has identified *causally interpretable relations* between specific instructional techniques and children's growth in lower- and higher-level language skills. In this section, we provide research-based techniques that have been shown to improve children's language abilities; these instructional techniques are included in Table 9.2.

Focused Stimulation

In focused stimulation, a common instructional technique used in early childhood settings (e.g., Ellis Weismer & Robertson, 2006), the targeted goal is repeated several times within an interaction, and the focus is on increasing the child's exposure to the form. Activities are arranged in such a way as to encourage, but not require, production of the target form. Focused stimulation is typically utilized during naturalistic conditions, such as play, to encourage generalization of the target. Researchers have found that a focused stimulation

TABLE 9.2. Empirically Validated Techniques Integrated for Language-Based Comprehension Instruction

Language skill	Instructional techniques	References
Syntax	• Focused stimulation	Fey, Cleave, Long, & Hughes (1993); Zevenbergen & Whitehurst (2003)
Morphology	• Focused stimulation • Cloze procedures	Bradshaw, Hoffman, & Norris (1998); Ellis Weismer & Robertson (2006)
Vocabulary	• Rich, extended instruction • Dialogic reading • Focused stimulation	Beck & McKeown (2007); Coyne, McCoach, & Kapp (2007); van Kleeck, Vander Woude, & Hammett (2006); Wasik & Bond (2001)
Inferencing	• Inferential questioning • Interpretative cloze	Bradshaw et al. (1998); van Kleeck (2006); van Kleeck, Vander Woude, & Hammett (2006)
Comprehension monitoring	• Self-questioning training • Think alouds	Glaubman, Glaubman, & Ofir (1997)
Text structure knowledge	• Clue words • Graphic organizers	Williams et al. (2005)

approach is an effective way to teach a variety of grammatical forms to young children (e.g., Fey, 1986; Zevenbergen & Whitehurst, 2003). Earlier, teaching the plural -*s* morpheme was identified as an appropriate instructional objective for young children; focused stimulation can be used to expose children to that target form. For example, during a free-play activity involving animals, an adult could provide many models of the plural form during conversation about the animals.

ADULT: I have a cat—oh, I have two *cats*.

ADULT: I will put the *cats* in the barn.

ADULT: And now I will put four *dogs* with the *cats*. Look—*dogs* and *cats* are both in the barn!

ADULT: Do you see any *animals*? What *animals* do you see?

During this short exchange the adult provided eight models of correct use of the target form. Again, the adult is not directly eliciting utterances from the child, although the context/activity provides ample opportunity for the child to produce plural forms. Focused stimulation has been utilized to address many aspects of language use, including grammar (e.g., Fey, 1986) and vocabulary (e.g., Girolametto, Pearce, & Weitzman, 1996).

Dialogic Reading

One evidence-based intervention for supporting language and literacy skills is dialogic reading (Whitehurst & Lonigan, 1998), which occurs during interactive storybook reading, with adults encouraging children to communicate verbally by asking questions, providing explicit feedback related to questions and comments, and gradually eliciting retells of the story. The assumption is that the feedback and practice will facilitate language development. When learning about dialogic reading, adults are encouraged to remember the PEER strategy (from Zevenbergen & Whitehurst, 2003):

Prompt: Prompt a response by asking a question about the story.
Evaluation: Evaluate the child's response and provide feedback.
Expand: Expand on what the child says.
Repeat: Repeat original prompt, encouraging the child to repeat or expand upon feedback.

Research has shown that dialogic reading can improve the language and literacy skills of young children (Wasik & Bond, 2001; Whitehurst et al., 1988), including those at high risk for reading disabilities (Valdez-Menchaca & Whitehurst, 1992).

Rich, Extended Instruction

Researchers have demonstrated that vocabulary gains in young children can be achieved by providing explicit instruction of word meanings (Beck, Perfetti, & McKeown, 1982; Coyne, McCoach, & Kapp, 2007; McKeown, Beck, Omanson, & Pople, 1985). Beck, McKeown, and Kucan (2002) stated that extended instruction "offers rich information about words and their uses, provides frequent and varied opportunities for students to think about and use words, and enhances students' language comprehension and production" (p. 2). Within this type of vocabulary instruction teachers provide explicit definitions for words that may be seen in storybooks but may be difficult for children to understand without assistance.

The definitions should be provided in child-friendly language; an example would be defining the word *dash* as "to run very fast." In addition to providing explicit instruction of the definitions, interactive opportunities to use the words should be set up in the classroom to extend students' understanding of the meanings of the target vocabulary words. In work by Coyne and colleagues (2007), teachers engaged kindergarten students in a variety of extension activities, such as recognizing examples of target words, answering questions about target words, and formulating sentences using the target words.

Inferential Questioning

Storybooks often contain details that are not explicitly stated, and for this reason it is crucial that children acquire the ability to make inferences from what they hear in text. Evidence suggests that young children need adult scaffolding and explicit instruction to learn to make inferences (Oakhill, Cain, & Bryant, 2003). Questions posed by adults during shared storybook reading provide a natural context in which to address inferencing. However, research has shown that although adults do ask questions during book reading, the majority of questions posed by both parents and teachers are literal in nature (van Kleeck, Gillam, Hamilton, & McGrath, 1997). Storybook reading is an ideal context in which to address objectives related to making inferences. One technique that has been utilized in research studies with young children includes embedding inferential questions during book-reading activities (e.g., van Kleeck, Vander Woude, & Hammett, 2006). Prior to reading aloud with children, teachers can identify locations within a story in which an inferential question should be asked. For example, if a main character in a story becomes angry based on another character's actions, a teacher could stop reading and ask, "Why is the boy mad?" Generating questions and embedding them within a story ahead of time (e.g., writing prompts on sticky notes and putting them in the book) prevent teachers from forgetting to ask such questions.

Self-Questioning Training

Accomplished readers consistently ask themselves questions about what they have read. Self-questioning helps readers make connections between what is read and identify gaps in comprehension. Glaubman, Glaubman, and Ofir (1997) found that kindergarten children were able to enhance their story comprehension when they learned to self-question. After reading aloud to children, teachers can model self-questioning by asking simple questions related to important components in the text. For example, after reading a story aloud, a teacher could ask aloud, "What did the boy do after his mother left?" The teacher could then turn to the portion of the story that answers that question, read it aloud, or show the picture to the students, and say, "Oh, I remember, he started walking to look for help."

Clue Words

The use of clue words can foster children's understanding of both narrative and expository text (e.g., Williams et al., 2005). For example, clue words can be very helpful in relation to expository text. Once young children understand the meaning of the words *same* and *different*, these words can be used in compare–contrast activities after reading expository text. Thus, in a lesson in which children learn about animals, teachers can use these words to help students dictate sentences using these clue words: "Giraffes and koala bears are the *same* because they both eat leaves. Giraffes and koala bears are *different* because giraffes are big and koala bears are small." Clue words such as *before, then*, and *next* are important within a narrative structure and may assist children in keeping track of important story elements.

For example, a teacher could scaffold a child's retelling of a story by prompting, "But what happened *before* the boy was late for school?"

Both the instructional objectives and the empirically validated techniques described in the previous sections can be incorporated into lesson plans to be used in preschool or primary grade classroom. An example of such a lesson plan is included in Figure 9.1.

Conclusions

Oral language abilities contribute greatly to children's social and academic success; therefore, early childhood educators should make a concerted effort to enhance these abilities in early childhood classrooms. In this chapter we have presented objectives and instructional techniques that early childhood educators can implement in a classroom setting. This information should support teachers in their efforts to increase the quantity and quality of language-based instruction, which should improve children's listening and reading comprehension as they move through the primary grades.

Weekly Objectives	Instructional Techniques
• Comprehend and produce grammatical morphemes • Use and respond to a variety of question types • Distinguish shades of meaning • Comprehend and produce questions about causes of events	• Focused stimulation • Dialogic reading • Clue words

Materials Needed

A Pocket for Corduroy by Don Freeman (Viking Press, 1978)

Prereading Activity

Hold the text so all children can see the cover. Remind the children that they read this book with you previously. Ask for volunteers to describe some of the things they recall about this book. **Expand** upon what individual children say by adding grammatical information to their utterances. For instance, if a child says, "She hug the bear," you could say: "That's right, the girl hugged Corduroy at the end of the story." Then say, "What did the girl do at the end of the story?" Encourage students to use correct tense in response. Continue this process as long as children are volunteering information.

During Reading

Stop and ask questions related to target vocabulary words. Prompt children to discuss the difference in meaning between similar words. For example, say, "The book says Corduroy was drowsy. Does drowsy mean the same thing as sleepy? Does it mean the same thing as really tired? Name one time that you have been drowsy." Engage children to discuss that drowsy is similar to sleepy but is not the same as really tired or exhausted.

After Reading

When the text is complete, say, "Now we are going to talk about the important parts in the story. Who can tell me what happened first in the story?" Scaffold the students to retell each part of the story either individually or as a group. Use clue words *before, then*, and *after* to facilitate children's answers and retellings. Provide many opportunities for students to use regular past tense -*ed* (i.e., "Corduroy smelled the soap," "The man washed his clothes").

FIGURE 9.1. Sample lesson for preschool.

References

Adlof, S. M., Catts, H. W., & Lee, J. (2010). Kindergarten predictors of second versus eighth grade reading comprehension impairments. *Journal of Learning Disabilities, 43*, 332–345.

American Psychiatric Association. (1994). *Diagnostic and statistical manual of mental disorders* (4th ed.). Washington, DC: Author.

American Speech–Language–Hearing Association. (2010). Social language use (pragmatics). Rockville, MD: Author. Retrieved August 2, 2010, from *www.asha.org/public/speech/development/pragmatics.htm*.

Beck, I., & McKeown, M. (2007). Increasing young low-income children's oral vocabulary repertoires through rich and focused instruction. *Elementary School Journal, 107*, 251–271.

Beck, I. L., McKeown, M. G., & Kucan, L. (2002). *Bringing words to life: Robust vocabulary instruction*. New York: Guilford Press.

Beck, I. L., Omanson, R. C., & McKeown, M. G. (1982). An instructional redesign of reading lessons: Effects on comprehension. *Reading Research Quarterly, 17*, 462–481.

Beck, I. L., Perfetti, C. A., & McKeown, M. G. (1982). Effects of long-term vocabulary instruction on lexical access and reading comprehension. *Journal of Educational Psychology, 74*, 506–521.

Biemiller, A., & Slonim, N. (2001). Estimating root word vocabulary growth in normative and advantaged populations: Evidence for a common sequence of vocabulary acquisition. *Journal of Educational Psychology, 93*, 498–520.

Bishop, D. V. M., & Adams, C. (1990). A prospective study of the relationship between specific language impairment, phonological disorders and reading retardation. *Journal of Child Psychology and Psychiatry, 31*, 1027–1050.

Bloom, L., & Lahey, M. (1978). *Language development and language disorders*. New York: Wiley.

Bloom, P. (2000). *How children learn the meanings of words*. Cambridge: MIT Press.

Botting, N. (2002). Narrative as a tool for the assessment of linguistic and pragmatic impairments. *Child Language Teaching and Therapy, 18*, 1–21.

Bradshaw, M., Hoffman, P., & Norris, J. (1998). The efficacy of expansions and cloze procedures in the development of interpretations by preschool children exhibiting delayed language development. *Language, Speech, and Hearing Services, 29*, 85–95.

Brown, R. (1973) *A first language: The early stages*. Cambridge, MA: Harvard University Press.

Cain, K., Oakhill, J., & Bryant, P. (2004). Children's reading comprehension ability: Concurrent prediction by working memory, verbal ability, and component skills. *Journal of Educational Psychology, 96*, 31–42.

Calfee, R. C., Lindamood, P., & Lindamood, C. (1973). Acoustic–phonetic skills and reading: Kindergarten through twelfth grade. *Journal of Educational Psychology, 64*, 293–298.

Carnine, D., & Kinder, D. (1985). Teaching low performing students to apply generative and schema strategies to narrative and expository materials. *Remedial and Special Education, 6*, 20–30.

Caswell, L. J., & Duke, N. K. (1998). Non-narrative as a catalyst for literacy development. *Language Arts, 75*, 108–117.

Catts, H., Adlof, S., Hogan, T., & Weismer, S. E. (2005). Are specific language impairment and dyslexia distinct disorders? *Journal of Speech, Language, and Hearing Research, 48*, 1378–1396.

Catts, H. W., Fey, M., Zhang, X., & Tomblin, J. B. (2001). Estimating risk for future reading difficulties in kindergarten children: A research-based model and its clinical implications. *Language, Speech, and Hearing Services in Schools, 32*, 38–50.

Coyne, M. D., McCoach, B., & Kapp, S. (2007). Vocabulary intervention for kindergarten students: Comparing extended instruction to embedded instruction and incidental exposure. *Learning Disability Quarterly, 30*, 74–88.

Dimino, J., Gersten, R., Carnine, D., & Blake, G. (1990). Story grammar: An approach for promoting at-risk secondary students' comprehension of literature. *Elementary School Journal, 91*, 19–32.

Dixon, J. A., & Marchman, V. A. (2007). Grammar and the lexicon: Developmental ordering in language acquisition. *Child Development, 78*, 190–212.

Ellis Weismer, S., & Robertson, S. B. (2006). Focused stimulation approach to language intervention. In R. McCauley & M. Fey (Eds.), *Treatment in language disorders in children: Conventional and controversial approaches* (pp. 175–202). Baltimore: Brookes.

Fey, M. E. (1986). *Language intervention with young children*. San Diego, CA: College-Hill Press.

Fey, M. E., Cleave, P. L., Long, S. H., & Hughes, D. L. (1993). Two approaches to the facilitation of grammar in children with language impairment: An experimental evaluation. *Journal of Speech and Hearing Research, 36*, 141–157.

Fujiki, M., Brinton, B., & Clarke, D. (2002). Emotion regulation in children with specific language impairment. *Language, Speech, and Hearing Services in Schools, 33*, 102–111.

Fujiki, M., Brinton, B., Isaacson, T., & Summers, C. (2001). Social behaviors of children with language impairment on the playground: A pilot study. *Language Speech and Hearing Services in Schools, 32*, 101–113.

Gersten, R., Fuchs, L. S., Williams, J. P., & Baker, S. (2001). Teaching reading comprehension strategies to students with learning disabilities: A review of the research. *Review of Educational Research Summary, 71*, 279–320.

Girolametto, L., Pearce, P. S., & Weitzman, E. (1996). The effects of focused stimulation for promoting vocabulary in young children with delays: A pilot study. *Journal of Children's Communication Development, 17*, 39–49.

Girolametto, L., & Weitzman, E. (2002). Responsiveness of child care providers in interactions with toddlers and preschoolers. *Language, Speech, and Hearing Services in Schools, 33*, 268–281.

Glaubman, R., Glaubman, H., & Ofir, L. (1997). Effects of self-directed learning, story comprehension, and self-questioning in kindergarten. *Journal of Educational Research, 90*, 361–374.

Hadley, P. A., & Rice, M. L. (1991). Conversational responsiveness of speech-impaired and language-impaired preschoolers. *Journal of Speech and Hearing Research, 34*(6), 1308–1317.

Hart, B., & Risley, T. R. (1995). *Meaningful differences in the everyday experiences of young American children*. Baltimore: Brookes.

Huttenlocher, J., Vasilyeva, M., Cymerman, E., & Levine, S. (2002). Language input at home and at school: Relation to syntax. *Cognitive Psychology, 45*, 337–374.

Individuals with Disabilities Education Improvement Act of 2004, Public Law 108-466 (2004).

Justice, L., Meier, J., & Walpole, S. (2005). Learning new words from storybooks: An efficacy study with at-risk kindergartners. *Language, Speech, and Hearing Services in Schools, 36*, 17–32.

Justice, L. M., Bowles, R. P., Pence Turnbull, K. L., & Skibbe, L. E. (2009). School readiness among children with varying histories of language difficulties. *Developmental Psychology, 45*, 460–476.

Kintsch, W., & Kintsch, E. (2005). Comprehension. In S. G. Paris & S. A. Stahl (Eds.), *Current issues in reading comprehension and assessment* (pp. 71–92). Mahwah, NJ: Erlbaum.

Kucan, L., & Beck, I. L. (1997). Thinking aloud and reading comprehension research: Inquiry, instruction, and social interaction. *Review of Educational Research, 67*, 271–299.

Leonard, L. B. (2000). *Children with specific language impairment*. Cambridge, MA: MIT Press.

Mandler, J., & Johnson, N. (1977). Remembrance of things parsed: Story structure and recall. *Cognitive Psychology, 9*, 111–151.

Mashburn, A. J., Pianta, R. C., Hamre, B. K., Down, J. T., Barbarin, O. A., Bryant, D., et al. (2008). Measures of classroom quality in prekindergarten and children's development of academic, language, and social skills. *Child Development, 79*, 732–749.

McKeown, M. G., Beck, I. L., Omanson, R. C., & Pople, M. T. (1985). Some effects of the nature and frequency of vocabulary instruction on the knowledge and use of words. *Reading Research Quarterly, 20*, 522–535.

Muter, V., Hulme, C., Snowling, M., & Stevenson, J. (2004). Phonemes, rimes, vocabulary, and grammatical skills as foundations of early reading development: Evidence from a longitudinal study. *Developmental Psychology, 40*, 665–681.

National Institute of Child Health and Human Development. (2000). *Report of the National Reading Panel: Teaching children to read: An evidence-based assessment of the scientific research literature on reading and its implications for reading instruction* (NIH Publication No. 00-4769). Washington, DC: U.S. Government Printing Office.

NICHD Early Child Care Research Network. (2005). Pathways to reading: The role of oral language in the transition to reading. *Developmental Psychology, 41*, 428–442.

Oakhill, J., Cain, K., & Bryant, P. E. (2003). The dissociation of word reading and text comprehension: Evidence from component skills. *Language and Cognitive Processes, 18*, 443–468.

Pappas, C. C. (1991). Fostering full access to literacy by including information books. *Language Arts, 68*, 449–462.

Pence, K. L., & Justice, L. M. (2007). *Language development from theory to practice.* Columbus, OH: Pearson.

Penno, J. F., Wilkinson, I. A. G., & Moore, D. W. (2002). Vocabulary acquisition from teacher explanation and repeated listening to stories: Do they overcome the Matthew effect? *Journal of Educational Psychology, 94*, 23–33.

Perfetti, C. A. (2007). Reading ability: Lexical quality to comprehension. *Scientific Studies of Reading, 11*, 357–383.

Perfetti, C. A., Landi, N., & Oakhill, J. (2005). The acquisition of reading comprehension skill. In M. J. Snowling & C. Hulme (Eds.), *The science of reading: A handbook* (pp. 227–247). Malden, MA: Blackwell.

Pressley, M., & Afflerbach, P. (1995). *Verbal protocols of reading: The nature of constructively responsive reading.* Hillsdale, NJ: Erlbaum.

Rice, M. L., Warren, S. E., & Betz, S. K. (2005). Language symptoms of developmental language disorders: An overview of autism, Down syndrome, fragile X, specific language impairment, and Williams syndrome. *Applied Psycholinguistics, 26*, 7–28.

Roberts, J., Price, J., & Malkin, C. (2007). Language and communication development in Down syndrome. *Mental Retardation and Development Disabilities Research Reviews, 13*, 26–35.

Scarborough, H. S. (1990). Very early language deficits in dyslexic children. *Child Development, 61*, 1728–1743.

Stanovich, K. E. (1986). Matthew effects in reading: Some consequences of individual differences in the acquisition of literacy. *Reading Research Quarterly, 21*, 360–406.

Stanovich, K. E., Cunningham, A. E., & Freeman, D. J. (1984). Intelligence, cognitive skills, and early reading progress. *Reading Research Quarterly, 19*, 120–139.

Stein, N., & Glenn, C. (1979). An analysis of story comprehension in elementary school children. In R. D. Freedle (Ed.), *Advances in discourse processes: Vol. 2. New directions in discourse processing* (pp. 53–119). Norwood, NJ: Ablex.

Stein, J., & Trabasso, T. (1982). What's in a story: An approach to comprehension and instruction. In R. Glaser (Ed.), *Advances in the psychology of instruction* (Vol. 2, pp. 213–267). Hillsdale, NJ: Erlbaum.

Tomblin, J. B., Records, N. L., Buckwalter, P., Zhang, X., Smith, E., & O'Brien, M. (1997). Prevalence of specific language impairment in kindergarten children. *Journal of Speech and Hearing Research, 40*, 1245–1260.

Torgesen, J., Wagner, R., & Rashotte, C. (1994). Longitudinal studies of phonological processing and reading. *Journal of Learning Disabilities, 27*, 276–286.

Valdez-Menchaca, M. C., & Whitehurst, G. J. (1992). Accelerating language development through picture book reading: A systematic extension to Mexican day care. *Developmental Psychology, 28*(6), 1106–1114.

van den Broek, P., Kendeou, P., Kremer, K., Lynch, J., Butler, J., White, M. J., et al. (2005). Assessment of comprehension abilities in young children. In S. G. Paris & S. A. Stahl (Eds.), *Children's reading comprehension and assessment* (pp. 107–130). Mahwah, NJ: Erlbaum.

van Kleeck, A. (2006). Fostering inferential language during book sharing with preschoolers: A foundation for later text comprehension strategies. In A. van Kleeck (Ed.), *Sharing books and stories to promote language and literacy* (pp. 269–318). San Diego, CA: Plural.

van Kleeck, A., Gillam, R., Hamilton, L., & McGrath, C. (1997). The relationship between middle-class parents' book sharing discussion and their preschoolers' abstract language development. *Journal of Speech, Language, and Hearing Research, 40*, 1261–1271.

van Kleeck, A., Vander Woude, J., & Hammett, L. (2006). Fostering literal and inferential language skills in head start preschoolers with language impairment using scripted book sharing discussions. *American Journal of Speech–Language Pathology, 15*, 1–11.

Wasik, B. A., & Bond, M. A. (2001). Beyond the pages of a book: Interactive book reading and language development in preschool classrooms. *Journal of Educational Psychology, 93*, 243–250.

Watkins, R., & Rice, M. L. (1994). *Specific language impairments in children*. Baltimore: Brookes.

Whitehurst, G. J., Falco, F. L., Lonigan, C. J., Fischel, J. E., DeBaryshe, B. D., Valdez-Menchaca, M. C., et al. (1988). Accelerating language development through picture book reading. *Developmental Psychology, 24*, 552–559.

Whitehurst, G. J., & Lonigan, C. J. (1998). Child development and emergent literacy. *Child Development, 69*, 848–872.

Williams, J. P. (2005). Instruction in reading comprehension for primary-grade students: A focus on text structure. *Journal of Special Education, 39*, 6–18.

Williams, J. P., Hall, K. M., Lauer, K. D., Stafford, K., Desisto, L., & deCani, J. (2005). Expository text comprehension in the primary grade classroom. *Journal of Educational Psychology, 97*, 538–550.

Williams, J. P., Stafford, K. B., Lauer, K. D., Hall, K. M., & Pollini, S. (2009). Embedding reading comprehension training in content-area instruction. *Journal of Educational Psychology, 101*, 1–20.

Zevenbergen, A., & Whitehurst, G. (2003). Dialogic reading: A shared picture book reading intervention for preschoolers. In A. van Kleeck, S. A. Stahl, & E. Bauer (Eds.), *On reading to children: Parents and teachers* (pp. 177–200). Mahwah, NJ: Erlbaum.

CHAPTER 10

Promoting Early Literacy and Language Development

Douglas R. Powell and Karen E. Diamond

The search for instructional practices and curricula that improve children's school readiness is at an all-time high as policymakers and educators bolster efforts to eliminate persistent achievement gaps in U.S. schools. Early literacy and language skills occupy a prominent spot in these efforts because they are strongly predictive of later abilities in reading and writing. Fortunately, there is a growing evidence base to inform instructional decisions about how to promote early childhood precursors to conventional literacy.

Scientific understandings of early literacy and language development have undergone numerous refinements since the concept of "emergent literacy" was introduced several decades ago to characterize literacy acquisition as a developmental process that starts well before formal instruction in reading (Teale & Sulzby, 1986). Currently there is recognition of the multidimensionality of both early literacy skills and early literacy instruction (Connor, Morrison, & Slominski, 2006) as investigators continue to identify distinct components of early literacy (e.g., Lonigan et al., 2009) and differences within and between teachers in the extent to which various types of literacy instruction are implemented (Powell, Diamond, Bojczyk, & Gerde, 2008). Research has led to attenuation of the long-standing idea that children's exploration of a literacy-rich environment is sufficient support for developing early literacy skills. Prominent guidelines on early literacy and language instruction now recommend explicit and intentional instruction as an essential complement to implicit approaches to promoting early literacy and language (Copple & Bredekamp, 2009).

This chapter reviews current research evidence on instructional practices and curricula designed to promote early literacy and language development. We focus chiefly on prekindergarten and kindergarten classrooms, while also acknowledging the importance of family practices that are linked to children's literacy and language outcomes. The chapter was prepared with keen interest in children at risk of reading difficulties due to family socioeconomic status or developmental disabilities. At the same time, the review includes many studies conducted with children from middle-class families and with children without disabilities.

We assume many readers are interested in the translation of research findings into practices and policies that improve school readiness and general well-being of young children. To facilitate the use of research findings in program improvement initiatives, we include brief descriptions of instructional practices and curricula highlighted in this chapter. Understandably, most curriculum titles provide a vague notion of content or pedagogy. The same instructional term can represent different types of practice. For example, the "shared book reading" label may mean the use of open questions, prompts, comments, and other forms of adult encouragement for children to be actively involved during a book reading (Mol, Bus, & de Jong, 2009). It also can be defined more broadly as an intervention that increases the frequency or style of reading activities with children by teachers, parents, or computer software (National Early Literacy Panel, 2008). Furthermore, shared book reading—typically associated with oral language outcomes—may be used to improve children's word awareness, segmentation, and print concepts by focusing on attributes of print during the book reading (Justice & Ezell, 2002).

Code-Related and Oral Language Skills

Our survey of instructional practices and curricula associated with early literacy and language skills is organized into children's code-related and oral language skills. These two broad domains increasingly are used to categorize early literacy and language outcomes. Instructional practices also may be sorted into code-focused and meaning-focused (largely oral language) domains (Connor et al., 2006). Our decision to emphasize children's skills as the organizing framework for this chapter reflects a practical consideration that some broadly defined instructional practices (e.g., shared book reading) can be employed to improve code-related and/or oral language skills, as described later in this chapter. We also subscribe to the perspective that an instructional practice is more effective when teachers have a clear eye on the child skill targeted by the practice (Epstein, 2007).

Code-related skills enable children to translate the alphabetic system (visual codes) into meaningful language. Central to this process is the task of decoding letters into corresponding sounds, then linking the sounds to single words (Whitehurst & Lonigan, 1998). We give attention to the following code-related skills: identifying letter names and letter sounds, phonological awareness, and writing. Oral language skills facilitate children's understanding of words and passages. Receptive and expressive language skills are central to this process. We review strategies for promoting the following oral language skills: vocabulary knowledge, syntactic skills, and comprehension. In addition to content distinctions, the skills differ in the scope of knowledge that children need to learn for mastery. Knowledge of the English alphabet (26 letters) is considerably smaller in scope and can be acquired in a relatively shorter period of time than vocabulary knowledge, for example (Paris & Paris, 2006).

Code-related and oral language skill sets contribute to the development of reading competence in unique ways at different points from preschool through elementary school (Storch & Whitehurst, 2002). The relation between code-related and oral language skills is especially strong in the preschool years (Storch & Whitehurst, 2002), and there is some evidence that phonological awareness is partly a product of vocabulary growth (Lonigan, 2007). However, investigators differ in their views of the relative importance of code-related and oral language skills, and whether oral language has an indirect or direct relation to later reading ability. The National Early Literacy Panel's (2008) meta-analysis aimed at identifying precursors of later literacy achievement found that a number of code-related skills (e.g., alphabet knowledge, phonological awareness, writing) had medium to large predictive relations with later literacy skills, whereas oral language skills, among others, were moderately correlated with later literacy achievement (decoding, reading comprehension, spelling). These findings prompted the publication of an alternative perspective on the centrality of language skills to reading achievement (Dickinson, Golinkoff, & Hirsh-Pasek, 2010) and a National Early Literacy Panel rebuttal (Lonigan & Shanahan, 2010).

In preparing this chapter, adherence to page limitations in the context of a robust literature that is spread across a wide range of journals in several well-established disciplines led to representative rather than inclusive use of research on code-related and oral language skills. We selected emergent literacy skills predictive of later reading competence that studies suggest are promoted with generally low levels of frequency or quality in early childhood classrooms (e.g., Justice, Mashburn, Hamre, & Pianta, 2008) and for which empirical evidence connects use of an instructional practice or curriculum to improvements in the skill.

Scope of the Evidence Base

Most of the studies that inform the content of this chapter employed experimental or quasi-experimental designs to determine the impact of an instructional practice(s) or curriculum on children's literacy outcomes. Fortunately, the past two decades have seen a substantial increase in the use of experiments involving real classrooms to identify effective approaches to improving children's early school outcomes. There has been a concomitant increase in attention to the methodological quality of education research (Mosteller & Boruch, 2002) such as the use of rigorous scientific standards for determining the inclusion of intervention studies in the What Works Clearinghouse sponsored by the U.S. Department of Education's Institute of Education Sciences (*ies.ed/ncee/wwc*). Nearly all of the studies included in this chapter were published in refereed scholarly outlets, although only one of the five meta-analyses we cite (National Early Literacy Panel, 2008) limited its review to published studies.

Results of intervention studies differ in the amount of specificity about practices that promote early literacy and language outcomes. Some studies systematically vary a discrete instructional practice (e.g., asking children to label a picture; Sénéchal, Thomas, & Monker, 1995), whereas other investigations compare a combination of instructional practices and conditions, such as group size to a business-as-usual approach (e.g., dialogic reading; Lonigan, Anthony, Bloomfield, Dyer, & Samwel, 1999). The latter type of investigation, including curriculum outcome research, yields beneficial information on effects of a package of intervention features but leaves unanswered the question of which feature(s) is the most influential or active ingredient. Adoption of an intervention that comprises a combination of strategies requires implementation of all features with a high degree of fidelity if the goal is to approximate results achieved in an outcome study of the intervention.

In addition to intervention studies, there is an informative line of correlational research on naturally occurring practices at home and school in relation to children's short-term (e.g., Connor et al., 2006) and long-term (e.g., Dickinson & Porche, 2011; Weizman & Snow, 2001) literacy and language outcomes. Studies that identify potentially modifiable correlates of a child skill are especially valuable in informing the design of subsequent intervention studies aimed at determining the causal role of specific practices. Research on naturally occurring practices also can inform the interpretation of results of intervention studies.

Calls for new and improved measures of literacy and language outcomes are prevalent in the scholarly literature (National Institute of Child Health and Human Development [NICHD], 2000). While there is some recent progress toward this end, considerable work remains to be done. Measures of vocabulary development are a case in point. Recent meta-analyses indicate that investigator-developed measures of vocabulary skill typically yield stronger intervention effects than standardized measures of vocabulary (Elleman, Lindo,

Morphy, & Compton, 2009; Marulis & Neuman, 2010; Mol et al., 2009), presumably because measures developed by intervention researchers are more sensitive than standardized measures to the vocabulary skills targeted in their respective interventions. A problem is the reliability and validity of new measures developed in the context of a specific intervention, and constraints on comparing outcomes across vocabulary interventions that employ customized measures. Elleman and colleagues (2009) note that nearly two-thirds of the studies included in their meta-analysis did not report any reliability information on investigator-developed measures.

Caveat Lector: *Some Nuances in Existing Findings*

Although major advances have occurred in the quantity and quality of research on how to promote early literacy and language outcomes, some nuances in the characteristics and findings of the extant research literature have implications for the adoption of practices or curricula found to be effective in outcome studies. The issues transcend the obvious limitation of generalizing the findings from a middle-class sample to a low-income population or incorporating into a whole-group format an instructional practice found to be effective in a one-to-one configuration.

First, we know considerably more about effective approaches to improving code-related outcomes than oral language outcomes. This is partly a function of the amount of research on interventions that target code-related versus oral language skills. For example, the National Early Literacy Panel (2008) identified 78 code-focused intervention studies but only 19 shared reading interventions, mostly focused on oral language outcomes for meta-analyses of instructional practices that enhance early literacy skills. What is more, there are speculative suggestions in the literature that it is challenging to help teachers improve their support of children's oral language skills because high-quality language instruction requires responsive linguistic input to children that cannot be readily included in a scripted curriculum or protocol (Justice, Mashburn, Hamre, et al., 2008) and cuts across a range of settings and times during the school day (Justice, Mashburn, Pence, & Wiggins, 2008). Consistent with this idea, some random assignment studies of intensive professional development interventions that targeted children's code-related and oral language skills have found effects on children's code-related skills but not language outcomes (Landry, Anthony, Swank, & Monseque-Bailey, 2009; Powell, Diamond, Burchinal, & Koehler, 2010).

A second, related nuance pertains to whether conditions that presumably contributed to positive intervention effects on children can be taken to scale. For example, in many early literacy and language intervention studies, the interventions are carried out by investigators or their closely supervised designees (e.g., graduate students). Can the teaching staff adopt the intervention's practices with the same level of effectiveness? Some indirect evidence on this question is available in meta-analyses results indicating that interventions implemented by researchers with children in laboratories or as special visitors in early childhood classrooms are significantly more effective than interventions implemented by teachers or child care staff (Marulis & Neuman, 2010; Mol et al., 2010). The quality of implementation of effective literacy and language instruction by a teaching staff can be highly variable and related to the magnitude of instructional effects on children (e.g., Hamre et al., 2010).

Third, consumers of intervention research findings need to be mindful of the contribution of child characteristics to intervention outcomes. Possible differential effects of instruction are most commonly examined in relation to children's initial ability level in the targeted skill area. A common finding in vocabulary acquisition studies, for example, is that children with weaker initial vocabulary knowledge gain significantly less from vocabulary instruction than children with stronger vocabulary knowledge (Marulis & Neuman, 2010). Still, there is scant experimental evidence on what types of instructional strategies are most help-ful to specific types of children. Fortunately, there is a fledgling line of research on effects of different literacy instruction approaches with English language learners (e.g., Farver, Lonigan, & Eppe, 2009; Silverman & Hines, 2009), and an emerging research literature on innovations in individualized instruction (Connor, Morrison, Fishman, Schatschneider, & Underwood, 2007) and progress monitoring (Landry et al., 2009).

Fourth, what we know about intervention effects is limited in part by the scope of variables assessed in an outcome study (Schickedanz & McGee, 2010). Not surprisingly, investigators usually give measurement priority to outcomes targeted by an intervention. Consequently, little is known about unintended effects on literacy or language skills not included in an intervention's theory of change. Yet information about intervention effects on both intended and unintended outcomes might broaden our understanding of an inter-vention's ripple effects. For example, in a randomized trial, Wasik, Bond, and Hindman (2006) found that an oral language intervention had strong, positive effects on children's oral language skills, all targeted by the intervention. Interestingly, the researchers also found that children in the control group gained more than the children in the intervention group in alphabet knowledge, a skill that was not targeted by the intervention. This type of find-ing raises practical questions—for which the field has scant empirical information—about trade-offs made in classrooms that implement well-defined interventions that focus on a few specific outcomes but do not explicitly address skills in other domains.

Code-Related Skills

Decoding skills help children to "crack" the alphabetic code in order to read combina-tions of letters (National Early Literacy Panel, 2008). A child who has developed decoding skills necessary for skilled reading is able to "read" letter combinations independent of their meaning (e.g., nonsense words). Decoding skills address auditory (phonological, phonemic) and written (orthographic) aspects of language and include phonological awareness, knowl-edge of letter names and letter sounds, and writing. Phonological and orthographic skills in preschool and kindergarten, along with an understanding of print conventions and book concepts (e.g., that we read from left to right in English, and that words rather than pictures tell a story), are related to children's performance on reading, spelling, and decoding tasks in early elementary grades (Ehri & Roberts, 2006). Although these skills are often discussed as though they are independent, and are discussed separately in this chapter, there is evidence for reciprocal relations among letter-name knowledge, letter-sound knowledge, and phono-logical awareness (Lonigan et al., 2009; Piasta & Wagner, 2010b).

Opportunities to engage in frequent naturalistic and meaningful interactions with literacy-related artifacts enhance children's literacy knowledge in an implicit manner and are an important component of best practices in early childhood classrooms (Justice, Chow, Capellini, Flanigan, & Colton, 2003). Yet such an implicit approach to helping children acquire decoding skills is insufficient for children who are at risk because they live in poverty, have an identified disability, or are learning English (Hair, Halle, Terry-Humen, Lavelle, & Calkins, 2006). More explicit approaches to teaching young children decoding skills include defining the concept or skill that is being taught (e.g., blending words, syllables, or sounds), demonstrating or modeling the skill, and providing multiple and repeated opportunities for children to engage in guided and then independent practice (Phillips, Clancy-Menchetti, & Lonigan, 2008). Explicit, intentional teaching requires planning and direct teacher guid-ance, along with instructional activities that are sequential and build on existing skills (Epstein, 2007). Children are likely to learn more when they are attentive (Yeh, 2003) and interested in the activity (Justice et al., 2003), and teaching of important decoding skills is likely to be most effective when skills are taught within meaningful and engaging activities (Phillips et al., 2008). There is evidence that explicit teaching of decoding skills with small groups of children results in more learning than does teaching with large groups (National Early Literacy Panel, 2008). As well, instruction is more effective in promoting learning when it is individualized and responsive to what children have already learned (Landry et al., 2009; Schuele et al., 2010).

As we noted earlier, decoding skills require an understanding of both auditory (phonological, phonemic) and written (orthographic) aspects of language and include knowledge of letter names and letter sounds, phonological awareness, and writing. Given the importance of decoding skills for learning to read (National Early Literacy Panel, 2008) and substantial disparities among preschool and kindergarten children in decoding and early reading skills (Denton Flanagan, & McPhee, 2009), what do we know about intervention content and instructional strategies that promote children's competence on decoding tasks? In the next section, we focus on interventions to promote young children's understanding of letter names and letter sounds, phonological awareness, and writing. Most of these approaches have been implemented with small groups of young children as pull-out instruction by researchers, perhaps because teacher-planned and -implemented small-group instruction occurs infrequently in early childhood classrooms in the United States (Pianta et al., 2005).

Letter Names and Letter Sounds

Young children's letter-name and letter-sound knowledge is one of the best predictors of early reading competence (National Early Literacy Panel, 2008). Teaching children letter names is a Congressionally mandated requirement for Head Start programs serving at-risk low-income children (U.S. Department of Health and Human Services, 2003). There has been debate about the value of teaching either letter names or letter sounds alone, compared to an approach in which letter names and sounds are taught together (Ellefson, Treiman, & Kessler, 2009), but current evidence points to the value of teaching letter names and sounds together (Piasta & Wagner, 2010a, 2010b).

In English, most letter names include the phoneme that the letter represents (Treiman & Kessler, 2003), and both typically developing children and children with speech-sound disorders and language impairments use their knowledge of letter names to learn the corresponding letter sound (Ellefson et al., 2009). There are significant correlations between young children's knowledge of letter names and their corresponding letter sounds, with evidence that the probability of knowing letter sounds increases substantially when children know letter names (Kim, Petscher, Foorman, & Chengfu, 2010). Share (2004) provided evidence from an experiment that knowledge of letter names had a significant, causal impact on kindergarten children's letter-sound learning.

Piasta and Wagner (2010b) examined the effects of three different instructional approaches (instruction in letter names and sounds, letter sounds only, or a control condition in which children were taught about numbers) on preschool children's letter name and letter sound learning. The eligibility criterion for participation was that the child produced fewer than 8 letter names on an uppercase letter name production task. An eight-week curriculum consisting of 34 10- to 15-minute lessons, delivered as a pull-out program to small groups of 3 to 5 children, was implemented in four private child care centers by a researcher and research assistants. Results revealed that children receiving the combined letter name–sound instruction showed accelerated learning of sounds of consonant–vowel (CV) and vowel–consonant (VC) letters when compared with children in either the letter name only or control group. In addition, children in the letter–sound instructional group learned the sounds of CV and VC letters to a greater extent than letters in which the name did not include the sound. These results are consistent with a "causal interpretation of the letter name-to-sound facilitation effect" (p. 337) and suggest that effective instruction includes teaching both letter names and sounds simultaneously. Piasta and Wagner note that instruction in letter names and sounds increased children's knowledge of letter sounds independently of their other phonological processing abilities (blending and elision); children who did not receive letter-sound instruction were unlikely to learn letter sounds if other phonological processing abilities were low.

Phonological Awareness

Phonological skills require a child to attend to, remember, and manipulate elements of spoken language across different sizes of sound pieces, ranging from words in sentences to phonemes in words (Phillips et al., 2008). There is evidence for a developmental continuum of phonological awareness over the preschool and early elementary years, beginning with children's awareness of larger units of sound (sentences are made of words) and continuing through awareness of syllables, initial sounds, and then phonemes (Phillips et al., 2008). Phonological processing, at least for preschool children, includes a substantial memory component (Lonigan et al., 2009), and although phonological awareness is an auditory skill, visual representations can be helpful in supporting children's early phonological competence. Phonological awareness is substantially related to children's decoding, reading, and spelling competence in early elementary grades (Ehri & Roberts, 2006) and is a skill that can be taught successfully to preschool and kindergarten children (National Early Literacy Panel, 2008). Phillips and her colleagues (2008) argue that key elements in promoting phonological awareness, particularly for children who are at risk and children with identified disabilities, include (1) individualized small-group instruction that (2) provides explicit attention to key phonological skills, along with (3) opportunities for children to practice new skills with (4) graduated support from their teachers.

Results of intervention studies suggest that explicit instruction in phonological awareness skills results in significant gains in children's learning. Justice and colleagues (2003) used an alternating treatments design to evaluate the effectiveness of an intervention that included phonological awareness games, and alphabet and writing activities with low-income preschool children, many of whom had identified oral language impairments. The intervention was implemented in small groups of six children for 30 minutes, twice each week for 6 weeks. The intervention was explicit and designed to promote children's attention to features of written and oral language. The comparison condition included shared storybook reading and retelling. Results revealed that children's scores increased significantly on measures of phonological awareness and alphabet knowledge when they participated in the intervention. Byrne and Fielding-Barnsley (1991, 2000) examined the effects of a 12-week focused intervention (Sound Foundations) in which preschoolers were taught a subset of English phonemes in small groups of four to six children. There were significant effects of the intervention on children's sensitivity to both trained and untrained phonemes when compared to a control group. Differences in children's nonword and irregular word reading continued to be apparent 3–6 years later. Similarly, O'Connor, Jenkins, Leicester, and Slocum (1993) found significant effects of small-group instruction in rhyming, blending, and segmenting for learning of these phonological skills in a random assignment intervention with preschool children with significant learning and developmental delays. Individual differences in children's initial skill levels were unique predictors of children's learning in each of these studies.

Vadasy and her colleagues examined the effectiveness of an 18-week intervention focused on phonics (including letter–sound correspondence, segmenting, phoneme blending, and alphabet naming) and assisted oral reading practice with kindergarten children who had identified delays in early reading performance. Participating children were selected using a two-step screening process that included teacher nomination and assessments of performance using Dynamic Indicators of Basic Early Literacy Skills (DIBELS) subtests. Quasi-random assignment was used within classrooms to assign children to a supplemental reading intervention or business-as-usual classroom reading instruction (including Title I and special education). The intervention included 70 scripted lessons implemented 4 days/week for 30 minutes each day by trained paraeducators. Intervention sessions were implemented with individual children (Vadasy, Sanders, & Peyton, 2006) or in dyads (Vadasy & Sanders, 2008) in a small area away from the classroom. Results revealed that tutored students outperformed nontutored students on measures of phonological awareness, oral reading fluency, spelling, word reading, and reading comprehension, with no significant differences in outcomes between children receiving tutoring in dyads or individually. A follow-up of students in the first study (Vadasy et al., 2006) revealed that students in the intervention group continued to make substantially greater growth than control group children on most measures when tested 1 year later (at the end of first grade; Vadasy & Sanders, 2008).

There is evidence of substantial, concurrent associations among young children's performance on letter name, letter sound, and phonological awareness skills (Lonigan et al., 2009). Integrating orthographic features of written language (e.g., letters) and phonological features of oral language in the context of early literacy instruction is important in both preschool (Justice et al., 2003) and early elementary (Ehri, 2004) settings. In a study that examined existing kindergarten literacy instruction using districtwide curricula, Foorman and colleagues (2003) reported that teachers' implementation of alphabetic instruction in conjunction with phonemic awareness activities was more effective than alphabetic instruction alone in promoting children's early reading competence. Preschool children participating in phonological awareness instruction coupled with instruction in letters also demonstrated greater gains on measures of print knowledge, phonological processing, and early reading when compared to a control group of children who received unrelated training (Gettinger, 1986).

Piasta and Wagner (2010a) analyzed results from 63 different studies that examined the effects of alphabet training with preschool and early elementary age children. Of those studies in their meta-analysis, most had multiple intervention components; phonological awareness in conjunction with alphabet training was most common (44 studies). Outcomes of interest included children's letter-name and letter-sound knowledge, letter-name and letter-sound fluency, and letter writing. Analyses revealed that instruction had a substantial effect on every outcome except for letter-name fluency. Larger effects were noted when alphabet and phonological awareness instruction were combined, although most effect sizes were small to moderate. Studies in which only letter-name instruction was provided showed reliable positive impacts on children's letter-sound knowledge, lending support to the argument that knowing letter names facilitates knowledge of letter sounds (see also Piasta & Wagner, 2010b). Effect sizes were not larger for interventions implemented with children at risk for reading problems, suggesting that "more intensive, explicit alphabet instruction may be needed to close the gap" (Piasta & Wagner, 2010a, p. 23) between lower-performing students and their peers. Moderator analyses revealed that while parent and home-based interventions were relatively ineffective, there were no differences in the effectiveness of interventions implemented by teachers in classrooms compared to those implemented by researchers.

As these investigators note, this is an important finding, suggesting that effective alphabet and phonological awareness interventions can be implemented by teachers in the ecologically valid context of the classroom setting. Understanding the "training and support [that teachers need] to secure these effects" (p. 23) remains an important research goal.

There are a number of commercially available curricula that focus on promoting young children's phonological awareness and knowledge of letters. Many are designed as "add-ons" to a broader developmental curriculum, with implementation of curriculum activities by teachers (e.g., Let's Begin With the Letter People®) or through computer-assisted instruction (e.g., Daisy Quest®, Waterford Early Reading®). Readily accessible, peer-reviewed published evaluations of these three curricula reveal inconsistent effects for children's learning outcomes.

Let's Begin With the Letter People consists of 26 units promoting children's understanding of letters and sounds, including attention to rhyming, alliteration, and segmentation. The curriculum includes instructional activities implemented in large-group (e.g., opening circle), interest-area, and small-group activities. Results of a random assignment study revealed no discernible effects of this curriculum on children's early reading, letter knowledge, or phonological awareness skills (Preschool Curriculum Evaluation Research Consortium [PCER], 2008). More recently, Fischel and her colleagues (2007), in a random assignment study, examined the effectiveness of Letter People in comparison to the business-as-usual classroom curriculum (High Scope) for promoting low-income preschool children's letter-name and letter-sound knowledge and phonological awareness. Results revealed few effects of Letter People for children's letter knowledge or phonological awareness in classrooms in which teachers were implementing the curriculum in the first year. There was some evidence for effects of Letter People on standardized measures of letter knowledge, dictation, and book conventions when analyses included data from children in classrooms in which teachers were implementing the curriculum for a second or third year (Fischel et al., 2007). It is difficult to interpret these differential effects because no data on the quality of teachers' implementation were provided.

Daisy Quest and Waterford Early Reading are both designed to promote children's phonological awareness through the use of individualized computer-assisted instruction. Daisy Quest promotes children's awareness of rhyme; initial, middle, and final sounds; and blending. Designed for use in early elementary grades, it has been used and evaluated in child care programs (Foster, Erickson, Foster, Brinkman, & Torgesen, 1994) and with preschool children who are at risk (Lonigan et al., 2003). Because the software is self-contained and tracks children's learning, it does not require teachers' active participation (other than to send children to use the computer). Results of random assignment studies with elementary children who are below average readers (Mitchell & Fox, 2001) and children in child care centers (Foster et al., 1994) revealed significant effects of Daisy Quest on measures of phonological awareness, when compared to business-as-usual reading or literacy instruction. Although not a randomized trial study, Lonigan and his colleagues (2003) provide evidence for the utility of Daisy Quest in promoting at-risk children's development of phonological awareness. In these studies, it is unclear the extent to which Daisy Quest provided children with additional instructional time and practice opportunities, a factor that might account for some of these intervention effects.

Waterford Early Reading is a computer-based intervention that focuses on print concepts, letter knowledge, and phonological awareness. There is a well-defined scope and sequence, and children are to participate in the program on a regular basis. Designed for kindergarten and first-grade classrooms, at least one study has evaluated its effectiveness for promoting learning among preschool children. Paterson, Henry, O'Quin, Ceprano, and Blue (2003) evaluated the effectiveness of Waterford Early Reading in a random assignment study with low-income, at-risk elementary-age children in an urban school district. Children participated in the program 15 minutes each day. Results revealed no significant impact of Waterford Early Reading compared with typical classroom instruction for any of the dependent variables associated with reading achievement. Similar evidence for few effects of Waterford Early Reading are reported by Fischel and colleagues (2007) in a study with at-risk preschool children, and by Llosa and Slayton (2009) in a study that included kindergarten children learning English. Importantly, Paterson and her colleagues (2003) found that teachers' instructional behaviors, including effective use of instructional time, learning activities that promoted high levels of student engagement, and opportunities for student practice, were critical for promoting student learning, independent of their use of Waterford.

Writing

Writing, including writing one's own name, has been identified as an important component of children's early literacy skills by the National Early Literacy Panel (2008). Children's writing competence has been linked to important decoding skills, particularly knowledge of letters (Diamond, Gerde, & Powell, 2008), letter-sound knowledge (Rieben, Ntamakiliro, Gonthier, & Fayol, 2005), and print conventions (Ukrainetz, Cooney, Dyer, Kysar, & Harris, 2000). Writing, including preschool children's ability to write both dictated letters and their own names, has been linked to conventional literacy outcomes in decoding, reading comprehension, and spelling (National Early Literacy Panel, 2008).

What is it that makes writing an important component in a child's development of literacy-related skills? Young children enjoy writing, and it is often a part of both teacher-planned and child-initiated activities in preschool (Neuman & Roskos, 1997). Writing integrates auditory (e.g., initial and final sound awareness) and orthographic (e.g., knowledge of letters and print conventions) skills critical for "cracking" the alphabetic code. Both name and letter writing provide an opportunity for children to make connections between orthographic and phonological representations of language (Diamond et al., 2008). Diamond and her colleagues found that as children became more sophisticated in writing their first names, their knowledge of letters also increased. In a recent study with Dutch children, Both-de Vries and Bus (2010) found that children's name writing was associated with their ability to spell phonetically simple words beginning with the first letter in their name. Writing reinforces children's understanding of procedures related to early reading, for example, that writing in English proceeds from left to right (Ukrainetz et al., 2000).

Little research has focused on the effectiveness of writing interventions with young children, and writing is only occasionally included as a dependent variable in phonological awareness interventions (National Early Literacy Panel, 2008). Rieben and his colleagues (2005) implemented a random assignment study designed to evaluate the effectiveness of three different teaching activities related to writing: children's letter knowledge, phoneme awareness, and word reading and word spelling. Children were 5-year-olds from Switzerland; all spoke French, and all were nonreaders. They were randomly assigned to one of three intervention groups (invented spelling, copied spelling, and invented spelling with individualized feedback on correct orthography) or to a drawing control group. Children participated in the intervention during school hours in small groups of three or four for approximately 6 hours total over a period of 6 months. The intervention was implemented by an experimenter in a small room away from the classroom. Using a pre- to posttest design, outcomes were assessed using multiple measures of orthographic (letter knowledge, spelling) and phonological (phoneme awareness, word reading) skills. Results revealed significant effects of the invented spelling plus feedback intervention on tasks assessing orthographic skills but not phonological skills (see also Ehri & Wilce, 1987). There was no evidence that either of the other interventions (invented spelling without feedback, copying words) were effective in enhancing children's phonological or orthographic skills. Rieben and his colleagues speculated that because feedback was designed to call attention to orthographic features (and correct spellings) rather than phonological features of words, the intervention had little impact on children's phonological skills. They speculate that feedback on phonological aspects of writing (e.g., linking written letters and their sounds) may be more effective for promoting children's phonological awareness. This study is important because the results suggest that classroom activities promoting preschool children's writing may be especially effective when teachers call children's attention to the letters they have written and link letter names with letter sounds when providing feedback. Thus, planned writing activities (e.g., signing up for center activities, labeling drawings, or writing in journals) may be most effective when adults monitor and provide feedback on the letters that children have written and the sounds those letters make.

Oral Language Skills

Although we examine vocabulary, syntax, and comprehension separately, there are some interdependencies among these oral language skills. Vocabulary knowledge impacts comprehension skills (Elleman et al., 2009) and, as noted by the National Early Literacy Panel (NELP; 2008), a child with strong grammatical knowledge but limited vocabulary would find it difficult to understand a text or produce meaningful narrative. Vocabulary skills have been targeted more frequently than other oral language skills in intervention studies, but the merits of a focus on vocabulary alone are now in question. Recent results indicate that broad-based oral language skills (NICHD Early Child Care Research Network, 2005) and more complex oral language skills such as grammar, the ability to define words, and listening comprehension skills (NELP, 2008) are stronger predictors of reading abilities than simple measures of receptive vocabulary.

Shared book-reading interventions are commonly employed to improve children's oral language outcomes. Book reading is particularly conducive to learning new words because the book narrative provides an immediate context for defining words and mapping novel words to shared referents. Recent meta-analyses have found significant moderate effects of book-reading interventions on children's oral language outcomes (Mol et al., 2009; NELP, 2008). The NELP (2008) meta-analysis did not find statistically significant differential effects of shared book-reading interventions on measures of simple vocabulary compared to composite measures of oral language.

Vocabulary Skills

The breadth and depth of young children's understanding of word meanings are strong predictors of subsequent reading skill. Vocabulary size in kindergarten predicts reading comprehension in middle school (Scarborough, 2001), and vocabulary knowledge at the end of first grade predicts reading comprehension 10 years later (Cunningham & Stanovich, 1997). Striking differences between young children's vocabulary knowledge are consistently linked to family socioeconomic status (e.g., Hart & Risley, 1995). Researchers often use the term "Matthew effect" (Stanovich, 1986), inspired by a biblical "the rich get richer" theme, to depict the idea that a broader and deeper understanding of words facilitates the ease of learning new words. Earlier in this chapter, we noted evidence that vocabulary interventions are less effective for children with weak initial vocabulary knowledge (Marulis &

Neuman, 2010). Deeper understanding of vocabulary entails a decontextualized knowledge of a word's meaning, including its relation to other words and appropriate use in novel contexts (Beck & McKeown, 2007).

What instructional practices are associated with gains in children's vocabulary knowledge? Existing studies point to positive outcomes of explicitly providing an explanation of a novel word, repeated readings of the same book, and asking questions that promote children's active engagement with target words. The instructional practices associated with improvements in children's vocabulary knowledge in early childhood classrooms generally mirror findings of the National Reading Panel's narrative review of vocabulary instruction studies involving school-age children (NICHD, 2000).

The benefits of explicit instruction described in our prior section on code-related outcomes are also evident in studies of vocabulary instruction (e.g., Justice, Meier, & Walpole, 2005). In the Marulis and Neuman (2010) meta-analysis, children made significantly higher gains in interventions that used an explicit method or a combination of explicit and implicit methods than in interventions that used implicit instruction only. Instruction was coded as explicit if it provided detailed definitions and examples of a word before, during, or after a book reading, plus a follow-up discussion to review target words. In implicit instruction, words were taught as an embedded part of an activity, without intentionally stopping the activity to teach a word meaning. One of the advantages of direct instruction of word meanings is simply drawing a child's attention to a novel word (Biemiller & Boote, 2006). It is difficult for a young listener to attend to a new word in a stream of speech and interrupt the speaker (especially in a large group) to inquire about its meaning.

Research supports the practice of repeated readings of the same book as a strategy for increasing the frequency of children's exposure to different word meanings. For example, Sénéchal (1997) found in an experimental study that 3- and 4-year-old middle-class children who experienced three readings of the same book over a 2-day period demonstrated stronger receptive and expressive vocabulary skills than children who participated in a single reading of the book. Sénéchal speculates that repeated exposure to a book increases the opportunity for children to encode contextual information about novel words, and to associate and store the novel word with its appropriate referent. The combination of repeated readings and teacher explanation of novel words has been found to be more effective than repeated readings without teacher explanation of novel words among children in the beginning stages of learning to read (Penno, Wilkinson, & Moore, 2002). In this study, teacher explanation of a target word occurred in the context of the book reading and included the use of a simpler synonym or role play of a word (e.g., buzzing action and sound of a hornet), or pointing to an illustration of the target word. On the first reading, one or two target words were introduced prior to the reading, then the reading occurred without interruption because anecdotal evidence indicated that some children disliked interruptions for the purpose of providing word meaning explanations during the first reading. Text was interrupted briefly to provide target word meanings on the second and subsequent readings. Biemiller and Boote (2006) found that kindergarten and first-grade but not second-grade students experienced significant gains in vocabulary knowledge when a text was read four times compared to two times within a week. Different words were taught on each reading (i.e., 12 word meanings from each book read twice, 24 word meanings from each book read four times).

Asking children questions related to a target word is helpful in improving vocabulary skill. Researchers have examined effects of different types of word- or book-related questions on vocabulary acquisition. Questions that place lower versus higher cognitive demand on children have been of special interest. Lower-demand questions pertain to concrete features of the text or illustrations, such as requests for children to label or point to a picture of a novel word, or to describe the action on a page. Higher-demand questions invite children to make inferences or predictions and generally come in the form of open-ended questions that encourage children to think more abstractly about the story (Blewitt, Rump, Shealy, & Cook, 2009).

In an experiment involving the use of lower-demand questions with middle-class 4-year-olds, children who actively labeled illustrations of target words in response to adult questions during individualized book reading comprehended and produced more words than children who listened passively to the same book. The book was read twice in each condition. Children with larger vocabularies prior to exposure to one of the two book reading conditions produced more new words than children with smaller vocabularies (Sénéchal et al., 1995). The investigators viewed the labeling questions, combined with repeated readings, as providing children with increased practice at retrieving novel words from memory. In a related experiment, they compared labeling questions to adult requests to point to pictures of novel words during book reading. Both labeling and pointing conditions were associated with improved comprehension skills, but children in the labeling condition performed better than children in the pointing condition in word production (Sénéchal et al., 1995). In a subsequent study Sénéchal (1997) also found that children's responding to what and where questions during repeated book reading was more helpful to expressive than to receptive vocabulary skills compared to a repeated reading condition without the questions.

Research support for the use of higher-demand questions during shared book reading with young children comes primarily from studies of teachers' (e.g., Dickinson & Smith, 1994) and parents' (e.g., van Kleeck, Gillam, Hamilton, & McGrath, 1997) naturally occurring approaches to book reading. For example, preschool teachers' use of analytic talk (discussion of characters' actions, events in the story, meanings of words), among other attributes of book reading behavior, has been linked to stronger vocabulary skill in kindergarten (Dickinson & Smith, 1994) and fourth grade (Dickinson & Porche, 2011). Results of experiments that systematically compare effects of lower- and higher-demand questions on children's vocabulary growth are less compelling, however. Random assignment studies with preschool children indicate that lower- and higher-demand questions have similar effects on children's vocabulary growth (Blewitt et al., 2009; Justice, 2002). An experimental study by Blewitt and colleagues (2009) suggests that a scaffolding arrangement, wherein low-demand questions (asking children to recall story elements or describe pictures) are asked when novel words first appear and high-demand questions (focused on inferences and predictions) are asked later in the book reading, facilitates a deeper understanding of word meanings. Blewitt and colleagues argue that high-demand questions can help children access more detailed aspects of a novel word's meaning only when the target word is already familiar.

Both lower- and higher-demand questions are among the instructional practices employed in the dialogic reading method of reading picture books to preschool-age children (Whitehurst et al., 1988). In dialogic reading, children are encouraged to become the storyteller, and the adult functions as an active listener, asking questions, adding information, and prompting the child to increase the sophistication of language used to describe events or pictures in the book. Results of randomized controlled trials of dialogic reading with children from low-income families point to significant, immediate intervention effects on children's expressive vocabulary skills (Lonigan et al., 1999; Whitehurst, Arnold, et al., 1994). Significant effects on expressive vocabulary also have been found 6 months after the intervention ended (Whitehurst, Arnold, et al., 1994). In an experimental study with children from low-income families, Wasik and Bond (2001) found immediate effects on children's receptive vocabulary skills in an interactive book reading intervention that built on dialogic reading plus emphasis on teaching vocabulary words and teachers' use of extension activities to reinforce vocabulary introduced in the book reading.

Studies of vocabulary and shared book-reading interventions in preschool classrooms differ according to who provides the intervention, as noted earlier. The Marulis and Neuman (2010) meta-analysis of vocabulary interventions found that training provided by an experimenter or teacher had similar effects on children's outcomes, but interventions delivered by child care providers had significantly weaker effects on children's vocabulary growth. Results of the Mol and colleagues (2009) meta-analysis of shared book-reading interventions indicated that child effects were stronger when an investigator versus a teacher carried out the intervention. In contrast, the National Early Literacy Panel's (2008) meta-analysis of shared book-reading interventions found no differential effects according to who did the reading.

The configuration of vocabulary and shared book-reading interventions also varies across studies, from one-to-one to whole group. Early literacy experts often recommend small groups (e.g., Wasik, 2008) and interventions such as the dialogic reading model (Whitehurst et al., 1988) call for five or fewer children per shared book-reading group. One of the few studies that systematically compared group size found that small groups (three children) were superior to one-to-one and whole-class settings regarding children's comprehension skills (Morrow & Smith, 1990). However, both the Marulis and Neuman (2010) and Mol and colleagues (2009) meta-analyses found no differences in the magnitude of child effects by group configuration.

There is some evidence to support the use of extension activities focused on words explicitly taught in a book reading. A study with kindergarten children found that extended vocabulary instruction resulted in more refined word knowledge than did embedded instruction (Coyne, McCoach, Loftus, Zipoli, & Kapp, 2009). In the extended instruction method, target words introduced and defined during a storybook reading were the focus of follow-up activities involving different contexts for use of the word. In the embedded instruction approach, target words were introduced prior to a book reading, then defined and discussed when they occurred during the book reading. Mol and colleagues (2009) reported that interactive book-reading interventions that included a book-related extension activity were no more effective than interactive book-reading sessions without an extension activity. This finding is not compelling, however, because the implementer of the intervention was a major confounder. Teachers implemented nearly all interventions with extension activities, whereas researchers generally carried out interventions with book-reading sessions only.

In spite of progress in identifying instructional practices that promote improvements in children's vocabulary outcomes, questions about some basic parameters of vocabulary instruction remain unsettled because they have not received systematic research attention. First, there is not an empirically derived list of words that children should master in early childhood as preparation for school success. Beck and her colleagues offer conceptually based guidance with the suggestion that children should be taught words used with high frequency by mature language users (Tier 2 words; Beck, McKeown, & Kucan, 2002). Second, research has not determined the optimal number of words to teach in an instructional session or week of lessons. Interventions vary considerably on this matter. For example, Beck and McKeown (2007) provided intensive instruction of six words per week for 7 weeks with kindergarten and first-grade children, whereas teachers taught four to six different word meanings at each reading in the Biemiller and Boote (2006) intervention with kindergarten, first-grade, and second-grade children. The latter researchers argue that because children know different words, a larger number of word meanings should be taught to provide opportunities for each child to learn new words. Third, the optimal number of exposures to target words (e.g., repeated readings) is not known. Useful guidance on this practical consideration likely will need to specify children's existing vocabulary ability.

Syntactic Knowledge

Young children's syntactic knowledge is a significant predictor of later reading ability (e.g., National Early Literacy Panel, 2008), as noted earlier, but little research has been conducted on instructional practices that promote syntax skills. Correlational studies have found links between specific aspects of teacher talk and children's oral language outcomes. For example, an investigation of the syntactic speech of teachers in preschool classrooms enrolling children from varied socioeconomic backgrounds found a significant relation between the proportion of complex sentences in teachers' speech and growth in children's comprehension of complex syntactic constructions (Huttenlocher, Vasilyeva, Cymerman, & Levine, 2002).

Research on experimental manipulation of adult language input indicates that 4-year-old children are more likely to use a particular form of syntax to describe a picture if an experimenter used the syntactic form in describing the picture (Huttenlocher, Vasilyeva, & Shimpi, 2004). In a random assignment study with 4-year-old children from diverse backgrounds enrolled in preschool classrooms, groups of about nine children listened to stories containing either a high proportion of passive voice sentences (e.g., "Sam got hit by the ball") or a high proportion of active voice sentences (e.g., "The giraffe caught the feather") read by a researcher 5 days a week over two consecutive weeks. The stories read in the passive condition also included sentences in an active form, in an effort to provide a natural-sounding narrative. At the end of the intervention, children who heard stories with a higher proportion of passive voice sentences produced more passive constructions and showed higher comprehension scores than children who heard stories with active voice sentences (Vasilyeva, Huttenlocher, & Waterfall, 2006).

An experimental study of the language-focused curriculum (Bunce, 1995) by Justice, Mashburn, Pence, and colleagues (2008) with at-risk preschool children included discourse-level child outcomes measured by coding transcripts of child language at the utterance level (e.g., child's most syntactically complex utterance). The curriculum promotes teachers' use of eight language stimulation techniques (e.g., repeat the child's utterance using varied syntax) and includes detailed daily lesson plans plus materials such as storybooks and props. Results indicated that teachers implemented the language stimulation techniques at relatively low levels (Pence, Justice, & Wiggins, 2008). Children's school attendance levels moderated the relation between exposure to the language stimulation techniques and children's language outcomes, including use of complex syntax. More regular school attendance was associated with positive outcomes of the intervention.

Listening Comprehension Skills

Children's understanding of a book or passage read aloud is a distinct component of early oral language skills that predicts later reading competence, as noted earlier. In addition to results of the NELP (2008) meta-analysis and the Storch and Whitehurst (2002) investigation cited earlier, we note a longitudinal study of middle-class children in Canada, which found that listening comprehension and receptive vocabulary skills in kindergarten uniquely predicted reading ability in third grade (Sénéchal & LeFevre, 2002). Sénéchal (2006) replicated these findings in a French-speaking sample followed to fourth grade. Feagans and Appelbaum (1986) found that a measure of story retelling was a better predictor of later reading achievement of children with learning disabilities than other dimensions of oral language, including vocabulary and syntax. Findings of research in New Zealand suggest that, in predicting later reading ability, the quality of a child's story recall (oral narratives) may depend on the child's age. Reese, Suggate, Long, and Schaughency (2010) found that the quality of narrative skill (e.g., recalling the internal state of a character) at approximately 5 years of age did not predict children's reading skill 1 year later, but in a subsample of children assessed at 7 years of age, quality of narrative skill uniquely predicted reading ability 1 year later after researchers controlled for receptive vocabulary and early decoding skills.

Findings of correlational research indicate that better story comprehension skills among preschoolers are linked to teachers' (Dickinson & Smith, 1994) and mothers' (Haden, Reese, & Fivush, 1996) use of higher-level questioning strategies during shared book reading (e.g., asking children to predict what will happen in the story, to draw inferences about story events). Higher-level questioning strategies are a component of a number of shared book-reading interventions examined in random assignment studies (e.g., Wasik et al., 2006), but comprehension skills are infrequently included in assessments of child outcomes. An exception to this general pattern is a dialogic reading intervention with preschool children by Zevenbergen, Whitehurst, and Zevenbergen (2003), who found significant positive effects of dialogic reading on a story-retelling task, notably, children's inclusion of evaluative information (i.e., references to internal states of story characters). In contrast, Lonigan and colleagues (1999) found that children who participated in a typical book reading performed better than children in a dialogic reading condition on a listening comprehension measure at postintervention. Book reading was conducted 10–15 minutes daily for 6 weeks by undergraduate students with small groups of children enrolled in child care centers. The listening comprehension measures of these respective studies are markedly different. Zevenbergen and colleagues used an adaptation of the Bus Story Test (Renfrew, 1969), whereas Lonigan and colleagues used a standardized listening comprehension measure in which children were verbally presented with an incomplete sentence and asked to complete the sentence with the correct word. The latter measure arguably pertains more to depth of vocabulary knowledge than to comprehension of book text.

A classroom-based story-reading intervention examined in a random assignment study by Morrow, O'Connor, and Smith (1990) with at-risk kindergarten children included teachers asking prediction questions about books read aloud to children, plus children engaging in role playing and retelling a story with use of puppets, felt board characters, and props, among other intervention components. Children in the experimental group scored significantly better than children randomly assigned to a book-reading-as-usual control condition on investigator-developed measures of story retelling and story comprehension.

Interventions Designed to Promote Code–Related and Oral Language Outcomes

Research evidence is available on the effectiveness of programs and curricula that target literacy and language skills related to both code-related and oral language outcomes. The interventions vary in comprehensiveness, from a combination of two well-established programs to more broadly comprehensive curricula that include science and mathematics, as well as literacy.

The dialogic reading intervention was combined with an adaptation of the Sound Foundations phonological awareness training program described earlier in this chapter (Byrne & Fielding-Barnsley, 1991; Byrne, Fielding-Barnsley, & Ashley, 2000) in a study by Whitehurst, Epstein, and colleagues (1994). Adaptations of Sound Foundations in the Whitehurst, Epstein, and colleagues study included a letter of the week, and games and extension activities. It was offered February through June. The dialogic reading intervention used 30 books across the school year, one per week, in the classroom. Books also were loaned to parents for use at home, and parents received dialogic reading training. Whitehurst, Epstein, and colleagues found positive intervention effects on children's writing, on print concepts, and on one linguistic awareness subtest (identification of first letter and first sound of words) at the end of the Head Start year. These results were replicated in a new cohort of children, but a follow-up study of the original cohort found no intervention effects at the end of first or second grade (Whitehurst et al., 1999).

Ladders to Literacy is a more comprehensive curriculum that focuses on print awareness, phonological awareness, and oral language skills (O'Connor, Notari-Syverson, & Vadasy, 2005). It was originally designed to supplement kindergarten reading curricula; a preschool version has been recently developed. Most of the intervention activities are designed to be implemented in large groups. Although the curriculum includes lesson plans and a theoretical framework, teachers have leeway in how and how often activities are implemented. O'Connor, Jenkins, Leicester, and Slocum (1999) report results of two random assignment studies of Ladders in kindergarten classrooms for children without disabilities, and for children at risk (including children with identified disabilities). In these classrooms, Ladders served as a supplement to the districtwide reading curriculum (used in both comparison and intervention classrooms). Children in classrooms in which teachers received professional development training in the use of Ladders made significantly greater gains on most measures of early reading, including blending, segmenting, and rapid letter naming, than children in comparison classrooms. There was evidence, as well, that greater intensity of professional development, including teacher learning groups and attention to individualized instruction, resulted in greater gains for children. Results of a subsequent random assignment study are consistent in demonstrating significant gains in phonological awareness skills for kindergarten children whose teachers used Ladders when compared with business-as-usual reading instruction (Fuchs et al., 2001). However, a recent random assignment evaluation of the preschool version of Ladders to Literacy revealed no significant effects on children's learning on a number of different measures of early literacy competence (PCER, 2008). We note, however, that teachers in the preschool evaluation were trained to implement 27 different Ladders activities at least once during the year. This is substantially fewer than the average of 135 different Ladders activities implemented by kindergarten teachers with typically developing children in the classrooms studied by O'Connor and her colleagues (1993), raising questions about whether the preschool intervention (PCER) was of sufficient intensity to promote accelerated learning.

Literacy Express is a comprehensive preschool curriculum that includes attention to science, mathematics and socioemotional development, as well as oral language and phonological competence. While we could find no published evaluations of the complete Literacy Express curriculum, components appear effective in promoting preschool children's early literacy skills. In a recent random assignment study, Farver and colleagues (2009) examined the effectiveness of the Literacy Express small-group activities designed to promote oral language (through dialogic reading), phonological awareness, and print knowledge. Participants were Spanish-speaking children enrolled in a Head Start program where they were learning English. Children were randomly assigned to one of three groups: a business-as-usual control, Literacy Express in English, and a Literacy Express transitional intervention with instruction in Spanish until midyear, then a transition to English. Intervention was provided as a pull-out, four times/week for approximately 20 minutes each session (21 weeks) by research assistants, and children were taught in small groups. Children in both intervention groups made substantially greater gains than children in the control group on measures of phonological awareness, print knowledge, and vocabulary administered in English; children in the transitional group made significantly greater gains than children in either the control or English-only intervention on measures administered in Spanish. This study is especially noteworthy because of its attention to the development of Spanish-speaking preschool children's phonological awareness, print knowledge, and vocabulary skills in English.

Summary

A growing scientific literature documents the effectiveness of instructional practices and curricula designed to improve young children's literacy and language skills. The recent publication of five meta-analyses related to different aspects of early literacy and language instruction indirectly attests to heightened interest in this critically important dimension of school readiness and the scope of available research. Studies point to positive outcomes of a range of teaching strategies, with a fledgling body of evidence suggesting that some instructional approaches are more effective than others. As noted in our chapter, the depth of investigation varies considerably, and some practices have the benefit of a stronger empirical foundation than others.

Advances in our understanding of how to improve children's early literacy and language competencies require movement on multiple fronts. The development of valid and reliable measures of discrete literacy and language skills is central to significant progress in evaluations of intervention outcomes and longitudinal investigations of early childhood precursors to later reading ability. Research on factors that facilitate use of evidence-based instruction and curricula in classrooms by teachers is needed to inform initiatives designed to promote widespread use of exemplary practices. Equally important, studies of the implementation of literacy and language instruction, including possible consequences for child outcomes and instruction not targeted by an intervention, hold promise to help policymakers refine guidelines and mandates regarding the desired pedagogy and outcomes of early education. In each of these lines of research, systematic attention to the growing diversity of early childhood populations and early education delivery systems would improve the utility of findings.

Acknowledgment

Preparation of this chapter was supported by Grant No. R305B070605 from the Institute of Education Sciences, U.S. Department of Education, to Purdue University.

References

Beck, I. L., & McKeown, M. G. (2007). Increasing young low-income children's oral vocabulary repertoires through rich and focused instruction. *Elementary School Journal, 107*, 251–271.

Beck, I. L., McKeown, M. G., & Kucan, L. (2002). *Bringing words to life: Robust vocabulary instruction*. New York: Guilford Press.

Biemiller, A., & Boote, C. (2006). An effective method for building meaning vocabulary in primary grades. *Journal of Educational Psychology, 98*, 44–62.

Blewitt, P., Rump, K. M., Shealy, S. E., & Cook, S. A. (2009). Shared book reading: When and how questions affect young children's word learning. *Journal of Educational Psychology, 101*, 294–304.

Both-de Vries, A. C., & Bus, A. G. (2010). The proper name as starting point for basic reading skills. *Reading and Writing, 23*, 173–187.

Bunce, B. H. (1995). *Building a language-focused curriculum for the preschool classroom: Volume II*. Baltimore: Brookes.

Byrne, B., & Fielding-Barnsley, R. (1991). Evaluation of a program to teach phonemic awareness to young children. *Journal of Educational Psychology, 83*, 451–455.

Byrne, B., Fielding-Barnsley, R., & Ashley, L. (2000). Effects of preschool phoneme identity training after six years: Outcome level distinguished from rate of response. *Journal of Educational Psychology, 92*, 659–667.

Connor, C. M., Morrison, F. J., Fishman, B. J., Schatschneider, C., & Underwood, P. (2007). The early years: Algorithm-guided individualized reading instruction. *Science, 315*, 464–465.

Connor, C. M., Morrison, F. J., & Slominski, L. (2006). Preschool instruction and children's emergent literacy growth. *Journal of Educational Psychology, 98*, 665–689.

Copple, C., & Bredekamp, S. (Eds.). (2009). *Developmentally appropriate practice in early childhood programs, third edition*. Washington, DC: National Association for the Education of Young Children.

Coyne, M. D., McCoach, D. B., Loftus, S., Zipoli, R., & Kapp, S. (2009). Direct vocabulary instruction in kindergarten: Teaching for breadth versus depth. *Elementary School Journal, 110*, 1–18.

Cunningham, A. E., & Stanovich, K. E. (1997). Early reading acquisition and its relation to reading experience and ability 10 years later. *Developmental Psychology, 33*, 934–945.

Denton Flanagan, K., & McPhee, C. (2009). *The children born in 2001 at kindergarten entry: First findings from the kindergarten data collections of the Early Childhood Longitudinal Study, Birth Cohort (ECLS-B)*. Washington, DC: National Center for Education Statistics, Institute of Education Sciences, U.S. Department of Education.

Diamond, K. E., Gerde, H., & Powell, D. R. (2008). Development in early literacy skills during the pre-kindergarten year in Head Start: Relations between growth in children's writing and understanding of letters. *Early Childhood Research Quarterly, 23*, 467–478.

Dickinson, D., & Smith, M. (1994). Long-term effects of preschool teachers' book readings on low-income children's vocabulary and story comprehension. *Reading Research Quarterly, 29*, 104–122.

Dickinson, D. K., Golinkoff, R. M., & Hirsh-Pasek, K. (2010). Speaking out for language: Why language is central to reading development. *Educational Researcher, 39*, 305–310.

Dickinson, D. K., & Porche, M. V. (2011). Relationship between language experiences in preschool classrooms and children's kindergarten and fourth grade language and reading abilities. *Child Development, 82*, 870–886.

Ehri, L. C. (2004). Teaching phonemic awareness and phonics: An explanation of the National Reading Panel metaanalyses. In P. McCardle & V. Chabra (Eds.), *The voice of evidence in reading research* (pp. 153–186). Baltimore: Brookes.

Ehri, L. C., & Roberts, T. (2006). The roots of learning to read and write: Acquisition of letters and phonemic awareness. In D. K. Dickinson & S. B. Neuman (Eds.), *Handbook of early literacy research* (Vol. 2, pp. 113–134). New York: Guilford Press.

Ehri, L. C., & Wilce, L. S. (1987). Does learning to spell help beginners learn to read words? *Reading Research Quarterly, 22*, 47–65.

Ellefson, M. R., Treiman, R., & Kessler, B. (2009). Learning to label letters by sounds or names: A comparison of England and the United States. *Journal of Experimental Child Psychology, 102*, 323–341.

Elleman, A. M., Lindo, E. J., Morphy, P., & Compton, D. L. (2009). The impact of vocabulary instruction on passage-level comprehension of school-age children: A meta-analysis. *Journal of Research on Educational Effectiveness, 2*, 1–44.

Epstein, A. S. (2007). *The intentional teacher: Choosing the best strategies for young children's learning*. Washington, DC: National Association for the Education of Young Children.

Farver, J. M., Lonigan, C. J., & Eppe, S. (2009). Effective early literacy skill development for young Spanish-speaking English language learners: An experimental study of two methods. *Child Development, 80*, 703–719.

Feagans, L., & Appelbaum, M. L. (1986). Validation of language subtypes in learning disabled children. *Journal of Educational Psychology, 78*, 308–364.

Fischel, J. E., Bracken, S. S., Fuchs-Eisenberg, A., Spira, E. G., Katz, S., & Shaller, G. (2007). Evaluation of curricula approaches to enhance preschool early literacy skills. *Journal of Literacy Research, 39*, 471–501.

Foorman, B. R., Chen, D.-T., Carlson, C., Moats, L., Francis, D. J., & Fletcher, J. M. (2003). The necessity of the alphabetic principle to phonemic awareness instruction. *Reading and Writing, 16*, 289–324.

Foster, K. C., Erickson, G. C., Foster, D. F., Brinkman, D., & Torgesen, J. K. (1994). Computer administered instruction in phonological awareness: Evaluation of the Daisy Quest program. *Journal of Research and Development in Education, 27*, 126–137.

Fuchs, D., Fuchs, L. S., Thompson, A., Al Otaiba, S., Yen, L., Yang, N. J., et al. (2001). Is reading important in reading-readiness programs?: A randomized field trial with teachers as program implementers. *Journal of Educational Psychology, 93*, 251–267.

Gettinger, M. (1986). Prereading skills and achievement under three approaches to teaching word recognition. *Journal of Research and Development in Education, 19*, 1–9.

Haden, C. A., Reese, E., & Fivush, R. (1997). Mothers' extratextual comments during storybook reading: Stylistic differences over time and across texts. *Discourse Processes, 21*, 135–169.

Hair, E., Halle, T., Terry-Humen, E., Lavelle, B., & Calkins, J. (2006). Children's school readiness in the ECLS-K: Predictions to academic, health, and social outcomes in first grade. *Early Childhood Research Quarterly, 21*, 431–454.

Hamre, B. K., Justice, L. M., Pianta, R. C., Kilday, C., Sweeney, B., Downer, J., et al. (2010). Implementation fidelity of MyTeachingPartner literacy and language activities: Association with preschoolers' language and literacy growth. *Early Childhood Research Quarterly, 25*, 329–347.

Hart, B., & Risley, T. R. (1995). *Meaningful differences in the everyday experience of young American children*. Baltimore: Brookes.

Huttenlocher, J., Vasilyeva, M., Cymerman, E., & Levine, S. (2002). Language input and child syntax. *Cognitive Psychology, 45*, 337–374.

Huttenlocher, J., Vasilyeva, M., & Shimpi, P. (2004). Syntactic priming in young children. *Journal of Memory and Language, 50*, 182–195.

Justice, L. M. (2002). Word exposure conditions and preschoolers' novel word learning during shared storybook reading. *Reading Psychology, 23*, 87–106.

Justice, L. M., Chow, S.-M., Capellini, C., Flanigan, K., & Colton, S. (2003). Emergent literacy intervention for vulnerable preschoolers: Relative effects of two approaches. *American Journal of Speech–Language Pathology, 12*, 320–332.

Justice, L. M., & Ezell, H. K. (2002). Use of storybook reading to increase print awareness in at-risk children. *American Journal of Speech–Language Pathology, 11*, 17–29.

Justice, L. M., Mashburn, A., Hamre, B. K., & Pianta, R. C. (2008). Quality of language and literacy instruction in preschool classrooms serving at-risk pupils. *Early Childhood Research Quarterly, 23*, 51–68.

Justice, L. M., Mashburn, A., Pence, K. L., & Wiggins, A. (2008). Experimental evaluation of a preschool language curriculum: Influence on children's expressive language skills. *Journal of Speech, Language, and Hearing Research, 51*, 983–1001.

Justice, L. M., Meier, J., & Walpole, S. (2005). Learning new words from storybooks: An efficacy study with at-risk kindergartners. *Language, Speech, and Hearing Services in Schools, 36*, 17–32.

Kim, Y.-S., Petscher, Y., Foorman, B. R., & Chengfu, Z. (2010). The contributions of phonological awareness and letter-name knowledge to letter-sound acquisition—a cross-classified multilevel model approach. *Journal of Educational Psychology, 102*, 313–326.

Landry, S. H., Anthony, J. L., Swank, P. R., & Monseque-Bailey, P. (2009). Effectiveness of comprehensive professional development for teachers of at-risk preschoolers. *Journal of Educational Psychology, 101*, 448–465.

Llosa, L., & Slayton, J. (2009). Using program evaluation to inform and improve the education of young English language learners in US schools. *Language Teaching Research, 13*, 35–54.

Lonigan, C. J. (2007). Vocabulary development and the developmental phonological awareness skills in preschool children. In R. K. Wagner, A. E. Muse, & K. R. Tannenbaum (Eds.), *Vocabulary acquisition: Implications for reading comprehension* (pp. 15–31). New York: Guilford Press.

Lonigan, C. J., Anthony, J. L., Bloomfield, B. G., Dyer, S. M., & Samwel, C. S. (1999). Effects of two shared-reading interventions on emergent literacy skills of at-risk preschoolers. *Journal of Early Intervention, 22,* 306–322.

Lonigan, C. J., Anthony, J. L., Phillips, B. M., Purpura, D. J., Wilson, S. B., & McQueen, J. D. (2009). The nature of preschool phonological processing abilities and their relations to vocabulary, general cognitive abilities, and print knowledge. *Journal of Educational Psychology, 101,* 345–358.

Lonigan, C. J., Driscoll, K., Phillips, B. M., Cantor, B. G., Anthony, J. L., & Goldstein, H. (2003). A computer-assisted instruction phonological sensitivity program for preschool children at-risk for reading problems. *Journal of Early Intervention, 25,* 248–262.

Lonigan, C. J., & Shanahan, T. (2010). Developing early literacy skills: Things we know we know and things we know we don't know. *Educational Researcher, 39,* 340–346.

Marulis, L. M., & Neuman, S. B. (2010). The effects of vocabulary intervention on young children's word learning: A meta-analysis. *Review of Educational Research, 80,* 300–335.

Mitchell, M. J., & Fox, B. J. (2001). The effects of computer software for developing phonological awareness in low-progress readers. *Reading Research and Instruction, 40,* 315–332.

Mol, S., Bus, A., & de Jong, M. (2009). Interactive book reading in early education: A tool to stimulate print knowledge as well as oral language. *Review of Educational Research, 79,* 979–1007.

Morrow, L. M., O'Connor, E. M., & Smith, J. K. (1990). Effects of a story reading program on the literacy development of at-risk kindergarten children. *Journal of Reading Behavior, 22,* 255–275.

Morrow, L. M., & Smith, J. K. (1990). The effects of group size on interactive storybook reading. *Reading Research Quarterly, 25,* 213–231.

Mosteller, F., & Boruch, R. (2002). *Evidence matters: Randomized trials in education research.* Washington, DC: Brookings Institution Press.

National Early Literacy Panel (NELP). (2008). *Developing early literacy: Report of the National Early Literacy Panel.* Washington, DC: National Institute for Literacy.

National Institute of Child Health and Human Development (NICHD). (2000). *Report of the National Reading Panel: Teaching children to read: An evidence-based assessment of the scientific research literature on reading and its implications for reading instruction.* Washington, DC: U.S. Government Printing Office.

Neuman, S. B., & Roskos, K. (1997). Literacy knowledge in practice: Contexts of participation for young writers and readers. *Reading Research Quarterly, 32,* 10–32.

NICHD Early Child Care Research Network. (2005). Pathways to reading: The role of oral language in the transition to reading. *Developmental Psychology, 41,* 428–442.

O'Connor, R. E., Jenkins, J. R., Leicester, N., & Slocum, T. A. (1993). Teaching phonological awareness to young children with learning disabilities. *Exceptional Children, 59,* 532–546.

O'Connor, R. E., Jenkins, J. R., Leicester, N., & Slocum, T. A. (1999). Teachers learning Ladders to Literacy. *Learning Disabilities Research and Practice, 14,* 203–214.

O'Connor, R. E., Notari-Syverson, A., & Vadasy, P. F. (2005). *Ladders to Literacy: A kindergarten activity book* (2nd ed.). Baltimore: Brookes.

Paris, S. G., & Paris, A. H. (2006). Assessments of early reading. In K. A. Renninger & I. E. Sigel (Vol. Eds.), W. Damon & R. M. Lerner (Eds.), *Handbook of child psychology: Vol. 4. Child psychology in practice* (6th ed., pp. 48–74). Hoboken, NJ: Wiley.

Paterson, W. A., Henry, J. J., O'Quin, K., Ceprano, M. A., & Blue, E. V. (2003). Investigating the effectiveness of an integrated learning system on early emergent readers. *Reading Research Quarterly, 38,* 172–207.

Pence, K., Justice, L. M., & Wiggins, A. K. (2008). Preschool teachers' fidelity in implementing a comprehensive language-rich curriculum. *Language, Speech, and Hearing Services in Schools, 39,* 329–341.

Penno, J. F., Wilkinson, I. A. G., & Moore, D. W. (2002). Vocabulary acquisition from teacher explanation and repeated listening to stories: Do they overcome the Matthew effect? *Journal of Educational Psychology, 94,* 23–33.

Phillips, B. M., Clancy-Menchetti, J., & Lonigan, C. J. (2008). Successful phonological awareness instruction with preschool children: Lessons from the classroom. *Topics in Early Childhood Special Education, 28,* 3–17.

Pianta, R., Howes, C., Burchinal, M., Bryant, D., Clifford, R., Early, D., et al. (2005). Features of pre-kindergarten programs, classrooms, and teachers: Do they predict observed classroom quality and child–teacher interactions? *Applied Developmental Science, 9,* 144–159.

Piasta, S. B., & Wagner, R. K. (2010a). Developing early literacy skills: A meta-analysis of alphabet learning and instruction. *Reading Research Quarterly, 45,* 8–38.

Piasta, S. B., & Wagner, R. K. (2010b). Learning letter names and sounds: Effects of instruction, letter type, and phonological processing skill. *Journal of Experimental Child Psychology, 105,* 324–344.

Powell, D. R., Diamond, K. E., Bojczyk, K. E., & Gerde, H. K. (2008). Head Start teachers' perspectives on early literacy. *Journal of Literacy Research, 40,* 422–460.

Powell, D. R., Diamond, K. E., Burchinal, M. R., & Koehler, M. J. (2010). Effects of an early literacy professional development intervention on Head Start teachers and children. *Journal of Educational Psychology, 102,* 299–312.

Preschool Curriculum Evaluation Research Consortium (PCER). (2008). *Effects of preschool curriculum programs on school readiness.* Washington, DC: U.S. Department of Education, Institute of Education Sciences, National Center for Education Research.

Reese, E., Suggate, S., Long, J., & Schaughency, E. (2010). Children's oral narrative and reading skills in the first 3 years of reading instruction. *Reading and Writing, 23,* 627–644.

Renfrew, C. (1969). *The bus story: A test of continuous speech.* Oxford, UK: Author.

Rieben, L., Ntamakiliro, L., Gonthier, B., & Fayol, M. (2005). Effects of various early writing practices on reading and spelling. *Scientific Studies of Reading, 9,* 145–166.

Scarborough, H. S. (2001). Connecting early language and literacy to later reading (dis)abilities: Evidence, theory, and practice. In S. B. Neuman & D. Dickinson (Eds.), *Handbook of early literacy research* (pp. 97–110). New York: Guilford Press.

Schickedanz, J. A., & McGee, L. M. (2010). The NELP report on shared story reading interventions (Chapter 4): Extending the story. *Educational Researcher, 39,* 323–329.

Schuele, C. M., Justice, L. M., Cabell, S. Q., Knighton, K., Kingery, B., & Lee, M. W. (2010). Field-based evaluation of two-tiered instruction for enhancing kindergarten phonological awareness. *Early Education and Development, 19,* 726–752.

Sénéchal, M. (2006). Testing the home literacy model: Parent involvement in kindergarten is differentially related to grade 4 reading comprehension, fluency, spelling, and reading for pleasure. *Scientific Studies of Reading, 10,* 59–87.

Sénéchal, M. (1997). The differential effect of storybook reading on preschoolers' acquisition of expressive and receptive vocabulary. *Journal of Child Language, 24,* 123–138.

Sénéchal, M., & LeFevre, J. (2002). Parental involvement in the development of children's reading skills: A five-year longitudinal study. *Child Development, 73,* 446–490.

Sénéchal, M., Thomas, E., & Monker, J. (1995). Individual differences in 4-year-old children's acquisition of vocabulary during storybook reading. *Journal of Educational Psychology, 87,* 218–229.

Share, D. L. (2004). Knowing letter names and learning letter sounds: A causal connection. *Journal of Experimental Child Psychology, 88,* 213–233.

Silverman, R., & Hines, S. (2009). The effects of multimedia-enhanced instruction on the vocabulary of English-language learners and non-English-language learners in pre-kindergarten through second grade. *Journal of Educational Psychology, 101,* 305–314.

Stanovich, K. E. (1986). Matthew effects in reading: Some consequences of individual differences in the acquisition of literacy. *Reading Research Quarterly, 21,* 360–407.`

Storch, S. A., & Whitehurst, G. J. (2002). Oral language and code-related precursors to reading: Evidence from a longitudinal structural model. *Developmental Psychology, 38,* 934–947.

Teale, W. H., & Sulzby, E. (Eds.). (1986). *Emergent literacy: Writing and reading.* Norwood, NJ: Ablex.

Treiman, R., & Kessler, B. (2003). The role of letter names in the acquisition of literacy. In R. V. Kail (Ed.), *Advances in child development and behavior* (Vol. 31, pp. 105–135). San Diego, CA: Academic Press.

Ukrainetz, T. A., Cooney, M. H., Dyer, S. K., Kysar, A. J., & Harris, T. J. (2000). An investigation into teaching phonemic awareness through shared reading and writing. *Early Childhood Research Quarterly, 15,* 331–355.

U.S. Department of Health and Human Services, Administration on Children, Youth and Families/ Head Start Bureau. (2003). *The Head Start path to positive child outcomes.* Washington, DC: Author.

Vadasy, P. F., & Sanders, E. A. (2008). Code-oriented instruction for kindergarten students at risk for reading difficulties: A replication and comparison of instructional groupings. *Reading and Writing, 21,* 929–963.

Vadasy, P. F., Sanders, E. A., & Peyton, J. A. (2006). Code-oriented instruction for kindergarten students at risk for reading difficulties: A randomized field trial with paraeducator implementers. *Journal of Educational Psychology, 98,* 508–528.

van Kleeck, A., Gillam, R. B., Hamilton, L., & McGrath, C. (1997). The relationships between middle-class parents' book-sharing discussion and their preschoolers' abstract language development. *Journal of Speech, Language, and Hearing Research, 40,* 1261–1271.

Vasilyeva, M., Huttenlocher, J., & Waterfall, H. (2006). Effects of language intervention on syntactic skill levels in preschoolers. *Developmental Psychology, 42,* 164–174.

Wasik, B. (2008). When fewer is more: Small groups in early childhood classrooms. *Early Childhood Education Journal, 35,* 515–521.

Wasik, B. A., & Bond, M. A. (2001). Beyond the pages of a book: Interactive book reading and language development in preschool classrooms. *Journal of Educational Psychology, 93,* 243–250.

Wasik, B. A., Bond, M. A., & Hindman, A. (2006). The effects of a language and literacy intervention on Head Start children and teachers. *Journal of Educational Psychology, 98,* 63–74.

Weizman, Z. O., & Snow, C. E. (2001). Lexical input as related to children's vocabulary acquisition: Effects of sophisticated exposure and support for meaning. *Developmental Psychology, 37,* 265–279.

Whitehurst, G. J., Arnold, D. S., Epstein, J. N., Angell, A. L., Smith, M., & Fischel, J. E. (1994). A picture book reading intervention in day care and home for children from low-income families. *Developmental Psychology, 30,* 679–689.

Whitehurst, G. J., Epstein, J. N., Angell, A. L., Payne, A. C., Crone, D. A., & Fischel, J. E. (1994). Outcomes of an emergent literacy intervention in Head Start. *Journal of Educational Psychology, 86,* 542–555.

Whitehurst, G. J., Falco, F. L., Lonigan, C., Fischel, J. E., DeBaryshe, B. D., Valdez-Menchaca, M., et al. (1988). Accelerating language development through picture book reading. *Developmental Psychology, 24,* 552–558.

Whitehurst, G. J., & Lonigan, C. J. (1998). Child development and emergent literacy. *Child Development, 69,* 848–872.

Whitehurst, G. J., Zevenbergen, A. A., Crone, D. A., Schultz, M. D., Velting, O. N., & Fischel, J. E. (1999). Outcomes of an emergent literacy intervention from Head Start through second grade. *Journal of Educational Psychology, 91,* 261–272.

Yeh, S. S. (2003). An evaluation of two approaches for teaching phonemic awareness to children in Head Start. *Early Childhood Research Quarterly, 18,* 513–529.

Zevenbergen, A. A., Whitehurst, G. J., & Zevenbergen, J. A. (2003). Effects of a shared-reading intervention on the inclusion of evaluative devices in narratives of children from low-income families. *Journal of Applied Developmental Psychology, 24,* 1–15.

CHAPTER 11

Mathematics Learning, Assessment, and Curriculum

Douglas H. Clements and Julie Sarama

Just after her fourth birthday, Abby was playing with three of the five identical toy train engines her father had brought home. Passing by, her mother asked, "Where are the other trains?" Although her mother had left the room, Abby answered to herself. "Oh, I have five. Ummm ... [pointing to each engine] you are one, two, three. I'm missing 'four' and 'five'— two are missing! [She played with the trains for another minute.] No, I have 'one,' 'three,' and 'five.' I'm missing 'two' and 'four.' I gotta find them two" (Clements & Sarama, 2009, p. 19).

What does this episode say to you about young children and mathematics? What should teachers know about mathematics learning, assessment, and curriculum to develop Abby's interest and competence in mathematics? We address these questions by synthesizing the substantial body of research on young children's learning of mathematics.

Learning What Counts: What Mathematics?

Throughout the majority of mathematics history, mathematics standards and specific "scope and sequences" have been based on traditional sequences of mathematics curricula (e.g., count in kindergarten, add in first grade). However, there have been increasing criticisms of these standards, with recommendations for improvement from a variety of perspectives.

Some reformers criticized traditional standards and curricula. Richard Skemp encapsulated much of that criticism by noting that there were different subjects taught under the name of mathematics. *Instrumental* knowledge of mathematics involved only "rules without reason" (Skemp, 1976). *Relational* understanding of mathematics included knowing not only how to solve problems—what to do—but also why. Relational understanding is based on mental, conceptual structures that permit the generation of a variety of solution strategies. The first curriculum and standards document from the National Council of Teachers of Mathematics (NCTM) similarly declared that the present elementary mathematics curriculum is narrow in scope; fails to foster mathematical insight, reasoning, and problem solving emphasizes rote activities. Even more significant is that students begin to lose their belief that learning mathematics is a sense-making activity. They become passive receivers of rules and procedures rather than active participants in creating knowledge. (1989, p. 15)

Unfortunately, this statement of vision was often misinterpreted. For example, the relative statements of "decreased attention" to objectives such as "isolated treatment of division facts" and instructional practices such as "rote memorization of rules" were misconstrued to mean "no attention to" certain topics and incorrectly generalized to mean no attention to fluency with arithmetic; that was never the intention.

A decade later, NCTM revised its statement to reflect current thought and research. The council spent years of substantial effort to develop *Principles and Standards for School Mathematics* (*PSSM*; NCTM, 2000). Grade bands were changed: Rather than grades K–4, the youngest band was PreK to grade 2 (NCTM was the first subject-matter organization to propose standards and the first to include preschool). The structure for the standards was reorganized. For the first time, the same five *content* categories were used across grade levels: numbers and operations, algebra, geometry, measurement, and data analysis and probability. For the first time, five *process* standards also were included: problem solving, reasoning and proof, communication, connections, and representation.

Also new were *principles*, fundamental propositions to guide decision making. The broad issues included equity, curriculum, teaching, learning, assessment, and technology.

The *PSSM* remained a vision. Even though it was carefully vetted to a wide variety of individuals and organizations,[1] its content was debated. Some believed that the *PSSM* deemphasized "rigorous" mathematics. Another criticism was that it did not give sufficient guidance to curriculum developers and teachers as to what should be taught at specific age or grade levels. These criticisms, and the need for consistency across the states, helped generate two additional projects.

First, we (Clements and Sarama) sought funding to hold a national conference on early mathematics standards (funded by the National Science Foundation [NSF] and the Exxon-Mobil Educational Foundation; see *gse.buffalo.edu/org/conference*). A gathering of experts from U.S. State Departments of Education, researchers from a variety of fields, teachers, policymakers, and so forth, attended this historic conference. The work, along with a massive review of research and expert practice, resulted in the book *Engaging Young Children in Mathematics: Standards for Early Childhood Mathematics Education* (Clements, Sarama, & DiBiase, 2004). In the conclusion, it was stressed that all standards should be *mathematically central and coherent, consistent with students' thinking, and generative of future learning* (p. 13). This work was disseminated to all state departments of education and also was used to support NCTM's next project, to which we now turn.

Second, the need for specificity also helped influence NCTM to produce the *Curriculum Focal Points for Prekindergarten through Grade 8 Mathematics* (*CFP*; NCTM, 2006; again, Clements was one of the writers), a concise description of the important mathematical topics for each grade level. Each age or grade level has exactly three content "focal points," cohesive clusters of related knowledge, skills, and concepts. The limited number of content focal points at each grade level was posited to allow deeper and better learning. Thus, the content focal points preceded the recommendation of President Bush's National Mathematics Advisory Panel (NMAP), which argued strongly that "the mathematics curriculum in Grades PreK–8 should be streamlined and should emphasize a well-defined set of the most critical topics in the early grades" (National Mathematics Advisory Panel, 2008, p. xiii).

Grade-level specificity and consistent application of standards across the U.S. were particular motivators for the development of the *Common Core State Standards for Mathematics* (*Common Core*; CCSSO/NGA, 2010)[2] by the National Governors Association (NGA) Center for Best Practices and the Council of Chief State School Officers (CCSSO). Although developed mainly by a new set of authors, the *Common Core* was influenced by the *CFP* (see the introductions to the K–8 grade levels in the *Common Core*). Most important, both the *Common Core* and the *CFP* were based to some extent on knowledge of how children learn specific mathematical ideas. Indeed, as the *Common Core* was being developed, we first wrote *learning trajectories* for each major topic—for example, the levels of thinking through which most children progress as they learn geometry. These were used to determine what the sequence would be and were "cut" into grade-level specific standards. (Learning trajectories are described in the following two sections.)

Before we address learning trajectories, however, we wish to raise two related points that emerge from the *Common Core* and the *CFP*. First, we must stress that questions such as "What is most important, teaching skills, concepts, or problem solving?" or "Should instruction for young children concentrate on facts or problem solving?" *are not the right questions*. Children at all ages need to develop mathematical skills, concepts, reasoning, and strategies (general and specific processes, including problem-solving competencies).

Second, other general educational goals must not be neglected. Productive dispositions include curiosity, imagination, inventiveness, risk taking, creativity, and persistence.

> As important as mathematical content are general mathematical processes such as problem solving, reasoning and proof, communication, connections, and representation; specific mathematical processes such as organizing information, patterning, and composing, and habits of mind such as curiosity, imagination, inventiveness, persistence, willingness to experiment, and sensitivity to patterns. All should be involved in a high-quality early childhood mathematics program. (Clements & Conference Working Group, 2004, p. 57)

Children need to view mathematics as sensible, useful, and worthwhile, and to view themselves as capable of thinking mathematically. Children should also come to appreciate the beauty and creativity that is at the heart of mathematics. With that in mind, we turn to the question of *how* children think about and learn mathematics.

Learning Trajectories: Illuminating Paths for Successful Learning

Research-based learning trajectories are powerful tools educators can use to improve mathematics learning and teaching. Children generally follow natural developmental trajectories, or paths, in learning mathematics. When teachers understand these trajectories, and sequences activities based on them, they can build powerful mathematics learning environments.

Each learning trajectory has three parts: a goal, a developmental progression, and instructional activities. To attain a certain mathematical competence in a given topic or domain (the goal), children learn each successive level (the developmental progression), aided by tasks (instructional activities) designed to build the mental actions-on-objects that enable thinking at each higher level (Clements & Sarama, 2004).

For example, consider one *goal* regarded as important in all the documents from the previous section: Young children should learn to be competent in whole-number addition and subtraction. More specifically—and beyond what many schools develop—they should learn to solve arithmetic problems of different *types* or *structures*. Type depends on the *situation* and the *unknown*. There are four different situations, shown in the four rows of Figure 11.1. In each of these situations, there are three quantities that play different roles in the problem, any one of which could be the unknown. In some cases, such as the unknown parts of part–part–whole problems, there is no real difference between the roles, so the unknown does not affect the difficulty of the problem. In others, such as result unknown, change unknown, or start unknown of join problems, the differences in difficulty are large. Result unknown problems are easy, change unknown problems are moderately difficult, and

Situation	Start/Part Unknown	Change/Difference Unknown	Result/Whole Unknown
Join ("change plus") An action of joining increases the number in a set.	*Start unknown* $\Box + 6 = 11$ Al had some balls. Then he got 6 more. Now he has 11 balls. How many did he start with?	*Change unknown* $5 + \Box = 11$ Al had 5 balls. He bought some more. Now he has 11. How many did he buy?	*Result unknown* $5 + 6 = \Box$ Al had 5 balls and gets 6 more. How many does he have in all?
Separate ("change minus") An action of separating decreases the number in a set.	*Start unknown* $\Box - 5 = 4$ Al had some balls. He gave 5 to Barb. Now he has 4. How many did he have to start with?	*Change unknown* $9 - \Box = 4$ Al had 9 balls. He gave some to Barb. Now he has 4. How many did he give to Barb?	*Result unknown* $9 - 5 = \Box$ Al had 9 balls and gave 5 to Barb. How many does he have left?
Part–part–whole ("collection") Two parts make a whole, but there is no action—the situation is static.	*Part ("partner") unknown* 10 / 6 Al has 10 balls. Some are blue, 6 are red. How many are blue?	*Part ("partner") unknown* 10 / 4 Al has 10 balls; 4 are blue, the rest are red. How many are red?	*Whole ("total") unknown* 4 / 6 Al has 4 red balls and 6 blue balls. How many balls does he have in all?
Compare The numbers of objects in two sets are compared.	*Smaller unknown* 7 / 2 Al had 7 balls. Barb has 2 fewer balls than Al. How many balls does Barb have? (More difficult language: "Al has 2 more than Barb.")	*Difference unknown* 7 / 5 Al has 7 dogs and 5 bones. How many dogs won't get a bone? Al has 6 balls. Barb has 4. How many more does Al have than Barb?	*Larger unknown* 5 / 2 Al has 5 marbles. Barb has 2 more than Al. How many balls does Barb have? (More difficult language: "Al has 2 balls less than Barb.")

FIGURE 11.1. Addition and subtraction problem types.

start unknown are the most difficult. This is due in large part to the increasing difficulty children have in modeling or "acting out" each type.

Thus, the main *goal* of the counting-based addition and subtraction learning trajectory is that children learn to solve arithmetic problems of the types in Figure 11.1. The second component of the learning trajectory is the "developmental progression," which describes a typical counting-based trajectory children follow in developing understanding and skill in arithmetic. The second column in Figure 11.2 describes several levels of thinking in the counting-based learning trajectory. (The first column is the approximate age at which children achieve each level of thinking. These are present-day averages and *not* the goal—with good education, children often develop these levels earlier.) The third column of Figure 11.2 provides an example of children's behavior and thinking for each level.

The fourth, right-most, column in Figure 11.2 provides examples of instructional tasks, matched to each of the levels of thinking in the developmental progression. These tasks are designed to help children learn the ideas and skills needed to achieve that level of thinking; that is, as teachers, we can use these tasks to promote children's growth from one level to the next. More complete learning trajectories provide multiple illustrations of tasks for each level (e.g., see Clements & Sarama, 2009); however, keep in mind that these illustrations are simply examples—many approaches are possible. Furthermore, curriculum developers and teachers must interpret these examples within their specific school contexts (see the later section on culture).

In summary, learning trajectories describe the goals of learning, the developmental progression through which children pass, and the learning activities in which students might engage. The *source* of the developmental progressions—the thinking and learning processes of children at various levels—is extensive research reviews and empirical work that cannot be presented here due to space constraints (but see Sarama & Clements, 2009). Also beyond the scope of this chapter are the complex, cognitive actions-on-objects that underlie all the example behaviors in Figure 11.2. Here we provide one illustration of both cognitive actions-on-objects and how different trajectories grow not in isolation but interactively.

Consider learning a critical competence—counting-on, used especially at the *Counting Strategies* level in Figure 11.2. Children need to develop competencies from three trajectories: counting, subitizing (not shown, but see Clements & Sarama, 2009; Sarama & Clements, 2009), and the addition and subtraction trajectory from Figure 11.2 to learn to count-on meaningfully. From the counting trajectory, they learn to count forward from any number. Then they learn to understand explicitly and apply the idea that each number in the counting sequence includes *the number before, hierarchically.* That is, 5 includes 4, which includes 3, and so forth. From the subitizing trajectory they quickly learn to recognize the number of—not just visual sets, but also *rhythmic patterns.* From the addition and subtraction trajectory, children learn to interpret situations mathematically, such as interpreting a real-world problem as a "part–part–whole" situation. They also learn to use counting to determine what is missing. The creative combination of these developments allows them to solve *meaningfully* problems such as "You have three green candies and six orange candies. How many candies do you have in all?" by counting-on. They understand that these numbers are two parts, and that they need to find the whole. They also understand that the order of numbers does not matter in addition. They know, in practice, that the sum is the number that results by starting at the first number and counting-on a number of iterations, equal to the second number. They can use counting to solve this, starting by saying "siiiiix ... " because they understand that word can stand for the counting acts from 1 to 6 (because 6 includes 5 ...). They know *how many more* to count because they use the subitized "rhythm of three" "Du de Du" ("Doo–Day–Doo"): "seven (du ...), eight (day ...), nine (*du*)—*nine!*"

Age	Developmental Progression	Example Behavior	Instructional Tasks
2–3	**Nonverbal +/–** Adds and subtracts very small collections nonverbally.	Shown 1 object then 1 object going under a napkin; identifies or makes a set of 2 objects to "match."	*Blocks in the Box.* Children play a game in which, for example, 2 blocks then 1 block go into a box, and they try to "guess" how many are in the box. The cover is taken off and the blocks are counted to check.
4	**Small Number +/–** Finds sums for joining problems up to 3 + 2 by counting-all with objects.	Asked, "You have 2 balls and get 1 more. How many in all?" Counts out 2, then counts out 1 more, then counts all 3: "1, 2, 3 … 3!"	*Join result unknown or separate, result unknown* (take-away) problems, numbers < 5 (see Figure 11.1). "You have 2 balls and get 1 more. How many in all?" *Finger word problems.* Tell children to solve simple addition problems with their fingers. Use very small numbers. Children should place their hands in their laps between each problem. To solve the problems above, guide children in showing 3 fingers on one hand and 2 fingers on the other and reiterate: "How many is that altogether?" Ask children how they got their answer and repeat with other problems.
4–5	**Find Result +/–** Finds sums for joining (you had 3 apples and get 3 more, how many do you have in all?) and part–part–whole (there are 6 girls and 5 boys on the playground, how many children were there in all?) problems *by direct modeling, counting-all, with objects.* Solves take-away problems by separating with objects.	Asked, "You have 2 red balls and 3 blue balls. How many in all?" Counts out 2 red, then counts out 3 blue, then counts all 5. Asked, "You have 5 balls and give 2 to Tom. How many do you have left?" Counts out 5 balls, then takes away 2, and then counts remaining 3.	*Word problems.* Children solving all the above problem types using manipulatives or their fingers to represent objects. For *separate, result unknown (take-away)*, "You have 5 balls and give 2 to Tom. How many do you have left?" Children might count out 5 balls, then take away 2, and then count remaining 3. For *part–part–whole, whole unknown* problems, they might solve "You have 2 red balls and 3 blue balls. How many in all?" *Places scenes (addition)—Part–part–whole, whole unknown problems.* Children play with toy on a background scene and combine groups. For example, they might place 4 tyrannosaurus rexes and 5 apatosauruses on the paper and then count all 9 to see how many dinosaurs they have in all.
	Find Change +/– Finds the missing addend (5 + _ = 7) by adding on objects.	Join-to—Count-All-Groups. Asked, "You have 5 balls and then get some more. Now you have 7 in all. How many did you get?" Counts out 5, then counts those 5 again starting at 1, then adds more, counting "6, 7," then counts the balls added to find the answer: 2.	*Join change unknown* problems such as, "You have 5 balls and then get some more. Now you have 7 in all. How many did you get?" Children solve using balls of two colors. *Part–part–whole, part unknown.* "There are 6 children on the playground. 2 are boys and the rest are girls. How many are girls?"

(cont.)

FIGURE 11.2. Samples from the learning trajectory for counting-based arithmetic.

Age	Developmental Progression	Example Behavior	Instructional Tasks
		(Some children may use their fingers, and attenuate the counting by using finger patterns.)	
5–6	**Counting Strategies +/–** Finds sums for joining ("You had 8 apples and get 3 more ... ") and part–part–whole (6 girls and 5 boys ...) problems with finger patterns and/or by counting-on.	Counting-on. "How much is 4 and 3 more?" "Fourrrrr ... five, six, seven [uses rhythmic or finger pattern to keep track]. Seven!" Counting-up-to. May solve missing addend (3 + _ = 7) or compare problems by counting up; for example, counts "4, 5, 6, 7" while putting up fingers; and then counts or recognizes the 4 fingers raised. Asked, "You have 6 balls. How many more would you need to have 8?" Says, "Six, seven [puts up first finger], eight [puts up second finger]. Two!"	*How many now?* Have the children count objects as you place them in a box. Ask, "How many are in the box now?" Add 1, repeating the question, then check the children's responses by counting all the objects. Repeat, checking occasionally. When children are ready, sometimes add 2, and eventually more, objects. Variations: Place coins in a coffee can. Declare that a given number of objects are in the can. Then have the children close their eyes and count on by listening as additional objects are dropped in. *Teaching counting-on skills.* If children need assistance to use counting-on, or do not spontaneously create it, explicitly teach the subskills. 1. Lay out the problem with numeral cards (e.g., 5 + 2). Count out objects into a line below each card. 2. Point to the last object of the first addend. When child counts that last object, point to numeral card and says, "See this is 5 also. It tells how many dots there are here." 3. Solve another problem. If children count the first set starting with 1 again, interrupt them sooner and ask what number they will say when they get to the last object in the first set. Emphasize that it will be the same as the numeral card. 4. Point to first dot of set and say (e.g., for 5 + 2) "See, there are fiiiiive here, so this one (exaggerated jump from last object in the first set to first object in the second set) gets the number *six*. 5. Repeat with new problems. If children need more assistance, interrupt their counting of the first set with questions: "How many are here (first set)? So *this* (last of first) gets what number? And what number for *this* one (first of second set)"?

(cont.)

FIGURE 11.2. *(cont.)*

Age	Developmental Progression	Example Behavior	Instructional Tasks
			Double compare. Students compare sums of cards to determine which sum is greater. Encourage children to use more sophisticated strategies, such as counting-on. *Join Result Unknown* and *Part–Part–Whole, Whole Unknown* "How much is 4 and 3 more?" "See, there are 5 here, so this one (exaggerated jump from last object in the first set to first object in the second set) gets the number *six*." Repeat with new problems. If children need more assistance, interrupt their counting of the first set with questions: "How many are here (first set)? So *this* (last of first) gets what number? And what number for *this* one (first of second set)?" *Easy as Pie:* Students add two numerals to find a total number (sums of 1 through 10), and then move forward a corresponding number of spaces on a game board. The game encourages children to count on from the larger number (e.g., to add 3 + 4, they would count "four … 5, 6, 7!")

(cont.)

FIGURE 11.2. *(cont.)*

Age	Developmental Progression	Example Behavior	Instructional Tasks
	Deriver +/– Uses flexible strategies and derived combinations (e.g., "7 + 7 is 14, so 7 + 8 is 15) to solve all types of problems. Includes Break-Apart-to-Make-Ten (BAMT). Can simultaneously think of 3 numbers within a sum, and can move part of a number to another, aware of the increase in one and the decrease in another.	Asked, "What's 7 plus 8?" thinks: $7 + 8 \rightarrow 7 + [7 + 1]$ $\rightarrow [7 + 7] + 1 = 14 + 1 =$ 15. Or, using BAMT, thinks 8 + 2 = 10, so separate 7 into 2 and 5, add 2 and 8 to make 10, then add 5 more, 15.	*Teach the BAMT strategy.* *All types* of single-digit problems. *Tic-Tac-Total.* Draw a tic-tac-toe board and write the numbers 1 to 10. Players take turn crossing out one of the numbers and writing it in the board. Whoever makes 15 first wins (Kamii, 1985). *21.* Play cards, where Ace is worth either 1 or 11 and 2 to 10 are worth their values. Dealer gives everyone 2 cards, including herself. On each round, each player, if sum is less than 21, can request another card, or "hold." If any new card makes the sum more than 21, the player is out. Continue until everyone "holds." The player whose sum is closest to 21 wins.
7	**Problem Solver +/–** Solves all types of problems, with flexible strategies and known combinations. Multidigit may be solved by incrementing or combining 10's and 1's (latter not used for join, change unknown).	Asked, "If I have 13 and you have 9, how could we have the same number?" Says, "Nine and one is ten, then three more to make 13. One and three is four. I need four more!" "What's 28 + 35?" Incrementer thinks: 20 + 30 = 50; +8 = 58; 2 more is 60, 3 more is 63. Combining 10's and 1's: 20 + 30 = 50. 8 + 5 is like 8 plus 2 and 3 more, so, it's 13. 50 and 13 is 63.	*All types* of problem structures for single-digit problems.

FIGURE 11.2. *(cont.)*

Persons often have several questions about learning trajectories, which we answer in the remainder of this section.

- *Why this emphasis on learning trajectories?* Learning trajectories allow teachers to build the *mathematics of children—the thinking of children as it develops naturally.* With an understanding of developmental progressions, we can be assured that all the goals and activities outlined are within the developmental capacities of children. We know that each level provides a natural *developmental building block* to the next level. Finally, we know that the activities provide the *mathematical building blocks* for school success because the research on which they are based typically involves children who have had educational advantages that allow them to do well at school.

- *When are children "at" a level?* Children are at a certain level when most of their behaviors reflect the thinking—ideas and skills—of that level. Often, they show a few behaviors from the next (and previous) levels as they learn. Levels are not "absolute stages." They are "benchmarks" of complex growth that represent distinct ways of thinking. So, another way to think of a level is as a sequence of different *patterns* of thinking and reasoning. Children are continually learning within levels and moving between them.

   • *How are learning trajectories different from just a scope and sequence?* They are related, of course. But they are *not* lists of everything children need to learn because they don't cover every single "fact"; rather, they emphasize the "big ideas." Furthermore, they are about children's *levels of thinking*, not just sequences of more and more content.

   • *There are ages in the charts. Should teachers plan to help children develop just the levels that correspond to their ages?* No, the ages in the table are typical ages at which children develop these ideas. *But these are rough guides only*—children differ widely. More importantly, children who are provided high-quality mathematics experiences are capable of developing beyond these averages to levels 1–2 years above those listed in the charts.

   • *How would teachers know at what levels their classes or, more challenging, individuals in their classes, are operating along a learning trajectory?* This question is so important that we respond to it in the next section.

Assessment

Learning trajectories may be embedded in standards (e.g., the *Common Core*) or curricula such as *Building Blocks*. However, the potentials of learning trajectories cannot be realized fully unless teachers explicitly understand *and* use learning trajectories to guide their teaching. We first discuss teachers' central role, then the use of learning trajectories to support that role.

Of the 10 instructional practices the NMAP (2008) researched, only a few had an adequate number of rigorous studies that consistently supported them. One of the most strongly supported was teachers' use of "formative assessment," which is the ongoing monitoring of children's learning to inform instruction. Teachers might monitor both their class as a whole and each individual in the class.

Although the NMAP's rigorous studies only included children as young as the upper primary grades, other studies confirm that regular assessment and individualization are key to effective early math education (Shepard, 2005; Thomson, Rowe, Underwood, & Peck, 2005). We believe that the key questions of formative assessment are answered best through the use of learning trajectories (see Table 11.1). To perform this kind of research-based formative assessment requires, of course, that teachers understand each component of the learning trajectory.

TABLE 11.1. Key Questions of Formative Assessment and Components of Learning Trajectories

Formative assessment question	Learning trajectory component
Where are you trying to go?	The goal—Describes the mathematical concepts, structures, and skills
Where are you now?	The developmental progression—Helps determine how the children are thinking now and what the next step, or level of thinking, would be.
How can you get there?	The instructional activities—Provide tasks linked to each level of the developmental progression that are designed to engender the kind of thinking that will form the next level. Suggests feedback for specific errors.

First, they have to understand the *goal*—the *mathematics*. Although that appears obvious, the U.S. culture has such a low level of mathematics understanding, *we often do not realize what we do not know.* The vast majority of early childhood educators in a recent survey claimed that they knew all the mathematics they needed to teach (Sarama, 2002). For example, they believe that they know how to count, and that is what they teach. However, many teachers do not fully understand the concepts and procedures that underlie counting, nor how counting connects to other areas of mathematics (Clements & Sarama, 2009; National Research Council, 2009). Primary-grade teachers may lack full understanding of place value and arithmetic (Clements & Sarama, 2009; Ma, 1999; National Research Council, 2009). Even if teachers have some understanding of the mathematics they teach, it is likely insufficient. Few educators or parents would be satisfied if teachers of fourth grade could read (only) at the fourth-grade level.

As one example, adequate knowledge of counting-based addition and subtraction involves understanding the *mathematical structure* of the problem types in Figure 11.1. It also involves knowing that the *sum* of $5 + 3$ is the whole number that results from counting 3 more numbers starting at 5. In general, for any two whole numbers a and b, the sum $a + b$ is the number that results by counting b more numbers, starting at the number a (Wu, 2007). Moving to multidigit operations involves multiple other concepts and procedures.

Second, performing effective formative assessment requires that teachers understand the developmental progression shown in Figure 11.2. They also need to know *how to assess* children in order to identify the level(s) at which children are thinking. This is what we discuss in the remainder of this section. (The third component, knowing what to do instructionally, is discussed in the following main section.) Of course, to assess effectively, the teacher must understand behavioral indicators at each level of a given developmental progression and what *distinguishes* them from behaviors at levels just before and after, especially those levels children are most likely to demonstrate in their classrooms. Our work with teachers has not only supported the usefulness of these competencies for teachers but it also has shown that it takes considerable work and time to develop these competencies (Clements, Sarama, Spitler, Lange, & Wolfe, 2011; Sarama & Clements, 2009; Sarama, Clements, Starkey, Klein, & Wakeley, 2008). We have developed a tool, the Building Blocks Learning Trajectories Web application, BBLT (for a demonstration, see *www.ubtriad.org*). BBLT presents and connects all components of the innovation, encouraging teachers to view the learning through a curriculum or developmental (children's thinking) perspective. Each view is linked to the others. That is, teachers might choose the "Instruction" view (see Figure 11.3), click an activity, and see not only an explanation and video of the activity "in action" but also the level of thinking that activity is designed to develop, within the context of the entire learning trajectory. Alternatively, the developmental progressions can be studied independently as the teacher moves up and down the levels, observing videos of clinical interviews in which text comments highlight the behavioral indicators of each level of thinking (Sarama & Clements [2009] provide additional details).

Assessment that supports early learning can draw upon a range of evidential sources of children's thinking development, as outlined in Table 11.2 (based on Chittenden, 1999). At appropriate ages, all of these sources can be useful. However, in early education, group-administered tests often are not adequate assessment tools and can actually do harm.

A positive approach to assessing children's strengths and needs starts with individually administered interview assessments based on developmental progressions ("mastery"-type tests that tell you what children can and cannot do; see Fuson, 2004). These are supplemented with frequent observations, documentation of children's talk, interviews, samples of children's work, and performance assessments that illuminate children's thinking. These strategies are more likely to illuminate children's background knowledge and emerging

The user reads the description that appears on the right. If she chooses "More info," the screen "slides over" to reveal the expanded view shown below.

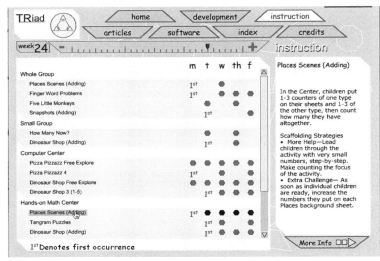

Here she can see multiple video examples, with commentary. Clicking on the related developmental level (child's level of thinking), ringed here, yields the view on the next page.

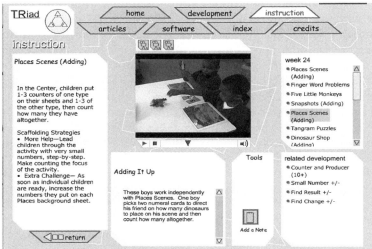

This developmental view likewise provides a description, video, and commentary on the developmental level—the video here is of a clinical interview task in which a child displays that *level of thinking*.

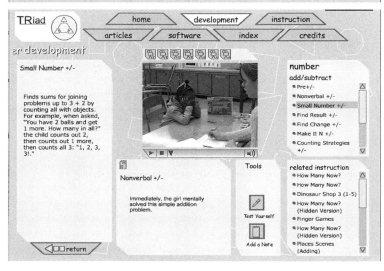

FIGURE 11.3. Sample screens from the Building Blocks Learning Trajectories (BBLT) Web application.

TABLE 11.2. Sources of Assessment Information

General observation and records of activities	Class discussions and conversations	Work samples	Performance tasks and curriculum-embedded assessments	Interviews and tests
• Anecdotal records • Checklists projects • Inventories of student activities	• Whole-group discussions • Student comments and questions about their work • Conferences and conversations	• Drawings • Writing and journal entries • Constructions	• Solving a problem, with explanation • Telling a story problem	• Teacher-made • Textbook/unit questions • Standardized, norm-referenced

Note. Based on Chittenden (1999).

ideas and skills, thus providing insight that teachers need to perform high-quality formative assessment. Careful assessment is especially important for instruction of children with special needs or disabilities. Our experience suggests that teachers should combine all appropriates sources, but that two are especially important in assessing children's progress through mathematical learning trajectories. They are the (1) structured interviews administered three times per year and (2) assessments embedded in small-group curriculum activities.

Effective and efficient teaching is possible when teachers know what their children do and do not already understand, and what they can and cannot already do. Gathering information from structured interview assessments near the beginning of the school year allows teachers to develop clear pictures of both the class and each individual, across multiple learning trajectories that are important for children in that age group. For example, *TEAM* (*Tools for Early Assessment in Math*; Clements, Sarama, & Wolfe, 2011) is an interview tool that teachers administer using a flipbook, manipulatives, and a laptop, iPad, iPod, or the like (Figure 11.4). The teacher interacts with each child individually and records both the child's responses and strategies. Thus, the teacher can see whether children understand and can explain their methods—critical goals for early mathematics learning (Fuson, 2004). At the conclusion, the teacher automatically receives profiles of individual children, including summary scores and information (correctness and strategies) for each trajectory, as well as reports on the class as a whole. Finally, the *TEAM* report also prescribes instructional activities for each child, connected to a variety of curricula. Teachers are encouraged to readminister the *TEAM* in the middle and at the end of the year.

The second important source of information lies in weekly assessments that are embedded in small-group activities throughout the year. For example, in the BBLT curriculum, the Small Group Record Sheets is used to record the concepts and skills children display during each week's small-group activity. For example, one beginning activity is matching and naming geometric shapes. This is an ideal point to see what shapes children already know, especially given research suggesting that kindergarten teachers often teach only those shapes most children in their classes already know (Thomas, 1982). Figure 11.5 is an example of how one teacher filled out the Small Group Record Sheet for that activity. Portions of the learning trajectory's developmental levels are listed in the table in the upper right corner. The teacher's notes show her strategic use of abbreviations and drawings to convey substantial information about her children, all the while guiding and participating in the instructional activity.

To sum up so far, in order to perform effective formative assessment, teachers need to understand the developmental progression shown in Figure 11.2. They also need to know

FIGURE 11.4. The TEAM (Tools for Early Assessment in Math; Clements, 2011) interview-based assessment in use.

how to assess children so as to identify the level(s) at which the child is thinking. We discuss the third component, knowing what to do instructionally, next.

Curriculum: Learning Trajectories' Instructional Tasks

As mentioned, to implement research-based formative assessment requires that teachers understand each component of the learning trajectory, including the instructional tasks. This goes beyond knowing how to enact instructional activities. Teachers also must know when to implement them, with whom, and why. That is, they need to know what specific instructional activities are appropriate for learners at a given level in a developmental progression, and how and why those activities may assist learning by building toward the next level of thinking.

Research highlights the importance of such knowledge, showing that educational benefits of formative assessment depend on teachers *adapting instruction* based on assessments (NMAP, 2008; Shepard, 2005; Thomson et al., 2005). Furthermore, teachers are more effective when they are offered advice about specific instructional activities to use. Learning trajectories, as defined here, *include* just such advice—instructional activities are linked to every level of thinking of each trajectory. Assessments based on learning trajectories, such as the *TEAM*, and strategies such as curriculum-embedded assessments, link directly to relevant instruction. Research also indicates that computer-assisted instruction can help make formative assessment more effective (NMAP, 2008).

Small Group Record Sheet
Building Blocks Math - PreK Assessment

Week: 4

Activity: Match & Name Shapes

Trajectory Name	Description
Shape Matcher	Matches basic shapes
Shape Recognizer, Typical	Recog. & name typical cr. Sq. & tri
Shape Recognizer, Circles, Squares, & Triangles +	Recog. Non-typical sq. & rect.
Shape Recognizer, All Rectangles	Recog. More rect. Sizer, shapes & orient.

	Child's Name	Shapes Known & Trajectory Level:	Child's explanation(s):	Comments
1	Michelle	Shape matcher	Confuses between different △s	unable to give properties
2	Alexis	Shape recognizer all ▭	able to give properties	
3	Carlos	Shape recognizer all shapes	"	
4	Karizma	Shape matcher	was able to recog. all △s	unable to give properties
5	Diego	Shape recognizer ○ ▢ ▭ △	# of sides # of angles	
6	Gabriella	"	"	
7	Angel	"	"	
8	Melanie	"	"	
9	Valerie	Shape recognizer	Lang. barrier to explain properties	○ △ ▢ ▭
10	Vianney	Shape matcher	"	○ ▨ ▨ ▭
11	Jonathan	Shape recognizer ○ ▢ ▭ △	unable to give properties	○ △ ▢ ▭
12	Anieya	Shape recognizer typical		○ △ ▢ ▭
13	Ciara			
14	Daniella	Shape recognizer all rectangles		Confused between △ ▭
15	Cynathia	"	can differentiate diff ▢ ▭	"
16	Michael	Shape recognizer all rectangles		able to recognize & describe all △ ▢ ◇

FIGURE 11.5. One teacher's classroom use of a Building Blocks' Small Group Record Sheet.

Of course, instructional tasks in learning trajectories are not the only way to guide children to achieve the levels of thinking embedded within the learning trajectories. However, they are specific examples of the type of instructional activity that helps promote thinking at the subsequent level. Thus, teachers implement them, or adapt them, or use them as a template to gauge the usefulness of other lessons, including those in their published curricula.

Furthermore, in many cases, there *is* research evidence that certain aspects of the instructional tasks are especially effective. We discuss two examples. First, *although* Figure 11.2 includes only samples of levels and activities, we included one elaborated example called "teaching counting-on skills" in the Counting Strategies level. Based on theory and empirical work (El'konin & Davydov, 1975; Fuson, 1992), these instructional procedures have been effective in teaching counting-on to children who have not yet developed this skill by creating and discussing counting strategies in the classroom. After setting up the problem situation (Step 1), the teacher guides children to connect the numeral signifying the first addend (5 in the example; see Figure 11.2) to the five objects in the first set; students then learn to recognize that the fifth object is assigned the counting word *five* (Step 2 and, as necessary, Step 3). Afterwards, the teacher helps the children understand that the first object in the second set will always be assigned the next counting number (*six*). These understandings and skills are reinforced with additional problems and focused questions.

Besides carefully addressing necessary ideas and subskills, this instructional activity is successful because it promotes "psychological curtailment" (Clements & Burns, 2000; Krutetskii, 1976). Curtailment is an encapsulation process in which one mental activity gradually "stands in for" another mental activity. Children must learn that it is not necessary to enumerate each element of the first set. The teacher explains this, then demonstrates by naming the number of that set with an elongated number word and a sweeping gesture of the hand before passing on to the second addend. El'konin and Davydov (1975) claim that such abbreviated actions are not eliminated but are transferred to the position of actions which are considered *as if* they were carried out and are thus "implicit." The sweeping movement gives rise to a "mental plan" by which addition is performed because only in this movement does the child begin to view the group as a unit. The child becomes aware of addition as distinct from counting. This construction of counting-on must be based on physically present objects. Then, through introspection (considering the basis of one's own ways of acting), the object set is transformed into a symbol (El'konin & Davydov, 1975).

Our second example of instructional activities backed by specific research evidence is found in the next level in Figure 11.2, Deriver +/−. *Teach the BAMT strategy* actually comprises a series of instructional activities involving several interrelated learning trajectories (see Sarama & Clements, 2009, for a full description). BAMT stands for Break-Apart-to-Make-Ten. Before lessons on BAMT, children work on several related learning trajectories. They develop solid knowledge of numerals and counting (i.e., move along the counting learning trajectory). This includes the number structure for teen numbers as 10 + another number, which, is more straightforward in Asian languages than in English ("thirteen" is "ten and three"—note that U.S. teachers must be particularly attentive to this competence). They learn to solve addition and subtraction of numbers with totals less than 10, often chunking numbers into 5 (e.g., 7 as 5-plus-2) and using visual models.

With these levels of thinking established, children develop several levels of thinking within the composition–decomposition developmental progression. For example, they work on "break-apart partners" of numbers less than or equal to 10. They solve addition and subtraction problems involving teen numbers using the 10's structure ($10 + 2 = 12$; $18 − 8 = 10$), and addition and subtraction with three addends using 10's (e.g., $4 + 6 + 3 = 10 + 3 = 13$ and $15 − 5 − 9 = 10 − 9 = 1$).

Teachers then introduce problems such as $8 + 6$. They first elicit, value, and discuss *child-invented strategies* and encourage children to use these strategies to solve a variety of problems. Only then do they proceed to the use of BAMT. They provide supports to connect visual and symbolic representations of quantities. In the example $9 + 4$, they show 9 counters (or fingers) and 4 counters, then move one counter from the group of four to make a group of 10. Next, they highlight the three left in the group. Then children are reminded that the 9 and 1 made 10. Last, children see 10 counters and 3 counters and think ten-three, or count on "ten-one, ten-two, ten-three." Later, representational drawings serve this role, in a sequence such as that shown in Figure 11.6.

Teachers spend many lessons ensuring children's understanding and skill using the BAMT strategy. Children are asked why the strategy works and what its advantages are. Extensive repeated experiencing (distributed practice) is used to develop fluency.

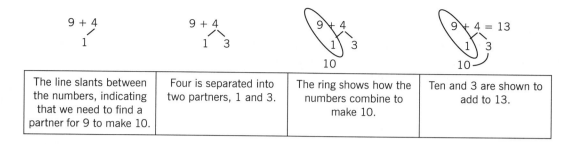

The line slants between the numbers, indicating that we need to find a partner for 9 to make 10.	Four is separated into two partners, 1 and 3.	The ring shows how the numbers combine to make 10.	Ten and 3 are shown to add to 13.

FIGURE 11.6. Teaching BAMT.

As mentioned previously, not all instructional tasks are as specific as these just outlined. In many cases, instructional tasks are simply illustrations of the kind of activity that would be appropriate to reach a certain level of thinking. For example, the problems suggested for each levels should be changed for different children, but the *type* of problem (see Figure 11.1) is important.

A final observation regarding our Figure 11.2 discussions is that learning trajectories promote learning skills and concepts together. Learning skills before developing understanding can lead to learning difficulties (Baroody, 2004a, 2004b; Fuson, 2004; Kilpatrick, Swafford, & Findell, 2001; Sophian, 2004; Steffe, 2004). Furthermore, effective curricula and teaching often build on children's thinking, provide opportunities for both invention and practice, and ask children to explain their various strategies (Hiebert, 1999). Such programs facilitate conceptual growth and higher-order thinking without sacrificing skills learning. Effective teachers also consistently integrate real-world situations, problem solving, and mathematical content (Fuson, 2004). Making connections to real-life situations also enhances children's knowledge and positive beliefs about mathematics (Perlmutter, Bloom, Rose, & Rogers, 1997). Thus, a critical task for teachers is to adapt activities, such as the example problems in Figure 11.2, so that they are relevant and appropriate to their own students.

One caveat is notable here; Figure 11.2 does not include multidigit arithmetic. As children work with larger numbers, the learning trajectory is extended (see Chapter 6 in each of the companion books; Clements & Sarama, 2009; Sarama & Clements, 2009). Children should apply new computational skills to a variety of problem types (Figure 11.1) using larger numbers, and also in solving two-step problems.

Overarching Concerns: Cultures and Individuals

Culture

All learning trajectories are "hypothetical," and this must be realized by teachers and their children. Thus, educators should remember that the instructional tasks of these learning trajectories are "bare bones" examples of the *type* of activity that might be adapted by a teacher. Contextual and cultural must be considered as they are brought to life (Wager & Carpenter, in press). If educators do not recognize the mathematical strategies children develop out of school and the mathematical knowledge that they bring to school, these competencies are not connected to school mathematics, and the gap between out-of-school and school mathematics grows.

This is important because teachers who use culturally specific pedagogical approaches help minority and poor children learn mathematics more effectively. For example, such teachers connect curriculum to children's out-of-school life (e.g., in playing dominoes) and allow children to create their own solution strategies (e.g., using rhythms from games and songs in mathematical activity from beginning counting multidigit addition) (Leonard, 2008). Using children's native language is also useful, but combining that with modifications of the problem within contexts reflecting out-of-school experiences, as well as communicating with families, may be even more effective (Celedón-Pattichis, Musanti, & Marshall, 2010; Wager & Carpenter, in press).

The U.S. Culture and Mathematics

The U.S. culture writ large is not a hospitable environment for the development of positive attitudes and beliefs about mathematics. For example, all it takes to raise math anxiety in approximately 17% of the population is to show them "17%" (Ashcraft, 2006). Many have negative affect and beliefs about mathematics.

Furthermore, a particularly destructive cultural belief is that achievement in mathematics depends mostly on native aptitude or ability. In contrast, people from other countries, such as Japan, believe that achievement comes from effort (Holloway, 1988). Even more disturbing, research shows that this U.S. cultural belief hurts children. However, and just as importantly, research indicates that the belief is groundless. Children who are led to understand the idea "I can learn if I try" work on tasks longer and achieve more throughout their school careers than do children who believe that people either "get math" or not (McLeod & Adams, 1989). This latter view leads to failure and "learned helplessness" (McLeod & Adams, 1989; Weiner, 1986).

Fortunately, most young children have positive feelings about math and are motivated to explore numbers and shapes (Middleton & Spanias, 1999). After only a couple of years in typical schools, however, they begin to believe that "only some people have the ability to do math." Children who experience math as a sense-making activity build positive feelings about math throughout their school careers.

Teachers can promote positive attitudes and beliefs about mathematics using several strategies (Anghileri, 2004; Clements et al., 2004; Cobb, 1990; Cobb, Yackel, & Wood, 1989; Fennema et al., 1996; Hiebert, 1999; Kutscher, Linchevski, & Eisenman, 2002; McClain, Cobb, Gravemeijer, & Estes, 1999). They can provide meaningful tasks that make sense to children and connect with their everyday interests and lives. The right degree of challenge and novelty can promote interest, and promoting and discussing skills improvement can promote a mastery orientation. Researchers have estimated that children should be successful about 70% of the time to maximize motivation (Middleton & Spanias, 1999). They can expect children to invent, explain, and critique their own solution strategies within a social context. They can encourage and support children's progress toward increasingly sophisticated and abstract mathematical methods and understandings, as well as the development of more efficient and elegant solution strategies.

Teachers also can greatly facilitate children's mathematical thinking by countering the typical U.S. cultural beliefs about mathematics. One such belief is that "academics" such as math and "play" are opposing and mutually exclusive foci for the early childhood classroom. A related belief is that mathematics and creativity are similarly at opposite poles. We believe the research in this chapter effectively shows the motivation and creativity children can bring to mathematics. As a final example, recall Abby's experience with the trains, introduced at the beginning of this chapter. We believe this illustrates the following:

- Young children may have more *intrinsic* interest in mathematics activity than most adults believe.
- Children may be—or at least have the potential to be—more competent in mathematics than many adults realize.

- Learning mathematics may take place in play situations.
- The likelihood of such learning is probably dependent on frequent informal, but interactive, and often guided and structured learning episodes with adults.
- Children do not just "do" mathematics while they play. In the right circumstances, they may *play with mathematics itself.*
- Again, the likelihood of such creative and impressively complex play probably depends on experiences with competent adults.

Before we move on, let us elaborate on some of these points. When Abby first figured out how many she was missing, she was using math in her play. But when she decided that she would renumber the three engines she had with her 'one,' 'three,' and 'five' and the missing engines 'two' and 'four' she was *playing with the notion that the assignment of numbers to a collection of objects is arbitrary.* She was also counting not just objects, but counting words themselves. She counted the words *four* and *five* to see that there were two missing, then figured that counting the renumbered counting words *two* and *four also* yielded the result of "two." She was *playing with the idea that counting words themselves could be counted. She was applying an abstract symbol system—recursively—to itself.*

What would Abby's teacher need to know to provide Abby with high-quality experiences that would foster this inventive girl's mathematical development? We believe the teacher would need to know about the research we review in this chapter. To serve all children, the teacher also would have to know about children with special needs.

Children with Special Needs

Children with special needs often do not fare well in mathematics. Children with mathematical difficulties (MD) are those who are struggling to learn math for any reason (even a reason such as lack of motivation; Berch & Mazzocco, 2007). As many as 35 to 40% of children may fall into that category. Children with specific mathematics learning disabilities (MLD) have memory or cognitive deficits that interfere with their ability to learn math (Geary, 2004). About 6–7% of children may have MLD (Berch & Mazzocco, 2007; Mazzocco & Myers, 2003). However, early diagnoses are not stable; only 63% of those classified as MLD in kindergarten were still so classified in third grade (Mazzocco & Myers, 2003).

One of the most consistent findings is that children with MLD have difficulty quickly retrieving basic arithmetic facts. This may be due to an inability to store or retrieve facts; impairments in visual–spatial representations; or limits in working memory and speed of cognitive processing, indicators that appear as early as kindergarten (Geary, Hoard, Byrd-Craven, Nugent, & Numtee, 2007).

Other possibilities include a lack of higher-order, or executive, control of verbal material, which may hamper learning basic arithmetic combinations or facts. As an example, children with MLD may have difficulty inhibiting irrelevant associations, such as hearing 5 + 4 and saying "six" because it follows 5. As late as second grade, children with MLD may not fully understand counting and may not recognize errors in counting. They persist in using immature counting strategies throughout elementary school (Ostad, 1998). For example, some still count "one-by-one" on their fingers at end of the elementary grades. This may help explain their difficulty learning basic arithmetic combinations (Geary, Bow-Thomas, & Yao, 1992). Other experts claim that lack of specific competencies, such as in subitizing, is more important (Berch & Mazzocco, 2007).

Especially because diagnoses are not stable, children should be labeled as "MLD" only with great caution and after good instruction has been provided. Learning trajectories can help identify children's level of thinking, and these children may then receive additional (not substitute) instruction to move along as fast and far as possible toward the level of thinking of their peers. Other adaptations can be made simultaneously; for example, some children who have MLD may simply need extra time to study and complete calculation tasks. The use of a calculator and other computational aids would enable these children to concentrate on developing their otherwise good problem-solving skills (Jordan & Montani, 1997). As another example, teachers might teach strategies more explicitly (not just "facts" or "skills"), encouraging children to think aloud, then provide feedback. Teacher could highlight carefully key aspects of each type of problem (not "key words"). In one research example, children with developmental delays who learned "$n + 1$" tasks ($4 + 1$, $6 + 1$) discovered "the number-after-n" rule, after which they spontaneously invented counting on (realizing, e.g., that if $7 + 1$ is 8, $7 + 2$ is two count words after 7).

As a final note, learning trajectories also can help identify and serve the needs of children who are gifted and talented; however, many such children are never identified. Moreover, even when these children are noticed, they rarely are exposed to more sophisticated topics, even though they have advanced knowledge about and interest in them (Wadlington & Burns, 1993). They need to solve engaging, difficult problems in the domains of number, operations, geometry, and spatial sense. They need to be challenged to engage in high-level mathematical reasoning, including abstract reasoning. Much work remains to help identify and promote the learning process for gifted children.

Final Words

Children in the preschool- through primary-grade years can learn more mathematics, in multiple ways that honor their unique ways of thinking, than was previously thought possible. Learning trajectories can support children's learning, as can assessment and curriculum development and enactment. Children whose teachers use research-based learning trajectories demonstrate higher levels of mathematical reasoning. Current research in learning trajectories points the way toward more effective and efficient, yet creative and enjoyable mathematics learning, through culturally relevant and developmentally appropriate curricula and assessment.

Acknowledgments

This chapter was based on work supported in part by the Institute of Education Sciences (U.S. Dept. of Education) under Grant No. R305K05157. Work on the research was also supported in part by the National Science Foundation under Grant Nos. DRL-1019925 and DRL-1020118. Any opinions, findings, and conclusions or recommendations expressed in this material are those of the authors and do not necessarily reflect the views of the funding agencies.

Notes

1. Drafts of the *PSSM* were disseminated widely through print (to members and associated organizations), the Web, journals, and presentations. Feedback was gathered from commissioned reviews (25 mathematicians, mathematics educators, and educators outside mathematics), associated review groups (14 groups; e.g., Mathematical Association of America), individuals, and mailings (e.g., leaders of state and national educational associations). Over 30,000 printed copies were mailed, and 20,000 copies were downloaded per month. Over 700 reviews were received. Data were analyzed as rigorously as any qualitative research (e.g., multiple raters for coding by multiple categories) using software that permitted the writing team to request specific, detailed reports (e.g., the query "What did reviewers say about geometry for preschoolers?" could be answered with a report giving all relevant text, each passage identified with its source, location, etc.).

2. Clements was a coauthor of all these reports, the *CFP*, NMAP report, and *Common Core*. However, comments here are our own and do not necessarily reflect the views of the organizations or other coauthors.

References

Anghileri, J. (2004). Disciplined calculators or flexible problem solvers? In M. J. Høines & A. B. Fuglestad (Eds.), *Proceedings of the 28th Conference of the International Group for the Psychology in Mathematics Education* (Vol. 1, pp. 41–46). Bergen, Norway: Bergen University College.

Ashcraft, M. H. (2006, November). *Math performance, working memory, and math anxiety; Some possible directions for neural functioning work.* Paper presented at the Neural Basis of Mathematical Development, Nashville, TN.

Baroody, A. J. (2004a). The developmental bases for early childhood number and operations standards. In D. H. Clements, J. Sarama, & A.-M. DiBiase (Eds.), *Engaging young children in mathematics: Standards for early childhood mathematics education* (pp. 173–219). Mahwah, NJ: Erlbaum.

Baroody, A. J. (2004b). The role of psychological research in the development of early childhood mathematics standards. In D. H. Clements, J. Sarama, & A.-M. DiBiase (Eds.), *Engaging young children in mathematics: Standards for early childhood mathematics education* (pp. 149–172). Mahwah, NJ: Erlbaum.

Berch, D. B., & Mazzocco, M. M. M. (Eds.). (2007). *Why is math so hard for some children?: The nature and origins of mathematical learning difficulties and disabilities.* Baltimore: Brookes.

Celedón-Pattichis, S., Musanti, S. I., & Marshall, M. E. (2010). Bilingual elementary teachers' reflections on using students' native language and culture to teach mathematics. In M. Q. Foote (Ed.), *Mathematics teaching and learning in K–12: Equity and professional development* (pp. 7–24). New York: Palgrave Macmillan.

Chittenden, E. (1999). Science assessment in early childhood programs. In G. D. Nelson (Ed.), *Dialogue on early childhood science, mathematics, and technology education* (pp. 106–114). Washington, DC: American Association for the Advancement of Science.

Clements, D. H., & Burns, B. A. (2000). Students' development of strategies for turn and angle measure. *Educational Studies in Mathematics, 41,* 31–45.

Clements, D. H., & Conference Working Group. (2004). Part one: Major themes and recommendations. In D. H. Clements, J. Sarama, & A.-M. DiBiase (Eds.), *Engaging young children in mathematics: Standards for early childhood mathematics education* (pp. 1–72). Mahwah, NJ: Erlbaum.

Clements, D. H., & Sarama, J. (2004). Learning trajectories in mathematics education. *Mathematical Thinking and Learning, 6,* 81–89.

Clements, D. H., & Sarama, J. (2009). *Learning and teaching early math: The learning trajectories approach.* New York: Routledge.

Clements, D. H., Sarama, J., & DiBiase, A.-M. (2004). *Engaging young children in mathematics: Standards for early childhood mathematics education.* Mahwah, NJ: Erlbaum.

Clements, D. H., Sarama, J., Spitler, M. E., Lange, A. A., & Wolfe, C. B. (2011). Mathematics learned by young children in an intervention based on learning trajectories: A large-scale cluster randomized trial. *Journal for Research in Mathematics Education, 42*(2), 127–166.

Clements, D. H., Sarama, J., & Wolfe, C. B. (2011). *TEAM—Tools for early assessment in mathematics.* Columbus, OH: McGraw-Hill Education.

Cobb, P. (1990). A constructivist perspective on information-processing theories of mathematical activity. *International Journal of Educational Research, 14,* 67–92.

Cobb, P., Yackel, E., & Wood, T. (1989). Young children's emotional acts during mathematical problem solving. In D. B. McLeod & V. M. Admas (Eds.), *Affect and mathematical problem solving: A new perspective* (pp. 117–148). New York: Springer-Verlag.

Council of Chief State School Officers and the National Governors Association Center for Best Practices (CCSSO/NGA). (2010). *Common core state standards for mathematics.* Washington, DC: Author.

El'konin, D. B., & Davydov, V. V. (1975). Children's capacity for learning mathematics. In L. P. Steffe (Ed.), *Soviet studies in the psychology of learning and teaching mathematics* (Vol. 7, pp. 1–11). Chicago: University of Chicago Press.

Fennema, E. H., Carpenter, T. P., Frank, M. L., Levi, L., Jacobs, V. R., & Empson, S. B. (1996). A longitudinal study of learning to use children's thinking in mathematics instruction. *Journal for Research in Mathematics Education, 27,* 403–434.

Fuson, K. C. (1992). Research on whole number addition and subtraction. In D. A. Grouws (Ed.), *Handbook of research on mathematics teaching and learning* (pp. 243–275). New York: Macmillan.

Fuson, K. C. (2004). Pre-K to grade 2 goals and standards: Achieving 21st century mastery for all. In D. H. Clements, J. Sarama, & A.-M. DiBiase (Eds.), *Engaging young children in mathematics: Standards for early childhood mathematics education* (pp. 105–148). Mahwah, NJ: Erlbaum.

Geary, D. C. (2004). Mathematics and learning disabilities. *Journal of Learning Disabilities, 37,* 4–15.

Geary, D. C., Bow-Thomas, C. C., & Yao, Y. (1992). Counting knowledge and skill in cognitive addition: A comparison of normal and mathematically disabled children. *Journal of Experimental Child Psychology, 54,* 372–391.

Geary, D. C., Hoard, M. K., Byrd-Craven, J., Nugent, L., & Numtee, C. (2007). Cognitive mechanisms underlying achievement deficits in children with mathematical learning disability. *Child Development, 78,* 1343–1359.

Hiebert, J. C. (1999). Relationships between research and the NCTM Standards. *Journal for Research in Mathematics Education, 30,* 3–19.

Holloway, S. C. (1988). Concepts of ability and effort in Japan and the United States. *Review of Educational Research, 58,* 327–345.

Jordan, N. C., & Montani, T. O. (1997). Cognitive arithmetic and problem solving: A comparison of children with specific and general mathematics difficulties. *Journal of Learning Disabilities, 30,* 624–634.

Kamii, C. (1985). *Young children reinvent arithmetic: Implications of Piaget's theory.* New York: Teaching College Press.

Kilpatrick, J., Swafford, J., & Findell, B. (2001). *Adding it up: Helping children learn mathematics.* Washington, DC: National Academy Press.

Krutetskii, V. A. (1976). *The psychology of mathematical abilities in schoolchildren.* Chicago: University of Chicago Press.

Kutscher, B., Linchevski, L., & Eisenman, T. (2002). From the Lotto game to subtracting two-digit numbers in first-graders. In A. D. Cockburn & E. Nardi (Eds.), *Proceedings of the 26th Conference of the International Group for the Psychology in Mathematics Education* (Vol. 3, pp. 249–256). Norwich, UK.

Leonard, J. (2008). *Culturally specific pedagogy in the mathematics classroom: Strategies for teachers and students.* New York: Routledge.

Ma, L. (1999). *Knowing and teaching elementary mathematics: Teachers' understanding of fundamental mathematics in China and the United States.* Mahwah, NJ: Erlbaum.

Mazzocco, M. M. M., & Myers, G. F. (2003). Complexities in identifying and defining mathematics learning disability in the primary school-age years. *Annuals of Dyslexia, 53,* 218–253.

McClain, K., Cobb, P., Gravemeijer, K. P. E., & Estes, B. (1999). Developing mathematical reasoning within the context of measurement. In L. V. Stiff & F. R. Curcio (Eds.), *Developing mathematical reasoning in grades K–12* (pp. 93–106). Reston, VA: National Council of Teachers of Mathematics.

McLeod, D. B., & Adams, V. M. (Eds.). (1989). *Affect and mathematical problem solving.* New York: Springer-Verlag.

Middleton, J. A., & Spanias, P. (1999). Motivation for achievement in mathematics: Findings, generalizations, and criticisms of the research. *Journal for Research in Mathematics Education, 30,* 65–88.

National Council of Teachers of Mathematics (NCTM). (1989). *Curriculum and evaluation standards for school mathematics.* Reston, VA: Author.

National Council of Teachers of Mathematics (NCTM). (2000). *Principles and standards for school mathematics*. Reston, VA: Author.

National Council of Teachers of Mathematics (NCTM). (2006). *Curriculum focal points for prekindergarten through grade 8 mathematics: A quest for coherence*. Reston, VA: Author.

National Mathematics Advisory Panel (NMAP). (2008). *Foundations for success: The final report of the National Mathematics Advisory Panel*. Washington, DC: U.S. Department of Education, Office of Planning, Evaluation and Policy Development.

National Research Council. (2009). *Mathematics in early childhood: Learning paths toward excellence and equity*. Washington, DC: National Academy Press.

Ostad, S. A. (1998). Subtraction strategies in developmental perspective: A comparison of mathematically normal and mathematically disabled children. In A. Olivier & K. Newstead (Eds.), *Proceedings of the 22nd Conference for the International Group for the Psychology of Mathematics Education* (Vol. 3, pp. 311–318). Stellenbosch, South Africa: University of Stellenbosch.

Perlmutter, J., Bloom, L., Rose, T., & Rogers, A. (1997). Who uses math?: Primary children's perceptions of the uses of mathematics. *Journal of Research in Childhood Education, 12*(1), 58–70.

Sarama, J. (2002). Listening to teachers: Planning for professional development. *Teaching Children Mathematics, 9*, 36–39.

Sarama, J., & Clements, D. H. (2009). *Early childhood mathematics education research: Learning trajectories for young children*. New York: Routledge.

Sarama, J., Clements, D. H., Starkey, P., Klein, A., & Wakeley, A. (2008). Scaling up the implementation of a pre-kindergarten mathematics curriculum: Teaching for understanding with trajectories and technologies. *Journal of Research on Educational Effectiveness, 1*, 89–119.

Shepard, L. A. (2005). Assessment. In L. Darling-Hammond & J. Bransford (Eds.), *Preparing teachers for a changing world* (pp. 275–326). San. Francisco: Jossey-Bass.

Skemp, R. (1976). Relational understanding and instrumental understanding. *Mathematics Teaching, 77*, 20–26.

Sophian, C. (2004). A prospective developmental perspective on early mathematics instruction. In D. H. Clements, J. Sarama, & A.-M. DiBiase (Eds.), *Engaging young children in mathematics: Standards for early childhood mathematics education* (pp. 253–266). Mahwah, NJ: Erlbaum.

Steffe, L. P. (2004). *PSSM* from a constructivist perspective. In D. H. Clements, J. Sarama, & A.-M. DiBiase (Eds.), *Engaging young children in mathematics: Standards for early childhood mathematics education* (pp. 221–251). Mahwah, NJ: Erlbaum.

Thomas, B. (1982). *An abstract of kindergarten teachers' elicitation and utilization of children's prior knowledge in the teaching of shape concepts*: Unpublished manuscript, School of Education, Health, Nursing, and Arts Professions, New York University, New York.

Thomson, S., Rowe, K., Underwood, C., & Peck, R. (2005). *Numeracy in the early years: Project Good Start*. Camberwell, Victoria: Australian Council for Educational Research.

Wadlington, E., & Burns, J. M. (1993). Instructional practices within preschool/kindergarten gifted programs. *Journal for the Education of the Gifted, 17*(1), 41–52.

Wagner, A. A., & Carpenter, T. P. (in press). Learning trajectories through a socio-cultural lens. In J. Carlson & J. R. Levine (Eds.), *Instructional strategies for improving students' learning*. Charlotte, NC: Information Age.

Weiner, B. (1986). *An attributional theory of motivation and emotion*. New York: Springer-Verlag.

Wu, H. (2007). *Whole numbers, fractions, and rational numbers*. Berkeley: University of California Press.

CHAPTER 12

Science and Early Education

Kathy Cabe Trundle and Mesut Saçkes

Children, during their earliest years, begin to develop important scientific thinking skills as well as basic understandings of natural phenomena (Eshach & Fried, 2005; Gallenstein, 2003; Lind, 1999). These fundamental science understandings and skills begin to develop as early as infancy, and children's competency continues to develop with age (Kuhn, Amsel, & O'Loughlin, 1988; Kuhn & Pearsall, 2000; Lind, 1999; Meyer, Wardrop, & Hastings, 1992; Piaget & Inhelder, 1928/2000). The results of recent developmental psychology and cognitive science studies indicate that early learning experiences are crucial for a child's cognitive development, and limited experiences and stimuli may result in a child not developing to his or her fullest potential (Brecht & Schmitz, 2008; Hadzigeorgiou, 2002; Lawson, 2003; Lindsey, 1997; Rushton & Larkin, 2001). The findings of research studies over the last two decades suggest that young children, if they are provided with the requisite opportunities, are capable of performing various cognitive tasks, including observing, inferring, and finding patterns, that are the basis of scientific thinking and learning (Carey, 2004; Carey & Spelke, 1994; Kuhn & Pearsall, 2000; Metz, 1997; Opfer & Siegler, 2004; Ruffman, Perner, Olson, & Doherty, 1993; Spelke, Breinlinger, Macomber, & Jacobson, 1992; Wellman & Estes, 1986; Zimmerman, 2000). Early science learning experiences have the potential to capitalize on children's natural abilities, and these learning opportunities seem to be essential for the development of children's core scientific knowledge and essential inquiry skills (Eshach & Fried, 2005; Patrick, Mantzicopoulos, & Samarapungavan, 2009; Samarapungavan, Mantzicopoulos, &Patrick, 2008). Quality science education during the early years is important to many aspects of child development. Thus, researchers suggest that science education should begin during the early years of preschool (Eshach, 2003; Eshach & Fried, 2005; Ginsburg & Golbeck, 2004; Kallery, 2004; Watters, Diezmann, Grieshaber, & Davis, 2000).

Early science learning opportunities allow children to develop their basic science inquiry skills, as well as understand fundamental science concepts, laying a foundation for the subsequent understanding of more complex science concepts. The *Atlas of Science Literacy* (American Association for the Advancement of Science [AAAS], 2001), which maps science concepts for grades K–12, suggests that the understanding of many complex science concepts is built on children's understanding of the more basic concepts in the early years. Recent studies on science learning progressions suggest the sequential development of conceptual understanding of science topics, as well as scientific reasoning skills (Duschl, Schweingruber, & Shouse, 2007; Hmelo-Silver & Duncan, 2009; Liu & Lesniak, 2006; Smith, Wiser, Anderson, & Krajcik, 2006). An understanding of basic science concepts may facilitate the learning of more complex and advanced concepts and scientific thinking skills (Plummer & Krajcik, 2010; Smith et al., 2006).

In addition to the potential for learning science concepts, children naturally enjoy observing and experiencing nature (Eshach & Fried, 2005; Patrick, Mantzicopoulos, Samarapungavan, & French, 2008; Ramey-Gassert, 1997), and science content and skills naturally complement the way young children explore their environments and try to understand them. Early science learning experiences can take advantage of young children's inclination to explore the world and be highly motivating (French, 2004; Patrick et al., 2009). Effective science experiences during the early years that help children develop positive attitudes toward science (Eshach & Fried, 2005; Patrick et al., 2008) have been linked to science achievement (Bruce, Bruce, Conrad, & Huang, 1997; Neathery, 1997; Osborne, Simon, & Collins, 2003). In summary, quality science learning experiences that are developmentally appropriate can support children's early development of science skills and knowledge, laying a foundation for science learning throughout their academic lives (Eshach & Fried, 2005; Gilbert, Osborne, & Fensham, 1982).

Science Content Standards for the Early Years

State and national academic content standards provide guidelines for the science content and process skills that are appropriate for children of different ages. The *National Science Education Standards* by the National Research Council (NRC; 1996) has been used by most U.S. states in the development of their state science standards. However, most science standards efforts have focused on kindergarten through 12th grade. Few states have developed and adopted science content standards for preschool. A review of the science content standards of all U.S. states found that only 17 states had science content standards for preschool–kindergarten. However, only 12 states had separate academic science content standards specifically for preschool (Saçkes, Trundle, & Flevares, 2009b). The review of preschool science content standards of those 12 states revealed three common content areas across the states: physical science, earth and space science, and life science. These content areas are derived from the *National Science Education Standards* for grades K–12. Within each common content area several common themes for preschool were also identified across the states.

There were six common themes for physical science: (1) physical properties of objects and materials (e.g., solid–liquid and hard–soft) was the most common theme (all 12 states); (2) classification of objects and materials based on qualities such as weight and shape (nine states); (3) movement of objects (six states); (4) sound; (5) light; and (6) physical changes. For the earth and space science content area, the four common themes were (1) weather (eight states), (2) day and night (four states), (3) earth materials (three states), and (4) season (three states). The five common themes for life science, the most emphasized content area in the preschool science content standards, included (1) life cycle of plants and animals (nine states), (2) plant and animal habitats (eight states), (3) classification of plants and animals (seven states), (4) common needs of plants and animals (six states), and (5) heredity (five states).

In addition to content areas, science process skills were included in the preschool standards (Saçkes, Trundle & Flevares, 2009a). Eleven common science process skills, the most emphasized across the states, were identified. These skills included asking questions (10 states); using basic tool (10 states); making observation (nine states); explaining cause and effect (nine states); making predictions (eight states); describing events and observations (seven states); collecting, organizing, and recording data (six states); communicating observations and findings (six states); ordering, sorting, and counting (six states); discussing and drawing conclusion (five states); and making comparison (five states).

Future science education reform efforts should include expectations for preschool in the *National Science Education Standards* or the common core standards, much like the mathematics standards (National Council of Teachers of Mathematics [NCTM], 2000). State-level reform efforts also should include standards for preschool science teaching and learning.

The State of Science Teaching in Early Childhood Classrooms

According to state and national standards and research findings, young children are capable of performing various cognitive skills, such as asking questions and making predictions, which are the basis for scientific thinking and learning (Carey & Spelke, 1994; Kuhn & Pearsall, 2000; Metz, 1997; Opfer & Siegler, 2004; Zimmerman, 2000). Despite these capabilities, children's emerging skills usually are not the target of instructional practices in typical early childhood classrooms (Tilgner, 1990; Tu, 2006). In other words, current classroom practices are inconsistent with young children's abilities and with educational reform documents.

Children seem to have fewer opportunities to learn science concepts than to learn literacy, mathematics, social studies, and art (Early et al., 2010; Greenfield et al., 2009; Tilgner, 1990). For example, the findings of a recent study with a nationally representative sample of kindergarten teachers indicated that the majority of teachers teach science only once or twice per week, for a total of up to 60 minutes of instruction (Saçkes, Trundle, Bell, & O'Connell, 2011).

When early childhood teachers do teach science they tend to utilize ineffective science teaching practices. For example, Tu (2006) reported that almost 87% of the activities teachers labeled or described as science activities in their preschool classroom were unrelated to science concepts. Although more than half of the classrooms observed in the Tu study had adequate science materials and teachers had high levels of education, along with many years of teaching experience, the teachers tended to not utilize these resources appropriately to teach science. In a similar study, Nayfeld (2008) found that the science areas in four preschools were rarely used by teachers or children. During the periods when science areas were observed, they were occupied by children only 15% of the time. In a more recent study, a total of 88.6% of teachers claimed to teach science at least once per week, while less than half of the teachers (44.9%) reported using science equipment that often (Saçkes et al., 2011). These results indicate that many early childhood teachers teach science concepts without the science equipment that is available to them. Contemporary science education literature suggests that teaching science as inquiry, including during the early years, essentially involves investigations in which children use developmentally appropriate materials to make observations and answer questions. Considering this definition of effective science teaching, the overall findings of these studies suggest that what early childhood teachers consider and practice as science teaching might not fit with the effective science instruction suggested in contemporary education research literature.

In addition to ineffective science instruction at the early childhood level, teachers also have limited resources to teach science in the early years due to a lack of validated science curricula for young children. Hence, early childhood teachers have very few scientifically based options for science instruction (French, 2004). Preschool Pathways to Science (PrePS; Gelman & Brenneman, 2004) and ScienceStart! (French, 2004) are the most recent examples of science curricula developed specifically for young children. These science curricula, however, are limited in that they introduce science concepts in isolation and not integrated with other content. Although they address the development of essential scientific process skills, these two science curricula exclude key science concepts, such as those in the earth and space sciences. For example, PrePS and ScienceStart! include a limited introduction to some physical and life science concepts but no earth or space science concepts, which are integral to national and state standards. Moreover, these curricula do not offer content support or professional development to assist teachers in effectively implementing the instruction.

There are widespread demands for improving student science learning. As previously mentioned, understandings of foundational science concepts in the early years can facilitate student learning of more sophisticated concepts and scientific thinking skills in later grades (Plummer & Krajcik, 2010; Smith et al., 2006). Previous longitudinal studies that examined the effect of early learning experiences on children's later academic achievement have provided evidence that experiences in kindergarten predict children's general academic achievement in elementary and upper grades (Bodovski & Farkas, 2007; Campbell, Pungello, Miller-Johnson, Burchinal, & Ramey, 2001; Gersten, Darch, & Gleason, 1988). For example, children who received quality early learning experiences in kindergarten performed significantly better on mathematics and reading achievement tests at ages 8, 15, and 21 years (Campbell et al., 2001). A similar long-term effect of kindergarten learning experiences on children's academic development was reported in another study in which the benefits of early learning experiences in kindergarten were detected 6 years after the program ended (Gersten et al., 1988).

Previous studies that have examined the impact of early literacy and mathematics experiences on academic achievement in kindergarten and later grades report statistically significant relationships between children's achievement and early literacy and mathematics experiences (e.g., Bodovski & Farkas, 2007; Byrnes & Wasik, 2009; National Center for Education Statistics [NCES], 2006). Results of these studies suggest that early childhood teachers are well equipped with effective instructional strategies to introduce basic mathematics concepts and literacy skills in the early years. However, results of a study that focused on science learning experiences in kindergarten differed from the mathematics and literacy findings. Early science experiences in kindergarten are not significant predictors of children's immediate and subsequent science achievement (Saçkes et al., 2011). Therefore, developing research-based high-quality curricula that include a range of supports to increase teacher knowledge and quality of implementation for the early years, and that have the potential to improve children's learning of science, should be a priority for educators.

Effective Science Teaching for Young Children

The *National Science Education Standards* (NRC, 1996, 2000) emphasize inquiry-based instruction as a "gold standard" for promoting conceptual understandings of science phenomena. Inquiry-based instruction aims to promote active learning through hands-on activities within small groups and sense-making discussions. A common expectation is that children are more likely to construct an understanding of content in an inquiry learning environment, where they have opportunities and guidance to use investigative skills such as observing, inferring, posing questions, forming hypotheses, and developing conclusions based on the analysis of data (Anderson, 2007). Indeed, asking questions, making predictions, planning and conducting basic investigations, collecting data by using appropriate tools and techniques, communicating and representing data, and establishing relation-ships between evidence and explanations are among the inquiry skills children across all grade levels are expected to develop (NRC, 1996). Researchers also have found that inquiry approaches allow teachers to support the development of children's explanatory language (Peterson & French, 2008).

Instructional approaches that are considered nontraditional (e.g., inquiry, discovery, and constructivist teaching) have been criticized for being ineffective (Kirschner, Sweller, & Clark, 2006; Mayer, 2004). Some researchers have suggested that inquiry-based instruc-tional approaches place a heavy cognitive load on learners, resulting in a diminished cogni-tive processing capacity that may limit the learner's ability to process novel information and thus hinder learning. Clearly, the involvement of a heavy cognitive load is more likely to be the case for young children who have a limited cognitive processing capacity. Minimal guidance in inquiry-based instruction, especially with young children, is not consistent with contemporary science education theories, which advocate selective structuring and scaf-folding for the learning of scientific concepts (Hatano & Inagaki, 2003; Kirschner et al., 2006; Vosniadou, 2007). Appropriate structuring and scaffolding are especially important for young children. Neither traditional instruction that presents information essentially in its final form nor nontraditional approaches that provide minimal guidance are likely to promote conceptual understandings of natural phenomena. Rather, inquiry-based instruc-tion for young children must be sufficiently structured and scaffolded so that children are motivated and able to investigate the natural world (Vosniadou, 1999, 2007; Vosniadou, Ioannides, Dimitrakopoulou, & Papademetriou, 2001).

Researchers make distinctions between the types of inquiry based on the complexity and the amount of information provided in the inquiry activities. These types include con-firmation, structured inquiry, guided inquiry, and open inquiry (Bell, Smetana, & Binns, 2005; Herron, 1971). Guided inquiry, in which teachers provided an appropriate level of scaffolding and guidance during the activities, seems to be the most appropriate for young children.

One of the approaches that successfully incorporates inquiry into the teaching of sci-ence concepts is a project approach, which is based on the fundamental idea of "learning by doing." Project approach or project-based learning basically involves an in-depth investiga-tion of a topic in which children are interested (Curtis, 2002; Katz & Chard, 2000). Learn-ing activities usually focus on child-generated questions or problems, which are carefully situated within central concepts or themes and guided by teachers. Children use various tools in their investigations, collect and analyze data, and produce artifacts (e.g., drawings, paintings, collages, and dramatic plays) to represent their understandings by collaborating with their peers (Krajcik, Blumenfeld, Marx, & Soloway, 1994; Youngquist & Pataray-Ching, 2004).

A project approach enhances children's collaboration skills, helps children make con-nections among other content areas, promotes conceptual understandings, facilitates chil-dren's reflective thinking, and increases motivation (Doppelt, 2003). Despite the advantages, there are some shortcomings of the project approach. For example, it is difficult simultane-ously to balance children's interests with the required curriculum. Implementing a project approach is a time-consuming task that requires more work of teachers. Designing assess-ments to measure children's understandings that may develop from a project is also a chal-lenge for many teachers (Curtis, 2002; Drake & Burns, 2004; Marx, Blumenfeld, Krajcik, & Soloway, 1997).

In summary, research literature and policy documents, despite the drawbacks, advocate for use of a project approach in the teaching of science in the early years (e.g., AAAS, 2001; Inan, Trundle, & Kantor, 2010; Morris, 2004).

Science and Young Children with Special Needs

National reform documents for science education also call for science for *all* children (AAAS, 2001; NRC, 1996). As increasing numbers of children with disabilities are in classrooms, individual education plans (IEPs), 504 Plans, and intervention plans are more frequent realities for science instruction. By including students with visual (low vision and blindness), hearing (limited hearing and deafness), mobility, emotional, and cognitive impairments in the development of classroom lessons, science instruction ultimately becomes more inclusive. Moreover, taking into account the needs of children with disabilities ensures that *all* students learn science content and processes as they become scientifically literate (NRC, 1996).

Science content provides the perfect context in which to engage and captivate all children, including those with disabilities (Trundle, 2008). Inquiry instruction, which is at the center of effective science teaching, can provide effective learning experiences that allow all children to participate in the investigations and learn science content (Mastropieri & Scruggs, 1992; Mastropieri et al., 1996; Scruggs, Mastropieri, & Boon, 1998). Inquiry involves objects to touch, see, and smell, and there are investigations to conduct. Since these opportunities exist naturally in the inquiry class, small revisions to the planned instruction and assessments can greatly enhance opportunities for children with disabilities to engage with the concepts. These modifications are not difficult to make and often require a small amount of preparation or the use of common equipment in novel ways (e.g., computers with larger text, meter sticks with raised lines). Once the modifications are made, children with disabilities can participate more fully in the learning experience, which impacts their overall performance and science learning. Moreover, providing these learning opportunities to children with disabilities sends a clear message that *all* students can and should participate in science, and all students can learn science.

The results of several studies indicate that inquiry-based science instruction benefits children who have a range of disabilities, including learning disabilities, mild mental retardation, autism (Mastropieri, Scruggs, Boon, & Butcher, 2001; Mastropieri et al., 1996), visual impairments (Erwin, Ayala, & Perkins, 2001), and hearing impairments or deafness (Borron, 1978). These results indicate that children with a wide range of disabilities were all able to participate successfully in and explain their results of inquiry experiences. These children also were likely to become proficient in using science process skills, develop skills to work independently, and be motivated to learn science (Barman & Stockton, 2002; Mastropieri et al., 1996). A more active environment associated with inquiry-based instruction can result in more effective learning of science concepts, as well as increase children's confidence in their capabilities to participate in science (Dalton, Morocco, Tivnan, & Mead, 1997; Palincsar, Magnusson, Collins, & Cutter, 2001). Also, students with disabilities who are taught in an inquiry setting are better able to participate and more successful in science achievement when compared to students taught in traditional settings (Mastropieri et al., 1996). Overall, a science as inquiry environment allows the greatest number of students to experience and learn about science.

Integration of Science with Mathematics and Literacy

Since early childhood teachers often feel uncomfortable teaching science and most of the curricular time in early childhood classrooms is usually devoted to mathematics and literacy, early childhood teachers can integrate science into other content areas (Early et al., 2010; Garbett, 2003; Odgers, 2007; Tilgner, 1990). Researchers suggest integrating mathematics and science because both content areas involve similar skills, such as discovering patterns and relationships, and both use similar cognitive processing skills (Berlin & White, 1994; Charlesworth, 2005; Czerniak, Weber, Sandmann, & Ahern, 1999; Ginsburg & Golbeck, 2004; Pang & Good, 2000). Integrating mathematics and science helps children to appreciate connections and applications that link mathematics and science concepts (Frykholm, 2005). Although educators and researchers have advocated the integration of mathematics and science at the elementary and middle school levels for years (Beatty, 2005; Berlin & White, 1994; Tu, 2006), there has been little effort to prepare teachers in the practice of curriculum integration (Furner & Kumar, 2007; Isaacs, Wagreich, & Gartzman, 1997; Jones, Lake, & Dagli, 2003; Pang & Good, 2000). Thus, early childhood teachers rarely attempt to integrate science and mathematics (Cady & Rearden, 2007; Douville, Pugalee, & Wallace, 2003; Koirala & Bowman, 2003).

A project approach, such as a weather or bird project, offers a context for integrating science and mathematics in early childhood classrooms (Flevares, Saçkes, Gonya, & Trundle, 2009). For example, whole-class sessions may focus on observations and representations of observations (data), formulating productive questions for inquiry, designing data collection, and connecting early childhood mathematics and science through measurement and data analysis. The National Association for the Education of Young Children's planning wheel model can be used to create an integrated unit of activities and resources across the curriculum (Conezio & French, 2002).

Literacy education in the early years offers another opportunity for science integration. Despite the limited number of prior research studies investigating the use of children's literature to teach science, evidence provided by these studies suggests that children's literature can be used as an effective instructional tool to teach young children science concepts (Bricker, 2005; Castle & Needham, 2007; Morrow, Pressley, Smith, & Smith, 1997).

Indeed, using children's literature as an instructional tool to introduce scientific concepts and develop inquiry skills in children's early years has gained popularity among teachers in recent years. This increase in popularity is due, in part, to teachers' familiarity with literature as an instructional tool. Children's literature has great potential to foster interest in and positive attitudes toward learning science (Broemmel & Rearden, 2006; Castle & Needham, 2007; Coskie, 2006). By presenting content knowledge in narrative form, children's literature can facilitate children's understanding of difficult science concepts (Morrow et al., 1997). This facilitation may result from the relevance given to the science concepts and process skills in a context that is more meaningful for children (Henriques & Chidsey, 1997). In this meaningful environment, children can find opportunities to develop scientific understandings of natural phenomena and practice inquiry skills such as making observations and predictions, raising questions, and reaching conclusions from evidence (Castle & Needham, 2007; Monhardt & Monhardt, 2006; Pringle & Lamme, 2005).

Teachers can use children's literature as a starting point for science activities as well as for a medium to support children's ongoing science projects in early childhood classrooms. Children's literature also offers a practical way to introduce science concepts that usually require observations in nature over extended periods of time. Pairing children's literature with observations in nature can help avoid situations that can make the observations difficult and frustrating, especially for young children. For example, using selected children's literature about the moon and stars or weather along with observations of the sky can help avoid unfavorable weather conditions, urban light pollution, and obstacles like tall trees and buildings that can interfere with observations in nature (Trundle & Saçkes, 2008, 2010; Trundle & Troland, 2005). Therefore, children's literature has great potential—both practical and conceptual—to be an effective tool for introducing science concepts and developing inquiry skills in the early years.

The benefits of using children's literature to teach science concepts and promote inquiry skills include the following:

- To make learning of science concepts and skills more meaningful.
- To offer a practical way to introduce science concepts that usually require observations in nature over extend periods of time.
- To facilitate children's understanding of difficult science concepts.
- To provide opportunities to develop and practice inquiry skills.
- To enrich children's ongoing science projects.
- To foster interest in and positive attitudes toward learning science.

Picture books and nonfiction books can be used to support children's science learning, but they should not be considered as substitutes for hands-on experiences or inquiry (Duke & Bennett-Armistead, 2003; Norris & Phillips, 2003). Previous studies demonstrated that children's books may include misconceptions and anthropomorphisms, as well as inaccurate illustrations and information (Broemmel & Rearden, 2006; Gomez-Zwiep & Straits, 2006; Kazemek, Louisell, & Wellike, 2004; Trundle & Troland, 2005). In selecting children's books, teachers should consider the science background of the author and illustrator (Pringle & Lamme, 2005) and if a science consultant was used. Examples of using children's books that include misconceptions and inaccurate illustrations can be found in recent publications (e.g., Trundle & Saçkes, 2008, 2010; Trundle & Troland, 2005). Nonfiction books should also be evaluated to determine whether they are scientifically accurate and developmentally appropriate for the targeted children.

Children's Ideas about Natural Phenomena

Research studies revealed that children have ideas, beliefs, and explanations of how things happen in the world around them, although they mostly diverge from scientific explanations. Piaget (1928/1972) used the term *naive ideas* to describe these types of understandings held by children. Children's ideas also have been variously referred to as *alternative conceptions* (Dove, 1998), *misconceptions* (Posner, Strike, Hewson, & Gertzog, 1982), *preconceptions* (Novak, 1977), and *initial explanatory frameworks* (Vosniadou, 2002) in the literature. A considerable amount of research have been conducted on children's understandings of the natural world (e.g., Baxter, 1989; Bryce & Blown, 2006; Carey, 1985; Hobson, Trundle, & Saçkes, 2010; Nussbaum, 1985; Osborne, Black, Wadsworth, & Meadows, 1994; Saçkes, Flevares, & Trundle, 2010; Trundle, Atwood, & Christopher, 2007; Tytler, 1998; Vosniadou & Brewer, 1992, 1994). These studies demonstrate that children have preconceptions or alternative ideas about many science concepts across the content areas of physical, biological, and earth and space sciences.

For example, young children mostly explain the flotation of an object in water as being caused by the air inside the object or the weight of the object (Havu-Nuutinen, 2005). Young children perceive force as a property of a physical object, and they relate force to the object's weight and size (Vosniadou, 2002). Young children tend to attribute substantiality to sound and believe that sound cannot pass through solids (Mazens & Lautrey, 2003). Although most young children believe that rain is water, they tend not to relate clouds with rain, and believe that rain simply comes from the sky, not clouds (Saçkes et al., 2011). Young children attribute the day–night cycle to movement of the sun in the sky, or they provide religious or supernatural explanations (Vosniadou & Brewer, 1994). Most young children believe that earth is flat and stationary, and that people cannot live on "the bottom of the earth" (i.e., the southern hemisphere) because they would fall off (Diakidoy & Kendeou, 2001; Vosniadou & Brewer, 1992). Young children see human action and supernatural forces as being responsible for the change in the moon's shape (e.g., the moon is born, cut by people, changed by fairies) (Hobson et al., 2010; Piaget, 1928/1972). In summary, young children hold a variety of alternative ideas that they use to explain natural phenomena, and these alternative ideas have been documented across all content areas of science (i.e., physical, life, and earth and space sciences).

Exploring Children's Ideas about Science Concepts

Researchers have developed and used various data collection methods for studying children's understandings of scientific concepts, and the most widely used data collection method is interviews. Commonly used interview protocols are based on Piaget's (1928/1972) clinical method, which was designed to achieve three goals: (1) to describe the child's genuine explanation for a given phenomenon, (2) to identify the reasoning processes that produced the child's explanation, and (3) to situate the explanation and reasoning processes in a mental context (Ginsburg, 1997). The clinical interview is a fruitful method for revealing children's understanding of the natural world. Thus, it has been adopted and modified by several researchers. Examples include the Interview-about-Instances (Osborne & Cosgrove, 1983) and the Interview-about-Events (Osborne & Freyberg, 1985) as viable options for studying children's conceptual understandings and identifying alternative conceptions. However, clinical interviews, whether structured or not, are not easy to conduct. They require extensive training and practice to master, and the analysis of data also can be difficult and time consuming. Therefore, researchers have sought alternative data collection techniques for studying children's understandings of science concepts. Children's drawings and the manipulation of physical models are two common data collection techniques used in studying children's conceptions of natural phenomena.

Drawings

Researchers have used drawings as a data-gathering method with young children. This technique requires children to draw all that they know about a given phenomenon. Then, they are asked to explain their drawings in writing or verbally. Alternatively, children may be given a specific prompt, such as "Draw all the phases of the moon that you have observed" or "Draw the shape of the earth" to focus and to initiate their drawings. Both the drawings and children's explanations of the drawings can be analyzed (Bell, 1993; White & Gunstone, 1992).

Drawings can provide a valuable means for data collection. They may allow young children to express their perspective in a productive and efficient way. Considering the limited vocabulary skills of young children and previous research findings that report possible language effects on the responses given by young children (Clerk & Rutherford, 2000; Dunlop, 2000; Miner, 1992; Russell & Watt, 1990), drawing techniques, when combined with a structured interview, may produce a more detailed description of children's perspectives. Drawings also may provide aspects of older participants' conceptual understandings that are not easily captured by other procedures (White & Gunstone, 1992).

Results obtained from participants' drawings can be used to interpret verbal responses to the interview questions. For example, in lunar studies, researchers found that participants who used an eclipse model (i.e., the shadow of the Earth) to explain the cause of the moon phases were more likely to draw a false gibbous shape, which was consistent with their verbal explanations (Trundle, Atwood, & Christopher, 2002, 2006). Drawings also can be used to clarify verbal explanations and identify false positives (i.e., a child selected the correct answer or provided responses in an interview that suggested a scientific understanding when, in fact, the child actually held an alternative understanding) (Trundle et al., 2002, 2006). In their study with young children, Vosniadou and Brewer (1992) found that many children were able to provide verbal explanations about the shape of the earth that sounded like scientific responses, but they drew nonscientific models of the earth. These children very likely used scientific language, while actually holding nonscientific views of the shape of the earth.

Ideally, drawings can be used in conjunction with other data-gathering methods. For example, children should always be asked to explain their drawings. Follow-up interviews can be conducted immediately after the drawing task or, alternatively, children can be asked to explain their drawings as they are producing them (Ehrlen, 2009). If the number of children involved in a study is large, researchers may select representative drawings and interview the children who produced them (Dove, Everett, & Preece, 1999). Drawings can provide rich information about children's conceptual understandings that may not be captured by other methods. In order to interpret children's drawings as representations of their conceptual understanding, researchers must ensure that drawings are not produced as an attempt to conform to cultural conventions. Rather, drawings should be derived from the way children see the natural world, which might be accomplished by requesting that children explain their drawing or by asking if there are other ways to represent the phenomenon (Ehrlen, 2009). Although children's drawings are valuable sources of their conceptual understandings of natural phenomena, drawings can be difficult to interpret and score objectively.

Construction Materials and Physical Artifacts

Construction materials (e.g., Play-Doh, modeling clay) and physical tools (e.g., globes, maps) can be used to investigate children's conceptions (Ivarsson, Schoultz, & Saljo, 2002; Vosniadou, Skopeliti, & Ikospentaki, 2004, 2005). With this method of data gathering, children are asked to manipulate or use materials (e.g., Play-Doh, globe) to express their ideas about a given phenomenon. exploring children's conceptions using Play-Doh may provide more accurate data about children's ideas, particularly when the investigated phenomenon is three dimensional (Vosniadou et al., 2004). Artifacts made by children can be used as supplementary evidence for the type of mental model they hold. These artifacts can offer aspects of children's conceptual understandings that are not evident in their verbal explanations or drawings.

Researchers, from the sociocultural perspective particularly, suggest the use of physical tools to investigate students' conceptions (Ivarsson et al., 2002). Since cognitive development is seen as a mastery of tool use, some researchers believe that data gathering must involve both cognitive and physical tool use in order to gain an accurate description of a child's thinking (Ivarsson et al., 2002; Tytler & Peterson, 2004). In other words, from a sociocultural perspective, physical tools such as maps or globes are seen as extensions of cognition. Therefore, children must have access to these mental tools during an interview process that focuses on their conceptual understandings of the shape of the earth (Schoultz, Saljo, & Wyndhamn, 2001).

Some researchers, however, argue that using a physical tool, such as a globe, in interviews about the shape of the earth provides information to the child and communicates the idea of Earth's spherical shape (Vosniadou et al., 2005). Thus, some researchers contend that the use of physical tools might not be appropriate when studying conceptual understanding because children's responses can be confounded or influenced by the presence of the models during the interview. Researchers from a cognitive development perspective suggest that the focus of conceptual change studies should be on the children's cognitive representations and the explanations they generate, without the aid of external objects.

Although this debate between cognitive and sociocultural researchers seems merely to be a methodological issue, the difference is based on a fundamental distinction between how these two perspectives define cognition. Thus, the different definitions of cognition offered by these two groups of researchers influence their conceptualization of appropriate methods to study cognition. Researchers, therefore, should carefully situate their research within a theoretical framework before deciding on the format of their data collection methods.

A Need for a Comprehensive Data Collection Protocol

A specific body of research literature suggests that data collection techniques, questions, and contextual clues during an interview might influence children's responses (Bar & Galili, 1994; Clerk & Rutherford, 2000; Tytler & Peterson, 2004; Vosniadou et al., 2004). A data collection protocol that combines various data collection methods, such as verbal responses, drawings, manipulation of three-dimensional models, and card sorting, into a single interview protocol could reduce the possible method effect on children's responses. The use of multiple data collection methods in studying children's conceptual understandings has been useful in studies with young children (Hobson et al., 2010; Trundle et al., 2007). Using multiple data collection techniques can provide more detailed information about children's conceptual understandings, as well as the way they represent scientific concepts. Results of such studies also might contribute to the ongoing debate in the field on coherency versus fragmentation of children's conceptions (Ivarsson et al., 2002; Schoultz et al., 2001; Vosniadou et al., 2004, 2005).

Summary and Discussion:
The Future of Science Education in the Early Years

Previous studies of early childhood teachers' practice and perceptions of teaching science offer several possible reasons for the reported ineffectiveness of science experiences in the early years. First of all, children seem to have fewer opportunities to learn science than literacy, mathematics, social studies, and art (Early et al., 2010). Children do not learn science in the early years because few science learning opportunities are provided for them (Greenfield et al., 2009; Tilgner, 1990).

Early childhood teachers spend less time on science instruction for several reasons, including a lack of time, self-confidence, materials, space, and science and pedagogical content knowledge (Appleton & Kindt, 1999, 2002). The lack of content knowledge in science has been reported to be one of the most important reasons that teachers of young children do not teach science (Appleton, 1992; Tobin, Briscoe, & Holman, 1990). For example, Kallery and Psillos (2001) reported that only about 22% of the early childhood teachers in their study felt that they had sufficient scientific content knowledge. Garbett (2003) found that many early childhood teachers have a limited understanding of the science concepts they are expected to teach, which makes them uncomfortable teaching science (Appleton, 1995; Pell & Jarvis, 2003; Schoon & Boone, 1998; Tilgner, 1990). Indeed, a recent study that investigated the reasons teachers do not teach science in the early years found that teachers do not feel confident in teaching science or using science equipment. Also, teachers reported that they feel pressured to teach language and literacy, and they are not able to find time in the school day also to teach science (Greenfield et al., 2009).

A lack of pedagogical content knowledge for teaching science to young children presents another major obstacle for early childhood teachers. Kallery and Psillos (2001) reported that many early childhood teachers have difficulty addressing children's science-related questions and devising inquiry-based science investigations in early childhood classrooms. Teachers use a variety of coping strategies to compensate for their lack of science and pedagogical content knowledge, which includes teaching as little of the subject as possible; teaching more biology versus physical science; relying on commercially developed lessons; using nonfiction children's trade books; and avoiding all but simple, hands-on activities (Akerson, 2004; Appleton & Kindt, 1999; Harlen, 1997).

The research literature suggests that early childhood teachers might not be well equipped with the effective instructional strategies needed to teach science to young children (Nayfeld, 2008; Saçkes et al., 2011; Tu, 2006). What early childhood teachers consider and practice as science teaching during the early years might not fit with the conceptualization of effective science instruction suggested in the contemporary science education literature (e.g., Minner, Levy, & Century, 2010).

Research studies suggest that current early childhood science instruction is not effective and support the need for improving early childhood teachers' knowledge of science and science pedagogy. A growing body of literature suggests that methods courses and inservice teacher training programs that incorporate science and pedagogical content knowledge can enhance preservice and inservice teachers' skills and knowledge of effective instructional strategies in teaching science to young children, and improve teachers' efficacy beliefs about teaching science (e.g., Huinker & Madison, 1997; Morrell & Carroll, 2003; Oliveira, 2010; Palmer, 2006). Therefore, early childhood preservice and inservice teacher education programs should focus on providing well-designed science methods instruction to improve science teaching practices of early childhood teachers.

Addressing teachers' limited knowledge of science and science pedagogy, supplying preschool and kindergarten classrooms with science materials, and building teachers' confidence in teaching science seem integral to improving science learning experiences for young children. Educational policy documents suggesting that children's literacy, language, and mathematics performance are the sole criteria for success should be revised. Bringing a balance to the educational policy documents might reduce the pressure teachers reportedly feel to teach specific content areas. Consequently, teachers might devote more time to teaching science to children in the early years.

Research studies are need to investigate what early childhood teachers consider to be science teaching, and how their perceptions and practices of teaching science relate to what the contemporary science education literature offers as effective science teaching for young children. Studies should seek to provide rich descriptions of what is going on during science lessons in preschool and kindergarten classrooms. These investigations should employ mixed methods and gather a variety of data, including observations of science teaching practices; artifacts produced by children during their science activities; and perceptions of teachers' needs, intentions, and practices in regard to teaching science. The results of these types of studies can help to describe the current state of teaching science in children's early years and inform teacher-educators, who can use the information to better address the needs of early childhood teachers.

Overall, research studies point to major concerns about the effectiveness of early childhood science instruction. If policymakers and educators aim to make a difference in children's learning by closing the gender and socioeconomic gaps in science achievement, it is essential for early childhood teachers to be better equipped with more useful science content knowledge and effective instructional strategies for teaching science to young children. Science learning should be included as another criterion for success in early education.

References

Akerson, V. L. (2004). Designing a science methods course for early childhood preservice teachers. *Journal of Elementary Science Education, 16*(2), 19–32.

American Association for the Advancement of Science (AAAS). (2001). *Atlas of science literacy.* Washington, DC: Author.

Anderson, R. D. (2007). Inquiry as an organizing theme for science curricula. In S. Abell & N. Lederman (Eds.), *Handbook of research on science education* (pp. 807–830). Mahwah, NJ: Erlbaum.

Appleton, K. (1992). Discipline knowledge and confidence to teach science: Self-perceptions of primary teacher education students. *Research in Science Education, 22*(1), 11–19.

Appleton, K. (1995). Student teachers confidence to teach science: Is more science knowledge necessary to improve self-confidence? *International Journal of Science Education, 17*(3), 357–369.

Appleton, K., & Kindt, I. (1999). Why teach primary science?: Influences on beginning teachers' practices. *International Journal of Science Education, 21*(2), 155–168.

Appleton, K., & Kindt, I. (2002). Beginning elementary teachers' development as teachers of science. *Journal of Science Teacher Education, 13*(1), 43–61.

Bar, V., & Galili, I. (1994). Stages of children's views about evaporation. *International Journal of Science Education, 16*(2), 157–174.

Barman, C. R., & Stockton, J. D. (2002). An evaluation of the SOAR-High Project: A Web-based science program for deaf students. *American Annals of the Deaf, 147*(3), 5–10.

Baxter, J. (1989). Children's understanding of familiar astronomical events [Special issue]. *International Journal of Science Education, 11*, 502–513.

Beatty, A. (2005). *Mathematical and scientific development in early childhood: A workshop summary.* Washington, DC: National Academies Press.

Bell, B. (1993). *Children's science, constructivism and learning in science.* Victoria: Deakin University.

Bell, R. L., Smetana, L., & Binns, I. (2005). Simplifying inquiry instruction. *Science Teacher, 72*(7), 30–33.

Berlin, D. F., & White, A. L. (1994). The Berlin–White integrated science and mathematics model. *School Science and Mathematics, 94*(1), 2–4.

Bodovski, K., & Farkas, G. (2007). Do instructional practices contribute to inequality in achievement?: The case of mathematics instruction in kindergarten. *Journal of Early Childhood Research, 5*(3), 301–322.

Borron, R. (1978). Modifying science instruction to meet the needs of the hearing impaired. *Journal of Research in Science Teaching, 15*(4), 257–262.

Brecht, M., & Schmitz, D. (2008). Rules of plasticity. *Science, 319*(4), 39–40.

Bricker, P. L. (2005). *Children's books and the nature of science: A multisite naturalistic case study of three elementary teachers in the rural southeast.* Unpublished doctoral dissertation, University of Tennessee.

Broemmel, A. D., & Rearden, K. T. (2006). Should teachers use the Teachers' Choice books in science classes? *Reading Teacher, 60*(3), 254–265.

Bruce, B. C., Bruce, S., Conrad, R., & Huang, H. (1997). Collaboration in science education: University science students in the elementary school classroom. *Journal of Research in Science Teaching, 34*, 69–88.

Bryce, T. G. K., & Blown, E. J. (2006). Cultural mediation of children's cosmologies: A longitudinal study of the astronomy concepts of Chinese and New Zealand children. *International Journal of Science Education, 28*(10), 1113–1160.

Byrnes, J. P., & Wasik, P. A. (2009). Factors predictive of mathematics achievement in kindergarten, first and third grades: An opportunity–propensity analysis. *Contemporary Educational Psychology, 34*, 167–183.

Cady, J. A., & Rearden, K. (2007). Pre-service teachers' beliefs about knowledge, mathematics, and science. *School Science and Mathematics, 107*(6), 237–245.

Campbell, F. A., Pungello, E. P., Miller-Johnson, S., Burchinal, M., & Ramey, C. T. (2001). The development of cognitive and academic abilities: Growth curves from an early childhood educational experiment. *Developmental Psychology, 37*(2), 231–242.

Carey, S. (1985). *Conceptual change in childhood.* Cambridge, MA: MIT Press.

Carey, S. (2004, Winter). Bootstrapping and the development of concepts. *Daedalus,* pp. 59–68.

Carey, S., & Spelke, E. S. (1994). Domain-specific knowledge and conceptual change. In L. A. Hirschfeld & S. A. Gelman (Eds.), *Mapping the mind: Domain specificity in cognition and culture* (pp. 169–201). New York: Cambridge University Press.

Castle, K., & Needham, J. (2007). First graders' understanding of measurement. *Early Childhood Education Journal, 35*(3), 215, 221.

Charlesworth, R. (2005). Prekindergarten mathematics: Connecting with standards. *Early Childhood Education Journal, 32*(4), 229–236.

Clerk, D., & Rutherford, M. (2000). Language as a confounding variable in the diagnosis of misconceptions. *International Journal of Science Education, 22*(7), 703–717.

Conezio, K., & French, L. (2002, September).Science in the preschool classroom: Capitalizing on children's fascination with the everyday world to foster language and literacy development. *Young Children,* 12–18.

Coskie, T. L. (2006). The synergy of science and reading. *Science and Children, 44*(3), 62–63.

Curtis, D. (2002). The power of projects. *Educational Leadership, 60*(1), 50–54.

Czerniak, C. M., Weber, W. B., Sandmann, A. J., & Ahern, J. (1999). A literature review of science and mathematics integration. *School Science and Mathematics, 99*(8), 421–430.

Dalton, B., Morocco, C., Tivnan, T., & Mead, P. (1997). Supported inquiry science: Teaching for conceptual change in urban and suburban science classrooms. *Journal of Learning Disabilities, 30*(6), 670–684.

Diakidoy, A., & Kendeou, P. (2001). Facilitating conceptual change in astronomy: A comparison of the effectiveness of two instructional approaches. *Learning and Instruction, 11,* 1–20.

Doppelt, Y. (2003). Implementing an assessment of project-based learning in a flexible environment. *International Journal of Technology and Design Education, 13,* 255–272.

Douville, P., Pugalee, D. K., & Wallace, J. D. (2003). Examining instructional practices of elementary science teachers for mathematics and literacy integration. *School Science and Mathematics, 103*(8), 388–396.

Dove, J. (1998). Alternative conceptions about weather. *School Science Review, 79,* 65–69.

Dove, J. E., Everett, L. A., & Preece, P. F. W. (1999). Exploring a hydrological concept through children's drawings. *International Journal of Science Education, 21*(5), 485–497.

Drake, S. M., & Burns, R. C. (2004). *Meeting standards through integrated curriculum.* Alexandria, VA: Association for Supervision and Curriculum Development.

Duke, N. K., & Bennett-Armistead, V. S. (2003). *Reading and writing informational text in the primary grades.* New York: Scholastic Teaching Resources.

Dunlop, J. (2000). How children observe the universe. *Publication of Astronomical Society of Australia, 17,* 194–206.

Duschl, R. A., Schweingruber, H. A., & Shouse, A. (Eds.). (2007). *Taking science to school: Learning and teaching science in grades K–8.* Washington, DC: National Academies Press.

Early, D. M., Iruka, I. U., Ritchie, S., Barbarin, O. A., Winn, D. C., Crawford, G. M., et al. (2010). How do pre-kindergarteners spend their time?: Gender, ethnicity and income as predictors of experiences in pre-kindergarten classrooms. *Early Childhood Education Quarterly, 25,* 177–193.

Ehrlen, K. (2009). Drawings as representations of children's conceptions. *International Journal of Science Education, 31*(1), 41–57.

Erwin, E., Ayala, J., & Perkins, T. (2001). You don't have to be sighted to be a scientist do you?: Issues and outcomes in science education. *Journal of Visual Impairment and Blindness, 95,* 338–352.

Eshach, H. (2003). Inquiry-events as a tool for changing science teaching efficacy belief of kindergarten and elementary school teachers. *Journal of Science Education and Technology, 12*(4), 495–501.

Eshach, H., & Fried, M. N. (2005). Should science be taught in early childhood? *Journal of Science Education and Technology, 14*(3), 315–336.

Flevares, L. M., Saçkes, M., Gonya, M., & Trundle, K. C. (2009, September 18–19). *Preservice early childhood teachers' sense of efficacy for integrating mathematics and science: Effectiveness of a methods course.* Paper presented at the annual meeting of the Association for Science Teacher Education Mid-Atlantic Regional Conference, Friendship, OH.

French, L. (2004). Science as the center of a coherent, integrated early childhood curriculum. *Early Childhood Research Quarterly, 19*(1), 138–149.

Frykholm, J. (2005). Connecting science and mathematics instruction: Pedagogical context knowledge for teachers. *School Science and Mathematics, 105*(3), 127–141.

Furner, J. M., & Kumar, D. D. (2007). The mathematics and science integration argument: A stand for teacher education. *Eurasia Journal of Mathematics, Science and Technology Education, 3*(3), 185–189.

Gallenstein, N. L. (2003). *Creative construction of mathematics and science concepts in early childhood.* Olney, MD: Association for Childhood Education International.

Garbett, D. (2003). Science education in early childhood teacher education: Putting forward a case to enhance student teachers' confidence and competence. *Research in Science Education, 33,* 467–481.

Gelman, R., & Brenneman, K. (2004). Science learning pathways for young children. *Early Childhood Research Quarterly, 19* (1), 150–158.

Gersten, R., Darch, C., & Gleason, M. (1988). Effectiveness of a direct instruction academic kindergarten for low-income students. *Elementary School Journal, 89*(2), 227–240.

Gilbert, J. K., Osborne, R. J., & Fensham, P. J. (1982). Children's science and its consequences for teaching. *Science Education, 66*(4), 623–633.

Ginsburg, H. P. (1997). *Entering the child's mind: The clinical interview in psychological research and practice.* Cambridge, UK: Cambridge University Press.

Ginsburg, H. P., & Golbeck, S. L. (2004). Thoughts on the future of research on mathematics and science learning and education. *Early Childhood Research Quarterly, 19*(1), 190–200.

Gomez-Zwiep, S., & Straits, W. (2006). Analyzing anthropomorphisms. *Science and Children, 44*(3), 26–29.

Greenfield, D. B., Jirout, J., Dominguez, X., Greenberg, A., Maier, M., & Fuccilo, J. (2009). Science in the preschool classroom: A programmatic research agenda to improve science readiness. *Early Education and Development, 20*(2), 238–264.

Hadzigeorgiou, Y. (2002). A study of the development of the concept of mechanical stability in preschool children. *Research in Science Education, 32*(3), 373–391.

Harlen, W. (1997). *The teaching of science in primary schools.* London: David Fulton.

Hatano, G., & Inagaki, K. (2003). When is conceptual change intended?: A cognitive–sociocultural view. In G. M. Sinatra & P. R. Pintrich (Eds.), *Intentional conceptual change* (pp. 407–427). Mahwah, NJ: Erlbaum.

Havu-Nuutinen, S. (2005). Examining young children's conceptual change process in floating and sinking from a social constructivist perspective. *International Journal of Science Education, 27*(3), 259–279.

Henriques, L., & Chidsey, J. L. (1997, January). *Analyzing and using children's literature to connect school science with parents and home.* Paper presented at the annual meeting of the Association for the Education of Teachers in Science, Cincinnati, OH.

Herron, M. D. (1971). The nature of scientific inquiry. *School Review, 79*(2), 171–212.

Hmelo-Silver, C. E., & Duncan, R. G. (2009). Learning progressions. *Journal of Research in Science Teaching, 46*(6), 606–609.

Hobson, S. M., Trundle, K. C., & Saçkes, M. (2010). Using a planetarium software program to promote conceptual change with young children. *Journal of Science Education and Technology, 19*(2), 165–176.

Huinker, D., & Madison, S. K. (1997). Preparing efficacious elementary teachers in science and mathematics: The influence of method courses. *Journal of Science Teacher Education, 8*(2), 107–126.

Inan, H. Z., Trundle, K. C., & Kantor, R. (2010). Understanding natural sciences education in a Regio Emilia–inspired school. *Journal of Research in Science Teaching, 47*(10), 1186–1208.

Isaacs, A., Wagreich, P., & Gartzman, M. (1997).The quest for integration: School mathematics and science. *American Journal of Education, 106,* 179–206.

Ivarsson, J., Schoultz, J., & Saljo, R. (2002). Map reading versus mind reading: Revisiting children's understanding of the shape of the earth. In M. Limon & L. Mason (Eds.), *Reconsidering conceptual change: Issues in theory and practice* (pp. 59–76). Dordrecht: Kluwer Academic.

Jones, I., Lake, V. E., & Dagli, U. (2003). Integrating mathematics and science in undergraduate early childhood teacher education programs. *Journal of Early Childhood Teacher Education, 24,* 3–8.

Kallery, M. (2004). Early years teachers' late concerns and perceived needs in science: An exploratory study. *European Journal of Teacher Education, 27*(2), 147–165.

Kallery, M., & Psillos, D. (2001). Pre-school teachers' content knowledge in science: Their understandings of elementary science concepts and of issues raised by children's questions. *International Journal of Early Years Education, 9*(3), 165–177.

Katz, L. G., & Chard, S. C. (2000). *Engaging children's minds: The project approach* (2nd ed.). Stamford, CT: JAI Press.

Kazemek, F., Louisell, R., & Wellike, J. (2004, April). *Children's stories about their natural worlds: An exploration from multiple perspectives (and an invitation to participate).* Paper presented at the annual meeting of the National Association of Research in Science Teaching, Vancouver, BC, Canada.

Kirschner, P., Sweller, J., & Clark, R. (2006). Why minimal guidance during instruction does not work: An analysis of the failure of constructivist, discovery, problem-based, experimental and inquiry-based teaching. *Educational Psychologist, 40,* 75–86.

Koirala, H. P., & Bowman, J. K. (2003). Preparing middle level preservice teachers to integrate mathematics and science: Problems and possibilities. *School Science and Mathematics, 10*(3), 145–154.

Krajcik, J. S., Blumenfeld, P. C., Marx, R. W., & Soloway, E. (1994). A collaborative model for helping middle grade science teachers learn project-based instruction. *Elementary School Journal, 94*(5), 483–498.

Kuhn, D., Amsel, E., & O'Loughlin, M. (1988). *The development of scientific thinking skills.* Orlando, FL: Academic Press.

Kuhn, D., & Pearsall, S. (2000). Developmental origins of scientific thinking. *Journal of Cognition and Development, 1,* 113–129.

Lawson, A. E. (2003). *The neurological basis of learning, development and discovery: Implications for science and mathematics instruction.* New York: Kluwer.

Lind, K. K. (1999). Science in early childhood: Developing and acquiring fundamental concepts and skills. In *Dialogue on early childhood science, mathematics, and technology education* (pp. 114–117). Washington, DC: American Association for the Advancement of Science.

Lindsey, G. (1997). Brain research and implications for early childhood education. *Childhood Education, 72*(2), 97–100.

Liu, X., & Lesniak, K. (2006). Progression in children's understanding of the matter concept from elementary to high school. *Journal of Research in Science Teaching, 43*(3), 320–347.

Marx, R. W., Blumenfeld, P. C., Krajcik, J. S., & Soloway, E. (1997). Enacting project-based science. *Elementary School Journal, 97,* 341–358.

Mastropieri, M., & Scruggs, T. (1992). Science for students with disabilities. *Review of Educational Research, 62*(4), 377–411.

Mastropieri, M., Scruggs, T., Boon, R., & Butcher, K. (2001). Correlations of inquiry learning in science. *Remedial and Special Education, 22*(3), 130–137.

Mastropieri, M. A., Scruggs, T. E., Mantzicopoulos, P., Sturgeon, A., Goodwin, L., & Chung, S. (1996). "A place where living things affect and depend on each other": Qualitative and quantitative outcomes associated with inclusive science teaching. *Science Education, 82*(2), 163–179.

Mayer, R. (2004). Should there be a three-strike rule against pure discovery learning?: The case for guided methods of instruction. *American Psychologist, 59,* 14–19.

Mazens, K., & Lautrey, J. (2003). Conceptual change in physics: Children's naive representation of sound. *Cognitive Development, 18,* 159–176.

Metz, K. E. (1997). On the complex relation between cognitive developmental research and children's science curricula. *Review of Educational Research, 67*(1), 151–163.

Meyer, L. A., Wardrop, J. L., & Hastings, J. N. (1992). *The development of science knowledge in kindergarten through second grade.* (ERIC Document Reproduction Service No. ED ED354146)

Miner, J. T. (1992). *An early childhood study of the water cycle.* Unpublished master's thesis, University of Nevada, Las Vegas.

Minner, D. D., Levy, A. J., & Century, J. (2010). Inquiry-based science instruction—what is it and does it matter?: Results from a research synthesis years 1984 to 2002. *Journal of Research in Science Teaching, 47*(4), 474–496.

Monhardt, L., & Monhardt, R. (2006). Creating a context for the learning of science process skills through picture books. *Early Childhood Education Journal, 34*(1), 67–71.

Morrell, P., & Carroll, J. B. (2003). An extended examination of preservice elementary teachers' science teaching self-efficacy. *School Science and Mathematics, 103*(5), 246–251.

Morris, M. (2004). Interacting science in early childhood—a project approach. *Teaching Science, 50*(3), 11–14.

Morrow, L. M., Pressley, M., Smith, J. K., & Smith, M. (1997). The effect of a literature-based program integrated into literacy and science instruction with children from diverse backgrounds. *Reading Research Quarterly, 32*, 54–76.

National Center for Education Statistics (NCES). (2006). *Teachers' qualifications, instructional practices, and reading and mathematics gains of kindergartners: Research and development report* (NCES Publication No. 2006-031). Washington, DC: U.S. Department of Education.

National Council of Teachers of Mathematics (NCTM). (2000). *Principles and standards for school mathematics.* Reston, VA: Author.

National Research Council (NRC). (1996). *National Science Education Standards.* Washington, DC: National Academy Press.

National Research Council (NRC). (2000). *Inquiry and the National Science Education Standards: A guide for teaching and learning.* Washington, DC: National Academy Press.

Nayfeld, I. (2008, April). *Science in the classroom: Finding a balance between autonomous exploration and teacher-led instruction in preschool settings.* Poster presented at the honor's program poster session, Rutgers University, New Brunswick, NJ.

Neathery, M. F. (1997). Elementary and secondary students' perceptions toward science and the correlation with the gender, ethnicity, ability, grade, and science achievement. *Electronic Journal of Science Education, 2*(1). Available online at *unr.edu/homepage/jcannon/ejse/neathery.html.*

Norris, S. P., & Phillips, L. M. (2003). How literacy in its fundamental sense is central to scientific literacy. *Science Education, 87*(2), 224–240.

Novak, J. (1977). *A theory of education.* Ithaca, NY: Cornell University Press.

Nussbaum, J. (1985). The earth as a cosmic body. In R. Driver, E. Guesne, & A. Tiberghien (Eds.), *Children's ideas in science* (pp. 170–192). Philadelphia: Open University Press.

Odgers, B. M. (2007). Elementary pre-service teachers' motivation towards science learning at an Australian university. *International Journal of Learning, 14*(3), 201–216.

Oliveira, A. W. (2010). Improving teacher questioning in science inquiry discussions through professional development. *Journal of Research in Science Teaching, 47*(4), 422–453.

Opfer, J. E., & Siegler, R. S. (2004). Revisiting preschoolers' living things concept: A microgenetic analysis of conceptual change in basic biology. *Cognitive Psychology, 49*, 301–332.

Osborne, J., Black, P. J., Wadsworth, P., & Meadows, J. (1994). *SPACE Research Report: The Earth in space.* Liverpool, UK: University of Liverpool.

Osborne, J., Simon, S., & Collins, S. (2003). Attitudes towards science: A review of the literature and its implications. *International Journal of Science Education, 25*(9), 1049–1079.

Osborne, R., & Freyberg, P. (1985). *Learning in science: The implications of children's science.* Portsmouth, NH: Heinemann.

Osborne, R. J., & Cosgrove, M. M. (1983). Children's conceptions of the changes of state of water. *Journal of Research in Science Education, 20*(9), 825–838.

Palincsar, A. S., Magnusson, S. J., Collins, K. M., & Cutter, J. (2001). Making science accessible to all: Results of a design experiment in inclusive classrooms, *Learning Disability Quarterly, 24*(1), 15–32.

Palmer, D. H. (2006). Durability of changes in self-efficacy of preservice primary teachers. *International Journal of Science Education, 28*(6), 655–671.

Pang, J., & Good, R. (2000). A review of the integration of science and mathematics: Implications for further research. *School Science and Mathematics, 100*(2), 73–82.

Patrick, H., Mantzicopoulos, P., & Samarapungavan, A. (2009). Motivation for learning science in kindergarten: Is there a gender gap and does integrated inquiry and literacy instruction make a difference. *Journal of Research in Science Teaching, 46*(2), 166– 191.

Patrick, H., Mantzicopoulos, P., Samarapungavan, A., & French, B. F. (2008). Patterns of young children's motivation for science and teacher–child relationship. *Journal of Experimental Education, 76*(2), 121–144.

Pell, A., & Jarvis, T. (2003). Developing attitude to science education scales for use with primary teachers. *International Journal of Science Education, 25*(10), 1273–1296.

Peterson, S. M., & French, L. (2008). Supporting young children's explanations through inquiry science in preschool. *Early Childhood Research Quarterly, 23*(3), 395–408.

Piaget, J. (1972). *The child's conceptions of the world* (J. Tomlinson & A. Tomlinson, Trans.). Lanham, MD: Littlefield Adams. (Original work published 1928)

Piaget, J., & Inhelder, B. (2000). *The psychology of childhood* (H. Weaver, Trans.). New York: Basic Books. (Original work published 1928)

Plummer, J. D., & Krajcik, J. (2010). Building a learning progression for celestial motion: Elementary levels from an earth-based perspective. *Journal of Research in Science Teaching, 47*(7), 768–787.

Posner, G. J., Strike, K. A., Hewson, P. W., & Gertzog, W. A. (1982). Accomodation of a scientific conception: Toward a theory of conceptual change. *Science Education, 66*(2), 221–227.

Pringle, R. M., & Lamme, L. L. (2005). Using picture story books to support young children's science learning. *Reading Horizons, 46*(1), 1–15.

Ramey-Gassert, L. (1997). Learning science beyond the classroom. *Elementary School Journal, 97*(4), 433–450.

Ruffman, T., Perner, J., Olson, D. R., & Doherty, M. (1993). Reflecting on scientific thinking: Children's understandings of the hypothesis–evidence relation. *Child Development, 64*, 1617–1636.

Rushton, S., & Larkin, E. (2001). Shaping the learning environment: Connecting developmentally appropriate practices to brain research. *Early Childhood Education Journal, 29*(1), 25–33.

Russell, T., & Watt, D. (1990). *Primary SPACE Project Research Report: Evaporation and condensation.* Liverpool, UK: Liverpool University Press.

Saçkes, M., Flevares, L., & Trundle, K. C. (2010). Four- to six-year-old children's conceptions of the mechanism of rainfall. *Early Childhood Research Quarterly, 25*(4), 536–546.

Saçkes, M., Trundle, K. C., Bell, R. L., & O'Connell, A. A. (2011). The influence of early science experience in kindergarten on children's immediate and later science achievement: Evidence from the Early Childhood Longitudinal Study. *Journal of Research in Science Teaching, 48*(2), 217–235.

Saçkes, M., Trundle, K. C., & Flevares, L. (2009a). Using children's books to teach inquiry skills. *Young Children, 64*(6), 24–31.

Saçkes, M., Trundle, K. C., & Flevares, L. M. (2009b). Using children's literature to teach standard-based science concepts in early years. *Early Childhood Education Journal, 36*(5), 415–422.

Samarapungavan, A., Mantzicopoulos, P., & Patrick, H. (2008). Learning science through inquiry in kindergarten. *Science Education, 92*, 368–908.

Schoon, K. J., & Boone, W. J. (1998). Self-efficacy and alternative conceptions of science of preservice elementary teachers. *Science Education, 82*(5), 553–568.

Schoultz, J., Saljo, R., & Wyndhamn, J. (2001). Heavenly talk: Discourse, artifacts, and children's understanding of elementary astronomy. *Human Development, 44*, 103–118.

Scruggs, T., Mastropieri, M., & Boon, R. (1998). Science education for students with disabilities: A review of recent research. *Studies in Science Education, 32*, 21–44.

Smith, C. L., Wiser, M., Anderson, C. W., & Krajcik, J. (2006). Implications of research on children's learning for standards and assessment: A proposed learning progression for matter and the atomic molecular theory. *Measurement: Interdisciplinary Research and Perspective, 14*(1–2), 1–98.

Spelke, E. S., Breinlinger, K., Macomber, J., & Jacobson, K. (1992). Origins of knowledge. *Psychological Review, 99*(4), 605–632.

Tilgner, P. J. (1990). Avoiding science in elementary school. *Science Education, 74*(4), 421–431.

Tobin, K., Briscoe, C., & Holman, J. R. (1990). Overcoming constraints to effective elementary science teaching. *Science Education, 74*(4), 409–420.

Trundle, K. C. (2008). Inquiry based instruction for students with disabilities. In J. Luft, R. L. Bell, &

J. Gess-Newsome (Eds.), *Science as inquiry in the secondary setting* (pp. 79–85). Washington, DC: National Science Teachers Association.

Trundle, K. C., Atwood, R. K., & Christopher, J. E. (2002). Preservice elementary teachers' conceptions of moon phases before and after instruction. *Journal of Research in Science Teaching, 39*(7), 633–658.

Trundle, K. C., Atwood, R. K., & Christopher, J. E. (2006). Preservice elementary teachers' knowledge of observable moon phases and pattern of change in phases. *Journal of Science Teacher Education, 17*(2), 87–101.

Trundle, K. C., Atwood, R. K., & Christopher, J. E. (2007). Fourth grade elementary students' conceptions of standards-based lunar concepts. *International Journal of Science Education, 29*(5), 595–616.

Trundle, K. C., & Saçkes, M. (2008). Sky observation by the book: Lessons for teaching young children astronomy concepts with picturebooks. *Science and Children, 46*(1), 36–39.

Trundle, K. C., & Saçkes, M. (2010). Look! It is going to rain: Using books and observations to promote young children's understanding of clouds. *Science and Children, 47*(8), 29–31.

Trundle, K. C., & Troland, T. H. (2005). The moon in children's literature. *Science and Children, 43*(2), 40–43.

Tu, T. (2006). Preschool science environment: What is available in a preschool classroom? *Early Childhood Education Journal, 33*(4), 245–251.

Tytler, R. (1998). Children's conceptions of air pressure: Exploring the nature of conceptual change. *International Journal of Science Education, 20*(8), 929–958.

Tytler, R., & Peterson, S. (2004). Young children learning about evaporation: A longitudinal perspective. *Canadian Journal of Science, Mathematics, and Technology Education, 4*(1), 111–127.

Vosniadou, S. (1999). Conceptual change research: State of the art and future directions. In W. Schnotz, S. Vosniadou, & M. Carretero (Eds.), *New perspective on conceptual change* (pp. 3–13). Amsterdam: Pergamon.

Vosniadou, S. (2002). On the nature of naive physics. In M. Limon & L. Mason (Eds.), *Reconsidering conceptual change: Issues in theory and practice* (pp. 61–76). Dordrecht: Kluwer Academic.

Vosniadou, S. (2007). The conceptual change approach and its reframing. In S. Vosniadou, A. Baltas, & X. Vamvakoussi (Eds.), *Reframing the conceptual change approach in learning and instruction* (pp. 1–15). Oxford, UK: Elsevier.

Vosniadou, S., & Brewer, W. F. (1992). Mental models of the earth: A study of conceptual change in childhood. *Cognitive Psychology, 24*, 535–585.

Vosniadou, S., & Brewer, W. F. (1994). Mental models of the day/night cycle. *Cognitive Science, 18*, 123–183.

Vosniadou, S., Ioannides, C., Dimitrakopoulou, A., & Papademetriou, E. (2001). Designing learning environments to promote conceptual change in science. *Learning and Instruction, 11*, 381–419.

Vosniadou, S., Skopeliti, I., & Ikospentaki, K. (2004). Modes of knowing and ways of reasoning in elementary astronomy. *Cognitive Development, 19*(2), 203–222.

Vosniadou, S., Skopeliti, I., & Ikospentaki, K. (2005). Reconsidering the role of artifacts in reasoning: Children's understanding of the globe as a model of the earth. *Learning and Instruction, 15*, 331–351.

Watters, J. J., Diezmann, C. M., Grieshaber, S. J., & Davis, J. M. (2000). Enhancing science education for young children: A contemporary initiative. *Australian Journal of Early Childhood, 26*(2), 1–7.

Wellman, H. M., & Estes, D. (1986). Early understanding of mental entities: A reexamination of childhood realism. *Child Development, 57*(4), 910–923.

White, R., & Gunstone, R. (1992). *Probing understanding.* London: Falmer Press.

Youngquist, J., & Pataray-Ching, J. (2004). Revisiting "play": Analyzing and articulating acts of inquiry. *Early Childhood Education Journal, 31*(3), 171–178.

Zimmerman, C. (2000). The development of scientific reasoning skills. *Developmental Review, 20*, 99–149.

CHAPTER 13

Teacher–Child Play Interactions to Achieve Learning Outcomes

Risks and Opportunities

Jeffrey Trawick-Smith

Play has long been viewed as a mediator in the development of cognitive, social, and language development of young children (Bergen, 2002; Garvey, 1993; Nichols & Stich, 2000; Vygotsky, 1976, 1978). Traditionally, long periods of playtime have been included in the daily schedules of preschool and kindergarten programs; play has been considered a cornerstone of the early childhood curriculum (Copple & Bredekamp, 2006). But things in American education have changed. The growing emphasis on standards, assessment, and accountability in schools has led to a concern that play-based programs do not adequately address important learning outcomes. In many preschools and centers, play has been reduced or even eliminated to make room for quieter, academic learning (Stipek, 2006). Preschools and kindergartens in public school settings have become particularly regimented and adult-directed, with teachers feeling compelled to increase literacy and numeracy instruction at the expense of playtime (Golinkoff, Hirsh-Pasek, & Eyer, 2004). In short, play in school has become an endangered species.

Play enthusiasts have responded in two ways to these modern threats to play. Some have argued, simply and strenuously, for a return of play to its rightful place in the early childhood classroom (Alliance for Childhood, 2009; Miller & Almon, 2009). Relying on early work on the relationship of play to physical and emotional well-being (Axline, 1947; Freud, 1961; Landreth, 2002), these authors urge school administrators and policymakers to restore playtime in school, arguing that children have a fundamental right to play.

A very different response to the reduction of play time in school is to argue that play contributes to learning (Singer, Golinkoff, & Hirsh-Pasek, 2006). From this view, teachers should carefully plan and implement play environments and experiences to address national and state standards and learning outcomes. This position has gained traction in the field because it recognizes the developmental contributions of play on the one hand, but acknowledges the need for teacher guidance and planning in play to meet specific learning outcomes on the other. This perspective emphasizes adult interactions in play. Through teacher involve-ment, from this view, play can become more useful for development and learning.

Questions and concerns about the use of play to promote learning goals abound. What are the effects on play of so much adult planning and intervention? What should be the pre-cise role of teachers when they interact with children who are playing? Can adults guide play, so that learning is achieved but play is not threatened? In this chapter, I first define play, then present three approaches to teacher–child play interactions in classrooms that can be found in the literature. I describe each approach and consider its unique risks and opportunities for learning and development. I then integrate ideas from all three approaches in order to construct a coherent model of adult play interactions in early childhood classrooms.

What Is Play?

Determining the best approach for including play in early childhood classrooms requires a clear understanding of what it is—a clarity that has never been fully achieved in the literature. Some play theorists have defined play quite narrowly to include four categories of activity—motor play, pretend play, construction play, and games—described by Piaget (1962). These categories have been elaborated by play researchers. For example, some have differentiated between social and nonsocial enactments of these types of play (Howes & Matheson, 1992).

It has been argued that these conventional definitions of play may be too narrow in scope, focusing only on childhood pastimes that are frequently observed within Western societies, while overlooking or undervaluing many developmentally significant play forms that are more common in non-Western cultures (Göncü, Mistry, & Mosier, 2000; McLoyd, 1986; Trawick-Smith, 2010b). Too, some researchers have found that these theoretically tidy categories of play cannot be easily teased apart in real life (Reifel & Yeatman, 1993; Trawick-Smith, 2010a). A child might integrate a make-believe play theme into a motor activity on the playground. Would this be an instance of pretend play, motor play, or both?

For this chapter, I have chosen to adopt a broader definition of play, based on the work of Bateson (1972) and Rubin, Fein, and Vandenberg (1983). These authors propose that "play" is an intellectual and emotional frame of mind in which children come to an agreement with one another that things are not to be taken literally. This detachment of experience from the very serious day-to-day life of classrooms is the defining quality of play. In order to be play, an activity must also be freely chosen, intrinsically motivated, and emo-tionally meaningful, according to this definition. Play, then, can take the form of almost any activity during free-choice time in a classroom. Building with blocks, pretending, making a puzzle, solving a math game, or even eating lunch could include play if this nonliteral frame has been established.

The Trust-in-Play Approach

One perspective on teacher–child play interactions, a "trust-in-play" approach, is reflected in the work of traditional scholars and educators who believe that play, itself—without adult involvement—leads to important developmental outcomes (Golinkoff et al., 2004; Landreth, 2002; Miller & Almon, 2009). When children play, according to this view, they naturally acquire social competence and language; think deeply about people, objects, and events; and solve problems. The more complex, symbolic, language-rich, and social play becomes, the more powerful will be its effect on learning. Adult involvement can do little to improve on the developmental outcomes of child-guided play from this perspective. Teachers should mainly prepare play environments and observe child-directed activities. If they are to intervene at all, according to this view, they should provide new materials, ask a few interesting questions, help to resolve disputes, and then quickly withdraw. Child-directed play is what produces positive outcomes; adults can only get in the way.

Advocates of a trust-in-play perspective find empirical support in studies showing the relationships of play itself to measures of general cognition, language and literacy, mathematical thinking, and overall academic success (Cohen & Uhry, 2007; Craig-Unkefer & Kaiser, 2003; DeKroon, Kyte, & Johnson, 2002; Fekonja, Marjanovic-Umek, & Kranjc, 2005; Hanline, Milton, & Phelps, 2009a, 2009b; Ingersoll & Schreibman, 2006; Lewis, Boucher, Lupton, & Watson, 2000; Mendez & Fogle, 2002; Neeley, Neeley, Justen, & Tipton-Sumner, 2001; Riojas-Cortez, 2001; Wolfgang, Standard, & Jones, 2001). Because these studies are largely correlational, questions can be raised about the direction of these associations: Which comes first, play ability (which promotes cognitive development) or cognitive development (which promotes play)? Trust-in-play advocates assume a linear, unidirectional relationship between play activities and learning outcomes.

Concerns have been raised about this approach to play. What happens if some children do not engage in useful forms of play activity? What if some are unable to play at all because of social or cognitive limitations, or other special needs? How can a teacher be certain that playing will help students learn to read, do math, or achieve other state and national academic standards? In addition, there is evidence that some adult guidance in play is beneficial. A host of "play training" studies have shown that adult intervention in children's activities can promote specific play abilities, as well as social, cognitive, and language development (Bennet, Wood, & Rodgers, 1997; Connolly & Doyle, 1984; Smilansky & Shefatya, 1990; Thorp, Stahmer, & Schreibman, 1995). When teachers and parents choose to trust in play, rather than interact with children, some authors contend, they are missing opportunities to foster early development.

Child care quality research has also shown that adult play interactions are useful (Howes, Ritchie, & Bowman, 2002). In one investigation, the frequency of adult engagement in children's play was found to be related both to attachment to caregivers and to the intellectual quality of children's activities (Howes & Smith, 1995). In another study, the nature and amount of adult–child interactions were found to be fundamental indicators of overall quality in child care (Howes, Phillips, & Whitebrook, 1992). Studies on inclusive classrooms have shown that adult intervention can significantly increase the frequency and complexity of play for children with special needs (Kok, Kong, & Bernard-Opitz, 2002; Lantz, Nelson, & Loftin, 2004).

Trusting in play, with little or no adult facilitation, is not fully supported by current research. Although play certainly contributes to child development, there is a risk that some children, without adult support, will not engage in the sustained, high-quality play activities needed to achieve important social and educational outcomes.

The Facilitate-Play Approach

Decades of research on adult involvement in children's play have led to a second approach to using play in early childhood classrooms. A "facilitate-play" perspective holds that play leads to important social and intellectual outcomes but requires elaboration and enrichment through adult intervention. The earliest of these studies were based on the assumption that children living in poverty are deprived of play opportunities. Their poor play skills may actually explain their relatively low academic performance (Feitelson & Ross,

1974; Smilansky, 1968). Since play enhances general cognitive abilities, they argue, teachers should intervene to teach play skills. The most didactic of these approaches involved training children to engage in make-believe and related behaviors (Saltz, Dixon, & Johnson, 1977). Children were presented with stories or experiences to later "play out" with props. Adults intervened to model role playing, make suggestions, or encourage social interaction and language. Children who participated in such programs were found to perform higher on measures of play ability, general intelligence, and creativity.

A more recent focus of facilitate-play theorists is on threats to play in modern American life. Overly academic preschools and kindergartens and the prevalence of computers and television in homes have produced a new generation of poor players (Bodrova & Leong, 2006). Children's play must be actively supported by adults, from this view, usually through not only brief entry into children's natural play activities in the classroom but also periodic direct guidance in how to pretend. Researchers in early childhood special education have also argued for a facilitate-play approach for children with disabilities (File & Kontos, 1993; Girolametto, Hoaken, & Weitzman, 2000). The number of play intervention studies on children with autism alone has burgeoned in the last few decades (Kok et al., 2002; Lantz et al., 2004; Thorp et al., 1995; Wolfberg, 2003).

Findings of studies on the effects of adult–child play interventions are quite compelling. Experimental investigations on children with special needs, for example, have shown that adult play intervention can promote greater social interaction, frequency of language, and task engagement (Kohler, Anthony, Steighner, & Hoyson, 2001; Kok et al., 2002; Lantz et al., 2004; Skellenger & Hill, 1994). An early childhood curriculum that enhances pretend play through adult instruction and play interactions has been found promote greater self-regulation and higher scores on language and literacy measures (Barnett et al., 2008; Bodrova & Leong, 2001; Diamond, Barnett, Thomas, & Munro, 2007).

According to some, the facilitate-play approach also poses risks. Sutton-Smith (1990) has warned that, too often, well-intentioned play intervention lapses into "didactic play bumblings" (p. 25), in which adults overdirect children's activities. Other theorists argue that play intervention imposes on children a single, correct way to play that may be incongruous with their interests, needs, and cultural traditions (Brown & Freeman, 2001; Trawick-Smith, 1994). Research has suggested that adult involvement in play can sometimes impede play behavior. Greater adult interaction in child care has been associated with lower levels of social play (File, 1994; File & Kontos, 1993; Harper & McCluskey, 2003; Wilcox-Herzog & Kontos, 1998). More cognitively oriented behaviors have been observed in children's self-guided play, compared with teacher-directed play activities (Gmitrova & Gmitrov, 2003).

Standards-oriented educators might raise very different concerns about a facilitate-play approach. Does adult-enriched play, they might ask, even if related to general cognitive or social outcomes, address specific areas of academic learning mandated by states and school districts? Do adult interactions to support play itself enhance literacy or mathematical thinking? Wouldn't interventions focused on specific academic standards be more efficient?

The Enhance-Learning-Outcomes-through-Play Approach

A third approach to using play in early education is to *enhance learning outcomes through play*. This approach is based on the assumption that teacher–child play interactions have their greatest impact on learning when they focus narrowly on learning goals in literacy, math, science, or other measurable outcomes. From this viewpoint, teachers' interactions in play should always be "intentional"—that is, carried out with one or several particular goals for learning in mind. The thinking is that meeting national or state standards is the overarching purpose of Head Start, child care, or public preschool programs. Focusing specifically on these standards, even in play interactions, is the most direct route to meeting them.

Support for this approach comes primarily from studies on facilitating literacy through play. A variety of investigations have examined the effects of adult play interactions on children's literacy activities and knowledge. In these studies, adults modeled "literacy routines," pointed out print, offered literacy props to children, or in other ways prompted literacy enactments in pretend play. Findings indicate that children have shown modest gains by participating in these programs in print awareness and literacy enactments (Dickinson & Smith, 1991; Neuman & Roskos, 1991, 1993; Roskos, Christie, Widman, & Holding, 2010; Roskos & Neuman, 2003; Vukelich, 1994; Wasik, Bond, & Hindman, 2006). Support for enhancing mathematics through play has been largely theoretical. Several researchers have speculated that the some of the features of play—pretending, building with blocks, spontaneously experimenting with numbers—make it a rich context for teaching mathematical thinking (Edo, Planas, & Badillo, 2009; Ginsberg, 2006).

Those with the trust-in-play perspective would obviously raise concerns about inserting such academic-oriented interventions into children's activities. No matter how skillful teachers might be in such interactions, they run the risk of interrupting play (Kuschner, 2010). Some researchers have asked whether math- or literacy-enriched play is even play anymore (Trawick-Smith, 1994; Trawick-Smith & Picard, 2003). When a child in a pretend post office discontinues her sorting and delivery of mail to join the teacher in writing and mailing a letter to her mother, is she still pretending? When the child writes, "I miss you, Mommy. When are you picking me up?" could she really be carrying out the role of a postal worker? Play, in this case, appears to have been turned into something else.

An Integrated, Responsive Model of Play Intervention

Each approach to play poses risks but also provides opportunities. Is there a way to reconcile these three seemingly disparate perspectives, borrowing the most effective elements from each? In this section, an integrated, responsive model of teacher–child play interactions is described. The model includes components of each play approach and provides a solution to the problem of heavy-handed adult intervention on the one hand, and too little play involvement on the other. Four assumptions underlie this model; the first three are related to each of the three approaches to play; the fourth assumption integrates the three perspectives.

Assumption 1: Autonomous Play Is Beneficial

Based on the work of Vygotsky (1976) and neo-Vygotskian researchers (Berk & Winsler, 1995; Bodrova & Leong, 2006; Lantz et al., 2004; Schuler & Wolfberg, 2000; Trawick-Smith, 1994, 1998; Winsler, 2003), this model is grounded on the assumption that autonomous play is necessary for child development—a fundamental premise of the trust-in-play perspective. From Vygotsky's view, self-guided play activities are an ideal context for thinking and learning because, as children play, they behave as if they are "a head taller" (Vygotsky, 1976, p. 542)—that is, they exhibit greater control over their own actions; engage in more mature thinking; and speak in longer, more complex sentences (Cohen & Uhry, 2007; Elias & Berk, 2002; Fekonja et al., 2005). This is particularly true during pretend play, in which children assume the roles of adults in their lives and strive for a higher level of maturity in speech and behavior (Hanline et al., 2009a, 2009b). This association between autonomous play and more mature language and behavior has been found to be most pronounced for children with disabilities (Brown, Rickards, & Bortoli, 2001; Craig-Unkefer & Kaiser, 2003; DeKroon et al., 2002; Ingersoll & Schreibman, 2006; Neeley et al., 2001; Schepis, Reid, Ownbey, & Clary, 2003) and those who are learning a second language (Riojas-Cortez, 2001).

Self-guided play can lead to desired child outcomes in early childhood classrooms in two ways, based on this assumption. First, it can support cognitive processes that are important for learning. For example, frequency and quality of play have been related to specific areas of "executive function"—the cognitive system that allows control and management of intellectual processes. Play experiences and abilities have been associated with areas of executive function such as self-regulation (Barnett et al., 2008; Diamond et al., 2007; Elias & Berk, 2002; Fantuzzo & McWayne, 2002), working memory, and processing speed (Piek, Dawson, Smith, & Gasson, 2008). Acquiring these fundamental cognitive abilities can, in turn, support learning in academic and social areas in classrooms.

A second way that self-guided play can contribute to early educational goals is by promoting children's direct acquisition of specific academic knowledge and skills as they interact with materials and peers. Ginsberg (2006) has argued that mathematical thinking is naturally embedded in many types of play. Other researchers and educators have observed that that child-directed play, without adult involvement, can include scientific thinking (Fleer, 2009a, 2009b) and literacy (Göncü & Klein, 2001; Pellegrini & Galda, 1990).

The model presented here, then, assumes that autonomous play is beneficial and a worthwhile goal in and of itself, in early childhood education.

Assumption 2: Not All Children Are Able to Play

A second assumption of this model is that many children, with certain developmental characteristics, or in certain contexts, have difficulty playing independently and in ways that support development. This view reflects a facilitate-play perspective. There is strong evidence that children who have a wide range of disabilities and certain temperamental characteristics, or who face family challenges, have difficulty engaging in meaningful, autonomous play (Roach, Barrat, Miller, & Leavitt, 1998; Van Berckelaer-Onnes, 2003). If play is critical for development, according to this assumption, some children will need to be assisted in learning how to engage in play activities.

Theories abound for why children with particular challenges or disabilities are unable to play. A play deprivation explanation is common in the literature; children who grow up in play-deficient environments—in multiple foster care placements or dangerous neighborhoods that don't allow outdoor activities, for example—may never acquire play abilities (Comfort, 2005). Children with disabilities that impair social understanding—such as those with autism spectrum disorders—may lack a theory of the mind (TOM) that helps them interpret the behaviors, motives, and emotions of others (Baron-Cohen, Leslie, & Frith, 2007; Rutherford & Rogers, 2003). Children lacking a TOM may not understand when a peer who is playing an angry mother is "just pretending" or what a make-believe firefighter would think, do, or say in a particular situation. Some children with disabilities are ignored or rejected by peers, which restricts social play (Odom et al., 2006). Regardless of the cause, some children will benefit from adult involvement in their play.

Assumption 3: Supporting Play Does Not Preclude Academic Learning

A third assumption of the model proposed here is that adults can enhance the learning of academic knowledge and skills without disrupting self-directed play. Consistent with the enhance-learning-outcomes-through-play approach, this assumption holds that sensitive and skillfully delivered teacher interactions—asking questions, giving hints, posing problems, or providing encouragement—can simultaneously extend thinking and learning, and enhance on-going play activities. Adult interactions to promote learning in math, literacy, science, and other areas—when these are meaningful and congruent with children play activities—do not threaten play and may even enrich it.

There has been little research on play intervention strategies to promote academic learning. A theoretical foundation for using such an approach has been laid by scholars from a variety of fields—language, literacy, and mathematics education. Theoretical arguments and descriptive data have been presented in support of using play intervention to promote oral language abilities, such as grammar and vocabulary, in young children with special needs (Gupta, 2009; Modica, 2010). Other researchers have formulated and, in some cases, empirically studied models for embedding literacy interactions in play and other routines (Justice & Kaderavek, 2004; Neuman & Roskos, 1991, 1993; Roskos et al., 2010; Roskos & Neuman, 2003; Vukelich, 1994; Wasik et al., 2006). Math educators have identified a variety of adult interactions that can enhance mathematical thinking in play and nonplay contexts. These include the use of "math talk" (Klibanoff, Levine, Huttenlocher, Vasilyeva, & Hedges, 2006) and promotion of specific mathematical skills in pretend and block play (Edo et al., 2009).

The emphasis of these interventions is on entering children's play with the intent of enhancing specific academic skills when these relate to activities in progress. Teachers ask children how many cards they won in a game of memory, whether a block structure is taller or shorter than the children who built it, what groceries a child has scribbled on a pretend grocery list, or what children predict about whether an object will float or sink. The assumption here is that such interactions will support play, as well as learning.

Assumption 4: Approaches to Play Are Not Incompatible If Teachers Are Responsive

The model presented here is based on the assumption that any sort of adult play interaction can promote development and learning if it is responsive to children's current needs. This assumption reflects the work of Vygotsky (1976, 1978), who argued that adults should tailor their interactions to the needs of individual children and the demands of the immediate environment. If children cannot play at all or are limited in their play by challenging conditions or insurmountable environmental obstacles (e.g., a toy that is too complex or a peer who is too aggressive), a direct method of guidance is most likely to result in productive thinking, learning, and play. If children are already playing independently and in useful and meaningful ways, adult intervention will not be helpful at all. A situation in which adults can be most effective in enhancing play and learning is when children are in Vygotsky's *zone of proximal development*—a time when children can play independently, with a little indirect guidance from an adult: a question, a hint, or a subtle prompt. This may include a situation in which a child needs just a little guidance in order to play in a more social, verbal, or symbolic way. It might also involve a teacher asking a question or posing a problem at just the right moment in a child's thinking to enhance literacy, math, or other academic areas.

The key to using to play to promote learning and development, according to this model, is observation and interpretation of what children are currently doing. It is only by fully understanding a child's play activities that a teacher can determine whether or not to intervene and, if so, whether general play support or interactions to enhance specific thinking and learning goals are appropriate. Such a responsive approach is difficult to implement, to be sure. It is quite common for adults to engage in those "didactic play bumblings" that Sutton-Smith describes. However, there is evidence that adults can accurately identify play needs and adapt their interactions accordingly (Damast, Tamis-LeMonda, & Bornstein, 1996; File, 1994; Freund, 1989; Girolametto et al., 2000; Wilcox-Herzog & Kontos, 1998).

Implementing the Model

In the model proposed here, shown in Figure 13.1, teachers begin this approach with careful observation of children's play. Based on these observations, they determine specific play needs. To do this, they ask two fundamental questions:

1. How much support do children need at this moment in their play?
2. What learning outcomes, if any, can be enhanced in these play activities?

Teachers then implement (or do not implement) a play interaction based on the answers to these questions. If children are playing in meaningful and independent ways, and there are no clear opportunities to promote academic learning, teachers observe or withdraw from the play area altogether. Noninvolvement is considered a "good fit" for children who have no need for adult guidance. Another possibility is that children need a certain level of support in play itself. Here, teachers must judge whether children need relatively direct guidance (e.g., making direct play suggestions) or indirect support (e.g., asking a question or giving a hint). In a third situation, children may be playing well but show a need for guidance in thinking and learning related to academic standards. In this case, teachers must decide on an approach that supports this learning without interrupting play.

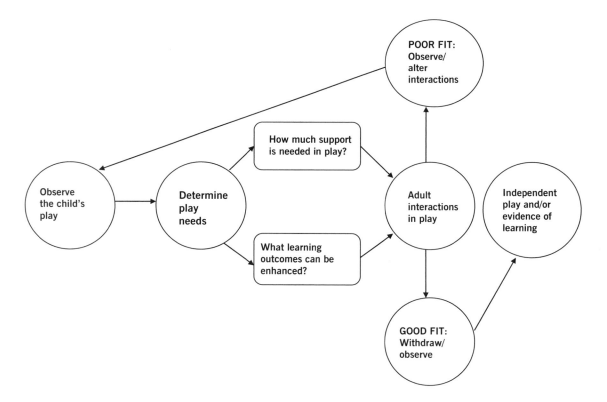

FIGURE 13.1. An integrated, responsive model of teacher–child play interactions.

These teacher decisions are complex and require careful reflection. For example, when deciding to support play, teachers must determine what aspect of play needs guidance. Should an interaction promote make-believe, greater engagement, social interaction, verbalization, or other play elements? They must then decide what degree of assistance is needed. A child who is wandering, watching peers from the periphery of a play area, or showing confusion about how to complete a play task, might be determined to need much support in play. Direct teacher guidance in play engagement would be warranted: "Why don't you sit with me, and we'll make this puzzle." This would be considered a good-fit interaction.

A child who is engaged in less elaborate pretend play—rocking a doll in a simple, repetitive fashion—might be viewed as needing some guidance. An indirect interaction—a simple question such as, "Why is your baby crying?"—would then be a good fit. A teacher might choose simply to observe a child who is playing independently in sustained, elaborate, and meaningful ways. What is critical, in this model, is not the specific type of interaction in and of itself that is selected, but whether the teacher's interaction matches the amount of support children need.

Decision making is equally complex when considering whether children need support in thinking and learning related to academic outcomes. As they simultaneously contemplate a child's need for support in play itself, teachers must also determine whether there is an opportunity to address learning in a specific area. Critical to this decision is to consider whether such a learning and thinking interaction can be implemented without disrupting ongoing play. If children building with blocks are discussing the height of their structure, a teacher might ask about whether the building is taller than those who built it. If children are shopping at a pretend grocery, a teacher could offer materials to make a grocery list. In this model, these outcomes-oriented interactions are considered a good fit if they are congruent with and supportive of what children are doing. An effort to teach academic skills that do not match children's play activities would be considered a poor-fit interaction. For example, a teacher who interrupts a make-believe dinner party to quiz children about the shapes of the plates and napkins would be engaging in a poor-fit interaction.

As shown in Figure 13.1, after implementing an intervention, teachers observe children's play to determine whether their strategy was successful. If the interaction was a good fit—in terms of amount of support, its promotion of learning outcomes, or both—children would be expected to show ongoing autonomous play and/or evidence of progress in learning outcomes. Teachers could withdraw altogether and trust in ongoing, child-directed activity. However, if the interactions chosen are a poor-fit, teachers would observe that children are still in need of support. They might continue wandering, show frustration over a material, or in other ways indicate that meaningful autonomous play is not possible. Also, children might show that they are still struggling with a learning outcome the teacher was trying to promote. In this case, the teacher would be required to repeat the process. As shown in Figure 13.1, the teacher would once again observe play, reflect on play needs, and interact with the child in ways that would hopefully comprise a better fit. In this model, the teacher would continue this intervention cycle until a good fit was reached and children show self-directed and enhanced play activities.

Preliminary Empirical Evidence

Colleagues and I have conducted three studies to test various aspects of this model of teacher–child play interactions. Preliminary findings suggest that teachers can (and frequently do) respond naturally to children's play in ways that are consistent with the model.

When interactions are a good fit, based on our data, children's play becomes more autonomous and some aspects of academic learning are enhanced.

Study 1: Good-Fit Interactions and Autonomous Play

In one study, we sought to determine whether a good fit between the amount of support children need in play and the degree of adult guidance would affect children's subsequent, autonomous play (Trawick-Smith & Dziurgot, 2010). We video-recorded eight adults—two head teachers, four assistant teachers, and two student assistants—as they interacted with 32 3- and 4-year-old children of culturally diverse backgrounds in naturally occurring free play in three full-day preschool classrooms. Five 30-minute observations were recorded for each adult over a 20-week period.

Segments of video in which an adult participant moved to within 5 feet of a child who was playing were identified and edited into separate subclips for transcription and analysis. Using video and transcripts, we coded child and teacher behaviors using an observation system developed for the study. For each teacher–child interaction, children's initial play need was first coded as *much, some,* or *none,* depending on the degree of support needed prior to an adult intervention. Teacher guidance was next coded for each interchange as *direct, indirect, observation,* or *no interaction.* Finally, subsequent play was coded for each interaction, using the same coding system used for initial play need: *much, some,* or *none.* Play coded as *none,* following an interaction, was considered to be autonomous play, since it did not require any form of adult support.

Frequencies of each level of initial child play need, level of teacher guidance, and subsequent child play need were entered into a loglinear analysis to examine relationships among these variables. The purpose was to determine whether a good-fit interaction between a child's initial need and a teacher's guidance would be associated with subsequent autonomous play, as predicted by the model. Good-fit interactions were considered to be one of the following: much child need followed by direct adult guidance, some child need followed by indirect adult guidance, and no child need followed by observation or no teacher interaction.

Findings of the study are represented in Figure 13.2. On the left side are standardized residuals that reveal the strength of all associations between initial child play need and level of adult guidance provided. The right side presents standardized residuals that show the strength of associations between different types of good- or poor-fit interactions and subsequent play that is in no need of support (i.e., autonomous play). Solid, bold arrows represent positive, significant relationships between variables. As shown in Figure 13.2, significant and positive relationships were found only for initial child play needs and teacher responses that were a good fit (much need–direct guidance, some need–indirect guidance, no need–observe, and no need–no interaction). This indicates that all adults studied were most likely to respond to children's play needs with good-fit guidance. Figure 13.2 also illustrates that only these good-fit child–teacher sequences were significantly, positively associated with subsequent autonomous play.

These findings provide preliminary support for an integrated, responsive model in three ways. First, they suggest that teachers often naturally provide for children the level of support they need when they intervene in play. This should assuage the concerns of trust-in-play theorists who are wary of adult play intervention. Furthermore, these data indicate that when good-fit interactions do occur they are more likely to lead to autonomous play—as facilitate-play theorists would predict. Finally, results show that sometimes no interaction or mere observation by teachers can be the most supportive response to independent play, as trust-in-play advocates contend. Overall, the study demonstrates that two approaches to play—trust-in-play and facilitate-play—can be complementary, if teachers are responsive to children's play needs.

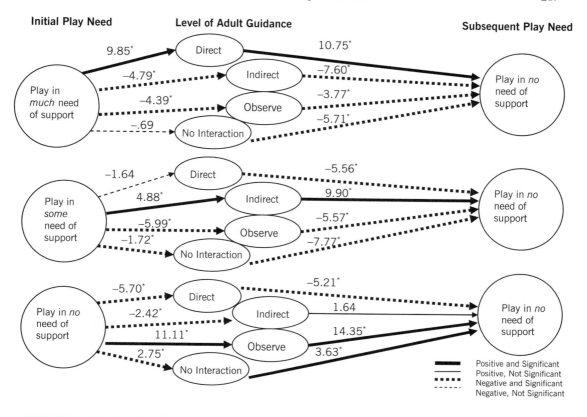

FIGURE 13.2. Standardized residuals for associations among initial play need, level of adult guidance, and subsequent play in *no need* of support (autonomous play).

Study 2: Good-Fit Interactions and Oral Language

Can an enhance-learning-outcomes-through-play approach also be compatible with trust-in-play and facilitate-play methods, as this model suggests? A colleague and I are completing final analyses on a second study, which examined whether good-fit interactions to support play itself or good-fit interactions to enhance specific learning outcomes would be most effective in enhancing specific outcomes in oral language (Trawick-Smith & Breen, 2010). We video-recorded 42 preschool-age children as they interacted during free-play periods in their classrooms over a 9-month period. For each child, we captured three separate 30-minute play interactions. As in Study 1, we then identified sections of video in which an adult—a teacher, assistant teacher, or student assistant—moved within 5 feet of a child in play. These were edited into separate subclips for analysis. We coded these clips to determine the frequency of two types of interactions. First, we coded initial child need and adult guidance behaviors, as in Study 1. From resulting data, we calculated the total frequency of general play interactions that were determined to be a good fit (much need–direct guidance, some need–indirect guidance, and no need–observation or no interaction).

Next, we coded two narrowly focused academic interventions that have been recommended in the literature for promoting oral language: asking open-ended questions to prompt verbal expression, and recasting children's utterances to extend grammatical structures (Dickinson & Smith, 1991; Fey & Proctor-Williams, 2000; Yifat & Zadunaisky-Ehrlich, 2008). When an interaction was found to include one of these two interventions, we additionally coded it as a good or poor fit based on the following question: "Is this interaction congruent with the child's current thinking and play actions?" If a teacher question was related to what a child was playing, it was considered to be a good fit. If such a question interrupted, distracted from, or in other ways interfered with play and thinking, it was coded as a poor fit. An attempt to recast a child's utterance that effectively furthered ongoing play and conversation was marked as a good fit. A recast that was highly exaggerated, obviously didactic, or in other ways interfered with authentic conversation and play was considered a poor fit. Frequencies of good-fit recasts and good-fit open-ended questions were tallied.

The Peabody Picture Vocabulary Test–4 (PPVT-4) was administered to children at the beginning of the study and again at its end, 1 year later. A multiple regression analysis was conducted with pretest language scores and each of the good-fit teacher–child interaction frequencies as independent variables and posttest language scores as dependent measures. Findings of this analysis are presented in Table 13.1.

As shown, two teacher–child interactions were significantly related to vocabulary growth. Good-fit interactions to support play itself were found to predict posttest PPVT-4 after we controlled for pretest performance. Good-fit open-ended questions also were significantly associated with posttest language measures, after we controlled for pretest scores. Frequency of good-fit expansions was not significantly related to language measures.

What are the implications of these findings for the model proposed here? They indicate that both general interactions to support play and a more focused oral language intervention—open-ended question asking—contribute to language development, if they are administered in a manner that matches what children need and are currently doing in play. Facilitate-play strategies, such as good-fit hint-giving or modeling and an enhance-learning-outcomes-through-play method, such as good-fit question asking, contribute independently and significantly to oral language growth. It is the responsive quality of these adult interactions, according to this model, that explains these findings.

Study 3: Good–Fit Interactions and Mathematical Thinking

A colleague and I also conducted a pilot study on teacher–child interactions related to mathematical thinking (Trawick-Smith, Swaminathan, Lui, & Yu, 2011). This was a descriptive investigation in which we recorded, transcribed, and analyzed four preschool teachers' natural interactions in play. Our purpose was to identify, categorize, and define specific interactions related to academic outcomes in mathematics. Teachers were recorded in their

TABLE 13.1. Summary of Regression Analysis with Pretest Language Scores (PPVT) and Teacher–Child Interactions as Independent Variables and Posttest PPVT Scores as the Dependent Variable

Model	B	Standard error	Beta	t
(Constant)	34.063	6.867		4.960*
PPVT pretest	.638	.070	.700	9.174*
Good-fit interactions	.358	.119	.270	3.009*
Open-ended questions	.340	.127	.247	2.672**
Good-fit recasts	.043	.156	.022	.278
R^2	.840			
Adjusted R^2	.819			

*$p < .001$; **$p < .01$.

own classrooms during four, separate, half-hour free-play sessions over a 6-month period. Videos were edited, as in the previous two studies; segments in which the teacher moved within 5 feet of a child or children at play were captured for analysis. Two researchers viewed these segments and their corresponding transcripts, and marked specific teacher behaviors that were determined to be efforts to prompt children's mathematical thinking. The two researchers, in constant consultation with one another, categorized these interactions. As categories of teacher behaviors were created, rules for inclusion were discussed and written. Throughout the analysis, previous categories were changed—divided, collapsed and/or renamed—and inclusion rules were modified, until a final categorization of both teacher and child play behaviors was constructed.

Four distinct math–play interactions were identified in this analysis:

1. *Interactions to support number.* Interactions by a teacher that guide children at play in thinking about "how many"; in using counting and other methods of quantification; in recognizing, comparing, or naming number words or numerals; and/or in connecting them to the quantities they represent.
2. *Interactions to support measurement.* Teacher behaviors that guide children at play in recognizing, comparing, ordering, or measuring objects or spaces using the attributes of length, volume, weight, area, and time, using standard or nonstandard units of measure.
3. *Interactions to support geometry.* Interactions that guide children at play in recognizing, building, comparing, drawing, sorting, naming, or describing the attributes' two- or three-dimensional shapes.
4. *Interactions to support problem solving in mathematical contexts.* Teacher behaviors that guide children at play in solving mathematical problems. A *problem* is defined as a dilemma or puzzle that is challenging to solve, a task that is difficult to complete, or an answer to a thought-provoking question that the child wishes to find. A *mathematical problem* is a problem that may be solved only by using clearly identified mathematical methods.

These four categories of teacher behavior could be further categorized as good- or poor-fit interactions. Goodness of fit for an interaction was determined by asking two questions:

1. Does amount of guidance provided by the adult (direct, indirect, observe, no interaction) match the level of a child's need for support in thinking mathematically (*much, some, none*)?
2. Does the content of the teacher's interaction (number, measurement, geometry, or problem solving) match what the child is currently thinking about or doing?

In order for an interaction to be considered a good fit, the answer to both questions must be *yes*.

Table 13.2 presents each category of math–play interaction, an example, and the percentage of each that was found to be a good fit in this study. As shown, there was variation in good-fit interactions across categories. Problem-solving interactions were highly likely to be a good fit; geometry interactions, less so. Although this study is limited in scope, it suggests that teachers can, and often do, interact with children in play to support mathematical thinking. Furthermore, it shows that, more often than not, these interactions are consistent with children's current thinking and play. A new investigation, with a larger number of children and teachers, is currently under way to examine the relationships of each type of interaction to performance on assessments of mathematical thinking.

TABLE 13.2. Categories of Math–Play Interactions, Examples, and Percentages of Each That Were a Good Fit

Math–play interaction	Example	% Good fit
Number interactions	Teacher: What did you roll? Child: (*Counts dots on a die.*) One, two three, four, five. Teacher: Five? So can you move your marker that many? Child: (*Counts squares on a board game.*)	76
Geometry interactions	Teacher: (*Points to blocks on a shelf.*) We don't have too many shapes left to use. What shape will you use next on your bridge? Child: (*Holds up a cylinder block.*) Teacher: Will a cylinder shape work? Child: Yep, a cylinder, I think. Like this one. (*Places the block on his structure.*)	61
Measurement interactions	Teacher: Does it take more squirts of water to fill up the jar or this shell? What would you guess? Child: Oh, the jar. (*Continues to squirt water into the jar with a baster.*) See? There's lots of squirts in here. (*Points to the jar.*) Teacher: What about the shell? Child: Not too many. See? (*Begins to squirt water into the shell.*) One, two, three … and it's all full.	81
Problem-solving interactions	Child: (*Placing beads on posts using a math game.*) How do you do this? Teacher: (*Points to a peer.*) See how Jamal is doing it? He puts five beads where it says five and four beads where it says four. So how many beads would go here? Can you figure this out? Child: Oh. I can do it. (*Begins to place beads on the posts.*)	84

Implication for Classroom Practice

Findings of these preliminary investigations are consistent with the model presented here. Good-fit play interactions—those in which a teacher's guidance matches a child's need for support—are associated with autonomous play—a general developmental outcome—and vocabulary growth—a specific academic outcome. Teachers naturally attempt to promote mathematical thinking in children's play as well.

This model suggests that purposes and strategies for interacting with children in play should be based on an understanding of what children are currently doing. Sometimes children should be left alone in play, as trust-in-play theorists advocate; other times interventions to enhance play itself are warranted, as prescribed by facilitate-play advocates. At the right moments, interactions to address specific academic standards can be effective, reflecting an enhance-learning-outcomes-through-play approach. According to the model, prior to an interaction, teachers should pause to study carefully the play in progress and consciously consider the amount and type of support, if any, children require. To do this effectively, teachers must hone skills of observation and the interpretation of children's play needs, which serve as the basis for successful intervention. They must also build a broad repertoire of play interaction strategies from which to draw when confronted with unique play situations that arise in the classroom. Skills are needed at supporting play itself in nonobtrusive ways—modeling a make-believe enactment, providing new play props, or encouraging children to interact with peers, for example. Strategies for smoothly implementing academic interventions without interrupting play must also be learned—asking a question or giving a hint precisely when it is needed, for example.

No adult observed in the studies cited here was able to implement good-fit interactions in every situation; and there was variability across individual teachers in how successfully they did so. This suggests that teacher preparation programs or professional development activities for teachers should focus on enhancing competence in observation and identification of play needs, and on decision making related to implementing play intervention strategies. Self-analysis of classroom video, peer coaching, journaling, and other methods of prompting that reflect on professional practice have been shown to be effective in teacher training studies on scaffolding children's play (Kohler et al., 2001; Kok et al., 2002; Skellenger & Hill, 1994; Wolfberg & Schuler, 1993; Young, 1997).

In summary, there is growing evidence that what is needed for effective teacher–child play interactions is what is needed for so many aspects of good teaching: observing, interpreting, and responding to what children need at a particular moment.

References

Alliance for Childhood. (2009). *The loss of children's play: A public health issue.* College Park, MD: Author.

Axline, V. (1947). *Play therapy.* New York: Ballantine.

Barnett, W. S., Jung, K., Yarosz, D. J., Thomas, J., Hornbeck, A., Stechuk, R., et al. (2008). Educational effects of the Tools of the Mind curriculum: A randomized trial. *Early Childhood Research Quarterly, 23,* 299–313.

Baron-Cohen, S., Leslie, A. M., & Frith, U. (2007). Does the autistic child have a theory of mind? In B. Gertler & L. Shapiro (Eds.), *Arguing about the mind* (pp. 310–318). New York: Routledge.

Bateson, G. (1972). *A theory of play and fantasy: Steps to an ecology of mind.* New York: Ballantine Books.

Bennet, N., Wood, L., & Rogers, S. (1997). *Teaching through play: Teacher's thinking in classroom practice.* Buckingham, UK: Open University Press.

Bergen, D. (2002). The role of pretend play in children's cognitive development. *Early Childhood Research and Practice, 4,* 1–12.

Berk, L., & Winsler, A. (1995). *Scaffolding children's learning: Vygotsky and early childhood education.* Washington, DC: National Association for the Education of Young Children.

Bodrova, E., & Leong, D. (2001). *Tools of the mind: A case study of implementing the Vygotskian approach in American early childhood and primary education.* Geneva: Geneva International Bureau of Education.

Bodrova, E., & Leong, D. (2006). *Tools of the mind: The Vygotskian approach to early childhood education* (2nd ed.). Columbus, OH: Merrill/Prentice-Hall.

Brown, M., & Freeman, N. (2001). "We don't play that way in school": The moral and ethical dimensions of controlling children's play. In S. Reifel & M. Brown (Eds.), *Advances in early education and day care: Vol. 11. Early education and care, and reconceptualizing play* (pp. 257–275). New York: JAI Press.

Brown, M., Rickards, F. W., & Bortoli, A. (2001). Structures underpinning pretend play and word production in young hearing children and children with hearing loss. *Journal of Deaf Studies and Deaf Education, 6,* 15–31.

Cohen, L., & Uhry, J. (2007). Young children's discourse strategies during block play: A Bakhtinian approach. *Journal of Research in Childhood Education, 21,* 302–316.

Comfort, R. L. (2005). Learning to play: Play deprivation among young children in foster care. *Zero to Three, 25,* 50–53.

Connolly, A., & Doyle, A. (1984). Relation of social fantasy play to social competence in preschoolers. *Developmental Psychology, 20,* 797–806.

Copple, C., & Bredekamp, S. (2006). *Basics of developmentally appropriate practice.* Washington, DC: National Association for the Education of Young Children.

Craig-Unkefer, L. A., & Kaiser, A. P. (2002). Increasing peer-directed social-communication skills of children enrolled in Head Start. *Journal of Early Intervention, 25,* 229–247.

Damast, A., Tamis-LeMonda, C., & Bornstein, M. (1996). Mother–child play: Sequential interactions and the relations between maternal beliefs and behaviors. *Child Development, 67,* 1752–1766.

DeKroon, D., Kyte, C., & Johnson, C. (2002). Partner influences on the social pretend play of children with language impairments. *Language, Speech, and Hearing Services in Schools, 33,* 253–267.

Diamond, A., Barnett, W. S., Thomas, J., & Munro, S. (2007). Preschool program improves cognitive control. *Science, 318,* 1387–1389.

Dickinson, D. K., & Smith, M. W. (1991). Preschool talk: Patterns of teacher–child interaction in early childhood classrooms. *Journal of Research in Childhood Education, 6,* 20–29.

Edo, M., Planas, N., & Badillo, E. (2009). Mathematics learning in a context of play. *European Early Childhood Education Journal, 17,* 325–341.

Elias, C. L., & Berk, L. E. (2002). Self-regulation in young children: Is there a role for sociodramatic play? *Early Childhood Research Quarterly, 17,* 216–238.

Fantuzzo, J., & McWayne, C. (2002). The relationship between peer-play interactions in the family context and dimensions of school readiness for low-income preschool children. *Journal of Educational Psychology, 94,* 79–87.

Feitelson, D., & Ross, G. S. (1974). The neglected factor—play. *Human Development, 16,* 202–223.

Fekonja, U., Marjanovic-Umek, L., & Kranjc, S. (2005). Free play and other daily preschool activities as a context for child's language development. *Studia Psychologica, 47,* 103–118.

Fey, M. E., & Proctor-Williams, K. (2000). Recasting, elicited imitation and modelling in grammar intervention for children with specific language impairments. In D. Bishop & L. B. Leonard (Eds.), *Speech and language impairments in children: Causes, characteristics, intervention and outcome* (pp. 177–194) New York: Psychology Press.

File, N. (1994). Children's play, teacher–child interactions, and teacher beliefs in integrated early childhood programs. *Early Childhood Research Quarterly, 9,* 223–240.

File, N., & Kontos, S. (1993). The relationship of program quality to children's play in integrated early intervention settings. *Topics in Early Childhood Special Education, 13,* 84–109.

Fleer, M. (2009a). Supporting scientific conceptual consciousness or learning in "a roundabout way" in play-based contexts. *International Journal of Science Education, 31,* 1069–1089.

Fleer, M. (2009b). Understanding the dialectical relations between everyday concepts and scientific concepts within play-based programs. *Research in Science Education, 39,* 281–306.

Freud, S. (1961). *Beyond the pleasure principle.* New York: Norton.

Freund, L. S. (1989). Maternal regulation of children's problem solving behavior and its impact on children's performance. *Child Development, 61,* 113–126.

Garvey, C. (1993). *Play.* Cambridge, MA: Harvard University Press.

Ginsberg, H. (2006). Mathematical play and playful mathematics: A guide for early education. In D. Singer, R. M. Golinkoff, & K. Hirsh-Pasek (Eds.), *Play = learning: How play motivates and enhances children's cognitive and social–emotional growth* (pp. 145–165). New York: Oxford University Press.

Girolametto, L., Hoaken, L., & Weitzman, E. (2000). Patterns of adult–child linguistic interactions in integrated day care groups. *Language, Speech, and Hearing Services in the Schools, 31,* 155–168.

Gmitrova, V., & Gmitrov, J. (2003). The impact of teacher-directed and child-directed pretend play on cognitive competence in kindergarten children. *Early Childhood Education Journal, 30,* 241–246.

Golinkoff, R., Hirsh-Pasek, K., & Eyer, D. (2004). *Einstein never used flashcards: How our children really learn—and why they need to play more and memorize less.* New York: Rodale Books.

Göncü, A., & Klein, E. L. (2001). *Children in play, story, and school.* New York: Guilford Press.

Göncü, A., Mistry, J., & Mosier, C. (2000). Cultural variations in the play of toddlers. *International Journal of Behavioral Development, 24,* 321–329.

Gupta, A. (2009). Vygotskian perspectives on using dramatic play to enhance children's development and balance creativity with structure in the early childhood classroom. *Early Child Development and Care, 179*, 1041–1054.

Hanline, M. F., Milton, S., & Phelps, P. (2009a). A longitudinal study exploring the relationship of representational levels of three aspects of preschool sociodramatic play and early academic skills. *International Journal of Early Childhood Education, 2*, 55–75.

Hanline, M. F., Milton, S., & Phelps, P. (2009b). The relationship between preschool block play and reading and maths abilities in early elementary school: A longitudinal study of children with and without disabilities. *Early Child Development and Care, 14*, 76–82.

Harper, L. V., & McCluskey, K. S. (2003). Teacher–child and child–child interactions in inclusive preschool settings: Do adults inhibit peer interactions? *Early Childhood Research Quarterly, 18*, 163–184.

Howes, C., & Matheson, C. (1992). Sequences in the development of competent play with peers: Social pretend play. *Developmental Psychology, 28*, 961–974.

Howes, C., Phillips, D., & Whitebrook, M. (1992). Thresholds of quality in child care centers and children's social and emotional development. *Child Development, 63*, 449–460.

Howes, C., Ritchie, S., & Bowman, B. (2002). *A matter of trust: Connecting teachers and learners in the early childhood classroom.* New York: Teachers College Press.

Howes, C., & Smith, E. (1995). Relations among child care quality, teacher behavior, children's play activities, emotional security, and cognitive activity in child care. *Early Childhood Research Quarterly, 10*, 381–404.

Ingersoll, B., & Schreibman, L. (2006). Teaching reciprocal imitation skills to young children with autism using a naturalistic behavioral approach: Effects on language, pretend play, and joint attention. *Journal of Autism and Developmental Disorders, 36*, 487–505.

Justice, L. M., & Kaderavek, J. N. (2004). Embedded–explicit emergent literacy intervention I: Background and description of approach. *Language, Speech, and Hearing Services in Schools, 35*, 201–211.

Klibanoff, R. S., Levine, S. C., Huttenlocher, J., Vasilyeva, M., & Hedges, L. V. (2006). Preschool children's mathematical knowledge: The effect of teacher "Math Talk." *Developmental Psychology, 42*(1), 59–69.

Kohler, F. W., Anthony, L. J., Steighner, S., & Hoyson, M. (2001). Teaching social interaction skills in the integrated preschool: An examination of naturalistic tactics. *Topics in Early Childhood Special Education, 21*, 93–103.

Kok, A., Kong, T., & Bernard-Opitz, V. (2002). A comparison of the effects of structured play and facilitated play approaches on preschoolers with autism: A case study. *Autism, 6*, 181–196.

Kuschner, D. (2010, March). *Play, the urban child, and the new developmentally appropriate practice.* Paper presented at the annual meeting of the Association for the Study of Play, Atlanta, GA.

Landreth, G. (2002). Therapeutic limit setting in the play therapy relationship. *Professional Psychology: Research and Practice, 33*, 529–535.

Lantz, J. E., Nelson, J. M., & Loftin, R. L. (2004). Guiding children with autism in play applying the integrated play group model in school settings. *Teaching Exceptional Children, 37*, 8–14.

Lewis, V., Boucher, J., Lupton, L., & Watson, S. (2000). Relationships between symbolic play, functional play, verbal and non-verbal ability in young children. *International Journal of Language and Communication Disorders, 35*, 117–127.

McLoyd, V. C. (1986). Social class and pretend play. In A. W. Gottfried & C. C. Brown (Eds.), *Play interactions: The contribution of play materials and parental involvement to children's development* (pp. 175–196). Lexington, MA: Heath.

Mendez, J. L., & Fogle, L. M. (2002). Parental reports of preschool children's social behavior: Relations among peer play, language competence, and problem behavior. *Journal of Psychoeducational Assessment, 20*, 370–385.

Miller, E., & Almon, J. (2009). *Crisis in the kindergarten: Why children need to play in school.* College Park, MD: Alliance for Childhood.

Modica, A. N. (2010). Using a play intervention to improve the skills of children with a language delay. *Dissertation Abstracts International. B: The Sciences and Engineering, 70*, 5208.

Neeley, P. M., Neeley, R. A., Justen, J. E., & Tipton-Sumner, C. (2001). Scripted play as a language intervention strategy for preschoolers with developmental disabilities. *Early Childhood Education Journal, 28,* 243–246.

Neuman, S., & Roskos, K. (1991). Peers as literacy informants: A description of young children's literacy conversations in play. *Early Childhood Research Quarterly, 6,* 233–248.

Neuman, S. B., & Roskos, K. (1993). Access to print for children of poverty: Differential effects of adult mediation and literacy-enhanced play settings on environmental and functional print tasks. *American Educational Research Journal, 30,* 95–122.

Nichols, S., & Stich, S. (2000). A cognitive theory of pretense. *Cognition, 74,* 115–147.

Odom, S. L., Zercher, C., Li, S., Marquart, J., Sandall, S., & Brown, W. H. (2006). Social acceptance and rejection of preschool children with disabilities: A mixed-method analysis. *Journal of Educational Psychology, 98,* 807–823.

Pellegrini, A. D., & Galda, L. (1990). Children's play, language, and early literacy. *Topics in Language Disorders, 10,* 76–88.

Piaget, J. (1962). *Play, dreams, and imitation in childhood.* New York: Norton.

Piek, J., Dawson, L., Smith, L., & Gasson, N. (2008). The role of early fine and gross motor development on later motor and cognitive ability. *Human Movement Science, 2,* 668–684.

Reifel, S., & Yeatman, J. (1993). From category to context: Considering classroom play. *Early Childhood Research Quarterly, 8,* 347–367.

Riojas-Cortez, M. (2001). Preschoolers' funds of knowledge displayed through sociodramatic play episodes in a bilingual classroom. *Early Childhood Education Journal, 29,* 35–40.

Roach, M., Barrat, M., Miller, J., & Leavitt, L. (1998). The structure of mother–child play: Young children with Down syndrome and typically developing children. *Developmental Psychology, 34,* 77–87.

Roskos, K., & Neuman, S. B. (2003). Environment and its influences for early literacy teaching and learning. In S. B. Neuman & D. K. Dickinson (Eds.), *Handbook of early literacy* (Vol. 1, pp. 281–294). New York: Guilford Press.

Roskos, K. A., Christie, J. F., Widman, S., & Holding, A. (2010). Three decades in: Priming for meta-analysis in play-literacy research. *Journal of Early Childhood Literacy, 10,* 55–96.

Rubin, K. H., Fein, G. G., & Vandenberg, B. (1983). Play. In E. M. Hetherington (Ed.) & P. H. Mussen (Series Ed.), *Handbook of child psychology: Vol. 4. Socialization, personality, and social development* (pp. 693–774). New York: Wiley.

Rutherford, M. D., & Rogers, S. J. (2003). Cognitive underpinnings of pretend play in austism. *Journal of Autism and Developmental Disorders, 33,* 289–302.

Saltz, E., Dixon, D., & Johnson, J. (1977). Training disadvantaged preschoolers on various fantasy activities: Effects on cognitive functioning and impulse control. *Child Development, 48,* 367–380.

Schepis, M. M., Reid, D. H., Ownbey, J., & Clary, J. (2003). Training preschool staff to promote cooperative participation among young children with severe disabilities and their classmates. *Research and Practice for Persons with Severe Disabilities, 28,* 37–42.

Schuler, A., & Wolfberg, P. (2000). Promoting peer play and socialization: The art of scaffolding. *Journal of Autism and Developmental Disorders, 23,* 467–489.

Singer, D., Golinkoff, R. M., & Hirsh-Pasek, K. (2006). *Play = learning: How play motivates and enhances children's cognitive and social–emotional growth.* New York: Oxford University Press.

Skellenger, A., & Hill, E. (1994). Effects of a shared teacher–child play intervention on the play skills of three young children who are blind. *Journal of Visual Impairment and Blindness, 88,* 33–45.

Smilansky, S. (1968). *The effects of sociodramatic play on disadvantaged preschool children.* New York: Wiley.

Smilansky, S., & Shefatya, L. (1990). *Facilitating play: A medium for promoting cognitive, socio-emotional, and academic development in young children.* Gaithersburg, MD: Psychosocial and Educational Publications.

Stipek, D. (2006). No Child Left Behind comes to preschool. *Elementary School Journal, 106,* 455–467.

Sutton-Smith, B. (1990). Dilemmas in adult play with children. In K. McDonald (Ed.), *Parent–child play* (pp. 15–42). Albany: State University of New York Press.

Thorp, D., Stahmer, A., & Schreibman, L. (1995). Effects of sociodramatic play training on children with autism. *Journal of Autism and Developmental Disorders, 25,* 265–282.

Trawick-Smith, J. (1994). *Interactions in the classroom: Facilitating play in the early years.* Upper Saddle River, NJ: Prentice-Hall.

Trawick-Smith, J. (1998). Why play training works: An integrated model for play intervention. *Journal of Research in Childhood Education, 12,* 117–129.

Trawick-Smith, J. (2010a). Drawing back the lens on play: A frame analysis of young children's play in Puerto Rico. *Early Education and Development, 21,* 1–32.

Trawick-Smith, J. (2010b). *Early childhood development: A multicultural perspective* (5th ed.). Columbus, OH: Merrill/Prentice-Hall.

Trawick-Smith, J., & Breen, M. (2010). [Teacher–child play interactions and oral language growth in preschool children]. Unpublished raw data.

Trawick-Smith, J., & Dziurgot, T. (2010). "Good-fit" teacher–child play interactions and subsequent autonomous play in preschool. *Early Childhood Research Quarterly, 26,* 110–123.

Trawick-Smith, J., & Picard, T. (2003). Literacy play: Is it really play anymore? *Childhood Education, 79*(4), 229–231.

Trawick-Smith, J., Swaminathan, S., Lui, X., & Yu, H. (2011, April). *How teacher–child play interactions promote intellectual development: An analysis and empirical test of three conceptual models.* Paper presented at the annual meeting of the American Educational Association, New Orleans, LA.

Van Berckelaer-Onnes, I. (2003). Promoting early play. *Autism, 7,* 415–423.

Vukelich, C. (1994). Effects of play interventions on young children's reading of environmental print. *Early Childhood Research Quarterly, 9,* 153–170.

Vygotsky, L. S. (1976). Play and its role in the mental development of the child. In J. Bruner, A. Jolly, & K. Sylva (Eds.), *Play: Its role in development and evolution* (pp. 536–552). New York: Basic Books.

Vygotsky, L. S. (1978). *Mind in society: Development of higher psychological processes.* Cambridge, MA: Harvard University Press.

Wasik, B. A., Bond, M. A., & Hindman, A. (2006). The effects of a language and literacy intervention on Head Start children and teachers. *Journal of Educational Psychology, 98,* 63–74.

Wilcox-Herzog, A., & Kontos, S. (1998). The nature of teacher talk in early childhood classrooms and its relationship to children's play with objects and peers. *Journal of Genetic Psychology, 159,* 65–109.

Winsler, A. (2003). Introduction to special issue: Vygotskian perspectives in early childhood education: Translating ideas into classroom practice. *Early Education and Development, 14,* 253–270.

Wolfberg, P. J. (2003). *Peer play and the autism spectrum: The art of guiding children's socialization and imagination.* Shawnee Mission, KS: Autism Asperger Publishing.

Wolfberg, P. J., & Schuler, A. L. (1993). Integrated play groups: A model for promoting the social and cognitive dimensions of play in children with autism. *Journal of Autism and Developmental Disorders, 23,* 467–489.

Wolfgang, C. H., Standard, L., & Jones, I. (2001). Block party performance among preschoolers as a predictor of later school achievement in mathematics. *Journal of Research in Childhood Education, 15,* 173–180.

Yifat, R., & Zadunaisky-Ehrlich, S. (2008). Teachers' talk in preschools during *circle time*: The case of revoicing. *Journal of Research in Childhood Education, 23* 211–227.

Young, K. S. (1997). Effects of teacher scaffolding on verbal communication in young children's dramatic play. *Korean Journal of Childhood Studies, 18,* 229–240.

CHAPTER 14

A Transactional Model
of Effective Teaching and Learning
in the Early Childhood Classroom

Claire E. Cameron

What are the precise mechanisms through which participation in formal schooling makes a meaningful difference in young children's learning and development? Successfully addressing this familiar question requires sustained and systematic inquiry, which has a new face with current emphases on randomized controlled trial (RCT) designs (McDonald, Keesler, Kauffman, & Schneider, 2006; Raudenbush, 2005). Experimental trials of the impacts of specific practices and programs on children's development have steadily contributed to the knowledge base about effective teaching in diverse skills domains (Barnett et al., 2008; Bierman, Nix, Greenberg, Blair, & Domitrovich, 2008; Jackson et al., 2006). As one example, a recent federally funded report described the unique effects of several specific curricula, tested in a collaborative multisite national evaluation, on preschoolers' progress in such skills domains as literacy, language, mathematics, and socioemotional competence (Preschool Curriculum Evaluation Research Consortium [PCER], 2008).

The PCER report and similarly focused, federally supported efforts (e.g., What Works Clearinghouse at *ies.ed.gov/ncee/wwc*) are designed to increase practitioner access to techniques with causally interpretable effects on specific child outcomes. As such, they are a potentially useful resource for improving the effectiveness of early childhood education. However, a consequent challenge concerns how a single teacher might feasibly incorporate a variety of disparate practices and programs into her everyday practice. To help synthesize and translate intervention results into *plausible* evidence-based recommendations, this chapter presents a model that serves as a lens through which to view key practices from effective interventions. The target audience is researchers, who are most proximal to interventions, and who also assist in training teachers to use practices in alignment with intervention findings. I take a bird's-eye view of the landscape of research and practice related to early childhood education, incorporating information on current funding trends (i.e., RCTs), research on typical classrooms in both early elementary and preschool settings, and theories from human development. This multidisciplinary, complex perspective approach is necessary for understanding the current state of instructional efforts in early childhood, in an attempt to illuminate the most important future directions.

I first describe the scope of the problem. Multiple RCTs—which are not featured here—show that teachers' fidelity of implementing the key ingredients of empirically validated programs and practices is an important and significant moderator of child outcomes (Davidson, Fields, & Yang, 2009; Hulleman & Cordray, 2009; Justice, Mashburn, Pence, & Wiggins, 2008). Yet teachers often find it challenging to integrate effectively then fully implement a set of practices, which can result in an attenuation of program effects on targeted child outcomes (Hulleman & Cordray, 2009). Given the growing number of empirically successful interventions, attempting to implement the host of specific recommendations from each one could quickly overwhelm even the most ambitious and accomplished of teachers.

This problem may be most acute in early childhood settings, where the school day is abbreviated, teachers often receive minimal professional training, and programs are expected to target a broad range of areas. Preschool teachers are charged with preparing children in many competencies (Administration on Children, Youth, and Families/Head Start Bureau, 2003, 2010), which are organized into five target skills domains in this chapter: (1) language and literacy; (2) social and emotional development, including children's approaches to learning; (3) content areas (mathematics, science, and social studies); (4) motor development including creative arts; and (5) physical health. Many of the programs and practices assessed within early childhood RCTs focus narrowly on only one or two of these domains, to adhere to robust scientific standards (Bierman, Domitrovich et al., 2008; Davidson et al., 2009; Farver, Lonigan, & Eppe, 2009; Justice, Mashburn, Pence, et al., 2008; PCER, 2008). Nonetheless, a myopic approach to intervention raises questions about how the early childhood field might best translate RCT results into effective and *integrated* teaching practices that can be adopted readily by practitioners.

At present, the bulk of scientific attention and funding is paid to two tasks in relation to this question: first, education scientists *create* theoretically derived practices and programs; second, research teams *assess* their efficacy and effectiveness. This chapter argues for attention to a third task. Researchers need to assist early childhood professionals better to *synthesize* research findings into a single set of recommendations for effective classroom practice. Without synthesis, many early childhood educators will be poorly equipped to manage the avalanche of emerging information about "what works" in classrooms. Furthermore, the field of early childhood education can make best use of emergent study findings by thoughtfully and theoretically integrating research results that are available now. Toward this end, this chapter introduces a conceptual model with synthesis as a goal. The model exemplifies two lessons from research: First, learning proceeds through transactions. Transactions include the frequency (how often), duration (for how long), and quality (what exactly happens) of the exchanges between teachers and children in a given skill domain. Second, learning is domain-specific, and the effects of certain experiences often depend on an individual child's current skills level within a given domain.

Transactional Model of Effective Teaching and Learning

The model posits that results from successful experimental trials may have a single pair of underlying explanations: First, enough transactions occur between teacher and child for learning to have the potential to occur; second, transactions are targeted to the child's current skill(s) level. Therefore, the central part of the model—both pictorially and conceptually—is the transactions that occur between teacher and child. The transactional model of effective teaching and learning, which represents interactions between a teacher and an individual child, is shown in Figure 14.1. Four primary components, which are briefly summarized here, comprise the model: (A) child attributes, (B) teacher attributes, (C) developmental domains, and (D) transactions between teacher and child (space of interactions).

At the foundation of the model is (A) child attributes, with which the child enters the classroom and which contribute to his or her functioning in that setting. Similarly, (B) teacher attributes comprise the top portion of the model to indicate teacher factors that contribute to his or her functioning in the classroom setting. Depending on one's view, the list of attributes could be endless; in the interest of space, a few examples are highlighted for both teacher and child.

In (C), developmental skills domains are represented with five boxes each for child and teacher. The height of each child box varies to represent symbolically that individual children enter school with both strengths (tall boxes) and weaknesses (short boxes). The height of each teacher box indicates that teachers also vary in their knowledge of these domains and of children's development in each domain.

Finally, in (D) space of interactions, the arrows represent teacher–child interactions within each domain. More arrows from teacher to child in one domain than another indicate more teacher efforts to teach (as in literacy compared to content areas); more arrows from child to teacher indicate more signals of child learning in that domain. Arrows that meet in the middle indicate effective transactions that result in learning; arrows that do not meet indicate ineffective transactions, where the teacher or child makes an attempt to interact, but this does not result in learning. Later in the chapter, I explore potential reasons for ineffective transactions and showcase an intervention that maximizes the number of effective and individualized teacher–child transactions.

(A) Child Attributes

Children in the United States enter the classroom exhibiting significant individual differences in how they process and act upon information, which is heavily influenced by variation in their prior experiences (Curby, Rimm-Kaufman, & Cameron Ponitz, 2009; Morrison,

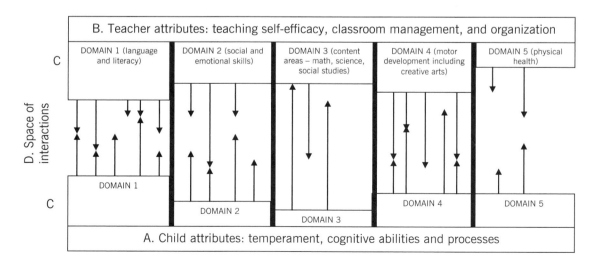

FIGURE 14.1. The transactional model of teaching and learning.

Bachman, & Connor, 2005). These individual differences shape the quality and quantity of the transactions that occur between teacher and child, and also affect the nature and degree of growth that children may derive from certain transactions. Thus, it is the entire child, with this host of unique attributes, to which teachers must accommodate their responses and instructional approaches. Two examples, temperament and cognitive abilities/processes, are described here. These examples are selected because they represent the strategies, resources, and capacities with which children approach the early childhood setting, in terms of external behavior and internal cognition.

Temperament

Children's temperament can be characterized as their baseline levels of tolerance for new situations, and their ability to control and redirect their impulses. These biologically based reactivity and regulatory aspects of behavior represent a well-researched developmental construct (Kagan, 1989; Rothbart & Jones, 1998). Temperament has significant implications in the classroom context; research indicates that children contribute to their own learning inasmuch as they are able to control their emotions and impulses, and effectively participate in classroom activity (Eisenberg et al., 2000; Ladd, Birch, & Buhs, 1999; Rimm-Kaufman et al., 2002). Children prone to intense negative reactions tend to have more school adjustment problems than those with lower negative emotionality (Lengua, 2002); however, even highly labile children who are able to focus their attention realize positive school-related outcomes (Belsky, Friedman, & Hsieh, 2001; National Institute for Child Health and Human Development Early Child Care Research Network, 2003). This suggests that children challenged by high temperamental reactivity can thrive if they are able to redirect their attention to positive or neutral aspects of a situation.

Cognitive Abilities and Processes

The cognitive abilities and processes with which children enter the classroom are considered indicators of their starting point and potential for learning, as well as another relevant child factor to which teachers must adapt. Children in the early childhood classroom vary considerably in the efficiency with which they perceive, accommodate, and manipulate new information. Many cognitive abilities and processes operate in early childhood; for purposes of brevity, two underlying constructs of recent interest to researchers are described, namely, executive function and motor development. *Executive function* refers to a complex of cognitively and affectively mediated processes that include focusing and shifting attention, inhibiting automatic responses, and keeping track of information in working memory (Blair & Diamond, 2008; Demetriou, Christou, Spanoudis, & Platsidou, 2002; McClelland, Cameron, Wanless, & Murray, 2007). *Motor development* refers to the physical actions that children exert in relation to the perceptual input that enters their awareness from the environment (Adolph & Berger, 2006). Both executive function and motor development have been linked to early achievement and are implicated in learning (Blair, 2002; Cameron et al., in press; Marr, Cermak, Cohn, & Henderson, 2003; Son & Meisels, 2006).

Some scholars consider executive function an indicator of children's ability to learn and to problem-solve (Zelazo, Carter, Reznick, & Frye, 1997). In addition, motor actions are beginning to be recognized as the interface through which learning proceeds (Willingham, 1998). In others words, children's ability to control and direct their motor actions; including moving their bodies in the classroom space, articulating new words, and learning to write; provide a foundation for learning other, increasingly sophisticated skills. As such, motor skill is a strong predictor of later learning and may be an underappreciated indicator of children's early learning potential (Grissmer, Grimm, Aiyer, Murrah, & Steele, 2010).

(B) Teacher Attributes

Early childhood teachers enter the classroom with their own set of psychological and behavioral resources that affect their actions in that context. I highlight two attributes while acknowledging that there are likely many more, that research has shown to be central to understanding the transactions between teachers and children: teaching self-efficacy or what teachers think they can do and teachers' ability to manage and organize a group of children or the behaviors that create a foundation for the instruction that teachers deliver.

Teacher Self-Efficacy

Self-efficacy generally refers to the belief in one's ability to attain a given outcome, which includes being able to plan and execute the discrete behaviors that will relate to that outcome (Bandura, 1977). Work related to children with learning difficulties in elementary school classrooms suggests that teachers with higher teaching self-efficacy are more likely to attribute children's learning difficulties to events and experiences external to the child, and thus realize the potential for good teaching to produce change (Brady & Woolfson, 2008). Though not explored here, self-efficacy tends to be domain-specific. For example, teachers may feel comfortable with early literacy instruction, but not mathematics (Brown, 2005). The important point to remember is that teacher perceptions of their own ability undergird their exchanges with children in the classroom.

Teacher Classroom Management and Organization

A large body of research indicates the importance of effective organization and classroom management strategies for both behavioral and academic outcomes. Instead of simple disciplinary strategies, the contemporary view of effective management is explicit, preventive, and proactive (Brophy, 1979, 1983, 1986). Empirical work indicates that strong classroom organization tends to minimize wasted time (Bohn, Roehrig, & Pressley, 2004; Cameron, Connor, & Morrison, 2005) and to predict learning and engagement in elementary school (Cameron et al., 2005; Cameron, Connor, Morrison, & Jewkes, 2008; Cameron Ponitz, Rimm-Kaufman, Brock, & Nathanson, 2009; Rimm-Kaufman, Curby, Grimm, Nathanson, & Brock, 2009). Relatively little attention has been paid to organizing at the preschool level, though preliminary findings indicate that spending more time organizing and orienting children to upcoming activities is associated with learning gains in multiple academic, as well as behavioral, domains (Cameron Ponitz & Morrison, 2011).

(C) Developmental Domains

The model's third element follows from the assumption that contemporary curricula and teachers' actual practices are organized around a discrete set of developmental skills domains, including the content or explicit focus of selected activities and instruction (Graue, 2003). *Content* refers to the subject of teacher–child learning interactions; *skills* refer to the type of competencies, including motor behaviors, language, and thought processes, that children exercise and develop through interactions with their teachers, peers, objects, and ideas in school.

Five Skills Domains

Five general developmental skills domains are proposed; this selection was informed by information from the leading organizations focused on young children's learning and development, including the Administration on Children, Youth, and Families/Head Start Bureau (2003), the National Association for the Education of Young Children (NAEYC), and Council for Exceptional Children—Early Childhood: language and literacy; social–emotional learning (SEL); content areas; motor development, including creative arts; and physical health. Due to space limitations, each area is briefly described.

LANGUAGE AND LITERACY

Of all the developmental domains, perhaps language and literacy have received the most attention in the last decade with respect to areas of instruction within the early childhood classroom (Dickinson, 2006; Justice, Mashburn, Hamre, & Pianta, 2008). Language and literacy, while often used interchangeably, are not synonyms. *Language* refers to a symbol-based, rule-governed, multidimensional system that is used to represent the world internally and to others through the process of communication (Pence, Justice, & Wiggins, 2008). Within the early childhood classroom, children's demonstration of skill competence refers to specific behaviors in the areas of morphology (e.g., to use plural and tense markings), syntax (e.g., to use compound sentences), phonology (e.g., to articulate words clearly), semantics (e.g., to use a precise vocabulary), and pragmatics (e.g., to use questions to seek more information).

Literacy, a domain distinct from but related to that of language, refers to the ability to produce and comprehend written language. Within the preschool classroom, because few children read and write in a conventional sense, teachers help children develop precursors to reading and writing, referred to as *emergent literacy* (Whitehurst & Lonigan, 2001). Emergent literacy skills typically targeted within the early childhood classroom include phonological awareness, alphabet knowledge, the concept of words in print, invented spelling, environment print recognition, and print awareness (Snow, Burns, & Griffin, 1999). Children's attainment of emergent literacy skills across these areas is seen as critical because of their well-established predictive relations with long-term outcomes in word recognition, spelling, and reading comprehension (National Early Literacy Panel, 2008).

SEL AND APPROACHES TO LEARNING

SEL represents a broad domain long emphasized in preschool settings. SEL can be articulated as five skills objectives (Bear & Minke, 2006). Two focus on children's relationship skills with others: social competence, or effective social exchanges with others, and social awareness, or knowledge of others as socioemotional beings with needs distinct from oneself. Two reflect children's skills in relation to themselves: self-concept, or ideas and feelings about oneself; and self-control, or the ability to control impulses. The fifth skill objective can be described as decision making, which refers to children's abilities to make constructive and ethical choices about both social and personal behavior. SEL helps children navigate social relationships and also manage and deploy their emotions, attention, and behavior toward the educational tasks afforded in the classroom (Blair, 2002; Bronson, 2001). Preschoolers who demonstrate concrete skills (i.e., approaches to learning) such as curiosity, persistence, focused attention, problem solving, impulse control, independence, and initiative, do better in the classroom, on learning assessments, and with peers (Fantuzzo, Bulotsky-Sheare, Fusco, & McWayne, 2005; Fantuzzo, Perry, & McDermott, 2004).

Some work points to the longitudinal relevance of this domain; for example, Duncan and colleagues (2007) found that attention consistently predicts achievement throughout elementary and middle school. Other research, including meta-analytic summaries, also shows that early childhood offers the period of the greatest plasticity in the development of SEL, especially for those children at risk for school failure (La Paro & Pianta, 2000; Zhou et al., 2007), suggesting the important role teachers and classrooms may play in shifting growth trajectories. Along these lines, intervention studies show the efficacy of explicit efforts to improve SEL. Children who participated in the Promoting Alternative Thinking Strategies (PATHS) intervention improved in their social competence, social skills, social interaction, and independence (Domitrovich, Cortes, & Greenberg, 2007). Other SEL-based interventions have shown similar results (Izard et al., 2008). Findings from an emotion-based prevention program showed improvement in children's social competencies and emotion regulation, as well as decreases in aggressive behavior as reported by their teachers. These findings were particularly evident in classrooms that achieved high levels of fidelity of implementation, suggesting the key role that teachers play in helping children adopt effective SEL strategies (Izard et al., 2008).

CONTENT AREAS (MATHEMATICS, SCIENCE, SOCIAL STUDIES)

Preschool teachers are charged with introducing children to the content areas that become prominent in elementary and secondary curricula: mathematics, science, and social studies. Literatures devoted to learning in each area (mathematics and science, especially) exist and are another example where research attempts to inform, yet has the potential to overwhelm, practitioner capacity (Newcombe et al., 2009). Children's acquisition of proficiency within these domains is increasingly recognized as a function of their prior experiences, developmental status, and instruction (National Research Council, 2007). No longer must American children simply recite memorized facts in school; they must be able to use these facts to solve problems. For children to attain proficiency in mathematics and science, experts emphasize the need for activities that require children to *integrate* new information with prior knowledge (sometimes requiring them to discard or modify their old knowledge) and *apply* this knowledge to real-world situations.

Specific concepts and overarching skills are necessary to excel in each of these domains; these overlap in ways that justify grouping them together in this model. Skills include being able to notice and describe; compare and contrast; and predict, explain, or manipulate objects or events. For example, in social studies, the elements that children are observing, describing, comparing, predicting, and manipulating are the people, systems, events, and relationships in the social world. In mathematics, the concepts of cardinality, ordinality, and the abilities to manipulate number quantities, including "subitizing" (breaking numbers into multiple subsets, such as noticing that 5 comprises 2 and 3) and estimating, are strong predictors of later mathematics achievement and are amenable to intervention (Clements & Sarama, 2007). Sarama, Clements, Starkey, Klein, and Wakeley (2008) found that children showed improvements over controls in a range of mathematics competencies when their teachers were trained in the Technology-enhanced, Research-based, Instruction, Assessment, and professional Development (TRIAD) mathematics curriculum. Children improved the most in the skills emphasized in the curriculum, indicating that instruction within a given area relates to skill development in that specific area. In other words, children tend to learn what they are taught.

In preschool science, most children enter school with a knowledge of cause and effect and the abilities to observe, describe, compare, predict, and experiment with objects in the natural world (Greenfield et al., 2009). Preschoolers are naive biologists, chemists, physicists, and psychologists in exploring the causes and motivations for events. Children recognize that animals are different from elements such as air and water, which are different from inanimate objects, which are different from people (Michaels, Shouse, & Schweingruber, 2008). Greenfield and colleagues' (2009) quasi-experimental work found that preschoolers whose teachers participated in focus group sessions on science-related classroom practice had greater competence in a range of outcomes relative to a control group from fall to spring, suggesting that an increase in the number of transactions (see arrows that meet in the middle of Figure 14.1) in one domain can be associated with improvement within and outside of that domain.

MOTOR DEVELOPMENT, INCLUDING CREATIVE ARTS

The creative arts include music, art, dramatic play, and movement. These have in common a focus on the coordination of motor behaviors and sequences embedded within a context, such as a song, artwork, play, or dance. Typically, within the early childhood classroom, children's experiences within these creative arts serve not only creative purposes but also as a vehicle to support more academically oriented domains. For instance, children may participate in singing activities to teach them phonological awareness (e.g., rhymes) or alphabet knowledge (e.g., the alphabet song). Or teachers may use dramatic play as a means to introduce children to new vocabulary words and related linguistic concepts (Justice, Mashburn, Pence, et al., 2008). Indeed, creative activities such as music, art, play, and movement can be used to serve a variety of other goals within the early childhood classroom because creative activities provide children a means to express themselves actively and practice their developing skills (e.g., producing new words within the context of a song). It is also important to point out that children's participation in creative arts need not be a means to another end; developing creative abilities is a worthy goal on its own. How creative activities facilitate motor development is a new area of investigation of potential contributors to academic competence. Recent work has indicated that fine motor skills in early childhood predict learning outcomes much later (e.g., eighth grade), with emerging rationales focusing on the interconnections between motor and cognitive processing (Diamond, 2000; Grissmer et al., 2010).

PHYSICAL HEALTH

Last but not least, early childhood educators are responsible for the health and well-being of preschoolers in their charge. For many children, preschool is the first setting in which they have the chance to label body parts, identify food groups, and engage in formal group exercise. A focus on physical health has heightened in recent years, with the sharp increase in obesity and weight-related health problems in Americans of all ages, including preschool-age children, where the prevalence of obesity exceeds 18% (Anderson & Whitaker, 2009). In response, some Head Start programs have made physical health a priority. One region adopted the "I Am Moving, I Am Learning" (IM/IL) curriculum, integrating movement throughout the day and providing nutritional information within and outside the classroom (Finkelstein et al., 2007).

Variation in Child Skills Domains

Preschoolers enter the classroom possessing unique knowledge and competencies within these five different domains. Regarding *intra*individual differences (within children), because of cultural emphases on literacy education in the United States, language and literacy skills are likely more advanced in the *average* preschooler than are numeracy skills (Miller, Kelly, & Zhou, 2005). Intraindividual variation in the five developmental domains is represented in Figure 14.1 by the varying heights of the domain-labeled boxes (note that the language and literacy box is the highest). Every child's unique profile includes boxes of varying height; one child may be extremely proficient in alphabet knowledge within emergent literacy but initiate awkward or inappropriate social interactions within SEL, whereas another may be skilled at interacting with others (SEL) but not yet understand cause and effect in relation to actions on objects (science within content areas).

Interindividual variation (among children) means that children show considerable individual differences in these skills, especially in the United States, where wide disparities in socioeconomic environments translate into vastly different early home learning environments (Hart & Risley, 1995; Morrison et al., 2005). This type of variation becomes apparent when one compares the box heights of developmental domains for multiple children. For example, children from sociodemographically disadvantaged backgrounds usually arrive at school with lower levels of knowledge in multiple skills areas compared to those from middle-class backgrounds (Fantuzzo, Rouse, et al., 2005; Sameroff, Bartko, Baldwin, Baldwin, & Seifer, 1998).

Similarly, teachers have varying knowledge of these domains. Teacher domain knowledge has emerged as a particularly important construct within the last decade. This emergence has been particularly evident as it relates to the teaching of literacy within preschool and early elementary classrooms (Cunningham, Perry, Stanovich, & Stanovich, 2004; Moats, 1994; Piasta, Connor, Fishman, & Morrison, 2009), with results suggesting that many teachers do not possess the level of disciplinary knowledge deemed important to teach certain skills within the classroom. Variation in knowledge across domains is represented in Figure 14.1 by varying heights of teacher boxes in the five domains, and is meant to reflect this contemporary research.

(D) Transactions

The conceptual model is intended to serve as a navigational tool between theory and practice. Alignment between theory and practice means researchers will be better equipped to understand why a particular education practice or program succeeds or fails. This focus on mechanism is often missing from experimental designs, which are meant to test the straightforward, relatively easy-to-analyze question of whether a curriculum modification works. The final part of the model attempts to describe the mechanisms and processes linking teachers and children.

An Argument for Transactions

The present focus on transactions follows from research that suggests external or structural factors such as materials and teacher credentials relate to child outcomes through what actually happens in the classroom (Bowman, Donovan, & Burns, 2001; Connor, Son, Hindman, & Morrison, 2005; Early et al., 2007; Mashburn et al., 2008; Rimm-Kaufman & Cameron Ponitz, 2009; Tudge, Odero, Hogan, & Etz, 2003). Though, for representational reasons, the conceptual model is based on a single child, readers might use their imagination to envision the myriad iterations of models that would exist for an entire classroom of children.

Transactional developmental models include a few key assumptions; the notion of reciprocal or bidirectional processes is highlighted here. The model prioritizes the exchanges that occur in classrooms, such as between teachers and children (emphasized in the model); or between child peers, and between children and objects/ideas (not emphasized in the model) (Bransford, Brown, & Cocking, 1999; Bronfenbrenner & Morris, 2006; Sameroff, 2000). Bronfenbrenner and Morris (2006) call these exchanges "proximal processes," and they can be thought of as the sustained interactions children have within their environments over time. In practical terms, proximal processes mean that one teacher can be successful in a disadvantaged school if his or her interactions put children at ease and engage them in the activity; another teacher will not succeed in even the wealthiest classroom setting if his or her behaviors alienate, embarrass, or dissuade children from learning. The transactional nature of these exchanges also means that while teachers can influence children, children can also influence teachers. Given space constraints and this chapter's focus on instructional approaches, how teachers respond to children in ways that might extend or limit their learning is highlighted. At the same time, the reader is encouraged to consider how children's responses may also extend or inhibit the teacher's ability to teach and interact effectively.

Representing Transactions

Given the number of possible inputs in a teacher–child interaction, modeling transactions among participants in the learning process is a representational dilemma. The model pictorially represents single interactions among teachers and individual children within different developmental domains of learning; this is shown in (D) Space of interactions. The number and length of the arrows signify teacher and child inputs within the learning system. Teachers' inputs include all actions and behaviors to which children can respond, and are represented with arrows that extend from the teacher's developmental domain downward toward the child. Child inputs, represented by arrows leading from a domain from the child up toward the teacher, signify inputs to the interactional system and represent the child's observable status (including emotional, verbal, or behavioral signals) within a skill domain. As an example, if Lawrence is very demanding and talks a lot to get attention, and elicits more conversation from the teacher than socially reticent Ellie, this would be represented with more arrows from Lawrence toward the teacher than from Ellie toward the teacher. Research has shown that learning happens during extended, rich interchanges whereby the teacher (or peers, or an object such as a book) provides stimulation, the child responds, and the teacher builds on this response (Wasik, Bond, & Hindman, 2006; Wood, Bruner, & Ross, 1976). In this model, such an interchange would be represented by many pairs of arrows between teacher and child that meet in the middle of (D).

EXAMPLES OF INEFFECTIVE TRANSACTIONS

To represent ineffective transactions in Figure 14.1, not all arrows from teacher to child (or from child to teacher) meet an arrow on the opposing side. Essentially, ineffective teaching efforts mean that the teacher's inputs (arrows) are not "taken up" or perceived by the child, and are represented by a short, unmet arrow leading from teacher to child. As one example of ineffective transactions, a teacher may provide an activity that is too difficult or too easy for the child's current level of competence in a given domain. As another example, children's behavior may go unnoticed, ignored, or misunderstood. For example, a child says "Post office" when the teacher asks children to name different types of containers. Instead of saying, "Do you mean a mailbox? A mailbox is a kind of container, and we can find mailboxes at the post office," the teacher says dismissively, "No, the post office is not a container." In this example, the child's question may have made the teacher feel impatient or distracted from the conversation, which may result in a cascade of other ineffective interactions.

Another type of ineffective transaction is where no arrows exist, which means the teacher does not provide any activities in a certain domain. Similarly, an absence of arrows from the child might occur if he or she is given no opportunity to demonstrate his or her competence in a given domain. If a science activity is never provided, children will not have an opportunity to demonstrate their learning in relation to science content (Greenfield et al., 2009). In Figure 14.1, more arrows meet between teacher and child in the area of literacy, reflecting research that indicates teachers in the early years of school tend to be more knowledgeable about literacy than about other content areas and to make more attempts to teach literacy than to teach other content areas (Miller et al., 2005; NICHD Early Child Care Research Network, 2002). In contrast, there are few arrows for mathematics or science in either direction because teachers tend to feel their knowledge of these areas is limited; solicit little child feedback that would tell them what children need to learn in these areas; and provide few opportunities for students to demonstrate their knowledge of numeracy or cause–effect, for example (Greenfield et al., 2009; Newcombe et al., 2009; Starkey, Klein, & Wakeley, 2004).

ENGAGEMENT AS AN INDICATOR OF INEFFECTIVE TRANSACTIONS

Importantly for teachers, ineffective efforts may have a common indicator that emerges over time—children's behavioral engagement. When teachers present an activity that does not match what individuals are interested in or able to learn at that moment, or when they fail to present it in an engaging manner or to respond appropriately to relevant inputs, young children indicate this with misbehavior, boredom, or frustration. The importance of engagement is beginning to be better understood as the mediator between teachers' instructional efforts and children's learning outcomes (Cameron Ponitz, Rimm-Kaufman, Grimm, & Curby, 2009; Greenwood, Horton, & Utley, 2002). Indeed, many of the behavior problems that plague early childhood classrooms may arise because of a mismatch between children's interests and the provided activities. For example, sitting for long periods, listening to a story without talking, or completing a center activity without the requisite peer interaction skills to successfully avoid altercation may reveal ineffective transactions, as evidenced by children's low engagement or off-task behavior. According to this view, a child who is wandering around the classroom may not be acting out intentionally, but instead may need an opportunity or explicit invitation to participate in an engaging activity.

Next Steps: Challenges and Applications of the Model

Successful teacher practices, including classroom-based interventions, are proposed to implicitly or explicitly address the model's four components: child attributes, teacher attributes, developmental domains, and transactions. Even without interventions, undoubtedly these classrooms already exist. They exist wherever teachers provide appropriate and engaging activities, feedback, and instruction in content areas, and wherever children have opportunities throughout the day to show what they know and what they still need to learn. In terms of the model, these classrooms increase the number of arrows (or effective exchanges) connecting teacher to child, and child to teacher, in a given skill area.

In addition to the right setting, creating many connections—or, in model terms, increasing the number of arrows that meet in (D) Space of interactions—requires a heightened level of teacher awareness (e.g., Guo, Piasta, Justice, & Kaderavek, 2009). Teachers who are highly aware of child inputs, who are able to respond to children's overtures, outbursts, and even omissions sensitively and appropriately, develop stronger relationships with students and have stronger self-efficacy (Jennings & Greenberg, 2009; Rimm-Kaufman, Voorhees, Snell, & La Paro, 2003). Furthermore, teaching effectively means being able to direct one's own reactions to create optimal learning conditions for individual children. In turn, this requires an exceptional degree of self-awareness. Teachers who are less aware may accidentally scare children, for example, by yelling not in anger but in excitement about a lesson. According to this model, becoming more aware of preschoolers' individual behavioral patterns, cognitive abilities, and domain-related competencies in each activity setting will in turn help teachers select the most appropriate learning experiences and responses for individual children.

Intervention Activity in Alignment with the Model

A central aim of future interventions might be to help teachers target multiple skills domains of learning in a single activity, rather than one at a time (as reports on domain-specific interventions, and the earlier examples, might have them do). Following is an example of an activity from an intervention that, while not explicitly designed with the five domains in mind, successfully targets multiple aspects of children's learning. Using a 1-week teacher training with weekly follow-up, the Tools of the Mind intervention, heretofore called Tools, targets executive function in the preschool context (Bodrova & Leong, 2007). Children are taught to use strategies and concrete tools that help remind them to take turns, listen patiently, and remember directions. Two separate experiments, with random assignment of classrooms or children to classrooms, indicate that, as intended, Tools participation improves preschoolers' executive function and related classroom skills (Barnett et al., 2008; Diamond, Barnett, Thomas, & Munro, 2007). One of these studies indicated program effects on both classroom processes, including a measure of quality of teacher–child interactions, and children's language and literacy skills and teacher-reported social skills (Barnett et al., 2008).

In Play Planning and Play, teachers help children draw or write a plan for their play, to which they refer throughout the day. In this activity the teacher sits down to converse with the individual child about his or her desired activities, which means the teacher must be in tune with the child's interests and inputs. In turn, children are required to think in advance about what they want to do, and to use language to talk with the teacher and emergent literacy skills to write or draw out the plan. The teacher is available to assist the child in the plan making. Finally, if the child forgets the plan, the teacher reminds him or her to refer to the plan.

It goes without saying that the successful implementation of Play Planning and Play depends on both the teacher and the child. However, this activity, by its definition, requires that teachers interact with children by assessing their interests and level of ability, and more specifically, "scaffolding children's thinking through language interactions and the development of daily play plans" (Barnett et al., 2008, p. 310). In contrast with a whole-group, lecture-style activity or book-reading without interaction, in which every child receives essentially the same dose of teacher input, Play Planning and Play maximizes teacher–child interaction and the incorporation of children's contributions in the activity. Furthermore, multiple domains are addressed, including language and emergent writing, and executive function (e.g., planning and self-control). It is important to note that individual activities have not been tested as the cause of the reported program effects shown for Tools. However, conceptually, interventions such as Tools may succeed because of their adherence to the conceptual model in Figure 14.2, in which effective interactions among teachers and children are maximized. Important to note is this example's emphasis on individual teacher–child

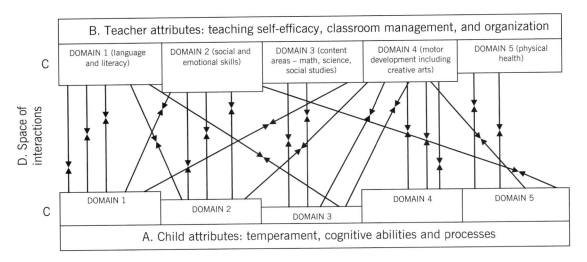

FIGURE 14.2. The transactional model of effective, cross-domain teaching and learning.

interactions, which can be challenging to create for an entire classroom of children. Creating not only an organized and calm classroom setting in which individual interactions become possible, but also whole-group activities in which individual contributions are recognized, may help to address this challenge.

Overall Summary and Conclusions

Two implications for future research follow: First, the literature base on each of the five developmental domains needs to be summarized by experts in each domain, *with the work of other-domain researchers as well as teachers in mind*. Meta-analyses or collections of studies that describe early childhood learning environments with a transactional approach (e.g., Rimm-Kaufman & Cameron Ponitz, 2009), and that distill the key aspects of effective instruction for individual learners in the five domains enable researchers and teachers to accommodate suggestions from outside their domain of interest/expertise and to recognize areas of overlap. Second, a self-assessment developed by researchers who work with teachers might focus on increasing the number of effective transactional exchanges that occur with individual children, especially those entering the classroom with challenging or unfamiliar child attributes. Depending on the intervention, the presence of transactional exchanges may serve as an index of fidelity of the intervention's implementation in that more frequent exchanges may indicate participant responsiveness, reflecting teachers' and children's engagement in the intervention (Dane & Schneider, 1998). This will require teachers' knowledge of the strengths and needs of individual children in their classrooms and an awareness of their own strengths and growth areas.

Somewhat alarmingly, early childhood teachers are among the least credentialed of teachers, especially in Head Start preschools and other settings that serve underresourced populations (Raver et al., 2008). As universal prekindergarten becomes increasingly advocated and implemented, the population of children served by preschool, and its diversity, will continue to grow. To teach effectively and to keep pace with emerging research in diverse content areas, preschool teachers' content knowledge, pedagogical knowledge, and pedagogical content knowledge in each domain must all deepen, and researchers must assist in meaningful and realistic ways (Shulman, 1987).

Education research in children's early years is experiencing a sea change as investigators across disciplines initiate inquiries on how to teach children the skills they need to succeed in school and in life. Advances are both promising and daunting, and require researchers to organize findings from diverse studies. RCTs afford us the privilege of knowing whether a practice or program works. Furthermore, transactional models drawn from human development research point toward a coherent model of learning that accounts for what is being taught, as well as how it is being taught; in other words, the social relationships and transactions within which teaching and learning happens. These findings illuminate new models of improved classroom environments, where teachers' efforts to teach in one area cross over to improve children's skills in another area.

Acknowledgments

This chapter was written while Claire E. Cameron was funded through a fellowship from the Institute of Education Sciences, U.S. Department of Education to the University of Virginia (R305B060009). The opinions expressed are those of the author, and do not represent views of the U.S. Department of Education.

I express the most sincere gratitude to Drs. Sara Rimm-Kaufman and Laura Justice for their support in encouraging and sustaining this work. Both scholars provided timely encouragement, clarity regarding the articulation of the conceptual model, and insights about issues relevant to teacher training and self-efficacy. In addition, invaluable expertise was offered by Dr. Rimm-Kaufman on children's socioemotional learning, and by Dr. Justice with regard to language and literacy development.

References

Administration on Children's Youth and Families/Head Start Bureau. (2003). *Head Start outcomes framework: The Head Start path to positive child outcomes.* Washington, DC: U.S. Department of Health and Human Services.

Administration on Children's Youth and Families/Head Start Bureau. (2010). *The Head Start child development and early learning framework: Promoting positive outcomes in early childhood programs serving children 3–5 years old.* Washington, DC: U.S. Department of Health and Human Services.

Adolph, K. E., & Berger, S. E. (2006). Motor development. In D. Kuhn, R. S. Siegler, W. Damon, & R. M. Lerner (Eds.), *Handbook of child psychology: Vol. 2. Cognition, perception, and language* (6th ed., pp. 161–213). Hoboken, NJ: Wiley.

Anderson, S. E., & Whitaker, R. C. (2009). Prevalence of obesity among US preschool children in different racial and ethnic groups. *Archives of Pediatrics and Adolescent Medicine, 163,* 344–348.

Bandura, A. (1977). Self-efficacy: Toward a unifying theory of behavioral change. *Psychological Review, 84,* 191–215.

Barnett, W. S., Jung, K., Yarosz, D. J., Thomas, J., Hornbeck, A., Stechuk, R., et al. (2008). Educational effects of the Tools of the Mind curriculum: A randomized trial. *Early Childhood Research Quarterly, 23,* 299–313.

Bear, G. G., & Minke, K. M. (2006). *Children's needs III: Development, prevention, and intervention.* Washington, DC: National Association of School Psychologists.

Belsky, J., Friedman, S. L., & Hsieh, K.-H. (2001). Testing a core emotion-regulation prediction: Does early attentional persistence moderate the effect of infant negative emotionality on later development? *Child Development, 72,* 123–133.

Bierman, K. L., Domitrovich, C. E., Nix, R. L., Gest, S. D., Welsh, J. A., Greenberg, M. T., et al. (2008). Promoting academic and social–emotional school readiness: The Head Start REDI program. *Child Development, 79*, 1802–1817.

Bierman, K. L., Nix, R. L., Greenberg, M. T., Blair, C., & Domitrovich, C. E. (2008). Executive functions and school readiness intervention: Impact, moderation, and mediation in the Head Start REDI program. *Development and Psychopathology, 20*, 821–843.

Blair, C. (2002). School readiness: Integrating cognition and emotion in a neurobiological conceptualization of children's functioning at school entry. *American Psychologist, 57*, 111–127.

Blair, C., & Diamond, A. (2008). Biological processes in prevention and intervention: The promotion of self-regulation as a means of preventing school failure. *Development and Psychopathology, 20*, 899–911.

Bodrova, E., & Leong, D. (2007). *Tools of the mind: The Vygotskian approach to early childhood education* (2nd ed.). Columbus, OH: Merrill/Prentice-Hall.

Bohn, C. M., Roehrig, A. D., & Pressley, M. (2004). The first days of school in the classrooms of two more effective and four less effective primary-grades teachers. *Elementary School Journal, 104*, 269–287.

Bowman, B. T., Donovan, M. S., & Burns, M. S. (Eds.). (2001). *Eager to learn: Educating our preschoolers*. Washington, DC: National Academy Press.

Brady, K., & Woolfson, L. (2008). What teacher factors influence their attributions for children's difficulties in learning? *British Journal of Educational Psychology, 78*, 527–544.

Bransford, J. D., Brown, A. L., & Cocking, R. R. (1999). *How people learn: Brain, mind, experience, and school*. Washington, DC: National Academy Press.

Bronfenbrenner, U., & Morris, P. A. (2006). The bioecological model of human development. In R. M. Lerner & W. Damon (Eds.), *Handbook of child psychology: Theoretical models of human development* (6th ed., Vol. 1, pp. 793–828). Hoboken, NJ: Wiley.

Bronson, M. B. (2001). *Self-regulation in early childhood: Nature and nurture*. New York: Guilford Press.

Brophy, J. E. (1979). Teacher behavior and its effects. *Journal of Educational Psychology, 71*, 733–750.

Brophy, J. E. (1983). Classroom organization and management. *Elementary School Journal, 83*, 265–285.

Brophy, J. E. (1986). Teacher effects research and teacher quality. *Journal of Classroom Interaction, 22*, 14–23.

Brown, E. T. (2005). The influence of teachers' efficacy and beliefs regarding mathematics instruction in the early childhood classroom. *Journal of Early Childhood Teacher Education, 26*, 239–257.

Cameron, C. E., Brock, L. L., Murrah, W. M., Bell, L. H., Worzalla, S. L., Grissmer, D., et al. (in press). Fine motor skills and executive function both contribute to kindergarten achievement. *Child Development*.

Cameron, C. E., Connor, C. M., & Morrison, F. J. (2005). Effects of variation in teacher organization on classroom functioning. *Journal of School Psychology, 43*, 61–85.

Cameron, C. E., Connor, C. M., Morrison, F. J., & Jewkes, A. M. (2008). Effects of classroom organization on letter–word reading in first grade. *Journal of School Psychology, 46*, 173–192.

Cameron Ponitz, C. E., & Morrison, F. J. (2011). Teacher activity orienting predicts preschoolers' academic and self-regulatory skills. *Early Education and Development, 22*, 620–648.

Cameron Ponitz, C. E., Rimm-Kaufman, S. E., Brock, L. L., & Nathanson, L. (2009). Early adjustment, gender differences, and classroom organizational climate in first grade. *Elementary School Journal, 110*, 142–162.

Cameron Ponitz, C. E., Rimm-Kaufman, S. E., Grimm, K. J., & Curby, T. W. (2009). Kindergarten classroom quality, behavioral engagement, and reading achievement. *School Psychology Review, 38*, 102–120.

Clements, D. H., & Sarama, J. (2007). Effects of a preschool mathematics curriculum: Summative research on the building blocks project. *Journal for Research in Mathematics Education, 38*, 136–163.

Connor, C. M., Son, S.-H., Hindman, A. H., & Morrison, F. J. (2005). Teacher qualifications, classroom practices, family characteristics, and preschool experience: Complex effects on first-graders' vocabulary and early reading outcomes. *Journal of School Psychology, 43,* 343–375.

Cunningham, A. E., Perry, K. E., Stanovich, K. E., & Stanovich, P. J. (2004). Disciplinary knowledge of K–3 teachers and their knowledge calibration in the domain of early literacy. *Annals of Dyslexia, 54,* 139–167.

Curby, T. R., Rimm-Kaufman, S. E., & Cameron Ponitz, C. (2009). Teacher–child interactions and children's achievement trajectories across kindergarten and first grade. *Journal of Educational Psychology, 101,* 912–925.

Dane, A. V., & Schneider, B. H. (1998). Program integrity in primary and early secondary prevention: Are implementation effects out of control? *Clinical Psychology Review, 18,* 23–45.

Davidson, M. R., Fields, M. K., & Yang, J. (2009). A randomized trial study of a preschool literacy curriculum: The importance of implementation. *Journal of Research on Educational Effectiveness, 2,* 177–208.

Demetriou, A., Christou, C., Spanoudis, G., & Platsidou, M. (2002). The development of mental processing: Efficiency, working memory, and thinking. *Monographs of the Society for Research in Child Development, 67,* vii–154.

Diamond, A. (2000). Close interrelation of motor development and cognitive development and of the cerebellum and prefrontal cortex. *Child Development, 71,* 44–56.

Diamond, A., Barnett, W. S., Thomas, J., & Munro, S. (2007). Preschool program improves cognitive control. *Science, 318,* 1387–1388.

Dickinson, D. K. (2006). Toward a toolkit approach to describing classroom quality. *Early Education and Development, 17,* 177–202.

Domitrovich, C. E., Cortes, R. C., & Greenberg, M. T. (2007). Improving young children's social and emotional competence: A randomized trial of the preschool "PATHS" curriculum. *Journal of Primary Prevention, 28,* 67–91.

Duncan, G. J., Dowsett, C. J., Claessens, A., Magnuson, K., Huston, A. C., Klebanov, P., et al. (2007). School readiness and later achievement. *Developmental Psychology, 43,* 1428–1446.

Early, D. M., Maxwell, K. L., Burchinal, M., Bender, R. H., Ebanks, C., Henry, G. T., et al. (2007). Teachers' education, classroom quality, and young children's academic skills: Results from seven studies of preschool programs. *Child Development, 78,* 558–580.

Eisenberg, N., Guthrie, I. K., Fabes, R. A., Shepard, S., Losoya, S., Murphy, B. C., et al. (2000). Prediction of elementary school children's externalizing problem behaviors from attention and behavioral regulation and negative emotionality. *Child Development, 71,* 1367–1382.

Fantuzzo, J., Perry, M. A., & McDermott, P. (2004). Preschool approaches to learning and their relationship to other relevant classroom competencies for low-income children. *School Psychology Quarterly, 19,* 212–230.

Fantuzzo, J. W., Bulotsky-Sheare, R., Fusco, R. A., & McWayne, C. (2005). An investigation of preschool classroom behavioral adjustment problems and social–emotional school readiness competencies. *Early Childhood Research Quarterly, 20,* 259–275.

Fantuzzo, J. W., Rouse, H. L., McDermott, P. A., Sekino, Y., Childs, S., & Weiss, A. (2005). Early childhood experiences and kindergarten success: A population-based study of a large urban setting. *School Psychology Review, 34,* 571–588.

Farver, J. A. M., Lonigan, C. J., & Eppe, S. (2009). Effective early literacy skill development for young Spanish-speaking English language learners: An experimental study of two methods. *Child Development, 80,* 703–719.

Finkelstein, D., Whitaker, R., Hill, E., Fox, M. K., Mendenko, L., & Boller, K. (2007). *Results from the "I Am Moving, I Am Learning" stage 1 survey.* Princeton, NJ: Mathematica Policy Research, Inc.

Graue, E. M. (2003). Kindergarten in the 21st century. In A. J. Reynolds, M. C. Wang, & H. J. Walberg (Eds.), *Early childhood programs for a new century* (pp. 143–162). Washington, DC: Child Welfare League of America.

Greenfield, D. B., Jirout, J., Dominguez, X., Greenberg, A., Maier, M., & Fuccillo, J. (2009). Science in the preschool classroom: A programmatic research agenda to improve science readiness. *Early Education and Development, 20,* 238–264.

Greenwood, C. R., Horton, B. T., & Utley, C. A. (2002). Academic engagement: Current perspectives on research and practice. *School Psychology Review, 31,* 328–349.

Grissmer, D., & Eiseman, E. (2008). Can gaps in the quality of early environments and non-cognitive skills help explain persisting black–white achievement gaps? In J. Waldfogel & K. Magnuson (Eds.), *Stalled progress: Inequality and the black–white test score gap.* New York: Russell Sage Foundation.

Grissmer, D., Grimm, K. J., Aiyer, S. J., Murrah, W. M., & Steele, J. S. (2010). Fine motor skills and early comprehension of the world: Two new school readiness indicators. *Developmental Psychology, 46,* 1008–1017.

Guo, Y., Piasta, S. B., Justice, L. M., & Kaderavek, J. N. (2009). Relations among preschool teachers' self-efficacy, classroom quality, and children's language and literacy gains. *Teaching and Teacher Education, 26,* 1094–1103.

Hart, B., & Risley, T. R. (1995). *Meaningful differences in the everyday experience of young American children.* Baltimore: Brookes.

Hulleman, C. S., & Cordray, D. S. (2009). Moving from the lab to the field: The role of fidelity and achieved relative intervention strength. *Journal of Research on Educational Effectiveness, 2,* 88–110.

Izard, C. E., King, K. A., Trentacosta, C. J., Morgan, J. K., Laurenceau, J.-P., Krauthamer-Ewing, E. S., et al. (2008). Accelerating the development of emotion competence in Head Start children: Effects on adaptive and maladaptive behavior. *Development and Psychopathology, 20,* 369–397.

Jackson, B., Larzelere, R., St. Clair, L., Corr, M., Fichter, C., & Egertson, H. (2006). The impact of HeadsUp!: Reading on early childhood educators' literacy practices and preschool children's literacy skills. *Early Childhood Research Quarterly, 21,* 213–226.

Jennings, P. A., & Greenberg, M. T. (2009). The prosocial classroom: Teacher social and emotional competence in relation to student and classroom outcomes. *Review of Educational Research, 79,* 491–525.

Justice, L. M., Mashburn, A., Pence, K. L., & Wiggins, A. (2008). Experimental evaluation of a preschool language curriculum: Influence on children's expressive language skills. *Journal of Speech, Language, and Hearing Research, 51,* 983–1001.

Justice, L. M., Mashburn, A. J., Hamre, B. K., & Pianta, R. C. (2008). Quality of language and literacy instruction in preschool classrooms serving at-risk pupils. *Early Childhood Research Quarterly, 23,* 51–68.

Kagan, J. (1989). Temperamental contributions to social behavior. *American Psychologist, 44,* 668–674.

La Paro, K. M., & Pianta, R. C. (2000). Predicting children's competence in the early school years: A meta-analytic review. *Review of Educational Research, 70,* 443–484.

Ladd, G. W., Birch, S. H., & Buhs, E. S. (1999). Children's social and scholastic lives in kindergarten: Related spheres of influence? *Child Development, 70,* 1373–1400.

Lengua, L. J. (2002). The contribution of emotionality and self-regulation to the understanding of children's response to multiple risk. *Child Development, 73,* 144–161.

Marr, D., Cermak, S., Cohn, E. S., & Henderson, A. (2003). Fine motor activities in Head Start and kindergarten classrooms. *American Journal of Occupational Therapy, 57,* 550–557.

Mashburn, A. J., Pianta, R. C., Hamre, B. K., Downer, J. T., Barbarin, O. A., Bryant, D., et al. (2008). Measures of classroom quality in prekindergarten and children's development of academic, language, and social skills. *Child Development, 79,* 732–749.

McClelland, M. M., Cameron, C. E., Wanless, S., & Murray, A. (2007). Executive function, behavioral self-regulation, and social–emotional competence: Links to school readiness. In O. N. Saracho & B. Spodek (Eds.), *Contemporary perspectives in early childhood education: Social learning in early childhood education* (Vol. 7, pp. 113–137). Greenwich, CT: Information Age.

McDonald, S.-K., Keesler, V. A., Kauffman, N. J., & Schneider, B. (2006). Scaling-up exemplary interventions. *Educational Researcher, 35,* 15–24.

Michaels, S., Shouse, A. W., & Schweingruber, H. A. (2008). *Ready, set, science!: Putting research to work in K–8 science classrooms* (Board on Science Education, Center for Education, Division of Behavioral and Social Sciences and Education). Washington, DC: National Academies Press.

Miller, K. F., Kelly, M., & Zhou, X. (2005). Learning mathematics in China and the United States: Cross-cultural insights into the nature and course of preschool mathematical development. In J. I. D. Campbell (Ed.), *Handbook of mathematical cognition* (pp. 163–177). New York: Psychology Press.

Moats, L. C. (1994). The missing foundation in teacher education: Knowledge of the structure of spoken and written language. *Annals of Dyslexia, 44*, 81–102.

Morrison, F. J., Bachman, H. J., & Connor, C. M. (2005). *Improving literacy in America: Guidelines from research.* New Haven, CT: Yale University Press.

National Association for the Assessment of Young Children. (2002). *Early learning standards: Creating the conditions for success* (A Joint Position Statement of the National Association for the Education of Young Children [NAEYC] and the National Association of Early Childhood Specialists in State Departments of Education [NAECS/SDE]). Washington, DC: Author.

National Early Literacy Panel. (2008). *Developing early literacy: A scientific synthesis of early literacy development and implications for intervention.* Jessup, MD: National Center for Early Literacy.

National Institute for Child Health and Human Development (NICHD) Early Child Care Research Network. (2002). The relation of global first-grade classroom environment to structural classroom features and teacher and student behaviors. *Elementary School Journal, 102*, 367–387.

NICHD Early Child Care Research Network. (2003). Do children's attention processes mediate the link between family predictors and school readiness? *Developmental Psychology, 39*, 581–593.

National Research Council. (2007). *Taking science to school: Learning and teaching science in grades K–8* (Committee on Science Learning, Kindergarten through Eighth Grade; Richard A. Duschl, Heidi A. Schweingruber, & Andrew W. Shouse, Eds.; Board on Science Education, Center for Education, Division of Behavioral and Social Sciences and Education). Washington, DC: National Academies Press.

Newcombe, N. S., Ambady, N., Eccles, J., Gomez, L., Klahr, D., Linn, M., et al. (2009). Psychology's role in mathematics and science education. *American Psychologist, 64*, 538–550.

Pence, K. L., Justice, L. M., & Wiggins, A. K. (2008). Preschool teachers' fidelity in implementing a comprehensive language-rich curriculum. *Language, Speech, and Hearing Services in Schools, 39*, 329–341.

Piasta, S. B., Connor, C. M., Fishman, B. J., & Morrison, F. J. (2009). Teachers' knowledge of literacy concepts, classroom practices, and student reading growth. *Scientific Studies of Reading, 13*, 224–248.

Preschool Curriculum Evaluation Research Consortium (PCER). (2008). *Effects of preschool curriculum programs on school readiness* (NCER 2008-2009, National Center for Education Research, Institute for Education Sciences, U.S. Department of Education). Washington, DC: U.S. Government Printing Office.

Raudenbush, S. W. (2005). How do we study "what happens next"? *Annals of the American Academy of Political and Social Science, 602*, 131–144.

Raver, C. C., Jones, S. M., Li-Grining, C. P., Metzger, M., Champion, K. M., & Sardin, L. (2008). Improving preschool classroom processes: Preliminary findings from a randomized trial implemented in Head Start settings. *Early Childhood Research Quarterly, 23*, 10–26.

Rimm-Kaufman, S. E., Curby, T. W., Grimm, K. J., Nathanson, L., & Brock, L. (2009). The contribution of children's self-regulation and classroom quality to children's adaptive behaviors in the kindergarten classroom. *Developmental Psychology, 45*, 958–972.

Rimm-Kaufman, S. E., Early, D. M., Cox, M. J., Saluja, G., Pianta, R. C., Bradley, R. H., et al. (2002). Early behavioral attributes and teachers' sensitivity as predictors of competent behavior in the kindergarten classroom. *Journal of Applied Developmental Psychology, 23*, 451–470.

Rimm-Kaufman, S. E., & Cameron Ponitz, C. E. (2009). Introduction to the special issue on data-based investigations of the quality of preschool and early child care environments. *Early Education and Development, 20*, 201–210.

Rimm-Kaufman, S. E., Voorhees, M. D., Snell, M. E., & La Paro, K. M. (2003). Improving the sensitivity and responsivity of preservice teachers toward young children with disabilities. *Topics in Early Childhood Special Education, 23,* 151–163.

Rothbart, M. K., & Jones, L. B. (1998). Temperament, self-regulation and education. *School Psychology Review, 27,* 479–491.

Sameroff, A. J. (2000). Developmental systems and psychopathology. *Development and Psychopathology, 12,* 297–312.

Sameroff, A. J., Bartko, W. T., Baldwin, A., Baldwin, C., & Seifer, R. (1998). Family and social influences on the development of child competence. In M. Lewis & C. Feiring (Eds.), *Families, risk, and competence* (pp. 161–185). Mahwah, NJ: Erlbaum.

Sarama, J., Clements, D. H., Starkey, P., Klein, A., & Wakeley, A. (2008). Scaling up the implementation of a pre-kindergarten mathematics curriculum: Teaching for understanding with trajectories and technologies. *Journal of Research on Educational Effectiveness, 1,* 89–119.

Shulman, L. S. (1987). Knowledge and teaching: Foundations of the new reform. *Harvard Educational Review, 57,* 1–22.

Snow, C. E., Burns, M. S., & Griffin, P. (1999). Preventing reading difficulties in young children. In Consortium on Reading Excellence (Ed.), *Reading research: Anthology: The why? of reading instruction* (pp. 148–155). Novato, CA: Arena Press.

Son, S.-H., & Meisels, S. J. (2006). The relationship of young children's motor skills to later reading and math achievement. *Merrill–Palmer Quarterly, 52,* 755–778.

Starkey, P., Klein, A., & Wakeley, A. (2004). Enhancing young children's mathematical knowledge through a pre-kindergarten mathematics intervention. *Early Childhood Research Quarterly, 19,* 99–120.

Tudge, J. R. H., Odero, D. A., Hogan, D. M., & Etz, K. E. (2003). Relations between the everyday activities of preschoolers and their teachers' perceptions of their competence in the first years of school. *Early Childhood Research Quarterly, 18,* 42–64.

Wasik, B. A., Bond, M. A., & Hindman, A. (2006). The effects of a language and literacy intervention on Head Start children and teachers. *Journal of Educational Psychology, 98,* 63–74.

Whitehurst, G., & Lonigan, C. (2001). Emergent literacy: Development from prereaders to readers. In S. B. Neuman & D. K. Dickinson (Eds.), *Handbook of early literacy research* (Vol. 1, pp. 11–29). New York: Guilford Press.

Willingham, D. B. (1998). A neuropsychological theory of motor skill learning. *Psychological Review, 105,* 558–584.

Wood, D., Bruner, J. S., & Ross, G. (1976). The role of tutoring in problem solving. *Journal of Child Psychology and Psychiatry, 17,* 89–100.

Zelazo, P. D., Carter, A., Reznick, J. S., & Frye, D. (1997). Early development of executive function: A problem-solving framework. *Review of General Psychology, 1,* 198–226.

Zhou, Q., Hofer, C., Eisenberg, N., Reiser, M., Spinrad, T. L., & Fabes, R. A. (2007). The developmental trajectories of attention focusing, attentional and behavioral persistence, and externalizing problems during school-age years. *Developmental Psychology, 43,* 369–385.

PART III

DEVELOPMENTAL PROCESSES, EARLY EDUCATION, AND FAMILIES

CHAPTER 15

An Ecological Perspective for Understanding the Early Development of Self-Regulatory Skills, Social Skills, and Achievement

Sara E. Rimm-Kaufman and Shannon B. Wanless

Interdisciplinary work on children's development from the past two decades points to the importance of the early childhood years to forecast later development of socioemotional and academic skills. Economists point to the cost-effectiveness of early childhood interventions; specifically, early interventions targeted toward disadvantaged children have higher rates of returns than later interventions (Heckman, 2006). Education researchers describe the intransigency of academic outcomes for children by the time they reach their eighth birthday such that interventions after that time point shift from a preventive to a remedial approach (Entwisle & Alexander, 1993). Neuroscientists describe rapid maturation and organization of the prefrontal cortex that initiate during the preschool years and result in enhanced performance on tasks critical for school success (Diamond, Kirkham, & Amso, 2002; Tsujimoto, 2008).

Evidence from these varied disciplines signals the same message: Children's early experiences at home, in child care, in schools, and in neighborhoods form a critically important basis for children's social and academic future. Furthermore, current research describes the period of early childhood as a "sensitive period" for children's development. By definition, the presence of a sensitive period implies that specific experiences (or absence of such experiences) wield disproportionate influence on children's later outcomes (Bornstein, 1989). Taken together, the confluence of findings from interdisciplinary perspectives and understanding of the salience of sensitive periods turns our attention toward the extent to which various early experiences can be encouraged in early childhood to prevent later school and societal problems. The purpose of this chapter is to examine evidence for the role of children's early contexts (e.g., families and early school environments in a cultural context) as contributors to children's self-regulatory, social, and academic skills. The approach is consistent with an ecological approach to human development and emphasizes the bidirectional interactions between children and the people and objects in their social environment.

Self-regulatory skills refer to children's ability to focus their attention, manage their thoughts and emotions, and inhibit some behaviors in favor of other, less dominant behaviors. These skills involve cognitive, behavioral, and, in some cases, emotional processes. Children's development of self-regulatory skills during the first 8 years of life reflects an interaction between children's genetic predispositions and their social environment during a period characterized by high levels of neural development and plasticity (Fox, Levitt, & Nelson, 2010; Glaser, 2000; Huttenlocher, 2002).

Young children experience situations that require them to use self-regulatory skills in many social contexts (e.g., home, early child care and school classroom, peer situations). When children play a game that requires them to stop when an adult says "go" or resist eating a tempting treat, they exhibit their self-regulatory skills. A teacher may say, "Gather up your worksheets, put them in your folders, and put your folder in your backpack." Alternatively, a teacher may establish a classroom routine that requires children to wait their turn, so their peers have opportunities to engage with interesting materials. In such situations, children exert self-regulatory skills as they inhibit their dominant response (to keep working or to touch the materials) and display a subdominant response (to put away their work or to resist touching the materials). Worth noting, some classroom experiences elicit emotional responses from children, whereas others do not. The teacher's instruction (mentioned earlier) to put worksheets away requires planning and remembering, but typical children would experience little or no emotional response to the situation. In contrast, the situation requiring children to wait and inhibit their tendency to engage with materials may elicit an emotional response (e.g., disappointment or anger). Situations that elicit cognitive versus cognitive and emotional processing appear to involve different patterns of neural activation and have different physiological correlates (Bush, Luu, & Posner, 2000; Lisonbee, Pendry, Mize, & Gwynn, 2010). However, both the cognitive and emotional processes underlying self-regulation support children's development because they foster opportunities for children's engagement in relationships and learning contexts.

Level and growth of self-regulatory skills in early childhood have been linked to academic performance. Self-regulation in preschool correlates with concurrent vocabulary, and emergent literacy and math skills (McClelland, Cameron, Connor, et al., 2007) and forecasts, kindergarten reading achievement (Howse, Calkins, Anastopoulos, Keane, & Shelton, 2003). Children who show better self-regulation upon kindergarten entry demonstrated higher mathematics, vocabulary, and early literacy skills in the spring of the kindergarten year (Ponitz, McClelland, Matthews, & Morrison, 2009), suggesting the usefulness of self-regulatory abilities in school contexts (Ponitz, Rimm-Kaufman, Grimm, & Curby, 2009). Preschool self-regulatory behavior has been shown to relate to later mathematics achievement in several national datasets (Duncan et al., 2007), as well as in other samples (Blair & Razza, 2007; Wanless, McClelland, Acock, et al., 2011). Research on the subconstructs serving as mechanisms underlying associations between self-regulation and achievement implicate the role of working memory (Blair & Razza, 2007; Duncan et al., 2007; Ponitz, McClelland, et al., 2009), attention, and inhibitory control in academic learning (Brock, Rimm-Kaufman, Nathanson, & Grimm, 2009; Clark, Pritchard, & Woodward, 2010).

Self-regulatory ability appears to contribute to social skills, as well as academic performance. Children with better self-regulatory skills (i.e., who were viewed by their preschool teachers as attentive, persistent, positive toward learning, and engaged) were observed as having more positive peer interactions by their teachers and parents compared to their counterparts with fewer self-regulatory skills (Fantuzzo, Perry, & McDermott, 2004). Higher levels of self-regulatory skills (rated as their mothers' perception of self-control) at age 4 related to less deviant behavior (lying, fighting) in preschool (Vazsonyi & Huang, 2010).

Furthermore, children's self-regulation (involving working memory and attention) was associated with less aggressive behavior and stronger prosocial skills (e.g., turn taking and sharing, empathy, social problem solving) in the classroom (Bierman, Nix, Greenberg, Blair, & Domitrovich, 2008). Self-regulatory skills (inhibitory control) are required to assess another person's mental state and to take someone else's perspective (Ciairano, Visu-Petra, & Settanni, 2007), offering one explanation for the role of early self-regulatory skills in forecasting peer relationship quality.

Growth, not just initial skill level, in self-regulation during early childhood appears to be important in children's efforts to navigate social relationships. For instance, teachers reported fewer conduct and peer problems among children showing greater growth in self-regulation (inhibitory control) between the ages of 4 and 6 (Hughes & Ensor, 2008). Furthermore, rate of growth appears to have long-term consequences, in that children demonstrating greater growth in self-regulation during middle childhood showed less deviant behavior in early adolescence compared to children on a slower growth trajectory (Vazsonyi & Huang, 2010).

Perhaps because of its links to children's academic and social performance, children's ability to self-regulate has become increasingly viewed as an indicator of readiness for school (Blair, 2002). Even in the earliest years of school, children's ability to inhibit a dominant response in favor of one that is less dominant, direct attention toward learning goals, stay on task, and participate actively in learning is associated with increased success in school (Greenwood, 1991; Ladd & Dinella, 2009). However, a national survey of kindergarten teachers describes the prevalence of self-regulatory problems and suggests that many children enter into formal school lacking skills in these areas. For instance, teachers reported that almost 50% of children experienced adjustment problems during the transition to kindergarten, and the ability to follow directions was the most frequently cited skill that children lacked. Adjustment problems appear to be more prevalent among children living in poverty and ethnic minority children, one factor that may contribute to the achievement gap in many American schools (Rimm-Kaufman & Pianta, 2000).

Self-Regulatory Skills in Context

Why study self-regulatory skills *in context*? We advance the premise that children's self-regulatory skills are critical for them to become *engaged* in the early academic opportunities, social relationships, and contexts that support their future development. Efforts to modify and improve social contexts (e.g., families, child care, schools) serve little purpose unless children *actively* interact with individuals and experiences in those contexts (Bronfenbrenner & Morris, 2006). The process of engaging with social contexts is one that may be initially adult-guided but ultimately requires children's self-direction of behavior and attention (Bronson, 2001; Kopp, 1982). Young children recruit their self-regulatory abilities when they play simple hiding games with their parents, heed a parent's request to wait to eat, wait to use a desirable toy because they are taking turns with a peer, and respond to a teacher's request to engage in a series of activities in a specific order (e.g., "First put away your materials, wash your hands, and then get in line at the door"). As a result of effective self-regulation, children create opportunities for positive engagement and social relationships in their proximal and distal social contexts. Children's application of their self-regulatory skills to engage in proximal contexts may explain growing evidence for children's self-regulatory skills as a foundation for their academic and social performance.

Self-regulatory skills may create *opportunities* for positive engagement, but stimulating environments need to be present in order for those opportunities to translate into academic and social learning. For example, observers may agree that a kindergartner who wanders aimlessly for an extended period (15 or more minutes) is showing evidence of low self-regulation. However, whether the behavior can be attributed primarily to child attributes, classroom affordances, or both depends on the provisions in the classroom. Are there age-appropriate, cognitively engaging learning activities available for the child? Is a teacher available to reengage the child? Has the teacher given explicit instructions about what activities are available if the child finishes an assignment early? In other words, the interaction between children's self-regulatory skills and the affordances in their classroom results in children's expression and frequency of self-regulated behaviors, as well as their consequent social and academic skills.

Levels of Analysis of Self-Regulation

Children's self-regulation has been defined and operationalized in many different ways, depending on whether researchers or practitioners are focused on its neurological, physiological, behavioral, or contextual level of analysis. We adhere to a hierarchical structure to define and analyze children's self-regulation, as described by Willingham and Lloyd (2007). Lower level constructs serve as "building blocks" to higher level constructs in this hierarchy of self-regulatory skills, and in many cases elements of the lower level constructs are nested within higher order constructs (see Table 15.1). At the lowest level, Level 1, children have *internal representations* of their experience; that is, they perceive symbols, objects, and people and their interrelation as they receive sensory input from the physical world. At Level 2, children recruit *cognitive and emotional processes* to manage internal representations; these involve inhibitory control, working memory, attention, and other cognitive and emotional processes. Level 3 is represented by *educationally relevant constructs*, corresponding to children's self-regulatory behaviors or demonstrated engagement in learning, so named because of their relevance to schools' achievement and socialization goals and reflecting a combination of various Level 2 processes. Level 4, which corresponds to the *individual child* characteristics as units of analysis, reflects combinations of educationally relevant constructs and may refer to a child's trait-level motivation, academic skills, or social skills, which draws upon one or more Level 3 elements. Level 5 corresponds to *interpersonal dynamics in children's proximal social contexts* that are comprised of the social interactions among the individual children (who vary in child-level attributes), and adults in children's lives. Level 6 relates to *children's distal social contexts*, reflecting a composite of children's various proximal social contexts, often reflected as a set of inculcated cultural values.

Higher-order constructs always implicate involvement of lower-order constructs. In the aforementioned classroom example, when the teacher asks children to stop working and put away worksheets, children's self-regulatory ability is implicated (a Level 3 educationally relevant construct), which in turn requires inhibitory control (a Level 2 cognitive construct) and assumes children's perception of their teacher and objects in their environment (a Level 1 internal representation). However, higher-order constructs cannot be fully explained as simply a composite of lower-order constructs. Lower-order constructs interact with one another; thus, the whole (higher-order construct) is greater than the sum of its constituent elements (lower-order constructs) (Willingham & Lloyd, 2007).

Over recent years, developmental researchers have developed a new and growing literature on proximal and distal social contexts that contribute to young children's self-regulatory ability. From an early age, children are exposed to culturally specific values and expectations, social dynamics and experiences (present in Levels 5 and 6) that contribute meaningfully to children's emergence of self-regulatory skills (Level 3) and the child-level characteristics that develop (Level 4). We define the educationally relevant construct of "self-regulation" (Level 3) as a set of related *cognitive and emotional constructs* (Level 2) involved in self-regulation,

TABLE 15.1. Behavioral Levels for the Hierarchical Definition and Analysis of Self-Regulation

	Level of analysis	Example constructs
Higher level	Level 6: Children's distal social contexts	Cultural expectations Cultural values
	Level 5: Interpersonal dynamics in children's proximal social contexts	Family interactions Early child care setting social dynamics Classroom composition Peer social dynamics
	Level 4: Child-level characteristics	Academic skills Social skills Trait-level motivation Student interest in learning
Lower level	Level 3: Educationally relevant constructs	Self-regulatory ability Engagement in learning Behavioral self-regulation Self-control Participation in learning Adaptive classroom behavior Approach to learning
	Level 2: Cognitive (and emotional) processes	Inhibitory control Working memory Attention Executive functioning Emotional processing Effortful control
	Level 1: Internal representations	Perception of symbols Perception of objects

particularly working memory, attentional shifting, and inhibitory control skills. We realize that the literature reflects extensive disagreement about the definitions and components of the self-regulation construct (McClelland, Cameron, Wanless, & Murray, 2007; Ponitz et al., 2008). Table 15.1 provides examples of the commonly used terms to describe constructs at varied levels of analysis.

Conceptual Model

This chapter draws upon the bioecological model of human development (Bronfenbrenner, 1979; Bronfenbrenner & Morris, 2006) and dialectical theory (Sameroff, 2010) to describe early experiences and their contribution to the development of self-regulatory abilities. Both frameworks explain children's development in terms of the increasingly complicated, bidirectional interactions between children and their social contexts over time.

The bioecological model of human development (Bronfenbrenner & Morris, 2006) frames the biological realities and the ecological context of child development. *Proximal processes* describe the increasingly complex interactions between children and the people or objects in their environment over the course of development. Some proximal processes have more influence on the developing child than others, depending on the child's personal characteristics, contexts for development, and amount of time of exposure. *Person* characteristics refer to the child's dispositional qualities, personal resources to which the child has access (including ability and previous experiences), as well as the demand characteristics of the child that relate to the way in which children evoke person-specific reactions from the environment (e.g., shy children evoke fewer responses from their teachers because of their shyness). *Context* refers to the proximal and distal systems in children's lives. Parents, teachers, or friends who interact with children regularly directly comprise microsystem influences, whereas parents' workplaces, neighborhoods, and religious groups encompass exosystem influences that indirectly influence children via their effect on microsystems. *Macrosystems* refer to cultural values and events that have indirect influence on children's development. *Mesosystems* refer to the combined influence of two or more microsystems that influence children. *Time* describes the frequency and duration of episodes of proximal processes that children experience over days, weeks, and years. Typically, proximal processes that occur with greater frequency and/or duration are more likely to impact development than those with lower frequency or duration. Furthermore, historical and societal changes that occur (e.g., entrance into the digital age) constrain the nature of proximal processes to which children are exposed.

A teacher's support for self-regulatory behavior in an early childhood classroom provides an example of a proximal process that influences self-regulatory development. Children bring person characteristics with them to the classroom, including their age and maturity, temperament, and other characteristics that elicit reactions from the people around them. Children's contexts, including families, child care providers, and teachers (individually or in combination with each other), have direct influence on their self-regulatory skills; family workplaces, community religious groups, cultural values about self-regulation (e.g., valuing independence over dependence), and policy decisions, such as the priority placed on early childhood in the Blueprint for Reform for the Elementary and Secondary Education Act (U.S. Department of Education & Office of Planning Evaluation and Policy Development, 2010), have indirect influences on development.

Dialectical theory explains the relation between children's genetically based personal attributes and the cultures in which they live in a way that acknowledges the complex, nonlinear interplay between nature and nurture over the course of development. Sameroff (2010) describes the "unity of opposites" stating that development involves nature and nurture in balance, as well as the "interpenetration of opposites," in that nature modifies nurture and nurture changes nature (p. 9). Applied to self-regulation, the unity of opposites posits that self-regulatory abilities are inherent to the child (nature), but if there were no social context (nurture) in which to operate, there would be no raw material (e.g., learning situations requiring attention, temptations to resist) to which a child could respond. The interpenetration of opposites, in contrast, states that children's self-regulatory abilities (directed by nature) lead to actions and changes to their physical and social world (nurture). In turn, children's experiences with their physical and social worlds (nurture) produce changes in their self-regulatory abilities (that are directed by nature).

Dialectical theory offers an approach to understanding the relation between children's self-regulatory behaviors in early childhood, their social contexts, as well as their broader culture. Self-regulatory abilities at the transition to kindergarten provide an example that exposes important transactions between children and their environment. In relation to the unity of opposites, when children come to school they display self-regulatory behaviors in reaction to the kindergarten classroom environment that reflect child characteristics and early learning experiences. In turn, the classrooms and schools into which children enter have a particular way of arranging physical and social features (e.g., coat hooks with names, routines for standing in line) to support and challenge the development of self-regulatory behaviors. The child and environment also show the interpenetration of opposites, in that children's self-regulatory abilities elicit different types of opportunities for practicing self-regulation in the classroom environment by, for instance, influencing teacher and peer behavior toward the child. In turn, the classroom environment socializes children in ways that either enhance or diminish self-regulatory abilities. As children develop, their self-regulatory skills reflect initial child characteristics, learning prior to school entry, and experiences in early school environments.

Figure 15.1 provides a conceptual framework to explain children's social and academic development. Children's macrosystem (e.g., cultural values, policies) and exosystem influences (e.g., community and family workplace) influence children's microsystems. Aspects of the microsystem (e.g., family, child care, school, peers) and mesosystems (e.g., family involvement in school) and child characteristics (e.g., biologically based attributes, including gender, age, temperament, cognitive ability) directly contribute to children's development of self-regulation, social skills, and academic skills. In addition, aspects of the microsystem and child attributes have indirect influence on children's social and academic skills via self-regulation. Children's attributes influence the types of microsystems to which they are exposed. For instance, children's gender and self-regulatory abilities elicit different reactions from caregivers (Deater Deckard & Petrill, 2004; Eisenberg, Valiente, & Eggum, 2010). The nature of the interactions among the systems and their consequences depends on sociohistorical time. Here, for brevity, we focus on family and early childhood classroom environments.

The Family Microsystem

Often recognized as "children's first teachers," families vary in the frequency and manner of interactions with children, resulting in a wide variety of acquired self-regulatory skills. Family influence on children's self-regulatory behavior begins prenatally as environmental factors (e.g., exposure to smoking, alcohol) curtail the development of cognitive constructs (working memory, attention) underlying self-regulation (Kodituwakku, Handmaker, Cutler, Weathersby, & Handmaker, 1995; Wiebe et al., 2009). Research on human infants and animals suggests a strong biobehavioral basis for self-regulatory behavior (Hinde, 1975). Family contributions to self-regulation continue through infancy and the toddler years, early childhood, and beyond; however, the manner by which families influence children's self-regulation changes through the course of development (Halgunseth, Ispa, & Rudy, 2006; Kopp, 1982).

Socioeconomic status has been associated with self-regulatory abilities in preschool (Wanless, McClelland, Tominey, & Acock, 2011) and kindergarten (Howse, Lange, Farran, & Boyles, 2003). Studies examining the relation between family income and self-regulation (behavioral regulation) suggest that children living in economically impoverished conditions show lower behavioral regulation than their middle-class peers (Evans & Rosenbaum, 2008; Mezzacappa, 2004; Mistry, Benner, Biesanz, & Clark, 2011; Sektnan, McClelland, Acock, & Morrison, 2010), a relation that has been attributed to less effective prefrontal functioning among children living in poverty (Kishiyama, Boyce, Jimenez, Perry, & Knight, 2009). Process features of family environments may explain the apparent impact of low socioeconomic status. Specifically, families constrained by the stressors associated with poverty and its accompanying hardships (parental depression, family conflict) often experience greater challenges in supporting children's ability to self-regulate consistently compared to those with more resources (Conger et al., 2002; Evans & Rosenbaum, 2008; McLoyd, 1998).

Home learning stimulation, assessed in terms of its provisions in the physical environment for children's opportunities to learn (e.g., number of books present, cuddly toys present) and the presence of social environments that promote young children's learning (e.g., parents' frequency of reading to, talking to, or teaching new skills to their children), plays an important role in children's self-regulation (Bradley, Corwyn, Burchinal, McAdoo, & García Coll, 2001; Christian, Morrison, & Bryant, 1998). As one example, among a group

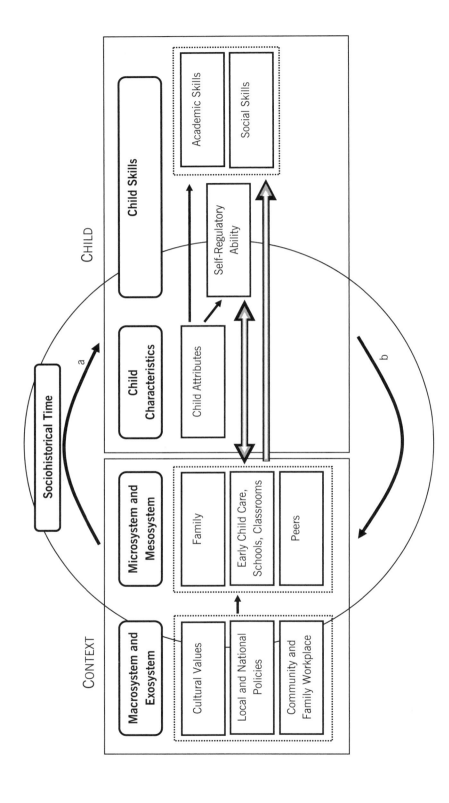

FIGURE 15.1. Conceptual framework for understanding the direct and indirect influences on children's self-regulatory ability and academic and social skills. The smaller arrows indicate potential direct and indirect effects. The dotted lines represent systems or constructs that relate to one another and act individually or in interaction with one another to predict children's outcomes. The large arrows represent the dialectical process between a child and his or her context. Context influences the child (a) and the child influences his or her context (b) through a dynamic, transactional process that occurs over the course of development. A child's self-regulatory abilities often reflect more of one of the influences—either contextual or child—but there is a continual dialectical process that occurs throughout development.

of preschoolers from urban, poor families, home-based learning stimulation (e.g., parents reading to children and asking their preschool children about school) showed stronger links to children's self-regulation (teacher-reported approach to learning, motivation, and persistence) than either school-based involvement or home–school communication (Fantuzzo, McWayne, Perry, & Childs, 2004). Furthermore, children's self-regulation (self-control) may mediate the relation between home learning stimulation and fewer externalizing problems at school (Bradley & Corwyn, 2005). Such findings suggest plausible mechanisms for the ways that families cultivate development of children's self-regulatory abilities, clearly implicating both opportunities for learning in stimulating environments and children's engagement in those stimulating situations. Self-regulatory skills children develop as a consequence of shared learning activities reflect explicit support for attention (e.g., when a parent directs a child's attention), modeling (e.g., when a parent persists at a challenging problem in the presence of a child), or implicit activities that exercise self-regulatory skills (e.g., when parents and children wait for one another or parents point out a salient detail of a book to a child, even in the presence of a distraction). The synchrony between parents and their children provides occasions for children to exercise their self-regulatory skills as they learn how to approach and structure challenging tasks (Eisenberg, Valiente, et al., 2010; Harrist & Waugh, 2002).

Parents vary in their style of parenting, particularly in relation to their warmth, support for autonomy, and control. In a study, parental warmth toward children, characterized by conveyance of security, little anger, and low dependence, contributed to steeper growth in self-regulation (self-control) from early childhood to age 10 than did less warm relationships (Vazsonyi & Huang, 2010). *Autonomy support*, defined as parents' use of practices that support and encourage independent problem solving, choice, and participation in decisions, has been contrasted with parenting styles that involve punitive and coercive approaches to discipline; children of parents who offered more autonomy support showed greater self-regulation (autonomy as rated by their teacher) than did children of punitive and coercive parents (Grolnick & Ryan, 1989). Some aspects of parental control are conveyed by parents' language, with implications for self-regulation. For example, preschool parents' use of demands during a structured play task (indicating high control) was associated with lower self-regulation than parents' use of suggestions (low-control) with their preschoolers (Worzalla, Hindman, Bowles, & Morrison, 2011).

Relationships between parents and children are transactional. Although the majority of research on parenting emphasizes the influence parents have on their children, children's self-regulatory ability influences the frequency and manner of parents' interaction with their children (Lengua & Kovacs, 2005). Several studies stand out as exemplars of these transactions. As one example, research using biological children and adopted siblings in the same family examined the extent to which parent–child mutuality developed as a function of the child's genetic characteristics or the shared genetic characteristics of the parent and child. Findings demonstrated that children who managed their own behaviors competently and directed their attention effectively (at approximately age 8) elicited more warm, sensitive, and responsive behaviors from their parents than did their counterparts who had difficulty with these self-regulatory competencies, a finding rooted in the genetic contribution to student behavior (Deater Deckard & Petrill, 2004). As another example, work by Eisenberg, Vidmar, and colleagues (2010) examined temperament-based elements of children's self-regulatory behavior (specifically, effortful control) three times between ages 18 and 42 months and their relation to mothers' behavior during a teaching task. The mothers' language was coded for maternal directives, questioning, and cognitive assistance. Findings from an autoregressive panel model suggest the presence of evocative genetic effects. Specifically, children with higher self-regulation (effortful control) at earlier ages elicited more cognitive assistance and questioning strategies, and fewer directives during later observations, even when researchers controlled for concurrent levels of self-regulation (effortful control).

Relationships between parents and their children do not exist in isolation from other social contexts. A rich understanding of the relation between social context and children's self-regulation requires attention to the influence of exosystems and macrosystems. Maternal stress experienced in the earliest years of life, often increased or reduced by contexts in children's exosystems (e.g., parent workplace, community supports), can contribute to poor self-regulation (lower frustration tolerance) and more externalizing in early childhood (Yates, Obradović, & Egeland, 2010). In contrast, aspects of children's exosystems can foster family strengths, and in turn, enhance self-regulatory abilities. Consider parents' religiosity and its potential to influence parenting practices and self-regulatory behavior. In a sample of rural, single-parent, African American mothers, most of whom lived in poverty, mothers who reported higher religiosity used more "no-nonsense parenting," had more positive mother–child relationships, and showed greater family–school involvement. Furthermore, mothers' religiosity had an indirect and positive effect on children's self-regulation via the quality of the mother–child interactions. In turn, higher-quality mother–child interactions were related to children's improved cognitive and social competence and less internalizing behavior, associations that were fully mediated by children's self-regulatory abilities (operationalized as self-control) (Brody & Flor, 1998). Viewing both challenges faced by families and the strengths present in their lives fosters improved understanding of the distal social contexts that contribute to children's success. Such work suggests avenues for intervention, particularly with culturally and socioeconomically diverse samples.

The family cultural context functions as a macrosystem, with indirect effects on children's self-regulation. Many parenting practices reflect culturally specific beliefs, thoughts, and knowledge (Shweder et al., 1998). Although variability within cultures can be as large as those between cultures, several examples help explain how culture constrains the nature of parenting, establishes parents' targets for what is considered "ideal" self-regulation, and contributes to central tendencies in children's self-regulatory abilities. For example, in the Taiwanese culture, parents focus on teaching children to control their behaviors, especially around elderly family members (Hsieh, 2004). Children are taught to eat quietly, to sit still, or not to speak when elderly family members are speaking. In China, cultural beliefs are also reflected in teaching behaviors where most lessons involve group activities during which children are all expected to do the same thing and independence is discouraged (Pang & Richey, 2007). In these examples, cultural behaviors rooted in Confucian beliefs lead to parenting practices that give children frequent possibilities to practice self-regulation. Children are expected to regulate their behaviors and follow the behaviors of the group, even when these behaviors may be in conflict with more dominant responses.

Culturally specific parenting practices within the United States show indirect effects on child outcomes. A national data collection effort identified developmental trends for young children from varied family backgrounds. As one example, Hispanic kindergartners appeared to show less social competence (involving emotional, behavioral, and attentional regulation) compared to non-Hispanic white kindergartners (Brown et al., 2004). As one possible explanation, some research on Hispanic American parents suggests an emphasis on strictness and child compliance in early childhood (Brooks-Gunn & Markman, 2005; Wasserman, Rauh, Brunelli, Garcia-Castro, & Necos, 1990). Cultural valuation of compliance may decrease children's ability for self-regulation. Albeit in non-Hispanic samples, parental emphasis on child compliance has been related to lower child self-regulation (Kochanska & Knaack, 2003; Wachs, Gurkas, & Kontos, 2004), in that children who passively comply with directions, rather than actively regulate their behaviors, may have difficulty later in school in situations requiring self-reliance and autonomy.

Such research may oversimplify Hispanic parents' views toward children. Integrative work (Halgunseth et al., 2006) suggests that Hispanic families are indulgent and permissive toward their children up to approximately age 6. Up to that point, Hispanic mothers have lower expectations for children's independent performance of behaviors (e.g., drinking from a cup), provide more physical nurturance and soothing of their young children, and create more opportunities for dyadic activity rather than self-regulation compared to European American mothers. At approximately age 6, Hispanic families appear to undergo a shift in their approach to parenting, characterized by greater strictness and intensified focus on compliance. One explanation for the shift suggests that Hispanic families begin to hold higher expectations for independent behavior around this age (Halgunseth et al., 2006).

Simply living a home life based in a different culture than school life opens up experiences that pertain to children's self-regulation. For instance, children who live in cultures in which they are expected to learn multiple languages may be at a distinct advantage for developing self-regulation. Learning a second language requires not only the skills implicated in learning a first language but also self-regulatory skills. Specifically, children must shift their attention between languages as their minds process information in one language but produce words in another. They must also inhibit the inclination to use their dominant language and instead activate the secondary language. Studies have demonstrated higher self-regulatory skills (inhibitory control) in bilingual children than in their monolingual counterparts (Bialystok, 1999; Bialystok & Craik, 2010; Bialystok & Martin, 2004; Bialystok & Viswanathan, 2009; Carlson & Meltzoff, 2008; Emmorey, Luk, Pyers, & Bialystok, 2008).

Understanding cultural differences in parenting practices fosters an understanding of the role of culture in children's developmental trajectories, particularly as home and school environments interface. Home and school cultures may differ, and what is considered well regulated in one context may not be perceived as well regulated in another. Furthermore, communication styles may differ between families and teachers. This effect may be especially pronounced when families speak a different language from that of their child's teacher, resulting in an inability to convey congruent and incongruent values about self-regulation. Research addressing interactions between family and school cultures shows, for example, that teachers may perceive parents that do not speak English to be less intelligent or less interested in their child's education (Tapia, 1992; Trueba, 1991). The central role of families and children's self-regulatory growth is a reality that requires recognition as policymakers and practitioners define school readiness in relation to children's self-regulatory competencies and think through optimal practices to support children's self-regulation during the transition from home to child care, or home to school settings.

Child Care and Classroom Environments as Microsystems

Caregivers, teachers, and peers are socializing agents who support and challenge children's regulatory skills in classrooms settings (McClelland, Cameron, Wanless, et al., 2007). Their influence may be particularly pronounced during the transition to kindergarten, as this time often represents great discontinuity and places large demands on self-regulatory skills. Upon kindergarten entry, children's academic performance becomes tethered to a set of expectations for achievement (Pianta, Cox, & Snow, 2007), and children's ability to self-regulate and engage in instruction becomes essential to meet achievement benchmarks and school expectations for social behavior. In addition to placing high demands on children, the transition to kindergarten is also critical because self-regulatory skills during this time have lasting consequences; children develop skills that are related to academic and social outcomes throughout adulthood (Ladd & Dinella, 2009; Moffitt et al., 2011). Because of the critical importance of self-regulatory abilities in early childhood classrooms, we focus our discussion on how preschool and early elementary classrooms, particularly teachers, contribute to or diminish growth in self-regulation. Children's engagement or participation in the classroom experience is the *educational construct* that most closely reflects the presence of children's self-regulatory skills in early childhood classroom settings.

Self-regulatory abilities become apparent in the classroom when children recruit their cognitive, emotional, and behavioral resources to meet the demands of classroom life. In child care and preschool settings, engagement has also been operationalized as cooperative, reciprocal, and creative play between peers (Fantuzzo, Sekino, & Cohen, 2004), repeated attempts at problem solving (McWilliam, Scarborough, & Kim, 2003), or participation in a learning activity (Early et al., 2010). In early elementary school, children appear engaged and "on task" when they resist interacting with a nearby peer during a teacher-directed learning experience that does not involve peer interaction, engage in positive reciprocal interactions with peers in a center setting, demonstrate self-reliance during a transition between activities, or take initiative to participate in classroom learning activities (Ladd & Dinella, 2009; Rimm-Kaufman, Curby, Grimm, Nathanson, & Brock, 2009).

Classrooms vary widely in the extent to which they support and challenge children's self-regulatory abilities. Effective teachers support the development of self-regulation by organizing their classrooms as a means of managing children's behavior, incorporating instructional strategies that are interesting and engaging to children, and cultivating emotionally supportive teacher–child relationships and peer interactions. Effective interactions between teachers and children appear to be even more influential than structural features of classrooms (e.g., class size and full- vs. part-day instruction in kindergarten) in predicting children's engagement (e.g., Finn & Pannozzo, 2004), and social skills and early achievement (Mashburn et al., 2008). Teachers use organizational, instructional, and relational strategies to "down-regulate" and direct attention of children who are loud and misbehaving and to "up-regulate" and connect to children who seem withdrawn and uninvolved (Rimm-Kaufman et al., 2002; Rimm-Kaufman & Kagan, 2005; Thompson, 1994).

"Classroom organization" refers to the strategies teachers use to proactively guide children's behavior and attention (Hamre, Pianta, Mashburn, & Downer, 2007). Many of the strategies teachers use to organize their classrooms, establish classroom routines, and prevent behavior problems provide external structures and supports that become internalized and foster children's self-regulatory behaviors (Rimm-Kaufman et al., 2009). Several classroom practices typify such classroom organization strategies. For example, organizing classrooms to be more child centered than teacher centered appears to support engagement (Pianta, La Paro, Payne, Cox, & Bradley, 2002). Setting up the classroom environment so that children can access needed materials without help from adults allows children to take responsibility for their actions and regulate the pace at which they work through available activities. Use of such child-centered practices (including support for self-reliance and child responsibility) has been related to greater engagement among kindergartners (Pianta et al., 2002). As another example, establishing routines clearly, particularly in the beginning of the year, appears to increase self-regulated behavior throughout the school year (Bohn, Roehrig, & Pressley, 2004). Furthermore, some teachers use routines to create clear expectations for behavior. For instance, they may regularly give children a verbal warning of the number of minutes before they will be expected to clean up, have containers available for returning materials, and make additional learning materials available should children finish an activity early (Cameron, Connor, Morrison, & Jewkes, 2008). In first-grade classrooms, teachers who allocated more time to establish routines, stated instructional goals, and oriented children to materials in the fall of the year showed more efficient transitions between activities later in the year and had students who spent more time engaged in child-managed activities (requiring self-direction of attention) in the spring (Cameron et al., 2008). Taken together, findings suggest that when children are offered age-appropriate situations to be self-reliant and are taught routines in the classroom early in the year, they show less dependency on the teacher and begin to internalize classroom rules.

Teacher language has often been implicated as a strategy to support children's self-regulatory skills and engagement. Teachers' use of language in the classroom, particularly verbal modeling in problem-solving situations and use of mental state words, is an aspect of instruction implicated in the support of children's self-regulatory abilities (Englert, Raphael, Anderson, Anthony, & Stevens, 1991; Hughes, Graham, & Grayson, 2004). It is possible that children internalize these verbal dialogues and use them in their own private speech when attempting to regulate themselves (Winsler, Fernyhough, & Montero, 2009). For example, a teacher may talk aloud as she struggles with a math problem on the board and remind herself to think about an estimation strategy that she used in a previous lesson. The children may then feel more comfortable talking themselves through challenging math problems, and, as a result, slow down and access previously learned strategies more effectively than they do without self-talk.

Effective instructional strategies play an important role in supporting children's self-regulation. Teachers who provide scaffolding; encourage choice, autonomy, and creativity in instruction; and engage children in one-on-one interactions were more likely to have their students be more engaged in literacy activities, based on research from a first-grade classroom (Bogner, Raphael, & Pressley, 2002). Furthermore, third-grade teachers who offered cognitively challenging tasks, created small-group work situations, and asked questions requiring careful thought and analysis of material were more likely to support children's engagement in learning (Dolezal, Welsh, Pressley, & Vincent, 2003; Downer, Rimm-Kaufman, & Pianta, 2007). Early childhood teachers use this type of instruction when they gather children into small groups and ask them to create hypotheses about what might happen next. Such approaches support self-regulatory development.

Teachers establish a climate in their classrooms, ranging from warm, positive, and emotionally supportive to negative, harsh, and critical. Positive classroom climates set the stage for the development of cooperative peer interactions and caring teacher–child relationships (Pianta et al., 2002). Positive teacher–child relationships, evidenced by teachers' report of little conflict, a high degree of closeness and support, and little dependency, have been shown to contribute to children's self-regulatory development and academic outcomes (Battistich, Schaps, & Wilson, 2004; Birch & Ladd, 1997; Borman & Overman, 2004; Hamre & Pianta, 2001). Moreover, teachers with close relationships to their students reported that these children were less avoidant toward school, appeared more self-directed, and were more cooperative and engaged in learning compared to peers without close relationships (Birch & Ladd, 1997; Klem & Connell, 2004). Positive communication and social engagement between teachers and children helps children modulate emotions effectively and foster a shared understanding of the behavioral expectations and norms of the classroom (Baker, Grant, & Morlock, 2008). Furthermore, positive teacher–child relationships foster feelings of attachment and emotional security, so that children are comfortable fully engaging in the learning process and taking risks as needed (Pianta, 1999). Children use their relationships with adults to organize their social experiences and develop "internal working models" for how teacher–child relationships operate. In turn, these working models may be applied to other relationships with future teachers and perpetuate themselves over time (Pianta, 2006).

Studies of classrooms of young children provide a consistent set of findings about the benefits of interpersonal warmth and sensitivity toward children in supporting self-regulatory skills. Affective warmth between teachers and children contributes to students' use of self-regulatory skills (classroom adjustment; Baker et al., 2008). First graders, for example, showed higher behavioral self-control, self-reliance, and engagement when their teachers offered emotional support (Merritt, Wanless, Ponitz, & Rimm-Kaufman, in press; National Institute of Child Health and Human Development [NICHD] Early Child Care Research Network, 2003). Furthermore, the way teachers use language when interacting with children, such as elaborating on behaviors that children are already exhibiting as opposed to issuing directives, contributes to higher levels of engagement in young children (McWilliam et al., 2003). Thus, by responding to children's cues for interaction as opposed to interrupting their engaged state, teachers support children's sustained joint attention with peers and higher levels of engagement in activities. High-quality instruction involves microadaptations of teacher behavior to meet the needs of individual students (Corno, 2008). Such microadaptations require that teachers know children individually and adapt their practices to scaffold children's self-regulatory, social, emotional, and academic growth.

Teachers' effective use of organizational, instructional, and relational strategies affords the types of classroom opportunities that promote engagement and, ultimately, student achievement and social competence. Time spent in deficient, uninteresting social and academic contexts is non-nutritive to a growing and developing child (Curby, Rimm-Kaufman, & Ponitz, 2009). In kindergarten, the relation between quality of teacher–child interactions (emotional support, classroom organization, and instructional support) and reading achievement appears to be fully explained by children's engagement in learning (Ponitz, Rimm-Kaufman, Grimm, et al., 2009). Likewise, children who had positive relationships with their teachers in first grade showed higher math and reading scores in third grade, an association that appears to be mediated via effortful engagement (reflecting persistence, attention, and effort) (Hughes, Luo, Kwok, & Loyd, 2008). Higher reading achievement among girls than among boys in kindergarten has been a very robust finding across samples, and this, too, appears to be mediated primarily by differences in engagement (attentiveness, persistence with difficult tasks) in the kindergarten classroom (Ready, LoGerfo, Burkam, & Lee, 2005). These findings demonstrate that self-regulated behavior in the classroom stands as an important mechanism linking high-quality teacher–student interactions to achievement.

Teacher–child relationships are transactional, a fact that calls attention to the importance of individual differences in child attributes in relation to school experiences. Teachers use strategies to socialize children and support self-regulatory development in the classroom; also, children with different self-regulatory abilities elicit different reactions and behaviors from their teachers. Child attributes have been shown to relate to the frequency of interactions children have with teachers, which may have implications for the development of such relationships. Specifically, shy children appear to initiate fewer interactions with their teachers than do outgoing children, a behavior that appears to contribute to less close relationships between teachers and children (Rudasill & Rimm-Kaufman, 2009). Furthermore, research on over 1,000 pairs of twins, ages 5–12, indicated that the genetic component of children's behavior explained differences between children requiring high teacher effort compared to those requiring very little effort. Children's self-regulatory abilities and behavioral difficulties, not IQ, appeared to be the factors that required the greatest amount of teacher attention (Houts, Caspi, Pianta, Arseneault, & Moffitt, 2010). Understanding the role of child attributes in the development of teacher–child relationships may allow teachers to individualize their relationship-building strategies best to fit each child.

Some children benefit more than others from high-quality organizational, instructional, and relational strategies in the classroom. Children who entered first grade with lower initial academic abilities showed benefits when teachers spent more time structuring activities and orienting individual children to tasks well into the school year, even after the majority of children had settled into the regular routines (Cameron et al., 2008). Children who are approach-oriented or show low effortful control appear to rely on teacher support to maintain their engagement in learning. Children who are bold in kindergarten appear to be more engaged in the presence of a sensitive and responsive teacher than in the presence of a less sensitive and less responsive teacher (Rimm-Kaufman et al., 2002), and first-grade children low in effortful control appeared to perform as high on math and reading achievement tests as children high in effortful control where their teachers were warm and responsive and showed little conflict toward students (Liew, Chen, & Hughes, 2010). In addition, boys tend to have fewer self-regulatory abilities to support their adaptation to the classroom. In fact, gender differences in teacher reports of self-control in spring of the first-grade year can be explained completely by their initial differences in the start of the year. Boys, perhaps because of their lower levels of self-regulatory abilities, may be more affected by high-quality organization and less chaotic classrooms because it appears that boys in poorly managed and chaotic classrooms show low levels of math achievement in the first grade, an association not evident among girls (Ponitz, Rimm-Kaufman, Brock, & Nathanson, 2009). Taken together, the research on differential effects of teacher–student interactions on children's self-regulatory skills suggests that children at risk for school performance problems (based on initial low self-regulatory ability, sociodemographic risk, or low initial achievement) benefit more from effective teachers than do those living with less adversity.

Research described in this section provides evidence that early school experiences contribute to children's development of self-regulatory skills, underscoring the need to intervene in early childhood classroom settings to improve these skills. Observational, descriptive research on early school settings exposes specific challenges that need to be addressed to improve school contexts. For example, a large-scale observational study of more than 600 state-funded preschool classrooms in 11 states demonstrated that almost half (44%) of children's time is spent in situations offering no learning activity. Also, preschool children received three times more teacher-directed, didactic instruction than scaffolded instruction (i.e., instruction that fully acknowledges children's preexisting knowledge and academic level; Early et al., 2010). Comparable observational techniques used to assess more than 700 kindergarten classrooms in six states revealed that, on average, children are exposed to moderate levels of classroom organization/classroom management and low levels of instructional support (La Paro et al., 2009). Studies examining quality in kindergarten, first-, and third-grade classrooms point to room for growth in classroom quality (NICHD Early Child Care Research Network, 2002, 2005; Pianta et al., 2002). Ratings of quality in these elementary school years suggest moderate levels of classroom organization and behavior management, moderate to high levels of emotional support for learning, and low levels of classroom instructional quality. These findings point to the need for classroom-based interventions to improve children's self-regulatory outcomes.

Interventions for Creating Change

National interest in school readiness and the increased focus on the salience of self-regulatory skills for adapting to classroom learning environments (Blair, 2002; Raver, 2002) have generated a line of work developing and evaluating interventions to improve children's self-regulatory competencies. School-based, preventive universal interventions have used varied tactics to achieve the same goal. Some interventions focus on the development of teachers, particularly the enhancement of classroom organization, management, and teacher–student relationships, whereas others attend to the instructional techniques, with the development of self-regulatory skills as an inherent or incidental by-product of the individualized instruction inherent to the intervention. Albeit brief, this section describes several classroom-based interventions focused on self-regulation in early childhood, with some synthesis identifying potential critical ingredients (see Domitrovich, Moore, Thompson, & the CASEL Preschool to Elementary School Social and Emotional Learning Assessment Workgroup, Chapter 19, this volume, for a review).

Several interventions have been examined using randomized controlled trials. The Chicago School Readiness Project offers coaching to Head Start teachers to manage children's problem behavior by supporting implementation of clear expectations, regular routines, reward systems for positive behaviors, and redirection of problem behaviors. Results demonstrated improvement in self-regulation (attention, impulse control), and children's self-regulatory abilities appeared partially to explain gains in academic skills (Raver et al., 2011). The Head Start REDI (Research-based, Developmentally Informed) program involves brief lessons with follow-up activities at school and home to improve children's social, emotional, language, and literacy skills. Teachers using this enriched approach to preschool instruction for one year improved preventative behavior management, classroom climate, and quality of verbal interactions with students (Domitrovich et al., 2009). In turn, children showed small gains in various domains tapping school readiness, as well as task engagement (Bierman, Domitrovich, et al., 2008). The Fast Track program provides both universal services through PATHS (Promoting Alternative Thinking Strategies) and selective services for children at risk for problems. Children exposed to this intervention for 3 consecutive years showed mild to moderate gains in academic engagement and improved self-control and on-task behavior, with largest effects in school with more disadvantaged students (Conduct Problems Prevention Research Group, 2010).

The Tools of the Mind curriculum (Bodrova & Leong, 1996), a preschool intervention rooted in Vygoskian theory, emphasizes socially mediated interactions among peers, and between teachers and children, as well as "tools" or activities designed to promote children's attention and self-regulatory skills. The intervention includes activities designed to foster sociodramatic play and encourage private speech, and it uses external aids that support attention. Results suggest that Tools of the Mind contributes to improved teacher sensitivity and productivity, fewer behavior problems in the classroom (Barnett et al., 2008), and improved self-regulation (Diamond, Barnett, Thomas, & Munro, 2007; see also Bodrova & Leong, Chapter 17, this volume). Individualized student instruction using the Assessment to Instruction (A2i) Web-based software (Connor, Morrison, Fishman, Schatschneider, & Underwood, 2007) focuses on instructional support and tailors first-grade reading instruction to individual children. Teachers' use of individualized instruction appeared to improve classroom management (e.g., smoother transitions, less classroom disruption, greater capability to use small-group instruction). Furthermore, use of A2i related to gains in self-regulation in children with low initial levels of self-regulation (in the lowest quartile at the beginning of the year), most likely a by-product of the individualized approach to instruction (Connor et al., 2010). A few critical ingredients appear in the aforementioned interventions, setting the stage for future innovation: (1) support for teachers to meet children at their developmental and academic level; (2) opportunities for children to practice self-regulatory skills repeatedly; and (3) teachers' establishment of well-organized, regular routines.

Closing Comments and Next Steps

The promotion of self-regulatory ability in early childhood stands as an approach to improve children's early adjustment to school and has potential as a point of leverage for policymakers eager to improve social and academic outcomes for children and youth. Efforts focused on children's self-regulatory abilities need to be based on theory and research, to reflect accurately lower-order constructs in the hierarchical analysis of self-regulation, and to realize the limitations to existing research. Efforts to produce change need to resource the many systems (macrosystem, exosystem, mesosystem, and microsystems) influential to young children. Typically, resources available to families with young children are fragmented because they are distributed across many social service agencies and varied child care and school environments. Often children outgrow services provided by one social service agency focused on birth through age 3, shift between various child care environments between ages 3 and 5, then move into schooling environments that may or may not be comprehensive enough (in terms of hours and services) to meet the needs of working families and young children (Rouse & Fantuzzo, 2009). One cause for this fragmentation is that funding for early childhood education is often distributed across local, state, and federal agencies, each bringing its own regulatory guidelines and eligibility criteria. Efforts to support children from birth to age 8 require community-specific approaches that take the perspective of the families and children being served. Such perspective taking requires practitioners to know the answers to key questions, for instance: How many transitions do children experience between various child care and school settings in the 5 years prior to school entry? How many transitions between child care settings do families need to negotiate prior to school entry? How many different agencies do families need to approach to provide high-quality health, early assessment services, and psychological services to their young children? To what extent does the culture at home match or mismatch the culture of the early childhood environments outside of the home?

Taking an ecological and dialectical perspective to early childhood experiences, children's self-regulatory abilities, and school performance reflects not only children's self-regulation but also the affordances in the classroom. Weighing available options, resources need to be in place to improve the quality of early childhood environments (including families, child care environments, and schools) to enhance the proximal processes between adults and children that promote self-regulatory growth and development. Interventions that build upon family strengths provide new directions. For instance, encouraging pride in children's cultural heritage appears to influence parenting practices (after controlling for general levels of parent involvement) and, in turn, relates to fewer problem behaviors in school, based on a sample of African American parents (Caughy, O'Campo, Randolph, & Nickerson, 2002). It is quite likely that self-regulatory behaviors play a role in such models, suggesting a strengths-based approach to intervention that acknowledges the exosystem and its indirect effect on children.

Nationally, the quality of early childhood environments is not sufficiently high to offer the provisions necessary for young children to engage and to learn optimally (La Paro et al., 2009). Thus, these environments require intervention to improve skills during a sensitive period of children's development. Descriptive research on early school settings exposes specific challenges that need to be addressed to improve school contexts. Progress requires enhancing the quality of adult interaction in early childhood directly and strengthening the supports available to caregiving adults, so that they are better able to meet the social, emotional, and instructional needs of young children.

Noting key limitations in current research is critical to next steps designed to improve children's self-regulatory efforts. The three listed here are illustrative. First, current measures of self-regulation and engagement serve as only coarse proxies for patterns of neural activation and physiological processes that are difficult to measure in classroom contexts. As a result, we have much to learn about how children's internal motivational and self-regulatory states show moment-to-moment correspondence to their parents' behavior at home or their teachers' behaviors in early classroom contexts. At present, the scientific understanding of self-regulatory behaviors in context is constrained by existing methods. Direct assessments of children's self-regulatory abilities, observed child engagement and participation in early childhood classrooms, and teachers' report of self-regulatory skills each offer a different lens on the development of self-regulation (Konold & Pianta, 2007; Mashburn, Hamre, Downer, & Pianta, 2006). Second, developmental science offers new statistical methods for analyzing children's growth and development that have not yet been fully applied to the study of self-regulation. New approaches to growth curve modeling can be used to model fluctuations in children's self-regulatory abilities over time (Nesselroade & Ram, 2004). Person-oriented rather than variable-oriented approaches to data analysis may help to examine the ways children's self-regulatory abilities are context-specific (to home, school, or peer) and may generate guidelines to individualize interventions (Denham & Brown, 2010). Autoregressive structural equation models offer effective means for modeling of the dialectical transactions between children's characteristics and the behaviors of their socializing agents, resulting in the detection of evocative genetic effects (Eisenberg, Vidmar, et al., 2010). Third, and perhaps most importantly, the contribution of self-regulatory abilities cannot be overstated. Self-regulation appears to be one important mechanism predicting children's academic and social outcomes in studies examining naturally occurring variation (Ponitz, Rimm-Kaufman, Grimm, et al., 2009), as well as interventions (Raver et al., 2011). However, existing work often points to "partial mediation" and, clearly, much of the child-level variance in predicting outcomes is accounted for by other, unmeasured constructs besides children's self-regulatory abilities that have yet to be determined (Raver et al., 2011).

The development of self-regulatory ability in early childhood stands as a malleable factor that can be enhanced. The Obama administration has prioritized early childhood programming by its explicit support for high-quality teachers of young children in schools with high need, continued use of Title I funds for high-quality preschools, commitment to evidence-based practices in early childhood, and recognition that the achievement gap that exists upon school entry starts at birth (see U.S. Department of Education & Office of Planning Evaluation and Policy Development, 2010). Incorporating evidence-based practices that address children's self-regulatory skills holds promise for improving children's early childhood experiences and better preparing them for school and life. An even more aggressive tactic would be to broaden accountability standards for schools to include children's socioemotional outcomes (e.g., ability to exhibit self-control, engage in learning, follow directions) as a metric of school success. Efforts focused on children's self-regulatory abilities based on developmental theory and contemporary research in early childhood education hold promise for building skills that serve as a foundation for social and academic performance.

References

Baker, J. A., Grant, S., & Morlock, L. (2008). The teacher–student relationship as a developmental context for children with internalizing or externalizing behavior problems. *School Psychology Quarterly, 23*, 3–15.

Barnett, W. S., Jung, K., Yarosz, D. J., Thomas, J., Hornbeck, A., Stechuk, R., et al. (2008). Educational effects of the Tools of the Mind curriculum: A randomized trial. *Early Childhood Research Quarterly, 23*, 299–313.

Battistich, V., Schaps, E., & Wilson, N. (2004). Effects of an elementary school intervention on students' "connectedness" to school and social adjustment during middle school. *Journal of Primary Prevention, 24*, 243–262.

Bialystok, E. (1999). Cognitive complexity and attentional control in the bilingual mind. *Child Development, 70*, 636–644.

Bialystok, E., & Craik, F. I. M. (2010). Cognitive and linguistic processing in the bilingual mind. *Current Directions in Psychological Science, 19,* 19–23.

Bialystok, E., & Martin, M. M. (2004). Attention and inhibition in bilingual children: Evidence from the dimensional change card sort task. *Developmental Science, 7,* 325–339.

Bialystok, E., & Viswanathan, M. (2009). Components of executive control with advantages for bilingual children in two cultures. *Cognition, 112,* 494–500.

Bierman, K. L., Domitrovich, C. E., Nix, R. L., Gest, S. D., Welsh, J. A., Greenberg, M. T., et al. (2008). Promoting academic and social emotional school readiness: The Head Start REDI program. *Child Development, 79,* 1802–1817.

Bierman, K. L., Nix, R. L., Greenberg, M. T., Blair, C., & Domitrovich, C. E. (2008). Executive functions and school readiness intervention: Impact, moderation, and mediation in the Head Start REDI program. *Development and Psychopathology, 20,* 821–843.

Birch, S. H., & Ladd, G. W. (1997). The teacher–child relationship and children's early school adjustment. *Journal of School Psychology, 35,* 61–79.

Blair, C. (2002). School readiness: Integrating cognition and emotion in a neurobiological conceptualization of children's functioning at school entry. *American Psychologist, 57,* 111–127.

Blair, C., & Razza, R. P. (2007). Relating effortful control, executive function, and false belief understanding to emerging math and literacy ability in kindergarten. *Child Development, 78,* 647–663.

Bodrova, E., & Leong, D. J. (1996). *Tools of the Mind: The Vygotskian approach to early childhood education.* Englewood Cliffs, NJ: Merrill.

Bogner, K., Raphael, L., & Pressley, M. (2002). How grade 1 teachers motivate literate activity by their students. *Scientific Studies of Reading, 6,* 135–165.

Bohn, C. M., Roehrig, A. D., & Pressley, M. (2004). The first days of school in the classrooms of two more effective and four less effective primary-grades teachers. *Elementary School Journal, 104,* 269–287.

Borman, G. D., & Overman, L. T. (2004). Academic resilience in math among poor and minority students. *Elementary School Journal, 104,* 177–195.

Bornstein, M. H. (1989). Sensitive periods in development: Structural characteristics and causal interpretations. *Psychological Bulletin, 105,* 179–197.

Bradley, R. H., & Corwyn, R. F. (2005). Caring for children around the world: A view from HOME. *International Journal of Behavioral Development, 29,* 468–478.

Bradley, R. H., Corwyn, R. F., Burchinal, M., McAdoo, H. P., & García Coll, C. (2001). The home environments of children in the United States: Part II. Relations with behavioral development through age thirteen. *Child Development, 72,* 1868–1886.

Brock, L. L., Rimm-Kaufman, S. E., Nathanson, L., & Grimm, K. J. (2009). The contributions of "Hot" and "Cool" executive function to children's academic achievement, learning-related behaviors, and engagement in kindergarten. *Early Childhood Research Quarterly, 24,* 337–349.

Brody, G. H., & Flor, D. L. (1998). Maternal resources, parenting practices, and child competence in rural, single-parent African American families. *Child Development, 69,* 803–816.

Bronfenbrenner, U. (1979). *The ecology of human development: Experiments by nature and design.* Cambridge, MA: Harvard University Press.

Bronfenbrenner, U., & Morris, P. A. (2006). The bioecological model of human development. In R. M. Lerner (Ed.), *Theoretical models of human development* (6th ed., Vol. 1, pp. 793–828). Hoboken, NJ: Wiley.

Bronson, M. B. (2001). *Self-regulation in early childhood: Nature and nurture.* New York: Guilford Press.

Brooks-Gunn, J., & Markman, L. B. (2005). The contribution of parenting to ethnic and racial gaps in school readiness. *The Future of Children, 15,* 139–168.

Brown, B., Weitzman, M., Bzostek, S., Kavanaugh, M., Aufseeser, D., Bagley, S., et al. (2004). *Early child development in social context: A chartbook.* New York: Commonwealth Fund.

Bush, G., Luu, P., & Posner, M. I. (2000). Cognitive and emotional influences in anterior cingulate cortex. *Trends in Cognitive Sciences, 4,* 215–222.

Cameron, C. E., Connor, C. M., Morrison, F. J., & Jewkes, A. M. (2008). Effects of classroom organization on letter–word reading in first grade. *Journal of School Psychology, 46,* 173–192.

Carlson, S. M., & Meltzoff, A. N. (2008). Bilingual experience and executive functioning in young children. *Developmental Science, 11,* 282–298.

Caughy, M. O. B., O'Campo, P. J., Randolph, S. M., & Nickerson, K. (2002). The influence of racial socialization practices on the cognitive and behavioral competence of African American preschoolers. *Child Development, 73,* 1611–1625.

Christian, K., Morrison, F. J., & Bryant, F. B. (1998). Predicting kindergarten academic skills: Interactions among child care, maternal education, and family literacy environments. *Early Childhood Research Quarterly, 13,* 501–521.

Ciairano, S., Visu-Petra, L., & Settanni, M. (2007). Executive inhibitory control and cooperative behavior during early school years: A follow-up study. *Journal of Abnormal Child Psychology, 35,* 335–345.

Clark, C. A. C., Pritchard, V. E., & Woodward, L. J. (2010). Preschool executive functioning abilities predict early mathematics achievement. *Developmental Psychology, 46,* 1176–1191.

Conduct Problems Prevention Research Group. (2010). Fast Track intervention effects on youth arrests and delinquency. *Journal of Experimental Criminology, 6,* 131–157.

Conger, R. D., Wallace, L. E., Sun, Y., Simons, R. L., McLoyd, V. C., & Brody, G. H. (2002). Economic pressure in African American families: A replication and extension of the family stress model. *Developmental Psychology, 38,* 179–193.

Connor, C. M., Morrison, F. J., Fishman, B. J., Schatschneider, C., & Underwood, P. (2007). The early years: Algorithm-guided individualized reading instruction. *Science, 315,* 464–465.

Connor, C. M., Ponitz, C. C., Phillips, B. M., Travis, Q., Glasney, S., & Morrison, F. J. (2010). First graders' literacy and self-regulation gains: The effect of individualizing student instruction. *Journal of School Psychology, 48,* 433–455.

Corno, L. (2008). On teaching adaptively. *Educational Psychologist, 43,* 161–173.

Curby, T. W., Rimm-Kaufman, S. E., & Ponitz, C. C. (2009). Teacher–child interactions and children's achievement trajectories across kindergarten and first grade. *Journal of Educational Psychology, 101,* 912–925.

Deater Deckard, K., & Petrill, S. A. (2004). Parent–child dyadic mutuality and child behavior problems: An investigation of gene–environment processes. *Journal of Child Psychology and Psychiatry, 45,* 1171–1179.

Denham, S. A., & Brown, C. (2010). "Plays nice with others": Social–emotional learning and academic success. *Early Education and Development, 21,* 652–680.

Diamond, A., Barnett, W. S., Thomas, J., & Munro, S. (2007). Preschool program improves cognitive control. *Science, 318,* 1387–1388.

Diamond, A., Kirkham, N., & Amso, D. (2002). Conditions under which young children can hold two rules in mind and inhibit a prepotent response. *Developmental Psychology, 38,* 352–362.

Dolezal, S. E., Welsh, L. M., Pressley, M., & Vincent, M. M. (2003). How nine third-grade teachers motivate student academic engagement. *Elementary School Journal, 103,* 239–267.

Domitrovich, C. E., Gest, S. D., Gill, S., Bierman, K. L., Welsh, J. A., & Jones, D. (2009). Fostering high-quality teaching with an enriched curriculum and professional development support: The Head Start REDI program. *American Educational Research Journal, 46,* 567–597.

Downer, J. T., Rimm-Kaufman, S. E., & Pianta, R. C. (2007). How do classroom conditions and children's risk for school problems contribute to children's behavioral engagement in learning? *School Psychology Review, 36,* 413–432.

Duncan, G. J., Dowsett, C. J., Claessens, A., Magnuson, K., Huston, A. C., Klebanov, P., et al. (2007). School readiness and later achievement. *Developmental Psychology, 43,* 1428–1446.

Early, D. M., Iruka, I. U., Ritchie, S., Barbarin, O. A., Winn, D. M. C., Crawford, G. M., et al. (2010). How do pre-kindergarteners spend their time?: Gender, ethnicity, and income as predictors of experiences in pre-kindergarten classrooms. *Early Childhood Research Quarterly, 25,* 177–193.

Eisenberg, N., Valiente, C., & Eggum, N. D. (2010). Self-regulation and school readiness. *Early Education and Development, 21,* 681–698.

Eisenberg, N., Vidmar, M., Spinrad, T. L., Eggum, N. D., Edwards, A., Gaertner, B., et al. (2010). Mothers' teaching strategies and children's effortful control: A longitudinal study. *Developmental Psychology, 46,* 1294–1308.

Emmorey, K., Luk, G., Pyers, J. E., & Bialystok, E. (2008). The source of enhanced cognitive control in bilinguals: Evidence from bimodal bilinguals. *Psychological Science, 19,* 1201–1206.

Englert, C. S., Raphael, T. E., Anderson, L. M., Anthony, H. M., & Stevens, D. D. (1991). Making strategies and self-talk visible: Writing instruction in regular and special education classrooms. *American Educational Research Journal, 28,* 337–372.

Entwisle, D. R., & Alexander, K. L. (1993). Entry into school: The beginning school transition and educational stratification in the United States. *Annual Review of Sociology, 19,* 401–423.

Evans, G. W., & Rosenbaum, J. (2008). Self-regulation and the income-achievement gap. *Early Childhood Research Quarterly, 23,* 504–514.

Fantuzzo, J., McWayne, C., Perry, M. A., & Childs, S. (2004). Multiple dimensions of family involvement and their relations to behavioral and learning competencies for urban, low-income children. *School Psychology Review, 33,* 467–481.

Fantuzzo, J., Perry, M. A., & McDermott, P. (2004). Preschool approaches to learning and their relationship to other relevant classroom competencies for low-income children. *School Psychology Quarterly, 19,* 212–230.

Fantuzzo, J., Sekino, Y., & Cohen, H. L. (2004). An examination of the contributions of interactive peer play to salient classroom competencies for urban Head Start children. *Psychology in the Schools, 41,* 323–336.

Finn, J. D., & Pannozzo, G. M. (2004). Classroom organization and student behavior in kindergarten. *Journal of Educational Research, 98,* 79–92.

Fox, S. E., Levitt, P., & Nelson, C. A., III. (2010). How the timing and quality of early experiences influence the development of brain architecture. *Child Development, 81,* 28–40.

Glaser, D. (2000). Child abuse and neglect and the brain—a review. *Journal of Child Psychology and Psychiatry, 41,* 97–116.

Greenwood, C. R. (1991). Longitudinal analysis of time, engagement, and achievement in at-risk versus non-risk students. *Exceptional Children, 57,* 521–534.

Grolnick, W. S., & Ryan, R. M. (1989). Parent styles associated with children's self-regulation and competence in school. *Journal of Educational Psychology, 81,* 143–154.

Halgunseth, L. C., Ispa, J. M., & Rudy, D. (2006). Parental control in Latino families: An integrated review of the literature. *Child Development, 77,* 1282–1297.

Hamre, B. K., & Pianta, R. C. (2001). Early teacher–child relationships and the trajectory of children's school outcomes through eighth grade. *Child Development, 72,* 625–638.

Hamre, B. K., Pianta, R. C., Mashburn, A. J., & Downer, J. T. (2007). Building a science of classrooms: Application of the CLASS framework in over 4,000 US early childhood and elementary classrooms. Retrieved from *www.icpsr.umich.edu/files/prek3rd/resources/pdf/buildingascienceofclassroomspiantahamre.pdf.*

Harrist, A. W., & Waugh, R. M. (2002). Dyadic synchrony: Its structure and function in children's development. *Developmental Review, 22,* 555–592.

Heckman, J. J. (2006). Skill formation and the economics of investing in disadvantaged children. *Science, 312,* 1900–1901.

Hinde, R. A. (1975). *Biological bases of human social behaviour.* New York: McGraw-Hill.

Houts, R. M., Caspi, A., Pianta, R. C., Arseneault, L., & Moffitt, T. E. (2010). The challenging pupil in the classroom. *Psychological Science, 21,* 1802–1810.

Howse, R. B., Calkins, S. D., Anastopoulos, A. D., Keane, S., P., & Shelton, T. L. (2003). Regulatory contributors to children's kindergarten achievement. *Early Education and Development, 14,* 101–119.

Howse, R. B., Lange, G., Farran, D. C., & Boyles, C. D. (2003). Motivation and self-regulation as predictors of achievement in economically disadvantaged young children. *Journal of Experimental Education, 71,* 151–174.

Hsieh, M.-F. (2004). Teaching practices in Taiwan's education for young children: Complexity and ambiguity of developmentally appropriate practices and/or developmentally inappropriate practices. *Contemporary Issues in Early Childhood, 5,* 309–329.

Hughes, C., & Ensor, R. (2008). Does executive function matter for preschoolers' problem behaviors? *Journal of Abnormal Child Psychology, 36,* 1–14.

Hughes, C., Graham, A., & Grayson, A. (2004). Executive functions in childhood: Development and disorder. In J. Oates & A. Grayson (Eds.), *Cognitive and language development in children* (pp. 206–230). Oxford, UK: Blackwell.

Hughes, J. N., Luo, W., Kwok, O. M., & Loyd, L. K. (2008). Teacher–student support, effortful engagement, and achievement: A 3-year longitudinal study. *Journal of Educational Psychology, 100,* 1–14.

Huttenlocher, P. R. (2002). *Neural plasticity: The effects of environment on the development of the cerebral cortex.* Cambridge, MA: Harvard University Press.

Kishiyama, M. M., Boyce, W. T., Jimenez, A. M., Perry, L. M., & Knight, R. T. (2009). Socioeconomic disparities affect prefrontal function in children. *Journal of Cognitive Neuroscience, 21,* 1106–1115.

Klem, A. M., & Connell, J. P. (2004). Relationships matter: Linking teacher support to student engagement and achievement. *Journal of School Health, 74,* 262–273.

Kochanska, G., & Knaack, A. (2003). Effortful control as a personality characteristic of young children: Antecedents, correlates, and consequences. *Journal of Personality, 71,* 1087–1112.

Kodituwakku, P., Handmaker, N., Cutler, S., Weathersby, E., & Handmaker, S. (1995). Specific impairments in self regulation in children exposed to alcohol prenatally. *Alcoholism: Clinical and Experimental Research, 19,* 1558–1564.

Konold, T. R., & Pianta, R. C. (2007). The influence of informants on ratings of children's behavioral functioning. *Journal of Psychoeducational Assessment, 25,* 222–236.

Kopp, C. B. (1982). Antecedents of self-regulation: A developmental perspective. *Developmental Psychology, 18,* 199–214.

Ladd, G. W., & Dinella, L. M. (2009). Continuity and change in early school engagement: Predictive of children's achievement trajectories from first to eighth grade? *Journal of Educational Psychology, 101,* 190–206.

La Paro, K., Hamre, B. K., LoCasale-Crouch, J., Pianta, R. C., Bryant, D., Early, D., et al. (2009). Quality in kindergarten classrooms: Observational evidence for the need to increase children's learning opportunities in early education classrooms. *Early Education and Development, 20,* 657–692.

Lengua, L. J., & Kovacs, E. A. (2005). Bidirectional associations between temperament and parenting and the prediction of adjustment problems in middle childhood. *Journal of Applied Developmental Psychology, 26,* 21–38.

Liew, J., Chen, Q., & Hughes, J. N. (2010). Child effortful control, teacher–student relationships, and achievement in academically at-risk children: Additive and interactive effects. *Early Childhood Research Quarterly, 25,* 51–64.

Lisonbee, J. A., Pendry, P., Mize, J., & Gwynn, E. P. (2010). Hypothalamic–pituitary–adrenal and sympathetic nervous system activity and children's behavioral regulation. *Mind, Brain, and Education, 4,* 171–181.

Mashburn, A. J., Hamre, B. K., Downer, J. T., & Pianta, R. C. (2006). Teacher and classroom characteristics associated with teachers' ratings of prekindergarteners: Relationships and behaviors. *Journal of Psychoeducational Assessment, 24,* 367–380.

Mashburn, A. J., Pianta, R. C., Hamre, B. K., Downer, J. T., Barbarin, O., Bryant, D. M., et al. (2008). Measures of classroom quality in pre-kindergarten and children's development of academic, language, and social skills. *Child Development, 79,* 732–749.

McClelland, M. M., Cameron, C. E., Connor, C. M., Farris, C. L., Jewkes, A. M., & Morrison, F. J. (2007). Links between behavioral regulation and preschoolers' literacy, vocabulary, and math skills. *Developmental Psychology, 43,* 947–959.

McClelland, M. M., Cameron, C. E., Wanless, S. B., & Murray, A. (2007). Executive function, self-regulation, and social-emotional competence: Links to school readiness. In O. N. Saracho & B. Spodek (Eds.), *Contemporary perspectives on research in social learning in early childhood education* (pp. 83–107). Charlotte, NC: Information Age.

McLoyd, V. C. (1998). Socioeconomic disadvantage and child development. *American Psychologist, 53*, 185–204.

McWilliam, R. A., Scarborough, A. A., & Kim, H. (2003). Adult interactions and child engagement. *Early Education and Development, 14*, 7–27.

Merritt, E. G., Wanless, S. B., Ponitz, C. C., & Rimm-Kaufman, S. E. (in press). The contribution of emotional support to social behaviors in first grade. *School Psychology Review.*

Mezzacappa, E. (2004). Alerting, orienting, and executive attention: Developmental and sociodemographic properties in an epidemiological sample of young, urban children. *Child Development, 75*, 1373–1386.

Mistry, R. S., Benner, A. D., Biesanz, J., & Clark, S. (2011). Family and social risk and parental investments during the early childhood years as predictors of low-income children's school readiness outcomes. *Early Childhood Research Quarterly, 25*, 432–449.

Moffitt, T. E., Arseneault, L., Belsky, D., Dickson, N., Hancox, R. J., Harrington, H. L., et al. (2011). A gradient of childhood self-control predicts health, wealth, and public safety. *Proceedings of the National Academy of Sciences, 108*, 2693–2698.

Nesselroade, J. R., & Ram, N. (2004). Studying intraindividual variability: What we have learned that will help us understand lives in context. *Research in Human Development, 1*, 9–29.

National Institute of Child Health and Human Development (NICHD) Early Child Care Research Network. (2002). The relation of global first grade classroom environment to structural classroom features and teacher and student behaviors. *Elementary School Journal, 102*, 367–387.

NICHD Early Child Care Research Network. (2003). Do children's attention processes mediate the link between family predictors and school readiness? *Developmental Psychology, 39*, 581–593.

NICHD Early Child Care Research Network. (2005). A day in third grade: A large-scale study of classroom quality and teacher and student behavior. *Elementary School Journal, 105*, 305–323.

Pang, Y., & Richey, D. (2007). Preschool education in China and the United States: A personal perspective. *Early Child Development and Care, 177*, 1–13.

Pianta, R. C. (1999). *Enhancing relationships between children and teachers.* Washington, DC: American Psychological Association.

Pianta, R. C. (2006). Schools, schooling, and developmental psychopathology. In D. Cicchetti & D. Cohen (Eds.), *Handbook of developmental psychopathology: Vol. 1. Theory and method* (2nd ed., pp. 494–529). Hoboken, NJ: Wiley.

Pianta, R. C., Cox, M. J., & Snow, K. L. B. (2007). *School readiness and the transition to kindergarten in the era of accountability.* Baltimore: Brookes.

Pianta, R. C., La Paro, K. M., Payne, C., Cox, M. J., & Bradley, R. (2002). The relation of kindergarten classroom environment to teacher, family, and school characteristics and child outcomes. *Elementary School Journal, 102*, 225–238.

Ponitz, C. C., McClelland, M. M., Jewkes, A. M., Connor, C. M., Farris, C. L., & Morrison, F. J. (2008). Touch your toes!: Developing a direct measure of behavioral regulation in early childhood. *Early Childhood Research Quarterly, 23*, 141–158.

Ponitz, C. C., McClelland, M. M., Matthews, J. S., & Morrison, F. J. (2009). A structured observation of behavioral self-regulation and its contribution to kindergarten outcomes. *Developmental Psychology, 45*, 605–619.

Ponitz, C. C., Rimm-Kaufman, S. E., Brock, L. L., & Nathanson, L. (2009). Early adjustment, gender differences, and classroom organizational climate in first grade. *Elementary School Journal, 110*, 142–162.

Ponitz, C. C., Rimm-Kaufman, S. E., Grimm, K. J., & Curby, T. W. (2009). Kindergarten classroom quality, behavioral engagement, and reading achievement. *School Psychology Review, 38*, 102–120.

Raver, C. C. (2002). *Emotional matter: Making the case for the role of young children's emotional development for early school readiness* (Social policy reports). Ann Arbor, MI: Society for Research in Child Development.

Raver, C. C., Jones, S. M., Li Grining, C., Zhai, F., Bub, K., & Pressler, E. (2011). CSRP's impact on low income preschoolers' preacademic skills: Self regulation as a mediating mechanism. *Child Development, 82,* 362–378.

Ready, D. D., LoGerfo, L. F., Burkam, D. T., & Lee, V. E. (2005). Explaining girls' advantage in kindergarten literacy learning: Do classroom behaviors make a difference? *Elementary School Journal, 106,* 21–38.

Rimm-Kaufman, S. E., Curby, T. W., Grimm, K., Nathanson, L., & Brock, L. L. (2009). The contribution of children's self-regulation and classroom quality to children's adaptive behaviors in the kindergarten classroom. *Developmental Psychology, 45,* 958–972.

Rimm-Kaufman, S. E., Early, D. M., Cox, M. J., Saluja, G., Pianta, R. C., Bradley, R. H., et al. (2002). Early behavioral attributes and teachers' sensitivity as predictors of competent behavior in the kindergarten classroom. *Applied Developmental Psychology, 23,* 451–470.

Rimm-Kaufman, S. E., & Kagan, J. (2005). Infant predictors of kindergarten behavior: The contribution of inhibited and uninhibited temperament types. *Behavioral Disorders, 30,* 331–347.

Rimm-Kaufman, S. E., & Pianta, R. C. (2000). An ecological perspective on the transition to kindergarten: A theoretical framework to guide empirical research. *Journal of Applied Developmental Psychology, 21,* 491–511.

Rouse, H. L., & Fantuzzo, J. W. (2009). Multiple risks and educational well-being: A population-based investigation of threats to early school success. *Early Childhood Research Quarterly, 24,* 1–14.

Rudasill, K. M., & Rimm-Kaufman, S. E. (2009). Teacher–child relationship quality: The roles of child temperament and teacher–child interactions. *Early Childhood Research Quarterly, 24,* 107–120.

Sameroff, A. (2010). A unified theory of development: A dialectic integration of nature and nurture. *Child Development, 81,* 6–22.

Sektnan, M., McClelland, M. M., Acock, A. C., & Morrison, F. J. (2010). Relations between early family risk, children's behavioral regulation, and academic achievement. *Early Childhood Research Quarterly, 25,* 464–479.

Shweder, R. A., Goodnow, J., Hatano, G., LeVine, R. A., Markus, H., & Miller, P. (1998). The cultural psychology of development: One mind, many mentalities. In R. M. Lerner (Ed.), *Handbook of child psychology: Vol. 1. Theoretical models of human development* (5th ed., pp. 865–937). New York: Wiley.

Tapia, M. R. (1992). Motivational orientations, learning, and the Puerto Rican child. In A. N. Ambert & M. D. Alvarez (Eds.), *Puerto Rican children on the mainland* (pp. 109–131). New York: Garland.

Thompson, R. A. (1994). Emotional regulation: A theme in search of definition. *Monographs of the Society for Research in Child Development, 59*(Serial No. 240), pp. 25–52.

Trueba, H. T. (1991). From failure to success: The roles of culture and cultural conflict in the academic achievement of Chicano students. In R. R. Valencia (Ed.), *Chicago school failure and success: Research and policy agendas for the 1990s* (pp. 151–163). Bristol, PA: Falmer Press.

Tsujimoto, S. (2008). The prefrontal cortex: Functional neural development during early childhood. *Neuroscientist, 14,* 345–358.

U.S. Department of Education & Office of Planning Evaluation and Policy Development. (2010, March). ESEA blueprint for reform. Retrieved from *www2.ed.gov/policy/elsec/leg/blueprint/blueprint.pdf.*

Vazsonyi, A., & Huang, L. (2010). Where self-control comes from: On the development of self-control and its relationship to deviance over time. *Developmental Psychology, 46,* 245–257.

Wachs, T. D., Gurkas, P., & Kontos, S. (2004). Predictors of preschool children's compliance behavior in early childhood classroom settings. *Journal of Applied Developmental Psychology, 25,* 439–457.

Wanless, S. B., McClelland, M., Acock, A., Ponitz, C. C., Son, S., Lan, X., et al. (2011). Measuring behavioral regulation in four societies. *Psychological Assessment, 23*(2), 364–378.

Wanless, S. B., McClelland, M. M., Tominey, S., & Acock, A. C. (2011). The influence of demographic risk factors on children's behavioral regulation in prekindergarten and kindergarten. *Early Education and Development, 22,* 461–488.

Wasserman, G. A., Rauh, V. A., Brunelli, S. A., Garcia-Castro, M., & Necos, B. (1990). Psychosocial attributes and life experiences of disadvantaged minority mothers: Age and ethnic variations. *Child Development, 61,* 566–580.

Wiebe, S. A., Espy, K. A., Stopp, C., Respass, J., Stewart, P., Jameson, T. R., et al. (2009). Gene–environment interactions across development: Exploring DRD2 genotype and prenatal smoking effects on self-regulation. *Developmental Psychology, 45,* 31–44.

Willingham, D. T., & Lloyd, J. W. (2007). How educational theories can use neuroscientific data. *Mind, Brain, and Education, 1,* 140–149.

Winsler, A., Fernyhough, C., & Montero, I. (2009). *Private speech, executive functioning, and the development of verbal self-regulation.* Cambridge, MA: Cambridge University Press.

Worzalla, S. L., Hindman, A. H., Bowles, R. P., & Morrison, F. J. (2011). *The contributions of parent management language to self-regulation in preschool children.* Manuscript submitted for publication.

Yates, T. M., Obradović, J., & Egeland, B. (2010). Transactional relations across contextual strain, parenting quality, and early childhood regulation and adaptation in a high-risk sample. *Development and Psychopathology, 22,* 539–555.

CHAPTER 16

Executive Functioning and Developmental Neuroscience

Current Progress and Implications for Early Childhood Education

Jelena Obradović, Ximena A. Portilla, and W. Thomas Boyce

Learning to self-regulate attention and behavior is one of the major developmental milestones of childhood, with substantial implications for educational opportunity and achievement. Initially, parents play an essential role in directing infants' and toddlers' attention and helping them inhibit impulsive, inappropriate, or dangerous behaviors. Out of this dyadic, parent–child coregulation, children develop a set of self-regulating abilities that enables them to function independently as they transition into school contexts. As children mature, they learn to focus attention on teacher-presented lessons, ignore distractions, wait for their turn in games and classroom activities, remember steps for solving math problems, and flexibly shift between different roles in pretend-play scenarios. These basic self-regulatory skills known as executive functions (EFs) are directly implicated in children's school readiness and in the subsequent achievement of academic and social competence. In recent years, EF research has surged forward, fueled by conceptual and technical advances in developmental and cognitive neuroscience. The purpose of this chapter is to provide an overview of the growing literature and its implications for researchers, educators, and policymakers. The chapter is divided into four sections addressing (1) the definition, structure, and measurement of EF components; (2) the importance of EFs for academic and social skills; (3) environmental influences on EFs; and (4) interventions designed to improve EFs.

Definition, Structure, and Measurement

EFs comprise a set of higher-order cognitive skills that fall under the broad conceptual rubric of self-regulatory abilities. Although researchers differ in their views of EF structure, which range from unitary to componential (see Garon, Bryson, & Smith, 2008, for a review of the differing perspectives), factor-analytic procedures corroborate the assertion that EFs consist of functionally distinct yet related sets of skills (Carlson & Moses, 2001; Lehto, Juujarvi, Kooistra, & Pulkkinen, 2003; Miyake et al., 2000). There is a growing consensus that *inhibitory control, working memory,* and *cognitive flexibility* constitute three major EF components.

Inhibitory control (IC) refers to a child's ability to suppress impulsive thoughts or behaviors and resist distractions and temptations. These impulses are often referred to as "prepotent" or "dominant" responses and can be motoric (e.g., reaching out for a desired object), verbal (e.g., blurting out a wrong answer), or oculomotoric (e.g., looking in the direction of a distracting stimulus). Basic response inhibition is present in infants, who can obey adult prohibitions and suppress perseverating actions with increasing success as they age (Diamond, 2006). Although 2-year-olds can successfully delay or withhold some prepotent responses, the ability to exercise IC according to complex rules emerges toward the end of the third year of life and develops rapidly in preschoolers (Carlson, 2005; Garon et al., 2008; Kochanska, Murray, & Harlan, 2000). IC is assessed using laboratory tasks that require various degrees of response inhibition. Go/no-go tasks measure children's ability to activate a certain behavior (e.g., press a button, move a body part) in response to "go" stimuli, while inhibiting the same behavior in response to "no-go" stimuli. For example, in the bear and dragon task, children are instructed to perform actions ordered by a bear puppet but to ignore orders from a dragon puppet (Carlson, 2005). IC also represents the ability to monitor interference and resolve conflicts between incongruent information. For example, in a child version of the Stroop task, children perform congruent trials by pointing to the picture of an animal that matches the sound played (i.e., hear meow, point to a cat) and perform incongruent trials by pointing to the picture of an animal that does not match the sound (i.e., hear meow, point to a dog) (Berger, Jones, Rothbart, & Posner, 2000). The incongruent trials thus require children to resolve a conflict between a familiar rule and a new rule that is contrary to the expected. Similarly, in a version of the flanker task, children are instructed to focus attention on the orientation of a central stimulus (e.g., feed the middle fish by pressing the button that corresponds with the direction the fish faces), while suppressing attention to distracting flankers that surround the central stimuli (e.g., ignore the orientation of adjacent fish) (Rueda et al., 2004). In congruent trials, the flanker fish point in the same direction as the central fish, but in incongruent trials they point in the opposite direction. The efficiency of IC in these laboratory tasks is indexed by the number of errors children make, or by the difference in reaction time between congruent and incongruent trials.

Although most IC tasks used by researchers employ neutral stimuli, some tasks have been designed to measure children's ability to delay or withhold a dominant response in the context of reward (e.g., candy, gift). In one classic delay-of-gratification task, children are offered the choice between taking a small reward immediately (a piece of candy) or waiting for a larger reward (more candy) (Mischel, Shoda, & Rodriguez, 1989). Similarly, in a gift delay task, children are left alone for a period of time and instructed not to peek at a gift they are told they will receive (Kochanska, Murray, & Coy, 1997). These "hot" tasks, as opposed to emotionally neutral "cold" tasks, also involve inhibition of proponent tendencies; however, neuroscience research indicates that different brain circuitry is involved in the inhibition of emotionally laden stimuli (Bush, Luu, & Posner, 2000). By examining performance on hot tasks, researchers shed some light on the role EFs play in emotion regulation. It is unclear, though, whether successful performance on hot tasks indicates less emotional arousal in the first place or better emotion regulation skills. In EF literature, emotions have primarily been conceptualized as sources of conflict that children must overcome and control using EF skills (Blair & Diamond, 2008). Future research needs to examine the transactional interplay between EF skills and various sources of positive and negative emotions. As Blair and

Diamond (2008) note, "Emotions both organize and are organized by cognitive control," and the "optimal relation between processes of emotionality and processes of cognitive control is one of balance and mutual reinforcement" (p. 904). Thus, researchers need to identify optimal levels of psychological and physiological arousal that promote rather than hinder EFs, as well as to examine how arousal and EFs interact to influence adaptive functioning.

Working memory (WM) refers to a child's ability to hold, update, and manipulate verbal or nonverbal information in the mind over short periods of time. Infants can briefly retain a single item or perform simple two-step procedures, but the capacity to hold and manipulate multiple units of information in the mind emerges in preschool children and continues to develop as children grow older (Diamond, 2006; Garon et al., 2008; Luciana, 2003). WM is assessed with laboratory tasks that measure children's accuracy at performing mental operations on an increasing number of items. In one version of the self-ordered pointing (SOP) task, children are asked to select an image from a group of pictures and keep that image in mind. In subsequent steps, they repeat this procedure with new groups of pictures, and each time they must select an image they have not previously selected (Luciana & Nelson, 1998). With each additional trial, the updating load as indexed by the number of previously selected images increases, compromising the child's accuracy in making new selections. In the backward digit span task, in which children must correctly manipulate a series of digits they hear by repeating the numbers backward, the number sequences grow longer with each trial (Casey, Trainor, Orendi, et al., 1997). To isolate children's ability to manipulate information from simple recall capacity, researchers frequently contrast performance on backward and forward digit span tasks, as indexed by number of errors and reaction time.

WM is frequently studied separately from other EF components, in part because it underlies and supports various cognitive abilities. Successful performance on most EF tasks requires some degree of WM, as children must keep in mind various complex task rules that guide their actions. In fact, WM is frequently used as a covariate when examining the effects of IC on achievement (e.g., Espy et al., 2004). Many studies of WM further differentiate the effects of two types of WM, the "phonological loop" and the "visuospatial sketch pad," involved in processing verbal and visuospatial information, respectively (for details, see Baddeley, 1986, 2003).

Cognitive flexibility (CF) refers to a child's ability to shift attention or responses between competing mental sets or rules. Switching between simple behavioral response strategies can be seen in older infants and in toddlers, but the ability to shift flexibly between complex rules and mental sets across different contexts requires good IC and WM skills and emerges later in preschool (Diamond, Carlson, & Beck, 2005; Garon et al., 2008). CF is assessed with tasks that establish one arbitrary rule, then introduce a second, opposing rule in order to measure the accuracy with which children can adjust their responses based on the second rule and avoid perseverating errors. For example, in the dimensional change card sort task (DCCS; Zelazo, 2006), children are taught first to play a "color game," placing all red cards in a box with a red rabbit and all blue cards in a box with a blue boat. After they learn the rules of the color game, they are asked to play a "shape game," placing all cards with blue or red rabbits in the box with the red rabbit and all cards with blue or red boats in the box with the blue boat. Performance is measured by the number of correctly sorted cards during the postswitch trials. More advanced CF skills can be assessed with tasks that rely on increasingly complex, hierarchically embedded sets of rules. One advanced version of the DCCS requires children to determine for each card whether to sort based on color or shape, depending on whether the card has a border or not (Zelazo, 2006). As with IC and WM, children's CF can be measured by the number of errors and the time needed to complete the task.

Tasks used to study EF in older children and adolescents often rely on all three types of EF skills, as they measure the individual's ability to make a plan, formulate strategy, and execute goal-oriented behaviors. For example, the Tower of London (TOL) task requires children to reposition a set of colored disks on three pegs in order to achieve a designated pattern using a limited number of moves. Success depends on the child's ability to inhibit impulsive moves, keep in mind the number of steps completed, and change strategy when the first strategy is not working. Despite growing research interest in EF, few studies have examined the development of EF skills in healthy children past early elementary school years (Best, Miller, & Jones, 2009). It is important to examine how the structure and function of these skills change with age and whether other skills contribute to performance on more complex tasks, above and beyond the contribution of the three core EF skills.

Terminology

With growing research interest in the role of EFs for children's development and adaptive functioning, the literature has been muddied by confounding terminology and overlapping constructs. Researchers have used terms such as *self-regulation, cognitive self-control, attentional control, effortful control, effortful attention, executive attention*, and *fluid cognition* to label constructs that include various EF components assessed via either laboratory tasks or questionnaires. Two terms in particular have been commonly used to describe skills that are conceptually analogous if not identical to EFs. *Executive attention* is a term used by Posner and colleagues to describe the functioning of the executive attention network, which supports abilities to monitor and resolve conflicting thoughts, feelings, and actions; to detect and correct errors; and to inhibit prepotent responses (Rueda, Posner, & Rothbart, 2005). Fundamentally, executive attention and IC are equivalent constructs assessed using the same neurocognitive tasks (e.g., flanker task; Rueda et al., 2004). Another frequently used term, *effortful control*, refers to a major temperamental control system that regulates children's genetically predisposed variability in emotional, behavioral, and attentional reactivity (Eisenberg, Smith, Sadovsky, & Spinrad, 2004; Rothbart, Posner, & Kieras, 2006). Although effortful control has frequently been defined as "the ability to inhibit a dominant response to perform a subdominant response" (Rothbart & Bates, 1998, p. 137)—a definition that is indistinguishable from IC—it is often measured by parent and teacher reports of behaviors in naturalistic settings that capture more than just basic IC skills. Moreover, in some earlier studies, indices of temperamental reactivity were composited with measures of effortful control behaviors, yielding a more powerful predictor but a less precise construct. On the other hand, the distinction between these constructs has been blurred by studies that employ EF laboratory tasks as more objective measures of effortful control (Kochanska et al., 2000; Obradović, 2010; Valiente et al., 2003). For the purposes of this review, we do not distinguish between studies employing EF versus effortful control terminology. We not only focus primarily on studies that rely on laboratory assessments because they provide more precise measures of distinct EF domains, but we also highlight important findings from a few studies that use adult report of EF behaviors. For a more detailed distinction between these and other similar terms, readers are encouraged to consult the insightful footnote in Diamond's (2010) commentary.

Neural Substrate

EFs are supported by the maturation and activation of the *prefrontal cortex* (PFC), a region of the brain that has a protracted period of development, extending from prenatal life through early adulthood (Casey, Giedd, & Thomas, 2000; Gogtay et al., 2004). Changes in the PFC occur dramatically over the course of early and middle childhood, supported by neurodevelopmental processes involving synaptogenesis (the early overproduction of points of contact and communication between neurons), pruning (the subsequent normative and systematic reduction of synapse numbers), and myelination (the formation of a lipid layer of insulation around neuronal axons, resulting in an increased conduction velocity of neural impulses). Synaptogenesis in the PFC peaks around 1 to 1.5 years of age, while pruning and myelination continue slowly through adolescence and up until about age 20 (Nelson & Jeste, 2009). Throughout early childhood, the PFC also changes structurally via increases in both white and grey matter, as well as proliferation of pyramidal cell dendritic trees (Tsujimoto, 2008). As with other areas where cortical function is associated with structural complexity and size, performance on tests of EF, such as response inhibition, is correlated with volumetric measures of PFC size (Casey, Trainor, Giedd, et al., 1997).

Neuroimaging studies have revealed specific subregions associated with different aspects of EFs (Fan, Flombaum, McCandliss, Thomas, & Posner, 2003; Farah et al., 2006). The *anterior cingulate cortex* (ACC) integrates information from different brain regions and supports monitoring and resolution of conflicting stimuli and responses. Performance on IC tasks (go/no-go and Stroop) has been linked to activation of the ACC (Adleman et al., 2002; Casey, Trainor, Orendi, et al., 1997). Specifically, the dorsal portion of the ACC is activated during "cool" or unemotional conflict tasks, whereas the ventral portion of the ACC is engaged during "hot" or emotionally laden tasks (Bush et al., 2000). The *ventromedial prefrontal cortex* is involved in processing and resisting reward stimuli, as in delay of gratification tasks (May et al., 2004). Particularly in regard to emotion regulatory functions, the *obitofrontal prefrontal cortex* has bidirectional linkages with limbic structures, such as the amygdala, and these linkages are implicated in the modulation of emotion and the regulation of stress hormones and neuroendocrine reactivity (Fisher, Gunnar, Dozier, Bruce, & Pears, 2006). The *lateral prefrontal cortex* supports processes such as the maintenance and use of complex rules and has been linked to performance on WM tasks (Casey et al., 1995; Thomas et al., 1999). Moreover, frontoparietal connectivity appears to underlie the development of WM, and the weaker links among PFC subregions may subserve the fractionated maturation of specific EFs (Tsujimoto, 2008). Finally, as in adults, children experiencing traumatic damage to the PFC sustain immediate and often lasting deficits in EF, including diminished WM and impairments in inhibitory control and attentional capacity (Nelson & Sheridan, 2011). For a more detailed account of how the different brain regions support EF components, see Zelazo, Carlson, and Kesek (2008). It is important to note that as performance on specific EF tasks has been linked to the activation of particular brain regions, most developmental researchers do not employ neuroimaging techniques when studying processes related to EFs, but use task performance as a proxy measure of neurocognitive systems (see Farah et al., 2006).

Developmental Course

Researchers hold differing views on how EF skills emerge in developing children (for details, see Garon et al., 2008; Zelazo et al., 2008). Some researchers argue that the development of EFs depends primarily on the strength of WM skills, which enable children to hold in mind a rule that is in conflict with prepotent or habitual responses (Munakata, 2001). Other researchers note that the ability to hold in mind a particular rule is a necessary but not sufficient condition, as the ability to resolve a conflict also requires a capacity to inhibit prepotent or perseverating tendencies (Diamond, Kirkham, & Amso, 2002). Yet others stress the importance of cognitive capacities that enable children to perceive multiple aspects of the same concept, such as color, shape, or size (Kloo & Perner, 2003), or to comprehend a hierarchically embedded sets of if–then rules (Zelazo, Mueller, Frye, & Marcovitch, 2003). The development of EFs also depends on children's ability to orient and sustain attention on a particular rule or task at hand (Rueda, Posner, et al., 2005).

Although developmental trajectories vary somewhat for the main EF components (Diamond, 2006), the general pattern includes significant improvement during early childhood between the ages of 3 and 6 (Carlson, 2005; Diamond, 2006). Rueda, Posner, and colleagues (2005) found that performance on a flanker task seemed to plateau after age 7, but other studies show improvements into middle childhood (Davidson, Amso, Anderson, & Diamond, 2006; Garon et al., 2008; Romine & Reynolds, 2005). Capacities to hold and manipulate larger numbers of items in WM and to shift between ever more complex sets of rules also increase linearly with age (Luciana & Nelson, 1998). As children become more accurate at switching between complex rules, initially their reaction times increase (Davidson et al., 2006; Huizinga, Dolan, & van der Molen, 2006; Huizinga & van der Molen, 2007). Similarly, the ability to detect and correct errors, which grows with age, is reflected in slower reaction times following an incorrect response (Jones, Rothbart, & Posner, 2003). This ability to self-correct is also revealed at the level of brain activation. Larger amplitudes on an event-related potential (ERP) component reflecting response monitoring (error-related negativity) have been linked to a lower error rate on incongruent trials (Santesso, Segalowitz, & Schmidt, 2006). As the number of errors that older children and adolescents make on incongruent trials plummets with development, individual differences in performance on EF task are best captured using variability in reaction times. Neuroimaging studies have shown that maturational improvements in behavioral measures of EFs parallel more focalized brain activation, more efficient neural activity, and increased connectivity of frontal brain regions (Durston et al., 2006; Lamm, Zelazo, & Lewis, 2006; Liston et al., 2006; Scherf, Sweeney, & Luna, 2006). There is a need for more longitudinal neuroimaging research differentiating how maturation and learning opportunities change the neural basis of EF skills over time. Such studies may shed more light on when and how deficit or delay in the development of EF skills causes maladaptive outcomes (Durston et al., 2006). Longitudinal work will be greatly aided by the creation of EF tasks that span multiple developmental periods (see *www.nihtoolbox.org*).

Implications of Executive Functioning for Academic and Social Competence

EFs have been linked to child development outcomes in a variety of areas, ranging from theory of mind to conscience (Carlson, Mandell, & Williams, 2004; Hughes & Ensor, 2007; Kochanska & Knaack, 2003). However, in this chapter we focus primarily on studies that demonstrate the significance of EFs for the development of early academic and social skills, the two domains of adjustment most relevant for early childhood educators and policymakers. Furthermore, we restrict our review to recent and representative studies of EF skills and adjustment in preschool and school-age children.

Academic Skills

In the last decade, studies examining the contribution of EFs for young children's attainment of fundamental academic skills, such as mathematical abilities, have proliferated (Andersson, 2007; Blair, Knipe, & Gamson, 2008; Bull & Scerif, 2001; Espy et al., 2004; St. Clair-Thompson & Gathercole, 2006). Most such work has focused on WM, since the capacity to hold, update, and transform information in the mind is essential to performing mathematical operations and calculations. As Blair and colleagues (2008) suggest, WM may contribute to the acquisition of mathematical knowledge by promoting variety of problem-solving strategies and by ensuring successful encoding and retrieval of mathematical facts. However, Bull and Scerif (2001) found that all three major EF components (IC, WM, and CF) uniquely contributed to mathematical skills in 6- to 8-year-olds, over and above IQ and vocabulary measures. Similar findings have been reported in preschool children, with both IC and WM linked to concurrent mathematical ability after adjustment for the effects of child age, vocabulary, and maternal education (Espy et al., 2004). In addition, both WM and CF skills were related to mathematical word-problem-solving ability, controlling for arithmetical calculation processes (Andersson, 2007). It is not hard to conceive how difficulties in inhibiting automatic response patterns or inability to switch flexibly between alternate sets of strategies could undermine performance on math tests. Blair and colleagues (2008) offer some insights into how mathematical errors may be interpreted in the light of EF demands and failures, although the specific mechanisms by which EFs contribute to math ability still need to be identified.

The development of language and EFs seem to be mutually codetermined. Vygotsky (1962) posited that children use "private speech" as a way to regulate behavior and follow complex rules. For example, while completing a difficult CF task, children may mouth to themselves the rules they need to follow in order to ensure better performance. As children grow older, this private speech becomes internalized. It is thus not surprising that numerous studies have linked children's performance on EF tasks to various language and literacy skills, such as expressive and receptive vocabulary (Blair & Razza, 2007; Carlson & Meltzoff, 2008; Wolfe & Bell, 2004), phonemic awareness and letter knowledge (Blair & Razza, 2007), written expression (Hooper, Swartz, Wakely, de Kruif, & Montgomery, 2002), and reading abilities (Blair & Razza, 2007; Gathercole, Alloway, Willis, & Adams, 2006; Swanson & Jerman, 2007). For example, IC was found to relate to phonemic awareness and letter knowledge in kindergartners (Blair & Razza, 2007), and the ability to regulate attention was found to relate to concurrent reading achievement in 5- to 6-year-olds, controlling for the significant contribution of vocabulary knowledge and teacher-reported motivation (Howse, Lange, Farran, & Boyles, 2003). Moreover, recent studies show that bilingualism is related to enhanced performance on EF tasks (Bialystok & Craik, 2010).

Although these cross-sectional studies have helped to chart concurrent correlations between EFs and academic skills, they reveal very little about the direction of the effect between EF processes and achievement. Increasingly, researchers are employing longitudinal study designs to determine whether EFs predict changes in academic achievement over time. In a study of low-income children attending Head Start programs, Blair and Razza (2007) reported that preschool levels of IC were associated with kindergarten levels of math but not literacy ability. Similarly, a study of kindergartners revealed that initial EFs at school entry predicted an increase in math skills from fall to spring, but not gains in literacy and vocabulary (Ponitz, McClelland, Matthews, & Morrison, 2009). In a 2-year study, performance on IC and shifting tasks, and observed EF behaviors at age 4, significantly predicted teacher report of mathematical achievement, and performance on standardized tests at age 6, controlling for IQ and reading ability (Clark, Pritchard, & Woodward, 2010).

Although these studies represent a step in the right direction, researchers need to conduct longer longitudinal follow-ups to examine the relative importance for achievement of initial EF skills versus later EF skills. Studies that address this question are rare. A growth curve analysis of achievement trajectories from preschool to third grade found not only that better IC and planning skills in 4- and 5-year-olds not only positively predicted initial math and reading abilities, but also that these EF-related advantages persisted until third grade (Bull, Espy, & Wiebe, 2008). McClelland and colleagues (2007) found that changes in EF skills from fall to spring of preschool significantly predicted greater gains in vocabulary, literacy, and math abilities. Together these findings suggest that although individual differences in EFs as early as preschool can put children on very different achievement trajectories, growth in EFs over the preschool year matters as well.

Interestingly, the relations between EFs and academic skills are not unidirectional. Using a path analysis, Welsh, Nix, Blair, Bierman, and Nelson (2010) found that an increase in preschool *numeracy* skills was predicted by initial EFs, while an increase in preschool EFs was predicted by initial numeracy skills. In contrast, EFs at the beginning of the preschool year predicted an increase in *literacy* skills across that year, but the opposite was not true. The authors also report that both initial EFs and domain-specific skills (i.e., numeracy and literacy) uniquely predicted math and reading achievement in kindergarten. More studies like this are needed to tease apart the transactional dynamics between EFs and achievement over longer periods of time and different developmental periods.

It will also be important to address how individual EF components contribute to longitudinal changes in achievement. Are WM, IC, and CF equally important for different academic skills? Does their relative importance change with age? Some studies suggest a degree of domain specificity, both concurrently and longitudinally (Blair & Razza, 2007; Bull et al., 2008; Holmes & Adams, 2006; Jarvis & Gathercole, 2003; Ponitz et al., 2009; Senn, Espy, & Kaufmann, 2004; St. Clair-Thompson & Gathercole, 2006). For example, WM may be a more important predictor of future math achievement than of reading abilities (Savage, Lavers, & Pillay, 2007), whereas visuospatial WM seems to be especially important for mathematical skills that rely on representing abstract constructs (Holmes & Adams, 2006). Differentiating the effect of various EF components on academic skills will help researchers better understand the processes implicated in knowledge acquisition and problem solving. For example, Blair and colleagues (2008) suggest that certain errors children make, such as when they know the right strategy but fail to implement it, may be failures of EFs.

However, it is also important to recognize that the effect of EFs on achievement may be partially due to EF contributions to general study habits and school engagement. Children with better EFs may find it easier to pay attention in class, to ignore distractions while studying or taking a test, and generally to take advantage of available resources in the school context. Blair and Peters (2003) found that performance on two EF tasks was associated with teacher ratings of "on-task" behaviors (e.g., ability to work hard, concentrate, pay attention, and stay focused) in a sample of 5-year-olds attending the Head Start program. Likewise, EFs in the fall of kindergarten were related to spring levels of classroom behavioral regulation, as indexed by children's ability to follow rules and directions, complete complex tasks in an organized fashion, concentrate, and persist (Ponitz et al., 2009). In addition, children with strong EFs may enjoy school more and feel more comfortable in a classroom environment. Obradović (2010) found that performance on EF tasks was associated with higher levels of teacher-reported school engagement in homeless 5- and 6-year-olds. As school engagement and success depend greatly on the quality of the child's social experiences, we turn next to the question of how EFs affect social skills and behaviors.

Social Skills

The ability to inhibit socially maladaptive behaviors and to switch between complex sets of rules is also important on the playground, where young children develop and practice social skills, form friendships, and negotiate their places in social hierarchies. However, studies examining the role of EFs for various measures of social competence have primarily relied on parent and teacher reports of EF behaviors rather than performance on laboratory EF tasks. Although parent and teacher reports of EF behaviors may be more ecologically valid predictors of social behavior, it is important to note that using the same informant for both EFs and social behaviors can inflate the significance of relations between the two constructs.

In a series of studies on the same longitudinal sample, Eisenberg and colleagues (1995, 1997) have shown how teacher report of attention shifting and focusing abilities in 4- to 6-year-olds relates to children's future social skills, prosocial behavior, and peer-rated sociometrics. Attentional control during preschool and kindergarten predicted socially appropriate behavior (e.g.. social skills, lack of disruptive behaviors) and prosocial/sociable behavior (e.g., popularity, sharing, perspective taking, leadership skills) 2 years and 4 years later (Eisenberg et al., 1995, 1997). In addition, the same team of investigators found that children who had consistently low or decreasing levels of social competence between the two follow-ups had the lowest levels of preschool/kindergarten attentional control (Eisenberg et al., 1997). In a study of 8- to 12-year-olds, Lengua (2002, 2003) found similar results, in that mother- and self-reported attention regulation and IC was linked to social competence, but mostly concurrently.

Some recent studies have also linked children's performance on laboratory EF tasks to adult reports of social competence. In a low-income, ethnically diverse sample of preschoolers, IC was related to teacher report of positive social skills, such as being cooperative and following directions (Rhoades, Greenberg, & Domitrovich, 2009). Similarly, Obradović (2010) found that performance on EF tasks was associated with teacher reports of peer acceptance and rejection in a homeless, high-risk sample of 5- and 6-year-olds. However, the longitudinal effects of EFs on social competence are not highly robust. In a preschool study group, for example, initial measures of IC predicted teacher reports of social competence 6 months later. However, this effect became nonsignificant after the inclusion of parenting measures (Lengua, Honorado, & Bush, 2007). In addition, 6-month changes in EFs were not related to social competence. Likewise, Ponitz and colleagues (2009) reported that performance on a behavior-regulation task in the fall of kindergarten did not predict spring levels of interpersonal skills. In a different short-term longitudinal study, the marginal relation of preschool EFs and kindergarten social competence became nonsignificant after researchers controlled for initial levels of social competence (Razza & Blair, 2009). In general, performance on EF tasks has emerged as a more consistent longitudinal predictor of negative social behaviors. For example, IC was concurrently related to both cooperative and noncooperative behaviors in elementary school students. However, initial IC predicted only noncooperative behaviors at the 1-year follow-up (Ciairano, Visu-Petra, & Settanni, 2007). A recent study also found that growth in EFs predicted teacher report of peer problems but had no effect on children's perceived social competence (Hughes & Ensor, 2011).

Consistent with these recent findings is the extensive literature documenting the effects of EFs on children's disruptive and emotional behavior problems. Performance on EF tasks as early as 22, 33, and 45 months of age was related to externalizing behavior problems when children were 6 years old (Kochanska & Knaack, 2003). The relation between EFs and externalizing behavior problems is robust and holds across diverse assessments, multiple informants, and different ages, even after controlling for important covariates, such as the child's cognitive ability, parenting styles, and family risks (Bierman, Torres, Domitrovich, Welsh, & Gest, 2009; Eisenberg et al., 1995, 1997; Hughes & Ensor, 2008; Olson, Sameroff, Kerr, Lopez, & Wellman, 2005). EFs have also been linked to short-term changes in problem behaviors between ages 3 and 4 (Hughes & Ensor, 2008). Similarly, Riggs, Blair, and Greenberg (2003) found that initial levels of IC in first and second graders predicted changes in reports of externalizing and internalizing symptoms across a 2-year period, controlling for common correlates such as IQ and sex. Changes in adult reports of EF behaviors over 2 years also differentiated 4- to 8-year-olds who changed or retained disorder status, as indicated by subclinical levels of externalizing symptoms (Eisenberg, Sadovsky, et al., 2005). However, the relation between EFs and disruptive behaviors is dynamic and bidirectional. For example, initial reports of EFs in 4- to 8-year-olds predicted lower levels of externalizing symptoms 2 years later, and initial reports of externalizing symptoms predicted lower levels of consequent EF, after accounting for the significant longitudinal stability and concurrent intercorrelations of both domains (Eisenberg, Spinrad, et al., 2004). Thus, changes in EFs may engender longitudinal change in psychopathology, but externalizing symptoms may also contribute to lower levels in EF behaviors over time.

In contrast to externalizing problems, the link between EFs and internalizing symptoms is not as strong or consistent (Davis, Bruce, & Gunnar, 2002; Eisenberg, Spinrad, et al., 2004; Eisenberg et al., 2009). Several conceptual and methodological issues may contribute to this pattern of findings. First, researchers often use EF tasks that test the inhibition of impulsive behaviors as prepotent responses, rather than the inhibition of withdrawn and shy behaviors. Accordingly, children who display high levels of internalizing symptoms tend to score higher on these tasks than children who display high levels of externalizing symptoms (Eisenberg, Spinrad, et al., 2004). Second, adults (especially teachers) are not good reporters of internalizing symptoms in young children, since symptoms of anxiety and depression are not as salient as disruptive and oppositional behaviors. Third, EF components may show some degree of specificity in predicting different types of symptoms. In a 1-year follow-up study of 8- to 12-year-olds, the initial level of reported attention regulation was related to subsequent internalizing and well-being, whereas the initial level of IC behaviors was related to externalizing symptoms (Lengua, 2003). Future studies need to ensure that measures of EFs are not biased for behaviorally inhibited children by developing more tasks that require the inhibition of passive and withdrawn tendencies. They also need to investigate how different EF components relate to the change of various social behaviors.

In summary, cross-sectional and longitudinal studies link EF skills to the development of both academic and social skills, as well as behavior problems known to undermine achievement and the formation of prosocial relationships. Although questions remain about the causality of this relation and specific underlying mechanisms by which EF components promote or hinder various aspects of academic and social functioning, it is hard to dismiss the abundant evidence that EFs relate to various indices of school readiness and early school adjustment. The growing number of longitudinal studies that control for within-time covariation of EFs and adaptation demonstrate convincingly how initial levels and growth in EFs predict changes in competence and symptoms over time. Children who enter the school system with poor EFs may be at increased risk for falling behind academically, while failing to engage in prosocial relationships. As early maladaptation tends to persist or worsen over time, it is important that educators and researchers work together to identify processes that foster the growth of EFs in young children. However, before we consider how to systematically improve EFs, we turn our review to naturally occurring antecedents and correlates of emergent EF skills.

Environmental Influences on Executive Functioning in Children

Family and School Environments

Although individual differences in executive functioning have a robust biological and genetic basis (Fan, Wu, Fossella, & Posner, 2001; Fossella, Posner, Fan, Swanson, & Pfaff, 2002; Rueda, Rothbart, McCandliss, Saccomanno, & Posner, 2005), EF skills are also shaped by the quality of the environments in which children are raised. Parents play an important role in helping young children regulate attention and behavior before they can do so on their own, and the quality of early parenting and the parent–child relationship influence the development of EF skills. Secure infant attachment and positive parenting styles during toddlerhood have been found to predict children's IC 6 years later (Olson, Bates, & Bayles, 1990). Similarly, observed maternal sensitivity and autonomy during parent–infant interactions predicted measures of toddlers' emergent WM, IC, and CF skills (Bernier, Carlson, & Whipple, 2010). In early and middle childhood, studies have linked the development of EFs, both concurrently and longitudinally, to various indicators of parenting quality, ranging from parental positive expressivity, warm responsiveness, and support, to punitive discipline and hostility (Brody & Ge, 2001; Eisenberg et al., 2001, 2003; McCabe, Cunnington, & Brooks-Gunn, 2004; Obradović, 2010; Olson et al., 2005). Furthermore, the quality of the home environment, as indicated by measures of physical and social resources present in the home, as well as maternal sensitivity and maternal stimulation, predicted levels of sustained attention and IC in first graders over and above stringent controls, including age, gender, ethnicity, income, maternal vocabulary, and the amount of hours in child care (National Institute of Child Health and Human Development [NICHD] Early Child Care Research Network, 2005). However, a recent study reveals that children's EF behaviors can also have an evocative effect on future maternal behavior. Mothers whose children displayed higher levels of EF behaviors used fewer directive and more assisting and questioning strategies during a short teaching task (Eisenberg et al., 2010).

In contrast to the family environment, researchers know very little about the effects of the school environment on EFs, despite the fact that classrooms are perhaps the most important context in which children rehearse and apply EF skills. An NICHD Early Child Care Research Network (2005) study showed that the quality of early child care, although significantly related, did not predict EF skills over and above the effect of family environment. Moreover, the quality of preschool and first-grade classroom environments was not even correlated with EF skills. On the other hand, Noble, McCandliss, and Farah (2007) reported unique effects of home literacy environment, quality of school environment, and time spent in day care/preschool on the WM of first graders. The measure of school context quality was based on publicly available information about attendance, school finances, and the percentage of students meeting state standards. Ardila, Rosselli, Matute, and Guajardo (2005) found that 5- and 6-year-old children in private schools outperformed those in public schools on an EF test, although these differences were partially due to factors unrelated to the school environment (i.e., parent education) and were not observed among older children. Given the importance of EFs for school readiness and success, future research needs to delineate better how early school and classroom environments contribute to the development of EFs. Researchers need to look beyond easily obtained measures of overall attendance and economic resources to examine the role of specific factors, such as classroom climate, management style, teacher expectations, and sense of efficacy. It is also important to examine whether individual–aggregate classroom levels of executive functioning moderate the quality of teacher–student relationships or evoke certain behaviors in teachers.

Socioeconomic Disadvantage and Adversity

Children who come from disadvantaged socioeconomic backgrounds tend to display lower levels of EF skills when compared to more advantaged peers. Howse and colleagues (2003) found that economically at-risk 5- and 6-year-olds performed significantly worse on an attention-regulation task than their agemates from middle- and upper-middle-income families, after controlling for age and race. Similarly, when compared to affluent peers, socioeconomically disadvantaged children in an ethnically diverse sample of 5- to 7-year-olds performed worse on an attention-shifting task (Mezzacappa, 2004). In a series of studies, Noble, Farah, and colleagues examined the association between socioeconomic status (SES)—as indexed by low parental occupation status, income, and education—and children's performance on behavioral tests reflecting the function of specific neurocognitive systems. In comparison to middle-class peers, low SES kindergartners performed worse on an overall EF test (Noble, Norman, & Farah, 2005), and low SES first graders and middle school children who were tested on more specialized EF tasks demonstrated deficits in both IC and WM (Farah et al., 2006; Noble et al., 2007). Low SES children also showed inferior language abilities, which mediated the association between SES and EFs (Noble et al., 2004, 2005, 2007). In particular Noble and colleagues (2007) reported that semantic processing rather than phonological processing mediated the relation between SES and EFs. These studies shed some light on possible processes by which SES undermines the development of specific EFs that need to be further examined using longitudinal studies.

In addition to examining associations with SES, which is a broad measure of disadvantage, researchers have found that exposure to specific adverse life experiences is related to individual differences in EFs. Prenatal exposure to teratogens, which are detrimental to healthy brain development, has been linked to inferior executive functioning later in life (Accornero et al., 2007; Eyler et al., 2009; Green et al., 2009; Korkman, Kettunen, & Autti-Rämö, 2003). Exposure to negative life events (e.g., serious illness or injury, moving, loss of friends, and changing schools) has been associated with reports of attention regulation, impulsivity, and inhibitory control in a community sample of 8- to 12-year-olds (Lengua & Long, 2002). Pears and Fisher (2005) found a significant negative association between maltreatment experience, namely, neglect and emotional abuse, and current levels of EF skills in 3- to 6-year-old foster children. However, when compared to a community sample of children with similar SES background, children in foster care had only a marginally lower EF score, indicating that poverty, as well as maltreatment, influenced development of attention and inhibitory skills. Variability in adversity exposure is associated with EFs even in high-risk samples, such as homeless kindergartners and first graders living in an emergency shelter (Obradović, 2010).

Several studies have examined the joint influences of different aspects of the childrearing environment. Lengua and colleagues (2007) reported that parental limit setting and scaffolding, which predicted an increase in EF levels in a community sample of preschoolers, also mediated the effect of cumulative risk exposure on EFs. Similarly, Noble and colleagues (2007) found that the quality of family and school environments mediated the effect of SES on WM in a kindergarten sample. In a low-income, predominantly minority group of preschoolers, Li-Grining (2007) showed that low birth weight, psychosocial risk (e.g., parental psychopathology, lack of social support, and domestic violence), and residential risk (e.g., housing and neighborhood problems) were all uniquely related to EFs. In the NICHD Early Child Care Research Network (2005) study, the quality of home environment during the first 3 years of life was related to EFs in first graders; however, the association was fully accounted for by the influence of the concurrent home environment. These studies highlight the need to investigate how the timing and chronicity of adversities in family and school settings influence the development EFs. Understanding the processes by which general socioeconomic disparities emerge in EFs among disadvantaged populations has important implications for ameliorating the risk of underdeveloped EF skills.

Environmental Effects on Neural Structure and Processing

Researchers have only recently turned to examining differences in brain structure and activation among low and high SES groups of children using electrophysiological and neuroimaging methods. For example, Raizada, Richards, Meltzoff, and Kuhl (2008) reported that children with low and high SES had marginal anatomical differences in the left inferior frontal gyrus, an area involved in language processing. In adults, low subjective social status has been associated with reduced grey matter volumes in the perigenual portion of the ACC, a cortical area involved in behavior regulation, and this relation was significant after controlling for objective measures of SES (Gianaros et al., 2007). As there are only a handful of studies examining SES differences in children's brain structure, it is hard to draw any but provisional conclusions. It is important that future research in this area pursues a developmental perspective, as brain regions associated with EFs have protracted developmental trajectories.

Researchers have employed simple auditory and visual stimuli to investigate SES disparities in functional brain activation patterns. Two recent studies, for example, investigated SES differences in children's selective attention by measuring electrophysiological response (i.e., ERPs) during the simultaneous presentation of two auditory stimuli (e.g., tones, stories)—one that children were instructed to attend to and another they were instructed to ignore (D'Angiulli, Weinberg, Grunau, Hertzman, & Grebenkov, 2008; Stevens, Lauinger, & Neville, 2009). In a group of 3- to 8-year-olds, Stevens and colleagues (2009) found that low SES children were unable to suppress their attention to a distracting story, as evidenced by similar early neural processing of both attended and unattended stimuli. D'Angiuli and colleagues (2008) reported similar results in older children. Although both of these studies demonstrated SES differences in neural processing, low and high SES groups did not differ in behavioral performance on tasks requiring them to detect the attended tone or recall the attended story. Electrophysiological data thus allowed researchers to identify SES differences in attentional modulation that could not be captured with behavioral tests. These studies emphasized that researchers and educators cannot assume that children use equally efficient and effective strategies just because they show no difference in test performance. Disparities in selective attention at the level of neural processing may not be captured by performance on a relatively simple laboratory task, but they may contribute to well-documented achievement disparities. The inability to filter out distracting stimuli may get in the way of learning and studying, especially for disadvantaged children who live in chaotic family, school, and neighborhood environments.

Differences in visual attention processing have been examined by Kishiyama, Boyce, Jimenez, Perry, and Knight (2009), who studied children's ERP responses to a visual-oddball task, in which children were instructed to press a button every time a low-probability stimulus appeared on a screen and to ignore randomly interspersed photographs that were actually used to measure their responses to novelty. They reported that low SES children displayed reduced early extrastriate (P1 and N1) and novelty related (N2) ERP responses. Although low and high SES groups did not differ in their accuracy and reaction times on the simple visual-oddball task, the low SES group performed worse on EF tasks than did the high SES group.

Several studies show SES differences in brain activation of children undergoing functional magnetic resonance imaging (fMRI) during challenges that measure abilities functionally related to children's EFs, such as language skills (Noble et al., 2005; Noble, Wolmetz, Ochs, Farah, & McCandliss, 2006). For example, a recent study shows that SES moderated the relation between brain activation during a language task and reading ability (Noble et al., 2006). Moreover, Raizada and colleagues (2008) found that low SES was linked to reduced specialization of language-related brain areas in 5-year-olds when they controlled for children's performance on language and cognitive tests. Researchers interested in examining SES-related variability in neural processing during reward-based EF tasks should consider that adults' lower parental education, independent of adults' own education, was related to reduced activation in brain regions involved in regulating impulses and processing reward-relevant information in response to positive feedback (Gianaros et al., 2011).

Understanding SES differences in the neural processing of cognitive challenges represents a nascent area of developmental neuroscience research. As researchers continue examining the neural fingerprint of exposure to early adversity and deprivation, it will be important that they conduct longitudinal studies focusing on important developmental transitions, such as school entry, and elucidate how both behavioral and neural indices of learning change in response to educational programs and interventions. Moreover, neuroscience researchers must expand their samples to include resilient children who show positive adjustment despite exposure to high risk and adversity. By comparing the neural structures and processing of resilient children with a competent low-risk group, as well as a maladaptive, high-risk group, we can learn more about the biological basis of protective and compensatory processes.

Executive Functioning and Resilience

Despite the fact that various sources of risk and adversity undermine the development of EF skills in children, EF skills have been found to moderate associations of adversity with other domains of adjustment (Lengua, 2002; Lengua, Bush, Long, Kovacs, & Trancik, 2008). In one study, for example, high levels of IC protected children's positive adjustment from the effects of adversity, whereas low levels of attention regulation and IC exacerbated the effects of adversity on behavior problems in third through fifth graders (Lengua, 2002). At a 3-year follow-up, adversity exposure predicted increases in internalizing and externalizing symptoms only in children with low EF behaviors, whereas a high level of EF behaviors buffered children against adversity influences (Lengua et al., 2008).

In addition, researchers have identified EFs as mediators of the effects of parenting quality and family environment on children's adaptation across different domains of functioning (Kochanska & Knaack, 2003; NICHD Early Child Care Research Network, 2003; Spinrad et al., 2007). For example, EF skills mediated the effect of maternal support on children's social competence, and internalizing and externalizing symptoms in toddlers (Spinrad et al., 2007). In a study of 1,002 first graders, the NICHD Early Child Care Research Network (2003) reported that children's ability to sustain attention and inhibit impulsive responses partially mediated the effect of family environment—a composite of home resource quality, maternal sensitivity, and cognitive stimulation—on 54-month and first-grade measures of cognitive, social, and emotional development. Using a rigorous test of mediation that controlled for longitudinal continuity and within-time covariation of parenting, EF behaviors, and externalizing symptoms, Eisenberg, Zhou, and colleagues (2005) found that maternal warmth and positive expressivity when children were 9 years old positively affected change in EF behaviors 2 years later, which in turn predicted a decline in externalizing symptoms in 13-year-olds.

Finally, person-centered analyses show that self-regulation, and EF skills in particular, can differentiate at-risk children who show resilient versus maladaptive outcomes (Buckner, Mezzacappa, & Beardslee, 2003; Obradović, 2010). In a logistic regression that included measures of parenting quality, family risk, and child IQ, performance on EF tasks emerged as the strongest correlate of whether 5- and 6-year-old homeless children were classified as resilient, as indexed by positive academic adjustment and peer relations, and a lack of psychopathological symptoms (Obradović, 2010). Together these studies demonstrate that the role of EFs for adaptive functioning is even more salient for children who face risk and adversity. Since EFs are implicated in fostering academic and social competence in children, as well as in buffering adaptive functioning from the effects of risk and adversity, we now look to promising new research that identifies methods for improving and fostering good executive functioning.

Promoting Executive Functioning in Children

In recent years, researchers have turned their attention to designing and evaluating methods aimed at improving EFs in children. Various approaches have emerged, ranging from short-term training sessions to more comprehensive classroom curricula. Some interventions focus directly on enhancing specific EF skills, whereas others seek to improve EFs indirectly by promoting children's general socioemotional well-being, mindfulness, or physical activity. We review several programs and studies that are representative of current efforts to promote EFs in normative, community samples of children.

Short-term training programs are a relatively simple and inexpensive way to boost EFs in young children who show early deficits. For example, Dowsett and Livesey (2000) assigned 3- to 5-year-olds who were initially identified as having difficulty inhibiting on a go/no-go task (i.e., failing more than 80% of inhibiting trials) to three experimental conditions. A practice group repeatedly rehearsed the same go/no-go task, while a training group was taught two sorting tasks designed to elicit acquisition of increasingly complex rules. After three intermediate sessions, both the practice and training groups performed significantly better than the control group on a retest of the go/no-go task. However, the greatest inhibitory control improvement was achieved via a more generalized training procedure that required greater attentional control and active processing of rule structures than the simple practice condition. This study highlights the importance of going beyond simple task rehearsal to promote broad-based EF skills.

Rueda, Rothbart, and colleagues (2005) demonstrated that a training program designed to improve EFs can produce a spillover effect on general intelligence and underlying neural processing. Three weeks after participating in a 5-day training program, 4- and 6-year-olds performed better than a control group on an EF task; however, these behavioral differences did not reach statistical significance. On the other hand, the effect of the training program was significant for an IQ test in 4-year-olds and a vocabulary test in 6-year-olds. Moreover, training produced a more mature electroencephalographic (EEG) pattern of frontal activation in response to conflict-related activity. The brain activation in trained 4-year-olds looked more like the brain activation of untrained 6-year-olds, whereas the trained 6-year-olds' brains exhibited an adult-like activation pattern. The training effects on IQ and brain activation were replicated in a small sample of Spanish preschoolers, who maintained these effects 2 months after the training and also showed improved performance on a delay of gratification task (Rueda, Checa, & Santonja, 2008), as reported in Rueda, Checa, and Rothbart (2010).

Several recent studies have further examined transfer effects of interventions on both behavioral indices and biological processes. Using two 5-week computerized training programs designed to improve either visuospatial WM or IC in preschoolers, Thorell, Lindqvist, Bergman Nutley, Bohlin, and Klingberg (2009) examined changes in children's performance on trained WM and IC tasks, as well as various nontrained EF tasks. Children who received daily 15-minute visuospatial WM training showed general improvements on both the visuospatial and verbal WM tasks. Moreover, the effect of WM training transferred to attention but not to IC or problem-solving skills. In contrast, daily 15-minute IC training produced improvements on some trained IC tasks but had no effect on the nontrained IC or other EF domains. Although this is only the first attempt to disaggregate the training effects of distinct EF components, the findings suggest that WM and IC may differ in their malleability and transferability properties. In addition, WM training was linked to changes in cortical dopamine receptor density in young adults (McNab et al., 2009), demonstrating that training can influence underlying brain biochemistry implicated in executive functioning. In addition, Stevens and colleagues (2008) reported that a computerized six-week language intervention improved children's selective auditory attention, as indexed by changes in neural processing of attended auditory stimuli (Stevens, Fanning, Coch, Sanders, & Neville, 2008). Children who were exposed to training showed significant increases in mean amplitude of ERP response only to the attended auditory probe. Given that deficits in selective auditory attention have been noted in socioeconomically disadvantaged children (Stevens et al., 2009), it is important to further examine implications and transfer effects of this training program.

In contrast to these discrete training efforts, Bodrova and Leong (2007) developed a kindergarten curriculum called Tools of the Mind (ToM), which promotes EF skills using strategies seamlessly incorporated into daily classroom routines and activities. For example, the ToM curriculum emphasizes (1) external aids that support the development of memory and attention (e.g., holding a drawing of an ear that reminds children to listen and not to talk); (2) private speech to regulate and scaffold new action (e.g., verbally reminding oneself of a particular rule); and (3) dramatic play that encourages advance planning, goal-directed behavior, and observance and monitoring of play rules and characters (Bodrova & Leong, 2007; Diamond, Barnett, Thomas, & Munro, 2007). Diamond and colleagues (2007) found that children who were randomly assigned to the ToM curriculum performed significantly better on EF tasks than children who attended preschool with a literacy-based curriculum. Moreover, the difference in performance between the two groups was the largest on tasks that required more advanced EF skills. However, this evaluation study lacked preintervention measures of EF, so it is unclear whether initial levels of EF skills moderated the effects of ToM. In another randomized trial, Barnett and colleagues (2008) reported that children in ToM classrooms had fewer behavior problems and marginally better language and literacy skills when compared to children in a control group. In addition, independent observers rated ToM classrooms as having overall higher quality and ToM teachers as being more sensitive to children's needs and more efficient with respect to the management of instructional time and routines.

Classroom interventions administered by teachers using brief lessons or activities several times a week also have been found to foster better EFs. The preventive intervention Promoting Alternative THinking Strategies (PATHS; Kusche & Greenberg, 1994) was designed to foster neurocognitive development by providing students with strategies for self-control and emotional understanding. The benefits of the PATHS intervention have been established for various aspects of socioemotional development (Domitrovich, Cortes, & Greenberg, 2007; Greenberg, Kusche, Cook, & Quamma, 1995), and a recent study links the efficacy of PATHS to improved IC in second and third graders. Children enrolled in PATHS had significantly higher levels of IC at a 9-month follow-up, which partially mediated the effect of PATHS on behavior problems at a 1-year follow-up (Riggs, Greenberg, Kusche, & Pentz, 2006).

Similar to the PATHS intervention, the Head Start REDI (Research-based Developmentally Informed) intervention is administered by trained teachers and consists of short lessons and activities that aim to improve preschoolers' school readiness skills across both the socioemotional and cognitive domains. A 1-year follow-up study of the randomized controlled trial revealed that 4-year-olds attending the Head Start REDI intervention had better social behavior, emotional understanding, vocabulary, literacy skills, and learning engagement than children who attended regular Head Start classrooms (Bierman, Domitrovich, et al., 2008). Moreover, initial levels of children's EF skills both moderated and mediated the effects of the Head Start REDI intervention on adjustment and school readiness skills (Bierman, Nix, Greenberg, Blair, & Domitrovich, 2008). The effect of the intervention on reducing aggression and improving social and literacy skills was significant only for children who displayed lower EFs at the onset of the study. The intervention also produced improvements in shifting abilities and experimenter-rated EF behaviors, which in turn partially mediated the effect of intervention on school readiness outcomes. Thus, EFs seem central to the underlying processes through which these classroom-based interventions influence children's adaptation.

Together, these intervention studies demonstrate that teachers can directly foster EF skills in preschoolers, kindergartners, and elementary schoolchildren through specialized lessons and activities. However, a recent intervention study showed that providing teachers with strategies and tools to offer individualized student instruction (ISI) can also improve EFs in first graders who entered school with the lowest level of skills (Connor et al., 2010). The gains in EFs among these children were linked to improved classroom learning environment, as indexed by ISI teachers' more effective teaching and management practices (e.g., more instructional time, less disruption), in comparison to a control group. This finding is consistent with literature showing that improving teachers' classroom management style can have a pervasive influence on children's socioemotional adjustment, especially among high-risk samples (Webster-Stratton & Reid, 2004; Webster-Stratton, Reid, & Hammond, 2004; Webster-Stratton, Reid, & Stoolmiller, 2008). It is important that future studies adopt a transactional and systemic view in examining how various strategies can improve children's EFs, as well as how gains in children's EFs can trigger a cascading effect on classroom climate, teachers' sense of efficacy, and teacher–child relationships. For example, an increase in EFs may not only enable children to pay better attention in the classroom and behave on the playground, but it also may affect the quality of the teacher–child relationship, a known predictor of children's adaptation and school success (Pianta, 2006; Pianta & Stuhlman, 2004).

Recently, alternative intervention approaches have emerged that focus on children's level of activity. One approach includes mindfulness training programs that teach children relaxation, breathing, and meditation techniques, and emphasize stillness and sensory awareness. After conducting a meta-analysis of 15 pioneering studies that implemented mindfulness training in clinical and community populations of children and adolescents, Burke (2009) concluded that current research provides evidence of feasibility and acceptability but lacks rigorous evaluation of efficacy. However, two randomized controlled trials with elementary schoolchildren offer initial insight into mindfulness training's effects on EF-related behaviors. Napoli, Krech, and Holley (2005) reported small to medium effects of participation in twelve 45-minute mindfulness sessions on measures of selective visual attention and teacher-reported attention behaviors in first and third graders. Flook and colleagues (2010) found that only children who had low teacher-reported EF behaviors showed gains in response to an 8-week mindfulness awareness program. As with other mindfulness studies, teacher reports in both of these studies may be biased, as teachers were not blind to intervention group status. Still, it is important that future studies more rigorously examine the effects of mindfulness training on EFs across both behavioral and neural levels, as meditation has been found to yield positive changes in the structure and function of adults' brains (Treadway & Lazar, 2009).

The other new approach examines vigorous physical activity and fitness as means of improving children's EFs (Hillman, Castelli, & Buck, 2005; Stroth et al., 2009). Kubesch and colleagues (2009) found that seventh graders performed better on an IC task following 30 minutes of anaerobic endurance exercise than children who only engaged in a 5-minute aerobic movement break. The authors stress the importance of daily physical education classes and argue that physical activity should be scheduled before, not after, academic classes, as it can enhance attention and learning. These findings suggest the possibility of promoting development of EFs not only with specialized lessons but also balanced grade curricula. Likewise, studies that link bilingualism to better EFs (Bialystok & Craik, 2010; Carlson & Meltzoff, 2008) also offer potential avenues to improve EFs through educational programs that offer foreign language study or support the development of native languages of bicultural and immigrant students.

Finally, it is important that researchers who evaluate these intervention effects conduct longitudinal follow-ups and test the long-term effects on growth of children's EFs. Studies that show changes in neural activity or structure should determine whether more mature activation yields lagging behavioral improvements. In addition, randomized controlled studies designed to improve EF skills need to test how changes in EF affect short- and long-term growth of specific academic and social skills. For example, it is surprising that children exposed to the ToM curriculum, known to improve EF skills, did not show more robust improvement in academic skills (Barnett et al., 2008) given the well-established links between EFs and academic competence. However, these spillover effects may take time to emerge and could be mediated by more immediate improvements in student behavior and classroom climate. Moreover, it important to examine how factors such as individual and relationship characteristics among students, teachers, and parents modify intervention effects. Future studies need to identify subgroups of children and classrooms for whom these intervention programs work the best.

Together these studies demonstrate the malleability of EF skills, which for many years were attributed solely to the age-related developmental maturation of underlying neural structures. The consequences of such training interventions could be far-reaching, due to the significant effects that EFs appear to have on early adjustment and school success. Disadvantaged children in particular may benefit from programs designed to foster better EF skills because risk and adversity exposure can undermine the development of emergent EFs and the successful achievement of academic and social skills.

Conclusion

Executive functioning represents a cornerstone of early childhood development, as it encompasses a set of core skills that enables children to exert control over their thoughts, feelings, and behavior. Established concurrent and longitudinal links between EF skills and various domains of adaptive functioning indicate that EFs can be conceptualized as basic underlying abilities that facilitate successful attainment of various salient developmental tasks. Although issues of causality still need to be addressed empirically, the fact that EF skills start to develop before children engage in any formal education or form sustained relationships with peers suggests that EFs can be seen as necessary precursors to achievement of academic and social competence.

Future research will need to elucidate the exact mechanisms by which EFs contribute to children's school readiness and the development of early numeracy and literacy skills. It remains to be seen whether effects of EFs are mediated by cognitive and/or socioemotional processes that enable children to thrive in school contexts. However, as children's school-entry attention, math, and reading abilities are the strongest predictors of later academic competences (Duncan et al., 2007), preschool EF skills could influence differences in long-term achievement trajectories. Thus, we believe that school readiness assessment batteries should include EF tasks that explicitly measure children's early IC, WM, and CF skills. Examining EF skills in the context of large-scale preschool screenings potentially would enable educators to prevent negative cascading effects that may result from children's inability to exert control over their attention and behavior as they transition to more demanding school settings.

Since recent research demonstrates that EFs are amenable to change at both neural and behavioral levels, we believe it is important to identify ways to promote growth of EF skills through a large-scale effort. Feasibility studies will determine whether this necessitates wide adoption of EF-focused preschool curricula or can be achieved through implementation of other classroom practices known to support EF development. Emerging intervention research suggests various avenues to incorporate EF training in school programs meaningfully by focusing on activities that encourage creative play, physical fitness, mindfulness, and emotion understanding.

Given the observed socioeconomic disparities in EF skills and related functioning, it is important to ameliorate differences as early as possible through subsidized high-quality targeted preschool programs like Head Start. As EF skills have also been shown to protect children against the deleterious effects of risk and adversity, early education curricula should be designed explicitly to support the development of executive functioning in disadvantaged children who may lack appropriate stimulation, resources, or guidance at home. Based on research that shows protective effects of native bilingualism on EFs in disadvantaged minority children (Carlson & Meltzoff, 2008), education policies can reflect the commitment to invest in young children's executive functioning by supporting bilingual education.

At the same time, educators need to be better prepared to promote growth in EF skills informally and reduce risks for developing poor executive functioning, such as disruptive classroom environments. Early childhood education teacher training programs and professional development courses should address both biological and behavioral aspects of EF development and the relative importance of EFs for classroom behaviors and academic achievement. It is also crucial that teachers learn how to model good executive functioning and to seamlessly incorporate the rehearsal of EF skills in everyday activities. In addition to promoting EF skills through engaging learning activities, educators need to ensure that their evaluations and tests rely on growth of EFs. There is a huge difference between rote memorization and WM, and if students' progress is measured only using tests of the former, we fail to reward and emphasize the importance of the latter.

As educators and policymakers turn to promoting EFs in classroom settings, researchers need to investigate the dynamic interplay between children's EF skills and classroom-level factors, such as classroom climate, quality of teacher–student relationships; and teacher burnout, efficacy and management style, and teachers' own EF skills. Future studies should also examine how the degree to which the classroom comprises students with high or low EF skills can moderate teacher effects on individual children's learning and behavior. Similarly, it is important to understand better the effects of peers and social networks on the development of EF skills, and how these interact to shape adaptation.

Examining EFs across and within different ecological systems will require researchers to measures children's EFs outside of a laboratory context. In order to understand better the role of EFs in naturalistic settings, researchers need to employ study paradigms that cross multiple levels of analysis and use longitudinal developmental design. The next generation of studies will aim to address how factors ranging from school district policies to children's biological arousal and reactivity influence EFs across different developmental periods. The interdisciplinary nature of such work necessitates that researchers, educators, and policymakers work together to identify and create the most optimal environments for promoting EF skills in young children.

Acknowledgments

Preparation of this chapter was supported in part by a research grant from the Canadian Institute for Advanced Research (CIFAR) to Jelena Obradović and by the Institute of Education Sciences (IES) Predoctoral Training Grant in Education Sciences at Stanford University to Ximena A. Portilla. Jelena Obradović is the Great-West Life Junior Fellow in the CIFAR's experience-based Brain and Biological Development Program and Junior Fellow Academy. W. Thomas Boyce is a Fellow of the CIFAR and holds the Sunny Hill Health Centre/BC Leadership Chair in Child Development at the University of British Columbia.

References

Accornero, V. H., Amado, A. J., Morrow, C. E., Xue, L., Anthony, J. C., & Bandstra, E. S. (2007). Impact of prenatal cocaine exposure on attention and response inhibition as assessed by continuous performance tests. *Journal of Developmental and Behavioral Pediatrics, 28*, 195–205.

Adleman, N. E., Menon, V., Blasey, C. M., White, C. D., Warsofsky, I. S., Glover, G. H., et al. (2002). A developmental fMRI study of the Stroop color–word task. *NeuroImage, 16*, 61–75.

Andersson, U. (2007). The contribution of working memory to children's mathematical word problem solving. *Applied Cognitive Psychology, 21*, 1201–1216.

Ardila, A., Rosselli, M., Matute, E., & Guajardo, S. (2005). The influence of the parents' educational level on the development of executive functions. *Developmental Neuropsychology, 28*, 539–560.

Baddeley, A. (2003). Working memory: Looking back and looking forward. *Nature Reviews, Neuroscience, 4*, 828–839.

Baddeley, A. D. (1986). *Working memory.* New York: Oxford University Press.

Barnett, W., Jung, K., Yarosz, D., Thomas, J., Hornbeck, A., Stechuk, R., et al. (2008). Educational effects of the Tools of the Mind curriculum: A randomized trial. *Early Childhood Research Quarterly, 23*, 299–313.

Berger, A., Jones, L., Rothbart, M. K., & Posner, M. I. (2000). Computerized games to study the development of attention in childhood. *Behavior Research Methods, Instruments, and Computers, 32*, 297–303.

Bernier, A., Carlson, S. M., & Whipple, N. (2010). From external regulation to self-regulation: Early parenting precursors of young children's executive functioning. *Child Development, 81*, 326–339.

Best, J. R., Miller, P. H., & Jones, L. L. (2009). Executive functions after age 5: Changes and correlates. *Developmental Review, 29*, 180–200.

Bialystok, E., & Craik, F. I. M. (2010). Cognitive and linguistic processing in the bilingual mind. *Current Directions in Psychological Science, 19*, 19–23.

Bierman, K. L., Domitrovich, C. E., Nix, R. L., Gest, S. D., Welsh, J. A., Greenberg, M. T., et al. (2008). Promoting academic and social-emotional school readiness: The Head Start REDI program. *Child Development, 79*, 1802–1817.

Bierman, K. L., Nix, R. L., Greenberg, M. T., Blair, C., & Domitrovich, C. E. (2008). Executive functions and school readiness intervention: Impact, moderation, and mediation in the Head Start REDI program. *Development and Psychopathology, 20*, 821–843.

Bierman, K. L., Torres, M. M., Domitrovich, C. E., Welsh, J. A., & Gest, S. D. (2009). Behavioral and cognitive readiness for school: Cross-domain associations for children attending Head Start. *Social Development, 18*, 305–323.

Blair, C., & Diamond, A. (2008). Biological processes in prevention and intervention: The promotion of self-regulation as a means of preventing school failure. *Development and Psychopathology, 20*, 899–911.

Blair, C., Knipe, H., & Gamson, D. (2008). Is there a role for executive functions in the development of mathematics ability? *Mind, Brain, and Education, 2*, 80–89.

Blair, C., & Peters, R. (2003). Physiological and neurocognitive correlates of adaptive behavior in preschool among children in Head Start. *Developmental Neuropsychology, 24*, 479–497.

Blair, C., & Razza, R. P. (2007). Relating effortful control, executive function, and false belief understanding to emerging math and literacy ability in kindergarten. *Child Development, 78*, 647–663.

Bodrova, E., & Leong, D. J. (2007). *Tools of the Mind: The Vygotskian approach to early childhood education* (2nd ed.). New York: Merrill/Prentice-Hall.

Brody, G. H., & Ge, X. (2001). Linking parenting processes and self-regulation to psychological functioning and alcohol use during early adolescence. *Journal of Family Psychology, 15*, 82–94.

Buckner, J. C., Mezzacappa, E., & Beardslee, W. R. (2003). Characteristics of resilient youths living in poverty: The role of self-regulatory processes. *Development and Psychopathology, 15*, 139–162.

Bull, R., Espy, K. A., & Wiebe, S. A. (2008). Short-term memory, working memory, and executive functioning in preschoolers: Longitudinal predictors of mathematical achievement at age 7 years. *Developmental Neuropsychology, 33*, 205–228.

Bull, R., & Scerif, G. (2001). Executive functioning as a predictor of children's mathematics ability: Inhibition, switching, and working memory. *Developmental Neuropsychology, 19*, 273–293.

Burke, C. A. (2009). Mindfulness-based approaches with children and adolescents: A preliminary review of current research in an emergent field. *Journal of Child and Family Studies, 19*, 133–144.

Bush, G., Luu, P., & Posner, M. I. (2000). Cognitive and emotional influences in anterior cingulate cortex. *Trends in Cognitive Sciences, 4*, 215–222.

Carlson, S. M. (2005). Developmentally sensitive measures of executive function in preschool children. *Developmental Neuropsychology, 28*, 595–616.

Carlson, S. M., Mandell, D. J., & Williams, L. (2004). Executive function and theory of mind: Stability and prediction from ages 2 to 3. *Developmental Psychology, 40*, 1105–1122.

Carlson, S. M., & Meltzoff, A. N. (2008). Bilingual experience and executive functioning in young children. *Developmental Science, 11*, 282–298.

Carlson, S. M., & Moses, L. J. (2001). Individual differences in inhibitory control and children's theory of mind. *Child Development, 72*, 1032–1053.

Casey, B. J., Cohen, J. D., Jezzard, P., Turner, R., Noll, D. C., Trainor, R. J., et al. (1995). Activation of prefrontal cortex in children during a nonspatial working memory task with functional MRI. *NeuroImage, 2*, 221–229.

Casey, B. J., Giedd, J. N., & Thomas, K. M. (2000). Structural and functional brain development and its relation to cognitive development. *Biological Psychology, 54*, 241–257.

Casey, B. J., Trainor, R., Giedd, J., Vauss, Y., Vaituzis, C., Hamburger, S., et al. (1997). The role of the anterior cingulate in automatic and controlled processes: A developmental neuroanatomical study. *Developmental Psychobiology, 30*, 61–69.

Casey, B. J., Trainor, R. J., Orendi, J. L., Schubert, A. B., Nystrom, L. E., Giedd, J. N., et al. (1997). A developmental functional MRI study of prefrontal activation during performance of a go–no-go task. *Journal of Cognitive Neuroscience, 9*, 835–847.

Ciairano, S., Visu-Petra, L., & Settanni, M. (2007). Executive inhibitory control and cooperative behavior during early school years: A follow-up study. *Journal of Abnormal Child Psychology, 35*, 335–345.

Clark, C. A. C., Pritchard, V. E., & Woodward, L. J. (2010). Preschool executive functioning abilities predict early mathematics achievement. *Developmental Psychology, 46*, 1176–1191.

Connor, C. M., Ponitz, C. C., Phillips, B. M., Travis, Q. M., Glasney, S., & Morrison, F. J. (2010). First graders' literacy and self-regulation gains: The effect of individualizing student instruction. *Journal of School Psychology, 48*, 433–455.

D'Angiulli, A., Weinberg, J., Grunau, R., Hertzman, C., & Grebenkov, P. (2008). Towards a cognitive science of social inequality: Children's attention-related ERPs and salivary cortisol vary with their socioeconomic status. *Proceedings of the 30th Cognitive Science Society Annual Meeting*, pp. 211–216.

Davidson, M., Amso, D., Anderson, L., & Diamond, A. (2006). Development of cognitive control and executive functions from 4 to 13 years: Evidence from manipulations of memory, inhibition, and task switching. *Neuropsychologia, 44*, 2037–2078.

Davis, E. P., Bruce, J., & Gunnar, M. R. (2002). The anterior attention network: Associations with temperament and neuroendocrine activity in 6-year-old children. *Developmental Psychobiology, 40*, 43–56.

Diamond, A. (2006). The early development of executive functions. In E. Bialystock & F. I. M. Craik (Eds.), *Lifespan cognition: Mechanisms of change* (pp. 70–95). New York: Oxford University Press.

Diamond, A. (2010). The evidence base for improving school outcomes by addressing the whole child and by addressing skills and attitudes, not just content. *Early Education and Development, 21*, 780–793.

Diamond, A., Barnett, S., Thomas, J., & Munro, S. (2007). Preschool program improves cognitive control. *Science, 318*, 1387–1388.

Diamond, A., Carlson, S., & Beck, D. (2005). Preschool children's performance in task switching on the dimensional change card sort task: Separating the dimensions aids the ability to switch. *Developmental Neuropsychology, 28*, 689–729.

Diamond, A., Kirkham, N., & Amso, D. (2002). Conditions under which young children can hold two rules in mind and inhibit a prepotent response. *Developmental Psychology, 38*, 352–362.

Domitrovich, C. E., Cortes, R. C., & Greenberg, M. T. (2007). Improving young children's social and emotional competence: A randomized trial of the Preschool "PATHS" Curriculum. *Journal of Primary Prevention, 28*, 67–91.

Dowsett, S. M., & Livesey, D. J. (2000). The development of inhibitory control in preschool children: Effects of "executive skills" training. *Developmental Psychobiology, 36*, 161–174.

Duncan, G., Dowsett, C., Claessens, A., Magnuson, K., Huston, A., Klebanov, P., et al. (2007). School readiness and later achievement. *Developmental Psychology, 43*, 1428–1446.

Durston, S., Davidson, M. C., Tottenham, N., Galvan, A., Spicer, J., Fossella, J. A., et al. (2006). A shift from diffuse to focal cortical activity with development. *Developmental Science, 9*, 1–8.

Eisenberg, N., Fabes, R. A., Murphy, B., Maszk, P., Smith, M., & Karbon, M. (1995). The role of emotionality and regulation in children's social functioning: A longitudinal study. *Child Development, 66*, 1360–1384.

Eisenberg, N., Fabes, R. A., Shepard, S. A., Murphy, B. C., Guthrie, I. K., Jones, S., et al. (1997). Contemporaneous and longitudinal prediction of children's social functioning from regulation and emotionality. *Child Development, 68*, 642–664.

Eisenberg, N., Gershoff, E. T., Fabes, R. A., Shepard, S. A., Cumberland, A. J., Losoya, S. H., et al. (2001). Mothers' emotional expressivity and children's behavior problems and social competence: Mediation through children's regulation. *Developmental Psychology, 37*, 475–490.

Eisenberg, N., Sadovsky, A., Spinrad, T. L., Fabes, R. A., Losoya, S. H., Valiente, C., et al. (2005). The relations of problem behavior status to children's negative emotionality, effortful control, and impulsivity: Concurrent relations and prediction of change. *Developmental Psychology, 41*, 193–211.

Eisenberg, N., Smith, C. L., Sadovsky, A., & Spinrad, T. L. (2004). Effortful control: Relations with emotion regulation, adjustment, and socialization in childhood. In R. F. Baumeister & K. D. Vohs (Eds.), *Handbook of self-regulation: Research, theory, and applications* (pp. 259–282). New York: Guilford Press.

Eisenberg, N., Spinrad, T. L., Fabes, R. A., Reiser, M., Cumberland, A., Shepard, S. A., et al. (2004). The relations of effortful control and impulsivity to children's resiliency and adjustment. *Child Development, 75*, 25–46.

Eisenberg, N., Valiente, C., Morris, A. S., Fabes, R. A., Cumberland, A., Reiser, M., et al. (2003). Longitudinal relations among parental emotional expressivity, children's regulation, and quality of socioemotional functioning. *Developmental Psychology, 39*, 3–19.

Eisenberg, N., Valiente, C., Spinrad, T. L., Cumberland, A., Liew, J., Reiser, M., et al. (2009). Longitudinal relations of children's effortful control, impulsivity, and negative emotionality to their externalizing, internalizing, and co-occurring behavior problems. *Developmental Psychology, 45*, 988–1008.

Eisenberg, N., Vidmar, M., Spinrad, T. L., Eggum, N. D., Edwards, A., Gaertner, B., et al. (2010).

Mothers' teaching strategies and children's effortful control: A longitudinal study. *Developmental Psychology, 46*, 1294–1308.

Eisenberg, N., Zhou, Q., Spinrad, T. L., Valiente, C., Fabes, R. A., & Liew, J. (2005). Relations among positive parenting, children's effortful control, and externalizing problems: A three-wave longitudinal study. *Child Development, 76*, 1055–1071.

Espy, K., McDiarmid, M. D., Cwik, M. F., Stalets, M. M., Hamby, A., & Senn, T. E. (2004). The contribution of executive functions to emergent mathematic skills in preschool children. *Developmental Neuropsychology, 26*, 465–486.

Eyler, F., Warner, T., Behnke, M., Hou, W., Wobie, K., & Garvan, C. (2009). Executive functioning at ages 5 and 7 years in children with prenatal cocaine exposure. *Developmental Neuroscience, 31*, 121–136.

Fan, J., Flombaum, J. I., McCandliss, B. D., Thomas, K. M., & Posner, M. I. (2003). Cognitive and brain consequences of conflict. *NeuroImage, 18*, 42–57.

Fan, J., Wu, Y., Fossella, J., & Posner, M. (2001). Assessing the heritability of attentional networks. *BMC Neuroscience, 2*, 14.

Farah, M., Shera, D., Savage, J., Betancourt, L., Giannetta, J., Brodsky, N., et al. (2006). Childhood poverty: Specific associations with neurocognitive development. *Brain Research, 1110*, 166–174.

Fisher, P., Gunnar, M., Dozier, M., Bruce, J., & Pears, K. (2006). Effects of therapeutic interventions for foster children on behavioral problems, caregiver attachment, and stress regulatory neural systems. *Annals of the New York Academy of Sciences, 1094*, 215–225.

Flook, L., Smalley, S., Kitil, M. J., Galla, B., Kaiser-Greenland, S., Locke, J., et al. (2010). Effects of mindful awareness practices on executive functions in elementary school children. *Journal of Applied School Psychology, 26*, 70–95.

Fossella, J., Posner, M. I., Fan, J., Swanson, J. M., & Pfaff, D. W. (2002). Attentional phenotypes for the analysis of higher mental function. *Scientific World Journal, 2*, 217–223.

Garon, N., Bryson, S. E., & Smith, I. M. (2008). Executive function in preschoolers: A review using an integrative framework. *Psychological Bulletin, 134*, 31–60.

Gathercole, S. E., Alloway, T. P., Willis, C., & Adams, A. M. (2006). Working memory in children with reading disabilities. *Journal of Experimental Child Psychology, 93*, 265–281.

Gianaros, P. J., Horenstein, J. A., Cohen, S., Matthews, K. A., Brown, S. M., Flory, J. D., et al. (2007). Perigenual anterior cingulate morphology covaries with perceived social standing. *Social Cognitive and Affective Neuroscience, 2*, 161–173.

Gianaros, P. J., Manuck, S. B., Sheu, L. K., Kuan, D. C. H., Votruba-Drzal, E., Craig, A. E., et al. (2011). Parental education predicts corticostriatal functionality in adulthood. *Cerebral Cortex, 21*(4), 896–910.

Gogtay, N., Giedd, J. N., Lusk, L., Hayashi, K. M., Greenstein, D., Vaituzis, A. C., et al. (2004). Dynamic mapping of human cortical development during childhood through early adulthood. *Proceedings of the National Academy of Sciences USA, 101*, 8174–8179.

Green, C., Mihic, A., Nikkel, S., Stade, B., Rasmussen, C., Munoz, D., et al. (2009). Executive function deficits in children with fetal alcohol spectrum disorders (FASD) measured using the Cambridge Neuropsychological Tests Automated Battery (CANTAB). *Journal of Child Psychology and Psychiatry, 50*, 688–697.

Greenberg, M. T., Kusche, C. A., Cook, E. T., & Quamma, J. P. (1995). Promoting emotional competence in school-aged children: The effects of the PATHS curriculum. *Development and Psychopathology, 7*, 117–136.

Hillman, C. H., Castelli, D. M., & Buck, S. M. (2005). Aerobic fitness and neurocognitive function in healthy preadolescent children. *Medicine and Science in Sports and Exercise, 37*, 1967–1974.

Holmes, J., & Adams, J. (2006). Working memory and children's mathematical skills: Implications for mathematical development and mathematics curricula. *Educational Psychology, 26*, 339–366.

Hooper, S. R., Swartz, C. W., Wakely, M. B., de Kruif, R. E. L., & Montgomery, J. W. (2002). Executive functions in elementary school children with and without problems in written expression. *Journal of Learning Disabilities, 35*, 57–68.

Howse, R. B., Lange, G., Farran, D. C., & Boyles, C. D. (2003). Motivation and self-regulation as predictors of achievement in economically disadvantaged young children. *Journal of Experimental Education, 71,* 151–174.

Hughes, C., & Ensor, R. (2007). Executive function and theory of mind: Predictive relations from ages 2 to 4. *Developmental Psychology, 43,* 1447–1459.

Hughes, C., & Ensor, R. (2008). Does executive function matter for preschoolers' problem behaviors? *Journal of Abnormal Child Psychology, 36,* 1–14.

Hughes, C., & Ensor, R. (2010). Individual differences in growth in executive function across the transition to school predict externalizing and internalizing behaviors and self-perceived academic success at 6 years of age. *Journal of Experimental Child Psychology, 108*(3), 663–676.

Huizinga, M., Dolan, C. V., & van der Molen, M. W. (2006). Age-related change in executive function: Developmental trends and a latent variable analysis. *Neuropsychologia, 44,* 2017–2036.

Huizinga, M., & van der Molen, M. W. (2007). Age-group differences in set-switching and set-maintenance on the Wisconsin Card Sorting Task. *Developmental Neuropsychology, 31,* 193–215.

Jarvis, H. L., & Gathercole, S. E. (2003). Verbal and non-verbal working memory and achievements on national curriculum tests at 11 and 14 years of age. *Educational and Child Psychology, 20,* 123–140.

Jones, L. B., Rothbart, M. K., & Posner, M. I. (2003). Development of executive attention in preschool children. *Developmental Science, 6,* 498–504.

Kishiyama, M. M., Boyce, W. T., Jimenez, A. M., Perry, L. M., & Knight, R. T. (2009). Socioeconomic disparities affect prefrontal function in children. *Journal of Cognitive Neuroscience, 21,* 1106–1115.

Kloo, D., & Perner, J. (2003). Training transfer between card sorting and false belief understanding: Helping children apply conflicting descriptions. *Child Development, 74,* 1823–1839.

Kochanska, G., & Knaack, A. (2003). Effortful control as a personality characteristic of young children: Antecedents, correlates, and consequences. *Journal of Personality, 71,* 1087–1112.

Kochanska, G., Murray, K., & Coy, K. C. (1997). Inhibitory control as a contributor to conscience in childhood: From toddler to early school age. *Child Development, 68,* 263–277.

Kochanska, G., Murray, K. T., & Harlan, E. T. (2000). Effortful control in early childhood: Continuity and change, antecedents, and implications for social development. *Developmental Psychology, 36,* 220–232.

Korkman, M., Kettunen, S., & Autti-Rämö, I. (2003). Neurocognitive impairment in early adolescence following prenatal alcohol exposure of varying duration. *Child Neuropsychology, 9,* 117–128.

Kubesch, S., Walk, L., Spitzer, M., Kammer, T., Lainburg, A., Heim, R., et al. (2009). A 30-minute physical education program improves students' executive attention. *Mind, Brain, and Education, 3,* 235–242.

Kusche, C. A., & Greenberg, M. T. (1994). *The PATHS curriculum.* Seattle, WA: Developmental Research and Programs.

Lamm, C., Zelazo, P. D., & Lewis, M. D. (2006). Neural correlates of cognitive control in childhood and adolescence: Disentangling the contributions of age and executive function. *Neuropsychologia, 44,* 2139–2148.

Lehto, J. E., Juujarvi, P., Kooistra, L., & Pulkkinen, L. (2003). Dimensions of executive functioning: Evidence from children. *British Journal of Developmental Psychology, 21,* 59–80.

Lengua, L. (2002). The contribution of emotionality and self-regulation to the understanding of children's response to multiple risk. *Child Development, 73,* 144–161.

Lengua, L. (2003). Associations among emotionality, self-regulation, adjustment problems, and positive adjustment in middle childhood. *Journal of Applied Developmental Psychology, 24,* 595–618.

Lengua, L., Bush, N. R., Long, A. C., Kovacs, E. A., & Trancik, A. M. (2008). Effortful control as a moderator of the relation between contextual risk factors and growth in adjustment problems. *Development and Psychopathology, 20,* 509–528.

Lengua, L., Honorado, E., & Bush, N. R. (2007). Contextual risk and parenting as predictors of effortful control and social competence in preschool children. *Journal of Applied Developmental Psychology, 28,* 40–55.

Lengua, L., & Long, A. C. (2002). The role of emotionality and self-regulation in the appraisal-coping process: Tests of direct and moderating effects. *Journal of Applied Developmental Psychology, 23,* 471–493.

Li-Grining, C. P. (2007). Effortful control among low-income preschoolers in three cities: Stability, change, and individual differences. *Developmental Psychology, 43,* 208–221.

Liston, C., Watts, R., Tottenham, N., Davidson, M. C., Niogi, S., Ulug, A. M., et al. (2006). Frontostriatal microstructure modulates efficient recruitment of cognitive control. *Cerebral Cortex, 16,* 553–560.

Luciana, M. (2003). Practitioner review: Computerized assessment of neuropsychological function in children: Clinical and research applications of the Cambridge Neuropsychological Testing Automated Battery (CANTAB). *Journal of Child Psychology and Psychiatry, 44,* 649–663.

Luciana, M., & Nelson, C. A. (1998). The functional emergence of prefrontally-guided working memory systems in four- to eight-year-old children. *Neuropsychologia, 36,* 273–293.

May, J. C., Mauricio, R. D., Ronald, E. D., Stenger, V. A., Neal, D. R., Julie, A. F., et al. (2004). Event-related functional magnetic resonance imaging of reward-related brain circuitry in children and adolescents. *Biological Psychiatry, 55,* 359–366.

McCabe, L. A., Cunnington, M., & Brooks-Gunn, J. (2004). The development of self-regulation in young children: Individual characteristics and environmental contexts. In R. F. Baumeister & K. D. Vohs (Eds.), *Handbook of self-regulation: Research, theory, and applications* (pp. 340–356). New York: Guilford Press.

McClelland, M. M., Cameron, C. E., Connor, C. M., Farris, C. L., Jewkes, A. M., & Morrison, F. J. (2007). Links between behavioral regulation and preschoolers' literacy, vocabulary, and math skills. *Developmental Psychology, 43,* 947–959.

McNab, F., Varrone, A., Farde, L., Jucaite, A., Bystritsky, P., Forssberg, H., et al. (2009). Changes in cortical dopamine D1 receptor binding associated with cognitive training. *Science, 323,* 800–802.

Mezzacappa, E. (2004). Alerting, orienting, and executive attention: Developmental properties and sociodemographic correlates in an epidemiological sample of young, urban children. *Child Development, 75,* 1373–1386.

Mischel, W., Shoda, Y., & Rodriguez, M. I. (1989). Delay of gratification in children. *Science, 244,* 933–938.

Miyake, A., Friedman, N. P., Emerson, M. J., Witzki, A. H., Howerter, A., & Wager, T. D. (2000). The unity and diversity of executive functions and their contributions to complex "frontal lobe" tasks: A latent variable analysis. *Cognitive Psychology, 41,* 49–100.

Munakata, Y. (2001). Graded representations in behavioral dissociations. *Trends in Cognitive Sciences, 5,* 309–315.

Napoli, M., Krech, P. R., & Holley, L. C. (2005). Mindfulness training for elementary school students. *Journal of Applied School Psychology, 21,* 99–125.

Nelson, C., & Jeste, S. (2009). Neurobiological perspectives on developmental psychopathology. In M. Rutter et al. (Eds.), *Rutter's child and adolescent psychiatry* (5th ed., pp. 145–159). Oxford, UK: Blackwell.

Nelson, C. A., & Sheridan, M. A. (2011). Lesson from neuroscience research for understanding causal links between family and neighborhood characteristics and educational outcomes. In G. Duncan & R. Murnane (Eds.), *Whither opportunity: Rising inequality, schools, and children life chances* (pp. 27–46). New York: Russell Sage Foundation Press.

NICHD Early Child Care Research Network. (2003). Do children's attention processes mediate the link between family predictors and school readiness? *Developmental Psychology, 39,* 581–593.

NICHD Early Child Care Research Network. (2005). Predicting individual differences in attention, memory, and planning in first graders from experiences at home, child care, and school. *Developmental Psychology, 41,* 99–114.

Noble, K. G., McCandliss, B. D., & Farah, M. J. (2007). Socioeconomic gradients predict individual differences in neurocognitive abilities. *Developmental Science, 10,* 464–480.

Noble, K. G., Norman, M. F., & Farah, M. J. (2005). Neurocognitive correlates of socioeconomic status in kindergarten children. *Developmental Science, 8*, 74–87.

Noble, K. G., Wolmetz, M. E., Ochs, L. G., Farah, M. J., & McCandliss, B. D. (2006). Brain-behavior relationships in reading acquisition are modulated by socioeconomic factors. *Developmental Science, 9*, 642–654.

Obradović, J. (2010). Effortful control and adaptive functioning of homeless children: Variable-focused and person-focused analyses. *Journal of Applied Developmental Psychology, 31*, 109–117.

Olson, S. L., Bates, J. E., & Bayles, K. (1990). Early antecedents of childhood impulsivity: The role of parent–child interaction, cognitive competence, and temperament. *Journal of Abnormal Child Psychology, 18*, 317–334.

Olson, S. L., Sameroff, A. J., Kerr, D. C. R., Lopez, N. L., & Wellman, H. M. (2005). Developmental foundations of externalizing problems in young children: The role of effortful control. *Development and Psychopathology, 17*, 25–45.

Pears, K. C., & Fisher, P. A. (2005). Emotion understanding and theory of mind among maltreated children in foster care: Evidence of deficits. *Development and Psychopathology, 17*, 47–65.

Pianta, R. C. (2006). Schools, schooling, and developmental psychopathology. In D. Cicchetti & D. J. Cohen (Eds.), *Developmental psychopathology: Vol. 1. Theory and method* (2nd ed., pp. 494–529). Hoboken, NJ: Wiley.

Pianta, R. C., & Stuhlman, M. W. (2004). Teacher–child relationships and children's success in the first years of school. *School Psychology Review, 33*, 444–458.

Ponitz, C. C., McClelland, M. M., Matthews, J. S., & Morrison, F. J. (2009). A structured observation of behavioral self-regulation and its contribution to kindergarten outcomes. *Developmental Psychology, 45*, 605–619.

Raizada, R., Richards, T., Meltzoff, A., & Kuhl, P. (2008). Socioeconomic status predicts hemispheric specialisation of the left inferior frontal gyrus in young children. *NeuroImage, 40*, 1392–1401.

Razza, R. A., & Blair, C. (2009). Associations among false-belief understanding, executive function, and social competence: A longitudinal analysis. *Journal of Applied Developmental Psychology, 30*, 332–343.

Rhoades, B. L., Greenberg, M. T., & Domitrovich, C. E. (2009). The contribution of inhibitory control to preschoolers' social–emotional competence. *Journal of Applied Developmental Psychology, 30*, 310–320.

Riggs, N., Blair, C., & Greenberg, M. T. (2003). Concurrent and 2-year longitudinal relations between executive function and the behavior of 1st and 2nd grade children. *Child Neuropsychology, 9*, 267–276.

Riggs, N., Greenberg, M. T., Kusche, C. A., & Pentz, M. A. (2006). The mediational role of neurocognition in the behavioral outcomes of a social–emotional prevention program in elementary school students: Effects of the PATHS curriculum. *Prevention Science, 7*, 91–102.

Romine, C. B., & Reynolds, C. R. (2005). A model of the development of frontal lobe functioning: Findings from a meta-analysis. *Applied Neuropsychology, 12*, 190–201.

Rothbart, M., Posner, M., & Kieras, J. E. (2006). Temperament, attention and the development of self-regulation. In K. McCartney & D. Phillips (Eds.), *The Blackwell handbook of early child development* (pp. 338–339). Malden, MA: Blackwell.

Rothbart, M. K., & Bates, J. E. (1998). Temperament. In N. Eisenberg & W. Damon (Eds.), *Handbook of child psychology* (5th ed., Vol. 3, pp. 105–176). New York: Wiley.

Rueda, M., Checa, P., & Rothbart, M. (2010). Contributions of attentional control to socioemotional and academic development. *Early Education and Development, 21*, 744–764.

Rueda, M. R., Checa, P., & Santonja, M. (2008, April). *Training executive attention in preschoolers: Lasting effects and transfer to affective self-regulation.* Paper presented at the annual meeting of the Cognitive Neuroscience Society, San Francisco.

Rueda, M. R., Fan, J., McCandliss, B. D., Halparin, J. D., Gruber, D. B., Lercari, L. P., et al. (2004). Development of attentional networks in childhood. *Neuropsychologia, 42*, 1029–1040.

Rueda, M. R., Posner, M. I., & Rothbart, M. K. (2005). The development of executive attention: Contributions to the emergence of self-regulation. *Developmental Neuropsychology, 28*, 573–594.

Rueda, M. R., Rothbart, M. K., McCandliss, B. D., Saccomanno, L., & Posner, M. I. (2005). Training, maturation, and genetic influences on the development of executive attention. *Proceedings of the National Academy of Sciences USA, 102,* 14931–14936.

Santesso, D., Segalowitz, S., & Schmidt, L. (2006). Error-related electrocortical responses are enhanced in children with obsessive–compulsive behaviors. *Developmental Neuropsychology, 29,* 431–445.

Savage, R., Lavers, N., & Pillay, V. (2007). Working memory and reading difficulties: What we know and what we don't know about the relationship. *Educational Psychology Review, 19,* 185–221.

Scherf, K. S., Sweeney, J. A., & Luna, B. (2006). Brain basis of developmental change in visuospatial working memory. *Journal of Cognitive Neuroscience, 18,* 1045–1058.

Senn, T. E., Espy, K. A., & Kaufmann, P. M. (2004). Using path analysis to understand executive function organization in preschool children. *Developmental Neuropsychology, 26,* 445–464.

Spinrad, T. L., Eisenberg, N., Gaertner, B., Popp, T., Smith, C. L., Kupfer, A., et al. (2007). Relations of maternal socialization and toddlers' effortful control to children's adjustment and social competence. *Developmental Psychology, 43,* 1170–1186.

St. Clair-Thompson, H. L., & Gathercole, S. E. (2006). Executive functions and achievements in school: Shifting, updating, inhibition, and working memory. *Quarterly Journal of Experimental Psychology, 59,* 745–759.

Stevens, C., Fanning, J., Coch, D., Sanders, L., & Neville, H. (2008). Neural mechanisms of selective auditory attention are enhanced by computerized training: Electrophysiological evidence from language-impaired and typically developing children. *Brain Research, 1205,* 55–69.

Stevens, C., Lauinger, B., & Neville, H. (2009). Differences in the neural mechanisms of selective attention in children from different socioeconomic backgrounds: An event-related brain potential study. *Developmental Science, 12,* 634–646.

Stroth, S., Kubesch, S., Dieterle, K., Ruchsow, M., Heim, R., & Kiefer, M. (2009). Physical fitness, but not acute exercise modulates event-related potential indices for executive control in healthy adolescents. *Brain Research, 1269,* 114–124.

Swanson, H. L., & Jerman, O. (2007). The influence of working memory on reading growth in subgroups of children with reading disabilities. *Journal of Experimental Child Psychology, 96,* 249–283.

Thomas, K. M., King, S. W., Franzen, P. L., Welsh, T. F., Berkowitz, A. L., Noll, D. C., et al. (1999). A developmental functional MRI study of spatial working memory. *NeuroImage, 10,* 327–338.

Thorell, L. B., Lindqvist, S., Bergman Nutley, S., Bohlin, G., & Klingberg, T. (2009). Training and transfer effects of executive functions in preschool children. *Developmental Science, 12,* 106–113.

Treadway, M. T., & Lazar, S. W. (2009). The neurobiology of mindfulness. In F. Didonna (Ed.), *Clinical handbook of mindfulness* (pp. 45–57). New York: Springer.

Tsujimoto, S. (2008). The prefrontal cortex: Functional neural development during early childhood. *The Neuroscientist, 14,* 345–358.

Valiente, C., Eisenberg, N., Smith, C. L., Reiser, M., Fabes, R. A., Losoya, S., et al. (2003). The relations of effortful control and reactive control to children's externalizing problems: A longitudinal assessment. *Journal of Personality, 71,* 1171–1196.

Vygotsky, L. S. (1962). *Thought and language.* Cambridge, MA: MIT Press.

Webster-Stratton, C., & Reid, M. J. (2004). Strengthening social and emotional competence in young children—the foundation for early school readiness and success: Incredible Years Classroom Social Skills and Problem-Solving Curriculum. *Infants and Young Children, 17,* 96–113.

Webster-Stratton, C., Reid, M. J., & Hammond, M. (2004). Treating children with early-onset conduct problems: Intervention outcomes for parent, child, and teacher training. *Journal of Clinical Child and Adolescent Psychology, 33,* 105–124.

Webster-Stratton, C., Reid, M. J., & Stoolmiller, M. (2008). Preventing conduct problems and improving school readiness: Evaluation of the Incredible Years Teacher and Child Training Programs in high-risk schools. *Journal of Child Psychology and Psychiatry, 49,* 471–488.

Welsh, J. A., Nix, R. L., Blair, C., Bierman, K. L., & Nelson, K. E. (2010). The development of cognitive skills and gains in academic school readiness for children from low-income families. *Journal of Educational Psychology, 102,* 43–53.

Wolfe, C. D., & Bell, M. A. (2004). Working memory and inhibitory control in early childhood: Contributions from physiology, temperament, and language. *Developmental Psychobiology, 44,* 68–83.

Zelazo, P. D. (2006). The dimensional change card sort (DCCS): A method of assessing executive function in children. *Nature Protocols, 1,* 297–301.

Zelazo, P. D., Carlson, S. M., & Kesek, A. (2008). The development of executive function in childhood. In C. A. Nelson & M. Luciana (Eds.), *Handbook of developmental cognitive neuroscience* (2nd ed., pp. 553–574). Cambridge, MA: MIT Press.

Zelazo, P. D., Mueller, U., Frye, D., & Marcovitch, S. (2003). The development of executive functioning in early childhood. *Monographs of the Society for Research in Child Development, 68,* 1–27.

CHAPTER 17

Scaffolding Self-Regulated Learning in Young Children

Lessons from Tools of the Mind

Elena Bodrova and Deborah J. Leong

As new data become available on the role of self-regulation in children's development and learning, researchers as well as educators, have expressed the need for instructional interventions that would strengthen development of self-regulation in typically developing children and/or prevent possible development delays in children with various risk factors. *Tools of the Mind* (Tools) is a program developed to facilitate this by engaging preschool and kindergarten children in a variety of experiences specifically designed to promote self-regulation in the authentic context of an early childhood classroom. In this chapter we describe the theoretical foundation of Tools, illustrate the implementation of these principles using examples of Tools instructional strategies, and discuss the curriculum impact on the development of self-regulation/executive functions in young children and their academic achievement. Tools is based on Lev Vygotsky's views on child development and learning, as well as work completed by his colleagues and students within a cultural–historical paradigm. Vygotskian and post-Vygotskian insights about the development and promotion of self-regulation form the basis for the Tools design of instructional activities and the pedagogy used by the Tools teachers.

Self-Regulation: A Critical Competency

Teachers have long known that one reason young children have trouble adjusting to school is lack of self-regulation. Many studies have found that kindergarten teachers rank the level of self-regulation as one of the most important indicators of child school readiness (e.g., Rimm-Kaufmann, Pianta, & Cox, 2000). In fact, for experienced teachers, self-regulation outweighs other factors, such as chronological age, overall background knowledge, or the child's mastery of specific academic skills (e.g., counting or letter recognition) as the most important skill set for school readiness (Lin, Lawrence, & Gorrell, 2003).

These responses, however inconsistent they may seem with the recent emphasis on "academic" school readiness, come as no surprise if one reflects on the demands of an elementary classroom. In school, children are required to control their attention by blocking distractions and focusing on specific elements of the classroom environment that are not the most obvious or engaging (Downer, Rimm-Kaufman, & Pianta, 2007). Young students are required to conform to a routine, which often means that they have to switch from something they are enjoying to something of less interest.

The start of formal schooling also means new demands on young children's ability to regulate not only their social–emotional but also cognitive processes. For example, starting in kindergarten, children are expected to be able to follow directions that sometimes have multiple, interrelated steps, so that skipping any one of them affects the ultimate outcome. Acquiring early literacy skills requires children to form associations between seemingly unrelated pieces of information, such as the association between a letter symbol and the name of a letter, and frequently to switch between similar but not identical tasks, such as separating words into syllables or individual phonemes. To meet these and other demands of elementary classrooms, children need to develop self-regulatory abilities associated with the development of executive functions (EFs). Executive functions refer to the "processes associated with holding information in mind in working memory, inhibiting automatic responses to stimulation and flexibly shifting attention between distinct but related pieces of information or aspects of a given task" (Blair, Protzko, & Ursache, 2011, p. 22). These processes can be used to regulate cognitive as well as social–emotional behaviors. Children who engage in cognitive self-regulation plans monitor and evaluate their behaviors and are able to adjust these behaviors when needed. On the other hand, social–emotional self-regulation is usually demonstrated in situations associated with the need to inhibit negative responses or to delay gratification. Certain situations, including the ones critical for school success, such as when a child keeps trying to solve a challenging problem in the face of repeated errors, require both aspects of self-regulation: cognitive and social–emotional. The exact mechanisms of the relationship between cognitive and social–emotional aspects of EFs are not yet clear; however, researchers are beginning to consider these to be parts of a more general regulatory system (Blair & Razza, 2007).

Teachers' observations about the relationship between self-regulation and school readiness have been confirmed by research data collected over the past several decades. Comprehensive reviews of research published in sources such as the *From Neurons to Neighborhoods* (Shonkoff & Phillips, 2000), *Eager to Learn* (Bowman, Donovan, & Burns, 2001), and *Ready to Enter* (Raver & Knitzer, 2002) discuss the importance of self-regulation for children's success in school. Recent research focuses on specific self-regulatory mechanisms that may contribute to children's school adjustment, including their effects on children's ability to establish relationships with peers and teachers, as well as to acquire certain academic competencies. For example, a growing body of research points out the importance of self-regulatory mechanisms in children's learning to read, write, and do mathematics (Escalón & Greenfield, 2009). Moreover, research indicates that the development of self-regulation in early childhood predicts children's academic success in primary grades better than children's IQ, socioeconomic background, or even their emerging knowledge in mathematics and literacy measured in preschool (Blair et al., 2011; Blair & Razza, 2007).

A strong relationship between self-regulation and school success is not limited to primary grades but is even more dramatically present in older children, whose inability to regulate their behavior also results in increased vulnerability to risks such as truancy, peer victimization, and substance use (Bandy & Moore, 2010). Emphasizing the cumulative effect of poor self-regulation over school years, Blair and Diamond (2008) compare it to the downward spiral awaiting unregulated young children when they start school: Each turn of the spiral results in behaviors that elicit "reactions from individuals that exacerbate that child's difficulties with regulation, and those interactions help to maintain a developmental course of poor regulation" (p. 901). This increasingly poor regulation, in turn, contributes to children's low engagement in academic tasks and may often result in school dropout and overall poor adaptive functioning (Buckner, Mezzacappa, & Beardslee, 2009).

The existence of strong connections between self-regulation and later cognitive and social outcomes draws attention to the alarming fact that the numbers of young children with poor self-regulation seem to be on the rise, with up to half of incoming kindergartners not being able to benefit from instruction (Rimm-Kaufmann et al., 2001). The number of children expelled from preschool is three times higher than that in grades K–12 (Gilliam, 2005), and teachers admit that the main reason for expulsion is children's out-of-control behaviors. The situation is most dramatic for low-income children, who consistently demonstrate lower levels of self-regulation and higher incidences of behavior problems than their middle-income peers (Evans & Rosenbaum, 2008).

Early childhood programs designed to promote school readiness, such as Head Start or preschool, do not appear to be particularly effective at supporting children's self-regulation (Skibbe, Connor, Morrison, & Jewkes, 2011). This has resulted in the development of supplemental curricula and interventions that focus specifically on this competency. Most of these programs address social–emotional aspects of self-regulation, and are designed to prevent and remediate challenging behaviors in young children (Domitrovich, Cortes, & Greenberg, 2007; Hemmeter & Fox, 2009). Other interventions target cognitive components of self-regulation, primarily attention (Rueda, Rothbart, & McCandliss, 2005; Stevens, Fanning, Coch, Sanders, & Neville, 2008). While these programs demonstrate positive impact on specific behaviors, they remain somewhat limited given the complex and intertwined nature of the self-regulation construct. In contrast, Tools is a systemic intervention that promotes multiple aspects of self-regulation in a synergistic manner for all children, not just those at risk for developing or already manifesting challenging behaviors or attention deficits.

Tools of the Mind Theoretical Foundations: The Vygotskian Approach to Development and Learning

Tools is grounded in Vygotsky's theory of child learning and development (Vygotsky, 1978, 1987, 1998). The curriculum also incorporates developmental and educational theories of post-Vygotskians such as Alexander Luria (1960, 1994, 1998), Daniel Elkonin (1977, 1978), and Alexander Zaporozhets (1986), whose ideas are less familiar to the Western audiences than the ideas of Vygotsky himself.

Tools is one of the first attempts in the United States to create a comprehensive Vygotskian-based curriculum for use in early childhood classrooms. Vygotskian-based curricula have previously been designed for elementary and middle school students (Campione & Brown, 1990; Newman, Griffin, & Cole, 1989; Tharp & Gallimore, 1989). Most of the attempts to use Vygotskian-based pedagogy with preschool- and kindergarten-age children were limited to individual instructional strategies (e.g., Elkonin blocks, widely used in reading remediation programs) or focused on only one type of scaffolding (primarily teacher-assisted learning in a one-on-one setting).

Vygotsky's Cultural–Historical Approach

One of the fundamental principles of the cultural–historical paradigm is the assertion that " a child's mental development is not a simple maturing of natural 'instincts,' but that it occurs in the process of objective activity and communication with adults" (Luria, 2002, p. 21). As children master the tools developed in human history, they learn to make use of culturally developed tools such as language or nonverbal external *stimuli-media* to organize their own behavior. The acquisition of these cultural tools—*tools of the mind*—does more than just allow a child to perform better on a specific task; it actually promotes the restructuring of the child's brain by connecting previously independent areas of the brain and forming what Vygotskians call a new "functional system" (Luria, 1973).

As a result of acquiring mental tools, children develop higher mental functions—*deliberate, mediated*, and *internalized* behaviors (Vygotsky, 1997). By characterizing higher mental functions as *deliberate*, it is believed that they are controlled by the person and not by the environment; their use is based on thought and choice. These deliberate behaviors become possible because they do not depend on the environment in an immediate and direct fashion but are instead *mediated* by the use of tools. By the time higher mental functions are fully developed, most of the tools used are not external but internal (e.g., mnemonics) and so are the processes involved in using these tools. Vygotsky describes this process as "internalization," emphasizing that when external behaviors *grow into the mind*, they maintain the same structure, focus, and function as their external precursors. It is the deliberate nature of higher mental functions that makes them central to the discussion of the development of self-regulation.

Vygotsky described the mechanism of the development of higher mental functions as their gradual transformation from "interpsychological"—shared by a child with two or more people—to "intrapsychological"—something that belongs to this child only. Vygotsky illustrated this process using an example of a voluntary action: First, the initiation and the execution of the action is distributed between two individuals—"I order, you execute." The next stage involves an individual issuing commands to him- or herself, then executing these self-commands. Finally, at the last stage, the voluntary action is formed. This Vygotskian view of the development of higher mental functions in general, and voluntary actions in particular, has guided the development of Tools of the Mind, in which children's experiences and teacher–child interactions are specifically designed to promote development of EFs.

Vygotsky's Theory of Development in Early Childhood

Further elaborating on the idea of human development as an interplay between the processes of natural development that are determined biologically and the processes of cultural development, Vygotsky proposed that this interplay takes different forms for children at different developmental stages defining their specific social situations of development. The social situation of development defined by Vygotsky (1998) as a "unique relation, specific to a given age, between the child and reality, mainly the social reality that surrounds him" (p. 198) propels development forward by providing new and more advanced mental tools that continue to shape children's growing competencies: "Neo-formations [developmental accomplishments] that arise toward the end of a given age lead to a reconstruction of the whole structure of the child's consciousness and in this way change the whole system of relations to external reality and to himself" (p. 199). The major changes in the structure of mental processes marking the end of early childhood are associated with their growing intentionality. This ability to engage in intentional behaviors enables preschool children to make the necessary transition from learning that "follows the child's own agenda" to learning that "follows the school agenda" (Vygotsky, 1956, p. 426).

Vygotsky's and Luria's Views on the Development of EFs and Self-Regulation

The construct of EFs per se was not used by Vygotsky or Luria, although the use of the term EFs by most current researchers is consistent with the idea of Vygotskian concepts of higher mental functions and the idea of psychological systems (Fernyhough, 2010). In the cultural–historical tradition, the constructs currently associated with EF and self-regulation have been primarily framed in terms of the development of voluntary behaviors and associated with children gaining control of their previously involuntary behaviors by using cultural tools, mostly of a linguistic nature.

For example, Luria (1959, 1960) analyzed the changes in the role speech plays in allowing young children to regulate their motor actions. In the beginning, the effects of speech on child behavior are limited to its excitatory function: A toddler gradually becomes able to follow verbal instructions and no longer needs to be guided by more salient visual stimuli. This excitatory aspect of speech remains strong until 4 to 4½ years. At this age, the semantic aspects of speech become more important when the meanings of the words continue to direct motor responses independent of whether the words themselves are audible. As a result of the further development of the executive functioning system, children gain even greater control of their behaviors as they become able to direct not only their physical behaviors but also their cognitive behaviors. In an experiment with school-age children, Luria studied children's ability to memorize a set of random words with and without the help of picture cards. Using picture cards allowed children to increase the number of items they were able to recall by 60%. In this experiment, picture cards served as cultural tools that enabled children to gain control over their memory by "replacing their direct application by a complicated cultural application" (Luria, 1994, p. 54).

Vygotsky's Views on the Role of Instruction in Child Development

The idea of a social situation driving child development is reflected in the position Vygotsky (1997) took in regard to childrearing practices in general and formal education in particular. Arguing with the proponents of "following a child's lead," he wrote:

> The old point of view ... assumed that it was necessary to adapt rearing to development (in the sense of time, rate, form of thinking and perception proper to the child, etc.). It did not pose the question dynamically. The new point of view ... takes the child in the dynamics of his development and growth and asks *where must the teaching bring the child.* (p. 224, emphasis added)

From Vygotsky's perspective, this new point of view called for a different approach to education, an approach that focused instruction not on the competencies already existing in a child, but on the competencies still under construction—the ones that exist in the child's zone of proximal development (ZPD). Vygotsky believed that the role of the teacher is more than teaching facts and skills—that teachers can actually shape children's development by helping them acquire the mental tools of their culture. In the pages that follow, we discuss the specific implications of this principle for early childhood education.

Applying Vygotskian and Post-Vygotskian Ideas
to Early Childhood Education

Tools builds on the work of Vygotsky and of post-Vygotskians who developed their own theories and continued to carry out the Vygotskian tradition. One of the most important concepts from post-Vygotskians used in the development of Tools is the idea of amplification of child development (Zaporozhets, 1986). The term "amplification" was coined to argue against the idea that the preschool classroom should be designed as a miniature copy of a primary classroom, with teaching methods and materials modeled after the ones used by elementary teachers. The idea of amplification also was intended as an alternative to the notion of spontaneous development of young children, which posited that development could not and should not be affected by instruction. Amplification focuses on the role of education in child development, emphasizing that properly designed educational interactions do not stifle but instead promote development of preschool children, thus presenting a logical extension of Vygotsky's principle of instruction leading development.

Make-Believe Play Is the Leading Activity of Preschool- and Kindergarten-Age Children

For Vygotskians, certain activities in which children engage, known as "leading activities," produce the greatest gains in development, with the magnitude of these gains being age dependent. Leading activities provide optimal conditions for children to learn the cognitive and social competencies most critical for child development in each age period (Chaiklin, Hedegaard, & Jensen, 1999; Elkonin, 1977; Leont'ev, 1978). They also provide the prerequisites necessary for the child to benefit from the leading activity to come at the next age level. Make-believe play is the leading activity of preschool- and kindergarten-age children, whereas the leading activity for students of primary grades is intentional learning (frequently referred to as the "learning activity"). Young children's engagement in high-level make-believe play contributes to the development of underlying cognitive skills such as symbolic thinking and self-regulation. However, the Vygotskian definition of high-level play is much narrower than that in popular culture. The definition of play does not include activities such as object manipulations and explorations that are considered precursors to play or activities, such as games and sports, that are considered an outgrowth of play. Rather, make-believe play happens only when children are able to create a joint imaginary situation, take on the roles of various pretend characters, and act these out using imaginary props, language, and symbolic gestures.

In addition, consistent with the foundational ideas of the cultural–historical theory, Vygotskians do not believe that play develops spontaneously in all children once they reach preschool age. High-level or "mature play," the level necessary to be a leading activity for preschoolers, emerges only with adult mediation or when young children are assisted by older children acting as play mentors. Not all play is equally beneficial for the development of self-regulation. Current studies of the relationship between play and self-regulation confirm Vygotsky's belief that make-believe play can improve self-regulation, especially in highly impulsive, hard-to-manage children (Berk, Mann, & Ogan, 2006; Elias & Berk, 2002; Krafft & Berk, 1998).

Scaffolded Interactions Are Essential to Children's Learning

Although the term "scaffolding" has a long history in the West of being associated with Vygotsky's paradigm (Wood, Bruner, & Ross, 1976), it is not a term used by either Vygotsky himself or the post-Vygotskians. In this chapter we use the term "scaffolding" to adhere to the Western tradition but specify some characteristics of this process that make it more consistent with the Vygotskian view on the relationship between instruction and development.

Scaffolding interactions are used in the course of teaching to help a child move from being assisted by an adult in performing a new task to being able to perform this and similar tasks independently (Bodrova & Leong, 2007). These interactions must fall within each individual's ZPD so that they support the very skills and knowledge that are on the edge of emergence (Vygotsky, 1978). When providing scaffolding, an adult does not make the task easier but instead makes the child's job easier by giving the child maximum support in the beginning stages, then gradually withdrawing support as the child's mastery of a new skill increases (Wood et al., 1976). An appropriate support is one that makes it easier for a child to complete a current task, brings to the surface behaviors most mature to date, and also supports the child's "construction of mind," influencing the development of mental categories and processes responsible for the child's performance on a variety of tasks. Thus, effective scaffolding should provide the temporary support needed until new mental processes and categories are fully developed, and be something the child can gradually use without any outside assistance. From this perspective, scaffolding may exist in different formats ranging from teacher–child interactions when they work on a task jointly, to teacher introduction of a strategy or a tool for later independent use by the child, to the teacher planning for a specific context or environment in which the child will be supported by other children (Bodrova & Leong, 2007; Campione & Brown, 1990; Wood et al., 1976). In Tools classrooms, teachers provide scaffolding in a variety of formats and across various contexts.

When applied to young children, scaffolding should focus on introducing the earliest strategies and tools that young children can use on their own. Among these are private speech, external mediators, and symbolic representations written or drawn by the child. According to Vygotsky (1987), private speech in young children is a precursor to verbal thinking and consequently serves as a carrier of thought at a time when most higher mental functions are not yet fully developed. As later discovered by Luria (1969) and confirmed by many studies within and outside the Vygotskian framework, private speech has another important function: Children can use it to regulate their own behaviors, both overt and mental (Berk, 1992; Winsler, de Leon, Wallace, Carlton, & Willson-Quayle, 2003). External mediators are another example of the first tools used by children. They include tangible objects, pictures of objects, and physical actions that children use to gain control over their own behavior. Finally, children's early representations—symbolic drawings (pictographs), scribbles, or writing—were also found by the Vygotskians to be the first tools that children use to support their memory (Luria, 1998). The Tools curriculum expands children's repertoire of tools and provides new opportunities for children to use them. For example, prior to going to the centers, children are asked to draw a picture of where they will be and what they will play to help them remember their play ideas.

Tools in an Early Childhood Classroom: Content and Pedagogy

Tools is a comprehensive curriculum that promotes the development of self-regulation and is designed to be used in typical early childhood (preschool and kindergarten) classrooms. Tools differs from other existing interventions that promote self-regulation in several ways. First, rather than focusing on children at risk for behavior problems or the ones already diagnosed with autism or attention-deficit/hyperactivity disorder (ADHD), Tools addresses all children. Second, unlike programs such as Promoting Alternative Thinking Skills (PATHS; Domitrovich et al., 2007) that target only the social–emotional component of self-regulation, Tools approaches the development of self-regulation in a systemic way, addressing social–emotional and cognitive aspects simultaneously. Finally, Tools activities that promote self-regulation do not require one-on-one adult–child interactions or pulling a child out of the classroom to play a computer game, as is the case with other interventions (e.g., Rueda et al., 2005). Furthermore, Tools activities are not limited to one specific time in the daily schedule or added to another curriculum already being implemented by teachers (e.g., Domitrovich et al., 2007; Neville et al., 2011).

Tools is designed as a systemic intervention addressing multiple facets of self-regulation throughout the day and in varying contexts found in a typical preschool or kindergarten program. The design of specific content and pedagogy implemented in Tools classrooms is guided by general principles of the cultural–historical approach and a set of specific Vygotskian principles pertaining to the development of self-regulation (Bodrova & Leong, 2007):

- Children's self-regulatory abilities originate in social interactions and only later become internalized and independently used by children (Vygotsky, 1978). It follows that to develop self-regulation, children need to have an opportunity to engage in other-regulation. Other-regulation implies that children act both as subjects of another person's regulatory behaviors and as actors regulating other person's behaviors.

- Play affects a young child's self-regulation through shared behaviors that result in internalized higher mental functions. The development of self-regulation in play becomes possible because of the inherent relationship that exists between the roles children play and the rules that they need to follow when playing these roles (Vygotsky, 1967).

- A necessary condition for the emergence of self-regulation is children's learning of specific cultural tools that allow them eventually to use self-regulatory behaviors independently. Among the first such tools children learn is self-talk or private speech (Berk, 1992; Vygotsky, 1987). Other kinds of tools used by young children are external mediators, that is, objects that assist them in carrying out intentional behaviors (Vygotsky, 1978), as in the use of external mediators in Buddy Reading, described later in this chapter.

- To be successful in school, children must develop general social and cognitive competencies that allow them to become deliberate, self-regulated learners, capable of establishing adequate social relationships with other participants in the teaching and learning process, as well as being able to adopt a specific position of a "student" characterized by things such as interest in learning, willingness to adhere to school rules, and readiness to follow the teacher's directions.

These principles guide the design of the Tools program as an integrated curriculum, in which *all* activities implemented throughout the day support both cognitive and social–emotional aspects of self-regulation. These activities fall into three main categories: (1) symbolic make-believe play and games, (2) focal activities in which self-regulation is the primary focus, and (3) activities in which self-regulation practice is embedded in academic content.

Symbolic Play as an Integrative Way to Promote Self-Regulation

Symbolic play is key feature of Tools that promotes self-regulation. Development of self-regulation in play becomes possible because of the inherent relations that exist between roles children play and rules they need to follow when playing these roles. This requires children to practice self-regulation both in its shared and individual forms. In play, the shared form of self-regulation exists as "other-regulation," as children monitor their play partners' playing by the rules, while at the same time following directions issued by other players. By engaging in other-regulation, young children gain awareness of the rules of the play situation that they can then apply to their own behavior at a later time.

According to the Vygotskian approach, make-believe play yields self-regulatory benefits only when it reaches its fully developed or mature stage (Elkonin, 1978, 2005). With dramatic changes in society today, many children do not get an opportunity to acquire play skills from other children acting as play mentors; thus, they may engage in play that never reaches its mature level (Karpov, 2005). As a result, many children, especially those from low socioeconomic status (SES) backgrounds, may not experience the benefits afforded by fully developed play (Chien et al., 2010; Farran & Son-Yarbrough, 2001). Therefore, in Tools preschool classrooms, teachers intentionally promote mature play by focusing on all of its essential aspects. These include (1) using toys and props in a symbolic way, (2) developing consistent and extended play scenarios based on the story, (3) taking on and staying in a pretend role for an extended play episode or a series of play episodes, and (4) consistently following the rules that determine what each pretend character can or cannot do.

By kindergarten age, most children can be expected to master the ability to regulate each other and themselves in the context of make-believe play. They become capable of engaging in a different kind of play, games with rules, where they abide by decontextualized and often arbitrary rules, which further promotes self-regulation. In reality, many children enter kindergarten not having higher levels of play that have been associated with the development of self-regulation (Berk et al., 2006; Elkonin, 1978); they are unprepared to conform their actions to mandatory rules and norms of a classroom. Therefore, teachers in Tools kindergarten classrooms support play in two ways: (1) by continuing to promote mature and intentional make-believe play as a part of daily activities, and (2) by facilitating children's transition from make-believe play to playing games with rules.

To facilitate children's transition from make-believe play to playing games with rules in kindergarten, Tools teachers engage children in learning games with increasingly complex rules. These games are designed to support learning of specific academic content, along with other competencies such as self-regulation or perspective taking, while at the same time engaging children in interactions that are playful and fun. For example, as children play Market Farm, a numerals game activity, one of them plays the role of a grocer and another plays that of a farmer. The grocer orders food items for the store (e.g., eggs and bacon) and writes the number on an order form. The farmer fills the order with manipulatives that represent the food items. Finally, by using a checking sheet, the grocer has to determine whether the farmer sent the right amount.

Focal Activities to Promote Self-Regulation

Activities designed to focus specifically on various components of EF are an essential component of Tools. One example is a version of a movement game, Freeze, in which children move freely as the music plays but have to stop and freeze, mimicking the position of a stick figure held by a teacher the moment the music stops. Although the stick figure is always visible to children, they are required to ignore it deliberately while the music is playing and attend to it only after the music stops. As the year progresses, the game becomes more difficult, with the stick figures appearing on different colored backgrounds that require children to remember as an additional step which of two figures they are to enact. If there are two figures, one on a pink background and one on a yellow background, the children must remember to freeze only in the position of the figure with the yellow background if the teacher holds up a yellow card or a pink card with a "no" symbol on it (meaning the "not pink" option). In this activity, children practice inhibitory control and learn to switch from one set of rules to another.

During Play Planning, another example of a focal activity, children orally plan and then represent on paper what they intend to do during their make-believe play. The primary goal of the activity is to enable children to describe intentions prior to enacting them and to follow through with a plan, with an additional goal of supporting children's oral and written language. When engaged in Play Planning, children display aspects of EF/self-regulation, such as the use of information and prior experience to manage behavior prospectively or the coordination of past experience with future action (Fuster, 1997). Children also practice monitoring their own actions by reviewing whether they followed the plan.

In conjunction with some props corresponding to the children's initial choice of a role or an activity, an additional function of Play Plans is that they allow children to engage in other-regulation and monitor their friends' compliance with the rules of play without teacher intervention. Another self-regulatory benefit is that Play Plans assist children in developing perspective-taking abilities (Carlson, Moses, & Breton, 2002) as they anticipate their friends' behaviors while composing their own Play Plans. For example, in noticing that many children want to be the fireman, the child who plans to play the role of firefighter makes sure to add details to his picture, so that he can later use his plan as the evidence that he is the one who gets to wear the disputed outfit.

As children move from preschool to kindergarten, Play Plans are gradually replaced by Learning Plans, which is also an example of an activity with the primary focus of self-regulation. Learning plans have three functions. First they serve as a simple calendar to help children remember which center to go to and the "must do" activity and work product in that center and in centers they have not yet visited, thus helping children stay on task when they finish with something in a given center. Second, the Learning Plans serve as means for children to learn to review their own work by checking to see that the work is finished. Third, the plans help children reflect on their own learning. At the end of the week the child, with the teacher's help, sets a learning goal that is placed at the bottom of the following week's Learning Plan. Setting learning goals involves adult-scaffolded reflection on one's own thought processes and promotes early reflective thinking in children, both because children write or draw something to help them remember the goal and read the goal prior to starting each activity each week. At the end of the week, the teacher has a learning conference with each child to discuss the effectiveness of the learning strategies, the child's progress on that week's learning goal, and next week's learning goal.

Activities in Which EF Is Embedded in Academic Content

The number of activities combining academic content with EF enhancement is greater in the kindergarten version of Tools than the preschool version; however, a number of such activities are implemented in preschool classrooms as well. These activities are designed both to retain the focus on literacy, math, science, and art, and to strengthen EF. An example of preschool literacy activity is Buddy Reading, in which children learn book handling skills and print concepts as they "read" books. Instead of each child reading the book alone, however, children read books to each other, which exercises self-regulation in turn taking and requires children to develop the ability to remain in the role of reader or listener for the entire activity. To support self-regulation in this activity, Tools teachers use visual representations (i.e., mediators) of lips and ears (*lips read and ears listen*) to help children enact the social norms of turn taking and remain in a given role. As children move from pretend reading in preschool to reading the words and actually decoding text in kindergarten, this activity changes, with additional mediators introduced for the listener whose role now involves prompting the reader to use a specific reading strategy when encountering an unfamiliar word (see Figure 17.1).

In a similar way, many math activities follow a Numerals Game format in which children alternate roles as "doers" and "checkers" with visual symbols (a picture of a hand, *doer*, and a picture of a checkmark, *checker*) assigned to each role, thus embedding self-regulation and performance-monitoring practice into learning math content. In the Numerals Game, the doer has a number card and counts out that number of small teddy bears into a cup. The checker takes the bears and puts them on a checking sheet with the numeral and

 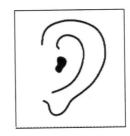

FIGURE 17.1. Examples of mediator cards used for Buddy Reading in kindergarten.

the corresponding number of dots. If the bears cover the dots with no extra ones showing, the children know that the number is correct. If there are more bears than dots, then there were too many counted into the cup. If there are more dots than bears, then the children know that there were too few counted.

By assuming doing or checking roles separately rather than simultaneously in activities such as Buddy Reading and Numerals Games, children are able to develop proficiency in performing various roles, while increasing their cognitive set-shifting ability. The idea of scaffolding children's learning through shared activity, such as when one child is the doer and the other is the checker (then switching roles) represents Vygotsky's (1997) principle that children gradually internalize mental tools that first exist in a shared or distributed state. This is also based on the work of post-Vygotskians, who applied this principle to study reflective thinking and metacognition in children as an outgrowth of specifically organized shared activities (Rubtsov, 1991; Zuckerman, 2003). By designing cooperative activities around different roles, thus engaging children in the state of shared activity, Tools accomplishes two goals. First, it maximizes children's engagement in the context of large- or small-group activities because children do not wait for the teacher's help but help each other or work as much as they can on their own. Second, by assuming strategically identified roles (e.g., checker), children learn to monitor and evaluate the actions of their partners, eventually internalizing criteria and actions they will be able to apply to their own work. With respect to the development of self-regulation and EF, such activities build cognitive and social competencies that are hallmarks of self-regulated learning in older children (Schunk, 1999). These activities also provide optimal contexts for children to practice perspective taking and to develop insights into a theory of mind, both of which are associated with the development of EF and social–emotional competence (Riggs, Jahromi, Razza, Dillworth-Bart, & Mueller, 2006).

The Pedagogy of Scaffolding

The pedagogy used by Tools teachers is based on the concept of individualized scaffolding within each child's ZPD that the teacher has determined through dynamic assessment. In Tools classrooms, teachers provide scaffolding in a variety of formats and across various contexts not limited to academic tasks. Likewise, they introduce children to a variety of tools or auxiliary means that promote the development of self-regulated behaviors.

One of the primary tools built into activities in the Tools classrooms is the encouragement of children's use of oral language, in not only social interactions but also as private speech, the mechanism of self-regulation. For example, teachers ask questions that require children to share their answers with other children instead of waiting to be called upon by a teacher. Unlike well-known "think–pair–share" formats, Tools recognizes that young children are not able to separate the "think" part from the "talk" part. Instead, young children "think as they talk" (Berk, 1992; Vygotsky, 1987). Distinctions between private and social speech are not clearly defined. Providing specifically designed opportunities for children to talk to each other has multiple benefits: It promotes the development of oral language as a tool for social interactions, creates the conditions for the emergence of private or inner speech that will serve as a mechanism for self-regulation, promotes social interaction and turn taking, and fosters early literacy development by providing for growth in knowledge of vocabulary and syntax.

Another category of tools includes a variety of visual aids specifically designed to help children practice their most mature self-regulated behaviors. These external mediators (Bodrova & Leong, 2007) are used primarily in activities where children cannot yet self-regulate independently or can do so for only a short time. Examples of such external mediators include the cards with "lips" and "ears" used in Buddy Reading, cards with a check and a hand used in the Numerals Game, or the use of "role tags" children wear to indicate the role they are playing. In all these cases, external mediators support self-regulation in two complementary ways: First, children use these mediators to regulate their friends, reminding them of the role in which they are supposed to be; and second, children use the mediators as reminders that allow them to remember their own roles better.

To provide guidance for teachers in identifying which scaffolds should be used for which children at which time, the procedures for dynamic assessment are written into the description of each Tools activity. Dynamic assessment "takes into account the results of an intervention" (Sternberg & Grigorenko, 2002, p. vii) and is used to establish both the child's current level of achievement and potential ability to attain higher levels. Dynamic assessment is an alternative to a typical assessment paradigm that measures only current competencies and renders as invalid any test involving intervention on the child's performance during the measurement session. In contrast, dynamic assessment treats the interactions between the child and the tester as a valuable source of information about a child's ability. In a Tools activity, dynamic assessment consists of a series of prompts and hints provided by the teacher to probe children's emerging skills and understandings. These prompts and hints are arranged in a developmental and learning trajectory for that skill and also have embedded in them different levels of teacher assistance. Teachers learn not only about developmental sequences, but also variable degrees of assistance from minimal (e.g., verbal hint) to maximal (walking the child through steps, hand over hand). Teachers use the information to decide the focus of their scaffolding going forward. Activities are designed so that teachers learn not only how to provide support but also how to gradually withdraw that support, making sure that children grow more independent over time. For example, as teachers assist with Play Planning, they mark the child's levels of independence (e.g., draws a picture) and assistance (e.g., plans her message by using lines) on the Play Plan (see Figure 17.2). Reviewing records from past Play Planning sessions allows the teacher to adjust the level of scaffolding to meet the child's growing mastery.

Effects of Tools Implementation on Children's Self-Regulation and Academic Achievement

While the number of programs currently using Tools is large, collecting data on its effectiveness presents logistical challenges due to the lack of common assessment instruments used across different sites. Therefore, at this point we are using these data primarily as a means of formative assessment of the curriculum rather than for reporting its effectiveness.

The first formal evaluation of the effectiveness of Tools was conducted by the National Institute for Early Education Research (NIEER) in a study employing a double-blind, randomized experimental design (Barnett et al., 2008). The control group experienced

FIGURE 17.2. Examples of Play Plans with the Dynamic Assessment form filled in by the teacher.

an established, district-created model described as a "balanced literacy curriculum with themes" (p. 299). The study was conducted in a school district with a high level of poverty and a predominantly non-English-speaking population. Teachers and students were randomly assigned either to treatment or to control classrooms. Children (88 in Tools and 122 controls ages 3 and 4) were compared on social behavior, language, and literacy growth. The Tools curriculum was found to improve classroom quality and children's executive functions, as indicated by lower scores on the Problem Behavior dimension of the Social Skills Rating Scale (Gresham & Elliot, 1990). In addition, there were gains in language development; however, these effects were smaller and did not reach conventional levels of statistical significance. Teachers trained in Tools scored higher in classroom management, use of classroom time, and appropriate engagement interactions that challenged children to learn at the next level.

A quasi-experimental study (Diamond, Barnett, Thomas, & Munroe, 2007) compared Tools children to control children on several measures of executive/inhibitory control administered by computer. The sample was based on the one used in the Barnett and colleagues (2008) study, reported earlier. At the time of the study, all children attended kindergarten and were on average 5 years of age. A stratified randomized sample was used to control for teacher effects. To test EF, children were assessed on the dots and flanker tasks, which have been used with individuals from age 4 to adult (Rueda et al., 2004). The results showed that on the test trials requiring minimal EF, children in the Tools and control conditions performed the same. In those conditions that taxed EF, children in Tools did significantly better than controls. Further analyses comparing the children's scores on the two EF tests and the academic achievement measures collected on the Tools children found that the higher the level of EF, the higher the achievement scores. In addition, results regarding the EF measures correlated with the teachers' ratings of behavior on the Social Skills Rating Scale.

Tools is currently the subject of a number of randomized controlled trials. Several more experimental and quasi-experimental studies are in the planning stages. In addition to determining the efficacy of the curriculum when implemented with children of different ages (preschool and kindergarten) and with different demographic characteristics (e.g., with dual language learners), these new studies will investigate the specific mechanisms involved in developing self-regulation and EFs. At the same time, data from various school districts that have been implementing Tools are being analyzed to track its effects on children's later academic achievement as measured on third- and fourth-grade standardized tests.

Implications

In the process of developing Tools, implementing it in a variety of early childhood settings, and conducting research on its effectiveness, we have learned several lessons than might be helpful for the others who develop and study self-regulation interventions or who work in the educational policy area.

Need for More Comprehensive Research on Self-Regulation

Most current research focuses on only cognitive or social–emotional aspects of self-regulation, and the question of how these aspects might be interrelated or affect each other is just now being addressed. In addition, given the dearth of longitudinal studies on the topic, very little is known about developmental trajectories of various aspects of self-regulation. Studies are needed that examine the relationship between attention and inhibitory control and later cognitive gains, as well as questions about the effects of emotion regulation and children's ability to control stress and anxiety, and later learning. The lack of longitudinal research also extends to the study of interventions that target self-regulation. Most investigations assess short-term gains at the end of 1 or 2 years and do not follow children for extended periods of time. This short-term orientation does not allow one to study possible "latent" outcomes of intervention that may not be manifest in the early school years but may surface as school demands on children increase or change.

Need for More Measures of Self-Regulation

The field is also in the earliest stages of developing assessments for self-regulation and investigating the relationship between these assessments and measures of academic achievement. Little is known about the self-regulation or EF measures that are most sensitive and predictive of later success. Many measures are applicable at one age but not another, making longitudinal evaluation difficult. Moreover, the discussion is still open about whether focusing primarily on academic outcomes accurately reflects the broader context of an individual's success in life when assessed many years after graduation.

Including Self-Regulation in State and National Standards

For self-regulation to be fostered, specific goals and objectives need to be required as a part of the standards and objectives in states' and districts' early learning and K–12 guidelines. These goals should not be relegated to the social–emotional domain, but the elements of cognitive self-regulation (attending and ignoring distractions, remembering on purpose) should be specified as a part of learning goals. Self-regulation expectations must be developmentally appropriate within and across grades to allow for further growth. Alignment on self-regulation goals throughout the grades is also important, with attention to changes in the manifestations of self-regulated behaviors in children of different ages.

There may be considerable experimentation in the manner in which self-regulation is emphasized over time in a classroom. Unlike content area standards, which may require consistent practice over the course of a year, it is our experience with implementing Tools in variety of settings that children benefit from concentrating on self-regulation at the beginning of the year. This is because once that it is in place, learning seems to more efficient, and children can reach and even exceed benchmarks in academic areas at the end of the year. However, the initial intensive work on self-regulation appears necessary to allow children to end the year with a strong foundation that carries forward into the next year. For self-regulation to become an attainable goal, emphasis must be placed on those behaviors associated with self-regulation, and the field may need to experiment with a more flexible timetable, with differing levels of dosage depending on the age and the level of self-regulation of the children.

Teacher Preparation and Professional Development That Includes an Understanding of Self-Regulation Development and How to Support It

More preservice and inservice training is needed for teachers in the area of children's self-regulation/EF and methods to support its development in the classroom. Although teachers are required to know about child development and learning, as pointed out in a recent report on teacher preparation (National Council for Accreditation of Teacher Education, 2010), in reality teachers have very limited knowledge of how self-regulation develops and how to scaffold children at different points in their developmental trajectories. In addition to this knowledge about self-regulation, teachers need to know how to assess children's level of self-regulation development within the classroom context. For example, techniques such as dynamic assessment yield information that translates directly into scaffolds for specific children. Assessments that do not provide immediate feedback are useful to ensure that growth is occurring in a general way but are not helpful for identifying specific instructional needs at a given moment.

Another critical aspect of promoting self-regulation in early childhood classrooms is helping teachers to learn strategies and techniques for supporting self-regulation. Vygotskian research shows that support is critical for play to become the more mature type of activity that develops regulated behavior. Whereas make-believe play is still an essential part of preschool classrooms, this is no longer the case in kindergarten. Moreover, many preschool teachers may think it is unnecessary for an adult to intervene in play unless children are fighting or arguing. Both preservice and inservice training should include information on how to use play, as well as other strategies to support self-regulation development.

Teachers need strategies and assessments not just for typically developing children but also for children with special needs, whose self-regulation skills do not respond to strategies one might use with typically developing children. These children become more obvious in classrooms that emphasize self-regulation development, and teachers and special education teams need strategies that go beyond the activities in programs like Tools.

As more and more interventions are developed that address the need to support and improve self-regulatory skills, we are entering a period with a new and growing understanding of self-regulation. As more researchers study the subject, our understanding of what works and how to improve teaching of self-regulation will also grow.

References

Bandy, T., & Moore, K. A. (2010). *Assessing self-regulation: A guide for out-of-school time program practitioners.* Washington, DC: Child Trends.

Barnett, W. S., Jung, K., Yarosz, D., Thomas, J., Hornbeck, A., Stechuk, R., et al. (2008). Educational effects of the Tools of the Mind curriculum: A randomized trial. *Early Childhood Research Quarterly, 23,* 299–313.

Berk, L. E. (1992). Children's private speech: An overview of theory and the status of research. In R. M. Diaz & L. E. Berk (Eds.), *Private speech: From social interaction to self-regulation* (pp. 17–53). Hillsdale, NJ: Erlbaum.

Berk, L. E., Mann, T. D., & Ogan, A. T. (2006). Make-believe play: Wellspring for development of self-regulation. In D. Singer, R. M. Golinkoff, & K. A. Hirsh-Pasek (Eds.), *Play = learning: How play motivates and enhances cognitive and social-emotional growth* (pp. 74–100). New York: Oxford University Press.

Blair, C., & Diamond, A. (2008). Biological processes in prevention and intervention: The promotion of self-regulation as a means of preventing school failure. *Development and Psychopathology, 20,* 899–911.

Blair, C., Protzko, J., & Ursache, A. (2011). Self-regulation and early literacy. In S. B. Neuman & D. K. Dickinson (Eds.), *Handbook of early literacy research* (Vol. 3, pp. 20–35). New York: Guilford Press.

Blair, C., & Razza, R. A. (2007). Relating effortful control, executive function, and false-belief understanding to emerging math and literacy ability in kindergarten *Child Development, 78,* 647–663.

Bodrova, E., & Leong, D. J. (2007). *Tools of the Mind: A Vygotskian approach to early childhood education* (2nd ed.). Columbus, OH: Merrill/Prentice-Hall.

Bowman, B. T., Donovan, M. S., & Burns, M. S. (Eds.). (2001). *Eager to learn: Educating our preschoolers.* Washington, DC: National Academy Press.

Buckner, J. C., Mezzacappa, E., & Beardslee, W. R. (2009). Self-regulation and its relations to adaptive functioning in low income youths. *American Journal of Orthopsychiatry, 79,* 19–30.

Campione, J. C., & Brown, A. L. (1990). Guided learning and transfer. In N. Fredricksen, R. Glaser, A. Lesgold, & M. G. Shafto (Eds.), *Diagnostic monitoring of skill and knowledge acquisition* (pp. 141–172). Hillsdale, NJ: Erlbaum.

Carlson, S. M., Moses, L. J., & Breton, C. (2002). How specific is the relation between executive function and theory of mind?: Contributions of inhibitory control and working memory *Infant and Child Development, 11,* 73–92.

Chaiklin, S., Hedegaard, M., & Jensen, U. J. (Eds.). (1999). *Activity theory and social practice: Cultural–historical approach.* Aarhus, Denmark: Aarhus University Press.

Chien, N. C., Howes, C., Burchinal, M., Pianta, R. C., Ritchie, S., Bryant, D. M., et al. (2010). Children's classroom engagement and school readiness gains in prekindergarten. *Child Development, 81*(5), 1534–1549.

Diamond, A., Barnett, S., Thomas, J., & Munro, S. (2007). Preschool program improves cognitive control. *Science, 318,* 1387–1388.

Domitrovich, C. E., Cortes, R. C., & Greenberg, M. (2007). Improving young children's social and emotional competence: A randomized trial of the preschool "PATHS" curriculum. *Journal of Primary Prevention, 28,* 67–91.

Downer, J. T., Rimm-Kaufman, S. E., & Pianta, R. C. (2007). How do classroom conditions and children's risk for school problems contribute to children's behavioral engagement in learning? *School Psychology Review, 36,* 413–432.

Elias, C., & Berk, L. E. (2002). Self-regulation in young children: Is there a role for sociodramatic play? *Early Childhood Research Quarterly, 17,* 216–238.

Elkonin, D. (1977). Toward the problem of stages in the mental development of the child. In M. Cole (Ed.), *Soviet developmental psychology* (pp. 538–563). White Plains, NY: Sharpe.

Elkonin, D. (1978). *Psychologija igry* [The psychology of play]. Moscow: Pedagogika.

Elkonin, D. (2005). *The psychology of play*: Preface. *Journal of Russian and East European Psychology, 43*(1), 11–21.

Escalón, X. D., & Greenfield, D. (2009). Learning behaviors mediating the effects of behavior problems on academic outcomes. *NHSA Dialog: A Research-to-Practice Journal for the Early Childhood Field, 12*, 1–17.

Evans, G. W., & Rosenbaum, J. (2008). Self-regulation and the income–achievement gap. *Early Childhood Research Quarterly, 23*, 504–514.

Farran, D. C., & Son-Yarbrough, W. (2001). Title I funded preschools as a developmental context for children's play and verbal behaviors. *Early Childhood Research Quarterly, 16*, 245–262.

Fernyhough, C. (2010). Vygotsky, Luria, and the social brain. In J. Carpendale, G. Iarocci, U. Mueller, B. Sokol, & A. Young (Eds.), *Self- and social-regulation: Exploring the relations between social interaction, social cognition, and the development of executive functions* (pp. 56–79). Oxford, UK: Oxford University Press.

Fuster, J. M. (1997). *The prefrontal cortex: Anatomy, physiology, and neuropsychology of the frontal lobe.* New York: Lippincott-Raven.

Gilliam, W. S. (2005). *Prekindergarteners left behind: Expulsion rates in state prekindergarten system.* New Haven, CT: Yale University Child Study Center.

Gresham, F., & Elliot, S. (1990). *Social Skills Rating Scale.* Circle Pines, MN: American Guidance Service.

Hemmeter, M. L., & Fox, L. (2009). The teaching pyramid: A model for the implementation of classroom practices within a program-wide approach to behavior support. *NHSA Dialogue, 12*, 133–147.

Karpov, Y. V. (2005). *The neo-Vygotskian approach to child development.* New York: Cambridge University Press.

Krafft, K., & Berk, L. E. (1998). Private speech in two preschools: Significance of open-ended activities and make-believe play for verbal self-regulation. *Early Childhood Research Quarterly, 13*, 637–658.

Leont'ev, A. (1978). *Activity, consciousness, and personality.* Englewood Cliffs, NJ: Prentice-Hall.

Lin, H.-L., Lawrence, F. R., & Gorrell, J. (2003). Kindergarten teachers' views of children's readiness for school. *Early Childhood Research Quarterly, 18*, 225–237.

Luria, A. R. (1959). The directive function of speech in development and dissolution: Pt. 1. Development of directive function of speech in early childhood. *Word, 15*, 341–352.

Luria, A. R. (1960). Experimental analysis of the development of voluntary action in children. In H. P. David & J. C. Brengelmann (Eds.), *Perspectives in personality research* (pp. 139–149). New York: Springer.

Luria, A. R. (1969). Speech development and the formation of mental processes. In M. Cole & I. Maltzman (Eds.), *Handbook of contemporary Soviet psychology* (pp. 121–162). New York: Basic Books.

Luria, A. R. (1973). *The working brain: An introduction to neuropsychology.* New York: Basic Books.

Luria, A. R. (1994). The problem of the cultural development of the child. In J. Valsiner (Ed.), *The Vygotsky reader* (pp. 46–56). Oxford, UK: Blackwell.

Luria, A. R. (1998). The development of writing in the child. In M. K. de Oliveira & J. Valsiner (Eds.), *Literacy in human development* (pp. 15–56). Stamford, CT: Ablex.

Luria, A. R. (2002). L. S. Vygotsky and the problem of functional localization. *Journal of Russian and East European Psychology, 40*(1), 17–25.

National Council for Accreditation of Teacher Education. (2010). *The road less traveled: How the developmental sciences can prepare educators to improve student achievement: Policy recommendations.* Washington, DC: Author.

Neville, H., Stevens, C., Klein, S., Fanning, J., Bell, T., Cakir, E., et al. (2011, April). *Improving behavior, cognition and neural mechanisms of attention in at-risk children.* Paper presented at the 18th annual meeting of the Cognitive Neuroscience Society, San Francisco.

Newman, D., Griffin, P., & Cole, M. (1989). *The construction zone: Working for cognitive change in school.* New York: Cambridge University Press.

Raver, C. C., & Knitzer, J. (2002). *Ready to enter: What research tells policymakers about strategies to promote social and emotional school readiness among three- and four-year-old children.*

New York: National Center for Children in Poverty, Mailman School of Public Health, Columbia University.

Riggs, N. R., Jahromi, L. B., Razza, R. P., Dillworth-Bart, J. E., & Mueller, U. (2006). Executive function and the promotion of social–emotional competence. *Journal of Applied Developmental Psychology, 27,* 300–309.

Rimm-Kaufman, S. E., Pianta, R. C., & Cox, M. J. (2000). Teacher's judgments of problems in the transition to kindergarten. *Early Childhood Research Quarterly, 15,* 147–166.

Rubtsov, V. (1991). *Learning in children: Organization and development of cooperative actions.* New York: Nova Science.

Rueda, M. R., Fan, J., McCandliss, B. D., Halparin, J. D., Gruber, D. B., Lercari, L. P., et al. (2004). Development of attentional networks in childhood. *Neuropsychologia, 42,* 1029–1040.

Rueda, M. R., Rothbart, M. K., & McCandliss, B. D. (2005). Training, maturation and genetic influences on the development of executive attention. *Proceedings of the National Academy of Sciences USA, 102,* 14931–14936.

Schunk, D. (1999). Social-self interaction and achievement behavior. *Educational Psychologist, 34,* 219–227.

Shonkoff, J. P., & Phillips, D. A. (Eds.). (2000). *From neurons to neighborhoods: The science of early childhood development.* Washington, DC: National Academy Press.

Skibbe, L. E., Connor, C. M., Morrison, F. J., & Jewkes, A. M. (2011). Schooling effects on preschoolers' self-regulation, early literacy, and language growth. *Early Childhood Research Quarterly, 26,* 42–49.

Sternberg, R. J., & Grigorenko, E. L. (2002). *Dynamic testing.* New York: Cambridge University Press.

Stevens, C., Fanning, J., Coch, D., Sanders, L., & Neville, H. (2008). Neural mechanisms of selective auditory attention are enhanced by computerized training: Electrophysiological evidence from language-impaired and typically developing children. *Brain Research, 1205,* 55–69.

Tharp, R. G., & Gallimore, R. (1989). *Rousing minds to life: Teaching, learning and schooling in social context.* Cambridge, UK: Cambridge University Press.

Vygotsky, L. S. (1956). *Izbrannye psychologicheskije trudy* [Selected psychological works]. Moscow: RSFSR Academy of Pedagogical Sciences.

Vygotsky, L. S. (1967). Play and its role in the mental development of the child. *Soviet Psychology, 5*(3), 6–18.

Vygotsky, L. S. (1978). *Mind in society: The development of higher mental processes.* Cambridge, MA: Harvard University Press.

Vygotsky, L. S. (1987). *Thinking and speech* (N. Minick, Trans., Vol. 1). New York: Plenum Press.

Vygotsky, L. S. (1997). *The history of the development of higher mental functions* (Vol. 4). New York: Plenum Press.

Vygotsky, L. S. (1998). *Child psychology* (M. J. Hall, Trans., Vol. 5). New York: Plenum Press.

Winsler, A., de Leon, J. R., Wallace, B. A., Carlton, M. P., & Willson-Quayle, A. (2003). Private speech in preschool children: Developmental stability and change, across-task consistency, and relations with classroom behaviour. *Journal of Child Language, 30,* 583–608.

Wood, D., Bruner, J. S., & Ross, G. (1976). The role of tutoring in problem solving. *Journal of Child Psychology and Psychiatry, 17,* 89–100.

Zaporozhets, A. (1986). *Izbrannye psychologicheskie trudy* [Selected works]. Moscow: Pedagogika.

Zuckerman, G. (2003). The learning activity in the first years of schooling. In A. Kozulin, B. Gindis, V. Ageyev, & S. Miller (Eds.), *Vygotsky's educational theory in cultural context* (pp. 177–199). Cambridge, MA: Cambridge University Press.

CHAPTER 18

Fostering Collaborative Partnerships between Early Childhood Professionals and the Parents of Young Children

Lisa L. Knoche, Keely D. Cline, and Christine A. Marvin

Relationships are the foundation for young children's development. Children's relationships with their parents and with other adult caregivers can shape the trajectory of their developmental outcomes. Concurrently, relationships between early childhood professionals (e.g., home visitors, early childhood educators, early interventionists) and parents are also important. Early intervention and prevention services for children at risk for developmental delays and/or later school failure can work to promote optimal outcomes for infants, toddlers, and preschoolers when programming takes advantage of these triadic (child–parent–professional) relationships and creates supportive connections across the settings and people in children's lives. Powerful and ample evidence suggests that linking early intervention providers with families does in fact result in better implementation of interventions and improved child outcomes. In this chapter we (1) establish the need for collaborative parent–professional partnerships in the interest of positive child outcomes, (2) outline and explain the effective characteristics of these collaborative partnerships, and (3) highlight a selection of intervention programs and approaches that reflect the components of collaborative parent–professional partnerships, including the Getting Ready intervention that focuses jointly on parent–child and parent–professional relationships to support development in young children.

Theoretical Rationale for Supporting Relationships and Creating Connections

A strong theoretical foundation exists for focusing on relationships (parent–child and parent–professional) and connections across settings associated with children's learning to ensure the effective implementation of early childhood intervention and prevention programs, and support positive outcomes for children and families. Rogoff's (1991) sociocultural theory places an emphasis on children's development in context. Children assume the role of apprentice in their early years and participate in cultural practices and relationships with adults and peers in natural learning contexts in the home and community that result in the development of functional skills and competencies (Rogoff, 1991). For young children, families constitute a primary source of influence, as do the relationships that children have with other adults in both home- and center-based early education and care settings.

Additionally, Bronfenbrenner's (1977) bioecological framework suggests that children's development occurs within the context of the constantly changing and interacting multilevel environments of family, home, school, community, and society. The children's relationships with parental caregivers and other family members, and their relationships with early childhood professionals while participating in early childhood intervention and prevention programs, are characterized as microsystems. According to this theory, the microsystems independently (e.g., parent–child, parent–professional, professional–child) influence children's development, as do the dynamic interactions among these microsystems (e.g., parent–child–professional). Interactions and influences across systems and settings (i.e., the mesosystem) are reciprocal in nature and cumulatively contribute to the positive or negative outcomes observed in young children in the early years of life. Similarly, high-quality parent–child interactions and high-quality professional–child interactions can influence and be influenced by the relationships that exist between the professionals and the parents (Bronfenbrenner, 1977). Collectively, sociocultural and bioecological theories provide a strong rationale for investing in the concurrent relationships between parent–child and parent–professional in early childhood intervention and prevention programs.

Parent Engagement in Children's Development

Children's earliest relationships with parents are critical for the establishment of cognitive, social–emotional, and self-regulatory competencies that set the stage for lifelong adaptation and functioning (Chazan-Cohen et al., 2009; El Nokali, Bachman, & Votruba-Drzal, 2010; National Research Council and Institute of Medicine, 2000; Thompson, 2002). Parental behavior can be categorized along three dimensions that relate to developmental outcomes for young children: (1) responsiveness and sensitivity; (2) support for autonomy; and (3) participation in learning (Edwards, Sheridan, & Knoche, 2010).

Interactions characterized with high degrees of parental warmth and sensitivity are associated with children's positive cognitive growth over time (Bradley, Corwyn, Burchinal, McAdoo, & Coll, 2001; Landry, Smith, Swank, Assel, & Vellet, 2001; Pungello, Iruka, Dotterer, Mills-Koonce, & Reznick, 2009). Furthermore, parental warmth during the early childhood years has also been linked to the structure and neuroanatomy of the adolescent brain (Rao et al., 2010). Additionally, parental support of autonomy in children's early years relates to positive cognitive and social outcomes for young children (Clark & Ladd, 2000; Grolnick & Farkas, 2002; Grolnick & Ryan, 1987, 1989; Ng, Kenney-Benson, & Pomerantz, 2004), including improved relationships with peers, and social assertiveness and self-directedness (Denham, Renwick, & Holt, 1991; McNamara, Selig, & Hawley, 2010). By supporting their independence and inviting children to participate in decision making, parents foster self-regulatory skills and intrinsic motivation in children, including task persistence (Kelley, Brownell, & Campbell, 2000). Finally, parents who provide a home environment rich in opportunities for learning through shared book reading, constructive play, and exploration have children who display higher language and cognitive skills in toddlerhood, preschool, and the primary years (Chazan-Cohen et al., 2009; Hood,

Conlon, & Andrews, 2008; National Institute of Child Health and Human Development [NICHD] Early Child Care Research Network, 2002; Raikes et al., 2006; Tamis-LeMonda & Bornstein, 2002). Parents' abilities to embed learning and problem-solving opportunities formally and informally in everyday family events and activities have been related to positive academic outcomes for young children (Bradley et al., 2001; Foster, Lambert, Abbott-Shim, McCarty, & Franze, 2005; Hill, 2001; Weigel, Martin, & Bennett, 2006a, 2006b).

Collectively, these findings unequivocally indicate the necessity and value of supporting the engagement of parents in their children's early learning. Interventions that target these parenting dimensions, and support positive parent engagement behaviors, will likely result in positive developmental outcomes for infants, toddlers, and preschoolers that last well past the early childhood period. Forming collaborative partnerships with parents in the intervention program is one approach to achieving such outcomes.

Collaborative Parent–Professional Partnerships

Early intervention and prevention models that focus on partnerships with families often have as their foundation a family-centered philosophy. Family-centered services aim to provide opportunities for parents and other familial caregivers to demonstrate their competence and confidence in (1) recognizing children's development, needs and interests; (2) recognizing pertinent learning opportunities in routine and preferred everyday activities; and (3) using or developing their own skills, interests, and abilities to support and implement plans to guide their children's growth in the context of family beliefs and values. A family-centered philosophy requires professionals to assist and, when appropriate, guide parents and those in parenting roles in using their existing strengths and supports to address needs and desires they have identified as important within the context of their lifestyle. Professionals assist and guide with full respect for the cultural traditions and values that parents hold for their family as a whole and for their children in particular (Dunst, 1997; Dunst & Deal, 1994). A recent meta-analysis of studies of help-giving practices indicates that family-centered programs and practices, including efforts to support the self-efficacy of families in meeting children's needs, yield significant positive effects on both children and parents (Trivette, Dunst, & Hamby, 2010).

Models of service delivery in home and community settings that focus on collaboration between caregivers and professionals provide a unique, strengths-based context for implementing family-centered early childhood intervention and prevention programming. Collaborative partnerships emphasize the unique perspectives and expertise offered by participants (e.g., parents, early educators, home visitors) to address mutually determined goals for children and families (Friend & Cook, 2006; Welch & Sheridan, 1995). In a partnership model, child observations, as well as ideas, opinions, values, and priorities, are shared by parents and professionals (Dunst, Trivette, & Deal, 1995; Hanft, Rush, & Shelden, 2004). These shared inputs determine the direction of decision making, and allow for the mutual selection and/or design of intervention strategies, and the use of supports that reflect unique contributions and interacting learning contexts for the children.

There are many potential benefits of a collaborative approach when partnering with families (Sheridan, Knoche, & Marvin, 2007). A collaborative partnership requires professionals and family members to communicate regularly with each other in a constructive manner, and to demonstrate mutual regard. Ongoing communication with family members is believed to enhance the professional's understanding of the family's values, practices, beliefs, and goals. The meaningful involvement of parents in joint action planning, ongoing problem solving, and decision making relative to children's services has been shown to increase family ownership, sense of control, and commitment to intervention goals

(Dempsey & Dunst, 2004; Dunst & Dempsey, 2007). Additionally, active participation by family members in the assessment and planning phases increases parental sense of control and commitment during the intervention stage (Trivette, Dunst, Boyd, & Hamby, 1996). Furthermore, this joint decision making can result in positive perceptions of professionals on the part of families, which can result in a greater benefit from intervention services (Korfmacher, Green, Spellman, & Thornburg, 2007).

Collaboration allows professionals and family members to pool knowledge and skills related to both process (i.e., how best to support children's development) and content (i.e., identifying primary or priority developmental skills and functional competencies), which results in more comprehensive, effective, and efficient early intervention programming and services to support children. When families' and professionals' beliefs and practices related to process and content have been congruent, improved child outcomes have been reported (Barbarin, Downer, Odom, & Head, 2010). A collaborative partnership approach takes advantage of the multiple perspectives and vantage points of both professionals and parents. Parents have unique information about their children that is important to children's developmental success. Typically, parents and other familial caregivers possess a particular understanding of their children that pervades time and place. They are able to comment on their children's likes, dislikes, preferred activities, toys, and playmates, and what they might find motivating or threatening. They also possess a historical and developmental perspective of their children that aids in determining appropriate developmental goals. As such, parents are especially instrumental partners for professionals who have only periodic (i.e., weekly or monthly home visits) or limited (i.e., 12–18 hours a week) opportunities for engagement with children.

Along with more complete interpretations and enhanced understanding of children's developing skills and abilities, collaboration between parents and professionals promotes the generation of (1) increased range and number of possible solutions to shared concerns (Welch & Sheridan, 1995) and (2) developmental goals or targets that are most appropriate for children. Family members are experts at knowing children's natural learning environments, how children like to spend their time, and the natural routines and schedules that they keep, whereas professionals are experts with information on recommended and/or evidence-based practices in child development and early intervention services. Collectively, parents' and professionals' perspectives yield plans and developmental goals that are most fitting and productive for children and their parents.

Additionally, collaborative partnerships between professionals and parents result in opportunities to incorporate familial beliefs, cultures, values, and traditions into programming designed to benefit children. Building relationships with parents helps professionals understand how families socialize and share information, and ensures continuity between home traditions and external expectations for young children. Intervention efforts incorporating processes that address family cultures and priority needs have been shown to be important in achieving maximum outcomes (Barbarin et al., 2010; DeGangi, Wietlisbach, & Poisson, 1994; Garcia Coll & Magnuson, 2000). Intervention efforts tailored to incorporate a family's unique cultural beliefs and styles of interacting are more instrumental in instituting change than approaches that are inconsistent with family values and practices (Boyce, Innocenti, Roggman, Norman, & Ortiz, 2010; Epps & Jackson, 2000).

Thus, collaborative partnerships between parents and professionals allow for an increased range and diversity of expertise and resources available to support children's development and functional competencies across a host of developmental domains (e.g., social, behavioral, cognitive) and settings (e.g., home, child care, community). In particular, collaboration yields interventions that are grounded in the strengths of all participants—parents, children, and professionals—and that ultimately are more likely to result in desired success (Chao, Bryan, Burstein, & Ergul, 2006).

Components of Effective Collaborative Parent–Professional Partnerships

Collaboration within early childhood intervention and prevention programs does not occur without a planful, systematic approach. There are requisite key components that characterize a collaborative, parent–professional partnership model in early childhood programs. To be effective, necessary components of a collaborative parent–professional partnership model include (1) a focus on parent–child interactions; (2) support and availability of learning opportunities in children's natural learning environments; (3) use of structured, data-based problem-solving approaches to guide consultation and collaboration; and (4) incorporation of evidence-based strategies into intervention program delivery (see Figure 18.1; Sheridan, Knoche, et al., 2007).

Parent–Child Interaction

The first key component to a collaborative partnership model of intervention is a focus on the interactions between parents and their children. Collaborative partnerships should include efforts to initiate, support, and enhance positive parent–child interactions as a means of promoting positive child outcomes. The presence of a secure relationship between parent and child (Ainsworth, Blehar, Waters, & Wall, 1978; Cohn, Patterson, & Christopoulos, 1991; Guralnick & Neville, 1997) is a universally accepted predictor of healthy child functioning. Direct and shared observations of children and parent–child interactions allow for an assessment of both children's natural abilities and tendencies, and parents' prompts and responses concerning children's behaviors. In addition, observation of parent–child interactions provides early childhood professionals opportunities to note and affirm parents' strengths (thereby building their confidence), focus parents' attention on important assets and behaviors children demonstrate, provide developmental information (including realistic

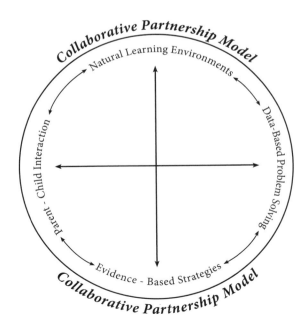

FIGURE 18.1. A collaborative partnership model of early childhood service delivery.

expectations), model strategies to support children's learning, and/or provide suggestions to aid parents in engaging their children successfully (thereby building competence in both parents and children; McCollum & Yates, 1994; Sheridan, Marvin, Knoche, & Edwards, 2008).

The degree to which parents view their role as an instrumental force in their children's development (i.e., their role construct) and possess positive beliefs in their abilities to support their children's learning (i.e., their self-efficacy) are also appropriate targets for collaborative interventions. Self-efficacy and clarity of roles contribute to parents' engagement with their children and ultimately to positive outcomes from intervention services (Trivette et al., 2010). Consultation efforts that help parents construct an active role for themselves and develop a sense of self-efficacy in relation to their children's learning (Sheridan et al., 2004) are important for supporting positive child outcomes, as well as a trajectory for positive parental involvement in the children's learning into the future (Hoover-Dempsey, Walker, & Sandler, 2005; Jones & Prinz, 2005).

Natural Learning Environments

A second key component to a collaborative parent–professional partnership model is the use of "natural learning environments" (Bruder & Dunst, 2000; McWilliam, 2010), defined as everyday activities (i.e., mealtimes, interactions with siblings, outdoor or indoor play) that take place in the settings frequented by young children of a similar age, culture, and geographic region. Natural learning environments that engage the interest of children with disabilities have been found to be associated with optimal behavioral changes (Dunst et al., 2001).

"Naturalistic teaching" utilizes children's momentary interest in unstructured and routine activities, materials, and interactions to facilitate learning (Brown & Odom, 1995; Pretti-Frontczak & Bricker, 2004). Embedded within the activity that currently holds children's interest, these naturalistic teaching strategies have potential to capture children's attention and elicit desired behaviors over time. Parents can be taught to identify natural incidental teaching and learning opportunities within routine activities at parks, restaurants, shopping malls, sporting events, and virtually any home- and community-based setting or function within which parents and children naturally participate (Dunst et al., 2001). Studies have shown that parents' use of contingent responsiveness and incidental teaching support young children's learning in routine activity settings (Dunst, 2006; Girolametto & Weitzman, 2006; Guralnick, 2001).

Empirical support is available for the use of natural environments and family members as change agents to advance children's developmental outcomes in the areas of secure attachments (Mahoney & Powell, 1988; van den Boom, 1994); communication/language (Santos & Lignugaris-Kraft, 1997; Woods, 2003; Woods, Kashinath, & Goldstein, 2004); motor skills (Tieman, Palisano, Gracely, & Rosenbaum, 2004); and adaptive skills, such as eating (Najdowski, Wallace, Doney, & Ghezzi, 2003; O'Reilly & Lancioni, 2001). Specifically, research reflects a use of guided participation, situated learning and instruction, apprenticeship, and responsiveness in everyday activities (Dunst, 2001). *Guided participation* includes actions taken by parents to maximize learning opportunities in natural settings by engaging with children in child-initiated activities and providing assistance as needed (Dunst, Raab, Trivette, & Swanson, 2010; Rogoff, Mistry, Goncu, & Mosier, 1993; Wertsch, 1985). In *situated learning*, children are provided opportunities to observe peers or other competent individuals participating in an activity of interest that sets a standard for expected behavior (Clark, 1998; Lancy, 1996). *Apprenticeship* involves the parent and child working with one another in close coordination as the parent prompts the child for an appropriate behavior or response (Dunst et al., 2007; Hancock & Kaiser, 2006). *Parental responsiveness*, which involves positive physical, social, and verbal attention and communication to the child as he or she demonstrates desirable behaviors, functions as a reinforcer to maintain, shape, and promote desired behavior (Mahoney, 1988; Zisser & Eyberg, 2010).

Data–Based Problem Solving

The use of a structured, data-based problem-solving approach for guiding the direction of developmental interventions for young children is another key feature of collaborative parent–professional partnerships. A structured service delivery approach that includes problem solving based on data has dual goals of promoting positive child outcomes, as well as enhancing skills and competencies of parents and other care providers for future independent problem solving. Data-based problem solving involves (1) identifying and prioritizing shared goals for children, (2) collecting data (i.e., observations and reports) and analyzing factors that may influence skill development or performance, (3) developing intervention strategies that can address concerns and achieve goals, and (4) evaluating the effectiveness of chosen strategies (Sheridan & Kratochwill, 2008; see Sheridan, Clarke, & Ihlo, Chapter 21, this volume). The process of data-based problem solving can be facilitated through a professional consultant (e.g., school psychologist, mental health professional, special education provider) working with parents and other caregivers (e.g., Kratochwill & Bergan, 1990; Sheridan & Kratochwill, 2008; Sheridan, Kratochwill, & Bergan, 1996), or it can be provided by an early childhood professional (e.g., classroom teacher, home visitor, special education educator) who works directly but collaboratively with family members (Buysse & Wesley, 2005; File & Kontos, 1992; Rush, Sheldon, & Hanft, 2003). Decades of research on this consultation-based approach (Sheridan, Clarke, & Burt, 2008; Sheridan & Kratochwill, 2008, Sheridan, Welch, & Orme, 1996) have yielded substantial empirical support for the use of data-based problem solving as an approach for supporting young children's positive outcomes.

Use of Evidence–Based Strategies and Practices

The final component of effective collaborative partnerships is the use of empirically established strategies and practices. This requires that early childhood professionals and parents ensure that core curricula and/or strategies included on the intervention plans are evidence-based, which means that empirical support attests to the efficacy of the strategies producing desired outcomes (Buysse & Wesley, 2006). We adopt the functional definition of *evidence-based practice* offered by Dunst, Trivette, and Cutspec (2002), and conceptualize these practices as those "that are informed by research, in which the characteristics and consequences of environmental variables are empirically established, and the relationship directly informs what a practitioner can do to produce a desired outcome" (p. 3). Professionals are responsible for sharing with parents their knowledge of evidence-based practices that may appropriately address children's goals and developmental targets, and encourage the review of relevant research literature when intervention plans require refinement.

Review of Select Intervention Programs

In an effort to provide a context for how collaborative partnerships operate in practice, five intervention programs and approaches characterized by some or all of the components

(Figure 18.1) of effective parent–professional partnerships are reviewed below. The intervention programs reviewed are Play and Learning Strategies (PALS; Landry, Smith, & Swank, 2006), parent–child interaction therapy (PCIT; Hembree-Kigin & McNeil, 1995), Incredible Years BASIC Parent Training Program (Webster-Stratton, 1992), Storytelling for Home Enrichment of Language and Literacy Skills (SHELLS; Boyce et al., 2010) and the Getting Ready intervention (Sheridan, Marvin, et al., 2008). This selection is not intended to be an exhaustive list but rather, a sampling of model collaborative partnership–based interventions focused on a range of targeted child outcomes, populations, and ages.

Play and Learning Strategies

The PALS curriculum (Children's Learning Institute, 2010; Landry et al., 2006) is a preventive intervention program for parents and their infants and toddlers, particularly those from at-risk families. The purpose of the program is to strengthen the parent–child bond; promote parents' mastery of interactional skills that support better child outcomes; and stimulate the child's early development in language, cognitive, and/or social domains. Current research findings that emphasize the unique developmental needs of children born prematurely form the basis for the PALS program. Topics addressed in PALS sessions include

> (a) attending to babies' and toddlers' communicative signals, (b) responding appropriately to children's positive and negative signals, (c) supporting infants' and toddlers' learning by maintaining their interest and attention rather than redirecting or over stimulating, (d) introducing toys and activities, (e) stimulating language development through labeling and scaffolding, (f) encouraging cooperation and responding to misbehavior, (g) incorporating these strategies and supportive behaviors throughout the day and during routine activities such as mealtimes, dressing, and bathing, as well as at play times. (Children's Learning Institute, 2010, paragraph 1)

There is also an emphasis on understanding that children of various ages demonstrate different typical behaviors.

PALS curricula are available for both parents of infants (approximately 5 months to 1 year) and toddlers (approximately 18 months to 3 years). PALS involves individualized weekly 1½ hour sessions with parents and children. The PALS Infant curriculum comprises 10 sessions and the PALS Toddler curriculum, 12 sessions. Each session involves a facilitator

> (a) asking mothers to review their experiences across the last week related to their efforts to try the targeted behaviors, (b) describing the current visit's targeted behavior, (c) watching and discussing with mothers the educational videotape of mothers from similar backgrounds, (d) videotaping mothers interacting with their infants in situations that the mothers selected (e.g., toy play, feeding, bathing) with coaching, (e) supporting mothers to critique their behaviors and the infants' response during the videotaped practice, and (f) planning with mothers as how to integrate responsive behaviors into their everyday activities with laminated cards defining the behavior and its importance provided to support practice. (Landry et al., 2006, p. 630)

The PALS videotaped exemplars depict actual mother–child dyads and are selected to resemble the families participating in the program in regard to background and child age.

Research with parents and their infants (6–10 months of age) has indicated significant increases in maternal responsiveness behaviors following participation in PALS in comparison to the control group. Additionally, significant increases in children's behaviors, including early communication, language, social interaction, and play skills, have been observed following completion of PALS in a controlled trial (Landry et al., 2006).

Characteristics that qualify PALS as an effective collaborative partnership program (Figure 18.1) include the fact that PALS is conducted in the families' natural (home) settings and involves parents practicing skills with facilitator coaching in everyday activities such as toy play, feeding, and bathing. PALS utilizes structured, data-based problem solving through the use of videotapes. Sessions include the facilitator asking parents to reflect on experiences with implementing the previous session's targeted behaviors, supporting parents in critiquing their own and their children's behaviors as they jointly observe a videotape of the parent–child interactions, and planning with parents how to integrate the session's targeted behavior into routine activities. Finally, PALS includes a focus on parent–child interaction because it encourages parents' responsiveness to their infants or toddlers. It is an evidence-based intervention grounded in current research about special needs of infants and toddlers born prematurely (Children's Learning Institute, 2010). The intervention focuses on behaviors related to four aspects of responsiveness behaviors previously found to be related to children's development: "(a) contingent responding, (b) emotional–affective support, (c) support for infant foci of attention, and (d) language input that supports developmental needs" (Landry et al., 2006, p. 627). Additionally, the program includes the following factors that Bakermans-Kranenburg, van IJzendoorn, and Juffer (2003) indicate are related to intervention efficacy: a short-term intervention period, implemented later in the child's first year of life, defined by a clear focus, and designed to link intervention goals to a theoretical model (as cited in Landry et al., 2006). PALS has been found to increase maternal responsiveness behaviors and child communication, language, social interaction and play skill behaviors effectively.

Parent–Child Interaction Therapy

PCIT (Hembree-Kigin & McNeil, 1995; McNeil & Hembree-Kigin, 2010; Zisser & Eyberg, 2010), a treatment for young children with disruptive behavior disorders, is based on a conceptual model informed by Baumrind's (1966) developmental theory of parenting. Both attachment and social learning principles are utilized to support development of an authoritative parenting style, which involves a high level of parental nurturance and control, and good parent–child communication. The underlying theory of PCIT is that a warm and nurturing parent–child relationship is foundational for establishing effective and consistent limit setting and disciplinary practices that are key to changing problematic parent and child behaviors. Consequently, the first phase of PCIT, child-directed interaction (CDI), focuses on helping parents learn to follow their children's lead during play, with the goal of building or strengthening a positive and mutually rewarding relationship between them. The parents receive instruction in using praise, reflection, imitation, description and enthusiasm (PRIDE) with their children. In the second phases of PCIT, parent-directed interaction (PDI), parents are taught to lead children's activities when needed, with the goal of decreasing problematic behaviors (e.g., noncompliance, aggression) while increasing prosocial behaviors. Parents learn to improve limit setting and use clearly stated commands and appropriate and consistent discipline.

The PCIT intervention typically lasts 10–16 weeks, meeting 1 hour each week individually with a clinician in a clinic setting. Both treatment phases begin with the clinician providing a training session that involves explaining, modeling, and role-playing CDI and PDI skills for the parent. This is followed by coaching sessions in which parents practice the skills with their child and receive coaching from the clinician in a play situation, often in a clinic setting. Before each session, each parent completes a brief rating scale to assess his or her child's behavior problem(s) at home. The session begins with a review of the previous week's experiences and a 5-minute coded observation of parent–child interactions. This information is used to determine which skills the parent has mastered and which should be the focus for the coaching session. The majority of the session time is then spent in coaching as the parent and child engage in play interactions. The session ends with the clinician summarizing for the parent how often the parent used each CDI or PDI skill in the initial 5-minute, coded observation. These summaries allow the parent to track his or her weekly progress and determine the skills on which to focus throughout the following week. The clinician and parent also review a graph charting the child's progress according to parent report on a weekly behavior rating scale.

Research has indicated significant improvements in parent–child interaction and declines in problem behaviors for children following PCIT compared to children in a control condition. Most studies investigating the outcomes of PCIT have focused on 3- to 6-year-old children with disruptive behavior disorders, although both younger and older children from other clinical populations have also been studied. Results have been found to generalize across multiple cultural groups, including Mexican American (McCabe & Yeh, 2009), Puerto Rican (Matos, Torres, Santiago, Jurando, & Rodriguez, 2006), Chinese (Leung, Tsang, Heung, & Yiu, 2009), and Australian families (Nixon, Sweeny, Erickson, & Touyz, 2003; Phillips, Morgan, Cawthorne, & Barnett, 2008). Findings also generalize to maltreating parent–child dyads (Timmer, Urquiza, Zebell, & McGrath, 2005), to school settings (Funderburk et al., 1998), and from clinic to home settings and to untreated siblings (Eyberg & Robinson, 1982). Furthermore, effects maintain for 3 to 6 years postintervention (Hood & Eyberg, 2003; see Zisser & Eyberg, 2010, for a review).

Components that characterize PCIT as an effective collaborative partnership model (Figure 18.1) include learning opportunities provided to children in the natural context of parent–child play, as well as a focus on parent–child interaction. Furthermore, while PCIT consists mostly of clinician-led didactic training and coaching of the parent, there are data-based problem-solving components that include summary sheets of CDI and PDI skills progress to help clinician and parents collaboratively problem-solve and determine skills on which to focus during the following week. Additionally, the clinician and parent review parent reports of child progress during each session. PCIT is based on a conceptual model informed by Baumrind's (1966) developmental theory of parenting and incorporates operant methods and play therapy techniques; the intervention is evidence-based, as it has been found to be related to improvements in parent–child interaction and declines in children's problem behaviors.

Incredible Years BASIC Parent Training Program

The Incredible Years Training Series (Webster-Stratton, 1992; Webster-Stratton & Reid, 2007, 2010) was developed to address parenting, family, child, and school factors that place children at risk for early-onset conduct disorders. The series consists of three training curricula designed for parents, teachers, and children between birth and age 13. One component of the series, the Incredible Years BASIC Parent Training Program, was originally developed as a trainer-led, interactive, video-based intervention for parents of children between the ages of 2 and 7. This program has been revised to target four separate age ranges: infant (0 to 1 year), toddler (1 to 3 years), preschool (3 to 6 years), and school age (6 to 13 years). The initial focus of the program is to support positive parent–child relationships by providing parents with instruction in using "(a) child-directed interactive play, (b) academic and persistence coaching, (c) social and emotional coaching, (d) praise, and (e) incentive programs" (Webster-Stratton & Reid, 2010, p. 196). This is followed by parents receiving guidance in developing predictable routines and rules in the home, using nonviolent discipline techniques, and teaching children problem-solving skills.

The Incredible Years BASIC Parent Training Treatment Program involves weekly, 2-hour group sessions for parents, with the typical number of sessions differing based on the age range of the children. The infant program typically consists of eight to nine sessions. The toddler program may require 12 sessions, and the preschool and school-age programs, 18–20 sessions. The program involves a trainer leading groups of eight to 10 parents in viewing and discussing videotapes that show vignettes of modeled parenting skills. More than three hundred 1- to 3-minute videos demonstrating age-appropriate examples of culturally diverse families and children with various temperamental characteristics are used. In addition to videotape modeling, other training methods include trainer role-play and behavioral rehearsal (i.e., with some parents acting the role of children and others the role of parent); parent homework assignments (i.e., reading and hands-on assignments); session evaluations to allow the trainer to understand better the parents' response to the training; and individualized behavior planning meetings. During the planning meetings, parents both identify child behaviors they want to increase and decrease and learn how to apply strategies to achieve goals with their children. Trainers are encouraged to adopt a collaborative approach to parent training (Webster-Stratton, 1998; Webster-Stratton & Herbert, 1994), but specific collaborative strategies are not scripted.

The developers of the Incredible Years BASIC Parent Training Treatment Program found that implementing the program with parents of children between ages 3 and 8 diagnosed with oppositional defiant disorder/conduct disorder resulted in improved parental attitudes and parent–child interactions, and a reduction in harsh discipline and child conduct problems, as compared to control group participants. Furthermore, replications by independent researchers have demonstrated that effects generalized beyond a university research clinic to applied mental health settings and high-risk (i.e., low-income) populations, and multiple cultural groups (i.e., families from Norway and the United Kingdom) (see Webster-Stratton & Reid, 2010, for a review).

In terms of key elements of an effective collaborative partnership approach (Figure 18.1), the Incredible Years BASIC Parent Training Treatment Program is relevant to families' natural settings; while the training is provided to parents in a group clinical setting and uses commercial videotapes as one method of instruction, parents are encouraged to implement new strategies through "hands-on" assignments in the home. The Incredible Years BASIC Parent Training Treatment Program begins with a focus on parent–child interaction. While collaboration between the trainer and parent is strongly encouraged and individual behavior planning meetings involve parents identifying and receiving instruction in how to achieve goals related to increasing and decreasing particular child behaviors, documentation of data is not systematically used for problem solving or to evaluate the effectiveness of the chosen strategies. The developers of the Incredible Years treatment programs indicate that because of evidence that intervening when children are younger results in more positive behavioral adjustments across home and school contexts, the interventions are designed to address behavior problems when they begin. The Incredible Years BASIC Parent Training Treatment Program is evidence-based, as research has demonstrated that participation in the intervention is related to improved parental attitudes and parent–child interactions, as well as reduced incidences of harsh discipline and child conduct problem.

Storytelling for Home Enrichment of Language and Literacy Skills

SHELLS (Boyce et al., 2010), an early language and literacy intervention, is based on current research literature on shared book reading and storytelling. It was originally designed for low-income Latino families whose children were English language learners, and who were more likely to spend little time reading or engaging in the types of extended conversations known to support the language and literacy development of young children. However, the SHELLS activities are intended to be individualized and flexible in order to be appropriate and engaging for all families. The program is culturally sensitive and strengths-based, building on the skills and abilities of families served. The basis of SHELLS is support of language and literacy activities, and growth through the natural context of the parent–child relationship. Parents and children are encouraged to engage together in activities and conversations that support children's language and literacy development. Three main aims of SHELLS are to "(a) increase parent–child conversation and narratives, (b) create the use of meaningful literacy materials, and (c) encourage continuing language and literacy activities for children at home" (Boyce et al. 2010, p. 348).

The SHELLS intervention is intended to be implemented by a home visitor. In the study conducted by Boyce and colleagues (2010), the number of home visits ranged from one to eight. SHELLS activities are intended to encourage parents and children to develop co-constructed narratives about familiar events in order to provide a context for families to engage in culturally appropriate and meaningful, extended conversations. These narratives are used to develop books that the families are able to keep using a digital camera and printer. The home visitor provides information on the importance of language and encourages the parent to incorporate specific evidence-based language and literacy strategies (i.e., *Support, Ask,* and *Expand*) as the parent and child develop the co-constructed narrative and make and share the book. The book-making process consists of seven steps:

(a) Planning ahead with the family to encourage parent to generate story/book ideas with their child; (b) encouraging parent–child conversation and interest in the book topic; (c) cooperatively illustrating the story through pictures or drawings; (d) facilitating written captions from words or sentences heard in the parent–child narrative; (e) helping organize and make the book; (f) observing the parent and child using the book; and (g) leaving the finished book. (Boyce et al., p. 351)

SHELLS has evidence supporting its use with Spanish-speaking parents and their preschoolers participating in Migrant Head Start programs (Boyce et al., 2010). Significant improvements in mothers' language-supporting behaviors and the quality of the home language and literacy environment were indicated for SHELLS participants as compared to mothers in a control condition. Furthermore, significant gains were identified in SHELLS children's total number of words and total number of different words used in an assessment as compared to children in a comparison condition.

As per key elements of an effective collaborative partnership model (Figure 18.1), SHELLS focuses on the natural environment by using families' co-constructed narratives of familiar events or activities as a basis for language and literacy activities and interactions. SHELLS emphasizes parent–child interaction as a context for supporting language and literacy, and encourages parent–child conversation and activities as means of promoting positive child language and literacy outcomes. While SHELLS does involve planning ahead to encourage parents and children to consider ideas for their book topic, the intervention does not use structured, data-based problem solving. SHELLS is based on current research literature on shared book reading and storytelling, and utilizes evidence-based strategies shown to support children's language and literacy; the intervention has been found to be related to increases in mothers' language-supporting behaviors and home language and literacy home environment, as well as the number of total words and different words that children used.

The Getting Ready Intervention

The intervention programs reviewed thus far, while characterized as effective collaborative partnership-based programs and approaches, are heavily focused on the parent–child relationship, with less intentional emphasis on the relationship between professional and parent. One additional program, the Getting Ready intervention, systematically incorporates the four components of a collaborative partnership model (Figure 18.1) and is equally focused on parent–child and parent–professional relationships. The Getting Ready intervention (Sheridan, Marvin, et al., 2008) was designed to provide an integrated, ecological, strengths-based approach to school readiness for families with children from birth to 5 years of age who are participating in early childhood intervention and prevention programs. In studies of efficacy, the Getting Ready intervention targeted low-income, ethnically and developmentally diverse children and families who were enrolled in infant–toddler or preschool early childhood programs (Sheridan, Knoche, Edwards, Bovaird, & Kupzyk, 2011; Sheridan, Knoche, Kupzyk, Edwards, & Marvin, 2011).

The intervention is constructed on the foundational belief that optimal school readiness for children and their families occurs through the development of positive relationships within the multiple interacting ecological systems of the home (i.e., parent–child relationships), and between the home and other supportive environments (i.e., parent–professional relationships). School readiness is understood to mean that children must develop certain capacities to be "ready" to participate in formal schooling; additionally, parents and other caregivers must also be ready to develop positive working relationships and partner with educational professionals to ensure consistent cross-setting supports, to encourage ongoing stimulation, and to promote positive developmental outcomes in children.

The Getting Ready intervention integrates principles of *triadic intervention* (McCollum & Yates, 1994) as a means of supporting the parent–child relationship, and *collaborative (conjoint) consultation models* (Sheridan & Kratochwill, 2008; Sheridan, Kratochwill, et al., 1996) in an effort to guide the parent–professional interaction. The Getting Ready intervention strategies are described in Table 18.1, and the dynamic relation between these strategies is depicted in Figure 18.2. This collective set of strategies is used in a fluid and dynamic way to (1) support parents in establishing warm and sensitive interactions with their children, promoting children's emerging autonomy, and participating actively in their children's learning; (2) promote parent–professional partnerships for guiding children's development; and ultimately (3) promote children's healthy social–emotional, cognitive, communicative, and behavioral development and parents' confidence and competence in influencing their children's learning in the future.

The Getting Ready intervention takes place during home visits or group socializations, with families scheduled as part of regular program activities (monthly or weekly). Trained early childhood professionals (ECPs; including home visitors, teachers, and other early interventionists) use the strategies dynamically in their interactions with families (see Table 18.1; Sheridan, Marvin, et al., 2008). Initially and throughout all interactions, ECPs work to establish and maintain relationships with parents and support the parent–child relationship. ECPs share and discuss observations about children with their families, and affirm parents' competence in supporting or advancing children's abilities. Furthermore, they discuss developmental expectations and appropriate targets by sharing developmental information and focusing parents' attention on their children's strengths. ECPs and parents brainstorm collaboratively around problems or issues related to children's social, motor, cognitive, or communicative development and learning. ECPs ask parents for their reflections and ideas related to children's recent learning needs and interests. When appropriate, ECPs make suggestions for possible modifications to intervention plans that might include new learning

TABLE 18.1. Getting Ready Intervention Strategies

Establish parent–child and parent–professional relationship.
- Establish a context for parent–child interaction
- Listen, respond to parent priorities, concerns, challenges

Share observations/knowledge of child over time.
- Share/seek information about child's progress
- Affirm parents' insights and competent observations

Identify mutually agreed-upon developmental expectations for child.
- Focus parents' attention on child strengths and developmental needs
- Share developmentally appropriate information

Share ideas and brainstorm methods for helping child meet expectations.
- Mutually identify natural learning opportunities in the home
- Identify current and potential parent behaviors that can support targeted learning
- Make suggestions when necessary

Observe parent–child interactions and provide feedback.
- Observe parent and child in meaningful context
- Identify current strengths related to developmental expectations
- Provide developmental information
- Model/suggest on the spot when necessary to support parent interactions with their child

Monitor the child's skill development and determine directions for continued growth.
- Engage parent in noting child's progress and measuring progression toward individualized developmental expectations
- Discuss needed adjustments in interactions and/or learning opportunities
- Cycle to new developmental expectations and learning opportunities as needed

Note. From "Getting Ready: Promoting School Readiness through a Relationship-Based Partnership Model," by S. M. Sheridan, C. A. Marvin, L. L. Knoche, & C. P. Edwards, 2008, *Early Childhood Services, 2*(3), pp. 149–172. Copyright 2008 by Plural Publishing, Inc. Reprinted with permission.

opportunities, and may also interact with the child to serve as a model for the parent. During visits and socializations, ECPs observe the parent–child interaction and provide feedback to draw parents' attention to the specific parental actions that resulted in positive responses from their children and provide suggestions when necessary. ECPs also support families in noting progress toward developmental targets, and help determine necessary modifications and learning opportunities to support the child's ongoing development.

Rather than representing an "add on" to current services, the Getting Ready intervention is integrated within established early childhood intervention services such as Early Head Start and Head Start, thereby augmenting existing curricula and services. The use of Getting Ready strategies in concert with the established early childhood programs strengthens the ongoing interactions with families in support of child and family school readiness. The Getting Ready intervention offers opportunities for professionals to support and enhance the quality of parent–child interactions in daily routines and creates a shared responsibility between parent and professional to influence child developmental success and school readiness. Results of efficacy studies of the Getting Ready intervention have indicated that the intervention effectively supports both social–emotional competencies (Sheridan et al., 2010) and language and literacy skills in preschool children (Sheridan, Knoche, Kupzyk, Edwards, & Marvin, 2011). Results also indicate positive treatment effects on parenting behaviors (Knoche et al., in press). Additionally, evidence suggests that the Getting Ready intervention can be implemented with fidelity, as indicated through both direct observations of ECPs' interactions with parents (Knoche, Sheridan, Edwards, & Osborn, 2010) and review of

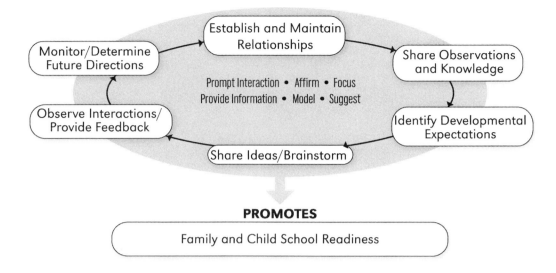

FIGURE 18.2. The Getting Ready intervention. The outer oval depicts the collaborative consultation structure that supports the parent–professional relationship, while the set of triadic strategies (parent–child–professional) indicated in the middle of the model are used by the ECP to support simultaneously the parent–child relationship during the collaborative parent–professional interactions. It is the tandem use of these triadic and collaborative strategies (further specified in Table 18.1) that characterizes the Getting Ready intervention. From "Getting Ready: Promoting School Readiness through a Relationship-Based Partnership Model," by S. M. Sheridan, C. A. Marvin, L. L. Knoche, & C. P. Edwards, 2008, *Early Childhood Services, 2*(3), pp. 149–172. Copyright 2008 by Plural Publishing, Inc. Reprinted with permission.

ECPs' documentation of interactions with families (Edwards, Hart, Rasmussen, Haw, & Sheridan, 2009).

The Getting Ready intervention is delivered as a collaborative effort; the intervention includes all of the key components of a collaborative partnership model. By design, the Getting Ready intervention supports children's learning in natural routines and events that are coidentified by parents and professionals in home or center-based infant–toddler or preschool settings. The intervention is targeted on enhancing the parent–child relationship via interactions between the parent and professional and quality parent–child interactions. Evidence-based curricula are used as part of Getting Ready programming for preschoolers (e.g., High/Scope; Hohmann & Weikert, 2002) and infants–toddlers (e.g., Beautiful Beginnings; Raikes & Whitmer, 2006; Parents as Teachers [PAT]; Parents as Teachers National Center, 2008). The intervention provides the process through which the evidence-based curricula are delivered and adds value to their efforts. Finally, data-based problem solving guides collaboration between parents and the early childhood professionals (Sheridan, Clarke, Knoche, & Edwards, 2006).

Conclusions

The reviewed programs are a selection of interventions and approaches that include some or all of the key components of collaborative parent–professional partnerships across a variety of target behaviors, populations, and child ages. The collaborative partnerships in early childhood prevention and intervention programs are intended simultaneously to support parent–child and parent–professional relationships, albeit to varying degrees. Intervention programs that can strengthen these relationships in support of children's early development are necessary given the associations reported with desired outcomes for both young children and families (Roggman, Boyce, & Cook, 2009).

Summary and Future Directions

Many early childhood prevention and intervention programs at their core aim to support healthy development of children. As an increased number of children and families are being served in a variety of early childhood settings and programs, the mechanism or approach to service delivery requires careful consideration. In addition to developmentally appropriate content, service delivery models that emphasize relationships and connections across people and settings are in critical need. Child development occurs in multiple contexts for infants, toddlers, and preschool-age children. These contexts include (1) the children's home, and their parents and family members; (2) the community events and settings families choose for themselves and their children; (3) early childhood education centers; and (4) the relationships with early childhood professionals associated with early childhood intervention and prevention programming, and the services they provide.

In this chapter we have advocated for a theoretically grounded model to service delivery, namely, a collaborative parent–professional partnership that places equal emphasis on the parent–child and parent–professional relationships in the early childhood intervention and prevention programs for young children and families. Substantial and clear-cut research exists on the critical associations between parent–child interactions and lifelong positive effects for children's development (Chazan-Cohen et al., 2009; National Research Council and Institute of Medicine, 2000; Rao et al., 2010). Similarly, strong relationships between parents and professionals dedicated to their children's development also result in benefits for children and families (Dunst, 1997). Consequently, intervention programs and approaches designed as collaborative parent–professional partnerships that create connections across the people (parents, professionals) and settings associated with children's learning are needed to support optimal outcomes for children, families, and professionals.

Collaborative parent–professional partnerships in early childhood intervention and prevention programs, as described, are based in a family-centered philosophy and have four core common components. Family-centered service for young children aims to ensure parental confidence and competence in positively influencing their children's development and school readiness within a family's own cultural framework and value set. The first core feature is an intentional focus on parent–child interaction. Second, the collaboration and planning that occurs between professionals and parents is structured and grounded in data-based decisions. Third, the curricula and interventions selected as part of collaborative planning are evidence-based, and fourth, interventions are designed to occur as natural learning opportunities and within common settings experienced by children.

The Getting Ready intervention (Sheridan, Marvin, et al., 2008), a collaborative partnership approach that focuses on both parent–child and parent–professional relationships, incorporates the four core components of a collaborative partnership model (Figure 18.1). It aims to advance both children's and parents' confidence and competence in being "ready" for school, and the ongoing parent–child and parent–professional interactions that ensure success once children begin formal schooling. A collaborative parent–professional partnership approach such as Getting Ready is not meant to replace evidence-based, child-focused early childhood curricula, but it is intended to complement child-focused intervention efforts in a way that meaningfully involves parents in decision making on behalf of their children.

A collaborative parent–professional partnership benefits all participants in early childhood programming—children, parents, *and* professionals. Professionals bring expertise in early childhood development and intervention to the interaction, and parents bring expertise on their children; the perspectives of both partners yield a greater quantity of solutions and strategies to benefit children (Welch & Sheridan, 1995). Additionally, the cultural preferences and practices of children and families have a meaningful place in collaborative partnerships and strengthen the intervention activities taking place in the natural setting of the home and community (Garcia Coll & Magnuson, 2000). Ultimately, the collaborative process results in strategies that are specifically tailored to the needs and preferences of individual children and families. These strategies have a greater likelihood of being implemented and, consequently, result in positive outcomes for children and their families.

As prevention and intervention programming in early childhood advances, systematic approaches to supporting collaboration that is grounded in relationships within and across settings are needed, given the inconsistencies inherent in early childhood services. Service delivery settings and approaches (home- or center-based), as well as the education, experience and skills of early childhood professionals and parents, are variable. Additionally, the characteristics and needs of children and families are unique and change over time. A collaborative parent–professional partnership is an approach to service delivery in early childhood intervention and prevention programs that can accommodate these complexities and incorporate them into programming that will benefit all participants and ultimately promote optimal outcomes for young children and their families.

References

Ainsworth, M. D. S., Blehar, M. C., Waters, E., & Wall, S. (1978). *Patterns of attachment*. Hillsdale, NJ: Erlbaum.

Bakermans-Kranenburg, M. J., van IJzendoorn, M. H., & Juffer, F. (2003). Less is more: Meta-analyses of sensitivity and attachment interventions in early childhood. *Psychological Bulletin, 129*, 195–215.

Barbarin, O. A., Downer, J., Odom, E., & Head, D. (2010). Home–school differences in beliefs, support, and control during public pre-kindergarten and their link to children's kindergarten readiness. *Early Childhood Research Quarterly, 3*, 358–372.

Baumrind, D. (1966). Effects of authoritative parental control on child behavior. *Child Development, 37*, 887–907.

Boyce, L. K., Innocenti, M. S., Roggman, L. A., Norman, V. K. J., & Ortiz, E. (2010). Telling stories and making books: Evidence for an intervention to help parents in migrant Head Start families support their children's language and literacy. *Early Education and Development, 21*, 343–371.

Bradley, R. H., Corwyn, R. F., Burchinal, M., McAdoo, H. P., & Coll, C. G. (2001). The home environments of children in the United States, Part II: Relations with behavioral development through age thirteen. *Child Development, 72*, 1868–1886.

Bronfenbrenner, U. (1977). Toward an experimental ecology of human development. *American Psychologist, 32*, 513–531.

Brown, W., & Odom, S. (1995). Naturalistic peer interventions for promoting preschool children's social interactions. *Preventing School Failure, 39*, 38–43.

Bruder, M. B., & Dunst, C. (2000). Expanding learning opportunities for infants and toddlers in natural environments. *Zero to Three, 20*(3), 34–36.

Buysse, V., & Wesley, P. (2005). *Consultation in early childhood settings*. Baltimore: Brookes.

Buysse, V., & Wesley, P. (Eds.). (2006). *Evidence-based practice in the early childhood field.* Washington, DC: Zero to Three Press.

Chao, P., Bryan, T., Burstein, K., & Ergul, C. (2006). Family-centered intervention for young children at-risk for language and behavior problems. *Early Childhood Education Journal, 34,* 147–153.

Chazan-Cohen, R., Raikes, H., Brooks-Gunn, J., Ayoub, C., Pan, B. A., Kisker, E. E., et al. (2009). Low-income children's school readiness: Parent contributions over the first five years. *Early Education and Development, 20,* 958–977.

Children's Learning Institute. (2010). Play and learning strategies. Retrieved from *www.childrenslearninginstitute.org/our-programs/program-overview/pals.*

Clark, K. E., & Ladd, G. W. (2000). Connectedness and autonomy support in parent–child relationships: Links to children's socioemotional orientation and peer relationships. *Developmental Psychology, 36,* 485–498.

Clark, S. (1998). Learning at the public bathhouse. In J. Singleton (Ed.), *Learning in likely places: Varieties of apprenticeship in Japan* (pp. 239–252). New York: Cambridge University Press.

Cohn, D. A., Patterson, C. J., & Christopoulos, C. (1991). The family and children's peer relations. *Journal of Social and Personal Relationships, 8,* 315–346.

Committee on Integrating the Science of Early Childhood Development, National Research Council and Institute of Medicine. (2000). *From neurons to neighborhoods: The science of early childhood development* (J. P. Shonkoff & D. A. Phillips, Eds.). Washington, DC: National Academy Press.

DeGangi, G. A., Wietlisbach, S., & Poisson, S. (1994). The impact of culture and socioeconomic status on family–professional collaboration: Challenges and solutions. *Topics in Early Childhood Special Education, 14,* 503–520.

Dempsey, I., & Dunst, C. J. (2004). Helpgiving styles and parent empowerment in families with a young child with a disability. *Journal of Intellectual and Developmental Disability, 29,* 40–51.

Denham, S. A., Renwick, S. M., & Holt, R. W. (1991). Working and playing together: Prediction of preschool social–emotional competence from mother–child interaction. *Child Development, 62,* 242–249.

Dunst, C. (1997). Conceptual and empirical foundations of family-centered practice. In R. J. Illback, C. T. Cobb, & H. M. Joseph, Jr. (Eds.), *Integrated services for children and families: Opportunities for psychological practice* (pp. 75–92). Washington, DC: American Psychological Association.

Dunst, C. (2001). Participation of young children with disabilities in community learning activities. In M. Guralnick (Ed.), *Early childhood inclusion* (pp. 307–336). Baltimore: Brookes.

Dunst, C. (2006). Parent-mediated everyday child learning opportunities: I. Foundations and operationalization. *CASEinPoint, 2,* 1–10. Retrieved from *www.fippcase.org/caseinpoint/caseinpoint_vol2_no2.pdf.*

Dunst, C., Bruder, M. B., Trivette, C., Hamby, D., Raab, M., & McLean, M. (2001). Characteristics and consequences of everyday natural learning opportunities. *Topics in Early Childhood Special Education, 21,* 68–92.

Dunst, C., & Deal, A. (1994). A family-centered approach to developing individualized family support plans. In C. Dunst, C. Trivette, & A. Deal (Eds.), *Supporting and strengthening families: Volume 1: Methods, strategies and practices* (pp.73–89). Cambridge, MA: Brookline Books.

Dunst, C., Trivette, C., & Deal, A. (1995). *Enabling and empowering families: Principles and guidelines for practice.* Cambridge, MA: Brookline Books.

Dunst, C. J., & Dempsey, I. (2007). Family professional partnerships and parenting competence, confidence and enjoyment. *International Journal of Disability, Development and Education, 54,* 305–318.

Dunst, C. J., Raab, M., Trivette, C. M., Parkey, C., Gatens, M., Wilson, L. L., et al. (2007). Child and adult social–emotional benefits of response-contingent child learning opportunities. *Journal of Early and Intensive Behavior Intervention, 4,* 379–391.

Dunst, C. J., Raab, M., Trivette, C. M., & Swanson, J. (2010). Community-based everyday child learning opportunities. In R. A. McWilliam (Ed.), *Working with families of young children with special needs* (pp. 60–87). New York: Guilford Press.

Dunst, C. J., Trivette, C. M., & Cutspec, P. A. (2002). Toward an operational definition of evidence-based practices. *Centerscope, 1*(1), 1–10.

Edwards, C. P., Hart, T., Rasmussen, K., Haw, Y. M., & Sheridan, S. M. (2009). Promoting parent partnership in Head Start: A qualitative case study of teacher documents from a school readiness intervention project. *Early Childhood Services: An Interdisciplinary Journal of Effectiveness, 3*, 301–322.

Edwards, C. P., Sheridan, S. M., & Knoche, L. (2010). Parent–child relationships in early learning. In E. Baker, P. Peterson, & B. McGaw (Eds.), *International encyclopedia of education* (Vol. 5, pp. 438–443). Oxford, UK: Elsevier.

El Nokali, N., Bachman, H. J., & Votruba-Drzal, E. (2010). Parent involvement and children's academic achievement and social development in elementary school. *Child Development, 81*, 988–1005.

Epps, S., & Jackson, B. J. (2000). *Empowered families, successful children: Early intervention program that work*. Washington, DC: American Psychological Association.

Eyberg, S. M., & Robinson, E. A. (1982). Parent–child interaction training: Effects on family functioning. *Journal of Clinical Child Psychology, 11*, 130–137.

File, N., & Kontos, S. (1992). Indirect service delivery through consultation: Review and implications for early intervention. *Journal of Early Intervention, 16*, 221–235.

Foster, M. A., Lambert, R., Abbott-Shim, M., McCarty, F., & Franze, S. (2005). A model of home learning environment and social risk factors in relation to children's emergent literacy and social outcomes. *Early Childhood Research Quarterly, 20*, 13–36.

Friend, M., & Cook, L. (2006). *Interactions: Collaboration skills for school professionals*. Boston: Allyn & Bacon.

Funderburk, B. W., Eyberg, S. M., Newcomb, K., McNeil, C. B., Hembree-Kigin, T., & Capage, L. (1998). Parent–child interaction therapy with behavior problem children: Maintenance of treatment effects in the school setting. *Child and Family Behavior Therapy, 20*, 17–38.

Garcia Coll, C., & Magnuson, K. (2000). Cultural differences as sources of developmental vulnerabilities and resources. In J. P. Shonkoff & S. J. Meisels (Eds.), *Handbook of early childhood intervention* (2nd ed., pp. 94–114). New York: Cambridge University Press.

Girolametto, L., & Weitzman, E. (2006). It Takes Two to Talk—The Hanen program for parents: Early language intervention through caregiver training. In R. McCauley & M. Fey (Eds.), *Treatment of language disorders in children* (pp. 77–104). Baltimore: Brookes.

Grolnick, W. S., & Farkas, M. (2002). Parenting and the development of children's self-regulation. In M. H. Bornstein (Ed.), *Handbook of parenting: Vol. 5. Practical issues in parenting* (pp. 89–110). Mahwah, NJ: Erlbaum.

Grolnick, W. S., & Ryan, R. M. (1987). Autonomy in children's learning: An experimental and individual difference investigation. *Journal of Personality and Social Psychology, 52*, 890–898.

Grolnick, W. S., & Ryan, R. M. (1989). Parent styles associated with children's self-regulation and competence in school. *Journal of Educational Psychology, 81*, 143–154.

Guralnick, M. (2001). Social competence with peers and early childhood inclusion: Need for alternative approaches. In M. J. Guralnick (Ed.), *Early childhood inclusion: Focus on change* (pp. 481–502). Baltimore: Brookes.

Guralnick, M., & Neville, B. (1997). Designing early intervention programs to promote children's social competence. In M. Guralnick (Ed.), *The effectiveness of early intervention* (pp. 579–610). Baltimore: Brookes.

Hancock, T., & Kaiser, A. (2006). Enhanced milieu teaching. In R. McCauley & M. Fey (Eds.), *Treatment of language disorders in children* (pp. 203–236). Baltimore: Brookes.

Hanft, B. E., Rush, D. D., & Shelden, M. L. (2004). *Coaching families and colleagues in early childhood*. Baltimore: Brookes.

Hembree-Kigin, T., & McNeil, C. B. (1995). *Parent–child interaction therapy*. New York: Plenum Press.

Hill, N. E. (2001). Parenting and academic socialization as they relate to school readiness: The roles of ethnicity and family income. *Journal of Educational Psychology, 93,* 686–697.

Hohmann, M., & Weikert, D. (2002). *Educating young children: Active learning practices for preschool and child care programs.* Ypsilanti, MI: High/Scope Press.

Hood, K. K., & Eyberg, S. M. (2003). Outcomes of parent–child interaction therapy: Mothers' reports of maintenance three to six years after treatment. *Journal of Clinical Child and Adolescent Psychology, 32,* 419–429.

Hood, M., Conlon, E., & Andrews, G. (2008). Preschool home literacy practices and children's literacy development: A longitudinal analysis. *Journal of Educational Psychology, 100,* 252–271.

Hoover-Dempsey, K. V., Walker, J. M. T., & Sandler, H. M. (2005). Parents' motivations for involvement in their children's education. In E. N. Patrikakou, R. P. Weisberg, S. Redding, & H. J. Walberg (Eds.), *School–family partnerships for children's success* (pp. 40–56). New York: Teachers College Press.

Jones, T. L., & Prinz, R. J. (2005). Potential roles of parental self-efficacy in parent and child adjustment: A review. *Clinical Psychology Review, 25,* 341–363.

Kelley, S. A., Brownell, C. A., & Campbell, S. B. (2000). Child development: Mastery motivation and self-evaluative affect in toddlers: Longitudinal relations with maternal behavior. *Child Development, 71,* 1061–1071.

Knoche, L. L., Edwards, C. P., Sheridan, S. M., Kupzyk, K. A., Marvin, C. A., Cline, K. D., et al. (in press). Getting ready: Results of a randomized trial of a relationship-focused intervention on the parent–infant relationship in rural Early Head Start. *Infant Mental Health Journal.*

Knoche, L. L., Sheridan, S. M., Edwards, C. P., & Osborn, A. Q. (2010). Implementation of a relationship-based school readiness intervention: A multidimensional approach to fidelity measurement for early childhood. *Early Childhood Research Quarterly, 25,* 299–313.

Korfmacher, J., Green, B., Spellman, M., & Thornburg, K. R. (2007). The helping relationship and program participation in early childhood home visiting. *Infant Mental Health Journal, 28,* 459–480.

Kratochwill, T. R., & Bergan, J. R. (1990). *Behavioral consultation in applied settings: An individual guide.* New York: Plenum Press.

Lancy, D. F. (1996). *Playing on the mother ground: Cultural routines for children's development.* New York: Guilford Press.

Landry, S. H., Smith, K. E., & Swank, P. R. (2006). Responsive parenting: Establishing early foundations for social, communication, and independent problem-solving skills. *Developmental Psychology, 42,* 627–642.

Landry, S. H., Smith, K. E., Swank, P. R., Assel, M. A., & Vellet, N. S. (2001). Does early responsive parenting have a special importance for children's development or is consistency across early childhood necessary? *Developmental Psychology, 37,* 387–403.

Leung, C., Tsang, S., Heung, K., & Yiu, I. (2009). Effectiveness of parent–child interaction therapy (PCIT) among Chinese families. *Research on Social Work Practice, 19,* 304–313.

Mahoney, G. (1988). Enhancing the developmental competence of handicapped infants. In K. Marfo (Ed.), *Parent–child interaction and developmental disabilities: Theory, research, and intervention* (pp. 203–219). Westport, CT: Praeger.

Mahoney, G., & Powell, A. (1988). Modifying parent–child interaction: Enhancing the development of handicapped children. *Journal of Special Education, 22,* 82–96.

Matos, M., Torres, R., Santiago, R., Jurando, M., & Rodriguez, I. (2006). Adaptations of parent–child interaction therapy for Puerto Rican families: A preliminary study. *Family Process, 45,* 205–222.

McCabe, K., & Yeh, M. (2009). Parent–child interaction therapy for Mexican Americans: A randomized clinical trial. *Journal of Clinical Child and Adolescent Psychology, 38,* 753–759.

McCollum, J. A., & Yates, T. J. (1994). Dyad as focus, triad as means: A family-centered approach to supporting parent–child interactions. *Infants and Young Children, 6,* 54–63.

McNamara, K. A., Selig, J. P., & Hawley, P. H. (2010). A typological approach to the study of parenting: Associations between maternal parenting patterns and child behaviour and social reception. *Early Child Development and Care, 180,* 1185–1202.

McNeil, C. B., & Hembree-Kigin, T. L. (2010). *Parent–child interaction therapy* (2nd ed.). New York: Springer.

McWilliam, R. A. (Ed.). (2010). *Working with families of young children with special needs.* New York: Guilford Press.

Najdowski, A., Wallace, M., Doney, J., & Ghezzi, P. (2003). Parental assessment and treatment of food selectivity in natural settings. *Journal of Applied Behavioral Analysis, 36,* 383–386.

Ng, F. F.-Y., Kenney-Benson, G. A., & Pomerantz, E. M. (2004). Children's achievement moderates the effects of mothers' use of control and autonomy support. *Child Development, 75,* 764–780.

NICHD Early Child Care Research Network. (2002). Early child care and children's development prior to school entry: Results from the NICHD Study of Early Child Care. *American Educational Research Journal, 39,* 133–164.

Nixon, R. D. V., Sweeny, L., Erickson, D. B., & Touyz, S. W. (2003). Parent–child interaction therapy: A comparison of standard and abbreviated treatments for oppositional defiant preschoolers. *Journal of Consulting and Clinical Psychology, 71,* 251–260.

O'Reilly, M., & Lancioni, G. (2001). Treating food refusal in a child with Williams Syndrome using a parent as therapist in the home setting. *Journal of Intellectual Disability Research, 45,* 41–46.

Parents as Teachers National Center. (2008). *Parents as Teachers Birth to Three: Program planning and implementation guide* (Rev. ed.). St. Louis, MO: Author.

Phillips, J., Morgan, S., Cawthorne, K., & Barnett, B. (2008). Pilot evaluation of parent–child interaction therapy delivered in an Australian community early childhood clinic setting. *Australian and New Zealand Journal of Psychiatry, 42,* 712–719.

Pretti-Frontczak, K., & Bricker, D. (2004). *An activity-based approach to early intervention* (3rd ed.). Baltimore: Brookes.

Pungello, L., Iruka, I., Dotterer, A. M., Mills-Koonce, R., & Reznick, S. (2009). The effects of income, race, and sensitive and harsh parenting on receptive and expressive language development in early childhood. *Developmental Psychology, 45,* 544–557.

Raikes, H., Alexander Pan, B., Luze, G., Tamis-LeMonda, C. S., Brooks-Gunn, J., & Constantine, J. (2006). Mother–child bookreading in low-income families: Correlates and outcomes during the first three years of life. *Child Development, 77,* 924–953.

Raikes, H., & Whitmer, J. M. (2006). *Beautiful beginnings: A developmental curriculum for infants and toddlers.* Baltimore: Brookes.

Rao, H., Betancourt, L. M., Giannetta, J. M., Brodsky, N. L., Korczykowski, M., Avants, B. B., et al. (2010). Early parental care is important for hippocampal maturation: Evidence from brain morphology in humans. *NeuroImage, 49,* 1144–1150.

Roggman, L. A., Boyce, L. K., & Cook, G. A. (2009). Keeping kids on track: Impacts of a parenting-focused Early Head Start program on attachment security and cognitive development. *Early Education and Development, 20,* 920–941.

Rogoff, B. (1991). *Apprenticeship in thinking: Cognitive development in social context.* New York: Oxford University Press.

Rogoff, B., Mistry, J., Goncu, A., & Mosier, C. (1993). Guided participation in cultural activities by toddlers and caregivers. *Monographs of the Society for Research in Child Development, 58*(8, Serial No. 236).

Rush, D., Shelden, M., & Hanft, B. (2003). Coaching families and colleagues: A process for collaboration in natural settings. *Infants and Young Children, 16*(1), 33–47.

Santos, R., & Lignugaris-Kraft, B. (1997). Integrating research on effective instruction with instruction in the natural environment for young children with disabilities. *Exceptionality, 7*(2), 97–129.

Sheridan, S. M., Clarke, B., Knoche, L. L., & Edwards, C. P. (2006). The effects of conjoint behavioral consultation in early intervention. *Early Education and Development, 17,* 593–617.

Sheridan, S. M., Clarke, B. L., & Burt, J. D. (2008). Conjoint behavioral consultation: What do we know and what do we need to know? In W. P. Erchul & S. M. Sheridan (Eds.), *Handbook of research in school consultation: Empirical foundations for the field* (pp. 171–202). Mahwah, NJ: Erlbaum.

Sheridan, S. M., Knoche, L. L., Edwards, C. P., Bovaird, J. A., & Kupzyk, K. A. (2010). Parent engagement and school readiness: Effects of the Getting Ready intervention on preschool children's social–emotional competencies. *Early Education and Development, 21,* 125–156.

Sheridan, S. M., Knoche, L. L., Kupzyk, K. A., Edwards, C. P., & Marvin, C. A. (2011). A randomized trial examining the effects of parent engagement on early language and literacy: The Getting Ready intervention. *Journal of School Psychology, 49,* 361–383.

Sheridan, S. M., Knoche, L. L., & Marvin, C. A. (2007). Competent families, competent children: Family-based interventions to promote social competence in young children. In W. H. Brown, S. L. Odom, & S. R. McConnell (Eds.), *Social competence of young children: Risk, disability, and intervention* (2nd ed., pp. 301–320). Baltimore: Brookes.

Sheridan, S. M., & Kratochwill, T. (2008). *Conjoint behavioral consultation: Promoting family–school connections and interventions.* New York: Springer.

Sheridan, S. M., Kratochwill, T. R., & Bergan, J. R. (1996). *Conjoint behavioral consultation: A procedural manual.* New York: Plenum Press.

Sheridan, S. M., Marvin, C., Knoche, L., & Edwards, C. (2008). Getting Ready: Promoting school readiness through a relationship-based partnership model. *Early Childhood Intervention Services, 2,* 149–172.

Sheridan, S. M., Warnes, E., Brown, M., Schemm, A., Cowan, R. J., & Clarke, B. L. (2004). Family-centered positive psychology: Building on strengths to promote student success. *Psychology in the Schools, 41,* 7–17.

Sheridan, S. M., Welch, M., & Orme, S. (1996). Is consultation effective?: A review of outcome research. *Remedial and Special Education, 17,* 341–354.

Tamis-LeMonda, C. S., & Bornstein, M. H. (2002). Maternal responsiveness and early language acquisition. In R. V. Kail & H. W. Reese (Eds.), *Advances in child development and behavior* (pp. 89–127). San Diego, CA: Academic Press.

Thompson, R. A. (2002). The roots of school readiness in social and emotional development. *Kauffman Early Education Exchange, 1,* 18–29.

Tieman, B., Palisano, R., Gracely, E., & Rosenbaum, P. (2004). Gross motor capability and performance of mobility in children with cerebral palsy: A comparison across home, school and outdoors/community settings. *Physical Therapy, 84,* 419–429.

Timmer, S. G., Urquiza, A. J., Zebell, N. M., & McGrath, J. M. (2005). Parent–child interaction therapy: Application to maltreating parent–child dyads. *Child Abuse and Neglect, 29,* 825–842.

Trivette, C. M., Dunst, C. J., Boyd, K., & Hamby, D. (1996). Family-oriented program models, helpgiving practices and parental control appraisals. *Exceptional Children, 62,* 237–248.

Trivette, C. M., Dunst, C. J., & Hamby, D. W. (2010). Influences of family-systems intervention practices on parent–child interactions and child development. *Topics in Early Childhood Special Education, 30,* 3–19.

van den Boom, D. (1994). The influence of temperament and mothering on attachment and exploration: An experimental manipulation of sensitive responsiveness among lower-class mothers of irritable infants. *Child Development, 65,* 1457–1477.

Webster-Stratton, C. (1992). *The Incredible Years: A trouble-shooting guide for parents of children ages 3–8 years.* Toronto: Umbrella Press.

Webster-Stratton, C. (1998). Parent training with low-income families: Promoting parental engagement through a collaborative approach. In J. Lutzker (Ed.), *Handbook of child abuse research and treatment* (pp. 183–210). New York: Plenum Press.

Webster-Stratton, C., & Herbert, M. (1994). *Troubled families—problem children: Working with parents: A collaborative process.* Chichester, UK: Wiley.

Webster-Stratton, C., & Reid, M. J. (2007). Incredible Years Parents and Teachers Training Series: A Head Start partnership to promote social competence and prevent conduct problems. In P. Tolan, J. Szapocznik, & S. Sambrano (Eds.), *Preventing youth substance abuse: Science based programs for children and adolescents* (pp. 67–88). Washington, DC: American Psychological Association.

Webster-Stratton, C., & Reid, M. J. (2010). The Incredible Years Parents, Teachers, and Children Training Series: A multifaceted treatment approach for young children with conduct disorders.

In J. R. Weisz & A. E. Kazdin (Eds.), *Evidence-based psychotherapies for children and adolescents* (2nd ed., pp. 194–210). New York: Guilford Press.

Weigel, D. J., Martin, S. S., & Bennett, K. K. (2006a). Contributions of the home literacy environment to preschool-aged children's emerging literacy and language skills. *Early Child Development and Care, 176,* 357–378.

Weigel, D. J., Martin, S. S., & Bennett, K. K. (2006b). Mothers' literacy beliefs: Connections with the home literacy environment and pre-school children's literacy development. *Journal of Early Childhood Literacy, , 6,* 191–211.

Welch, M., & Sheridan, S. M. (1995). *Educational partnerships: Serving students at-risk.* San Antonio, TX: Harcourt Brace Jovanovich.

Wertsch, J. V. (1985). *Vygotsky and the social formation of mind.* Cambridge, MA: Harvard University Press.

Woods, J. (2003). When the toddler takes over: Changing challenging routines into conduits for communication. *Focus on Autism and Other Developmental Disabilities, 18,* 176–181.

Woods, J., Kashinath, S., & Goldstein, H. (2004). Effects of embedding caregiver-implemented teaching strategies in daily routines on children's communication outcomes. *Journal of Early Intervention, 26,* 175–193.

Zisser, A., & Eyberg, S. M. (2010). Parent–child interaction therapy and the treatment of disruptive behavior disorders. In J. R. Weisz & A. E. Kazdin (Eds.), *Evidence-based psychotherapies for children and adolescents* (2nd ed., pp. 179–193). New York: Guilford Press.

CHAPTER 19

Interventions That Promote Social–Emotional Learning in Young Children

Celene E. Domitrovich, Julia E. Moore, Ross A. Thompson, and the CASEL Preschool to Elementary School Social and Emotional Learning Assessment Workgroup

Children who enter school without requisite social, behavioral, and cognitive skills continue to fall behind over the early elementary years and are at risk for a range of poor elementary and adolescent outcomes, including school failure, dropout, and adjustment problems (Alexander, Entwisle, & Olson, 2001; Downey, von Hippel, & Broh, 2004; Duncan et al., 2007; McClelland, Acock, & Morrison, 2006; Ryan, Fauth, & Brooks-Gunn, 2006). Whereas research suggests that cognitive assessments are significant predictors of standardized reading and math achievement scores in elementary school (Duncan et al., 2007), readiness to engage in learning is highly dependent on their social–emotional skills, and social–emotional competencies are crucial for positive school adjustment and success (Durlak, Weissberg, Dymnicki, Taylor, & Schellinger, 2011). The preschool period is marked by significant growth in children's emotion knowledge and self-regulatory capacities, psychological understanding of the self and others, and their perspective-taking abilities (Thompson & Raikes, 2007). Individual differences in these skills play a role in children's school readiness and success, as they influence how well the child is able to adapt to the demands of formal schooling (Campbell & von Stauffenberg, 2008; Coolahan, Fantuzzo, Mendez, & McDermott, 2000; Ladd, Birch, & Buhs, 1999; Welsh, Nix, Blair, Bierman, & Nelson, 2010).

The first several years of formal education involve increasing demands on children that include the need to sit still and maintain attention for increasing periods of time, challenging learning and social situations that require high levels of emotion regulation, and the need to work collaboratively with others. In addition, there are changes in classroom structures, including larger class sizes, lower teacher–student ratios, longer days, and less structured routines, than what is typical in preschool. It is important to recognize that school readiness is not limited to skills or knowledge within children but also includes characteristics of the environments around them. At the classroom level, teacher–student interactions and classroom environments also have the potential to promote or challenge children's social–emotional development (Pianta, Steinberg, & Rollins, 1995; Pianta & Stuhlman, 2004). Children's personal competencies and the quality of their environments work interactively to foster both healthy social development and successful academic outcomes. Jennings and Greenberg (2009) propose that children's positive behavioral adaptation, growth in social–emotional skills and academic achievement, requires healthy classroom environments. These types of environments are characterized by positive teacher–student relationships, effective behavior management, and high-quality implementation of social–emotional interventions. As a result both children and teachers have become targets of preventive interventions designed to improve school readiness outcomes.

Our purpose in this chapter is to provide an overview of the current literature regarding high-quality, evidence-based interventions that promote school readiness in young children by focusing on the enhancement of children's social–emotional skills either directly with explicit classroom curricula, or indirectly through interventions with teachers. Only interventions with evidence of effectiveness are included. In addition to reviewing specific interventions, we discuss several critical issues to consider when implementing interventions in early childhood settings to ensure the highest quality and effectiveness.

Definitions of School Readiness

In 1995, a National Educational Goals Panel was convened to establish benchmarks for children's achievement. One of the primary goals was that, by 2010, all children would enter school ready to learn. Educational goals and legislation to date reflect this national priority (Bowman, Donovan, & Burns, 2000; National Education Goals Panel, 1997; No Child Left Behind Act, 2002). The federal emphasis on school readiness is because children who are successful during the early elementary years are more likely to perform well over time and to graduate from high school than children who suffer delays in school readiness. Children who enter school without the necessary social, behavioral, and cognitive skills continue to fall behind relative to national norms and are at risk for a range of poor adolescent outcomes, including school failure and dropout.

There are numerous definitions of *school readiness*. Initially the term was used in reference to reading readiness, but it has evolved into a broader construct, dependent upon the perspective of the individual or organization using it. Most definitions of school readiness emphasize early academic indicators. Language and emergent literacy skills, including vocabulary, phonemic awareness, and letter identification, are strong predictors of later achievement (Snow, Burns, & Griffin, 1998). Recent research indicates that cognitive assessments are the strongest predictors of standardized reading and math achievement scores in elementary school (Duncan et al., 2007). However, there is increased recognition by researchers and policymakers of the importance of social–emotional development for children's school readiness (Blair, 2002; Denham & Weissberg, 2004; National School Readiness Indicators Initiative, 2005; Raver, 2002; Thompson, 2002). The social and self-regulatory skills necessary to meet the behavioral demands of formal classroom settings are sometimes referred to as "behavioral school readiness" (Campbell & von Stauffenberg, 2008). When kindergarten teachers are asked to describe what children need to succeed in school, this aspect of school readiness is given an emphasis equal to early academic skills (Rimm-Kaufman & Pianta, 2000).

Learning standards in early childhood settings have been a part of public education for over a decade. They represent the mechanism through which the necessary skills and knowledge for academic success are defined, and they are used to guide the educational process, from selecting curricula to academic priorities and decisions about instructional practices. In the past few years, as public preschool education has expanded and accountability for government expenditures has grown, federal and state agencies have responded by developing early learning standards (National Association for the Education of Young Children, 2005). There was already a long-standing tradition of standards in early care and education, but these tended to focus on the structural features of those settings, and to some degree, the nature of children's experiences (Lamb, 1998). A 2006 content analysis of the early learning standards in 46 states revealed that the majority of states include core language, literacy, and numeracy skill indicators in their standards (Scott-Little, Kagan, & Frelow, 2006). Social–emotional development and approaches to learning were also well represented, but with fewer indicators and in less systematic ways compared to cognitive skills.

One of the most importance advances in school readiness research was the recognition that definitions of readiness should not be limited to skills or knowledge within children, but should also include characteristics of the environments around them; this includes the family, educational setting, and neighborhood. High-quality relationships, in particular, serve important protective functions for children throughout development (Luthar, 2006), and the ability to form these types of relationships with peers and adults is included in the early learning standards of a number of states. Developmental research in this area clearly suggests that relationships evolve out of transactional processes (Hamre & Pianta, 2001; Ladd & Burgess, 2001).

Early Predictors of Academic Success

Educational research has identified patterns of observable learning behaviors in kindergarten and the early elementary school years associated with achievement (McClelland & Morrison, 2003). Children who are engaged and participate in class score higher on cognitive assessments in preschool than those who are disengaged or who do not participate (Reynolds, 1991; Reynolds & Bezruczko, 1993). When researchers control for prior achievement, higher levels of participation at the beginning of kindergarten predict higher achievement test scores at the end of the academic year (Ladd et al., 1999).

High-quality classroom participation requires skills such as listening and following directions, cooperating in groups, and working independently. It also includes mastery behaviors such as the ability to plan, organize, and complete tasks (McClelland & Morrison, 2003). These behaviors are sometimes considered early indicators of social responsibility (Wentzel, 1991). Several studies have shown that these "work-related" skills are predictive of achievement (Cooper & Farran, 1988; McClelland et al., 2006; McClelland, Morrison, & Holmes, 2000). One study that included a sample of students ages 6–17 demonstrated that these behaviors were associated with student achievement even after researchers controlled for cognitive ability (Yen, Konold, & McDermott, 2004). Some early research suggests that girls with deficits in work-related behavior may be especially vulnerable to poor school performance (Swartz & Walker, 1984). In addition to work-related behaviors, kindergarten children's attitudes (affective and cognitive) toward school are associated with their concurrent and future performance in the classroom setting (Hauser-Cram, Durand, & Warfield, 2007; Ladd, Buhs, & Seid, 2000; Ramey, Lanzi, Phillips, & Ramey, 1998; Yen et al., 2004).

Researchers interested in early behavioral indicators of academic success have highlighted the importance of social–emotional competence for school success by distinguishing between interpersonal skills and work-related skills, and showing that both contribute to early school performance (Cooper & Farran, 1988; McClelland et al., 2000, 2006). In these studies, the measures of work-related skills are similar to those described earlier, and the interpersonal skills include aspects of self-regulation and social competence that are needed for compliance and cooperation. Using latent growth curve analyses, both work-related and interpersonal skills have been shown to predict growth in reading and math achievement between kindergarten and second grade, and the level of achievement in both areas between third and sixth grade (McClelland et al., 2006). While this research represents an important step toward recognizing the role that social–emotional learning plays in facilitating academic achievement, the narrow way in which social–emotional skills are conceptualized in these studies fails to capture the complexity of the skills that undergird social competence. In the next section, we present a description of the individual skills that comprise social–emotional learning, and the empirical literature linking each of them to academic outcomes.

Individual Social–Emotional Competencies

The Collaborative for Academic, Social, and Emotional Learning (CASEL) has identified five domains of social–emotional learning that include the individual skills essential to both social and cognitive aspects of school readiness, and academic success more generally. These include self-awareness, self-management, social awareness, relationships skills, and responsible decision making (Payton et al., 2001). Children's self-concept or awareness of self has implications for learning as it relates to their motivation, approach to challenging tasks, and self-evaluation of performance (Marsh, Ellias, & Craven, 2002). *Self-management*, often referred to as *self-regulation* in the research literature, includes the overlapping but distinct constructs of emotional regulation, cognitive regulation (also called executive functions), and behavioral regulation (Smith-Donald, Raver, Hayes, & Richardson, 2007). Executive functions, which include working memory, inhibitory control, and mental flexibility, are considered the building blocks of both academic and social competence (Center on the Developing Child, 2011). Self-regulation is critical for school readiness and engagement in learning because children who are impulsive and distractible are more often noncompliant in the classroom, have difficulty following directions, and become overwhelmed in emotionally arousing situations. This undermines their ability to engage in learning and to benefit from instruction. The regulatory skills that are essential for self-management also indirectly impact the learning process by influencing children's ability to form and maintain positive relationships with adults and peers.

Social awareness includes emotion knowledge skills, such as the ability to identify and label emotions accurately, and perspective taking (e.g., empathy), skills in young children that predict academic competence in the early years of schooling (Izard et al., 2001; Leerkes, Paradise, O'Brien, Calkins, & Lange, 2008; Trentacosta & Izard, 2007). Awareness of oneself and others, and self-regulation skills that support sharing and cooperation in kindergarten are associated with concurrent literacy skills and predict reading achievement in later elementary grades (Miles & Stipek, 2006; National Institute of Child Health and Human Development [NICHD] Early Child Care Research Network, 2004). Children who have the social–emotional skills to sustain satisfying interactions with others, and who avoid or resolve conflicts when they occur, are more likely to develop high-quality friendships and be accepted by the larger peer group (Ladd et al., 1999). Positive peer relations are associated with academic success, while rejection and victimization are linked with underachievement (Ladd & Burgess, 2001).

There are several different mechanisms through which this social process is thought to impact learning. One is the positive emotional effect of having friends, which can buffer the stress of entering a new environment and facilitate a positive attitude toward school.

Another hypothesis about the role of positive peer relations for academic success is the opportunity these types of relationships provide for involvement in cooperative learning activities (Ladd, Kochenderfer, & Coleman, 1997). Children's social skills have implications for the quality of relationships that they form with teachers, relationships that have been shown to be important for both short- and long-term academic success (Pianta & Stuhlman, 2004). Teacher–student relationships characterized by high levels of conflict or dependency increase student risk for behavioral and academic problems, whereas high levels of closeness predict growth in social skills over time (Burchinal, Peisner-Feinberg, Pianta, & Howes, 2002; Ladd & Burgess, 1999). In the same way children's skills increase the likelihood that they are able to engage with peers in social experiences that promote learning, these skills have the potential to elicit certain patterns of behavior from the adults around them. Teachers who have positive relationships with students may spend more time interacting, show more patience, or be more willing to adjust instruction to meet the individual needs of those students (Pianta & Stuhlman, 2004).

The final domain of social–emotional competence is responsible decision making. Although this domain may seem more relevant for older children, it also applies to younger children, as it captures the importance of moral values and the social-cognitive skills that undergird responsible behavior and absence of aggressive behavior. Children's ability to engage in complex social problem solving has as much potential to impact their academic learning as it does their social success because this process requires executive functions such as cognitive flexibility and anticipatory planning.

The five social–emotional domains advanced by CASEL are represented in many of the social–emotional early learning standards currently used by early educators. Table 19.1 presents the most common standards organized according to these domains.

Contextual Factors

Participation in an early education program by itself is not sufficient to improve children's school-readiness skills. Exposure to a high-quality classroom experience is also essential (NICHD Early Child Care Research Network, 2004). Improving the quality of teaching practices in early childhood is a crucial strategy for improving children's school readiness (Clifford et al., 2005; Raikes et al., 2006). A growing body of research suggests that proximal features of teaching quality, including instructional practices, the way the classroom is organized and student behavior is managed, and the provision of emotional support by the teacher, are what determine the extent to which participation in the classroom results in social–emotional and cognitive skills development (Burchinal et al., 2008; Mashburn et al., 2008). High-quality teachers use engaging instructional techniques that scaffold student learning in key content areas and promote flexible, higher-order thinking. They manage the classroom effectively by creating predictable routines, monitoring their students and preventing negative behavior in positive ways, and refraining from overly authoritarian discipline techniques (Arnold, McWilliams, & Arnold, 1998; Jennings & Greenberg, 2009; Yates & Yates, 1990). Teachers who interact with students in a warm, sensitive, and responsive way validate their students' emotional experiences and create a secure environment that supports active engagement in classroom and learning activities (Howes & Smith, 1995; Kontos & Wilcox-Herzog, 1997; NICHD Early Child Care Research Network, 1998). These types of interactions between students and teachers result in high-quality relationships and a positive classroom climate.

In addition, several specific teaching strategies promote children's emotional understanding, emotion regulation, and social competence. These include "emotion coaching,"

TABLE 19.1. Examples of Common Early Social–Emotional Learning Standards Organized by Domain

Domains	Examples of social–emotional learning standards
Self-awareness	<ul><li>Perceives and values self as a unique individual</li><li>Demonstrates awareness of abilities, preferences, and characteristics</li><li>Demonstrates belief in abilities, self-confidence</li><li>Expresses appropriately a range of emotion</li></ul>
Self-management	<ul><li>Demonstrates growing awareness of and ability to control emotions</li><li>Shows capabilities in impulse control with adult guidance</li><li>Pays attention when needed to classroom activities</li><li>Initiates constructive activities with other children and adults; proposes new ideas</li><li>Shows curiosity, persistence in problem-solving, self-direction</li></ul>
Social awareness	<ul><li>Expresses feelings and opinions appropriately in difficult situations</li><li>Demonstrates caring for others and a desire to be helpful to those in need</li><li>Shows sensitivity to and respect for others' feelings, opinions, desires</li><li>Shows an interest in people and their feelings and behavior</li><li>Recognizes, appreciates, and respects similarities and differences between people</li><li>Demonstrates a sense of belonging to the program, family, and community</li><li>Uses language to communicate thoughts, feelings, and needs</li><li>Communicates well with others using language</li></ul>
Relationship skills with adults	<ul><li>Initiates and maintains relationships with adults</li><li>Seeks security and support from classroom teacher, especially when upset</li><li>Shares activities, demonstrates skills, and otherwise seeks approval from a special teacher</li><li>Participates in one-on-one conversations with adults</li><li>Seeks assistance from adults when needed</li><li>Cooperates with adult and follows instructions readily</li></ul>
Relationship skills with peers	<ul><li>Cooperates with peers in play and resolves conflicts easily</li><li>Interacts easily with one or more peers</li><li>Resolves conflict with peers constructively, using words to express feelings</li><li>Takes turns, negotiates, articulates preferences and accepts compromises</li><li>Uses play (especially pretend play) as a vehicle for building relationships and developing self-confidence</li><li>Shows pleasure in being friends; seeks the company of friends for shared activities</li></ul>
Responsible decision making	<ul><li>Seeks to comply with adult instructions and requests</li><li>Understands and cooperates with classroom rules and routines</li><li>Follows rules and routines, and understands role as a group member</li><li>Shows concern about fairness to others</li><li>Develops an understanding of consequences of negative behavior</li><li>Uses classroom materials carefully</li><li>Comprehends responsibilities as a member of the group</li></ul>

which involves empathetic and nonjudgmental responses to children's emotional expressions (Gottman, Katz, & Hooven, 1997), and social problem-solving dialogue, which provides children with "online" support to manage conflicts (Denham & Burton, 2003). Child self-control is encouraged when teachers provide support for self-regulation, including clear expectations, predictable and appropriate routines (La Paro, Pianta, & Stuhlman, 2004), and "induction strategies," which provide children with teacher and peer feedback to encourage self-control efforts (Bierman, 2004; Bierman, Greenberg, & the Conduct Problem Prevention Research Group [CPPRG], 1996). When teachers manage the inevitable conflicts and negative behaviors in preschool classrooms using positive discipline techniques rather than harsh and directive strategies, children display more positive behavior and higher levels of language development (Arnold et al., 1998; Whitebook, Howes, & Phillips, 1990). Hence, sensitive responding, proactive and preventive support, emotion coaching, induction strategies, and positive behavioral management all increase the level of emotional–behavioral support in the preschool classroom, which in turn is associated with stronger cognitive and language skills in preschool (NICHD Early Child Care Research Network, 2000a, 2000b) and higher levels of achievement in early elementary school (NICHD Early Child Care Research Network, 2004; Peisner-Feinberg et al., 2001).

Promoting Social–Emotional Learning with Classroom Interventions

For decades researchers have known that experiencing a classroom-based educational program prior to entering elementary school has a positive impact on children's school readiness and later academic and life success (Niles, Reynolds, & Roe-Sepowitz, 2008; Ramey & Ramey, 2004; Reynolds & Temple, 1998; Weikart & Schweinhart, 1997). More recently the focus has shifted from determining whether a preschool education is beneficial to understanding how best to improve the quality of practices in these settings to improve specific aspects of children's school readiness (Bierman, Torres, Domitrovich, Welsh, & Gest, 2009; Lonigan, Burgess, & Anthony, 2000; Sarama & Clements, 2004). Strategies include the increased dissemination of evidence-based curricula that target social–emotional skills and enhanced professional development regarding high quality teacher–child interactions. Although there are fewer interventions for preschool-age populations compared to older children, the number being developed and tested in randomized clinical trials is growing.

The majority of the evidence-based, social–emotional interventions available to early educators are universal models designed to be infused into preexisting, comprehensive educational curricula such as High Scope or Creative Curriculum. The term "universal," drawn from the public health literature, signifies that an intervention is appropriate for use with the general population (National Research Council and Institute of Medicine, 2010). It is important to recognize that there are limitations to the potential impact of universal interventions for young children who are exposed to high levels of risk. Children growing up in underresourced or neglectful environments, or who have emerging mental health problems or disabilities (i.e., disruptive behavior), are likely to need more intensive early intervention, in addition to being exposed to universal interventions in the classroom setting (Hemmeter & Conroy, Chapter 20, this volume).

Random assignment of subjects to condition is one of the most useful design strategies to address potential biases in intervention research and increase confidence in the interpretation of study outcomes. However, it is also important to consider several other methodological features that strengthen a study. These include the use of both pre- and posttest assessments, multiple methods, and statistical techniques that account for the clustering of students within classrooms (Flay et al., 2005). In the next section, we review studies of interventions designed to improve children's social–emotional learning. All of the studies utilized randomization but they vary in the degree to which additional elements of high-quality research were used. Findings from studies indicate that both explicit social–emotional curricula and interventions that target teacher–student interactions and quality of relationships can improve children's skills in the five domains of social and emotional development identified by CASEL.

Child-Focused Interventions

Child-focused interventions typically involve teachers delivering explicit lessons aimed at improving children's emotion knowledge, self-awareness, social-awareness and problem solving skills. While some are domain specific, most are comprehensive with components designed to impact a variety of skills.

I Can Problem Solve

One of the pioneer child-focused, social–emotional interventions is the I Can Problem Solve (ICPS) program by Shure and Spivack (1982). Classroom teachers implement the ICPS program with small groups, first teaching children fundamental skills related to language, thinking, and listening. The program then focuses on solving complex interpersonal problems through dialogues and role playing. Children are taught to identify multiple options to overcome obstacles they are facing and to evaluate and use each of the options in a step-by-step manner.

In one trial with preschool students, the intervention promoted gains in children's social problem-solving abilities and teacher-rated improvements in frustration tolerance, impulsivity, and task engagement (Shure & Spivack, 1982). These findings were replicated in other randomized studies (Feis & Simons, 1985). In a meta-analysis, Denham and Almeida (1987) found that preschool children who participated in ICPS programs successfully acquired ICPS skills and experienced positive behavior change.

Denham and Burton (1996) tested the impact of ICPS in an expanded intervention model for preschool children that also included teacher implementation of a relationship-building component, an understanding and regulating emotions component, the Turtle Technique (Robin, Schneider, & Dolnick, 1976) and the Dialoguing Technique (Shure, 1981). The goal of the relationship-building component was to have children develop a consistently positive relationship with teachers to support emotional growth. In an effort to help children to understand, express, and regulate their emotions, they were taught to recognize actions that cause certain emotions, and identify and label their own emotions. When using the Turtle Technique, children were instructed to imagine that they were turtles going inside their shells when they felt overwhelmed by emotion. In the Dialoguing Technique, the teacher identified a problem (e.g., two children who wanted to play with the same toy) and discussed feelings and possible solutions to the problem. The intervention had a positive impact on participants, based on both teacher ratings and classroom observations of student affect and behavior (Denham & Burton, 1996).

Emotion Course

Izard, Trentacosta, King, and Mostow (2004) developed an emotion-focused intervention based on differential emotions theory, which targets the skills related to children's understanding, regulation, and utilization of emotions through interactive experiences. The

Emotion Course consists of 22 lessons centered on emotional experiences, including happiness, sadness, anger and fear. Other emotions, such as motivation and contempt, are also covered. During lessons, children are first taught to recognize and label emotions, then to regulate their own emotions. The lessons include puppet vignettes, interactive reading, emotion expression posters, and games and emotion-focused techniques for regulating emotions.

In a randomized trial of the Emotions Course in 16 Head Start classrooms, children who received the curriculum were more likely to have better emotion knowledge and to be better able to regulate their emotions (Izard et al., 2008). No differences were found on receptive emotion vocabulary and teacher reports of social and academic competence. The program was subsequently tested in a randomized trial in 26 urban Head Start classrooms (Izard et al., 2008). Using hierarchical linear modeling (HLM) to account for the clustering of students within classrooms, intervention students were compared to a group of students receiving ICPS. Findings were assessed by the emotion matching task, the Emotion Regulation Checklist, the Emotion Expression Ratings Scale, and the Preschool Competence Questionnaire (Izard et al., 2008). Intervention students gained significantly more emotion knowledge and regulation, as well as social competence in terms of interpersonal relationships, compliance, and emotion expression.

Tools of the Mind

The Tools of the Mind (Tools) curriculum (Bodrova & Leong, 2007) applies the theories of Luria and Vygotsky to build preschool children's executive function (EF) skills and self-regulation. It strategically structures classroom activities to include a process that scaffolds, trains, and challenges the development of these skills, including inhibitory control, working memory, and cognitive flexibility. The core intervention includes 40 activities that often involve children working in pairs or engaging in pretend play. The program teaches children to make plans for their activities and to execute these plans through multiple types of activities, including make-believe play, focal self-regulation activities (e.g., the "Freeze" game) or embedded self-regulation activities (e.g., Buddy Reading).

A team of independent researchers evaluated the Tools curriculum in a PreK program serving primarily low-income students (Diamond, Barnett, Thomas, & Munro, 2007). Children were exposed to the Tools curriculum for 1–2 years in the intervention classrooms. Their performance on two measures of EF (the dots task and a flanker task) and teacher assessments of internalizing and externalizing behavior were compared to students from comparison classrooms in which teachers delivered the district's standard balanced literacy program. On both EF measures, intervention children performed significantly better than controls at the end of the intervention period. Similarly, children in the intervention group displayed fewer internalizing and externalizing problems than those who did not receive the intervention. Unfortunately, this study failed to assess students' pretest functioning, which is standard practice for inclusion in analyses. In addition, the clustering of students within classrooms was not controlled. A follow-up study found that the Tools curriculum improved children's self-regulatory behavior and social conduct but did not significantly improve language and literacy skills (Barnett et al., 2008).

Al's Pals: Kids Making Healthy Choices

Al's Pals: Kids Making Healthy Choices curriculum (Wingspan LLC, 1999) is based on resiliency research and geared toward children from preschool through early elementary school. Al's Pals has two major goals: to increase children's social–emotional competence, and to influence the risk factors for antisocial and aggressive behavior. The program includes lessons designed to promote children's social competence, problem solving, autonomy, and positive beliefs about themselves and their future, implemented in 47 lessons delivered over the course of 23 weeks. Each lesson lasts 15–20 minutes and addresses children's need to be active, imaginative, and to have fun, while engaging in focused activities (e.g., puppet-led discussions, brainstorming, role play, reading, and music) that promote prosocial behavior and express norms that violence and drug and alcohol use are not acceptable behaviors. In addition, teachers are also asked to infuse these concepts into their daily practices.

Al's Pals has been evaluated in the context of several replications across Virginia, Michigan, and Missouri. In a randomized study of 33 Head Start classrooms, the program produced significant effects on teacher ratings of child behavior problems, social competence, and independent functioning (Lynch, Geller, & Schmidt, 2004). Intervention students were rated as more socially independent and were better able to use coping skills than were students who did not participate in the program. From pre- to posttest, children in the intervention group maintained the same number of problem behaviors, whereas children in the control group became more disruptive over the course of the school year.

Learning with Purpose: A Lifelong Learning Approach to Self-Determination

Another classroom-based intervention model designed to increase students' adaptive skills (e.g., problem-solving skills, self-determination, social skills, and ability to cope with stress) is the *Learning with Purpose: A Lifelong Learning Approach to Self-Determination* (Serna & Lau-Smith, 1995) program. This 12-week program was tested in the context of a small randomized trial with 53 intervention children and 31 control children from three intervention Head Start classrooms and two control classrooms (Serna, Nielsen, Lambros, & Forness, 2000). Teachers presented concepts to children in the intervention classrooms through stories and songs. The researchers did not conduct direct child assessments; however, according to teacher and parent ratings of child skills and behavior, the intervention students exhibited higher levels of adaptive behavior after participation compared to students in the control classrooms (Serna et al., 2000).

Preschool PATHS (Promoting Alternative THinking Strategies)

Preschool PATHS (Domitrovich, Greenberg, Kusche, & Cortes, 2005) is another universal, social–emotional curriculum that has demonstrated positive effects in two randomized trials involving implementation by teachers in Head Start classrooms. The primary goals of the curriculum include developing children's ability to label and recognize emotions in themselves and others, improving self-control, promoting positive peer relationships, enhancing problem-solving skills, and fostering a positive classroom environment. The curriculum consists of 33 lessons that target four domains: (1) prosocial friendship skills, (2) emotional understanding and emotional expression skills, (3) self-control, and (4) problem-solving skills. Children are also taught the Turtle Technique. In addition, teachers are encouraged to incorporate social–emotional development in teachable moments throughout the day.

In the first study, Head Start children who received Preschool PATHS showed higher levels of emotional understanding and were rated more socially competent by teachers and parents than were children in the control group (Domitrovich, Cortes, & Greenberg, 2007). More recently, Preschool PATHS was integrated with evidence-based language and literacy intervention components to create a comprehensive curriculum and tested against "usual practice." The program, referred to as Head Start REDI (*R*esearch-based, *D*evelopmentally

Informed), involved brief lessons, hands-on extension activities, and specific teaching strategies, all linked empirically with the promotion of social–emotional competencies, language development, and emergent literacy skills. Analyses were conducted to account for the clustering of students within classrooms. Results revealed significant differences favoring children in the enriched intervention classrooms on measures of vocabulary, emergent literacy, emotional understanding, social problem solving, social behavior, and learning engagement (Bierman et al., 2008). Follow-up analyses indicated that these effects were sustained into kindergarten (Bierman et al., 2010).

Incredible Years Dinosaur School

A similar universal, social–emotional curriculum, Incredible Years Dinosaur School (Webster-Stratton, 1990), is based on cognitive social learning theory and focuses on social learning behavior change through the use of modeling, role play, and reinforcement. Teachers taught 30 biweekly lessons across seven units that targeted learning school rules, how to be successful at school, emotional literacy, perspective taking, prosocial skills, emotional understanding, self-regulation, social problem-solving skills, and communication skills. Teachers also received 4 days of training monthly that focused on effective classroom management, discipline, and coaching to promote social competence.

In an evaluation of the program, Incredible Years was combined with a teacher training component and tested in a randomized trial with preschool, kindergarten and first grade classrooms in Head Start programs and schools that served primarily low-income students (Webster-Stratton, Reid, & Stoolmiller, 2008). Students in the intervention group displayed higher levels of self-regulation and social competence, and fewer conduct problems compared to those in the control group, and the effects were stronger in classrooms that started with higher rather than lower levels of problems in these areas (Webster-Stratton et al., 2008). The high-risk students exposed to the program also provided more positive than negative solutions on the problem-solving task and showed greater accuracy identifying feelings compared to high-risk control students. It is impossible to know the specific effect of the intervention uniquely for preschool children because the outcomes were presented for the total sample and not specific age levels.

Banking Time

Banking Time is a preschool intervention designed to build a supportive and positive teacher–child relationship (Driscoll & Pianta, 2010). It is based on a component of Barkley's (1987) parent consultation program, in which parents were taught to interact and play with their children to increase parent–child communication, positive emotional experiences, and the child's motivation. The program is designed to complement existing social–emotional curricula in the preschool classroom. Teachers and children interact during one-on-one regularly scheduled play sessions led by the child. During the interaction, the teacher has four roles: Observe the child, narrate what the child is doing without directing the child, label emotions and feeling, and develop relational themes.

A randomized control trial of Banking Time was conducted in Head Start classrooms (Driscoll & Pianta, 2010). There were three conditions: (1) children who were randomized to receive the intervention; (2) children who were randomized not to receive the intervention but were in classrooms with children who received the intervention; and (3) classrooms that did not receive the intervention. Children who received the intervention had better teacher-reported frustration tolerance, task orientation, and social competence, and they exhibited fewer conduct problems than peers in the same classroom who did not participate in the program. Compared to classrooms in which no children received the program, those in the intervention conditions had a closer relationship with their teachers.

Teacher-Focused Interventions

As described previously, conceptual models of early education (Mashburn et al., 2008) and social–emotional learning specifically (Jennings & Greenberg, 2009) posit that changes in student outcomes evolve out of key interactions between teachers and students. As a result of research establishing the link between specific teacher–child interactions and children's school readiness outcomes across a variety of domains (Burchinal et al., 2008), professional development interventions have targeted these teaching behaviors. Randomized trials testing these interventions assess teacher behavior as an outcome, but some also include assessments of child outcomes in an effort to capture distal impacts of the intervention. It is important to note that most of the universal, child-focused curricular interventions are delivered by teachers, and an assumption is that when these approaches are implemented with fidelity, they improve the quality of teacher–student interactions and student behavior. Given this assumption, we have included a description of the teacher outcomes of one child-focused intervention in this section.

The Incredible Years Parents, Teachers, and Children's Training Series

The Incredible Years Teacher Training Program, a module within the Incredible Years Series, provides teachers with professional development in positive classroom management, discipline strategies, and ways to promote social competence in the classroom (Webster-Stratton, Reid, & Hammond, 2004). In an evaluation of the program, Webster-Stratton and colleagues provided intervention teachers in Head Start classrooms with six monthly, 1-day workshops that used videotape vignettes and group discussion for training. Postintervention observations indicated that, compared to control teachers, intervention teachers used more praise and effective discipline techniques, and fewer harsh and critical techniques.

Child School Readiness Project

The Child School Readiness Project (CSRP), a teacher-focused, multicomponent intervention, designed to improve low-income children's school readiness by fostering their emotional and behavioral self-regulation (Raver et al., 2011). CSRP includes professional development training in behavior management based on the Incredible Years Teacher Training Program, stress-reduction workshops, and classroom-based mental health consultation regarding student behavior. One of the primary goals of the intervention is to prevent escalating cycles of dysregulated behavior in children by enhancing teachers' use of clear rules and routines, rewards for positive behavior, and redirection of negative behavior.

Over the course of the academic year, both the lead and the assistant teacher in each of the intervention classrooms were provided with five training sessions, each of which lasted 6 hours. Additionally, teachers were paired with a mental health consultant who had a master's degree in social work. These individuals also served as coaches throughout the year, supporting teachers as they applied the techniques introduced in the training, and providing standardized, child-focused mental health consultation. The mental health consultants also conducted stress reduction workshops for teachers that were designed to reduce burnout.

Results of a randomized trial in 18 Head Start sites with 94 teachers indicated significantly higher levels of positive climate, teacher sensitivity, and behavior management in intervention classrooms at the end of the year (Raver et al., 2008). The intervention also had positive effects on child outcomes (Raver et al., 2009). Children in classrooms of intervention teachers exhibited fewer internalizing and externalizing behavior problems according to both independent observers and teacher ratings (Raver et al., 2009). Children who received the CSRP intervention also scored significantly better on preacademic and self-regulatory skills by the end of preschool than children in the control group. Specifically, intervention participants outperformed control participants on vocabulary, letter naming, early math skills, and measures of executive functioning and attention/impulsivity.

Head Start REDI

In addition to the enhanced curricular components in Head Start REDI, referred to previously in the section on PATHS, the program included an extensive professional development model that integrated enriched social–emotional and emergent literacy components (Domitrovich, Gest, Gill, Bierman, et al., 2009). Teachers received 3 days of inservice training prior to the school year; during the school year, teachers also received 1 day of booster training. In addition, Head Start teachers in the intervention classrooms received weekly mentoring from coaches to support their implementation of the curriculum model. The coaches observed each classroom for 3 hours each week, then held 1-hour meetings in which they provided feedback and introduced specific teaching strategies to the teacher teams (e.g., positive behavior management strategies, social–emotional skill promotion, and problem-solving prevention strategies).

The randomized trial, which included 44 Head Start teachers, was not designed to disentangle the effects of the curriculum components from the professional development support. When evaluated as a whole, significant effects were found for multiple domains of teaching quality (Domitrovich, Gest, Gill, Bierman, et al., 2009). Both intervention lead and assistant teachers talked with children more frequently and in more cognitively complex ways, established a more positive classroom climate, and used more preventive behavior management strategies compared to control teachers.

My Teaching Partner

My Teaching Partner (MTP) is a Web-mediated professional development intervention for teachers (Pianta, Mashburn, Downer, Hamre, & Justice, 2008). The intervention is grounded in the Classroom Assessment Scoring System (CLASS; Pianta, La Paro, & Hamre, 2008), an observation of teaching quality indicated by instructional practices, delivery of emotional support, and behavior management. An evaluation of the program compared two conditions that varied in the degree of support provided. All teachers had access to online versions of the MTP lesson materials that included language and literacy activity Web pages developed by the authors and a Web version of Preschool PATHS (Domitrovich et al., 2005). Teachers in the Web-only condition (low support) had access to video examples of high-quality teacher–student interactions, and teachers in the consultation condition (high support) were assigned to work with a consultant for 1 year. Teachers in the consultation condition submitted videotapes of their lesson delivery, which were reviewed by the consultants and edited into short examples that were given back, along with written feedback and questions to encourage teacher reflection (Pianta, Mashburn, et al., 2008). Teachers in both conditions submitted to the research team tapes that were coded using the CLASS observation system.

The efficacy of the program was evaluated in a randomized trial consisting of 113 prekindergarten teachers from state-funded programs (Pianta, Mashburn, et al., 2008).

Compared to teachers in the Web-only condition, teachers in the consultation condition had more positive growth for teacher sensitivity, instructional learning formats, and language modeling, as assessed by the CLASS. Teachers who viewed more of the activity Web pages experienced more growth in behavior management skills than those less exposed to activity Web pages. Moderation analyses indicated that the program effects were greater in classrooms in which a larger number of students came from families with lower socioeconomic status (SES) compared to classrooms with a greater proportion of children from middle-SES families.

Ensuring the Effectiveness of Evidence-Based Social–Emotional Interventions

Choosing to adopt an evidence-based intervention for a follow-up research trial does not guarantee that an early education program will produce the same kinds of effects as were achieved in the original research trial, but this is usually the goal. Multiple factors have the potential to impact the effectiveness of programs delivered in community settings (e.g., available resources, the nature of the intervention, how it is introduced into the program, characteristics of the individuals delivering it, and the nature of the setting where it is being used; Domitrovich, Gest, Gill, Jones, & DeRousie, 2009). Predominantly these factors operate through their effect on implementation quality and also have implications for whether interventions are successfully sustained.

High-quality, evidence-based interventions are grounded in theory regarding specific mechanisms required for change in participants (Greenberg, Domitrovich, Graczyk, & Zins, 2005). These include content and practices that are represented in the program's logic model. "Implementation quality" is the degree to which a program is implemented as originally defined in the logic model, or at least as achieved in the original efficacy trial. Monitoring implementation should be a priority whenever an evidence-based intervention is adopted. The variety of ways to assess implementation include gathering information on how much of the intervention is delivered (i.e., dosage), the degree to which core elements of the model are followed (i.e., fidelity), or the quality with which the intervention is delivered (Dane & Schneider, 1998). Typically, published programs have developed self-report ratings or observational measures that can be used in the field to assess quality and provide a source of information for quality improvement.

Evidence-based interventions that are well implemented (i.e., closer to the original model) have stronger outcomes but are rarely replicated with complete adherence (Durlak, 2010; Durlak & DuPre, 2008). One of the best strategies for ensuring high-quality implementation is to prepare and support the individuals delivering the program (Fixsen, Naoom, Blase, Friedman, & Wallace, 2005; Greenberg, Domitrovich, & Bumbarger, 2001). In the next section, we discuss research-based methods for supporting effective program implementation.

The Importance of Professional Development

One of the greatest challenges to implementing evidence-based interventions in preschool settings is to ensure that the individuals charged with delivering the interventions are prepared and have adequate skills to fulfill their role. High-quality interventions are standardized in terms of both their materials and training, but they vary as to whether they are broadly available. Interventions that have an adequate evidence base are typically published, enabling dissemination to broad community settings.

Individual preschool centers or programs have limited budgets and frequently only have the funds for purchasing materials, not for training in their use. Research suggests that training is important and associated with higher-quality implementation (Durlak & DuPre, 2008; O'Donnell, 2008). For curricular enhancements in early childhood settings, training is especially important, as it typically focuses on improvement in quality of teacher interactions with students, as well as specific use of program materials. In light of the importance of teacher–student interaction to intervention efficacy, it is professional development that appears necessary to promote improvement in both teaching quality and student outcome (Justice, Mashburn, Hamre, & Pianta, 2008).

Professional training by an individual certified in a specific program model is often an expensive, additional cost beyond program materials. The majority of effective interventions, however, are tested under conditions in which participants received this type of intensive training and, in many cases, also received ongoing support (Bierman et al., 2008; Pianta, Mashburn, et al., 2008; Raver et al., 2008). Mentoring that includes in-classroom coaching and out-of-classroom collaborative meetings is gaining attention as an effective professional development strategy compared to typical inservice workshops that are often time limited and didactic (Haskins & Loeb, 2007; International Reading Association & National Association for the Education of Young Children, 1998). In a study that compared four professional development models, the condition that was the most comprehensive—involving the combination of online coursework, mentoring, and detailed feedback—resulted in the greatest improvements in teacher behavior and student outcomes (Landry, Anthony, Swank, & Monseque-Bailey, 2009).

There is very little empirical research regarding the most effective models for ongoing implementation support or methods that should be used by coaches (Sheridan, Edwards, Marvin, & Knoche, 2009). Theory suggests that coaches serve multiple roles, including that of emotional support provider, facilitator, and technical assistant (Ryan & Hornbeck, 2004). Many teachers experience high levels of work-related emotional stress (Montgomery & Rupp, 2005; Tsouloupas, Carson, Matthews, Grawitch, & Barber, 2010) that can undermine motivation and performance, and contribute to negative interactions with children (Osher et al., 2007). Descriptive studies suggest that the support and encouragement provided by coaches is one of the most important elements of this form of professional development (Brooks, 1996; McCormick & Brennan, 2001).

It is difficult for teachers to evaluate their own practices given the inherent biases in this process. Likewise there are individual differences in teachers' knowledge and experience that can affect their practice. Ideally, coaches are nonevaluative facilitators who have "expert" knowledge, yet develop collaborative relationships with the teachers they support, enabling them to deliver accurate information about the teacher's performance in a way that is nonthreatening and facilitates learning. For example, in the REDI intervention, the professional development model included a weekly in-classroom observation and meetings outside of the classroom (Domitrovich, Gest, Gill, Bierman, et al., 2009).

In addition to providing emotional support, coaches are technical assistants who facilitate learning by helping teachers gain a deeper understanding of the intervention theory. They also provide suggestions regarding program delivery and integration between the intervention and the existing curriculum, and troubleshoot problems encountered by teachers while using the intervention (Dusenbury et al., 2007). There is some research to suggest that the use of feedback is especially important to this process (Leach & Conto, 1999; Rose & Church, 1998). Based on a study examining growth over time in the teaching quality of lead teachers, the coach's rating of the teacher's "openness to consultation" was found to be the most consistent predictor across different dimensions of behavior (Domitrovich, Gest, Gill, Jones, et al., 2009).

Planning for Sustainability

Sustainability, the process of maintaining an innovation so that it continues to benefit the stakeholders (Johnson, Hays, Center, & Daley, 2004; Kellam & Langevin, 2003), is a multifaceted, ongoing, and cyclical process (Johnson et al., 2004) that involves (1) institutionalizing the program or practice within the funded organization, (2) continuing benefit to participants, (3) maintaining capacity to support the innovation, and (4) continuing an organizational focus on the relevant intervention goals (Scheirer, Hartling, & Hagerman, 2008). Sustaining evidence-based interventions in community settings can be challenging for a number of reasons, and although research on this issue is still in its infancy, there is evidence that planning predicts later success (Elliott & Mihalic, 2004; Tibbits, Bumbarger, Kyler, & Perkins, 2010). Some of the barriers to sustaining programs or practices are present when a program is selected and adopted. The acceptability of an intervention by those implementing it is critical in predicting the quality with which it is implemented (Rohrbach, Graham, & Hansen, 1993). Thus it is important to consider carefully the process of introducing an intervention into an early childhood program. Ideally, the program that is selected fits with the philosophy of the organization and is seen as necessary and effective.

Although professional development is essential for ensuring high-quality implementation, programs often make an investment in staff training only to find that, with turnover, the number of formally trained individuals disappears quickly. One way that knowledge and experience associated with a program can be sustained is to develop structures that formalize and incorporate training and support into the existing professional development system of the organization. Similarly, implementation monitoring systems are most effective when they are part of the usual documentation process, and when the data are used as part of everyday practice, from planning within the classroom to supervision by the administration and quality reviews of the program.

Conclusions

Early education programs interested in enhancing their existing practices with evidence-based curricula to promote social-emotional learning have a number of options from which to choose. Several comprehensive models have been shown to be effective in elevating teacher performance and improving children's social–emotional school readiness. These types of interventions are increasingly recognized by state and federal initiatives designed to promote children's mental health and school readiness (Kellam & Langevin, 2003). The key to achieving positive outcomes with evidence-based interventions is maintaining high-quality implementation. An investment in professional development, implementation monitoring, and thoughtful planning regarding sustainability makes this possible. The field of prevention is focused on understanding the issues related to bridging science and practice, and the next several years of research should provide important information needed to guide this process and benefit early educators replicating these interventions in community settings.

Acknowledgments

This work was completed as part of Celene E. Domitrovich's participation in the Collaborative for Academic, Social, and Emotional Learning (CASEL) Preschool to Elementary School Social and Emotional Learning Assessment Workgroup funded by the Bill & Melinda Gates Foundation, the Kirlin Charitable Foundation, the Rauner Family Foundation, and the University of Illinois at Chicago. The opinions expressed are those of the authors and do not necessarily reflect those of the funders.

Authors' Note

Celene E. Domitrovich is the author of the PATHS Curriculum and has a royalty agreement with Channing-Bete, Inc. She receives income from PATHS Training LLC. This has been reviewed and managed by Penn State's Individual Conflict of Interest Committee.

References

Alexander, K. L., Entwisle, D. R., & Olson, L. S. (2001). Schools, achievement and inequality: A seasonal perspective. *Educational Evaluation and Policy Analysis, 23*, 171–191.

Arnold, D. H., McWilliams, L., & Arnold, E. H. (1998). Teacher discipline and child misbehaviour in day care: Untangling causality with correlational data. *Developmental Psychology, 34*, 276–287.

Barkley, R. (1987). *Defiant children: A clinician's manual for parent training.* New York: Guilford Press.

Barnett, W. S., Jung, K., Yarosz, D. J., Thomas, J., Hornbeck, A., Stechuk, R., et al. (2008). Educational effects of the Tools of the Mind curriculum: A randomized trial. *Early Childhood Research Quarterly, 23*, 299–313.

Bierman, K. L. (2004). *Peer rejection: Developmental processes and intervention strategies.* New York: Guilford Press.

Bierman, K. L., Domitrovich, C., Nix, R. L., Gest, S. D., Welsh, J. A., Greenberg, M. T., et al. (2008). Promoting academic and social–emotional school readiness: The Head Start REDI program. *Child Development, 79*, 1802–1817.

Bierman, K. L., Greenberg, M. T., & the Conduct Problems Prevention Research Group. (1996). Social skill training in the FAST Track program. In R. DeV. Peters & R. J. McMahon (Eds.), *Preventing childhood disorders, substance abuse, and delinquency* (pp. 65–89). Newbury Park, CA: Sage.

Bierman, K. L., Nix, R. L., Domitrovich, C., Welsh, J. A., Gest, S. D., Jones, D. E., et al. (2010, June). *Promoting kindergarten adjustment: Dual impact of REDI Head Start enrichment and kindergarten classroom quality.* Paper presented at the annual meeting of the Society for Prevention Research, Denver, CO.

Bierman, K. L., Torres, M. M., Domitrovich, C., Welsh, J. A., & Gest, S. D. (2009). Behavioral and cognitive readiness for school: Cross-domain associations for children attending Head Start. *Social Development, 18*, 305–323.

Blair, C. (2002). School readiness: Integrating cognition and emotion in a neurological conceptualization of children's functioning at school entry. *American Psychologist, 57*, 111–127.

Bodrova, E., & Leong, D. J. (2007). *Tools of the Mind: The Vygotskian approach to early childhood education* (2nd ed.). Upper Saddle River, NJ: Prentice-Hall.

Bowman, B. T., Donovan, M. S., & Burns, M. S. (Eds.). (2000). *Eager to learn: Educating our preschoolers* (Report of the Committee on Early Childhood Pedagogy, National Research Council). Washington, DC: National Academy Press.

Brooks, V. (1996). Mentoring: The interpersonal dimension. *Teacher Development, 5*, 5–10.

Burchinal, M., Howes, C., Pianta, R., Bryant, D., Early, D., Clifford, R., et al. (2008). Predicting child outcomes at the end of kindergarten from the quality of pre-kindergarten teacher–child interactions and instruction. *Applied Developmental Science, 12*, 140–153.

Burchinal, M. R., Peisner-Feinberg, E., Pianta, R., & Howes, C. (2002). Development of academic skills from preschool through second grade: Family and classroom predictors of developmental trajectories. *Journal of School Psychology, 40*, 415–436.

Campbell, S. B., & von Stauffenberg, C. (2008). Child characteristics and family processes that predict behavioral readiness for school. In A. Crouter & A. Booth (Eds.), *Early disparities in school readiness: How families contribute to transitions into school* (pp. 225–258). Mahwah, NJ: Erlbaum.

Center on the Developing Child at Harvard University. (2011). Building the brain's "air traffic control" system: How early experience shape the development of executive function (Working Paper No. 11). Retrieved from *www.developingchild.harvard.edu.*

Clifford, R. M., Barbarin, O., Chang, F., Early, D., Bryant, D., Howes, C., et al. (2005). What is pre-kindergarten?: Characteristics of public pre-kindergarten programs. *Applied Developmental Science, 9,* 126–143.

Coolahan, K., Fantuzzo, J. W., Mendez, J., & McDermott, P. A. (2000). Preschool peer interactions and readiness to learn: Relationships between classroom peer play and learning behavior and conduct. *Journal of Educational Psychology, 92,* 458–465.

Cooper, D. H., & Farran, D. C. (1988). Behavioral risk factors in kindergarten. *Early Childhood Research Quarterly, 3,* 1–19.

Dane, A. V., & Schneider, B. H. (1998). Program integrity in primary and early secondary prevention: Are implementation effects out of control? *Clinical Psychology Review, 18,* 23–45.

Denham, S. A., & Almeida, M. C. (1987). Children's social problem-solving skills, behavioral adjustment, and interventions: A meta-analysis evaluating theory and practice. *Journal of Applied Developmental Psychology, 8,* 391–409.

Denham, S. A., & Burton, R. (1996). A social–emotional intervention for at-risk 4-year-olds. *Journal of School Psychology, 34,* 225–245.

Denham, S. A., & Burton, R. (2003). *Social and emotional prevention and intervention programming for preschoolers.* New York: Springer.

Denham, S. A., & Weissberg, R. P. (2004). Social–emotional learning in early childhood: What we know and where to go from here. In E. Chesebrough, P. King, T. P. Gullotta, & M. Bloom (Eds.), *A blueprint for the promotion of prosocial behavior in early childhood* (pp. 13–50). New York: Kluwer Academic.

Diamond, A., Barnett, W. S., Thomas, J., & Munro, S. (2007). Preschool program improves cognitive control. *Science, 318,* 1387–1388.

Domitrovich, C., Cortes, R. C., & Greenberg, M. T. (2007). Improving young children's social and emotional competence: A randomized trial of the preschool "PATHS" curriculum. *Journal of Primary Prevention, 28,* 67–91.

Domitrovich, C. E., Gest, S. D., Gill, S., Bierman, K. L., Welsh, J. A., & Jones, D. (2009). Fostering high quality teaching with an enriched curriculum and professional development support: The Head Start REDI Program. *American Educational Research Journal, 46,* 567–597.

Domitrovich, C. E., Gest, S. D., Gill, S., Jones, D., & DeRousie, R. S. (2009). Individual factors associated with professional development training outcomes of the Head Start REDI program. *Early Education and Development, 20,* 402–430.

Domitrovich, C. E., Greenberg, M. T., Kusche, C., & Cortes, R. (2005). *The Preschool PATHS Curriculum.* South Deerfield, MA: Channing Bete.

Downey, D. B., von Hippel, P. T., & Broh, B. (2004). Are schools the great equalizer?: Cognitive inequality during the summer months and the school year. *American Sociological Review, 65,* 613–635.

Driscoll, K. C., & Pianta, R. C. (2010). Banking Time in Head Start: Early efficacy of an intervention designed to promote supportive teacher–child relationships. *Early Education and Development, 21,* 38–64.

Duncan, G. J., Dowsett, C. J., Claessens, A., Magnuson, K., Huston, A. C., Klebanov, P., et al. (2007). School readiness and later achievement. *Developmental Psychology, 43,* 1428–1446.

Durlak, J. A. (2010). The importance of doing well in whatever you do: A commentary on the special section, "Implementation Research in Early Childhood Education." *Early Childhood Research Quarterly, 25,* 348–357.

Durlak, J. A., & DuPre, E. P. (2008). Implementation matters: A review of research on the influence of implementation on program outcomes and the factors affecting implementation. *American Journal of Community Psychology, 41,* 327–350.

Durlak, J. A., Weissberg, R. P., Dymnicki, A. B., Taylor, R. D., & Schellinger, K. B. (2011). The impact of enhancing students' social and emotional learning: A meta-analysis of school-based universal interventions. *Child Development, 82,* 405–432.

Dusenbury, L., Hansen, W., Jackson-Newsom, J., Ringwalt, C., Pankratz, M., & Giles, S. (2007,

May). *Coaching to implementation quality.* Paper presented at the annual meeting of the Society for Prevention Research, Washington, DC.

Elliott, D. S., & Mihalic, S. (2004). Issues in disseminating and replicating effective prevention programs. *Prevention Science, 5,* 47–53.

Feis, C. L., & Simons, C. (1985). Training preschool children in interpersonal cognitive problem-solving skills: A replication. *Prevention in Human Services, 3,* 59–70.

Fixsen, D. L., Naoom, S. F., Blase, K. A., Friedman, R. M., & Wallace, F. (2005). *Implementation research: A synthesis of the literature.* Tampa: University of South Florida.

Flay, B. R., Biglan, A., Boruch, R. F., Castro, F. G., Gottfredson, D., Kellam, S., et al. (2005). Standards of evidence: Criteria for efficacy, effectiveness and dissemination. *Prevention Science, 6,* 151–175.

Gottman, J., Katz, L. F., & Hooven, C. (1997). *Meta-emotion.* Hillsdale, NJ: Erlbaum.

Greenberg, M. T., Domitrovich, C., Graczyk, P. A., & Zins, J. E. (2005). The study of implementation in school-based preventive interventions: Theory, research and practice. *Promotion of Mental Health and Prevention of Mental Behavioral Disorders, 3,* 1–62.

Greenberg, M. T., Domitrovich, C. E., & Bumbarger, B. (2001). The prevention of mental disorders in school-aged children: Current state of the field. *Prevention and Treatment, 4,* Article 1. Retrieved March 1, 2002, from *http://journals.apa.org/prevention/volume4/pre0040001a.html.*

Hamre, B. K., & Pianta, R. C. (2001). Early teacher–child relationships and the trajectory of children's school outcomes through eighth grade. *Child Development, 72,* 625–638.

Haskins, R., & Loeb, S. (2007). A plan to improve the quality of teaching in American schools. *Future of Children, 17,* 1–8.

Hauser-Cram, P., Durand, T. M., & Warfield, M. E. (2007). Early feelings about school and later academic outcomes of children with special needs living in poverty. *Early Childhood Research Quarterly, 22,* 161–172.

Howes, C., & Smith, E. W. (1995). Relations among child care quality, teacher behavior, children's play activities, emotional security, and cognitive activity in child care. *Early Childhood Research Quarterly, 10,* 381–404.

International Reading Association & National Association for the Education of Young Children. (1998). Learning to read and write: Developmentally appropriate practices for young children. *Young Children, 53,* 30–46.

Izard, C. E., Fine, S. E., Schultz, D., Mostow, A. J., Ackerman, B. P., & Youngstrom, E. (2001). Emotion knowledge as a predictor of social behavior and academic competence in children at risk. *Psychological Science, 12,* 18–23.

Izard, C. E., King, K. A., Trentacosta, C. J., Morgan, J. K., Laurenceau, J., Krauthamer-Ewing, E. S., et al. (2008). Accelerating the development of emotion competence in Head Start children: Effects on adaptive and maladaptive behavior. *Development and Psychopathology, 20,* 369–397.

Izard, C. E., Trentacosta, C. J., King, K. A., & Mostow, A. J. (2004). An emotion-based prevention program for Head Start children. *Early Education and Development, 15,* 407–422.

Jennings, P. A., & Greenberg, M. T. (2009). The prosocial classroom: Teacher social and emotional competence in relation to student and classroom outcomes. *Review of Educational Research, 79,* 491–525.

Johnson, K., Hays, C., Center, H., & Daley, C. (2004). Building capacity and sustainable prevention interventions: A sustainability-planning model. *Evaluation and Program Planning, 27,* 135–149.

Justice, L. M., Mashburn, A. J., Hamre, B. K., & Pianta, R. C. (2008). Quality of language and literacy instruction in preschool classrooms serving at-risk pupils. *Early Childhood Research Quarterly, 23,* 51–68.

Kellam, S., & Langevin, D. J. (2003). A framework for understanding "evidence" in prevention research and programs. *Prevention Science, 4,* 137–153.

Kontos, S., & Wilcox-Herzog, A. (1997). Influences on children's competence in early childhood classrooms. *Early Childhood Research Quarterly, 12,* 247–262.

Ladd, G. W., Birch, S. H., & Buhs, E. S. (1999). Children's social and scholastic lives in kindergarten: Related spheres of influence? *Child Development, 70,* 1373–1400.

Ladd, G. W., Buhs, E. S., & Seid, M. (2000). Children's initial sentiments about kindergarten: Is school liking an antecedent of early classroom participation and achievement? *Merrill–Palmer Quarterly, 46,* 255–279.

Ladd, G. W., & Burgess, K. B. (1999). Charting the relationship trajectories of aggressive, withdrawn, and aggressive/withdrawn children during early grade school. *Child Development, 70,* 910–929.

Ladd, G. W., & Burgess, K. B. (2001). Do relational risk and protective factors moderate the linkages between childhood aggression and early psychological and school adjustment? *Child Development, 72,* 1579–1601.

Ladd, G. W., Kochenderfer, B. J., & Coleman, C. C. (1997). Classroom peer acceptance, friendship, and victimization: Distinct relational systems that contribute uniquely to children's school adjustment? *Child Development, 68,* 1181–1197.

Lamb, M. E. (1998). Nonparental child care: Context, quality, correlates. In W. Damon (Ed.) & I. E. Sigel & K. A. Renninger (Vol. Eds.), *Handbook of child psychology: Vol. 4. Child psychology in practice* (5th ed., pp. 73–134). New York: Wiley.

Landry, S. H., Anthony, J. L., Swank, P. R., & Monseque-Bailey, P. (2009). Effectiveness of comprehensive professional development for teachers of at-risk preschoolers. *Journal of Educational Psychology, 101,* 448–465.

La Paro, K. M., Pianta, R. C., & Stuhlman, M. (2004). The classroom assessment scoring system: Findings from the prekindergarten year. *Elementary School Journal, 104,* 409–426.

Leach, D. J., & Conto, H. (1999). The additional effects of process and outcome feedback following brief in-service training. *Educational Psychology, 19,* 441–462.

Leerkes, E. M., Paradise, M., O'Brien, M., Calkins, S. D., & Lange, G. (2008). Emotion and cognition processes in preschool children. *Merrill–Palmer Quarterly, 54,* 102–124.

Lonigan, C. J., Burgess, S. R., & Anthony, J. L. (2000). Development of emergent literacy and early reading skills in preschool children: Evidence from a latent-variable longitudinal study. *Developmental Psychology, 36,* 596–613.

Luthar, S. S. (2006). Resilience in development: A synthesis of research across five decades. In D. J. Cohen & D. Cicchetti (Eds.), *Developmental psychopathology: Vol. 3. Risk, disorder, and adaptation* (2nd ed., pp. 739–795). Hoboken, NJ: Wiley.

Lynch, K. B., Geller, S. R., & Schmidt, M. G. (2004). Multi-year evaluation of the effectiveness of a resilience-based prevention program for young children. *Journal of Primary Prevention, 24,* 335–353.

Marsh, H. W., Ellias, L. A., & Craven, R. G. (2002). How do preschool children feel about themselves?: Unraveling measurement and multidimensional self-concept structure. *Developmental Psychology, 38,* 376–393.

Mashburn, A. J., Pianta, R. C., Hamre, B. K., Downer, J. T., Barbarin, O. A., Bryant, D., et al. (2008). Measures of classroom quality in prekindergarten and children's development of academic, language, and social skills. *Child Development, 79,* 732–749.

McClelland, M. M., & Morrison, F. J. (2003). The emergence of learning-related social skills in preschool children. *Early Childhood Research Quarterly, 18*(2), 206–224.

McClelland, M. M., Acock, A. C., & Morrison, F. J. (2006). The impact of kindergarten learning-related skills on academic trajectories at the end of elementary school. *Early Childhood Research Quarterly, 21,* 471–490.

McClelland, M. M., Morrison, F. J., & Holmes, D. L. (2000). Children at risk for early academic problems: The role of learning-related social skills. *Early Childhood Research Quarterly, 15,* 307–329.

McCormick, K., & Brennan, S. (2001). Mentoring the new professor in interdisciplinary early childhood education: Kentucky teacher internship program. *Topics in Special Education, 21,* 131–150.

Miles, S. B., & Stipek, D. (2006). Contemporaneous and longitudinal associations between social ·

behavior and literacy achievement in a sample of low-income elementary school children. *Child Development, 77*, 103–117.

Montgomery, C., & Rupp, A. A. (2005). A meta-analysis for exploring causes and effects of stress in teachers. *Canadian Journal of Education, 28*, 458–486.

National Association for the Education of Young Children. (2005). Position statements of NAYYC. Retrieved from *www.naecy.org/about/positions.asp*.

National Education Goals Panel. (1997). *The National Education Goals Report, 1997: Building a nation of learners*. Washington, DC: U.S. Government Printing Office.

National Research Council and Institute of Medicine. (2010). *Preventing mental, emotional, and behavioral disorders*. Washington, DC: Author.

National School Readiness Indicators Initiative. (2005). *Getting ready: Findings from the National School Readiness Indicators Initiative*. Providence: Rhode Island Kids Count.

NICHD Early Child Care Research Network. (1998). Early child care and self-control, compliance and problem behavior at twenty-four and thirty-six months. *Child Development, 69*, 1145–1170.

NICHD Early Child Care Research Network. (2000a). Characteristics and quality of child care for toddlers and preschoolers. *Applied Developmental Science, 4*, 116–135.

NICHD Early Child Care Research Network. (2000b). The relation of child care to cognitive and language development. *Child Development, 71*, 960–980.

NICHD Early Child Care Research Network. (2004). Multiple pathways to early academic achievement. *Harvard Educational Review, 74*, 1–29.

Niles, M. D., Reynolds, A. J., & Roe-Sepowitz, D. (2008). Early childhood intervention and early adolescent social and emotional competence: Second-generation evaluation evidence from the Chicago Longitudinal Study. *Educational Research, 50*, 55–73.

No Child Left Behind Act of 2001, Public Law No. 107-110, 115 Stat. 1425. (2002). Available from *www.ed.gov/policy/elsec/leg/esea02/107-110.pdf*.

O'Donnell, C. L. (2008). Defining, conceptualizing, and measuring fidelity of implementation and its relationship to outcomes in K–12 curriculum intervention research. *Review of Educational Research, 78*(1), 33–84.

Osher, D., Sprague, S., Axelrod, J., Keenan, S., Weissberg, R., Kendziora, K., et al. (2007). A comprehensive approach to addressing behavioral and academic challenges in contemporary schools. In J. Grimes & A. Thomas (Eds.), *Best practices in school psychology* (5th ed., pp. 1263–1278). Bethesda, MD: National Association of School Psychologists.

Payton, J. W., Wardlaw, D. M., Graczyk, P. A., Bloodworth, M. R., Tompsett, C. J., & Weissberg, R. P. (2001). Social and emotional learning: A framework for promoting mental health and reducing risk behavior in children and youth. *Journal of School Health, 70*(5), 179–185.

Peisner-Feinberg, E. S., Burchinal, M. R., Clifford, R. M., Culkin, M. L., Howes, C., Kagan, S. L., et al. (2001). The relation of preschool child-care quality to children's cognitive and social developmental trajectories through second grade. *Child Development, 72*, 1534–1553.

Pianta, R. C., La Paro, K. M., & Hamre, B. K. (2008). *Classroom Assessment scoring System: Manual K–3*. Baltimore: Brookes.

Pianta, R. C., Mashburn, A. J., Downer, J. T., Hamre, B. K., & Justice, L. (2008). Effects of web-mediated professional development resources on teacher–child interactions in pre-kindergarten classrooms. *Early Childhood Research Quarterly, 23*, 431–451.

Pianta, R. C., Steinberg, M. S., & Rollins, K. B. (1995). The first two years of school: Teacher–child relationships and deflections in children's classroom adjustment. *Development and Psychopathology, 7*, 295–312.

Pianta, R. C., & Stuhlman, M. W. (2004). Teacher–child relationships and children's success in the first years of school. *School Psychology Review, 33*, 444–458.

Raikes, H. H., Torquati, J. C., Hegland, S., Raikes, H. A., Scott, J., Messner, L., et al. (2006). Studying the culture of quality early education and care: A cumulative approach to measuring characteristics of the workforce in four Midwestern states. In M. Zaslow & I. Martinez-Beck (Eds.), *Critical issues in early childhood professional development* (pp. 111–136). Baltimore: Brookes.

Ramey, C. T., & Ramey, S. L. (2004). Early learning and school readiness: Can early intervention make a difference? *Merrill–Palmer Quarterly, 50,* 471–491.

Ramey, S. L., Lanzi, R. G., Phillips, M. M., & Ramey, C. T. (1998). Perspectives of former Head Start children and their parents on school and the transition to school. *Elementary School Journal, 98,* 311–327.

Raver, C. C. (2002). Emotions matter: Making the case for the role of young children's emotional development for early school readiness. *Social Policy Report, 16,* 3–18.

Raver, C. C., Jones, S. M., Li-Grining, C. P., Metzger, M., Champion, K. M., & Sardin, L. (2008). Improving preschool classroom processes: Preliminary findings from a randomized trial implemented in Head Start settings. *Early Childhood Research Quarterly, 23,* 10–26.

Raver, C. C., Jones, S. M., Li-Grining, C. P., Zhai, F., Bub, K., & Pressler, E. (2011). CSRP's impact on low-income preschoolers' pre-academic skills: Self-regulation as a mediating mechanism. *Child Development, 82,* 362–378.

Raver, C. C., Jones, S. M., Li-Grining, C. P., Zhai, F., Metzger, M., & Solomon, B. (2009). Targeting children's behavior problems in preschool classrooms: A cluster-randomized controlled trial. *Journal of Consulting and Clinical Psychology, 77,* 302–316.

Reynolds, A. J. (1991). Early schooling of children at risk. *American Educational Research Journal, 28,* 392–422.

Reynolds, A. J., & Bezruczko, N. (1993). Early schooling of children at risk through fourth grade. *Merrill–Palmer Quarterly, 39,* 457–480.

Reynolds, A. J., & Temple, J. A. (1998). Extended early childhood intervention and school achievement: Age thirteen findings from the Chicago Longitudinal Study. *Child Development, 69,* 231–246.

Rimm-Kaufman, S. E., & Pianta, R. C. (2000). Teachers' judgments of problems in the transition to kindergarten. *Early Childhood Research Quarterly, 15,* 147–166.

Robin, A. L., Schneider, M., & Dolnick, M. (1976). The Turtle Technique: An extended case study of self-control in the classroom. *Psychology in the School, 13,* 449–453.

Rohrbach, L. A., Graham, J. W., & Hansen, W. B. (1993). Diffusion of a school-based substance abuse prevention program: Predictors of program implementation. *Preventive Medicine, 22,* 237–260.

Rose, D. J., & Church, R. J., (1998). Learning to teach: The acquisition and maintenance of teaching skills. *Journal of Behavioral Education, 8,* 5–35.

Ryan, R. M., Fauth, R. C., & Brooks-Gunn, J. (2006). Childhood poverty: Implications for school readiness and early childhood education. In B. Spodek & O. N. Saracho (Eds.), *Handbook of research on the education of children* (2nd ed., pp. 323–346). Mahwah, NJ: Erlbaum.

Ryan, S., & Hornbeck, A. (2004). Mentoring for quality improvement: A case study of a mentor teacher in the reform process. *Journal of Research in Childhood Education, 19,* 79–96.

Sarama, J., & Clements, D. H. (2004). Building blocks for early childhood mathematics. *Early Childhood Research Quarterly, 19,* 181–189.

Scheirer, M. A., Hartling, G., & Hagerman, D. (2008). Defining sustainability outcomes of health programs: Illustrations from an on-line survey. *Evaluation and Program Planning, 31,* 335–346.

Scott-Little, C., Kagan, S. L., & Frelow, V. S. (2006). Conceptualization of readiness and the content of early learning standards: The intersection of policy and research? *Early Childhood Research Quarterly, 21,* 153–173.

Serna, L., Nielsen, E., Lambros, K., & Forness, S. (2000). Primary prevention with children at risk for emotional or behavioral disorders: Data on a universal intervention for Head Start classrooms. *Behavioral Disorders, 26,* 70–84.

Serna, L. A., & Lau-Smith, J. A. (1995). Learning with a purpose: Self-determination skills for students who are at risk for school and community failure. *Intervention in School and Clinic, 30,* 142–146.

Sheridan, S. M., Edwards, C. P., Marvin, C., & Knoche, L. L. (2009). Professional development in early childhood programs: Process issues and research needs. *Early Education and Development, 20,* 377–401.

Shure, M. B. (1981). Interpersonal problem solving: A cog in the wheel of social cognition. In D. J. Wine & M. D. Smye (Eds.), *Social competence* (pp. 158–185). New York: Guilford Press.

Shure, M. B., & Spivack, G. (1982). Interpersonal problem-solving in young children: A cognitive approach to prevention. *American Journal of Community Psychology, 10,* 341–356.

Smith-Donald, R., Raver, C. C., Hayes, T., & Richardson, B. (2007). Preliminary construct and concurrent validity of the Preschool Self-Regulation Assessment (PSRA) for field-based research. *Early Childhood Research Quarterly, 22,* 173–187.

Snow, C. E., Burns, M. S., & Griffin, P. (1998). *Preventing reading difficulties in young children: A report of the National Research Council.* Washington, DC: National Academy Press.

Swartz, J. P., & Walker, D. K. (1984). The relationships between teacher ratings of kindergarten classroom skills and second-grade achievement scores: An analysis of gender differences. *Journal of School Psychology, 22,* 209–217.

Thompson, R. A. (2002). The roots of school readiness in social and emotional development. *Kauffman Early Education Exchange, 1,* 8–29.

Thompson, R. A., & Raikes, H. A. (2007). The social and emotional foundations of school readiness. In D. F. Perry, R. F. Kaufmann, & J. Knitzer (Eds.), *Social and emotional health in early childhood: Building bridges between services and systems* (pp. 13–35). Baltimore: Brookes.

Tibbits, M., Bumbarger, B. K., Kyler, S., & Perkins, D. (2010). Sustaining evidence-based interventions under real-world conditions: Results from a large-scale diffusion project. *Prevention Science, 11,* 252–262.

Trentacosta, C. J., & Izard, C. E. (2007). Kindergarten children's emotion competence as a predictor of their academic competence in first grade. *Emotion, 7*(1), 77–88.

Tsouloupas, C. N., Carson, R. L., Matthews, R., Grawitch, M. J., & Barber, L. K. (2010). Exploring the association between teachers' perceived student misbehavior and emotional exhaustion: The importance of teacher efficacy beliefs and emotion regulation. *Educational Psychology, 30,* 173–189.

Webster-Stratton, C. (1990). Dina Dinosaur's Social Skills and Problem-Solving Curriculum. Seattle: The Incredible Year. Available from *www.incredibleyears.com/program/child.asp.*

Webster-Stratton, C., Reid, M. J., & Hammond, M. (2004). Treating children with early-onset conduct problems: Intervention outcomes for parent, child, and teacher training. *Journal of Clinical Child and Adolescent Psychology, 33,* 105–124.

Webster-Stratton, C., Reid, M. J., & Stoolmiller, M. (2008). Preventing conduct problems and improving school readiness: Evaluation of the Incredible Years teacher and child training programs in high-risk schools. *Journal of Child Psychology and Psychiatry, 49,* 471–488.

Weikart, D. P., & Schweinhart, L. J. (1997). High/Scope Perry Preschool Program. In G. Albee & T. P. Gullotta (Eds.), *Primary prevention works* (pp. 146–166). Thousand Oaks, CA: Sage.

Welsh, J. A., Nix, R. L., Blair, C., Bierman, K. L., & Nelson, K. E. (2010). The development of cognitive skills and gains in academic school readiness for children from low-income families. *Journal of Educational Psychology, 102,* 43–53.

Wentzel, K. R. (1991). Social competence at school: Relation between social responsibility and academic achievement. *Review of Educational Research, 61,* 1–24.

Whitebook, M., Howes, C., & Phillips, D. (1990). *Who cares?: Child care teachers and the quality of care in America* (Final Report of the National Child Care Staffing Study). Oakland, CA: Child Care Employee Project.

Wingspan, LLC. (1999). *Al's Pals: Kids Making Healthy Choices.* Richmond, VA: Author.

Yates, G. C. R., & Yates, S. M. (1990). Teacher effectiveness research: Towards describing user-friendly classroom instruction. *Educational Psychology, 10,* 225–238.

Yen, C.-J., Konold, T. R., & McDermott, P. A. (2004). Does learning behavior augment cognitive ability as an indicator of academic achievement? *Journal of School Psychology, 42,* 157–169.

CHAPTER 20

Supporting the Social Competence of Young Children with Challenging Behavior in the Context of the Teaching Pyramid Model

Research-Based Practices and Implementation in Early Childhood Settings

Mary Louise Hemmeter and Maureen A. Conroy

Findings from a national survey of teachers in state-funded early childhood programs indicate the rate of expulsion among preschool-age children who exhibit challenging behaviors to be three times that of children in grades K–12 (Gilliam, 2005). While this study drew the attention of national news media and federal and state policymakers, it was not altogether surprising to early childhood educators and researchers, who for the last decade have noted the increasing frequency and severity of challenging behavior in early childhood settings (Brown, Odom, & McConnell, 2008; Burchinal, Peisner-Feinberg, Pianta, & Howes, 2002). Early childhood educators, researchers, and policymakers have become increasingly concerned about the social–emotional development and challenging behavior of young children, and the impact of social and behavioral issues on children's success during the early childhood years and their transition into school (Hamre & Pianta, 2001; Loeber, Farrington, & Petchuk, 2003; Missall & Hojnoski, 2008). Children who have significant social and behavioral issues during preschool are likely to continue to exhibit challenging behavior that increases in intensity and interferes with their transition to and success in elementary school and beyond (Burchinal et al., 2002; Howes, Calkins, Anastopoulos, Keane, & Shelton, 2003).

Although prevalence estimates vary, there is evidence that somewhere between 10 and 21% of preschool children exhibit moderate to severe levels of challenging behavior (Campbell, 1995, Lavigne et al., 1996; West, Denton, & Germino-Hausken, 2000) depending on the population of children being studied. The prevalence of challenging behavior among children who have disabilities is also high. Data from the 27th Annual Report to Congress on the Individuals with Disabilities Education Act (IDEA; U.S. Department of Education, Office of Special Education and Rehabilitative Services, Office of Special Education Programs, 2007) revealed that 1.3% of 3- to 5-year-old children served under IDEA had a primary diagnosis of emotional disturbance. In addition to those children who have a diagnosed emotional disorder, a significant number of children with other types of disabilities require individualized supports related to their social and behavioral needs. For example, 46.4% of children served under IDEA have a primary diagnosis of language or communication delay, and a significant number of these children also have challenging behavior (Gallagher, 1999). A recent meta-analysis found that children with language delays are far more likely to have challenging behavior than their typically developing peers (Kaiser, Roberts, Feeney-Kettler, Frey, & Hemmeter, 2009). Furthermore, 14.4% of preschool children served under IDEA required some type of behavior management plan. Many believe that emotional–behavioral disorders are underdiagnosed in the preschool population (Conroy & Brown, 2004).

Many children with challenging behavior exhibit externalizing behaviors such as aggression, defiance, or property destruction. Also, a significant number of children have social deficits that result in internalizing or withdrawn behaviors (for a discussion, see Brown et al., 2008). Whereas internalizing behaviors are less apparent than externalizing behaviors, these social skill deficits are also likely to have a significant impact on children's developmental trajectory, particularly in their peer-related social interactions and the development of friendships (Brown et al., 2008). Many children's socially withdrawn behaviors may be related to other disabilities, such as intellectual disabilities or autism spectrum disorders; however, children who are typically developing also exhibit a range of withdrawn behaviors that may be problematic (Brown et al., 2008). Regardless of etiology, children who have either externalizing or internalizing behaviors are less likely to initiate or respond appropriately to social bids from their peers (Brown et al., 2008; Odom, McConnell, & McEvoy, 1992), and this has significant implications for the developmental trajectory related to their social competence.

Social competence in young children has been defined in many ways and includes many different aspects of development. "Social competence," often described as a composite of an individual's adaptive behavior and social skills (Gresham & Elliott, 1987), interacts with cognitive, social, and communication abilities (Guralnick, 2010; Masten et al., 1995). Social competence develops over time, and for young children is typically reflected by successful interactions with adults and early development of friendships with their peers (Brown et al., 2008; Buysse, Goldman, West, & Hollingsworth, 2008). Children who are socially competent are able to interact appropriately with others, even during difficult situations, and are less likely to engage in challenging behaviors and/or exhibit socially withdrawn behaviors (Brown et al., 2008). When we focus on strengthening and improving children's social competence, our goal is to equip children with the skills necessary for being successful in school and life, and to reduce the likelihood that they will engage in challenging behavior (Sutherland, Conroy, Abrams, & Vo, 2010). To be most effective for children who have significant social and behavioral issues, interventions must focus on both reducing challenging behavior and promoting social competence.

For the last 30 years, researchers have examined the effectiveness of an array of practices focused on promoting social and behavioral competence in young children with challenging behavior (for reviews, see Brown et al., 2008; Conroy, Brown, & Olive, 2008; Conroy, Dunlap, Clarke, & Alter, 2005). Some practices have focused on promoting skills related to social competence, and others have focused on promoting behavioral competence through increasing the likelihood that children will be meaningfully engaged in classroom activities, routines, and interactions. Both of these approaches reduce the likelihood of challenging behavior. In order to address both the social and behavioral competence of this population of children, researchers have proposed the need for a continuum of practices that includes environmental supports to promote engagement and interactions with peers, instruction focused on teaching new social skills, and teacher practices that support children's appropriate social behaviors without inadvertently maintaining children's challenging behaviors (Brown, Odom, & Conroy, 2001; Fox, Dunlap, Hemmeter, Joseph, & Strain, 2003).

Because children who need supports and interventions often attend early childhood programs with their typically developing peers, these strategies should be implemented within the context of a comprehensive approach to addressing the social, emotional, and behavioral needs of all children. A classroomwide model for addressing social–emotional development and challenging behavior must include strategies to address the range of skills seen across all children in the classroom. In most preschool classrooms, some children are learning complex social skills and emotional competencies, and need relatively little support to navigate the classroom environment and routines without engaging in challenging behavior. Other children have varying levels of challenging behavior, including those whose behavior responds to consistent, developmentally appropriate guidance strategies, as well as children whose behavior persists despite those guidance strategies. A critical aspect of the classroomwide model is to ensure that the needs of the increasing number of children who have persistent social and behavioral difficulties are effectively addressed.

A Classroomwide Model for Promoting Social–Emotional Development and Addressing Challenging Behavior in Preschool Children

The Teaching Pyramid (Fox, Carta, Strain, Dunlap, & Hemmeter, 2010; Fox et al., 2003; Hemmeter, Ostrosky, & Fox, 2006) is a comprehensive classroomwide model designed to address the social and behavioral competence of all children in a preschool setting. It reflects a public health model of promotion, prevention, and intervention (Simeonsson, 1991) as well as the tiered model used in the work on School-Wide Positive Behavior Supports (Horner, Sugai, Todd, & Lewis-Palmer, 2005). Consistent with principles of Positive Behavior Support (Dunlap, Sailor, Horner, & Sugai, 2009), the Teaching Pyramid provides early childhood educators with universal strategies for supporting social–emotional development and preventing challenging behavior in all children, secondary strategies for providing targeted social–emotional supports for children at risk, and tertiary supports for children whose behaviors are persistent and ongoing (see Figure 20.1). Universal strategies focus on building relationships with children, creating a positive climate in the classroom, implementing a consistent and predictable schedule, structuring routines so children know what to do and what is expected of them, designing and implementing developmentally appropriate and engaging activities, and using other developmentally appropriate guidance strategies such as giving clear directions, providing positive feedback, and redirection. At the secondary level, the focus is on systematically and intentionally teaching social skills and emotional competencies. Information is provided on what skills should be taught, procedures for teaching those skills, and strategies for ensuring children have adequate opportunities to practice the skills in a variety of contexts. At the tertiary level, a team conducts a functional assessment and develops and implements a behavior support plan for an individual child. The plan includes strategies for preventing challenging behaviors from occurring, teaching new social behaviors that replace the challenging behaviors, and changing how adults respond to the new skills and challenging behaviors. The top of the Teaching Pyramid represents a systematic approach to addressing the social and behavioral needs of children with the most

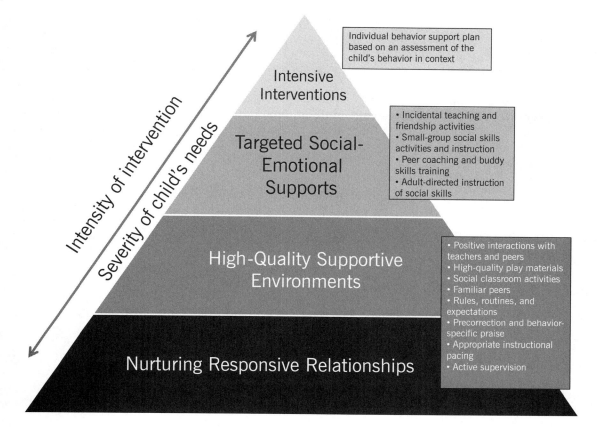

FIGURE 20.1. The Teaching Pyramid.

persistent and significant challenging behavior; however, practices at each level of the Teaching Pyramid have been shown to affect social outcomes positively for children with challenging behavior. The type and intensity of the practice that is used vary based on the needs of individual children. As illustrated in Figure 20.1, the intensity of each level of practice should be matched to individual children's social and behavioral skills and ability levels.

In the following section we describe each level of the Teaching Pyramid, with a specific emphasis on practices that have been shown to be effective for children with ongoing social and behavioral needs. These include both social competence and behavioral support practices. Although the practices we describe in the following section reflect only a subset of the Teaching Pyramid practices, the assumption is that they would be implemented in the context of the comprehensive model.

Universal Promotion: Nurturing and Responsive Relationships and High-Quality Supportive Environments

The foundation for promoting social and behavioral competence in all young children is providing a high-quality early childhood classroom with nurturing, responsive relationships that promote active engagement and learning (Mashburn & Pianta, 2006; Peisner-Feinberg & Burchinal, 1997; Pianta & Stuhlman, 2004). Relationships with teachers and peers provide the context in which all children learn classroom expectations and routines, social skills, and appropriate behavioral competencies. Practices associated with the base of the Teaching Pyramid focus on providing a nurturing environment, creating a predictable classroom routine, teaching the expectations of the environment, and implementing activities that are both developmentally appropriate and appropriately challenging based on children's skills levels.

Positive relationships with children, family members, and colleagues are the foundation for all other practices, and they represent the universal conditions that are necessary for promoting the social and behavioral competence of all children. The focus at the universal level is on teacher–child relationships, partnerships with families, and collaboration and teaming among professionals and families. This level of the Teaching Pyramid also includes child-focused practices that are linked to positive social and behavioral outcomes (Birch & Ladd, 1998; Cox, 2005; Kontos, 1999; Mill & Romano-White, 1999; National Research Council, 2001). They include, but are not limited to, facilitating children's play, having meaningful conversations with all children, providing positive descriptive feedback to promote social skills and appropriate behavior, and supporting children's positive interactions with their peers.

The other set of practices that is foundational to the Teaching Pyramid relates to providing high-quality supportive environments and interactions that promote children's meaningful engagement in classroom activities and routines (DeKlyen & Odom, 1989; Holloway & Reichart-Erickson, 1988; Jolivette, Wehby, Canale, & Massey, 2001; National Research Council, 2001). When children are supported to actively engage in ongoing classroom activities and routines, they are less likely to engage in inappropriate or challenging behavior (Conroy, Sutherland, Haydon, Stormont, & Harmon, 2008) and more likely to engage in the type of peer-related interactions that lead to increased social competence. This level of the Teaching Pyramid includes practices related to types of materials and activities that are provided, design of the classroom environment, schedule and routine of the classroom, transitions, and instructional methods. The practices described below are the subset of Teaching Pyramid practices that are particularly effective for children who have challenging behavior.

A number of variables that relate to classroom materials and activities have been examined to determine their relationship to promoting positive social interactions between children with challenging behavior and social skills needs and their peers. For example, studies have examined how different types of toys affect social interactions among young children. Research suggests that some toys, such as books and art materials, promote isolate behaviors, whereas other toys, such as dramatic play materials, blocks, and water play, are more likely to foster cooperative play between children (Ivory & McCollum, 1999). The relationship between social interactions and toys and materials is probably more complex than just the type of toy, but the type of toy appears to set the stage for more sophisticated interactions (Sainato, Jung, Salmon, & Axe, 2008). In addition to toys and materials, there appears to be a relationship between type of activity and children's peer-related social behaviors. Social behaviors are most likely to occur in activities such as free play, cleanup (Odom, Peterson, McConnell, & Ostrosky, 1990), center time (Kontos, Moore, & Giogretti, 1998), and snack time (Kohl & Beckman, 1984). The relationship between the type of activity and peer interactions may be mediated by the role of the adult in that activity. Children who have social deficits may be more likely to engage with their peers during free-play activities when teachers are available to provide structure and support.

The composition of the peer group also has an influence on interactions between children with challenging behavior and their socially competent peers. In general, research has indicated that familiarity of peers is an important factor in increasing the occurrence and complexity of social interactions (Doyle, Connolly, & Rivest, 1980; Harper & Huie, 1985) between children with social and behavioral deficits and their peers. The ratio of children with and without disabilities can also influence play interactions. Classrooms that have a more balanced ratio of children with and without disabilities increase the likelihood of positive social interactions (Hauser-Cram, Bronson, & Upshur, 1993). Social opportunities increase when children with disabilities have access to a higher proportion of children who are socially competent (Buysse, Goldman, & Skinner, 2002).

A number of practices are important to promoting children's engagement in classroom activities and routines. Children are more likely to be engaged when instruction is delivered at a developmentally appropriate level, the classroom environment includes high-quality materials, and activities and opportunities are organized and planned to promote learning. This, in exchange, decreases the likelihood of challenging behaviors (Conroy et al., 2008). Appropriate instructional pacing, which provides opportunities for children to actively respond, is important for promoting engagement and behavioral competence (Conroy et al., 2008; Sutherland et al., 2010). Another important practice is the use of explicit classroom rules and routines that communicate expectations to children and provide the structure for teaching and promoting appropriate behavioral expectations and competence (Conroy & Sutherland, 2011). Additionally, the use of precorrective statements, or reminders related to the classroom rules and social expectations (e.g., "Remember to keep your hands to yourself"), and descriptive praise (e.g., "Good for you! You kept your hands to yourself during group!") directed at individual children have been observed to reduce challenging behavior (Conroy & Sutherland, 2011; Stormont, Smith, & Lewis, 2007). For example, Fullerton, Conroy, and Correa (2009) found that teacher's use of behavior-specific praise increased children's appropriate engagement during transition times. Teacher's use of active supervision in early childhood settings is likely to decrease young children's challenging behavior as well (Benedict, Horner, & Squires, 2007; Conroy & Sutherland, 2011). When teachers closely monitor children's behavior, and use precorrective statements and descriptive praise, young children's appropriate behavior and engagement are likely to increase (Conroy, Sutherland, et al., 2008).

Practices related to nurturing and responsive relationships and high-quality, supportive environments are designed to promote the social–emotional competence of all children and prevent challenging behavior. In this section, we have described a number of practices and how they specifically support social development and prevent challenging behavior in children with social and behavioral needs. Although these practices are likely to lead to increased engagement and fewer challenging behaviors, these children also need systematic instruction around social skills and emotional competencies.

Targeted Social–Emotional Supports

The targeted level of the Teaching Pyramid involves the use of intentional and planned instruction focused on social skills and emotional competencies (Denham & Burton, 1996; National Research Council, 2001; Serna, Nielsen, Lambros, & Forness, 2000; Webster-Stratton, Reid, & Hammond, 2001). A wide range of teaching practices and/or social–emotional curricula can help children learn important social skills and emotional competencies (Joseph & Strain, 2003). Young children often need adult guidance to learn to express their emotions, play with their peers, and solve social problems in constructive ways. Effective strategies for promoting social skills in all children include teaching the concept, modeling the skill, providing opportunities to practice the skill, role playing, scaffolding children's use of the skill in context, and providing positive descriptive feedback when appropriate social behaviors occur (Fox & Lentini, 2006; Grisham-Brown, Hemmeter, & Pretti-Frontczak, 2005).

A key feature of this level of the Teaching Pyramid is the provision of instruction targeted for children who have social, emotional, and/or behavioral challenges. For these children, a range of instructional strategies can be used in the context of ongoing classroom activities and routines (e.g., naturalistic strategies), small-group instruction, or intensively and systematically in a one-on-one context. These strategies vary in terms of intensity and the extent to which the teacher is directly involved. No single strategy is most appropriate for use with all children; rather, strategy selection should be based on the skills and abilities of individual children.

Naturalistic instructional strategies are designed to teach skills within the context of typically occurring classroom activities and routines (see Brown et al., 2001; Rule, Losardo, Dinnebeil, Kaiser, & Rowland, 1998). At this level, these strategies are more intense than the universal practices and general social skills instruction used for all children. They are designed to provide frequent and systematic opportunities for children to learn new skills in the context of ongoing classroom activities and routines. Two naturalistic instructional strategies, incidental teaching and friendship activities, have been found to be effective for children with social and behavioral challenges. Children with social deficits have been found to increase their positive peer-related interactions when teachers used incidental teaching practices (McGee, Almeida, Sulzer-Azaroff, & Feldman, 1992; McGee & Daly, 2007). Specifically, when teachers used incidental teaching strategies that included (1) following the child's lead during socially oriented activities (e.g., free play, lunch), (2) providing systematic prompting to engage in social behaviors, and (3) elaborating on the child's social initiations and responses, the focal children's peer-related social skills increased. Additionally, McGee and Daly (2007) found that when children learned skills through incidental teaching, they were able to use them in unprompted social situations.

Friendship activities have also been found to be an effective naturalistic intervention strategy for teaching appropriate social skills (Brown, Ragland, & Fox, 1988; Frea, Craig-Unkefer, Odom, & Johnson, 1999; McEvoy et al., 1988; Twardosz, Nordquist, Simon, & Botkin, 1983). Similar to incidental teaching, friendship activities provide increased opportunities for engaging in positive social interactions; however, the nature of the strategy differs from incidental teaching, in that the teacher modifies existing classroom activities specifically to promote interactions between peers. For example, a song like "If You're Happy and You Know It" would include verses related to interacting with a friend (e.g., "If you're happy and you know it, hug your friend"). Friendship activities have resulted in increases in the frequency and duration of reciprocal social interactions between young children with social deficits and their peers (Frea et al., 1999; McEvoy et al., 1988) and target children's social initiations to their peers and peers' initiations to target children (Brown et al., 1988; McEvoy et al., 1988; Twardosz et al., 1983). Additionally, researchers have found that social behaviors learned through friendship activities generalize to activities other than those in which the friendship activities were conducted (Brown et al., 1988; McEvoy et al., 1988).

Peer coaching and buddy skills training are two approaches to instruction that have been used with small groups to promote social skills in children with social and behavioral challenges. Stanton-Chapman and her colleagues (Stanton-Chapman, Kaiser, Vijay, & Chapman, 2008; Stanton-Chapman & Snell, 2011) investigated the effectiveness of a social communication intervention on the social interactions and communication of young children with, and at risk for, language delays, behavioral disorders, and social skills deficits. In this intervention, dyads are taught in pairs to play with specific toy sets. The intervention includes reading to children a book about how they can play, supporting the children's play in context, and reviewing with children in the dyad how they played during the previous session. Across the studies, changes were observed in children's positive initiations and responses to each other, which is an important social skill for children who have or are at risk for challenging behavior. Furthermore, for some children, positive changes were observed in appropriate social interactions, type of play interactions, and challenging behavior. Although the findings in this study were mixed, they provide initial evidence of an approach that could be used to promote the social skills of children with challenging behavior.

Goldstein and colleagues (English, Goldstein, Shafer, & Kaczmarek, 1997; Goldstein, English, Shafer, & Kaczmarek, 1997) have developed an approach to peer-related social interaction training referred to as "buddy skills." This program employs peers as the interventionists. Typically developing peers are taught specific social initiation behaviors (e.g., gaining proximity, gaining attention, and organizing play), as well as skills that maintain social interactions (e.g., persisting and reinforcing). Overall findings indicate that both the target children (with behavioral challenges) and the peers increase their successful social initiations and interactions following the implementation of the buddy skills training program.

In addition to naturalistic and small-group instructional practices, teachers may choose to use individualized, systematic, adult-directed instruction for children who need additional help and intensive practice opportunities. Similar to naturalistic strategies described earlier, teachers provide direct instruction (including instructional prompting and reinforcement) during activities that are likely to promote social and behavioral competence. The difference in type of intervention is in the intensity and level of adult engagement. At this level, teachers systematically arrange *repeated* social opportunities and provide direct instruction focused on *teaching* and *strengthening* social and behavioral competence. Research has documented the effectiveness of systematic adult instruction for increasing children's positive social interactions (see DeKlyen & Odom, 1989; Odom et al., 1988). Additionally, this more intensive level of adult engagement (in comparison to less intense interventions) may be necessary for children with developmental delays who are at risk for, or who have, social and behavioral challenges (Brown et al., 2008; Odom et al., 1999).

Although the majority of children in early childhood programs are socially and behaviorally competent and respond well to universal practices, there are likely to be children who continue to demonstrate challenging behavior even when high-quality universal practices are in place. The practices we described in this section are designed for children who need more targeted interventions to help them learn appropriate ways of socially interacting and behaving in their classrooms. These types of interventions are often adequate to support the development of social competence in children who require more targeted support. However, there will be a small percentage of children whose social and behavioral needs persist and who will need more intensive interventions. Strategies to address these children's behaviors are discussed next.

Intensive Interventions

For children who demonstrate persistent and intensive challenging behaviors, researchers have found that a systematic process of individualized positive behavior supports (PBS) is often required (Dunlap & Fox, 2009; Dunlap et al., 2006). There is a growing body of evidence on the effectiveness of PBS with preschool-age children (Duda, Clarke, Fox, & Dunlap, 2008; Duda, Dunlap, Fox, Lentini, & Clarke, 2004). PBS is an approach designed to provide children with the supports they need to be successful in their daily routines and environments (Dunlap & Fox, 2009).

The process of PBS with young children has been described in a number of publications (e.g., Dunlap & Fox, 2009). The implementation of PBS involves a team-based process that at a minimum should include classroom teaching staff, a behavior support person, and the family. PBS involves the development of a behavior support plan based on a comprehensive assessment of children's developmental strengths and needs, as well as environmental factors that may contribute to and maintain the child's challenging behaviors (Dunlap et al., 2006).

Individualized behavior support plans generally have three components: (1) strategies for preventing the challenging behavior from occurring, (2) teaching the child new skills that can be used in place of the challenging behavior, and (3) responding to the child in a way that supports the use of new skills and does not maintain the challenging behavior. Prevention strategies are designed to decrease the likelihood that a child will engage in challenging behavior. They include practices such as choice making, embedding preferences into difficult tasks, self-monitoring strategies, and curricular modifications matched to the environmental events that trigger the child's challenging behavior. Second, instructional strategies are used to teach the child an appropriate social skill that can take the place of the challenging behavior. For example, if a child is aggressive toward other children when he wants something they are playing with, we might teach him to use his words to ask for the toy, to offer to trade for another toy, or to ask an adult for assistance. Finally, strategies that teachers can use to respond to behavior in a way that strengthens the new social skill and decreases the likelihood of the challenging behavior are included.

The goal of the behavior support planning process is to decrease the likelihood that challenging behavior will occur and to teach the child more appropriate social behaviors. When children's appropriate behaviors and skills are strengthened and their challenging behaviors are reduced, they have more opportunities to engage in positive peer interactions and meaningful learning opportunities. The PBS process is designed to be positive and supportive for children and does not include punitive procedures (Dunlap & Fox, 2009).

Behavior support plans are implemented in the context of ongoing activities and routines and thus are designed to be consistent with high-quality, developmentally appropriate practices. Many of the strategies on behavior support plans are practices used with all children, but they are implemented in a more intensive or individualized manner. The effectiveness of a behavior support plan depends on the extent to which all components of the plan are implemented consistently. The implementation of these plans can be challenging and may require support and training to caregivers who are involved in delivering the plan.

In summary, we have described the Teaching Pyramid, a classroomwide model for addressing social–emotional competence and challenging behavior in preschool settings. Although many children in early childhood programs need only minimal support to navigate social situations, some children require more intensive or individualized supports and instruction to be successful. Fortunately, the literature contains a host of effective practices that can be implemented to promote the social and behavioral competence of children with challenging behavior and social skills deficits. Our goal in this section was to describe practices associated with the Teaching Pyramid that can be individualized to meet the needs of children with challenging behavior in the context of supporting the social–emotional development of all children in a preschool classroom.

Implementation of a Comprehensive Framework for Addressing the Social and Behavioral Needs of All Children in Early Childhood Settings

One challenge with comprehensive frameworks such as the Teaching Pyramid is ensuring their implementation with fidelity in early childhood settings. There are many factors that influence the extent to which early childhood teachers implement these practices, including the skills, abilities, and attitudes of the provider, as well as programmatic policies and procedures that support implementation.

Despite our knowledge of research-based practices for addressing the social and behavioral needs of young children with challenging behaviors, there is evidence that many teachers are not implementing comprehensive social and behavioral practices with fidelity. Studies on training and coaching teachers in the use of specific strategies for promoting social and behavioral competence (e.g., praise, precorrection) often include baseline or preintervention data showing that teachers are not implementing these practices prior to being trained (Barton & Wolery, 2007; Fox, Hemmeter, Snyder, Binder, & Clarke, 2011; Hemmeter, Snyder, Kinder, & Artman, 2011). Recent studies on the Teaching Pyramid provide evidence that teachers' use of the Teaching Pyramid practices is relatively low before training. Across three studies on the Teaching Pyramid, we found that teachers on average were implementing less than 40% of the practices associated with the model prior to training (Artman, 2010; Hemmeter, Snyder, & Fox, 2009, 2010). In addition to data demonstrating that teachers are not using these practices with fidelity, teachers report that learning how to handle challenging behavior is one of their most significant training needs, and that it affects their job satisfaction (Buysse, Wesley, Keyes, & Bailey, 1996; Hemmeter, Corso, & Cheatham, 2006).

Given these findings, it is important to consider the supports necessary to ensure that these practices are implemented with fidelity by teachers in early childhood settings. To maximize outcomes for children, it is necessary that all active components of an intervention be implemented and that they be implemented with fidelity. This becomes a complex issue with comprehensive interventions (e.g., the Teaching Pyramid) that require teachers to implement a wide range of practices for all children, as well as targeted and individualized practices for children who do not respond to the universal practices. Furthermore, this involves helping teachers learn strategies for determining the supports children need and methods for delivering instruction in a way that responds to individualized needs.

Fortunately, the professional development literature suggests that teachers can be trained to use a range of social, emotional, and behavioral support practices with fidelity. In a recent review, Artman (2009) identified 21 studies in which early childhood professionals had been trained to use practices, strategies, or approaches to address the social, emotional, and behavioral needs of young children. The majority of the studies focused on training teachers to use specific practices (e.g., descriptive praise, precorrections) or a specific curriculum (e.g., PATHS). However, none of the studies in this review focused on training teachers to use a comprehensive framework of promotion, prevention, and intervention strategies such as the Teaching Pyramid.

Across studies on early childhood professional development, one common strategy to support teachers in implementing practices with fidelity has been coaching with performance-based feedback (Crow & Snyder, 1998). *Performance-based feedback* refers to the use of information about the teacher's performance in the classroom in the provision of feedback. Recent studies have found coaching with performance-based feedback to be effective in changing teacher practice related to promoting social skills and/or addressing challenging behavior in the classroom (cf. Fox et al., 2011; Fullerton et al., 2009; Hemmeter et al., 2011; Stormont et al., 2007). Across studies on coaching with performance-based feedback, teachers have been taught to use many of the strategies described in this chapter, including incidental teaching, descriptive praise, and precorrections. In addition, coaching with performance feedback has been used successfully to support teachers in the use of general teacher–child interaction strategies and instructional processes (Pianta, Mashburn, Downer, Hamre, & Justice, 2008), embedded instruction (Snyder, Hemmeter, McLaughlin, et al., 2011), behavior management strategies (Raver et al., 2008), and multiple strategies associated with the Teaching Pyramid model (Fox et al., 2011). Finally, research has demonstrated the effectiveness of coaching on teachers' use of specific curricula (Domitrovich et al., 2009). Across these studies, coaching has been successfully delivered through a variety of means, including live interactions between a coach and a teacher, via the Internet using e-mail, and via the Internet using interactive approaches.

Although coaching has been demonstrated to be beneficial for helping teachers learn and implement these practices in their classrooms, several factors related to coaching are important to consider, including the amount or dosage of coaching the teacher receives (Domitrovich, Gest, Jones, Gill, & Sanford DeRousie, 2010; Dusenbury, Brannigan, Hansen, Walsh, & Falco, 2005). The amount or dosage of coaching that is necessary to support teachers in implementing practices, strategies, or approaches depends on a number of factors. First, dosage may be influenced by the complexity of the intervention practice or program. Helping teachers learn to use a specific strategy is likely to take less time than helping them implement a curriculum that includes a range of strategies and practices. Second, the amount of coaching needed to achieve fidelity on a practice or set of practices varies based on individual differences in teachers. These factors may include the teacher's attitude toward the practice, the fit of the practice with the teacher's philosophy, the teacher's baseline level of implementation, and the teacher's competing priorities. Finally, the amount of coaching needed might vary based on the extent to which other programwide supports for implementation are in place. When an entire program or center is working on the same curriculum, practice, or program, there are likely to be additional supports (e.g., peer supports, administrative support) for a teacher's use of the practice(s).

Fixsen, Blasé, Duda, Naoom, and Van Dyke (2010) suggest that it is the combination of effective intervention practices and programs *and* effective implementation strategies that results in positive outcomes for children and families. Implementation research and, more specifically, research on professional development has found that some of the most common strategies used to provide professional development to teachers (e.g., dissemination of products about effective practices, training in the absence of follow-up support, mandating the implementation of a program or practice) do not result in the implementation of effective practices in classroom settings (Blasé & Fixsen, 2006; Fixsen, Naoom, Blasé, Friedman, & Wallace, 2005; Joyce & Showers, 2002; Snyder, Hemmeter, Artman, Kinder, & Pasia, in press). On the other hand, these bodies of research suggest that the following may be necessary to change practice: (1) organizational commitment; (2) professional development that is ongoing, individualized, and includes support in the practice setting; and (3) an ongoing plan for monitoring implementation and outcomes, and using that information to inform decision making about professional development and other program supports and processes.

Although there is a substantial body of literature on schoolwide approaches to implementing tiered models in kindergarten through secondary schools, the literature on implementation of these models in early childhood settings is just emerging (Fox & Hemmeter, 2009; Frey, Boyce, & Tarullo, 2009; Stormont, Lewis & Beckner, 2005). Work on programwide models in early childhood settings suggests the following components may be necessary to ensure that the full range of social–emotional teaching and behavior support strategies is implemented with fidelity and are effective for addressing the needs of all children in a preschool program: administrative support, policies, and procedures that define roles and responsibilities related to addressing the social, emotional, and behavioral needs of the children; ongoing training and coaching for classroom staff; a behavior-support planning process for children whose behavior is persistent; and an ongoing process for monitoring implementation and outcomes of the approach. Although these components may not vary significantly from those recommended in the K–12 schoolwide literature, the manner in which they are implemented varies significantly because of the unique features of early childhood programs (Fox & Hemmeter, 2009).

Unlike K–12 education, in which the majority of children are served in public schools, preschool children are served in a variety of settings, including Head Start, public school, and child care programs. A 2007 report on the Early Childhood Longitudinal Study found the following relative to preschool children being served: (1) 20% were in no regular early care or education arrangement, (2) 44.8% were in a center-based program (non–Head Start), (3) 12.7% were in a Head Start setting, (4) 13.1% were in a home-based relative care setting, and (5) 7.6% were in a home-based nonrelative care setting. The range of settings is even broader in that the 44.8% of children in center-based programs could be in public preschools or child care centers. These settings vary in a number of ways that influence how implementation supports are provided. For example, across early care and education settings, the educational and training requirements of teachers and caregivers range from no formal training or education beyond high school to certification in early childhood or early childhood special education. The extent to which these settings include professionals who can provide ongoing support and training to teachers varies significantly. Public school and Head Start settings are likely to have behavior support or mental health professionals on staff; however, many child care programs do not have access to these professionals. Finally, the hours that children spend in these programs can vary from 3 hours in a half-day PreK program to 10 or more hours in a child care setting. In recent studies, rates of preschool expulsion varied across types of early childhood setting, with the lowest rates in public school and Head Start classrooms, and the highest rates in faith-based and for-profit child care centers. The challenge in building a model of programwide supports for early childhood settings is how to design a model that is based on sound implementation principles and flexible enough to address the unique characteristics of different early childhood settings (Fox & Hemmeter, 2009).

Directions for Practice, Research, and Policy

In this chapter we have described individualized research-based practices and presented strategies for addressing the social and behavioral needs of young children with challenging behavior. We have suggested that because of the range of social, emotional, and behavioral needs of children in a typical preschool setting, these practices should be implemented in the context of a comprehensive approach that addresses the needs of all children, not just those with social and behavioral challenges. The Teaching Pyramid model (Fox et al., 2003; Hemmeter et al., 2006) provides one framework for integrating the practices into an approach for all children. Although we have evidence that early childhood teachers can be trained to use the range of practices associated with this approach, we also have evidence that they do not generally implement these practices with fidelity in the absence of training and supports. Professional development that includes coaching with performance feedback provides one approach for supporting teachers to use these practices. However, it is likely that for this approach to be effective, programwide supports must be in place, including policies and procedures related to behavior, clearly articulated procedures for supporting teachers around children with the most challenging behavior, and procedures for monitoring the implementation of practices and the effects of the intervention on children. A challenge for the field is how to design and implement programwide supports in the full range of early childhood settings.

To meet the challenges we have described, a number of research and policy issues must be addressed, including but certainly not limited to the following:

1. Although programwide approaches to behavior support in early childhood settings have been proposed and described (Fox & Hemmeter, 2009; Frey et al., 2009), there are no empirical studies of the implementation of programwide approaches in early childhood settings and the impact on teachers, classrooms, and children.
2. Despite the range of available strategies for addressing the social and behavioral needs of young children with challenging behavior, more research is needed on the effects of moderating variables, such as risk factors and developmental delays (i.e., intellectual disabilities, autism spectrum disorders), on the efficacy of these interventions. Furthermore, research is needed on the use and effects of these interventions across various settings in which these children spend their time (e.g., home, community, school).
3. Additional research is needed on effective approaches to professional development and how the dosage, type, and delivery of professional development is mediated by characteristics of the teacher (e.g., training, experience, match of intervention to teacher's philosophy), the type of intervention or intervention practice the teacher is being trained to use, and the extent to which program policies and procedures are in place to support the teacher's use of the intervention practices over time.

Finally, we have described in this chapter a comprehensive framework (i.e., the Teaching Pyramid) of practices for addressing the social–emotional development and/or challenging behavior of all children in a preschool classroom. However, we know neither the most salient ingredients of such an approach nor how the effects of a model such as the Teaching Pyramid compare to the effects of a specific social–emotional curriculum. The Teaching Pyramid was designed to be a comprehensive approach that addresses the needs of all children, including those with the most significant social and behavioral challenges. It is not clear how the Teaching Pyramid and curricula supporting social–emotional development would compare in terms of their effects on different groups of children served in preschool programs (e.g., typically developing children, children at risk, children with emotional and behavioral disorders or conduct problems).

In addition to implications for research, the information in this chapter raises a number of policy and practice issues. First, effective approaches for supporting teachers in implementing practices with fidelity will require a commitment of program resources. It is clear that short-term training is not likely to increase teachers' abilities to implement comprehensive approaches with fidelity. A major challenge will be identifying resources to provide the level of coaching needed by individual teachers. Second, a number of resources suggest the need for behavioral support or mental health consultation for children with the most significant challenging behaviors. For example, individualized PBS has been found to be effective with young children with ongoing, persistently challenging behavior. However, it requires that a person with behavior support expertise be available to support the process. Furthermore, in Gilliam's work (2005, 2007) on preschool expulsion, access to a behavior support or a mental health consultant was associated with decreased rates of expulsion. Again, the challenge for early childhood programs will be identifying the resources to ensure that this type of support is available to teachers and caregivers working directly with families and children.

In summary, many young children in early childhood programs demonstrate social and behavioral challenges of varying degrees. Not only do these behaviors impact children's learning and development, but they also present many challenges for early childhood teachers. Fortunately, programwide models that include specific research-based strategies are available to help teachers address the needs of all children in a preschool setting (Fox & Hemmeter, 2009; Frey et al., 2009; Stormont et al., 2005). Although there is evidence of the benefit of these individual strategies, our field is only in the early stages of identifying variables that can help teachers learn to implement these strategies with high levels of adherence and quality, and sustain their use over time. If teachers have the necessary knowledge and skills to address these social and behavioral deficits effectively early on, the short- and long-term outcomes for these children will be more promising.

Acknowledgments

The preparation of this chapter was supported by the Institute of Education Sciences (Grant Nos. R324A07212 and R324A080074), the Center on the Social and Emotional Foundations for Early Learning, U.S. Department of Health and Human Services (Grant No. 90YD0215/01), and the Technical Assistance Center on Social Emotional Intervention, Office of Special Education Programs, U.S. Department of Education (Grant No. H326B070002). We would like to thank Adrienne Golden for her assistance with the manuscript.

References

Artman, K. (2009). *Supporting children's social–emotional competence and preventing challenging behavior: A systematic review of the professional development literature.* Unpublished manuscript, Vanderbilt University, Nashville, TN.

Artman, K. (2010). *Effects of distance coaching on teachers' use of a tiered model of intervention and relationships with child behavior and social skills.* Unpublished doctoral dissertation, Vanderbilt University, Nashville, TN.

Barton, E. E., & Wolery, M. (2007). Evaluation of e-mail feedback on the verbal behaviors of preservice teachers. *Journal of Early Intervention, 30,* 55–72.

Benedict, E. A., Horner, R. H., & Squires, J. (2007). Assessment and implementation of positive behavior support in preschools. *Topics in Early Childhood Special Education, 27,* 174–192.

Birch, S. H., & Ladd, G. W. (1998). Children's interpersonal behaviors and the teacher–child relationship. *Developmental Psychology, 34,* 934–946.

Blasé, K. A., & Fixsen, D. L. (2006, November). *Scaling up: From research to national implementation.* Paper presented at the Center for Evidence Based Practice: Policy Makers' Summit, Washington, DC.

Brown, W. H., Odom, S. L., & Conroy, M. A. (2001). An intervention hierarchy for promoting preschool children's peer interactions in natural environments. *Topics in Early Childhood Special Education, 21,* 162–175.

Brown, W. H., Odom, S. L., & McConnell, S. R. (2008). *Social competence of young children: Risk, disability, and intervention.* Baltimore: Brookes.

Brown, W. H., Ragland, E., & Fox, J. (1988). Effects of group socialization procedures on the social interactions of preschool children. *Research in Developmental Disabilities, 9,* 359–376.

Burchinal, M. R., Peisner-Feinberg, E., Pianta, R., & Howes, C. (2002). Development of academic skills from preschool through second grade: Family and classroom predictors of developmental trajectories. *Journal of School Psychology, 40,* 415–436.

Buysse, V., Goldman, B. D., & Skinner, M. (2002). Setting effects on friendship formation among young children with and without disabilities. *Exceptional Children, 68,* 503–517.

Buysse, V., Goldman, B. D., West, T., & Hollingsworth, H. (2008). Friendships in early childhood: Implications for early education and intervention. In W. H. Brown, S. L. Odom, & S. R. McConnell (Eds.), *Social competence of young children: Risk, disability, and intervention* (pp. 77–97). Baltimore: Brookes.

Buysse, V., Wesley, P., Keyes, L., & Bailey, D. (1996). Assessing comfort zone of child care teachers in serving young children with disabilities. *Journal of Early Intervention, 20,* 189–203.

Campbell, S. B. (1995). Behavior problems in preschool children: A review of recent research. *Journal of Child Psychology and Psychiatry, 36,* 113–149.

Conroy, M. A., & Brown, W. H. (2004). Early identification, prevention, and early intervention with young children at risk for emotional/behavioral disorders: Issues, trends, and a call for action. *Behavioral Disorders, 29,* 224–236.

Conroy, M. A., Brown, W. H., & Olive, M. (2008). Social competence interventions for young children with challenging behaviors. In W. H. Brown, S. L. Odom, & S. McConnell (Eds.), *Social competence of young children: Risk, disability, and intervention* (2nd ed., pp. 205–232). Baltimore: Brookes.

Conroy, M. A., Dunlap, G., Clarke, S., & Alter, P. J. (2005). A descriptive analysis of positive behavioral intervention research with young children with challenging behavior. *Topics in Early Childhood Special Education, 25,* 157–166.

Conroy, M. A., Sutherland, K., Haydon, T., Stormont, M., & Harmon, J. (2008). Preventing and ameliorating young children's chronic problem behaviors: An ecological classroom-based approach. *Psychology in the Schools, 46,* 3–17.

Conroy, M. A., & Sutherland, K. S. (2011, March). *BEST in CLASS: Development of a classroom-based intervention aimed at reducing problem behavior of young high-risk children.* Paper presented at the annual meeting of the Society for Research on Educational Effectiveness, Washington, DC.

Cox, D. D. (2005). Evidence-based interventions using home–school collaboration. *School Psychology Quarterly, 20,* 473–497.

Crow, R., & Snyder, P. (1998). Organizational behavior management in early intervention: Status and implications for research and development. *Journal of Organizational Behavior Management, 18,* 131–156.

DeKlyen, M., & Odom, S. L. (1989). Activity structure and social interactions with peers in developmentally integrated play groups. *Journal of Early Intervention, 13,* 342–352.

Denham, S. A., & Burton, R. (1996). A social–emotional intervention for at-risk 4-year olds. *Journal of School Psychology, 34,* 225–245.

Domitrovich, C. E., Gest, S. D., Gill, S., Bierman, K. L., Welsh, J. A., & Jones, D. (2009). Fostering high quality teaching with an enriched curriculum and professional development support: The Head Start REDI program. *American Educational Research Journal, 46,* 567–597.

Domitrovich, C. E., Gest, S. D., Jones, D., Gill, S., & Sanford DeRousie, R. M. (2010). Implementation quality: Lessons learned in the context of the Head Start REDI trial. *Early Childhood Research Quarterly, 25,* 284–298.

Doyle, A., Connolly, J., & Rivest, L. (1980). The effect of playmate familiarity on the social interactions of young children. *Child Development, 51,* 217–223.

Duda, M. A., Clarke, S., Fox, L., & Dunlap, G. (2008). Implementation of positive behavior support with a sibling set in the home environment. *Journal of Early Intervention, 30,* 213–236.

Duda, M. A., Dunlap, G., Fox, L., Lentini, R., & Clarke, S. (2004). An experimental evaluation of positive behavior support in a community preschool program. *Topics in Early Childhood Special Education, 24,* 143–155.

Dunlap, G., & Fox, L. (2009). Positive behavior support and early intervention. In W. Sailor, G. Dunlap, G. Sugai, & R. Horner (Eds.), *Handbook of positive behavior support* (pp. 49–71). New York: Springer.

Dunlap, G., Sailor, W., Horner, R. H., & Sugai, G. (2009). Overview and history of positive behavior support. In W. Sailor, G. Dunlap, G. Sugai, & R. Horner (Eds.), *Handbook of positive behavior support* (pp. 3–16). New York: Springer.

Dunlap, G., Strain, P. S., Fox, L., Carta, J., Conroy, M., Smith, B., et al. (2006). Prevention and intervention with young children's challenging behavior: A summary of current knowledge. *Behavioral Disorders, 32,* 29–45.

Dusenbury, L., Brannigan, R., Hansen, W. B., Walsh, J., & Falco, M. (2005). Quality of implementation: Developing measures crucial to understanding the diffusion of preventive interventions. *Health Education Research, 20,* 308–313.

English, K., Goldstein, H., Shafer, K., & Kaczmarek, L. (1997). Promoting interactions among preschoolers with and without disabilities: Effects of a buddy skills-training program. *Exceptional Children, 63,* 229–243.

Fixsen, D. L., Blasé, K. A., Duda, M. A., Naoom, S. F., & Van Dyke, M. (2010). Implementation of evidence-based treatments for children and adolescents: Research findings and their implications for the future. In J. R. Weisz & A. E. Kazdin (Eds.), *Evidence-based psychotherapies for children and adolescents* (2nd ed., pp. 435–450). New York: Guilford Press.

Fixsen, D. L., Naoom, S. F., Blasé, K. A., Friedman, R. M., & Wallace, F. (2005). *Implementation research: A synthesis of the literature.* Tampa: University of South Florida, Louis de la Parte Florida Mental Health Institute.

Fox, L., Carta, J., Strain, P. S., Dunlap, G., & Hemmeter, M. L. (2010). Response-to-intervention and the Pyramid Model. *Infants and Young Children, 23,* 3–13.

Fox, L., Dunlap, G., Hemmeter, M. L., Joseph, G. E., & Strain, P. S. (2003). The Teaching Pyramid: A model for supporting social competence and preventing challenging behavior in young children. *Young Children, 58,* 48–52.

Fox, L., & Hemmeter, M. L. (2009). A program-wide model for supporting social emotional development and addressing challenging behavior in early childhood settings. In W. Sailor, G. Dunlap, G. Sugai, & R. Horner (Eds.), *Handbook of positive behavior support* (pp. 177–202). New York: Springer.

Fox, L., Hemmeter, M. L., Snyder, P., Binder, D., & Clarke, S. (2011). Coaching early childhood special educators to implement a comprehensive model for the promotion of young children's social competence. *Topics in Early Childhood Special Education, 31*(3), 178–192.

Fox, L., & Lentini, R. H. (2006). You got it!: Teaching social and emotional skills. *Young Children, 61,* 36–42.

Frea, W., Craig-Unkefer, L., Odom, S. L., & Johnson, D. (1999). Differential effects of structured social integration and group friendship activities for promoting social interaction with peers. *Journal of Early Intervention, 22,* 230–242.

Frey, A. J., Boyce, C. A., & Tarullo, L. B. (2009). Integrating a positive behavior support approach within Head Start. In W. Sailor, G. Dunlap, G. Sugai, & R. Horner (Eds.), *Handbook of positive behavior support* (pp. 125–148). New York: Springer.

Fullerton, E. K., Conroy, M., & Correa, V. I. (2009). Early childhood teachers' use of specific praise statements with young children at risk for behavioral disorders. *Behavioral Disorders, 34,* 118–135.

Gallagher, T. M. (1999). Interrelationships among children's language, behavior, and emotional problems. *Topics in Language Disorders, 19,* 1–15.

Gilliam, W. S. (2005). *Prekindergarteners left behind: Expulsion rates in state prekindergarten systems.* New Haven, CT: Yale University Child Study Center.

Gilliam, W. S. (2007). *Early childhood consultation partnership: Results of a random-controlled evaluation: Final report and executive summary.* New Haven, CT: Yale University Child Study Center.

Goldstein, H., English, K., Shafer, K., & Kaczmarek, L. (1997). Interaction among preschoolers with and without disabilities: Effects of across-the-day peer intervention. *Journal of Speech, Language, and Hearing Research, 40,* 33–48.

Gresham, F. M., & Elliott, S. N. (1987). The relationship between adaptive behavior and social skills: Issues in definition and assessment. *Journal of Special Education, 21,* 167–181.

Grisham-Brown, J. L., Hemmeter, M. L., & Pretti-Frontczak, K. L. (2005). *Blended practices in early childhood and early childhood special education.* Baltimore: Brookes.

Guralnick, M. J. (2010). Early intervention approaches to enhance the peer-related social competence of young children with developmental delays: A historical perspective. *Infants and Young Children, 23,* 73–83.

Hamre, B. K., & Pianta, R. C. (2001). Early teacher–child relationship and the trajectory of children's school outcome through eighth grade. *Child Development, 72,* 625–638.

Harper, L. V., & Huie, K. S. (1985). The effects of prior group experience, age, and familiarity on the quality and organization of preschoolers' social relationships. *Child Development, 56,* 704–717.

Hauser-Cram, P., Bronson, M. B., & Upsur, C. C. (1993). The effects of the classroom environment on the social and mastery behavior of preschool children with disabilities. *Early Childhood Research Quarterly, 8,* 479–497.

Hemmeter, M. L., Corso, R., & Cheatham, G. (2006, February). *A national survey of early childhood educators: Training needs and strategies.* Paper presented at the Conference on Research Innovations in Early Intervention, San Diego, CA.

Hemmeter, M. L., Ostrosky, M., & Fox, L. (2006). Social and emotional foundations for early learning: A conceptual model for intervention. *School Psychology Review, 35,* 583–601.

Hemmeter, M. L., Snyder, P., & Fox, L. (2009, June). *Examining the potential efficacy of a classroom-wide model for promoting social–emotional development and addressing challenging behavior in preschool children.* Poster presented at the Fourth Annual Institute of Education Sciences Research Conference, Washington, DC.

Hemmeter, M. L., Snyder, P., & Fox, L. (2010, June). *Examining the potential efficacy of a model for addressing social–emotional development and challenging behavior.* Poster presented at the Fifth Annual Institute of Education Sciences Research Conference, National Harbor, MD.

Hemmeter, M. L., Snyder, P., Kinder, K., & Artman, K. (2011). Impact of performance feedback delivered via electronic mail on preschool teachers' use of descriptive praise. *Early Childhood Research Quarterly, 26,* 96–109.

Holloway, S. D., & Reichart-Erickson, M. (1988). The relationship of day care quality to children's free play behavior and social problem-solving skills. *Early Childhood Research Quarterly, 3,* 39–53.

Horner, R. H., Sugai, G., Todd, A. W., & Lewis-Palmer, T. (2005). Schoolwide positive behavior support: An alternative approach to discipline in schools. In L. M. Bambara & L. Kern (Eds.), *Individualized supports for students with problem behaviors: Designing positive behavior plans* (pp. 359–390). New York: Guilford Press.

Howes, R., Calkins, S. D., Anastopoulos, A., Keane, S., & Shelton, T. (2003). Regulatory contributors to children's kindergarten achievement. *Early Education and Development, 14,* 101–119.

Ivory, J. J., & McCollum, J. A. (1999). Effects of social and isolate toys on social play in an inclusive setting. *Journal of Special Education, 32,* 238–243.

Jolivette, K., Wehby, J. H., Canale, J., & Massey, N. G. (2001). Effects of choice making opportunities on the behaviors of students with emotional and behavioral disorders. *Behavioral Disorders, 26,* 131–145.

Joseph, G. E., & Strain, P. S. (2003). Comprehensive evidence-based social emotional curricula for young children: An analysis of efficacious adoption potential. *Topics in Early Childhood Special Education, 23,* 65–76.

Joyce, B. J., & Showers, B. (2002). *Student achievement through staff development* (3rd ed.). Alexandria, VA: Longman.

Kaiser, A., Roberts, M., Feeney-Kettler, K., Frey, J., & Hemmeter, M. (2009, October). *The relationship between language and behavior in preschool children: Evidence from a meta-analysis.* Paper presented at the annual meeting of the Division for Early Childhood, Albuquerque, NM.

Kohl, F. L., & Beckman, P. J. (1984). A comparison of handicapped and nonhandicapped preschoolers' interactions across classroom activities. *Journal of Early Intervention, 8,* 49–56.

Kontos, S. (1999). Preschool teachers' talk, roles, and activity settings during free play. *Early Childhood Research Quarterly, 14,* 363–383.

Kontos, S., Moore, D., & Giogretti, K. (1998). The ecology of inclusion. *Topics in Early Childhood Special Education, 18,* 38–48.

Lavigne, J. V., Gibbons, R. D., Christoffel, K. K., Arend, R., Rosenbaum, D., Binns, H., et al. (1996). Prevalence rates and correlates of psychiatric disorders among preschool children. *Journal of the American Academy of Child and Adolescent Psychiatry, 35,* 204–214.

Loeber, R., Farrington, D. P., & Petchuk, D. (2003). *Child delinquency: Early intervention and prevention* (Child Delinquency Bulletin Series). Washington, DC: Department of Justice.

Mashburn, A. J., & Pianta, R. C. (2006). Social relationships and school readiness. *Early Education and Development, 17,* 151–176.

Masten, A. S., Coatsworth, J. D., Neemann, J., Gest, S. D., Tellegen, A., & Garmezy, N. (1995). The structure and coherence of competence from childhood through adolescence. *Child Development, 66,* 1635–1659.

McEvoy, M., Nordquist, V. M., Twardosz, S., Heckaman, K., Wehby, J. H., & Denny, R. K. (1988). Promoting autistic children's peer interaction in an integrated early childhood setting using affection activities. *Journal of Applied Behavior Analysis, 21,* 193–200.

McGee, G. G., Almeida, C., Sulzer-Azaroff, B., & Feldman, R. S. (1992). Promoting reciprocal interactions via peer incidental teaching. *Journal of Applied Behavior Analysis, 25,* 117–126.

McGee, G. G., & Daly, T. D. (2007). Incidental teaching of age-appropriate phrases to children with autism. *Research and Practice for Persons with Severe Disabilities, 32,* 112–123.

Mill, D., & Romano-White, D. (1999). Correlates of affectionate and angry behavior in child care educators of preschool-aged children. *Early Childhood Research Quarterly, 14,* 155–178.

Missall, K. N., & Hojnoski, R. L. (2008). The critical nature of young children's emerging peer-related social competence for transition to school. In W. H. Brown, S. L. Odom, & S. R. McConnell (Eds.), *Social competence of young children: Risk, disability, and intervention* (pp. 117–137). Baltimore: Brookes.

National Research Council. (2001). *Eager to learn: Educating our preschoolers* (Committee on Early Childhood Pedagogy, Commission on Behavioral and Social Sciences and Education; B. T. Bowman, M. S. Donovan, & M. S. Burns, Eds.). Washington, DC: National Academy Press.

Odom, S. L., Bender, M. K., Stein, M. L., Doran, L. P., Houden, P. M., McInnes, M., et al. (1988). *The integrated preschool curriculum: Procedures for socially integrating handicapped and non-handicapped children.* Seattle: University of Washington Press.

Odom, S. L., McConnell, S. R., & McEvoy, M. A. (Eds.). (1992). *Social competence of young children with disabilities: Issues and strategies for intervention.* Baltimore: Brookes.

Odom, S. L., McConnell, S. R., McEvoy, M. A., Peterson, C., Ostrosky, M., Chandler, L. K., et al. (1999). Relative effects of interventions supporting the social competence of young children with disabilities. *Topics in Early Childhood Special Education, 19,* 75–91.

Odom, S. L., Peterson, C., McConnell, S., & Ostrosky, M. (1990). Ecobehavioral analysis of early education/specialized classroom settings and peer social interaction. *Education and Treatment of Children, 13,* 316–330.

Peisner-Feinberg, E., & Burchinal, M. (1997). Concurrent relations between child care quality and child outcomes: The study of cost, quality, and outcomes in child care centers. *Merrill–Palmer Quarterly, 43,* 451–477.

Pianta, R., Mashburn, A., Downer, J., Hamre, B., & Justice, L. (2008). Effects of web-mediated professional development resources on teacher–child interactions in pre-kindergarten classrooms. *Early Childhood Research Quarterly, 23,* 431–451.

Pianta, R. C., & Stuhlman, M. W. (2004). Teacher–child relationships and children's success in the first years of school. *School Psychology Review, 33,* 444–458.

Raver, C. C., Jones, S. M., Li-Grining, C., Metzger, M., Smallwood, K., & Sardin, L. (2008). Improving preschool classroom processes: Preliminary findings from a randomized trial implemented in Head Start settings. *Early Childhood Research Quarterly, 23,* 10–26.

Rule, S., Losardo, A., Dinnebeil, L., Kaiser, A., & Rowland, C. (1998). Translating research on naturalistic instruction into practice. *Journal of Early Intervention, 21,* 283–293.

Sainato, D. M., Jung, S., Salmon, M. D., & Axe, J. B. (2008). Classroom influences on young children's emerging social competence. In W. H. Brown, S. L. Odom, & S. R. McConnell (Eds.), *Social competence of young children: Risk, disability, and intervention* (pp. 99–116). Baltimore: Brookes.

Serna, L., Nielsen, E., Lambros, K., & Forness, S. (2000). Primary prevention with children at risk for emotional or behavioral disorders: Data on a universal intervention for Head Start classrooms. *Behavioral Disorders, 26,* 70–84.

Simeonsson, R. J. (1991). Primary, secondary, and tertiary prevention in early intervention. *Journal of Early Intervention, 15,* 124–134.

Snyder, P., Hemmeter, M. L., Artman, K., Kinder, K., & Pasia, C. (in press). Characterizing key features of the early childhood professional development literature. *Early Education and Development.*

Snyder, P., Hemmeter, M. L., McLaughlin, T., Algina, J., Sandall, S., & McLean, M. (2011, April).

Impact of professional development on preschool teachers' use of embedded-instruction practices. Paper presented at the annual meeting of the American Educational Research Association, New Orleans, LA.

Stanton-Chapman, T. L., Kaiser, A. P., Vijay, P., & Chapman, C. (2008). Teaching social interaction skills to children at-risk for emotional and behavioral disorders. *Journal of Early Intervention, 30,* 188–212.

Stanton-Chapman, T. L., & Snell, M. E. (2011). Promoting turn-taking events in preschool children with disabilities: The effects of a peer-based social communication based intervention. *Early Childhood Research Quarterly, 11,* 303–319.

Stormont, M., Lewis, T. J., & Beckner, R. (2005). Positive behavior support systems: Applying key features in preschool settings. *Teaching Exceptional Children, 37,* 42–49.

Stormont, M. A., Smith, S. C., & Lewis, T. J. (2007). Teacher implementation of precorrection and praise statements in Head Start classrooms as a component of a program-wide system of positive behavior support. *Journal of Behavioral Education, 16,* 280–290.

Sutherland, K. S., Conroy, M., Abrams, L., & Vo, A. (2010). Improving interactions between teachers and young children with problem behavior: A strengths-based approach. *Exceptionality, 18,* 70–81.

Twardosz, S., Nordquist, V. M., Simon, R., & Botkin, D. (1983). The effect of group affection activities on the interaction of socially isolate children. *Analysis and Intervention in Developmental Disabilities, 3,* 311–338.

U.S. Department of Education, Office of Special Education and Rehabilitative Services, Office of Special Education Programs. (2007). 27th annual report to Congress on the Individuals with Disabilities Act 2005 (Vol. 1). Retrieved from *www.eric.ed.gov:80/pdfs/ed499021.pdf.*

Webster-Stratton, C., Reid, M. J., & Hammond, M. (2001). Preventing conduct problems, promoting social competence: A parent and teacher training partnership in Head Start. *Journal of Clinical Child Psychology, 30,* 283–302.

West, J., Denton, K., & Germino-Hausken, E. (2000). *America's kindergartener: Findings from the Early Childhood Longitudinal Study, kindergarten class of 1998–99, fall 1998.* Washington, DC: U.S. Department of Education, National Center for Educational Statistics.

CHAPTER 21

Promoting Young Children's Mental Health through Early Childhood Consultation

Ecological Advances and Research Needs

Susan M. Sheridan, Brandy L. Clarke, and Tanya B. Ihlo

Educational, neurobiological, and intervention research conducted in the context of early childhood over recent decades has yielded a convincing set of findings, all leading to the unequivocal conclusion that social–emotional development, and related mental health correlates, begins early and impacts almost every aspect of a young child's life. For most children, development proceeds along an expected trajectory. For other children, however, challenges exist or disruptions occur that interfere with a typical course. In these latter cases, early childhood educators and interventionists are becoming concerned with identifying both programs and processes to redirect developmental pathways and promote positive mental health and social–emotional outcomes. Consultation-based services, providing collegial assistance and support to individuals responsible for children's daily care, are receiving increased attention in the early childhood literature. In this chapter, we first define early childhood mental health and chart its developmental course. Second, we offer early childhood consultation as a means to address challenges to positive social–emotional and mental health development. Third, we provide a brief review of challenges to the research base in early childhood consultation, stemming from both conceptual and procedural limitations. Fourth, we suggest advances in conceptualizing and delivering early childhood consultation from an ecological perspective and present a model of early childhood consultation incorporating several theoretically sound, developmentally appropriate, empirically supported features for use in early childhood education settings. Finally, we indicate directions for the future of research in early childhood consultation.

What Is Early Childhood Mental Health?

Early childhood mental health is a relatively new area of interest that was borne out of developmental, neurocognitive, and educational advances recognizing the role of children's affect and social–emotional skills as significant contributors to their overall functioning. In early childhood, the term "mental health" is typically considered synonymous with "social–emotional" health. For infants and toddlers from birth to age 3, it is considered "the developing capacity of … young children to experience, manage, and express emotion; form close, secure relationships; and actively explore the environment and learn" (Duran et al., n.d., p. 2). In the preschool years (ages 3–5), social–emotional health concerns "the capacity [of the young child] to recognize and manage emotions, solve problems effectively, and establish positive relationships with others" (Zins & Elias, 2006, p. 1). This includes a full spectrum of behaviors that characterize social and emotional functioning, ranging from the ability to connect with and form meaningful relationships with others, interact reciprocally in play and communication, take advantage of the myriad of learning opportunities present within the environment, learn social rules and manage one's behaviors within socially defined parameters, and identify and express basic emotions. It includes both self-awareness and self-regulation within intra- and interpersonal domains.

The notion of children's mental health is often associated with their skills and abilities vis-à-vis self- and social–emotional learning. *Social–emotional learning* (SEL) occurs when children experience maturational processes enabling them to coordinate and regulate their emotional, cognitive, and behavioral responses. This requires a complex set of behaviors and cognitions, all enacted simultaneously (i.e., engaging positively with others, managing one's emotions, and maintaining positive manifestations of oneself and one's skills in the social realm). Specifically, SEL involves self-awareness, self-management, emotional expressiveness, social awareness, and responsible decision making (Denham & Weissberg, 2004). It is now recognized as a pivotal skill set that is predictive of important school readiness outcomes (Carlton & Winsler, 1999).

Understanding what is appropriate within the social–emotional arena requires a developmental framework. In infancy, young children are developing the capacity to interact with others in a basic sense. Within the first year of life they respond positively when touched by a caregiver, smile and show pleasure, pay attention to others and to social overtures, mimic simple actions, and show anxiety when separated from their primary caregiver. By the time children reach their second birthday they become more aware of themselves and their ability to act on the environment with purpose. Most children show intense positive and negative emotions, imitate adult behaviors, gain assertiveness and self-direction, and demonstrate efforts at cooperation and helpfulness. In their third year of life children can be expected to begin evaluating themselves and their actions, show increased awareness of others' feelings, talk about feelings, engage in parallel play, and participate in simple group activities. Most 3-year-olds can follow simple directions, complete simple tasks, and perform basic self-help skills. Around the age of 4, children begin showing more interest in other children. They share toys, take turns, initiate or join in social interactions, engage in dramatic play, and show some moral reasoning ability (i.e., identify what is good, bad, fair). By the age of 5, children are very interested in peer relationships. They develop friendships, express greater levels of awareness of others' feelings, and enjoy complex play interactions, including imaginative and dramatic play.

Unfortunately, for some children, the path of healthy social–emotional development is diverted, and early manifestations of social–emotional problems become a reality. Between 9.5 and 14.2% of children below the age of 5 suffer from social–emotional problems that interfere with their healthy development and learning (Brauner & Stephens, 2006).

Prevalence appears greatest for oppositional defiant disorder, with estimates suggesting that up to 26% of children through age 5 experience this disorder (Cooper, Masi, & Vick, 2009). Behavioral problems appear to peak around age 4 years, with an estimated 13% of young children in pediatric primary care facilities experiencing behavioral problems, followed by 10% of 5-year-olds (Lavigne et al., 1996). Almost half (45%) of children under the age of 6 who are treated in mental health agencies meet criteria for serious emotional problems (Bean, Biss, & Hepburn, 2007), pointing to the significance of impairment and need for attention to both the symptoms and precursors of childhood emotional disturbance.

A host of factors contribute to the poor trajectory of social–emotional skills development in young children who manifest such problem behaviors. Research on neural stimulation during the early years has identified the significant role of early experiences in shaping a child's capacity to control his or her emotions and form relationships with others. Specifically, lack of nurturing relationships, thwarted cognitive stimulation, and chronic stress affect a young child's early brain development in detrimental ways (Shonkoff & Phillips, 2000). Dysfunctional parent–child interaction patterns have been shown to develop into coercive cycles that are predictive of later psychosocial problems, including behavioral disabilities and delinquency (Patterson, DeBaryshe, & Ramsey, 1989). Alternatively, warm and caring relationships with adults can subvert the deleterious effects of cumulative risk. Positive and nurturing attachments with significant adults serve as a protective mechanism for young children, building their resiliency and ability to circumvent the negative trajectory often experienced among children growing up in highly vulnerable circumstances. Furthermore, early intervention targeting the significant adults in a child's life—most notably, parents and teachers who are positioned to create positive and nurturing environments within and across home and school settings—is important for establishing a course of healthy social–emotional development.

Consultation as a Means to Promote Social–Emotional Learning: What Is It?

Consultation in early childhood provides a method for supporting young children's social–emotional functioning and other areas of development by working with the adults who are responsible for their learning and development. A highly cited and generally acknowledged definition of *consultation* in early childhood was offered by Cohen and Kaufmann (2005) who coined it as

> a problem-solving and capacity-building intervention implemented within a collaborative relationship between a professional consultant with mental health expertise and one or more individuals, primarily child care center staff, with other areas of expertise. ... [It] aims to build the capacity of staff, families, programs, and systems to prevent, identify, treat, and reduce the impact of mental health problems among children from birth to age 6 and their families. (p. 4)

Alternative approaches to consultation are available in the literature. Driven by the work of Gerald Caplan (1963), *mental health consultation* has historically focused attention on the teacher's or service provider's difficulties managing work-related challenges. Theoretically, mental health consultation stems from psychodynamic interpretations of professional behavior. Rather than pinpointing the causes underlying a child's problem, the mental health consultant has been concerned with reasons a consultee may struggle with providing services to the child (e.g., lack of knowledge, skill, self-confidence, or objectivity).

Furthermore, in mental health consultation, both case-centered and programmatic consultation is prominent. From a *case-centered* perspective, a focus on children and families is characteristic. In this case, the help of an expert consultant is solicited to address children's needs (e.g., challenging behaviors), typically by attending to teachers' emotional reactions to them (e.g., frustration, stress). *Programmatic* mental health consultation focuses on improving the overall quality of an early childhood agency, such as at a center or district level.

Behavioral consultation is driven theoretically by an orientation toward determining contingencies maintaining a child's behaviors. Seminal work by Bergan (1977), Bergan and Kratochwill (1990), and others led practitioners and researchers to consider specific, observable behaviors of children and alterable conditions in their environments as the foci of consultation. Procedurally, behavioral consultation follows a stagewise progression from the initial steps of identifying a focal concern to developing, implementing, and evaluating plans intended to address the problem behavior and establish desirable alternatives to it. As an extension, *ecological consultation* (and related models) attends to the interactions of persons, environments, and behaviors; interventions are determined only upon understanding the manner in which a child's behaviors intersect with conditions within his or her environments (Sheridan & Gutkin, 2000).

Regardless of the theoretical approach espoused by individual researchers, there are a number of features that characterize the practice of consultation. First, it is an indirect practice, wherein a consultant works with a consultee who is responsible for providing direct services to a child. This approach is presumed to provide a broader and potentially more extensive effect. Specifically, it provides opportunities for effective programs to be delivered to a target child over extended time and place, and for consultees to learn and generalize effective practices to children for whom they may have similar concerns (Sheridan, Kratochwill, & Bergan, 1996). Second, consultees engage in consultation on a voluntary basis. In this way, consultation is differentiated from supervision and evaluation. It is believed that the open and deliberate nature of the consultation practice allows learning and personal growth to occur. Third, it is practiced within the context of a collegial relationship between the consultant and consultee. Although consultants typically guide the consultation process, it is now understood that teachers and other consultees have important information to share, and it is elicited within the context of a positive and constructive relationship.

The State of Research in Early Childhood Consultation

Several seminal sources in the school-based literature articulate key features that are necessary to advance both the science and practice of consultation. Resources such as textbooks (e.g., Dougherty, 2008; Erchul & Martens, 2010), handbooks (e.g., Erchul & Sheridan, 2008), and journals (*Journal of Educational and Psychological Consultation*) are devoted to the topic. Such attention and scrutiny have resulted in much clearer understandings of the practice and its scientific foundation in elementary programs. Despite the long-standing recognition of consultation as an important and viable educational service delivery feature, its appearance in early childhood programs is relatively recent. Attention to the mental health needs of young children has prompted a variety of practices, such as coaching and mentoring, that have been introduced as examples of early childhood consultation. This has led to inconsistencies in specificity and operational understandings within the early childhood education field. With the proliferation of attention to the topic, increasing numbers of reviews are available and will not be repeated here. Rather, we present a brief summary of findings and issues in the current literature on early childhood consultation, followed by recommendations for advancing its research base. Readers interested in extensive research reviews are referred to Brennan, Bradley, Allen, and Perry (2008); Duran and colleagues (n.d.); and Perry, Allen, Brennan, and Bradley (2010). A few noteworthy studies described below demonstrate the desired effects of early childhood consultation as evidenced via highly regarded research methods.

Variations of practice exist under a broad umbrella of early childhood consultation. Of the various approaches appearing in the early childhood educational literature, those espousing a mental health orientation and framework are most prominent. As an example, Raver and colleagues (2009) tested the effects of the Chicago School Readiness Project (CSRP), in which mental health consultants provided teacher training, direct observation, coaching, stress reduction workshops, and direct child services in high-poverty Head Start classrooms. Thirty-five classrooms within 18 sites (approximately two classrooms per site) were randomly assigned to treatment and control conditions. Using standardized measures and direct child observations, CSRP was found to yield a statistically significant effect on reducing both externalizing and internalizing behaviors. The use of a randomized clinical trial and multilevel modeling are clear research strengths; however, the breadth of activities comprising the mental health intervention creates uncertainty in unpacking the operative elements of the consultation model.

Another model of early childhood consultation—albeit very different in both form and function—is My Teaching Partner (MTP), a Web-based professional development and consultation model focused on supporting teacher–student interactions in the classroom (Pianta, Mashburn, Downer, Hamre, & Justice, 2008). In a randomized control trial examining the efficacy of MTP, 113 teachers from 24 school districts were assigned to either a Web-only condition or a consultation condition. Teachers in both conditions had access to Web-based materials, including curricular resources for promoting positive social relationships (Promoting Alternative Thinking Strategies (PATHS; Greenberg, Kusche, Cook, & Quamma, 1995) and language and literacy development (MTP Language and Literacy Curriculum; Justice, Pullen, Hall, & Pianta, 2003), as well as videoclips of high-quality teacher–student interactions (Pianta, Mashburn, et al., 2008).

Teachers in the consultant condition submitted videotapes of implementation of study curricula and participated in biweekly, Web-based consultation focused on examination of teacher–student interactions using the Classroom Assessment Scoring System (CLASS; Pianta, La Paro, & Hamre, 2008), an observation system designed to measure teachers' instructional, organizational, and emotional interactions with children. Consultants provided targeted feedback and facilitated problem solving with teachers based on the targeted teacher–student interactions identified using the CLASS.

Results after the first year of implementation indicated that teachers participating in the consultation condition had greater gains on all dimensions of teacher–child interactions assessed by the CLASS, including significantly greater gains on the three dimensions of interaction quality (Teacher Sensitivity, Instructional Learning Formats, and Language Modeling) when compared to teachers in the Web-only condition (Pianta, Mashburn, et al., 2008). After the second year of implementation, results of an examination of teacher usage of and satisfaction with the Web-based resources indicated that teachers in both conditions found the resources easy to use and helpful in improving their interactions with students (Downer, Kraft-Sayre, & Pianta, 2009). Additionally, teachers in the consultant condition reported that the components of the project related to working with their consultant were the most helpful. Preliminary findings based on analysis of teacher outcomes suggest promise in the use of a Web-mediated systematic consultation process to improve teacher–student interactions, particularly in classrooms with a large number of students living in socioeconomic disadvantage. Further analysis is needed to examine the impact on student outcomes (Pianta, Mashburn, et al., 2008).

Other studies reporting positive outcomes of consultation utilized nonrandomized designs. For example, Upshur, Wenz-Gross, and Reed (2009) demonstrated decreases in classroom aggressive and maladaptive behavior, and improvements in adaptive behavior. Again, services included a range of disparate support activities, with no clear operational definition of the independent variable (i.e., mental health consultation). In this study, the consultation model included classroom observation, teacher training, individual child assessment and therapy, family assessment and support, and referrals for family needs. Using a more focused consultation model, Williford and Shelton (2008) provided individual consultation to teachers to support their use of behavior management strategies (via the Incredible Years approach; Webster-Stratton, Reid, & Hammond, 2001). Using this targeted and well-defined model of consultation, positive between-group differences were found for both child disruptive behaviors and teachers' use of effective behavior management strategies.

In addition to consultation research focused on teachers as consultees, the triadic model of early childhood consultation (McCollum & Yates, 1994) is a research-based model in which parents are consultees. The triadic model has been validated with parents of infants and young children with disabilities to promote responsive parent–child interactions (Mahoney & MacDonald, 2007; Mahoney & Powell, 1988). During parent–child interactions, consultants employ strategies such as modeling, providing information, enhancing parental competence by using parents' ideas and expanding on them, and focusing parents' attention on their child's actions (McCollum & Yates, 1994). Triadic consultation models have found that consultants are able to promote children's development through helping parents become more responsive in observing and interacting with their children (Mahoney & Powell, 1988; McCollum, Gooler, Appl, & Yates, 2001).

Challenges to the Early Childhood Consultation Research Base

Intentional scientific inquiry in the area of early childhood consultation is still in its infant stages. It is apparent that clarity in virtually all aspects of the practice is needed to understand, from an empirical standpoint, the processes and outcomes associated with early childhood consultation. This includes clarity in definition, procedural details, roles and relationships, and theoretical frameworks. Furthermore, research on the efficacy of consultation in early childhood is characterized by a range of studies utilizing designs of variable rigor that assess teacher and program effects primarily, and child effects less frequently.

Definitional Inconsistencies

Several definitions of consultation have been advanced in the early childhood sector, with emphases spanning from individual children to teachers, or sets of teachers, to entire programs. The myriad studies that evaluate early childhood consultation services use inconsistent definitions, making the empirical base difficult to pinpoint. In intervention research, definitions of the independent variable (in this case, early childhood consultation) often determine a study's focus, roles, and procedures; therefore, inconsistencies or confusions obfuscate findings and advances in multiple ways. Even programs that purport to espouse a similar mental health orientation promote different definitions. The traditional focus of mental health consultation has involved program-level efforts to support early childhood education programs as they served children with social, emotional, or behavioral challenges (Brennan et al., 2008). However, other articulations of mental health consultation—including the historical mental health consultation framework advanced in the Caplanian tradition—indicate a focus on teacher behaviors, affect, or knowledge.

Because different definitions and approaches to mental health consultation exist, targets vary significantly. Targets of consultation intervention, such as improving early childhood classroom environments (Gilliam, 2007) and enhancing program capacity (Alkon, Ramler, & MacLennan, 2003), are common in the early childhood consultation literature. Many studies report outcomes at the provider level, such as professional burnout, stress, confidence, knowledge, and skills. Some studies evaluate the effects of mental health consultation at the level of the agency or program service delivery unit (see Brennan et al., 2008, for a review). In these cases, foci such as improving communication among staff or discussing workplace conflicts are common. Fewer assess improvements in target children's behaviors or social–emotional functioning (for an exception, see Williford & Shelton, 2008).

Roles and Relationships

Also as a result of the various definitions of consultation in the early childhood literature, the consultant role and subsequent responsibility is defined in a variety of ways including a coach, a mentor, and a direct service provider. Consultants are typically viewed as experts observing in classrooms and providing teachers with interventions (Perry, Dunne, McFadden, & Campbell, 2008), but they also report being confused about their role and unsure of where to place their efforts (Wesley, Buysse, & Skinner, 2001). Some suggest that expert-driven consultation models lack social validity because they may not be responsive to the needs of stakeholders and may lead to a lack of investment in the prescribed intervention (Nastasi et al., 2000; Schulte & Osborne, 2003). In contrast, collaborative, partnership-driven consultation involves consultants and consultees engaged in a systematic process to address a child's concerns. Parents and teachers are actively involved in development of interventions for children, and consultants "give away" the process for addressing problem behaviors. This builds the capacity of parents and teachers to address future concerns (Gutkin & Curtis, 1990). Additionally, a collaborative partnership-driven model of consultation is associated with higher levels of adherence to interventions (Kelleher, Riley-Tillman, & Power, 2008) than a purely expert model.

Relatedly, roles of key participants are also narrowly conceived in much of the early childhood consultation literature. Consultation in traditional mental health consultation involves an expert delivering a service to consultees who are also professionals or providers. Very rarely are roles for parents described in early childhood mental health consultation, despite the fact that they control the environments within which children spend the majority of their time.

Procedural Inconsistencies

The lack of clearly operationalized definitions across studies is compounded by procedural inconsistencies in what constitutes the practice of early childhood consultation. Despite an assumption of indirect services as a defining feature of consultation, case-centered mental health consultation often includes related services such as assessment, individual and group therapy, referrals for family services, and teacher support groups. Programmatic mental health consultation may support implementation of a range of systemwide supports, such as programs to support children's social–emotional development, engage in staff training, or address issues of burnout or workplace conflict (Cohen & Kauffman, 2005). Thus, some models of early childhood mental health consultation combine indirect and direct services to children and families (e.g., California's Early Childhood Mental Health program; James Bowman Associates & Kagan, 2003), others incorporate structured curricula (e.g., Webster-Stratton & Reid's Incredible Years program; 1999a, 1999b), and still others consider all services geared toward social–emotional functioning (including child screening, assessment, development of individualized plans, and family mental health services; e.g., Gilliam, 2007) within the realm of consultation. In many instances, one study or evaluation includes several services and activities that collectively constitute the mental health consultation program (e.g., Alkon et al., 2003). The inclusion of a range of activities that defines consultation within and across studies complicates conclusions regarding the practice and its effects.

Narrow Scope and Conceptual Foundation

The conceptual foundation from which consultation services are offered or delivered has tended to be nonspecified, or narrow in scope. In the vast majority of the early childhood consultation literature, consultants reportedly work with other professionals (teachers, early childhood providers) to support their understanding or practice. However, children learn and develop within and across multiple settings through their interactions with multiple caregivers who influence and are influenced by one another. Such interactions call for interventions, including those emanating from consultation processes, which account for interdependencies between the developing child and the systems and settings within which he or she lives.

Consultation-based programs that encompass the entirety of children's learning environments, and most notably the home and the school, recognize the interrelatedness and interactions among socializing systems. Despite the unequivocal research support attesting to the significant role of families and family members in a young child's early social–emotional development, and the relationships between negative parent–child interactions and poor outcomes, the role of families in the early childhood consultation literature has been neglected. The consultant role in relation to parents is often described as providing parents with information (Mahoney, Boyce, Fewell, Spiker, & Wheeden, 1998), engaging them in direct clinical service (Alkon et al., 2003), or providing parent training (Williford & Shelton, 2008). In the majority of early childhood mental health studies, parents are not included as partners in the consultation process even though "early mental health services are most effective when family members are viewed as an important part of the intervention team and given appropriate and adequate supports to care for their children in their home and other early childhood environments" (Nikkel, 2007, p. 151).

Ecological approaches to early childhood consultation take advantage of the benefits of active parent participation and home–school partnerships, recognizing that positive and constructive relationships between systems are important for children's functioning. The essential role of parents in promoting learning is unequivocal (Henderson & Mapp, 2002). Parents' valuation of education, provision of a literacy-rich home environment, and establishment of high-quality relationships with preschool teachers have been shown to be positively related to young children's academic performance (Hill, 2001; Weigel, Martin, & Bennett, 2006). Creating conditions in early childhood for parents to develop positive roles in learning and development may pave the way for continued participation over time. During the elementary years, parent participation is associated with prosocial behavior (Comer & Haynes, 1991; McWayne, Hampton, Fantuzzo, Cohen, & Sekino, 2004), positive approaches to learning (perseverance and mastery motivation; Turner & Burke, 2003), participation in learning activities (Sattes, 1985), and academic achievement (Fan & Chen, 2001; Senechal, 2006).

The potential for parents to have a significant positive role in their children's education through consultation and other partnership approaches has been empirically established. Using a large, nationally representative sample (Early Childhood Longitudinal Study— Kindergarten Cohort; ECLS-K), parent involvement was found to partially mediate the relation between kindergarten transition practices and achievement (Schulting, Malone,

& Dodge, 2005). Continuity across caregiving systems (e.g., family and school), involvement of key stakeholders, and positive relationships among parents and professionals (e.g., early childhood teachers) contribute to the effectiveness of preschool intervention (Rimm-Kaufman & Pianta, 2000). Discontinuities across home, school, and peer worlds place children at significant risk for social–emotional and academic concerns (Phelan, Davidson, & Yu, 1998), pointing to the importance of creating connections between home and school. Promoting high-quality partnerships among caregivers through relationship-building strategies, such as perspective taking, joint decision making, and collaborative plan development and implementation, are some of the ways partnerships can be developed through ecologically focused early childhood consultation.

Conjoint Behavioral Consultation

Conjoint behavioral consultation (CBC; Sheridan & Kratochwill, 2008), an ecologically based model of early childhood consultation, focuses on improving mental health outcomes on behalf of young children by engaging primary caregivers across important systems in a conjoint decision-making process. CBC is presented as an exemplar model of early childhood consultation that addresses several of the presenting limitations discussed with other models. The following is a description of the how CBC addresses these concerns as an evidence-based early childhood consultation model.

CBC is an extension of traditional behavioral consultation models wherein parents, educators, and other professionals engage in the consultation process jointly on behalf of a child. CBC is defined as "a strength-based, cross-system problem-solving and decision-making model wherein parents, teachers, and other caregivers or service providers work as partners and share responsibility for promoting positive and consistent outcomes related to a child's academic, behavioral, and social–emotional development" (Sheridan & Kratochwill, 2008, p. 25). Its goals are to (1) address academic, behavioral, developmental, and/or social–emotional concerns for the child; (2) engage parents meaningfully in children's education; and (3) promote a home–school partnership between parents and educators. As such, both content (i.e., improving outcomes on behalf of children) and process objectives (promoting home–school partnerships) are articulated. See Table 21.1 for a summary of CBC's primary goals and objectives. The goals and objectives are further operationalized in practice via semistructured interviews among trained consultants, parents, and teachers.

Conceptual Framework

CBC is based on two foundational theories that guide implementation of the consultation process and services provided: ecological and behavioral theories. *Ecological theory* (Bronfenbrenner, 1977) focuses on the many systems, environments, and contexts that influence children's development and the interconnections among them. The *microsystem* is the primary ecosystem and setting within which children reside, such as home, preschool, and day care. Each system influences the other in a bidirectional manner; the relationships, communication patterns, and other influences among these systems comprise the *mesosystem*. For example, families' implicit or explicit expectations for children influence behaviors and performance in the preschool or day care setting. The exosystem comprises those settings that act indirectly on children through their influence on the microsystems, such as school district decisions regarding funding or curriculum, and parental work schedules influencing participation in preschool learning activities. Overall cultural influences that subsume all other systems and settings (e.g., federal educational policies) are part of the *macrosystem*.

TABLE 21.1. Goals and Objectives of CBC as an Early Childhood Consultation Model

Overarching goals

- Promote positive mental health or social emotional *outcomes on behalf of young children* via joint, collaborative, cross-system planning
- Promote *meaningful parent engagement* in their child's learning and development
- Develop and enhance *partnerships* between parents and educators or service providers on behalf of children's mental health that can be maintained over time

Content objectives

- Gather observational data of the child's functioning across settings
- Develop comprehensive intervention programs across settings
- Build skills, knowledge, and capacities of all parties (i.e., child, family, educators)
- Monitor child's progress and potential side effects of intervention plans over time
- Promote generalization and maintenance of positive outcomes utilizing cross-setting resources
- Promote conjoint problem-solving and collaboration skills and competencies among family members and educators

Process objectives

- Enhance communication patterns, knowledge, and understanding of child, family and educational system
- Establish a shared ownership and responsibility for the child's development and problem solving
- Increase perspective taking to promote a greater conceptualization of the needs and concerns for the child and the systems
- Promote continuity and consistency by addressing needs and concerns for child across, rather than within, settings
- Increase commitment from family members and educators toward fostering child's mental health

Whereas ecological theory elucidates important environmental and contextual variables influencing young children's developmental progress and the role of home–school partnerships, it does not specify means for providing ecological services. *Behavioral theory* focuses on behavioral principles of learning that can be applied in practice within an ecological framework (Sheridan et al., 1996). It is based on learning principles that guide human behavior. Behaviors are thought to be learned through interactions with the environment. The focus is on observable behaviors and identifying events that precede and maintain behaviors, rather than underlying "root" causes of behavior or personality traits. Of primary importance are efforts to understand environmental contingencies that maintain patterns of learning and behavior. Clearly defining target behaviors; setting specific, measurable goals; and implementing intervention strategies with empirical support are key features of behavioral approaches.

Combining ecological and behavioral approaches infuses behavioral assumptions and principles for addressing problem behaviors with a systemic focus on the contextual variables that influence a child's learning patterns. The primary objectives of an ecological–behavioral approach to early childhood consultation include (1) using a data-based approach to plan development, (2) implementing effective plans to address child-focused goals while meeting the needs of parents and educators, and (3) sustaining positive changes beyond termination of consultation (Sheridan & McCurdy, 2005).

Given the ecological approach to CBC, families are recognized as primary systems whose influence is not only recognized but also fostered. A family-centered approach to early childhood mental health and social–emotional services focuses on building strengths and capacities within families (Dunst, 2002). Furthermore, the unique and bidirectional influences of home and educational systems together are embraced in CBC. Thus, CBC employs a partnership-centered approach that fosters the unique roles and capacities of families, educators, and the relationships between the two. Within conjoint consultation, collaborative partnerships across home and school facilitate joint decision making and problem solving. Strengths of all parties and the strengths of the partnership are used to develop plans to promote behavioral change on behalf of the child. Through the establishment of a collegial partnership between parents and teachers, CBC consultants strive to create meaningful roles for families to support young children's learning, to promote continuity and consistency across systems, and to strengthen capacities on behalf of all participants (Sheridan & Kratochwill, 2008).

Parental engagement in early experiences has important implications for children's school readiness (Lamb-Parker, Boak, Griffin, Ripple, & Peay, 1999) and future academic success (Dieterich, Assel, Swank, Smith, & Landry, 2006; Hart & Risley, 1995). Especially for low-income, low-achieving children, Crosnoe, Leventhal, Wirth, Pierce, and Pianta (2010) found that stimulation in the home environment appears to be pivotal for changing negative achievement trajectories; these children benefited most from stimulation at home, in combination with other early childhood settings. Conditions within the home setting that establish opportunities for learning have been referred to as the "curriculum of the home" (Walberg, 1984). Providing opportunities for families to establish a meaningful role in making decisions for their children's education and learning strategies to enhance the curriculum of the home is a central feature of the CBC process. Engaging in the collaborative decision-making process, jointly setting child-related goals, and codeveloping plans to be carried out at both home and school are the means by which parents develop a meaningful role construct for engaging in their child's education through CBC.

Promoting continuity across home and school settings by establishing consistent expectations and endorsing similar values is an important aspect of the CBC process. Continuity across settings, characterized by smooth transitions across systems and high-quality relationships among important caregivers (e.g., families and educators), may serve as a protective factor for young children (Pianta & Walsh, 1996; Weissberg & Greenberg, 1998). Consistencies in positive stimulation across caregiving systems (i.e., family and school) and positive relationships among parents and professionals (e.g., early childhood teachers) may establish or deflect trajectories of early achievement (Crosnoe et al., 2010; Rimm-Kaufman & Pianta, 2000). High rates of early learning have been found among children who experienced consistencies in cognitive stimulation across multiple settings, but only when one of these settings was the home (Crosnoe et al., 2010). Jointly establishing goals and implementing collaboratively developed plans are methods used within the CBC process to help establish cross-setting consistency. Consultation strategies that allow participants to discuss differences in perspectives, encourage shared understanding of concerns, and point out and build on similarities across settings are additional methods used to promote continuity.

Procedural Specification

CBC is defined as an indirect model of service delivery whereby consultants facilitate the decision-making process and provide information, guidance, or training to promote capacity building on behalf of consultees. CBC is procedurally operationalized via a four-stage process implemented through consultant-led semistructured interviews. CBC procedural details have been documented in a manualized form (Sheridan & Kratochwill, 2008); the following section describes the content and process objectives of each stage.

Conjoint Needs Identification Stage

The initial stage of CBC focuses on identifying and prioritizing a child's target needs, operationally defining the target concern and developing data collection techniques. This stage is operationalized via the Conjoint Needs Identification Interview (CNII).

Determining the focus of consultation is a primary objective achieved by jointly select-ing priority behaviors across settings. Priority concerns are clearly specified and operation-ally defined in objective, measurable, behavioral terms to allow for direct observation of the target behavior. Data collection procedures that are feasible for parents and teachers to use in natural settings are specified to gather baseline levels from which goals are established and progress is evaluated. Identifying children's strengths, as well as the strengths and assets of the consultation team, is an important aspect of this stage. Pointing out similarities across settings, sharing perspectives, and building on strengths of the working relationship are critical to establishing partnerships. Identifying meaningful roles for parents in the decision-making process is accomplished by eliciting parents' perspectives on children's strengths and needs, and jointly determining priorities. Parents also participate in the data collection process by gathering information on the children's behaviors in the home setting as relevant to the consultation goals.

Conjoint Needs Analysis Stage

During the second stage of CBC, data are analyzed, a functional assessment identifying contextual and situational variables influencing the target concern is conducted, and home and school plans are developed. This stage is operationalized via the Conjoint Needs Analy-sis Interview (CNAI). Plans are codeveloped to address variables believed to be maintain-ing the target behavior across home and school settings. The role of the consultant is to ensure that research-based strategies are introduced to the consultation team; all members identify methods for implementing effective strategies in their own settings. Specific proce-dures for plan implementation are documented to promote fidelity of treatment implementa-tion. Establishing means for continued communication across home and school is critical to maintaining the partnership and facilitating continuity across contexts. As a result, home–school communication plans are routinely integrated into treatment plans.

Plan Implementation

As an indirect service model, parents and teachers serve as the primary treatment agents and are responsible for implementing treatment plans developed in consultation. The consultant serves to aid in treatment implementation by providing training around plan components as necessary, and monitoring treatment integrity and treatment effectiveness, as well as any potential side effects. Data continue to be collected throughout this stage to determine the effects of the treatment plan. Consultants help to identify potential barriers to treatment integrity, such as lack of clarity or competing events (e.g., other children in the home or classroom), and plans for addressing them. There is no formal CBC interview for the plan implementation stage; however, the aforementioned consultant activities are practiced to promote effective plan implementation. Frequent contact and communication with consult-ees is key during this stage.

Plan Evaluation

The last stage of CBC is the plan evaluation stage. During this stage, data collected through baseline and treatment phases are evaluated to determine progress toward consultation goals. The effectiveness and feasibility of the plan are evaluated, and plans for modification, generalization, and/or maintenance are discussed. Social validity (i.e., perceived effective-ness, goal attainment, satisfaction, acceptability) of the treatment plan, as well as the con-sultation process, is considered. The consultation team determines whether to terminate the consultation process or to continue with formal meetings. Plans for continued communication and partnering among the consultees are discussed. This final stage is operationalized via the Conjoint Plan Evaluation Interview (CPEI). Consultation teams may have several evaluation meetings until they determine that the previously agreed-upon goals have been met. They may also recycle through the previous stages of the process to address new behaviors, conduct another functional assessment to determine possible hypotheses for target behaviors, or develop new plans to address behaviors if goals have not been met.

Although the procedures specified here provide a concrete mechanism for implementing CBC, communication and interpersonal relationship-building strategies are critical to implementing early childhood consultation and CBC in a collaborative manner that will establish a working relationship among consultees. The manner by which consultation is provided is often overlooked, but it plays an important role in the effectiveness and social validity of the process. Interpersonal communication skills provide the means through which individuals create shared meanings via multiple and reciprocal communication channels (Friend & Cook, 2007). Such skills include summarizing and paraphrasing key statements, asking open questions to elicit information and perspective sharing, reflecting on underlying messages to convey understanding, perspective taking, and modeling positive communication. These strategies and others are specified within the CBC manual (Sheridan & Kratochwill, 2008).

A unique aspect of the CBC model is its focus on building home–school partnerships through a collaborative decision-making process. Along with assumptions targeting mechanisms of change inherent in the behavioral paradigm, it is presumed that the quality of the relationship between parents and teachers is responsible for (mediates) positive outcomes on behalf of the child. This suggests that desirable changes experienced by children as a result of consultation are due in part to the strength of the relationship that parents and teachers develop or exhibit throughout the process. Preliminary research has tested this theory. In a study of the effects of CBC for young children experiencing behavioral concerns, the parent–teacher relationship was found to mediate the effects of CBC on children's increased adaptive and social skills. The relationship was marginally significant as a mediator for children's improved externalizing behaviors (Sheridan, Glover, Bovaird, Garbacz, & Kwon, 2009). Based on these theories and the supporting evidence, change occurs for the child when the CBC process carefully identifies environmental variables that are manipulated through functional assessment and plan development, accomplished via enhanced home–school partnerships.

Research on CBC

Research has demonstrated that CBC is a socially valid, evidence-based consultation approach. Its clarity in both theoretical and procedural details provides a mechanism for specifying implementation of the CBC process with integrity and formal evaluation via efficacy studies. Meta-analyses and case studies have demonstrated that CBC is efficacious at addressing a range of primary learning and developmental concerns in early childhood (Sheridan, Clarke, Knoche, & Edwards, 2006) and school-age samples (Sheridan, Eagle, Cowan, & Mickelson, 2001). A review of parent consultation research conducted under the criteria specified in the *Procedural and Coding Manual of the Division 16 Task Force on Evidence-Based Intervention in School Psychology* (Kratochwill & Stoiber, 2002) found that CBC held promise as an evidence-based consultation model (Guli, 2005). Results of 4 years of federally funded CBC research demonstrated favorable outcomes for children using effect sizes calculated for home and school target behaviors, with an overall average effect size of 1.10 (*SD* = 1.07), home effect size of 1.08 (*SD* = 0.82), and school effect size of 1.11 (*SD* = 1.24) across various behavioral, academic, and social–emotional concerns (Sheridan et al., 2001). CBC has also been found to be an effective and socially valid consultation approach for diverse children (Sheridan, Eagle, & Doll, 2006).

One of the primary goals of CBC is to enhance and strengthen partnerships among primary caregivers through the process of consultation. Research investigating the process has revealed that CBC establishes a collaborative consultation process that promotes shared decision making, problem solving, and planning (Erchul et al., 1999; Sheridan, Meegan, & Eagle, 2002). CBC has also been found to be an acceptable (Freer & Watson, 1999; Sheridan & Steck, 1995; Sladeczek, Elliott, Kratochwill, Robertson-Mjaanes, & Stoiber, 2001) and helpful (Sheridan et al., 2004) consultation model by parents, teachers, and school psychologists. Goal attainment research revealed that parents and teachers perceive CBC to be effective in meeting consultation goals on behalf of the child (Sheridan et al., 2001).

As an early childhood consultation model, CBC has also been shown to be effective at addressing the behavioral, social–emotional, developmental, and preacademic concerns of young preschool children at-risk for future school difficulties. In a large meta-analysis testing the effects of CBC and generating effect sizes at home and school, Sheridan and colleagues (2001) found a significant interaction between child age and problem severity. Specifically, relative to older children (ages 8–10, and 11 and older) with varying levels of symptom severity, younger children (below the age of 8) with severe behavioral or social–emotional symptoms experienced the highest school-based effect sizes (2.33; *SD* = .84), followed by young children with moderately severe symptoms (effect size = 1.28; *SD* = .50). In a second study, single-subject designs were used to evaluate the effects of CBC for 48 individual children ages 6 and younger (Sheridan, Clarke, et al., 2006). Average effect sizes across home and school settings were 1.09. Median effect sizes were 0.97 at home (*SD* = 1.78) and 1.13 at school (*SD* = 1.44). Significant changes in parents' ratings of communication with teachers, and their overall relationship with teachers, were found as a function of CBC (*p*'s < .01). Furthermore, parents and teachers reported high levels of acceptability and satisfaction with the process.

These reviews demonstrate the effectiveness of CBC as a collaborative process that can be used in early childhood. Further examination of the CBC in a randomized clinical trial addressing behavioral concerns for young children (range, 5–8 years of age; *M* = 6 years) yielded similar results (Sheridan et al., in press). When compared to a control group, children who received CBC to address behavioral concerns had significant improvements in teacher-reported behavior problems. They also demonstrated significant improvements in externalizing problems and in adaptive and social skills (all *p*'s < .05) relative to control children. Parents who participated in CBC reported significant improvement in parent engagement in their children's education and home–school communication compared to parents who did not participate. Teachers also reported improvements in parent–teacher relationships and beliefs about parent participation (Sheridan et al., 2009).

Aims for the Future

Children's social–emotional development impacts all aspects of their lives and there is considerable evidence linking these to the quality of teacher–child and parent–child relationships. Therefore, when concerns or problem behaviors arise, meaningful participation of adults (parents and teachers) who have the most influence on children's development is critical. Early childhood consultation provides a framework for professionals to partner with caregivers to address child-focused concerns systematically.

Empirical support for early childhood consultation has increased in recent years. Nevertheless, inconsistent definitions, procedural questions, and quasi-experimentation plague the literature. Only recently has the inclusion of rigorous studies evaluating the efficacy of consultation for young children been evident in the peer-reviewed literature. As evidenced, early childhood consultation is a promising practice for addressing the social, emotional, and behavioral needs of young children. However, much more targeted research is necessary. Below we articulate an agenda for future research in early childhood consultation.

Perhaps the first essential step for both research and practice is to define early childhood consultation operationally. Research reviews suggest the current use of highly eclectic approaches, in which consultation is often a menu of possible activities and services. This creates complications from a research perspective, as it becomes difficult to tease out critical elements of consultation that impact teacher, student, or family outcomes. From a practice perspective, it creates difficulties for consultants who are uncertain where to place their efforts and often fall into the role of a coach or a direct service provider.

Rigorous research methods, including randomized controlled trials to examine the effectiveness of early childhood consultation, can help answer questions related to defining an effective model of consultation for early childhood settings. Researchers interested in studying early childhood consultation should develop a theory of change articulating *how* consultation impacts outcomes. Many studies currently describe a range of consultation activities, including teacher stress reduction, direct therapy for children and parents, teacher training, and coaching. Often there is not a clear description of the intended link between the consultation focus and potential outcomes, for whom, and under what conditions. A well-developed theory of change can help as researchers try to identify the causal features or critical aspects (mediators) influencing consultation's effects, as well as indicate characteristics of and roles for effective consultants.

The lack of well-developed measures for monitoring outcomes and assessing the early childhood consultation process also plagues consultation research. Many tools currently being used to measure processes and outcomes are teacher surveys and teacher or parent ratings of child behaviors. There are few direct measures of teacher, student, and parent outcomes. Additionally, there is a need for more tools to measure other aspects that may impact consultation's effects (e.g., changes in teacher knowledge, perceptions of the process, and perception of self-efficacy in addressing concerns), and factors that may moderate its effectiveness (e.g., teacher, child, or parent characteristics; plan implementation fidelity).

In addition to research on the efficacy of early childhood consultation in general, further research on innovative modes for providing consultation services is critical as the number of young children in early childhood settings grows each year, creating a need to support larger numbers of teachers and staff. Preliminary evidence on MTP suggests promise for Web-based consultation. As discussed throughout this chapter, involvement of parents as partners in the process of problem solving and development of plans to address children's needs is critical. As researchers further examine the efficacy of Web-based consultation, it will be important to consider the potential for inclusion of parents.

In practice, early childhood settings can capitalize on what is known from current research and provide training and support to consultants. Research from school-age consultation is more developed than that available in the early childhood literature, and can provide some insight. Use of an indirect model of consultation that incorporates a systematic process for defining and analyzing concerns in context, for natural treatment agents (teachers and parents) to develop a plan and systematically evaluate its effects, can have a broader impact than provision of direct services alone. Indeed, one of the intended outcomes of consultation is to build the capacity of consultees to address future concerns. A collaborative partnership-driven role versus an expert-driven one may facilitate engagement of consultees in the process and improve adherence to intervention plans. It is also well accepted that involving parents in the process of defining children's concerns, examining the factors that may be impacting behavior, and developing a plan for addressing them are highly valued, effective practices that build parental capacity to deal with early childhood developmental concerns (Sheridan, Clarke, et al., 2006).

Consultation practice requires specialized skills and knowledge. Often consultants in early childhood settings are ill-prepared to work with teachers and parents through a systematic process for addressing children's needs (Wesley et al., 2001). It is essential that early childhood settings clearly define the role of the consultant, and provide training and support to carry out their role. Researchers should continue to explore consultation elements most predictive of desired effects for children's learning and behavior, as well as for parents' and teachers' skills development and practice.

In this chapter, we have presented CBC as a potential model of early childhood consultation. CBC incorporates theoretically sound, developmentally appropriate, empirically supported features and addresses some of the current issues with consultation in early childhood settings. It provides a clear definition of consultation, defines the role of the consultant, and outlines procedures for the consultation process. Additionally, it provides a family-centered approach that brings together school and home systems to support children. Initial research on the application of CBC in early childhood settings has produced favorable effect sizes for child behavioral outcomes and high social validity ratings on acceptability of the process by parents and teachers. Though further research on its utilization in early childhood settings is needed, CBC shows promise as a model of early childhood consultation to support the academic, behavioral, and social development of young children.

References

Alkon, A., Ramler, M., & MacLennan, K. (2003). Evaluation of mental health intervention in child care centers. *Early Childhood Education Journal, 31*, 91–99.

Bean, B. J., Biss, C. A., & Hepburn, K. S. (2007). Vermont's Children UPstream Project: Statewide early childhood mental health services and supports. In D. Perry, R. Kaufmann, & J. Knitzer (Eds.), *Social and emotional health in early childhood* (pp. 169–188). Baltimore: Brookes.

Bergan, J. R. (1977). *Behavioral consultation.* Columbus, OH: Merrill.

Bergan, J. R., & Kratochwill, T. R. (1990). *Behavioral consultation in applied settings.* New York: Plenum.

Brauner, C. B., & Stephens, C. B. (2006). Estimating the prevalence of early childhood serious emotional/behavioral disorders: Challenges and recommendations. *Public Health Report, 121,* 303–310.

Brennan, E. M., Bradley, J. R., Allen, M. D., & Perry, D. F. (2008). The evidence base for mental health consultation in early childhood settings: Research synthesis addressing staff and program outcomes. *Early Education and Development, 19*, 982–1022.

Bronfenbrenner, U. (1977). Toward an experimental ecology of human development. *American Psychologist, 32*, 513–531.

Caplan, G. (1963). Types of mental health consultation. *American Journal of Orthopsychiatry, 33*, 470–481.

Carlton, M. P., & Winsler, A. (1999). School readiness: The need for a paradigm shift. *School Psychology Review, 28*, 338–352.

Cohen, E., & Kaufmann, R. (2005). *Early childhood mental health consultation.* Washington, DC: Center for Mental Health Services of the Substance Abuse and Mental Health Services Administration and the Georgetown University Child Development Center.

Comer, J. P., & Haynes, N. M. (1991). Parent involvement in schools: An ecological approach. *Elementary School Journal, 91*, 271–277.

Cooper, J. L., Masi, R., & Vick, J. (2009). *Social–emotional development in early childhood: What every policymaker should know*. New York: National Center for Children in Poverty, Mailman School of Public Health, Columbia University. Retrieved from *www.nccp.org/publications/pdf/text_882.pdf*.

Crosnoe, R., Leventhal, T., Wirth, R. J., Pierce, K. M., & Pianta, R. C. (2010). Family socioeconomic status and consistent environmental stimulation in early childhood. *Child Development, 81*, 972–987.

Denham, S. A., & Weissberg, R. P. (2004). Social–emotional learning in early childhood: What we know and where to go from here. In E. Chesebrough, P. King, T. P. Gullotta, & M. Bloom (Eds.), *A blueprint for the promotion of prosocial behavior in early childhood* (pp. 13–50). New York: Kluwer Academic/Plenum Press.

Dieterich, S., Assel, M., Swank, P., Smith, K., & Landry, S. (2006). The impact of early maternal verbal scaffolding and child language abilities on later decoding and reading comprehension skills. *Journal of School Psychology, 43*, 481–494.

Dougherty, M. (2008). *Psychological consultation and collaboration in school and community settings: A casebook* (5th ed.). Belmont, CA: Brooks/Cole.

Downer, J. T., Kraft-Sayre, M., & Pianta, R. C. (2009). On-going, web-mediated professional development focused on teacher–child interactions: Feasibility of use with early childhood educators. *Early Education and Development, 20*, 321–345.

Dunst, C. J. (2002). Family-centered practices: Birth through high school. *Journal of Special Education, 36*(3), 139–147.

Duran, F., Hepburn, K., Kaufmann, R., Le, L., Allen, M. D., Brennan, E., et al. (n.d.). *Research synthesis: Early childhood mental health consultation*. Nashville, TN: Center on the Social and Emotional Foundations for Early Learning.

Erchul, W. P., & Martens, B. K. (2010). *School consultation: Conceptual and empirical bases of practice*. New York: Springer.

Erchul, W. P., & Sheridan, S. M. (Eds.). (2008). *Handbook of research in school consultation: Empirical foundations for the field*. New York: Erlbaum.

Erchul, W. P., Sheridan, S. M., Ryan, D. A., Grissom, P. F., Killough, C. E., & Mettler, D. W. (1999). Patterns of relational control in conjoint behavioral consultation. *School Psychology Quarterly, 14*, 121–147.

Fan, X., & Chen, M. (2001). Parental involvement and students' academic achievement: A meta-analysis. *Educational Psychology Review, 13*, 1–22.

Freer, P., & Watson, T. S. (1999). A comparison of parent and teacher acceptability ratings of behavioral and conjoint behavioral consultation. *School Psychology Review, 28*, 672–684.

Friend, M., & Cook, L. (2007). *Interactions: Collaboration skills for school professionals* (5th ed.). Boston: Allyn & Bacon.

Gilliam, W. S. (2007). *Early childhood consultation partnership: Results of a random-controlled evaluation: Final report and executive summary*. New Haven, CT: Yale School of Medicine.

Greenberg, M. T., Kusche, C. A., Cook, E. T., & Quamma, J. P. (1995). Promoting emotional competence in school-aged children: The effects of the PATHS curriculum. *Development and Psychopathology, 7*, 117–136.

Guli, L. A. (2005). Evidence-based parent consultation with school-related outcomes. *School Psychology Quarterly, 20*, 455–472.

Gutkin, T. B., & Curtis, M. J. (1990). School-based consultation: Theory, techniques, and research. In T. B. Gutkin & C. R. Reynolds (Eds.), *The handbook of school psychology* (2nd ed., pp. 577–611). New York: Wiley.

Hart, T., & Risley, B. (1995). *Meaningful differences in the everyday experiences of young American children*. Baltimore: Brookes.

Henderson, A. T., & Mapp, K. L. (2002). *A new wave of evidence: The impact of school, family, and community connections on student achievement*. Austin, TX: Southwest Educational Development Laboratory.

Hill, N. E. (2001). Parenting and academic socialization as they relate to school readiness: The roles of ethnicity and family income. *Journal of Educational Psychology, 93*, 686–697.

James Bowman Associates, & Kagan, S. L. (2003). *Evaluation report on mental health consultation to childcare centers.* San Francisco: Jewish Family and Children's Services.

Justice, L., Pullen, P., Hall, S., & Pianta, R. (2003). *Curry School Curriculum for Early Literacy and Oral Language Support.* Unpublished document, University of Virginia, Charlottesville.

Kelleher, C., Riley-Tillman, T. C., & Power, T. J. (2008). An initial comparison of collaborative and expert-driven consultation on treatment integrity. *Journal of Educational and Psychological Consultation, 18,* 294–324.

Kratochwill, T. R., & Stoiber, K. C. (2002). Evidence-based interventions in school psychology: Conceptual foundations of the procedural and coding manual of Division 16 and the Society for the Study of School Psychology Task Force. *School Psychology Quarterly, 17,* 341–389.

Lamb-Parker, F., Boak, A. Y., Griffin, K. W., Ripple, C., & Peay, L. (1999). Parent–child relationship, home learning environment, and school readiness. *School Psychology Review, 28,* 413–425.

Lavigne, J. V., Gibbons, R. D., Christoffel, K. K., Arend, R., Rosenbaum, D., Binns, H., et al. (1996). Prevalence rates and correlates of psychiatric disorders among preschool children. *Journal of the American Academy of Child and Adolescent Psychiatry, 35,* 204–214.

Mahoney, G., Boyce, G., Fewell, R. R., Spiker, D., & Wheeden, C. A. (1998). The relationship of parent–child interaction to the effectiveness of early intervention services for at-risk children and children with disabilities. *Topics in Early Childhood Special Education, 18,* 5–17.

Mahoney, G., & MacDonald, J. (2007). *Autism and developmental delays in young children: The Responsive Teaching curriculum for parents and professionals.* Austin, TX: Pro-Ed.

Mahoney, G., & Powell, A. (1988). Modifying parent–child interaction: Enhancing the development of handicapped children. *Journal of Special Education, 22,* 82–96.

McCollum, J. A., Gooler, F., Appl, D., & Yates, T. J. (2001). PIWI: Enhancing parent–child interaction as a foundation for early intervention. *Infants and Young Children, 14,* 34–45.

McCollum, J. A., & Yates, T. J. (1994). Dyad as focus, triad as means: A family-centered approach to supporting parent–child interactions. *Infants and Young Children, 6,* 54–63.

McWayne, C., Hampton, V., Fantuzzo, J., Cohen, H., & Sekino, Y. (2004). A multivariate examination of parent involvement and the social and academic competencies of urban kindergarten children. *Psychology in the Schools, 41,* 1–15.

Nastasi, B., Varjas, K., Schensul, S. L., Silva, K. T., Schensul, J. J., & Ratnayake, P. (2000). The participatory intervention model: A framework for conceptualizing and promoting intervention acceptability. *School Psychology Quarterly, 15,* 207–232.

Nikkel, P. (2007). Building partnerships with families. In D. F. Perry, R. K. Kaufmann, & J. Knitzer (Eds.), *Social and emotional health in early childhood: Building bridges between services and systems* (pp. 151–172). Baltimore: Brookes.

Patterson, G. R., DeBaryshe, B. D., & Ramsey, E. (1989). A developmental perspective on antisocial behavior. *American Psychologist, 44,* 329–335.

Perry, D. F., Allen, M. D., Brennan, E. M., & Bradley, J. R. (2010). The evidence base for mental health consultation in early childhood settings: A research synthesis addressing children's behavioral outcomes. *Early Education and Development, 21,* 795–824.

Perry, D. F., Dunne, M. C., McFadden, L., & Campbell, D. (2008). Reducing the risk for preschool expulsion: Mental health consultation for young children with challenging behaviors. *Journal of Child and Family Studies, 17,* 44–54.

Phelan, P., Davidson, A. L., & Yu, H. C. (1998). *Adolescents' worlds: Negotiating family, peers, and schools.* New York: Teachers College Press.

Pianta, R., Mashburn, A., Downer, J., Hamre, B., & Justice, L. (2008). Effects of web-mediated professional development resources on teacher–child interactions in pre-kindergarten classrooms. *Early Childhood Research Quarterly, 23,* 431–451.

Pianta, R. C., La Paro, K. M., & Hamre, B. K. (2008). *Classroom Assessment Scoring System (CLASS).* Baltimore: Brookes.

Pianta, R. C., & Walsh, D. J. (1996). *High risk children in the schools: Creating sustaining relationships.* New York: Routledge.

Raver, C. C., Jones, S. M., Li-Grining, C., Zhai, F., Metzger, M. W., & Solomon, B. (2009). Targeting children's behavior problems in preschool classrooms: A cluster-randomized controlled trail. *Journal of Consulting and Clinical Psychology, 77,* 302–316.

Rimm-Kaufman, S. E., & Pianta, R. C. (2000). An ecological perspective on the transition to kindergarten: A theoretical framework to guide empirical research. *Journal of Applied Developmental Psychology, 21,* 491–511.

Sattes, B. D. (1985). *Parent involvement: A review of the literature.* Charleston, WV: Appalachia Educational Laboratory.

Schulte, A. C., & Osborne, S. S. (2003). When assumptive worlds collide: A review of definitions of collaboration in consultation. *Journal of Educational and Psychological Consultation, 14,* 109–138.

Schulting, A. B., Malone, P. S., & Dodge, K. A. (2005). The effect of school-based kindergarten transition policies and practices on child academic outcomes. *Developmental Psychology, 41,* 860–871.

Senechal, M. (2006). Testing the home literacy model: Parent involvement in kindergarten is differentially related to grade 4 reading comprehension, fluency, spelling, and reading for pleasure. *Scientific Studies of Reading, 10,* 59–87.

Sheridan, S. M., Bovaird, J. A., Glover, T. A., Garbacz, S. A., Witte, A., & Kwon, K. (in press). A randomized trial examining the effects of conjoint behavioral consultation and the mediating role of the parent–teacher relationship. *School Psychology Review.*

Sheridan, S. M., Clarke, B. L., Knoche, L. L., & Edwards, C. P. (2006). The effects of conjoint behavioral consultation in early childhood settings. *Early Education and Development, 17,* 593–617.

Sheridan, S. M., Eagle, J. W., Cowan, R. J., & Mickelson, W. (2001). The effects of conjoint behavioral consultation: Results of a four-year investigation. *Journal of School Psychology, 39,* 361–385.

Sheridan, S. M., Eagle, J. W., & Doll, B. (2006). An examination of the efficacy of conjoint behavioral consultation with diverse clients. *School Psychology Quarterly, 21,* 396–417.

Sheridan, S. M., Erchul, W. P., Brown, M. S., Dowd, S. E., Warnes, E. D., Marti, D. C., et al. (2004). Perceptions of helpfulness in conjoint behavioral consultation: Congruity and agreement between teachers and parents. *School Psychology Quarterly, 19,* 121–140.

Sheridan, S. M., Glover, T., Bovaird, J. A., Garbacz, S. A., & Kwon, K. (2009, June). *Conjoint behavioral consultation: Effects on student behaviors and family–school outcomes.* Paper presented at the Annual Research Conference of the Institute of Education Sciences, U.S. Department of Education, Washington, DC.

Sheridan, S. M., & Gutkin, T. B. (2000). The ecology of school psychology: Examining and changing our paradigm for the 21st century. *School Psychology Review, 29,* 485–502.

Sheridan, S. M., & Kratochwill, T. R. (2008). *Conjoint behavioral consultation: Promoting family-school connections and interventions.* New York: Springer.

Sheridan, S. M., Kratochwill, T. R., & Bergan, J. R. (1996). *Conjoint behavioral consultation: A procedural manual.* New York: Plenum Press.

Sheridan, S. M., & McCurdy, M. (2005). Ecological variables in school-based assessment and intervention planning. In R. Brown-Chidsey (Ed.), *Assessment for intervention: A problem-solving approach* (pp. 43–64). New York: Guilford Press.

Sheridan, S. M., Meegan, S., & Eagle, J. W. (2002). Exploring the social context in conjoint behavioral consultation: Linking processes to outcomes. *School Psychology Quarterly, 17,* 299–324.

Sheridan, S. M., & Steck, M. (1995). Acceptability of conjoint behavioral consultation: A national survey of school psychologists. *School Psychology Review, 24,* 633–647.

Shonkoff, J. P., & Phillips, D. (2000). *From neurons to neighborhoods.* Washington, DC: National Academy Press.

Sladeczek, I. E., Elliott, S. N., Kratochwill, T. R., Robertson-Mjaanes, S., & Stoiber, K. C. (2001). Application of goal attainment scaling to a conjoint behavioral consultation case. *Journal of Educational and Psychological Consultation, 12,* 45–59.

Turner, L. A., & Burke, J. (2003). A model of mastery motivation for at-risk preschoolers. *Journal of Educational Psychology, 95,* 495–505.

Upshur, C., Wenz-Gross, M., & Reed, G. (2009). A pilot study of early childhood mental health consultation for children with behavioral problems in preschool. *Early Childhood Research Quarterly, 24*, 29–45.

Walberg, H. (1984). Families as partners in educational productivity. *Phi Delta Kappan, 65*, 397–400.

Webster-Stratton, C., & Reid, M. J. (1999a, November). *Treating children with early-onset conduct problems: The importance of teacher training.* Paper presented at the annual meeting of the American Association of Behavior Therapy, Toronto, ON, Canada.

Webster-Stratton, C., & Reid, M. J. (1999b, June). *Effects of teacher training in Head Start classrooms: Results of a randomized controlled evaluation.* Paper presented at the annual meeting of the Society for Prevention Research, New Orleans, LA.

Webster-Stratton, C., Reid, M. J., & Hammond, M. (2001). Preventing conduct problems, promoting social competence: A parent and teacher training partnership in Head Start. *Journal of Clinical Child Psychology, 30*, 283–302.

Weigel, D. J., Martin, S. S., & Bennett, K. K. (2006). Contributions of the home literacy environment to preschool-aged children's emerging literacy and language skills. *Early Child Development and Care, 176*, 357–378.

Weissberg, R. P., & Greenberg, M. T. (1998). School and community competence-enhancement and prevention programs. In I. Siegel & A. Renninger (Eds.), *Handbook of child psychology* (5th ed., pp. 877–954). New York: Wiley.

Wesley, P. W., Buysse, V., & Skinner, D. (2001). Early interventionists' perspectives on professional comfort as consultants. *Journal of Early Intervention, 24*, 112–128.

Williford, A. P., & Shelton, T. L. (2008). Using mental health consultation to decrease disruptive behaviors in preschoolers: Adapting an empirically-supported intervention. *Journal of Child Psychology and Psychiatry, 49*, 191–200.

Zins, J. E., & Elias, M. J. (2006). Social and emotional learning. In G. G. Bear & K. M. Minke (Eds.), *Children's needs III: Development, prevention, and intervention* (pp. 1–13). Bethesda, MD: National Association of School Psychologists.

PART IV

BUILDING SYSTEMS OF EFFECTIVE EARLY INTERVENTION SUPPORTS

Meeting the Needs of Diverse Children and the Adults Who Serve Them

CHAPTER 22

Implications of Research on Postinstitutionalized Children for Practice and Policy in Early Education

Jamie M. Lawler and Megan R. Gunnar

T he fields of early child development and education have a rich history of drawing inspiration from studies of institutionally reared infants and toddlers. Early studies by Dennis, Spitz, Provence and Lipton, and Tizard (for reviews, see Gunnar, 2001; Rutter, 1981) documented the poor development of infants and young children in institutions, and contributed to our understanding of the importance of attachment relationships for early social development, and stimulation for motor and cognitive development. Regarding policy, these early studies formed the basis for the establishment of foster care and the closing of baby homes and orphanages in the United States and other Western countries.

Nonetheless, the lessons learned in earlier eras sometimes need relearning. We are relearning these lessons on several fronts. First, increases of infants and toddlers in child protection and decreases in availability of foster homes have led some jurisdictions to establish residential nurseries. Although these are supposed to be temporary placements, infants and toddlers sometimes stay from 6 months to over a year. Recent studies have once again shown that, compared to children in foster care, infants and toddlers in residential nurseries have delayed mental development and adaptive skills (Harden, 2002). Second, in the 1990s, families began to adopt increasing numbers of children from institutions overseas in a "natural" experiment of the potential for families to reverse any negative impact of early institutional care (Gunnar, Bruce, & Grotevant, 2000). At its peak in the United States, nearly 23,000 international children were adopted in 1 year (2004), with the vast majority coming from countries using institutional care. The economic recession and changing practices in several key referring countries have slowed this flow, with 2009 seeing only 12,800 international adoptions into the United States (U.S. Department of State, 2009). Although the majority (80–90%) of these children are adopted under age 4, rarely do those adopted from institutional settings reach their families before 10–12 months of age, and most have spent nearly all of their preadoption lives in some kind of institutional setting (Gunnar et al., 2000).

The children from this new wave of institutional adoption have been the focus of considerable research. In this chapter we review current findings, placing them in the context of earlier work. Although results of current research largely confirm earlier findings, the use of standardized instruments and meta-analytic procedures, and the increasing use of methods from developmental behavioral neuroscience have helped to hone our understanding of both the promise and the limits of the young child's capacity to rebound once removed from institutional deprivation. A theme that runs throughout this review is that if placed in supportive families within the first 6 months or so, postinstitutionalized (PI) children are often indistinguishable on measures of cognitive and social development from never-institutionalized children. Beyond 6 months, differences are increasingly reported even years following adoption. These findings support the idea that many of the higher-order processes being studied do have sensitive periods in early development. However, it is not at all clear what these periods are, how long they extend, how they may relate to the degree of and specific components of deprivation experienced, and, critically for intervention, whether particular postadoption intervention strategies might mitigate noted deficits. As would be expected given our current understanding of brain development, what does seem apparent is that the adoption age beyond which long-term impacts of early institutional care are likely to be observed differs for different outcomes, being strikingly early for some (e.g., optimal development of attention regulation and inhibitory control) and strikingly late (if there is one at all) for others (e.g., the capacity to form discriminating attachments to adoptive parents). There is another theme that also runs through all of the research, both old and new; specifically, virtually regardless of how affected the child appears to be at adoption, unless there is evidence of frank neurological defects (e.g., fetal alcohol syndrome, cerebral palsy, Down syndrome), the range of outcomes is as striking as the increase in risk of poorer outcomes with duration and degree of deprivation. Even under conditions of horrifically deprived early care, a remarkable percentage of children appear to have no significant problems several years postadoption. This speaks to the power of families in the healthy development of children (van IJzendoorn & Juffer, 2006).

The heterogeneity of outcomes for PI children reflects a well-known phenomenon termed "multifinality" in developmental psychopathology (Cicchetti & Rogosch, 1996). Multifinality is the concept that one etiological factor can lead to any of many possible outcomes, depending on the person and context. This heterogeneity has occasioned recent interest in genes and gene × experience interactions in explaining these individual differences. Because these studies are still few and there are no replications of findings that we know of, we do not review this work. The heterogeneity of outcomes, however, also cautions us to avoid limiting expectations for the development of the individual PI child based on evidence from group analyses. Although we continue throughout this review to point out the variability in outcomes in each domain we discuss, it is all too easy to fall into a shorthand that fosters expectations that *all* PI children exhibit the deficits or delays that have been identified.

With these points in mind, we attempt in the following review very succinct overviews of three domains of development for PI children: health issues and physical effects, cognitive development, and socioemotional development. Once we have reviewed all three domains, we end with a section on policy, research, and practice implications.

Physical Effects of Institutionalization

At adoption, PI children often have numerous physical problems. These problems include medical issues, growth delays, altered endocrine activity, and immature brain wave activity. Many of these issues ameliorate within a year or two after adoption; some, however, persist.

Institutional care clearly contributes to these problems, as physical problems are more common among children adopted from institutions than from foster care, even from the same native country (Miller, Chan, Comfort, & Tirella, 2005). Here we briefly summarize key findings.

Physical Health and Growth

The likelihood of serious medical problems varies with the degree of preadoption deprivation. In one study of children adopted from conditions of profound institutional deprivation, 85% had one or more medical problem (Fisher, Ames, Chisholm, & Savoie, 1997). Common problems include intestinal parasites, infectious diseases (e.g., hepatitis B) and iron deficiency (Johnson, 2001). Although most medical problems improve with treatment, PI children have been reported to have more health issues than family-reared children several years after adoption (Fisher et al., 1997; Groze & Ileana, 1996). Some of these problems are related to prenatal alcohol exposure, which is relatively common, especially for children adopted from Russia and Eastern Europe (e.g., Landgren et al., 2006; Miller et al., 2007). For some of the cognitive and neurological outcomes discussed in this chapter, disentangling the effects due to alcohol exposure from those due to institutional deprivation is challenging, particularly when exposure is suspected but cannot be verified.

PI children are often small for their age at adoption, with a significant number being extremely small. Indeed, it is common to find an average two standard deviations below the mean, which meets criteria for stunted growth (Loman, Wiik, Frenn, Pollak, & Gunnar, 2009; Rutter and the English and Romanian Adoptees Study Team, 1998). Both the degree and duration of deprivation are related to growth delay, with children falling behind by 1 month in growth for every 3 months in institutional care by one estimate (Miller & Hendrie, 2000). The typical pattern is for weight to be proportional to height, but for height to be stunted; this pattern is sometimes termed "psychosocial dwarfism" to reflect evidence that lack of attention and affection are as much the cause as lack of adequate nutrition (Johnson, 2000).

Once adopted, PI children grow rapidly, achieving growth parameters within the normal range, albeit still smaller than the mean for age, within a year or two (Johnson, 2000; Loman et al., 2009). Examining a series of cross-sectional studies, Van IJzendoorn, Bakermans-Kranenburg, and Juffer (2007) concluded that catch-up growth continues throughout childhood; however, when children are followed longitudinally into adolescence, it appears that their continued catch-up actually may have been due to an earlier pubertal growth spurt (Sonuga-Barke, Schlotz, & Rutter, 2010; see also Virdis et al., 1998). Especially for girls, puberty onset may be advanced 1 or more years (Mason & Narad, 2005b). Once through puberty, PI children tend to reach an adult height that is significantly shorter than their peers (Sonuga-Barke, Scholtz, & Rutter, 2010).

Neuroendocrine Effects

Studies of the effects of institutional care on endocrine function are just beginning; although these effects would be expected given growth stunting (i.e., growth-related hormones) and early puberty (i.e., pubertal hormones; see Teilmann, et al., 2009). The hypothalamic–pituitary–adrenocortical (HPA) system, a stress-sensitive neuroendocrine system, has been the most studied. At basal levels, the HPA system plays multiple roles in supporting healthy functioning of the body and brain. In response to physical or emotional threat, this system increases its activity in support of shifting the brain and body into an immediate defense mode and ensures that other threat-activated systems do not overshoot. Both hyper- and hypofunctioning of the HPA system impairs health and cognitive functioning (Gunnar, Bruce, & Hickman, 2001). Long-term stress and chronic early deprivation alter the functioning of the HPA system in animal models (e.g., Higley & Suomi, 1992). Children living in poverty (Lupien, King, Meaney, & McEwen, 2001), as well as maltreated children (De Bellis et al., 1999), show abnormal functioning of the HPA system, indicated by measures of cortisol, the hormone it produces. Abnormal regulation of the HPA axis is also observed in depression and posttraumatic stress disorder (Gunnar & Fisher, 2006).

The HPA system exhibits a daily rhythm, with peak levels around awakening that decrease to very low levels by bedtime. Children living in institutions do not show the typical daily cortisol rhythm (Carlson & Earls, 1997). After adoption, the normal rhythm begins to be reestablished, but adopted children from the most deprived conditions produce higher levels of this hormone than do nonadopted children or children adopted very early in life (Gunnar, Morison, Chisholm, & Schuder, 2001). Elevated levels are most often observed in children with severe growth delays at the time of adoption (Kertes, Gunnar, Madsen, & Long, 2008).

Not only everyday levels but also stress responses of the HPA system may be greater in PI children. In one study, PI preschoolers were assessed after interacting with either a parent or an unfamiliar adult. Cortisol levels increased after parent–child interaction and remained elevated up to several hours (Wismer Fries, Shirtcliff, & Pollak, 2008). These researchers also examined levels of oxytocin and vasopressin, hormones associated with social bonding (Wismer Fries, Ziegler, Kurian, Jacoris, & Pollak, 2005). PI children, compared to nonadopted children, had lower levels of vasopressin and failed to exhibit an oxytocin increase following interaction with their mothers. These neuroendocrine abnormalities likely mediate some of the effects of institutional deprivation. For example, the HPA system has a profound influence on growth processes and is likely one of the mechanism causing psychosocial dwarfism in institutionalized children (Mason & Narad, 2005a).

Neurobiological Effects

Despite its importance for understanding why some children show persisting effects of institutional deprivation and others do not, researchers have only recently begun examining brain structure and functioning in PI children. In the past, head circumference was used as a rough estimate of the effect of deprivation on the brain. As already noted, children adopted from institutions often have smaller head growth. Although there is considerable catch-up in head growth following adoption, it is less so than that for height and weight, and is far from complete for some children. Indeed, head circumference of PI children adopted from extremely severe institutional deprivation at 15 years remained on average nearly a full standard deviation below age norms (Sonuga-Barke, Schlotz, & Rutter, 2010).

Recently researchers have begun to use structural brain imaging to study the effects of early institutional deprivation. PI children, who as a group scored poorly on tasks of executive functioning and emotion regulation, also showed less brain activity (i.e., decreased glucose metabolism) in regions of the prefrontal cortex and medial temporal region (e.g., hippocampus; Chugani et al., 2001). They also showed less white matter in areas of the brain that provide connections between regions involved in emotion regulation (Eluvathingal et al., 2006). PI children also had significantly smaller superior-posterior cerebellar lobes, with volume of this area mediating performance on neuropsychological test. Taken together these studies underscore the profound effect that institutional deprivation may have on the developing brain.

Further neurobiological evidence comes from the Bucharest Early Intervention Project (BEIP; Zeanah et al., 2003). This is a remarkable study involving the random assignment of institutionalized children, ages 6–31 months, to "care as usual" versus placement in foster care designed and supported by the research study. It was possible to do this study because, at the time of random assignment, Romania had no foster care system. A comparison group of Romanian never-institutionalized children was also assessed (Zeanah et al., 2003). Just prior to randomization, measures were obtained of brain electrical activity [i.e., electroencephalography (EEG) and event-related potentials (ERPs)]. At 6–31 months the children in the institution showed less brain activity in higher EEG frequencies than comparison children, suggesting either hypoactivation of the brain or delayed brain development (for a review, see Nelson, 2007). Children who remained in the institution continued to demonstrate a general cortical hypoactivation compared to community children; however, foster care was at least partially effective in ameliorating this problem (Moulson, Fox, Zeanah, & Nelson, 2009; Moulson, Westerlund, Fox, Zeanah, & Nelson, 2009). At 8 years, foster placement resulted in higher EEG frequencies, especially for children placed before age 24 months (Vanderwert, Marshall, Nelson, Zeanah, & Fox, 2010).

Summary of Physical Effects

The physical effects of institutionalization are extensive, and resent research suggests that they are more persistent than previously thought. PI children are at heightened risk for a plethora of medical problems and experience psychosocial growth delays. Although post-adoption catch-up in height and weight seems nearly complete by middle childhood, this may be a function of earlier pubertal onset in PI children. Early deprivation has a profound effect on the developing HPA stress axis, with abnormalities in both basal and stress responses of this system that may continue years after adoption. Children adopted from institutions also show smaller head circumference (a marker of total brain volume) and structural abnormalities in several brain areas associated with higher cognitive functions and emotions. Finally, institutionalization decreases children's overall brain activity, which is somewhat, but not completely, ameliorated by removal from the institution. However, as with all the other data reported in this chapter, there are large individual differences, and not all PI children exhibit these effects.

Cognitive Effects of Institutionalization

Considering the significant effects of early institutional care on brain development, it is not surprising that PI children are at risk for cognitive deficits. Deficits have been documented in language, executive function, and scholastic achievement. Recovery of these competencies is profound following adoption, but the degree of initial deficit and the extent to which children recover vary greatly by child. Heterogeneity in outcome means that averages are not always representative; whereas some PI children show above average intelligence, others remain significantly impaired. Nonetheless, averages help us to see areas where PI children are at heightened risk for delays.

Cognitive and Language Delays

Studies in the 1930s and 1940s found that children who had experienced institutional care showed profound deficits in IQ (e.g., Spitz, Goldfarb; see a review by MacLean, 2003). These studies led to the view that institutional care necessarily suppresses cognitive development. This is not the case. If the institution provides its charges with high-quality intellectual and social stimulation, intellectual development proceeds fairly typically. This was shown by Tizard and colleagues (see a review by Gunnar, 2001), who studied children living in residential nurseries in Great Britain. These institutions provided adequate nutrition, medical care, appropriate levels of stimulation, and relatively low caregiver–child ratios. As a training site for nurses, however, the turnover rate of the caregivers was quite high, and the caregivers were instructed to avoid forming attachments to the children. Tizard and colleagues found that children in these institutions had normal language development and IQ, and this continued to be the case when they were followed up to 16 years after foster care or adoption at about age 2.

What about institutions that do not provide adequate stimulation and those in which developmentally appropriate physical and social stimulation is profoundly lacking? Frequently cited is the claim that children adopted before age 24 months are capable of making a full recovery in IQ, while children adopted after 2 years never fully catch up; however, this has not been adequately tested (MacLean, 2003). A long-term longitudinal study, led by Michael Rutter, followed children adopted between birth and 42 months of age from Romania immediately after the fall of communism in 1989. The comparison group in this study consisted of domestically adopted children, all of whom were adopted before 6 months of age (Rutter & the ERA Study Team, 1998). At adoption, the PI children showed severe cognitive and motor delays. By 4 years of age, nearly all had IQs within the normal range, although IQs were lower than those in the comparison group for children adopted after 6 months of age. At 6 years, while cognitive growth continued, the pattern did not change, with IQ being predicted by duration of institutional care and, in addition, by the amount of individualized care and exposure to toys and other stimulation children received in the institution (Castle et al., 1999; see also the review by MacClean, 2003). Little change in IQ was seen from 6 to 15 years of age, except for continued modest gains in the children with the lowest IQs (Beckett, Castle, Rutter, & Sonuga-Barke, 2010).

Children who end up in institutions likely experience a relatively poor prenatal environment and more perinatal complications (e.g., low birthweight, premature birth) that also compromise IQ. When compared to children raised in homes by parents with education and income comparable to those of the children's adoptive families, even PI children adopted very early may have somewhat lower IQs (Loman et al., 2009). The BEIP study compared children placed in foster care to never-institutionalized children in homes with more "average" resources. Here they found that after several years in the foster home, children placed before age 2 were comparable in IQ to never-institutionalized children, while those placed later in foster care still showed IQ deficits nearly comparable to those in the "care as usual" group (Nelson et al., 2007). Because this study used random assignment, the difference between children placed early and those placed later in foster care could not be due to prenatal or perinatal factors.

Because of the importance of IQ to children's successful functioning, it is important to quickly identify children who will benefit from cognitive intervention. Notably, for children who are old enough to be developing language (i.e., 12 months or older), language development in the initial months postadoption does predict later IQ (Croft et al., 2007). Importantly, language development was even more important than stunted physical growth and head size at the time of adoption for cognitive and behavioral outcomes (Sonuga-Barke et al., 2008).

As this suggests, many PI children exhibit deficits in language development. Although this may partly be due to children's need to switch from their native language to the language of the adoptive home, in fact, the development of the native language is also severely delayed, with many institutionalized children producing no intelligible language in their native tongue even by 30 months of age (Windsor, Glaze, Koga, & the BEIP Core Group, 2007). After a year in a family, productive and receptive language nearly approach age norms; however, the use of complex grammatical construction still lags behind. As with cognitive impairment, language delays years after adoption are correlated with age at adoption. Years after adoption, PI children often still fall behind in understanding and use of complex grammatical sentences, language pragmatics, and the ability to use language to guide behavior (Loman et al., 2009; Schoenbrodt, Carran, & Preis, 2007). Schoenbrodt and colleagues (2007) point out that it is important not to ignore language delays in PI children or to attribute them simply to learning a new language because their difficulties may reflect more substantive and long-lasting challenges that will impact their scholastic achievement.

Specific Cognitive Processes

Even when IQ is normal or even high, PI children are at risk for delays/deficits in executive function and theory of mind that can affect how well they do in school and in relationships with others (Bos, Fox, Zeanah, & Nelson, 2009; Colvert et al., 2008; Pollak et al., 2010). As in other areas, children adopted from institutions by 6 months of age typically do not show these delays, and those adopted later do not always show them. Executive functions include abilities such as working memory, cognitive flexibility, and cognitive inhibitory control. This means that PI children score more poorly than same-age nonadopted children on tasks in which they must search for targets in the shortest number of moves without returning to the same place twice (working memory), learn a sorting rule (e.g., sort by color), then, when they are used to doing that, switch to another rule (e.g., sort by shape; cognitive flexibility), or press a bar for every letter as fast as they can, but not for the letter *X* (cognitive inhibition). Theory of mind, a core deficit in autism, contributes to the autistic-like behavior shown by some PI children (Colvert et al., 2008), but delays on theory of mind tasks are seen even in PI children who do not exhibit autistic-like behaviors (Tarullo, Bruce, & Gunnar, 2007). All of these functions depend on development of the prefrontal cortex; thus, the fact that PI children often show deficits or delays in these cognitive abilities is consistent with the neuroimaging data discussed earlier.

Scholastic Achievement

Because PI children show delays in numerous areas of functioning deemed essential for school readiness, including attention, executive function, and sensory skills (Jacobs, Miller, & Tirella, 2010), it follows that school is difficult for many of them. PI children demonstrate more learning disabilities (Tirella, Chan, & Miller, 2006), utilize more special educational services (Groze & Ileana, 1996), and are more often held back a grade in school (Beckett et al., 2010) than family-reared children. Some researchers have argued that children's educational problems go beyond what would be expected for their cognitive level, implying that these problems are perhaps due to behavioral and attentional issues as opposed to cognitive ability. In a meta-analysis of cognitive recovery and school function, van IJzendoorn, Juffer, and Poelhuis (2005) found a full recovery of IQ in many PI children but continuing deficits in school performance. In contrast, in a Swedish study school performance was above what would be predicted by IQ in a PI group (Dalen et al., 2008), and the English and Romanian Adoptee study that followed children to age 15 reported that scholastic achievement was comparable to what would be expected, based on the children's IQ (Beckett et al., 2010). This controversy is far from settled. Nonetheless, there is also evidence that, in addition to IQ, problems with attention regulation and hyperactivity may compromise scholastic attainment among PI children (Beckett et al., 2007).

Summary of Cognitive Effects

Many of the cognitive effects of institutional care are related to deprivation of physical, social, and linguistic stimulation; when institutions provide more stimulation, then IQ and language develop more normally. However, most institutions do not provide sufficient stimulation, and children arrive in their adopted families significantly delayed. Rebound is remarkable in the first year or so postadoption; however, it is often incomplete, particularly for children who experience prolonged institutionalization prior to adoption. For these children, compared to never-institutionalized children living in comparable homes, persistently lower IQ, suppressed language competence, and specific cognitive abilities (e.g., executive functions) are observed, along with lower academic achievement and greater need for services. Early intervention in the preschool years might be needed to help these children increase their chances for later academic success.

Socioemotional Development

As the earlier sections imply, institutionalization has a profound impact on all aspects of development. Some of these effects are ameliorated with adoption into supportive families, while others persist years after children leave institutional care. The most persistent and sometimes profound effects are seen in children's socioemotional development. Parents rate emotional/interpersonal functioning as the area in which children make the least progress following adoption (Fisher et al., 1997). Children adopted from institutions show deficits or delays in emotion understanding, attachment, and social behavior, as well heightened rates of psychopathology, including attention-deficit/hyperactivity disorder (ADHD) and quasi-autistic features. Although these problems sometimes cluster together (Kumsta et al., 2010), the mechanisms linking them are still unknown.

Face Processing and Emotion Understanding

One of the basic skills necessary for social interaction is the ability to process faces and recognize emotions. Children reared in normative environments develop these skills rapidly over the first years of life. By 7 months of age, typically developing children can distinguish between facial expressions such as happy, sad, angry, and fearful (Nelson, Parker, & Guthrie, 2006). By age 3, most children can match a facial expression to an emotion, as well as choose the expression that would typically accompany different emotional situations (Denham, 1986). Children raised in institutions experience a poverty of face-to-face interactions, limiting their experience with facial expressions of emotions.

In the BEIP study, institutionalized infants did not demonstrate behavioral differences in face processing compared with community children (Nelson et al., 2006); however, ERP data (measures of brain electrical activity) suggested differences at the neural level (for a review, see Nelson, 2007). Removal from the institution into quality foster care ameliorated some of the effects of institutionalization on the neural systems underlying face processing. Two studies that examined face recognition and discrimination of facial expressions found that the foster care group had ERP levels intermediate between those of the institutionalized group and the community controls (Moulson, Fox, et al., 2009; Moulson, Westerlund, et al., 2009).

Once children are able to recognize faces and expressions, they begin to understand the different emotions and situations in which emotions arise. Children still residing in an institution performed significantly worse than community children on an emotion understanding task (Sloutsky, 1997). Several studies of PI children have confirmed that these deficits continue postadoption. In one such study, Wismer Fries and Pollak (2004) examined 4- and 5-year-old children raised for the first years of their lives in Russian and Eastern European orphanages before adoption into U.S. families, and compared them with U.S.-born children matched on socioeconomic status. PI children performed more poorly on both identifying and labeling facial expression and on matching emotions to emotional situations. Delays or deficits in reading emotions and understanding how they relate to situations may underlie some of the other social challenges that PI children experience.

Attachment

Many researchers believe that the source of most of the problems faced by PI children is their lack of a stable attachment figure early in life (Rutter, 1981). According to attachment theory (Bowlby, 1969), human infants are evolutionarily primed to form a close, lasting bond to one or a few primary caregivers. This bond serves to protect the infant from harm, provide a secure base for exploration, and ingrain regulatory abilities in the child. Virtually all children form selective attachments in the second half of their first year of life. Children reared for more than 6 months in severely deprived conditions, such as those found in institutions with poor caregiver–child ratios and high turnover rates of staff, may not have the opportunity to form this enduring bond. Attachment theory suggests that this will be detrimental to the children's development in numerous areas of functioning.

Researchers have been studying this issue ever since Spitz first drew attention to the detrimental effects of institutionalization. In fact, studies of children in institutions significantly influenced Bowlby as he developed his theory of attachment. Early studies focused primarily on whether or not children were able to form attachments after a period of institutionalization. These early studies painted a dismal picture. The later study of model institutions in Britain found contrasting results (see a review of Tizard's work in Gunnar, 2001). In institutions that provided sufficient nutrition and stimulation, Tizard was able to study the specific socioemotional repercussions of the lack of a primary attachment figure for the first several years of life. Tizard found that while still in the institution, children appeared to have shallow ties to all of their caregivers, and not to care deeply about anyone. However, once placed in a family, most of these children were able to form discriminating attachments with their new parents within a year, according to parent report. However, none of these early studies used standardized measures of attachment to assess the parent–child relationships, which makes it hard to compare results. More recent research has used modified separation–reunion procedures and standardized coding schemes to assess attachment observationally in PI children, giving us more confidence in the results and making it possible to compare across studies. However, there is still some debate as to how to classify children who show behavior patterns outside the established organized patterns. Organized attachment classifications include secure, resistant (sometimes referred to as ambivalent–dependent), and avoidant attachment patterns. A small proportion of the general population also demonstrates a disorganized attachment pattern (also known as the disorganized–controlling pattern), which is associated with pathological caregiving conditions, such as maltreatment. This pattern suggests that the child does not have an organized strategy for using the caregiver as a secure base to manage stress, and instead becomes behaviorally disorganized in the caregiver's presence. Finally the insecure–other category is used when the child's behavior exhibited in the separation–reunion procedure is clearly not secure-base behavior, nor did it fit into the established insecure categories. This category is almost exclusively used for foster care, adopted, and institutionalized children. Often researchers (e.g., Chisholm, 1998; Smyke, Zeanah, Fox, Nelson, & Guthrie, 2010) combine the disorganized pattern with the insecure–other pattern to form an "atypical" attachment group because both are uncommon in normative samples and predict increased risk for negative outcomes (Sroufe, Carlson, Levy, & Egeland, 1999). We use this distinction unless otherwise noted.

Before children leave institutions, many have no attachment to any caregiver (Zeanah, Smyke, Koga, & Carlson, 2005). Caregiving quality is associated with socioemotional deficits in institutionalized children (Smyke et al., 2007). Adoption marks a radical change in the caregiving context. PI children adopted internationally do form attachments to their adoptive parents, with more than one-third of PI children in one study showing secure attachments (Chisholm, 1998; Chisholm, Carter, Ames, & Morison, 1995; Marcovitch et al., 1997). This evidence expands on Tizard's results because not only were these children deprived of a primary caregiver–child relationship prior to adoption, but they were also exposed to an extremely high level of general privation (Chisholm, 1998). The English and Romanian Adoptee study has also examined attachment longitudinally in a group of children adopted out of Romanian institutions, compared with children adopted within the UK before age 6 months (O'Connor, Marvin, Rutter, Olrick, & Britner, 2003). Attachment to their adoptive parents was measured when the children were 4 years old by a modified separation–reunion procedure. These researchers also found that children were able to form attachments to their adoptive parents, with approximately 30% showing secure attachment patterns.

The most promising results for PI children have come from recent evaluation of attachment in the BEIP study. As previously mentioned, the BEIP study is a randomized controlled trial comparing a quality foster care system to care as usual in an institution (Zeanah et al., 2003). Children's social and emotional functioning, including attachment, were evaluated in the institution prior to randomization, and several follow-up evaluations were conducted, including an evaluation of attachment at 42 months of age. PI children who had been assigned to foster care showed vast improvements in their attachment quality, with nearly 50% showing secure attachments to their foster parent (Smyke et al., 2010).

It is important to point out, however, that in all of these cases there are abnormally high proportions of atypical attachment classifications in the PI children (O'Connor et al., 2003). Most studies of children adopted out of institutions find atypical patterns in approximately half of the attachment relationships. The recent data from the BEIP study showed more promising results, with only 23% of the children in foster care showing atypical attachment patterns (Smyke et al., 2010).

PI children are able to form attachments to their new caregivers; however, these attachments are less likely to be secure and more likely to be atypical. Despite this, a substantial minority (and in one case nearly half) of the children studied were able to form secure attachment relationships. Organized forms of insecurity (avoidant, resistant patterns) do not seem to be associated with institutionalization. It may be the case that the older the child is when forming the primary attachment, the harder it is to form a secure relationship. Correlates of secure attachment to adoptive parents included higher IQ and fewer behavioral problems (Chisholm, 1998; Marcovitch et al., 1997). It is likely that these child characteristics affect the ability of the parent to be sensitively responsive and therefore affect attachment quality.

Indiscriminate Friendliness

The relation between attachment and other effects of deprivation is complex. Researchers have long debated the association between attachment and indiscriminate friendliness. The core feature of indiscriminate friendliness is a general lack of developmentally appropriate reticence around unfamiliar adults. Other, related characteristics include a propensity frequently to approach and attempt to engage strangers, failure to check back with a care-giver in novel situations, and willingness to go away with a stranger. Once the child is verbal, age-inappropriate levels of asking intrusive, personal questions is also observed, consistent with the idea that the child is struggling to conform to social boundary norms. This behavior is often seen among children with severe IQ deficits, but, notably, it is not correlated with IQ among PI children because it is seen even among children with normal or even high IQs (see a review by Gunnar, 2001). Notably, the behavior is neither completely indiscriminate nor truly friendly. Instead, it is superficial, impersonal, and shallow, and while children show a strong initial approach to strangers, they *do* in fact show some prefer-ence for known caregivers (e.g., O'Connor, Bredenkamp, Rutter, & the ERA Study Team, 1999). Other researchers have referred to this behavior as disinhibited attachment behavior (a form of attachment disorder), nonattachment, or diffuse attachment; however, recent research in indiscriminate friendliness (discussed below) suggests that this behavior may not be evidence of attachment problems.

Stranger reticence is a normative developmental milestone that appears between ages 6 and 12 months. Though variability in stranger reticence exists in normally developing children, those demonstrating indiscriminate friendliness also show very little or no wari-ness of strangers, even under unfamiliar circumstances. These behaviors could be danger-ous for the children (e.g., going off with a stranger) and could also prove deleterious to the caregiver–child relationship. Many PI children show varying degrees of indiscriminately friendly behaviors. Parents report that children adopted from institutions exhibit signifi-cantly more of this behavior than do family-reared or early-adopted children (Chisholm et al., 1995; O'Connor et al., 1999; O'Connor & Rutter, 2000). PI children also demonstrated more indiscriminately friendly behavior in an observational laboratory procedure (Bruce, Tarullo, & Gunnar, 2009). This behavior continued to be evident at least 3 years after adoption (Chisholm, 1998), with some researchers finding that aspects of this behavior persist into adolescence in nearly half of PI children (ERA Study Team, 2010; Kreppner et al., 2010). Duration of deprivation predicts severity of indiscriminate friendliness; however, some children who had been institutionalized for more than 2 years showed no evidence of these behaviors (O'Connor & Rutter, 2000). Notably, Tizard and colleagues (as discussed in Gunnar, 2001) even described this behavior in children adopted out of the high-quality institutional settings, and Zeanah and colleagues (2005) found that the severity of these behaviors was unrelated to institutional care quality. This, plus the fact that it is seen even among PI children with normal IQs, suggests that it is not due solely or primarily to depri-vation, but may instead be related to disruption in relationships and/or a high turnover of caregivers. Consistent with this argument, indiscriminate friendliness is also seen among preschoolers in child protective service in the United States, and here it is predicted by the number of different foster homes children have been in rather than the severity of maltreat-ment they experienced (Pears, Bruce, Fisher, & Kim, 2010).

On the surface, this behavior seems incompatible with a secure attachment. In fact, it is the core feature of the *Diagnostic and Statistical Manual of Mental Disorders* (DSM-IV) diagnosis of reactive attachment disorder: disinhibited type (American Psychiatric Associa-tion, 1994). O'Connor and colleagues used this diagnosis in their studies of PI children and conceptualized this problem as a failure of the attachment system to organize itself properly (O'Connor et al., 1999; O'Connor & Rutter, 2000). Recent research, however, suggests that indiscriminate friendliness and attachment security are not mutually exclusive. For exam-ple, some PI children with secure attachments to their adoptive parents continue to show significant indiscriminate friendliness (Chisholm, 1998; O'Connor et al., 2003). Children still living in an institution showed equally high levels of these behaviors despite differences in attachment relationships (Zeanah, Smyke, & Dumitrescu, 2002). In addition, despite improvements in attachment over time, indiscriminate friendliness remains evident in PI children for years following adoption (Chisholm, 1998; Smyke, Zeanah, Fox, & Nelson, 2009; Smyke et al., 2010). The concept of attachment disorders, particularly the disinhibited type, has also come under recent scrutiny. Zeanah and Gleason (2010) have argued that the cluster of behaviors described by the current disinhibited type is not an attachment disorder at all and have recommended that it be reformulated for the DSM-V revision and renamed "disinhibited social engagement disorder." They stated, "It is not necessarily attachment behaviors that are disinhibited but rather social engagement or affiliative behaviors that are expressed non-selectively" (p. 28).

Because the attachment-related etiology for this cluster of behaviors is under debate, researchers have begun examining other reasons for the persistence of indiscriminately friendliness after the child is placed in a family. Chisholm (1998) suggested that while children are in institutional care, being overly friendly helps to get them attention and affectionate contact; thus, it is adaptive. The behavior is hard to extinguish after adoption, she argued, because parents report enjoying the fact that their child is so friendly with everyone. Although continued reinforcement of the behavior may be involved, there is growing evidence that it also may be related to some of the persistent cognitive deficits described earlier, particularly attention regulation and inhibitory control (Bruce et al., 2009; O'Connor et al., 1999; Pears et al., 2010; Roy, Rutter, & Pickles, 2004). So, for example, children who had more difficulty stopping themselves from pressing the button on the no-go trials of a go/no-go task (Bruce et al., 2009) or those who had more difficulty on the day–night Stroop task (Pears et al., 2010) also exhibited more indiscriminately friendly behavior. It is possible that problems with inhibitory control more generally underlie indiscriminately friendly behaviors. Interestingly, there is some evidence that turnover in caregivers also influences inhibitory control, and it is the impact on inhibitory control that influences preschool-age children's ability to regulate social engagement appropriately (Pears et al., 2010). Thus, indiscriminately friendly behavior may not reflect problems in the parent–child attachment relationship; instead, it may represent deficient neurocognitive regulatory capacities that have their basic building blocks established within stable, early, caregiver–child relationships.

Emotional and Behavioral Problems

PI children are at a heightened risk for developing emotional and behavioral problems. This is a probabilistic rather than deterministic effect; however, many PI children show none of these problems (e.g., Gunnar & van Dulmen, 2007; Rutter, Kreppner, & O'Connor, 2001). What type of problems do they exhibit? Much attention has been paid to the wide range of problems in children with difficult early histories, specifically, internalizing (anxiety, depression) and externalizing (aggression, conduct) problems. To some extent, the answer to whether PI children exhibit elevated rates of internalizing and externalizing symptoms and are at risk for clinical levels of difficulty in these domains depends on the comparison group. When the comparison is to domestic adoptees, during early and middle childhood, PI children are not at greater risk, and indeed, are seen to have fewer internalizing and externalizing symptoms (Juffer & van IJzendoorn, 2005; Sonuga-Barke, Schlotz, & Kreppner, 2010). When PI children are compared to children adopted internationally from foster care, likewise during early and middle childhood, they do not differ in either of these domains (Gunnar & van Dulmen, 2007), especially when parents are the informants (Wiik et al., 2010). In middle childhood, when children report on their own symptoms, PI children report more internalizing symptoms than do children adopted early from foster care overseas (Wiik et al., 2010). Interestingly, separation anxiety is the most elevated internalizing symptom and it correlates positively with duration of institutional care (Wiik et al., 2010). Notably, for both children adopted from foster care overseas and those adopted from institutions, being over age 2 at adoption is associated with greater risk of internalizing and externalizing problems (Gunnar & van Dulmen, 2007).

The clearest evidence of elevated rates of internalizing and externalizing problems comes from studies comparing PI children to children born and raised in families with the same education and high income as the families who adopt internationally (Ames, 1997; Fisher et al., 1997; Juffer & van IJzendoorn, 2005; Marcovitch et al., 1997; Wiik et al., 2010). Although there are many reasons that nonadopted, high socioeconomic class children are a poor comparison group if the question is the impact of early institutional care, such comparisons nonetheless do inform us about comparisons that parents of PI children may be making. That is, nonadopted, high-resource children are the types who will be in the PI child's neighborhood and school classrooms. If the PI child stands out as having more anxiety, aggression, or conduct problems than such children, it may be tempting to attribute that to their experiences of early institutional care. Because of the evidence that internalizing and externalizing problems may not differ (or may be less) for PI children than for domestically adopted children and/or children adopted from foster care overseas, there is little reason to think that the institutional care has affected them. Critically, though, for institutionalized children and children in domestic or international foster care, the likelihood of significant internalizing and externalizing problems increases the longer the children live without a consistent, supportive family and, thus, with age at adoption.

Unlike internalizing and externalizing problems, there is considerable evidence that PI children are at risk for ADHD. This is true for PI children adopted beyond age 6 months, compared to both PI children and domestically adopted children who reach their families before age 6 months; furthermore when studied longitudinally, this risk persists from ages 4 to 15 (Kreppner et al., 2010). The BEIP study confirmed high rates of inattention in institutionalized children and demonstrated that foster care intervention was effective in increasing attention levels, as measured during emotion-eliciting tasks (Ghera et al., 2009). Ames (1997) examined children 3 years postadoption and found that children who had experienced institutional care showed elevated levels of attention problems, according to parent report, compared with family-reared children, as well as higher levels of parent-reported distractibility and hyperactivity. These same children continued to show attention problems 8 years after adoption, and 29% of them had been diagnosed as having ADHD (Le Mare & Audet, 2002, as cited in MacLean, 2003). Length of institutionalization is associated with attention problems. Some researchers have questioned whether the inattention/overactivity seen in PI children is the same as "typical" attention and activity problems, or whether it is specific to institutional deprivation (e.g., Kumsta et al., 2010). This issue has not yet been resolved.

Stereotypies, especially rocking, are often reported for PI children at the time of adoption. For children adopted from profound deprivation, nearly half (47%) to nearly all (87%) have been described as exhibiting stereotypies at adoption (Beckett et al., 2002; Fisher et al., 1997). For most children these behaviors resolve over the first year or two postadoption (Beckett et al., 2002; Fisher et al., 1997). For some children, though, they persist and co-occur with other problems, particularly autistic symptoms. In their study of children adopted from profound deprivation, Rutter and colleagues (1999) noted that 6% of the sample met criteria for autism, while another 6% showed milder and usually isolated autistic features. They noted that both greater cognitive impairment and longer durations of profound deprivation were associated with autistic features. Although, with time in the adoptive families many of the children no longer met criteria for autism, 14.9% of those who did so initially would still be classified this way by early adulthood (18–20 years; Kumsta et al., 2010). One thing that set these PI children with autistic features apart quite radically from typical children with autism was that their autistic features coexisted with intense interest in social interaction. Given this and the improvements seen for many children who initially exhibited autistic features, these researchers labeled the phenomenon "quasi-autism," with the strong presumption that it arose from early experiences of profound deprivation. Quasi-autistic symptoms have also been noted in other studies of PI children (Hoksbergen, ter Laak, Rijk, van Dijkum, & Stoutjesdijk, 2005).

Another problem noted for PI children is difficulty in regulating their responses to auditory and tactile stimulation. This may be why some PI children appear so dysregulated, as problems in processing stimulation can manifest as hyperactivity, feeding problems, and emotional lability. Parents of PI children report both sensory overresponsiveness and accompanying avoidance of stimulation, and unusual sensory-seeking behavior (Cermak & Groza, 1998). Nearly all of the studies showing elevated rates of sensory-processing problems have depended on parent report; however, recently 8- to 12-year-old PI children who had been in their adoptive families for many years were administered a standardized sensory processing test (Wilbarger, Gunnar, Schneider, & Pollak, 2010). Compared to children adopted early from foster care overseas and nonadopted children, PI children were more likely to react with either high aversion or high pleasure to tactile stimulation. As with other behavior problems, sensory-processing problems increase with more prolonged and profound deprivation prior to adoption. When these problems are pervasive the child may be classified as having a sensory-processing (or integration) disorder.

Summary of Socioemotional Development

Rutter and colleagues (Rutter et al., 2001; Rutter & Sonuga-Barke, 2010) have argued that PI children do not show the garden variety of problems typically seen in children reared in difficult circumstances (e.g., see Cicchetti & Toth, 1995). As reviewed, during preschool and middle childhood, elevated risk of internalizing and externalizing disorders does not characterize these children when compared with maltreated and other high-adversity groups. Contrary to early theories, PI children are able to form attachments to adoptive and foster parents after even a prolonged time in an institution; however, although many do form secure relationships, there is an increased risk of insecure and atypical attachments. Many PI children do find it difficult to regulate their behavior. They are at risk for disinhibited responses and may be overly motivated to approach strangers and seek social contact indiscriminately. They are at increased risk of reacting to stimulation with either high aversion or atypical interest. As a group, PI children have more problems than other children in regulating attention, and they are also at an increased risk of meeting criteria for ADHD. In the preschool and early school years, they have difficulty identifying emotion in faces and matching facial emotions to situations, which, in addition to delays in theory of mind, may make it difficult for them be successful in social relations with peers. In addition, a significant but still small percentage of PI children meet classification criteria for autism, which, because it often coexists with intense interest in social interaction, is an atypical or "quasi" form of autism. While many PI children do quite well in all of these domains, others express problems in one or more of them. Whether these difficulties co-occur often enough to justify the label of postinstitutionalized or deprivation-specific syndrome is currently being debated (Gunnar, 2010; Sonuga-Barke, Schlotz, & Kreppner, 2010). If such a syndrome is confirmed, it could prove useful in clinical interventions. However, there is also the issue of prematurely labeling children with a disorder, which may lead to its own problems.

Implications for Policy, Research, and Practice

The work we have described has implications for policy, research, and practice in early education and beyond. Despite an overall remarkable recovery in function following adoption, PI children continue to show numerous deficits that warrant further investigation and attention. With thousands of children being adopted internationally each year, this group will continue to grow and to need services and support from policymakers and educators.

Policy

Given the evidence that institutionalization causes drastic deleterious effects on development, the most obvious policy implication of this work is that we should avoid institutional care for young children. In countries where it is possible, this means the best policy is to establish and maintain the infrastructure and intervention strategies to allow young children to stay safely in their families and, when this is not possible, to place them in foster family care. We need to be cautious about calling for the immediate dismantling of all orphanages/institutions before the infrastructure to support adequate alternatives is in place (Groze, Bunkers, & Gamer, in press). In the interim, improving institutional care through staff training and reorganization of staffing schedules to reduce the number of different individuals caring for each child may be options (see, e.g., St. Petersburg–USA Orphanage Research Team, 2008). Another equally obvious policy implication based on the relative developmental outcomes discussed for early-adopted children is that early, permanent placement in a supportive family is the best option for children. With increasing age at placement, there is increased risk that optimal functioning will not be achieved, and that deficits in one or more domains are more likely. Of course, this is the same policy implication that comes from work on children in foster care.

Work on institutionalized and PI children also speaks to the importance of early stimulation. We cannot directly extrapolate to children reared in poverty or to neglected children in the child welfare system, but when combined with other intervention studies of early stimulation, evidence of the power of intervention (in this case, adoption) to improve functioning and the risks that accrue when intervention is delayed may inform early intervention policies for at-risk children.

Finally, there are policy implications related to adoption. Because of the substantial burden of these ongoing developmental problems, families need to be informed of the risks of adopting a child who has experienced prolonged institutional care in his or her first year(s) of life, and they need ongoing support once they bring the child home. Unfortunately, not all adoption agencies adequately prepare parents for the challenges of rearing a child adopted from institutional care, and fewer still provide adequate postadoption services (Gunnar & Pollak, 2007). The failure to inform and support parents can have tragic consequences, as in the recent case in which a family shipped a boy back to Russia, claiming that no one told them about his problems, and that they were getting no help in dealing with them.

However, even agencies that offer postadoption services can do only so much. Also needed is an increase in the number of physicians, psychologists, and educators knowledgeable about the development and needs of PI children. It was not until 2000 that the American Academy of Pediatrics established a Section on Adoption and Foster Care Medicine. While there are increasing numbers of international adoption medical clinics, these are typically associated with medical schools, and it is still the case that relatively few physicians in most communities understand the special medical and behavioral needs of children adopted from institutional care. The same is also true of other professionals to whom parents turn for evaluation and treatment. As a result, parents get conflicting advice, including everything from "love will take care of the problem" to encouragement to seek expensive and unproven treatments (Gunnar et al., 2000). We need policies that support the development of medical, mental health, and education professionals with knowledge of the needs of PI children. As with the American Academy of Pediatrics, it makes sense that this training also administer to the needs of domestically adopted and fostered children.

Research

We increasingly understand the impact of early deprivation on neurobehavioral development. Research on PI children shows that even such a massive intervention as removing children from poor-quality institutions and placing them in supportive families is not enough. The question is, where do we intervene, and which interventions are effective for which aspects of the child's functioning? To date, to our knowledge, the only intervention for PI adopted children being studied in a randomized trial targets improvement of parenting by facilitating parents' understanding of the children's attachment needs, and strategies to reduce indiscriminate sociability and improve attention regulation. Quasi-autistic behaviors are also targeted. Preliminary results indicate an increase in attachment security in PI children compared to a control group exposed to a physical and occupational therapy condition (M. Dozier, personal communication, March 10, 2011). Although parenting interventions assume that parenting can shift the odds for PI children, there are remarkably few studies of parenting and the development of PI children on which to base this assumption. Castle, Beckett, Rutter, and Sonuga-Barke (2010) reported that they found no relation between family factors typically associated with poorer outcomes for children and the presence of deprivation-specific, pervasive problems among their PI Romanian children. These researchers also found that initially following adoption, children who were more delayed had parents who were less supportive of them in a problem-solving laboratory task. Over time, as the children's functioning improved, parenting improved as well. And it appeared that the improvement in the children influenced parental behavior, rather than parental behavior influencing how much improvement was seen in the children (Croft, O'Connor, Keavene, Groothues, & Rutter, 2001). It would be surprising to find that parental sensitivity, responsiveness, and appropriate limit setting had no influence on the development of PI children, but it would not be surprising to find that even superlative parenting is insufficient to overcome some of the neurobehavioral effects of early institutional deprivation. Thus, we need further research to help us understand the relations between parenting and the development of PI children, and to identify which domains need additional interventions. Because attention regulatory problems, inhibitory control, and working memory appear to be an issue for many PI children, it would be helpful to know whether training interventions designed to foster improvements in executive functioning might be particularly helpful for PI children. For example, would PI children benefit from preschool programs, such as Tools of the Mind, that have been shown to benefit low-income children, who also are often delayed in the development of executive functions (Diamond, Barnett, Thomas, & Munro, 2007), or might they need more focused training (e.g., Rueda, Rothbart, McCandliss, Saccomanno, & Posner, 2005)?

Early Education Practice

There are several layers of influence in terms of early education practice. The first is at the national policy level. The Individuals with Disabilities Education Act (IDEA) is a federal law that governs how states and school districts provide early intervention and special education services to children with disabilities. This policy applies not only to services for school-age children but also to early intervention services for disabled children, starting at birth. The current incarnation of this policy makes it difficult to obtain needed services for PI children. Under the category of "learning disorder," IDEA specifically excludes problems cause by "cultural, environmental or economic disadvantage" (U.S. Department of Education, 2006, p. 2). Therefore, PI children's difficulties with specific academic areas may be deemed a result of their poor early environment, and they are therefore not eligible for services. PI children sometimes qualify under the category "other health impaired or emotionally disturbed"; however, parents of PI children have continued trouble obtaining the necessary services for their children (Gindis, 2011). In the case of children who were adopted at or near school age, parents are often told to wait until the child learns English before completing an educational evaluation, despite the need for immediate services (Gindis, 2009). The research reviewed here clearly shows that many PI children are in need of additional services to help with the cognitive and language issues many of them face. IDEA should be modified to allow PI children to obtain the needed educational and intervention services.

In addition, there are implications at the level of the individual teachers. Notably, there are no observational studies of PI children interacting with peers or teachers in child care or preschool settings. These are needed before we can confidently draw implications for practice. However, we know that, at this point, teacher preparedness for work with PI children is limited to sensitivity training at best (Gindis, 2009). While PI children have some things in common with children experiencing other adversity (e.g., children in extreme poverty, or maltreated children), such as higher rates of attention problems, the PI group has a unique set of needs that require intervention. In order for teachers to have the most positive impact, program modifications and support for teachers have to be specific to this group of children and need to include information on the most common disabilities and their implications for instruction.

First, because language development in the first years postadoption appears to predict cognitive outcomes for PI children, tracking language development is extremely important. PI children who are still struggling with language a year or more after adoption likely require intervention. Second, because of an increased likelihood that PI children with be either hyperaversive or highly attracted to stimulation, for PI children who appear to be having problems with behavior and emotion regulation in the classroom, it would be wise to consider whether sensory processing issues are contributing the child's regulatory problems. If so, then it might be wise to consider implementing classroom strategies for managing sensory-processing problems in the preschool classroom (e.g., Rudman, 2009). In addition, although strategies to reduce indiscriminate friendly behavior have not been subjected to randomized trials, it would seem reasonable to notice these behaviors and avoid their reinforcement, and to help the child learn alternative behaviors, to differentiate unfamiliar from familiar people, and to practice not going off with friendly strangers. In addition, knowing the effects of attachment issues, indiscriminate friendliness, and inattention/hyperactivity on child development and educational processes would be beneficial. Teacher training for the application of specific behavior interventions and instructional strategies is important. Most importantly, teachers need to work closely with parents to ensure positive educational and social development of the child.

Acknowledgments

We wish to thank the many parents and children who have participated in Minnesota International Adoption Project (MnIAP) research that has contributed to information reviewed in this chapter, along with our thanks to the MnIAP research team. We also thank Barbara Murphy for help with implications for practice. The writing of this chapter was supported by grants from the National Institute of Mental Health (Nos. R01MH080905 and P50MH078105).

References

American Psychiatric Association. (1994). *Diagnostic and statistical manual of mental disorders* (4th ed.). Washington, DC: American Psychiatric Association.

Ames, E. W. (1997). *The development of Romanian orphanage children adopted to Canada* (Final Report to the National Welfare Grants Program: Human Resources Development Canada). Burnaby, Canada: Simon Frasier University.

Beckett, C., Bredenkamp, D., Castle, J., Groothues, C., O'Connor, T. G., & Rutter, M. (2002). Behavior patterns associated with institutional deprivation: A study of children adopted from Romania. *Journal of Developmental Behavior Pediatrics, 23*(5), 297–303.

Beckett, C., Castle, J., Rutter, M., & Sonuga-Barke, E. J. (2010). VI. Institutional deprivation, specific cognitive functions, and scholastic achievement: English and Romanian Adoptee (ERA) study findings. *Monographs of the Society for Research in Child Development, 75*(1), 125–142.

Beckett, C., Maughan, B., Rutter, M., Castle, J., Colvert, E., Groothues, C., et al. (2007). Scholastic attainment following severe early institutional deprivation: A study of children adopted from Romania. *Journal of Abnormal Child Psychology, 35*(6), 1063–1073.

Bos, K. J., Fox, N., Zeanah, C. H., & Nelson, C. A. (2009). Effects of early psychosocial deprivation on the development of memory and executive function. *Frontiers in Behavioral Neuroscience, 3,* 16.

Bowlby, J. (1969). *Attachment and loss: Vol. 1. Attachment.* New York: Basic Books.

Bruce, J., Tarullo, A. R., & Gunnar, M. R. (2009). Disinhibited social behavior among internationally adopted children. *Development and Psychopathology, 21*(1), 157–171.

Carlson, M., & Earls, F. (1997). Psychological and neuroendocrinological sequelae of early social deprivation in institutionalized children in Romania. *Annals of the New York Academy of Sciences, 807,* 419–428.

Castle, J., Beckett, C., Rutter, M., & Sonuga-Barke, E. J. (2010). VIII. Postadoption environmental features. *Monographs of the Society for Research in Child Development, 75*(1), 167–186.

Castle, J., Groothues, C., Bredenkamp, D., Beckett, C., O'Connor, T. G., & Rutter, M. (1999). Effects of qualities of early institutional care on cognitive attainment. *American Journal of Orthopsychiatry, 69*(4), 424–437.

Cermak, S., & Groza, V. (1998). Sensory processing problems in post-institutionalized children: Implications for social work. *Child Adolescent Social Work Journal, 15*(1), 5–37.

Chisholm, K. (1998). A three year follow-up of attachment and indiscriminate friendliness in children adopted from Romanian orphanages. *Child Development, 69*(4), 1092–1106.

Chisholm, K., Carter, M. C., Ames, E. W., & Morison, S. J. (1995). Attachment security and indiscriminately friendly behavior in children adopted from Romanian orphanages. *Development and Psychopathology, 7,* 283–294.

Chugani, H. T., Behen, M. E., Muzik, O., Juhasz, C., Nagy, F., & Chugani, D. C. (2001). Local brain functional activity following early deprivation: A study of postinstitutionalized Romanian orphans. *NeuroImage, 14*(6), 1290–1301.

Cicchetti, D., & Rogosch, F. A. (1996). Equifinality and multifinality in developmental psychopathology. *Development and Psychopathology, 8,* 597–600.

Cicchetti, D., & Toth, S. L. (1995). A developmental psychopathology perspective on child abuse and neglect. *Journal of the American Academy of Child Adolescent Psychiatry, 34,* 541–565.

Colvert, E., Rutter, M., Kreppner, J., Beckett, C., Castle, J., Groothues, C., et al. (2008). Do theory of mind and executive function deficits underlie the adverse outcomes associated with profound early deprivation?: Findings from the English and Romanian adoptees study. *Journal of Abnormal Child Psychology, 36*(7), 1057–1068.

Croft, C., Beckett, C., Rutter, M., Castle, J., Colvert, E., Groothues, C., et al. (2007). Early adolescent outcomes of institutionally-deprived and non-deprived adoptees: II. Language as a protective factor and a vulnerable outcome. *Journal of Child Psychology and Psychiatry, 48*, 31–44.

Croft, C., O'Connor, T. G., Keavene, L., Groothues, C., & Rutter, M. (2001). Longitudinal change in parenting associated with developmental delay and catch-up. *Journal of Child Psychology and Psychiatry, 42*, 649–659.

Dalen, M., Hjern, A., Lindblad, F., Odenstad, A., Ramussen, F., & Vinnerljung, B. (2008). Educational attainment and cognitive competence in adopted men—A study of international and national adoptees, siblings and a general Swedish population. *Children and Youth Services Review, 30*, 1211–1219.

De Bellis, M. D., Baum, A. S., Birmaher, B., Keshavan, M. S., Eccard, C. H., Boring, A. M., et al. (1999). A. E. Bennett Research Award: Developmental traumatology: Part I. Biological stress systems. *Biological Psychiatry, 45*(10), 1259–1270.

Denham, S. A. (1986). Social cognition, prosocial behavior, and emotion in preschoolers: Contextual validation. *Child Development, 57*(1), 194–201.

Diamond, A., Barnett, W. S., Thomas, J., & Munro, S. (2007). Preschool program improves cognitive control. *Science, 318*, 1387–1388.

Eluvathingal, T. J., Chugani, H. T., Behen, M. E., Juhasz, C., Muzik, O., Maqbool, M., et al. (2006). Abnormal brain connectivity in children after early severe socioemotional deprivation: A diffusion tensor imaging study. *Pediatrics, 117*(6), 2093–2100.

English and Romanian Adoptees (ERA) Study Team. (2010). II. Methods and measures used for follow-up at 15 years of the English and Romanian Adoptee (ERA) study. *Monographs of the Society for Research in Child Development, 75*(1), 21–47.

Fisher, L., Ames, E. W., Chisholm, K., & Savoie, L. (1997). Problems reported by parents of Romanian orphans adopted to British Columbia. *International Journal of Behavioral Development, 20*(1), 67–82.

Ghera, M. M., Marshall, P. J., Fox, N. A., Zeanah, C. H., Nelson, C. A., Smyke, A. T., et al. (2009). The effects of foster care intervention on socially deprived institutionalized children's attention and positive affect: Results from the BEIP study. *Journal of Child Psychology and Psychiatry, 50*(3), 246–253.

Gindis, B. (2009, February/March). Children left behind: International adoptees in our schools. *Adoption Today*, pp. 42–45.

Gindis, B. (2011, January 28). Educational classification for your internationally adopted child: How important is it? Retrieved from *www.adoptionarticlesdirectory.com*.

Groze, V., Bunkers, K. M., & Gamer, G. N. (in press). Ideal components and current characteristics of alternative care options for children outside of parental care in low-resource countries. *Monographs of the Society for Research in Child Development*.

Groze, V., & Ileana, D. (1996). A follow-up study of children adopted from Romania. *Child and Adolescent Social Work Journal, 13*(6), 541–565.

Gunnar, M. R. (2001). Effects of early deprivation: Findings from orphanage-reared infants and children. In C. A. Nelson & M. Luciana (Eds.), *Handbook of developmental cognitive neuroscience* (pp. 617–629). Cambridge, MA: MIT Press.

Gunnar, M. R. (2010). A commentary on deprivation-specific psychological patterns: Effects of institutional deprivation. *Monographs of the Society for Research in Child Development, 75*, 232–247.

Gunnar, M. R., Bruce, J., & Grotevant, H. D. (2000). International adoption of institutionally reared children: Research and policy. *Development and Psychopathology, 12*, 677–693.

Gunnar, M. R., Bruce, J., & Hickman, S. E. (2001). Salivary cortisol response to stress in children. *Advances in Psychosomatic Medicine, 22*, 52–60.

Gunnar, M. R., & Fisher, P. A. (2006). Bringing basic research on early experience and stress neurobiology to bear on preventive interventions for neglected and maltreated children. *Development and Psychopathology, 18*(3), 651–677.

Gunnar, M. R., Morison, S. J., Chisholm, K., & Schuder, M. (2001). Salivary cortisol levels in children adopted from Romanian orphanages. *Development and Psychopathology, 13*(3), 611–628.

Gunnar, M. R., & Pollak, S. D. (2007). Supporting parents so that they can support their internationally adopted children: The larger challenge lurking behind the fatality statistics. *Child Maltreatment, 12,* 381–382.

Gunnar, M. R., & van Dulmen, M. H. (2007). Behavior problems in postinstitutionalized internationally adopted children. *Development and Psychopathology, 19*(1), 129–148.

Harden, B. J. (2002). Congregate care for infants and toddlers: Shedding new light on an old question. *Infant Mental Health Journal, 23,* 476–495.

Higley, J., & Suomi, S. J. (1992). A longitudinal assessment of CSF monoamine metabolite and plasma cortisol concentrations in young rhesus monkeys. *Biological Psychiatry, 32,* 127–145.

Hoksbergen, R., ter Laak, J., Rijk, K., van Dijkum, C., & Stoutjesdijk, F. (2005). Post-institutional autistic syndrome in Romanian adoptees. *Journal of Autism and Developmental Disorders, 35,* 615–623.

Jacobs, E., Miller, L. C., & Tirella, L. G. (2010). Developmental and behavioral performance of internationally adopted preschoolers: A pilot study. *Child Psychiatry and Human Development, 41,* 15–29.

Johnson, D. E. (2000). Long-term medical issues in international adoptees. *Pediatric Annals, 29*(4), 234–241.

Johnson, D. E. (2001). Medical and developmental sequelae of early childhood institutionalization in Romania. In C. A. Nelson (Ed.), *The Minnesota Symposia on Child Psychology: Vol. 31. Effects of early adversity on neurobehavioral development* (pp. 113–162). Mahwah, NJ: Erlbaum.

Juffer, F., & van IJzendoorn, M. H. (2005). Behavior problems and mental health referrals of international adoptees: A meta-analysis. *Journal of the American Medical Association, 293*(20), 2501–2515.

Kertes, D. A., Gunnar, M. R., Madsen, N. J., & Long, J. D. (2008). Early deprivation and home basal cortisol levels: A study of internationally adopted children. *Development and Psychopathology, 20*(2), 473–491.

Kreppner, J., Kumsta, R., Rutter, M., Beckett, C., Castle, J., Stevens, S., et al. (2010). IV. Developmental course of deprivation-specific psychological patterns: Early manifestations, persistence to age 15, and clinical features. *Monographs of the Society for Research in Child Development, 75*(1), 79–101.

Kumsta, R., Kreppner, J., Rutter, M., Beckett, C., Castle, J., Stevens, S., et al. (2010). III. Deprivation-specific psychological patterns. *Monographs of the Society for Research in Child Development, 75*(1), 48–78.

Landgren, M., Andersson Gronlund, M., Elfstrand, P. O., Simonsson, J. E., Svensson, L., & Stromland, K. (2006). Health before and after adoption from Eastern Europe. *Acta Paediatrica, 95*(6), 720–725.

Loman, M. M., Wiik, K. L., Frenn, K. A., Pollak, S. D., & Gunnar, M. R. (2009). Postinstitutionalized children's development: Growth, cognitive, and language outcomes. *Journal of Developmental Behavioral Pediatrics, 30*(5), 426–434.

Lupien, S. J., King, S., Meaney, M. J., & McEwen, B. S. (2001). Can poverty get under your skin?: Basal cortisol levels and cognitive function in children from low and high socioeconomic status. *Development and Psychopathology, 13*(3), 653–676.

MacLean, K. (2003). The impact of institutionalization on child development. *Develoment and Psychopathology, 15*(4), 853–884.

Marcovitch, S., Goldberg, S., Gold, A., Washington, J., Wasson, C., Krekewich, K., et al. (1997). Determinants of behavioural problems in Romanian children adopted in Ontario. *International Journal of Behavioral Development, 20*(1), 17–31.

Mason, P., & Narad, C. (2005a). International adoption: A health and developmental prospective. *Seminars in Speech Language, 26*(1), 1–9.

Mason, P., & Narad, C. (2005b). Long-term growth and puberty concerns in international adoptees. *Pediatric Clinics of North America, 52*(5), 1351–1368.

Miller, L. C., Chan, W., Comfort, K., & Tirella, L. (2005). Health of children adopted from Guatemala: Comparison of orphanage and foster care. *Pediatrics, 115*(6), 710–717.

Miller, L. C., Chan, W., Litvinova, A., Rubin, A., Tirella, L., & Cermak, S. (2007). Medical diagnoses and growth of children residing in Russian orphanages. *Acta Paediatrica, 96*, 1765–1769.

Miller, L. C., & Hendrie, N. W. (2000). Health of children adopted from China. *Pediatrics, 105*(6), E76.

Moulson, M. C., Fox, N. A., Zeanah, C. H., & Nelson, C. A. (2009). Early adverse experiences and the neurobiology of facial emotion processing. *Development and Psychology, 45*(1), 17–30.

Moulson, M. C., Westerlund, A., Fox, N. A., Zeanah, C. H., & Nelson, C. A. (2009). The effects of early experience on face recognition: An event-related potential study of institutionalized children in Romania. *Child Development, 80*(4), 1039–1056.

Nelson, C. A. (2007). A neurobiological perspective on early human deprivation. *Child Development Perspectives, 1*(1), 13–18.

Nelson, C. A., Parker, S. W., & Guthrie, D. (2006). The discrimination of facial expressions by typically developing infants and toddlers and those experiencing early institutional care. *Infant Behavior and Development, 29*(2), 210–219.

Nelson, C. A., Zeanah, C. H., Fox, N. A., Marshall, P. J., Smyke, A. T., & Guthrie, D. (2007). Cognitive recovery in socially deprived young children: The Bucharest Early Intervention Project. *Science, 318*, 1937–1940.

O'Connor, T. G., Bredenkamp, D., Rutter, M., & the ERA Study Team. (1999). Attachment disturbances and disorders in children exposed to early severe deprivation. *Infant Mental Health Journal, 20*(1), 10–29.

O'Connor, T. G., Marvin, R. S., Rutter, M., Olrick, J. T., & Britner, P. A. (2003). Child–parent attachment following early institutional deprivation. *Development and Psychopathology, 15*(1), 19–38.

O'Connor, T. G., & Rutter, M. (2000). Attachment disorder behavior following early severe deprivation: Extension and longitudinal follow-up. *Journal of the American Academy of Child Adolescent Psychiatry, 39*(6), 703–712.

Pears, K. C., Bruce, J., Fisher, P. A., & Kim, H. K. (2010). Indiscriminate friendliness in maltreated foster children. *Child Maltreatment, 15*, 64–75.

Pollak, S. D., Nelson, C. A., Schlaak, M. F., Roeber, B. J., Wewerka, S. S., Wiik, K. L., et al. (2010). Neurodevelopmental effects of early deprivation in postinstitutionalized children. *Child Development, 81*(1), 224–236.

Roy, P., Rutter, M., & Pickles, A. (2004). Institutional care: Associations between overactivity and lack of selectivity in social relationships. *Journal of Psychology and Psychiatry, 45*(4), 866–873.

Rudman, R. (2009). Managing sensory processing disorder in the preschool classroom. *Pacing and Clinical Electrophysiology, 3*(1), 23–29.

Rueda, M. R., Rothbart, M. K., McCandliss, B. D., Saccomanno, L., & Posner, M. (2005). Training, maturation, and genetic influences on the development of executive attention. *Proceeds of the National Academy of Sciences USA, 102*(41), 14931–14936.

Rutter, M. (1981). *Maternal deprivation reassessed.* New York: Penguin.

Rutter, M., Andersen-Wood, L., Beckett, C., Bredenkamp, D., Castle, J., Groothues, C., et al. (1999). Quasi-autistic patterns following severe early global privation. *Journal of Child Psychology and Psychiatry, 40*(4), 537–549.

Rutter, M., Kreppner, J., & O'Connor, T. G. (2001). Specificity and heterogeneity in children's responses to profound institutional privation. *British Journal of Psychiatry, 179*, 97–103.

Rutter, M., & Sonuga-Barke, E. J. (2010). X. Conclusions: overview of findings from the era study, inferences, and research implications. *Monographs of the Society for Research in Child Development, 75*(1), 212–229.

Rutter, M., & the English and Romanian Adoptees (ERA) Study Team. (1998). Developmental catch-up, and deficit, following adoption after severe global early privation. *Journal of Child Psychology and Psychiatry, 39*(4), 465–476.

Schoenbrodt, L. A., Carran, D. T., & Preis, J. (2007). A study to evaluate the language development of post-institutionalised children adopted from Eastern European countries. *Language, Culture and Curriculum, 20*(1), 52–69.

Sloutsky, V. M. (1997). Institutional care and developmental outcomes of 6- and 7-year-old children: A contextual perspective. *International Journal of Behavioral Development, 20*, 131–151.

Smyke, A. T., Koga, S. F., Johnson, D. E., Fox, N. A., Marshall, P. J., Nelson, C. A., et al. (2007). The caregiving context in institution-reared and family-reared infants and toddlers in Romania. *Journal of Child Psychology and Psychiatry, 48*(2), 210–218.

Smyke, A. T., Zeanah, C. H., Fox, N. A., & Nelson, C. A. (2009). A new model of foster care for young children: The Bucharest Early Intervention Project. *Child Adolescent Psychiatry Clinics of North America, 18*(3), 721–734.

Smyke, A. T., Zeanah, C. H., Fox, N. A., Nelson, C. A., & Guthrie, D. (2010). Placement in foster care enhances quality of attachment among young institutionalized children. *Child Development, 81*(1), 212–223.

Sonuga-Barke, E. J., Beckett, C., Kreppner, J., Castle, J., Colvert, E., Stevens, S., et al. (2008). Is subnutrition necessary for a poor outcome following early institutional deprivation? *Developmental Medicine and Child Neurology, 50*(9), 664–671.

Sonuga-Barke, E. J., Schlotz, W., & Kreppner, J. (2010). V. Differentiating developmental trajectories for conduct, emotion, and peer problems following early deprivation. *Monographs of the Society for Research in Child Development, 75*(1), 102–124.

Sonuga-Barke, E. J., Schlotz, W., & Rutter, M. (2010). VII. Physical growth and maturation following early severe institutional deprivation: Do they mediate specific psychopathological effects? *Monographs of the Society for Research in Child Development, 75*(1), 143–166.

Sroufe, L. A., Carlson, E. A., Levy, A. K., & Egeland, B. (1999). Implications of attachment theory for developmental psychopathology. *Development and Psychopathology, 11*(1), 1–13.

St. Petersburg–USA Orphanage Research Team. (2008). The effects of early social–emotional and relationship experience on the development of young orphanage children. *Monographs of the Society for Research in Child Development, 73*(3), 1–262.

Tarullo, A., Bruce, J., & Gunnar, M. R. (2007). False belief and emotion understanding in post-institutionalized children. *Social Development, 16*, 57–78.

Teilmann, G., Peterson, J. H., Gormsen, M., Damgaard, K., Skakkebæk, N. E., & Kold Jenson, T. (2009). Early puberty in internationally adopted girls: Hormonal and clinical markers of puberty in 276 girls examined biannually over two years. *Hormone Research in Paediatrics, 72*, 236–246.

Tirella, L., Chan, P. K., & Miller, L. (2006). Educational outcomes of children adopted from Eastern Europe, now ages 8–12. *Journal of Research in Childhood Education, 20*, 245–254.

U.S. Department of Education. (2006, October 4). IDEA regulations: Identification of specific learning disabilities. Retrieved from *idea.ed.gov*.

U.S. Department of State. (2009). Adoption visa issuance for FY-2009. Retrieved from *www.adoption.state.gov*.

Vanderwert, R. E., Marshall, P. J., Nelson, C. A., Zeanah, C. H., & Fox, N. A. (2010). Timing of intervention affects brain electrical activity in children exposed to severe psychosocial neglect. *PLS ONE, 5*(7), e11415.

van IJzendoorn, H. W., & Juffer, F. (2006). Adoption as intervention: Meta-analytic evidence for massive catch-up and plasticity in physical, socio-emotional, and cognitive development. *Journal of Child Psychology and Psychiatry, 27*, 1228–1245.

van IJzendoorn, M. H., Bakermans-Kranenburg, M. J., & Juffer, F. (2007). Plasticity of growth in height, weight, and head circumference: Meta-analytic evidence of massive catch-up after international adoption. *Journal of Developmental Behavior Pediatrics, 28*(4), 334–343.

van IJzendoorn, M. H., Juffer, F., & Poelhuis, C. W. (2005). Adoption and cognitive development: A meta-analytic comparison of adopted and nonadopted children's IQ and school performance. *Psychological Bulletin, 131*(2), 301–316.

Virdis, R., Street, M. E., Zampolli, M., Radetti, G., Pezzini, B., Benelli, M., et al. (1998). Precocious puberty in girls adopted from developing countries. *Archives of Diseases in Childhood, 78*(2), 152–154.

Wiik, K. L., Loman, M. M., Van Ryzin, M. J., Armstrong, J. M., Essex, M. J., Pollak, S. D., et al.

(2010). Behavioral and emotional symptoms of post-institutionalized children in middle childhood. *Journal of Child Psychology and Psychiatry, 56–63.*

Wilbarger, J., Gunnar, M. R., Schneider, M. L., & Pollak, S. D. (2010,). Sensory Processing in Internationally-adopted, Post-institutionalized Children. *Journal of Child Psychology and Psychiatry, 51*(10), 1105–1114.

Windsor, J., Glaze, L. E., Koga, S. F., & the Bucharest Early Intervention Project Core Group. (2007). Language acquisition with limited input: Romanian institution and foster care. *Journal of Speech, Language, and Hearing Research, 50,* 1365–1381.

Wismer Fries, A. B., & Pollak, S. D. (2004). Emotion understanding in postinstitutionalized Eastern European children. *Development and Psychopathology, 16*(2), 355–369.

Wismer Fries, A. B., Shirtcliff, E. A., & Pollak, S. D. (2008). Neuroendocrine dysregulation following early social deprivation in children. *Develomental Psychobiology, 50*(6), 588–599.

Wismer Fries, A. B., Ziegler, T. E., Kurian, J. R., Jacoris, S., & Pollak, S. D. (2005). Early experience in humans is associated with changes in neuropeptides critical for regulating social behavior. *Proceedings of the National Academy of Sciences USA, 102*(47), 17237–17240.

Zeanah, C. H., & Gleason, M. M. (2010). Reactive attachment disorder: A review for DSM-V. Retrieved from *www.dsm5.org/proposedrevisions/pages/proposedrevision.*

Zeanah, C. H., Nelson, C. A., Fox, N. A., Smyke, A. T., Marshall, P., Parker, S. W., et al. (2003). Designing research to study the effects of institutionalization on brain and behavioral development: The Bucharest Early Intervention Project. *Development and Psychopathology, 15,* 885–907.

Zeanah, C. H., Smyke, A. T., & Dumitrescu, A. (2002). Attachment disturbances in young children: II. Indiscriminate behavior and institutional care. *Journal of the American Academy of Child and Adolescent Psychiatry, 41*(8), 983–989.

Zeanah, C. H., Smyke, A. T., Koga, S. F., & Carlson, E. (2005). Attachment in institutionalized and community children in Romania. *Child Development, 76*(5), 1015–1028.

CHAPTER 23

Access, Participation, and Supports

A Framework for Improving Inclusive Early Education Opportunities for Children with Disabilities

Virginia Buysse

Today, ever-increasing numbers of infants and young children with disabilities in the United States have opportunities to develop and learn in many different types of *inclusive* and *natural* settings. This represents a stark contrast to previous educational practices, prior to inclusion, in which children with disabilities generally were isolated and separated from their typically developing peers. Generally positive views toward early childhood inclusion as an appropriate practice reflect broader societal values about the importance of helping each child reach his or her full potential, and promoting every child's sense of belonging as a full member of a family and a community.

But reaching consensus on the value of inclusion in early childhood does not mean that there is universal agreement on the best way to implement and support this approach in early care and education programs. Implementing early childhood inclusion in an effective manner entails a complex set of related policies and practices that are designed to have an impact on different aspects of the early childhood system: the individual child and family, programs and settings, professional development, program quality standards and accountability, and the entire service delivery system. It means ensuring that an individual child and his or her family have positive experiences and outcomes related to inclusion, while also recognizing the need for a broader system of services and supports that address the individual needs of many other young children with disabilities and their families in ways that are consistent and predictable across different contexts.

Not surprisingly, the early childhood field faces enormous challenges in this regard. Fortunately, the field can turn to a body of knowledge amassed through research, as well as consensus wisdom on inclusion, as a framework for identifying the key components of high-quality inclusive programs. This knowledge in turn can be used to shape the educational policies and practices that support the implementation of inclusion across a wide variety of early childhood places and contexts—homes, early care and education programs, neighborhoods, recreational programs, and a host of other community-based settings.

This chapter describes current knowledge about early childhood inclusion, summarizing the research literature and consensus wisdom contained within the joint Division for Early Childhood/National Association for the Education of Young Children (DEC/NAEYC; 2009) position statement, and identifying specific educational practices that promote *access*, *participation*, and *supports*—the defining features of high-quality inclusive services for young children with disabilities and their families. This information is intended for multiple purposes. It can be used by families and other consumers to advocate for quality inclusive services and supports, by practitioners and administrators to create a program philosophy on inclusion and to support program quality improvement efforts, by professional development (PD) providers to inform the development of professional competencies and the content of PD, and by policymakers and researchers to advance knowledge and understanding on all of these issues. The chapter ends with ideas about new opportunities on the horizon for promoting high-quality inclusion.

Research on Early Childhood Inclusion

Research on early childhood inclusion in the United States stretches over a period of more than 30 years. The National Professional Development Center on Inclusion (NPDCI; 2009) summarized what is currently known about early childhood inclusion, drawing on published articles, books, critical reviews, and syntheses on this topic (Buysse & Hollingsworth, 2009a). The summary offered succinct conclusions from this body of literature, referred to as research synthesis points, along with a list of references to support each of the key conclusions, including both primary sources in the form of reports of original studies and several published reviews and syntheses (Guralnick, 2001; Odom, 2002; Odom et al., 2004). Rather than being an exhaustive review of the literature, the NPDCI summary provided the most current and representative studies on specific topics related to inclusion to support the broad conclusions drawn from this body of research (see NPDCI, 2009, for a complete list of supporting references). The research synthesis points consist of the following:

1. *Inclusion takes many forms.* Currently, states are required to report annually to the U.S. Department of Education the number of children with disabilities who participate in inclusive programs. However, current reporting requirements do not provide information about the quality of these services and supports for children and families. What is known is that inclusion can occur in a wide variety of organizational and community contexts (e.g., homes, child care, Head Start, recreational programs, PreK programs). Furthermore, there are many ways in which inclusive services can be designed and implemented (e.g., itinerant services, blended programs, coteaching, home visiting, family supports, community-based services). Regardless of what form inclusion takes, the defining features of inclusion (access, participation, and supports) serve as the foundation for ensuring high-quality early care and education to achieve its desired results for children and families.

2. *Universal access to inclusive programs for children with disabilities is far from a reality.* According to the most recent annual report to Congress in 2007, approximately 51% of children from 3 to 5 years old with disabilities spend at least some time in an inclusive setting with typically developing peers, while 35% receive services in specialized or self-contained settings (U.S. Department of Education, 2010). The vast majority of infants and toddlers (approximately 83%) receive early intervention services through home visiting,

while approximately 4% of these children receive services in other types of settings that also serve typically developing peers. A national longitudinal study found that 57% of parents of prekindergartners with disabilities reported that their child participated at least once a month in play groups, story hours, church- or synagogue-affiliated activities, lessons, athletics, and other children's organizations (Carlson, Bitterman, & Daley, 2010). Much more work is needed to ensure that all young children with disabilities (particularly infants and toddlers in center-based programs and child care homes) and their families have access to the highest quality inclusive programs and services.

3. *Inclusion can benefit children with and without disabilities.* Strong research evidence shows that children with disabilities enrolled in inclusive settings make at least as much developmental progress as they do in noninclusive settings. Furthermore, there is some evidence to suggest that children with disabilities in inclusive programs make greater progress in the areas of social development, communication, and perhaps play. There is also limited evidence to suggest that inclusion does not impede learning for typically developing children, and that it may help these children develop tolerance and acceptance of individual differences in their peers. Due to the variation in how inclusion has been defined and implemented across studies, it is difficult to identify specific aspects of programs (e.g., the percentage of children, with and without disabilities, enrolled; the curriculum used; the specific practices adults use to facilitate play and learning) that likely influenced the positive outcomes reported in young children.

4. *Factors such as child characteristics, policies, resources, and attitudes influence the acceptance and implementation of inclusion.* This body of research suggests that beliefs and practices related to inclusion are based on many factors, and all of these factors can influence how well inclusion is accepted and implemented. Some of these influencing factors identified in the literature include the nature and severity of a child's disability, professional attitudes toward inclusion, parental preferences and priorities for various types of services, financial incentives for inclusion, and professional and program standards.

5. *Specialized instruction is an important component of inclusion and a factor affecting child outcomes.* A variety of research-based instructional strategies support child development and learning in the context of inclusion. These include curricular modifications (e.g., adding visual prompts, reinforcing key vocabulary words), adapting the learning environment (e.g., using assistive technology, rearranging the furniture to accommodate a wheelchair or walker), peer supports (e.g., pairing a child with disabilities and a more competent peer during a small-group activity), embedded interventions (i.e., addressing learning goals within the context of daily routines and activities), and individualized scaffolding strategies (e.g., response prompting, modeling, corrective feedback), among others. Other approaches have little empirical evidence but represent promising practices based on preliminary studies, research conducted with school-age children, or strong conceptual frameworks. These include tiered models of instruction and intervention, and universal design for learning (UDL) that involves multiple and varied formats for learning.

6. *Collaboration among parents, teachers, and specialists is a cornerstone of high-quality inclusion.* Collaboration has been identified as an essential component of high-quality inclusion by families and professionals. Promising models for effective communication and collaboration described in the literature include technical assistance, consultation, coaching, mentoring, and various team-based approaches (e.g., inter-, multi-, and transdisciplinary teams; communities of practice; professional learning communities). At this time, the empirical evidence for the effectiveness of many of these approaches in early childhood can best be characterized as nonexistent.

7. *Families of young children with disabilities generally view inclusion favorably, although some express concerns about the quality of early childhood programs and services.* Some of the issues that families have identified in the literature include concerns that general education teachers may not be qualified to work with their children, that their children may not receive sufficient adult attention and support, and that their children may not experience positive peer relationships. However, most families have expressed positive attitudes toward inclusion and report that their children have benefited from inclusion in a variety of ways.

8. *The quality of early childhood programs that enroll children with disabilities is as good as, or slightly better than, the quality of programs that do not enroll these children.* There is limited research indicating that the quality of inclusive programs is as good as, or slightly better than, the quality of programs that do not enroll children with disabilities. However, it is important to note that much of the research supporting this conclusion was based on general measures of program quality. Few studies have evaluated the quality of programs on the basis of inclusive practices for individual children with disabilities and their families. At least some evidence suggests that inclusive programs rated higher on general classroom practices also had more qualified teachers. The field needs additional measures of program quality that assess dimensions of quality inclusion related to access, participation, and supports.

9. *Early childhood professionals may not be adequately prepared to serve young children with disabilities and their families in inclusive programs.* The little research evidence that exists in this area suggests that few early childhood teacher education programs require one or more courses in working with children with disabilities. Furthermore, related research has found that a large proportion of early childhood professionals located in community-based early care and education programs reported a lack of knowledge or comfort regarding their work with children with disabilities, particularly children with severe disabilities. Existing studies lack information about whether specific inclusive practices such as embedded interventions or scaffolding strategies reflect core competencies and the content of teacher education programs in early childhood.

Defining Features of High-Quality Early Childhood Inclusion

In 2009 the DEC of the Council for Exceptional Children (CEC) and the NAEYC released a joint position statement on early childhood inclusion. Facilitated by the NPDCI, the process of developing and validating the joint position statement included multiple opportunities for members of both organizations and the field at large to provide input and feedback (for additional information see Buysse, Hollingsworth, & Catlett, 2009). A total of 753 members of the early childhood field participated in an online validation survey, and 457 members provided written comments, ranging from one or two sentences to two to three pages in length, that were used to make final revisions to the joint position statement. Respondents included practitioners (35%), state and local administrators (22%), family members (4%), higher education faculty and professional development providers (19%), students (11%), and others (9%). Ratings were obtained for the quality ($M = 4.40$, $SD = 0.81$), relevance ($M = 4.40$, $SD = 0.82$), and utility ($M = 4.27$, $SD = 0.83$) of the joint position statement on a scale of 1 (very low) to 5 (very high) on each dimension. A total of 94% of respondents indicated that they endorsed the joint position statement.

The development and validation of a joint position statement on inclusion was a historic event within the early childhood field for several reasons. For one, federal legislation on inclusion under the Individuals with Disabilities Education Act (IDEA) enacted over the past three decades (reauthorized as the Individuals with Disabilities Education Improvement Act of 2004, Public Law No. 108-446) had fundamentally changed the way early childhood services could be designed and delivered for young children with disabilities and their families, but, surprisingly, there was not an agreed-upon definition of *early childhood inclusion*. The lack of a shared definition contributed to misunderstandings about inclusion and served as an obstacle to reaching agreement among stakeholder groups on what types of services and supports were necessary to implement inclusion in early care and education settings. For example, cross-sector state teams had consistently mentioned the need for an agreed-upon definition of *inclusion* in conjunction with their efforts to create an integrated, statewide professional development system (Buysse, Winton, & Rous, 2009). Consequently, reaching consensus on the meaning of *inclusion* and its implications for practice constituted an important milestone. Additionally, it was the first time that these leading, national professional organizations representing the general and special early childhood education fields had worked together to produce a consensus position statement. This collaboration helped pave the way for a subsequent effort to work together on a joint DEC/NAEYC position statement on response to intervention (RTI) in early childhood (*community.fpg.unc. edu/resources/community-contributed-content/plan-for-joint-position-statement-on-rti. pdf/view*), this time in collaboration with a third professional organization—the National Head Start Association (NHSA). Perhaps most indicative of the extent to which the joint position statement on inclusion has influenced thinking on this issue is the impact it has had at different levels in the field. For example, the national discussions that ensued as part of the process of developing a joint position statement on inclusion have continued and prompted some states to revise their quality rating and improvement systems (QRISs) to include dimensions of high-quality inclusion. Other examples of the impact of the joint position statement can be found in the creation of new resources on inclusion organized around the concepts of access, participation, and supports. These include Web-based professional development modules, assessment tools, and even a blog called *Christine's Chronicles*, written by the mother of a young child with disabilities, with the goal of sharing her family's unique experiences with inclusion (Lindauer, 2009).

Defining High-Quality Inclusion

The DEC/NAEYC (2009) joint position statement defines inclusion in the following way:

> Early childhood inclusion embodies the values, policies, and practices that support the right of every infant and young child and his or her family, regardless of ability, to participate in a broad range of activities and contexts as full members of families, communities, and society. The desired results of inclusive experiences for children with and without disabilities and their families include a sense of belonging and membership, positive social relationships and friendships, and development and learning to reach their full potential. The defining features of inclusion that can be used to identify high quality early childhood programs and services are access, participation, and supports.

Using the Joint Position Statement on Inclusion to Shape Policies and Practices

In addition to providing a definition of inclusion, the DEC/NAEYC (2009) joint position statement provided six recommendations for how the information can be used by families and professionals alike to shape educational policies and practices that support high-quality inclusion. These included the following:

1. *Create high expectations for every child to reach his or her full potential.* The joint position statement was designed to assist families and professionals in their efforts to advocate for young children with disabilities. Having shared expectations that every child should reach his or her potential was described as the first step in selecting appropriate learning goals, and ensuring that families and professionals reach consensus on the best way of organizing services and supports to accomplish them.

2. *Develop a program philosophy on inclusion.* As part of an overall mission statement, programs were advised to develop a program philosophy on inclusion to ensure that program staff operate under a similar set of assumptions, values, and beliefs about the best ways to support the development and learning of children with disabilities in the context of inclusion. It was suggested that agreement on these broad-based principles would in turn lead to the identification of specific teaching and intervening practices aimed at ensuring that children with disabilities are full members of a community and have multiple opportunities to learn, develop, and form positive relationships. For example, the principles of access and participation align with the practice of embedding learning opportunities within daily routines and the general education curriculum, rather than providing pull-out services and isolated therapies for children with disabilities.

3. *Establish a system of services and supports.* Reaching consensus on the meaning of inclusion was intended to inform the creation of a continuum of services and supports that respond to the individual characteristics and needs of children with various types of disabilities (including children at risk for learning difficulties) enrolled in early care and education programs. Such services and supports can include home visiting programs, itinerant services, family support, specialized programs and interventions, therapies, assistive technology, and equipment. Regardless of the nature or severity of the disability, specialized services and therapies should be coordinated and integrated with general early childhood services to ensure access, participation, and the supports needed to achieve the desired results related to inclusion. Furthermore, the joint position statement encouraged the principle of natural proportions to guide the design of inclusive early childhood programs. The "principle of natural proportions" means that, to the extent that it is possible, the composition of early childhood settings should reflect the proportion of children with disabilities that exists within the general population.

4. *Revise program and professional standards.* Existing program and professional standards in early childhood primarily reflect the needs of the general population of young children and their families, a fundamentally essential but insufficient framework to promote high-quality inclusion for children with disabilities and their families. The joint position statement can be used to incorporate the defining features of inclusion (i.e., access, participation, and supports) that can be used to identify dimensions of quality inclusive programs and the competencies of professionals who work with children, with and without disabilities, in these settings.

5. *Achieve an integrated professional development system.* The joint position statement was intended to promote the move toward the creation of integrated, cross-sector professional development systems to support the early care and education of diverse young learners, including children with disabilities, and their families. Toward this end, the joint position statement was intended to help designers determine who would benefit from professional development, what practitioners need to know and be able to do, and how learning opportunities can be organized and delivered as part of an integrated professional development system to produce the desired results for children and families.

6. *Influence federal and state accountability systems.* The joint position statement was intended to influence federal and state accountability standards. Policymakers were encouraged to move away from only requiring states to report annually the number of children with disabilities who received services in inclusive settings and to emphasize instead the quality and intensity of the services experienced by children and families, and the outcomes of these services.

Practices That Promote Access, Participation, and Supports

The DEC/NAEYC (2009) joint position statement on inclusion offered the early childhood field clear, consensus wisdom on the meaning of inclusion and the defining features (access, participation, and supports) that distinguish high-quality inclusive programs, services, and supports from those that do not reflect these features. But the position statement accomplished even more. It identified particular practices that could be used to promote access and participation of young children and families in the context of inclusion, and the kinds of necessary infrastructure to support the implementation of inclusion systemwide. In this way, the joint position statement shifted the focus from the myriad issues and challenges related to inclusion that preoccupied the field previously to specific practices for implementing and supporting inclusion at all levels of the system, beginning with practical strategies that have empirical evidence of effectiveness (or show promise in this regard) for use with individual children and their families. In keeping with standards for establishing the evidence base for instructional and intervention practices now widely embraced as part of the evidence-based practice movement, the following sections present a description of specific practices related to access and participation that incorporate core elements from research (if available) that can be used to appraise the evidence base of these practices (Buysse & Wesley, 2006; National Research Council, 2002; Sackett, Straus, Richardson, Rosenberg, & Haynes, 2000). These core elements for determining the evidence base of specific practices include an operational definition of the practice, the settings and contexts in which the practice is implemented, the characteristics of the target group for whom the practice is intended, the qualifications of those who implement the practice, and the outcomes associated with using the practice (Horner, Sugai, & Anderson, 2010). Table 23.1 reflects efforts undertaken by NPDCI to summarize the most promising or effective practices related to access, participation, and supports within inclusion.

Access

Access means providing a wide range of activities and environments for every child, removing physical or structural barriers, and offering multiple ways to promote learning and development. Access means something different for each child. For example, the first step in promoting the social development of a young child with developmental delays who has no, or limited, opportunities to play with typically developing peers would be to create such opportunities (e.g., by arranging playdates or enrolling the child in an inclusive early childhood program), prior to intervention using a social skills curriculum. For a child with significant communication delays who is already enrolled in an inclusive classroom, access would mean ensuring that this child has a way to communicate his or her wants and needs to primary caregivers, teachers, and other children (e.g., using sign language or a communication device). The joint position statement identified universal design (UD), universal design for learning (UDL), and assistive technology (AT) as promising or effective practices for promoting access to inclusion.

TABLE 23.1. Practices and Activities That Promote Access, Participation, and Supports

Defining feature of inclusion	Instructional/intervention practices or activities	Description
Access: removing physical barriers, providing a wide range of activities and environments, and making necessary adaptations to create opportunities for optimal development and learning for individual children.	Universal design (UD)/ Universal design for learning (UDL)	• Supports access to early care and education environments through the removal of physical and structural barriers (UD). • Provides multiple and varied formats for instruction and learning (UDL).
	Assistive technology (AT)	• Involves a range of strategies to promote a child's access to learning opportunities, from making simple changes to the environment and materials to helping a child use special equipment and technology.
Participation: using a range of instructional and intervention approaches to promote engagement in play and learning activities, and a sense of belonging for each child.	Embedded instruction/ interventions (related terms include routines-based or activity-based instruction/interventions and integrated therapy)	• Strategies that address specific developmental or learning goals within the context of everyday activities, routines, and transitions at home, at school, or in the community.
	Scaffolding strategies	Providing the following types of strategies across a wide range of teaching and learning contexts for children who require intensive learning supports: • Modeling: demonstrating how to do something • Response prompting: providing assistance to elicit a response • Variations of prompting and modeling: increasing–decreasing the level of assistance, adding wait time, or combining strategies • Peer supports: enlisting peers to support another child in learning • Corrective feedback: responses that reinforce correct responses and address incorrect responses or nonresponses
	Tiered models of instruction/intervention	• Involves gathering assessments on children's behavior or learning to plan and organize instruction/ interventions and to monitor progress.
Supports: creating an infrastructure of systems-level supports for implementing high-quality inclusion.	Professional development	• Teaching and learning activities designed to support the acquisition of professional knowledge, skills, and dispositions related to inclusion, as well as the application of this knowledge in practice. The content of the PD should include evidence-based practices that define high-quality early childhood inclusion.
	Models of collaboration, communication, and coordination	• Approaches that promote multiple opportunities for collaboration among key stakeholders (families, practitioners, specialists, administrators) to support implementation of high-quality inclusive practices. Models that support this type of collaboration include technical assistance, consultation, coaching, mentoring, IEP/IFSP teams, collaborative problem solving, and communities of practice/professional learning communities.
	Policies	• Quality frameworks (e.g., early learning standards, professional competencies, program standards, QRISs) that reflect and guide high-quality inclusive practices as well as addressing the needs of the general population of young children and families.

(cont.)

TABLE 23.1. *(cont.)*

Defining feature of inclusion	Instructional/intervention practices or activities	Description
	Resources	• Funding approaches that support the appropriation of resources across health and human service agencies and the strategic use of financial incentives to increase universal access to high-quality inclusive opportunities.
	Research and program evaluation	• Research and program evaluation that advance knowledge and understanding about the most effective ways of implementing inclusion, develop and evaluate research-based practices that promote children's development and learning and family support, and identify strategies for improving the quality of inclusive services for children and families.

Note. IEP/IFSP, individualized education plan/individualized family service plan; QRIS, quality rating and improvement system. From the National Professional Development Center on Inclusion (2011). Reprinted by permission.

UD and UDL

UD is a concept that means supporting the access of children with disabilities to many different types of environments and settings through the removal of physical and structural barriers, whereas UDL reflects practices that provide multiple and varied formats to promote wider access to teaching and learning activities (DEC/NAEYC, 2009). The Center for Applied Special Technology (CAST) provides an array of resources that can be used by teachers and families to expand learning opportunities for all individuals, with a particular focus on school-age children with disabilities, almost exclusively through UDL (for more information on CAST, see *www.cast.org*). According to the National Universal Design for Learning (UDL) Task Force, the Higher Education Opportunity Act of 2008 (Section 103 [a] [24]) defined UDL as

> a scientifically valid framework for guiding educational practice that (a) provides flexibility in the ways information is presented, in the ways students respond or demonstrate knowledge, and in the ways students are engaged; and (b) reduces barriers in instruction; provides appropriate accommodations, supports, and challenges; and maintains high achievement expectations for all students, including students with disabilities and students who are limited English proficient. (*www.advocacyinstitute.org/udl/nclb.shtml*)

In 2007, the DEC published a set of recommendations as a companion to a NAEYC position statement that explained how UD and UDL principles could be translated into practices that promote the development and learning of children with disabilities. DEC identified three essential principles of UDL in this regard: (1) multiple means of representation (i.e., learning opportunities provided in various formats and at different levels of complexity to address a range of ability levels and learning characteristics); (2) multiple means of engagement (i.e., using a range of strategies for arousing and maintaining children's attention, curiosity, and motivation in learning); and (3) multiple means of expression (i.e., providing a variety of options and formats for children to respond, demonstrate what they know, and express their ideas and feelings). The DEC publication noted that applying UD and UDL principles means building universal access components from the beginning rather than after the fact as an adaptation. In this way, UDL can be distinguished from other approaches for promoting access and participation for children with disabilities that rely on strategies such as embedded interventions or the use of scaffolding to modify existing physical environments or add instructional approaches not originally designed to address the needs of children with varying learning abilities. With respect to removing physical or structural barriers to buildings, UD would mean addressing access issues at the design stage, creating ramps, rails, and accessible entrances from inception. With respect to early childhood curricula or developmental approaches, UDL would mean incorporating accommodations (e.g., modifications in the instructional level, assessments, content, and performance criteria to include alternative assessments and instructional accommodations for children who need them) that address the full range of diversity in the children and families who might participate—from the beginning, as part of the development phase.

The DEC recommendations provided many examples of how UDL principles of multiple means of representation, engagement, and expression can be incorporated into early care and education practices with young children with disabilities. However, at this time, the early childhood field is at a very early stage in defining and evaluating the specific practices that reflect UD principles. Consequently, these practices represent a promising but as yet unproven approach for promoting access within inclusion. Additional research is needed to determine the target population for whom these practices will be most effective and most feasible, the types of settings and contexts in which these practices work best, the professional development required to ensure that practitioners can implement these practices appropriately and with fidelity, and the benefits of using these strategies with young children and families.

Assistive Technology (AT)

Provisions within IDEA (2004) differentiate between AT and AT services. AT is defined as "any item, piece of equipment, or product system, whether acquired commercially off the shelf, modified, or customized, that is used to increase, maintain, or improve functional capabilities of a child with a disability" (p. 15, cited in Moore & Wilcox, 2006). By contrast, AT services are defined as "any service that directly assists a child with a disability in the selection, acquisition, or use of an assistive technology device" (p. 16, cited in Moore & Wilcox, 2006). Such services within IDEA include (1) evaluation of the needs of the child; (2) purchasing, leasing, or providing for the acquisition of the device; and (3) training or technical assistance in the use of the device for a child or for professionals. These two related definitions point both to the importance of the hardware or specialized technology associated with the term *AT* and the specific practices designed to help children with disabilities use the technology to access their physical and social surroundings and to promote their development and learning. Project Connect (the Center to Mobilize Early Childhood Knowledge) proposed yet another term, *AT interventions*, which combines these two critical dimensions (i.e., technology and adult support) and also recognizes that these strategies are designed for use by practitioners and families, in addition to the "services" provided by specialists. The Project Connect definition is as follows: "AT interventions involve a range of strategies to promote a child's access to learning opportunities, from making simple changes to the environment and materials to helping a child use special equipment (Winton, Buysse, Rous, Epstein, & Pierce, 2011)."

Adaptations and devices that are easy to find and use are considered low-tech because they include items such as bath seats and other baby equipment that are readily available at low cost to most families. At the other end of the continuum are specialized, high-tech devices that are more complex and include augmentative communication, switches, power wheelchairs, and computerized toys not readily available for use by the general population.

Practitioners and families support children's use of all of these devices in a variety of ways, first, by evaluating a child's need for such approaches; second, by identifying appropriate adaptations and technologies; and third, by teaching children and families how to use these devices. It is important to note that some low-tech AT devices require very little teaching or technical assistance for children and families to incorporate them into their daily routines (e.g., special spoons or plates, picture symbols, hand grips, positioning supports), whereas most high-tech devices (e.g., augmentative communication devices, motorized wheelchairs, computerized toys), require demonstration and coaching to ensure that the AT equipment and devices will be used appropriately and effectively. A list of AT resources and related websites appears in Table 23.2.

A research synthesis reviewed 104 articles published from 1980 through 2004 about AT with infants and young children (Campbell, Milbourne, Dugan, & Wilcox, 2006). Of these, 77 were descriptive or discussion-oriented articles about recommended AT practices with infants and young children, and 27 reported the results of studies examining the effectiveness of AT practices or interventions (four of these that focused on experiments to teach the use of prosthetic limbs, generally viewed as medical devices rather than as AT, were subsequently dropped, leaving a total of 23 articles on the effectiveness of AT for young children). The majority of the 23 studies examining the effectiveness of AT employed single-participant designs; only one study used a group design with random assignment to condition; and the remaining studies used quasi-experimental designs, case studies, or qualitative methods. Across all studies, the infants and young children ranged in age from 2½ to 60 months and were reported as having cerebral palsy, severe multiple disabilities, physical disabilities, global developmental delays, mild mental retardation, speech and language delays, and Down syndrome. Most of the 23 studies examining effectiveness focused on teaching children switch activation. As a whole, these studies provided relatively strong evidence that children as young as 1 year old with various types of physical disabilities and developmental delays could be taught to operate switches to activate toys and other devices. Only one of the 23 studies reported on the effectiveness of teaching young children to use augmentative communication devices, and it revealed that all of the children demonstrated increased communications following the intervention using a naturalistic instructional strategy implemented by teachers. The results of studies examining strategies to teach young children to use power mobility devices and computers were inconclusive due to methodological weaknesses. Across all AT devices, the review found that the primary teaching strategy was providing opportunities for children to access the device and to practice using it, either independently or with some adult or peer involvement. For example, children learned power mobility simply through opportunities to experiment with moving the power mobility device and through trial-and-error learning rather than receiving instruction in how to use the devices.

TABLE 23.2. Resources for Using AT with Young Children and Families

- AT for infants and toddlers: *www.fape.org/pubs/fape-12.pdf*
- Family Center on Technology and Disability (FCTD): *www.fctd.info*
- Developmental Research for the Effective Advancement of Memory and Motor Skills (DREAMMS) for Kids: *www.dreamms.org*
- Tots-n-Tech Research Institute (TnT): *tnt.asu.edu*
- AT for infants, toddlers, and young children: *www.nectac.org/topics/atech/atech.asp*
- Early Childhood Technology Integrated Instructional System (EC-TIIS): *www.wiu.edu/users/ectiis*
- CONNECT: The Center to Mobilize Early Childhood Knowledge: *community.fpg.unc.edu/connect*
- Cara's Kit: *www.dec-sped.org/store/additional_resources*

The authors of the review called for further research on AT with young children that focuses on not only evaluating intervention effectiveness for performance of isolated skills but also promoting children's successful participation within the context of a variety of everyday activities and routines. A related review of 19 studies on the effectiveness of adaptations to the environment, materials, and activities in young children with disabilities found that all three types of adaptations were related to positive changes in child behavior, particularly with respect to communication and cognition (e.g., utterances, toy play), and, to a lesser extent, social behavior (e.g., self-care, social functioning) (Trivette, Dunst, Hamby & O'Herin, 2010). Furthermore, the adaptations were most effective when used for 10 or more sessions. Moore and Wilcox (2006) cited both limited previous research indicating that the majority of early childhood practitioners were unprepared to provide AT interventions with young children and their own research showing that early childhood practitioners lacked confidence in their ability to obtain and use AT resources and support services.

Participation

Ensuring that environments and programs provide each child with access to learning opportunities does not guarantee that every child will be able to participate fully in those learning opportunities. For example, removing physical barriers and providing a communication device could promote access to learning for a child with cerebral palsy, but this child almost certainly will need additional individualized accommodations and supports to participate fully in play and learning activities with peers and adults. Participation means using a range of instructional and intervention approaches to promote engagement in both play and learning activities, and a sense of belonging for each child. The DEC/NAEYC (2009) joint position statement identified practices such as embedded interventions, scaffolding, and tiered models of instruction and intervention, as promising or effective for promoting the participation of children, with and without disabilities, within inclusive settings.

Embedded Instruction and Interventions

Embedded instruction and interventions—and related practices such as embedded learning opportunities, routines-based intervention, activity-based instruction and intervention, and integrated therapy—embody the idea of supporting a child's development and learning (regardless of ability level) within the context of the natural environment. Embracing these practices is linked to key assumptions that have direct implications for how services and supports for young children with disabilities and their families will be organized and delivered. For example, the belief that children learn best through everyday experiences and routines with familiar people in familiar contexts suggests that early intervention services should occur in places that are part of the child's and family's normal life, and be woven throughout their daily routines and activities rather than being delivered in specialized programs or clinical settings (McWilliam, 2010).

Embedded instruction and interventions are implemented in different ways and across different contexts depending on the age of the child targeted for these services. For infants and toddlers with disabilities who receive Part C early intervention services, the most common location for such services is the child's own home, with a smaller number of children receiving services in a group-care setting. The embedded learning for infants and toddlers within a home-visiting context is commonly referred to as "routines-based intervention" and takes the form of supporting families in helping their children learn throughout the day, rather than working directly with the child with materials introduced by the home visitor as parents observe (McWilliam, 2010).

Most prekindergarten children (3- to 5-year-olds) with disabilities receive special education services in center-based early childhood programs or home-based child care settings. Project Connect developed a module on embedded interventions that offered the following definition of this practice: "strategies that address specific learning goals within the context of everyday activities, routines, and transitions at home, at school, or in the community" (Winton, Buysse, Turnbull, Rous, & Hollingsworth, 2010). Other researchers refer to these interventions as "embedded learning opportunities" (Horn, Lieber, Li, Sandall, & Schwartz, 2000) or "activity-based instruction" (Pretti-Frontczak, Barr, Macy, & Carter, 2003). Embedded interventions can occur naturally anytime and anyplace; they build on children's interests and extend learning by offering multiple opportunities to practice new skills. Adult support is the essential ingredient in the effective use of any embedded intervention. Examples of embedded interventions include making environmental changes, such as adding signs and labels in the classroom to support the development of concepts of prints, or modifying aspects of the curriculum, such as adding a picture-naming game to centers to support vocabulary development.

In contrast to pull-out therapy, *integrated therapy* is a term that means the provision of specialized instruction or therapy (e.g., speech–language, physical, occupational, and developmental therapies) that occurs at school, home, or in community-based settings within the context of daily routines and activities when other children are present (McWilliam, 1996). In a widely viewed video that has become a classic exemplar of the use of integrated therapy in early childhood, a physical therapist engages a group of toddlers in a group-care setting in a game of "Up, Up," in which all of the children are encouraged to lie on their backs and lift their legs as the therapist works with a young child with motor delays to strengthen his leg muscles.

Taken together, approaches that involve embedding interventions within children's natural environments, daily routines, and activities have been labeled and described in various ways by researchers, but overall, these strategies have more features in common than features that might distinguish them. Noting the growing body of research-based knowledge on this topic, Pretti-Frontczak and her colleagues (2003) created an annotated bibliography of key research studies and resources related to all of these "naturalistic" teaching approaches. These authors concluded that there are two general types of embedded intervention strategies: those using specific, targeted interventions, and those in which generic learning opportunities are employed. In the first approach, the learning activity generally is more structured and the teacher's role is more directive and involved; in the second, in which a learning opportunity might be created for multiple children within the general curriculum or a daily activity, the teacher's role is more likely to consist of monitoring children's responses to these learning opportunities, and redirecting, encouraging, and facilitating learning for children who either do not or cannot take advantage of them. The Connect Project summarized a research synthesis of 38 studies that examine the effectiveness of embedded interventions for 2- to 7-year-old children with disabilities in early childhood settings (Snyder, Hemmeter, Sandall, & McLean, 2007). This research indicated that practitioners (e.g., teachers, teaching assistants) rather than specialists (e.g., speech–language pathologists, physical therapists) were the ones who most often implemented the embedded interventions. Significantly, almost every study showed that children who received embedded interventions acquired targeted skills or made progress across a number of areas, including language and communication, motor and adaptive skills, cognitive development, academic learning, and social–emotional development. Furthermore, the findings of the synthesis suggest that there are a variety of ways of implementing embedded interventions, such as making changes to the curriculum or learning environment, taking advantage of natural learning opportunities throughout the day, using systematic instructional procedures, and enlisting support from children's peers.

Scaffolding Strategies

Scaffolding strategies are structured, targeted approaches that practitioners, families, and specialists can use with children who require more intensive supports across a wide variety of teaching and learning contexts, and in combination with other approaches (e.g., as part of embedded interventions and tiered models). The research literature is replete with information on the effectiveness of different types of scaffolding strategies, and various combinations and hybrids of these for use with infants and preschoolers with disabilities (e.g., Chiara, Schuster, Bell, & Wolery, 1995; Craig-Unkefer & Kaiser, 2002; Gibson & Schuster, 1992; Girolametto, Weitzman, & Greenberg, 2004; Hancock & Kaiser, 2006; Hawkings & Schuster, 2007; Kaiser, Hemmeter, & Ostrosky, 1996; Kaiser, Hester, & McDuffie, 2001; Kouri, 2005; Ostrosky & Kaiser, 1995; Ross & Greer, 2003; Walker, 2008; Wolery, 2000). All of these individual scaffolding strategies can be organized under several broad categories to create a more practical framework for applying these approaches to promote children's participation within inclusion. These categories include modeling, response prompting, variations of modeling and prompting, peer supports, and corrective feedback (Buysse, Soukakou, Peisner-Feinberg, & Benshoff, 2011).

MODELING

Modeling is an instructional strategy in which an adult demonstrates a response. There are two types of modeling: verbal and nonverbal. In verbal modeling, an adult uses language to demonstrate how to say or do something (e.g., as part of a word game with an infant, a parent looks at an object, then at the child and says, "Cup"). In nonverbal modeling, an adult uses physical movements, signs, or gestures to demonstrate how to say or do something (e.g., during a rhyming activity, a teacher demonstrates how to find two picture cards that show the words *log* and *dog*).

RESPONSE PROMPTING

Response prompting is an instructional strategy in which an adult offers assistance to elicit a response from a child. In verbal prompting, a teacher uses questions (i.e., mand-model) or verbal cues to help a child give a response (e.g., during an alphabet hunt, a parent says, "I see the letter *A* in this word. Can you find the letter *A*?"). In nonverbal prompting, an adult uses gestures, expectant looks, and physical assistance to help a child give a response (e.g., during the same alphabet hunt in which the child is asked to find the letter *A*, the parent points to the word and looks expectantly at the child).

VARIATIONS OF MODELING AND PROMPTING

There are many variations and combinations of approaches involving modeling and prompting. One variation of response prompting involves gradually increasing assistance to help a child perform a task: For example, when a toddler has difficulty with a shape puzzle, a parent might ask, "Where does the circle go?" If the child still can't give the correct response, then the parent might show the child where the circle goes and say, "The circle goes here. Put the circle here." Another variation of response prompting involves gradually decreasing assistance to help a child perform a task: For example, during the same activity with a shape puzzle, the parent might hand the circle to the child, point to the place where the circle goes, and say, "The circle goes here. Put the circle here." If the child is successful, the next time the parent might simply hand a triangle to the child, but not point to the place where the triangle goes. Delay procedures involve waiting a few seconds for a child's response, while looking expectantly at the child to create a prompt–wait–prompt sequence: For example, a teacher asks a child to identify the first sound in the word *dog* and waits for a few seconds. If there is no response, the teacher might prompt by saying, "*Dog* starts with the same letter as *Dakota*. Dakota starts with a. . . . " It is also possible to combine response prompting, wait time, and modeling to create a prompt–wait–show sequence: For example, while engaging in a finger play activity, a teacher tells a child that it is her turn to clap and waits for a response. If there is no response, then the teacher shows the child how to clap at the appropriate time.

PEER SUPPORTS

Peer supports involve enlisting a target child's peers to encourage the child to participate in a learning activity or demonstrate a correct response: For example, a more proficient peer is prompted to invite a target child to join him in playing a matching game, or a more proficient peer joins a target child in a small-group activity and demonstrates the use of key vocabulary words introduced during storytime.

CORRECTIVE FEEDBACK

Corrective feedback is a critical component of all teaching and learning contexts and frequently is combined with other scaffolding strategies, embedded interventions, and tiered models. It is used to reinforce correct responses (e.g., "That's right. You pointed to the dog") and address incorrect responses and nonresponses (e.g., the adult points to the correct picture and says, "Here is the dog. Point to the dog").

Although empirical evidence demonstrates the efficacy of many of these approaches with young children with disabilities when implemented under carefully controlled conditions by researchers, there is a need for additional research to show that these approaches can be implemented effectively by teachers and families in inclusive settings, without a high level of support by researchers. Although parents and teachers frequently use many of these approaches naturally in their interactions with young children, additional guidance would be helpful in determining which approaches may be more appropriate and effective for some children, and when and how to use them to systematically support high-quality inclusion.

Tiered Models of Instruction and Intervention

Tiered instructional approaches in early childhood are based largely on response to intervention (RTI), an approach that is gaining widespread acceptance in public schools throughout the United States for use in kindergarten through 12th grade. The key features of school-age RTI models involve (1) gathering information on students' skills to plan and organize instruction and targeted interventions, and (2) monitoring progress in learning to support data-based decision making. In the past several years, RTI has become a more familiar phrase within the early childhood field. Current provisions within IDEA address the use of RTI for school-age students, with a particular emphasis on students in kindergarten through third grade. However, there are no provisions within IDEA or any other federal legislation addressing the use of RTI for younger children in prekindergarten, child care, and early intervention, and only general references to the concept of early intervening within

Head Start legislation reauthorized in 2007 (Public Law No. 110-134). In 2010, the Office of Special Education Programs (OSEP) offered informal guidance on issues related to using RTI to determine eligibility for special education but did not address broader questions about the appropriate use of RTI with children who may not be eligible for special education services (*www.nectac.org/idea/clarfctnltrs.asp*). At the same time, the use of RTI practices prior to kindergarten (particularly in programs for 3- to 5-year-olds) has generated widespread interest in the early childhood field, with some programs beginning to implement this approach with PreK children. Consequently, RTI can be considered an emerging practice when it is implemented prior to kindergarten.

At this time, an agreed-upon definition of RTI in early childhood does not exist. However, the joint position statement on inclusion identified the use of tiered models such as RTI as a promising approach for helping practitioners scaffold learning and participation in children with and without disabilities in the context of high-quality inclusion. Three national professional organizations (the Division for Early Childhood of the Council for Exceptional Children, DEC; the National Association for the Education of Young Children, NAEYC; and the National Head Start Association, NHSA) are collaborating to address the need for a definition and guidance on implementation through a joint position statement on RTI in early childhood (*community.fpg.unc.edu/resources/community-contributed-content/plan-for-joint-position-statement-on-rti.pdf/view*).

As an initial step in advancing understanding about how RTI might be applied to work with younger children, it is possible to examine the most familiar and widely used tiered models in early childhood to determine what these approaches have in common. Figure 23.1 shows a conceptual framework for a tiered model in early childhood focused on social–emotional development. Figure 23.2 shows a conceptual framework for a tiered model in early childhood focused on academic learning. Models such as First Step to Success (Walker et al., 1997, 2008) and the Teaching Pyramid (Fox, Dunlap, Hemmeter, Joseph, & Strain, 2003; Hemmeter, Ostrosky, & Fox, 2006; see also *NHSA Dialog*, 2009b) provide explicit guidance on classroomwide foundational and prevention-oriented practices regarding

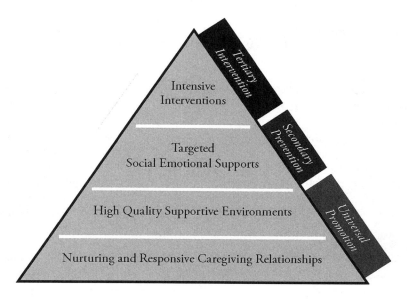

FIGURE 23.1. Conceptual framework for the teaching pyramid. From Fox, Carta, Strain, Dunlap, and Hemmeter (2009).

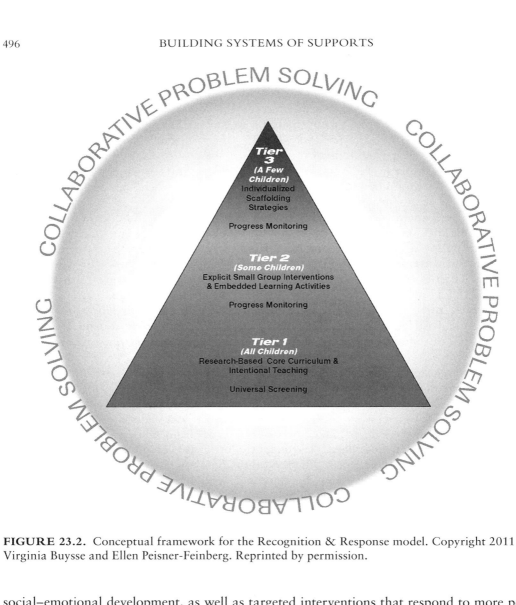

FIGURE 23.2. Conceptual framework for the Recognition & Response model. Copyright 2011 by Virginia Buysse and Ellen Peisner-Feinberg. Reprinted by permission.

social–emotional development, as well as targeted interventions that respond to more persistent needs of some children with respect to regulating behaviors, controlling impulses, focusing attention, and maintaining engagement in learning activities (Frey, 2009; Hemmeter & Fox, 2009; *NHSA Dialog*, 2009b). The building blocks model primarily focuses on instructional strategies that support the participation and engagement of children with disabilities in the context of inclusion (Sandall & Schwartz, 2008). Recognition & Response (R&R) addresses academic learning (e.g., language, literacy, and math) for young children with diverse learning characteristics and includes the key RTI components (universal screening and progress monitoring, research-based tiered interventions, and collaborative problem solving to support data-based decision making; Buysse & Peisner-Feinberg, 2010; *NHSA Dialog*, 2009a; Peisner-Feinberg, Buysse, Benshoff, & Soukakou, 2011).

Across all of these models, the primary emphasis is on helping practitioners (e.g., general early educators and specialists) organize the way in which they gather information and deliver instruction and targeted interventions to respond effectively to children's learning and social–emotional needs. Tiered models provide practitioners with a system for linking children's assessment results to specific instructional approaches and behavioral supports.

In tiered models, the assessment component (i.e., universal screening for all children and progress monitoring for some children who receive targeted interventions) differs from the way in which assessment typically is used in early childhood programs and settings. Unlike most standardized assessment tools currently available, early childhood assessment within an RTI context is designed to be conducted repeatedly throughout the school year. As a result, the assessment tools need to be brief (e.g., 5–10 minutes to administer per child) and easy to use by practitioners (e.g., relying on computer-assisted devices and Web-based assessment systems). Furthermore, assessment within an RTI framework measures both children's *level* and *rate* of growth (i.e., how well a child performs at any given point and the amount of gain in learning over time), and is not tied to a specific curriculum. Instead, these assessments measure specific skills within key domains of behavior and learning that predict later school adjustment and academic achievement when children enter kindergarten and the elementary grades. In tiered models, instructional and intervention strategies are arranged from least to most intensive to reflect how directive and involved a practitioner must be to help individual children learn specific skills or new behaviors. The foundation of all tiered approaches involves providing a high-quality, effective core curriculum, along with intentional teaching of key school readiness skills (i.e., both academic learning and social–emotional skills). Tiered interventions are layered on top of this foundation of teaching and learning to help practitioners make adjustments to their instruction for *some* children who require additional supports to learn beyond the general curriculum and classroom activities provided for *all* children at Tier 1.

With respect to empirical evidence for RTI, a growing body of research suggests that RTI is effective in the early grades and that it can yield positive learning outcomes and reduce the need for special education services. A meta-analysis of 24 studies concluded that students attending schools implementing RTI demonstrated greater growth in academic skills, more time on task, and better task completion compared to those attending schools not implementing RTI (Burns, Appleton, & Stehouwer, 2005). The schools implementing RTI also had fewer referrals to special education, fewer students placed in special education, less student retention, and fewer students identified as having a specific learning disability. Two Institute of Education Sciences (IES) Practice Guides, one in reading and the other in math, offered further empirical evidence to support the efficacy of RTI with school-age children (Gersten et al., 2008, 2009). These syntheses concluded that universal screening in reading and math can predict children's future performance, and that progress monitoring can have a positive effect on teachers' instructional decision making. The authors of both reports found strong evidence for the effectiveness of Tier 2 small-group interventions for students identified as being at risk for learning difficulties in these areas. Although preliminary evidence from at least one study suggests that RTI holds promise for supporting academic learning in PreK, additional research is needed with larger samples and across other content areas to provide further evidence of the effectiveness of this approach in PreK settings (Buysse & Peisner-Feinberg, 2009). The Center for Response to Intervention in Early Childhood (CRTIEC), funded by the U.S. Department of Education, is conducting a program of research to develop and validate assessments and tiered interventions that are appropriate for children prior to kindergarten, and that can be used within an RTI framework.

Supports

As defined within the DEC/NAEYC (2009) joint position statement on inclusion, "supports" refer to broader aspects of the infrastructure or system that must be in place to undergird the efforts of individuals and organizations providing inclusive services to children and families.

At a minimum, such systems-level supports would include ongoing professional development, collaboration and coordination among key stakeholders, public policy, resources, and research and evaluation. Given the depth and breadth of information available on each of these topics, the purpose of this section is to highlight a few examples of how each of these areas could serve as a support to high-quality inclusion, rather than to provide a comprehensive overview for each one.

Professional Development

Professional development (PD) is widely viewed as the most effective approach in preparing practitioners to work in early childhood education and to improve their practices once they enter the workforce. Furthermore, there is consensus in the early childhood education field about various components of program quality for young children in general, and a number of states now have a program quality rating and improvement system (QRIS) in place to guide professional practice in this regard. However, because improving the overall quality of an early childhood program might not be sufficient to address the individual needs of children with disabilities and their families, there is a need to reach consensus on dimensions of program quality that define high-quality inclusion (e.g., access, participation, and supports), and to reflect these dimensions in both program standards and PD efforts (Buysse & Hollingsworth, 2009a). In response to concerns about the fragmented nature of PD and the absence of an agreed-upon definition of PD in early childhood, NPDCI (2008) proposed a definition and framework for PD—along with related resources such as the Landscape PD survey; the Who, What, and How (WWH) Matrix; and the Big Picture Planning Guide (NPDCI, 2011)—that would apply to all sectors of the early childhood field (see also Buysse, Winton, et al., 2009). Figure 23.3 shows the NPDCI framework for PD. The core of the NPDCI framework aimed at promoting highly effective teaching and intervening consists of the *Who* (the characteristics and contexts of the learners and the children and families they serve), the *What* (the content of PD that defines what professionals should know and be able to do), and the *How* (the approaches, models, and methods used to support teaching and learning, and the application of new knowledge in practice). The WWH framework can be used to plan and organize PD on a broad range of topics, including quality inclusive practices, and therefore is presented to illustrate how PD can serve as an infrastructure support to implementing high-quality inclusion in early childhood. For example, addressing the *Who* would lead PD planners to consider not only the characteristics and contexts of the primary end users in inclusive programs and settings—the teachers, paraprofessionals, specialists, and others who work directly with young children and families in a variety of home- and center-based programs—but also those who work indirectly with children and families through the provision of PD, consultation, and technical assistance aimed at helping others improve the quality of their inclusive programs and practices. The *What* of PD should help planners redefine the content of PD to reflect what is currently known about quality inclusive programs, practices, and measures related to high-quality inclusion. Finally, the *How* should guide planners to use the most effective methods, such as guided practice with corrective feedback and models of collaboration (e.g., technical assistance; consultation; coaching; mentoring; and team-based approaches, such as communities of practice and professional learning communities), to facilitate experientially oriented learning and the transfer of new skills to applied work with children and families (Zaslow, Tout, Halle, Whittaker, & Lavelle, 2010).

Underlying the WWH organizing framework is another important concept: the shift from focusing on general knowledge topics to emphasizing specific research-based practices as the foundation for PD. Historically, PD in early childhood (and in the broader field of

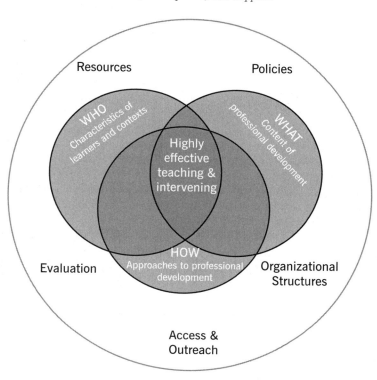

FIGURE 23.3. NPDCI conceptual framework for professional development. From the National Professional Development Center on Inclusion (2008). Reprinted by permission.

education) has focused on a range of general knowledge issues, such as induction to organizational policies and procedures, compliance to health and safety standards, and information about particular curricula, whereas only a relatively small proportion of time in PD has been spent on improving professional practice related to organizing teaching and learning for young children, and collaborating with families (Lambert, Sibley, & Lawrence, 2010). In response to this need for content focused on evidence-based practice in early childhood, Project Connect has developed Web-based modules on research-based practices to support the implementation of quality inclusion in early childhood settings (Winton, 2010). Content on specific practices such as embedded interventions, transition practices, and tiered models of instruction is organized around a five-step learning cycle adapted from the five-step decision-making process widely used in evidence-based medicine (Buysse & Wesley, 2006). The sequence is designed to help learners acquire skills that can be applied to an endless number of future problems in practice through a process that involves considering an authentic practice dilemma, posing an answerable question related to the practice, consulting the best available research and other sources of evidence to determine the effectiveness of the practice, integrating sources of evidence to make a decision about whether to use the practice in relation to a particular situation or context, and developing a plan to implement and evaluate the practice. Infusing a practice-oriented, evidence-based approach in PD holds promise for creating a highly effective early childhood workforce and improved outcomes for young children and their families in the context of inclusion. Future research is needed to evaluate the effectiveness of this approach to PD in early childhood education compared to traditional PD approaches in which an evidence-based approach is not used.

Models of Collaboration

The joint position statement on inclusion noted that collaboration among key stakeholders (e.g., families, practitioners, specialists, administrators) is a cornerstone for implementing high-quality inclusion. Furthermore, it recommended that resources and program policies are needed to promote multiple opportunities for communication and collaboration among these groups. Recently, a variety of approaches (e.g., technical assistance, coaching, consultation, mentoring, and team-based) have gained prominence as a key component of PD. Many of the same approaches can be used to support collaboration in conjunction with ongoing, effective professional practice, and actually were created originally as help-giving or indirect service delivery models rather than as components of PD. For example, consultation in early childhood education had its origins in mental health (and later, school-based consultation) and has been defined as an indirect, triadic service delivery model in which a consultant and consultee work together to address an area of concern or a goal for change (Buysse & Wesley, 2005). Coaching and mentoring, among the fastest growing approaches for supporting PD in early childhood and in education more broadly, had their origins in athletics and reflective supervision, respectively, and were originally used to enhance specific on-the-job skills in ways that were unrelated to traditional notions of coursework or training within PD.

In view of the growing emphasis on strengthening early childhood practices directly rather than focusing on increasing general knowledge and awareness of a topic, these approaches to improving professional practice through effective collaboration show a great deal of promise. However, there is little agreement on what each of these approaches means, how and when they can be used to enhance PD, and whether they are actually effective in improving professional practice (Dinnebeil, Buysse, Rush, & Eggbeer, 2008; Sibley, Lawrence, & Lambert, 2010). The terms "technical assistance," "consultation," "mentoring," and "coaching" are used interchangeably in the early childhood education literature, with little to distinguish them in terms of professional competencies, roles and activities, and the goals and processes associated with each approach. Furthermore, most early childhood education professionals who function as consultants, coaches, or mentors have received little, if any, formal preparation in approaches that are predicated on knowing how to on apply a systematic process for working with others and that involve sharing content expertise and negotiating differences to reach mutually determined goals for improving early childhood services. Zaslow and colleagues (2010) reviewed studies in early childhood education that often combine coursework or training with individualized modeling and feedback in early childhood settings, and concluded that there is promising, but somewhat mixed, evidence on the effectiveness of these approaches. Broader reviews of the literature on coaching also have found mixed results, along with little evidence for the value of coaching relative to teacher performance, and have concluded that more rigorous research is needed on this topic (Deussen, Coskie, Robinson, & Autio, 2007). There is a particular need in future studies to distinguish specific features of these approaches that contribute most to improving practices in early childhood settings, and to determine whether these approaches work best independently or in combination with formal PD.

Policies and Resources

Policies and resources are critical systems-level supports for implementing high-quality inclusion. The joint position statement has offered several examples of how this would work in practice. One such example is the creation of "blended programs" to achieve natural proportions of children with and without disabilities in early childhood classrooms (i.e., the inclusion of children with disabilities in proportion to their presence in the general population). Blended programs integrate key components (e.g., funding, eligibility criteria, curricula) of two or more different early childhood programs (e.g., the federally funded program for preschoolers with disabilities [Part B-619] and Head Start, public PreK, and/ or child care). The goal of blended programming is to serve a broader group of children and families within a single program to reflect the principle of natural proportions and improve the quality of inclusive services and experiences for children with and without disabilities and their families. States that prohibit this type of blending at the local level may inadvertently create disincentives for improving the quality of inclusion. To incentivize inclusion, states should promote the appropriation of resources across agencies and use incentives such as adjusted child–staff ratios and increased child care subsidies for children with disabilities who are served in inclusive settings and programs. Another example of how policies can support high-quality inclusion is through the creation of quality frameworks in early childhood, such as program quality standards, quality rating and improvement systems, early learning standards and guidelines, and professional competencies and standards. All of these frameworks for defining and regulating quality should reflect and guide dimensions of quality inclusive practices to ensure that all early childhood programs and practitioners are prepared to address the needs of every child and family, including young children with disabilities.

Research and Evaluation

Research creates interest and momentum on a particular topic and inevitably leads to advances in knowledge and infrastructure supports in ways that are difficult to accomplish in its absence. The Early Childhood Research Institute on Inclusion (ECRII), a 5-year national research project funded by the U.S. Department of Education (Office of Special Education Programs), ended in 2000. The project developed, tested, and disseminated strategies to support the participation of children (birth to 5 years) with disabilities and their families in classrooms and communities (Odom, 2002). In the decade that has passed since ECRII ended, the field has benefited from the contributions of this work with respect to defining the various forms of inclusion, understanding factors that inhibit or support its implementation, identifying models that assist in individualizing instruction, and recognizing the importance of collaborative relationships among adults that support inclusive practices, among other contributions. In an edited volume that summarized what was known at the time about early childhood inclusion, Guralnick (2001) outlined a program of research that he acknowledged would require a long-term investment in model development and evaluation, starting with small-scale studies to test iterations and refinements of new approaches, eventually moving to large randomized controlled trials to evaluate the effectiveness of new practices and to understand the mechanisms through which such interventions operate, and finally, translating research-based practices for use in a wide range of early childhood programs and settings. He noted that this translation would require the development of supporting materials such as guidelines for using assessments, linked interventions, and program evaluation strategies to make these approaches acceptable and feasible to practitioners with varying levels of preparation and experience in working with children with disabilities and their families. Little has changed in the decade since Guralnick and Odom and his colleagues (2004) completed their research and outlined new research directions for the field. Although research on specific aspects of inclusion is occurring, there continues to be a need for a large-scale, comprehensive program of research that develops and tests new approaches, then integrates these research-based practices and supports within a single framework that can be used to guide implementation of these inclusive practices in states, communities, and local programs.

New Opportunities to Promote High-Quality Inclusion on the Horizon

This chapter presented current knowledge about early childhood inclusion, summarizing the research literature and consensus wisdom contained within the DEC/NAEYC (2009) joint position statement. The chapter also described effective or promising educational practices that promote access, participation, and supports—the defining features of high-quality inclusion. With respect to advancing the cause to improve inclusive practices in the future, research in this area needs to evolve from focusing on what works on average to help the field predict with more precision which practices work best with particular subgroups of children and families, and under what conditions.

Furthermore, rather than working in isolation, advocates of inclusion would do well to find new ways of connecting the principles and practices of inclusion to broader early childhood initiatives. Efforts to improve the quality of inclusion must begin to connect research-based practices such as AT or embedded interventions with the broader systems-level supports related to program quality improvement such as QRISs, early learning standards, measurement and accountability, and PD. Otherwise, inclusion will continue to exist as a separate service delivery system, apart from programs and services designed for the general population of young children and families.

In the future, there will be a number of opportunities to seek ways to move toward a better interface between early childhood inclusion and program quality for all children (Wesley & Buysse, 2010; Winton, 2010). One area that seems ripe for developing these connections is the movement under way to customize teaching and learning to address the needs of an increasingly diverse population of young children and families (Buysse & Wesley, 2010). Just as in the broader field of K–12 education, there is a growing realization in early childhood education that we need to customize teaching and learning to ensure that practitioners are equipped to help every child—including children with identified disabilities, those at risk for learning or behavioral difficulties, and those from diverse cultural and linguistic backgrounds—reach his or her full potential. The customization of early education will require new technologies and research-based practices, as well as changes to organizational structures related to teaching, intervening, and monitoring progress. One indication that the early childhood field is moving in this direction is growing interest in the use of tiered models of instruction. The disability field contains a wealth of knowledge, resources, and technologies related to customizing education for individual children and their families, but many times the application of this knowledge does not occur within an inclusive teaching and learning context. Tiered models incorporate specific intervention strategies developed within special education and use them within a general early childhood context to address the needs of a broader group of young children with varying abilities and needs. In the end, efforts to improve inclusive practices and better outcomes for children and families will depend on the field's ability to recognize what it has already accomplished through research, policy, and practice over more than three decades, and to build on these accomplishments by posing new questions and seeking new solutions for the future.

References

Burns, M. K., Appleton, J. J., & Stehouwer, J. D. (2005). Meta-analytic review of responsiveness-to-intervention research: Examining field-based and research-implemented models. *Journal of Psychoeducational Assessment, 23*(4), 381–394.

Buysse, V., & Hollingsworth, H. L. (2009a). Program quality and early childhood inclusion:

Recommendations for professional development. *Topics in Early Childhood Special Education,* 29(2), 119–128.

Buysse, V., & Hollingsworth, H. L. (2009b). Research synthesis points on early childhood inclusion: What every practitioner and all families should know. *Young Exceptional Children Monograph Series, 11,* 18–30.

Buysse, V., Hollingsworth, H., & Catlett, C. (2009). *Early childhood inclusion: The validation process.* Chapel Hill: University of North Carolina, FPG Child Development Institute, National Professional Development Center on Inclusion (NPDCI). Retrieved February 23, 2011, from *community.fpg.unc.edu/resources/articles/files/ips/earlychildhoodinclusion-thevalidationprocess2009.pdf.*

Buysse, V., & Peisner-Feinberg, E. (2009). Recognition & response: Findings from the first implementation study. Retrieved October 2009, from *randr.fpg.unc.edu/sites/randr.fpg.unc.edu/files/keyfindingshandout.pdf.*

Buysse, V., & Peisner-Feinberg, E. (2010). Recognition & Response: Response to intervention for pre-K. *Young Exceptional Children, 13*(4), 2–13.

Buysse, V., Soukakou, E., Peisner-Feinberg, E., & Benshoff, L. M. (2011). *Recognition & Response: Effective ways of responding to children who need additional supports to learn.* Manuscript submitted for publication.

Buysse, V., & Wesley, P. W. (2005). *Consultation in early childhood settings.* Baltimore: Brookes.

Buysse, V., & Wesley, P. W. (2006). *Evidence-based practice in the early childhood field.* Washington, DC: Zero to Three Press.

Buysse, V., Winton, P. J., & Rous, B. (2009). Reaching consensus on a definition of professional development for the early childhood field. *Topics in Early Childhood Special Education, 28*(4), 235–243.

Campbell, P. H., Milbourne, S., Dugan, L. M., & Wilcox, M. J. (2006). A review of evidence on practices for teaching young children to use assistive technology devices. *Topics in Early Childhood Special Education, 26*(1), 3–13.

Carlson, E., Bitterman, A., & Daley, T. (2010). Access to educational and community activities for young children with disabilities: Selected findings from the pre-elementary education longitudinal study. Rockville, MD: Westat. Retrieved from *ies.ed.gov/ncser/pubs/20113000.*

Chiara, L., Schuster, J. W., Bell, J. K., & Wolery, M. (1995). Small-group massed-trial and individually distributed-trial instruction with preschoolers. *Journal of Early Intervention, 19,* 203–217.

Craig-Unkefer, L. A., & Kaiser, A. P. (2002). Improving the social communication skills of at-risk preschool children in a play context. *Topics in Early Childhood Special Education, 22,* 3–13.

DEC/NAEYC. (2009). *Early childhood inclusion: A joint position statement of the Division for Early Childhood (DEC) and the National Association for the Education of Young Children (NAEYC).* Chapel Hill: University of North Carolina, FPG Child Development Institute. Retrieved December 12, 2010, from *community.fpg.unc.edu/resources/articles/files/earlychildhoodinclusion-04-2009.pdf.*

Deussen, T., Coskie, T., Robinson, L., & Autio, E. (2007). "Coach" can mean many things: Five categories of literacy coaches in Reading First (Issues & Answers Report, REL 2007-No. 005). Washington, DC: U.S. Department of Education, Institute of Education Sciences, National Center for Education Evaluation and Regional Assistance. Retrieved from *ies.ed.gov/ncee/edlabs/regions/northwest/pdf/rel_2007005.pdf.*

Dinnebeil, L., Buysse, V., Rush, D., & Eggbeer, L. (2008). Becoming an effective collaborator and change agent. In P. Winton, J. McCollum, & C. Catlett (Eds.), *Practical approaches to early childhood professional development: Evidence, strategies, and resources* (pp. 227–245). Washington, DC: Zero to Three Press.

Division for Early Childhood (DEC). (2007). Promoting positive outcomes for children with disabilities: Recommendations for curriculum, assessment, and program evaluation. Missoula, MT: Author. Retrieved December 12, 2010, from *www.naeyc.org/positionstatements/cape.*

Fox, L., Carta, J., Strain, P., Dunlap, G., & Hemmeter, M. L. (2009). *Response to intervention and the pyramid model.* Tampa: University of South Florida, Technical Assistance Center on Social Emotional Intervention for Young Children. Retrieved from *cfs.fmhi.usf.edu/publications/detail.cfm?id=217.*

Fox, L., Dunlap, G., Hemmeter, M. L., Joseph, G. E., & Strain, P. S. (2003). The teaching pyramid: A model for supporting social competence and preventing challenging behavior in young children. *Young Children, 58*(4), 48–52.

Frey, A. (2009). Positive behavior supports and interventions in early childhood education. *NHSA Dialog, 12*(2), 71–74.

Gersten, R., Beckman, S., Clarke, B., Foegen, A., Marsh, L., Star, J. R., et al. (2009). Assisting students struggling with mathematics: Response to intervention (RTI) for elementary and middle schools (NCEE 2009-4060). Washington, DC: National Center for Education Evaluation and Regional Assistance, Institute of Education Sciences, U.S. Department of Education. Retrieved October 1, 2010, from *ies.ed.gov/ncee/wwc/publications/practiceguides.*

Gersten, R., Compton, D. L., Connor, C. M., Dimino, J., Santoro, L., Linan-Thompson, S., et al. (2008). Assisting students struggling with reading: Response to intervention and multi-tier intervention for reading in the primary grades: A practice guide (NCEE 2009-4045). Washington, DC: National Center for Education Evaluation and Regional Assistance, Institute of Education Sciences, U.S. Department of Education. Retrieved October 1, 2010, from *ies.ed.gov/ncee/wwc/publications/practiceguides.*

Gibson, A. N., & Schuster, J. W. (1992). The use of simultaneous prompting for teaching expressive word recognition to preschool children. *Topics in Early Childhood Special Education, 12,* 247–267.

Girolametto, L., Weitzman, E., & Greenberg, J. (2004). The effects of verbal supports on small-group peer interactions. *Language, Speech, and Hearing Services in Schools, 35,* 254–268.

Guralnick, M. J. (Ed.). (2001). *Early childhood inclusion: Focus on change.* Baltimore: Brookes.

Hancock, B., & Kaiser, A. P. (2006). Enhanced milieu teaching. In R. McCauley & M. Fey (Eds.), *Treatment of language disorders in children* (pp. 203–236). Baltimore: Brookes.

Hawkings, S. R., & Schuster, J. W. (2007). Using a mand-model procedure to teach preschool children initial speech sounds. *Journal of Developmental and Physical Disabilities, 19*(1), 65–80.

Hemmeter, M. L., & Fox, L. (2009). The teaching pyramid: A model for the implementation of classroom practices within a program-wide approach to behavior support. *NHSA Dialog, 12*(2), 133–147.

Hemmeter, M. L., Ostrosky, M., & Fox, L. (2006). Social and emotional foundations for early learning: A conceptual model for intervention. *School Psychology Review, 35*(4), 583–601.

Horn, E., Lieber, J., Li, S., Sandall, S., & Schwartz, I. (2000). Supporting young children's IEP goals in inclusive settings through embedded learning opportunities. *Topics in Early Childhood Special Education, 20,* 208–224.

Horner, R. H., Sugai, G., & Anderson, C. (2010). Examining the evidence base for school-wide positive behavior support. *Focus on Exceptional Children, 42*(8), 1–14.

Individuals with Disabilities Education Act of 2004 (IDEA), P.L. No. 108-446. Available at *idea.ed.gov.*

Kaiser, A. P., Hemmeter, M. L., & Ostrosky, M. M. (1996). The effects of teaching parents to use responsive interaction strategies. *Topics in Early Childhood Special Education, 16,* 375–406.

Kaiser, A. P., Hester, P. P., & McDuffie, A. S. (2001). Supporting communication in young children with developmental disabilities. *Mental Retardation and Developmental Disability Research Reviews, 7,* 143–150.

Kouri, T. A. (2005). Lexical training through modeling and elicitation procedures with late talkers who have specific language impairment and developmental delays. *Journal of Speech, Language, and Hearing Research, 48,* 157–171.

Lambert, R. G., Sibley, A., & Lawrence, R. (2010). Choosing content. In S. B. Neuman & M. L. Kamil (Eds.), *Preparing teachers for the early childhood classroom: Proven models and key principles* (pp. 67–85). Baltimore: Brookes.

Lindauer, C. (2009). Christine's chronicles: Inclusion starts at home. Retrieved November 2, 2010, from *community.fpg.unc.edu/discussions/blog-speaking-of-inclusion/christines-chronicles.*

McWilliam, R. A. (1996). *Rethinking pull-out services in early intervention: A professional resource.* Baltimore: Brookes.

McWilliam, R. A. (2010). *Routines-based early intervention supporting young children and their families.* Baltimore: Brookes.

Moore, H. W., & Wilcox, M. J. (2006). Characteristics of early intervention practitioners and their confidence in the use of assistive technology. *Topics in Early Childhood Special Education, 26*(1), 15–23.

National Professional Development Center on Inclusion. (2008). *What do we mean by professional development in the early childhood field?* Chapel Hill, NC: Author.

National Professional Development Center on Inclusion. (2009). Research synthesis points on early childhood inclusion. Chapel Hill, NC: Author. Retrieved November 5, 2010, from *community. fpg.unc.edu/resources/articles/ndpci-researchsynthesis-9-2007.pdf/view.*

National Professional Development Center on Inclusion. (2011). *The Big Picture Planning Guide: Building cross-sector professional development systems in early childhood* (3rd ed.). Chapel Hill: University of North Carolina, FPG Child Development Institute, Author. Available at *community.fpg.unc.edu/resources/planning-and-facilitation-tools/npdci_big-picture-planning-guide_2008.pdf.*

National Research Council. (2002). *Scientific research in education.* Washington, DC: National Academy Press.

NHSA Dialog. (2009a). Approaches to individualizing supports for high-risk preschoolers [Special issue]. Vol. 12(3).

NHSA Dialog. (2009b). Positive behavior supports and interventions in early childhood education [Special issue]. Vol. 12(2).

Odom, S. L. (Ed.), (2002). *Widening the circle: Including children with disabilities in preschool programs.* New York: Teachers College Press.

Odom, S. L., Vitztum, J., Wolery, R., Lieber, J., Sandall, S., Hanson, M., et al. (2004). Preschool inclusion in the United States: A review of research from an ecological systems perspective. *Journal of Research in Special Educational Needs, 4*(1), 17–49.

Ostrosky, M., & Kaiser, A. P. (1995). The effects of a peer-mediated intervention on the social communicative interactions between children with and without special needs. *Journal of Behavioral Education, 5*(2), 151–171.

Peisner-Feinberg, E., Buysse, V., Benshoff, L., & Soukakou, E. (2011). Recognition & Response: Response to intervention for pre-kindergarten. In C. Groark, S. M. Eidelman, L. Kaczmarek, & S. Maude (Eds.), *Early childhood intervention: Shaping the future for children with special needs and their families: Vol. 3. Emerging trends in research and practice* (pp. 37–53). Santa Barbara, CA: Praeger.

Pretti-Frontczak, K. L., Barr, D. M., Macy, M., & Carter, A. (2003). Research and resources related to activity-based intervention, embedded learning opportunities, and routines-based instruction: An annotated bibliography. *Topics in Early Childhood Special Education, 23*, 29–40.

Ross, D. E., & Greer, R. D. (2003). Generalized imitation and the mand: Inducing first instances of speech in young children with autism. *Research in Developmental Disabilities, 24*, 58–74.

Sackett, D. L., Straus, S. E., Richardson, W. S., Rosenberg, W., & Haynes, R. B. (2000). *Evidence-based medicine: How to practice and teach EBM.* Edinburgh, UK: Churchill Livingstone.

Sandall, S. R., & Schwartz, I. S. (2008). *Building blocks for teaching preschoolers with special needs* (2nd ed.). Baltimore: Brookes.

Sibley, A., Lawrence, R., & Lambert, R. G. (2010). Mentoring: More than a promising strategy. In S. B. Neuman & M. L. Kamil (Eds.), *Preparing teachers for the early childhood classroom: Proven models and key principles* (pp. 105–122). Baltimore: Brookes.

Snyder, P., Hemmeter, M. L., Sandall, S., & McLean, M. (2007). *Impact of professional development on preschool teachers' use of embedded instructional practices.* Gainesville: University of Florida, College of Education.

Trivette, C. M., Dunst, C. J., Hamby, D., & O'Herin, C. E. (2010). Effects of different types of adaptations on the behavior of young children with disabilities (Research Brief, Vol. 4, No. 1). Available at *www.tnt.asu.*

U.S. Department of Education, Office of Special Education and Rehabilitative Services, Office of Special Education Programs. (2010). 29th annual report to Congress on the implementation of the Individuals with Disabilities Education Act 2007. Washington, DC: Author. Retrieved February 23, 2011, from *ww2.ed.gov/about/reports/annual/osep/index.html*.

Walker, H. M. (2008). Constant and progressive time delay procedures for teaching children with autism: A literature review. *Journal of Autism and Developmental Disorders, 38,* 261–275.

Walker, H. M., Kavanagh, K., Stiller, B., Golly, A., Severson, H. H., & Feil, E. G. (1997). *First Step to Success: An early intervention program for antisocial kindergarteners.* Longmont, CO: Sopris West.

Walker, H. M., Seeley, J. R., Small, J., Golly, A., Severson, H., & Feil, E. G. (2008). The First Step to Success program for preventing antisocial behavior in young children: Update on past, current, and planned research. *Emotional and Behavioral Disorders in Youth, 8*(1), 17–23.

Wesley, P. W., & Buysse, V. (Eds.). (2010). *The quest for quality: Promising innovations for early childhood programs.* Baltimore: Brookes.

Winton, P., Buysse, V., Rous, B., Epstein, D., & Pierce, P. (2011). *CONNECT Module 5: Assistive technology interventions* (Web-based professional development curriculum). Chapel Hill: University of North Carolina, FPG Child Development Institute, CONNECT: The Center to Mobilize Early Childhood Knowledge. Available at *community.fpg.unc.edu/connect-modules/learners/module-5*.

Winton, P. J. (2010). Professional development and quality initiatives: Two essential components of an early childhood system. In P. W. Wesley & V. Buysse (Eds.), *The quest for quality: Promising innovations for early childhood programs* (pp. 113–129). Baltimore: Brookes.

Winton, P. J., Buysse, V., Turnbull, A., Rous, B., & Hollingsworth, H. (2010). *CONNECT Module 1: Embedded interventions.* Chapel Hill: University of North Carolina, FPG Child Development Institute, CONNECT: The Center to Mobilize Early Childhood Knowledge. Available at *community.fpg.unc.edu/connect-modules/learners/module-1*.

Wolery, M. (2000). Behavioral and educational approaches to early intervention. In J. P. Schonkoff & S. J. Meisels (Eds.), *Handbook of early childhood intervention* (2nd ed., pp. 179–203). Cambridge, UK: Cambridge University Press.

Zaslow, M., Tout, K., Halle, T., Whittaker, J. E., & Lavelle, B. (2010). Emerging research on early childhood professional development. In S. B. Neuman & M. L. Kamil (Eds.), *Preparing teachers for the early childhood classroom: Proven models and key principles* (pp. 19–47). Baltimore: Brookes.

CHAPTER 24

Enhancing Teachers' Intentional Use of Effective Interactions with Children

Designing and Testing Professional Development Interventions

Bridget K. Hamre, Jason T. Downer, Faiza M. Jamil,
and Robert C. Pianta

The success of early childhood programs in the United States depends largely on the quality of its workforce (Zaslow & Martinzez-Beck, 2006; Zaslow, Tout, Halle, Whittaker, & Lavelle, 2010). It is the teachers in these programs who bear the greatest responsibility for supporting children's social and academic development on a daily basis (Hamre & Pianta, 2007). Yet data from large national and statewide studies suggest that this workforce is far from fully prepared to provide the types of classroom experiences that young children need to be ready for kindergarten (Maxwell et al., 2009; Phillips, Gormley, & Lowenstein, 2009).

There are many factors contributing to the lack of preparation of the early childhood workforce. Two of the most salient are an underdeveloped and disjointed teacher preparation system that does little to teach the types of knowledge and skills most needed in today's classrooms (Early & Winton, 2001) and a professional development system that is "inconsistent, fragmented, and often chaotic" (Bowman, Donovan, & Burns, 2001, p. 276).

Yet, each year, millions of dollars are being spent on educating and training early childhood professionals. School districts report spending between $2,100 and $7,900 per teacher, per year (Miles, Odden, Fermanich, & Archibald, 2004). Over a 5-year period, First 5 California and local county First 5 commissions spent more than $157 million providing incentives for more than 58,000 early childhood providers to take coursework and professional development—equaling an average of over $2,700 per teacher. Many quality rating and improvement systems devote a significant amount of their total resources to the improvement component (Tout et al., 2010). There is little evidence regarding the extent to which these expenditures lead to systematic and sustained improvements in program quality or children's outcomes (Bridges, Fuller, Huang, & Hamre, 2011).

If these investments are to have the intended impact of improving outcomes for young children, the field needs to move rapidly to articulate what types of educational and professional development experiences are most likely to enhance teachers' effectiveness and, ultimately, children's development and learning. Although there is growing consensus around a general set of parameters for "effective" professional development (Garet, Porter, Andrew, & Desimone, 2001; Yoon, Duncan, Lee, Scarloss, & Shapley, 2007), these broad categorizations do not provide enough specificity to inform the rapidly expanding creation of new professional development programs or to help state, district, and program administrators choose among the many programs the ones that will be most effective.

For example, most recommendations around professional development suggest that effective programs should focus explicitly on practice (Zaslow et al., 2010). But on which practices should they focus, and how can this content be delivered in ways that ultimately impact teaching and learning? Similarly, most recommendations state that programs should be more than 1- or 2-hour workshops (Garet et al., 2001)—but how long is long enough and how can administrators make decisions to invest wisely in these programs?

Despite a growing body of work on specific professional development programs that are effective or ineffective (see Zaslow et al., 2010, for a review), there is very limited theory or research to inform these types of questions about the process of professional development (see Clarke & Hollingsworth, 2002, for an exception in K–12 research). This problem was summarized in a recent conceptual paper by Sheridan, Edwards, Marvin, and Knoche (2009):

> The early childhood field is at a place where professional development practice and craft knowledge require a larger and firmer platform of theoretical and empirical expertise in order to guide planning and implementation of the ambitious kinds of school and child care reforms that are demanded in the current era of services expansion and accountability. Indeed, the field is acquiring a body of findings about the effects of various forms, levels, and organizations of professional development on early childhood educators' knowledge bases and skill sets (e.g., findings about the outcomes of different trainings, coaching, consultation, and other models of staff support). However, we need to know more about the dynamic and transactional teaching and learning processes underlying these effects as they function in real-world early childhood settings. (p. 378)

This chapter addresses this gap in knowledge by describing a set of professional development resources targeting teachers' use of effective teacher–child interactions, as well as a new conceptualization of intentional teaching that we believe underlies the process through which the interventions have their effect. We first describe the basis for choosing this particular content area on which to focus by briefly summarizing literature on how and why teacher–child interactions are critical to effective teaching. Next we outline a new conceptualization of intentional teaching that serves as our theory of change and the foundation for development of our professional development programs. We then present findings from several recent randomized controlled trials demonstrating the potential efficacy of these approaches and providing some initial evidence in support of the theory of change. We conclude with a discussion of implications for future research on effective models of professional development.

Focusing Professional Development on Effective Teacher–Child Interactions

A first step in the development of any intervention is the identification of the problem to be solved. Our work has focused on improving the effectiveness of teachers' daily interactions with young children, due to a wealth of evidence about the importance of these interactions (e.g., Burchinal et al., 2008; Howes et al., 2008), as well as the results from large observational studies demonstrating a clear need for improvement (e.g., Maxwell et al., 2009; Phillips et al., 2009; Pianta et al., 2005). Theory and research in classroom and familial contexts suggest that the interactions of children with their peers and with adults are a key part of learning and development (see Hamre & Pianta, 2010, for a review). Consistent with these studies, Teaching Through Interactions (TTI; Hamre, Pianta, Downer, Hakigmi, & Mashburn, 2011) is a theoretically and empirically driven framework for organizing the wide range of interactions that take place in classrooms and are associated with children's academic and social outcomes. Drawing from observations conducted in over 4,000 classrooms, this conceptual framework focuses on the proximal processes, or moment-to-moment classroom interactions (Bronfenbrenner & Morris, 1998), which, TTI posits, fall into three broad domains: emotional support, classroom organization, and instructional support. The following sections briefly describe each of these domains of classroom interactions and summarize some of the more recent findings in the educational and developmental literature that support their importance as a focus for teacher professional development.

Emotional Support

The emotional support domain of the TTI framework is grounded in two broad areas of developmental theory, attachment (Ainsworth, Blehar, Waters, & Wall, 1978; Bowlby, 1969) and self-determination (Connell & Wellborn, 1991; Ryan & Deci, 2000). Teacher–child interactions that contribute to emotional support are posited to create a sense of security and relatedness, allowing children to explore and motivating them to learn (Downer, Sabol, & Hamre, 2010). The TTI framework views classroom interactions related to emotional support according to three dimensions, each of which focuses on different features of emotional support in the classroom: classroom climate, teacher sensitivity, and regard for student perspectives (see Table 24.1 for details on dimensions).

Research findings in recent years suggest that children who experience positive, supportive classroom environments and close relationships with their teachers show greater academic gains (O'Connor & McCartney, 2007), exhibit fewer behavior problems (McClelland, Cameron, Wanless, & Murray, 2007) and demonstrate better social skills (Brophy-Herb, Lee, Nievar, & Stollak, 2007; Curby et al., 2009). Whereas a positive classroom climate can moderate the effects of insecure maternal attachment on achievement (O'Connor & McCartney, 2007) and protect at-risk children from developing conflictual relationships with their teachers (Buyse, Verschueren, Doumen, Van Damme, & Maes, 2008), negative teacher–child interactions can place children at increased risk for poor academic and behavioral outcomes (Decker, Dona, & Christenson, 2007). Similarly, children who experience caregiving that is sensitive to their needs and supportive of their autonomy display increased social competence (Burchinal, Roberts, Zeisel, Hennon, & Hooper, 2006; Stipek & Byler, 2004) and fewer behavior problems (Kern & Clemens, 2007; Kern, Gallagher, Starosta, Hickman, & George, 2006), as well as stronger academic skills, suggesting that teacher awareness and responsiveness may be important for children's social and academic outcomes (Connor, Morrison, & Katch, 2004; Connor, Morrison, & Petrella, 2004; Connor, Son, Hindman, & Morrison, 2005).

Classroom Organization

The classroom organization domain of the TTI framework is theoretically based in the work of developmental psychologists interested in children's self-regulatory skills (Raver, 2004; Tobin & Graziano, 2006), and the relevance of these skills to social and academic success in

TABLE 24.1. Teaching through Interactions Framework Dimensions

Domain	Dimension	Description
Emotional support	Classroom climate	Reflects the overall emotional tone of the classroom and the connection between teachers and students. Considers the warmth and respect displayed in teachers and students interactions with one another as well as the degree to which they display enjoyment and enthusiasm during learning activities.
	Teacher sensitivity	Encompasses teachers' responsivity to students' needs and awareness of students' level of academic and emotional functioning. The highly sensitive teacher helps students see adults as a resource and creates an environment in which students feel safe and free to explore and learn.
	Regard for student perspectives	The degree to which the teacher's interactions with students and classroom activities places an emphasis on students' interests, motivations, and points of view, rather than being very teacher-driven. This may be demonstrated by the teacher's flexibility within activities and respect for students' autonomy to participate in and initiate activities.
Classroom organization	Behavior management	Encompasses the teacher's ability to use effective methods to prevent and redirect misbehavior, by presenting clear behavioral expectations and minimizing time spent on behavioral issues.
	Productivity	Considers how well teachers manages instructional time and routines so that students have the maximum number of opportunity to learn. Not related to the quality of instruction, but rather to teachers' efficiency.
	Instructional learning formats	The degree to which teachers maximize students' engagement and ability to learn by providing interesting activities, instruction, centers, and materials. Considers the manner in which the teacher facilitates activities so that students have opportunities to experience, perceive, explore, and utilize materials.
Instructional support	Concept development	The degree to which instructional discussions and activities promote students' higher-order thinking skills versus focus on rote and fact-based learning.
	Quality of feedback	Considers teachers' provision of feedback focused on expanding learning and understanding (formative evaluation), not correctness or the end product (summative evaluation).
	Language modeling	The quality and amount of teachers' use of language-stimulation and language-facilitation techniques during individual, small-group, and large-group interactions with children. Components of high-quality language modeling include self- and parallel-talk, open-ended questions, repetition, expansion/extension, and use of advanced language.

school. The proactive management strategies, instructional planning, and engaging materials and activities used by instructionally supportive teachers are posited to help emotionally dysregulated children develop higher levels of self-regulation (Raver et al., 2008), and ensure that children are spending enough time engaged in learning activities to master new skills and concepts (Phillips, Clancy-Menchetti, & Lonigan, 2008). Classroom interactions in this domain are classified into the dimensions of behavior management, productivity, and instructional learning formats (see Table 24.1 for details on dimensions).

High levels of classroom organization have been shown to predict changes in preschool children's learning behaviors (Domínguez, Vitiello, Maier, & Greenfield, 2010). Findings from several school intervention studies have found that when teachers consistently monitor their classes and use positive and proactive classroom management strategies, their students not only exhibit more social competence and emotional self-regulation (Bierman & Erath, 2006; Webster-Stratton, Reid, & Stoolmiller, 2008), but they are also more engaged in learning tasks and making academic gains (Rimm-Kaufman & Chiu, 2007; Tingstrom, Sterling-Turner, & Wilczynski, 2006). Classrooms in which more time is spent in organizational activities in the beginning of the school year have been associated with higher student achievement in reading (Cameron, Connor, Morrison, & Jewkes, 2008) and children's greater behavioral and cognitive self-control, engagement, and time on-task (Rimm-Kaufman, Curby, Grimm, Nathanson, & Brock, 2009). Furthermore, exposing children to exciting, creative, and novel academic experiences, such as learning games (Raab et al., 2009), can help to foster the development of positive learning behaviors (Hyson, 2008), and to capitalize on newly developed interests to motivate student engagement in academic tasks (Neitzel, Alexander, & Johnson, 2008).

Instructional Support

The instructional support domain of the TTI framework is theoretically grounded both in research on children's cognitive and language development that emphasizes the importance of learning information that is interconnected and organized in ways that make it useful in the future and the important role that adults play in supporting children's development of complex skills (Davis & Miyake, 2004; Skibbe, Behnke, & Justice, 2004; Vygotsky, 1991). Among the three dimensions comprising this domain of the TTI framework are concept development, quality of feedback, and language modeling (see Table 24.1 for details on dimensions).

Empirical research suggests that the significant classroom interactions that fall within these three dimensions are important for child outcomes. In a six-state study of 240 randomly selected preschool programs, Burchinal and colleagues (2008) found that in instructionally supportive classroom environments, in which students were encouraged to use language to develop reasoning skills and provided with clear and positive feedback, students appeared to learn more and sustain their achievements. More specifically, classrooms with the highest levels of concept development have been shown to promote gains in vocabulary development and math problem solving (Curby et al., 2009; Peterson & French, 2008). Teachers' effective use of hints and assistance, and of back-and-forth exchanges with the intention of expanding students' engagement and understanding, is associated with increases in children's language and social development (Barnett, Yarosz, Thomas, & Hornbeck, 2008; Pence, Justice, & Wiggins, 2008; Phillips et al., 2008), as well as functioning, in areas such as literacy and general knowledge (Howes et al., 2008). In addition, when teachers elicit child language and target vocabulary development by using a variety of words and connecting them to more familiar words, children show significant growth in vocabulary, communication, and language use at school and at home (Bierman et al., 2008).

Intentional Teaching: Developing Interventions That Systematically Target Teacher Improvement

Once we have a target for professional development, in this case teachers' use of the types of interactions described by the TTI framework, how do we decide how to go about actually promoting change in that target? Those designing interventions need a clear theory of change that specifies the processes through which they anticipate initiating improvement in the targeted outcome. As we have worked on a variety of interventions targeting teachers' use of effective classroom interactions, we have begun to articulate a process through which our interventions may have effects—we refer to this process as intentional teaching. We hypothesize that our interventions, and many others, have their effects in part by helping to make teachers much more purposeful and deliberate about their practice.

Before describing this model in more detail it is important to take a moment to explain the process through which it is being developed. Changing behavior is incredibly complex, and we cannot reasonably expect to articulate a comprehensive model for changing teaching behavior that accounts for all components of the system (Glaser, 1992). However, we do feel it is important to draw from the rich empirical and theoretical work conducted within developmental and educational research, as well as from other disciplines, to begin to articulate and test specific models for change. Our current model draws from several literatures—including work in teacher education and work from cognitive science on adult learning. This model is not complete, and we expect it to evolve as we gather more qualitative and quantitative data from our work. However, it provides a useful heuristic that guides the refinement of our interventions and the measures used to test their effects. In this section, we briefly summarize the components of this model, and the theoretical and empirical foundations on which it was built.

What Is Intentional Teaching?

Many others have written about what it means to be an intentional teacher. Ann Epstein in her book *The Intentional Teacher* (2007) writes:

> The intentional teacher ... acts with knowledge and purpose to ensure that young children acquire the knowledge and skills (content) they need to succeed in school and in life. Intentional teaching does not happen by chance; it is planful, thoughtful, and purposeful. Intentional teachers use their knowledge, judgment, and expertise to organize learning experiences for children; when an unexpected situation arises (as it always does), they can recognize a teaching opportunity and are able to take advantage of it, too. (p. 1)

Our approach to understanding intentional teaching shares much with Epstein's definition. However, we have tried to create a more tangible definition that can serve as both a basis for our design of professional development programs and a guide for the development and testing of measures to use in our research.

Components of Intentional Teaching

We conceptualize four major elements to intentional teaching: knowing, seeing, doing, and reflecting. Table 24.2 provides a summary of each component, along with some examples. We first describe each of these components of intentional teaching, then present a conceptual model for how they work together to help produce improvements in teacher effectiveness.

Knowing

DESCRIPTION AND THEORETICAL BACKGROUND

Early childhood teachers bring a wealth of knowledge and expertise into the classroom. Some of this may be learned in teacher education programs, some in on-the-job training, and some in professional development experiences. Lee Shulman has conducted the preeminent work on teacher knowledge—though most of this has been applied to K–12 rather than early childhood teaching. Shulman is particularly well known for coining the term "pedagogical content knowledge" (Shulman, 1987). He defines this as the extent to which teachers know the specific teaching strategies associated with a given content area—in other words, a math teacher needs to understand not only math content but also how to teach students math. Although much of Shulman's work focuses on pedagogical content knowledge, he also articulated other types of knowledge required of teachers (Shulman, 1987), including

TABLE 24.2. Components of Intentional Teaching

	Definition	Examples
Knowing	Understanding current information on how to interact with children in ways that promote social, behavioral, and cognitive development.	Knowledge of child development, knowledge of a range of effective teaching practices, knowledge of individual children's needs, content knowledge, knowledge of self
Seeing	Identifying effective teacher–child interactions in action—both in others' as well as in one's own interactions.	Analysis of videos of effective teachers and of self to identify when things are going well or not well in interactions with children
Doing	Enacting effective teacher–child interactions in the classroom.	Effective implementation of curricula, ability to modify plans as needed in the moment to meet specific goals
Reflecting	Engaging in self-observation and critical analysis of teaching with goal of becoming more effective.	Guided reflections, coaching/mentoring

content knowledge, general pedagogical knowledge, knowledge of learners, and knowledge of educational contexts and purposes. Clearly there are many types of knowledge that early childhood teachers need. Because our work has focused on teachers' daily interactions with children, with a particular focus on the development of positive relationships and early literacy and language skills, we have focused on two types of knowledge—teachers' knowledge of children's development and their knowledge about specific teaching practices.

Teachers of young children need to have a depth of knowledge about children's development and *how* they learn. This type of understanding provides a critical foundation for all of a teacher's interactions with children. For example, knowing that even 2- and 3-year-olds have the capacity to understand and use complex language may change the way a teacher intentionally provides opportunities to scaffold this language in the classroom. Similarly, knowing that young children need concrete, hands-on experiences to learn should inform the way a teacher plans for and delivers instructional opportunities. Teachers need to know basic principles of children's development, such as the ways in which children learn through adult interactions and play, as well as more content-specific developmental knowledge (e.g., how and when children develop specific language skills).

Teachers need more than just abstract theory about children's development and content knowledge—they need a deep understanding of classroom practices that are effective and ineffective. This encompasses both general pedagogical knowledge (how to teach) and knowledge about how to teach specific content areas, or pedagogical content knowledge. With regard to general pedagogical knowledge, the TTI framework suggests that teachers need knowledge about how to provide emotionally supportive interactions, how to manage children's time and behavior in the classroom, and how to support cognitive and language development through the provision of instructional interactions. Because our work focuses on children's literacy and language development, we also expect that teachers need specific knowledge about how to teach young children early literacy and language skills. Similar knowledge is needed in other content areas, such as math and science.

EMPIRICAL SUPPORT FOR THE IMPORTANCE OF KNOWLEDGE TO TEACH EFFECTIVELY

There is very little evidence regarding either type of teacher knowledge among early childhood teachers. We know almost nothing about what early childhood teachers know, or do not know, and we know even less about the ways in which this knowledge may be associated with teachers' practices in the classroom. One exception to this relates to teachers' knowledge of language and literacy skills and teaching. Recently Neuman and Cunningham (2009) have articulated the importance of teachers' knowledge about literacy and language development. Cunningham, Zibulsky, and Callahan (2009) discuss the ways in which many early childhood teachers lack foundational knowledge of early literacy development and point out that many teachers overestimate their knowledge in ways that may keep them from seeking out new information and learning opportunities. There is no similar information regarding teachers' knowledge of children's social or self-regulatory development, but this is clearly an area needing attention.

Seeing

DESCRIPTION AND THEORETICAL BACKGROUND

Effective teacher–child interactions are complex, and it is insufficient just to know what they are. To become effective, teachers need to be able to see effective practices (and ineffective practices) in action. Teachers may know that they should individualize instruction and be sensitive to the diverse needs of all children in their classrooms—but what does this actually look like? We view this ability to see effective practice as a discrete skill that can be improved in teachers through systematic exposure to and analysis of video examples from real classrooms. It is important to note that this component of intentional teaching likely also capitalizes on other aspects of the perceptual system, such as hearing and feeling, and the use of the term "seeing" in our work stems from our application of classroom observation.

As suggested by Moreno and Valdez (2007), the theoretical foundation for the role of seeing effective practice lies in work on social learning theory (e.g., Bandura, 1986) as well as cognitive models of learning, such as dynamic memory theory (Schank, 1982). Social learning theory suggests that people learn how to behave in large part through observation of others (Bandura, 1986). These observations may occur through not only live experience but also observation of other media, such as video. Dynamic memory theory (Schank, 1982, 1997) extends this work by suggesting that the schemas and scripts that people develop based on experiences are an important component of learning how to behave in a particular moment. This work suggests that teachers should learn a lot about how to teach from watching examples of teaching.

However, just watching lots of video likely will not lead to changes in practice; teachers also need structured opportunities to engage in and analyze this video. We have found that an initial step to helping teachers really "see" classroom experiences is to help them objectively describe, at a very behavioral level, what is happening in the classroom. We often find that when people first watch classroom videos, they make very global statements (e.g., "That teacher is boring" or "He's mean") rather than clearly observing the actual behaviors that are in evidence (e.g., "The teacher's voice is flat and she does not look at students when they talk to her" or "The teacher raises his voice when a student comes in late"). Thus, a part of the work focuses on helping teachers be more objective observers of teaching practice.

We also find that teachers benefit greatly from having a specific lens though which to view practice. This is where the TTI framework comes into our work. When teachers are asked simply to watch classroom video without a particular lens, we find that they struggle to articulate what is going on in specific ways. For example, they may say, "She's doing a great job of behavior management," but struggle to articulate the specific behaviors that indicate effective behavior management. By introducing a specific framework for viewing practice, teachers are more clearly able to identify, describe, and see specific practices in ways that we expect are important to their ability to enact these practices in the classroom.

EMPIRICAL SUPPORT FOR THE IMPORTANCE OF SEEING TO TEACH EFFECTIVELY

A growing literature base demonstrates the value of using video case examples as a way to support teacher learning (e.g., Borko, Jacobs, Eiteljorg, & Pittman, 2008; Hatch & Grossman, 2009; Santagata, Zannoni, & Stigler, 2007). Even more importantly, a small body of research suggests that the ability to "see" effective interactions may be foundational to the ability to demonstrate these skills in the classroom consistently (Hamre, Pianta, Burchinal, et al., in press; Koran, Snow, & McDonald, 1971; Moreno & Valdez, 2007). In the 1970s, Mary Lou Koran and her colleagues (1971) conducted an interesting line of research in an attempt to validate social learning theory in teaching—demonstrating that teachers learn how to teach in part through video observations of teaching. In one study (Koran et al., 1971), 121 teacher education students were divided into three groups: The first group received video modeling of a specific teaching skill (use of analytic questioning strategies), the second received a written transcript of this video, and the third group was the control condition. Each group was asked to teach a short "micro-lesson" with four high school students before and after receiving the materials on teaching skills. Results suggested that teachers in both modeling treatment groups demonstrated more growth in the use of frequent and high-quality analytic questioning in the micro-lessons between the pre- and postassessment. Furthermore, the video modeling group demonstrated significantly larger gains in observed teaching skill than did the group only provided with written instructions. Moreno and Valdez (2007) have recently reinvigorated this work in K–12 teaching contexts, but we know of no work, outside of that discussed below, that focuses on observation of teaching skills in early childhood teachers.

Doing

DESCRIPTION AND THEORETICAL BACKGROUND

Enactment of effective teaching exists on a continuum from practicing brand new skills in an isolated fashion, such as role playing during a workshop, to engaging in intentional effective teaching in the classroom with ease. Theory and research on experiential learning (Kolb, Boyatzis, & Mainemelis, 2000), as well as the literature on expertise (e.g., Ericsson & Charness, 1994), suggest that practice is an essential component to becoming more effective at any task, and that learning occurs in part through doing.

Experiential learning theory suggests that learning occurs not just through obtaining abstract knowledge, or through observation, but through experience itself (Kolb et al., 2000). Kolb and colleagues (2000) argue that people learn through "experiencing the concrete, tangible, felt qualities of the world, relying on our senses and immersing ourselves in concrete reality" (p. 194). This theory has been widely applied to disciplines such as higher education, management, nursing, and medicine, with considerable evidence to support the value of experience on performance across disciplines. Ericsson and Charness (1994) similarly emphasize the importance of practice, as summarized in their review of literature on expertise:

> The effects of extended deliberate practice are more far-reaching than is commonly believed. Performers can acquire skills that circumvent basic limits on working memory capacity and sequential processing. Deliberate practice can also lead to anatomical changes resulting from adaptations to intense physical activity. The study of expert performance has important implications for our understanding of the structure and limits of human adaptation and optimal learning. (p. 725)

Particularly in relation to complex interpersonal and dynamic skills, such as those involved in teaching, it seems quite obvious that learning to be effective requires practice; however, there has traditionally been less emphasis on this as an important component of teacher education than one might expect.

Once again, the TTI framework provides the basis for our work with teachers as they attempt to enact new teaching interactions. Teachers are asked to practice new classroom interactions in a particular TTI dimension (e.g., concept development). Here, the specificity of the TTI framework has been helpful to teachers. It is often hard for them simply to engage in interactions that foster "higher-order thinking skills." However, if they are given some very explicit examples of the types of behaviors that they can use to meet this goal (e.g., making real-world connections, asking children to compare and contrast, connecting new learning to prior knowledge), then they are better able to enact these practices.

EMPIRICAL SUPPORT FOR THE EFFECT OF "DOING" ON TEACHING EFFECTIVELY

Despite years of qualitative work suggesting the importance of field experiences and other opportunities to practice teaching in the development of teacher knowledge and expertise (e.g., Darling-Hammond, 2010), surprisingly little empirical evidence links the quality or amount of teaching practice to later effectiveness. One recent study does suggest a link. Boyd, Grossman, Lankford, Loeb, and Wyckoff (2009) found that among teacher education experiences linked to later teacher performance, as assessed by student value-added scores, field experiences were among the most important. Clearly there is a need for more evidence in this domain.

Reflecting

DESCRIPTION AND THEORETICAL BACKGROUND

The final component of intentional teaching is reflection. *Reflection* is a word that is used often in teacher education programs and research, and as with teacher knowledge, there is a vast descriptive and qualitative literature suggesting its importance to effective teaching (see Marcos & Tillema, 2006, for a review). Theoretical work on the importance of reflection goes back to early work by Dewey (1933) and has also been the source of a great deal of controversy, with critiques from many directions (e.g., Gore, 1987; Pearson & Smith, 1985). We find that this concept is a useful one because it implies an intentional process of thinking that we think is critical to behavioral change. However, it is also clear that we need to provide a clear definition of this term in relation to our work.

We suggest that "reflection" involves active examination of teaching practice and the factors that may influence it, including the knowledge and skills described earlier—with the aim of improvement. As stated by Kottkamp (1990), reflection is "a cycle of paying deliberate attention to one's own actions in relation to intentions ... for the purpose of ... making decisions about improved ways of acting in the future, or in the midst of the action itself" (p. 182).

There are several important pieces of this definition of reflection. First, reflection is not something that happens one time; rather, a *cycle* of ongoing reflection is required to enact clear change in teaching practices. Second, it requires paying *deliberate attention to one's own actions*. In the case of teaching, this means that teachers need to spend time watching themselves teach. As we discussed earlier in relation to "seeing," this process is greatly enhanced through the use of video—a point to which we return throughout this chapter. Third, the goal of reflection should be to *improve ways of acting in the future*. In relation to teaching, this suggests that reflection activities should directly focus teachers on attempts to improve the effectiveness of their teaching and daily interactions with students. Too often teachers are asked to reflect, but without being urged to take these reflections back into the classroom. Finally, Kottkamp's definition notes that reflection can lead to changes not only in the planning of future teaching episodes but also in the *midst of action*. Teachers who consistently engage in a cycle of observation and reflection about their teaching practices are more likely to be able to make the right decisions in the moment of teaching.

Our work focuses on four major components of reflection: observation, assessment, analysis, and planning for change. A part of the reflective process is simple observation. Obviously this overlaps with the seeing component of the system, but we reemphasize it here due to its critical nature as the first step in motivating change. Assessment is another important part of reflection; teachers need to be aware of their own strengths and weaknesses (Ross & Bruce, 2007). Intentional teachers engage in ongoing assessment of their own effectiveness and are open to the feedback and assessments of others, such as administrators, parents, students, peers, and mentors or coaches. How does one go about conducting self-assessment on something as complex as teaching? A first step is to gain knowledge about a specific lens through which to view practice—here, the TTI framework. We then encourage teachers to videotape themselves and look for specific evidence that they are enacting the practices described by that framework. We also suggest that it is helpful to get feedback on strengths and weaknesses from a colleague or mentor, who might provide a different perspective, or from a more standardized source, such as a formal evaluation conducted as a part of a QRIS.

Once observation and assessment have occurred, effective reflection requires a process of analysis. *Analysis* is the process of taking a complex idea or process, such as teaching, and breaking it into smaller parts to gain a better understanding of it. During our analytic work with teachers, we encouraged them to ask questions. For example, why did a particular interaction work or not work? And what other factors may be influencing the tendency to interact with a child in a particular way? During analysis we try to stay focused on the teaching itself rather than on the contextual influences on that teacher (e.g., lack of administrator support or unengaged families). We find that, given the limited amount of time that teachers have to reflect on their practice, this type of practice-based reflection is more effective. It helps teachers feel that they have more control over what happens in the classroom and leads to positive changes that they can see for themselves.

The final step in the process is for teachers to use their observation, assessment, and analysis of practice and make a plan to change the way they are interacting in the classroom. As with the other steps in reflection, we find that these plans work best if they are very specific and target just one or two dimensions of teaching practice.

EMPIRICAL SUPPORT FOR THE EFFECT OF REFLECTION ON TEACHING EFFECTIVELY

Despite the abundance of research on teacher reflection, most of the research linking reflection to changes in teachers' practice is qualitative, in the form of descriptive case studies. The lack of a complementary quantitative research base may in large part be due to definitional and measurement issues that limit our understanding of when and how reflection has occurred. As Hatton and Smith (1995) stated:

> Definitions of reflection … are often inappropriate or inadequate, and it is clear that the terms are extremely difficult to render operational in questionnaires and other research instruments. Then it would appear that it has been a considerable challenge to develop means for gathering and analysing data so that the evidence shows unequivocally that reflection has taken place. (pp. 38–39)

This problem was not rectified in more recent work by Marcos and Tillema (2006), and there is very little writing about reflective practice among early childhood teachers specifically (Howes, James, & Ritchie, 2003). Given this state of the evidence, we are somewhat tentative in our inclusion of reflection in the intentional teaching process. It is important to operationally define and measure "reflection" within our work in ways that may inform future iterations of this model of intention teaching. In particular, we are interested in examining the potential components of reflection (e.g., analysis and planning for change), as defined earlier, to assess the extent to which they may be particularly important.

Properties of the Intentional Teaching System

Most of the research described earlier has progressed in an isolated fashion. We know very little about how these components of knowledge, perception, action, and reflection work together to produce changes in teaching practice. This problem is not unique to teaching. Schwartz, Martin, and Nasir (2005) describe the ways in which most of our knowledge about how people learn has developed in isolation rather than in clear articulation of the ways these systems may interact to produce learning.

Figure 24.1 is an initial illustration of how we hypothesize this system of intentionality may operate to produce more effective teaching. The know, see, and do components of the system operate together like cogs in a motor. Reflection that occurs is somewhat removed from, but closely linked to, this system. In our work, the reflection occurs through the very specific lens of the TTI framework, which helps teachers observe, assess, and analyze their knowledge, perceptions, and practices in a particular way that leads to more effective teaching or plans to change. However, it is important to note that we hypothesize that this system is not unique to our work, and that the system of intentional teaching would operate in similar ways in cases in which a particular professional development program had a different lens through which to view teaching. Below we briefly discuss some of proposed features of this system.

1. There is no single starting place for intentional teaching—it operates as a system. Teachers may first activate knowledge that informs their behavior—or they may simply enact practices and use their experience of those practices to change or update their knowledge.

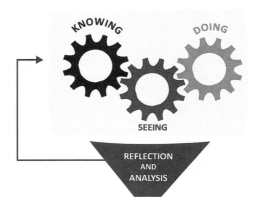

FIGURE 24.1. A model of intentional teaching.

2. Similarly, although "seeing" in this representation lies between "knowing" and "doing," we expect that the ordering of these cogs may be interchangeable. In other words, sometimes a teacher's knowledge may directly impact that teacher's practice, without the teacher having the ability to see it.

3. In new teachers or in teachers working to change a specific set of teaching practices, these systems are somewhat more disconnected from one another. Knowledge, for example, may be very disconnected from what teachers do in the classroom. As teachers work through a process of becoming more intentional, the components of this system become more tightly linked, and the whole system begins to operate in such a fluid fashion that it reaches a state of automaticity (Feldon, 2007). Thus, teachers' active mental attention is no longer required for them to produce effective teaching.

4. We can think about this system as it applies "in the moment" of teaching, as well as in the context of professional development or other activities in which teachers are gaining new knowledge or experiences that may influence the system. In the moment, teachers may access particular types of knowledge, see various interactions occurring, and/or enact particular types of teaching practices. They may engage in quick reflective actions that lead them to change their behavior in the classroom or seek out new knowledge (e.g., quickly reading through a lesson plan). This process also occurs outside of the classroom as teachers gain knowledge, spend time observing themselves and others, and try out new practices through activities such as role plays. Our expectation is that the more experience teachers get working on this system outside of the classroom, the more they will internalize it, and the better they will be at applying it in the moment.

5. Though not depicted here, we anticipate that many factors influence the efficiency of this system. We hypothesize that characteristics of teachers, such as working memory, emotional regulatory capacities, and personalities, as well as larger contextual variables (e.g., administrative support), may influence their abilities to be intentional (Raver, Blair, & Li-Grining, in press; Rimm-Kaufman & Hamre, 2010).

The hypothesized structure, components, and features of this system have formed the basis of our development work in recent years. However, it has been, and will continue to be, an iterative process in which initial theory informs the development of interventions for teachers and the results of research on those interventions-informed modifications to the theory. The next section describes some of the professional development research that has informed our theory to date.

Initial Validation of the Intentional Teaching Process from Randomized Controlled Trials

Over the past decade, we have developed several professional development (PD) resources for early childhood educators that map onto the intentional teaching process. In the following sections, we describe these teacher supports, outline how they align with the elements of practice that lead to intentional teaching through interactions (i.e., seeing, knowing, doing, and reflecting), and report findings from several randomized controlled trials that provide evidence in support of the framework.

MyTeachingPartner: The Early Years

Initially, we developed two PD resources as part of the MyTeachingPartner (MTP) project: (1) the MTP Video Library and (2) Web-mediated MTP Consultation—with the ultimate goal of facilitating teachers' use of effective interactions with the children in their class-rooms. The MTP Video Library provided over 200 videoclips of effective implementation of instructional activities in literacy, language, and social development in an online, on-demand format (Kinzie et al., 2006; Pianta, Mashburn, Downer, Hamre, & Justice, 2008). These 1- to 2-minute videos were organized (and searchable) by the TTI dimensions (Figure 24.2), and each one included an explicit behavioral description of what was happening in the video footage that reflected a high-quality teacher–child interaction (Figure 24.3). Early childhood educators are often isolated within their own classrooms and rarely have the opportunity to see authentic, real-time examples of effective interactions and teaching. The idea behind the MTP Video Library was to provide opportunities for these teachers to learn more about what types of interactions are important for student learning (knowing) and to understand exactly what these interactions look like when enacted by others (seeing).

MTP Consultation involved observation-based analysis and feedback during a regular cycle of Web-mediated interaction (both synchronous and asynchronous) between a teacher and consultant (see Figure 24.4). Every 2 weeks, teachers videotaped their instruction in lit-eracy, language, and social skills, and sent this footage to their consultant. In the intentional teaching process, this is represented by the doing cog; teachers were trying out new ways of interacting with the children in their classrooms and capturing it on videotape. The consul-tant then edited the tape into three segments that highlighted a specific TTI dimension (e.g.,

FIGURE 24.2. CLASS (Teaching through Interactions) video library.

FIGURE 24.3. Sample page with video and annotation.

concept development) and focused on (1) identification of instances of effective behavior, (2) analysis of alternatives, and (3) implementation of instructional activities. These video segments were then paired with written feedback (i.e., "prompts") and posted to a secure website, where teachers viewed the segments and responded to the prompts. Similar to watching other teachers in the Video Library, it was our intention to have teachers improve their ability to detect visual cues through guided practice watching their own classroom footage (seeing). For example, prompts focused attention on specific aspects of teacher–child interaction (e.g., "What did you do here to help J. pay attention, and what did he do in response?") in which child and teacher behaviors were contingent on one another. After the online contact, teachers and consultants met by video conference or phone to discuss the feedback in prompts and responses, followed by efforts to problem-solve and develop an action plan for future instructional activities. Both the response to consultant feedback online and the conversations during conferences were set up to encourage teacher reflection on observed interactions. Namely, teachers were challenged to analyze how their own actions were linked to certain child behaviors, and vice versa. With these moments identified, the consultant then

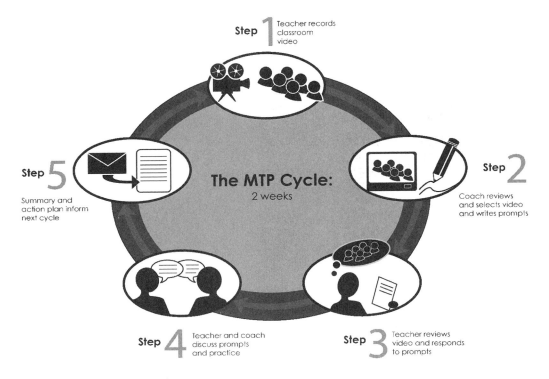

Step 1 Teacher records classroom video

Step 2 Coach reviews and selects video and writes prompts

Step 3 Teacher reviews video and responds to prompts

Step 4 Teacher and coach discuss prompts and practice

Step 5 Summary and action plan inform next cycle

The MTP Cycle: 2 weeks

FIGURE 24.4. MTP cycle.

pushed teachers a step further to plan and create future learning opportunities to replicate successful interactions or to try out new ways of engaging children in learning through interactions (which feeds back into doing). This MTP Consultation cycle was spread over 2 weeks and repeated continually across 2 years, with gradually deepening reflective analysis around interactions that are more difficult to detect and enact. All told, these loops of video-taping, feedback, and conferencing were designed to encourage seeing, doing, and reflecting, and the linkages among them.

Once developed, we tested these MTP teacher resources in a randomized controlled trial with over 240 state-funded PreK teachers to determine whether a PD focus on the components of the intentional teaching process would result in improved instruction and child outcomes. Two approaches to PD were implemented and compared (Pianta et al., 2008): (1) Web Only, in which teachers had access to the MTP Video Library, and (2) MTP Consultation, in which teachers had consultation and access to the Video Library. Encouragingly, we found that teachers assigned to Consultation made significant gains compared to the Web Only teachers in reading and responding to students' cues ($d = 0.82$), using a variety of formats to engage children actively in instruction, ($d = 0.77$), and intentionally stimulating language development ($d = 0.97$). And in classrooms with 100% of the children enrolled from families at or below 2.0 in the federal poverty guidelines, there were remarkable differences in teachers' rates of changes in sensitivity and responsiveness ($d = 2.29$) and facilitating engagement and enthusiasm in learning ($d = 2.13$), in favor of those receiving Consultation. In addition, comparisons of child outcomes between the two intervention conditions and an attention-only control group indicated that children in Consultation classrooms made greater gains in receptive vocabulary ($d = 0.27$; Mashburn et al., 2010), task orientation, and assertiveness ($d = 0.21$ and $d = 0.28$; Hamre, Pianta, Mashburn, & Downer, in press) than did children in the other conditions.

Clearly, the evidence was in favor of the Consultation condition, which had a comprehensive focus on all elements of the intentional teaching process. However, there were hints in post hoc analyses and anecdotal feedback from participants to suggest that the knowing and seeing cogs played an explicit role in changing instructional practice. For example, teachers who only had access to video exemplars (Web Only condition) and made regular use of these exemplars were observed to be more sensitive and responsive to children's needs, more proactive and effective at managing behavior, and more skilled at maximizing children's learning time (Pianta et al., 2008). Teachers who spent more time watching video exemplars online also had children who experienced greater gains in social development during the PreK year ($d = 0.23–0.36$; Hamre, Pianta, Mashburn, et al., in press). And, indications of the importance of observing video footage were not exclusive to exemplars in the MTP Video Library; teachers who spent more time watching and analyzing their own classroom video footage online as part of Consultation also had children who experienced greater gains in vocabulary development during the PreK year ($d = 0.30$; Mashburn et al., 2010). These findings suggest that the act of watching oneself and others interact with children in a classroom (seeing) in and of itself may contribute to changes in instruction and children's learning. Additionally, in focus groups at the end of the project, many of the teachers, particularly those receiving Consultation, felt that they could have taken better advantage of reflection work with their consultant if they had had a greater understanding of what constituted effective teacher–child interactions at the beginning of the year. They needed more knowledge about these practices and more time to see what they looked like in classrooms.

Although these quasi-experimental and qualitative findings offered encouraging evidence in favor of certain components of the intentional teaching process, this initial trial of MTP was designed only to test the model comprehensively, leaving many open questions about which elements of the theory of teacher change are necessary targets of PD.

The Next Iteration of MTP: NCRECE Professional Development Study

Building on the promise of the initial study of MTP, the Institute of Education Sciences (IES)– funded National Center for Research on Early Childhood Education (NCRECE) recently embarked on a professional development study that begins experimentally to unpack the components of the intentional teaching process. This project involved 440 preschool teachers who participated in an 18-month study of two forms of professional development—a 14-week course and yearlong MTP consultation. We designed the course to increase teachers' knowledge about the vital role that teacher–child interactions play in children's learning and to build their specific skills for observing these interactions. When contrasted with the underutilized, teacher-initiated viewing of the MTP Video Library (as described earlier), this was an explicit attempt to ramp up the intensity of focus on the knowing and seeing components of the system. Initially, NCRECE teachers were randomly assigned to participate in the course or a business-as-usual control group; at the conclusion of this phase of intervention, all teachers were then rerandomized into either a yearlong MTP Consultation experience or a control group. The following sections describe the course in greater detail, summarize initial findings during the course phase, and acknowledge how future analysis can further speak to the validity of the intentional teaching process.

The course, entitled Support of Language and Literacy Development in Preschool Classrooms through Effective Teacher–Child Interactions and Relationships, targeted two major clusters of belief, knowledge and skill. The former focused on effective teacher–child interactions, and the latter focused specifically on teaching of literacy and language in early childhood classrooms. With regard to teacher–child interactions, the course was designed to advance the belief that teachers need to be actively engaged in interactions with children in order for learning to occur. The course also provided very specific knowledge about effective interactions and used TTI (Hamre, Pianta, Downer, et al., 2011) as the framework for this knowledge. Teachers were taught to make explicit links between behavioral actions and intended consequences for children. For example, when learning about quality of feedback, teachers were encouraged to watch and analyze videos that highlighted the ways specific teacher actions led to children spending more or less time thinking about and analyzing a problem. The course also targeted teachers' skills in detecting effective teacher–child interactions though video analysis. We hypothesized that it was not sufficient for teachers to be able to gain knowledge about effective interactions; they needed actual skills involving identification of effective interactions with a high degree of specificity in order to be most likely to transfer the coursework into changes in their instructional practice. Therefore, a primary emphasis in the course was analysis of videotapes from real classrooms to develop skills of identifying effective (and ineffective) interactions and articulating specific behavioral evidence to support these judgments.

In terms of logistics, the course was delivered in 14, 3-hour-long sessions, through collaborations with local colleges and universities in 10 sites across the country. There were between five and 15 teachers in each course section. Instructors ($N = 15$) were provided with standardized manuals that included PowerPoint presentations, videos, and written assignments for each course section. Instructors attended weeklong training and were provided with ongoing implementation support by NCRECE staff, including weekly phone calls from course developers. Videotape coding of course sections indicated high levels of implementation fidelity (LoCasale-Crouch et al., 2011).

Compared to teachers in the control condition, those in the course condition reported more intentional teaching beliefs (effect size = 0.43) and demonstrated greater knowledge of ($d = 0.77$) and skills in detecting effective teacher–child interactions ($d = 0.60$; Hamre, Pianta, Burchinal, et al., in press). Teachers in the course condition also reported stronger beliefs about the importance of teaching children early literacy and language skills ($d = 0.65$) and demonstrated greater knowledge about these skills ($d = 0.49$). Importantly, teachers who took the course demonstrated more effective emotional ($d = 0.41$) and instructional ($d = 0.66$) practices in interactions with children. Importantly, teachers' skills in detecting effective interactions partially mediated the effects of the coursework on teachers' actual practices.

These findings substantiate the proposed intentional teaching process in several ways. First, a course focused almost exclusively on knowing and seeing can be effective at improving teacher knowledge about teacher–child interaction and children's language/literacy development, as well as teacher's skill at detecting behavioral cues in videotape footage of teachers and children interacting with one another. Second, despite the course's narrow intent to alter teacher beliefs, knowledge, and skill at observing teacher–child interactions, course participation was also associated with improvements in actual teaching practice. Third, and perhaps most interesting, there was some indication that changes in teachers' instructional practices came about as a function of improvements in detecting the nuances of teacher–child interactions during observation. It is possible that the portions of the course that focused on having teachers analyze classroom video in very specific ways were among the most important for helping teachers enact these practices in their classrooms. This suggests PD that targets the "seeing" cog may result in movements of the "doing" cog, and even produce elements of effective teaching.

Once data are available to examine the full four-condition design of the NCRECE study, we will be poised to answer several other questions about the intentional teaching process.

Teachers who only received the course will be compared to those who only received MTP Consultation, which sets up several interesting contrasts. One involves the way in which the "seeing" cog is addressed; the course provides opportunities for seeing in relation to exemplars of other teachers' practice, whereas the consultation adds an element of watching one's own teaching. In addition, consultation explicitly activates the "doing" and "reflection" cogs by asking teachers to try out new ways of interacting with their students, then offering opportunities to analyze these experiences on video to plan for future interactions. Given that the course and consultation target different aspects of the intentional teaching process, do they produce equal or differentiated impacts on teachers' effective instructional practice? On a different note, some teachers will receive both interventions to determine whether an exponential gain in teacher effectiveness occurs when all four elements of the intentional teaching process are targeted. These tests of the intentional teaching process are, of course, all imprecise to some degree given that certain aspects of knowing are targeted during MTP consultation (e.g., Classroom Assessment Scoring System [CLASS] dimension guides) and elements of doing are a minor focus of the course (e.g., one assignment to practice a certain teacher–child interaction in the classroom). However, the NCRECE professional development study is an example of how experimental studies can be designed to contribute to theory development and in this case has already generated findings that are helping to refine our thinking about the intentional teaching process.

Implications and Directions for Future Research

The work described here provides one example of evidenced-based professional development programs targeting improvement in teachers' daily interactions with children. There are many other recent examples of effective PD programs (Zaslow et al., 2010). The question is, *why* are these approaches effective? What are the common elements of programs that work to change teachers' behavior? We argue that answering this question requires us to move beyond the identification of PD program structures (e.g., length and type of intervention) to articulate clearly and test the theories of change that underlie these successful programs. The work reported here provides initial evidence in support of the model of intentional teaching and highlights the importance of teacher knowledge, perception, action, and reflection. However, there is clearly much more to learn.

There are many unanswered questions about how this intentional teaching system may operate. Are some of these cogs easier to turn than others, and do some have stronger effects on others? In other words, is it easier to change teacher knowledge in ways that modify practice, or should we work on directly changing practice as a way of altering knowledge? We also need to understand the component parts of each cog. For example, among all the types of teacher knowledge, which is the most important in helping teachers enact effective practices? As noted earlier, we expect that child development knowledge is important, but we have very little evidence to support this claim. Online coursework provides an opportunity to design efficient experiments in which teachers are randomly assigned to course components designed specifically to answer these questions. Some teachers may get a course on just children's literacy and language development, whereas others may get a course only on literacy and language teacher practices. Another group may get both. We can then examine the differential effects of these types of interventions.

We also need to understand more about the factors that influence how the intentional teaching system works. Raver, Blair, and Li-Grining (in press) have written about the ways in which teachers' own emotional regulatory capabilities may influence both their teaching and their ability to take advantage of professional development opportunities. Belief systems may also be important moderators of effectiveness. Although initial evidence suggests the NCRECE course was effective across a broad spectrum of teachers, teachers with more authoritarian beliefs were less engaged in course content (Hamre, Pianta, Burchinal, et al., in press). To develop the most effective programs for teachers, we need to understand which of these factors may moderate their effectiveness, and develop alternative approaches to meet the needs of different types of teachers.

We also need to understand better how time factors into the system. At what point in teachers' development should they be introduced to various aspects of the intentional teaching system? For example, what aspects of this system are most useful for teacher education students? The NCRECE team (Scott-Little et al., 2011) examined this issue in part by offering the same course through the Institutes of Higher Education (IHE). Compared to teachers in the main study, who were all in service, teachers in the IHE courses were a mix of in service and preservice teachers. Although students did report liking the course, in general, their reports on the helpfulness of the video examples were more mixed than reports in the main study. Our experience suggests that those without experience teaching ("doing") may have more difficulty engaging in opportunities to see others teach. They are more inclined to make comments such as "Oh sure, I get that—it's easy," whereas teachers with more experience may be able to glean more from these types of experiences.

A major weakness of PD research specifically, and educational research in general, is that very few studies follow teachers over time (Rimm-Kaufman & Hamre, 2010). Most studies, including ours, are intended to assess the efficacy of a specific approach or program. We know very little about the long-term impact of our interventions, and even less about how teachers develop knowledge and expertise over the course of their careers. How do they integrate what they have learned in teacher education with ongoing professional development and with what they learn every day on the job during interactions with children? Several large-scale, longitudinal studies have great potential in this area—for example, the Teacher Pathways Project in New York City (Boyd et al., 2009), the Teacher Quality Partnership Study (2006) in the state of Ohio, and the Fit-Choice Study in Australia (Watt & Richardson, 2007). None of these studies, however, follow early childhood education teachers.

Although we have now been doing this work for almost a decade, we are still just beginning to understand the processes underlying effects. Not only do we need to understand more about what is working, but we also need to continue to critically examine what is not working. Similar to other PD studies in early childhood education, our effects on teachers are modest to large, but the effects on children are small. We see the effects on child outcomes as a good starting place, but we need to take seriously the challenge put forth by government agencies, such as the Office of Head Start and state legislatures, to show meaningful impacts on children. Future revisions of our PD programs need to take on this challenge more explicitly. We hope that we can use the intentional teaching process as a guide as we make some of these changes. For example, if we continue to find evidence that "seeing" is important to improving practice, are there ways in which we can provide teachers with a greater dosage of this aspect within our PD programs?

Implications for Practice

Practitioners now have the option to engage in PD programs with proven efficacy. However, we also know that many PD programs will be developed and disseminated without such evidence. It will be important, therefore, for us to draw conclusions from our work and the work of others that inform the development of those programs and that can help practitioners make informed decisions about programs that are more likely to be effective. For example, there is clearly evidence supporting the value of providing teachers with video examples of effective practice. However, this does not mean that every PD program that uses video will be effective. Our work suggests that teachers need opportunities and support to analyze video in ways that allow them to focus on the moment-to-moment interactions in the classroom. The more we can understand the underlying components and processes of effective PD, the more refined our work will be going forward.

One unique implication for teachers is that the intentional teaching model brings attention to multiple avenues for development as an effective teacher. More importantly, it does so in ways that align with typical teacher feedback about inservice PD opportunities. PD for teachers has a long history of reliance on static, stand-alone informational sessions focused on knowledge expansion, while teachers often report desire for PD that is better linked to their practice and experiential in nature. A strength of this intentional teaching model is that it recognizes the need for development of teacher knowledge yet fully acknowledges that knowledge in isolation is unlikely to result in effective teaching. By highlighting several interwoven elements of intentional teaching, this model provides teachers with a guide for evaluating their current PD experiences and selecting future PD that both touches on complementary aspects of the intentional teaching process and supplies a platform from which to advocate for more PD that addresses the seeing, doing, and reflecting part of improving teaching practice.

Conclusions

The recent proliferation of evidence-based PD programs for early childhood education teachers is an encouraging step toward realizing the promise of early childhood education programs. Unfortunately, the creation of these effective programs seems to have far outpaced the development of accompanying theory about the mechanisms through which PD works. This has the potential to handicap progress in the field by making it difficult to compare results across programs and isolate essential (and nonessential) components. This chapter makes an effort to outline a unifying model of intentional teaching that draws from developmental, cognitive, and education science literatures to pinpoint the core elements of a process that results in effective teaching. This model is the product of our own PD work, as well as that of others, yet it is only a starting point in the iterative generation of a deeper understanding about the ways in which teachers become intentional and effective in their practices.

Acknowledgments

The research reported here was supported by the Institute of Education Sciences, U.S. Department of Education, through Grant No. R305A060021 to the University of Virginia, funding the National Center for Research on Early Childhood Education (NCRECE), and by the National Institute of Child Health and Human Development and the Interagency Consortium on School Readiness. The opinions expressed are those of the authors and do not represent views of the funders.

References

Ainsworth, M. D., Blehar, M. C., Waters, E., & Wall, D. (1978). *Patterns of attachment: A psychological study of the strange situation*. Hillsdale, NJ: Erlbaum.

Bandura, A. (1986). *Social foundations of thought and action: A social cognitive theory.* Englewood Cliffs, NJ: Prentice-Hall.

Barnett, S., Yarosz, D., Thomas, J., & Hornbeck, A. (2008). Educational effectiveness of a vygotskian approach to preschool education: A randomized trial. *Early Childhood Research Quarterly, 23,* 299–313.

Bierman, K. L., Domitrovich, C. E., Nix, R. L., Gest, S. D., Welsh, J. A., Greenberg, M. T., et al. (2008). Promoting academic and social–emotional school readiness: The Head Start REDI program. *Child Development, 79*(6), 1802–1817.

Bierman, K. L., & Erath, S. A. (2006). Promoting social competence in early childhood: Classroom curricula and social skills coaching programs. In K. McCartney & D. Phillips (Eds.), *Blackwell handbook on early childhood development* (pp. 595–615). Malden, MA: Blackwell.

Borko, H., Jacobs, J., Eiteljorg, E., & Pittman, M. E. (2008). Video as a tool for fostering productive discussions in mathematics professional development. *Teaching and Teacher Education, 24*(2), 417–436.

Bowlby, J. (1969). *Attachment and loss: Vol. 1. Attachment.* New York: Basic Books.

Bowman, B., Donovan, S., & Burns, M. S. (Eds.). (2001). *Eager to learn: Educating our preschoolers* (National Research Council, Committee on Prevention of Reading Difficulties in Young Children). Washington, DC: National Academy Press.

Boyd, D., Grossman, P. L., Lankford, H., Loeb, S., & Wyckoff, J. (2009). Teacher preparation and student achievement. *Educational Evaluation and Policy Analysis, 31*(4), 416–440.

Bridges, M., Fuller, B., Huang, D. S., & Hamre, B. R. (2011). Strengthening the early childhood workforce: How wage incentives may boost training and job stability. *Early Education and Development, 22*(6), 1009–1029.

Bronfenbrenner, U., & Morris, P. A. (1998). The ecology of developmental processes. In W. Damon & R. M. Lerner (Eds.), *Handbook of child psychology: Theoretical models of human development* (5th ed., Vol. 1, pp. 993–1029). New York: Wiley.

Brophy-Herb, H. E., Lee, R. E., Nievar, M. A., & Stollak, G. (2007). Preschoolers' social competence: Relations to family characteristics, teacher behaviors and classroom climate. *Journal of Applied Developmental Psychology, 28*(2), 134–148.

Burchinal, M., Howes, C., Pianta, R., Bryant, D., Early, D., Clifford, R., et al. (2008). Predicting child outcomes at the end of kindergarten from the quality of pre-kindergarten teacher–child interactions and instruction. *Applied Developmental Science, 12*(3), 140–153.

Burchinal, M., Roberts, J. E., Zeisel, S. A., Hennon, E. A., & Hooper, S. (2006). Social risk and protective child, parenting, and child care factors in early elementary school years. *Parenting, 6*(1), 79–113.

Buyse, E., Verschueren, K., Doumen, S., Van Damme, J., & Maes, F. (2008). Classroom problem behavior and teacher–child relationships in kindergarten: The moderating role of classroom climate. *Journal of School Psychology, 46*(4), 367–391.

Cameron, C. E., Connor, C. M. D., Morrison, F. J., & Jewkes, A. M. (2008). Effects of classroom organization on letter–word reading in first grade. *Journal of School Psychology, 46*(2), 173–192.

Clarke, D. J., & Hollingsworth, H. (2002) Elaborating a model of teacher professional growth. *Teacher and Teacher Education, 18,* 947–967.

Connell, J. P., & Wellborn, J. G. (1991). Competence, autonomy, and relatedness: A motivational analysis of self-system processes. In R. Gunnar & L. A. Sroufe (Eds.), *Minnesota Symposia on Child Psychology* (Vol. 23, pp. 43–77). Hillsdale, NJ: Erlbaum.

Connor, C., Son, S., Hindman, A. H., & Morrison, F. J. (2005). Teacher qualifications, classroom practices, family characteristics, and preschool experience: Complex effects on first graders' vocabulary and early reading outcomes. *Journal of School Psychology, 43*(4), 343–375.

Connor, C. M., Morrison, F. J., & Katch, L. E. (2004). Beyond the reading wars: Exploring the effect of child-instruction interactions on growth in early reading. *Scientific Studies of Reading, 8*(4), 305–336.

Connor, C. M., Morrison, F. J., & Petrella, J. N. (2004). Effective reading comprehension instruction: Examining child × instruction interactions. *Journal of Educational Psychology, 96*(4), 682–698.

Cunningham, A. E., Zibulsky, J., & Callahan, M. (2009). Starting small: Building preschool teacher knowledge that supports early literacy development. *Reading and Writing: An Interdisciplinary Journal, 22*(4), 487–510.

Curby, T. W., LoCasale-Crouch, J., Konold, T. R., Pianta, R. C., Howes, C., Burchinal, M., et al. (2009). The relations of observed pre-K classroom quality profiles to children's achievement and social competence. *Early Education and Development, 20*(2), 346–372.

Darling-Hammond, L. (2010). Teacher education and the American future. *Journal of Teacher Education, 61*, 35–47.

Davis, E. A., & Miyake, N. (2004). Explorations of scaffolding in complex classroom systems. *Journal of the Learning Sciences, 13*(3), 265–272.

Decker, D. M., Dona, D. P., & Christenson, S. L. (2007). Behaviorally at-risk African American students: The importance of student–teacher relationships for student outcomes. *Journal of School Psychology, 45*(1), 83–109.

Dewey, J. (1933). *How we think: A restatement of the relation of reflective thinking to the educative process.* Boston: Heath.

Domínguez, X., Vitiello, V. E., Maier, M. F., & Greenfield, D. B. (2010). A longitudinal examination of young children's learning behavior: Child-level and classroom-level predictors of change throughout the preschool year. *School Psychology Review, 39*(1), 29–47.

Downer, J., Sabol, T. J., & Hamre, B. K. (2010). Teacher–child interactions in the classroom: Toward a theory of within- and cross-domain links to children's developmental outcomes. *Early Education and Development, 21*(5), 699–723.

Early, D. M., & Winton, P. J. (2001). Preparing the workforce: Early childhood teacher preparation at 2- and 4-year institutions of higher education. *Early Childhood Research Quarterly, 16*, 285–306.

Epstein, A. S. (2007). *The intentional teacher: Choosing the best strategies for young children's learning.* Washington, DC: National Association for the Education of Young Children.

Ericsson, K. A., & Charness, N. (1994). Expert performance: Its structure and acquisition. *American Psychologist, 49*(8), 725–747.

Feldon, D. F. (2007). Cognitive load and classroom teaching: The double-edged sword of automaticity. *Educational Psychologist, 42*, 123–137.

Garet, M., Porter, S., Andrew, C., & Desimone, L. (2001). What makes professional development effective?: Results from a national sample of teachers. *American Educational Research Journal, 38*, 915–945.

Glaser, R. (1992). Learning, cognition, and education: Then and now. In H. L. Pick, Jr., P. Van Den Broek, & D. C. Knill (Eds.), *Cognition: Conceptual and methodological issues* (pp. 239–266). Washington, DC: American Psychological Association.

Gore, J. (1987). Reflecting on reflective teaching. *Journal of Teacher Education, 38*(2), 33–39.

Hamre, B., & Pianta, R. C. (2007). Learning opportunities in preschool and early elementary classrooms. In R. Pianta, M. Cox, & K. Snow (Eds.), *School readiness and the transition to kindergarten in the era of accountability* (pp. 49–84). Baltimore: Brookes.

Hamre, B., Pianta, R., Burchinal, M., Field, S., LoCasale-Crouch, J., Downer, J. T., et al. (in press). Supporting effective teacher–child interactions through coursework: Effects on teacher beliefs, knowledge, and observed practice. *American Educational Research Journal.*

Hamre, B. K., & Pianta, R. C. (2010). Classroom environments and developmental processes: Conceptualization and measurement. In J. Meece & J. Eccles (Eds.), *Handbook of research on schools, schooling, and human development* (pp. 25–41). New York: Routledge.

Hamre, B. K., Pianta, R. C., Downer, J. T., Hakigmi, A., & Mashburn, A. J. (2011). *Teaching through interactions—testing a developmental framework of teacher effectiveness in over 4,000 classrooms.* Manuscript submitted for publication.

Hamre, B. K., Pianta, R. C., Mashburn, A. J., & Downer, J. T. (in press). Promoting young children's social competence through the Preschool PATHS curriculum and MyTeachingPartner professional development resources. *Early Education and Development.*

Hatch, T., & Grossman, P. (2009). Learning to look beyond the boundaries of representation: Using technology to examine teaching (Overview for a digital exhibition: Learning from the Practice of Teaching). *Journal of Teacher Education, 60*(1), 70–85.

Hatton, N., & Smith, D. (1995). Reflection in teacher education: Towards definition and implementation. *Teaching and Teacher Education, 11*(1), 33–49.

Howes, C., Burchinal, M., Pianta, R., Bryant, D., Early, D., Clifford, R., et al. (2008). Ready to learn?: Children's pre-academic achievement in pre-kindergarten programs. *Early Childhood Research Quarterly, 23*(1), 27–50.

Howes, C., James, J., & Ritchie, S. (2003). Pathways to effective teaching. *Early Childhood Research Quarterly, 18*(1), 104–120.

Hyson, M. (2008). *Enthusiastic and engaged learners: Approaches to learning in the early childhood classroom.* New York: Teachers College Press.

Kern, L., & Clemens, N. H. (2007). Antecedent strategies to promote appropriate classroom behavior. *Psychology in the Schools, 44*(1), 65–75.

Kern, L., Gallagher, P., Starosta, K., Hickman, W., & George, M. (2006). Longitudinal outcomes of functional behavioral assessment-based intervention. *Journal of Positive Behavior Interventions, 8*(2), 67–78.

Kinzie, M. B., Whitaker, S. D., Neesen, K., Kelley, M., Matera, M., & Pianta, R. C. (2006). Innovative web-based professional development for teachers of at-risk preschool children. *Educational Technology and Society, 9*(4), 194–204.

Kolb, D. A., Boyatzis, R. E., & Mainemelis, C. (2000). Experiential learning theory: Previous research and new directions. In R. J. Sternberg & L. E. Zhang (Eds.), *Perspectives on cognitive, learning and thinking styles* (pp. 193–210). Mahwah, NJ: Erlbaum.

Koran, M. L., Snow, R. E., McDonald, F. J. (1971). Teacher aptitude and observational learning of a teaching skill. *Journal of Education Psychology, 62,* 219–228.

Kottkamp, R. (1990). Means of facilitating reflection. *Education and Urban Society, 22*(2), 182–203.

LoCasale-Crouch, J., Kraft-Sayre, M., Pianta, R. C., Hamre, B. K., Downer, J. T., Burchinal, M., et al. (2011). Implementation of an early childhood professional development course in nine settings and fifteen sections. *NHSA Dialog, 14*(4), 275–292.

Marcos, J. J., & Tillema, M. (2006). Studying studies of teacher reflection and action: An appraisal of research contributions. *Educational Research Review, 1,* 112–132.

Mashburn, A. J., Downer, J. T., Hamre, B. K., Justice, L. M., & Pianta, R. C. (2010). Consultation for teachers and children's language and literacy development during pre-kindergarten. *Applied Developmental Science, 14,* 179–196.

Maxwell, K. L., Early, D. M., Bryant, D., Kraus, S., Hume, K., & Crawford, G. (2009). *Georgia study of early care and education: Findings from Georgia's pre-k program.* Chapel Hill: University of North Carolina at Chapel Hill, FPG Child Development Institute.

McClelland, M. M., Cameron, C. E., Wanless, S., & Murray, A. (2007). Executive function, behavioral self-regulation, and social–emotional competence: Links to school readiness. In O. N. Saracho & B. Spodek (Eds.), *Contemporary perspectives in early childhood education: Social learning in early childhood education* (Vol. 7, pp. 113–137). Greenwich, CT: Information Age.

Miles, K. H., Odden, A., Fermanich, M., & Archibald, S. (2004). Inside the black box of school district spending on professional development: Lessons from comparing five urban districts. *Journal of Education Finance, 30*(1), 1–26.

Moreno, R., & Valdez, A. (2007). Immediate and delayed learning effects of presenting classroom cases in teacher education: Are video cases or case narratives more effective? *Journal of Educational Psychology, 99,* 194–206.

Neitzel, C., Alexander, J. M., & Johnson, K. E. (2008). Children's early interest-based activities in the home and subsequent information contributions and pursuits in kindergarten. *Journal of Educational Psychology, 100*(4), 782–797.

Neuman, S., & Cunningham, L. (2009). The impact of professional development and coaching on early language and literacy instructional practices. *American Educational Research Journal, 46*(2), 532–566.

O'Connor, E., & McCartney, K. (2007). Examining teacher–child relationships and achievement as part of an ecological model of development. *American Educational Research Journal, 44*(2), 340–369.

Pearson, M., & Smith, D. (1985). Debriefing in experience-based learning. In D. Boud, R. Keogh, & D. Walker (Eds.), *Reflection: Turning experience into learning* (pp. 69–84). New York: Nichols.

Pence, K. L., Justice, L. M., & Wiggins, A. K. (2008). Preschool teachers' fidelity in implementing a comprehensive language-rich curriculum. *Language, Speech, and Hearing Services in Schools, 39*, 329–341.

Peterson, S. M., & French, L. (2008). Supporting young children's explanations through inquiry science in preschool. *Early Childhood Research Quarterly, 23*(3), 395–408.

Phillips, B. M., Clancy-Menchetti, J., & Lonigan, C. J. (2008). Successful phonological awareness instruction with preschool children. *Topics in Early Childhood Special Education, 28*(1), 3–17.

Phillips, D., Gormley, W., & Lowenstein, A. (2009). Inside the pre-kindergarten door: Classroom climate and instructional time allocation in Tulsa's pre-k programs. *Early Childhood Research Quarterly, 24*(3), 213–228.

Pianta, R., Howes, C., Burchinal, M., Bryant, D., Clifford, R., Early, D., et al. (2005). Features of pre-kindergarten programs, classrooms, and teachers: Do they predict observed classroom quality and child–teacher interactions? *Applied Developmental Science, 9*(3), 144–159.

Pianta, R., Mashburn, A., Downer, J., Hamre, B., & Justice, L. (2008). Effects of web-mediated professional development resources on teacher–child interactions in pre-kindergarten classrooms. *Early Childhood Research Quarterly, 23*, 431–451.

Raab, M., Dunst, C. J., Wilson, L. L., Parkey, C., Admas, F., Rinaldi, C., et al. (2009). Early contingency learning and child and teacher concomitant social–emotional behavior. *International Journal of Early Childhood, 1*, 1–14.

Raver, C. C. (2004). Placing emotional self-regulation in sociocultural and socioeconomic contexts. *Child Development, 75*(2), 346–353.

Raver, C. C., Blair, C., & Li-Grining, C. (in press). Extending models of emotional self-regulation to classroom settings: Implications for professional development. In C. Howes, B. K. Hamre, & R. C. Pianta (Eds.), *Effective early childhood professional development*. Baltimore: Brookes.

Raver, C. C., Jones, S. M., Li-Grining, C. P., Metzger, M., Smallwood, K., & Sardin, L. (2008). Improving preschool classroom processes: Preliminary findings from a randomized trial implemented in Head Start settings. *Early Childhood Research Quarterly, 23*(1) 10–26.

Rimm-Kaufman, S. E., & Chiu, Y. J. I. (2007). Promoting social and academic competence in the classroom: An intervention study examining the contribution of the responsive classroom approach. *Psychology in the Schools, 44*(4), 397–413.

Rimm-Kaufman, S. E., Curby, T. W., Grimm, K. J., Nathanson, L., & Brock, L. L. (2009). The contribution of children's self-regulation and classroom quality to children's adaptive behaviors in the kindergarten classroom. *Developmental Psychology, 45*, 958–972.

Rimm-Kaufman, S. E., & Hamre, B. K. (2010). The role of psychological and developmental science in efforts to improve teacher quality. *Teacher College Record, 112*(12), 2988–3023.

Ross, J. A., & Bruce, C. D. (2007). Teacher self-assessment: A mechanism for facilitating professional growth. *Teaching and Teacher Education, 23*(2), 146–159.

Ryan, R. M., & Deci, E. L. (2000). Self-determination theory and the facilitation of intrinsic motivation, social development, and well-being. *American Psychologist, 55*, 68–78.

Santagata, R., Zannoni, C., & Stigler, J. W. (2007). The role of lesson analysis in pre-service teacher education: An empirical investigation of teacher learning from a virtual video-based field experience. *Journal of Mathematics Teacher Education, 10*(2), 123–140.

Schank, R. (1982). *Dynamic memory: A theory of reminding and learning in computers and people.* New York: Cambridge University Press.

Schank, R. (1997). *Virtual learning.* New York: McGraw-Hill.

Schwartz, D. L., Martin, T., & Nasir, N. (2005). Designs for knowledge evolution: Towards a prescriptive theory for integrating first- and second-hand knowledge. In P. Gardenfors & P. Ohansson (Eds.), *Cognition, education, and communication technology* (pp. 21–54). Mahwah, NJ: Erlbaum.

Scott-Little, C., La Paro, K. M., Thomason, A. C., Pianta, R. C., Hamre, B., Downer, J., et al. (2011). Implementation of a course focused on language and literacy within teacher–child interactions:

Instructor and student perspectives across three institutions of higher education. *Journal of Early Childhood Teacher Education, 32*(3), 200–224.

Sheridan, S., Edwards, C., Marvin, C., & Knoche, L. (2009). Professional development in early childhood programs: Process issues and research needs. *Early Education and Development, 20*(3), 377–401.

Shulman, L. S. (1987). Knowledge and teaching: Foundations of the new reform. *Harvard Educational Review, 57*, 1–22.

Skibbe, L., Behnke, M., & Justice, L. M. (2004). Parental scaffolding of children's phonological awareness skills: Interactions between mothers and their preschoolers with language difficulties. *Communication Disorders Quarterly, 25*(4), 189–203.

Stipek, D., & Byler, P. (2004). The early childhood classroom observation measure. *Early Childhood Research Quarterly, 19*(3), 375–397.

Teacher Quality Partnership Study. (2006). Developing profile of Ohio future teachers. Retrieved from *www.teacherqualitypartnership.org/pdf/newsmedia/newsletters/spring06newsletter.pdf.*

Tingstrom, D., Sterling-Turner, H., & Wilczynski, S. (2006). The good behavior game: 1969–2002. *Behavior Modification, 30*(2), 225–253.

Tobin, R. M., & Graziano, W. G. (2006). Development of regulatory processes through adolescence. In D. K. Mroczek & T. D. Little (Eds.), *Handbook of personality development* (pp. 263–283). Mahwah, NJ: Erlbaum.

Tout, K., Starr, R., Soli, M., Moodie, S., Kirby, G., & Boller, K. (2010). *Compendium of quality rating systems and evaluations.* Washington, DC: U.S. Administration for Children and Families, Office of Planning, Research and Evaluation.

Vygotsky, L. S. (1991). Genesis of the higher mental functions. In P. Light, S. Sheldon, & M. Woodhead (Eds.), *Learning to think* (pp. 32–41). Florence, KY: Taylor & Frances/Routledge.

Watt, H. M. G., & Richardson, P. W. (2007). Motivational factors influencing teaching as a career choice: Development and validation of the FIT-Choice Scale. *Journal of Experimental Education, 75*(3), 167–202.

Webster-Stratton, C., Reid, M. J., & Stoolmiller, M. (2008). Preventing conduct problems and improving school readiness: Evaluation of the incredible years teacher and child training programs in high-risk schools. *Journal of Child Psychology and Psychiatry, 49*(5), 471–488.

Yoon, K. S., Duncan, T., Lee, S. W. Y., Scarloss, B., & Shapley, K. (2007). *Reviewing the evidence on how teacher professional development affects student achievement* (Issues and Answers Report, REL 2007-033). Washington, DC: U.S. Department of Education, Regional Educational Laboratory Southwest.

Zaslow, M., & Martinez-Beck, I. (2006). *Critical issues in childhood professional development.* Baltimore: Brookes.

Zaslow, M., Tout, K., Halle, T., Whittaker, J., & Lavelle, B. (2010). *Toward the identification of features of effective professional development for early childhood educators: Literature review.* Washington, DC: U.S. Department of Education, Office of Planning, Evaluation, and Social Development.

CHAPTER 25

Improving Language
and Literacy Outcomes in Child Care

Susan B. Neuman

"It all comes down to the teacher," parents often say when describing the quality of their child's school experience. Nothing can replace the power of a high-quality teacher during children's formative years (Barnett, 2004). Studies (e.g., Burchinal, Cryer, Clifford, & Howes, 2002) confirm that the quality of early education programs is strongly associated with the qualifications of the programs' teachers, and that quality programs are especially important if we are to improve children's readiness skills, especially for children in poverty, who are at increased risk for school failure.

Nevertheless, while our research base on teaching and learning for young children, particularly in language and literacy, has grown considerably in recent years, our knowledge about how to prepare quality teachers has grown far less. Although enhanced teacher education has been identified as a key strategy for improving children's learning in PreK, the link from evidence about teacher education to quality practices to children outcomes has required a fairly high level of inference (Strickland, Snow, Griffin, & Burns, 2002). One promising professional development practice to help teachers implement quality instruction is coaching, an ongoing, job-embedded approach with training on specific concepts and techniques (Sheridan, Edwards, Marvin, & Knoche, 2009). Despite its increasing adoption in the field, however, myriad questions remain on its utility for creating language-rich classrooms that have measurable, high-quality effects on children.

In this chapter, we first briefly review coaching as a model for professional development in early childhood. Then, we describe Project Great Start, a coaching model that has demonstrated powerful effects on early childhood educators' language and literacy instruction. In particular, we focus on the aspects of our model that promote teachers' implementation of best practices in early literacy. We then highlight key findings, as well as remaining questions, about the use of coaching as an effective professional development approach in early childhood.

Coaching as a Model for Professional Development

Recent research (Zaslow, 2009) suggests that professional development that provides authentic, situated learning experiences is more likely to succeed in influencing practice than traditional approaches, such as workshops or conferences. Change is most likely to occur within the context of practice (Ball & Cohen, 1999), where teachers can try out new practices and observe their effects on children, which can in turn motivate teachers to continue making changes. Even when these conditions are met, however, changing teachers' practices can be challenging, especially when prior experiences present obstacles for seeing content in new ways (Hodgen & Askew, 2007).

It is for these reasons that coaching has received a groundswell of interest as a professional development model for bolstering teachers' practices in classrooms (Neuman & Kamil, 2010). The primary features of the approach include (1) providing teachers with a clear rationale for the adoption of certain research-based practices; (2) modeling or demonstrating techniques in their own setting (classroom; center; home-based child care); (3) encouraging teachers to practice; and (4) providing corrective feedback and review. As a practice-based approach, coaching offers the opportunity to individualize the presentation of evidence-based practices, and provides for feedback to improve instruction. In optimal situations, it encourages educators to reflect on and to challenge their beliefs (Joyce & Showers, 2002), to analyze their teaching practices, and to experiment with new ideas in a safe environment. Moreover, coaching has the potential to address within-school teacher differences that in the past may have been masked in large group settings. For example, it is not uncommon for teachers within the same building to have widely different educational backgrounds, content specializations, previous workshops, and years of experience, all of which may influence their interests and motivations toward large-group professional development delivered at the school level.

However, a closer look at the coaching research literature suggests that coaching models may vary distinctly in their emphases, their methods of delivery, and their intensity. For example, Landry, Swank, Smith, Assel, and Gunnewig (2006) have provided teachers with instruction over the course of 1–2 years, as well as training and in-person coaching in their classrooms, through which they receive feedback on target practices. A full implementation of the professional development included the use of a mobile device for monitoring children's language and literacy progress. Results of the program indicated that teachers' and children's skills grew most substantially when the comprehensive program was used—training, coaching, as well as progress-monitoring information about children's skills. Children in this most comprehensive program demonstrated significant, medium-size gains in language and literacy (Landry, Anthony, Swank, & Monseque-Bailey, 2009).

Powell, Diamond, Burchinal, and Koehler (2010), on the other hand, as well as Pianta and his research team (Pianta, Mashburn, Downer, Hamre, & Justice, 2008), have shown exciting results for the use of a distance-based coaching approach. Powell and Diamond (2011) created a hypermedia approach for helping teachers better integrate language and literacy instructional practices. After biweekly coaching sessions that focus on code-based skills and vocabulary, teachers who received either Web-mediated or onsite coaching demonstrated stronger language and literacy environments than control group teachers. Furthermore, children in classrooms where teachers were coached performed better on alphabetic skills compared to controls. Pianta and his colleagues (2008) as well have shown strong support for a Web-mediated model of professional development (MyTeachingPartner), in which coaches provide teachers with extensive feedback through the Internet. In their study, those who received coaching made greater gain in instructional quality, as well as in sensitivity and organization, than colleagues who had access to the videos but did not receive coaching.

In short, these studies and others (Dickinson & Caswell, 2007; Wasik & Hindman, 2011) suggest that coaching may be an efficient and effective approach for enhancing teachers' knowledge and practices in early language and literacy. Still, because programs differ from one another, we have limited information on the active ingredients—intensity of delivery, modes, and so forth—that may account for their effectiveness. If we are to advance our understanding of what works in the complex array of early childhood settings, we must begin to understand what aspects of coaching may account for changes in practice and ultimately help to improve children's language and literacy instruction.

Although no standard model of coaching is used across these different educational settings, there is consensus in the literature on the basic characteristics of a coaching relationship in education; that is, "coaching" is typically a supportive, collaborative relationship between an expert (coach) and a practitioner that facilitates the practitioner's professional self-reflection and the development of knowledge and skills necessary to improve the quality of practice (Joyce & Showers, 2002). In some cases, coaching approaches help to implement particular curriculum supplements (Bierman et al., 2008; Wasik & Hindman, 2011) and use tools to monitor children's progress (Landry et al., 2006). In other cases, the coaching model's targeted focus is to help teachers translate research-based knowledge into global quality in early childhood (Zaslow, 2009). In still other approaches, coaching is designed to focus on and improve particular skills or sets of strategies in areas of literacy development. Studies by our team (Koh & Neuman, 2009; Neuman & Cunningham, 2009; Neuman & Wright, 2010), as well as others (Powell & Diamond, 2011; Wasik & Hindman, 2011), are representative of this tradition.

This is the approach we use in Project Great Start. Our onsite model is intensive, involving teachers in weekly 1½- to 2-hour onsite sessions for an extended period of time, rather than a temporary infusion of professional development activities to enhance evidence-based practices in language and literacy. In the following section, we first describe our coaching model, Project Great Start, which has been shown to improve language and literacy practices effectively in child care centers and home-based settings. We then examine what we have learned about our coaching model, and how it might differ from traditional professional development for early childhood educators.

Project Great Start Professional Development Initiative

Project Great Start is a professional development model that uses individualized coaching to train early childhood education teachers serving in high-poverty settings to apply literacy knowledge in practice. Funded through the Early Childhood Educator Professional Development Grant (U.S. Department of Education), the approach is based on a diagnostic/ prescriptive coaching model. The model builds on the substantial research, over 200 studies in teacher training, by Joyce and Showers (2002) and includes the following: Coaches engage teachers in reflection and goal setting; they help to identify desired outcomes and strategies to achieve these outcomes; collaboratively, coaches and teachers develop an action plan for the implementation of new practices the following week, which become the source of further reflection and action.

The content of our professional development program targets the skills and best practices that serve as the foundation for reading and writing ability, and not overall quality improvements. A growing consensus of research (National Early Literacy Panel, 2008; National Reading Panel Report, 2000; Snow, Burns, & Griffin, 1998), indicates that skills associated with early literacy include helping children develop a rich language and conceptual knowledge base, a broad and deep vocabulary, code-related skills, an understanding that spoken words are composed of smaller elements of speech (phonological awareness) and that letters represent these sounds (the alphabetic principle), and an understanding of the role that teachers and parents play in its development. Core competencies include oral language comprehension, phonological awareness, letter knowledge, print conventions, strategies for working with second language learners, assessment techniques, parental involvement, and developing literacy and a content-rich curriculum (see Figure 25.1 for core competencies of professional development).

In contrast to other coaching approaches that help to implement particular curriculum supplements (Bierman et al., 2008; Wasik & Hindman, 2011), our coaching model's focus is to help teachers translate research-based knowledge about literacy development and instruction for use in classrooms. It is onsite and intensive, and involves teachers in the infusion of professional development activities.

Project Great Start is designed to be a scalable model of professional development that can be implemented across various communities within a state or a large region. Therefore, to scale up required us to (1) operationalize with sufficient precision our definitions of

---

I. Oral language comprehension
- Recognizes that language skills play a prominent role in early literacy development.
- Recognizes the central contributions of vocabulary, syntax, and discourse skills to children's literacy development.

II. Phonological awareness
- Recognizes the role of phonological awareness in early literacy development.

III. Letter knowledge
- Recognizes the importance of letter knowledge in helping children discover the alphabetic principle.

IV. Print convention
- Recognizes the importance of print convention in helping children to predict, comprehend, retell stories, and recall important information.

V. Strategies for working with second language learners
- Recognizes that second language learners have unique language and literacy development needs.
- Identifies features of a supportive learning environment for second language learners.
- Understands the importance of engaging second language learners in storybook reading, literacy and play, developmental writing, and small-group instruction.

VI. Literacy assessments
- Recognizes the importance of observation, documentation, and other appropriate assessment tools and strategies in early language and literacy.
- Recognizes that language and literacy assessment for young children should occur in a natural setting.

VII. Parental role in language and literacy development
- Recognizes that parents are their child's first early language and literacy teacher.
- Identifies parent involvement activities.
- Recognizes the importance of children's home background.

VIII. Literacy and other aspects of the curriculum
- Understands importance of incorporating literacy activities throughout the curriculum.
- Identifies ways to incorporate literacy activities throughout curriculum.

FIGURE 25.1. Core competencies for language and literacy course.

quality literacy practices; (2) identify the time commitment and the necessary conditions for full implementation of our model; and (3) receive continuous feedback targeted to our outcomes (Carnine, 1997). As the model evolved through both piloting and experimentation, we addressed many of these issues by standardizing some of our procedures; however, our model continues to evolve as we learn from our providers.

Project Great Start is based on the approach that community colleges can serve as regional service centers, providing continuing education courses and professional development to teachers in a wide array of early childhood settings. Consequently, within key cities throughout Michigan, we work with community college early childhood coordinators to create our ongoing support system for coaches to be trained, scheduled to work with child care and home-based child care settings, and supervised throughout the year.

Coaching and Training

Our project has worked in six urban cities to provide professional development for over 800 early childhood educators. While our team at the University of Michigan is responsible for overall management of the project, community college coordinators play a central role in our program. They are responsible for recruiting from their local community, hiring, and supervising coaches. All coaches are required to have a bachelor's degree in early childhood education, experience working with adults, previous early childhood teaching in the priority urban area, and knowledge of early language and literacy research-based practices.

Before coaches go out in the field with teachers, they receive extensive training from our team. We gather coaches from all locations and hold a 2-day coaching institute at a central location to provide an overview of our diagnostic/prescriptive approach to coaching. We provide readings related to the core competencies, and research-based practices that are considered essential for children's success. We also focus on the social etiquette of coaching, reminding coaches that they are neither a friend nor a supervisor but a professional 'guest' in the setting. Coaches role-play specific scenarios, and brainstorm solutions to common problems. This training is conducted early in the fall to allow coaches to meet as a large team with the project coordinators and the lead research team to discuss the issues related to teachers, classrooms and children.

The gist of our diagnostic/prescriptive approach can be seen in Figure 25.2. The coach first engages in reflection with the practitioner; together they set goals on what are the most outstanding issues and areas of needed change. We use evidence from either Early Language and Literacy Classroom Observation (ELLCO) or the Child–Home Environmental Language Observation (CHELLO; described later) to inform the coach about what we see are the most needed issues. Along with this documented information and the goals the practitioner is interested in working on, they form a plan and the steps needed to achieve the desired outcomes. The coach works with the practitioner on instructional strategies, often modeling or coteaching techniques in classrooms. This is followed by the teacher practicing the technique and getting feedback from the coach. The cycle then continues to establish the next goals.

Project Great Start coaches begin to work with educators in the field after this orientation. But our training doesn't stop there. From then on, coaches meet with their coordinators at the community college for weekly debriefing sessions. These meetings are designed for discussion of issues that may not have been anticipated and to brainstorm new strategies for helping practitioners. For example, in some cases, coaches found that the structural characteristics in the classroom or home-based care setting prevented children from actively engaging in literacy-related play. Together, coaches and coordinator develop strategies to help overcome these challenges. Sometimes the weekly sessions turn into workshops to help coaches promote skills such as oral language and vocabulary development. These weekly

FIGURE 25.2. Project Great Start professional development coaching cycle.

sessions continue throughout the coaching intervention and provide a strategy for ongoing training for the coaches.

Because our coaching model is designed for large-scale implementation, we needed a strategy to ensure fidelity to our diagnostic/prescriptive model. Coaches diagnose what they consider to be the greatest impediments of change in each setting; at the same time, however, coaches address certain research-based practices in order to promote changes in children's progress. To measure fidelity, we first used a rather simple reflection form, asking coaches to document their daily progress with practitioners. On this form, they were asked to specify the language and literacy content area(s) being addressed, the goals set, and the strategies and action plans for completing next steps. These reflection sheets were reviewed each week at their debriefing meetings with coordinators at the community colleges.

Nevertheless, we found that these reflections did not provide fidelity of information to the research team at the University of Michigan. We too often felt we were in the dark regarding the actual implementation of coaching in the field. Furthermore, we found great variation among coaches. Some, for example, wrote only brief notes, whereas others detailed their activities more extensively. We recognized that a more systematic method was needed to record coach activity in the field. As the program evolved, we moved toward a more explicit definition of our focused outcomes, specific to language and literacy development; greater standardization in terms of the amount of time spent providing feedback to the educator; and a greater percentage of time devoted to planning, modeling, and demonstrating lessons rather than observation alone. For example, we found that coaches sometime did not leave enough time in their visit for discussion with their provider; consequently, we asked that coaches fill out action plans that we could examine prior to the next visit.

Based on the work of Rowan, Camburn, and Correnti (2004), we designed a coaching log (see Figure 25.3) to measure the active ingredients of each coaching session (Wright, 2010). Following each session with practitioners, the coach fills out a log on SurveyMonkey to indicate the date and duration of sessions, the coaching techniques used during the session, as well as the coach's key goal for the session. Aligned with research-based practices, coaches are asked to check "Focus of Session," indicating the activity that is their prime focus; "Touched on Briefly," suggesting more of a teachable moment; or "Not Discussed." Sections include general environment, assessment, book reading, writing, teacher–child interactions, and oral language and vocabulary development. Validated through observations in our previous research (Wright, 2010), the log takes only about 5 minutes to fill out and provides us with an instant record of the activities in each session across the entire project. The log essentially opens up the "black box" of intervention.

We also make unannounced visits to watch how coaches work with practitioners. Detailed observations from these visits in center-based and home-based settings give us a rich set of observations on the quality of the coaching sessions, and the interactions among the coach, caregiver, children, and the occasional parent volunteers that work in these settings.

Part I: Coaching Methods (coach only)

Which coaching techniques did you use during today's session? Check all that apply:

_____ Setting goals and objectives with teacher

_____ Engaging teacher in professional self-reflection

PART II: Teacher–Coach Session Summary

What areas did you work on or discuss today?

_____ **General Environment** – creating an appropriate setting for 3 to 5-year-old children

_____ **Activities and Assessment** – using assessment to create developmentally appropriate activities

What are your goals for next week's session?

_____

PART III: Teacher–Coach Session Elaboration

For each of the areas indicated on page 1, please specify what skills or concepts you worked on or discussed during today's session.

Today we worked on or discussed . . .

Focus of Session	Touched on Briefly	Not Discussed	
O	O	O	**GENERAL ENVIRONMENT**
O	O	O	Creating a space that is clean, safe, and in good repair
O	O	O	Creating a space that is intentionally organized to be appropriate for 3- to 5-year-old children (interest areas, place to play, place to rest, etc.)
O	O	O	Other:
O	O	O	**ACTIVITIES AND ASSESSMENT**
O	O	O	Planning activities to encourage children's interest and engagement in learning
O	O	O	Planning activities based on children's interests
O	O	O	Planning activities based on children's individual needs
O	O	O	Creating/using assessment (observation, portfolios, etc.) to monitor children's progress

FIGURE 25.3. Sample coaching log, on SurveyMonkey (see Wright, 2010).

In summary, the logs provide us with a means to examine the key features of our coaching model. Focused on enhancing evidence-based language and literacy practices, our model emphasizes a diagnostic/prescriptive approach to practice that includes coach–provider collaborative reflection and goal setting to establish key instructional strategies that may improve child outcomes.

Assessments of Teachers' Knowledge and Practice

Based on our theoretical model of teacher development, we assumed that content knowledge expertise in early language and literacy aligned with practice-sensitive professional development might represent the most powerful approach for transforming teachers' knowledge and instructional practices. To our knowledge, however, there were no measures of teachers' content knowledge in early language and literacy.

Consequently, we developed Teacher Knowledge Assessment of Early Language and Literacy Development, a multiple-choice, true–false assessment to allow us to better track teachers' growth in knowledge of early language and literacy (Neuman & Cunningham, 2009). From our perspective, it was imperative that high-quality early language and literacy instruction be embedded within sound child development principles. We constructed items on the eight core competencies in language and literacy described earlier and foundational knowledge in child development based on National Association for the Education of Young Children (NAEYC) standards. Items were designed to assess knowledge encountered in the work or practice of teaching language and literacy. Our effort was to place the focus on identifying the knowledge that teachers would *use* in practice. Grounding examples in activities that might occur in center- and home-based care settings, items were developed to tap the type of content knowledge most likely associated with successful early literacy practices (Phelps & Schilling, 2004). For example, this might entail the knowledge of how to help a child learn the letters of his or her name, or how to construct a play setting that could support language and literacy development. Several sample items are shown in Figure 25.4 that describes these efforts to embed knowledge in practice.

---

2. During group time, Ms. Betty is about to read a book to her 5-year-olds. As she reads, she runs her finger along underneath the text. Why does she do this?
   a. To help children connect sounds and letters.
   b. To keep children's attention.
   c. To help children understand how print works.*
   d. To improve children's letter knowledge.

26. Four-year-old Sarah has drawn a picture. As Sarah tells her about the picture, the teacher writes down her words, and then reads them back to her. This activity promotes literacy development by:
   a. Helping the child learn more about narratives and their structure.
   b. Reinforcing the child's understanding of the parts of a story.
   c. Increasing the child's awareness of the relationship between written and oral language.*
   d. Expanding the child's understanding that there are many ways to write letters.

1. Children's vocabulary in the early years is a strong predictor of their later reading achievement.   True*   False

5. It is more important to have small teacher–child ratios in the toddler years, when children are beginning to talk, than in early infancy, when children spend most of their time napping.   True*   False

---

FIGURE 25.4. Sample items (asterisks indicate correct answers).

This assessment was reviewed by several experts in the field of early literacy to ensure that the content was accurate and research-based, and subsequently validated with several early childhood groups. Each community college instructor reviewed the assessment for content validity and alignment with the course syllabus. On the basis of their comments, revisions were made. The Teacher Knowledge Assessment of Early Language and Literacy Development was then administered to 302 second-year early childhood education students. Results from this pilot were analyzed using item analysis to identify the best items for further analysis and inclusion in the assessment of teacher knowledge. Final forms of the assessment were administered to a sample of 146 child care providers. Results indicated excellent overall reliability (Cronbach's alpha = .96). These results indicated that the assessments worked well together to define a corpus of early language and literacy knowledge that could be assessed accurately by this instrument.

We used this measure to examine changes in teacher knowledge of our project.

Global Measures of Quality Practices

Because our goal was to improve the quality of language and literacy practices in an array of early childhood settings, we also needed tools to assess these changes accurately. ELLCO (Smith & Dickinson, 2002) serves as a useful measure of classroom quality, gauging the language and literacy opportunities in the classroom, such as children's access to books and writing experiences. However, this measure is not appropriate for the home-based care setting. In these settings, one does not find a traditional structural array of characteristics. Furthermore, home-base care often involves children of multiple ages, which calls upon the practitioner to adapt activities in ways that can enhance the development of infants and preschoolers. It is also difficult to compare gains in the quality of practices from classroom- and home-based settings.

Therefore, we developed CHELLO to assess quality practices in family care (Neuman, Dwyer, & Koh, 2007; Neuman, Koh, & Dwyer, 2008). Designed to gauge many of the same environmental characteristics as ELLCO, CHELLO examines language and literacy practices specific to the contextual features of family- and home-based child care settings. CHELLO is composed of two interdependent research tools: the Literacy Environment Checklist, and the Observation and Provider Interview. The former measures the presence or absence of 22 items in the environment, including the accessibility of books, writing materials, and displays of children's work. The latter focuses on the psychological supports in the educational environment, including teacher–child interactions in storybook reading, vocabulary development, and play. Similar to ELLCO, CHELLO uses a rubric ranging from a 1 (*deficient*) to 5 (*exemplary*).

We piloted CHELLO with a small sample of home-based providers to examine the validity of each section. Home-based providers, based on our observations, reviewed the instrument for accuracy, clarity, and inclusiveness, and provided detailed written comments. Additional reviews were solicited from directors of four local resource and referral agencies. This feedback was used to clarify and revise items. Following this review, the authors each piloted the revised instrument in three family day care settings in three cities to refine the instructions and descriptors. The final version of the Literacy Environment Checklist and the Group/Family Observation was designed to take approximately 1½ to 2 hours to complete. Psychometric properties show good internal consistency, with a Cronbach's alpha of .82 for the checklist and .91 for the observation (for a review of psychometric properties, see Neuman et al., 2008).

Designed to focus on the unique characteristics of each environment (e.g., center, home), the toolkits share complementary features. For the Literacy Environment Checklist in both toolkits, items are used to rate settings for the presence or absence of literacy related materials, using a yes–no response format (e.g., "Is an area set aside for books?"). For example, the Books subscale is the summed score of items that describe the area, book condition, and book use (ELLCO = 12; CHELLO = 10). Similarly the Writing subscale is the summed score of items that describe the use and accessibility of writing tools (ELLCO = 12; CHELLO = 6). The overall checklist is the sum of both subscales.

Both instruments require trained, certified observers (i.e., with an average of 8 hours of training) who are knowledgeable in early childhood education and early literacy development. Scores are derived after visits during planned activity/instructional time, with a brief follow-up interview with the teacher. Average observation times for both instruments lasts between 1½ to 2 hours. Although CHELLO is a more recent addition to a corpus of environmental tools (e.g., Early Childhood Environmental Rating Scale; Harms & Clifford, 2008), ELLCO has been used substantially in Early Reading First programs to provide information about the quality of environmental support for children's language and literacy development.

Although both ELLCO and CHELLO were designed as independent measures of the quality of language and literacy practices, they share a common set of 16 items. Five items evaluate the book area; four items, the writing area on the checklist, and seven items evaluate adult teaching strategies on the observation. By examining this subset of items (across all sections of the tool), we were able to compare and contrast language and literacy practice outcomes across these different educational settings, as well as to measure changes over time in these environments.

Having the tools to measure teacher knowledge and teacher practice, we then conducted studies to examine how our practice-sensitive approach to professional development might work on a large scale. Below we briefly detail our findings.

Program Findings

To date, Project Great Start has been subjected to two large-scale trials (Neuman & Cunningham, 2009; Neuman & Wright, 2010). In the first quasi-experimental study, 85 treatment teachers from four urban cities in Michigan received 64 hours of weekly coaching (32 weeks × 2 hours) plus a professional development course (3 credit hours) compared to a comparison group ($N = 89$) that received the professional development course or a group that received no professional development at all ($N = 100$). The weekly intervention was provided by coaches, trained by our research team, who had qualifications and experiences equivalent to master teachers (e.g., a bachelor's degree; more than 5 years experience in early childhood). Sessions were conducted in the morning, with a maximum caseload of five teachers per coach. During their visits, coaches engaged in reflection, planning, side-by-side modeling and teaching, and corrective feedback. Each of the 32 visits had two to three fidelity site visits conducted by the research team. Coaches met weekly with their supervisors to debrief and review teachers' progress to focus on how best to influence language and literacy practices.

Prior to and following the intervention, we examined teachers' knowledge of language and literacy using our specially developed and validated instrument (e.g., Teacher Knowledge Assessment of Early Language and Literacy Development) and measured the quality of teachers' language and literacy practices using ELLCO and CHELLO.

The results of our first quasi-experimental study with teachers (midcareer, with a high school or Child Development Associate [CDA] degree) showed significant and educationally meaningful improvements in practice for those who received our coaching intervention, with an average effect size of 0.75, compared to a control group. Professional development coaching seems to matter. Participants who received coursework and coaching demonstrated higher-quality practices, after we took into account pretest measures of quality, than their counterparts who received no treatment or course-based professional development only. These findings were consistent across the entire sample in two very different educational settings. Effect sizes further highlighted the educational benefits. By engaging in practice, and reflecting on that practice with a more experienced colleague, teachers appeared to incorporate new physical design features, supports for learning, and teaching strategies into their daily routines.

What most surprised us were the benefits for home care providers. Previous research on the effects of training to improve family child care quality has been sparse, and the methodology is fraught with problems such as correlational designs and self-reported outcome measures (Kontos, 1992). Although a small number of studies on family care training have shown that frequent coaching visits can be part of successful training, professional development programs have traditionally emphasized the classroom component over these more individualized, expensive, and time-consuming approaches. However, Kontos, Howes, and Galinsky (1996) have demonstrated that while training based on workshops and classrooms sessions increased family care providers' knowledge and awareness, they were not potent mechanisms for behavioral changes in practice.

Figure 25.5 illustrates the pre- and posttest quality scores for Group 2—those teachers who received our coaching intervention. Prior to the start of our project, language and literacy practices in home-based settings were substantially lower in quality than center-based practices, confirming previous reports on quality (Fuller, Kagan, Loeb, & Chang, 2004). Following the intervention, the gap closed between home-based and center-based care for teachers who received professional development coursework plus coaching. Strikingly, by the end of the treatment, coached providers in home-based care were essentially equal to those in center-based care in provision of quality language and literacy practices, suggesting that the addition of coaching appeared particularly to benefit home-based teachers in our sample (Koh & Neuman, 2009).

Especially of interest to us, it suggests that coaching as a means of professional development can be facilitative in multiple contexts. Classroom-based care and child care in family settings both gained in terms of quality practices. Given the sheer number of children who attend home-based care (nationally over 1.5 million receive care *exclusively* in home-based day care), these results are particularly heartening for improving language and literacy development, and for providing greater opportunities for children to engage in activities known to support early literacy learning.

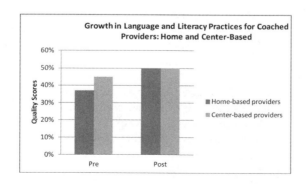

FIGURE 25.5. Pre- and posttest scores for teachers receiving the coaching intervention.

These promising results led to our second study, a randomized controlled trial to examine the active ingredients of coaching sessions. Here, we used a mixed-method design, randomly assigning teachers to one of three groups: coaching; traditional coursework at a community college; and a control "business as usual" group. We also conducted extensive observations and interviews to analyze how the treatment was enacted and its influence on ongoing practices. Participants from six urban communities with 146 center-based teachers (associate's degree or less) were included in the study.

The professional development intervention comprised a 30-hour program in early language and literacy development. Participants randomly assigned to Group 1 received a professional development course held at one of six locations closest in proximity to the child care site. Participants randomly selected for Group 2 received professional development through onsite individualized coaching. Participants in Group 3, the waiting-list comparison, received no professional development. Each intervention is described below.

Language and Literacy Course

Working collaboratively with faculty partners at a multisite community college, we adapted a three-credit course in early language and literacy to be consistent with the research and best practices model described earlier. The course was designed to provide students with the content knowledge and pedagogical skills considered by experts to be essential for quality early language and literacy practice.

Each site used a common course syllabus. All lectures and assignments were taken from the seventh edition of the text *Early Childhood Experiences in Language Arts* (Machado, 2003) and *Nurturing Knowledge* (Neuman, Roskos, Wright, & Lenhart, 2007). Specifically, the course focused on developing providers' knowledge in the following areas: oral language comprehension; phonological awareness; letter knowledge and the alphabetic principle; print convention; strategies for working with second language learners; literacy assessments; parental role in early language and literacy development; and linkages between literacy and other aspects of the curriculum.

Each class used a lecture format to present the week's topic, followed by simulation and hands-on activities designed to link theory to practice. Instructors used videotape examples frequently in class to augment instruction and to demonstrate examples of quality practices.

Assignments required participants to use course content in their instructional practice and to reflect on their effectiveness. For example, teachers were asked to record themselves engaging with one or two children in a storybook reading situation, and to reflect on children's responses to the story, their interests, and their uses of sophisticated vocabulary. Similarly, another assignment required teachers to encourage a child or children to write a story "their way" and to examine the products for evidence of developmental writing. These assignments were then used in class discussions to help instructors create linkages between their understanding of child development and early literacy development, and their current practices with children.

The courses were taught by experienced early childhood education faculty members, who also served as coordinators for each of the six community colleges. Instructors covered the topics in weekly 3-hour classes over a 10-week period. At each site, classes included participants in the study, as well as other students enrolled in the course (course instructors were not informed of which students were participating in the study). Class size varied between 18 and 25 students.

Given that the six sites were widely dispersed across the state, we used several indirect methods to determine fidelity of instructional implementation. First, attendance was taken at all sites to ensure that students participated in at least 8 of the 10 sessions. (Given that Teacher Education and Compensation Helps [T.E.A.C.H.] stipends were dependent on attendance and completion of the course, there was high attendance throughout sessions—overall attrition was less than 2%.) Second, weekly conference calls with instructors were conducted to ensure that the pacing of content and materials was maintained throughout the course. Third, unannounced observations by their supervisor, who served as a site manager for the project, were conducted in each class and reported high fidelity to the course syllabus. Fourth, instructors were required to send us products from the same four specified assignments (related to reading, writing, oral language, and play) in each class to indicate that students had participated and completed work in these areas. And fifth, evidence from student grades, reviewed by instructors and site manager, indicated that they had completed the course requirements according to the guidelines on the syllabus.

Coaching Intervention

Similar to our previous project, we employed a diagnostic/prescriptive model of coaching that focused on helping participants apply research-based strategies to improve child outcomes in language and literacy. Based on a review of best practices (International Reading Association, 2004; Joyce & Showers, 2002; Koh & Neuman, 2006), the model was designed to include the following elements: Coaching was onsite, involving teachers in ongoing practice rather than just a temporary infusion of activities. It was designed to facilitate reflection, not to dictate "a right answer." Furthermore, it emphasized coteaching through modeling and demonstration—highly interactive strategies—rather than observation and postfeedback. Coaches were encouraged to establish rapport, build trust, and provide useful suggestions rather than evaluate or judge teachers' performance. And in each case, coaches were encouraged to help teachers prioritize, to focus on those activities that might best benefit children's outcomes (Herll & O'Drobinak, 2004).

To ensure an equal dosage of treatment, sessions were weekly, one-on-one, and onsite for approximately for 3 hours. Coaches were provided with the course syllabus and readings, and encouraged to emphasize similar content and skills in a manner appropriate to the needs of their participants. For example, if their observations clearly indicated that changes in the physical environment were needed due to safety concerns or noise level, then this area might take priority over creating a daily schedule. Therefore, although content plans were highly consistent across settings, coaches were encouraged to make adjustments to meet teachers' needs. Coaching session occurred weekly over a 10-week period.

A number of common procedures were used to ensure fidelity of coaching across sites. Coaches were required to meet weekly in debriefing sessions with the instructional coordinator at each site. These meetings were designed so that coaches could discuss the challenges and successes of their weekly efforts and determine goals, strategies, and action plans for completing next steps. These debriefing sessions gave coaches opportunities to review their notes with others and to share experiences and resources. They also served as an accountability mechanism for us, providing information on any missed or rescheduled sessions, as well as the number of hours coaches worked.

Coaches, therefore, followed similar procedures as in our first study; however, the number of sessions was reduced substantially to be equivalent to the number of contact hours of the comparison group (e.g., those who received traditional coursework in a 10-week semester). Consequently, coaching sessions were longer but fewer in number, with both groups receiving 30 hours (10 weeks × 3 hours) of training compared to none for the control group.

The findings from our first study were replicated; that is, there were significant gains for coaching (Cohen's $d = 0.57$) though smaller than those in our previous study immediately following the intervention. Furthermore, these gains were sustained 6 months later (Cohen's $d = 0.42$). Most revealing, however, was the analysis of the active ingredients of coaching sessions. In the example below, we found that, for some teachers, some aspects of the content of professional development clearly took longer to instantiate than others. In Figure 25.6, for example, we found that this particular coach was able to address a teacher's weaknesses in the literacy environment, supporting quality shared-reading strategies, early on in her work with relative efficiency; however, it took far longer than expected, so that even at the end of their professional development, she still needed continued coaching in this area.

This figure highlights differences in teacher skill sets and their abilities to make changes in their classrooms. It also led us to yet another issue about coaching: It argues strongly against a "one-size-fits-all" model of professional development. Moreover, coaching has the potential to address within-school teacher differences (Powell et al., 2010) that in the past may have been masked in large-group settings. For example, it is not uncommon for teachers' within the same building to have widely different educational backgrounds, content specializations, previous workshops, and years of experience, all of which may influence their interests and motivations toward professional development. Nevertheless, a closer look at the coaching research literature (Neuman & Kamil, 2010; Zaslow & Martinez-Beck, 2006) suggests that we may not have taken full advantage of the potential that this model provides for individualizing professional development.

Coaching from a Participant's Point of View

Interviews with participants of both traditional professional development and coaching have helped us to understand better the additional benefits of this practice-based approach. As the reader might recall, some of our teachers engaged in traditional professional development through an interactive course at the community college, while others had coaching. The content on instructional best practices in early language and literacy, therefore, was basically the same; rather, it was the delivery system that significantly differed. As a research

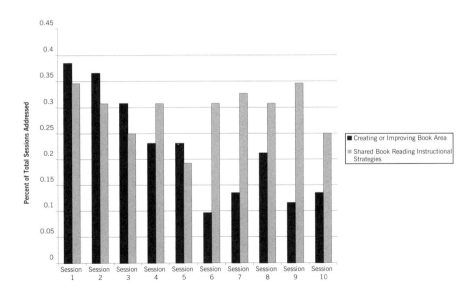

FIGURE 25.6. Differential focus of coaching strategies over sessions: Reading.

team, we asked: Why did the teachers who received traditional coursework not improve either in knowledge or in quality classrooms? In other words, in what ways did the delivery system of coaching influence their ability to make significant changes in their classroom practices?

In these interviews, it was clear that all participants enjoyed their professional development, whether it was through traditional coursework or coaching. Nevertheless, many participants had difficulties with traditional coursework. Teachers struggled with the literacy demands of the course, the translation from theory to practice, and the translation from what they were learning in their class to their individual instructional context.

Literacy Demands

Many teachers in early education are midcareer (Zaslow & Martinez-Beck, 2006). They may be new to college instruction or formal education. Some found the pacing of a course, the reading requirements, and the information itself very demanding. One participant stated, "In that book we went through the names of people that did certain things in child care. And that just didn't sink in my head. I couldn't comprehend it. I can't even remember what they did and their names and stuff."

Some teachers found that the textbook reading was difficult and had trouble keeping up with the assignments (Neuman & Wright, 2010). In some cases, the reading expectations were very high. One teacher commented: "It was a big-sized book [textbook] but it was too short of time we had to do it." Furthermore, teachers often did not see the relevance of the readings to their practice. For example, one participant indicated that "there was a ton of reading that I felt, you know, wasn't necessary. I found that projects were more beneficial than reading."

Too Theoretical

Sometimes it was not just the literacy demands of the textbook that the teachers question about traditional coursework (Doescher & Beudert, 2011). It was also *what* they were reading and learning about that they questioned. Traditional coursework sometimes appeared to focus more on the "why we do certain literacy practices," rather than the "what and how to do them." For example, one teacher commented that she learned why it was a good idea to put a word and a picture label together, and why children should be allowed to handle books, but when asked what she would like to learn more about, she turned to examples of the concrete materials they made in the classroom. One teacher reported, "The instructor gave us time to ask questions and she'd tell us the why of everything. And I'd say, oh, well, yeah, that explains why I need to do this." But when asked what was most helpful about the course, that same teacher replied, "I would say how we took stories and we made flannel boards and different props to go along with it. What really stood out for me was learning about felt stories and making props for stories."

Teachers seemed to enjoy the sharing of ideas in a traditional course. They liked the social interaction. At the same time, they reported that it was the making of concrete materials—flannel board stories, puppets, homemade books—that seemed to be most relevant and most closely tied to their practice. While instructors encouraged teachers to use these materials in their classroom instruction and to report back on their use, neither the activity enactment nor its quality of implementation were monitored, other than through class assignments and discussion.

Consequently, the course presented several challenges to these nontraditional students (Zaslow, 2009). The literacy demands were high, and concepts were relatively abstract, requiring a strong translation to classroom practice. Although teachers believed they learned about many new activities, these were not consistently translated into literacy practices that they felt they could use.

Coaching Practices

On the other hand, teachers who received coaching also praised their professional development training. All had high marks for their coach, but unlike participants in the coursework group, it was the practicality of the training to which they appeared to refer in their comments. Especially effective, the intervention was onsite, context-specific, and held teachers accountable for making changes in their classrooms.

Individualized and Context-Specific

Teachers appeared to appreciate the individualized attention and the special focus on making improvements in their environment (Koh & Neuman, 2009). Many contrasted their experience with previous professional development. As one teacher put it: "You know, you go to a conference and you're bombarded with so many things it's hard to remember ... it's hard to take it all in. And you go through your notes and say, 'Oh my gosh, I don't remember what that was about.'" In contrast, coaches helped teachers try out strategies immediately in their own environment and get instant feedback for their efforts. One teacher said: "You get the one-on-one, hands-on attention. You know you go to a seminar or something and you go and learn and you come back. But you may not be doing it the way that it would be best. You know, you may think that you learned it right when you were there. And then you come home and you think, 'Oh I forgot how to do this.' Where she [the coach] is here to work with you on things."

New Resources

Many times, without specific directions, coaches would bring and demonstrate new resources to teachers. For example, coaches would show the teachers websites that provided useful lesson plans and materials. The coaches also made journals for the children, so that teachers could better implement writing in their daily curriculum, and they brought catalogues to support literacy-related play. In some contexts, coaches literally flooded their sites with new materials and resources. One teacher commented: "She would always bring some sort of resource, whether it was a book or an article, things like that. She would go over it, bit by bit, answer any questions that I had. And she would give me some advice or recommendations."

In this respect, it was the practice-based nature of coaching—directly tied to the context in which these teachers worked with children—that appeared to be its most distinctive feature (Koh & Neuman, 2009). Coaches talked about ideas and the *why's* of literacy not in a vacuum but in the context of practice.

Informal Accountability

Even though coaches had no supervisory role, there was inherent accountability in the coaching cycle (Zaslow & Martinez-Beck, 2006). With coaches visiting weekly, teachers often wanted to be responsive and make the changes they had discussed the previous week. As one teacher articulated, "If you have a one-to-one relationship with someone, you don't want to disappoint them. So whether or not you like it, you do the work." In addition, the weekly goal setting appeared to help teachers focus on particular practices. By establishing priorities, the changes made each week could be more attainable. One teacher put it this way:

> "I think it's worthwhile to have somebody come in. You can go and learn something. That doesn't mean that you're going to come back and implement it. Where if there's somebody coaching you on, and you're making the goal that next week, OK, we're going to *A* and she comes back and *A* is not done, you're going to feel pretty crummy that we talked ... yes I told you that I would do *A* and I didn't do *A*, you know. Where if I took the classes and I said to myself, yeah, I'm going to do this next week, well, I'll wait until the following week and then it'll be put off for a month or whatever."

These and other comments reveal that coaching appears to support individualized, context-specific practices, along with an informal accountability cycle that provides real-time feedback to teachers. As a model of professional development, it is practice-based, focusing on the more immediate translation of ideas to classroom practice. It is less about evaluation and more about the improvement of quality practices.

In summary, our coaching model has shown through two large-scale trials are highly effective in enhancing and sustaining quality practices in center-based care and family-based care settings. These are the components of our model that seem to matter:

- Onsite: Successful coaches meet teachers "where they are"—in their own practice settings to help providers learn through modeling and demonstrating practices (Poglinco & Bach, 2004).
- Balanced and sustained: Coaches involve teachers in ongoing continuing education rather than just a temporary infusion or a rapid-fire string of professional development activities (Darling-Hammond, 1997; Guiney, 2001; Speck, 2002).
- Facilitative of reflection: Effective coaches observe, listen, and support instructional practices that improve child outcomes; they don't dictate "the right answer" (Harwell-Kee, 1999).
- Highly interactive: Coaches establish rapport, build trust, and engender mutual respect among practitioners and interact extensively to benefit children's outcomes (Herll & O'Drobinak, 2004).
- Corrective feedback: Coaches provide descriptive, not evaluative or judgmental, feedback based on observable events in settings that enable practitioners to engage in collaborative problem-solving to improve practice (Gallacher, 1997; Schreiber, 1990).
- Prioritizes: Coaches assist teachers in identifying priorities and developing action plans to improve children's language and literacy practices (Neuman & Cunningham, 2009).

Lessons Learned about Professional Development for Early Childhood Educators

In the past few years, we have made significant progress in identifying some of the mechanisms that can improve teacher quality. We now know that teachers who receive significant dosages of training can improve their classroom instructional practices (Neuman & Kamil, 2010). We also know that coaching is a viable strategy for providing job-embedded professional development that can improve child outcomes in language and literacy development (Landry et al., 2009; Powell & Diamond, 2011), and more global quality practices in early childhood (Pianta et al., 2008).

Still, further research is needed to evaluate the relative contributions of professional development in early childhood. Specifically, we need more empirical evidence to determine what works, for whom, within which contexts, and at what cost. If we are to establish a scientific base for early childhood professional development, vital questions must be addressed to enhance evidence-based exemplars for best practice. Research is needed to determine more specifically the characteristics of effective coaches. Furthermore, we need to know which activities or strategies effective coaches use appear to result in the positive changes. In addition, dosage remains an issue. Given that coaching tends to be an individual, one-on-one approach to professional development and therefore is likely to be more costly than other techniques, we need to understand better how much time and effort may be necessary to reach the goal of improving practice. Therefore, we need studies that examine the impact of professional development over time. Such studies could provide vital information on the "real costs" of professional development. Studying the cost–benefit ratio of professional development, particularly in the field of early childhood, where turnover has been high, is essential to determine its overall capacity to improve the quality of early childhood programs.

In addition, research is needed to determine the most efficient and effective means for promoting changes in teachers' knowledge skills and dispositions. We need to better understand how to alter hard-to-change practices. We also need to understand institutional supports and how they help or thwart innovative practices. Exploring these and other factors in future research can help elucidate the potential effects of professional development efforts with greater precision to better ensure evidence-based practice.

References

Ball, D., & Cohen, D. (1999). Developing practice, developing practitioners: Toward a practice-based theory of professional development (pp. 3–32). In G. Sykes & L. Darling-Hammond (Eds.), *Teaching as the learning profession: Handbook of policy and practice*. San Francisco: Jossey-Bass.

Barnett, W. S. (2004). *Better teachers, better preschools: Student achievement linked to teacher qualifications*. New Brunswick, NJ: National Institute for Early Education Research.

Bierman, K., Domitrovich, C., Nix, R., Gest, S., Welsh, J., Greenberg, M., et al. (2008). Promoting academic and social–emotional school readiness: The Head Start REDI program. *Child Development, 79*, 1802–1817.

Burchinal, M. R., Cryer, D., Clifford, R. M., & Howes, C. (2002). Caregiver training and classroom quality in child care centers. *Applied Developmental Science, 6*(1), 2–11.

Carnine, D. (1997). Bridging the research-to-practice gap. *Exceptional Children, 63*, 513–521.

Darling-Hammond, L. (1997). *Doing what matters most: Investing in quality teaching*. New York: National Commission on Teaching and America's Future.

Dickinson, D., & Caswell, L. (2007). Building support for language and early literacy in preschool classrooms through in-service professional development: Effects of the Literacy Environment Enrichment Program (LEEP). *Early Childhood Research Quarterly, 22*, 243–260.

Doescher, S., & Beudert, J. (2011). Professional development in the community college setting. In S. B. Neuman & M. Kamil (Eds.), *Professional development for early childhood educators: Principles and strategies for improving practice* (pp. 165–180). Baltimore: Brookes.

Fuller, B., Kagan, S., Loeb, S., & Chang, V. (2004). Centers and home settings that serve poor families. *Early Childhood Research Quarterly, 19*, 505–527.

Gallacher, K. (1997). Supervision, mentoring and coaching. In P. J. Winton, J. A. McCollum, & C. Catlett (Eds.), *Reforming personnel in early intervention* (pp. 191–214). Baltimore: Brookes.

Guiney, E. (2001). Coaching isn't just for athletes: The role of teacher leaders. *Phi Delta Kappan, 82*, 740–743.

Harms, T., & Clifford, R. (2008). *Early Childhood Environmental Rating Scale-R.* New York: Teachers College Press.

Harwell-Kee, K. (1999). Coaching. *Journal of Staff Development, 20*(3), 28–29.

Herll, S., & O'Drobinak, B. (2004). Role of a coach: Dream keeper, supporter, friend. *Journal of Staff Development, 25*(2), 42–46.

Hodgen, J., & Askew, M. (2007). Emotion, identity, and teacher learning: Becoming a primary mathematics teacher. *Oxford Review of Education, 33*, 469–487.

International Reading Association. (2004). *The role and qualifications of the reading coach in the United States: A position statement of the International Reading Association.* Newark, DE: Author.

Joyce, B., & Showers, B. (2002). *Student achievement through staff development* (3rd ed.). Alexandra, VA: Association for Supervision and Curriculum Development.

Koh, S., & Neuman, S. B. (2006). *Research-based evidence on coaching.* Unpublished manuscript, University of Michigan.

Koh, S., & Neuman, S. B. (2009). The impact of professional development on family child care: A practice-based approach. *Early Education and Development, 20*(3), 537–562.

Kontos, S. (1992). *Family day care: Out of the shadows and into the limelight.* Washington, DC: National Association for the Education of Young Children.

Kontos, S., Howes, C., & Galinsky, E. (1996). Does training make a difference to quality in family child care? *Early Childhood Research Quarterly, 11*, 427–445.

Landry, S., Anthony, J., Swank, P., & Monseque-Bailey, P. (2009). Effectiveness of comprehensive professional development for teachers of at-risk preschoolers. *Journal of Educational Psychology, 101*, 448–465.

Landry, S., Swank, P., Smith, K., Assel, M., & Gunnewig, S. (2006). Enhancing early literacy skills for preschool children: Bringing a professional development model to scale. *Journal of Learning Disabilities, 39*, 306–324.

Machado, J. (2003). *Early childhood experiences in the language arts* (7th ed.). New York: Delmar.

National Early Literacy Panel. (2008). *Developing early literacy.* Washington, DC: National Institute for Literacy.

National Reading Panel Report. (2000). *Teaching children to read.* Washington, DC: National Institute of Child Health and Development.

Neuman, S. B., & Cunningham, L. (2009). The impact of professional development and coaching on early language and literacy practices. *American Educational Research Journal, 46*, 532–566.

Neuman, S. B., Dwyer, J., & Koh, S. (2007). *Child/Home Environmental Language and Literacy Observation.* Baltimore: Brookes.

Neuman, S. B., & Kamil, M. (2010). *Preparing teachers for the early childhood classroom: Proven models and key principles.* Baltimore: Brookes.

Neuman, S. B., Koh, S., & Dwyer, J. (2008). CHELLO: The Child/Home Environmental Language and Literacy Observation. *Early Childhood Research Quarterly, 23*, 159–172.

Neuman, S. B., Roskos, K., Wright, T., & Lenhart, L. (2007). *Nurturing knowledge: Linking literacy to math, science, social studies and much more.* New York: Scholastic.

Neuman, S. B., & Wright, T. (2010). Promoting language and literacy development for early childhood educators: A mixed-methods study of coursework and coaching. *Elementary School Journal, 111*, 63–86.

Phelps, G., & Schilling, S. (2004). Developing measures of content knowledge for teaching reading. *Elementary School Journal, 105*, 31–48.

Pianta, R., Mashburn, A., Downer, J., Hamre, B., & Justice, L. (2008). Effects of web-mediated professional development resources on teacher–child interactions in pre-kindergarten classrooms. *Early Childhood Research Quarterly, 23*, 431–451.

Poglinco, S., & Bach, S. (2004). The heart of the matter: Coaching as a vehicle for professional development. *Phi Delta Kappan, 85*(5), 398–402.

Powell, D., & Diamond, K. (2011). Improving the outcomes of coaching-based professional development interventions. In S. B. Neuman & D. K. Dickinson (Eds.), *Handbook of early literacy research* (Vol. 3, pp. 295–307). New York: Guilford Press.

Powell, D., Diamond, K., Burchinal, M., & Koehler, M. (2010). Effects of an early literacy professional development intervention on Head Start teachers and children. *Journal of Educational Psychology, 102*, 299–312.

Rowan, B., Camburn, E., & Correnti, R. (2004). Using teacher logs to measure the enacted curriculum in large-scale surveys: A study of literacy teaching in 3rd grade classrooms. *Elementary School Journal, 105*, 75–102.

Schreiber, B. (1990). Colleague to colleague: Peer coaching for effective in-house training. *Education Libraries, 15*(1–2), 30–35.

Sheridan, S., Edwards, C., Marvin, C., & Knoche, L. (2009). Professional development in early childhood programs: Process issues and research needs. *Early Education and Development, 20*(3), 377–401.

Smith, M., & Dickinson, D. (2002). *Early Language and Literacy Classroom Observation*. Baltimore: Brookes.

Snow, C., Burns, M. S., & Griffin, P. (1998). *Preventing reading difficulties in young children*. Washington, DC: National Academy Press.

Speck, M. (2002). Balanced and year-round professional development: Time and learning. *Catalyst for Change, 32*, 17–19.

Strickland, D., Snow, C., Griffin, P., & Burns, M. S. (2002). *Preparing our teachers: Opportunities for better reading instruction*. Washington, DC: John Henry Press.

Wasik, B., & Hindman, A. (2011). Identifying critical components of an effective preschool language and literacy coaching intervention. In S. B. Neuman & D. K. Dickinson (Eds.), *Handbook of early literacy research* (Vol. 3, pp. 322–336). New York: Guilford Press.

Wright, T. (2010). Online Logs: A tool to monitor fidelity of implementation in large-scale interventions. In S. B. Neuman & M. Kamil (Eds.), *Professional development for early childhood educators: Principles and strategies for improving practice* (pp. 207–220). Baltimore: Brookes.

Zaslow, M. (2009). Strengthening the conceptualization of early childhood professional development initiatives and evaluations. *Early Education and Development, 20*(3), 527–536.

Zaslow, M., & Martinez-Beck, I. (Eds.). (2006). *Critical issues in early childhood professional development*. Baltimore: Brookes.

CHAPTER 26

Higher Education for Early Childhood Educators and Outcomes for Young Children

Pathways toward Greater Effectiveness

Marilou Hyson, Diane M. Horm, and Pamela J. Winton

Although it is only one of many avenues for the delivery of early childhood professional development, higher education's role is significant and growing. State prekindergarten (PreK) programs, the U.S. federal government, and accreditation systems have raised the bar for early childhood teachers' formal education. Based on national average graduation rates, college and university programs are producing great numbers of degreed early childhood educators—at least 40,000 per year. In turn, a growing pool of degreed teachers has the potential to improve outcomes for great numbers of children.

Numbers, however, do not equal effectiveness. The potential of higher education to be a consistently *effective* component of a professional development delivery system, capable of improving teachers' practices and child outcomes, is far from being realized. By calling into question the relations between teachers' degrees and both classroom quality and children's outcomes, the Early and colleagues (2007) synthesis paper has had the unintended benefit of shifting the higher education focus. Rather than simply debating the merits of degrees versus no degrees, many in the early childhood field are now calling for a closer analysis of the key features and relative quality of higher education programs. In this chapter we aim to contribute to that analysis.

The model outlined in Figure 26.1 illustrates the approach we take in the chapter. Presumably, teachers' higher education should result in better developmental and learning outcomes for the children whom graduates teach and the families with whom they work. However, as the model suggests, the relationships are complex.

Many factors, including the resources and supports afforded by teachers' current work environments, make it easier or more difficult for graduates to implement what they have learned in their college years; that is, teachers' practices, and the outcomes of those

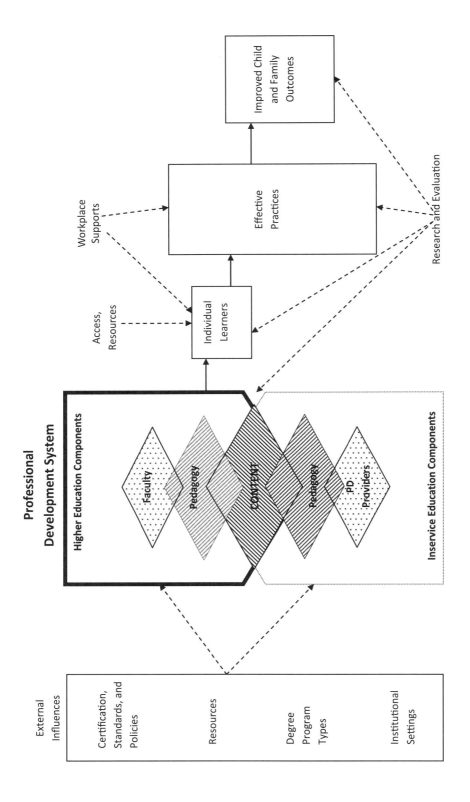

FIGURE 26.1. Professional development system, practices, and outcomes: Contexts and pathways. (The higher education component of the early childhood professional development system is the focus of this chapter.)

practices, are not simply a direct product of teachers' experiences within higher education. Additionally, practices are implemented by individuals who differ from one another in many ways: by culture and ethnicity, experience and skills, beliefs and dispositions, readiness for change, and other factors. These individuals also differ in their access to financial and other resources that facilitate or hamper their entrée into and experience within the higher education system.

The potential of the higher education system to affect learners positively is equally complex. Within the "proximal" higher education system—that which most directly affects learners' practices—are the interconnected elements of *faculty, content,* and *pedagogy*—in a sense, the "who," the "what," and the "how" (National Professional Development Center on Inclusion, 2008) of the delivery of higher education. Each of these elements varies in quality and defining features, and each, separately and together, may influence how higher education shapes college graduates' practices in early childhood education settings.

From a more distal perspective, the preparation of early childhood educators within higher education programs is also influenced by each program's institutional setting, specific program/degree type, and available resources. Preparation programs also operate within an array of regulations and professional expectations, ranging from state teacher licensure requirements to national standards used in accreditation, to degree requirements enacted by state and federal bodies.

As Figure 26.1 illustrates, it is also important to note that higher education does not— or rather, should not—operate in isolation. Higher education is part of a larger system of early childhood professional development (Hyson & Whittaker, 2012), which includes community-based training or "inservice" education. And, in turn, early childhood professional development is only one part of a complex and evolving early childhood system (Kagan & Kauerz, 2012).

An ecological perspective is necessary to represent this complexity. Accordingly, we begin by providing a description of the multiple settings and contexts for early childhood higher education today. With that context in place, we take a closer look at what is inside the higher education "black box"—the content and delivery of early childhood higher education, and the role of professional preparation standards and accreditation. Next, we focus on faculty, beginning with a description of the higher education workforce. Drawing on several recent surveys, we describe what is known about the knowledge base, beliefs, and attitudes of early childhood faculty. This section concludes with a discussion of professional development for higher education faculty.

The critical issue of higher education's impact on educators' practices and child outcomes is the focus of the next section of this chapter. We briefly review what is known about the general association between degrees, program quality, and child outcomes, but we spend more time analyzing what is known and not yet known about the impact of specific features of higher education on the outcomes of interest.

Next we note a few examples of recent reforms and innovations in early childhood higher education that may have potential to produce more effective practices in the future. Examples include systems-level innovations, national resources to build faculty capacity, and innovations in individual higher education programs.

In the final section of the chapter we summarize current gaps in the research base and policies needed to improve early childhood educators' preparation. This discussion leads to specific recommendations for addressing these issues.

Throughout this chapter certain themes recur. Perhaps the major theme is the sheer lack of research evidence on most of the critical issues in early childhood higher education. This was the case more than a decade ago (Horm-Wingerd, Hyson, & Karp, 2000) and it continues today, with recent surveys of higher education programs providing some new information but carrying all the limitations of self-report data. A second recurring theme is the continuing mismatch between "business as usual" in higher education and the evolving, diverse characteristics of faculty, students, children and families, and the programs that serve those children and families. Yet another theme is early childhood teacher education's frequent isolation from both the larger system of early childhood professional development and the general field of teacher education, including early childhood's ambivalent relationship with the often-overlapping domain of elementary teacher education.

Settings and Contexts for Higher Education Today

In the past, preparation to work with preprimary-age children was based in a range of academic units, including home economics, child development, child psychology, education, and allied fields such as nursing. Similar diversity continues today. However, the higher education landscape has changed in other, important ways. Today's context includes an increased demand for personnel with specialized early childhood knowledge; more potential work roles and settings for graduates; more states with stand-alone teaching licenses for early childhood educators; and an increased number of licenses/certificates and other credentials that further complicate the demands for transfer and articulation between 2- and 4-year institutions of higher education (IHEs). In fact, the contexts for early childhood teacher preparation appear more complex than those for elementary- or secondary-level preparation (Whitebook, Gomby, Sakai, & Kipnis, 2009), challenging the field's attempts both to describe and improve current practices.

The early childhood field continues to strive for recognition as a profession. This effort provides a context for, and raises questions about, the current and future role of higher education in that profession. For instance, do the policies, career pathways, and professional development systems—including the teacher education system—that have evolved for the K–12 teacher workforce provide the right model for early childhood? In light of the movement to create a seamless educational system from PreK through third grade, and the beginning policy discussions of a preschool to college (P–16) approach (Education Commission of the States, 2010), the obvious answer would be "yes." Yet the loosely configured early childhood system, with multiple sectors having distinct histories, funding, policies, and standards, creates a different context than that within which traditional K–12 public school teachers have been educated. In this more complex early childhood context, even something as seemingly simple as defining who is an early childhood "practitioner" becomes fraught with differing definitions and opinions. Models from fields other than education may need to be taken into consideration. To that end, a recently convened Committee of the National Academies/Institute of Medicine on the Early Childhood Care and Education (ECCE) Workforce is examining issues of how to define and support the ECCE workforce as a profession, drawing from a model developed for evaluating emerging health professions (Dower, O'Neil, & Hough, 2001). These and other contextual issues have clear implications for discussions about the role of higher education for the early childhood field, and we return to them in later sections of this chapter.

Number of Programs and Students

Based on data collected in 2004, Maxwell, Lim, and Early (2006) estimate that approximately 1,350 IHEs offer some type of early childhood education degree program. Maxwell and colleagues report that approximately 44% of these IHEs offer baccalaureate (BA)[1] and/ or graduate degrees, and 56% offer associate degrees.

Associate Degree Programs

Maxwell and colleagues (2006) found that most of the 750 associate degree programs were housed in community colleges, located in an academic department called "Early Childhood" or "Child Development," and offered a range of degrees, including Associate of Arts in Sciences (AAS), Associate of Arts (AA), or the newer Associate of Arts in Teaching (AAT). Usually, the AA degree is designed for students planning to transfer to a 4-year institution; thus, the focus is on general education. The AAS and AAT degrees are often referred to as "workforce" degrees that prepare students to enter child care, Head Start, or other work settings immediately after attaining the associate's degree. Given this goal, the primary focus of these degrees' courses and fieldwork is on building specialized knowledge in child development and early childhood education theory and practice, not on general education.

In meeting the needs of the workforce, community colleges are increasingly involved with the Child Development Associate (CDA) credential, a national credential created in 1971 by the Council for Professional Recognition to improve the quality of child care and Head Start, and to recognize staff competencies acquired through work experience (Council for Professional Recognition, 2006; Winton & West, 2011). Although the CDA was initially developed outside of higher education, one current path to achieve the credential is though the CDA Professional Preparation Program. This program, designed for early childhood practitioners without degrees, combines college courses with fieldwork and mentoring. The credential is awarded to candidates who demonstrate competency in six areas relevant to all early childhood settings serving children from birth to age 5 (Winton & West, 2011). Hyson, Tomlinson, and Morris (2009) found that 80% of associate degree programs reported offering the CDA or other nondegree certificate. Potentially strengthening the link to higher education, many community colleges also make it possible for CDA candidates to translate their CDA into academic credit, although the number of credits is usually quite limited.

BA Programs: Influence of Teacher Licensure and Institutional Home

Based on the Maxwell and colleagues (2006) data, approximately 600 BA-level early childhood education programs exist within IHEs. These programs are diverse in their content, orientation, and goals for graduates in part because of differences in state teacher licensure[2] requirements (Hyson et al., 2009) and in institutional characteristics. States vary greatly in the scope of early childhood licensure, encompassing birth to age 5, birth to age 8, PreK to grade 3, PreK to grade 4, and numerous other configurations—with equally great variations in expected competencies and coursework. The New America Foundation's recent report (Bornfreund, 2011) on early childhood licensing and preparation describes variations across states as well as many instances of licensure overlap within a single state. In Wyoming, for example, there are four different teacher licensure options (birth to age 5; ages 3–5; age 3 to third grade; and K–6). Depending on the license a student seeks, exposure to specific early childhood content may vary considerably (Bornfreund, 2011).

Especially at the BA level, programs that prepare early childhood educators are frequently housed in one of two institutional homes—in a unit allied with the study of human development, or in a department, school, or college of education. Traditionally, these two affiliations have produced programs with different orientations, with the human development programs emphasizing child development and ecological contexts, and the education programs emphasizing pedagogy and academic content. Although the early childhood field now sees all these bodies of knowledge as essential in professional preparation (National Association for the Education of Young Children [NAEYC], 2009), interprogram divides remain. For example, in survey and interview responses from early childhood education program faculty members at 40 major public research universities, Johnson, Fiene, McKinnon, and Babu (2010) found that half of the respondents said that their institution's early childhood and elementary education programs functioned as completely separate entities. The remaining 50% of respondents reported a range of interprogram relationships, with only 15% of those relationships described as positive.

This summary of higher education in early childhood education (ECE) contexts reflects the same complexity and fragmentation that is seen in other aspects of the early childhood field. Early childhood higher education programs serve a range of purposes and constituencies, occur in diverse and often "siloed" settings, and overlap with but are not identical to other professional preparation systems.

Policy Trends and Cost Issues

Policy and cost issues are also key to understanding higher education's role in the early childhood field. These include trends in degree requirements, the costs of meeting those requirements, and efforts to provide support to those seeking higher education and those aiming to improve the system.

Policy Expectations for Degrees and Credentials

Federal and state policymakers have increased requirements for teachers of young children to have degrees, with the BA becoming the new target. A notable example is the recent reauthorization of the Head Start Act, requiring that by 2013 all Head Start teachers will have a minimum of an associate degree and 50% of those teachers will have earned a BA in early childhood (Improving Head Start for School Readiness Act, 2007). Barnett, Epstein, Friedman, Sansanelli, and Hustedt (2009) reported that 26 of 51 state-funded PreK initiatives now require the BA. Other higher education policy levers are found within state quality rating and improvement systems (QRIS) that tie higher ratings to higher levels of staff formal education and credentials (LeMoine, 2008).

Costs of and Support for Acquiring a Degree

A report from the National Center for Education Statistics (Knapp, Kelly-Reid, & Ginder, 2009) found that average 2008–2009 academic year tuition and required fees for full-time, in-state undergraduates in 4-year programs at public IHEs totaled $6,070; in 2-year programs, in-state tuition and fees were $2,830. For out-of-state undergraduates in 4-year programs, the charges averaged $14,378, and in 2-year programs, $6,118. Private not-for-profit 4-year IHEs reported charging $20,112, and private not-for-profit 2-year programs averaged $9,987. Finally, private for-profit 4-year IHEs reported charging an average of $15,521, with 2-year IHEs in this category charging $13,073. These charges are for one academic year only; also, the estimates do not include books and other nonrequired but often essential expenses.

Those seeking higher education in the early childhood field are often returning adult students with low salaries and multiple work/family responsibilities, with associated extra costs such as child care. LeMoine (2008) emphasizes that the costs of both initial preparation and ongoing professional development pose an "enormous financial burden" for individuals and for early childhood programs that attempt to support further education for their staff. Ackerman (2004) estimated that an average PreK teacher would need to spend more than one-third of his or her salary to attain a BA. In addition to tuition costs, early childhood educators must also consider the opportunity costs of delaying employment or taking time off to complete training while employed full time (Bueno, Darling-Hammond, & Gonzales, 2010).

Initiatives such as T.E.A.C.H. (Teacher Education and Compensation Helps) aim to address this issue by providing scholarships and guaranteeing that those who complete their associate or BA degrees receive either salary increases or bonuses. As of spring 2010, 20 states had adopted the T.E.A.C.H. strategies (T.E.A.C.H. Early Childhood Assistance & Quality Assurance Center, 2010). With a similar aim, the Higher Education Opportunity Act contains provisions for states to implement loan forgiveness and compensation incentives for early childhood educators who obtain associate or BA degrees (LeMoine, 2008). Head Start programs often have financial assistance and supports available for staff to seek higher education. The Office of Special Education Programs (OSEP), U.S. Department of Education, has a long history of providing stipend support for undergraduate and graduate students as part of their grant program to improve the quality and quantity of special education personnel (Kleinhammer-Tramill, Tramill, & Brace, 2010). Some of these OSEP stipends have supported students in early childhood programs with a focus on inclusion. Private philanthropy also contributes through scholarships or loan forgiveness, although these programs typically target individuals or small groups of students in specific geographic regions (e.g., see Goble & Horm, 2009). Although foundations fund professional development to enhance early childhood programs (National Child Care Information Center [NCCIC], 2009), no estimates of the scope or reach of these efforts are currently available.

Early childhood advocates have called attention to the need for higher education mandates to be accompanied by adequate funding. LeMoine (2008) identifies four specific targets: (1) funding to enable early childhood professionals to obtain the expected level of education; (2) funding for programs and workplaces to facilitate professional development through release time, substitute staff, and other forms of assistance; (3) a system of rewards and compensation parity initiatives to promote attainment of additional education; and (4) funding for statewide infrastructure, with components such as data systems, support to colleges and universities, quality assurance systems, and other related systems. Some progress has been made. For example, Pennsylvania has recently increased state support for T.E.A.C.H. scholarships and has begun a voucher reimbursement program to help teachers earn degrees (Hyson & Whittaker, 2012); Maine used ARRA (American Recovery and Reinvestment Act) funds to support scholarships for early childhood practitioners; Ohio has created a Center for Early Childhood Development to reduce duplication and to align standards and quality improvement across sectors (NAEYC, 2011); and the state of Montana funds the Early Childhood Project at Montana State University, which in turn supports a higher education consortium that oversees the state's professional development plans and activities (LeMoine, 2008).

Even if such supports are in place, a cautionary note is sounded by data from Herzenberg, Price, and Bradley (2005) documenting a decline in the percentage of BA-level teachers and administrators in center-based settings, from 43% in 1983–1985 to 30% in 2002–2004. Interpreting these findings, the authors note that the decline coincided with rapid increases in education levels of the U.S. workforce as a whole, highlighting the negative impact of ECE working conditions, especially compensation, as competing work options became available. Additionally, in 2005, Herzenberg and colleagues projected the most educated generation of ECE teachers was due to retire over the following 15 years, further exacerbating a severe personnel shortage. In light of these broad labor force trends, Herzenberg and colleagues urge policymakers to combine their calls for enhanced teacher credentials with pragmatic strategies such as phase-in periods and differentiated staffing models.

Program Content, Professional Preparation Standards, and Program Delivery Issues

With the diverse contexts of the early childhood higher education system in mind, and with these policy issues as background, we turn to a description of what is taught in early childhood higher education programs. We outline content priorities and use the results of several surveys to describe how these are included in professional preparation programs. Next we discuss the standards or student competencies that professional associations use to describe and assess higher education program quality. We conclude the section by outlining some issues in program delivery, including distance learning and opportunities for student engagement in class and field experiences.

Program Content

Content Priorities

Analysis of program content is essential when assessing the quality and relevance of higher education. Research reviews and national reports underscore several key priorities, including (1) content related to current knowledge in the developmental sciences—child and adolescent development, cognitive science, and neuroscience—and its implications for teaching and learning (Pianta, Hitz, & West, 2010); (2) content related to current knowledge and pedagogy in core academic disciplines, including early mathematics and literacy (National Early Literacy Panel, 2009; National Research Council, 2009; Strickland & Riley-Ayers, 2006); (3) content related to the characteristics and needs of the growing number of young children with disabilities in ECE settings (U.S. Department of Education, 2010), who are ethnically and linguistically diverse (U.S. Census Bureau, 2005), or who have challenging behaviors (Dunlap et al., 2006); and (4) especially for BA and graduate programs, content on the characteristics and needs of adult learners (Snyder & Wolfe, 2008).

Having identified these priorities, one must ask whether they have penetrated the content of early childhood higher education programs. The primary source of information on this issue comes from national- and state-level surveys in which respondents have been early childhood program faculty or administrators (e.g., Early & Winton, 2001; Hyson et al., 2009; Johnson et al., 2010; Lobman, Ryan, & McLaughlin, 2005; Maxwell et al., 2006; Ray, Bowman, & Robbins, 2006). Besides having the limitations of self-report data, the survey results also do not yield much information about the depth or quality of content; for the most part, the studies simply have asked respondents whether certain courses were offered or topics were "covered." Additionally, research provides no guidance about how much "coverage" is adequate, and there is only limited information from K–12 teacher education (e.g., Kim, Andrews, & Carr, 2004) about the relative merits of integrating topics throughout a teacher preparation program rather than addressing them in separate courses or field experiences. Finally, discussions of content "coverage" do not address the question of whether the content is consistent with current research, or whether it is well taught—issues that we address in a later section of this chapter.

Keeping these limitations in mind, the results from these surveys and other sources indicate that although certain broad topics (e.g., the education and care of preschool-age children) are likely to be covered in coursework and practica in most programs, other content receives uneven and inadequate coverage. The following examples are organized around the content priorities outlined earlier.

Developmental Sciences

As compared to elementary and secondary teacher education, traditionally ECE programs have had a strong emphasis on child development knowledge—although aspects of this emphasis have been criticized (Goffin, 1996). Yet even in this content area there is evidence that coverage may be mismatched to the developmental scope of the early childhood field: For example, in a national survey of all CDA, associate degree, BA, and graduate teacher education programs (Maxwell et al., 2006), only 49% of the bachelor's programs that claimed to include the birth to age 3 range in their degree program required at least one infant/toddler course.

Content in Literacy and Mathematics

The strong emphasis on literacy in state early learning and licensure standards has ensured that—at least in terms of number of courses—coverage is extensive, with 77% of BA programs reportedly offering at least one dedicated course on this topic (Maxwell et al., 2006). However, Early and Winton (2001) found that fewer than 10% of the programs required a course in working with young dual language learners, and this was the least likely content area to be required during a practicum experience. Coverage of this topic did not substantially improve by the time of the Maxwell and colleagues' (2006) follow-up, when fewer than 15% of programs reported requiring such a course. Mathematics continues to receive less coverage than literacy, with 77% of BA and 65% of associate degree programs requiring a literacy course, compared with 59% (BA) and 49% (AA) requiring a numeracy or math course for young children.

Disabilities and Challenging Behavior

Concerns about adequate emphasis also arise when examining course offerings related to children with disabilities or challenging behaviors. Of the large percentage (80%) of BA programs that indicate their primary mission includes preparing early childhood special educators/early interventionists, only 60% require one or more courses on working with children who have disabilities (Chang, Early, & Winton, 2005; Early & Winton, 2001). Ray and colleagues (2006) report similar findings. They conducted a website analysis of the program and course descriptions of 226 BA early childhood programs to ascertain the content foci of these programs, with specific reference to diversity issues, and found that, on average, disability content was addressed in only 12.8% of total required semester hours, with time devoted to this content ranging from 0 to 43 semester hours.

With respect to coverage of issues around young children's challenging behavior, Maxwell and colleagues (2006) found that slightly more than half of BA (53%) and associate degree programs (53%) required a separate course on social and emotional development, where this content may likely be addressed. Additionally, 65% of BA programs and 57% of associate degree programs required a course on classroom or behavioral management.

Cultural and Linguistic Diversity

The area of cultural and linguistic diversity appears to lack adequate emphasis, especially in light of changing demographics. Maxwell and colleagues (2006) found that that the majority of programs did not require even one course on working with children and families from diverse ethnic and cultural environments. Again, with a specific focus on diversity, the Ray and colleagues (2006) study of BA programs found a similar lack of attention to this content area, with only 12.5% of the total required semester hours specifically targeted toward diversity education, and only 7% of the programs requiring student teaching in a setting described as diverse or multicultural.

Adult Development and Learning

The coverage of content on adult learning is also worthy of examination, especially at the BA and graduate levels. Over time, some graduates of these programs may move into higher education faculty positions, most often serving the growing number of nontraditional students pursuing higher education (Zaslow, Tout, Halle, Whittaker, & Lavelle, 2010). Often motivated by higher salaries, other graduates may move out of positions in child care to work with adult learners as supervisors and professional development providers or in resource and referral agencies (Whitebook, Sakai, & Kipnis, 2010). The Maxwell and colleagues (2006) survey found that about 40% of BA or graduate programs did not require any coursework in adult learning and development.

The preceding section describes coverage in some critical content areas, identifying possible gaps or inadequate coverage. As noted earlier, however, we do not know what "thresholds" determine sufficient content coverage, or whether exposure to specific content results in improved practices. The next section moves us closer to the practice issues by examining outcome standards or student competencies for professional preparation programs and how those are used in program accreditation.

Links from Content to Competencies through Standards and Accreditation

Focusing on course content alone provides a very limited picture of higher education programs' effectiveness or adequacy. Of greater importance is whether programs are building competencies in early educators. Two distinct but related sets of standards, which include specific competencies organized within key content areas, have been developed by national organizations to guide the preparation of early childhood practitioners. NAEYC has standards for programs preparing "general" early childhood educators to work with children from birth to age 8 (Hyson, 2003; NAEYC, 2009), and the Council for Exceptional Children/Division of Early Childhood (CEC/DEC; 2008) has standards specific to programs preparing early childhood special educators and early interventionists serving children from birth to age 8. The standards from both associations are organized by content domain and are differentiated by level (e.g., "initial" vs. "advanced" teacher preparation). Within each content domain are specific competencies that describe what graduates must know and be able to do to meet the standards.

Using Standards for Program Review and Accreditation

Although the standards provide important guidance for higher education programs, their use is voluntary. The primary way that national standards shape higher education programs is through accreditation. Using its standards, NAEYC recognizes early childhood BA and advanced-degree programs in schools of education accredited by the National Council for Accreditation of Teacher Education (NCATE) (NAEYC, 2009; Willer, Lutton, & Ginsberg, 2011). NAEYC standards are organized around six areas in which programs' graduates must demonstrate competence: (1) promoting child development and learning; (2) building family and community relationships; (3) observing, documenting, and assessing young children; (4) using developmentally effective approaches to connect with children and families; (5) using content knowledge to build meaningful curriculum; and (6) becoming a professional (NAEYC, 2009). In reviewing programs, both NAEYC and other professional associations that participate in accreditation or similar credentialing systems (e.g., the CEC/DEC; the National Board for Professional Teaching Standards) have moved toward a strongly performance-based approach that relies less on counting courses and credits than on valid documentation by a program that its graduates have gained knowledge, skills, and professional dispositions aligned with the relevant professional standards. Independent of NCATE (which only accredits at BA and graduate levels), NAEYC has recently established a system to review and accredit associate degree programs through the NAEYC Commission on Early Childhood Associate Degree Accreditation (ECADA). Using the same NAEYC core standards and a review process comparable to that of NCATE, this accreditation system not only promotes the use of NAEYC standards to guide personnel preparation in 2-year degree granting programs but also helps to promote the articulation or transfer of credits from 2-year to 4-year degree-granting IHEs.

Seven states have "blended" licensure or certification for early educators, usually as one of several licensure options (Bornfreund, 2011).[3] Blended licensure is intended to combine preparation in general early childhood education and early childhood special education (Stayton et al., 2009). In states offering a blended licensure options, a number of IHEs have designed blended preparation programs at the BA and master's levels. Those blended programs undergoing NCATE review must meet the review criteria for both NAEYC and CEC/DEC personnel standards.

Accreditation and Higher Education Quality

Only 363 BA and graduate programs have received NAEYC/NCATE accreditation, approximately two-thirds of the total number of BA programs with an early childhood emphasis (Bornfreund, 2011). The question of whether early childhood program accreditation is associated with other indicators of quality has been addressed in a few studies. Hyson and colleagues (2009) examined the association between NCATE accreditation and faculty-reported program climate, priorities, and other factors, and found no significant differences between accredited and nonaccredited programs. Lim, Maxwell, Able-Boone, and Zimmer (2009) and Ray and colleagues (2006) did a similar comparison, looking specifically at the relationship between diversity coverage and NCATE/NAEYC accreditation. Again they found no significant differences between accredited and nonaccredited programs. Obviously, these findings raise questions about accreditation as a potential measure of program quality, yet many institutions are not members of NCATE and so are not eligible for NAEYC's program review. Other institutions may be eligible yet choose not to participate for varied reasons.

Although simple comparisons of accredited versus nonaccredited programs are problematic for the reasons just outlined, it is possible to sample only those programs reviewed for accreditation, comparing those that were or were not successful in terms of critical outcomes such as graduates' teaching practices. Such research would also have the benefit of identifying ways in which the accreditation process might be improved. Comments by faculty in Hyson and colleagues' (2009) study suggest that most see benefits in the accreditation process; for example, creating a shared focus on standards and quality improvement. Anecdotal reports also suggested that faculty members view accreditation as instrumental in securing program resources. Additional research could verify whether these self-reported benefits indeed are reflected in changes in programs' priorities, structure, or instructional practices. More generally, the recent creation by NCATE and TEAC (Teacher Education

Accreditation Commission) of a new accrediting body, the Council for Accreditation of Educator Preparation (CAEP), affords an opportunity to conduct research on accreditation standards and accreditation options in light of their potential impact on teaching practices and learning outcomes for early childhood education, as well as other areas.

It appears that the competencies presented in national standards for preparing personnel in higher education have potential to help programs move beyond courses and credits, focusing on what graduates should know and be able to do. Yet again we see that lack of research leaves the early childhood field uncertain about whether that potential is being realized.

Program Delivery

Having examined program content and standards, we conclude this section with a brief discussion of some options and issues in program delivery.

Online Program Delivery

Online ECE program delivery has become a frequent option at both 2- and 4-year IHEs. Johnson and colleagues (2010) report that 72.5% of the 40 ECE BA programs surveyed use some form of online learning, and several respondents stated that new online master's programs are being developed. However, the study did not probe these issues further. A national review of distance learning programs in early childhood professional development (Center for the Child Care Workforce, 2007) identified a number of entirely online ECE degree programs. Of the 73 educational institutions and training programs surveyed for that report (all of which were known to offer distance learning programs), 27 offered distance coursework leading to the associate's degree and 42 had online BA or MA degree options. It has been noted anecdotally that faculty barriers may stand in the way of continuing growth in the implementation of distance learning programs. Some early childhood faculty members seem unwilling to teach online because of their strong preference for personal relationships with students; many believe that early childhood content cannot be adequately delivered online; and many are "digital immigrants" who are unfamiliar and uncomfortable with online learning (C. Donohue, personal communication, July 21, 2010). However, little systematic information is available about these tendencies, and even less is known about the effectiveness of various distance education and technology systems in early childhood teacher preparation—making these topics ripe for research.

We also lack data on the extent to which students in higher education programs are actively engaged in content, exposed to video or live demonstrations of research-based instructional strategies, or have opportunities to develop and practice applying these strategies in real settings with guided feedback. Effective professional development is characterized by these kinds of learning opportunities for students (Pianta et al., 2010; Trivette, 2005; Winton, 2010), yet it seems that textbooks and coursework continue to focus heavily on general content knowledge, with inadequate attention to research-based teaching and intervention strategies. Child development laboratory schools, whose missions include early childhood teacher preparation, offer a potentially effective environment for modeling and coaching theory- and research-based practice. However, not all teacher preparation programs have access to a lab school and, similar to other initiatives discussed, little research has focused on the efficacy of lab schools in fulfilling their teacher preparation mission (Monroe & Horm, in press).

More generally, solid descriptive information is not available on hours and settings used for early childhood field experiences, including student teaching. Additionally, there is little evidence that field experiences are meeting the need for students to observe, implement, and receive feedback on effective practices. Reflecting the more general concerns in NCATE's (2010) report on clinical practice, the Johnson and colleagues (2010) survey and interview study of higher education programs for early educators in 40 states found that relatively few programs linked content topics (e.g., science) directly with clinical practice/fieldwork. The study also found that the absence of high-quality field placement sites and lack of supervisors was a major faculty concern. Finally, some early childhood teacher candidates do their student teaching at their own workplace, an arrangement that does not often provide students with strong coaching or mentoring (Whitebook, Gomby, Bellm, et al., 2009).

Looking back at this section of the chapter, clearly there is much to learn about the content, professional preparation standards, and delivery of higher education programs for early educators. Survey research highlights content areas that may need strengthening. However, the implications of different patterns of content coverage, the effects of national standards and accreditation on program quality, and the effects of variations in program delivery are far from being understood.

Faculty in ECE Programs

Whatever the overall program content and delivery systems, what students get out of their experiences in higher education depends to a great extent on the characteristics of those who are teaching, supervising, and mentoring them. These characteristics include not only the demographics of faculty training, experience, and ethnicity but also faculty knowledge, beliefs, and pedagogical skills. Decisions made by individual instructors (e.g., how much time to spend on mathematics within a general early childhood curriculum course) and by program or department faculty (e.g., how much to emphasize infant/toddler programming) influence teacher education quality and may increase or decrease the likelihood of graduates' implementing practices that can positively affect child and family outcomes. Unfortunately, except for demographic descriptions, information on early childhood faculty members, such as their knowledge, professional beliefs, and pedagogical skills, is limited.

What Is Meant by "Early Childhood Faculty"?

Definitional issues have perplexed the early childhood field (Maxwell, Feild, & Clifford, 2005), and the definition of "faculty" is one more example. In K–12 teacher education, Cochran-Smith (2003) has proposed that the term "teacher educator" should include all those with responsibility for preparing future teachers. However, demographic information on early childhood faculty has typically been collected only on those full- and part-time instructors who are part of the core early childhood program, rather than on general education faculty, field supervisors, and school-based cooperating teachers. This data gap limits our knowledge of the full range of "faculty" characteristics.

Demographics of the Early Childhood Faculty

Keeping those limitations in mind, the most recent higher education data on early childhood faculty were collected in 2004 by an FPG (Frank Porter Graham) Child Development Institute team (Maxwell et al., 2006), replicating the methods and expanding the sample used in a previous FPG study (Early & Winton, 2001). Information was gathered from telephone interviews with early childhood program heads from 1,179 institutions of higher education offering certificates or degrees ranging from CDA to the master's degree, about many characteristics of the higher education work force, including full-time/part-time status, number of students served, race/ethnicity, educational background, and work experience. Noteworthy findings include the following: (1) Across ECE degree levels, 57% of faculty were part time, with significantly more (69%) associate degree faculty being part time; (2) ECE program faculty members included significantly more part-time faculty and had substantially greater teaching and supervising responsibilities than faculty members across all disciplines at their institution (Early & Winton, 2001); (3) 80% of full-time faculty members were white and non-Hispanic, with only slightly more diversity among part-time faculty; (4) education varied by type of program, with over half of faculty in BA programs having a doctorate, compared with less than 10% of associate degree program faculty; (5) compared with faculty in BA programs, substantially more faculty in associate degree programs had direct experience working with children under age 4, and substantially more had an academic degree specifically focused on birth to age 4.

Implications of Data on Faculty Characteristics

Although these data were collected a number of years ago, other studies continue to examine their implications. For example, data from these studies have been used to explore ethnic disparities between the composition of the faculty and their college/university students (especially at community colleges), and the diversity of young children and families (e.g., Chang et al., 2005; Lim et al., 2009; Ray et al., 2006). For example, one follow-up study using the FPG data (Lim et al., 2009) found significant correlations between the proportion of nonwhite faculty in early childhood programs and the extent to which courses on diversity were provided, although the study could not identify causal relationships or underlying mechanisms.

What Should Early Childhood Teacher Educators Know and Be Able to Do?: Faculty Competencies

The early childhood field has identified competencies for graduates of professional preparation programs (NAEYC, 2009), and many states have also identified competencies for teachers of young children (Center for the Study of Child Care Employment, 2008; Winton & West, 2011). Beyond requirements for ECE faculty degree specializations (NAEYC, 2010), little attention has been given to defining competencies for early childhood faculty. The Association of Teacher Educators (ATE; 2008) has developed standards applying to all teacher educators, along with a discussion of their implications (Klecka, Odell, Houston, & McBee, 2009). However, the ATE standards have not been endorsed by ECE-specific professional organizations such as NAEYC and the National Association of Early Childhood Teacher Educators.

What Do Early Childhood Teacher Educators Actually Know and Do?

Although there is not yet consensus about desired competencies for early childhood teacher educators, a number of studies provide information about their knowledge, beliefs, and attitudes, and pedagogical skills.

Faculty Knowledge

A number of authors have expressed concerns about faculty members' knowledge in specific content areas (e.g., Daniel & Friedman, 2005; Hemmeter, Santos, & Ostrosky, 2008;

Hyson et al., 2009; Lobman et al., 2005; Ryan & Hyland, 2010). Direct evidence on this issue is limited, however.

A few studies of self-reported faculty knowledge have identified apparent knowledge gaps in areas such as brain development (Gilkerson, 2001) and mathematics education (Hyson, 2008). Additional insight is provided by a recent survey of early childhood teacher education faculty and administrators about their programs' quality improvement efforts (Hyson et al., 2009). Some responses suggested that the faculty knowledge base is not always consistent with the current developmental and educational research. For example, only 35% of BA program faculty prioritized the goal of helping students to have "more frequent and developmentally supportive interactions with individual children," despite strong evidence for this practice's importance (e.g., Pianta & Stuhlman, 2004). In the same study, faculty members were asked an open-ended question about what theories and research they rely on in making decisions about their programs' overall content. Many respondents chose not to answer this question; the responses of some who did answer it reflected an outdated or limited knowledge base (e.g., Piaget was a frequently cited influential theorist, while Vygotsky and others with more recent theoretical perspectives were underrepresented). Some other faculty members—not the majority—gave answers such as "developmentally appropriate practice" or "Reggio Emilia" as the sources of influential research for their program.

In a similar faculty survey about early childhood mathematics education (Hyson, 2008), many faculty members gave vague responses to a question about what they teach students about specific math curricula, suggesting that perhaps students are not introduced to any curriculum models. Many respondents were also vague in responding to a question about what math-related competencies they want their students to gain, suggesting a lack of precision in their own knowledge.

Obviously, the whole domain of faculty knowledge is critically important. Yet beyond a few self-report studies that do raise concerns, evidence about this domain is lacking.

Faculty Beliefs and Attitudes

Like faculty knowledge, the beliefs and attitudes of early childhood faculty have received little attention from researchers. As part of a recent study (Johnson et al., 2010), faculty in 40 public research-intensive institutions across the United States were surveyed on a range of issues, including faculty attitudes about the impact within their institutions of state PreK and the PreK–grade 3 movement. Another relatively large-scale study (Forer, Rochon Flanagan, & Beach, n.d.) surveyed Canadian ECE faculty members on their attitudes toward the quality of students, the national ECE curriculum, and the quality of child care. Other research, usually with small samples, has focused on faculty members' beliefs about issues such as behavior management (La Paro, Siepak, & Scott-Little, 2009), team teaching (Hestenes et al., 2009), and diversity constructs (Maude et al., 2010). Although some insights can be gained from these studies, they have not been part of a comprehensive, programmatic approach to understanding faculty beliefs and attitudes, or the relation between those beliefs and other aspects of higher education.

Skills of ECE Faculty

Research on faculty skills is even more limited than that on faculty knowledge and beliefs. As noted earlier, the early childhood field has not identified specific skills for early childhood faculty, although general faculty standards have been developed by the ATE (2008) and presented in its *Standards for Teacher Educators*. The first category within ATE's standards is Teaching. Faculty should "model teaching that demonstrates content and professional knowledge, skills, and dispositions reflecting research, proficiency with technology and assessment, and accepted best practices in teacher education." The ATE standards also delineate desired faculty skills in eight other standards categories (Cultural Competence, Scholarship, Professional Development, Program Development, Collaboration, Public Advocacy, Teacher Education Profession, and Vision). No systematic efforts have yet been made to assess early childhood faculty on these dimensions.

Another potentially important dimension for future research, not captured by the ATE categories, is skill in creating supportive faculty–student relationships. In K–12 teacher education research, Darling-Hammond, Holtzman, Gatlin, and Heilig (2005) cite evidence that these relationships can be significant contributors to teachers' development. In early childhood teacher education such relationships may be especially important because the students are often more diverse and older than college students in general. Many of these students are likely to need strong support from faculty (Ackerman, 2005). Yet early childhood programs have greater percentages of part-time faculty, and greater demands on faculty time for student advisement, than do higher education faculty as a whole (Early & Winton, 2001), limiting the time available to build such relationships.

Beyond specific faculty skills, there is converging evidence that a strong practice focus— not just transmission of knowledge—is essential for effective professional development (NCATE, 2010; Sheridan, Edwards, Marvin, & Knoche, 2009; U.S. Department of Education, 2010; Zaslow, Tout, Halle, & Starr, 2010). In its report *Preparing Teachers: Building Evidence for Sound Policy*, the National Research Council (NRC; 2010) described this focus ("clinical preparation" or "field experiences") as one of the components of teacher education that has the greatest likelihood of improving child outcomes. With this evidence and consensus in mind, it seems critical for future research to examine faculty skills in building students' ability to implement specific practices. In its recent report on revamping teacher education through clinical practice, NCATE outlined skills for "clinical faculty"—those who supervise future teachers in the field, urging that they "should know how adults learn, know mentoring strategies and how to use them, have a portfolio of assessment approaches, and a complement of personal skills for building trust, rapport, and communication with candidates" (2010, p. 21). If a strong practice focus is to become a reality, such skills should be part of the repertoire of all faculty members, not just those with direct responsibility for field experiences. Yet research sheds no direct light on these or other pedagogical skills—in part because of the previously discussed lack of consensus around what those skills ought to be for early childhood faculty.

Professional Development for Faculty

In contrast to extensive reviews and discussions of professional development for classroom teachers, including early childhood educators (e.g., Hyson & Whittaker, 2012; U.S. Department of Education, 2010; Zaslow & Martinez-Beck, 2006), relatively little attention has been paid to the need for, the content of, or the effects of professional development for faculty who are teacher educators, at least within the United States. Interestingly, a much more extensive literature exists on faculty development for those who teach future physicians, nurses, and other health professionals, including research on the effectiveness of different approaches to faculty development (Steinert et al., 2006).

Many early childhood teacher educators seem keenly interested in their own professional development but report being constrained by budget issues and the availability of professional resources (e.g., Gilkerson, 2001; Hemmeter et al., 2008; Hyson et al., 2009). For example, 46% of those surveyed about early childhood mathematics reported that faculty members were "eager" to improve students' preparation, but they needed more professional development (Hyson, 2008). Several faculty development initiatives have recently tried to build capacity in content areas such as diversity (Maude et al., 2010), inclusion (Winton & Catlett, 2009), and brain development (Gilkerson, 2001). Methods have included summer institutes, online discussions, and the development of modules for faculty to integrate into their courses. Such initiatives have not yet been rigorously evaluated, and their scale-up appears limited by institutional budget cuts—for example, only 50% of respondents to a faculty survey (Hyson et al., 2009) identified "building faculty capacity" as a programwide priority.

Beyond the Individual Faculty Member: The Role of Organizational Climate

As pointed out early in this chapter, ECE teachers' work environments are likely to influence the extent to which they are able to implement what they learn in higher education (Whitebook, Gomby, Sakai, & Kipnis, 2009). Similarly, the environment within which higher education faculty members work, and the level of support they receive, may influence their ability to implement effective practices. Many ECE faculty members work in programs with high ratios of students to full-time faculty—on average, 60% higher in an IHE's ECE program than in the IHE as a whole (Early & Winton, 2001). Other evidence of institutional obstacles is found in faculty responses to a survey that asked faculty to characterize the climate in which their program currently operates (Hyson et al., 2009). Almost 20% reported functioning in a negative climate, predominantly "survival mode—just keeping our heads above water." Programs also reported the extent of philosophical and financial support from upper administration. Not surprisingly, significant associations were found between level of administrative support and self-reported program climate. Further exploration of such issues may help us understand the faculty supports needed to promote effective practices for future early childhood educators.

The Impact of Higher Education

Of all the issues concerning early childhood higher education, the question "What are the effects of higher education on graduates and on the children and families with whom they work?" is arguably the most important. Yet here the research is most inadequate. Despite the limitations of the data, we know much more about the characteristics of institutions, students, faculty, and programs than about higher education's impact on (a) graduates' knowledge, skills, dispositions, and professional lives; (b) their classroom practices; and (c) developmental and learning outcomes for children who are taught by those graduates, let alone outcomes for the families with whom early childhood graduates may work.

Dimensions of Higher Education with Potential Impact

Table 26.1 outlines a number of dimensions of higher education; the impact of each could be investigated through research. With these dimensions in mind, multiple kinds of outcomes or potential impacts of higher education on graduates and the children and families with whom they work can be generated. Table 26.2 lists some examples of such outcomes, including graduates' content knowledge, observed classroom quality and teaching practices, graduates' career paths, and children's academic and developmental outcomes.

Reflecting on these tables, one can see rich opportunities for researchers to link features of early childhood higher education programs with a variety of potential outcomes for graduates' knowledge, beliefs, and practices and, in turn, to link those outcomes with

TABLE 26.1. Sample Dimensions of Higher Education with Potential Impact on Graduates and Children

1. Amount of higher education (e.g., none/some/associate/baccalaureate)
2. Extent and type of specialization (e.g., general college degree vs. elementary vs. ECE/child development degree vs. blended ECE/ECSE)
3. Delivery mode (e.g., online vs. face-to-face vs. mixed)
4. Academic home and philosophical orientation of program
5. Variations in specific program content and preparation emphases (e.g., number and type of courses in literacy; mathematics; diversity; amount and type of field experience)
6. Variations in quality of teacher education programs (e.g., as measured by accreditation or other indicators such as faculty qualifications)

associated outcomes for young children and their families. But it is also clear that few of these opportunities have been taken.

Impact of Teachers' Degrees on Classroom Quality and Child Outcomes

The limited research on higher education's impact has mainly asked whether observed classroom quality and child outcomes differ as a function of whether teachers do, or do not, have college degrees (including which degree levels and in what specializations). Many reviews of earlier research (e.g., Bowman, Donovan, & Burns, 2001; Whitebook, 2003) indicate that higher levels of teacher education generally predict better classroom quality and more positive cognitive and social child outcomes, and a 2007 meta-analysis (Kelley & Camilli, 2007) comparing impacts on quality for teachers with and without a BA found consistently positive impacts of the BA, although with relatively small effect sizes. However, a recent review of research on effective professional development (U.S. Department of Education, 2010) concluded that secondary analyses of large-scale studies by a consortium of researchers (Early et al., 2007) "provided little indication that degree, highest education level among those with an early childhood major, or having an early childhood major among those with a bachelor's degree were related either to observed classroom quality or to children's gain scores on measures of academic achievement" (U.S. Department of Education, 2010, pp. 11–12).

TABLE 26.2. Potential Outcomes for Early Childhood Graduates and Children

Outcomes for early childhood graduates

1. Content knowledge (e.g., Praxis scores)
2. Overall observed classroom quality (e.g., Early Childhood Environment Rating Scale, Infant/Toddler Environment Rating Scale, CLASS scores)
3. Observed skills in specific domains (e.g., observed competence in teaching mathematics or literacy; use of inclusive practices; addressing challenging behavior; responses to diversity)
4. Attitudes and beliefs in specific domains (graduates' self-perceived readiness to implement inclusive programs, work with linguistically and culturally diverse children, etc.)
5. Graduates' career development (e.g., turnover; seeking further education)

Outcomes for children

1. Academic outcomes (e.g., literacy, mathematics)
2. Other dimensions of positive development and school readiness (e.g., physical health and well-being; mental health; self-regulation; social and emotional competence)
3. Grade retention and assignment to special education

Although discussion continues about the relative merits of various studies and syntheses on the impact of teachers' education, both the consortium members (Early et al., 2007) and others (e.g., Bogard, Traylor, & Takanishi, 2008; Burchinal, Hyson, & Zaslow, 2008; Hyson et al., 2009; U.S. Department of Education, 2010; Washington, 2008; Whitebook, Gomby, Bellm, et al., 2009) acknowledge many limitations in this line of research, including the correlational nature of the studies and the narrow range of outcomes that have been investigated. At the same time, many of these authors call for reframing and expanding the research questions, going beyond the "degree or not" question to examine more of the variables outlined in Table 26.1, as well as the array of classroom and child outcomes highlighted in Table 26.2.

This call is only beginning to be answered. A few examples illustrate the kinds of studies that have been conducted recently, followed by brief comments on their limitations.

The Effects of Features of Higher Education on ECE Students' Current Knowledge, Beliefs, and Practices

There are numerous studies of this kind, for the most part by individual faculty members who have implemented an innovation such as a mentoring experience (Trepanier-Street, Adler, & Taylor, 2007), service learning (Szente, 2008), a practicum in infant care (Recchia & Shin, 2010), or a curricular emphasis on active listening strategies (McNaughton, Hamlin, McCarthy, Head-Reeves, & Schreiner, 2007), either in one course or across a program. Effects on students' knowledge and beliefs are then examined, often with qualitative methods. Data are usually gathered at one point in time, but a few studies have followed students over the course of their years in the ECE program (e.g., La Paro et al., 2009; Recchia, Beck, Esposito, & Tarrant, 2009; Vartuli & Rohs, 2009). One other approach (File & Gullo, 2002) has been to compare pedagogical beliefs about teaching in the early primary grades held by students in either elementary education or early childhood programs. In this study, although differences were not large, elementary education students were significantly more likely to hold positive beliefs about teacher-directed instruction, the use of formal tests, and behavior management through the use of extrinsic rewards.

The Effects of Features of Higher Education on ECE Graduates' Beliefs and Practices

Except for the follow-up surveys usually required for institutional accreditation, few studies have examined graduates' beliefs as a function of variations in their preparation. A few investigators have studied graduates' beliefs about the adequacy of their preparation to address issues such as cultural and linguistic diversity (e.g., Ray et al., 2006). Similarly, Miller and Losardo (2002) examined the perceptions of teachers who had graduated from seven blended early childhood education/early childhood special education programs about their programs' strengths (in child development and general ECE) and gaps (working with families and meeting the needs of children with moderate to severe disabilities). None of these studies has ventured into graduates' classrooms to investigate variations in practices related to variations in the content or quality of their higher education programs.

The Effects of Features of Higher Education on Child or Family Outcomes

Beyond the studies referred to earlier, which simply look at child outcomes as a function of whether teachers have degrees or not, research has not yet examined whether better outcomes result for those children who are taught by graduates from teacher education programs that differ in specific features, or for families with whom those graduates interact.

For example, one might ask whether children fare better on specific outcomes when their teachers have had a specific kind of literacy emphasis in their undergraduate program, or have graduated from a blended ECE/ECSE (early childhood education/early childhood special education) program, or have graduated from an NCATE/NAEYC accredited program. One might also ask whether family outcomes are improved if teachers or early interventionists have had family-focused field experiences practica or have had family members as course co-instructors. Such crucial questions remain to be addressed.

Limitations of Research on the Impacts of Higher Education in the Early Childhood Field

The preceding paragraphs clearly indicate the major limitation—the absence of programmatic, rigorous, fine-grained studies that tease apart how different features of higher education programs may affect both teachers' practices and child/family outcomes. Those studies that have tried to address a few of these issues have mostly been conducted in one institution, often by one faculty member, using small numbers of students, and for the most part have been limited to descriptive or qualitative methods. Together, the studies do not add up to a systematic program of research in which findings from one study lead to new studies, and in which consistent, valid, and reliable instruments are used across settings. Although existing research may prompt reflection on individual practices and may generate ideas for future studies, it cannot yet be used to guide higher education practices or policies on a large scale.

Research in K–12 teacher education, while sharing many of the same challenges and limitations (Kennedy, 1996; Wilson, Floden, & Ferrini-Mundy, 2001), has made somewhat better progress in examining a complex and nuanced set of higher education features for their possible effects on both teaching practices and student outcomes (e.g., Boyd, Grossman, Lankford, Loeb, & Wyckoff, 2009; Cochran-Smith, Feiman-Nemser, McIntyre, & Demers, 2008; Darling-Hammond et al., 2005; Florez, 2009). This body of work may offer some models for future early childhood research. For example, using a value-added methodology, Boyd and colleagues (2009) have examined relations between variations in the nature of preparation in 31 elementary education programs and the math and reading learning gains of students taught by the programs' graduates in the New York City public schools. Going beyond simply counting credit hours, the researchers used multiple measures of program content, including document analysis, surveys, and interviews. The results clearly demonstrate that some IHEs are more effective than others in producing graduates whose students make greater progress. Specifically, graduates of those IHEs with a stronger practice focus (e.g., stronger supervision of student teaching and a practice-focused capstone project) had better outcomes, at least during their first year of teaching. This kind of research is both feasible and important to conduct for early childhood teacher preparation programs.

Toward More Effective Higher Education: Recent Innovations and Promising Practices

Increasing the effectiveness of early childhood teacher preparation requires innovative thinking—a difficult process in higher education, a system often accused of deep resistance to change (Diamond, 2006). Some such efforts have been noted elsewhere in this chapter; here we highlight recent examples in three key areas: systems-level innovations; national efforts to build faculty capacity; and innovations in higher education coursework and program delivery. Again, it is important to note that few innovations have been rigorously evaluated, making this a high priority for the future.

Systems–Level Innovations

NAEYC's Early Childhood Workforce Systems Initiative is promoting states' design of policies for an integrated, cross-sector professional development system, including policies related to higher education (LeMoine, 2008). Interviews with state leaders (Hyson & Whittaker, 2012) reveal a number of emerging efforts to strengthen higher education's role. The state of Delaware, for example, recently established an "Institute for Excellence in Early Childhood" at the University of Delaware, with responsibility for coordinating the state QRIS and Delaware's overall professional development efforts. The decision to house this body at an IHE was intended to increase and institutionalize higher education's involvement in all aspects of Delaware's ECE quality improvement efforts.

More generally, the Improving Head Start for School Readiness Act of 2007 includes a significant mandate for states to establish Early Childhood Advisory Councils (ECACs). Because representation of higher education on these councils is required, ECACS afford another opportunity to strengthen links between higher education and other sectors of early childhood professional development.

Time and careful evaluation are needed to see whether such innovations result in meaningful participation and integration of higher education into the broader professional development system. Furthermore, without an equal focus on improving higher education content, pedagogy, and faculty capacity, simply focusing on process (i.e., merely having higher education represented "at the table") is unlikely to result in sustainable improvements.

National Resources to Build Faculty Capacity

Recognizing gaps in the knowledge base and resources of many faculty members (exacerbated by limited professional development funds for professional development and heavy teaching loads), several federally funded projects have developed free, easy-to-use, materials to use infuse current, research-based information into early childhood courses. The Research Connections Faculty Teaching Modules (*www.researchconnections.org*) provide suggested assignments and in-class activities to help faculty orient their students to Research Connections' search functions, and to help students make thoughtful connections between research and practice. Similarly, the Center to Mobilize Early Childhood Knowledge (CONNECT) is developing detailed, practice-focused modules, including rich video examples, to build faculty members' capacity to promote students' use of evidence-based practice in inclusive settings (*http://community.fpg.unc.edu/connect-modules)*. To date, the impact of such resources on the practices of faculty and students has not been studied, although CONNECT has evaluation built into its design.

Innovations in Higher Education Programs and Instructional Models

One promising innovation has been the development of ECE cohort programs to promote success among nontraditional students new to higher education. In California, for example, a cohort approach is being used in six BA completion programs, with small groups of adult students already teaching in ECE, moving together through the program, taking courses together, and providing mutual support (Whitebook et al., 2008). The University of Oklahoma–Tulsa's Bachelor's Completion Program admits students in cohort groups, offers courses during evenings and weekends, and provides attractive loan forgiveness and scholarship programs to support students throughout the academic program and during student teaching (Goble & Horm, 2009). Their nontraditional students report that while the financial aid and scheduling first attracted them to the program, the cohort organization is essential for their success and program completion. Ongoing research aims to assess the effectiveness of such programs in supporting successful degree completion and effective classroom practices.

Specific to innovations in higher education instruction, there are promising applications of CLASS (Classroom Assessment Scoring System) and MTP (MyTeachingPartner, a professional development component of the CLASS system). First used as part of inservice training, MTP engages participants in learning about and analyzing high-quality teacher–child interactions and applying these insights to their own practice. Efforts to incorporate this work into higher education include (1) using the CLASS categories in evaluating student teachers (La Paro, Maynard, Scott-Little, & Thomason, 2010) and (2) creating an MTP-related, 14-week course that has now been implemented with a small sample of preservice students (Scott-Little et al., 2011) and with a greater number of practicing teachers (Hamre et al., in press)—both delivered by college-level instructors. Again, more evaluation is needed, and is under way, to track impacts beyond participants' knowledge, beliefs, and concurrent practices to see what the longer-term outcomes may be for teachers and children.

Along with course-related innovations already mentioned earlier in this chapter, other promising examples may be cited, usually originating within one IHE. Although these individual program improvement efforts are quite diverse, most of them aim to strengthen the *practice* component of the teacher education program through enhanced field experiences, better collaboration between college/university faculty and early childhood program staff, or expanded use of coaching and mentoring as part of preservice teacher education. A continuing question is how some of these innovations might be brought to scale. The culture of higher education has typically been one of individual effort, with each program or institution taking pride in its "unique," homegrown program features. Greater state and federal leadership in early childhood teacher preparation may create incentives to remove those barriers.

Toward the Improvement of Higher Education: Gaps, Challenges, and Actions

This chapter has offered ample evidence of the obstacles facing efforts to improve higher education. Here we summarize these obstacles before outlining some urgently needed actions.

Research Gaps and Challenges

A major theme identified at the beginning of this chapter, and echoed throughout, is the lack of research in early childhood teacher education. We have observed specific, significant research gaps in every one of the major components of early childhood higher education depicted in Figure 26.1. Much of the research to date has been descriptive, and even this descriptive literature is far from complete. We do not yet have descriptions of all the components outlined in Figure 26.1; for example, we do not have comprehensive descriptive data on content or pedagogy across early childhood teacher education. Statistics about coverage of specific topics (e.g., diversity) in separate courses does not get at more complex questions about the value of embedding such content across courses and field experiences versus "delivering" content via discrete courses. As we have seen, except for a few larger surveys, most descriptive studies have been conducted by individual or small groups of faculty members, focused on specific features of their own programs with relatively small samples, and have covered only brief periods of time.

Moving beyond description, the existing literature does offer insights into the relations between and among some components of Figure 26.1, such as relations between teachers' implementation of effective practices and short- and long-term child outcomes. Yet few empirical studies have attempted to make systematic connections between the higher education system and these later teaching practices and outcomes, with the recent college-level implementation of aspects of the CLASS and MTP being a promising exception. The domain of family outcomes remains entirely unstudied.

To move into the next generation of early childhood higher education research, the field has numerous challenges to overcome. Challenges include (1) the absence of an overall research agenda that can serve as a road map for guiding future research efforts; (2) assessment tools and methods that are not adequate to capture the complexities of early childhood teacher education programs; the knowledge, skills, and attitudes of graduates; characteristics of effective early childhood program and classroom practices; and the learning and development of young children and their families; (3) limited faculty capacity to conduct high-quality early childhood research because of an inadequate pipeline of well-prepared future researchers and limited institutional supports for early childhood faculty to embrace and conduct research; and (4) a dearth of interdisciplinary teams that use rigorous methods and are able to design, conduct, analyze, and interpret research on critical higher education issues from multiple perspectives.

Policy Gaps and Challenges

One of the most pervasive and complicated policy challenges is the fragmentation of professional development initiatives at national, state, and local levels. This fragmentation has had a direct impact on the effectiveness of higher education. Each sector, including higher education, has a different funding stream for professional development, and a variety of standards, licensure and certification programs, and other quality assurance initiatives, each with its own related professional development components. Further complicating the fragmentation are the diverse professional development funds and requirements across early childhood disciplines—including education, special education, and allied health—and service providers—including Head Start, child care, health, mental health, and PreK. All of this impacts both resources for and integration of professional preparation within higher education. This challenge is long-standing, has been decried in the literature (Winton, McCollum, & Catlett, 1997, 2008), and still manages to elude solutions. The increased attention to early childhood professional development has meant the availability of more state money, mostly in the form of nonrecurring ARRA dollars, but too often that has meant additional disconnected efforts, without sufficient attention to quality or collaboration, including collaboration between higher education and other parts of the professional development system. Policymakers have not taken steps to overcome the traditions and turf issues that continue to isolate higher education and that keep cross-sector collaboration at the level of lip service.

A second and related policy challenge is the lack of agreement across sectors on a set of national and state professional preparation standards and related competencies,[4] based on the best available research on effective practices and interventions for educating and supporting the development of each child (Winton & West, 2011). Despite promising efforts at coordination and alignment, the existence of separate professional preparation standards (also called "personnel preparation standards") for general early childhood education (NAEYC) and early childhood special education (DEC/CEC) persists. A further concern surrounds the alignment of various state standards with those of the relevant national organizations.

In Stayton and colleagues' (2009) review of state licensure/certification standards for early childhood special educators, most state personnel said they used national standards as the basis for their state standards. However, content analysis of the state standards found little to no correlation with NAEYC and CEC/DEC standards. Furthermore, state competencies developed within the child care sector seldom align either with state teacher licensure standards or with national standards for personnel preparation.

This complex and often confusing context makes it difficult for early childhood educators to understand the professional development system and to know how to move across different parts of the system within and beyond higher education. It also creates obstacles in developing common measures and tools for assessing teachers' and teacher educators' practices. In turn, this limits our ability to measure the impact of higher education on learners' performance, or to examine the impact of higher education compared with, or linked to, other professional development activities.

A third challenge is presented by the lack of policies that create and support expectations for faculty professional development. Expectations for "highly qualified teachers" have not been accompanied by similar expectations for faculty. State and federal resources have not been directed toward helping faculty members to update their knowledge and skills about (1) emerging research-based approaches and strategies for working with children and families, and (2) research-based approaches for teaching early educators. In earlier sections of this chapter we have referred to some promising approaches for providing this kind of faculty support; however, such approaches need rigorous evaluation in light of differing characteristics of institutions, faculty, and learners. Linking back to the discussion of research challenges, significant investments will be needed to scale up "promising practices" and to ensure the fidelity of their implementation.

Taking Action

Daunting obstacles require bold, creative solutions. The continuing lack of research on a broad range of higher education issues should not prevent action, although it makes rigorous evaluation of these action steps especially important. The following steps are likely to move us forward in improving higher education's impact on future teachers, young children, and their families:

1. Convene a federal interagency collaborative and interdisciplinary experts to jointly develop and fund a comprehensive *research agenda* on early childhood higher education, and a grants program to support higher education innovation, similar to what the U.S. Department of Education's OSEP has done for personnel preparation in early childhood special education.
2. Make significant, systematic investments in ongoing support and *professional development for higher education faculty*, targeting the content knowledge, attitudes, pedagogical skills, and research expertise that are most likely to be linked to graduates' ability to implement evidence-based practices with children most at risk of negative outcomes, and to positively influence their families.
3. Invest in a *pipeline of diverse, well-prepared future faculty* with competence to positively influence students and the broader early childhood field through robust preparation in content, pedagogy, and research and evaluation. This requires attention to expanding the number of doctoral programs, linking with existing interdisciplinary programs in early childhood special education, and expanding support for graduate students.

4. Engage leadership and provide funding to ensure that higher education has a meaningful role in *cross-sector professional development systems*, and that preservice and inservice professional development are viewed as an integrated whole.
5. Continue to create *higher education pathways and incentives* for early childhood teachers to participate in degree programs that are accessible, affordable, *and* of high quality.

Young children in Head Start, PreK, and child care programs have no idea whether their teachers went to college, let alone what kind of program they attended or what courses they took. Young children do have a sense, however, about whether their teachers enjoy being with them and their families; challenge them with new ideas and activities; talk with them about interesting things; and create a safe, organized environment. Parents and policymakers expect these same behaviors and competencies from teachers of young children. These and related competencies can be promoted by higher education programs if those programs, in turn, have the support they need to implement effective approaches to educating future early childhood teachers—and if they are part of a comprehensive system of professional development.

Notes

1. Although there are several different kinds of baccalaureate degrees (e.g., BS), in this chapter the term "BA" is used as a shorthand descriptor for all baccalaureate degrees and programs.
2. The terms "licensure" and "certification" are sometimes used interchangeably. However, the National Council for Accreditation of Teacher Education (NCATE) reserves the term "licensure" for a state government agency's official recognition that an individual is approved to practice because the person has met specific professional qualifications. "Certification" is sometimes granted by nongovernmental organizations or associations; an example would be the "Accomplished Teacher Certification" of the National Board for Professional Teaching Standards (NBPTS).
3. Although not in Bornfreund's (2011) list, the state of North Carolina also offers a blended license, birth through kindergarten (Myers, Griffin, Telekei, Taylor, & Wheeler, 1998).
4. The terminology itself gets in the way of consistency and coordination, with the term "personnel preparation standards" used by CEC/DEC; "professional preparation program standards" used by NAEYC; "licensure" or "certification standards" used by state agencies; and "competencies" used by various groups, including state child care/professional development groups.

References

Ackerman, D. J. (2004). States' efforts in improving the qualifications of early care and education teachers. *Educational Policy, 18*, 311–337.

Ackerman, D. J. (2005). Getting teachers from here to there: Examining issues related to an early care and education teacher policy. *Early Childhood Research and Practice, 7*(1). Retrieved from *ecrp. uiuc.edu/v7n1/ackerman.html*.

Association of Teacher Educators. (2008). Standards for teacher educators. Washington, DC: Author. Retrieved from *www.ate1.org/pubs/uploads/tchredstds0308.pdf*.

Barnett, W. S., Epstein, D. J., Friedman, A. H., Sansanelli, R. A., & Hustedt, J. T. (2009). *The state of preschool 2009*. Princeton, NJ: National Institute for Early Education Research. Retrieved from *www.researchconnections.org/childcare/resources/18557?q=barnett+frede+sansanelli*.

Bogard, K., Traylor, F., & Takanishi, R. (2008). Teacher education and PK outcomes: Are we asking the right questions? *Early Childhood Research Quarterly, 23*(1), 1–6.

Bornfreund, L. (2011). *Getting in sync: Revamping the preparation of teachers in preK, kindergarten, and the early grades*. Washington, DC: New America Foundation.

Bowman, B. T., Donovan, M. S., & Burns, M. S. (2001). *Eager to learn: Educating our preschoolers.* Washington, DC: National Academies Press.

Boyd, D. J., Grossman, P. L., Lankford, H., Loeb, S., & Wyckoff, J. (2009). Teacher preparation and student achievement. *Educational Evaluation and Policy Analysis, 31*(4), 416–440.

Bueno, M., Darling-Hammond, L., & Gonzales, D. M. (2010). *A matter of degrees: Preparing teachers for the Pre-K classroom.* Washington, DC: Pre-K Now.

Burchinal, M., Hyson, M., & Zaslow, M. (2008). Competencies and credentials for early childhood educators: What do we know and what do we need to know? *NHSA Dialog Brief, 11*(1), 1–7.

Center for the Child Care Workforce. (2007). *EC E-learning: A national review of early childhood education distance learning programs.* Washington, DC: Author.

Center for the Study of Child Care Employment. (2008). *Early childhood educator competencies: A literature review of current best practices, and a public input process on next steps for California.* Berkeley: Center for the Study of Child Care Employment, Institute for Research on Labor and Employment, University of California at Berkeley. Retrieved from *www.irle.berkeley.edu/cscce/pdf/competencies_report08.pdf.*

Chang, F., Early, D. M., & Winton, P. J. (2005). Early childhood teacher preparation in special education at 2- and 4-year institutions of higher education. *Journal of Early Intervention, 27*(2), 110–124.

Cochran-Smith, M. (2003). Learning and unlearning: The education of teacher educators. *Teaching and Teacher Education, 19,* 5–28.

Cochran-Smith, M., Feiman-Nemser, S., McIntyre, D. J., & Demers, K. E. (2008). *Handbook of research on teacher education: Enduring questions in changing contexts* (3rd ed.). New York: Routledge.

Council for Exceptional Children/Division for Early Childhood (CEC/DEC). (2008). Early childhood special education/early intervention (birth to age 8) specialist standards with CEC advanced common core. Retrieved August 11, 2009, from *www.dec-sped.org/uploads/docs/about_dec/position_concept_papers/dec%20ecse-ei%20w_cec%20advanced%20standards%2010-08.pdf.*

Council for Professional Recognition. (2006). *The Child Development Associate assessment system and competency standards.* Washington, DC: Author.

Daniel, J., & Friedman, S. (2005). Taking the next step: Preparing teachers to work with culturally and linguistically diverse young children. *Young Children, Beyond the Journal.* Retrieved from *journal.naeyc.org/btj/200511/danielfriedmanbtj1105.pdf.*

Darling-Hammond, L., Holtzman, D. J., Gatlin, S. J., & Heilig, J. V. (2005). Does teacher preparation matter?: Evidence about teacher certification, Teach for America, and teacher effectiveness. *Education Policy Analysis Archives, 13,* 1–47.

Diamond, R. M. (2006, September 8). Why colleges are so hard to change. *Inside Higher Ed.* Retrieved from *www.insidehighered.com/views/2006/09/08/diamond.*

Dower, C., O'Neil, E. H., & Hough, H. J. (2001, September). *Profiling the professions: A model for evaluating emerging health professions.* San Francisco: University of California, Center for the Health Professions.

Dunlap, G., Strain, P. S., Fox, L., Carta, J., Conroy, M., Smith, B., et al. (2006). Prevention and intervention with young children's challenging behavior: A summary of current knowledge. *Behavioral Disorders, 32,* 29–45.

Early, D. M., Maxwell, K. L., Burchinal, M., Alva, S., Bender, R. H., Bryant, D., et al. (2007). Teachers' education, classroom quality, and young children's academic skills: Results from seven studies of preschool programs. *Child Development, 78*(2), 558–580.

Early, D. M., & Winton, P. J. (2001). Preparing the workforce: Early childhood teacher preparation at 2- and 4-year institutions of higher education. *Early Childhood Research Quarterly, 16*(3), 285–306.

Education Commission of the States. (2010). *P–16.* Denver, CO: Author. Retrieved from *www.ecs.org/html/issue.asp?issueid=76.*

File, N., & Gullo, D. F. (2002). A comparison of early childhood and elementary education students' beliefs about primary classroom teaching practices. *Early Childhood Research Quarterly, 17*(1), 126–137.

Florez, I. R. (2009). *The effects of instructional method on preservice teachers' learning, cognitive processes, and decision-making skills.* Doctoral dissertation, available from Dissertation Express database (UMI No. 3354943).

Forer, B., Rochon Flanagan, K., & Beach, J. (n.d.). *Faculty survey report: Prepared for the Child Care Human Resources Sector Council Training Strategy Project.* Ottawa: Child Care Human Resources Sector Council.

Gilkerson, L. (2001). Integrating an understanding of brain development into early childhood education. *Infant Mental Health Journal, 22*(1–2), 174–187.

Goble, C. B., & Horm, D. M. (2009). Infant–toddler services through community collaboration. *Zero to Three, 29*(6), 18–22.

Goffin, S. G. (1996). Child development knowledge and early childhood teacher preparation: Assessing the relationship—A special collection. *Early Childhood Research Quarterly, 11*, 117–133.

Hamre, B. K., Pianta, R. C., Burchinal, M., Field, S., Locasale-Crouch, J., & Downer, J. (in press). A course on supporting early language and literacy development through effective teacher–child interactions: Effects on teacher beliefs, knowledge, and practice. *American Education Research Journal.*

Hemmeter, M. L., Santos, R. M., & Ostrosky, M. (2008). Preparing early childhood educators to address young children's social–emotional development and challenging behavior: A survey of higher education programs in nine states. *Journal of Early Intervention, 30*(4), 321–340.

Herzenberg, S., Price, M., & Bradley, D. (2005). *Losing ground in early childhood education: Declining workforce qualifications in an expanding industry.* Washington, DC: Economic Policy Institute.

Hestenes, L. L., La Paro, K. M., Scott-Little, C., Chakravarthi, S., Lower, J. K., Cranor, A., et al. (2009). Team teaching in an early childhood interdisciplinary program: A decade of lessons learned. *Journal of Early Childhood Teacher Education, 30*(2), 172–183.

Horm-Wingerd, D., Hyson, M., & Karp, N. (2000). Introduction. *New teachers for a new century: The future of early childhood professional preparation.* Washington, DC: U.S. Department of Education.

Hyson, M. (Ed.). (2003). *Preparing early childhood professionals: NAEYC's standards for programs.* Washington, DC: National Association for the Education for Young Children.

Hyson, M. (2008). *Preparing teachers to promote young children's mathematical competence.* Unpublished report to National Research Council's Committee on Early Childhood Mathematics. Washington, DC: National Research Council.

Hyson, M., Tomlinson, H. B., & Morris, C. A. S. (2009). Quality improvement in early childhood teacher education: Faculty perspectives and recommendations for the future. *Early Childhood Research and Practice, 11*(1). Retrieved from *ecrp.uiuc.edu/v11n1/hyson.html.*

Hyson, M., & Whittaker, J. (2012). Professional development in early childhood systems. In S. L. Kagan & K. Kauerz (Eds.), *Early childhood systems: Transforming early learning* (pp. 104–118). New York: Teachers College Press.

Improving Head Start for School Readiness Act, Public Law No. 110-134 (2007).

Johnson, J., Fiene, R., McKinnon, K., & Babu, S. (2010). *A study of ECE pre-service teacher education at major universities in 38 PreK states* (Final Report to the Foundation for Child Development). State College: Pennsylvania State University.

Kagan, S. L., & Kauerz, K. (Eds.). (2012). *Early childhood systems: Transforming early learning.* New York: Teachers College Press.

Kelley, P. J., & Camilli, G. (2007). *The impact of teacher education on outcomes in center-based early childhood education programs: A meta-analysis* (NIEER Working Paper). New Brunswick, NJ: National Institute of Early Education Research. Retrieved from *nieer.org/docs/?docid=185.*

Kennedy, M. (1996). Research genres in teacher education. In F. Murray (Ed.), *The teacher educator's handbook: Building a knowledge base for the preparation of teachers* (pp. 120–152). San Francisco: Jossey-Bass.

Kim, M. M., Andrews, R. L., & Carr, D. L. (2004). Traditional versus integrated preservice teacher education curriculum: A case study. *Journal of Teacher Education, 55*(4), 341–356.

Klecka, C. L., Odell, S. J., Houston, W. R., & McBee, R. H. (Eds.). (2009). *Visions for teacher educators: Perspectives on the Association of Teacher Educators' standards.* Lanham, MD: Rowman & Littlefield.

Kleinhammer-Tramill, J., Tramill, J., & Brace, M. (2010). Contexts, funding history, and implications for evaluating the Office of Special Education Programs' investment in personnel preparation. *Journal of Special Education, 43,* 195–205.

Knapp, L. G., Kelly-Reid, J. E., & Ginder, S. A. (2009). *Postsecondary institutions and price of attendance in the United States: Fall 2008, degrees and other awards conferred: 2007–08, and 12-month enrollment: 2007–08* (NCES 2009-165). Washington, DC: National Center for Education Statistics, Institute of Education Sciences, U.S. Department of Education.

La Paro, K. M., Maynard, C., Scott-Little, C., & Thomason, A. (2010, June). *Assessing pre-service teachers' classroom practices: Using the CLASS in teacher education.* Paper presented at the National Association for the Education of Young Children Professional Development Institute, Phoenix, AZ.

La Paro, K. M., Siepak, K., & Scott-Little, C. (2009). Assessing beliefs of preservice early childhood education teachers using Q-sort methodology. *Journal of Early Childhood Teacher Education, 30* (1), 22–36.

LeMoine, S. (2008). *Workforce designs: A policy blueprint for state early childhood professional development systems.* Washington, DC: National Association for the Education of Young Children.

Lim, C., Maxwell, K. L., Able-Boone, H., & Zimmer, C. R. (2009). Cultural and linguistic diversity in early childhood teacher preparation: The impact of contextual characteristics on coursework and practica. *Early Childhood Research Quarterly, 24*(1), 64–76.

Lobman, C., Ryan, S., & McLaughlin, J. (2005). Reconstructing teacher education to prepare qualified preschool teachers: Lessons from New Jersey. *Early Childhood Research and Practice, 7* (2). Retrieved from *ecrp.uiuc.edu/v7n2/lobman.html.*

Maude, S. P., Catlett, C., Moore, S., Sanchez, S. Y., Thorp, E. K., & Corso, R. M. (2010). Infusing diversity constructs in preservice teacher preparation: The impact of a systematic faculty development strategy. *Infants and Young Children, 23*(2), 103–121.

Maxwell, K. L., Feild, C. C., & Clifford, R. M. (2005). Defining and measuring professional development in early childhood research. In M. Zaslow & I. Martinez-Beck (Eds.), *Critical issues in early childhood professional development* (pp. 21–48). Baltimore: Brookes.

Maxwell, K. L., Lim, C. I., & Early, D. M. (2006). *Early childhood teacher preparation programs in the United States: National report.* Chapel Hill: University of North Carolina, FPG Child Development Institute.

McNaughton, D., Hamlin, D., McCarthy, J., Head-Reeves, D. M., & Schreiner, M. (2007). Learning to listen: Teaching an active listening strategy to preservice education professionals. *Topics in Early Childhood Special Education, 27*(4), 223–231.

Miller, P. S., & Losardo, A. (2002). Graduates' perceptions of strengths and needs in interdisciplinary teacher preparation for early childhood education: A state study. *Teacher Education and Special Education, 25,* 309–319.

Monroe, L., & Horm, D. (in press). Using a logic model to evaluate undergraduate instruction in a laboratory preschool. *Early Education and Development.*

Myers, V. L., Griffin, H. C., Telekei, J., Taylor, J., & Wheeler, L. (1998). Birth through kindergarten teacher training. *Childhood Education, 74*(3), 154–159.

National Association for the Education of Young Children. (2009). *NAEYC standards for early childhood professional preparation programs: Position statement.* Washington, DC: Author.

National Association for the Education of Young Children. (2010). *Accreditation handbook: NAEYC Early Childhood Associate Degree Accreditation.* Washington, DC: Author.

National Association for the Education of Young Children. (2011). *State early care and education public policy developments: FY 2011.* Washington, DC: Author. Retrieved from *www.naeyc.org/files/naeyc/file/policy/state/state%20ece%20public%20policy%20developments%202_11_2.pdf.*

National Child Care Information Center (NCCIC). (2009). Foundations supporting early childhood care and education. Fairfax, VA: Author. Retrieved from *nccic.acf.hhs.gov/poptopics/foundations.html*.

National Council for Accreditation of Teacher Education (NCATE). (2010). *Transforming teacher education through clinical practice: A national strategy to prepare effective teachers.* Washington, DC: Author.

National Early Literacy Panel. (2009). *Developing early literacy: Report of the National Early Literacy Panel* (Executive Summary). Washington, DC: National Institute for Literacy.

National Professional Development Center on Inclusion, University of North Carolina, FPG Child Development Institute. (2008). *What do we mean by professional development in the early childhood field?* Chapel Hill, NC: Author. Retrieved from *www.fpg.unc.edu/~npdci*.

National Research Council. (2010). *Preparing teachers: Building evidence for sound policy.* Washington, DC: National Academies Press.

National Research Council, Division of Behavior and Social Sciences and Education, Center for Education, and Committee on Early Childhood Mathematics. (2009). *Mathematics learning in early childhood: Paths toward excellence and equity.* Washington, DC: National Academies Press.

Pianta, R., Hitz, R., & West, B. (2010). *Increasing the application of development sciences knowledge in educator preparation: Policy and practice issues.* Washington, DC: National Council for Accreditation of Teacher Education.

Pianta, R. C., & Stuhlman, M. (2004). Teacher–child relationships and children's success in the first years of school. *School Psychology Review, 33*(3), 444–458.

Ray, A., Bowman, B. T., & Robbins, J. (2006). *Preparing early childhood teachers to successfully educate all children: The contribution of four-year undergraduate teacher preparation programs.* New York: Foundation for Child Development.

Recchia, S. L., Beck, L., Esposito, A., & Tarrant, K. (2009). Diverse field experiences as a catalyst for preparing high quality early childhood teachers. *Journal of Early Childhood Teacher Education, 30*(2), 105–122.

Recchia, S. L., & Shin, M. (2010). "Baby teachers": How pre-service early childhood students transform their conceptions of teaching and learning through an infant practicum. *Early Years: An International Journal of Research and Development, 30*(2), 135–145.

Ryan, S., & Hyland, N. (2010). Preparing early childhood teachers to enact social justice pedagogies. In O. Saracho & B. Spodek (Eds.), *Contemporary perspectives on language and cultural diversity in early childhood education* (pp. 235–249). Charlotte, NC: Information Age.

Scott-Little, C., La Paro, K., Thomason, A. C., Pianta, R., Hamre, B., Downer, J., et al. (2011). Implementation of a course focused on language and literacy within teacher–child interactions: Instructor and student perspectives across three institutions of higher education. *Journal of Early Childhood Teacher Education, 32*, 200–224.

Sheridan, S. M., Edwards, C. P., Marvin, C. A., & Knoche, L. (2009). Professional development in early childhood programs: Process issues and research needs. *Early Education and Development, 20*(3), 377–401.

Snyder, P., & Wolfe, B. (2008). The big three process components of effective professional development: Needs assessment, evaluation, and follow-up. In P. J. Winton, J. A. McCollum, & C. Catlett (Eds.), *Practical approaches to early childhood professional development: Evidence, strategies, and resources* (pp. 13–51). Washington, DC: Zero to Three.

Stayton, V. D., Dietrich, S. L., Smith, B. J., Bruder, M. B., Mogro-Wilson, C., & Swigart, A. (2009). State certification requirements for early childhood special educators. *Infants and Young Children, 23*(1), 4–12.

Steinert, Y., Mann, K., Centeno, A., Dolmans, D., Spencer, J., Gelula, M., et al. (2006). A systematic review of faculty development initiatives designed to improve teaching effectiveness in medical education: BEME Guide No. 8. *Medical Teacher, 28*(6), 497–526.

Strickland, D. S., & Riley-Ayers, S. (2006). *Early literacy: Policy and practice in the preschool years.* New Brunswick, NJ: National Institute for Early Education Research.

Szente, J. (2008). Preparing preservice teachers to work with culturally and linguistically diverse children: A service learning experience. *Journal of Early Childhood Teacher Education, 29*(2), 140–145.

T.E.A.C.H. Early Childhood Assistance and Quality Assurance Center. (2010, Spring). *T.E.A.C.H. times*. Chapel Hill, NC: Author. Retrieved from *www.childcareservices.org/_downloads/teach-timesspring_10.pdf*.

Trepanier-Street, M., Adler, M. A., & Taylor, J. (2007). Impact of a mentoring experience on college students' beliefs about early childhood development. *Early Childhood Education Journal, 34*(5), 337–343.

Trivette, C. M. (2005). Effectiveness of guided design learning strategy on the acquisition of adult problem-solving skills. *Bridges, 3*(1), 1–18.

U.S. Census Bureau. (2005). American Community Survey 2005. Retrieved November 10, 2010, from *www.census.gov*.

U.S. Department of Education, Office of Special Education and Rehabilitative Services, Office of Special Education Programs. (2010). *29th Annual Report to Congress on the Implementation of the Individuals with Disabilities Education Act, 2007* (Vol. 1). Washington, DC: Author.

U.S. Department of Education, Policy and Program Studies Service. (2010). *Toward the identification of features of effective professional development for early childhood educators: Literature review*. Washington, DC: Author.

Vartuli, S., & Rohs, J. (2009). Early childhood prospective teacher pedagogical belief shifts over time. *Journal of Early Childhood Teacher Education, 30*(4), 310–327.

Washington, V. (2008). *Role, relevance, reinvention: Higher education in the field of early care and education*. Boston: Wheelock College.

Whitebook, M. (2003). *Early education quality: Higher teacher qualifications for better learning environments: A review of the literature*. Berkeley: University of California, Berkeley, Center for the Study of Child Care Employment.

Whitebook, M., Gomby, D., Bellm, D., Sakai, L., & Kipnis, F. (2009). *Preparing teachers of young children: The current state of knowledge, and a blueprint for the future: Executive summary*. Berkeley: University of California, Berkeley, Center for the Study of Child Care Employment.

Whitebook, M., Gomby, D., Sakai, L., & Kipnis, F. (2009). *Teacher preparation and professional development in grades K–12 and in early care and education: Differences and similarities, and implications for research*. Berkeley: University of California, Berkeley, Center for the Study of Child Care Employment, Institute for Research on Labor and Employment.

Whitebook, M., Sakai, L., & Kipnis, F. (2010). *Beyond homes and centers: The workforce in three California early childhood infrastructure organizations: Executive summary*. Berkeley: Center for the Study of Child Care Employment, Institute for Research on Labor and Employment, University of California at Berkeley.

Whitebook, M., Sakai, L., Kipnis, F., Almaraz, M., Suarez, E., & Bellm, D. (2008). *Learning together: A study of six B.A. completion cohort programs in early care and education: Year I report*. Berkeley: Center for the Study of Child Care Employment, University of California at Berkeley.

Willer, B. A., Lutton, A., & Ginsberg, M. (2011). The importance of early childhood teacher preparation: The perspectives and positions of the National Association for the Education of Young Children. In E. Zigler, W. S. Gilliam, & W. S. Barnett (Eds.), *Current debates and issues in preschool education* (pp. 77–83). Baltimore: Brookes.

Wilson, S., Floden, R., & Ferrini-Mundy, J. (2001). *Teacher preparation research: Current knowledge, gaps, and recommendations*. Seattle: Center for the Study of Teaching and Policy, University of Washington. Retrieved August 6, 2008, from *depts.washington.edu/ctpmail/pdfs/teacherprep-Wwffm-02-2001.pdf*.

Winton, P. (2010). Professional development and quality initiatives: Two essential components of an early childhood system. In P. W. Wesley & V. Buysse (Eds.), *The quest for quality: Promising innovations for early childhood programs* (pp. 113–129). Baltimore: Brookes.

Winton, P., McCollum, J., & Catlett, C. (Eds.). (1997). *Reforming personnel preparation in early intervention: Issues, models and practical strategies*. Baltimore: Brookes.

Winton, P. J., & Catlett, C. (2009). Statewide efforts to enhance early childhood personnel preparation programs to support inclusion: Overview and lessons learned. *Infants and Young Children, 22*(1), 63–70.

Winton, P. J., McCollum, J. A., & Catlett, C. (Eds.). (2008). *Practical approaches to early childhood professional development: Evidence, strategies and resources.* Washington, DC: Zero to Three Press.

Winton, P. J., & West, T. (2011). Early childhood competencies: Sitting on the shelf or guiding professional development? In C. Howes & R. C. Pianta (Eds.), *Foundations for teaching excellence: Connecting early childhood quality rating, professional development, and competency systems in states* (pp. 69–92). Baltimore: Brookes.

Zaslow, M., & Martinez-Beck, I. (Eds.). (2006). *Critical issues in early childhood professional development.* Baltimore: Brookes.

Zaslow, M., Tout, K., Halle, T., & Starr, R. (2010). *Professional development for early educators: Reviewing and revising conceptualizations.* Unpublished document.

Zaslow, M., Tout, K., Halle, T., Whittaker, J. E. V., & Lavelle, B. (2010). Emerging research on early childhood professional development. In S. B. Neuman & M. L. Kamil (Eds.), *Preparing teachers for the early childhood classroom: Proven models and key principles* (pp. 17–47). Baltimore: Brookes.

CHAPTER 27

Making the Case

Why Credentialing and Certification Matter

Sue Bredekamp and Stacie G. Goffin

Within the field of early childhood education, and to some extent outside of it, the value of formal preparation for early childhood teachers is being hotly debated. Presently, this debate focuses on baccalaureate degrees and whether they are necessary for effective preschool teaching (Early et al., 2007; Kelley & Camilli, 2007; Whitebook & Ryan, 2011). Although attention is appropriately shifting to the content of degrees, credentialing and certification usually are afterthoughts in these discussions.

This chapter challenges this long-standing tendency. It takes the stance that early childhood teacher credentialing and certification matter greatly. We acknowledge that much needs to be done to strengthen the preparation of early childhood education (ECE) teachers, so the foundation upon which credentials and certifications rest has merit, yet credentialing and certification requirements *drive* the content of preparation and the qualifications expected of early childhood educators, giving these systems the power to create a unified and aligned approach to teachers' preparation and ongoing development. Crucially, they can play a key role in decisions that affect *all* teachers and children—not just those participating in publicly funded programs.

As a result, ECE teacher credentials and certification are more important than generally recognized. Ultimately, they are central to the accountability of the ECE teaching profession and its responsibility to children, families, and the general public. This is so because, first, and most importantly, they impact (often negatively) the quality of practice, and consequently, children's learning and developmental outcomes. This influence derives from the fact that credentials and certifications significantly impact the configuration, content, and quality of teacher preparation programs and the competency of graduates. In turn, these requirements expand and/or limit employment opportunities available to ECE teachers, which directly affect the occupational options available to individuals and the teaching pool available to the ECE field. Thus, credentials and certification requirements involve high

Authors are listed in alphabetical order.

stakes for children, teachers, and programs—both teacher preparation programs and those that educate and care for young children.

No other time in history has seen ECE as high on the national agenda as it now is. Preschool education, in particular, is widely touted for its short-term ability to enhance school readiness and its long-term potential to close the achievement gap, lessen crime, and improve the school and life success of children from low-income families. At the same time, it is clear that the quality and effectiveness of the large majority of early childhood programs are inadequate to the task (Burchinal et al., 2008; Early et al., 2005; Hamre & Pianta, 2007; Howes et al., 2008). To accomplish the lofty goals now associated with ECE, attention must shift to the content knowledge and pedagogical skills practitioners need when assuming the responsibility of teaching young children.

Yet a singular focus on degrees (at whatever level) is not sufficient. The time has come to examine the question of teacher qualifications within the broader framework of discipline-specific certification and credentialing systems. As currently configured, these two systems contribute to the problem of inadequately prepared ECE teachers and poor quality ECE programs because of their structures and lack of consensus regarding the requisite knowledge and skills of early childhood teacher educators, resulting in uneven coverage of relevant content and pedagogy, and reliance on theoretical frameworks viewed by some as outdated. Teacher credentials and certifications need to be transformed so they can become effective parts of a solution.

Toward this end, this chapter argues the value of certification and credentialing as systemic, strategic levers for strengthening the overall effectiveness of ECE. Our goal is to make the case for specialized ECE teacher licensure and age-focused credentials. This recommendation is consistent with long-held positions of the National Association for the Education of Young Children (NAEYC), as expressed in a joint position paper with the Association of Teacher Educators (ATE & NAEYC, 1991), and with the National Association of Early Childhood Teacher Educators (2008), as well as with policy statements from the New America Foundation (Bornfreund, 2011) and American Association of Colleges for Teacher Education (AACTE; 2004). Given this volume's emphasis, we give special focus to preschoolers, 3–5 years old, in center- and school-based settings.

We begin by offering definitions and an overview of current ECE credentials and certifications. Then we discuss the importance of credentialing and certification systems—including what we currently know about their effectiveness—and highlight the high-stakes decisions that emerge from these systems. The context of credentials and certification in ECE's evolution follows. We conclude with a vision for the future that makes the case for the critical role of credentialing and certification in improving the quality of ECE teacher performance, and consequently, children's learning and development.

ECE Teacher Credentials and Certifications

One of many challenges in discussing ECE credentials and certification is lack of shared definitions. To minimize confusion, we begin by defining general terminology. We then describe ECE credentials and certifications having greatest impact in the field.

A Word about Definitions

Early childhood covers the developmental period from birth through age 8, during which time children are cared for and educated by adults in diverse settings. Regardless of sponsorship of the program in which children are served, we use the word *teacher* to refer to those adults with primary responsibility for a group of children (NAEYC, 2005, p. 12). *Assistant teachers* are defined as those adults who work under the direct supervision of a teacher (NAEYC, 2005, p. 12).

The terms "certification," "licensure," and "credentialing" refer to an official document, permit, or authorization to practice. In public education, the term "teacher licensure" is commonly used because teachers are obligated to have a *license* in order to practice. In the ECE field, the term "certification" tends to be used when referring to teacher licensure, while the term "licensing" usually refers to regulation of programs rather than individuals. Still, since in ECE the term "certification" is intended to convey an authorization to practice, we use "licensure" and "certification" interchangeably.

"Credential" is a more general term and is used in ECE to refer to a specialized qualification, including various certificates and licenses (Kagan, Kauerz, & Tarrant, 2008, p. 29). Holding a credential, such as a bachelor's degree, may be required to obtain certification and/or to be employed in a particular teaching position or by a particular auspice, such as a public school setting. Teacher preparation programs typically are authorized by states to grant teaching certificates to their graduates, though usually an additional test administered by the state is required for legal authorization to teach. As a result, credentialing and certifying ECE teachers tend to be inextricably linked.

ECE Credential and Certification Systems and Their Use

Credentialing and certification systems have the most direct impact on individual teachers, and their career options and employment opportunities. Three primary credential and certification systems address the early childhood period: the Child Development Associate (CDA) National Credential; state teacher licensure requirements; and National Board for Professional Teaching Standards certification. Their stature and infrastructure offer the greatest potential for influencing the quality and effectiveness of teacher preparation and programs for children.

In some ECE sectors, the trend is toward increased preparation requirements, driven by program evaluation findings that demonstrate minimal or no effects on children's learning and development. Head Start, for example, has significantly raised teacher and assistant teacher qualifications. In 1988, after decades during which Head Start teachers were only required to have a CDA credential, Head Start began requiring 50% of teachers to have an associate degree. The most recent reauthorization of the Head Start Act in 2007 again raised the bar. By 2013, 50% of Head Start teachers must have a baccalaureate (BA) degree in early childhood education or coursework equivalent to a major in preschool teaching. Similarly, at least 50% of teacher assistants are required to have at least a CDA credential or be enrolled in an associate or BA degree program.

More recently, infant/toddler teachers in Early Head Start centers are now required to hold an infant/toddler CDA credential. Although Early Head Start is a relatively small part of the federal program, it is expected to grow significantly in the future as more states provide prekindergarten and Head Start serves increasing numbers of younger children. Finally, reflecting a national trend, Head Start is recognizing alternative certification (discussed below), specifically that offered by Teach for America (TFA). Future Head Start teachers may meet qualification requirements by earning a non-ECE-related BA, admission to TFA, passing a rigorous ECE exam such as Praxis II, and participating in TFA's preschool summer training and ongoing professional development.

Public school prekindergarten (PreK) programs demand the most in terms of ECE teacher qualifications. Of the 40 states that offer state-funded preschool, 27 require teachers to have a BA degree, although not necessarily in ECE (National Institute for Early Education

Research [NIEER], 2009). The remaining states employ PreK teachers holding an associate degree, CDA, or other state-approved credential. Only 16 of 40 states require a minimum of a CDA or equivalent for assistant teachers (Barnett et al., 2010). Interestingly, the *State of Preschool Yearbook*, produced by NIEER, does not document state information on teacher licensure.

At the other end of the continuum, child care centers, which are licensed by states as separate entities, have significantly lower teacher (usually called "staff") qualifications. Although 39 states have some minimum qualification, most often it is a high school diploma and experience (National Child Care Information and Technical Assistance Center [NCCI-TAC] & National Association for Regulatory Administration [NARA], 2010). Although some states list alternative minimum qualifications, of which a CDA credential is the most common, these are not requirements. With Head Start and PreK trending toward increasing teacher credentials, the historic divide between child care and early education is growing wider.

Each of the three major ECE credentialing systems is described next. Despite variation in the age range or level of qualification for which each of these credentials or certifications is granted, all are based on multiple sources of information. Each rests on educational and experiential prerequisites and requires demonstrated competence and knowledge of what and how to teach.

Child Development Associate National Credential

In ECE, the word *credential* almost inevitably is associated with the CDA National Credential. A CDA is an individual who has successfully completed the CDA assessment and demonstrated competence in the CDA competency goals through her or his work in a center-based, family child care, or home visitor program (Council for Professional Recognition, 2011). Center-based CDAs are credentialed by age group, either preschool (3- to 5-year-olds) or infant/toddler (birth to 36 months). A bilingual Spanish specialization also is available.

Eligibility requirements for the CDA credential include completion of 120 clock hours of formal training distributed across six competency goals and 13 functional areas, and 480 hours of experience working with children in the applicable group setting (Council for Professional Recognition, 2011). Formal education hours may or may not be credit bearing. The assessment process requires candidates to demonstrate competence through multiple sources of evidence: (1) a Professional Resource File; (2) parent opinion questionnaires; (3) observation of practice; (4) a written test; and (5) an oral interview.

Administered by the Council for Professional Recognition (Council) in Washington, DC, approximately 20,000 CDA credentials and 12,000 renewals are awarded annually. Although Head Start developed the CDA in the early 1970s, it was conceptualized from the outset as a new credential for the entire ECE field. Unfortunately, similar consensus did not—and does not now—exist regarding the professional role for which CDAs are qualified. Both the Council and the larger field as represented by NAEYC (1993) identify the CDA as the *first step* on an early childhood career pathway. The goal and expectation is that CDAs will be motivated and supported to pursue higher education in early childhood education. Despite this intent, the CDA is used by different sectors of the field and by policymakers as a qualification for roles that clearly demand different levels of competence, including assistant teacher, teacher, and center director.

CDA's largest client is private child care, presumably because licensing standards recognize (but do not require) CDA as a staff qualification. Additionally, as of 2011, NAEYC's early childhood program accreditation criteria require at least a CDA for assistant teachers. Bright Horizons Family Solutions, one of the largest companies providing employer-sponsored child care, uses CDA to qualify its staff because the national credential is recognized in virtually every state, as well as by NAEYC accreditation (*www.brighthorizons.com*). Approximately 24 states include CDA in their quality rating and improvement systems (QRIS; state- and/or community-based systems that offer structured and incremental steps for recognizing higher levels of program quality), and it also is part of the U.S. Department of Labor's Child Development Specialist Apprenticeship Program.

CDA also plays a significant role in U.S. military child care, the largest employer-sponsored child care system in the world. All branches of the military use CDA as the foundation for their child care teacher career ladder. The 1989 Military Child Care Act requires child care centers to implement a career ladder linking compensation to teachers' qualifications and professional development, as well as to become NAEYC accredited. Conveniently, CDA, a national (and potentially international) credential, is portable for teachers in military centers who frequently relocate.

While CDA credentialing decisions affect employment options to a lesser extent than state teacher licensure, CDA credentials are now required by some sectors of the ECE field. Furthermore, the number of CDAs who report receiving salary increases or promotions as a result of earning the credential has increased over time (Bailey, 2004).

Due to growing demand and the changing knowledge base, in 2011, the Council for Professional Recognition began the process of revising CDA candidate assessment instruments and procedures, and strengthening its infant/toddler assessment in response to the needs of Early Head Start. In addition, the Council is updating its home visitor credentialing process in anticipation of the demand for qualified home visitors as a result of new funding from the Administration for Children and Families.

On a smaller scale, the National Child Care Association, an organization of for-profit child care programs, offers a credential called the Certified Child Care Professional, with training and experience qualifications comparable to CDA. Several states have also developed their own child care certificates.

State Licensure of Early Childhood Teachers

In K–12 public education, teacher licensure is almost universally required. The process of teacher certification typically requires three components: (1) completion of a BA degree in a teacher preparation program, (2) a passing score on an examination (e.g., Praxis II) that usually covers general knowledge, content knowledge, and pedagogy; and (3) experience in clinical practice, whether during student teaching or the induction year. Importantly for this discussion, teacher licensure for early childhood teachers is based on auspice—in this instance, public schools.

Certification configurations vary considerably from state to state. They are typically defined by the grades for which candidates are eligible to teach, such as elementary education certificates that cover K–6. Early childhood teacher licensure configurations are extremely diverse, including birth through age 8, PreK to third grade, and almost everything in between, as illustrated in Figure 27.1 (Bornfreund, 2011). Today all but four states (California, Montana, Oregon, and Utah) offer specialized ECE certification covering *some portion* of the birth through 8 age range (Bornfreund, 2011). Yet rarely is an ECE teacher license *required* as a prerequisite to practice in the early grades.

NAEYC Standards for Early Childhood Professional Preparation Programs, which define ECE as birth through age 8, are designed to guide both teacher education programs and state licensure (ATE & NAEYC, 1991; NAEYC, 2010). As part of the National Council for Accreditation of Teacher Education's (NCATE) accreditation process, ECE teacher education programs must document compliance with NAEYC standards.

Comparing Licenses for Teaching in an Elementary School

State	Licenses Available	State	Licenses Available
AL	B-K; K-5; P-3	MT	K-8
AK	P-3; K-6; K-8	NE	B-3; K-6; K-8
AZ	B-3; K-8	NV	B-K; B-2; K-8
AR	P-4; 4-8	NH	P-3; K-6; K-8
CA	P-12 (in self-contained classroom)	NJ	P-3; K-5
CO	P-3; K-6	NM	B-3; K-8
CT	B-K; N-3; K-6	NY	B-2; 1-6
DC	P-3; 1-6; 4-8	NC	B-K; K-6
DE	B-2; K-6	ND	B-3; K-6; 1-6; K-8; 1-8
FL	B- Age 4; Age 3 – 3rd; K-6	OH	P-3; 4-9
GA	B- Age 5; P-5; 4-8	OK	B- Age 3; P-3; 1-8
HI	P-3; K-6	OR	K-8 (in self-contained classrooms)
ID	B-3*; K-8	PA	P-4; 4-8
IL	B-3; K-9**	RI	P-2; 1-6
IN	B-K; K-3; 4-6	SC	P-3; 2-6
IA	B-3; P-K; K-6	SD	B- Age 4; B-3; K-8
KS	B-K*; B-3*; K-6	TN	B-K*; P-3; K-6; 4-8
KY	B-K*; K-5	TX	P-4; P-6; 4-8
LA	P-3; 1-5; 4-8	UT	1-8***
ME	B- Age 5; K-3, K-8	VT	B-3; B- Age 6* K-3; K-6
MD	P-3; 1-6; 4-8	VA	P-3; P-6
MA	P-2; 1-6	WA	P-3; K-8
MI	B-3; K-5	WV	B-P; P-K; K-4
MN	B-3; K-6	WI	B- Age 8; B – Age 11; Age 6 – Age 12
MS	N-1; P-K; K-3; 4-8; K-6	WY	B- Age 5*; Ages 3-5; Age 3- 3rd; K-6; 7-8
MO	B-3; 1-6		(in self-contained classroom)

The number represents a grade level, unless otherwise specified: B = birth; P = pre-k; K = kindergarten; N = nursery
* = Blended Program ECE/Special Ed   ** = Additional Requirements to Teach Middle Grades
*** = To teach kindergarten, teachers who have a 1-8 license can obtain a K-3 endorsement.
Note: In self-contained classrooms, students have the same teacher for all core subject areas.
SOURCE: New America Foundation reporting based on state teacher licensure web pages.

FIGURE 27.1. State licensure: A national perspective. From Bornfreund (2011). New America Foundation, Creative Commons License. *www.newamericafoundation.net*. Reprinted by permission.

As more states begin to offer early childhood teacher licensure, though, the number of possible age/grade configurations for certification is increasing. Some licenses are birth through age 5, or birth through age 8, while others begin at age 3 or 4 and go through grades 2, 3, or even 4. Pennsylvania, for example, recently adopted an early childhood specialized certificate covering PreK through grade 4, despite the fact that fourth grade has never been considered part of the early childhood period. Additionally, some states offer joint early childhood and special education licenses to achieve better the goal of inclusion of children with disabilities and special needs (Stayton et al., 2009).

Beyond this certification labyrinth, it is important to note that many early childhood educators, particularly those working in programs serving children from birth to age 5, typically obtain degrees that do not lead to certification/licensure. These programs tend to reside in departments of child development and family studies or human ecology. While individual faculty members in these programs may use NAEYC's professional preparation standards to guide their program content, they are not overseen by a system of accountability comparable to NCATE.

Furthermore, the majority of ECE teacher preparation programs are in associate-degree-granting institutions (Early & Winton, 2001). Although no mandate exists for external oversight, these programs are eligible for accreditation by NAEYC (2010). And, as of 2011, 113 associate degree programs in 24 states are accredited, with 100 more in another 14 states in the process (*www.naeyc.org/ecada*). No formal connection exists between associate degree preparation and state teacher licensure systems. Some state governors, however, are mandating NAEYC accreditation of associate degree programs and articulation agreements between 2-year and 4-year institutions to ensure transferability of credit, a trend that should enable individuals to pursue higher education and teacher licensure more easily.

The enormous variation in teacher preparation and licensure across states means that early childhood teacher credentials and licenses are by no means equal from place to place, creating a significant barrier to developing a shared conceptual framework regarding the content knowledge, pedagogical skills, and dispositions needed of competent ECE teachers. On a practical level, this variation also undermines reciprocity (transferability of licensure to another state). In a highly mobile society, lack of reciprocity can further discourage prospective teachers from pursuing ECE study (Egertson, 2008).

Alternative Certification

A trend exists toward alternative certification, with almost 20% of teachers entering the K–12 teaching profession through this route, particularly in underserved geographic areas or among high-need populations (Boyd, Goldhaber, Lankford, & Wyckoff, 2007; Whitebook et al., 2009). Alternate route program requirements vary but typically include having a bachelor's degree, participating in a preservice training program ranging from 4 to 12 weeks, and experiencing ongoing mentoring and supervision (Whitebook, Gomby, Bellm, Sakai, & Kipnis, 2009). Teach for America, one of the better-known alternative systems, added an early childhood initiative in 2007 that is rapidly expanding in major urban districts throughout the country (see *www.teachforamerica.org*).

At this point, it should be noted that limited research exists at *any* level on the effectiveness of teacher licensure per se. Research on K–12 certification essentially finds no effects on the quality of teaching practice or student outcomes (Boyd et al., 2007). Like so many other aspects of education, it is difficult to isolate the effects of certification from variations in the quality of teacher preparation programs, the strengths of individual teachers, and the diverse characteristics of students and school environments.

This also holds true for teachers trained though alternative routes, although some studies find that teachers certified through alternative routes perform as well or better than traditionally certified teachers (Decker, Mayer, & Glazerman, 2004). An evaluation of the effectiveness of Teach For America PreK teachers in the District of Columbia found that children made significant progress in vocabulary and early mathematics, and exceeded national norms in letter recognition by the end of the school year (Zill, 2008). Results such as these undoubtedly influenced Head Start's inclusion of Teach for America in its new teacher qualification requirements.

National Board for Professional Teaching Standards

Founded in 1987, the National Board for Professional Teaching Standards (NBPTS) certifies highly accomplished teachers who successfully complete a rigorous evaluation process to assess the quality and effectiveness of their teaching (Gundling & Hyson, 2002; NBPTS, 2009). Prerequisites include a BA degree, valid teacher certificate, and at least 3 years of teaching experience with the age group for which one is seeking recognition.

The assessment includes several components. Candidates must submit a portfolio that includes (1) videotapes of their classroom interactions with students; (2) student work samples; and (3) a demonstration of how their work outside the classroom, with parents or in the community, impacts student learning (NBPTS, 2009). Additionally, candidates must complete six online assessment center exercises that measure their knowledge of content and pedagogy.

NBPTS offers an Early Childhood Generalist certificate covering ages 3–8; this certificate accounts for almost a one-fourth of Board-certified teachers (AACTE, Focus Council on Early Childhood Education, 2004). NAEYC actively participated in the development of this certificate, the standards for which are congruent, though not totally aligned, with NAEYC's initial teacher preparation standards (Gundling & Hyson, 2002; NBPTS, 2009).

Given the variations in school structures, NBPTS made a conscious decision to define certificates using ages rather than grades. Their Middle Childhood certificate covers ages 7–12, creating minimal overlap with their specialized ECE credential.

Although NBPTS certification is voluntary, 49 states recognize it, and 37 provide financial incentives for its achievement (Boyd et al., 2007). In some situations, NBPTS certification qualifies teachers for different roles, such as mentor teachers for new inductees or coaches for struggling teachers in their content area. NBPTS certification requires considerable investment of time and hard work by candidates, but it also accords significant public recognition, respect, and prestige—accolades rarely afforded public school teachers in America today.

Although research results on the efficacy of NBPTS certification are mixed, a majority of the studies find positive effects (NBPTS, 2007). These studies, however, do not tease out the effects of Early Childhood Generalist teachers. Under Congressional mandate, the National Research Council (NRC; 2008) conducted a rigorous and comprehensive review of this research and concluded that students taught by Board-certified teachers had higher achievement gains than those taught by teachers who did not apply for or achieve certification. The NRC also concluded that the NBPTS certification process has a positive impact on teacher retention and professional development. According to the report, NBPTS has elevated teaching to a higher level by creating national standards for the profession.

The Importance of ECE Teacher Credentials and Certification

Never has more been expected of the early care and education field and its teachers. More children than ever participate in ECE programs; as a result, more has never been at stake. ECE is expected to provide a level playing field in kindergarten and beyond for children from diverse backgrounds; elevate the results that can be achieved from K–12 education; and help to undergird the nation's future global competiveness. Yet despite the field's own role in fueling these expectations, program evaluation studies too often reveal that these expectations are unfilled.

Current attention to the effectiveness of ECE teachers is driven by a number of factors. First, a dramatic increase in knowledge from the developmental sciences (Barbarin & Wasik, 2009; Bredekamp, 2011; NCATE, 2010a; National Scientific Council on the Developing Child, 2007) is largely being ignored in practice. Second, recent research on the impact of teacher–child interactions and instructional strategies on child outcomes has raised the bar on expectations for early childhood practice (Barnett, 2011; Burchinal et al., 2008; Howes et al., 2008; Pianta, La Paro, & Hamre, 2008). Finally, evaluation studies of ECE programs have added to the knowledge base of what is necessary to promote children's learning and development in ECE settings, both in the near and long term (Pianta, Barnett, Burchinal, & Thornburg, 2009).

Additionally, forces beyond a burgeoning research and evaluation base are fostering expanded thinking about what early educators need to know and be able to do. Political powers are placing pressure on the field to provide consistently effective programs worthy of the level of public investment in ECE and capable of fulfilling public expectations—and in the process are raising the ante. The latter is perhaps most cogently seen in Congressional debates regarding fiscal year 2012–2013 funding for Head Start.

At this point, it is important to note that most ECE public policy in America targets children and families living below or near the poverty level. Certification and credentialing systems escape this social services orientation. They apply to teachers of *all* children, allowing every child to experience the potential benefit achieved through strong, effective teacher credentials and certificates.

Additionally, the delivery of ECE programs is becoming increasingly complex, making it ever more difficult to rely on discrete program standards for improving program quality. Plus, as is well known, the historical reliance on program standards as the vehicle for achieving and maintaining quality, typically in association with disconnected federal and state funding policies, has only added to the ECE field's fragmentation and inconsistencies in quality and outcomes across programs. We also now know that these particular distal signifiers are not strong predictors of quality or child outcomes.

Instead, teacher interactions and instructional practices are the most salient determinants of children's outcomes (Pianta et al., 2009). Therefore, it is crucial to find systematic ways to target teacher competencies. The dramatic increase in children enrolled in ECE programs across a wide range of settings and auspices requires shifting attention away from programs and toward teachers and their practice. Well-structured and empirically based credentialing and certification offer the chance to systematically promote consistently improved quality through systems specialized for those who teach ECE on the scale now required—as is the case in other professional fields of practice (Dower, O'Neil, & Hough, 2001; Goffin, 2009). As Dower and colleagues (2001) outline in their assessment of emerging professions, "Regardless of the particular track one follows or portal one uses to enter a profession, the profession should be able to demonstrate (through clearly described methods) that its members are competent to provide the care they offer when they enter the profession" (p. 16).

Given their potential, it is frustrating that so little is known about ECE credentials and certifications. Yet, as Barnett (2011) expressed at a workshop on the ECE workforce, sponsored by the Institutes of Medicine National Research Council, advancing the value of credentials and certification should not rest solely on available empirical findings. Kagan and colleagues (2008) drew a similar conclusion following their extensive review of ECE professional preparation and development. Critically, even Early and colleagues (2006), who brought the disconnect between teachers' education and children's learning to the public's attention, concluded:

> Requiring a degree and compensating the teachers accordingly professionalizes the early childhood workforce. More can be expected of professional teachers who are credentialed. These individuals have made a commitment to this field by seeking out the appropriate education and are likely to stay in the field longer ... participating in on-going training, and meeting the challenges of the ever-changing requirements of early childhood education. (p. 192)

How ECE Credentials and Licensure Currently Contribute to Uneven Teacher Performance

Pianta (2007) has argued that "accountability is firmly entrenched in early childhood policy and practice" (p. 4). The consistent use of credentials and certification in conjunction with well-designed, evidence-based preparation programs offers a systematic—and systemic—method for making sure the field is accountable to children and families, as well as to its performance as a field of practice. In their absence, we help perpetuate the field's notorious and uneven performance.

As currently designed, however, credentialing and certifying systems contribute to the problem of inadequately prepared early care and education teachers and poor quality ECE programs. Their structures and the lack of consensus regarding the requisite knowledge and skills of early childhood educators result in uneven coverage of relevant content and pedagogy, and reliance on outdated theoretical frameworks.

Hyson, Horm, and Winton (Chapter 26, this volume) address the above issues. In this section, we focus on structural issues and their consequences for teacher preparation programs and for teachers. The scope of credentialing and certification systems and the availability of high performing teacher preparation programs affect the quantity and competence of early educators who can be trusted to positively influence—through the quality of their practice—children's learning and developmental outcomes.

How Teacher Credentials and Certification Impact Preparation Programs

Certification and credentialing systems drive the existence, design, and content of professional preparation programs. When early childhood teacher licensure does not exist, early childhood teacher preparation programs are unlikely to exist either. To underscore this point, in 1991, the ATE and NAEYC (1991) called for specialized teacher certification in every state covering the period from birth through age 8 that was "distinctive from and independent of" elementary and secondary certifications (p. 17). They justified their position as follows:

> Because institutions typically plan programs to meet state certification standards, it is impossible in some states to major in early childhood education. Other states may only provide an endorsement program that consists of two courses and a kindergarten student teaching placement. As a result, there is a shortage of well-qualified early childhood teachers to meet current needs, much less anticipate future demand as programs expand. (p. 17)

This statement remains essentially true two decades later. New Jersey is a case in point. In 1998, in the now famous Abbott school finance case, the New Jersey Supreme Court ordered widespread reform in its highest poverty school districts, including the provision of high-quality PreK programs for 3- and 4-year-old children (Ryan & Lobman, 2006). The ruling dramatically affected the state's early education systems, most especially the infrastructure of teacher preparation (Mead, 2009). In 2000, Abbott districts were required to hire teachers with BA degrees and PreK–3 certification. At the time, however, the state lacked a specialized early childhood teacher license, and only two early childhood teacher preparation programs were in existence.

In response to the court order, the state immediately created a PreK–3 license, and now, 13 New Jersey institutions of higher education offer ECE degrees (Mead, 2009; Ryan & Lobman, 2006). To expedite the process, alternative certification paths also became available, and within 4 years all Abbott districts had met the deadline for having qualified ECE teachers.

Another example of the effects of credentialing systems comes from the results of Head Start's development of the CDA competency goals and functional areas (standards) that guide the training and assessment system (Council for Professional Recognition, 2011). For many years, these competencies have served widely as an organizational framework in basic training for early childhood practitioners and have influenced preparation frameworks at higher levels as well (Bredekamp, 2000; Bredekamp & Willer, 1992).

These two examples demonstrate that credentials and certification have the power to influence professional preparation on a large scale, and thus have tremendous potential to function as a systemic change agent. As currently configured and implemented, however, state teacher licensure, in particular, contributes to the lack of quality and consistency in early childhood teacher preparation (Bornfreund, 2011; NAECT, 2008; Pianta et al., 2009) and ultimately, in teacher performance and child outcomes.

How Credentialing and Certification Impact Teacher Performance

Licensure structures have the most direct consequences for individual teachers and their career options, including employability. While credentialing systems affect individuals to varying degrees, state teacher licensure systems carry the highest stakes in terms of individual career options and the pool of applicants available to ECE programs.

Age/grade configurations of state licensure requirements tend to reflect elementary school grade divisions, such as K–6 or K–8. Licensing configurations almost always overlap (as is evident in Figure 27.1). With the intent of facilitating flexibility in hiring, teachers in most states can obtain a K–6 *or* a K–3 license, and an increasing number of states now include PreK on these licenses. These overlapping configurations discourage specialized preparation, however. An elementary school PreK–6 license is obligated to focus on breadth versus depth of preparation. Yet, currently, either license qualifies teachers for teaching in kindergarten (Bornfreund, 2011).

Given its scope, the broader license is less capable of focusing on the unique learning and development of younger children. In turn, preparation programs are less likely to offer targeted courses or hire qualified ECE faculty. Additionally, anecdotal evidence suggests that the scope of existing licenses undermines some teachers' pursuit of early childhood degrees when they are interested in teaching younger children.

Presently, only 14 states require kindergarten teachers to have a license focused on the early years, and only four states—Arkansas, Georgia, Ohio, and Pennsylvania—require an ECE license to teach kindergarten through third grade (Bornfreund, 2011). Especially pertinent to this discussion, PreK teachers are rarely required to be ECE certified.

The licensure held by teachers directly affects hiring and placement decisions (Bornfreund, 2011). Without a valid teaching license, unless granted a waiver—which typically is time-defined—individuals cannot achieve or maintain employment as a public school teacher. Teachers are therefore more likely to pursue degrees and licenses that grant them the greatest number of employment options, even if their preference is to teach younger children. Similarly, principals are more likely to hire teachers whose qualifications offer them the greatest flexibility in terms of assignment.

The Question of Effectiveness

In 2006 and again in 2007, articles by Early and colleagues called into question the effectiveness of teacher education in promoting classroom quality and child outcomes, setting off a frenzy of introspection and debate regarding the value of degrees, which at the time were increasingly viewed as the way toward improving the results of ECE programs. Although we think the time has come to examine the question of teacher qualifications within the broader framework of discipline-specific certification and credentialing systems, the issue of effectiveness cannot, and should not, be bypassed. In this section we turn to what is known about the effectiveness of the CDA credential and teacher licensure. (The effectiveness of alternative certification systems and of NBPTS were discussed earlier.)

Effectiveness of the CDA Credential

Notwithstanding the long history of CDA as a recognized ECE credential, little research exists on its effectiveness. Similar to teacher licensure, CDA assessment rests on a highly variable training system. The requirement states that candidates must obtain 120 clock hours in a "formal" training program (e.g., as opposed to attending conferences) distributed across the goals and functional areas of the CDA competency structure. Despite the Council's strong encouragement, fewer than 50% of applicants receive college credit for CDA training, and without credit, quality control is lacking and articulation into associate degree programs is unlikely. While there are no hard data regarding the number of CDAs who continue their education, considerable anecdotal evidence suggests that many do.

Early studies suggest that staff members with a CDA credential positively affect the quality of care in centers and family child care homes (Howes, 1997; Howes et al., 1996; Weaver, 2002). One of the difficulties in this research, however, is that requiring CDA-credentialed staff typically occurs as part of a larger system, as is the case in military child care, and, as a result, cannot easily be discretely evaluated (Tout, Zaslow, & Berry, 2006). Although CDA is only one component, large-scale evaluations have found that the Military Child Care Act significantly improved program quality and learning outcomes for children (Zellman & Johansen, 1998), elevating military child care as a model for employer-sponsored care (Campbell, Appelbaum, Martinson, & Martin, 2000).

Effectiveness of ECE Teacher Licensure

Likewise, teacher licensure is seldom evaluated for its effectiveness, and little is known specifically about early childhood teacher licensure. One model from which lessons can be learned, however, is Oklahoma's state-funded universal, voluntary PreK program, which enrolls a higher percentage of 4-year-olds of all income levels than any other state PreK program (Barnett et al., 2010). Oklahoma requires lead teachers in PreK to have a BA degree and to be certified in ECE; they also earn the same wages and benefits as other public school teachers. Although most classes are located in public schools, some classes are located in Head Start and child care programs that meet the same standards for quality.

ECE-certified teachers are but one aspect of the program, but they are considered a vital one. Large-scale program evaluations have found strong positive effects on children's language and cognitive test scores, regardless of their economic status or ethnicity. Still, poor children of color show the strongest gains, with Hispanic children making the most learning progress (Gormley, 2008; Gormley, Gayer, Phillips, & Dawson, 2005).

The Abbott school districts in New Jersey, described earlier, provide additional evidence in support of specialized preparation and certification. At kindergarten entry, children who attended Abbott preschools showed gains in oral language, literacy, and mathematics, with nearly twice the gains for children who attended for 2 years compared to those who attended only 1 year (Frede, Jung, Barnett, & Figueras, 2009). Strong positive effects on oral language, literacy, and especially math continued through second grade, and grade retention was reduced by half (Frede et al., 2009). While these two examples are encouraging, far more research is needed to determine whether these findings can be generalized.

Understanding the Current Status Quo

It hasn't always been the case that a broad constituency clamors for an examination of the qualifications needed for early childhood educators to promote children's learning and development effectively, although a burst of energy in this regard was evident during the 1960s (Lane, 1967). Effectively making a case for elevating the importance of ECE credentials and certification requires us to understand why this is so by placing the issue of credentials and certification in the context of ECE's evolution as a field of practice.

Those in the ECE field always have believed that practitioner training is important. From the beginning of its history as an emerging field, kindergarten teachers trained in the tenets and practices of Froebel crisscrossed late 19th- and early 20th-century America to transfer their knowledge (Snyder, 1972). Eventually, formal training programs were developed, including the Bureau of Educational Experiments (which eventually became Bank Street College in New York City), Teachers College at Columbia University, and Chicago Teaching Kindergarten Training School (now early childhood education in the School of Education) at National Louis University.

Yet this long-term commitment to training and education has been translated only erratically into formal credentials and certifications, both of which provide vehicles for systematizing what teachers know and are able to do. In addition, the field's first consensually developed credential—the Child Development Associate Credential—was not clearly identified with a particular teaching role (Bredekamp, 2000). As late as 1991, only half of the states had some form of an ECE-specialized certification (ATE & NAEYC, 1991). And the status of specialized ECE certification, while more prevalent, remains haphazard in form and content across the 50 states and the District of Columbia, as described earlier.

Historically, we can look to the comingling of several factors as laying the foundation for ECE as a field focused on children's overall development and well-being without also incorporating an instructional focus: the status of women in the 20th century; emergence in the late 1890s of the new perception of children as a distinct group and in need of "saving"; the split among women regarding the role of activism in legalizing women's right to vote that led to a break between political and social reform feminism; and early educators' interest in elevating the importance of children and their development in the context of social reform (Antler, 1987; Cahan, 1989; Cravens, 1985; Finkelstein, 1988). Over time, these motives have been expressed in the formation of discrete programs and policies (e.g., child care, Head Start, PreK) that have burdened the field with fragmented practices.

As explained by Antler (1987) in her biography of Lucy Sprague Mitchell, the founder of the Bureau of Educational Experiments and an important contributor to the field's child-centered approach to early education, "Lucy Sprague Mitchell and her colleagues were drawn to early childhood education as a career ... because of their eagerness for social reform" (p. xviii). Emotionally secure and healthy children—" 'whole' children were the best guarantors of a progressive, humanistic society" (p. xviii). Finkelstein (1988) clarifies further: In its early years, ECE was intended to "raise the status of children and child rearing, mothers and motherhood; to dignify social service; and to solidify the roles of women as moral and cultural authorities; and as agents of social control and transformation" (p. 11). Turning to kindergarten, Beatty (1990) argues that "unlike other types of teaching which began as masculine occupations and were then 'feminized,' kindergarten teaching began as a feminine vocation, with different ideals from masculine occupations evolving at the same time" (p. 35), a point also highlighted by Finkelstein (1988).

Collectively, these ideals espoused a voluntaristic view of work, a gender-linked definition of qualifications and expertise, and what Finkelstein (1988) called "moral evangelicism" (p. 13; see also Beatty, 1990). As articulated in 1929 by the Committee on Nursery Schools (which eventually formed the National Association for Nursery Educators, the forerunner of NAEYC) under the heading of Training in its *Minimum Essentials for Nursery School Education*, "Teaching is essentially an art. The ability to teach successfully is found sometimes in a person with a minimum of formal training, and no amount of training can be guaranteed to make a good teacher" (Davis, Johnson, & Richardson, 1929).

Finally, as noted by Cahan (1989), while the expertise surrounding nursery schools came largely from university-based child development researchers, when it came to child care (then labeled "day nurseries"), the professionalizing field of social work exerted the greatest influence. Thus, the field has a history of not only fragmented programs and policies but also of splintered purposes and identities—an uncertainty that exists to this day and permeates the field's response to setting fixed entry qualifications (Goffin & Washington, 2007).

Kagan and Kauerz (2007) label the current transformation being experienced by ECE as a progression of "educationalizing and systematizing early childhood education" (p. 11). This transformation provides impetus for revisiting the value of ECE credentials and certification as a forethought—versus as an afterthought, which too often has been the case. Beyond findings from numerous polls arguing that the term "education" has greater public resonance than the term "care," the widespread substitution of "early education and care" for early "care" and education—and, increasingly, the growing omission of the word *care*—reflects elevation of the field's educational/instructional function. In turn, uplifting education as a primary focus has generated concern over the uneven—and often poor—results coming from publicly funded PreK programs and escalating interest in the qualifications of the teachers in these programs (Barnett, 2011; Bogard, Traylor, & Takanishi, 2008; Bueno, Darling-Hammond, & Gonzales, 2010; Pianta et al., 2009; Whitebook, 2003a, 2003b).

The transformation of ECE also is seen in the redirection of attention away from an almost total focus on structural elements and curriculum models (see, e.g., Goffin & Wilson, 2001) to scrutiny of ECE practitioners and their performance, both as individuals and as a workforce. So, for example, with funding from the U.S. Department of Health and Human Services, the NRC recently convened a workshop focused on the early childhood workforce in hope of finding definitional clarity, a consistent framework for data collection, and increased consensus on how best to build the field's capacity to create a higher level of teacher quality (see *www.iom.edu/activities/children/earlychildcareeducation/2011-feb-28.aspx*).

Clearly, the need now exists for consistently high-performing early childhood educators. The scale and complexity of ECE and their consequences for teacher competence need to be tackled differently. The field's approach needs to move from discrete programmatic and policy solutions to a systemic approach focused on specialized credentials and certificates. The number of children and families whose daily lives are being influenced by the quality of their interactions with ECE teachers has raised the stakes for all of us—and created a sense of urgency that should no longer be ignored.

Specialized ECE Licensure: Making It Part of the Solution

While minimal evidence is presently available about the efficacy of credentialing and certification, we have ample evidence that ECE programs are not good enough, and that most teachers, including certified teachers, are not implementing effective practices. Given that current licensure systems are large-scale, existing systems that already affect the quality of early education in significant ways, it is nonsensical not to employ them to the fullest extent possible in reforming early education.

Teacher licensure is the strongest gatekeeping system available for managing entry into the teaching profession; yet it is a relatively unhinged portal. Despite its current weaknesses, ECE licensure has great potential to help ECE fulfill its promise to children and families. To do so, every state should adopt *and require* specialized early childhood licenses that achieve the following interconnected goals.

- Cover the early childhood developmental period from birth through age 8 (third grade), providing certification options of birth through age 5 or age 3 through grade 3. This combination of licenses will ensure that children in all forms of early childhood programs, regardless of auspice or funding stream, can have access to teachers with specialized preparation for their roles.
- Focus preparation programs for these ECE licenses on the skills and knowledge necessary to work across the scope encompassed by the license, whether the degree program comes under the auspices of education, child development and family studies/human ecology, or crosses these departments.
- Configure state's ECE licensure structure to ensure minimal or no overlap with elementary credentials.
- Increase the rigor of ECE teacher preparation and the award of teacher licensure by providing stronger focus on teacher competence.

Making the Case for Specialized ECE Teacher Licensure

Specialized ECE credentials and certification can help justify and sustain growing public expectations for the accountability of ECE programs. Expectations have steadily grown as one national report after another touts the potential of ECE as a public good both to close the achievement gap and to prepare all students to contribute in a global economy.

Dramatic growth in the ECE knowledge base justifies a 4-year degree plus specialized ECE certification because there is now so much more that teachers need to know and to be able to do—though associate degree programs should continue to play an integral role in ECE teacher preparation. Teachers of young children need not only a broad base of scientific knowledge about child development and learning but also wide content knowledge and skills, accompanied by a significant amount of supervised clinical practice (NCATE, 2010a, 2010b). Add to this the skills needed to work effectively with diverse families, dual language learners, and children with disabilities and special needs, and it becomes clear that initial preparation cannot be covered in less than 4 years or without specialization.

As evident in comparable fields such as nursing (Benner, Sutphen, Leonard, & Day, 2010; Goffin, 2009), 21st-century technological knowledge and shifting demands require more highly educated practitioners. It is ironic that just as the ECE knowledge base is exploding, the field's commitment to a highly qualified, well-educated workforce is imploding. Only ECE seems to question whether 4-year degrees and sanctioned licenses to practice are essential ingredients in defining professionalism. Teacher licensure exists to serve a gatekeeping function for sectors and individuals. It is essential that those who pass through that gate possess the knowledge and skills that a professional license represents.

Deciding the Age Range of an ECE Teacher License

One of the oldest continuing debates in the ECE field is the definition of its age span (Goffin & Washington, 2007). Although NAEYC's definition—birth through age 8—is now more widely accepted, it remains a broad age span for which to prepare teachers in a 4-year degree program—as broad as a K–6 credential, in fact. Nevertheless, early childhood educators are reluctant to compromise by "giving up" either end of the developmental period, not wishing to abdicate K–3 to elementary education nor neglect the essential importance of the first 3 years of life.

Teacher licensure configurations drive preparation programs. Therefore, it is essential that licenses adequately cover the full age range of early childhood and also provide the depth required for effective practice. Two current trends also must be considered in creating licensure structures for the present and future of the field. The first is the call for PreK–3 alignment (Foundation for Child Development, 2008; Guernsey & Mead, 2010). Given the tendency for the elementary curriculum to creep down into earlier grades, an age 3–grade 3 certificate must be designed that can promote developmentally appropriate, effective practices for each age group along this continuum.

The second trend is the anticipated growth in infant/toddler programs. The number of infant/toddler CDA credentials has almost doubled since 2006 (D. Jordan, April 7, 2011, personal communication). While colleges of education have traditionally not prepared teachers for work with babies and toddlers, 29 states already have at least one license on the books that begins at birth (see Figure 27.1). Oklahoma offers an interesting innovation in this regard. In 2010, it launched an Infant/Toddler–3-year-old (IT3) license to qualify teachers to work in its state-funded pilot program for very young children. While the state already requires that all lead teachers of 3-year-olds have a bachelor's degree and an ECE license, IT3 preparation programs are housed in departments such as Family and Consumer Science (rather than schools of education) and offer degrees in child development or family relations with an emphasis on infants through 3-year-olds (Bornfreund, 2011).

Decades ago, Jimmy Hymes (1988), former president of NAEYC and an important field leader, lamented that ECE gave up too soon on a birth through age 5 teacher credential because at the time too few jobs existed for it. He believed strongly that in a "marriage" between "under 6" and "over 6" as required by a PreK–3 credential, primary grade practices would always dominate. Bolstered by the history of kindergarten (Tyack & Cuban, 1995), many today would agree with him. Yet, at the same time, early childhood educators desperately want to hold on to kindergarten and primary grades to protect the ECE field's traditional focus on child development, families, and active learning.

Given the current and future demand for highly qualified teachers of children across the early childhood age span, states need to offer teacher licenses that cover both options— birth through age 5 and PreK to grade 3. The option to choose one of these and then to add coursework and clinical practice should be made available so teachers could modify the scope of their expertise, if they so desired.

Making Teacher Licensure Obligatory

If credentials and certification are to have any clout, teachers must be required to be licensed to practice. When states require ECE licensure for public school teachers of children from age 3 to grade 3, for example, as Oklahoma and New Jersey have done, systemic change is more likely.

Focusing on teachers' qualifications and credentials is challenging, and the ECE field resisted such an attempt in the past (National Institute for Early Childhood Professional Development, 1991). As a result, we, as early childhood leaders, are at least partially to blame for poor quality. As Barbara Bowman (2001) points out, "Most professions are organized along a career ladder with clear demarcations regarding the kind and amount of training required at each level. A license to practice (based on a standard program of study) is the baseline. ... This is not the model used in preschool education" (p. 176).

Focusing on Teacher Competence in Program Approval

States license teachers to practice in two ways: by approving teacher preparation programs to grant licenses and by reviewing individuals' transcripts to determine whether they have met requirements. When approving programs, states deem them to act in their stead. Consequently, the approval process needs to be as rigorous as possible. The content of courses, depth and breadth of coverage, currency of knowledge, clinical practice experiences, opportunities to interact with diverse children and families, and the specialized expertise of faculty all warrant greater attention than they currently receive (Bornfreund, 2011; Maxwell, Lim, & Early, 2006; NCATE, 2010b).

Moreover, program approval processes are trending toward evaluation of teacher performance rather than relying solely on input such as course content. This trend is especially pertinent to ECE because we now know that interactions and instructional practices are such strong predictors of child outcomes (e.g., Pianta et al., 2009). NCATE, the traditional accreditation body for teacher preparation programs, with which NAEYC has collaborated for many years, has joined forces with the Teacher Education Accreditation Council to form the Council for the Accreditation of Educator Preparation (CAEP; n.d.). The new accreditation process, presently under development, will focus on three standards: (1) Candidates demonstrate knowledge, skills, and professional dispositions for effective work in schools; (2) data drive decisions about candidates and programs; and (3) resources and practices support candidate learning (CAEP, n.d.). Furthermore, as of this writing, Congress is initiating the reauthorization process for the Elementary and Secondary Education Act (ESEA; i.e., No Child Left Behind), and giving serious consideration to replacing the requirement for "qualified" teachers with "effective" teachers—offering further evidence of the emphasis being given to teacher performance.

Moving Forward

The word *credential*, has the same origin as words such as *credibility, credence*, and *credo*. Each of these words communicates an element of trust, believability, and authority. Earning a credential and license to practice in a particular field of endeavor communicates that one is worthy of the public's trust. Caring for and educating other people's children, particularly during the early years when their development and learning are so foundational and readily influenced by both positive and negative experiences, is an enormous responsibility. Families and society place great trust in the hands of early childhood educators.

This makes it is all the more *incredible* that there are not consistently required, rigorously defined credentials that grant to every early childhood educator permission to practice. As evident by the chapters in this handbook, we know a great deal more than we did in the past about effective early education. At the same time, it is readily apparent that a large gap exists between this information and current practice. Improvement on the scale needed requires a systemic approach. Yet focusing only on how new knowledge is incorporated into degree programs fails to respond to the issue of ensuring that the ECE field has a sufficient quantity of teachers with demonstrable knowledge and the skills to apply it in their practice.

The state of affairs in credentialing and certification is discouraging. Yet it also offers a silver lining—the opportunity to think strategically and systemically about possible ways to resolve the gap between ECE's aspirations and its realities.

Moving forward will not be easy, in no small measure because of the multiple state structures that have to be navigated to achieve recognition of the credential and license being recommended (Egertson, 2008), and the effort that will be required to galvanize the ECE field to endorse this change (Goffin, 2009). Nevertheless, credentialing and certification should no longer be an afterthought. They should be a strong, viable part of the profession's efforts to improve the quality of care and education for all children.

References

AACTE Focus Council on Early Childhood Education. (2004, June). *The early childhood challenge: Preparing high-quality teachers for a changing society.* Washington, DC: American Association of Colleges for Teacher Education.

Antler, J. (1987). *Lucy Sprague Mitchell: The making of a modern woman.* New Haven, CT: Yale University Press.

Association of Teacher Educators & National Association for the Education of Young Children. (1991). Early childhood teacher certification: A position statement of the Association of Teacher Educators & National Association for the Education of Young Children. Retrieved March 13, 2011, from *www.naeyc.org.*

Bailey, C. T. (2004). *The 2004 survey of Child Development Associates.* Unpublished paper. Washington, DC: Council for Professional Recognition.

Barbarin, O. A., & Wasik, B. H. (Eds.). (2009). *Handbook of child development and early education: Research to practice.* New York: Guilford Press.

Barnett, W. S. (2011, March 1). *Preparing highly effective pre-k teachers.* Presentation at the Early Childhood Care and Education Workforce: A workshop. Washington, DC: Institute of Medicine and National Research Council Board on Children, Youth, and Families.

Barnett, W. S., Epstein, D. J., Carolan, M. E., Fitzgerald, J., Ackerman, D. J., & Friedman, A. (2010). *The state of preschool 2010: State preschool yearbook.* New Brunswick, NJ: National Institute for Early Education Research.

Beatty, B. (1990). "A vocation from on high": Kindergartening as an occupation for American women. In J. Antler & S. K. Biklen (Eds.), *Changing education: Women as radicals and conservators* (pp. 35–50). Albany: State University of New York Press.

Benner, P., Sutphen, M., Leonard, V., & Day, L. (2010). *Educating nurses: A call for radical transformation* (Carnegie Foundation for the Advancement of Teaching's Preparation for the Professions series). San Francisco: Jossey-Bass.

Bogard, K., Traylor, F., & Takanishi, R. (2008). Teacher education and Pre-K outcomes: Are we asking the right questions? *Early Childhood Research Quarterly, 23*(1), 1–6.

Bornfreund, L. A. (2011). *Getting in sync: Revamping licensing and preparation for teachers in Pre-K, kindergarten, and the early grades.* Washington, DC: New America Foundation. Available at *www.newamerica.net.*

Bowman, B. (2001). Facing the future. In *NAEYC at 75: Reflections on the past: Challenges for the future* (pp. 167–182). Washington, DC: NAEYC.

Boyd, D., Goldhaber, D., Lankford, H., & Wyckoff, J. (2007). The effect of certification and preparation on teacher quality. *The Future of Children, 17*(1), 45–64.

Bredekamp, S. (2000). CDA at 25: Reflections on the past and projections for the future. *Young Children, 55*(5), 15–19.

Bredekamp, S. (2011). *Effective practices in early childhood education: Building a foundation.* Boston: Pearson.

Bredekamp, S., & Willer, B. (1992). Of ladders and lattices, cores and cones: Conceptualizing an early childhood professional development system. *Young Children, 47*(3), 47–50.

Bueno, M., Darling-Hammond, L., & Gonzales, D. (May 2010). *A matter of degrees: Preparing teachers for the pre-k classroom.* Washington, DC: Pew Center on the States. Retrieved March 14, 2011, from *www.preknow.org/documents/teacherquality_march2010.pdf.*

Burchinal, M., Howes, C., Pianta, R., Bryant, D., Early, D., Clifford, R., et al. (2008). Predicting child outcomes at the end of kindergarten from the quality of pre-kindergarten teacher–child interactions and instruction. *Applied Developmental Science, 12*(3), 140–153.

Cahan, E. D. (1989). *Past caring: A history of U.S. preschool care and education for the poor, 1820–1965.* New York: National Center for Children in Poverty.

Campbell, N. D., Appelbaum, J. C., Martinson, K., & Martin, E. (2000). *Be all that you can be: Lessons from the military for improving our nation's child care system.* Washington, DC: National Women's Law Center.

Council for the Accreditation of Educator Preparation (CAEP). (n.d.). Report and Recommendation of the NCATE/TEAC Design Team to our respective Boards of Directors. Retrieved April 21, 2011, from *www.caepsite.org/documents/designteamreport.pdf.*

Council for Professional Recognition. (2011). *The Child Development Associate assessment system and competency standards: Preschool caregivers in center-based programs* (Rev. 3rd ed.). Washington, DC: Author.

Cravens, H. (1985). Child-saving in the age of professionalism, 1915–1939. In J. M. Hawes & N. R. Hiner (Eds.), *American childhood: A research guide and historical handbook* (pp. 415–488). Westport, CT: Greenwood Press.

Davis, M. D., Johnson, H., & Richardson, A. E. (1929). *Minimum essentials for nursery school education.* New York: National Committee on Nursery Schools.

Decker, P. T., Mayer, D. P., & Glazerman, S. (2004). *The effects of Teach for America on students: Findings from a national evaluation.* Princeton, NJ: Mathematica Policy Research, Inc. Retrieved April 10, 2011, from *www.teachforamerica.org/assets/documents/mathematica_results_6.9.04.pdf.*

Dower, C., O'Neil, E., & Hough, H. (2001). *Profiling the professions: A model for evaluating emerging health professions.* San Francisco: Center for the Health Professions, University of California, San Francisco.

Early, D. M., Barbarin, O., Bryant, D., Burchinal, M., Chang, F., Clifford, R., et al. (2005). Pre-kindergarten in eleven states: NCEDL's Multi-State Study of Prekindergarten and Study of State-Wide Early Education Programs (SWEEP)—Preliminary descriptive report (NCEDL Working Paper). Retrieved June 30, 2005, from *www.fpg.unc.edu/~ncedl/pdfs/SWEEP_MS_summary_final.pdf.*

Early, D. M., Bryant, D. M., Pianta, R. C., Clifford, R.M., Burchinal, M. R., Ritchie, S., et al. (2006). Are teachers' education, major, and credentials related to classroom quality and children's academic gains in pre-kindergarten? *Early Childhood Research Quarterly, 21,* 174–195.

Early, D., Maxwell, K., Burchinal, M., Alva, S., Bener, R., Bryant, D., et al. (2007). Teachers' education, classroom quality, and young children's academic skills: Results from seven studies of preschool programs. *Child Development, 58,* 558–580.

Early, D., & Winton, P. (2001). Preparing the workforce: Early childhood teacher preparation at 2- and 4-year institutions of higher education. *Early Childhood Research Quarterly, 16*(3), 285–306.

Egertson, H. (2008). Critical steps in advocating for stronger ECE certification/endorsement at the state level: An open letter to advocates from an Emerita early childhood state specialist and veteran of the fray. Retrieved March 15, 2011, from *www.naecte.org.*

Finkelstein, B. (1988). The revolt against selfishness: Women and the dilemmas of professionalism in early childhood education. In B. Spodek, O. N. Saracho, & D. L. Peters (Eds.), *Professionalism and the early childhood practitioner* (pp. 10–28). New York: Teachers College Press.

Foundation for Child Development. (2008). *America's vanishing potential: The case for Prek–3rd education.* New York: Author.

Frede, E., Jung, K., Barnett, W. S., & Figueras, A. (2009). The APPLES blossom: Abbott Preschool Program Longitudinal Effects Study (APPLES): Preliminary results through 2nd grade interim report. Retrieved April 8, 2011, from *www.nieer.org/pdf/apples_second_grade_results.pdf.*

Goffin, S. G. (2009). *Field-wide leadership: Insights from five fields of practice.* Washington, DC: Goffin Strategy Group.

Goffin, S. G., & Washington, V. (2007). *Ready or not: Leadership choices in early care and education.* New York: Teachers College Press.

Goffin, S. G., & Wilson, C. S. (2001). *Curriculum models and early childhood education: Appraising the relationship* (2nd ed.). Upper Saddle River, NJ: Prentice-Hall.

Gormley, W. T. (2008). *The effects of Oklahoma's Universal Pre-Kindergarten Program on Hispanic children.* Washington, DC: Center for Research on Children in the U.S. (CROCUS) at Georgetown University.

Gormley, W. T., Gayer, T., Phillips, D., & Dawson, B. (2005). The effects of universal pre-k on cognitive development. *Developmental Psychology, 41*(6), 872–884.

Guernsey, L., & Mead, S. (2010). *The next social contract for the primary years of education.* Washington, DC: New America Foundation.

Gundling, R., & Hyson, M. (2002). National board certification: The next professional step. *Young Children, 57*(5), 60–61.

Hamre, B. K., & Pianta, R. C. (2007). Learning opportunities in preschool and early elementary classrooms. In R. C. Pianta, M. J. Cox, & K. Snow (Eds.), *School readiness, early learning, and the transition to kindergarten* (pp. 49–83). Baltimore: Brookes.

Howes, C. (1997). Children's experiences in center-based care as a function of teacher background and adult–child ratio. *Merrill–Palmer Quarterly, 43*(3), 404–425.

Howes, C., Burchinal, M., Pianta, R., Bryant, D., Early, D., Clifford, R., et al. (2008). Ready to learn?: Children's pre-academic achievement in pre-kindergarten programs. *Early Childhood Research Quarterly, 23*(1), 27–50.

Howes, C., Galinsky, E., Shinn, M., Gulcur, L., Clements, M., Sibley, A., et al. (1996). *The Florida Child Care Quality Improvement Study: 1996 Report.* New York: Families and Work Institute.

Hymes, J. (1988, Spring). *A teaching credential for the under six years: Notes and comments by James Hymes.* Carmel, CA: Hacienda Press.

Kagan, S. L., & Kauerz, K. (2007). Reaching for the whole: Integration and alignment in early education policy. In R. C. Pianta, M. J. Cox, & K. L. Snow (Eds.), *Early education in transition in school readiness and the transition to kindergarten in the era of accountability* (pp. 11–30). Baltimore: Brookes.

Kagan, S. L., Kauerz, K., & Tarrant, K. (2008). *The early care and education workforce at the fulcrum.* New York: Teachers College Press.

Kelley, P. J., & Camilli, G. (2007). *The impact of teacher education on outcomes in center-based early childhood education programs: A meta-analysis* (NIEER Working Paper). New Brunswick, NJ: National Institute of Early Education Research. Retrieved October 4, 2010, from *nieer.org/docs/?docid=185.*

Lane, D. (1967, October). Certification of teachers … A part of improving the quality of education of young children. *Young Children, 23*(1), 3–13.

Maxwell, K. L., Lim, C.-I., & Early, D. M. (2006). *Early childhood teacher preparation programs in the United States* (National Report). Chapel Hill: University of North Carolina, FPG Child Development Institute.

Mead, S. (2009). *Education reform starts early: Lessons from New Jersey's PreK–3rd reform efforts.* Washington, DC: New America Foundation.

National Association for the Education of Young Children (NAEYC). (1993). *A conceptual framework for early childhood professional development: A position statement.* Washington, DC: Author. Retrieved April 8, 2011, from *www.naeyc.org/positionstatements.*

National Association for the Education of Young Children (NAEYC). (2005). *NAEYC early childhood program standards and accreditation criteria: The mark of quality in early childhood education.* Washington, DC: Author.

National Association for the Education of Young Children (NAEYC). (2010). *NAEYC standards for initial and advanced early childhood professional preparation programs.* Washington, DC: Author.

National Association of Early Childhood Teacher Educators (NAECTE). (2008). Position statement on early childhood teacher certification for teachers of children 8 years old and younger in public school settings. Retrieved March 15, 2011, from *www.naecte.org.*

National Board for Professional Teaching Standards (NBPTS). (2007). A research guide on National Board certification. Washington, DC: Author. Retrieved April 8, 2011, from *www.nbpts.org/resources/research/impact_of_certification.*

National Board for Professional Teaching Standards (NBPTS). (2009). *Early childhood generalist assessment at a glance.* Retrieved April 2, 2011, from *www.nbpts.org/userfiles/file/ec_gen_assessataglance.pdf.*

National Child Care Information and Technical Assistance Center (NCCITAC) & National Association for Regulatory Administration (NARA). (2010). The 2008 Child Care Center Licensing Study. Retrieved March 15, 2011, from *naralicensing.org.*

National Council for Accreditation of Teacher Education (NCATE). (2010a). *The road less traveled: How the developmental sciences can prepare educators to improve student achievement: Policy recommendations.* Washington, DC: Author.

National Council for Accreditation of Teacher Education (NCATE). (2010b). *Transforming teacher education through clinical practice: A national strategy to prepare effective teachers* (Report of the Blue Ribbon Panel on Clinical Preparation and Partnerships for Improved Student Learning). Washington, DC: Author.

National Institute for Early Childhood Professional Development. (1991). A vision for early childhood professional development. *Young Children, 47*(1), 35–37.

National Research Council (NRC). (2008). *Assessing accomplished teaching: Advanced-level certification programs.* Washington, DC: Author.

National Scientific Council on the Developing Child. (2007). The science of early childhood development. Retrieved April 21, 2011, from *www.developingchild.net.*

Pianta, R. C. (2007). Early education in transition. In R. C. Pianta, M. J. Cox, & K. L. Snow (Eds.), *Early education in transition in school readiness and the transition to kindergarten in the era of accountability* (pp. 3–10). Baltimore: Brookes.

Pianta, R. C., Barnett, W. C., Burchinal, M., & Thornburg, K. (2009). The effects of preschool education: What we know, how public policy is or is not aligned with the evidence base, and what we need to know. *Psychological Science in the Public Interest, 10*(2) 49–88.

Pianta, R. C., La Paro, K., & Hamre, B. K. (2008). *Classroom Assessment Scoring System (CLASS).* Baltimore: Brookes.

Ryan, S., & Lobman, C. (2006). *Carrots and sticks: New Jersey's effort to create a qualified PreK–3 workforce* (Foundation for Child Development Policy Brief No. 6, Advancing Pre-K–3). New York: Foundation for Child Development.

Snyder, A. (1972). *Dauntless women in childhood education: 1856–1931.* Washington DC: Association for Childhood Education International.

Stayton, V. D., Dietrich, S. L., Smith, B. J., Bruder, M. B., Mogro-Wilson, C., & Swigart, A. (2009). State certification requirements for early childhood special educators. *Infants and Young Children, 22*(1), 4–12.

Tout, K., Zaslow, M., & Berry, D. (2006). Quality and qualifications: Links between professional development and quality in early care and education settings. In M. Zaslow & I. Martinez-Beck (Eds.), *Critical issues in early childhood professional development* (pp. 77–110). Baltimore: Brookes.

Tyack, D., & Cuban, L. (1995). *Tinkering toward utopia: A century of public school reform.* Cambridge, MA: Harvard University Press.

Weaver, R. H. (2002). Prediction of quality and commitment in family child care: Provider education, personal resources, and support. *Early Education and Development, 13*(3), 265–282.

Whitebook, M. (2003a). *Bachelor's degrees are best: Higher qualifications for pre-kindergarten teachers lead to better learning environments for children.* Washington, DC: Trust for Early Education.

Whitebook, M. (2003b). *Early education quality: Higher teacher qualifications for better learning environments—a review of the literature.* Berkeley: Center for the Study of Child Care Employment, Institute for Research on Labor and Employment, University of California.

Whitebook, M., Gomby, D., Bellm, D., Sakai, L., & Kipnis, F. (2009). *Preparing teachers of young children: The current state of knowledge, and a blueprint for the future* (Executive Summary). Berkeley: Center for the Study of Child Care Employment, Institute for Research on Labor and Employment, University of California.

Whitebook, M., & Ryan, S. (2011). *Degrees in context: Asking the right questions about preparing skilled and effective teachers of young children.* New Brunswick, NJ: National Institute for Early Education Research & Center for the Study of Child Care Employment.

Zellman, G. I., & Johansen, A. S. (1998). *Examining the implementation and outcomes of the Military Child Care Act of 1989.* Santa Monica, CA: RAND Corporation.

Zill, N. (2008). *Achievement levels and growth in D.C.: Preschool and Pre-K classes taught by Teach for America teachers.* Rockville, MD: Westat.

Author Index

Subject Index

Page numbers followed by *f* indicate figure; *n*, note; and *t*, table

622